CYBERSPACE LAW

COMMENTARIES AND MATERIALS

Second Edition

YEE FEN LIM

BSc, LLB, LLM (Hons), University of Sydney

OXFORD
UNIVERSITY PRESS

D1400571

OXFORD

UNIVERSITY PRESS

253 Normanby Road, South Melbourne, Victoria 3205, Australia

Oxford University Press is a department of the University of Oxford.
It furthers the University's objective of excellence in research,
scholarship, and education by publishing worldwide in

Oxford New York

Auckland Cape Town Dar es Salaam Hong Kong Karachi
Kuala Lumpur Madrid Melbourne Mexico City Nairobi
New Delhi Shanghai Taipei Toronto

with offices in

Argentina Austria Brazil Chile Czech Republic France Greece
Guatemala Hungary Italy Japan Poland Portugal Singapore
South Korea Switzerland Thailand Turkey Ukraine Vietnam

OXFORD is a trade mark of Oxford University Press
in the UK and in certain other countries

First published 2002
Reprinted 2003, 2004, 2006
Second edition published 2007

National Library of Australia Cataloguing-in-Publication data:

Lim, Yee Fen.

Cyberspace law : commentaries and materials.
2nd ed.
Bibliography.
For tertiary law and IT students.

ISBN 9780195558616.
ISBN 0 19 555861 8.

1. Information technology - Social aspects. 2. Internet -
Law and legislation. 3. Computer networks - Law and
legislation - Australia. I. Title.

343.940999

Edited by Trischa Baker
Proofread and indexed by Puddingburn Publishing Services
Typeset by OUPANZ
Printed in Hong Kong by Sheck Wah Tong Printing Press Ltd

Contents

Foreword

This book of commentaries and materials will assist all lawyers, whether they be judges, legal practitioners, law teachers or students at law, in coming to grips with a vast range of issues generated by the creation of the internet and the development of what is now called cyberspace.

For example, what is the nature of the World Wide Web; who, if anyone, controls it at a technical and a policy level? To what extent are electronic or digital signatures to be treated in the law as analogous to paper-based authentications, particularly the manuscript signature? What issues of construction are presented in Australia by the provisions of the *Electronic Transactions Act 1999* (Cth) respecting the electronic agent? How should the common law respond in developing a tort for the protection of privacy and what changes may be appropriate to legislative schemes for protection of personal data? What is the role of the criminal law in policing what legislatures consider abuse of the freedom of communication engendered by the Internet?

The author rightly stresses the need for the law, statutory and judge-made, as it develops in this area, to balance the diverse interests at play, governmental, corporate and individual, and the goals of international comity and effective economic regulation.

The law of intellectual property, in particular the traditional legislative divisions between trade marks, patents and copyright, is challenged by this new technology, as it earlier was in Australia by the decision in *Computer Edge Pty Ltd v Apple Computer Inc.*[1] So also are the principles controlling jurisdiction, choice of law and transnational litigation. The controversy respecting situs of publication which was considered in *Dow Jones & Company Inc v Gutnick*[2] is a harbinger of litigation to come.

All of these matters, and many more, are considered in this work. Judicial decisions and scholarly writings are extracted and considered. The commentary is lively and to the point. The materials are from sources which extend from the United States and the European Union to Singapore and Australia. It was in the last-mentioned jurisdiction that the author received her tertiary education. This shows in her writing, to the mutual advantage of the author and the University of Sydney.

The Hon Justice WMC Gummow, AC
Canberra
October 2006

---

1   (1986) 161 CLR 171.
2   (2002) 210 CLR 575.

Table of Cases

Table of Statutes and International Instruments

CANADA

NEW ZEALAND

SINGAPORE

UNITED STATES

Introduction

- -

1   Introduction

As the world moves into the new century we are faced with an ever-increasing reliance upon technology, and particularly the Internet, in our day-to-day lives. The nature of the Internet means that it is impossible accurately to estimate the number of people with access to it. However, its importance and pervasiveness are certain to continue to expand.

Given the exponential growth of the Internet, legal institutions face serious questions, not only about how to regulate the Internet, but also about whether it should be regulated at all. As was the case with all of the previous technological revolutions throughout history, the law has been, and will continue to be, stretched to its practical and theoretical limits in its efforts to overcome the challenges raised by the Internet. It is these efforts, and these challenges, which form the foundation for the materials in this book.

The smooth continued operation of human relationships depends upon functional institutions, be they formal or customary, written or oral. As the relationships grow in number and complexity, so too must the institutions. Currently, 'Internet law' is still little more than an embryonic collection of laws and principles which, through

•   1

design or necessity, have been applied to the Internet. Despite the publicity surrounding the growth of the Internet, there are still very few professionals who can credibly call themselves 'Internet lawyers'. Indeed, it might be argued by some that there is in fact still no firm jurisprudence which can be collectively referred to as 'Internet law'.

Some scholars have suggested that the existing law can be stretched to encompass Internet-related issues, hence negating the need for a separate 'field' known as 'Internet law'.[1] There is certainly a developing body of statutory law, with numerous individual pieces of legislation aimed at separate aspects of Internet relationships. However, the effectiveness of legislation of this sort is limited because it must balance the large number of interests at play: those of the government itself; of corporations; of consumers; of the economy generally; and finally, the interests of international parties as expressed through international obligations. Governments around the world are pressed by these competing interests, and the resulting legislative results are frequently ill-considered and reactionary.

International cooperation offers a chance to develop institutions which might assist in the regulation of Internet relationships. In this approach we find the second major branch of scholarship. The call for an 'Internet law', a call manifested in a variety of models, has increasing support. New legal institutions, both conceptual and practical, might flow from direct international negotiations, as can be observed in the EU, or they might be generated by existing institutions such as the United Nations or the Organisation for Economic Cooperation and Development. These models provide some options for creating the most effective means of facing the challenges of the Internet.

Regardless of the legal or jurisprudential model used, often the solutions to Internet problems will lie in a combination of legal and technical innovation. As will be outlined in the extract that follows, the phenomenon known as the Internet has several components. The most well known of these is referred to as the World Wide Web. The World Wide Web has many definitions; in fact there are almost as many definitions as there are definers. In keeping with this trend, the following definition will be the foundation for discussions of the web throughout this book:

> The World Wide Web is a mechanism, or system, for linking together millions of electronic documents, or web pages, each of which can be accessed through a unique, yet changeable, Universal Resource Locator (URL). A website is simply a collection of web pages.

The websites developed in the early 1990s were mostly public: anyone could visit them. As technology developed, so did password-protected sites, as people realised that access to their documents could be restricted. Today we also have private sites in the form of intranets and extranets. Intranets are extremely useful within organisations such as universities and law firms, as they allow information to be shared within the organisations without the rest of the world being able to access the data or information. Common

---

1   See some of the discourse in L Lessig, 'The Law of the Horse: What Cyberlaw Might Teach', 113 *Harvard Law Review* 501, also available at <http://cyber.law.harvard.edu/works/lessig/finalhls.pdf> 12 January 2001.

information shared in this context would include meeting agendas, meeting minutes and leave entitlements. Extranets are an extension of the Internet system, in which large networks, generally created and utilised by large institutions and corporations, are partially open for general access. Access might be through an interface with the World Wide Web, or it might be through a separate system of networks with public access portals. The simplest example of extranets is the system used by airlines for booking seats on flights. The networks once used by airlines to check seat availability and prices can now be accessed not only by travel agents but also by members of the public.

One of the most significant aspects of the Internet concerns the question of ownership and control: Who owns and who controls the Internet? The answer, simply, is no one. Ownership of the physical infrastructure is spread between governments, individuals, corporations and telecommunications utilities. The networks within a country are funded and managed according to the individual country's policies, and the links between countries are managed by the agreements between telecommunications providers. Therefore, the Internet is the first major global institution that has no government. This is simultaneously its main strength and its main weakness, and is possibly the single most important point in relation to the study of Internet law. This point is further amplified once non-physical Internet property is considered, namely the intellectual property rights attached to the content of the documents contained on both the World Wide Web specifically, and the Internet generally.

Although no single body can claim to control the Internet, it would be misleading to suggest that it is a completely untamed, uncontrolled entity. In fact, there are numerous cooperative groups, with varying degrees of formality, which play important roles in the ongoing administration of the Internet. To simplify, these bodies operate on two distinct levels: technical and policy. Three organisations which demand mention:

- Internet Architecture Board. The Board has two separate and distinct operations: the Internet Engineering Task Force (IETF) and the Internet Research Task Force. As their names suggest, these bodies are concerned with the technical requirements of the Internet. On its web page at <http://www.ietf.org/overview.html>, the IETF describes itself as a large international community of network designers, operators, vendors and researchers concerned with the evolution and betterment of Internet architecture, and it invites any interested individuals to become members.
- Internet Corporation for Assigned Names and Numbers (ICANN). This is a non-profit-making corporation which assumed responsibility for Internet domain name system management in the late 1990s.
- World Wide Web Consortium. This is an international industry association involved in developing interoperable technologies for the Internet to reach its full potential as a communications medium and tool.

These bodies and others make up what could resemble an Internet executive. However, their operation is informal and highly dynamic. Their relationships with each other are ad hoc and quasi-democratic, and they rely on a mixture of commercial contracts, memoranda of understanding and other private arrangements.

So, as we begin our studies of the Internet and its legal consequences, we find relationships similar to those which have existed and operated in society for centuries, but with some wholly new characterisations and contexts. At the same time, we see institutions similar to those which have existed and operated in society for centuries, but which are not reinforced by a foundation in the sovereign nation state as we have come to expect. In this new combination we find a set of unprecedented challenges which provoke new ways of thinking about our new, global society. Faced with this complexity and uncertainty, and the embryonic nature of the field, students of 'Internet law' are likely to find more questions than answers as they progress through the materials in this book.

----

2 Nature of the Internet

The extract below is from the *Reno* decision's Statement of Fact which, in turn, reproduced a Stipulation the parties filed with the court. The court noted that '[t]he history and basic technology of this medium are not in dispute' and therefore there was no need for the court to add to the information set out below.

(a) The creation of the Internet and the development of cyberspace

---

American Civil Liberties Union, et al v Janet Reno, Attorney General of the United States

929 F Supp 824 (1996)

The United States District Court for the Eastern District of Pennsylvania,
Civil Action No 96-963, 11 June 1996

Available at <http://www.vtw.org/speech/decision.html> 30 August 2001

Sloviter CJ, Buckwalter and Dalzell JJ:

1   The Internet is not a physical or tangible entity, but rather a giant network which interconnects innumerable smaller groups of linked computer networks. It is thus a network of networks. This is best understood if one considers what a linked group of computers—referred to here as a 'network'—is, and what it does. Small networks are now ubiquitous (and are often called 'local area networks'). For example, in many United States Courthouses, computers are linked to each other for the purpose of exchanging files and messages (and to share equipment such as printers). These are networks.

2   Some networks are 'closed' networks, not linked to other computers or networks. Many networks, however, are connected to other networks, which are in turn connected to other networks in a manner which permits each computer in any network to communicate

with computers on any other network in the system. This global Web of linked networks and computers is referred to as the Internet.

3   The nature of the Internet is such that it is very difficult, if not impossible, to determine its size at a given moment. It is indisputable, however, that the Internet has experienced extraordinary growth in recent years. In 1981, fewer than 300 computers were linked to the Internet, and by 1989, the number stood at fewer than 90,000 computers. By 1993, over 1,000,000 computers were linked. Today, over 9,400,000 host computers worldwide, of which approximately 60 per cent are located within the United States, are estimated to be linked to the Internet. This count does not include the personal computers people use to access the Internet using modems. In all, reasonable estimates are that as many as 40 million people around the world can and do access the enormously flexible communication Internet medium. That figure is expected to grow to 200 million Internet users by the year 1999.

4   Some of the computers and computer networks that make up the Internet are owned by governmental and public institutions, some are owned by non-profit organizations, and some are privately owned. The resulting whole is a decentralized, global medium of communications—or 'cyberspace'—that links people, institutions, corporations, and governments around the world. The Internet is an international system. This communications medium allows any of the literally tens of millions of people with access to the Internet to exchange information. These communications can occur almost instantaneously, and can be directed either to specific individuals, to a broader group of people interested in a particular subject, or to the world as a whole.

5   The Internet had its origins in 1969 as an experimental project of the Advanced Research Project Agency ('ARPA'), and was called ARPANET. This network linked computers and computer networks owned by the military, defense contractors, and university laboratories conducting defense-related research. The network later allowed researchers across the country to access directly and to use extremely powerful supercomputers located at a few key universities and laboratories. As it evolved far beyond its research origins in the United States to encompass universities, corporations, and people around the world, the ARPANET came to be called the 'DARPA Internet', and finally just the 'Internet'.

6   From its inception, the network was designed to be a decentralized, self-maintaining series of redundant links between computers and computer networks, capable of rapidly transmitting communications without direct human involvement or control, and with the automatic ability to re-route communications if one or more individual links were damaged or otherwise unavailable. Among other goals, this redundant system of linked computers was designed to allow vital research and communications to continue even if portions of the network were damaged, say, in a war.

7   To achieve this resilient nationwide (and ultimately global) communications medium, the ARPANET encouraged the creation of multiple links to and from each computer (or computer network) on the network. Thus, a computer located in Washington, DC, might be linked (usually using dedicated telephone lines) to other computers in neighboring states or on the Eastern seaboard. Each of those computers could in turn be linked to other computers, which themselves would be linked to other computers.

8   A communication sent over this redundant series of linked computers could travel any of a number of routes to its destination. Thus, a message sent from a computer in Washington, DC, to a computer in Palo Alto, California, might first be sent to a computer in Philadelphia, and then be forwarded to a computer in Pittsburgh, and then to Chicago, Denver, and Salt Lake City, before finally reaching Palo Alto. If the message could not travel along that path (because of military attack, simple technical malfunction, or other reason), the message would automatically (without human intervention or even knowledge) be re-routed, perhaps, from Washington, DC to Richmond, and then to Atlanta, New Orleans, Dallas, Albuquerque, Los Angeles, and finally to Palo Alto. This type of transmission, and re-routing, would likely occur in a matter of seconds.

9   Messages between computers on the Internet do not necessarily travel entirely along the same path. The Internet uses 'packet switching' communication protocols that allow individual messages to be subdivided into smaller 'packets' that are then sent independently to the destination, and are then automatically reassembled by the receiving computer. While all packets of a given message often travel along the same path to the destination, if computers along the route become overloaded, then packets can be re-routed to less loaded computers.

10 At the same time that ARPANET was maturing (it subsequently ceased to exist), similar networks developed to link universities, research facilities, businesses, and individuals around the world. These other formal or loose networks included BITNET, CSNET, FIDONET, and USENET. Eventually, each of these networks (many of which overlapped) were themselves linked together, allowing users of any computers linked to any one of the networks to transmit communications to users of computers on other networks. It is this series of linked networks (themselves linking computers and computer networks) that is today commonly known as the Internet.

11 No single entity—academic, corporate, governmental, or non-profit—administers the Internet. It exists and functions as a result of the fact that hundreds of thousands of separate operators of computers and computer networks independently decided to use common data transfer protocols to exchange communications and information with other computers (which in turn exchange communications and information with still other computers). There is no centralized storage location, control point, or communications channel for the Internet, and it would not be technically feasible for a single entity to control all of the information conveyed on the Internet.

 NOTES AND QUESTIONS

1   The extract above highlights the central role of academic and non-commercial interests in the initial set-up period of the Internet. How have these interests been maintained as the Internet has grown in popularity? What aspects of this intellectual history are still apparent in the way the Internet operates today?

2   List some of the organisations that helped to develop the Internet. Explain what each of the acronyms, in the genealogy of the Internet, means. You may wish to examine section (d) below, which provides a discussion of the history of the

World Wide Web specifically. See also Matisse Enzer, 'Glossary of Internet Terms', available at <http://www.matisse.net/files/glossary.html> 17 August 2006 and Barry A Leiner et al, 'A Brief History of the Internet', available at <http://www.isoc.org/internet/history/brief.shtml> 17 August 2006.

3 Describe in detail the method by which individual e-mail messages are sent through the infrastructure of the Internet. Why might this particular method of transmission might be significant in a legal context?

(b) How individuals access the Internet

American Civil Liberties Union, et al v Janet Reno, Attorney General of the United States

929 F Supp 824 (1996)

The United States District Court for the Eastern District of Pennsylvania, Civil Action No 96-963, 11 June 1996

Available at <http://www.vtw.org/speech/decision.html> 30 August 2001

Sloviter CJ, Buckwalter and Dalzell JJ:

12 Individuals have a wide variety of avenues to access cyberspace in general, and the Internet in particular. In terms of physical access, there are two common methods to establish an actual link to the Internet. First, one can use a computer or computer terminal that is directly (and usually permanently) connected to a computer network that is itself directly or indirectly connected to the Internet. Second, one can use a 'personal computer' with a 'modem' to connect over a telephone line to a larger computer or computer network that is itself directly or indirectly connected to the Internet. As detailed below, both direct and modem connections are made available to people by a wide variety of academic, governmental, or commercial entities.

13 Students, faculty, researchers, and others affiliated with the vast majority of colleges and universities in the United States can access the Internet through their educational institutions. Such access is often via direct connection using computers located in campus libraries, offices, or computer centers, or may be through telephone access using a modem from a student's or professor's campus or off-campus location. Some colleges and universities install 'ports' or outlets for direct network connections in each dormitory room or provide access via computers located in common areas in dormitories. Such access enables students and professors to use information and content provided by the college or university itself, and to use the vast amount of research resources and other information available on the Internet worldwide.

14 Similarly, Internet resources and access are sufficiently important to many corporations and other employers that those employers link their office computer networks to the

Internet and provide employees with direct or modem access to the office network (and thus to the Internet). Such access might be used by, for example, a corporation involved in scientific or medical research or manufacturing to enable corporate employees to exchange information and ideas with academic researchers in their fields.

15 Those who lack access to the Internet through their schools or employers still have a variety of ways they can access the Internet. Many communities across the country have established 'free-nets' or community networks to provide their citizens with a local link to the Internet (and to provide local-oriented content and discussion groups). The first such community network, the Cleveland Free-Net Community Computer System, was established in 1986, and free-nets now exist in scores of communities as diverse as Richmond, Virginia; Tallahassee, Florida; Seattle, Washington; and San Diego, California. Individuals typically can access free-nets at little or no cost via modem connection or by using computers available in community buildings. Free-nets are often operated by a local library, educational institution, or non-profit community group.

16 Individuals can also access the Internet through many local libraries. Libraries often offer patrons use of computers that are linked to the Internet. In addition, some libraries offer telephone modem access to the libraries' computers, which are themselves connected to the Internet. Increasingly, patrons now use library services and resources without ever physically entering the library itself. Libraries typically provide such direct or modem access at no cost to the individual user.

17 Individuals can also access the Internet by patronizing an increasing number of storefront 'computer coffee shops', where customers—while they drink their coffee—can use computers provided by the shop to access the Internet. Such Internet access is typically provided by the shop for a small hourly fee.

18 Individuals can also access the Internet through commercial and non-commercial 'Internet service providers' that typically offer modem telephone access to a computer or computer network linked to the Internet. Many such providers—including the members of plaintiff Commercial Internet Exchange Association—are commercial entities offering Internet access for a monthly or hourly fee. Some Internet service providers, however, are non-profit organizations that offer free or very low cost access to the Internet. For example, the International Internet Association offers free modem access to the Internet upon request. Also, a number of trade or other non-profit associations offer Internet access as a service to members.

19 Another common way for individuals to access the Internet is through one of the major national commercial 'online services' such as America Online, CompuServe, the Microsoft Network, or Prodigy. These online services offer nationwide computer networks (so that subscribers can dial in to a local telephone number), and the services provide extensive and well-organized content within their own proprietary computer networks. In addition to allowing access to the extensive content available within each online service, the services also allow subscribers to link to the much larger resources of the Internet. Full

access to the online service (including access to the Internet) can be obtained for modest monthly or hourly fees. The major commercial online services have almost twelve million individual subscribers across the United States.

20 In addition to using the national commercial online services, individuals can also access the Internet using some (but not all) of the thousands of local dial-in computer services, often called 'bulletin board systems' or 'BBSs'. With an investment of as little as $2000 and the cost of a telephone line, individuals, non-profit organizations, advocacy groups, and businesses can offer their own dial-in computer 'bulletin board' service where friends, members, subscribers, or customers can exchange ideas and information. BBSs range from single computers with only one telephone line into the computer (allowing only one user at a time), to single computers with many telephone lines into the computer (allowing multiple simultaneous users), to multiple linked computers each servicing multiple dial-in telephone lines (allowing multiple simultaneous users). Some (but not all) of these BBS systems offer direct or indirect links to the Internet. Some BBS systems charge users a nominal fee for access, while many others are free to the individual users.

21 Although commercial access to the Internet is growing rapidly, many users of the Internet—such as college students and staff—do not individually pay for access (except to the extent, for example, that the cost of computer services is a component of college tuition). These and other Internet users can access the Internet without paying for such access with a credit card or other form of payment.

 NOTES AND QUESTIONS

1 Consider how different studying, at any level, has become since the advent of the Internet. How many of your friends and acquaintances do *not* have access to the Internet? How do you access the Internet? Since the decision in *ACLU v Reno*, the usage of modems has expanded beyond those described in that case to ADSL modems as well as cable modems and wireless. Free or paid wireless access can be found in places such as airports, libraries, universities, convention centres, hotels, and in some cafes and offices.

2 Do you think the Internet is likely to have as significant an impact upon non-Western, non-consumer cultures as it has upon ours?

3 Even within Western nations, and despite the grand predictions of its proponents, not all people can access the Internet. Might this result in another social dichotomy: those with and those without access? Are there implications to be drawn from this?

4 Find a comparison of uptake figures between the Internet and telephone, radio, television in the early years. Can you draw any conclusions from these comparisons? Do these conclusions alter the way you might answer question 3?

(c)   Methods of communicating over the Internet

American Civil Liberties Union, et al v Janet Reno, Attorney General of the United States

929 F Supp 824 (1996)

The United States District Court for the Eastern District of Pennsylvania,
Civil Action No 96-963, 11 June 1996

Available at <http://www.vtw.org/speech/decision.html> 30 August 2001

Sloviter CJ, Buckwalter and Dalzell JJ:

22   Once one has access to the Internet, there are a wide variety of different methods of communication and information exchange over the network. These many methods of communication and information retrieval are constantly evolving and are therefore difficult to categorize concisely. The most common methods of communications on the Internet (as well as within the major online services) can be roughly grouped into six categories:

(a)   one-to-one messaging (such as 'e-mail'),

(b)   one-to-many messaging (such as 'listserv'),

(c)   distributed message databases (such as 'USENET newsgroups'),

(d)   real time communication (such as 'Internet Relay Chat'),

(e)   real time remote computer utilization (such as 'telnet'), and

(f)   remote information retrieval (such as 'ftp', 'gopher', and the 'World Wide Web').

Most of these methods of communication can be used to transmit text, data, computer programs, sound, visual images (ie pictures), and moving video images.

23   One-to-one messaging. One method of communication on the Internet is via electronic mail, or 'e-mail', comparable in principle to sending a first class letter. One can address and transmit a message to one or more other people. E-mail on the Internet is not routed through a central control point, and can take many and varying paths to the recipients. Unlike postal mail, simple e-mail generally is not 'sealed' or secure, and can be accessed or viewed on intermediate computers between the sender and recipient (unless the message is encrypted).

24   One-to-many messaging. The Internet also contains automatic mailing list services (such as 'listservs'), [also referred to by witnesses as 'mail exploders'] that allow communications about particular subjects of interest to a group of people. For example, people can subscribe to a 'listserv' mailing list on a particular topic of interest to them. The subscriber can submit messages on the topic to the listserv that are forwarded (via e-mail), either automatically or through a human moderator overseeing the listserv, to anyone who has subscribed to the mailing list. A recipient of such a message can reply to the message and have the reply also distributed to everyone on the mailing list. This service provides the capability to keep abreast of developments or events in a particular subject area. Most listserv-type mailing lists automatically forward all incoming messages to all mailing

list subscribers. There are thousands of such mailing list services on the Internet, collectively with hundreds of thousands of subscribers. Users of 'open' listservs typically can add or remove their names from the mailing list automatically, with no direct human involvement. Listservs may also be 'closed,' ie, only allowing for one's acceptance into the listserv by a human moderator.

25 Distributed message databases. Similar in function to listservs—but quite different in how communications are transmitted—are distributed message databases such as 'USENET newsgroups'. User-sponsored newsgroups are among the most popular and widespread applications of Internet services, and cover all imaginable topics of interest to users. Like listservs, newsgroups are open discussions and exchanges on particular topics. Users, however, need not subscribe to the discussion mailing list in advance, but can instead access the database at any time. Some USENET newsgroups are 'moderated' but most are open access. For the moderated newsgroups, all messages to the newsgroup are forwarded to one person who can screen them for relevance to the topics under discussion. USENET newsgroups are disseminated using ad hoc, peer to peer connections between approximately 200,000 computers (called USENET 'servers') around the world. For unmoderated newsgroups, when an individual user with access to a USENET server posts a message to a newsgroup, the message is automatically forwarded to all adjacent USENET servers that furnish access to the newsgroup, and it is then propagated to the servers adjacent to those servers, etc. The messages are temporarily stored on each receiving server, where they are available for review and response by individual users. The messages are automatically and periodically purged from each system after a time to make room for new messages. Responses to messages, like the original messages, are automatically distributed to all other computers receiving the newsgroup or forwarded to a moderator in the case of a moderated newsgroup. The dissemination of messages to USENET servers around the world is an automated process that does not require direct human intervention or review.

26 There are newsgroups on more than fifteen thousand different subjects. In 1994, approximately 70,000 messages were posted to newsgroups each day, and those messages were distributed to the approximately 190,000 computers or computer networks that participate in the USENET newsgroup system. Once the messages reach the approximately 190,000 receiving computers or computer networks, they are available to individual users of those computers or computer networks. Collectively, almost 100,000 new messages (or 'articles') are posted to newsgroups each day.

27 Real time communication. In addition to transmitting messages that can be later read or accessed, individuals on the Internet can engage in an immediate dialogue, in 'real time', with other people on the Internet. In its simplest forms, 'talk' allows one-to-one communications and 'Internet Relay Chat' (or IRC) allows two or more to type messages to each other that almost immediately appear on the others' computer screens. IRC is analogous to a telephone party line, using a computer and keyboard rather than a telephone. With IRC, however, at any one time there are thousands of different party lines available, in which collectively tens of thousands of users are engaging in conversations on a huge range of subjects. Moreover, one can create a new party line to discuss a different topic at any time. Some IRC conversations are 'moderated' or include 'channel operators'.

28 In addition, commercial online services such as America Online, CompuServe, the Microsoft Network, and Prodigy have their own 'chat' systems allowing their members to converse.

29 Real time remote computer utilization. Another method to use information on the Internet is to access and control remote computers in 'real time' using 'telnet'. For example, using telnet, a researcher at a university would be able to use the computing power of a supercomputer located at a different university. A student can use telnet to connect to a remote library to access the library's online card catalog program.

30 Remote information retrieval. The final major category of communication may be the most well-known use of the Internet—the search for and retrieval of information located on remote computers. There are three primary methods to locate and retrieve information on the Internet.

31 A simple method uses 'ftp' (or file transfer protocol) to list the names of computer files available on a remote computer, and to transfer one or more of those files to an individual's local computer.

32 Another approach uses a program and format named 'gopher' to guide an individual's search through the resources available on a remote computer.

 ## NOTES AND QUESTIONS

1 Describe, in your own words, the various forms of communications available on the Internet. Which of these are real-time communications?

2 Can you think of circumstances where each of these separate forms of communications would be the best form of communication? If so, outline why each particular option is superior in each instance. Can you draw conclusions regarding the flexibility of the Internet from these investigations?

3 *ACLU v Reno* listed the following services and methods of communicating on the internet: email; listserv; USENET newsgroups; Internet Relay Chat; telnet; remote information retrieval (ftp, 'gopher', and the World Wide Web). Notes 4–8 describe other services that can now be identified.

4 A peer-to-peer (or P2P) computer network is a network that utilises the computing power and bandwidth of the users in the network, each generally regarded as a 'peer'. The participants on the network support roughly equivalent capabilities. This is in contrast to client–server networking, where the server has the responsibility for providing or 'serving' network information and the client consumes or otherwise act as 'clients' of those servers. In a P2P network, each peer acts as a client and as a server. In a pure P2P network, there is no central server managing the network and there is no central router.

5 In hybrid P2P networks, a central server maintains information on peers and responds to requests for such information. The peers are still responsible for hosting the information and for informing the central server of what files and resources are available for sharing and downloading.

6 Some P2P networks use stronger peers called 'super-peers' or 'super-nodes' as servers; client peers are then connected to a single super-peer. See further

<http://en.wikipedia.org/wiki/Peer_to_peer>. P2P networks will be further considered in Chapter 9.

7   Voice over Internet Protocol (VoIP) enables calls to be made over the Internet. Some services using VoIP work only between users of the same service; others enable calls to be made to anyone who has a standard telephone number. Some VoIP systems use a computer, while others use a special VoIP phone. Some systems can even use a traditional phone with an adaptor.[2]

8   Instant messaging (IM) is a modern form of the traditional UNIX 'talk' messaging system that allows instant communication between two or more people over the Internet in real time. Each IM service requires the user to have specific IM software to communicate with other users of that same IM service, who must also be logged on at the same time.

(d)   The World Wide Web

American Civil Liberties Union, et al v Janet Reno, Attorney General of the United States

929 F Supp 824 (1996)

The United States District Court for the Eastern District of Pennsylvania,
Civil Action No 96-963, 11 June 1996

Available at <http://www.vtw.org/speech/decision.html> 30 August 2001

Sloviter CJ, Buckwalter and Dalzell JJ:

33 A third approach, and fast becoming the most well-known on the Internet, is the 'World Wide Web'. The Web utilizes a 'hypertext' formatting language called hypertext markup language (HTML), and programs that 'browse' the Web can display HTML documents containing text, images, sound, animation and moving video. Any HTML document can include links to other types of information or resources, so that while viewing an HTML document that, for example, describes resources available on the Internet, one can 'click' using a computer mouse on the description of the resource and be immediately connected to the resource itself. Such 'hyperlinks' allow information to be accessed and organized in very flexible ways, and allow people to locate and efficiently view related information even if the information is stored on numerous computers all around the world.

34 Purpose. The World Wide Web (W3C) was created to serve as the platform for a global, online store of knowledge, containing information from a diversity of sources and accessible to Internet users around the world. Though information on the Web is contained in individual computers, the fact that each of these computers is connected to the

---

2   See further the US Federal Communications Commission <http://www.fcc.gov/voip/>.

Internet through W3C protocols allows all of the information to become part of a single body of knowledge. It is currently the most advanced information system developed on the Internet, and embraces within its data model most information in previous networked information systems such as ftp, gopher, wais, and Usenet.

35 History. W3C was originally developed at CERN, the European Particle Physics Laboratory, and was initially used to allow information sharing within internationally dispersed teams of researchers and engineers. Originally aimed at the High Energy Physics community, it has spread to other areas and attracted much interest in user support, resource recovery, and many other areas which depend on collaborative and information sharing. The Web has extended beyond the scientific and academic community to include communications by individuals, non-profit organizations, and businesses.

36 Basic Operation. The World Wide Web is a series of documents stored in different computers all over the Internet. Documents contain information stored in a variety of formats, including text, still images, sounds, and video. An essential element of the Web is that any document has an address (rather like a telephone number). Most Web documents contain 'links'. These are short sections of text or image which refer to another document. Typically the linked text is blue or underlined when displayed, and when selected by the user, the referenced document is automatically displayed, wherever in the world it actually is stored. Links for example are used to lead from overview documents to more detailed documents, from tables of contents to particular pages, but also as cross-references, footnotes, and new forms of information structure.

37 Many organizations now have 'home pages' on the Web. These are documents which provide a set of links designed to represent the organization, and through links from the home page, guide the user directly or indirectly to information about or relevant to that organization.

38 As an example of the use of links, if these Findings were to be put on a World Wide Web site, its home page might contain links such as these:

- The nature of cyberspace
- Creation of the Internet and the development of cyberspace
- How people access the Internet
- Methods to communicate over the Internet

39 Each of these links takes the user of the site from the beginning of the Findings to the appropriate section within this Adjudication. Links may also take the user from the original web site to another web site on another computer connected to the Internet. These links from one computer to another, from one document to another across the Internet, are what unify the Web into a single body of knowledge, and what makes the Web unique. The Web was designed with a maximum target time to follow a link of one-tenth of a second.

40 Publishing. The World Wide Web exists fundamentally as a platform through which people and organizations can communicate through shared information. When information is made available, it is said to be 'published' on the Web. Publishing on the Web simply requires that the 'publisher' has a computer connected to the Internet and that the computer is running W3C server software. The computer can be as simple as a small

personal computer costing less than $1500 or as complex as a multimillion-dollar mainframe computer. Many Web publishers choose instead to lease disk storage space from someone else who has the necessary computer facilities, eliminating the need for actually owning any equipment oneself.

41 The Web, as a universe of network accessible information, contains a variety of documents prepared with quite varying degrees of care, from the hastily typed idea, to the professionally executed corporate profile. The power of the Web stems from the ability of a link to point to any document, regardless of its status or physical location.

42 Information to be published on the Web must also be formatted according to the rules of the Web standards. These standardized formats assure that all Web users who want to read the material will be able to view it. Web standards are sophisticated and flexible enough that they have grown to meet the publishing needs of many large corporations, banks, brokerage houses, newspapers and magazines which now publish 'online' editions of their material, as well as government agencies, and even courts, which use the Web to disseminate information to the public. At the same time, Web publishing is simple enough that thousands of individual users and small community organizations are using the Web to publish their own personal 'home pages', the equivalent of individualized newsletters about that person or organization, which are available to everyone on the Web.

43 Web publishers have a choice to make their web sites open to the general pool of all Internet users, or close them, thus making the information accessible only to those with advance authorization. Many publishers choose to keep their sites open to all in order to give their information the widest potential audience. In the event that the publishers choose to maintain restrictions on access, this may be accomplished by assigning specific user names and passwords as a prerequisite to access to the site. Or, in the case of web sites maintained for internal use of one organization, access will only be allowed from other computers within that organization's local network.

44 Searching the Web. A variety of systems have developed that allow users of the Web to search particular information among all of the public sites that are part of the Web. Services such as Yahoo, Magellan, Altavista, Webcrawler, and Lycos are all services known as 'search engines' which allow users to search for web sites that contain certain categories of information, or to search for key words. For example, a Web user looking for the text of Supreme Court opinions would type the words 'Supreme Court' into a search engine, and then be presented with a list of World Wide Web sites that contain Supreme Court information. This list would actually be a series of links to those sites. Having searched out a number of sites that might contain the desired information, the user would then follow individual links, browsing through the information on each site, until the desired material is found. For many content providers on the Web, the ability to be found by these search engines is very important.

45 Common standards. The Web links together disparate information on an ever-growing number of Internet-linked computers by setting common information storage formats (HTML) and a common language for the exchange of Web documents (HTTP). Although the information itself may be in many different formats, and stored on computers which are not otherwise compatible, the basic Web standards provide a basic set of standards

which allow communication and exchange of information. Despite the fact that many types of computers are used on the Web, and the fact that many of these machines are otherwise incompatible, those who 'publish' information on the Web are able to communicate with those who seek to access information with little difficulty because of these basic technical standards.

46 A distributed system with no centralized control. Running on tens of thousands of individual computers on the Internet, the Web is what is known as a distributed system. The Web was designed so that organizations with computers containing information can become part of the Web simply by attaching their computers to the Internet and running appropriate World Wide Web software. No single organization controls any membership in the Web, nor is there any single centralized point from which individual web sites or services can be blocked from the Web. From a user's perspective, it may appear to be a single, integrated system, but in reality it has no centralized control point.

47 Contrast to closed databases. The Web's open, distributed, decentralized nature stands in sharp contrast to most information systems that have come before it. Private information services such as Westlaw, Lexis/Nexis, and Dialog, have contained large storehouses of knowledge, and can be accessed from the Internet with the appropriate passwords and access software. However, these databases are not linked together into a single whole, as is the World Wide Web.

48 Success of the Web in research, education, and political activities. The World Wide Web has become so popular because of its open, distributed, and easy-to-use nature. Rather than requiring those who seek information to purchase new software or hardware, and to learn a new kind of system for each new database of information they seek to access, the Web environment makes it easy for users to jump from one set of information to another. By the same token, the open nature of the Web makes it easy for publishers to reach their intended audiences without having to know in advance what kind of computer each potential reader has, and what kind of software they will be using.

 NOTES AND QUESTIONS

1 How important has the Internet been, and how important will it be, in shaping the future of the dissemination of information and ideas? Can you think of any historical parallels to this particular (r)evolution in information? How has the World Wide Web contributed to this?

2 Explain the role and importance of hyperlinks to publishing on the Internet.

3 Is the random, non-linear, and non-hierarchical system of hyperlinks more conducive to learning and searching than, say, the ordered and hierarchical method employed in libraries? Why or why not? See also the special issue of the *Akron Law Review,* Volume 30 (Winter 1996) which discusses aspects of print and web-based law reviews.

(e) Restricting access to unwanted on-line material

American Civil Liberties Union, et al v Janet Reno, Attorney General of the United States

929 F Supp 824 (1996)

The United States District Court for the Eastern District of Pennsylvania,
Civil Action No 96-963, 11 June 1996

Available at <http://www.vtw.org/speech/decision.html> 30 August 2001

Sloviter CJ, Buckwalter and Dalzell JJ:

49 With the rapid growth of the Internet, the increasing popularity of the Web, and the existence of material online that some parents may consider inappropriate for their children, various entities have begun to build systems intended to enable parents to control the material which comes into their homes and may be accessible to their children. The World Wide Web Consortium launched the PICS ('Platform for Internet Content Selection') program in order to develop technical standards that would support parents' ability to filter and screen material that their children see on the Web ...

 NOTES AND QUESTIONS

The issue of content regulation is perhaps the most controversial and well-publicised of all the issues surrounding the rise of the Internet. As such, it is an issue which extends far beyond the mere introductory context of the present extract. For present purposes, the 'Notes and questions' following section (f) below provide an adequate introduction to issues that will be revisited later in the book.

(f) Content on the Internet

American Civil Liberties Union, et al v Janet Reno, Attorney General of the United States

929 F Supp 824 (1996)

The United States District Court for the Eastern District of Pennsylvania, Civil Action No 96-963, 11 June 1996

Available at <http://www.vtw.org/speech/decision.html> 30 August 2001

Sloviter CJ, Buckwalter and Dalzell JJ:

74 The types of content now on the Internet defy easy classification. The entire card catalogue of the Carnegie Library is online, together with journals, journal abstracts, popular magazines, and titles of compact discs. The director of the Carnegie Library, Robert Croneberger, testified that online services are the emerging trend in libraries generally. Plaintiff Hotwired Ventures LLC organizes its web site into information regarding travel, news and commentary, arts and entertainment, politics, and types of drinks. Plaintiff America Online, Inc, not only creates chat rooms for a broad variety of topics, but also allows members to create their own chat rooms to suit their own tastes. The ACLU uses an America Online chat room as an unmoderated forum for people to debate civil liberties issues. Plaintiffs' expert Scott Bradner estimated that 15,000 newsgroups exist today, and he described his own interest in a newsgroup devoted solely to Formula 1 racing cars. America Online makes 15,000 bulletin boards available to its subscribers, who post between 200,000 and 250,000 messages each day. Another plaintiffs' expert, Harold Rheingold, participates in 'virtual communities' that simulate social interaction. It is no exaggeration to conclude that the content on the Internet is as diverse as human thought.

75 The Internet is not exclusively, or even primarily, a means of commercial communication. Many commercial entities maintain web sites to inform potential consumers about their goods and services, or to solicit purchases, but many other web sites exist solely for the dissemination of non-commercial information. The other forms of Internet communication—e-mail, bulletin boards, newsgroups, and chat rooms—frequently have non-commercial goals. For the economic and technical reasons set forth in the following paragraphs, the Internet is an especially attractive means for not-for-profit entities or public interest groups to reach their desired audiences. There are examples in the parties' stipulation of some of the non-commercial uses that the Internet serves. Plaintiff Human Rights Watch, Inc offers information on its Internet site regarding reported human rights abuses around the world. Plaintiff National Writers Union provides a forum for writers on issues of concern to them. Plaintiff Stop Prisoner Rape, Inc posts text, graphics, and statistics regarding the incidence and prevention of rape in prisons. Plaintiff Critical Path AIDS Project, Inc offers information on safer sex, the transmission of HIV, and the treatment of AIDS.

76 Such diversity of content on the Internet is possible because the Internet provides an easy and inexpensive way for a speaker to reach a large audience, potentially of millions. The start-up and operating costs entailed by communication on the Internet are significantly lower than those associated with use of other forms of mass communication, such as television, radio, newspapers, and magazines. This enables operation of their own web sites not only by large companies, such as Microsoft and Time Warner, but also by small, not-for-profit groups, such as Stop Prisoner Rape and Critical Path AIDS Project. The Government's expert, Dr Dan R Olsen, agreed that creation of a web site would cost between $1000 and $15,000, with monthly operating costs depending on one's goals and the web site's traffic. Commercial online services such as America Online allow subscribers to create Web pages free of charge. Any Internet user can communicate by posting a message to one of the thousands of newsgroups and bulletin boards or by

engaging in an online 'chat', and thereby reach an audience worldwide that shares an interest in a particular topic.

77 The ease of communication through the Internet is facilitated by the use of hypertext markup language (HTML), which allows for the creation of 'hyperlinks' or 'links'. HTML enables a user to jump from one source to other related sources by clicking on the link. A link might take the user from web site to web site, or to other files within a particular web site. Similarly, by typing a request into a search engine, a user can retrieve many different sources of content related to the search that the creators of the engine have collected.

78 Because of the technology underlying the Internet, the statutory term 'content provider', which is equivalent to the traditional 'speaker', may actually be a hybrid of speakers. Through the use of HTML, for example, Critical Path and Stop Prisoner Rape link their web sites to several related databases, and a user can immediately jump from the home pages of these organizations to the related databases simply by clicking on a link. America Online creates chat rooms for particular discussions but also allows subscribers to create their own chat rooms. Similarly, a newsgroup gathers postings on a particular topic and distributes them to the newsgroup's subscribers. Users of the Carnegie Library can read online versions of *Vanity Fair* and *Playboy*, and America Online's subscribers can peruse *The New York Times*, *Boating*, and other periodicals. Critical Path, Stop Prisoner Rape, America Online and the Carnegie Library all make available content of other speakers over whom they have little or no editorial control.

79 Because of the different forms of Internet communication, a user of the Internet may speak or listen interchangeably, blurring the distinction between 'speakers' and 'listeners' on the Internet. Chat rooms, e-mail, and newsgroups are interactive forms of communication, providing the user with the opportunity both to speak and to listen.

80 It follows that unlike traditional media, the barriers to entry as a speaker on the Internet do not differ significantly from the barriers to entry as a listener. Once one has entered cyberspace, one may engage in the dialogue that occurs there. In the argot of the medium, the receiver can and does become the content provider, and vice versa.

81 The Internet is therefore a unique and wholly new medium of worldwide human communication.

 NOTES AND QUESTIONS

1 Explain some of the arguments for and against the regulation of Internet content. In particular you might note the role of American intellectual traditions in the philosophical frameworks of the Internet.

2 Can you foresee any practical or logistical problems arising from calls to regulate Internet content?

Now that we have considered the basic workings of the Internet, there are a number of general points worth considering. The following questions deal with issues that will be revisited throughout this book. Their presence here is designed to stimulate the reader to consider the implications prior to reading about them. This, it is hoped, will aid understanding and facilitate a deeper contemplation of the issues as they arise.

3　Can you conceptualise the Internet in terms of any other communication tools? How credible are claims that it is entirely novel and unprecedented? If it cannot be described in terms of what has come before it, what do you think would be the best approach to providing the legal or social institutions required to regulate and support it?

4　Can you think of a list of 'harms' that might be perpetrated using the Internet? They might be financial, criminal, personal, or even military.

Innovation presents opportunities to reconsider our methods and ideas in other realms, and sometimes demands that we do so. Such a flow-on can be seen in terms of the Internet's implications for the concept of jurisdiction. The issues involved here will be discussed in more detail in subsequent chapters. For present purposes, consider the following questions in order to begin your musings.

5　Given the description of the Internet, and particularly the World Wide Web, in the extract above, what problems do you foresee in countering the harms that might be perpetrated by means of the Internet?

6　In the longer term, which method of institution-building—for example, stretching existing law or creating an entirely new field—do you think might best tackle the problems we face?

7　Can you provide a brief definition of jurisdiction? What does the concept encompass? How significant is it in the matrix of the Western legal tradition? How significant, then, are the challenges to it?

Jurisdiction

----

1   Introduction

As we saw in Chapter 1, materials posted on the World Wide Web can be accessed by anyone in the world even though it is physically hosted in only one place. Content can also be easily moved from one place to another and content can be hosted in one place and directed to users in another place. Parts of a website can be hosted in one jurisdiction while other parts are hosted in another jurisdiction. This chapter examines the concept of jurisdiction as it applies to the Internet. Questions of jurisdiction are extremely complex even before the added challenges of the Internet are considered. Notions of jurisdiction are territorially based and they are difficult to translate to the Internet. In many ways, to speak simply of the 'jurisdiction' problem is to oversimplify matters. The word 'jurisdiction' means many things to many people. The following is a non-exhaustive list of concepts which come under this umbrella term:

- power to legislate;
- ability to validly serve a defendant with notice of proceedings;
- power to hear;
- power to adjudicate;
- subject-matter jurisdiction;
- personal jurisdiction;
- forum conveniens or forum non conveniens;
- governing law or choice of law; and
- enforcement of judgments.

To complicate matters further, once we have identified the component parts of the jurisdictional matrix, it must be noted that different legal systems have different rules regarding the interrelationships of these parts. For example, under Australian (and British) law, personal jurisdiction depends largely on the valid service on the defendant. If the defendant cannot be validly served with notice of proceedings, there can be no proceedings. Of course, there are rules and exceptions regarding even this most basic threshold issue. And the rules and exceptions continue throughout the process and across all legal systems. It is not the intention here to attempt an analysis of jurisdiction, which could easily be found in a conflict of laws text. Readers are encouraged to read widely in this area if they intend to pursue these concepts further. The extract below outlines, from an American perspective, the basic structure of the jurisdictional matrix.

Throughout any reading on this subject, the reader should be keenly aware of the differences between jurisdictional matters within a nation and international jurisdictional matters. The two may produce similar discourse; however, there are subtle and important differences which cannot be ignored. The following extract provides an introduction to some of the more important parts of the matrix, as they relate to the Internet.

David G Post, 'Personal Jurisdiction on the Internet: An Outline for the Perplexed'

Temple University Law School/Cyberspace Law Institute, June 1998

Available at <http://www.temple.edu/lawschool/dpost/outline.htm> 28 August 2001

To understand what courts and commentators are saying about the rules regarding the scope of courts' 'personal jurisdiction' over participants in Internet transactions requires (unfortunately, perhaps) disentangling a number of closely related and oft-commingled legal doctrines, all of which speak to the same, fundamental question: What is the scope (and derivation) of a court's power to hear particular disputes and to compel the individuals involved to obey its commands? To illustrate, consider the prototypical civil lawsuit:

> Alice, a resident of Place 1, has suffered some injury to person or property. She believes that, under the law of Place 2, she is entitled to some form of compensation from Bob, a resident of Place 3, for this injury. Alice files suit against Bob in Place 4, asking the court in Place 4 to compel Bob to deliver that compensation.

Place 1 through Place 4 might, for example, be different countries, or different States within the United States, or different counties within a particular State. Regardless, the question Alice must ask herself—can the court do what she wants it to do, viz compel Bob to compensate her for the injury she has suffered?—is generally broken down into the following components:

- *Personal jurisdiction.* Personal jurisdiction refers to the Place 4 court's ability to exercise dominion over the parties to this lawsuit so that it can compel their obedience to its judgment in the case. Our legal system (and most others) recognize certain limitations on any court's power to compel defendants to appear and defend themselves. It is a fundamental principle of United States law that a court cannot validly act if it does not have personal jurisdiction over the parties to the suit. If the court in Place 4 cannot, in accordance with these various limitations, exercise personal jurisdiction over Bob, it must dismiss Alice's lawsuit; if it nonetheless goes ahead and hears the case and issues a judgment, that judgment is *not* entitled to respect by other courts elsewhere.

- *Subject matter jurisdiction.* Courts are not only restricted in terms of the persons over whom they can exercise power, they may be restricted in terms of the kinds of disputes that they can adjudicate. Courts are creatures of statute—the legislature vests them with power, and may condition that grant of power on their ability to hear only certain kinds of disputes. The US federal courts, for example, have had their subject matter jurisdiction limited in this way; the Constitution, in Article III Section 2 clause 1, provides that federal courts can only hear a specified range of cases, most importantly those (a) 'arising under this Constitution, the Laws of the United States, and Treaties made', and (b) 'between Citizens of different States'. Similarly, many States have specialized courts (traffic court, small claims court, etc) along with courts of so-called 'general jurisdiction' empowered to hear all lawful claims.

  As is the case for personal jurisdiction, subject matter jurisdiction is necessary for a court to act in a valid manner; courts that do not have subject matter jurisdiction over the particular dispute brought to it must dismiss such claims when they are presented before it. Thus, even if our Place 4 court possesses personal jurisdiction over Bob, it may not be able to grant Alice the relief she seeks because it may lack subject matter jurisdiction over the claim that Alice has made; if Alice's claim arises under, say, the law of defamation and she has filed suit in Newark traffic court, the court must dismiss the suit, inasmuch as the legislative grant of authority covered only certain matters (traffic disputes) and no others.

- *Venue.* Even if the court that Alice has chosen can exercise personal jurisdiction over Bob and has subject matter jurisdiction over Alice's claim, it may be the 'wrong' forum because of additional restrictions imposed on precisely where Alice needs to file her lawsuit—so-called 'venue' rules. These are, generally speaking, designed to protect defendants against being sued in 'inconvenient' places. Thus, the law of Place 4 may provide that lawsuits of the kind Alice has brought can only be heard in the court of the county in which Bob resides, or the county in which the events giving rise to the injury occurred.

Venue rules are not 'fundamental' in the same way that rules regarding personal jurisdiction and subject matter jurisdiction are; that is, while a court is directed not to hear cases brought in the wrong venue (and, generally, is directed to transfer the suit to the correct venue), judgments issued in such cases are not considered null and void in the way that judgments issued in cases where the court lacked jurisdiction are.

- *Choice of law.* If (and only if) the court that Alice has chosen determines (a) that it can exercise personal jurisdiction over Bob, (b) that it possesses subject matter jurisdiction over Alice's claim, and (c) that it is a proper forum under the venue rules governing such claims, it must then decide what body of law to apply to the dispute—the so-called 'choice of law' problem. There may be a number of plausible candidates—the law where Alice lives, where Bob lives, where the court sits, the transaction that is the basis of Alice's claim arose, etc. Alice, as noted, believes that she is entitled to relief under the substantive law of Place 2; she now needs to persuade the court in Place 4 that, under its own choice of law rules and principles, it should apply the law of Place 2 to the dispute she has brought to it.

- *Enforcement of judgments.* Finally, if Alice has obtained a judgment against Bob (for money damages, say), she then will enlist the support of the Place 4 court in enforcing her judgment against Bob. This may be a complex undertaking if, for example, neither Bob nor his assets are physically located within the boundaries of Place 4. In that case, Alice may need to take evidence of her favorable judgment to a different jurisdiction—one where Bob has assets, for example—and seek to have that jurisdiction honor the judgment she has obtained and enforce it against those assets.

In the United States federal system, this problem is dealt with by the 'full faith and credit clause' of the Constitution; each State, in other words, is bound to respect and enforce judgments duly entered by courts in other States (unless the party against whom enforcement is sought (Bob) can demonstrate that the original judgment is somehow infirm, because, for example, the court issuing it lacked either personal jurisdiction over Bob or subject matter jurisdiction over Alice's claim). Internationally, however, things are considerably more complicated; there is nothing equivalent to a 'full faith and credit clause' applicable to relations between sovereign nations, and while some countries have bilateral treaties obligating them to reciprocally honor each other's judgments, more frequently this problem is dealt with by reference to principles of international 'comity' [which Perritt describes in the following terms]: 'A valid judgment rendered in a foreign nation after a fair trial in a contested proceeding will be recognized in the United States so far as the immediate parties and the underlying cause of action are concerned'.

 NOTES AND QUESTIONS

1   Does the applicable law have to be the law of the venue?

2   Can judgments be enforced in jurisdictions other than the venue?

3   What is the difference between personal and subject-matter jurisdiction?

4   The concept of jurisdiction may well be easily subdivided into distinct component parts within the confines of academia; however, once we enter the courtroom,

the judge has a range of other factors to consider. The cases discussed below highlight these added complexities.

----

2   United States case law

The cases extracted and discussed in this chapter illustrate the difficulties courts have in transferring the theoretical doctrines on jurisdiction into coherent jurisprudence relating to the Internet. The following case is one of an increasing body of US case law tackling the challenges of the Internet. The reader should compare the extract with the cases discussed in the Notes and Questions in order to appreciate the spectrum of judicial reaction.

(a)   *People v World Interactive Gaming Corporation*

The People of the State of New York v World Interactive Gaming Corporation

714 NYS 2d 844 (NY County Sup Ct 1999)

Supreme Court of the State of New York, County of New York: Commercial Part 53
Index No 404428/98

Available at <http://www.courts.state.ny.us/nycdlr/issue2-4/Internet.htm> 4 August 2001

Charles Edward Ramos, JSC:
This proceeding is brought by the Attorney General of the State of New York (the 'Attorney General' or the 'State of New York'), pursuant to New York's Executive Law s 63(12) and General Business Law Article 23-A, to enjoin the respondents, World Interactive Gaming Corporation ('WIGC'), Golden Chips Casino, Inc ('GCC'), and their principals, officers, and directors from operating within or offering to residents of the State of New York State gambling over the Internet. The State also seeks to enjoin respondents from selling unregistered securities in violation of New York State's General Business Law s 352 (also known as 'The Martin Act').

The central issue here is whether the State of New York can enjoin a foreign corporation legally licensed to operate a casino offshore from offering gambling to Internet users in New York. At issue is Section 9(1), Article 1 of the New York State Constitution which contains an express prohibition against any kind of gambling not authorized by the state legislature. The prohibition represents a deep-rooted policy of the state against unauthorized gambling (*Intercontinental Hotel Corp v Golden* 18 AD 2d 45 [1st Dept 1963]; revd on other grounds, 15 NY 2d 9 [1964]).

WIGC is a Delaware corporation that maintains corporate offices in New York. WIGC wholly owns GCC, an Antiguan subsidiary corporation which acquired a license from the government of Antigua to operate a land-based casino. Through contracts executed by WIGC, GCC developed interactive software, and purchased computer servers which were installed in Antigua to allow users around the world to gamble from their home computers. GCC promoted its casino at its web site, advertised on the Internet and in a national gambling magazine. The promotion was targeted nationally and was viewed by New York residents.

In February 1998, the Attorney General commenced an investigation into the practices of WIGC. The investigation was prompted by an inquiry from the Texas State Securities Board which informed the Attorney General that WIGC was making unsolicited telephone calls to the public and disseminating offering materials for WIGC's securities. The petition alleges that respondents were attempting to sell what they termed a 'private subscription offering', which consisted of 700,000 shares of 'convertible preferred stock' at a price of $5.00 per share. The respondent's primary method of selling units of WIGC stock involved cold-calling prospective investors. The prospective investors were located throughout the United States, including New York. Respondents do not dispute that the calls originated from WIGC's headquarters in Bohemia, New York. At no time was this offering or the cold-callers registered with New York state as required by law.

During telephone solicitation, respondents claimed that investors would earn twenty per cent (20%) annual dividend on their investment, twenty-five per cent (25%) profit sharing and an initial public offering ('IPO') of WIGC's stock, which would likely take place within one year. Respondents also compared WIGC's projected stock price and earnings to that of land-based casinos. Respondents represented the profit margins of other Internet casinos at around eighty to eighty-five per cent (80–85%). Respondents told investors that WIGC would earn an estimate of up to $100,000 in revenue during the first year. Respondents claimed that the investment was conservative.

Together, respondents sold approximately $1,843,665 worth of shares to approximately 114 investors throughout the country, including approximately $125,000 worth of shares to 10 New York state residents.

In June 1998, the Attorney General furthered its investigation by logging onto respondents' web site, downloading the gambling software, and in July 1998, placed the first of several bets. Users who wished to gamble in the GCC Internet casino were directed to wire money to open a bank account in Antigua and download additional software from GCC's web site. In opening an account, users were asked to enter their permanent address. A user which submitted a permanent address in a state that permitted land-based gambling, such as Nevada, was granted permission to gamble. Although a user which entered a state such as New York, which does not permit land-based gambling, was denied permission to gamble. [B]ecause the software does not verify the user's actual location, a user initially denied access could easily circumvent the denial by changing the state entered to that of Nevada, while remaining physically in New York State. The user could then log onto the GCC casino and play virtual slots, blackjack or roulette. This raises the question if this constitutes a good faith effort not to engage in gambling in New York.

The Attorney General commenced this action pursuant to Executive Law s 63(12) and General Business Law Article 23-A. Petitioner seeks: (1) to enjoin respondents from conducting a business within the State of New York until they are properly registered with the Secretary of State to conduct business in New York; (2) to enjoin respondents from running any aspect of their Internet gambling Business within the State of New York; (3) to be awarded restitution and damages to injured investors; and (4) to be awarded penalties and costs to the State of New York for violations of New York State's Securities Law (GBL s 352, also known as 'The Martin Act'), federal and state laws prohibiting gambling, and New York State's Executive Law.

Respondents move to dismiss the petition on the grounds that (1) the Attorney General lacks the authority to bring a proceeding under Executive Law s 63(12), where a pattern of repeated or persistent fraud or illegal conduct is absent; (2) lack of personal jurisdiction over WIGC and GCC; and (3) lack of subject matter jurisdiction to prosecute alleged violations of the *Federal Interstate Wire Act* 18 USC s 1084(a) ('The Wire Act'), the *Interstate and Foreign Travel or Transportation in Aid of Racketeering Enterprising Act* 18 USC s 1952 ('The Travel Act'), and the *Wagering and Paraphernalia Act* 18 USC s 1953 ('The Paraphernalia Act').

Respondents contend that the transactions occurred offshore and that no state or federal law regulates Internet gambling.

They claim that they were operating a duly licensed legitimate business fully authorized by the government of Antigua and in compliance with that country's rules and regulations of a land-based casino. They further argue that the federal and state laws upon which the State relies either do not apply to the activities of WIGC or are too vague and ambiguous to criminalize the activity of Internet gambling, when such activity is offshore in Antigua ...

Personal jurisdiction over WIGC and GCC

Although at first glance, Internet transactions may appear novel, 'traditional jurisdictional standards have proved to be sufficient to resolve all civil Internet jurisdictional issues' (*People v Lipsitz* 174 Misc 2d 571, 578 [Sup Ct New York County 1997]).

The Internet is at least a medium through which individuals may obtain and transmit text, sound, pictures, moving video images, and interactive services using various methods. The Internet also allows individuals to trade securities, execute banking transactions, purchase consumer merchandise, and engage in many other types of business and personal dealings not possible using more traditional means. What makes Internet transactions shed their novelty for jurisdictional purposes, is that similar to their traditional counterparts, they are all executed by and between individuals or corporate entities which are subject to a court's jurisdiction.

Whether the exercise of personal jurisdiction comports with due process requirements depends, as in any case, upon a finding that respondent has purposefully engaged in significant activities such that he has 'availed himself of the privilege of conducting business [in the forum state]'. (*Burger King Corp v Rudzewicz* 472 US 462 at 475–6 [1985]). 'The test, though not "precise", is a simple pragmatic one [cites omitted]: it's the aggregate of the corporation's activities in the State such that it may be said to be "present" in the State, "not occasionally or casually, but with a fair measure of permanence and continuity[.]' (*Laufer v Ostrow* 55 NY 2d 305 at 310 [1982], citing *Tauza v Susquehanna Coal Co* 220 NY 259 [1917]; see also *American Dental Co-op v Attorney General* 127 AD 2d 274 at 280 [1st Dept 1987]).

Respondents in this case are clearly doing business in New York for purposes of acquiring personal jurisdiction. Although WIGC was incorporated in Delaware, WIGC operated its entire business from its corporate headquarters in Bohemia, New York. All administrative and executive decisions as well as the computer research and development of the Internet gambling web site were made in New York. The cold-calls to investors to buy WIGC stock were made by WIGC agents employed and operating from this location. Thereafter, respondents sent its prospectus and other solicitation materials about Internet gambling from the Bohemia, New York location. WIGC's continuous and systematic contacts with New York established their physical presence in New York.

Moreover, even without physical presence in New York, WIGC's activities are sufficient to meet the minimum contact requirement of *International Shoe Co v Washington* 326 US 310 at 316 [1945]. The nature and quality of the defendant's activity must be such that 'the defendant purposefully avails itself of the privilege of conducting activities within the forum state, thus invoking the benefits and protections of its laws' (*Agrashell, Inc v Bernard Sirotta Co* 344 F 2d 583, 591 [2nd Cir 1965]). The use of the Internet is more than the mere transmission of communications between an out-of-state defendant and a plaintiff within the jurisdiction.

WIGC and the other respondents are doing business in New York. They worked from New York in conjunction with another New York-based company, Imajix Studios, to design the graphics for their Internet gambling casino. From their New York corporate headquarters, they downloaded, viewed, and edited their Internet casino web site. Furthermore, respondents engaged in an advertising campaign all over the country to induce people to visit their web site and gamble. Knowing that these ads were reaching thousands of New Yorkers, respondents made no attempt to exclude identifiable New Yorkers from the propaganda. Phone logs from respondents' toll-free number (available to casino visitors on the GCC web site) indicate that respondents had received phone calls from New Yorkers. Respondents cannot dispute that they do business in New York and that the acts complained of are subject to this court's jurisdiction.

To establish *in personam* jurisdiction over GCC, the petitioner must show that GCC functioned merely as the alter ego of WIGC. The corporate form will be pierced only if one corporation is so controlled by the other as to be a mere agent, department or alter ego of the other. See, eg, *Frummer v Hilton Hotels International* 19 NY 2d 533 at 537 (1967); see also *Gonzalez v Amtek* 50 Misc 2d 62 at 65–7 (4th Dept 1966); *ABKCO Industries, Inc v Lennon* 52 AD 2d 435 at 440 (1st Dept 1976). There must be some proof that the parent company dominates or controls the daily activities of the subsidiary (*Delagi v Volkswagenwerk* 29 NY 2d 426 [1972]; *Taca International Airlines, SA v Rolls-Royce of England, Ltd* 15 NY 2d 97 [1965]; *Billy v Consolidated Machine Tool Corporation* 51 NY 2d 152 [1980]).

The evidence indicates that GCC is a corporation completely dominated by WIGC. Aside from it being a wholly owned subsidiary of WIGC, GCC's primary asset, the web site, was purchased by WIGC pursuant to a corporate decision by WIGC's CEO respondent, Mr Burton. The use of the GCC casino web site was handled from WIGC's corporate headquarters. From WIGC's New York office, respondents also actively solicited investors to buy WIGC shares. Although WIGC was conducting operations from New York, WIGC failed to register with the State: as a foreign corporation doing business in New York, the stock offering, the brokers, dealers, issuers, or salespersons for the offering. All GCC top employees were hired by and reported to WIGC. WIGC itself contracted to buy GCC casinos web site servers from AIE.

Whenever GCC's servers required servicing, AIE provided GCC with services pursuant to a contract executed between WIGC and AIE. Furthermore, the licensing agreement with AIE was executed by respondent Burton as CEO of WIGC and GCC. At no time were any formalities observed to maintain a financial distinction between the two entities. GCC did not repay WIGC for the purchase of computer servers, nor did GCC execute any formal documents to commemorate the transfer sale of the servers. Therefore, the corporate form is disregarded and GCC will be deemed an alter ego of WIGC.

 NOTES AND QUESTIONS

1   In the above paragraphs, Ramos JSC approved the following quote: 'traditional jurisdictional standards have proved to be sufficient to resolve all civil Internet jurisdictional issues' (*People v Lipsitz* 174 Misc 2d 571 at 578 [Sup Ct New York County 1997]). How accurate do you think the assessment from *Lipsitz* is?
2   What reasoning did the court employ regarding the relationship between the two companies?

(b)   Subject matter jurisdiction and application of New York law

The People of the State of New York v World Interactive Gaming Corporation

714 NYS 2d 844 (NY County Sup Ct 1999)

Supreme Court of the State of New York County of New York: Commercial Part 53
Index No 404428/98

Available at <http://www.courts.state.ny.us/nycdlr/issue2-4/Internet.htm> 4 August 2001

Ramos J:
Respondents argue that the Court lacks subject matter jurisdiction, and that Internet gambling falls outside the scope of New York state gambling prohibitions, because the gambling occurs outside of New York state. However, under New York Penal Law, if the person engaged in gambling is located in New York, then New York is the location where the gambling occurred [see Penal Law s 225.00(2)]. Here, some or all of those funds in an Antiguan bank account are staked every time the New York user enters betting information into the computer. It is irrelevant that Internet gambling is legal in Antigua. The act of entering the bet and transmitting the information from New York via the Internet is adequate to constitute gambling activity within the New York state.

Wide-range implications would arise if this Court adopted respondents' argument that activities or transactions which may be targeted at New York residents are beyond the state's jurisdiction. Not only would such an approach severely undermine this state's deep-rooted policy against unauthorized gambling, it also would immunize from liability anyone who engages in any activity over the Internet which is otherwise illegal in this state. A computer server cannot be permitted to function as a shield against liability, particularly in this case where respondents actively targeted New York as the location where they conducted many of their allegedly illegal activities. Even though gambling is legal where the bet was accepted, the activity was transmitted from New York. Contrary to respondents' unsupported allegation of an Antiguan management company managing GCC, the evidence also indicates that the individuals who gave the computer commands operated from WIGC's New York office. The respondents enticed Internet users, including New York residents, to play in its casino.

As for respondents' claim that none of the federal statutes apply to operation of an Internet casino licensed by a foreign government, there is nothing in the record or the law to support their contentions. To the contrary, the Wire Act, Travel Act and Wagering Paraphernalia Act all apply despite the fact that the betting instructions are transmitted from outside the United States over the Internet. The scope of each of these statutes clearly extends to the transmission of betting information to a foreign country (see the Wire Act, which prohibits 'use of a wire communication facility for the transmission in interstate or foreign commerce of bets or wagers ...' [18 USC s 1084(a)]; the Travel Act which prohibits the use of 'any facility in interstate or foreign commerce' with intent to promote any unlawful activity [18 USC s 1952]). Nor can it be convincingly argued by respondents that the federal statutes are unconstitutionally vague (see *Turf Center, Inc v US* 325 F2d 793 at 795 [9th Cir 1963], *Katz v United States* 369 F 2d 130 at 135 [9th Cir 1966], *United States v Mendelsohn* 896 F 2d 1183 at 1186 [9th Cir 1989]). Because the Wire [A]ct, the Travel Act and the Wagering Paraphernalia Act have all been found to be constitutionally valid, and have been found not to be overly broad or vague, and because respondents' conduct falls within the scope of New York's prohibition against gambling, all of these statutes apply to respondents' activities.

The evidence demonstrates that respondents have violated New York Penal law which states that 'a person is guilty of promoting gambling ... when he knowingly advances or profits from unlawful gambling activity' (Penal Law s 225.05). By having established the gambling enterprise, advertised, solicited investors to buy its stock, to gamble through its online casino, respondents have 'engage[d] in conduct which materially aids ... gambling activity', in violation of New York law (Penal Law s 225.00(4) which states 'conduct includes but is not limited to conduct directed toward the creation or establishment of a particular game, contest, scheme, device ... [or] toward the solicitation or inducement of persons to participate therein'). Moreover, this Court rejects respondents' argument that it unknowingly accepted bets from New York residents. New York users can easily circumvent the casino software in order to play by the simple expedient of entering an out-of-state address. Respondents' violation of the Penal Law is that they persisted in continuous illegal conduct directed toward the creation, establishment, and advancement of unauthorized gambling. The violation had occurred long before a New York resident ever staked a bet. Because all of respondents' activities illegally advanced gambling, this Court finds that they have knowingly violated Penal Law s 225.05.

Not only are respondents guilty of violating New York state's gambling laws but they have also violated several federal laws. Like the great majority of states, federal law also proscribes gambling. Statutes such as the Wire Act, the Travel Act and the Interstate Transportation of Wagering Paraphernalia Act are just three examples of the federal government's policy against gambling. As the Wire Act's legislative history states:

> The purpose of the Bill is to assist various States and the District of Columbia in the enforcement of their laws pertaining to gambling, bookmaking, and like offenses and to aid in the suppression of organized gambling activities by prohibiting the use of wire communication facilities which are or will be used for the transmission of bets or wagers and gambling information in interstate and foreign commerce.

HR Rep No 967, 87th Cong 1st Sess (1961), US Code Congressional and Administrative News 1961, p 2631; see also *Telephone News Systems, Inc v Illinois Bell Telephone Co* 220 F Supp 621 (1963), affirmed 376 US 782.

The Wire Act bars citizens from engaging '[i]n the business of betting or wagering knowingly using a wire communication for the transmission of interstate or foreign commerce of bets or wagers or information assisting in the placing of bets or wagers'. 18 USC 1084(a). A Wire Act violation occurs when a defendant is in the business of betting or wagering (see *US v Anderson, CA Wisconsin* 542 F 2d 428 [7th Cir 1976]).

Furthermore, the Travel Act, 18 USC s 1952 proscribes similar interstate gambling activity by stating:

> ... the use of any facility in interstate or foreign commerce, including the mail, with intent to (1) distribute the records of any unlawful activity ... or (3) otherwise promote, manage, establish, carry on, or facilitate the promotion, management, establishment, or carrying on of any unlawful activity ... shall be fined not more than $10,000 or imprisoned for not more than five years or both.

Respondents' interstate use of the Internet to conduct their illegal gambling business violates federal law. As the legislative history behind the Wire Act indicates, the purpose of these federal controls is to aid the states in controlling gambling. Like a prohibited telephone call from a gambling facility, the Internet is accessed by using a telephone wire. When the telephone wire is connected to a modem attached to a user's computer, the user's phone line actually connects the user to the Internet server and then the user may log onto this illegal gambling web site from any location in the United States. After selecting from the multitude of illegal games offered by respondents, the information is transmitted to the server in Antigua. Respondents' server then transmits betting information back to the user, which is against the Wire Act. The Internet site creates a virtual casino within the user's computer terminal. By hosting this casino and exchanging betting information with the user, an illegal communication in violation of the Wire Act and the Travel Act has occurred.

Respondents attempt to circumvent federal law by asserting that none of these statutes apply to the operation of an Antiguan casino. Moreover, they allege the federal government has not explicitly ruled on Internet gambling; therefore it is an unregulated field. Respondents disregard that the Interstate Commerce Clause gives Congress the plenary power to regulate illegal gambling conducted between a US and a foreign location (see *Champion v Ames* 188 US 321 at 334 [1903]). Gambling conducted via the Internet from New York to Antigua is indistinguishable from any other form of gambling, since both the Wire and Travel Acts apply to the transmission of information into a foreign country See 18 USC 1084(a); 18 USC 1953(a). Therefore, the respondents are culpable for violating the Wire Act and the Travel Act.

Additionally, respondents violated the Interstate Transportation of Wagering Paraphernalia Act. Under this Act: '[w]hoever, except a common carrier in the usual course of business, knowingly carries or sends in interstate or foreign commerce any record, paraphernalia, ticket, certificate, bills slip, token, paper, writing or other device under, or to be used, or adapted, devised, designed for use in (a) bookmaking; or (b) wagering pools with respect to a sporting event or (c) in a numbers, policy, bolita, or similar game shall be fined not more than $10,000 or imprisoned for more than five years, or both' [18 USC s 1953(a)].

The respondents intentionally sent records of gambling activity from the GCC location in Antigua through international and interstate commerce into various United States locations, among them New York. When respondents solicited perspective investors, they sent them a multitude of materials which were specifically to be utilized for the setting up and advancing of the Internet gambling business through US mail. Furthermore, the actual computers which would be used for gambling between the United States and Antigua were bought and delivered through US mail from Florida to GCC's location in Antigua.

The respondent's total activities unambiguously advance gambling in direct violation of the explicit safeguards that New York and the federal laws have placed against unauthorized gambling activity.

In addition, several of New York's registration requirements have been violated. For instance, under BCL s 1301(a), a 'foreign corporation shall not do business in this state until it has been authorized to do so ...' by submitting an application to the Department of State. WIGC is a foreign corporation, incorporated in Delaware, operating out of offices in Bohemia, New York. Since WIGC failed to apply for approval from the Department of State, the respondents were repeatedly operating illegally in New York State.

Moreover, pursuant to the Martin Act, the issuer, dealer, salesmen of securities must all be registered with the Attorney General prior to the solicitation of investors. GBL s 359(e) defines a dealer as 'a person, firm, association or corporation selling or offering for sale from or to the public within or from this state securities issued by it'. Respondents acted as the issuer, dealer and salesmen when they sold units of WIGC stock from their office in New York without registering. Respondents frivolously claim they are exempt from registering under the Martin Act due to due GBL s 359(f). However, they fail to point to any applicable exception under GBL s 359(f). Furthermore, although a company failing to register is normally penalized with a fine and subsequently the company is often allowed to file for registration, the violation still constitutes a fraudulent practice under New York law (see GBL s 359-e(14)(l)).

This Court further finds that respondents also violated the Martin Act's prohibition against the use of deception, misrepresentations, or concealment in the sale of securities (see GBL s 352(1)). It is well settled that fraud exists not only where there has been an affirmative misstatement of a material fact, but also where there has been an omission of a material fact (see GBL s 352-c(1); *TSC Industries, Inc v Northway, Inc* 426 US 438 [1976]; *State of New York v Rachmani Corp* 71 NY 2d 718, 727 [1988]). While the evidence does not conclusively show that respondents misrepresented to investors certain facts about the potential return on their investment, the likelihood of an IPO, or the legality of Internet gambling, respondents did misrepresent and failed to disclose facts regarding the use of proceeds raised in the offering.

It is undisputed that approximately 46% of the investors' funds were used to pay respondents' commissions, salaries, and consulting fees. Without disclosing to investors, individual respondent Jeffery Burton, CEO and Director of WIGC, received a personal loan of $84,000 from the corporation. Respondent Cynthia Burton, Jeffery Burton's wife and a secretary at WIGC, drew a salary of $93,439 from WIGC over a mere seven-month period. Respondent Lawrence Blocker, President and Director at WIGC, received $135,864 in salary, commissions and fees. Respondents Gregory Flemming Sr, Gerald Varland, and Howard Toomer, all Vice Presidents of Marketing, took substantial salaries of $242,260, $109,650, and $71,260 respectively. In addition the individual respondents created various business entities through which they paid themselves undisclosed consultant fees.

Not only were none of these salaries disclosed to investors, the respondents' offering materials indicated that only 18% of the offering proceeds would be used as working capital and to pay commissions. Had investors known that 46% of the funds raised were being paid to respondents in the form of salaries, commissions and consulting fees, they might well have chosen to forego the investment (compare *People v Tellier* 7 Misc 2d 43 [NY County Sup Ct 1956]; *Grandon v Merrill Lynch & Co* 147 F 3d 184 [2nd Cir 1998]).

Because of the clear illegality present in respondents' actions, and absence of any triable issue of fact, respondents are found liable under Executive Law s 63(12) for their state and federal law violations.

Remedies

The Attorney General is entitled to injunctive relief which is routinely granted in special proceedings under Executive Law s 63(12) (*People v Apple Health Sports Clubs, Ltd, Inc* 206 AD 2d 266 [1st Dept 1994], affd, 84 NY 2d 1004 [1994]). The requirement of a bond to assure future proper behavior on the part of an enjoined party traditionally accompanies such an injunction (see *People v Empyre Inground Pool* 227 AD 2d 731 [3rd Dept 1996]; *People v Helena VIP Personal Introductions Servs* 199 AD 2d 186 [1st Dept 1993]). This Court finds the request for an injunction warranted, and directs fixing of the amount be incorporated in an order to be settled.

As for the Attorney General's request for restitution, penalties, and costs, which are available under Executive Law s 63(12) and GBL s 353(3), this Court finds the circumstances warrant awarding them in this case. The manner of the accounting, the mechanism for restitution, and the amount in penalties and costs to be awarded shall be resolved at a hearing. Because each respondent is individually liable for the actions conducted by both WIGC and GCC (see, eg, *Matter of State of New York v Daro Chartours* 72 AD 2d 872, 873 [3rd Dept 1979]; see also, *Marine Midland Bank v Russo Produce Co* 50 NY2d 31, 44 [1980] [finding that corporate veil can be pierced to hold corporate officers liable for a tort regardless of whether they acted in conjunction with the corporation and in the course of their corporate duties], and shall be fined appropriately, all parties including individual respondents are directed to appear for a preliminary conference before this Court on September 9, 1999, at 9:30 am, to resolve any issues regarding, the scope of the accounting, discovery, or scheduling of the hearing.

Respondents are further directed not to destroy any personal or business records relating to this matter.

This constitutes the decision and order of this Court. Settle order on notice.

 NOTES AND QUESTIONS

1　A US state court can exercise jurisdiction over a defendant of another jurisdiction in the USA via the state's 'long arm statute' as long as the limits set out in the Due Process Clause of the Fourteenth Amendment of the US Constitution is not exceeded. This test was developed in *International Shoe v Washington*[1] and it asks whether the foreign defendant has certain 'minimum contacts' with the state and whether, if the state were to exercise jurisdiction, it would offend 'traditional notions of fair play and substantial justice.' The court in *International Shoe* also stated that much will also depend on the nature and quality of the party's contacts with the relevant state.

2　In *Bensusan Restaurant Corp v King* 937 F Supp 295 (SDNY 1996) the New York Court of Appeals decided that a jazz clubowner in Missouri with an allegedly trade mark infringing website had not purposefully availed himself of the benefits of New York, so the plaintiffs' case failed.

Note the different factual circumstances between *WIGC* and *Bensusan*. It appears that the US courts have sought to base their decisions on the nature and existence, or otherwise, of tangible actions of defendants which are related to the offending website, not just the website itself. See also *Blumenthal v Drudge* 992 F Supp 44 (1998) and *Digital Equipment Corporation v Altavista Technology Inc* 960 F Supp 456 (1997). Ramos JSC, in *WIGC*, clearly looks to the business activities of the respondent which lay behind the website in question. However, look carefully at his examination of US federal law. Here, there is a marked shift. In his analysis of the Wire Act, do you perceive any problems with the breadth of the argument he presents? Does this reasoning suggest that every Internet casino is illegal in the USA as soon as a single person interacts with it? If so, do you foresee any problems in combating this illegality?

3　Professor David Post, elsewhere in the piece extracted above,[2] highlights the importance of the US Constitutional landscape. In *American Network Inc v Access America/Connect Atlanta, Inc* 975 F Supp 494 (1997), the court held that asserting jurisdiction over the defendant would not violate the limitations of the Fourteenth Amendment, which are, according to Post, fourfold:

(a) Purposeful availment. The court declined to hold that the establishment of a web page accessible to NY residents was alone sufficient to demonstrate 'some act by which the defendant purposefully avails [itself] of the privilege of conducting activities with the forum state', citing *Hanson v Denckla* 357 US 235 at 253 (1958).

1　326 US 310 (1945).
2　<http://www.temple.edu/lawschool/dpost/jurisdictioncases.htm> 29 August 2001.

(b) The plaintiff must also show that 'the defendant's contacts with the forum are continuous and systematic, or that the suit arises out of or is related to those contacts', citing *Helicopteros Nacionales de Colombia v Hall* 466 US 408 at 415–16 (1984).

(c) Due process requires 'that the defendant's conduct and connection with the forum state are such that he should reasonably anticipate being haled into court there' (*WorldWide Volkswagen Corp v Woodson* 444 US 286 at 297 (1980)).

(d) Finally, as to the 'other factors' that a court 'may evaluate' in determining whether the assertion of jurisdiction over a party is so unreasonable as to violate due process—such as the burden on the defendant, the forum state's interest in adjudicating the dispute, the plaintiff's interest in obtaining convenient and effective relief, the interstate judicial system's interest in obtaining the efficient resolution of controversies, and the shared interest of the states in furthering fundamental substantive social policies—see *Burger King Corp v Rudzewicz* 471 US 462 at 476–7 (1985).

4   The 'minimum contacts' test, first clearly articulated in *International Shoe v Washington* 326 US 310 (1945), has become the generally accepted framework for judicial decisions in Internet-related matters in the USA. Professor Post outlines the three types of 'contact' that constitute the test:[3]

The first type of contact is when the defendant clearly does business over the Internet 'If the defendant enters into contracts with residents of a foreign jurisdiction that involve the knowing and repeated transmission of computer files over the Internet, personal jurisdiction is proper' (*Zippo Manufacturing Company v Zippo Dot Com, Inc* 952 F Supp 1119 (WD Pa, 16 January 1997) at 1124, citing *CompuServe, Inc v Patterson* 89 F3d 1257 (6th Cir 1996); *Weber v Jolly Hotels* 977 F Supp 327 at 333 (DNJ 1997)).

The second type of contact occurs when 'a user can exchange information with the host computer. In these cases, the exercise of jurisdiction is determined by examining the level of interactivity and commercial nature of the exchange of information that occurs on the website' (*Zippo* at 1124 (citing *Maritz, Inc v Cybergold, Inc* 947 F Supp 1328 (ED Mo 1996); Weber at 333).

The third type of contact involves the posting of information or advertisements on an Internet website 'which is accessible to users in foreign jurisdictions'. (*Zippo* at 1124; see *Weber* at 333; *Bensusan Restaurant Corp v King*, 937 F Supp 295 (SDNY 1996)). Personal jurisdiction is not exercised for this type of contact because 'a finding of jurisdiction ... based on an Internet website would mean that there would be nationwide (indeed, worldwide) personal jurisdiction over anyone and everyone who establishes an Internet website. Such nationwide jurisdiction is not consistent with personal jurisdiction case law ...' (*Weber* at 333 (quoting *Hearst Corp v Goldberger*, 1997)).

---

3   <http://www.temple.edu/lawschool/dpost/jurisdictioncases.htm> 29 August 2001.

Therefore, the minimum contacts test is essentially a sliding scale which seeks to measure the level of interactivity and the commercial nature of the website.

5   In *Bensusan Restaurant Corp v King*,[4] Bensusan was the owner of a jazz club in New York called 'The Blue Note'. He was also the owner of the trade mark, 'The Blue Note'. King was a resident of Missouri who operated a jazz club in Missouri also called 'The Blue Note'. King had set up a website that advertised his jazz club and used a logo that was very similar to the trade mark belonging to Bensusan. King did, however, place a disclaimer on the website to explain that this website was not for or related to The Blue Note in New York. There was also a telephone number on the website for users to order tickets. The New York court found that it could not exercise jurisdiction over the Missouri club because the Missouri website was simply supplying information. While the court acknowledged that it did supply a large quantity of information, it could not find the requisite level of interactivity. Creating a site, the court said, like placing a product into the stream of commerce, may be felt nationwide—or even worldwide—but, without more, it is not an act purposefully directed toward the forum state. Bensusan's argument that King should have foreseen that users could access the site in New York and be confused as to the relationship of the two Blue Note clubs was held insufficient to satisfy due process. There were no allegations that King actively sought to encourage New Yorkers to access his site, or that he conducted any business—let alone a continuous and systematic part of its business—in New York to satisfy general jurisdiction.[5] There had been no ticket sales made in New York nor was it King's practice to send tickets to residents who rang up to order them. So even if a New York resident (or any resident for that matter) had ordered tickets using the advertised number, she still would have had to travel to Missouri to pick them up, thereby transferring the conduct of business to Missouri. Because of this, the court said it had no specific or general jurisdiction.

6   The above cases and tests seem to be coherent and useful in providing some degree of certainty in the event of a dispute relating to the Internet. However, consider the following two cases. In *Inset Systems, Inc v Instruction Set, Inc*, 937 F Supp 161 (D Conn 1996), a Connecticut Court found jurisdiction over a defendant whose only contact with Connecticut was a website and the inclusion within that website of a nationwide toll-free phone number. In *Maritz, Inc v CyberGold, Inc* 947 F Supp 1328 (ED Mo 1996) jurisdiction was found in Missouri over a site hosted in California, simply on the basis that the website provided information about CyberGold's new upcoming Internet service that could be accessed in Missouri. What conclusions would you draw from these decisions? Two other decisions that employ similarly broad readings of the minimum contacts doctrine are *Bunn-O-Matic Corp v Bunn Coffee Service Inc*

---

4   *Bensusan Restaurant Corp v King* 937 F Supp 295 (1996).
5   Ibid, 301.

1998 US Dist Lexis 7819 (CD IL 1998), and *Minnesota v Granite Gates Resorts, Inc* 568 NW 2d 715 (Minn Ct App 1997).

7   Rather than suggest that there has been universally broad interpretation of the minimum contacts doctrine, the intention here is to demonstrate the spectrum of judicial reaction. In the USA in cases such as *Desktop Technologies, Inc v Coloworks Reproduction & Design, Inc* Civ Act No 98-5029, 1999 US Dist Lexis 1934 (D Pa, 24 February 1999) and *Stephen C Edberg, et al v Neogen Corporation,* No 3:98CV00717 GLG, 1998 US Dist Lexis 12311 (D Conn, 4 August 1998), courts have held that there was a lack of jurisdiction over plaintiffs in strikingly similar fact situations as those discussed in the previous paragraph. In Australia, there have been similarly divergent approaches to the question of jurisdiction in Internet-related areas and these will be examined below.

8   The majority of US cases deal with jurisdiction in terms of intra-nation disputes. These disputes are tempered by the fact that they take place between states that operate under a common constitution. Without this common foundation, do you think the judges may be more wary of extending the reach of their law? In the light of this, how much weight can be placed on the intra-nation jurisprudence when looking at an inter-nation dispute?

---

3   Australian case law

An Australian court may decline jurisdiction over a foreign defendant if it considers that the forum is 'clearly inappropriate' (See *Voth v Manilda Flour Mills* (1990) 171 CLR 538). Some factors to consider include whether there is any significant connection between the court and the dispute and whether there is any legitimate juridical advantage to the plaintiff such as greater recovery (*Oceanic Sun Line Special Shipping Co v Fay* (1988) 165 CLR 197, *Spiliada Maritime Corporation v Cansulex Ltd* [1987] 1 AC 460). In the area of exercising jurisdiction over matters concerning the Internet, the courts in Australia have moved from a position of timidity to one of boldness in the space of a few years. The cases extracted below are by no means exhaustive on the topic of jurisdiction and Internet-related disputes but they highlight the shift in the courts' jurisprudence.

(a)   *Macquarie Bank v Berg*

Macquarie Bank Limited and Anor v Berg

[1999] NSWSC 526

Supreme Court of NSW

Available at
<http://www.austlii.edu.au/au/cases/nsw/supreme_ct/1999/526.html> 16 August 2006

Simpson J:

1   By summons filed on 26 May 1999 the plaintiffs, Macquarie Bank Limited ('MBL') and Andrew James Downe, seek an order restraining the defendant, Charles Joseph Berg, from publishing certain material on the Internet. The summons first came before B M James J who abridged the time for service and directed that service be effected by delivering a copy of the documentation on Messrs Hickson Wisewoulds (solicitors acting for the defendant in other proceedings between the parties) and by sending copies of the documents, marked for the attention of the defendant, to a specified e-mail address. When the matter came before me on 28 May 1999 I was satisfied that the plaintiffs had complied with the directions as to service. Mr Dalgleish of counsel appeared, as a courtesy to the court, to acknowledge receipt of the documents by Hickson Wisewoulds. He did not appear for the purpose of representing the defendant and the matter proceeded ex parte.

2   It is convenient at this point to set out, as briefly as possible, the circumstances in which the application is made.

3   Some time before December 1997 MBL engaged the defendant to work in its business. Whether that engagement created a relationship of employer and employee is a matter of contention between the parties but is immaterial for present purposes. The relationship terminated in circumstances that gave rise to litigation in other courts. The defendant has commenced proceedings against MBL in both the Industrial Relations Commission of NSW ('IRC') and the Federal Court of Australia ('FCA'). MBL challenges the jurisdiction of the IRC. On 17 August 1998 an order was made for separate determination of that question. The defendant unsuccessfully appealed the order. There is no evidence as to when a hearing on the jurisdictional question might be expected. On 23 April 1999 MBL filed a summons in the Equity Division of this court claiming an order, under s 8 of the *Jurisdiction of Courts (Cross-Vesting) Act 1987*, that the IRC proceedings be removed to this court. Messrs Hickson Wisewoulds, although they are the solicitors acting for the defendant in the IRC proceedings, were instructed not to accept service of the summons. It has not been served on the defendant. MBL is also contemplating seeking a similar order in relation to the FCA proceedings, with a view to having all matters between the parties litigated in a single forum.

4   From at least January 1999 material relating to the relationship and the litigation has appeared on the Internet on a web site, the address of which is 'www. brgvsmbl. com'. The defendant's name appears prominently in the material which includes a document headed 'Letter From Charles Berg'. It is a reasonable inference that this material has been placed on the site by the defendant. No complaint is made about this publication.

5   However, since at least 24 May 1999, material has been appearing on another web site, the address of which is 'macquarieontrial.com'. This material, like the other, is transmitted to and can be received in NSW. It is the publication of this material that the plaintiffs seek to restrain. It is unnecessary to go into the detail of its contents. I am satisfied that the material on the site conveys imputations defamatory of each plaintiff.

6　While there is nothing in this material that specifically accepts or acknowledges that it is published by the defendant, there are sufficient similarities with that on the previously mentioned web site to permit an inference that the defendant is also, if not the author, at the very least involved in and associated with its publication.

7　It is reasonably clear that the defendant is not present in NSW, and that any acts done by him that result in publication of the material in NSW are done from outside the state. The evidence as to his whereabouts suggests that he is in the United States of America.

8　A question of jurisdiction is therefore raised. There is authority that a court is empowered to restrain conduct occurring or expected to occur outside the territorial boundaries of the jurisdiction: *Helicopter Utilities v Australian National Airlines Commission* (1963) 80 WN (NSW) 48 at 51; *Dunlop Rubber Company v Dunlop* [1921] 1 AC 367; *Tozier and Wife v Hawkins* (1885) 15 QBD 680.

9　Whether that power should be exercised is a question of discretion. Factors relevant to the exercise of the discretion include the potential enforceability of any orders made, and whether another court is a more appropriate forum: *Helicopter Utilities* (p 51).

10　Any order made by this court would be enforceable only if the defendant were voluntarily to return to NSW. He cannot be compelled to do so for the purpose of enforcement. Senior counsel for the plaintiff urged that, having regard to the litigation he has initiated in NSW, there is every prospect that he will return. If and when he does so he will immediately become amenable to the enforcement processes of this court that would be set in train in the event of disobedience of any orders made. Unenforceability should not, therefore, be seen as a factor contraindicating the grant of the relief sought.

11　I am not fully persuaded by this argument. It seems to me unsatisfactory to make orders the effectiveness of which is solely dependent upon the voluntary presence, at a time of his selection, of the person against whom the orders are made. The uncertainty of unenforceability is a factor adverse to the exercise of discretion in the plaintiff's favour. It is unnecessary further to consider this. There are other, more compelling, factors that militate against the making of the order sought.

12　The first and most significant of these concerns the nature of the Internet itself. No evidence was adduced to explain the mechanics of the operation of the Internet. It is reasonably plain, I think, that once published on the Internet, material is transmitted anywhere in the world that has an Internet connection. It may be received by anybody, anywhere, having the appropriate facilities. Senior counsel conceded that to make the order as initially sought would have the effect of restraining publication of all the material presently contained on the web site to any place in the world. Recognising the difficulties associated with orders of such breadth, he sought to narrow the claim by limiting the order sought to publication or dissemination *'within NSW'*. The limitation, however, is ineffective. Senior counsel acknowledged that he was aware of no means by which material, once published on the Internet, could be excluded from transmission to or receipt in any geographical area. Once published on the Internet material can be received anywhere, and it does not lie within the competence of the publisher to restrict the reach of the publication.

13 The consequence is that, if I were to make the order sought (and the defendant were to obey it) he would be restrained from publishing anywhere in the world via the medium of the Internet.

14 The difficulties are obvious. An injunction to restrain defamation in NSW is designed to ensure compliance with the laws of NSW, and to protect the rights of plaintiffs, as those rights are defined by the law of NSW. Such an injunction is not designed to superimpose the law of NSW relating to defamation on every other state, territory and country of the world. Yet that would be the effect of an order restraining publication on the Internet. It is not to be assumed that the law of defamation in other countries is coextensive with that of NSW, and indeed, one knows that it is not. It may very well be that, according to the law of the Bahamas, Tazhakistan, or Mongolia, the defendant has an unfettered right to publish the material. To make an order interfering with such a right would exceed the proper limits of the use of the injunctive power of this court.

15 For this reason alone, I would refuse the order sought.

16 It may be that what I have said above expresses merely a technological update of a long standing line of authority concerning the discretion to restrain defamatory publications. Such a power is to be exercised with great caution, and only in very clear cases: *Stocker v McElhinney (No 2)* (1961) 79 WN (NSW) 541; *Church of Scientology of California Inc v Reader's Digest Services Pty Limited* [1980] 1 NSWLR 344; *Chappell v TCN Channel Nine Pty Limited* (1988) 14 NSWLR 153. This, as I understand it, is largely for two reasons of principle. The first is that, while it may be relatively easy to establish, prima facie, that a publication is defamatory, the key to a defamation action very often lies in the defences advanced, and these cannot ordinarily be determined at the stage of an interlocutory injunction application. To restrain the publication would unduly override the rights of a publisher and pre-empt the resolution of legitimate issues which arise in claims for defamation. The second reason concerns the fundamental public interest in freedom of speech and freedom of information. An injunction will ordinarily not lie where it would have the effect of restraining discussion in the media of matters of public interest or concern: *Chappell*, p 158.

17 Contrary to the argument initially advanced (but, I think, abandoned) by senior counsel, the public interest in freedom of speech is not more deeply embedded in the protection of the publications of the organs of the mass media than in protection of publication by individuals. The courts will not be more reluctant to enjoin a publication by a media outlet than one by an individual. The fact that the publication the plaintiffs seek to restrain is publication by an individual and not a media outlet adds nothing to the plaintiffs' case.

18 Senior counsel placed heavy emphasis on the decision of Hunt J (as he then was) in *Chappell*. That was a case in which his Honour, having considered the history of, and the reasons for, the caution exercised in relation to applications for injunctions in defamation cases, nevertheless proceeded to make such an order.

19 In that case the statement of claim had been filed, and the imputations upon which reliance was to be placed had been formulated. The defendants, who were represented, had identified the defences upon which they proposed to rely. His Honour was therefore able to embark upon an examination of the defendants' realistic prospects of success in defending the defamatory imputations. A single focal issue emerged—whether the defendants would be able to show that publication of the material was on a matter of

public interest. He held that it was not, and, in effect, that any other conclusion would have been untenable. There was therefore no impediment to granting the injunction.

20 In the present case, on the first day of hearing no statement of claim had been prepared, although senior counsel formulated the imputations which were to be pleaded. By the second day of hearing a statement of claim had been prepared, but not filed or served. Accordingly, the defendant had no notice of the precise imputations on which the plaintiffs proposed to rely, and was not in a position (even if he had appeared or been represented on the proceedings) to identify his defences, and therefore isolate the issues for determination.

21 Counsel for the plaintiffs referred also to *National Mutual Life Association of Australasia Limited v GTV Corporation Pty Limited* [1989] VR 747, but it does not seem to me that the judgments in this case advance the argument. The issue to be determined, and the principles to be applied, are clearly stated in *Chappell* ...

27 The order I make is that the application for interlocutory injunction is refused.

 NOTES AND QUESTIONS

1 How compelling do you find the reasoning of Simpson J? Do you regard her decision as an example of well-founded judicial circumspection, or rather of mere judicial timidity? Explain your critique of the judgment by referring both to Australian and to overseas jurisprudence as well as to the nature of the Internet generally.

2 The case discussed immediately below highlights a different outcome in a similar fact situation. What, if anything, do these results suggest about the state of Australian Internet jurisprudence? Can any conclusions be drawn for future cases where the courts may be faced with similar Internet-related issues?

(b)   *ASIC v Matthews*

This matter was heard before the Federal Court in 1999 and the Supreme Court of NSW in 2000. The issue was the content of material published on a website which breached the Australian *Corporations Law*.

Australian Securities and Investments Commission v Matthews

[1999] FCA 164 (19 February 1999)

Federal Court of Australia

Available at
<http://www.austlii.edu.au//cgi-bin/disp.pl/au/cases/nsw/supreme_ct/1999/763.html>
16 August 2006

Ex tempore reasons for interlocutory judgment

O'Connor J:

1   This is an application pursuant to s 1324 of the *Corporations Law* brought by the applicant, the Australian Securities and Investments Commission. The respondent is Stephen Lewis Matthews. The application today seeks a series of orders by way of interlocutory relief in respect of the total matter. I have in fact made five orders which will appear with these reasons.

2   The applicant tendered a number of affidavits to which there were no objection. These affidavits are firstly one sworn by Jeremy Stephen Simpson, an Internet analyst, and in that affidavit, by means of annexure, are a number of hard copy depictions of material which appear, it is deposed, on an Internet site called 'The Chimes'. The material that is included in these hard copies I will return to later in these reasons. ...

4   The fifth affidavit is sworn by James Hunter Berry, the manager (surveillance) of the Australian Stock Exchange ('ASX') and this affidavit deals with a matter relating to trading in shares in a company called CMC Power Systems Limited whose securities are listed and whose ASX code is CSY. None of this material is challenged. This witness expressed the opinion that the trading in CSY in the period 9 to 11 February 1999 had changed from an earlier period. He deposes as to the reception of two calls, one of which was anonymous, giving information about statements made by unknown persons on a bulletin board that appeared on an Internet site called 'The Chimes'.

5   The site, 'The Chimes', was examined and the statement which appeared on the web site has been placed at 21:29 p.m. on 10 February by the publisher in relation to an announcement from CSY. That announcement was released on 9 February 1999, according to the web site and subsequently, and the other evidence shows that the date of materials in relation to this matter was corrected on the web site by the publisher (which the respondent today admitted was he) having corrected the date to demonstrate that the report on which he was commenting was in fact a 1998 report and not a 1999 report.

6   There was evidence that in the period concerned, there was increased activity in the stock on the exchange and, subsequently, when the mistake was acknowledged, a decline in the price of the shares. The relevant sections of the *Corporations Law* that govern this matter are s 18 which provides that the provisions of the law apply to a person who carries on business not necessarily for profit. The heading is 'Otherwise than for Profit'. Section 77 is relevant in relation to an investment advice business. The respondent, again, in submission, suggested that he could have the benefit of s 77(6). However, the case put by the applicant is that he is prevented from doing so because he fits within the provisions of s 77(7). Persons in that category are not given the benefit of the exemption from s 77 that is provided in s 77(6). The penultimate section that is relevant is s 781 of the *Corporations Law*, which provides that a person must not carry on an investment advice business or hold out that person as an investment adviser unless the person is a licensee or an exempt investment adviser.

7   As I have already pointed out, the respondent has conceded that he does not hold a licence and he is not an exempt investment adviser. The respondent did not provide

any evidence for the court to consider in opposing the interlocutory orders; however, he made a number of submissions. The first of them was that the provision of material on the screen of an Internet of the kind which is reproduced in the affidavits is not a publication of this material and, after some interchange with him, he agreed that the description of what he was doing was equivalent to having an 'electronic sandwich board'.

8   I do not think that (even putting what he said at its highest) the use of an 'electronic sandwich board' falls outside the description of publishing and, more particularly, a publishing business because Mr Matthews also concedes that his web site is conducted continuously and systematically so that it does fit within the description, 'to carry on business', as explained in *Hyde v Sullivan and Anor* [1956] 56 NSWLR 113, a decision of the New South Wales Court of Appeal. No quarrel was taken by Mr Matthews with that definition and it is my view that in relation to the activity taken by Mr Matthews in respect of his web site, as he describes it, he is carrying on a business.

9   The question of whether this business is carried on for profit does not arise because that is not necessary to be demonstrated for the purpose of the application. It, however, certainly fits within the definition of carrying on a business contained in *Hyde v Sullivan (supra)*. Mr Matthews put to me that he wasn't in a commercial relationship with subscribers but, as I said, he has admitted to all the other characteristics of carrying on a business.

10   He also submitted that he was not giving advice in the conduct of his electronic site. I do not accept that submission. The parts of the evidence presented by the applicant to which counsel referred, used phrases and words that are all directed to evaluation and encouragement to those reading the site to deal in the share market. It is certainly couched in the ordinary terminology of advice, and I so find.

11   I therefore find that the respondent, who is not licensed or authorised to do so, is carrying on an investment advice business without determining whether that is being done for profit and in the course of conducting the web site, 'The Chimes', is holding himself out as an investment adviser. Unless he is licensed or given an exemption as an investment adviser, this activity is, in my view, *prima facie* in contravention of the *Corporations Law* and it was for that reason, having taken into account all of the material to which I was referred, that I made the orders sought by the applicant.

12   If Mr Matthews, of course, had been earning his living in conducting the site or could have demonstrated today that there were serious financial or other consequences to him in making the orders, it might have been necessary to have considered both in relation to making interlocutory orders and also the consequences of them. For example, expedition or other orders could have been made to prevent any damage being too acute. Counsel for the applicant rightly points out that his client is exempt from any order as to undertaking for damages should Mr Matthews be successful in the main proceeding.

13   However, I am comforted by Mr Matthews' submissions that this activity, in conducting the web site, is done for pleasure only and the consequences of his complying with the orders will be to curb that pleasurable activity. The only other consequence he could point to was perhaps press comment on the activities that have been restrained by the order which I described in the context of the hearing of only having an effect on Mr Matthews' ego and would not, in my view, create too much of a burden upon him.

14 The respondent, apart from the submissions about publishing advice and other matters that I have already referred to in these reasons gave no other reason for resisting the injunctive relief. What I have particularly been concerned about and have put great weight upon is the incident which is part of the evidence in relation to the engine company CSY and the serious consequences which are deposed to from that acknowledged mistake contained in Mr Matthews' web site. For those reasons I have made the orders.

15 I propose to make a further order and that is that this matter be now referred to the registrar to be assigned, in the ordinary course, to a docket of a judge of the court for hearing of the application for final relief. The applicant has assured me that it is ready to proceed. It really will be a matter for Mr Matthews to consider any application he may care to make.

The Court orders that:

1 Until further order the respondent, Stephen Lewis Matthews, be restrained from advising either directly or indirectly other persons about securities.

2 Until further order the respondent, Stephen Lewis Matthews, be restrained from publishing either directly or indirectly reports about securities.

3 Until further order the respondent, Stephen Lewis Matthews, be restrained from advising other persons about securities on the Internet including but not limited to the Internet site known as 'The Chimes' and situated at http://www.chimes.com.au.

4 Until further order the respondent, Stephen Lewis Matthews, be restrained from publishing reports or allowing to be published reports about securities on the Internet including but not limited to the Internet site known as 'The Chimes' and situated at http://www.chimes.com.au.

5 The costs of this application be costs of the cause.

 NOTES AND QUESTIONS

1 O'Connor J's judgment is more significant for what it does not say than for what it does. What is your opinion on the ramifications of her Honour's orders? Do you consider that she demonstrated an awareness of the consequences of the orders? How do the orders contrast with those in *Macquarie Bank v Berg*?

2 Significantly, in the Federal Court case, the website in question was actually hosted in Australia. Subsequent to O'Connor J's orders, Matthews took the site down from its Australian host (http://www.chimes.com.au) and lodged it with a New Zealand server (http:// www.chimes.co.nz). These acts were tantamount to an overt challenge to the reach of the Australian legal system—a challenge which, one might have thought, provided the perfect opportunity to strike new ground in the Australian jurisprudence on the Internet. The extract following is a judgment relating to this New Zealand site.

(c) *ASIC v Matthews*

Australian Securities and Investments Commission v Matthews

[2000] NSWSC 392 (4 May 2000)

Supreme Court of NSW

Available at
< http://www.austlii.edu.au//cgi-bin/disp.pl/au/cases/nsw/supreme_ct/2000/392.html>
17 August 2006

Windeyer J:

1   On 23 March 2000 I gave judgment in which I determined that the defendant, Mr Matthews, was in contempt of court by failing to comply with orders made by O'Connor J in the Federal Court of Australia on 19 February 1999, which orders were confirmed as orders of this court by Austin J by a decision of 26 July 1999, the contempt being that he allowed to be published certain securities reports on a particular Internet site.

2   In the statement of charge and amended notice of motion the plaintiff, Australian Securities and Investments Commission, charged that a series of reports or if you like publications on the Internet site <www.chimes.co.nz> were reports on securities and that in breach of the orders of O'Connor J, particularly Order 4, the defendant Mr Matthews had allowed these reports to be published.

3   I found that nine of what I will call postings on the site were reports on securities and I found that Mr Matthews had allowed them to be published and therefore was in contempt of court for breach of the orders originally made by O'Connor J. I should say that five of those postings are now accepted by Mr Matthews as having been posted by him, he being 'the publisher', the other four being postings by other persons.

4   I have set out the history of this matter in my judgment of 23 March 2000 and I do not intend to go through the matters set out there again. The question before the court is the question of the penalty which should be imposed as a result of the contempt.

5   It is of some relevance to re-state that there were earlier proceedings for contempt for breach of the same orders heard by Sackville J in the Federal Court in June 1999 and that as a result of the contempt there admitted and in fact proved, he imposed a penalty of committal to jail for a period of two months but ordered that the warrant for committal be issued and lie in the office for a period of 12 months. It was assumed that if there were no further breach within that time then the term of the imprisonment would not have to be served.

6   The contempts, the subject of the charges before Sackville J, were different from the contempts which I have found. After the judgment and orders of Sackville J on 16 June, as I have stated in the earlier judgment, Mr Matthews closed down his Australian site and

in July opened a similar site in New Zealand on which it was clearly intended material of the same sort as was posted on the Australian site, when it was open, would be posted and in fact that is what took place.

7　The matters which are the subject of the plaintiff's charge in the proceedings before me related to postings taking place at the end of July and beginning of August 1999. Some of those matters charged I determined were not reports on securities but some of them were and thus having found that Mr Matthews allowed them to be published and in fact he did publish, having stated in evidence today that he in fact was the publisher of five of them, there was a clear breach of the orders which are now treated as orders of this court making the defendant liable to be dealt with for contempt of those orders.

8　It is clear from the transcript of proceedings before Sackville J that Mr Matthews was well aware of the risk he took in keeping a web site open, as that would enable other persons to post reports on securities to that web site. It is also clear that in so far as he has published reports to that web site he was well aware of what he was doing. It is equally clear that while he may not have had the technical expertise to remove from that site reports on securities, he is in a position to have that take place.

9　It is, I think, perfectly clear, that what he did in moving the site from Australia to New Zealand was a predetermined course of conduct to enable what had been happening in Australia to continue to happen on the New Zealand site. In other words, having been sufficiently warned, one would have thought, by what was said by Sackville J in his judgment on 16 June, he went ahead and engaged in precisely the same sort of conduct as had been the subject of the proceedings for contempt heard before Sackville J in the Federal Court.

10　The only thing which might be put in mitigation against this was the view which Mr Matthews maintains that what was being published by him were not reports about securities. I do not accept that he considered that was a view the court would agree with and it is relevant to point out that he does accept that material which he publishes may have an effect on the share price of the securities about which reports are published on that site. That is of course the conduct which the plaintiff is at pains to prevent.

11　Mr Matthews in oral evidence and again in submissions put forward some matters as to what was an appropriate penalty and as to whether any penalty should be imposed. Those matters were: first, that he had been punished enough as he had already received a jail sentence; second, that any jail sentence would have a serious effect on his family and that he has suffered substantial humiliation which is apparent when he makes any application for employment; thirdly, that he has already suffered serious financial penalty as a result of the orders for costs which have been made against him to date; and fourthly, he says that there is a wider public interest in this matter in that numerous other persons in the community are conducting themselves in the same manner as he has conducted himself and yet they are not being punished; and fifthly, he says that there is no evidence that anybody has suffered from the conduct in respect of which he is subject to the charges of contempt.

12　I do not think it is necessary to go through these matters in detail other than to set them out, so that it can be shown that I understand them. These matters all arose from conduct of Mr Matthews and have little to do with mitigation. Mr Matthews insisted on saying that he had been to jail or received a jail sentence well knowing of course that it has been suspended. So far as the other matters are concerned, while he is subject to the orders for costs he has not paid them; to some extent his financial position is brought about by the fact that he is not a licensed investment adviser and finally the fact that other persons are involved, if they are involved, in relation to securities reports, is no excuse for the conduct of the defendant in breaching the orders.

13 Mr Matthews did say, and this I did not regard as being disrespectful in any way, that there was a disagreement between him and myself as to whether or not the postings I found were a contempt were reports on securities. Whether that is so or not it is proper to say that no evidence was given by Mr Matthews, except on a voir dire matter, on the original hearing, and I do not think that it would be possible to suggest that he was in any way surprised at my decision on the question of whether or not these matters complained of were reports on securities.

14 The defendant is in a different position from that of persons charged with contempt for the first time because as a result of the first hearing before Sackville J he was made perfectly aware of his responsibilities and perfectly aware of the requirements necessary for him to obey the orders of the court. Thus it is perfectly clear in my view that he has purposely breached those orders and there has been a deliberate continuation of the conduct which was the subject of the original orders.

15 The question then is what ought to be the penalty. For the reasons which I have already set out, Mr Matthews submits that there should be no penalty at all and that the plaintiff Commission should pay the costs of these proceedings. The plaintiff Commission argues that there should be a term of imprisonment imposed.

16 It is necessary, I think, to say when the earlier proceedings for contempt were before Sackville J he said that there were some mitigating factors in that Mr Matthews had pleaded guilty, that he did not publish his own reports but put reports from other people on the site, and that those were reports prepared by licensed investment advisers. None of those mitigating factors is present in respect of the proceedings before me, there having been no plea of guilty and the proceedings actually having taken a considerable time, there having been publishing by Mr Matthews of some of the reports and the others which were allowed to be published I think can be safely assumed were not reports of licensed investment advisers.

17 I have come to the clear view in this matter that there are no mitigating circumstances. Mr Matthews said that he was not sorry about breaching the orders; he said that he was aware that he was a person who had an influence on the market through the site, and he said five of the reports were published by him. He was clearly well aware of what he was doing; he was clearly well aware that his continuing conduct was a breach of the orders originally made by O'Connor J.

18 I do not consider a fine would be appropriate and it is unlikely Mr Matthews could pay any substantial fine. In my view it is necessary to impose a term of imprisonment. The system of justice depends upon persons, the subject of court orders, obeying those orders and it depends upon the court making it perfectly clear that it will enforce in a proper way its own orders so as to make the system of justice, upon which the community relies, effective and recognised as being effective by members of the community.

19 Deliberate renewed breach of a court order in respect of which there has been no apology and no contrition shown, make it necessary for a term of imprisonment to be imposed, regrettable though that may be. In the circumstances I consider that an appropriate term of imprisonment in respect of the contempts, the subject of the proved charges before me, is a period of three months and I propose to make an order for the issue of a warrant forthwith.

20 I make the following orders:

1 The defendant, Stephen Lewis Matthews, is guilty of contempt of court by his conduct in disobeying an order made by O'Connor J on 19 February 1999 in proceedings in the Federal Court and treated as proceedings of this court pursuant to the *Federal Courts (State Jurisdiction) Act 1999* (NSW) by order of Austin J on 26 July 1999, in that he:

(a) Between about 26 July 1999 and 29 July 1999 allowed publication of a securities report, entitled 'Re: My physicals list', on the web site known as the Chimes and situated at <http://www.chimes.co.nz>;

(b) Between about 27 July 1999 and 1 August 1999 allowed publication of a securities report, entitled 'News Report #215: "Spike Radio is the bleeding edge of an ambitious transformation of Spike" ', on the web site known as the Chimes and situated at <http://www.chimes.co.nz>;

(c) Between about 27 July 1999 and 1 August 1999 allowed publication of a securities report, entitled 'SECRET TELSTRA ANALYSIS!!! THIS IS HOT!!!', on the web site known as the Chimes and situated at <http://www.chimes.co.nz>;

(d) Between about 27 July 1999 and 29 July 1999 allowed publication of a securities report, entitled 'Wait a minute ...', on the web site known as the Chimes and situated at <http://www.chimes.co.nz>;

(e) Between about 27 July 1999 and 29 July 1999 allowed publication of a securities report, entitled 'Telstra can hit $20 if ...', on the web site known as the Chimes and situated at <http://www.chimes.co.nz>;

(f) On or about 29 July 1999 allowed publication of a securities report, entitled 'News Report #216: Chimes Index buys Macquarie Bank and One.Tel at their all-time highs', on the web site known as the Chimes and situated at <http://www.chimes.co.nz>;

(g) Between about 30 July 1999 and 1 August 1999 allowed publication of a securities report, entitled 'News report #217: Murdoch factor to influence One.Tel's global ambitions', on the web site known as the Chimes and situated at <http://www.chimes.co.nz>;

(h) Between about 5 August 1999 and 6 August 1999 allowed publication of a securities report, entitled 'Tensions in Lucent contract oblige early exit from One.Tel', on the web site known as the Chimes and situated at <http://www.chimes.co.nz>; and

(i) On or about 10 August 1999 allowed publication of a securities report, entitled 'News Report #220: Emperor's credentials can't be denied', on the web site known as the Chimes and situated at <http://www.chimes.co.nz>.

2

   (a) The defendant be imprisoned for a fixed term of three months to commence
        on 4 May 2000 and conclude on 3 August 2000.
   (b) A warrant for the defendant's committal to prison for a fixed term of three
        months issue.
   (c) The warrant for the defendant's committal to prison be executed forthwith.

3   I order the defendant pay the plaintiff's costs of and incidental to the motion
    for contempt.

 NOTES AND QUESTIONS

1   In the Supreme Court of NSW, much as in the Federal Court, there was little,
    if any, discussion by Windeyer J of the mechanics of the Internet. Nor was it
    mentioned that the material violating Australian law might not violate the laws
    of another country which would nevertheless be affected by the order. The issue
    of avoiding the long arm of the Australian law was ever so slightly touched upon
    in paragraph 9, yet no comment of substance was made.

2   How does the result in this case contrast with the result in *Berg*? Although the
    result is the opposite, is the reasoning any more concrete?

3   Is it an oversimplification to suggest that Matthews was jailed for creating an
    Internet site and posting it in New Zealand? Why or why not?

4   What, if anything, would American free speech advocates say about this
    decision?

5   Consider again the quote approved by Ramos JSC: 'traditional jurisdictional
    standards have proved to be sufficient to resolve all civil Internet jurisdictional
    issues' (*People v Lipsitz*, 174 Misc 2d 571 at 578 [Sup Ct New York County
    1997]). In the light of the *Berg* and *Matthews* decisions, can the confidence of
    this statement be applied to Australian 'civil Internet jurisdictional issues'?

(d) *Gutnick v Dow Jones*

Gutnick v Dow Jones & Co Inc

[2001] VSC 305 (28 August 2001)

Supreme Court of Victoria, Australia

Available at <http://www.austlii.edu.au/au/cases/vic/VSC/2001/305.html> 16 August 2006

Hedigan J:

1   The defendant Dow Jones & Co Inc (hereinafter called 'the defendant' or 'Dow Jones' or
    'the applicant/defendant') is the publisher of the *Wall Street Journal*, an internationally

known and respected financial daily newspaper, much concerned with information concerning United States stocks and shares and other events that might affect their prices on the American market. The defendant is also the publisher of *Barrons* Magazine which, according to Mr G Robertson, QC, who with Mr T Robertson appeared on behalf of the defendant, is even more obsessively concerned with those matters. Mr Robertson also claimed that the plaintiff, Mr Joseph Gutnick, was a prominent business identity with a reputation in philanthropic, sporting and religious circles and that he was an international entrepreneur with substantial connections in the United States. The edition of *Barrons* of Monday, 30 October 2000 (which appears likely to have come out on Saturday, 28 October) contained an article written by a journalist working for the defendant, one William Alpert, headed 'Unholy Gains' and sub-headed 'When stock promoters cross paths with religious charities, investors had better be on guard'. The first page of the article also contained a large photograph of Mr Gutnick. The article of some 7000 words contained a number of different photographs of different persons, including one of Nachum Goldberg. *Barrons* is a weekly with a substantial circulation in the United States primarily among investors and those interested in money matters. It was claimed without objection in the hearing before me that this relevant copy of *Barrons* Magazine sold 305,563 copies. A very small number of the actual print copy of *Barrons* came to Australia, but a number of them were sold in Victoria. *Barrons*, however, is customarily put online and this article went on the defendant's web site on Sunday 29 October. The defendant Dow Jones operates from its so-called corporate campus in New Jersey where its web site is located. There is, as I understood it, no web site in Barrons' name and the web site is in the name 'wsj.com'. This is, however, a subscriber web site with some 550,000 subscribers. It was claimed in the opening by Mr Robertson that the defendant could not identify where they all were but it was conceded that 1700 of them paid by way of credit cards from Australia.

2   Ultimately (T139) the defendant made a formal admission that several hundred subscribers to wsj.com were from Victoria and that they included significant persons from finance, business and stockbroking, some of whom the Court might infer, for the purposes of these interlocutory proceedings, downloaded the article. This submission was to be seen in conjunction with the admission effectively made in the opening that there were 1700 subscribers from Australia. Notwithstanding this submission, it did not obviate the necessity to call the only witness who was called on the application, Mr Robert Sichler, a Dow Jones executive to parts of whose evidence I will briefly refer.

3   The plaintiff commenced his proceeding in the Supreme Court of Victoria by writ on 27 November 2000. By the statement of claim endorsed on the writ, the plaintiff asserted that the defendant Dow Jones was at all times the publisher of an Internet business and financial journal and news service entitled *Barrons Online* and that it caused to be published in Victoria by means of the Internet in permanent form an article entitled 'Unholy Gains' which was published on the Internet and available to all persons in Victoria connected to the Internet who could and/or did on or after 28 October 2000 obtain access to the article, including brokers, financial advisers and such persons ...

6   The defendant was served in the United States with the original proceeding and has made application to this Court to stay or dismiss the proceeding on a number of bases.

My description now of the bases of the applications will in effect identify the issues that were the subject of argument before me and they will also identify some other submissions subsidiary to the main themes. The first issue was the issue of jurisdiction, that is, the argument advanced on behalf of the applicant/defendant that the online article was not published in Victoria but in New Jersey, the location of the defendant's web server. I will develop the arguments as presented to me at a later stage but it is sufficient to say that the argument advanced by the defendant with respect to the online publication of *Barrons* would have no effect on the legal consequences of the sale of the hard copies, minimal as they were, in this State. However, it is likely that my decision on this aspect would, as a matter of practicality, dispose of this dispute concerning the paper sales of *Barrons* ...

59 I move to attempt to draw together this mass of material, voluminous authority (to a relatively modest proportion of which I have found it necessary to refer) and elaborate argument into a meaningful conclusion. The first matter to address is whether or not the pre-Internet law was that with respect to defamatory material, it was published at the time and in the place where it was made manifest in a form capable of being comprehended by a third party, or whether it was published when it was delivered 'whether its contents were understood, comprehended or known notwithstanding'. I emphasise that the question is in this case not simply where was it published but was it published in the State of Victoria? Embedded in either or both of those questions is the critical issue which is where and by whom it was published *for the purposes of the law of defamation*. It is not a question of where a scientist believes it was published for scientific purposes, or an executive of the defendant, nor for that matter the plaintiff himself. I have already referred to the attempt in the defendant's experts' affidavits to hijack the answer to the question by claiming it was published in New Jersey and not Victoria for legal purposes.

60 I have concluded that the law in defamation cases has been for centuries that publication takes place where and when the contents of the publication, oral or spoken, are seen and heard (ie made manifest to) and comprehended by the reader or hearer. I reject the defendant's submissions that the *Duke of Brunswick* case or *Burdett* established then or now any different rule for publication for the purposes of civil defamation. My preference is for the long and steady line of authority referred to over these errant authorities, asked by Mr Robertson to bear a greater burden than they can support alongside the mainstream of long applied and respected cases. I therefore conclude that delivery without comprehension is insufficient and has not been the law. On this basis, then, I uphold the plaintiff's contention that the article 'Unholy Gains' was published in the State of Victoria when downloaded by Dow Jones subscribers who had met Dow Jones's payment and performance conditions and by the use of their passwords. It is also absolutely clear that Dow Jones intended that only those subscribers in various States of Australia who met their requirements would be able to access them, and they intended that they should.

61 With respect to the print copy sold, the same proposition must apply although none of the Internet features are relevant. Not only, in my judgment, is that the law, but I am also of the view that it is a correct and just law, and that the arguments advanced against

it are primarily policy-driven, by which I mean policies which are in the interests of the defendant and, in a less business-centric vein, perhaps, by a belief in the superiority of the United States concept of the freedom of speech over the management of freedom of speech in other places and lands. It is, of all concepts, a simple and just one that no one could be heard to complain of a publication that diminishes reputation unless its contents, the very features that lead to the arguable diminution in reputation and standing, are known and understood by readers. Publication in this context is neither a scientific proposition nor a narrow philosophical debate. It is dealing with on the ground realities or, perhaps in this case, in cyberspace realities as well.

62 But even if I were not of the view that publication only occurred upon the contents of *Barrons Online* being downloaded by readers, I believe I would be of no different opinion that there has been publication in Victoria, basing that conclusion as being one reasonably open, having regard to the way in which the defendant formulated its case.

63 The key submission of the defendant is that the Internet publication of 'Unholy Gains' occurred when and where the material was uploaded in New Jersey, that is, when it was pulled from the server in New Jersey by the request emanating from the Victorian web browser. I ignore for the present purposes what appears to me to be a fallacious statement that the downloading was the result of an independent action for which Dow Jones cannot, to use counsel for the defendant's language, be 'properly responsible'. The denial of the plaintiff's case that it is only published when it is made intelligible to a third party by showing it and making it comprehensible is managed by an analysis of the manner of function of the unique and revolutionary Internet.

64 I have, in the course of dealing with the arguments, made some observations about some misleading aspects of the 'buying the book and taking it home analogies', doubtless, to some extent drawn from statements which at least made an appearance in the reasons of Moreland J in *Godfrey*, that were doubtless employed to assist the mind of any judge to understand the proposition. I will not revisit the substance of the way in which the technical steps of the operation of the Internet in this context operate. Much of it is dominated by the contrast between pull and push technology which may highlight differences between some of the features of the Internet such as e-mail and the World Wide Web but does not provide an answer to the legal inquiry as to when and where the words are published.

65 Mr Robertson's argument was that the act of delivery, on which he relied, was completed without the necessity for understanding as soon as the material was uplifted as a consequence of the web server request. He did not contend that it was published or delivered while quietly sitting in the web server. Of course, neither at that time nor on the instance of uplifting was it capable of being understood, but his argument was that at that time of uplifting it was delivered. One accepts that delivery of an electronic document onto the plaintiff's web site will only occur if the electronic request is met and the electronic message is sent. It may be that the web server cannot distinguish between the location of the web browser seeking to access the web page or the search engines which were used in conjunction with the hyperlinks necessary because of the quantity of material.

66 I have referred to counsel's assertion that those seeking to access the web site were 'publishing it to themselves'. In one way this is always so even when one buys a book.

The question is still, however, where and when is it published? The contrast between e-mail and the Web aspect of the Internet was defined as being a contrast between the absence of choice about the reception of e-mail and the situation in the case of accessing the web site in which case the choice is made not by the sender but by the one seeking the access. The claim that those pulling the web browser publish it for themselves by seeking it out and ordering it confuses acquisition and publication. There is only publication, as I have indicated, when it is published to a third party. Moreover, I do not accept the proposition that the web server is totally passive, as was pressed strongly by Mr Robertson. The web server's technology is a participant in the process. Two activities are required. The browser request and the server's response. Moreover, in the case of Dow Jones's *Barrons Online* site, the server's response will be to knock you back if you use the wrong password or you have a delinquent account. It is not, as he suggested, just a repository and is not just a 'pull' method. Dow Jones sets conditions specifically applicable to each client and its web browser. The 'pull' technology only operates on the defendant's terms. When the so-called knock on the door comes it is a web server that opens.

67 Without their web servers and electronic cooperation, nothing will occur. If the computers were down or turned off nothing will occur. But assuming the request is decoded and accepted, the response in the form of electronic bursts is made. In the same nanosecond it enters into cyberspace in New Jersey and arrives in Victoria. In my view, for the law's purposes, the operation of this phenomenon is not a divisible operation. If understanding or comprehension of the message is not a feature of publication, as the defendant claims, and that the act of delivery is the essential characteristic of publication, the better view would appear to be that the information is published in both places at the same time. Not perhaps at the same time for a scientist counting in milli-seconds but, for the law's purposes, no distinction can be sensibly drawn. If this is correct, even setting aside the view I have expressed that publication requires manifestation and comprehension, then, on the defendant's concept of publication, it is as much published and delivered in Victoria as it is sent for delivery from New Jersey. However, I decide this case on the basis that publication takes place on downloading.

68 Mr Robertson claims that the place of publication was in New Jersey and no other place, as I understood his argument, claiming that that follows from the unchallenged expert evidence. I reject this proposition. He claimed that the World Wide Web was an information repository and delivery system unlike any other and which defies traditional analysis. That may be so, but the law must nevertheless cope with it and one of the things about this is that this is an Internet publication, not a World Wide Web publication.

69 In my judgment, undue concentration was placed upon 'the force of the searcher's own action', the fact that it is his click that rests on the server and brings back a copy to the screen located in Victoria, that is, that he pulls the information off the server in New Jersey. It may be that these are meaningful descriptions of what occurs but none of them produce the consequence contended for.

70 As I have indicated the claims of the scientific experts do not control the legal context nor the proper conclusions. Bold assertions that the Internet is unlike other systems do not lead to the abandonment of the analysis that the law has traditionally and reasonably followed to reach just conclusions. The trumpeting of cyberspace miracles does not add

much to the sphere of debate here and occasionally degenerated into sloganeering, which decides nothing. Dr Clarke and Mr Hammond's affidavits merely describe the process and do not, challenged or unchallenged, dominate the legal conclusions which must accommodate much more than the employed scientists' assertions.

71 Mr Robertson's arguments, attractively presented as they were, became enmeshed in the pop science language of 'get' messages, 'pulling off', 'firewalls', and were also disfigured by the statement that the Dow Jones had no capacity to control the pulling off of the information by the get message. It clearly had. The suggestion is, because the recovery of the article awaiting the knock of the web server's door depends on the independently exercised will of the user, that the sending of the message and the obtaining of the information all occur in New Jersey. In my judgment, the information is released and received virtually instantaneously and the attempt to separate them for the law's purpose is a fallacy. The fact that the relevant web server responds to a request simply does not produce the result that publication takes place only in the place where the request is received. Reliance upon the Clarke and Hammond affidavits does not produce the legal consequence argued for although both, as I have already said, attempted to travel beyond their field of scientific expertise and into the realm of proper legal conclusions without success. At one point, Dr Clarke purported to give expert evidence as to what would be the effect of my decision on the world, if it did not establish the State of New Jersey as the place of publication.

72 The defendant's argument really is that liability for cyberspace defamation must be determined by the jurisdiction of the web site. It was virtually admitted that the reason for this is the claimed policy of the law to assist free speech, apparently including defamatory free speech resorting to some statements by Lord Keith in *Derbyshire County Court v Times Newspapers* (1993) AC 534. Counsel also prayed in aid the decision in *Ballina* (1994) 3 NSWLR 681 to little effect since the reason for the decision in *Ballina* was because of the possible inhibition upon the key electoral process by the spectre of being sued for what was said in the course of the electoral democratic process that decided it. It is a case about freedom of speech in elections, the core democratic process.

73 It has never been suggested that that the professional publisher of a magazine like *Barrons* was exempt from the law of defamation and the defendant did not suggest so here. The cases do not support the elusive policy considerations articulated by counsel for the defendant as proper to dominate the forum issue. To say that the country where the article is written, edited and uploaded and where the publisher does its business must be the forum is an invitation to entrench the United States, the primary home of much of Internet publishing, as the forum. The applicant's argument that it would be unfair for the publisher to have to litigate in the multitude of jurisdictions in which its statements are downloaded and read, must be balanced against the worldwide inconvenience caused to litigants, from Outer Mongolia to the Outer Barcoo, frequently not of notable means, who would at enormous expense and inconvenience have to embark upon the formidable task of suing in the USA, with its different fee and costs structures and where the libel laws are, in many respects, tilted in favour of defendants, or, if you will, in favour of the constitutional free speech concepts and rights developed in the USA which originated in the liberal construction by the courts of the First Amendment. Dow Jones controls

access to its material by reason of the imposition of charges, passwords and the like, and the conditions of supply of material on the Internet. It can, if it chooses to do so, restrict the dissemination of its publication of *Barrons* on the Internet in a number of respects. For that matter, the freedom to learn from the Internet of the statements of Mr Alpert in 'Unholy Gains' is restricted to those who pay for it.

74 As I have stated, it is contended that in the age of globalization the rule for which the defendant argues is appropriate. I observe that Mr Robertson referred to the European Community Rules but there are matters in that respect which escaped his attention. Under the draft Hague Convention, a plaintiff will be able to recover the whole of the damages suffered by reason of defamatory Internet publication by suing in the courts of the State in which either the defendant (Article 3) or the plaintiff (Article 10.14) is habitually resident. Counsel for the defendant admitted his argument was 'a business convenient' approach. This is not surprising since his instructions come from Dow Jones, whose interest in having any unpleasant litigation take place in New Jersey is too self-evident to require elaboration.

Mr Robertson advanced an argument which he called 'the parish pump argument' critical of a statement made by Mr Sher that the article was written about a Melburnian, a citizen of another country, and that the defendant did not bother to check up on the local laws of defamation before embarking upon publication. He attacked this relatively passing remark of counsel for the plaintiff, saying that

> As a policy argument for the development of the common law, the heritage of many advanced nations, this invited an unacceptable degree of insularity ... To suggest that US publications must not critically examine Australians except by reference to the defamation law in the State of origin or else erect a firewall to block that critical coverage, so that fellow Australians will not know what is being said about their compatriots elsewhere in the world, is not a proposition that a common law court should accept.

75 This latter observation was directed presumably more to me than to Mr Sher. However, in my judgment, this submission misses the point because it is concerned to articulate high-minded concepts rather than address the critical legal issues. Counsel was free to say what he chose when deploring the possibility that the Court should reach a conclusion which threw a *cordon sanitaire* around the country to prevent its citizens receiving information available everywhere else. But the claim reeks of overstatement. About these relatively self-indulgent submissions, the court says nothing, having neither the power or inclination to censor anything. The point simply is that if you do publish a libel justiciable in another country with its own laws (not mere copies of the US law as the defendant's submissions appear to favour, perhaps because they are tilted in favour of the defendant), then you may be liable to pay damages for indulging that freedom.

76 Counsel for the defendant's submissions as to the horrors of the so-called 'parish pump' insular approach, strongly warned against, lacked the conviction and quality of his other contentions. Paradoxically, his submission, if accepted, produces the greatest insularity of all, namely that every hit on a US website that unearthed a defamatory statement simultaneously created the US forum to decide the issue, if it arose. This was, I estimate, not so much driven by his argument that my decision ought to be informed by devotion

to securing unchecked freedom of speech as his client's interest in securing the comfort of the US forum in the event of any affronted foreigner, the subject of a Dow Jones publication, going to law.

77 The United States courts would generally exercise jurisdiction in defamation actions over defendants domiciled outside the jurisdiction of the court only where the defendant's conduct targeted the forum. Moreover, most American States have a single publication rule so that only one cause of action arises out of any single publication.

78 Many of the matters which were prayed in aid to support the policy imperatives urged on the Court also have a substantial role to play in Mr Robertson's submissions on the *forum non conveniens* issue. His claim that it is an attraction to litigation to be able to get global damages in New Jersey may or may not be true, depending on the circumstances. If it is, then plaintiffs can sue in the USA and presumably are welcome to do so. It is quite another thing to say that everyone libelled on the Internet by a US-based publication must sue in the publicist's domain and not in the place where the victim believes that his reputation lay and was damaged. Moreover, in this case the plaintiff is not interested in global damages. He confined his claim to publication in Victoria and has undertaken to the Court not to sue in the USA, Israel or anywhere other than in the State of Victoria. This will also be a matter to which I will refer when dealing with the issue of *forum non conveniens*.

79 I see no purpose in elaborating my reasons on this aspect further. I conclude that the State of Victoria has jurisdiction to entertain this proceeding.

[Footnotes omitted]

 NOTES AND QUESTIONS

1   This was an interlocutory proceeding involving materials on a subscriber-only website. Within what context was Hedigan J required to consider jurisdiction?

2   What is the significance of the evidence on 'pull and push' technology? What is Hedigan J's attitude towards the bulk of scientific information presented during the hearing? How much of the scientific information was relied upon in his decision?

3   Much of Hedigan J's analysis of jurisdiction was driven by the arguments presented by counsel for each party. Compare this analysis with the approach taken in the United States—in particular, the minimum contacts test.

4   How did Hedigan J deal with the issue of freedom of speech? Did he tackle it, or did he sidestep the issue?

5   The draft Hague Convention referred to in paragraph 74 is the *Preliminary Draft Convention on Jurisdiction and Foreign Judgments in Civil and Commercial Matters* released by the Hague Conference on Private International Laws in October 1999. This was adopted as the *Convention on Choice of Court Agreements* 2005, concluded in June 2005. See further <http://www.hcch. net/>. For a good overview of jurisdictional issues, see the Chicago-Kent Internet Jurisdiction Project, available at <http://www.kentlaw.edu/cyberlaw/docs/> 17 August 2006.

6   An application by Dow Jones for special leave to the Court of Appeal of Victoria was refused. By special leave Dow Jones appealed to the High Court of Australia, where it was joined by a number of interveners. The High Court of Australia dismissed the appeal and all members of the court rejected the argument that the Victorian Court was clearly an inappropriate forum.

(e)   *Dow Jones v Gutnick*

Dow Jones & Co Inc v Gutnick

[2002] HCA 56 (10 December 2002)

High Court of Australia, Australia

Available at <http://www.austlii.edu.au/au/cases/cth/HCA/2002/56.html> 26 January 2006

Gleeson CJ, McHugh, Gummow and Hayne JJ:

44 In defamation, the same considerations that require rejection of locating the tort by reference only to the publisher's conduct, lead to the conclusion that, ordinarily, defamation is to be located at the place where the damage to reputation occurs. Ordinarily that will be where the material which is alleged to be defamatory is available in comprehensible form assuming, of course, that the person defamed has in that place a reputation which is thereby damaged. It is only when the material is in comprehensible form that the damage to reputation is done and it is damage to reputation which is the principal focus of defamation, not any quality of the defendant's conduct. In the case of material on the World Wide Web, it is not available in comprehensible form until downloaded on to the computer of a person who has used a web browser to pull the material from the web server. It is where that person downloads the material that the damage to reputation may be done. Ordinarily then, that will be the place where the tort of defamation is committed ...

48 As has been noted earlier, Mr Gutnick has sought to confine his claim in the Supreme Court of Victoria to the damage he alleges was caused to his reputation in Victoria as a consequence of the publication that occurred *in that State*. The place of commission of the tort for which Mr Gutnick sues is then readily located as Victoria. That is where the damage to his reputation of which he complains in this action is alleged to have occurred, for it is there that the publications of which he complains were comprehensible by readers. It is his reputation in *that State*, and only that State, which he seeks to vindicate. It follows, of course, that substantive issues arising in the action would fall to be determined according to the law of Victoria. But it also follows that Mr Gutnick's claim was thereafter a claim for damages for a tort committed in Victoria, not a claim for damages for a tort committed outside the jurisdiction. There is no reason to conclude that the primary judge erred in the exercise of his discretion to refuse to stay the proceeding.

49 More difficult questions may arise if complaint were to be made for an injury to reputation which is said to have occurred as a result of publications of defamatory material in a number of places. For the reasons given earlier, in resolving those difficulties, it may be necessary to distinguish between cases where the complaint is confined to publications made in Australia, but in different States and Territories, and cases where publication is alleged to have occurred outside Australia, either with or without publication within Australia. Several kinds of difficulty may arise and each requires separate identification and consideration, even if the treatment of one may have consequences for some other aspect of the matter.

50 First, there may be some question whether the forum chosen by the plaintiff is clearly inappropriate. If there is more than one action brought, questions of vexation may arise and be litigated either by application for stay of proceedings or application for anti-suit injunction.

51 Secondly, a case in which it is alleged that the publisher's conduct has all occurred outside the jurisdiction of the forum may invite attention to whether the reasonableness of the publisher's conduct should be given any significance in deciding whether it has a defence to the claim made. In particular, it may invite attention to whether the reasonableness of the publisher's conduct should be judged according to all the circumstances relevant to its conduct, including where that conduct took place, and what rules about defamation applied in that place or those places. Consideration of those issues may suggest that some development of the common law defences in defamation is necessary or appropriate to recognise that the publisher may have acted reasonably before publishing the material of which complaint is made. Some comparison might be made in this regard with the common law developing by recognising a defence of innocent dissemination to deal with the position of the vendor of a newspaper and to respond to the emergence of new arrangements for disseminating information like the circulating library.

52 In considering any of these matters, it should go without saying that it is of the first importance to identify the precise difficulty that must be addressed. In particular, in cases where the publisher of material which is said to be defamatory has acted in one or more of the United States, any action that is brought in an Australian court in respect of publications that were made in America, would, in applying the law of the place of commission of the tort, have to give effect to the rather different balance that has been struck in the United States between freedom of speech and the individual's interest in reputation. Furthermore, it may well be that the resolution of a claim for publications made in one or more of the United States would be affected by the application by the law of the relevant state of a form of the single publication rule.

53 Three other matters should be mentioned. In considering what further development of the common law defences to defamation may be thought desirable, due weight must be given to the fact that a claim for damage to reputation will warrant an award of substantial damages only if the plaintiff has a reputation in the place where the publication is made. Further, plaintiffs are unlikely to sue for defamation published outside the forum unless a judgment obtained in the action would be of real value to the plaintiff. The value that

a judgment would have may be much affected by whether it can be enforced in a place where the defendant has assets.

54 Finally, if the two considerations just mentioned are not thought to limit the scale of the problem confronting those who would make information available on the World Wide Web, the spectre which Dow Jones sought to conjure up in the present appeal, of a publisher forced to consider every article it publishes on the World Wide Web against the defamation laws of every country from Afghanistan to Zimbabwe is seen to be unreal when it is recalled that in all except the most unusual of cases, identifying the person about whom material is to be published will readily identify the defamation law to which that person may resort …

[Footnotes omitted]

 NOTES AND QUESTIONS

1　Despite the outcry from publishers at the time the decisions in *Gutnick* were handed down, the decisions are rather unexceptional when the facts are considered. The plaintiff limited his claim to his home state, the claim was in defamation and not some other branch of law, and most importantly, the on-line service was one via paid subscription. As Dow Jones restricted access to paid subscribers only, it must surely be possible for Dow Jones to further restrict access to particular articles according to some other criteria.

2　Following the High Court decision in *Gutnick*, Canada's Ontario Court of Appeal handed down the decision of *Barrick Gold Corporation v Lopehandia* [2004] OJ No 2329, which adopted a similar approach.

3　In the United Kingdom, however, the decision of *Dow Jones & Co Inc v Jameel* [2005] EWCA Civ 75 (03 February 2005), where the court declined to exercise jurisdiction, should also be considered. The approach taken by the *Jameel* court discourages 'forum shopping' and points towards claimants having to bring their claim in the jurisdiction where the publication is most widely read, and presumably where the greatest damage occurred. See futher K Howard & YF Lim, 'Defamation and the Internet one more time: *Dow Jones v Yousef Abdul Latif Jameel*' (2005) 8(2) *Internet Law Bulletin* 21.

4　Europe

The *Matthews* case demonstrates the apparent ease with which the complexities of the Internet can be glossed over and simplified in the judicial context. The same potential exists within the academic context. The following extract is a discussion of e-commerce in the EU. As you read it, consider carefully the significance of the assumptions made at the beginning of the piece, and assess whether the hurdles faced when attempting a clear and coherent treatment of jurisdiction are cleared, or merely avoided.

Morten Foss and Lee Bygrave, 'International Consumer Purchases through the Internet: Jurisdictional Issues Pursuant to European Law'

(2000) 8(2) *International Journal of Law and Information Technology* 99

Introduction

... **[100]** [T]he crucial question [is] the degree to which the existing rules of the Brussels Convention, together with the rules in other instruments of private international law, may be sensibly applied in the context of e-commerce. This paper is primarily an attempt to address aspects of [this] question.

The scope of analysis in this paper is delimited along the following lines:

1   only contracts for the purchase of goods or services by consumers are analysed;
2   it is assumed that the vendors of the goods or services are not, in the context of the contracts concerned, consumers themselves;
3   it is further assumed that the vendors are not, in the context of the contracts concerned, public authorities acting in exercise of their powers;
4   consideration is only given to contracts entered into by parties that are domiciled or established within the European Economic Area (EEA);
5   it is assumed that the vendor is based in an EEA State other than that in which the consumer is domiciled;
6   only contracts in which the contract has been concluded over the Internet are canvassed;
7   there is no discussion of choice-of-law issues (ie issues as to which country's law should be applied to resolve the dispute in question);
8   discussion of issues concerned with cross-national enforcement of judicial decisions is also omitted.

It follows from the above delimitation that the basic point of departure for discussion in the paper of jurisdictional issues is the legal systems of Western Europe. More specifically, attention is directed to the provisions of the Brussels Convention of 1968, together with those of the Lugano Convention of 1988. The former Convention contains, *inter alia*, rules for the resolution of jurisdictional issues arising between Member States of the European Union (EU) with respect to civil and commercial matters—including the type of consumer contracts that are the focus of this paper—while the Lugano Convention addresses these issues also for Member States of the European Free Trade Association (EFTA). The provisions of each Convention are identical with respect to consumer contracts. For the sake of brevity, reference in the following is made only to the provisions of the Brussels Convention.

The basic jurisdictional rule laid down in the Convention is that a defendant shall be sued in the State where he/she/it is domiciled (Art 2(1)). The application of this rule—and most of the rules treated below (Arts 5(5), 13–15)—presupposes that the defendant is domiciled in a Contracting State to the Convention. If the defendant is not so domiciled, the issue of jurisdiction is to be determined by domestic law (Art 4).

The Convention allows for some derogation from the rule in Art 2(1). One important derogation is in order to give effect to what is commonly termed the principle of party autonomy; ie that parties are free to make a binding agreement as to which country's courts shall be competent to judge a dispute between them. If such agreement has been reached (and fulfils certain formal requirements), it shall be determinative of jurisdiction (Art 17(1)).

However, a multiplicity of other rules in the Convention take precedence over such an agreement. One set of rules (Arts 13–15) concerns particular kinds of consumer contracts. Another set (Art 5(5)) concerns disputes arising out of branch operations. Both sets lay down special rules on jurisdiction which also permit derogation from the rule in Art 2(1). Article 13 read[s] as follows:

> In proceedings concerning a contract concluded by a person for a purpose which can be regarded as being outside his trade or profession, hereinafter called 'the consumer', jurisdiction shall be determined by this Section, without prejudice to the provisions of Articles 4 and 5(5), if it is:
>
> 1   A contract for the sale of goods on instalment credit terms, or
> 2   A contract for a loan repayable by instalments, or any other form of credit, made to finance the sale of goods, or
> 3   Any other contract for the supply of goods or a contract for the supply of services, and
>   (a) in the state of the consumer's domicile the conclusion of the contract was preceded by a specific invitation addressed to him by advertising; and
>   (b) the consumer took in that State the steps necessary for the conclusion of the contract ...

... **[103]** [T]he effect of Arts 13–15 is that, in relation to disputes connected to consumer contracts falling within the ambit of Art 13, the vendor may only sue the consumer in the country where the latter is domiciled, while the consumer may always sue the vendor in the consumer's country of domicile. Further, these rules cannot be altered by agreement between the parties unless the agreement fulfils one or more of the conditions laid down in Art 15. Once the dispute has been settled by the court in question, a variety of rules in Title III of the Convention (see especially Arts 26, 28 and 31) are applicable to ensure the efficacious recognition and enforcement of the court's judgment in the State where the defendant/vendor is situated.

As for Art 5(5), this states that the defendant party to a dispute 'arising out of the operations of a branch, agency or other establishment' may be sued 'in the courts for the place in which the branch, agency or other establishment is situated'. It should be noted that Arts 13–15 do not limit application of the rule in Art 5(5) ...

... **[104]** When analysing the proper reach of Arts 13 and 5(5) *de lege lata*, it is endeavoured to adopt the method and perspective typical of the European Court of Justice (ECJ). The ECJ has been accorded jurisdiction to rule on interpretation of the Brussels Convention. The case law of the ECJ on this Convention also carries significant weight in interpretation of the Lugano Convention, though is not wholly determinative for construing the latter.

In its case law on the Brussels Convention, the ECJ has taken the purposive, teleological approach to rule interpretation that characterises its decision making generally. The Court holds that the concepts employed in the Convention are to be interpreted, as a point of departure, autonomously of the meaning they are given in the domestic law of one or more of the Contracting States. They are to be construed 'by reference, first, to the objectives and scheme of the Convention and, secondly, to the general principles which stem from the corpus of the national legal systems'. In contrast, though, to its general approach to rule interpretation, the ECJ also tends to place significant weight on the intentions of the drafters of the Brussels Convention as evidenced in several published reports by *rapporteurs of Convention* drafting groups ...

The scope of Articles 13(1)(1) and 13(1)(2)

[107] Articles 13(1)(1) and 13(1)(2) cover two types of contracts:

* contracts for the sale of goods on instalment credit terms; and
* contracts for loans repayable by instalments, or any other form of credit, made to finance the sale of goods.

The main issue arising with respect to the application of these two provisions in the context of e-commerce concerns the meaning of the term 'goods'. In many instances, interpretation and application of the term 'goods' will not be difficult in an e-commerce context. For instance, an Internet-based contract for the sale and purchase of a boat will clearly remain a contract for the sale and purchase of a good. However, more complex questions arise when products that have been traditionally delivered in the form of a physically tangible object (good) are instead delivered through the Internet in digital, non-tangible form. Such transactions are hereinafter termed as (online) delivery of digitized products. To spell out the obvious, a digitized product is a product that has been transformed from a physically tangible object to a purely digital combination of binary code.

Not all physically tangible objects—nor, concomitantly, all goods—can become *digitized products*, only those objects/goods that essentially have no other function than to serve as a physical medium for information. Typical examples of objects/goods that can be digitized are books, videos, CDs, cassette tapes, and computer programs. Common for such products is that intellectual property rights tend to attach to them. What is of concern in the following is the appropriate legal status of the digitized product itself, not the physical medium to which it was linked before digitization or to which it might later be linked ...

... To sum up so far, a differentiated, individualized approach should be taken when resolving the question at hand. Such an approach should attempt to analyse each product and product transaction in order to identify their principal features. It should also be wary of making a priori assumptions. Hence, for instance, just because a product and transaction linked to it are difficult to classify as goods in the traditional sense of the term should not automatically mean that they can easily be classified as services. Concomitantly, just because the product being purchased and delivered online, functionally equates with or replaces a physically tangible object that is traditionally classified as a good, should not automatically mean that the digital product can or should also be classified as such. It needs to be kept in mind that some offline transactions qualifying as sale and purchase of goods can, when carried out online, end up resembling more closely the provision of services. For example, a consumer's purchase of an encyclopaedia in paper form is clearly a purchase of a good, whereas if the consumer enters into a contract with, say, Britannica.com Inc for online access to the latter's database, he/she seems rather to be purchasing a service.

At the same time, when subjecting the various types of digitized products and product transactions to closer analysis, it is by no means easy to subsume any of them under any one of the aboFve-mentioned classifications. In view of this difficulty, one could argue that transactions involving digitized products cannot fall within the scope of Arts 13(1)(1) and 13(1)(2), and that an appropriate amendment to extend these provisions must be effected before such transactions can be covered. Such a result is far from satisfactory given the length of time typically taken to amend treaties like the Brussels Convention and given the fact that the sale and purchase of digitized products are rapidly growing in popularity and economic significance. If a regulatory vacuum is to be avoided, one must attempt to determine which of the existing legal classifications is best suited to apply to digitized products.

In doing so, account should firstly be taken of any existing consensus among policy-makers as to which classification is most appropriate. In the present context, however, no such consensus exists. The closest one comes to finding such consensus is in the area of taxation, but even in that field there has been criticism of the idea that digitized products should be seen as services. Given the lack of consensus, one is forced to move on to considering which classification is best in light of the purposes of Arts 13(1)(1) and 13(1)(2) and the needs of the parties involved in selling/buying digitized products.

When purchasing (on credit) digitized products from foreign vendors, consumers' need for protection pursuant to Arts 13(1)(1) and 13(1)(2) is not significantly different from when they purchase (on credit) traditional goods. Moreover, the principle that like cases should be treated alike speaks in favour of classifying digitized products as goods pursuant to Arts 13(1)(1) and 13(1)(2). Comparing the sale and purchase of digitized products with the sale and purchase of traditional goods, both sorts of transactions are essentially similar in terms of their functional and economic purposes. For example, when a consumer buys and receives a computer program online, he/she is usually interested in attaining a tool for the processing of data in various ways, and the program's basic function is to facilitate such processing. The medium by which the program is delivered to the consumer is of relatively marginal consequence for the ability of the program to meet the consumer's wants and expectations. Given this marginality, it would seem unreasonable to make the choice of medium for delivery determinative of whether or not the transaction falls under Art 13(1)(1) or 13(1)(2). Indeed, most consumers would probably be unaware of, and hence surprised over, such a result ...

The scope of Article 13(1)(3)

... [113] In order to fall within the scope of Art 13(1)(3), a contract must not only be of a certain type, it must also have arisen in a designated manner. Regarding contract type, this is formulated as 'any other contract for the supply of goods or a contract for the supply of services'. Of primary importance for electronic commerce is determining what is meant by the expression 'supply of goods or ... services'... In light of that discussion, there are solid grounds for concluding that the sale and purchase of digitized products may qualify as a 'supply of goods' pursuant to Art 13(1)(3).

Even if the sale of digitized products may not qualify as a 'supply of goods', it is highly likely to qualify as a 'supply of services'. There can be little doubt that the expression 'supply of goods or ... services' is largely commensurate with the expression 'supply of goods or services' commonly used in EU law. Thus, in working out the meaning of the expression employed in Art 13(1)(3), the ECJ is likely (implicitly, if not explicitly) to have recourse to its rulings on the scope of the expression 'supply of goods or services' in EU/EC treaty provisions. A basic premise of these rulings is that the expression is intended to cover all activities of a commercial nature. The sale of digitized products is clearly a commercial activity.

Moreover, it is likely that the ECJ will be moved to conclude that such a sale may fall within the scope of Art 13(1)(3) by the fact that an opposite conclusion (extending also to the scope of Arts 13(1)(1) and 13(1)(2)) would leave consumers of digitized products without any protection pursuant to Arts 13–15 of the Brussels Convention. The latter result would be difficult to justify in light of the basic purpose of these provisions as a whole.

As for the manner in which a contract arises, Art 13(1)(3) lists two cumulative requirements:

(a) in the State of the consumer's domicile the conclusion of the contract was preceded by a specific invitation addressed to him or by advertising; and

(b) the consumer took in that State the steps necessary for the conclusion of the contract.

These requirements are intended to ensure that the special protection accorded by Arts 13–15 applies only to consumer contracts that have an adequate connection with the consumer's place of domicile. The basic assumptions upon which the rules build are that a consumer may only sue a vendor in the courts of his/her own State when

(i) the vendor has directed his/her/its commercial activity towards the State of the consumer's domicile,

(ii) the consumer resided in that State at the time when he/she entered into the contract, and, accordingly,

(iii) there is a close connection between the contract and the State of the consumer's domicile, such that

(iv) the consumer has a reasonable expectation of being able to sue in his/her local courts in the event of a dispute ...

The scope of Article 13(2)

... **[125]** It will be recalled that a basic point of departure for the Brussels Convention is that its provisions only apply when the defendant is domiciled in one of the Convention's Contracting States. An exception to this rule is provided by Art 13(2), which reads:

> Where a consumer enters into a contract with a party who is not domiciled in a Contracting State but has a branch, agency or other establishment in one of the Contracting States, that party shall, in disputes arising out of the operations of the branch, agency or establishment, be deemed to be domiciled in that State.

Article 13(2) will only apply if the consumer contract meets the criteria in Art 13(1).

In the context of e-commerce, an important issue arises in the case of a vendor who/which is not domiciled in any of the contracting States but offers products via a web site that is supported by a server situated in one of those States. Can the vendor be properly deemed to be domiciled in that State pursuant to Art 13(2)? The answer to this question hinges on whether the operations of the web site and/or server can properly qualify as the operations of a 'branch, agency or other establishment' ...

... **[127]** Functionally, a web site can play much the same role as a branch or agency—particularly if it utilises advanced intelligent-agent software to process and execute customer orders. Moreover, it should be relatively easy for a web site to meet the control criterion laid down by the Court in the *De Bloos* case, especially when the site is supported by a server that is owned, run or otherwise controlled by the vendor. But even when the web site is supported by a server that is not owned, run or otherwise controlled by the vendor, the control criterion is probably still fulfilled if the vendor determines the content and functions of the site. The fact that the vendor does not determine where the site is located on the server is of relatively little importance. At the same time, a server (as opposed to a web site) which is not owned, run or otherwise controlled by the vendor cannot meet the control criterion and cannot, accordingly, qualify as a branch, agency or other establishment of the vendor.

What of the criteria laid down by the ECJ in its *Somafer* decision and elaborated upon in the *Blanckaert* decision? To begin with, a server per se probably cannot be said to meet the requirement 'materially equipped to negotiate business', as it is analogous to an empty business office. Only when the server is equipped with software (ie develops a web site) allowing a person/organisation to transact with the vendor is it possible for the requirement to be met. Thus, the next question is whether a web site can meet the requirement. The answer to this question is most likely to be in the affirmative if the web site has the necessary software allowing for either the setting of terms for, or the execution of, business transactions between the vendor and consumer (and not merely the transmission of orders). At-the same time, there is no necessity for the web site to be able to handle all sorts of enquiries (eg enquiries from persons/organisations wishing to place advertisements on the web site).

It should be emphasised that the web pages transferred (downloaded from the vendor's web site to the server of the customer upon the latter's request will not satisfy the requirement. Such pages do not contain the necessary software permitting the vendor and customer to enter into a business agreement. The pages are analogous to, inter alia, advertisement material. It is trite that the presence of such material in a foreign country cannot amount to the existence of agency, branch or other establishment for the vendor.

The next question is whether a web site can properly be regarded as 'a place of business which has the appearance of permanency'. If this expression is construed as requiring an agency etc to be continuously situated in the same physical place, a web site will probably be unable to meet the criterion if it is moved about on the server of the host provider or moved from one server to another (such movement does occur). However, such movement should not be decisive for answering the question as it has no significant consequence for the ability of a web site to function commercially with potential purchasers and is usually not apparent to the latter (or the vendor). Of far greater importance is whether the web site continuously operates under one unique domain name through which it appears to purchasers as a 'place of business'. And it is the degree of apparent permanency of this area which should be decisive for answering the question at hand.

To sum up so far on this question, a web site that continuously operates under one domain name would seem capable of qualifying as 'a place of business which has the appearance of permanency'. If the web site also meets the other criteria laid down by the ECJ in the *Somafer* and *Blanckaert* decisions, it would seem capable of qualifying as an 'agency, branch or establishment' pursuant to Arts 5(5) and 13(2). However, this does not mean that such a web site should qualify as such, either *de lege lata* or *de lege ferenda*...

... **[135]** [E]-commerce is unlikely to flourish if consumers lack confidence in their ability to expeditiously maintain and pursue their domestic legal rights. Even if there is empirical evidence indicating that the current jurisdictional rules for consumer contracts frequently fail to result in effective protection for consumers in the event of cross-border legal disputes, these rules are likely to be of significant *symbolic* value for consumer confidence. Nevertheless, there can be little doubt that the rules need to be supplemented by serious efforts to improve the efficacy of transnational dispute resolution procedures, particularly when small claims are at stake.

What is most problematic with the provisions of the proposed Regulation, along with the Commission commentary on them, is that they fail to resolve—let alone address—many of the major issues that are dealt with in this paper. To begin with, there is a failure to provide detailed guidance on the meaning of the expression 'directs such activities' (Art 15(1)(3)) in the context of Internet-based marketing and contracting. Recital 13 in the preamble to the proposed Regulation seems to indicate that the mere fact that a vendor's web site is accessible from a particular state is sufficient to deem the vendor as having 'directed' activity to that state for the purposes of Art 15(1)(3). In its explanatory memorandum, however, the Commission appears to limit inclusion of such activities within the scope of Art 15(1)(3) to those carried out via *interactive* web sites:

> [t]he concept of activities pursued in or directed towards a Member State is designed to make clear that point (3) applies to consumer contracts concluded via an interactive web site accessible in the State of the consumer's domicile. The fact that a consumer simply had knowledge of a service or possibility of buying goods via a passive web site accessible in his country of domicile will not trigger the protective jurisdiction. The contract is thereby treated in the same way as a contract concluded by telephone, fax and the like, and activates the grounds of jurisdiction provided for by Article 16.

Unfortunately, the Commission does not elaborate on what is exactly meant by an 'interactive' web site. It seems safe to assume, though, that interactivity entails a facility for exchange of information between the web site and those visiting it, including a facility for placement of purchase orders.

A second major uncertainty concerns the vexed issue of whether digitized products may constitute goods. The proposed provisions do not bring any clarity to this issue, neither does the Commission's explanatory memorandum. Admittedly, the issue loses some of its significance in relation to the proposed Art 15 given that Art 15(1)(3) refers to 'all other cases'; ie even if digitized products are found not to constitute 'goods' pursuant to Arts 15(1)(1) and 15(1)(2), their purchase may still fall within the ambit of Art 15(1)(3). This notwithstanding, it would be advantageous for consumers that such products were found to be 'goods', as the purchase of the products could then fall under either of the first two (relatively uncomplicated) paragraphs of Art 15 (granted, of course, that the purchases also satisfy the other conditions of these paragraphs).

One possible strategy worth pursuing would be to make it clear in the *travaux preparatoires* and/or recitals to the proposed Regulation that the concept of 'goods' in Art 15 covers digitized products. Another possible strategy would be to include a specific reference to digitized products in the proposed provision, such that references to 'goods' become references to 'goods and digitized products'.

Other unfortunate omissions in the proposed Regulation and Commission commentary on it include:

1   failure to address whether a web site may constitute a 'branch, agency or other establishment' (Art 15(2)) and
2   failure to address the issue of protection of the vendor's good faith (including the extent of such protection).

At the same time, the proposed provisions dispense with the requirement set down in Art 13(1)(3)(b) of the Brussels Convention ('the consumer took in that State the steps necessary for the conclusion of the contract'). This omission breaks with the basic assumptions upon which current law builds and will probably enable a consumer who is situated in, eg, the vendor's State when he/she enters into an electronic contract with the vendor, to enjoy the special protection extended by Art 15 even when it is doubtful that the consumer expects or should be entitled to expect that he/she can sue in the court of the State where he/she is domiciled. For instance, under the proposed Art 15, a consumer who is domiciled in Germany but who travels to Italy and, while there, accesses an Italian web site (using, eg, a portable computer), then orders and picks up a product from that site, and subsequently takes the product back to Germany, will apparently still be able to sue in a German court with respect to a dispute over the product or contract. Such a result is problematic, as it is extremely doubtful that the consumer in that scenario would expect or should be entitled to expect that he/she could sue in a German court.

Conclusion

This paper shows that the provisions of Art 13 of the Brussels and Lugano Conventions can be interpreted in a such a manner that they are able to satisfactorily meet the legitimate interests of both vendors and consumers in the context of e-commerce. This possibility notwithstanding, much uncertainty surrounds the exact scope of these provisions in such a context. Concomitantly, much uncertainty accompanies how the provisions will be construed by the ECJ or other judicial bodies with respect to Internet transactions. Hence, it cannot be taken for granted that the judiciary will interpret Art 13 in the manner argued for in this paper. Unfortunately, Art 15 of the proposed Regulation on jurisdiction fails to significantly roll back the uncertainty. In the interests of establishing secure legal parameters for both vendors and consumers in an e-commerce environment, this failure must be rectified in the future work on reform of the Brussels and Lugano Conventions.

[Footnotes omitted]

NOTES AND QUESTIONS

1   One of the most significant challenges of the Internet is that as soon as we attempt to analyse it, we are forced to simplify it. However, once we simplify our theoretical model, its predictability for practical purposes is immediately hampered. Consequently we are left with either exceedingly complex intellectual matrices which defy understanding or with simplistic models with limited practical value.

2   Look again at the limiting assumptions set out at the beginning of the extract above. What do you consider to be the effect of these assumptions upon wider use of the Internet and upon the analysis that makes those assumptions? How convincing is the interpretation presented?

----

5   Jurisdictional issues

Jurisdiction on the Internet is an all-pervasive issue. Regardless of what substantive legal issue one is dealing with, whether it be copyright or defamation or privacy, jurisdiction is an issue that is constantly looming—so much so that it has been said that the Internet is one big jurisdictional problem. It allows individuals to cross state and international boundaries in a matter of seconds, and without being aware of the transition or the foreign jurisdiction. Under the theory of general jurisdiction, the Internet user who initiates a communication into a foreign jurisdiction (state or nationality) may be subject to its jurisdiction.

State and national borders are no longer relevant in cyberspace.[6] The Internet lacks physical boundaries and communities and communications that exist on the Internet do not exist in any particular jurisdiction. In some instances, it can also be said that jurisdiction exists in many places. This anomaly poses a problem that current jurisdiction law cannot solve. Pre-World Wide Web jurisdictional jurisprudence was not designed to deal with the intricacies and nuances of the cyber-world. Existing law on jurisdiction evaluates physical movement or presence. Communication on the Internet, on the other hand, does not involve any physical movement.

As David R Johnson and David Post have pointed out,[7] events on the Internet occur everywhere but nowhere in particular. Communications are engaged in by on-line personae who are human and real, but who are at the same time 'unreal' in that they might not be traceable to any particular person. No physical jurisdiction has a more compelling claim than any other to subject these communications and events exclusively to its laws. It is for these reasons that in the infancy of the World Wide Web, calls were

---

6   See D Post and D Johnson, 'Law and Borders', available at <http://www.temple.edu/lawschool/dpost/Borders.html> 28 January 2001; D Burk, 'Jurisdiction in a World Without Borders', available at <http://vjolt.student.virginia.edu/graphics/vol1/home_art3.html> 28 January 2001.

7   'Law and Borders: The Rise of Law in Cyberspace', (1996) 48 *Stanford Law Review* 1367.

made for the Internet to have its own jurisdiction, governed by its own laws.[8] These calls have not been heeded. Further, some jurisdictions have attempted to enforce their laws on the Internet as a result of enforcing their laws in their own jurisdictions. In November 2000, a French court ordered Yahoo! to prevent French citizens from accessing on-line auctions of Nazi memorabilia that occurred on Yahoo!'s US servers. Yahoo! argued that the auctions were protected by US free speech laws and that the Yahoo! site based in France was free of such auctions. The court was not interested.[9]

---

8   See also D W Post, 'Anarchy, State and the Internet: An Essay on Law-Making in Cyberspace',' (1995) *Journal of Online Law* Art 3, available at <http://warthog.cc.wm.edu/law/publications/jol/post.html> 28 January 2001; D. Loundy, 'Internet Governance through Self-Help Remedies', available at <http://www.loundy.com/CPSR-Self-Help.html> 28 January 2001.

9   A Jesdanun, 'Yahoo: No Nazis Here: New Rules Dovetail With French Court Ruling', The Associated Press, available at <http://www.abcnews.go.com/sections/scitech/DailyNews/yahoo010103.html> 03 September 2001; BBC News, 'Yahoo hits back at Nazi Ruling,' available at <http://news.bbc.co.uk/hi/english/world/europe/newsid_1032000/1032605.stm> 03 September 2001. Yahoo! countered with a lawsuit of its own in the USA, saying that the French ruling violated US free speech rights. In November 2001, a US District Court agreed with Yahoo!, but in December 2001, two French civil rights groups appealed the decision to the US Ninth Circuit Court of Appeals. See Matt Beer, 'Back to Court for Yahoo Nazi Case', available at <http://australianit.news.com.au/articles/0, 7204,3384201%5e15319%5 e%5enbv%5e15306,00.html> . In 2005, the Paris Court of Appeal has confirmed the former president of Yahoo!, Timothy Koogle, has been cleared of 'justifying war crimes and crimes against humanity', for having permitted the sale of Nazi objects on its auction site. One of the charges had already been rejected in 2003. The court of appeal used the same arguments to order the acquittal of the former Yahoo! CEO. See further ZDNet France staff 'Yahoo! Nazi auction trial finally reaches an end' available at <http://networks.silicon.com/webwatch/0,39024667,39129362,00.htm>.

Electronic Contracting

1   Introduction

E-commerce is the buzzword of the new millennium, and inherent in any consideration of e-commerce are electronic contracts. The Internet is the fastest growing commercial market in the world at any point in history. The United Kingdom Department of Trade and Industry had estimated the 2000 value of Internet commerce at $12 billion per annum. In the USA the Federal Trade Commission reported that total on-line sales for 1999 were between $20 and $30 billion. Of course, if measuring current amounts is difficult, predicting future amounts is near impossible. Nevertheless, in the USA alone, some projections have estimated the value of Internet commerce to be as much as $184 billion by 2004. Estimates of global value reach up to $3.2 trillion globally by 2003.[1] It is for these reasons that any book on Internet law must address electronic contracts to some degree.

The key to understanding electronic contracting is to regard the Internet simply as another tool of communication. Until now, new modes or tools of communication have been adequately incorporated into the legal system: the mail, the telex, the fax machine and so on. In theory, therefore, there is no reason why the law should not be capable of incorporating Internet communications. How does the Internet differ from the technologies preceding it, and how can the law accommodate these differences? In order to answer these questions we need to consider, first, the practicalities of contract formation on the Internet and second, the common law of contracts. We must then examine how the latter applies to the former.

The first step is simply to ask the question 'How do people contract over the Internet?' There are two main methods: e-mail and click-wrap.

(a)   E-mail

The text of an e-mail message is simply the digital equivalent of a letter. One may attach things to it, it needs to be addressed, and it needs to be sent to the desired recipient. E-mail is capable of performing all the functions of normal mail (or 'snail mail' as it has been dubbed). E-mail can be used to send advertisements as well as offers and acceptances. However, there are some technicalities which complicate any comparison between standard mail delivery systems and electronic mail delivery systems. First, each e-mail message is actually split into 'packets' which take individual paths to the recipient's computer. The message text is not sent as an uninterrupted whole. Second, e-mail messages are generally regarded as instantaneous, where letters are not. This, however, can also be disputed, as it is quite possible for an e-mail message to be delayed, or even to be completely lost for a host of reasons such as system crashes.

---

1   A number of these projections are taken from J Catchpole, 'The Regulation of Electronic Commerce: A Comparative Analysis of the Issues Surrounding the Principles of Establishment' (2001) 9(1) *International Journal of Law and Information Technology* 4.

(b) Click-wrap

Click-wrap contracts are most commonly found on the World Wide Web. The usual process of formation of such a contract begins with the web vendor placing information about a product on the web. This information could be in the form of an advertisement (webvertisement), an invitation to treat, or an offer of a product or service for a sum of money. There is usually a hypertext order form within close electronic proximity which the consumer fills out and this form will contain a button labelled 'I Accept', 'Submit', 'Purchase', or some such phrase. When the consumer clicks on this button, the order is sent to the vendor, who usually reserves the right to proceed or not to proceed with the transaction. In many instances, however, the order will be processed automatically and in this respect, it is analogous to purchasing goods in a normal shop. Communications in this manner on the World Wide Web have generally been regarded as instantaneous.

(c) Invitations, offers and acceptance

Before we investigate the details of electronic contracting, we must first consider whether or not these contracts are legal and binding at all. In general, the common law will enforce almost any form of contract supported by consideration, whether oral or written, formal or informal, as long as the intention of the parties can be clearly discerned. There are only a few circumstances where contracts are required to be in a specific form, such as those for the sale of land. There seems, therefore, to be no reason in principle to prevent the enforcement of an electronic contract.

In theoretical terms, a traditional contract will be formed when there is a meeting of minds between the parties. This is usually found in a clear and unambiguous offer followed by a similarly clear and unambiguous acceptance. An important distinction needs to be made here between an offer, an invitation to treat, and an advertisement. An offer is a proposed set of terms that can form the basis of a contract. An invitation to treat is simply an invitation to make an offer for a product or service. Hence an advertisement, as a form of an invitation to treat, also acts as the carrier of information upon which contracting decisions might be based. Significantly, an offer will always contemplate acceptance and, therefore, it must always be something capable of being accepted. This is particularly important in the Internet context because the distinction between advertisements, invitations to treat, and offers included in websites are often blurred by vendors. If there is an offer, an affirmative response means a contract is formed. If a statement looks like an offer but it is not capable of being accepted, it is only an invitation to treat, and then an affirmative response is, in reality, only an offer. A well-established real-world example of an invitation to treat can be found in the case of the supermarket. Goods on the shelves are presented by the shop as an invitation to treat, and goods subsequently taken to the cash register are presented by the shopper as an offer.[2]

Applying these principles to the World Wide Web, the electronic proximity between the webvertisement and the actual point of sale is likely to render the status of a message

---

2   *Pharmaceutical Society of Great Britain v Boots Cash Chemists (Southern) Ltd* [1953] 1 QB 401.

closer to an invitation to treat in a shop than to an advertisement that we might see in a magazine. Hence, a consumer who clicks on a form in a click-wrap situation is generally making an offer and the vendor will be the party accepting the offer. This, of course, is not universally the case, as it is quite possible for a vendor to make a clear and unambiguous offer on the World Wide Web and the consumer, through the click of the mouse, accepts the offer.

(d)   Terms of a contract

Terms can be incorporated into a contract in a number of ways. A contract can contain these three distinct types of terms:

- express terms;
- terms incorporated by reference; and
- implied terms.

Before a contract can be formally concluded, all its terms must be brought to the attention of the parties.[3] Otherwise, there cannot be a meeting of minds and the terms may not form part of the contract. This is crucial in terms of both e-mail and click-wrap contracts. In the former, parties must take care to avoid contradiction and confusion if negotiations of terms are held using e-mail; this is especially so if the negotiations are lengthy and protracted. Parties must also take care to identify the documents intended to form part of the contract. In the event that the terms of a contract are imprecise, the effect of the contract may be substantially altered through a different interpretation of the terms from that originally intended. In the case of click-wrap contracts, website designers must take care to ensure that all terms are brought to the attention of the consumer before they are presented with the opportunity to purchase a product. Often the terms of click-wrap contracts are incorporated by reference.

Incorporating terms by reference is most important for on-line contracts. This means that the terms of the contracting parties are set out in a different document and incorporated by reference. In click-wrap contracts, the terms and conditions of the contract are usually located on a separate web page, rather than being embedded in the contract page. The problem with this is that both parties must know that these terms are part of the binding contract. The vendor must take all reasonable steps to bring the terms to the attention of the other party. As webvertisements are invitations to treat and not contractual documents, potential consumers would not expect to find terms and conditions of contracts contained in the webvertisements. Hence the design of the website must be such that before the consumer has the opportunity to click 'Submit' or 'I accept', the terms must be clearly brought to her or his attention. The onus is upon the web designers to ensure that consumers read and acknowledge the terms and conditions. In order to do this effectively, the usual practice has been to require consumers to tick a box on the order form or to click an acknowledgment that the terms and conditions have been read. If the consumer checks the box or clicks on the acknowledgment, the

---

3   *Thornton v Shoe Lane Parking* [1971] 2 QB 163.

terms will be incorporated (regardless of whether they have actually been read); if this is not done, the purchase order or other agreement will not proceed. See further *Specht v Netscape Communications Corp* 150 F Supp 2d 585 (SDNY July5 2001).[4]

Implied terms usually arise separately from the contract formation process and are usually localised. This means that, in the event of a dispute, the governing law of the contract would be of central concern, as would be the type of contract at issue. So this becomes removed from the method of contract formation in general. Terms may be implied by fact, on the basis of custom or usage, by statute, or by construction of the contract. Questions of implied terms are extremely case-specific and will turn on the particular relevant laws of a particular jurisdiction, such as of unconscionable conduct or business efficacy or on the subject matter of the contract.

(e)   Formation of a contract: the postal acceptance rule

The final step in our brief examination of the common law of contracts is the issue of when and where the contract is formally made, or concluded. The general rule of contract law is that the contract is made when the acceptance is communicated from the offeree to the offeror. The location of the formation is decided according to where the offeror receives notification of the acceptance. However, there is a well-known exception which is relevant to our present concern—the postal acceptance rule. This rule states that where it is contemplated that an acceptance is to be sent by post, a contract is deemed to have been concluded once the acceptance is posted and not when it is received. The rule is designed to provide certainty for the offeree that once an acceptance is posted, the contract is formed irrespective of delays in the postal delivery. After all, if the offeror does not wish to utilise this form of acceptance through the post, he or she is at liberty to stipulate the form of the acceptance.

There have been some twelve theories or explanations offered for the postal acceptance rule.[5] Two of these are particularly relevant to the Internet context. First, it has been argued that the postal acceptance rule applies because the communication has been entrusted to a trusted third party such as the postal system. Second, some have argued that the reason the postal acceptance rule applies to acceptances is because the postal system is a non-instantaneous form of communication. The question, then, is whether the postal acceptance rule applies to the two main ways of electronic contract formation outlined above, and what implications this carries for electronic contracting.

---

4   There have been numerous cases in the US concerning click-wrap and email contracts, see further *Csx Transp, Inc v Recovery Express, Inc,* 2006 US Dist LEXIS 3770 (D Mass., 2006); *Comb v PayPal, Inc* 218 F Supp 2d 1165 (District Court for the Northern District of California, 2002); *Forrest v Verizon Communications, Inc* 805 A 2d 1007 (District of Columbia Court of Appeals, 2002); *Motise v Am Online, Inc,* 346 F Supp (DNY, 2004); *Recursion Software, Inc v Interactive Intelligence, Inc,* 2006 US Dist LEXIS 7314 (ND Tex Feb 27, 2006); *Davidson & Assocs. v Internet Gateway,* 334 F Supp 2d 1164 (D Mo, 2004); *DeJohn v TV Corp Int'l,* 245 F Supp 2d 913 (D Ill, 2003); *Siedle v Nat'l Assoc of Sec Dealers, Inc,* 248 F Supp 2d 1140 (D Fla, October 30, 2002); *Roger Edwards, LLC v Fiddes & Son, Ltd,* 245 F Supp 2d 251 (D Me, 2003); *DeJohn v TV Corp Int'l,* 245 F Supp 2d 913, (D Ill, 2003); *Siedle v Nat'l Assoc of Sec Dealers, Inc,* 248 F Supp 2d 1140 (D Fla, 2002).

5   D Evans, 'The Anglo-American Mailing Rule: Some Problems of Offer and Acceptance in Contracts by Correspondence' (1966) *International and Comparative Law Quarterly* 553; R Posner, *Economic Analysis of Law,* Aspen Law and Business, New York, 1998, pp 113–14.

When applied to e-mail, technical considerations come to the fore. The balance of academic opinion is that e-mail acceptances should benefit from the postal acceptance rule due to the 'trusted third party' line of reasoning. However, this is also open to question because of the technical mechanism of e-mail: if we cannot know exactly where the packets of an e-mail message are routed, how can an unknown system gain our trust as a third party? Nevertheless, the fact remains that e-mail is not instantaneous; the packets may not all arrive, there may be congestion on the networks, some of the servers may malfunction, there may be a power outage, and so on. E-mail is also fragmented when compared to a telephone call, and the sender has no way of knowing whether the receiver will actually get the message. However, the question of the applicability of the postal acceptance rule to e-mail acceptances has not been judicially settled.

In relation to click-wrap, a different communication method is involved. The communication between the web client and the server is instantaneous. If the communication between the two parties is broken, for whatever reason, the other party will be immediately notified. This is due to the built-in self-checking mechanism known as a 'checksum', which maintains constant communication between computers and servers. Therefore, when dealing with click-wrap contracts, the postal acceptance rule is deemed not to apply because the line of communication is continually verified, which implies that a communiqué, once sent, will be instantly received.

 NOTES AND QUESTIONS

1   How does the formation of a click-wrap contract differ from that of an e-mail contract?

2   How are terms incorporated in click-wrap contracts? What precautions must vendors take? In *Specht v Netscape Communications Corp* 2001 WL 755396 (SDNY, 5 July 2001), the court had to consider a link leading to terms and conditions appearing on the same web page but below the 'download' icon. Do you think the court held that Internet users who downloaded the software were bound by the terms? See <http://www.wilmerhale.com/publications/whPubsDetail. aspx?publication=172> 17 August 2006. Compare *Steven J Caspi et al v The Microsoft Network, LLC, et al* 1999 WL 462175, 323 NJ Super 118 (NJ App Div, 2 July 1999) available at <http://legal.web.aol.com/decisions/dlother/caspi. html> 17 August 2006 and *Hotmail Corporation v Van Money Pie Inc, et al*, C98-20064 (NDCa, 20 April 1998) <http://www.phillipsnizer.com/library/cases/ lib_case21.cfm> 17 August 2006.

3   When do web pages amount to offers and when are they invitations to treat?

(f)   Pre-Internet analogies: *Entores* and *Brinkibon*

The central point to remember is that the Internet is a medium, or a collection of media, which can be used for contracting. The law has developed rules to deal with all of the new media it has been confronted with thus far. However, the law as it applies to the Internet is, at this stage, far from settled. The reasoning which began with *Entores*, and which was reinforced in *Brinkibon v Stahag,* is probably the most useful precedent. The reader is encouraged to contemplate the application of Lord Denning's reasoning to the modern context.

Entores Ltd v Miles Far East Corporation

[1955] 2 QB 327

Court of Appeal, United Kingdom

Lord Denning:

[332] When a contract is made by post it is clear law throughout the common law countries that the acceptance is complete as soon as the letter is put into the post box, and that is the place where the contract is made. But there is no clear rule about contracts made by telephone or by telex. Communications by these means are virtually instantaneous and stand on a different footing.

The problem can only be solved by going in stages. Let me first consider a case where two people make a contract by word of mouth in the presence of one another. Suppose, for instance, that I shout an offer to a man across a river or a courtyard but I do not hear his reply because it is drowned by an aircraft flying overhead. There is no contract at that moment. If he wishes to make a contract, he must wait till the aircraft is gone and then should shout back his acceptance so that I can hear what he says. Not until I have his answer am I bound ...

Now take a case where two people make a contract by telephone. Suppose, for instance, that I make an offer to a man by telephone and, in the middle of his reply, the line goes 'dead' so that I do not hear his words of acceptance. There is no contract at that moment. The other man may not know the precise moment when the line failed. But he will know that the telephone conversation was abruptly broken off: because people usually say something to signify the end of the conversation. If he wishes to make a contract, he must therefore get through again so as to make sure that I heard. Suppose, next, that the line does not go dead, but it is nevertheless so indistinct that I **[333]** do not catch what he says and I ask him to repeat it. He then repeats it and I hear his acceptance. The contract is made, not on the first time when I do not hear, but only the second time when I do hear. If he does not repeat it, there is no contract. The contract is only complete when I have his answer accepting the offer.

Lastly, take the telex. Suppose a clerk in a London office taps out on the teleprinter an offer which is immediately recorded on a teleprinter in a Manchester office, and a clerk at that end taps out an acceptance. If the line goes dead in the middle of the sentence of acceptance, the teleprinter motor will stop. There is obviously no contract. The clerk at Manchester must get through again and send his complete sentence. But it may happen that the line does not go dead, yet the message does not get through to London. Thus the clerk at Manchester may tap out his message of acceptance and it will not be recorded in London because the ink at the London end fails, or something of that kind. In that case, the Manchester clerk will not know of the failure but the London clerk will know of it and will immediately send back a message 'not receiving'. Then, when the fault is rectified, the Manchester clerk will repeat his message. Only then is there a contract. If he does not repeat it, there is no contract. It is not until his message is received that the contract is complete.

In all the instances I have taken so far, the man who sends the message of acceptance knows that it has not been received or he has reason to know it. So he must repeat it. But suppose that he does not know that his message did not get home. He thinks it has. This may happen if the listener on the telephone does not catch the words of acceptance, but nevertheless does not trouble to ask for them to be repeated: or the ink of the teleprinter fails, but the clerk does not ask for the message to be repeated: so that the man who sends an acceptance reasonably believes that his message has been received. The offeror in such circumstances is clearly bound, because he will be estopped from saying that he did not receive the message of acceptance. It is his own fault that he did not get it. But if there should be a case where the offeror without any fault on his part does not receive the message of acceptance—yet the sender of it reasonably believes it has got home when it has not—then I think there is no contract ...

[334] The contract is only complete when the acceptance is received by the offeror: and the contract is made at the place where the acceptance is received.

 NOTES AND QUESTIONS

1   Denning LJ tackles the problem before him by 'going in stages'. Is all that is required simply the development of a further stage (dealing with the Internet media) accompanied by explication of the attendant problems which will accompany it?
2   What is the key to all of Lord Denning's 'stages'?
3   In Lord Denning's 'stages', humans are at both ends of the communication devices. Would there be any problems with his argument if there were no human at one end? Or at both ends?

Brinkibon Ltd v Stahag Stahl GmbH

[1983] 2 AC 34

House of Lords, United Kingdom

Lord Wilberforce:
[42] Where the condition of simultaneity is met, and where it appears to be within the mutual intention of the parties that contractual exchanges should take place in this way, I think it a sound rule, but not necessarily a universal rule.

Since 1955, the use of telex communications has been greatly expanded, and there are many variants on it. The senders and recipients may not be the principals to the contemplated contract. They may be servants or agents with limited authority. The message may not reach, or be intended to reach, the designated recipient immediately: messages may be sent out of office hours, or at night, with the intention, or upon the assumption, that they will be read at a later time. There may be some error or default at the recipient's end which prevents receipt at a time contemplated and believed by the sender. The message may have been sent and/or received through machines operated by third persons. And many other variations may occur. No universal rule can cover all such cases: they must be resolved by reference to the intentions of the parties, by sound business practice and in some cases by a judgment of where the risks should lie ...

Lord Fraser of Tullybelton:

[43] [A]n acceptance sent by telex directly from the acceptor's office to the offeror's office should be treated as if it were an instantaneous communication between principals, like a telephone conversation. One reason is that the decision to that effect in *Entores v Miles Far East Corporation* [1955] 2 QB 327 seems to have worked without leading to serious difficulty or complaint from the business community. Secondly, once the message has been received on the offeror's telex machine, it is not unreasonable to treat it as delivered to the principal offeror, because it is his responsibility to arrange for prompt handling of messages within his own office. Thirdly, a party (the acceptor) who tries to send a message by telex can generally tell if his message has not been received on the other party's (the offeror's) machine, whereas the offeror, of course, will not know if an unsuccessful attempt has been made to send an acceptance to him. It is therefore convenient that the acceptor, being in the better position, should have the responsibility of ensuring that his message is received. For these reasons I think it is right that in the ordinary simple case, such as I take this to be, the general rule and not the postal rule should apply.

 NOTES AND QUESTIONS

1   To extend Lord Fraser's comments, could we reasonably hold a company responsible for the orderly receipt of electronic communications at that company? Are there any implications arising from the use of electronic sorting systems over which the intended recipient might have little or no control?

2   How does Lord Wilberforce's view differ from Lord Fraser's view? Which is the more just?

(g)   Post-Internet analogies: *Eastern Power Ltd*

The following is a Canadian case which endorses the *Brinkibon* decision. This case is useful because it indicates an ongoing endorsement of the rules set out decades ago. Despite the fact that it discusses facsimile transmissions, and not contracting over the Internet, the case provides a useful step in the development of an Internet jurisprudence.

Eastern Power Ltd v Azienda Communale Energia and Ambiente

[1999] OJ No 3275 Docket No C31224

Ontario Court of Appeal, Toronto, Ontario, Canada

Macpherson JA: ...

15 The issues on this appeal are:

- Was the motions judge correct to stay EP's action in Ontario on the basis of *forum non conveniens*?
- Was the motions judge correct to set aside service in Italy of EP's statement of claim?
- Was the motions judge correct to award ACEA costs of the motion fixed at $44,000?

16 In the view I take of the appeal, the disposition of the first issue makes it unnecessary to consider the second issue. Accordingly, in these reasons I will address only the *forum non conveniens* and costs issues ...

(a) Location where the contract was signed

21 The contract which forms the basis of EP's action in contract and tort against ACEA is the Cooperation Agreement: see Statement of Claim, paragraphs 5, 26, 30 and 31. The motions judge found that the Cooperation Agreement was made in Italy because 'acceptance was communicated to Italy'. Since EP's acceptance was communicated by facsimile transmission, this raises the interesting question of the legal relationship between a faxed acceptance of an offer and the place where a contract is formed.

22 The general rule of contract law is that a contract is made in the location where the offeror receives notification of the offeree's acceptance: see Fridman, *The Law of Contract in Canada* (3rd ed, 1994), at p 65; and *Re Viscount Supply Co* [1963] 1 OR 640 (SC). However, there is an exception to this general rule. It is the postal acceptance rule. As expressed by Ritchie J in *Imperial Life Assurance Co of Canada v Colmenares* [1967] SCR 443 at 447:

> It has long been recognized that when contracts are to be concluded by post the place of mailing the acceptance is to be treated as the place where the contract was made.

See also Fridman, *The Law of Contract in Canada*, *supra*, at pp 67–8.

23 EP contends that the rule with respect to facsimile transmissions should follow the postal acceptance exception. With respect, I disagree. EP has cited no authority in support of its position. There is, however, case authority for the proposition that acceptance by facsimile transmission should follow the general rule, which would mean that a contract is formed when and where acceptance is received by the offeror.

24 In *Brinkibon Ltd v Stahag Stahl GmbH* [1983] 2 AC 34 (HL), a contract was concluded when the buyer in London transmitted its acceptance to the seller in Vienna. The mode of acceptance was a message sent by telex, a form of instantaneous communication like the telephone. The law lords were unanimous in concluding that the contract was formed in Vienna where the acceptance was received by the offeror. Lord Brandon of Oakbrook analyzed the issue in this fashion, at p 48:

> Mr Thompson's second and alternative case that the contract was concluded by the buyers transmitting to the sellers their telex of May 4, 1979, seems to me to be the correct analysis of the transaction

25 In my view, this analysis is equally applicable to facsimile transmissions, another form of instantaneous communication. Indeed, there is at least one Canadian authority that has reached this conclusion. In *Joan Balcom Sales Inc v Poirier* (1991) 49 CPC (2d) 180 (NS Co Ct), an acceptance of a real estate listing offer was communicated by two vendors in Ottawa to a real estate company in Berwick, Nova Scotia. The mode of communication was a facsimile transmission. The vendors' position was that the contract was formed in Ottawa; they argued that the 'mailbox doctrine' should be applied to communication by facsimile transmission.

26 Haliburton Co Ct J did not accept the vendors' argument. He reviewed the English academic writing about the postal acceptance exception to the general rule of contract formation. He then concluded, at p 187:

> The writers then discuss the practical need of special rules to be applied to contracts entered into by post in the age when post was the primary method of commercial communication. The considerations which made it highly practical, if not imperative, in the interests of commerce, for the offeree to have knowledge in a timely fashion that he had a firm contract do not apply to facsimile transmissions. The communication is instantaneous. The offeree could easily have confirmed within minutes that they had a binding contract.

> I, therefore, find that the contract was executed at Berwick.

27 I agree with this analysis, and with the analysis of the law lords in *Brinkibon*. I would hold that in contract law an acceptance by facsimile transmission should follow the general rule of contract formation, not the postal acceptance exception.

28 I do not say that this rule should be an absolute one; like Lord Wilberforce in his separate speech in *Brinkibon*, 'I think it a sound rule, but not necessarily a universal rule' (p 42). Lord Wilberforce discussed some of the factors that might suggest caution about applying the general rule to telex communications in all cases, including the many variants in such communications and whether the message was sent and received by the principals to the contemplated contract. However, he concluded, at p 42:

> The present case is ... the simple case of instantaneous communication between principals, and, in accordance with the general rule, involves that the contract (if any) was made when and where the acceptance was received.

29 In my view, the present appeal is also 'the simple case'. The acceptance was faxed by the principals of EP in Ontario to the principals of ACEA in Italy. There is nothing to suggest that the communication between these principals was not instantaneous. Hence, applying the general rule, the contract was formed in Italy ...

 NOTES AND QUESTIONS

1   Lord Wilberforce in *Brinkibon* and Macpherson JA in *Eastern Power* both stress that the rule in question is not universal. Can the same reasoning be applied to e-mail contracts and click-wrap contracts? Why or why not?

2   The rules regarding acceptance, receipt, and conclusion are crucial in determining the governing law of the contract. Differences among governing laws around the world could, if known, affect the decisions of contractors. Differences could also

influence the outcome of a dispute where the laws between the two jurisdictions differ significantly. Contemplation of these issues leads directly to the attempts to overcome the problems, which we will examine presently.

----

2   A coordinated legislative approach?

The United Nations Commission on International Trade Law (UNCITRAL) was established by the General Assembly in 1966 (Resolution 2205(XXI) of 17 December 1966). The UNCITRAL Model Law on Electronic Commerce (UNCITRAL Model Law) was drafted in 1996 to assist countries in the framing of legislation which would enable and facilitate electronic contracting, and thus to eliminate the need for trading partner agreements. The peculiar nature of the Internet demands a general cross-border approach to contracting. Hence it was also the intention to harmonise domestic laws and to eliminate barriers so as to take advantage of computers and computer networks. The UNCITRAL Model Law adopts a limited framework approach. It is not intended to be a comprehensive code of rules for electronic transactions, nor is it intended to govern every aspect of e-commerce. Rather, the aim is to provide essential procedures and principles for electronic contracting. At the same time, the UNCITRAL Model Law offers the enacting states a very broad discretion to regulate beyond what the model law itself specified in certain areas, in order to tailor it to individual country specifications.

The underlying analytical approach of the UNCITRAL Model Law is the 'functional equivalence' approach. This approach evaluates the underlying purposes and functions of traditional paper-based legal requirements and assesses to what extent electronic transactions can meet these purposes and functions. Where electronic transactions can satisfy the purposes and functions, the UNCITRAL Model Law requires that they be given equal status. Therefore, rather than rewriting the law, the UNCITRAL Model Law seeks to extend the scope of standard legal definitions of 'writings', 'signatures' and so on to encompass their electronic counterparts.

The UNCITRAL Model Law has been influential in educating lawmakers about the legal ramifications of electronic transactions and it has served as a useful framework for drafters of national e-commerce legislation. Indeed, the e-commerce laws in countries such as Australia, members of the EU, and Singapore have been heavily influenced by the UNCITRAL Model Law. Uniform legislation influenced by the UNCITRAL Model Law, and the principles on which it is based, has been prepared in Canada (*Uniform Electronic Commerce Act*, adopted in 1999 by the Uniform Law Conference of Canada) and in the USA (*Uniform Electronic Transactions Act*, adopted in 1999 by the National Conference of Commissioners on Uniform State Law) and enacted as law by a number of jurisdictions in those countries.[6]

The UNCITRAL Model Law actually governs a number of technologies, including faxes. Article 2(a) was inserted to settle the debate that had been raging as to whether a faxed document was a legally binding document. As technology advanced, the line

---

6   The most up-to-date information regarding adoption of the UNCITRAL Model Law can be found on the Internet at <http://www.uncitral.org> 18 September 2001.

between fax technology and electronic computing technology became blurred. It was possible for faxes to be sent, received, and stored on a computer instead of a fax machine. At the outset of the UNCITRAL Model Law development process, the focus was on electronic data interchange (EDI). EDI is a structured system whereby one party agrees to send data in a certain specified format and the other party agrees to receive data in that format. By the time the project was several years old, the drafters realised the EDI concept was outmoded. EDI was certainly popular at one time but technology had moved on, even though it was not immediately clear where it was headed next. The drafters realised that they could not place restrictions on technology to which the law would apply. They therefore deliberately formulated a 'technology-neutral' document so that it would not have to be re-drafted as new technologies came into use.

In order for any model law to be effective, it must be enacted and interpreted in a consistent manner across jurisdictions. Further, as some jurisdictions place a strong emphasis on party autonomy, the UNCITRAL Model Law contains both mandatory provisions, which provide the substantive floor of the document, as well as flexible provisions, which, in keeping with the desire for flexibility and party autonomy, can be altered by agreement between the parties to a transaction.

Held up here for comparison with the UNCITRAL Model Law are the *Electronic Transactions Act* (Australia, Cth), the *Electronic Transactions Act* (Singapore), and the *Uniform Electronic Transactions Act* (USA). The US legislation is not actually a piece of federally enacted legislation. It was drafted by the National Conference of Commissioners on Uniform State Laws for enactment by the individual state legislatures.[7] In some respects, therefore, the UETA is a second-generation model law.

These pieces of legislation serve as useful examples of national attempts to incorporate the UNCITRAL Model Law into legislation, and of the problems and issues faced in the process. The following sections are structured so as to facilitate a direct comparison between the four instruments extracted. It is crucial that the reader understands the importance of comparing the framework law with enacted legislation. The reader should scrutinise the UNCITRAL Model Law and its progeny to see whether and how the outcomes have met the stated objectives, as well as any objectives that it perhaps should have stated, but did not.

(a)   The UNCITRAL Model Law

United Nations Commission on International Trade Law (UNCITRAL) Model Law on Electronic Commerce

1996 with additional article 5 bis as adopted in 1998

---

7   For information regarding the progress of individual state enactments, visit <http://www. uetaonline. com> 28 September 2001.

ARTICLE 1. SPHERE OF APPLICATION*

This Law** applies to any kind of information in the form of a data message used in the context*** of commercial**** activities.

NOTES AND QUESTIONS

The following notes are included as footnotes to the original UNCITRAL Model Law text.

* The Commission suggests the following text for States that might wish to limit the applicability of this Law to international data messages: 'This Law applies to a data message as defined in paragraph (1) of article 2 where the data message relates to international commerce.'

** This Law does not override any rule of law intended for the protection of consumers.

*** The Commission suggests the following text for States that might wish to extend the applicability of this Law: 'This Law applies to any kind of information in the form of a data message, except in the following situations: [...].'

**** The term 'commercial' should be given a wide interpretation so as to cover matters arising from all relationships of a commercial nature, whether contractual or not. Relationships of a commercial nature include, but are not limited to, the following transactions: any trade transaction for the supply or exchange of goods or services; distribution agreement; commercial representation or agency; factoring; leasing; construction of works; consulting; engineering; licensing; investment; financing; banking; insurance; exploitation agreement or concession; joint venture and other forms of industrial or business cooperation; carriage of goods or passengers by air, sea, rail or road.

What do you think is the purpose of the first note? Can the second note and the fourth note be reconciled?

(b)   Interpretation, construction and purpose

UNCITRAL Model Law on Electronic Commerce

ARTICLE 3. INTERPRETATION

(1) In the interpretation of this Law, regard is to be had to its international origin and to the need to promote uniformity in its application and the observance of good faith.

(2) Questions concerning matters governed by this Law which are not expressly settled in it are to be settled in conformity with the general principles on which this Law is based.

Electronic Transactions Act 1999 (Cth)

3. OBJECT

The object of this Act is to provide a regulatory framework that:

(a) recognises the importance of the information economy to the future economic and social prosperity of Australia; and
(b) facilitates the use of electronic transactions; and
(c) promotes business and community confidence in the use of electronic transactions; and
(d) enables business and the community to use electronic communications in their dealings with government.

Electronic Transactions Act 1998 (Singapore)

3. PURPOSES AND CONSTRUCTION

This Act shall be construed consistently with what is commercially reasonable under the circumstances and to give effect to the following purposes:

(a) to facilitate electronic communications by means of reliable electronic records;
(b) to facilitate electronic commerce, eliminate barriers to electronic commerce resulting from uncertainties over writing and signature requirements, and to promote the development of the legal and business infrastructure necessary to implement secure electronic commerce;
(c) to facilitate electronic filing of documents with government agencies and statutory corporations, and to promote efficient delivery of government services by means of reliable electronic records;
(d) to minimise the incidence of forged electronic records, intentional and unintentional alteration of records, and fraud in electronic commerce and other electronic transactions;
(e) to help to establish uniformity of rules, regulations and standards regarding the authentication and integrity of electronic records; and
(f) to promote public confidence in the integrity and reliability of electronic records and electronic commerce, and to foster the development of electronic commerce through the use of electronic signatures to lend authenticity and integrity to correspondence in any electronic medium.

Uniform Electronic Transactions Act 1999 (US)

SECTION 6. CONSTRUCTION AND APPLICATION

This [Act] must be construed and applied:

(1) to facilitate electronic transactions consistent with other applicable law;

(2) to be consistent with reasonable practices concerning electronic transactions and with the continued expansion of those practices; and

(3) to effectuate its general purpose to make uniform the law with respect to the subject of this [Act] among States enacting it.

 NOTES AND QUESTIONS

1   The UNCITRAL Model Law is intended to be read in conjunction with the *Guide to Enactment* <http://www.uncitral.org/uncitral/en/uncitral_texts.html> 17 August 2006. The Introduction to the *Guide* includes the following in its statement of objectives:

> [2]   … The purpose of the Model Law is to offer national legislators a set of internationally acceptable rules as to how a number of such legal obstacles may be removed, and how a more secure legal environment may be created for what has become known as 'electronic commerce'.

> [6]   The objectives of the Model Law, which include enabling or facilitating the use of electronic commerce and providing equal treatment to users of paper-based documentation and to users of computer-based information, are essential for fostering economy and efficiency in international trade. By incorporating the procedures prescribed in the Model Law in its national legislation for those situations where parties opt to use electronic means of communication, an enacting State would create a media-neutral environment.

The *Guide* also has a section titled 'History and Background of the Model Law', which includes the following statement:

> [123] … The UNCITRAL Model Law on Electronic Commerce was adopted by the United Nations Commission on International Trade Law (UNCITRAL) in 1996 in furtherance of its mandate to promote the harmonization and unification of international trade law, so as to remove unnecessary obstacles to international trade caused by inadequacies and divergences in the law affecting trade.

2   Do you think the objectives outlined above are broad enough? If so, why? If not, what further objectives might be included? If you add objectives, what are the consequences for the text of the above instruments?

3   How significant is UNCITRAL Model Law Article 3 when read in isolation? How important does it become when viewed in the overall context of the goals of the UNCITRAL Model Law and the other provisions of the Model Law? Is this provision a veiled admission of impotence, or is it a provision crucial to the coherence of the UNCITRAL Model Law?

4   Notice that none of the national legislation quoted above explicitly includes a reference to the 'international origin' of the UNCITRAL Model Law, and

that the Australian legislation says nothing about interpretation at all. What does this indicate about the commitment of national governments to the goals of UNCITRAL?

(c) Variation by agreement

UNCITRAL Model Law on Electronic Commerce

ARTICLE 4. VARIATION BY AGREEMENT

(1) As between parties involved in generating, sending, receiving, storing or otherwise processing data messages, and except as otherwise provided, the provisions of chapter III may be varied by agreement.
(2) Paragraph (1) does not affect any right that may exist to modify by agreement any rule of law referred to in chapter II.

Electronic Transactions Act 1998 (Singapore)

5. VARIATION BY AGREEMENT

As between parties involved in generating, sending, receiving, storing or otherwise processing electronic records, any provision of Part II or IV may be varied by agreement.

Uniform Electronic Transactions Act 1999 (US)

SECTION 5. USE OF ELECTRONIC RECORDS AND ELECTRONIC SIGNATURES; VARIATION BY AGREEMENT

(d) Except as otherwise provided in this [Act], the effect of any of its provisions may be varied by agreement. The presence in certain provisions of this [Act] of the words 'unless otherwise agreed', or words of similar import, does not imply that the effect of other provisions may not be varied by agreement.

 NOTES AND QUESTIONS

1 Which of these gives the broadest scope for variation? Explain why.
2 How is the effectiveness of the Model Law and the national legislation affected by allowing parties to vary? Can you see any problems if the power to vary is excessive?

(d)   Data messages and evidence

UNCITRAL Model Law on Electronic Commerce

ARTICLE 5. LEGAL RECOGNITION OF DATA MESSAGES

Information shall not be denied legal effect, validity or enforceability solely on the grounds that it is in the form of a data message.

ARTICLE 9. ADMISSIBILITY AND EVIDENTIAL WEIGHT OF DATA MESSAGES

(1) In any legal proceedings, nothing in the application of the rules of evidence shall apply so as to deny the admissibility of a data message in evidence:

(a) on the sole ground that it is a data message; or,

(b) if it is the best evidence that the person adducing it could reasonably be expected to obtain, on the grounds that it is not in its original form.

(2) Information in the form of a data message shall be given due evidential weight. In assessing the evidential weight of a data message, regard shall be had to the reliability of the manner in which the data message was generated, stored or communicated, to the reliability of the manner in which the integrity of the information was maintained, to the manner in which its originator was identified, and to any other relevant factor.

Electronic Transactions Act 1999 (Cth)

8. VALIDITY OF ELECTRONIC TRANSACTIONS

(1) For the purposes of a law of the Commonwealth, a transaction is not invalid because it took place wholly or partly by means of one or more electronic communications.

(2) The general rule in subsection (1) does not apply in relation to the validity of a transaction to the extent to which another, more specific provision of this Part deals with the validity of the transaction.

EXEMPTIONS

(3) The regulations may provide that subsection (1) does not apply to a specified transaction.

(4) The regulations may provide that subsection (1) does not apply to a specified law of the Commonwealth.

Electronic Transactions Act 1998 (Singapore)

6. LEGAL RECOGNITION OF ELECTRONIC RECORDS

For the avoidance of doubt, it is declared that information shall not be denied legal effect, validity or enforceability solely on the ground that it is in the form of an electronic record.

Uniform Electronic Transactions Act 1999 (US)

SECTION 7. LEGAL RECOGNITION OF ELECTRONIC RECORDS, ELECTRONIC SIGNATURES, AND ELECTRONIC CONTRACTS

(a) A record or signature may not be denied legal effect or enforceability solely because it is in electronic form.

(b) A contract may not be denied legal effect or enforceability solely because an electronic record was used in its formation.

SECTION 13. ADMISSIBILITY IN EVIDENCE

In a proceeding, evidence of a record or signature may not be excluded solely because it is in electronic form.

 NOTES AND QUESTIONS

1   Notice the lack of evidential provisions in the Australian and Singapore legislation. What do you think is the reason for this? How might these omissions affect the operation of the legislation? What reasons can you give for leaving out such provisions? Would this sort of provision be better placed here or in other pieces of legislation such as the *Evidence Act*?

2   These provisions effectively give electronic documents the same status as something written on paper. Why do you think the Australian legislation contains exemptions?

3   Is there such a thing as an original and a copy when it comes to electronic documents?

(e)   Formation and validity of electronic contracts

UNCITRAL Model Law on Electronic Commerce

ARTICLE 11. FORMATION AND VALIDITY OF CONTRACTS

(1) In the context of contract formation, unless otherwise agreed by the parties, an offer and the acceptance of an offer may be expressed by means of data messages. Where a data

message is used in the formation of a contract, that contract shall not be denied validity or enforceability on the sole ground that a data message was used for that purpose.

(2) The provisions of this article do not apply to the following: [...].

Electronic Transactions Act 1999 (Cth)

8. VALIDITY OF ELECTRONIC TRANSACTIONS

(1) For the purposes of a law of the Commonwealth, a transaction is not invalid because it took place wholly or partly by means of one or more electronic communications.

(2) The general rule in subsection (1) does not apply in relation to the validity of a transaction to the extent to which another, more specific provision of this Part deals with the validity of the transaction.

EXEMPTIONS

(3) The regulations may provide that subsection (1) does not apply to a specified transaction.

(4) The regulations may provide that subsection (1) does not apply to a specified law of the Commonwealth.

Electronic Transactions Act 1998 (Singapore)

11. FORMATION AND VALIDITY OF CONTRACTS

(1) For the avoidance of doubt, it is declared that in the context of the formation of contracts, unless otherwise agreed by the parties, an offer and the acceptance of an offer may be expressed by means of electronic records.

(2) Where an electronic record is used in the formation of a contract, that contract shall not be denied validity or enforceability on the sole ground that an electronic record was used for that purpose.

Uniform Electronic Transactions Act 1999 (US)

SECTION 7. LEGAL RECOGNITION OF ELECTRONIC RECORDS, ELECTRONIC SIGNATURES, AND ELECTRONIC CONTRACTS

(b) A contract may not be denied legal effect or enforceability solely because an electronic record was used in its formation.

NOTES AND QUESTIONS

Are these provisions necessary? Is it not obvious that offers and acceptances can be in electronic form? The mischief these provisions target lies in the fact that often, expressions of offer and acceptance are generated by computers without immediate human intervention—that is, electronic agents are used. These raise doubts as to the expression of intent by the parties, particularly as there is no paper document.

(f)   Terms of the electronic contracts

UNCITRAL Model Law on Electronic Commerce

ARTICLE 5 BIS. INCORPORATION BY REFERENCE
(as adopted by the Commission at its thirty-first session, in June 1998)
Information shall not be denied legal effect, validity or enforceability solely on the grounds that it is not contained in the data message purporting to give rise to such legal effect, but is merely referred to in that data message.

 NOTES AND QUESTIONS

Is any significance to be placed in the fact that none of the three national pieces of legislation includes a provision mirroring Article 5 bis? Refer to the earlier discussions on terms.

(g)   Writing

UNCITRAL Model Law on Electronic Commerce

ARTICLE 6. WRITING

(1) Where the law requires information to be in writing, that requirement is met by a data message if the information contained therein is accessible so as to be usable for subsequent reference.
(2) Paragraph (1) applies whether the requirement therein is in the form of an obligation or whether the law simply provides consequences for the information not being in writing.
(3) The provisions of this article do not apply to the following: [...].

Electronic Transactions Act 1999 (Cth)

9. WRITING

REQUIREMENT TO GIVE INFORMATION IN WRITING

(1) If, under a law of the Commonwealth, a person is required to give information in writing, that requirement is taken to have been met if the person gives the information by means of an electronic communication, where:

    (a) in all cases—at the time the information was given, it was reasonable to expect that the information would be readily accessible so as to be usable for subsequent reference; and

    (b) if the information is required to be given to a Commonwealth entity, or to a person acting on behalf of a Commonwealth entity, and the entity requires that the information be given, in accordance with particular information technology requirements, by means of a particular kind of electronic communication—the entity's requirement has been met; and

    (c) if the information is required to be given to a Commonwealth entity, or to a person acting on behalf of a Commonwealth entity, and the entity requires that particular action be taken by way of verifying the receipt of the information—the entity's requirement has been met; and

    (d) if the information is required to be given to a person who is neither a Commonwealth entity nor a person acting on behalf of a Commonwealth entity—the person to whom the information is required to be given consents to the information being given by way of electronic communication.

PERMISSION TO GIVE INFORMATION IN WRITING

(2) If, under a law of the Commonwealth, a person is permitted to give information in writing, the person may give the information by means of an electronic communication, where:

    (a) in all cases—at the time the information was given, it was reasonable to expect that the information would be readily accessible so as to be usable for subsequent reference; and

    (b) if the information is permitted to be given to a Commonwealth entity, or to a person acting on behalf of a Commonwealth entity, and the entity requires that the information be given, in accordance with particular information technology requirements, by means of a particular kind of electronic communication—the entity's requirement has been met; and

    (c) if the information is permitted to be given to a Commonwealth entity, or to a person acting on behalf of a Commonwealth entity, and the entity requires that particular action be taken by way of verifying the receipt of the information—the entity's requirement has been met; and

(d) if the information is permitted to be given to a person who is neither a Commonwealth entity nor a person acting on behalf of a Commonwealth entity—the person to whom the information is permitted to be given consents to the information being given by way of electronic communication.

CERTAIN OTHER LAWS NOT AFFECTED

(3) This section does not affect the operation of any other law of the Commonwealth that makes provision for or in relation to requiring or permitting information to be given, in accordance with particular information technology requirements:

(a) on a particular kind of data storage device; or

(b) by means of a particular kind of electronic communication.

GIVING INFORMATION

(4) This section applies to a requirement or permission to give information, whether the expression *give*, *send* or *serve*, or any other expression, is used.

(5) For the purposes of this section, giving information includes, but is not limited to, the following:

(a) making an application;

(b) making or lodging a claim;

(c) giving, sending or serving a notification;

(d) lodging a return;

(e) making a request;

(f) making a declaration;

(g) lodging or issuing a certificate;

(h) making, varying or cancelling an election;

(i) lodging an objection;

(j) giving a statement of reasons.

Electronic Transactions Act 1998 (Singapore)

7. REQUIREMENT FOR WRITING

Where a rule of law requires information to be written, in writing, to be presented in writing or provides for certain consequences if it is not, an electronic record satisfies that rule of law if the information contained therein is accessible so as to be usable for subsequent reference.

Uniform Electronic Transactions Act 1999 (US)

SECTION 7. LEGAL RECOGNITION OF ELECTRONIC RECORDS, ELECTRONIC SIGNATURES, AND ELECTRONIC CONTRACTS

(c) If a law requires a record to be in writing, an electronic record satisfies the law.

NOTES AND QUESTIONS

Carefully examine the provisions of the Australian Act (above). Compare its wording with that of the other three instruments. Look also at similarly worded provisions below. Are the qualifications for accepting data in the place of writing more rigorous in the national instruments? If so, how? What might the consequences of this added rigour be?

(h) Signatures

Electronic signatures are of such importance that they demand particular and focused attention. A more thorough treatment of these issues, both legal and technical, is provided in Chapter 6. For the moment, it must suffice to say that the UNCITRAL Model Law regime attempts to provide some guidance in this area; however, the attempt is less than comprehensive and the national legislation less than harmonised. Signatures are absolutely essential for the conduct of commerce. A paper signature is a mark carrying an expression of authenticity and intent, both essential for the formation of contracts. If electronic contracting is to become effective and frequent, secure signature mechanisms, both legal and technical, are essential. The UNCITRAL Model Law and the national statutes are extracted and discussed in Chapter 6.

(i) Documents: originals, production, retention

UNCITRAL Model Law on Electronic Commerce

ARTICLE 8. ORIGINAL

(1) Where the law requires information to be presented or retained in its original form, that requirement is met by a data message if:

   (a) there exists a reliable assurance as to the integrity of the information from the time when it was first generated in its final form, as a data message or otherwise; and

   (b) where it is required that information be presented, that information is capable of being displayed to the person to whom it is to be presented.

(2) Paragraph (1) applies whether the requirement therein is in the form of an obligation or whether the law simply provides consequences for the information not being presented or retained in its original form.

(3) For the purposes of subparagraph (a) of paragraph (1):

   (a) the criteria for assessing integrity shall be whether the information has remained complete and unaltered, apart from the addition of any endorsement and any change which arises in the normal course of communication, storage and display; and

(b) the standard of reliability required shall be assessed in the light of the purpose for which the information was generated and in the light of all the relevant circumstances.

(4) The provisions of this article do not apply to the following: [...].

ARTICLE 10. RETENTION OF DATA MESSAGES

(1) Where the law requires that certain documents, records or information be retained, that requirement is met by retaining data messages, provided that the following conditions are satisfied:

    (a) the information contained therein is accessible so as to be usable for subsequent reference; and

    (b) the data message is retained in the format in which it was generated, sent or received, or in a format which can be demonstrated to represent accurately the information generated, sent or received; and

    (c) such information, if any, is retained as enables the identification of the origin and destination of a data message and the date and time when it was sent or received.

(2) An obligation to retain documents, records or information in accordance with paragraph (1) does not extend to any information the sole purpose of which is to enable the message to be sent or received.

(3) A person may satisfy the requirement referred to in paragraph (1) by using the services of any other person, provided that the conditions set forth in subparagraphs (a), (b) and (c) of paragraph (1) are met.

Electronic Transactions Act 1999 (Cth)

11. PRODUCTION OF DOCUMENT

REQUIREMENT TO PRODUCE A DOCUMENT

(1) If, under a law of the Commonwealth, a person is required to produce a document that is in the form of paper, an article or other material, that requirement is taken to have been met if the person produces, by means of an electronic communication, an electronic form of the document, where:

    (a) in all cases—having regard to all the relevant circumstances at the time of the communication, the method of generating the electronic form of the document provided a reliable means of assuring the maintenance of the integrity of the information contained in the document; and

    (b) in all cases—at the time the communication was sent, it was reasonable to expect that the information contained in the electronic form of the document would be readily accessible so as to be usable for subsequent reference; and

    (c) if the document is required to be produced to a Commonwealth entity, or to a person acting on behalf of a Commonwealth entity, and the entity requires that an electronic form of the document be produced, in accordance with particular information technology requirements, by means of a particular kind of electronic communication—the entity's requirement has been met; and

(d) if the document is required to be produced to a Commonwealth entity, or to a person acting on behalf of a Commonwealth entity, and the entity requires that particular action be taken by way of verifying the receipt of the document—the entity's requirement has been met; and

(e) if the document is required to be produced to a person who is neither a Commonwealth entity nor a person acting on behalf of a Commonwealth entity—the person to whom the document is required to be produced consents to the production, by means of an electronic communication, of an electronic form of the document.

PERMISSION TO PRODUCE A DOCUMENT

(2) If, under a law of the Commonwealth, a person is permitted to produce a document that is in the form of paper, an article or other material, then, instead of producing the document in that form, the person may produce, by means of an electronic communication, an electronic form of the document, where:

(a) in all cases—having regard to all the relevant circumstances at the time of the communication, the method of generating the electronic form of the document provided a reliable means of assuring the maintenance of the integrity of the information contained in the document; and

(b) in all cases—at the time the communication was sent, it was reasonable to expect that the information contained in the electronic form of the document would be readily accessible so as to be usable for subsequent reference; and

(c) if the document is permitted to be produced to a Commonwealth entity, or to a person acting on behalf of a Commonwealth entity, and the entity requires that an electronic form of the document be produced, in accordance with particular information technology requirements, by means of a particular kind of electronic communication—the entity's requirement has been met; and

(d) if the document is permitted to be produced to a Commonwealth entity, or to a person acting on behalf of a Commonwealth entity, and the entity requires that particular action be taken by way of verifying the receipt of the document—the entity's requirement has been met; and

(e) if the document is permitted to be produced to a person who is neither a Commonwealth entity nor a person acting on behalf of a Commonwealth entity—the person to whom the document is permitted to be produced consents to the production, by means of an electronic communication, of an electronic form of the document.

INTEGRITY OF INFORMATION

(3) For the purposes of this section, the integrity of information contained in a document is maintained if, and only if, the information has remained complete and unaltered, apart from:

(a) the addition of any endorsement; or
(b) any immaterial change:

which arises in the normal course of communication, storage or display.

CERTAIN OTHER LAWS NOT AFFECTED

(4) This section does not affect the operation of any other law of the Commonwealth that makes provision for or in relation to requiring or permitting electronic forms of documents to be produced, in accordance with particular information technology requirements:

(a) on a particular kind of data storage device; or

(b) by means of a particular kind of electronic communication.

...

12. RETENTION

RECORDING OF INFORMATION

(1) If, under a law of the Commonwealth, a person is required to record information in writing, that requirement is taken to have been met if the person records the information in electronic form, where:

(a) in all cases—at the time of the recording of the information, it was reasonable to expect that the information would be readily accessible so as to be usable for subsequent reference; and

(b) if the regulations require that the information be recorded, in electronic form, on a particular kind of data storage device—that requirement has been met.

RETENTION OF WRITTEN DOCUMENT

(2) If, under a law of the Commonwealth, a person is required to retain, for a particular period, a document that is in the form of paper, an article or other material, that requirement is taken to have been met if the person retains an electronic form of the document throughout that period, where:

(a) in all cases—having regard to all the relevant circumstances at the time of the generation of the electronic form of the document, the method of generating the electronic form of the document provided a reliable means of assuring the maintenance of the integrity of the information contained in the document; and

(b) in all cases—at the time of the generation of the electronic form of the document, it was reasonable to expect that the information contained in the electronic form of the document would be readily accessible so as to be usable for subsequent reference; and

(c) if the regulations require that the electronic form of the document be retained on a particular kind of data storage device—that requirement has been met.

(3) For the purposes of subsection (2), the integrity of information contained in a document is maintained if, and only if, the information has remained complete and unaltered, apart from:

(a) the addition of any endorsement; or

(b) any immaterial change;

which arises in the normal course of communication, storage or display.

RETENTION OF ELECTRONIC COMMUNICATIONS

(4) If, under a law of the Commonwealth, a person (the first person) is required to retain, for a particular period, information that was the subject of an electronic communication, that requirement is taken to be met if the first person retains, or causes another person to retain, in electronic form, the information throughout that period, where:

    (a) in all cases—at the time of commencement of the retention of the information, it was reasonable to expect that the information would be readily accessible so as to be usable for subsequent reference; and

    (b) in all cases—having regard to all the relevant circumstances at the time of commencement of the retention of the information, the method of retaining the information in electronic form provided a reliable means of assuring the maintenance of the integrity of the information contained in the electronic communication; and

    (c) in all cases—throughout that period, the first person also retains, or causes the other person to retain, in electronic form, such additional information obtained by the first person as is sufficient to enable the identification of the following:

        (i)   the origin of the electronic communication;

        (ii) the destination of the electronic communication;

        (iii) the time when the electronic communication was sent;

        (iv) the time when the electronic communication was received; and

    (d) in all cases—at the time of commencement of the retention of the additional information covered by paragraph (c), it was reasonable to expect that the additional information would be readily accessible so as to be usable for subsequent reference; and

    (e) if the regulations require that the information be retained, in electronic form, on a particular kind of data storage device—that requirement is met throughout that period.

(5) For the purposes of subsection (4), the integrity of information that was the subject of an electronic communication is maintained if, and only if, the information has remained complete and unaltered, apart from:

    (a) the addition of any endorsement; or

    (b) any immaterial change;

which arises in the normal course of communication, storage or display.

Electronic Transactions Act 1998 (Singapore)

9. RETENTION OF ELECTRONIC RECORDS

(1) Where a rule of law requires that certain documents, records or information be retained, that requirement is satisfied by retaining them in the form of electronic records if the following conditions are satisfied:

    (a) the information contained therein remains accessible so as to be usable for subsequent reference;

    (b) the electronic record is retained in the format in which it was originally generated, sent or received, or in a format which can be demonstrated to represent accurately the information originally generated, sent or received;

    (c) such information, if any, as enables the identification of the origin and destination of an electronic record and the date and time when it was sent or received, is retained; and

    (d) the consent of the department or ministry of the Government, organ of State or the statutory corporation which has supervision over the requirement for the retention of such records has been obtained.

(2) An obligation to retain documents, records or information in accordance with subsection (1)(c) shall not extend to any information necessarily and automatically generated solely for the purpose of enabling a record to be sent or received.

(3) A person may satisfy the requirement referred to in subsection (1) by using the services of any other person, if the conditions in paragraphs (a) to (d) of that subsection are complied with.

(4) Nothing in this section shall—

    (a) apply to any rule of law which expressly provides for the retention of documents, records or information in the form of electronic records; or

    (b) preclude any department or ministry of the Government, organ of State or a statutory corporation from specifying additional requirements for the retention of electronic records that are subject to the jurisdiction of such department or ministry of the Government, organ of State or statutory corporation...

Uniform Electronic Transactions Act 1999 (US)

SECTION 8. PROVISION OF INFORMATION IN WRITING; PRESENTATION OF RECORDS

(a) If parties have agreed to conduct a transaction by electronic means and a law requires a person to provide, send, or deliver information in writing to another person, the requirement is satisfied if the information is provided, sent, or delivered, as the case may be, in an electronic record capable of retention by the recipient at the time of receipt. An electronic record is not capable of retention by the recipient if the sender or its information processing system inhibits the ability of the recipient to print or store the electronic record.

(b) If a law other than this [Act] requires a record (i) to be posted or displayed in a certain manner, (ii) to be sent, communicated, or transmitted by a specified method, or (iii) to contain information that is formatted in a certain manner, the following rules apply:

(1) The record must be posted or displayed in the manner specified in the other law.

(2) Except as otherwise provided in subsection (d)(2), the record must be sent, communicated, or transmitted by the method specified in the other law.

(3) The record must contain the information formatted in the manner specified in the other law.

(c) If a sender inhibits the ability of a recipient to store or print an electronic record, the electronic record is not enforceable against the recipient.

(d) The requirements of this section may not be varied by agreement, but:

(1) to the extent a law other than this [Act] requires information to be provided, sent, or delivered in writing but permits that requirement to be varied by agreement, the requirement under subsection (a) that the information be in the form of an electronic record capable of retention may also be varied by agreement; and

(2) a requirement under a law other than this [Act] to send, communicate, or transmit a record by [first-class mail, postage prepaid] [regular United States mail], may be varied by agreement to the extent permitted by the other law.

SECTION 12. RETENTION OF ELECTRONIC RECORDS; ORIGINALS

(a) If a law requires that a record be retained, the requirement is satisfied by retaining an electronic record of the information in the record which:

(1) accurately reflects the information set forth in the record after it was first generated in its final form as an electronic record or otherwise; and

(2) remains accessible for later reference.

(b) A requirement to retain a record in accordance with subsection (a) does not apply to any information the sole purpose of which is to enable the record to be sent, communicated, or received.

(c) A person may satisfy subsection (a) by using the services of another person if the requirements of that subsection are satisfied.

(d) If a law requires a record to be presented or retained in its original form, or provides consequences if the record is not presented or retained in its original form, that law is satisfied by an electronic record retained in accordance with subsection (a).

(e) If a law requires retention of a check, that requirement is satisfied by retention of an electronic record of the information on the front and back of the check in accordance with subsection (a).

(f) A record retained as an electronic record in accordance with subsection (a) satisfies a law requiring a person to retain a record for evidentiary, audit, or like purposes, unless a law enacted after the effective date of this [Act] specifically prohibits the use of an electronic record for the specified purpose.

(g) This section does not preclude a governmental agency of this State from specifying additional requirements for the retention of a record subject to the agency's jurisdiction.

NOTES AND QUESTIONS

1   What are the tests for being 'original' in each of these instruments? Are these tests sufficiently defined? Why? Is there scope for fraud under each of these?
2   Read carefully the national provisions for retention of electronic records. Do they all follow the UNCITRAL Model Law? Would it matter if the information was compressed or decoded?

(j)   Recognition

UNCITRAL Model Law on Electronic Commerce

ARTICLE 12. RECOGNITION BY PARTIES OF DATA MESSAGES

(1) As between the originator and the addressee of a data message, a declaration of will or other statement shall not be denied legal effect, validity or enforceability solely on the grounds that it is in the form of a data message.
(2) The provisions of this article do not apply to the following: [...].

Electronic Transactions Act 1998 (Singapore)

12. EFFECTIVENESS BETWEEN PARTIES

As between the originator and the addressee of an electronic record, a declaration of intent or other statement shall not be denied legal effect, validity or enforceability solely on the ground that it is in the form of an electronic record.

Uniform Electronic Transactions Act 1999 (US)

SECTION 7. LEGAL RECOGNITION OF ELECTRONIC RECORDS, ELECTRONIC SIGNATURES, AND ELECTRONIC CONTRACTS

(a) A record or signature may not be denied legal effect or enforceability solely because it is in electronic form.

 NOTES AND QUESTIONS

What circumstances are these provisions intended to address? Would these provisions be applicable to information concerning the performance of contractual obligations?

(k) Attribution

UNCITRAL Model Law on Electronic Commerce

ARTICLE 13. ATTRIBUTION OF DATA MESSAGES

(1) A data message is that of the originator if it was sent by the originator itself.

(2) As between the originator and the addressee, a data message is deemed to be that of the originator if it was sent:

(a) by a person who had the authority to act on behalf of the originator in respect of that data message; or

(b) by an information system programmed by, or on behalf of, the originator to operate automatically.

(3) As between the originator and the addressee, an addressee is entitled to regard a data message as being that of the originator, and to act on that assumption, if:

(a) in order to ascertain whether the data message was that of the originator, the addressee properly applied a procedure previously agreed to by the originator for that purpose; or

(b) the data message as received by the addressee resulted from the actions of a person whose relationship with the originator or with any agent of the originator enabled that person to gain access to a method used by the originator to identify data messages as its own.

(4) Paragraph (3) does not apply:

(a) as of the time when the addressee has both received notice from the originator that the data message is not that of the originator, and had reasonable time to act accordingly; or

(b) in a case within paragraph (3)(b), at any time when the addressee knew or should have known, had it exercised reasonable care or used any agreed procedure, that the data message was not that of the originator.

(5) Where a data message is that of the originator or is deemed to be that of the originator, or the addressee is entitled to act on that assumption, then, as between the originator and the addressee, the addressee is entitled to regard the data message as received as being what the originator intended to send, and to act on that assumption. The addressee is not so entitled when it knew or should have known, had it exercised reasonable care or used any agreed procedure, that the transmission resulted in any error in the data message as received.

(6) The addressee is entitled to regard each data message received as a separate data message and to act on that assumption, except to the extent that it duplicates another data message and the addressee knew or should have known, had it exercised reasonable care or used any agreed procedure, that the data message was a duplicate.

Electronic Transactions Act 1999 (Cth)

15. ATTRIBUTION OF ELECTRONIC COMMUNICATIONS

(1) For the purposes of a law of the Commonwealth, unless otherwise agreed between the purported originator and the addressee of an electronic communication, the purported originator of the electronic communication is bound by that communication only if the communication was sent by the purported originator or with the authority of the purported originator.

(2) Subsection (1) is not intended to affect the operation of a law (whether written or unwritten) that makes provision for:

   (a) conduct engaged in by a person within the scope of the person's actual or apparent authority to be attributed to another person; or

   (b) a person to be bound by conduct engaged in by another person within the scope of the other person's actual or apparent authority.

EXEMPTIONS

(3) The regulations may provide that this section does not apply to a specified electronic communication.

(4) The regulations may provide that this section does not apply to a specified law of the Commonwealth.

CERTAIN PROVISIONS OF THE EVIDENCE ACT 1995 ETC NOT AFFECTED

(5) This section does not affect the operation of:

   (a) section 87 or 88 of the *Evidence Act 1995*; or

   (b) a law of a State or Territory that corresponds to section 87 or 88 of the *Evidence Act 1995*; or

   (c) a law of a State or Territory, or a rule of common law, that provides for a statement made by a person to be treated as an admission made by a party to a proceeding in a court.

Electronic Transactions Act 1998 (Singapore)

13. ATTRIBUTION

(1) An electronic record is that of the originator if it was sent by the originator himself.

(2) As between the originator and the addressee, an electronic record is deemed to be that of the originator if it was sent—

   (a) by a person who had the authority to act on behalf of the originator in respect of that electronic record; or

   (b) by an information system programmed by or on behalf of the originator to operate automatically.

(3) As between the originator and the addressee, an addressee is entitled to regard an electronic record as being that of the originator and to act on that assumption if—

  (a) in order to ascertain whether the electronic record was that of the originator, the addressee properly applied a procedure previously agreed to by the originator for that purpose; or

  (b) the data message as received by the addressee resulted from the actions of a person whose relationship with the originator or with any agent of the originator enabled that person to gain access to a method used by the originator to identify electronic records as its own.

(4) Subsection (3) shall not apply—

  (a) from the time when the addressee has both received notice from the originator that the electronic record is not that of the originator, and had reasonable time to act accordingly;

  (b) in a case within subsection (3)(b), at any time when the addressee knew or ought to have known, had it exercised reasonable care or used any agreed procedure, that the electronic record was not that of the originator; or

  (c) if, in all the circumstances of the case, it is unconscionable for the addressee to regard the electronic record as being that of the originator or to act on that assumption.

(5) Where an electronic record is that of the originator or is deemed to be that of the originator, or the addressee is entitled to act on that assumption, then, as between the originator and the addressee, the addressee is entitled to regard the electronic record received as being what the originator intended to send, and to act on that assumption.

(6) The addressee is not so entitled when the addressee knew or should have known, had the addressee exercised reasonable care or used any agreed procedure, that the transmission resulted in any error in the electronic record as received.

(7) The addressee is entitled to regard each electronic record received as a separate electronic record and to act on that assumption, except to the extent that the addressee duplicates another electronic record and the addressee knew or should have known, had the addressee exercised reasonable care or used any agreed procedure, that the electronic record was a duplicate.

(8) Nothing in this section shall affect the law of agency or the law on the formation of contracts.

Uniform Electronic Transactions Act 1999 (US)

SECTION 9. ATTRIBUTION AND EFFECT OF ELECTRONIC RECORD AND ELECTRONIC SIGNATURE

(a) An electronic record or electronic signature is attributable to a person if it was the act of the person. The act of the person may be shown in any manner, including a showing of the efficacy of any security procedure applied to determine the person to which the electronic record or electronic signature was attributable.

(b) The effect of an electronic record or electronic signature attributed to a person under subsection (a) is determined from the context and surrounding circumstances at the time of its creation, execution, or adoption, including the parties' agreement, if any, and otherwise as provided by law.

 ## NOTES AND QUESTIONS

1   The UNCITRAL Model Law does not discuss the common law concepts of actual authority, apparent authority, and agency by estoppel but Article 13 sets out the electronic agency provisions. It effectively provides that an electronic agent is as much an agent as a human agent. Does this mean that an originator is responsible for all the electronic agent's errors?
2   Does the common law of agency make sense when applied to electronic agents? How could one guard against liability under agency by estoppel or apparent authority when faced with a forger?
3   Are there any differences between the operation of the national legislation and the operation of the UNCITRAL Model Law?

(I)   Receipt

UNCITRAL Model Law on Electronic Commerce

ARTICLE 14. ACKNOWLEDGMENT OF RECEIPT

(1) Paragraphs (2) to (4) of this article apply where, on or before sending a data message, or by means of that data message, the originator has requested or has agreed with the addressee that receipt of the data message be acknowledged.
(2) Where the originator has not agreed with the addressee that the acknowledgment be given in a particular form or by a particular method, an acknowledgment may be given by

(a) any communication by the addressee, automated or otherwise, or
(b) any conduct of the addressee,

sufficient to indicate to the originator that the data message has been received.

(3) Where the originator has stated that the data message is conditional on receipt of the acknowledgment, the data message is treated as though it has never been sent, until the acknowledgement is received.
(4) Where the originator has not stated that the data message is conditional on receipt of the acknowledgment, and the acknowledgment has not been received by the originator within the time specified or agreed or, if no time has been specified or agreed, within a reasonable time, the originator:

    (a) may give notice to the addressee stating that no acknowledgment has been received and specifying a reasonable time by which the acknowledgment must be received; and

    (b) if the acknowledgment is not received within the time specified in subparagraph (a), may, upon notice to the addressee, treat the data message as though it had never been sent, or exercise any other rights it may have.

(5) Where the originator receives the addressee's acknowledgment of receipt, it is presumed that the related data message was received by the addressee. That presumption does not imply that the data message corresponds to the message received.

(6) Where the received acknowledgment states that the related data message met technical requirements, either agreed upon or set forth in applicable standards, it is presumed that those requirements have been met.

(7) Except in so far as it relates to the sending or receipt of the data message, this article is not intended to deal with the legal consequences that may flow either from that data message or from the acknowledgment of its receipt.

Electronic Transactions Act 1998 (Singapore)

14. ACKNOWLEDGMENT OF RECEIPT

(1) Subsections (2), (3) and (4) shall apply where, on or before sending an electronic record, or by means of that electronic record, the originator has requested or has agreed with the addressee that receipt of the electronic record be acknowledged.

(2) Where the originator has not agreed with the addressee that the acknowledgment be given in a particular form or by a particular method, an acknowledgment may be given by —

    (a) any communication by the addressee, automated or otherwise; or

    (b) any conduct of the addressee, sufficient to indicate to the originator that the electronic record has been received.

(3) Where the originator has stated that the electronic record is conditional on receipt of the acknowledgment, the electronic record is treated as though it had never been sent, until the acknowledgment is received.

(4) Where the originator has not stated that the electronic record is conditional on receipt of the acknowledgment, and the acknowledgment has not been received by the originator within the time specified or agreed or, if no time has been specified or agreed within a reasonable time, the originator—

    (a) may give notice to the addressee stating that no acknowledgment has been received and specifying a reasonable time by which the acknowledgment must be received; and

    (b) if the acknowledgment is not received within the time specified in paragraph (a), may, upon notice to the addressee, treat the electronic record as though it has never been sent or exercise any other rights it may have.

(5) Where the originator receives the addressee's acknowledgment of receipt, it is presumed, unless evidence to the contrary is adduced, that the related electronic record was received by the addressee, but that presumption does not imply that the content of the electronic record corresponds to the content of the record received.

(6) Where the received acknowledgment states that the related electronic record met technical requirements, either agreed upon or set forth in applicable standards, it is presumed, unless evidence to the contrary is adduced, that those requirements have been met.

(7) Except in so far as it relates to the sending or receipt of the electronic record, this Part is not intended to deal with the legal consequences that may flow either from that electronic record or from the acknowledgment of its receipt.

 NOTES AND QUESTIONS

In order to protect itself from forgers giving the appearance of authority, the originator can protect itself by requiring an acknowledgment of receipt by the recipient. If the originator notices a falsified receipt, the originator can notify the recipient. How far do the extracted provisions go in achieving this protection for originators?

(m) Time and place

UNCITRAL Model Law on Electronic Commerce

ARTICLE 15. TIME AND PLACE OF DISPATCH AND RECEIPT OF DATA MESSAGES

(1) Unless otherwise agreed between the originator and the addressee, the dispatch of a data message occurs when it enters an information system outside the control of the originator or of the person who sent the data message on behalf of the originator.

(2) Unless otherwise agreed between the originator and the addressee, the time of receipt of a data message is determined as follows:

(a) if the addressee has designated an information system for the purpose of receiving data messages, receipt occurs:

(i) at the time when the data message enters the designated information system; or

(ii) if the data message is sent to an information system of the addressee that is not the designated information system, at the time when the data message is retrieved by the addressee;

(b) if the addressee has not designated an information system, receipt occurs when the data message enters an information system of the addressee.

(3) Paragraph (2) applies notwithstanding that the place where the information system is located may be different from the place where the data message is deemed to be received under paragraph (4).

(4) Unless otherwise agreed between the originator and the addressee, a data message is deemed to be dispatched at the place where the originator has its place of business, and is deemed to be received at the place where the addressee has its place of business. For the purposes of this paragraph:

  (a) if the originator or the addressee has more than one place of business, the place of business is that which has the closest relationship to the underlying transaction or, where there is no underlying transaction, the principal place of business;
  (b) if the originator or the addressee does not have a place of business, reference is to be made to its habitual residence.

(5) The provisions of this article do not apply to the following: [...].

Electronic Transactions Act 1999 (Cth)

14. TIME AND PLACE OF DISPATCH AND RECEIPT OF ELECTRONIC COMMUNICATIONS

TIME OF DISPATCH

(1) For the purposes of a law of the Commonwealth, if an electronic communication enters a single information system outside the control of the originator, then, unless otherwise agreed between the originator and the addressee of the electronic communication, the dispatch of the electronic communication occurs when it enters that information system.

(2) For the purposes of a law of the Commonwealth, if an electronic communication enters successively 2 or more information systems outside the control of the originator, then, unless otherwise agreed between the originator and the addressee of the electronic communication, the dispatch of the electronic communication occurs when it enters the first of those information systems.

TIME OF RECEIPT

(3) For the purposes of a law of the Commonwealth, if the addressee of an electronic communication has designated an information system for the purpose of receiving electronic communications, then, unless otherwise agreed between the originator and the addressee of the electronic communication, the time of receipt of the electronic communication is the time when the electronic communication enters that information system.

(4) For the purposes of a law of the Commonwealth, if the addressee of an electronic communication has not designated an information system for the purpose of receiving electronic communications, then, unless otherwise agreed between the originator and the addressee of the electronic communication, the time of receipt of the electronic communication is the time when the electronic communication comes to the attention of the addressee.

PLACE OF DISPATCH AND RECEIPT

(5) For the purposes of a law of the Commonwealth, unless otherwise agreed between the originator and the addressee of an electronic communication:

  (a) the electronic communication is taken to have been dispatched at the place where the originator has its place of business; and

  (b) the electronic communication is taken to have been received at the place where the addressee has its place of business.

(6) For the purposes of the application of subsection (5) to an electronic communication:

  (a) if the originator or addressee has more than one place of business, and one of those places has a closer relationship to the underlying transaction—it is to be assumed that that place of business is the originator's or addressee's only place of business; and

  (b) if the originator or addressee has more than one place of business, but paragraph (a) does not apply—it is to be assumed that the originator's or addressee's principal place of business is the originator's or addressee's only place of business; and

  (c) if the originator or addressee does not have a place of business—it is to be assumed that the originator's or addressee's place of business is the place where the originator or addressee ordinarily resides.

EXEMPTIONS

(7) The regulations may provide that this section does not apply to a specified electronic communication.

(8) The regulations may provide that this section does not apply to a specified law of the Commonwealth.

Electronic Transactions Act 1998 (Singapore)

15. TIME AND PLACE OF DESPATCH AND RECEIPT

(1) Unless otherwise agreed to between the originator and the addressee, the despatch of an electronic record occurs when it enters an information system outside the control of the originator or the person who sent the electronic record on behalf of the originator.

(2) Unless otherwise agreed to between the originator and the addressee, the time of receipt of an electronic record is determined as follows:

  (a) if the addressee has designated an information system for the purpose of receiving electronic records, receipt occurs—

    (i) at the time when the electronic record enters the designated information system; or

    (ii) if the electronic record is sent to an information system of the addressee that is not the designated information system, at the time when the electronic record is retrieved by the addressee; or

(b) if the addressee has not designated an information system, receipt occurs when the electronic record enters an information system of the addressee.

(3) Subsection (2) shall apply notwithstanding that the place where the information system is located may be different from the place where the electronic record is deemed to be received under subsection (4).

(4) Unless otherwise agreed to between the originator and the addressee, an electronic record is deemed to be despatched at the place where the originator has its place of business, and is deemed to be received at the place where the addressee has its place of business.

(5) For the purposes of this section—

(a) if the originator or the addressee has more than one place of business, the place of business is that which has the closest relationship to the underlying transaction or, where there is no underlying transaction, the principal place of business;

(b) if the originator or the addressee does not have a place of business, reference is to be made to the usual place of residence; and

(c) 'usual place of residence', in relation to a body corporate, means the place where it is incorporated or otherwise legally constituted.

(6) This section shall not apply to such circumstances as the Minister may by regulations prescribe.

Uniform Electronic Transactions Act 1999 (US)

SECTION 15. TIME AND PLACE OF SENDING AND RECEIPT

(a) Unless otherwise agreed between the sender and the recipient, an electronic record is sent when it:

(1) is addressed properly or otherwise directed properly to an information processing system that the recipient has designated or uses for the purpose of receiving electronic records or information of the type sent and from which the recipient is able to retrieve the electronic record;

(2) is in a form capable of being processed by that system; and

(3) enters an information processing system outside the control of the sender or of a person that sent the electronic record on behalf of the sender or enters a region of the information processing system designated or used by the recipient which is under the control of the recipient.

(b) Unless otherwise agreed between a sender and the recipient, an electronic record is received when:

(1) it enters an information processing system that the recipient has designated or uses for the purpose of receiving electronic records or information of the type sent and from which the recipient is able to retrieve the electronic record; and

(2) it is in a form capable of being processed by that system.

(c) Subsection (b) applies even if the place the information processing system is located is different from the place the electronic record is deemed to be received under subsection (d).

(d) Unless otherwise expressly provided in the electronic record or agreed between the sender and the recipient, an electronic record is deemed to be sent from the sender's place of business and to be received at the recipient's place of business. For purposes of this subsection, the following rules apply:

(1) If the sender or recipient has more than one place of business, the place of business of that person is the place having the closest relationship to the underlying transaction.

(2) If the sender or the recipient does not have a place of business, the place of business is the sender's or recipient's residence, as the case may be.

(e) An electronic record is received under subsection (b) even if no individual is aware of its receipt.

(f) Receipt of an electronic acknowledgment from an information processing system described in subsection (b) establishes that a record was received but, by itself, does not establish that the content sent corresponds to the content received.

(g) If a person is aware that an electronic record purportedly sent under subsection (a), or purportedly received under subsection (b), was not actually sent or received, the legal effect of the sending or receipt is determined by other applicable law. Except to the extent permitted by the other law, the requirements of this subsection may not be varied by agreement.

 # NOTES AND QUESTIONS

1 When is a message deemed to have been sent? When is a message deemed to have been received? Can you think of any rationales for these stipulations?

2 From where are messages deemed to have been sent? Why is this significant?

In the introduction to this chapter, the rules of traditional contracts were briefly discussed. The stated aim of the UNCITRAL Model Law is to facilitate electronic commerce between nations. This area is complicated by the nature of the concept of jurisdiction, which immediately becomes an issue once cross-border contracting takes place. You should consider each of the following questions in turn, noting that each question depends on the answers to those before it.

3 What might be some of the barriers to international trade as a phenomenon independent of the Internet?

4 How might the Internet amplify pre-existing problems of international contracting? How might it create new problems?

5 Consider the notion of jurisdiction. What significance, if any, does this notion have for the discussion of problems with international contracting? In your answer you should construe the notion of jurisdiction as widely as possible. Many of the complexities of electronic contracting are directly related to the complexities arising out of the concept of jurisdiction.

6   Is it a reasonable critique of the UNCITRAL Model Law to argue that it does little to solve the jurisdictional problems of e-commerce? If so, why? If not, can you provide some arguments outlining how the UNCITRAL Model Law might overcome the jurisdictional problems that arise specifically because of electronic commerce?

7   In light of the jurisdictional issues raised elsewhere in this book, how significant is the lack of an explicit provision outlining guidelines on the choice of law in the event of a disputed contract? Does 'Article 4: Variation by Agreement' simply serve the same ends, rendering an explicit clause redundant?

8   Despite any criticisms that might be directly levelled at the UNCITRAL Model Law, the true test lies in the performance of its progeny. As noted in the introduction to the UNCITRAL Model Law, around the globe several pieces of legislation have been enacted that follow it to varying degrees. In essence, the comparison should be between the objectives of the UNCITRAL Model Law on the one hand, and the outcomes manifested in national (or sub-national) legislation around the world on the other hand.

9   Willis owns a CD store. He has decided to expand his business onto the Internet. His website, williscds.com.au, allows customers to select a CD, then purchase it using the click-wrap method. A customer, Arnold in Bermuda, surfs onto the site. Arnold decides to purchase a rare CD of Classic Tangos. After providing his details he reads the Terms and Conditions (which are viewable on the same page), then purchases the CD by clicking on the 'PURCHASE' icon. The next page that appears states: 'You have purchased Classic Tangos.' When the CD arrives, Arnold thinks Willis has breached the contract because the tracks on the CD are not as he was led to believe. The law of contract is significantly different between Bermuda and Australia (NSW). There was no choice of law clause in the terms and conditions. The terms and conditions do not exonerate Willis.

In this process, which act is the offer, and which is the acceptance? Using the reasoning of *Entores* and *Brinkibon*, where and when was the contract formed? Does this result differ when using the rules outlined in the UNCITRAL Model Law? If so, where and when was the contract formed in this case?

10 How significant is the federal system of government in the formation of the Australian Act? Consider also the structure of the US legislative approach to the question of electronic commerce, transactions and contracting. Do you think our federal system of government operates as yet another hurdle on the path to harmonisation? In order to achieve uniformity, all Australian States and Territories have passed Electronic Transactions Acts that complement the Commonwealth legislation, being designed to cover private sector transactions. There have been very few cases dealing with the *Electronic Transactions Act* (Cth) and they have applied the legislation in an uncontroversial manner: see for example, *SZAEG Ors v Minister for Immigration* [2003] FMCA 258 (4 July 2003) and *Finlayson and Migration Agents Registration Authority* [2005] AATA 1127 (16 November 2005).

3 E-procurement

Governments around the world have been moving to the use of the Internet to buy and sell goods and services. The Australian Government has declared its commitment to using e-commerce for procurement. The government's policy for simple procurement, that of purchasing commodities from catalogues or pre-arranged contracts for example, is that Government agencies should be able to trade electronically with all suppliers that wish to do so, using open standards. For complex procurement such as those involving the purchase of complex or strategic requirements, usually via a tendering process, the Australian Government has established the AusTender system.[8]

While it has often been said that e-commerce results in streamlined purchasing processes and lowered cost of transacting business for both large and small companies, there has been few empirical studies on the subject. One such study was commissioned by the Australian Government Information Management Office (AGIMO). The *Case Studies on E-procurement Implementations* research report was released in 2005.[9] One of the key findings was that public sector e-procurement is a complex socio-technical system requiring inter-agency cooperation, as well as cooperation between government agencies and technology service providers and between users, buyers, suppliers and support staff. Importantly, technical tools alone are not sufficient to ensure success. Four other important factors established by the report were:[10]

- an effective procurement policy and practice;
- strategies that enable buyers and suppliers to adopt and use the e-procurement system;
- effective communication program that communicates the value of e-procurement to all stakeholders; and
- well-devised change management program to integrate these diverse parts.

These conclusions reflect the socio-legal framework within which e-commerce must be located. While technology is required for the e-commerce mechanisms to operate, the socio-legal framework is equally important.

4 United Nations Convention on the Use of Electronic Communications in International Contracts

The United Nations Convention on the Use of Electronic Comunications in International Contracts was adopted by the General Assembly on 23 November 2005. The Convention

---

8   See the web site of the Australian Government Information Management Office (AGIMO) <http://www.agimo.gov.au/business/e-procurement>.

9   This report is available online at <http://www.agimo.gov.au/publications/2005/may/e-procurement_research_reports>.

10   Ibid at 12–13.

complements and builds upon earlier instruments prepared by the UNCITRAL, including the UNCITRAL Model Law on Electronic Commerce and the UNCITRAL Model Law on Electronic Signatures. The Convention is aimed at enhancing legal certainty and commercial predictability where electronic communications are used in relation to international contracts, and thus, the provisions of the convention deal with many of the issues dealt with by the UNCITRAL Model Law on Electronic Commerce. These include issues such as determining a party's location in an electronic environment; the time and place of dispatch and receipt of electronic communications; and the use of automated message systems for contract formation.

The Convention also adopts the two underlying principles of the UNCITRAL Model Law on Electronic Commerce of functional equivalence and media neutrality. The move towards using a convention to regulate electronic contracts from the flexible and adaptable model laws is a reflection of the increased use, familiarity, and acceptance of electronic contracting. Moreover, it demonstrates a level of international consensus on the underlying legal rules and regulatory approach that should be used to ensure effective electronic transactions. While the large majority of the Convention reflect the provisions of the UNCITRAL Model Law on Electronic Commerce, the two documents are by no means identical. Readers should refer to the full text of the Convention available at <http://www.uncitral.org/uncitral/en/uncitral_texts/electronic_commerce/2005Convention.html>.

----

5   E-commerce and the jurisdiction question

The UNCITRAL Model Law and its progeny are but one example of the attempts to meet and embrace the challenges of the Internet. It was noted in the introduction to Chapter 1 that international cooperation was one, and arguably the most effective, path to practical Internet institutions. The following extract examines the progress of the OECD and the EU in their work towards developing institutions to regulate the conduct of e-commerce. The article provides a useful analysis of the jurisdictional problems of e-commerce.

James Catchpole, 'The Regulation of Electronic Commerce: A Comparative Analysis of the Issues Surrounding the Principles of Establishment'

(2000) 9(1) *International Journal of Law and Information Technology* 1 (pp 4–20 extracted)

3. Electronic commerce and the permanent establishment concept

[4] As may be envisaged, those regional authorities and national governments encouraging e-commerce's development also acknowledge the benefits derived from e-commerce's commercial growth. The obvious must be stated at this juncture: regional authorities and national governments, while keen to enjoy the enhanced economic and social benefits of

e commerce, also appreciate, although they do not always openly express it as such, that there is a need to clarify the issue of establishment in order that they may reap the consequential tax revenues brought by e-commerce. It must also be noted that the determination of establishment may also assist in the enforcement of other matters receiving regulatory attention, as it will permit greater ease to exert jurisdictional control over those areas subject to such regulation.

In relation to determining establishment, much may be drawn from those heavily regulated areas of activities involving financial services and income tax regulation. However, this is another area in which e-commerce and the Internet again challenge the application of traditional jurisdictional concepts and rules. An essential element of any tax system is the ability of taxpayers to discern their potential tax liabilities. Accordingly, an inability to distinguish boundaries in e-commerce has produced difficulties in identifying the location of the services or products being used, or in knowing with any degree of certainty where they might be subject to taxation. Hence, establishment and the surrounding issues are receiving increasing attention.

The question is thus, in which jurisdiction does a permanent establishment exist for e-commerce businesses? While there is no doubt that e-commerce is challenging traditional jurisdictional concepts, the Organisation for Economic Cooperation and Development's (OECD) Committee on Fiscal Affairs has suggested that the principles underlying international norms in tax treaties are capable of being applied to e-commerce, and so may provide a solution for determining establishment.

3.1. THE APPLICATION OF 'COMITY'

To start, while national governments may possibly be able to claim the application of their laws and regulations to e-commerce activities originating in different jurisdictions, the principle of comity is applied to limit the extraterritorial effect of such laws—ie the requirement that states should not apply their laws to persons in other states unless it is reasonable to do so. The United States Supreme Court, in *Hilton v Guyot*, defined comity as 'the recognition which one nation allows within its territory to the legislative ... Acts of another nation, having due regard both to international duty and convenience'. However, as Reed notes, the legislator's ability to maintain comity to activities within a jurisdiction is challenged by the Internet, particularly in association with establishment, which, Reed further notes, is an elastic concept.

3.2. THE EUROPEAN COURT'S APPROACH TO ESTABLISHMENT

To assist in the clarification of the issue of establishment, the European Court of Justice (ECJ), in the *Somafer* case, provided a definition:

> [t]he concept of branch, agency or other establishment implies a place of business which has the appearance of permanency, such as the extension of a parent body, has a management and is materially equipped to negotiate business with third parties, so that the latter, although knowing that there will if necessary be a legal link with the parent body, the head office of which is abroad, do not have to deal directly with such parent body but may transact business at the place of business constituting the extension.

The ECJ reaffirmed the application of establishment as a right for corporations under Article 52 of the EEC Treaty, as was held in the *Daily Mail* case. It is also worth noting that the *Daily Mail* case found that it does not follow that a corporation has the right to transfer its place of central management to another state, particularly if the aim is to move the fiscal residence of a head office—an important clarification should e-commerce businesses be seeking to take advantage of the difficulties in determining establishment to implement tax avoidance schemes. It must also be noted that determining the existence of a permanent establishment is a separate inquiry from revenue characterisation or source of income, a matter this paper does not intend to investigate.

Following the ECJ decisions, three components are generally required for the determination of establishment, namely:

- the use of fixed premises or equipment in a jurisdiction;
- the presence of staff (including possibly intermediaries); and
- the ability of those staff to undertake business transactions with customers within that jurisdiction.

While such criteria may be suitable for the physical world, invariably requiring an establishment *'plus'* component—ie in the sense that a business will not only be required to have a presence within a jurisdiction (whether that be premises, equipment or staff), but will also need to be undertaking some form of activity within that jurisdiction—it is becoming apparent that such criteria are not necessarily suitable for e-commerce and the Internet. For instance, the ECJ's decision in relation to gaming machines in *Berkholz v Finanzamt Hamburg-Mitte-Altstadt,* that an installation can only constitute a fixed establishment where there are also staff permanently present in the jurisdiction to operate the installation, has been interpreted to mean that this would apply equally to other forms of machines. E-commerce immediately raises new and difficult questions in the context of the application of the concept of permanent establishment. While it may be possible in the case of equipment that may be easily determined as *fixed*, it will not always be possible, or appropriate, to determine establishment on such basis for e-commerce operators.

To determine the application of establishment to e-commerce operators it will be necessary to decide: whether a web site on a server owned or used by a [foreign] enterprise, accounting for the fact that there may not necessarily be employees present in the source country (ie where the revenue is acquired), amounts to establishment; whether such web sites constitute a place of business; whether a server can then be said to be *fixed*; and whether the undertaking of periodic automated business functions (ie advertising, ordering, or payment) constitutes the carrying on of a business through such a fixed place of business.

3.3. HAS LEGISLATION ASSISTED IN DETERMINING ESTABLISHMENT?

Legislation, rather than assisting, has already raised a number of queries in the interpretation of the principles of establishment. For instance, the EU's Data Protection Directive (Article 4(1)(c)) requires that data controllers (when established on the territory of several Member States or, if not established in the EU, but processing personal data in a Member State) comply with the appropriate national legislation. The application of the term 'establishment' is unclear in the context of e-commerce, although Recital 19 to the Directive does provide that 'establishment ... implies the effective and real exercise of activity through stable arrangements'.

While both the Recital and Article 4(1)(c) appear to assist in clarifying some difficulties, bringing foreign data processors into the ambit of the Data Protection Directive's provisions, as they will be using equipment situated in the EU, it fails to address some of the potential issues that e-commerce poses. For example, it has been argued that the placing of cookies may even constitute establishment. Clarification is obviously required in the context of e-commerce in this particular example as it is difficult to fully understand the application of this proposition. E-commerce web sites viewed on a user's computer are not sufficient to create a virtual branch, such as for banks, since the e-commerce operator may have neither premises nor staff within the jurisdiction and the user's computer is only used temporarily. Is, therefore, the placing of cookies any different? Arguably not, since cookies are text file mechanisms by which server side connections may store and retrieve user-related and preference information, such as passwords or user-preferred destination pages in web sites, on the client side of a web-based connection. However, should their function exceed the mere recognition of users, and be used to collect/process additional user information, it would be questionable whether they would be afforded the exemption under the OECD Model Income Tax Convention on Income and on Capital 1998 (Article 5(4)(d)), discussed below. While this argument may be supported by the proposition that a cookie's life-span, normally set for 12 months, permits cookies to be re-activated upon the user's return to a web site, they are, however, not fixed, as a user may decline their placement or delete them. Nor do they perform any discernible activity in the execution of a business transaction.

4. The OECD's reconciliation of establishment with electronic commerce

Turning again to the issue of taxation, it has already been suggested that supranational and double taxation treaties may provide a solution by which establishment may be determined. However, the application of tax concepts of residence and permanent establishment to cross-border business, designed upon principles dating back to the international tax treaties following the League of Nations draft conventions (1927–33), and more recently to the OECD, have been placed under considerable pressure by the emergence of e-commerce.

The ECJ's interpretation of establishment is consistent with definitions contained in most double taxation treaties, which require that a business must have a permanent establishment in a jurisdiction before that jurisdiction is able to tax the business profits of the enterprise. When determined to be so established, a business will be subject to the corporate income tax of that jurisdiction, but the existence of permanent establishments in multiple countries may create cash flow disadvantages for e-commerce businesses. Thus the issue is, to what extent do business operations utilising the Internet create a permanent establishment for the participants?

4.1. THE OECD'S MODEL INCOME TAX CONVENTION ON INCOME AND ON CAPITAL

Of the treaties in place, the OECD's Model Income Tax Convention on Income and on Capital 1998 is one of the most highly regarded and has influenced many of the double taxation treaties currently in existence. It is, therefore, an appropriate focus for the determination of establishment. In assigning taxing rights over business operations, the OECD Convention's concept of permanent establishment is used to determine whether the enterprise has brought itself within any particular taxing jurisdiction. Under Article 7 a jurisdiction may tax an enterprise's business profits attributable to a permanent establishment located in that country, regardless of the enterprise's country of residence for tax purposes.

Permanent establishment is defined under Article 5 as a 'fixed place of business through which the business of an enterprise is wholly or partly carried on', including specifically an office, branch or place of management. The Convention additionally provides guidance for excluding from permanent establishment status:

> the use of facilities solely for the purpose of storage, display or delivery of goods or merchandise belonging to the enterprise, the maintenance of a stock of goods or merchandise belonging to the enterprise solely for the purpose of storage, display, delivery, processing by another enterprise, maintaining a fixed place of business solely for the purpose of purchasing goods or merchandise or of collecting information, for the enterprise, to carry on any other activity of a preparatory or auxiliary character.

Whether the application of these exemptions to e-commerce activities is possible is open to question, thus rendering many of them inappropriate. In addition, the Convention and its exemptions are further undermined by the fact that they are dependent upon a jurisdiction's own view and interpretation.

The Convention also provides that an enterprise will not be deemed to have a permanent establishment as a result of carrying on a business through brokers, general commission agents, or other independent agents acting in the ordinary course of their business. On the other hand, a dependent agent who has and who habitually exercises the authority to conclude contracts in the name of an enterprise will create a permanent establishment for the enterprise on whose behalf the agent is acting.

The Commentary to Article 5 of the earlier 1992 Model Income Tax Treaty appeared to provide additional guidance that may have been applicable to the emerging e-commerce industry. It stated that a permanent establishment might exist if the business of the enterprise is carried on 'mainly through automatic equipment', with the activities of personnel restricted to setting up, operating, controlling, and maintaining such equipment. However, this early Commentary is illustrative of the challenges that e-commerce has posed. The Commentary was initially developed in response to gaming and vending machines, where the user's entire transaction is conducted by interaction with the machine, but it has proved to be of limited application to e-commerce, and is currently being amended.

4.2. THE DETERMINATION OF 'FIXED PLACES OF BUSINESS'

Thus, the determination of whether an e-commerce operator will be deemed to have a particular fixed place of business as a result of Internet-generated sales, and thereby establishment, will need to be considered in the light of:

4.2.1. WHETHER THE LOCATION OF COMPUTER FILES CONSTITUTING A WEB SITE ON A SERVER LOCATED IN A JURISDICTION IS A PARTICULAR SITE AND THUS A PLACE OF BUSINESS WITH SUFFICIENT PERMANENCE TO BE A FIXED PLACE OF BUSINESS?

It is important to distinguish between the server and the web site. The latter does not, in itself, involve any tangible property and therefore may not constitute a place of business, as there is no facility such as premises or, in certain circumstances, machinery or equipment in accordance with Article 5. In addition, being visible in a jurisdiction is not synonymous with, nor does it entail, a physical presence in a jurisdiction. A web site's server, on the other hand, is equipment having a physical location and, combined with the web site's software contributing to the function performed in relation to the business, it may, in theory, constitute a place of business.

In order that servers may constitute a permanent establishment, it will be necessary that they meet the requirement of being fixed under Article 5(1)—ie that a server is located at a certain place for a sufficient period of time. However, the manner in which servers are used will not necessarily make the application of the test or the Article 5 straightforward. For instance, servers may be located in buildings situated in countries in which enterprises have no other presence; or on a portable computer used in different places within a building or moved from city to city. Further, the use of linked servers in different jurisdictions switching signals from one to another during the performance of a service, thus avoiding being fixed, makes it harder to determine which server in which jurisdiction is used for which portion of the activity for the purposes of determining establishment. Should an e-commerce operator wish to implement a scheme by which to ensure that its enterprise does not fulfil the requirement of being fixed, it would only have to have one web site which is electronically transferred in total, every so often, to new servers in different buildings, cities, or countries. In addition, it is not uncommon for a number of mirror web sites to exist on different servers located in different countries, directing customers to any of them for any function in order not to be subjected to congestion arising in Internet traffic. The UK's Inland Revenue has already stated that servers used solely for advertising would not likely be a permanent establishment, further noting the practical realities in that web sites held on servers may be switched to alternative servers.

Consequently, it may be necessary to apply a contrasting view to that which believes servers may constitute establishment, as noted by the OECD. In relation to the core functions of an enterprise, it is stated that the communication tools used in the selling process should be of no consequence. Whether the transaction is concluded by mail order, by telephone or through a server-based web site, the form in which a product is delivered (physically or electronically) should make no difference to the way in which it is taxed. Thus, only in exceptional cases would a permanent establishment exist, for example where the relevant transaction (the conclusion of a contract, the payment and the delivery of the goods) is handled fully (automatically) by the server itself. However, commentary on this view, which also expresses the opinion that the presence of a server (including one that hosts a web site) in a jurisdiction could not give rise to a permanent establishment, must to some extent be flawed. The argument that a server is not typically the type of equipment through which business is carried on cannot be sustained, since it is obviously not the case as far as e-commerce is now concerned. Consequently, while this view may be appropriate in some circumstances, as technologies develop permitting a greater proportion of a business to operate via a server, it must be a view that should not necessarily prevail; rather, it is one that will become outdated.

4.2.2. WHO OWNS THE WEB SITE CONTENTS AND/OR THE SERVER?
The enterprise that operates the server may be different from the enterprise that carries on business through the web site. For example, an e-commerce operator may own the web

site but lease the server from a service provider, lease both the web site and server from the service provider, or lease the web site and server and share various functions with the service provider.

Where a web site is hosted on an Internet Service Provider's (ISP) server, although the fees paid may be based on the amount of disk space used to store the web site's software and data, such arrangements do not typically give the web site operator any right to particular space or control over the operation of the server. Consequently, the server and its location are not at the web site operator's disposal, even if agreement has been reached that the web site should be hosted on a particular server at a particular location. Since the web site operator will not have a physical presence at that location, and because a web site should not be viewed as tangible assets, the web site operator cannot be considered to have acquired a place of business by virtue of that hosting arrangement. The OECD has suggested that where the e-commerce operator owns, or leases, and operates the web site's server, then, provided the other requirements of Article 5 are satisfied, the operator could constitute a permanent establishment.

In addition, it must also be considered whether ISPs may constitute permanent establishments for e-commerce operators by virtue of the web sites operated through the servers owned and operated by ISPs. The only application under which this may be possible is under Article 5(5) of the OECD Convention, which states that:

> where a person is acting on behalf of an enterprise and has ... an authority to conclude contracts in the name of the enterprise, [it] shall be deemed to have a permanent establishment in that State in respect of any activities which that person undertakes for the enterprise ...

In practice, ISPs will not constitute an agent, as they will invariably have neither authority to conclude contracts on behalf of e-commerce operators, nor will they constitute independent agents acting in the ordinary course of their business, as they will most likely host web sites for many e-commerce operators. Additionally, since a web site is obviously not in itself a 'person' as defined by Article 3 of the Convention, Article 5(5) cannot therefore deem a permanent establishment to exist by virtue of the web site being an agent of the enterprise.

4.2.3. WHETHER A WEB SITE MAY BE CONSIDERED SOLELY AN EXEMPT DISPLAY OF GOODS—AND SO SEEK EXEMPTION IN ACCORDANCE WITH THE OECD'S ARTICLE 5 EXEMPTIONS, OR MAY BE CONSIDERED AS THE TAX EQUIVALENT OF A MAIL-ORDER CATALOGUE, OR IS REGARDED AS AN ENTIRE SALES OUTLET LOCATED IN A JURISDICTION—IE DOES A WEB SITE GO BEYOND THE TYPES OF PREPARATORY AND AUXILIARY ACTIVITIES WHICH, UNDER ARTICLE 5(4), WOULD NOT RESULT IN A PERMANENT ESTABLISHMENT?

Assisting in this analysis, New York case law draws the analogy between conventional media and Internet advertising, suggesting that a web site containing information that simply advertises (solicits) business in New York does not amount to 'transaction of business' and would not subject a host to personal jurisdiction under the New York Civil Practice Laws and Rules. It is also worth considering the application of Atkin IJ's test in *FL Smidth and Co v Greenwood* for determining where a trade is being carried on. Although the test may have a limited application to the activities of e-commerce, it poses the question: 'where do the operations take place from which the Profits in substance arise?' In that the substance of the operation is invariably the conclusion of a contract, it may be appropriate to look for the end result of the online commercial activity. The OECD's own guidance on this matter lists a number of activities which, by themselves, would generally be regarded as preparatory or auxiliary; namely, the provision of communications links between suppliers and customers; advertising of goods or services; and/or relaying information through a mirror server for security and efficiency purposes.

In addition, the language used by the OECD Convention suggests that the mere solicitation of orders (in essence, the purpose for which a mail-order catalogue is used) via the Internet is unlikely to give rise to a permanent establishment, and would arguably fall under the auxiliary or preparatory activity exemption of Article 5. Should service companies be employed to process orders and clear payments, it may be concluded that such service providers have sufficient authority to bind a foreign enterprise in the activity and, if exercised habitually, give rise to permanent establishment. Although, it must be noted, that the exemption under Article 5(6) may apply to such activities as 'it [is] [carrying] on business ... through a broker, general commission agent or any other agent of an independent status ... acting in the ordinary course of their business'.

However, this issue has to consider the various functions (or combination of functions) that can be automated, such as advertising, ordering, payment, storage and digital delivery, and the extent to which a database of digital contents may constitute a stock of goods and, if that is the case, whether the database may be said to be maintained 'solely for the purposes of storage, display or delivery' if it also has a search and reporting facility (eg, if a customer can select the contents of the database merely for viewing). Should jurisdictions determine that any such functions form an essential and significant part of the commercial activity of e-commerce operators, or other core functions of the enterprise are carried on through the computer equipment, such functions must be deemed to go beyond the auxiliary or preparatory activities. If the equipment constituted a fixed place of business, then e-commerce could find that some of its activities may be determined sufficient for establishment in those jurisdictions. This may also be applicable in relation to what may be considered as the core function of the e-commerce operator and the equipment itself. If, for example, the sales functions are performed through the computer equipment (whether the product is delivered online or otherwise), the equipment would constitute a place of business and thereby be a permanent establishment. But again, this would need the certainty that the equipment is fixed.

In addition, in respect of the exception included under Article 5(4)(d) concerning the collection of information, it is unclear at what point mere collection of information substantially becomes processing of raw information that is collected. For example, should the EU's Data Protection Directive be applicable, its broad definition of processing (that includes any operation performed upon personal data, including collection, storage, adaptation or alteration, disclosure by transmission and dissemination) will, most likely, encompass anything that is done with personal data as processing, and will probably exceed the threshold for the mere collection of information permitted under the exemption, thus rendering it inapplicable to e-commerce operators.

4.2.4. THE EXTENT TO WHICH HUMAN INTERVENTION IS REQUIRED TO DETERMINE A PERMANENT ESTABLISHMENT

As the OECD notes, there appear to be two schools of thought in relation to whether some form of human intervention is required. Where it is stated that some human intervention is necessary, the interpretation of the exact parameters of that requirement differs. The OECD list three differences, namely:

- whether the intervention must necessarily take place in the country or can be done from abroad;
- whether the intervention needs to be that of employees of the enterprise or of any person, whether or not employed by the enterprise;
- what level of human intervention is required.

In relation to the first, the view put forward is that only when intervention by persons present in the country where the equipment is located takes place may the e-commerce operator be regarded as participating in the economic life of that jurisdiction. Obviously, when it is not possible to maintain or operate equipment remotely, there will be a greater assumption of establishment in the location of the personnel. The second issue is that an operator may only be said to be carrying on business activities in a jurisdiction through equipment located in that country if the equipment is operated by persons, whether or not employed by the enterprise. The third raises the question of how to distinguish between the operation of equipment and its maintenance, especially when databases or software are upgraded, and the level of human intervention required for each for a permanent establishment to exist.

An approach that appears to be both more logical and appropriate to e-commerce is that automated equipment, which does not require human intervention for its operation, may constitute a permanent establishment. The question thus becomes the nature of the business and whether the activities performed through the equipment are the core income-generating activities of that business. In this respect, e-commerce activities can be analogous to other activities in which equipment operates automatically, as applied by the German Supreme Tax Court. The German Court's pipeline decision found permanent establishment when a Dutch company owned and used German underground pipelines and provided, through computers, pressure to transport the oil by remote control from the Netherlands to the German oil companies. By analogy, it would appear that a sale or service provided to customers over the Internet through the use of a server in the customer's jurisdiction by a foreign supplier is generated by a permanent establishment in the customer's jurisdiction. Although commentary upon this analogy has limited its application to the provision of Internet services, rather than to the sale of, say, jeans etc, it would appear that personnel are not necessary for a permanent establishment when no personnel are in fact necessary to generate income. Further support for this conclusion may be drawn from the fact that no explicit reference for a requirement for human intervention is included in the OECD Convention's definition of 'fixed place of business', and paragraph 10 of the existing Commentary to Article 5 already recognises that automatic equipment may constitute a permanent establishment.

4.3. HAS THE OECD KEPT PACE?

As demonstrated by the OECD Convention, it may be assumed that many traditional tax laws and treaties by which establishment is determined envisage a single web site or server being responsible for the entire contracting purpose and are in fact struggling to keep pace with the actual operation of e-commerce. The OECD, in issuing its latest revisions, anticipates to clarify the application of permanent establishment and to address the difficulties that e-commerce has created in the interpretation of previous double taxation treaties, and to some extent, case law. Of importance is the OECD's recognition that a distinction must be made between computer equipment, such as servers (which may constitute permanent establishment under certain circumstances), and data and software which are used by, or stored on, that equipment, particularly as the entity operating a server may be different from that carrying on business through a web site. However, it must therefore be questioned whether the traditional approaches for determining establishment under long-standing principles such as the OECD's, which are invariably based on a requirement of activity (in order that tax may be collected), need to be overhauled and replaced with a concept that is more applicable to e-commerce.

5. The European Union's approach

5.1. THE EU'S ELECTRONIC COMMERCE DIRECTIVE

The EU, in specifically targeting its legislation at the Internet and e-commerce, has been the latest legislative body to address the issue of establishment, and has attempted to produce a coherent approach. The EU's Electronic Commerce Directive, approved by the European Parliament on 4 May 2000, is regarded as preparatory for Europe's transition to a knowledge-based economy, by ensuring that Information Society services benefit from EU Internal Market principles of free movement of services and freedom of establishment. The Directive's primary aim is the harmonisation of areas such as where operators are established, transparency obligations for operators and commercial communications, conclusion and validity of electronic contracts, Internet intermediaries' liabilities, online dispute settlement, and the role of national authorities.

While it is not the specific aim of the Directive, the EU's approach to establishment is both interesting and new. Further, the Directive also makes an important step in the actual regulation of the Internet and e-commerce activities. By virtue of Article 4 and Recital 22, the Directive provides that Information Society services should be supervised at the source of the activity in order to ensure an effective protection of public interest objectives; thus, the Directive has taken steps to ensure regulatory certainty by providing that once an e-commerce operator is established within a jurisdiction, it is that jurisdiction that regulates its activities. This will, in theory, eliminate a number of difficulties that have been experienced in everyday activities, such as commercial promotions and offers (such as '2-for-1' promotions) that contravene German competition laws.

The Directive's definition of established service provider states that establishment is where a service provider:

... effectively pursues an economic activity using a fixed establishment for an indefinite period. The presence and use of the technical means and technologies required to provide the service do not, in themselves, constitute an establishment of the provider ...

It is intended that this definition, stated as being in line with ECJ case law, will remove legal uncertainty and ensure that operators cannot evade supervision, as they will be subject to supervision in the Member State where they are established (the Directive will not apply to service providers established outside the EU). However, the definition cannot be read alone. As is becoming a common requirement in the interpretation of EU legislation, it is necessary to turn to the Recitals for additional guidance. Recital 19 states:

> The place at which a service provider is established should be determined in conformity with the case law ... according to which ... establishment involves the actual pursuit of an economic activity through a fixed establishment for an indefinite period; ... also fulfilled where a company is constituted for a given period, the place of establishment of a company providing services via an Internet web site is not the place at which the technology supporting its web site is located or the place at which its web site is accessible but the place where it pursues its economic activity; in cases where a provider has several places of establishment it is important to determine from which place of establishment the service concerned is provided; in cases where it is difficult to determine from which of several places of establishment a given service is provided, this is the place where the provider has the centre of his activities relating to this particular service ...

Thus, the EU has sought to rely upon established EC Treaty principles and ECJ case law and defines the place of establishment as the place where an operator actually pursues an economic activity through a fixed establishment, irrespective of where web sites or servers are situated or where the operator may have a mailbox. It has sought to remove some of the difficulties currently experienced in the adaptation of the physical world's legislation for the determination of establishment to the *online* world. Further assistance in determining establishment is provided by the obligation upon service providers to make available basic information concerning their activities, of which the most significant is the provision of the geographic address at which the service provider is established.

By clearly stating its parameters, and requiring service providers to state where they are established, thereby removing some of the requirements for various authorities to undertake the exercise of that determination, the Directive has moved away from previous models of establishment that encompass a establishment 'plus' element. It will no longer be necessary, as is required under various national legislation, such as the United Kingdom's *Income and Corporations Taxes Act 1998*, to show additional requirements of activity within a jurisdiction. However, while the scope of the Directive is not intended to apply to the field of tax, the application of rules established in existing double taxation treaties will no doubt assist in resolving some issues for some e-commerce operators.

5.2. THE EMERGENCE OF A NEW CONCEPT OF ESTABLISHMENT?

The important result of the Directive is that it is promulgating a new concept for the regulation of commercial activities within a region. Thus, once determined as established within a

Member State of the EU, e-commerce operators will, without question, be subjected to regulatory control within those Member States. The possible underlying tone of the Directive is the emergence of a principle by which a commercial activity, for which it may not necessarily be possible to determine that their activities etc are confined to one geographic jurisdiction, will ultimately be determined on a regional basis.

6. Conclusion

While there can be no doubt that e-commerce has and will continue to challenge many of the pre-existing rules and regulations that are commonplace within geographic areas and jurisdictions, the ability to embrace and control the Internet and e-commerce will depend upon authorities and legislative bodies to determine where such activities take place. Obviously, establishment is one such area of concern, of significant importance for ensuring that regulatory controls are applicable to the Internet and e-commerce and that the consequential social and economic benefits (of which, the collection of tax revenues is one factor) are obtained.

However, e-commerce has proved itself apt at not following the expected norms and capable of being able to circumnavigate pre-Internet models of establishment. In the physical world, vendors who change locations regularly would undoubtedly lose customers; in contrast, the location of a server is irrelevant to e-commerce customers, as they will have access to the business's goods or services wherever they have Internet access. Given the expected progress of cable and satellite technology, a further complication is anticipated once bandwidth limitations are overcome, making it possible to locate most, if not all, of the functions of an Internet business in any country. In fact, the consequences are so profound that the OECD has acknowledged that the concept of permanent establishment may be ill-adapted to e-commerce and that many bilateral and multilateral tax treaties may have to be amended or scrapped in order to accommodate international e-commerce taxation regimes. Obviously a coherent approach is required to ensure that establishment may be determined.

The EU's Electronic Commerce Directive appears to be implementing a new approach that would determine establishment on a regional basis, thus overcoming many of the geographical constraints experienced by national legislation and double taxation treaties. In fact, this notion of approaching such an issue on a regional basis is one that has already received some consideration. In relation to taxation at source, discussions have raised the issue that it could be expanded and liberalised to ensure that all countries receive a fair share of electronic commerce tax revenue. This is illustrated by the tension between two broad, but potentially incompatible, policy goals of the OECD. In October 1998 the OECD's Committee on Fiscal Affairs policies stated that existing tax principles should apply to the taxation of electronic commerce, but another policy goal, the maintenance of sovereignty and fairness, could conflict with the preservation of existing principles.

The consequence is that the OECD appears to be stating that the fiscal sovereignty of countries and a fair sharing of the tax base generated by e-commerce are more important than a strict (or possibly even loose) adherence to existing technical tax principles. In addition, e-commerce's removal of the middleman from business transactions, resulting in lost tax revenue, is receiving increasing concern. Whether these concerns will result in far-reaching changes to the international tax regime or a material reallocation of the world's tax revenue remains to be seen. The challenge that such changes will have to address will be preventing businesses without a permanent establishment (as that term is currently understood) in a particular country being subjected to taxation in that country. However, what is clear is that the governance of e-commerce will have to be consistently applied, of which establishment is only one issue. The EU's approach may appear to be the start of a process whereby, at least for e-commerce, establishment is determined on a regional basis with the consequential tax revenue and legislative responsibility being shared proportionately between regional members.

[Footnotes omitted]

 ## NOTES AND QUESTIONS

1   The European Union Electronic Commerce Directive is designed to cover business-to-business and consumer transactions as well as advertising and sponsorship. It applies to all 'information society services', which are defined as all services normally provided against remuneration and at a distance by electronic means and on request, including the on-line sale of goods and services and the licensing of information. EU member states were required to implement the Directive in national laws by 17 January 2002.

2   What are the fixed place of business and server problems raised by Catchpole? Does the EU Directive resolve the problems and issues as well as Catchpole thinks? Why, or why not? Can you see any problems with the EU Directive approach to establishment?

3   Compile a list, in point form, of all of the problems or issues that arise in relation to electronic commerce. How many points in your list are solely the result of the nature of the Internet (as opposed to being merely the result of a transboundary commercial dispute and conflicts of laws)?

4   How many of the problems listed in response to question 3 can be resolved using existing legal institutions, or existing mechanisms for building institutions?

5   If we assume that existing legal institutions and mechanisms are unable to solve all the problems, can you think of any innovative means by which other solutions might be reached? Your answer might be either technically or legally based, and you are encouraged to think beyond the four walls of traditional Western legal doctrine in your attempt.

4

Privacy and the Internet

1   Introduction

We saw in Chapter 3 the prevalence and importance of the role of e-commerce on the Internet. In order for consumers and businesses to engage in e-commerce, there must be a certain level of confidence in the privacy of their transactions. After all, it would be unworkable if confidential business deals or even credit card numbers were disclosed to the whole world. In this and the next few chapters, we look at the issues which affect the usage of the Internet as an e-commerce tool. Consumers want to be able to go about their Internet dealings in private, without others knowing about, for example, their sexual orientation. They want to purchase items with security and they want to be able to ascertain the identity and integrity of those they deal with. Each of these needs raises legal issues. The first deals with privacy, the second deals with encryption technology, and the third deals with issues of electronic signatures. However, this is not to say that these legal issues are solely relevant to commerce on the Internet. Indeed, they are relevant to the general use of the Internet irrespective of whether or not one is engaging in commerce. We will look at each of these against the background of e-commerce, as it provides a useful focal point.

Many people assume that use of the Internet is anonymous, private, not tracked, and not watched. This idea arises because users are rarely if ever asked explicitly to provide personal information as they use the Internet, and when they are the request is usually accompanied by a convincingly worded privacy or security guarantee. However, the assumption is misplaced. The Internet has many data collection mechanisms able to collect a variety of information about surfers: goods purchased, sites visited, personal information, and so on. It is possible to create personal profiles from information collected from a range of sources, which can be paired with information about the user's computer. This leads to the creation of a personal profile attached (in a database somewhere) to a particular computer. Therefore, it is possible to collect, organise, buy, and utilise much more information than might first be thought. Two recent examples illustrate these points.

During the confirmation hearings in the nomination process of Robert Bork for a seat on the US Supreme Court, a journalist was able to obtain a computerised record of 146 videos hired by Bork and his wife. While this might seem to be innocuous enough, it has wider implications for the security of personal data.

An American naval officer had utilised the services of America Online (AOL). A colleague accessed the AOL profile of the officer and discovered the word 'gay' among a list of search terms. The officer was subsequently discharged under the 'don't ask, don't tell' policy against homosexuality in the US military.[1]

All sorts of information can be gathered to create an individual user's on-line profile to reveal intimate details about his or her personal interests. This profile can be linked

---

[1]   See Hon Justice M Kirby, 'Privacy in Cyberspace' (1998) *UNSW Law Journal* available at <http://www. law.unsw.edu.au/unswlj/ecommerce/kirby.html> 26 September 2001.

to, or include, information about health, education, credit history, sexual or political orientation, and then used later to predict targeted advertising or to act as a quasi-credit rating. Of concern is the fact that much of this activity occurs without the knowledge of the subject. The consequence of this is that the subject has very little power to correct incorrect information once it enters the information flow, or to object to and opt out of the collection process. Incorrect information can be perpetuated and magnified. There are three main methods of data collection.

(a) Cookies

Cookies are small text files placed on a user's computer when a website is accessed. They contain information sent by the website server to the user's browser. If desired, a web user can sometimes view cookies in the source code of the header of a web page. However, generally, the information collected is not displayed to the user, but is recorded, tracked, and stored by the user's computer and browser. If a user returns to the website, the user's web browser will send the previously stored information to the website. In this way, the cookie can tell the website that this is the same computer that was here some time ago, thus tracking the movements of users of particular computers.

Cookies can also be set in the meta-tags of a web page, as well as being set and read using java script (a computer language). Here, the cookie will only be visible if the user inspects the underlying code of the web page. Generally speaking, cookies contain code or other data that uniquely identifies a user's computer; this enables the site to track and profile the user's activities on that site as well as other sites. While it is often claimed that cookies only pass on information that does not personally identify the user, this is not always so. The cookie itself may not contain personally identifying information, but the website may know the identity of the user whose browser sends the cookie. For example, a website that collects users' names or e-mail addresses from on-line enquiries, registration, or sales is readily able to connect personally identifying information to a cookie sent by the user's browser and to other information obtained about the user.

The second way cookies can collect personal information that can identify the user is through html-enabled e-mail programs, such as Microsoft Outlook. In this instance, the sender of an e-mail message can include personally identifying information about the recipient hidden in the code of the e-mail. When the reader reads the message or accesses a page mentioned in the e-mail, a cookie is set, and the site then receives details of the person associated with the cookie.

Some have said that cookies are not an entirely negative technology. They allow innovations such as the 'shopping cart' and the customisation of websites. After all, users are now able to disable cookies in the set-up of their browser programs. However, the lack of information accompanying a cookie means it is difficult to know whether to accept or not accept a particular cookie. Furthermore, some sites will simply not operate if cookies have been disabled, leaving the Internet user with little choice.

Frederic Debussere, 'The EU E-Privacy Directive: A Monstrous Attempt to Starve the Cookie Monster?'

(2005) 13 *International Journal of Law and Information Technology* 70

2. Cookie Technology in a Nutshell

If an individual wants to visit a website or navigate from webpage to webpage within a website, then his webbrowser (for instance, Microsoft Internet Explorer or Netscape Navigator) sends a request to the server that operates the website. Upon receiving the request, the server then transmits to the individual's webbrowser the information that constitutes the requested website or webpage. The communication between the individual's webbrowser and the server that operates the website occurs by means of a protocol called HyperText Transfer Protocol ('HTTP'). The file sent by the server to the webbrowser is preceded by an HTTP header, which is a set of ASCII strings following a special language called HyperText Markup Language ('HTML') and containing information about the server and the document being sent.

HTTP differs from other protocols such as the File Transport Protocol ('FTP') in that it is a 'stateless' protocol, which means that each visit to a website and even each click within a website is seen by the website's server as the first visit by the individual. Consequently, the server 'forgets' everything after each request, unless it can 'mark' a visitor to help remember it. It is at this point that cookies come into the picture: their technical purpose is to 'maintain state' between stateless HTTP communications. In other words, they help a server to remember an individual's activities on the website(s) concerned.

As mentioned above, the cookie technology was invented in the midnineties by Lou Montulli, at that time a programmer at Netscape Communications. The term 'cookies' comes from the computer science term 'magic cookie' used by Unix programmers.

A cookie is a text file of typically less than four kilobytes of memory that the server which operates the visited website places on the individual's hard drive by means of an additional line added to the HTTP header. Contrary to some newspaper reports and US court opinions, a cookie is thus not an executable computer program or code and cannot function like a program. The syntax of the additional line in the HTTP header of an HTML document is as follows: 'Set-Cookie: NAME = VALUE; expires = DATE; path = PATH; domain = DOMAIN_NAME; secure'.

NAME = VALUE is the name of the cookie and its value. This is the only required attribute in the Set-Cookie header; the others are optional. This is the globally unique identifier ('GUID') that the server specifically assigns to an individual and is the main component in the cookie's tracking system; it is through this number that companies are able to identify exactly which websites or webpages an individual has visited before. In other words, it is the data that the website's server wants passed back to it when a browser requests another page. It is this GUID that DoubleClick uses to target individual Web surfers and ensure that they do not see the same advertisement banner over and over again.

DATE is an attribute that determines how long the cookie persists on the individual's hard drive. Its format is: 'Wdy, DD-Mon-YYYY HH:MM:SS GMT'. If there is no expiration date, then the cookie is stored in memory only and is automatically erased when the individual unloads or closes his webbrowser; the cookie is then called a 'session' (or 'transient') cookie. Session cookies only store information in the form of a session identification and do thus not store any personally identifiable information. However, if the DATE attribute refers to a date in the future, then the cookie is a so-called 'persistent' (or 'permanent' or 'stored') cookie and is saved in a file. Only such persistent cookies can be used to track an individual at several visits of one or more websites or webpages. Setting the date for an existing cookie to be some day in the past deletes the cookie.

DOMAIN_NAME is an attribute that contains the address of the server that sent the cookie and that will receive a copy of the cookie when the webbrowser requests a file from that server. It defaults to the server that set the cookie if it is not explicitly set in the 'Set-Cookie:' line. This attribute may be set to equal the subdomain that contains the server so that multiple servers in the same subdomain will receive the cookie from the webbrowser. This allows larger websites to co-ordinate multiple servers in the same subdomain. For instance, if the DOMAIN_NAME equals www.company.com, then machines named one.company.com, two.company.com and three.company.com all receive the cookie from the webbrowser. The value of DOMAIN_NAME is limited such that only hosts within the indicated subdomain may set a cookie for that subdomain.

PATH is an attribute that is used to further refine when a cookie is sent back to a server. When the PATH attribute is set, a cookie is only sent back to the server if both the DOMAIN_NAME and the PATH match for the requested file.

'Secure' is an attribute that specifies that the cookie is only sent if a secure HTTP ('HTTPS') is being used. Since most websites do not require secure connections, this attribute defaults to false.

When applying the above to surfing to, for instance, the URL http://www.google.com, then the HTTP header (in HTML) of the response that Google's server sends to the individual's webbrowser may look like this:

```
HTTP/1.1 200 OK
Content-Length: 3059
Server: GWS/2.0
Date: Sat, 11 Jan 2003 02:44:04 GMT
Content-Type: text/html
Cache-control: private
Set-Cookie:
PREF = ID = 73d4aef52e57bae9:TM = 1042253044:LM = 1042253044:S = SMCc-
HRPCQiqy
x9j; expires = Sun, 17-Jan-2038 19:14:07 GMT; path =/; domain = .google.com
Connection: keep-alive
(followed by other HTML text)
```

Once a cookie is installed on an individual's hard drive for a particular website, then each time that individual surfs to and navigates through that website and requests a different webpage, the website's server gains access to the current cookie. The information stored in the cookie is attached to every subsequent request from the webbrowser to the website's server for a different webpage. After receiving the cookie's information attached to the web browser's request, the server may modify that information to reflect new or updated information. Together with the new webpage the individual requested, the server sends a revised cookie that replaces the old one. Thus, once installed on an individual's hard drive, cookies facilitate a flow of communication back and forth between that hard drive and the website's server.

3. Why Do Cookies Threaten Privacy?

The technical purpose of cookies is thus to make it possible that the server which operates a website can 'remember' that an individual visited that website or a webpage before; cookies allow websites to 'tag' their visitors with unique identifiers so that they can be identified each time they visit the website or webpage. In this way, cookies can be very useful things. For instance, if an individual wants to check his e-mail box via the World Wide Web, then the username and password that have to be typed, can be stored in a cookie, so that these data are automatically filled out the subsequent occasions the individual wants to check his e-mail and that he thus only has to type them once. In the case of electronic commerce, cookies can be used to retain a record of the items that one has ordered the previous time, so that one can view one's shopping basket over a certain period of time. Cookies can also be used to personalise a website; for instance when an individual visits a multi-language website, a cookie can be used to remember the individual's language preference.

In this context, it is important to distinguish between two separate types of information that can be stored in cookies: personally identifiable information and non-personally identifiable information. Personally identifiable information consists of data that is used to identify an individual and is mostly provided to the website by the individual himself, for instance in the context of electronic commerce. Such information, also called 'transaction generated information', can include, for instance, an individual's name, address, phone number, e-mail address, credit card number, age, gender, income, marital status, number of children, health, political affiliation, social security number, occupation, lifestyle dimensions, leisure activities, type of car, Internet Protocol address, etc. Non-personally identifiable information is not linked to any particular personal information and typically consists of so-called 'clickstream data', for instance the number of times that an individual clicks on an on-line advertisement ('banner').

The potential harm of cookies does not lie in the information stored on the user's computer itself, but in what companies can do with the information. It is a fact that a company that retrieves some personally identifiable information via cookies, for instance via electronic commerce, may have some knowledge of some characteristics of individuals. This is a legitimate concern, but in most cases the individual has provided the information himself and has consented to giving the information. In addition, since most websites have only the limited capability to read cookies from an individual's hard drive that that website itself sent on a previous visit, it is hard for single information collecting companies to come to a real 'dossier effect'. The real danger rather lies in so-called 'on-line profiling' by means of data mining. This consists of recording an individual's on-line behaviour through the accumulation of clickstream and other forms of data into vast databases and the subsequent construction of 'profiles' of individuals based upon that record. In this context, a third party, usually an advertising agent, places cookies on individuals' hard drives from its own servers. The clickstream data collected by such third parties is in some ways more comprehensive than those of single website owners because third parties serve material on a number of different websites. If company A, company B and company C all enter into an agreement with third party D to place advertisements on each of their respective websites, then third party D can use the same cookie irrespective of which of the three websites an individual is visiting. In other words, whereas companies A, B and C only know what individuals do when they are on their respective websites, third party D can link behaviour of a given individual on any of these websites to that individual's behaviour on any of the other websites. In this way, third party D can associate non-personally identifiable information retrieved from a cookie of company A's website with personally identifiable information retrieved from a cookie of company B's website.

This cookie-facilitated interaction for advertising purposes, such as that of DoubleClick, works as follows. When an individual visits website X, then the HTML code underlying the webpage at website X tells the individual's webbrowser that it needs to display several advertisements on the webpage, and it refers the individual's browser to server Y, ie the server of the advertising placement service's website. When the request from the individual's webbrowser arrives at server Y, the latter determines whether or not the individual has one of Y's cookies (or one of Y's network of associates). If there is no such cookie, then server Y installs a cookie on the individual's hard drive. If there is already such a cookie on the individual's hard drive, then server Y accesses it, analyses the stored clickstream data, combines that data with data about the individual previously retrieved and finds out what kind of advertisement the individual should be interested in. Server Y then responds to the request from the individual's webbrowser by filling the advertising space on website X's webpage with advertisement banners targeted to the individual's profile. The owner of website X is paid for displaying the banner ads (each view is called a 'hit') and receives more revenue if the individual clicks through on the banner to the sponsor's website (a 'click'). The owner of server Y earns money from the advertisers for placing the targeted banner advertisements on the requested webpage.

In addition, it has to be pointed out that the scope and penetration of data-profiling activities will probably increase with a new technology initiative aimed at facilitating the sharing of data among several businesses. It is currently rather difficult for companies to exchange customer data, because there is no uniform standard method for compiling and collecting such data, so that a company can share such data with another company only if it first transforms the data into a form that the other company can read. The creation of the Customer Profile Exchange ('CPEX') and the advent of Extensible Markup Language ('XML') will make this possible. CPEX, formed in 1999, is an alliance of technology companies dedicated to developing 'a vendor-neutral, open standard for facilitating the privacy-enabled interchange of customer information across disparate enterprise applications and applications'. To achieve this goal, CPEX is developing a common language based on XML that will allow different companies to exchange data more easily. XML is similar to HTML, but unlike HTML, XML has a greater capacity for facilitating the sharing of data. HTML currently allows website owners to use only a limited array of tags to designate whether Web text should be, for example, a certain font, size or colour. A characteristic of HTML tags is that they identify whether the text is a name, zip code or e-mail address. XML, in contrast, can attach identifying tags to any type of text, allowing it to be recognised. Because anyone can define XML tags, XML cannot by itself facilitate exchanges of customer data among companies; a standard format must exist for the tags. CPEX wants to develop common specifications of XML so that companies collecting customer data can quickly transfer that data to other companies.

There are several possible self-help measures against the installing of cookies. First, webbrowsers permit their users to set their 'preferences' to accept or reject cookies, to notify the user before accepting a cookie or to accept only cookies that will be returned to the originating website. A second possibility is to manually delete all cookies installed in the 'cookie jar' after having finished surfing the World Wide Web. Third, there is also software for examining, editing, blocking or eradicating cookies, such as Cookie Pal, Cookie Master 2, Cookie Crusher, Crumbler 97, and Cookie Cutter. However, it is perceived that self-help does not seem to be sufficient and that there should also be a legal framework with respect to the use of cookies. Below, we turn to an analysis of the new EU legal framework for the use of cookies ...

 NOTES AND QUESTIONS

1 Why are cookies important for the mechanics of the Internet? How do they function and what was their original purpose?

2 Do you believe that more good than harm comes of cookies?

3 It would be a reasonably straightforward task to reconfigure cookies to provide information more comprehensible than that highlighted in the above extract. Why do you think programmers and companies have not taken steps to make these changes?

4 The PGP Cookie Cutter concept is simply a tool for managing cookies when using the Internet. It allows a user to refuse selected cookies (that is, to reject them outright) or to block them (stop them from being set and allowing a user to examine them).

5 At this point there has been no authoritative ruling on the legality of cookies. Is there a legal solution to cookie management? Is there a technical solution? See *In re Doubleclick Inc Privacy Litigation*, 00 Civ 0641 (SDNY, 28 March 2001) for a US perspective on some of the issues.

6 The text, operation and implications of the European Directive will be examined in more detail later in this chapter.

(b) Web bugs

These are quite a recent innovation. They are also known as clear GIFs, or 1x1 GIFs. A web bug is a tiny graphic, included in a web page or e-mail message, used to identify who or how many people are viewing the material. They are generally about the size of a small full stop but they are clear images and they have no visible content. They can be placed in the image tags of the underlying HTML code of the page and they can also be placed in HTML-enabled e-mail messages.

When a bug is viewed the following information is sent to the web server:

- the Internet protocol address of the computer
- the URL of the web page
- the URL of the web bug image
- the time viewed
- the type of browser used
- the previously set cookie value.

Web bugs can be used for various purposes. Firstly, they can be used on web pages to compile information about the sites that a particular user visits. Advertising networks can place their web bugs on other companies' sites to enable them to record which sites and which pages a user visits and add the information to a user profile. Some or all of the information is then passed on, either to the site viewed, or to other companies or other people. This technology is especially useful in banner advertisements. Web bugs can track a user's movements through websites that are connected through banner advertisements. As soon as a user clicks on a banner, the information trail begins. This information is then given to the host websites and the advertisers, so that the next time that person logs in they can target the advertisements based on what the person has been attracted to in the past.

The second way web bugs can be used is to provide independent accounting of how many people visit a site. Third, they are used to compile information about which browsers are being used to visit which sites.

In relation to HTML-enabled e-mail messages, they can be used to gather all sorts of information. They can be used to determine whether the message has been read by the recipient, which is not possible otherwise. They can be used to obtain the Internet Protocol address of the recipient of an e-mail message. This is useful if the recipient is attempting to remain anonymous. In an organisation, you can tell how many times a message has been forwarded on and read, because as each new person receives it, the sender gets notification. If there is a website mentioned in an e-mail message and the recipient visits the site, even at a later date, the sender can be notified of the visit through the use of cookies.[2]

(c)   HTTP technology

Each time a user accesses a page, the browser will send information to the server site without the user's knowledge, and this step is part and parcel of the http protocol.

Types of information that can be sent include:

- The remote address variable and the remote host variable, which may provide information about the user's location.
- The 'HTTP From' and 'remote_user' variable, which can pass on the user's e-mail address or other indications of identity.

---

2   See further R M Smith, 'Web Bugs: FAQ' available at <http://www.privacyfoundation.org/resources/webbug.asp> 25 September 2001.

- The 'HTTP Referrer', which discloses the web page the user was viewing before accessing the current page. If the prior page was a search engine, the entire query in the search (the search term) is passed on. If the prior page was a banner advertisement, the URL of the advertisement is then sent to the site. If the URL clicked on was a private file on a hard disk, then the file name is passed on to the site. If the file was an e-mail message viewed in an e-mail program, the information passed on might be so detailed as to include the user's name, e-mail address, program used, and even file directories and file space.
- The 'User Agent' variable, which discloses information about the software and hardware being used, for example the browser name and the platform of the system such as Windows or Unix.
- The 'Remote-indent' variable may disclose the identity of the user, depending on whether the user's Internet Service Provider disables the function. Most do, but some do not. If not, then your real world name is visible to the website.[3]

(d)   Other technologies

Recently, there has been an increase in the different types of tracking technology available. Some of these are loosely termed spyware or adware and sometimes even malware. Spyware is essentially any form of technology that aids in gathering information about a person or an organisation without their knowledge or informed consent. They can comprise of software or hardware devices that simply track a user's access of web pages or they can comprise keystroke monitors that record every keystroke typed on a given computer. Keystroke monitors can be used by hackers to acquire passwords, credit card numbers, and even financial information.

Adware is similar to spyware to some extent because its purpose is to track the user's Internet usage and deliver targeted advertising. Adware can easily become spyware if the user has not adequately consented to the installation of the software. The litigation involving WhenU.com's SaveNow software illustrates the workings of adware. The SaveNow software is usually downloaded as part of a bundle of free software. Once installed, the SaveNow software launches whenever the user's browser is active. The software scans data from a browsing session, including URLs, search terms typed into a search engine, and the contents of a requested page. This data is compared with terms in SaveNow's proprietary database. If there is a match, then contextual pop-up advertising is triggered. See further *U-Haul International v WhenU.com, Inc*, 279 F Supp 2d 723 (ED Va 2003); *Wells Fargo & Co v WhenU.com, Inc*, 293, F Supp. 2d 734 (ED Mich 2003); 1-800 *Contacts, Inc v WhenU.com, et al*, 02 Civ 8043 (SDNY Dec 22, 2003). These cases are discussed in more detail in the chapter on Trade Marks.

These various technologies all invade the privacy of the Internet user, some with more serious consequences than others. No doubt more advanced and developed mechanisms will be employed in the future.

---

3   See further 'JUNKBUSTERS: Alert on Web Privacy' available at <http://www.junkbusters.com/cgibin/privacy> 26 September 2001.

NOTES AND QUESTIONS

1   The above outline, although brief, serves to highlight the mechanisms by which personal data can be collected and collated, and on-line profiles subsequently created. Has this information, if it is new to you, coloured your view of using the Internet? Would you change your Internet choices in light of this? Furthermore, could you change your actions to avoid these mechanisms?

2   Do you think the diligence required of individuals to monitor collection of their own personal data is realistically possible? Can you think of any alternatives to this diligence?

3   As you read the materials in this chapter compare the legal responses with the technological realities outlined above.

2   Privacy and e-commerce

A number of revealing surveys regarding consumer reactions to the Internet have been conducted. In an Australian Bureau of Statistics Survey of the twelve months prior to August 1999,[4] it was estimated that 41 per cent of the Australian adult population accessed the Internet. However, less than 5 per cent used it for on-line shopping. So the development of e-commerce had clearly not kept pace with Internet usage. This was due to users' reluctance to supply information about themselves over the Internet. Survey subjects were worried about security of personal information disclosed, and uncertain as to how it might be used, or whether it would be disclosed to others by the recipient organisations. They were also concerned about unsolicited advertising material and other intrusions into their personal cyberspace.

According to an Internet Privacy Survey carried out by the Australian law firm Freehill Hollingdale and Page in 2000,[5] Australians were quite justified in their concerns. Only 18 per cent of website operators offered users the option of increased security to protect personal privacy. Only 12 per cent of website operators had an accessible privacy statement. And only 6 per cent utilised independent external auditors to monitor compliance with privacy standards.

In contrast, the results pertaining to the collection of the information were promising. The survey found that 77 per cent of the website operators offering electronic payment facilities provided secure and encrypted transmission of data, and 80 per cent had adopted either an industry-based or some other recognised privacy protection code. Most respondents (97 per cent) said they do not disclose personal information obtained

---

4   Australian Bureau of Statistics, *Use of the Internet by Householders, Australia, August 1999* (AGPS, Canberra, November 1999).

5   The survey is available for download from their web site at <http://www.freehills.com.au/4A25682400258290/Lookup/pdfguides/$file/Freehills_internet_privacy_survey.pdf> 15 September 2001.

through their websites to other organisations, although there was no guarantee that they would not do so in the future.

The activities of the US company toysmart.com provide an example of the potential problems in this area.[6] Toysmart.com was an on-line toy retailer largely owned by Walt Disney. The website included a request for children's details, including their names, birthdays, wish lists, and so on. This information was collected through competitions, giveaways, and other means. Accompanying the requests was a privacy statement which included a 'guarantee' that the information would not be shared with any third parties. The retailer collected 250,000 children's details. In June 2000 the company encountered financial difficulties and decided to raise revenue by advertising its databases and customer files for sale. Despite the promises in the privacy statement, when financial trouble loomed, the information was used in an attempt to pay off creditors. This activity led to outcry from numerous quarters. The US Federal Trade Commission and a battery of lawyers brought a suit for misleading and deceptive practices. The dispute was settled by a deal with the US Federal Trade Commission, in which the company promised to destroy the databases in return for a payment of US$50,000 by an Internet subsidiary in the Walt Disney Group.

The *Toysmart* case has raised questions about the extent to which consumers can rely on self-regulation measures, particularly in cases where Internet companies are facing huge financial failures. In light of this, some options, such as self-help or codified law setting minimum standards for industry self-regulation, have been proposed to increase consumer confidence. Although far from perfect, the more feasible of these options is co-regulation. This involves implementing voluntary industry codes to provide standards of privacy protection and institutions to support and enforce them. The rationale for these moves is to try to foster confidence in e-commerce. However, considering the example of toysmart.com, it appears that self-regulation by companies is by no means a guaranteed success. Companies, like people, cannot always be trusted. Therefore, there needs to be a protocol for collection and use of information, including standards of protection that cannot simply be ignored when it does not suit a particular company's needs at a given time.

 NOTES AND QUESTIONS

1   It is often said that 'privacy is about control, not secrecy'. This is an important observation, especially when we consider that 'control' applies both to the individual's control and to the control exercised by the state—and in light of the encryption materials later in this book.

2   What preconceived ideas did you hold regarding the nature of privacy? Does a notion such as control fit within these ideas? Do you agree that this is how we should regard questions of personal privacy?

---

6   See further the US Federal Trade Commission's web site at <http://www.ftc.gov/opa/2000/07/toys-mart.htm> 16 September 2001.

3   The following extract examines the American response to the privacy challenge. The response has come at a number of levels and will be revisited later in this chapter in relation to the Safe Harbor principles. For the moment, the extract below highlights the position of the Federal Trade Commission—a position that was and is central to the Safe Harbor policy.

Prepared Statement of the Federal Trade Commission on 'Self-Regulation and Privacy Online', before the Subcommittee on Communications of the Committee on Commerce, Science, and Transportation, United States Senate, 27 July 1999

Available at <http://www.ftc.gov/os/1999/9907/privacyonlinetestimony.pdf>
10 September 2001

The current state of online privacy regulation

... The Commission believes that self-regulation is the least intrusive and most efficient means to ensure fair information practices online, given the rapidly evolving nature of the Internet and computer technology. During the past year the Commission has been monitoring self-regulatory initiatives, and the Commission's 1999 Report finds that there has been notable progress. Two new industry-funded surveys of commercial web sites suggest that online businesses are providing significantly more notice of their information practices than they were last year. Sixty-six percent of the sites in the Georgetown Internet Privacy Policy Survey ('GIPPS') post at least one disclosure about their information practices. Forty-four percent of these sites post privacy policy notices. Although differences in sampling methodology prevent direct comparisons between the GIPPS findings and the Commission's 1998 results, the GIPPS Report does demonstrate the real progress industry has made in giving consumers notice of at least some information practices. Similarly, 93% of the sites in the recent study commissioned by the Online Privacy Alliance ('OPA Study') provide at least one disclosure about their information practices. This, too, represents continued progress since last year, when 71% of the sites in the Commission's 1998 'Most Popular' sample posted an information practice disclosure.

The new survey results show, however, that, despite the laudable efforts of industry leaders, significant challenges remain. The vast majority of the sites in both the GIPPS and OPA surveys collect personal information from consumers online. By contrast, only 10% of the sites in the GIPPS sample, and only 22% of the sites in the OPA study, are implementing all four substantive fair information practice principles of Notice/Awareness, Choice/Consent, Access/Participation, and Security/Integrity. In light of these results, the Commission believes that further improvement is required to effectively protect consumers' online privacy.

In the Commission's view, the emergence of online privacy seal programs is a particularly promising development in self-regulation. Here, too, industry faces a considerable challenge.

TRUSTe, launched nearly two years ago, currently has more than 500 licensees representing a variety of industries. BBBOnLine, a subsidiary of the Council of Better Business Bureaus, which launched its privacy seal program for online businesses last March, currently has 54 licensees and more than 300 applications for licenses. Several other online privacy seal programs are just getting underway. Together, the online privacy seal programs currently encompass only a handful of all web sites. It is too early to judge how effective these programs will ultimately be in serving as enforcement mechanisms to protect consumers' online privacy.

Conclusion

The self-regulatory initiatives discussed above, and described in greater detail in the 1999 Report, reflect industry leaders' substantial effort and commitment to fair information practices. They should be commended for these efforts.

In addition, companies like IBM, Microsoft and Disney, which have recently announced, among other things, that they will forgo advertising on sites that do not adhere to fair information practices, should be recognized for their efforts, which we hope will be emulated by their colleagues. Similarly, the Direct Marketing Association (DMA) is now requiring its members to follow a set of consumer privacy protection practices, including providing notice and an opportunity to opt out, when identifying information is shared with other marketers, and to use the DMA's two national services for removing consumers' names from marketing lists.

Enforcement mechanisms that go beyond self-assessment are also gradually being implemented by the seal programs. Only a small minority of commercial web sites, however, have joined these programs to date. Similarly, although the results of the GIPPS and OPA studies show that many online companies now understand the business case for protecting consumer privacy, they also show that the implementation of fair information practices is not widespread among commercial web sites.

As stated previously, the Commission believes that legislation to address online privacy is not appropriate at this time. Yet, we also believe that industry faces some substantial challenges. Specifically, the present challenge is to educate those companies which still do not understand the importance of consumer privacy and to create incentives for further progress toward effective, widespread implementation.

First, industry groups must continue to encourage widespread adoption of fair information practices. Second, industry should focus its attention on the substance of web site information practices, ensuring that companies adhere to the core privacy principles discussed earlier. It may also be appropriate, at some point in the future, for the FTC to examine the online privacy seal programs and report to Congress on whether these programs provide effective privacy protections for consumers.

Finally, industry must work together with government and consumer groups to educate consumers about privacy protection on the Internet. The ultimate goal of such efforts, together with effective self-regulation, will be heightened consumer acceptance and confidence. Industry should also redouble its efforts to develop effective technology to provide consumers with tools they can use to safeguard their own privacy online.

The Commission has developed an agenda to address online privacy issues throughout the coming year as a way of encouraging and, ultimately, assessing further progress in self-regulation to protect consumer online privacy:

- The Commission will hold a public workshop on 'online profiling', the practice of aggregating information about consumers' preferences and interests gathered primarily by tracking their movements online. The workshop, jointly sponsored by the US Department of Commerce, will examine online advertising firms' use of tracking technologies to create targeted, user profile-based advertising campaigns.
- The Commission will hold a public workshop on the privacy implications of electronic identifiers that enhance web sites' ability to track consumers' online behavior.
- In keeping with its history of fostering dialogue on online privacy issues among all stakeholders, the Commission will convene task forces of industry representatives and privacy and consumer advocates to develop strategies for furthering the implementation of fair information practices in the online environment.
- One task force will focus upon understanding the costs and benefits of implementing fair information practices online, with particular emphasis on defining the parameters of the principles of consumer access to data and adequate security.
- A second task force will address how incentives can be created to encourage the development of privacy-enhancing technologies, such as the World Wide Web Consortium's Platform for Privacy Preferences (P3P).
- The Commission, in partnership with the US Department of Commerce, will promote private sector business education initiatives designed to encourage new online entrepreneurs engaged in commerce on the Web to adopt fair information practices.
- Finally, the Commission believes it is important to continue to monitor the progress of self-regulation, to determine whether the self-regulatory programs discussed in the 1999 Report fulfill their promise. To that end, the Commission will conduct an online survey to reassess progress in web sites' implementation of fair information practices, and will report its findings to Congress.

The Commission is committed to the goal of full implementation of effective protections for online privacy in a manner that promotes a flourishing online marketplace, and looks forward to working with the Subcommittee as it considers the Commission's 1999 Report.

 NOTES AND QUESTIONS

1   This statement is a condensed adaptation of the full Federal Trade Commission Report (FTC) of 1999, *Self-Regulation and Privacy Online: A Report to Congress*[7] which provides, in a formal structure, the same information as the above extract. It also contains the testimony of two of the Commissioners discussing their views on the report.

2   It is perhaps no surprise that the US position would favour a self-regulatory approach, as opposed to a legislative or code-based agenda. The final sections of

---

7   <http://www.ftc.gov/os/1999/9907/privacy99.pdf> 20 September 2001.

this chapter deal with Australia, which, for now, can also be described as having a hybrid approach based both on legislation and on code. Which of these models do you prefer, and why?

3   Is it safe to assume that companies will act in accordance with their obligations even if these obligations are imposed by legislation?

4   Private sector privacy endorsements (also known as privacy seals), such as those run by organisations like TRUSTe, are becoming increasingly popular. How much faith would you put in an audit from such an organisation? Do you think that these organisations will prevent a repeat of the toysmart.com controversy? Are they designed for such a purpose?

5   Do you think that the FTC's conclusion against legislative action is well-founded? Do you think that its privacy goals are achievable in the short to medium term?

3   The privacy discourse

The concept of informational privacy or personal data privacy was a topic of discussion well before the rise of the personal computer or the wider area network or the Internet. However, the processing power of the computer, the speed of networks, and the global nature of the Internet have taken the topic from the realms of high theory into the sphere of legislative activity.

The materials in this chapter focus on the regulation of personal data flows in the private sector. This is not to say the public sector is not worthy of consideration, as it is clear that governments are the major collectors of information. Further, it is not to deny that personal data information flows are problematic in the public sector. Rather, the focus is based on a belief that the public sector is more easily regulated than the private and, therefore, is not as prone to difficulties.

Over the last twenty-five years a number of social, political, economic, and technological factors have elevated private enterprises to the point where, collectively, they now pose the largest threat to personal privacy.[8] There are a number of reasons why the private enterprise is the bigger threat:[9]

- Private enterprises are better at data processing. As technology has become cheaper and more widespread, private enterprises have surpassed the public sector in their ability to gather information.
- Private enterprises, which arise from and are operated with a profit motive, have more motivation and inclination to push the envelope of privacy in search of greater rewards.
- There is only limited public control of private enterprise. Governments are subjected to at least some degree of democratic oversight, whereas corporations are accountable only to their shareholders, and traditionally judged according to the profit motive.

---

8   A Charlesworth, 'Data Privacy in Cyberspace: Not *National vs International* but Commercial vs Individual', in L Edwards L & C Waelde (eds), *Law and the Internet: A Framework for Electronic Commerce* second edition (Hart Publishing, Oxford, 2000).

9   Charlesworth, op cit, pp 81–2.

- The free market and deregulation ethos of recent years have operated to the benefit of corporations as governments gradually remove themselves from the role of regulator. The emphasis has, therefore, shifted towards methods of sectoral self regulation.
- Private enterprises have been given a larger role to play in international organisations. The reduction in government intervention at the national level has increased the activity of corporations at the international level. This inevitably reduces the influence of citizens, as governments are replaced by unelected and unaccountable private interest groups.
- Private enterprises are often able to relocate internationally with relative ease. Businesses can alter their choice of legal obligations by moving location.
  In light of the above it can be stated that:
- some sections of the private sector are better equipped to collect information than the public sector;
- private enterprises often have more reasons to collect information;
- private enterprises have limited reasons to respect the information they collect;
- increasingly, they do have control over some types of dispute resolution between commercial bodies and citizens; and
- when regulation is mooted, private enterprises are able to relocate, or threaten to relocate, to non-regulated jurisdictions.

Over the past five or ten years, the dominant academic discourse regarding privacy regulation has been one of convergence and divergence. On the one hand, convergence represents the drive to harmonise the laws of privacy internationally, and, on the other, divergence represents nations' desires to legislate according to predominantly national influences and ideologies. The discourse has been reformulated outside the boundaries of national versus transnational interests to take account of:

- the non-geographical nature of the Internet;
- the decline of the desire by certain nation states to engage in certain types of regulation; and
- the development of truly multinational corporations.

The earliest attempts to harmonise laws of privacy according to an international framework came with the OECD in the 1970s.

----

4   Privacy and the OECD

As the importance of personal data privacy became understood several decades ago the Organisation for Economic Cooperation and Development (OECD) produced a set of guidelines. These guidelines have remained the touchstone of privacy discourse since then. The OECD is an organisation focused predominantly on economic matters. The member countries are quite diverse and combined they produce approximately two-thirds of world goods and services. Consequently, concerns about the potential effects of the rise of the private enterprise were central to the OECD's interest in privacy.

During the 1970s, fears mounted that disparities between national laws on personal data might discourage or restrict the cross-border flow of information, and that these restrictions might cause disruptions in important sectors of the economy. To offset the risk, the OECD decided to outline some basic principles to serve as a basis for legislation in member countries, especially those which did not have any privacy legislation. The instrument is a set of guidelines and not a convention. It merely recommends that countries take its basic principles into account. They are not obligatory; countries need not apply all or any of the rules. The nature of an aspirational document is such that it often lacks detail and uses broad, flexible language. This is not necessarily a criticism of the OECD Guidelines; rather, this feature has enabled it to stand the test of time, and it remains one of the seminal documents in the privacy discourse.

Organisation for Economic Cooperation and Development, Guidelines Governing the Protection of Privacy and Transborder Flows of Personal Data

© OECD. Available at <http://www.oecd.org//dsti/sti/it/secur/prod/PRIV-EN.HTM> 10 September 2001

Part One. General

DEFINITIONS

1   For the purposes of these Guidelines:

(a) 'data controller' means a party who, according to domestic law, is competent to decide about the contents and use of personal data regardless of whether or not such data is collected, stored, processed or disseminated by that party or by an agent on its behalf:

(b) 'personal data' means any information relating to an identified or identifiable individual (data subject);

(c) 'transborder flows of personal data' means movements of personal data across national borders.

SCOPE OF GUIDELINES

2   These Guidelines apply to personal data, whether in the public or private sectors, which, because of the manner in which they are processed, or because of their nature or the context in which they are used, pose a danger to privacy and individual liberties.

3   These Guidelines should not be interpreted as preventing:

(a) the application, to different categories of personal data, of different protective measures depending upon their nature and the context in which they are collected, stored, processed or disseminated;

(b) the exclusion from the application of the Guidelines of personal data which obviously do not contain any risk to privacy and individual liberties; or

(c) the application of the Guidelines only to automatic processing of personal data.

4 Exceptions to the Principles contained in Parts Two and Three of these Guidelines, including those relating to national sovereignty, national security and public policy ('ordre public'), should be:

(a) as few as possible, and

(b) made known to the public.

5 In the particular case of Federal countries the observance of these Guidelines may be affected by the division of powers in the Federation.

6 These Guidelines should be regarded as minimum standards which are capable of being supplemented by additional measures for the protection of privacy and individual liberties.

Part Two. Basic Principles of National Application

COLLECTION LIMITATION PRINCIPLE

7 There should be limits to the collection of personal data and any such data should be obtained by lawful and fair means and, where appropriate, with the knowledge or consent of the data subject.

DATA QUALITY PRINCIPLE

8 Personal data should be relevant to the purposes for which they are to be used, and, to the extent necessary for those purposes, should be accurate, complete and kept up-to-date.

PURPOSE SPECIFICATION PRINCIPLE

9 The purposes for which personal data are collected should be specified not later than at the time of data collection and the subsequent use limited to the fulfilment of those purposes or such others as are not incompatible with those purposes and as are specified on each occasion of change of purpose.

USE LIMITATION PRINCIPLE

10 Personal data should not be disclosed, made available or otherwise used for purposes other than those specified in accordance with Paragraph 9 except:

(a) with the consent of the data subject; or

(b) by the authority of law.

SECURITY SAFEGUARDS PRINCIPLE

11 Personal data should be protected by reasonable security safeguards against such risks as loss or unauthorised access, destruction, use, modification or disclosure of data.

OPENNESS PRINCIPLE

12 There should be a general policy of openness about developments, practices and policies with respect to personal data. Means should be readily available of establishing the existence and nature of personal data, and the main purposes of their use, as well as the identity and usual residence of the data controller.

INDIVIDUAL PARTICIPATION PRINCIPLE

13   An individual should have the right:

(a)   to obtain from a data controller, or otherwise, confirmation of whether or not the data controller has data relating to him;

(b)   to have communicated to him, data relating to him
   - within a reasonable time;
   - at a charge, if any, that is not excessive;
   - in a reasonable manner; and
   - in a form that is readily intelligible to him;

(c)   to be given reasons if a request made under subparagraphs*(a)* and *(b)* is denied, and to be able to challenge such denial; and

(d)   to challenge data relating to him and, if the challenge is successful to have the data erased, rectified, completed or amended.

ACCOUNTABILITY PRINCIPLE

14   A data controller should be accountable for complying with measures which give effect to the principles stated above.

Part Three. Basic Principles of International Application

FREE FLOW AND LEGITIMATE RESTRICTIONS

15   Member countries should take into consideration the implications for other Member countries of domestic processing and re-export of personal data.

16   Member countries should take all reasonable and appropriate steps to ensure that transborder flows of personal data, including transit through a Member country, are uninterrupted and secure.

17   A Member country should refrain from restricting transborder flows of personal data between itself and another Member country except where the latter does not yet substantially observe these Guidelines or where the re-export of such data would circumvent its domestic privacy legislation. A Member country may also impose restrictions in respect of certain categories of personal data for which its domestic privacy legislation includes specific regulations in view of the nature of those data and for which the other Member country provides no equivalent protection.

18   Member countries should avoid developing laws, policies and practices in the name of the protection of privacy and individual liberties, which would create obstacles to transborder flows of personal data that would exceed requirements for such protection.

Part Four. National Implementation

19   In implementing domestically the principles set forth in Parts Two and Three, Member countries should establish legal, administrative or other procedures or institutions for the protection of privacy and individual liberties in respect of personal data. Member countries should in particular endeavour to:

(a) adopt appropriate domestic legislation;

(b) encourage and support self-regulation, whether in the form of codes of conduct or otherwise;

(c) provide for reasonable means for individuals to exercise their rights;

(d) provide for adequate sanctions and remedies in case of failures to comply with measures which implement the principles set forth in Parts Two and Three; and

(e) ensure that there is no unfair discrimination against data subjects.

Part Five. International Cooperation

20 Member countries should, where requested, make known to other Member countries details of the observance of the principles set forth in these Guidelines. Member countries should also ensure that procedures for transborder flows of personal data and for the protection of privacy and individual liberties are simple and compatible with those of other Member countries which comply with these Guidelines.

21 Member countries should establish procedures to facilitate:

- information exchange related to these Guidelines, and
- mutual assistance in the procedural and investigative matters involved.

22 Member countries should work towards the development of principles, domestic and international, to govern the applicable law in the case of transborder flows of personal data.

NOTES AND QUESTIONS

1   The OECD has not been silent on the issue of privacy or related matters. In 1998 the OECD Working Party on Information Security and Privacy produced a *Ministerial Declaration on the Protection of Privacy on Global Networks*. This declaration came out of a Ministerial meeting in Ottawa, Canada. It is both a reaffirmation and a 'goal document'. It highlights the continuing importance of the OECD Guidelines while outlining the need for their continuing implementation, and the need for increased focus on privacy issues by national governments.

　　The declaration was followed in 1999 by the Recommendation of the OECD Council Concerning Guidelines for Consumer Protection in the Context of Electronic Commerce.[10] The OECD describes these Guidelines as being:

> ... designed to help ensure that consumers are no less protected when shopping online than they are when they buy from their local store or order from a catalogue. By setting out the core characteristics of effective consumer protection for online business-to-consumer transactions, the Guidelines are intended to help eliminate some of the uncertainties that both consumers and businesses encounter when buying and selling online. The result of 18

---

10   <http://www.oecd.org/dsti/sti/it/consumer/prod/CPGuidelines_final.pdf> 18 September 2001.

months of discussions among representatives of OECD governments and business and consumer organisations, the Guidelines will play a major role in assisting governments, business and consumer representatives to develop and implement online consumer protection mechanisms without erecting barriers to trade.

These documents are likely to have played a role in the formation of government policy both in Australia and elsewhere. It is significant that the Privacy Guidelines are still a benchmark for judging legislation two decades later.

2   These guidelines are important because they established eight privacy principles which, although inadequate, formed part of the earliest attempts to codify privacy principles across national boundaries. The principles were motivated by the protection of business activity rather than the protection of personal privacy, so the focus was on facilitating commerce rather than on individuals' privacy concerns. Furthermore, they reflect the technology of the late 1960s and early 1970s.

-----

5   Convergence and divergence: *EU v United States*

The modern model for personal data privacy has been an economic and commercial construct, rather than a human rights construct.[11] In the USA, this appears to be due to the acquiescence of the US government. Ironically, this commercial notion is also, in part, a product of the credence given to it by cyberspace civil libertarians. The US government is unwilling to enact uniform and holistic legislation because of the perceived difficulties in harmonising regulation, and also because the lobbyists push the point that such regulation would harm the development of e-commerce. The libertarians base their human rights approach on the somewhat tired claim that the Internet cannot be regulated.

There are parallels here with the debate that took place over intellectual property rights on the Internet over the past ten years. In that instance, the 'unregulatable' argument was advanced by those predicting the demise of intellectual property on the Internet. However, in subsequent years, these rights have grown stronger at the expense of society and the individual. So the question arises: if intellectual property rights can prosper and grow stronger on the Internet, why not personal data property rights? The answer lies in the vested interests at stake. Commercial entities won out in the intellectual property law war, and commercial entities are poised to win in the privacy law war. Therefore, unless governments protect personal data privacy rights, they will continue to be eroded by commercial interests seeking to protect their profits.[12]

The EU, on the other hand, has been relatively active in its work on personal data privacy. It issued its Directive on the Protection of Individuals with regard to the

---

11   Charlesworth, op cit.
12   Charlesworth, op cit.

Processing of Personal Data and on the Free Movement of Such Data (Data Protection Directive) in 1995. The continuing debate over the Directive, and the reaction of the US government and American corporations, can be viewed as an example of the classic convergence and divergence debate.

On the convergence side, there is a struggle between two different convergence ideologies: a multinational commercial convergence, and the weakening push for rights-based convergence.[13]

The divergence discourse, for its part, no longer centres merely on protecting the national interests, ideologies, or preferences of individual countries, but rather on the struggle between two competing models of international personal data protection regulation. Therefore, the issue becomes not whether to legislate, but how.

The first divergence model is based on the theory that governments must ensure that individuals' privacy is protected. This model is exemplified by European approaches to government and regulation. The legislation passed under the Directive (although obviously retaining aspects of convergence in this respect) embodies the notion of the state as protector, providing individual rights and mechanisms for their enforcement in both public and private sectors. The second model is based on the theory that government intervention is unnecessary. Represented in the patchwork legislative quilt of the USA, it provides few positive rights except perhaps regarding the secondary use of information by governments. It relies on self-regulation and market forces to ensure that private enterprises adopt practices acceptable to the public. Although the collective European response is an example of converging standards and legislation, individually, the foundations of European countries' legislation can be held up as an example of the one ideology underlying the divergence discourse.[14]

The overall goal in privacy legislation is to provide a workable balance between the demands of individual personal privacy and the wider society's interests in the free flow of information. The parameters of the problem will be identified through a series of questions aimed at establishing a data privacy protection regime in cyberspace:

* What do we seek to protect?
* How do we seek to protect it?
* Why does society determine that it is worthy of protection? and
* What are the interests involved in the free flow of information?

The obvious next step is to pursue workable solutions to these questions. In this endeavour some issues can be identified:

* The first issue to be faced is the social, political and legal understanding of personal privacy, on which Europe and the USA differ.
* The second issue arises from the fact that in order to operate efficiently, the free market requires that some types of information are publicly available.

---

13   Charlesworth, op cit.
14   Charlesworth, op cit.

- The third issue is whether it is necessary for governments to regulate commercial activities to protect individuals.
- The fourth issue, the significance of which has been vastly amplified by the Internet, is whether governments can, or should, try to regulate cross-border data flows.

These issues are central to the following examination of the EU and US approaches.

(a)   European Union Data Protection Directive, 1995

National governments may not impede the flow of goods, services, people, money, and information within the EU, as there is a single market. However, member states often have policies that they are unwilling to sacrifice outright to the common market principles. Some countries are bound by international agreements which place restrictions on the extent to which they can remove protections in certain areas.

The unrestricted and unregulated flow of personal data information was first regulated by the 1981 Council of Europe's Convention on the Automated Processing of Personal Data, to which all the EU members were signatories. This convention required the signatories to protect the privacy rights of individuals in circumstances where information about them was to be processed automatically. It also required the facilitation of a common international standard for the protection of individuals so that the free flow of information could proceed without impediment.

The goal was to provide a level playing field within the EU. However, the means of achieving this outcome was not so simple. Some countries such as Germany and France saw significant human rights issues. Others, such as the United Kingdom, were concerned primarily with ensuring that minimum standards were met. As a result, there were many and varied laws among the signatories—the exact opposite of the goals of the original process. It became evident by the early 1990s that this lack of consistency was a serious impediment to attaining a common market, exacerbated by the increased use of information technology within the EU. It was feared that countries with strict privacy laws would restrict the movement of information into those whose laws were less so, or that companies would relocate to countries with the more lax laws. From these fears grew the directive on personal data. The main purpose of the directive was to harmonise the level of protection given to personal data within all member states. It was also in part designed to prevent the erection of trade barriers based on the protection of personal privacy.

Formulating the directive was a very long and arduous process. There were significant disagreements over early drafts of the agreement, with some countries refusing to accept any measures that reduced the level of protection and others maintaining that no directive was required. There was also intensive lobbying by certain business groups, which complicated any easy or early compromise on the directive. The first draft was released in 1990 but it was not adopted until October 1995. The final version does not favour a particular approach and it applies where data is processed partly or wholly by automatic means.

Directive 95/46/EC of the European Parliament and of the Council of 24 October 1995 on the Protection of Individuals with regard to the Processing of Personal Data and on the Free Movement of Such Data

Available at <http://europa.eu.int/eur-lex/en/lif/dat/1995/en_395L0046.html>
10 September 2001

Chapter I: General Provisions

ARTICLE 1: OBJECT OF THE DIRECTIVE

1   In accordance with this Directive, Member States shall protect the fundamental rights and freedoms of natural persons, and in particular their right to privacy with respect to the processing of personal data.

2   Member States shall neither restrict nor prohibit the free flow of personal data between Member States for reasons connected with the protection afforded under paragraph 1.

ARTICLE 2: DEFINITIONS

For the purposes of this Directive:

(a) 'personal data' shall mean any information relating to an identified or identifiable natural person ('data subject'); an identifiable person is one who can be identified, directly or indirectly, in particular by reference to an identification number or to one or more factors specific to his physical, physiological, mental, economic, cultural or social identity;

(b) 'processing of personal data' ('processing') shall mean any operation or set of operations which is performed upon personal data, whether or not by automatic means, such as collection, recording, organization, storage, adaptation or alteration, retrieval, consultation, use, disclosure by transmission, dissemination or otherwise making available, alignment or combination, blocking, erasure or destruction;

(c) 'personal data filing system' ('filing system') shall mean any structured set of personal data which are accessible according to specific criteria, whether centralized, decentralized or dispersed on a functional or geographical basis;

(d) 'controller' shall mean the natural or legal person, public authority, agency or any other body which alone or jointly with others determines the purposes and means of the processing of personal data; where the purposes and means of processing are determined by national or Community laws or regulations, the controller or the specific criteria for his nomination may be designated by national or Community law;

(e) 'processor' shall mean a natural or legal person, public authority, agency or any other body which processes personal data on behalf of the controller;

(f) 'third party' shall mean any natural or legal person, public authority, agency or any other body other than the data subject, the controller, the processor and the persons who, under the direct authority of the controller or the processor, are authorized to process the data;

(g) 'recipient' shall mean a natural or legal person, public authority, agency or any other body to whom data are disclosed, whether a third party or not; however, authorities which may receive data in the framework of a particular inquiry shall not be regarded as recipients;

(h) 'the data subject's consent' shall mean any freely given specific and informed indication of his wishes by which the data subject signifies his agreement to personal data relating to him being processed.

ARTICLE 3: SCOPE

1 This Directive shall apply to the processing of personal data wholly or partly by automatic means, and to the processing otherwise than by automatic means of personal data which form part of a filing system or are intended to form part of a filing system.

2 This Directive shall not apply to the processing of personal data:

- in the course of an activity which falls outside the scope of Community law, such as those provided for by Titles V and VI of the Treaty on European Union and in any case to processing operations concerning public security, defence, State security (including the economic well-being of the State when the processing operation relates to State security matters) and the activities of the State in areas of criminal law,

- by a natural person in the course of a purely personal or household activity.

ARTICLE 4: NATIONAL LAW APPLICABLE

1 Each Member State shall apply the national provisions it adopts pursuant to this Directive to the processing of personal data where:

(a) the processing is carried out in the context of the activities of an establishment of the controller on the territory of the Member State; when the same controller is established on the territory of several Member States, he must take the necessary measures to ensure that each of these establishments complies with the obligations laid down by the national law applicable;

(b) the controller is not established on the Member State's territory, but in a place where its national law applies by virtue of international public law;

(c) the controller is not established on Community territory and, for purposes of processing personal data makes use of equipment, automated or otherwise, situated on the territory of the said Member State, unless such equipment is used only for purposes of transit through the territory of the Community.

2 In the circumstances referred to in paragraph 1(c), the controller must designate a representative established in the territory of that Member State, without prejudice to legal actions which could be initiated against the controller himself.

NOTES AND QUESTIONS

1　The definition of processing extends to non-automated means of processing. Is this a significant extension?

2　Article 3 outlines the exceptions to the application of the Directive. Examine the language of this section. Do you consider that this provision is consistent with the goal of personal data privacy protection?

3　In the next chapter, the debate surrounding government use and control of encryption is studied. A significant point in this debate is a government's right to monitor its citizens. Article 3 provides for similar rights. Are there sufficient checks and balances in the operation of Article 3? Consider your answer in the light of Article 13, below.

4　Examine the definition of 'processing of data', above. In your opinion, do cookies fall within this definition? What implications might this have for those who derive benefit from the operation of cookies?

Directive 95/46/EC of the European Parliament and of the Council of 24 October 1995 on the Protection of Individuals with regard to the Processing of Personal Data and on the Free Movement of Such Data

Available at <http://europa.eu.int/eur-lex/en/lif/dat/1995/en_395L0046.html>
10 September 2001

Chapter II: General Rules on the Lawfulness of the Processing of Personal Data

ARTICLE 5
Member States shall, within the limits of the provisions of this Chapter, determine more precisely the conditions under which the processing of personal data is lawful.

Section I: Principles Relating to Data Quality

ARTICLE 6
1　Member States shall provide that personal data must be:

　(a)　processed fairly and lawfully;

　(b)　collected for specified, explicit and legitimate purposes and not further processed in a way incompatible with those purposes. Further processing of data for historical, statistical or scientific purposes shall not be considered as incompatible provided that Member States provide appropriate safeguards;

　(c)　adequate, relevant and not excessive in relation to the purposes for which they are collected and/or further processed;

(d) accurate and, where necessary, kept up to date; every reasonable step must be taken to ensure that data which are inaccurate or incomplete, having regard to the purposes for which they were collected or for which they are further processed, are erased or rectified;

(e) kept in a form which permits identification of data subjects for no longer than is necessary for the purposes for which the data were collected or for which they are further processed. Member States shall lay down appropriate safeguards for personal data stored for longer periods for historical, statistical or scientific use.

2 It shall be for the controller to ensure that paragraph 1 is complied with.

Section II: Criteria for Making Data Processing Legitimate

ARTICLE 7

Member States shall provide that personal data may be processed only if:

(a) the data subject has unambiguously given his consent; or

(b) processing is necessary for the performance of a contract to which the data subject is party or in order to take steps at the request of the data subject prior to entering into a contract; or

(c) processing is necessary for compliance with a legal obligation to which the controller is subject; or

(d) processing is necessary in order to protect the vital interests of the data subject; or

(e) processing is necessary for the performance of a task carried out in the public interest or in the exercise of official authority vested in the controller or in a third party to whom the data are disclosed; or

(f) processing is necessary for the purposes of the legitimate interests pursued by the controller or by the third party or parties to whom the data are disclosed, except where such interests are overridden by the interests for fundamental rights and freedoms of the data subject which require protection under Article 1(1).

 NOTES AND QUESTIONS

1 A balance is clearly required between 'legitimate interests pursued by the controller' and 'the fundamental rights and freedoms of natural persons, and in particular their right to privacy with respect to the processing of personal data'. Do you have faith that this balance will be struck in the best interests of the data subject?

2 Article 7(a) requires the unambiguous consent of the data subject. How meaningful is this requirement in the light of articles 7(b)–(f)? If the need for consent is overridden by the 'legitimate interests pursued by the controller', what purpose does the provision serve?

3 How important is it that Article 6 so clearly places the onus on the controller for compliance with the principles relating to data quality?

Section III: Special Categories of Processing

ARTICLE 8: THE PROCESSING OF SPECIAL CATEGORIES OF DATA

1   Member States shall prohibit the processing of personal data revealing racial or ethnic origin, political opinions, religious or philosophical beliefs, trade-union membership, and the processing of data concerning health or sex life.

2   Paragraph 1 shall not apply where:

   (a) the data subject has given his explicit consent to the processing of those data, except where the laws of the Member State provide that the prohibition referred to in paragraph 1 may not be lifted by the data subject's giving his consent; or

   (b) processing is necessary for the purposes of carrying out the obligations and specific rights of the controller in the field of employment law in so far as it is authorized by national law providing for adequate safeguards; or

   (c) processing is necessary to protect the vital interests of the data subject or of another person where the data subject is physically or legally incapable of giving his consent; or

   (d) processing is carried out in the course of its legitimate activities with appropriate guarantees by a foundation, association or any other non-profit-seeking body with a political, philosophical, religious or trade union aim and on condition that the processing relates solely to the members of the body or to persons who have regular contact with it in connection with its purposes and that the data are not disclosed to a third party without the consent of the data subjects; or

   (e) the processing relates to data which are manifestly made public by the data subject or is necessary for the establishment, exercise or defence of legal claims.

3   Paragraph 1 shall not apply where processing of the data is required for the purposes of preventive medicine, medical diagnosis, the provision of care or treatment or the management of health-care services, and where those data are processed by a health professional subject under national law or rules established by national competent bodies to the obligation of professional secrecy or by another person also subject to an equivalent obligation of secrecy.

4   Subject to the provision of suitable safeguards, Member States may, for reasons of substantial public interest, lay down exemptions in addition to those laid down in paragraph 2 either by national law or by decision of the supervisory authority.

5   Processing of data relating to offences, criminal convictions or security measures may be carried out only under the control of official authority, or if suitable specific safeguards are provided under national law, subject to derogations which may be granted by the Member State under national provisions providing suitable specific safeguards. However, a complete register of criminal convictions may be kept only under the control of official authority.

   Member States may provide that data relating to administrative sanctions or judgments in civil cases shall also be processed under the control of official authority.

6   Derogations from paragraph 1 provided for in paragraphs 4 and 5 shall be notified to the Commission.

7   Member States shall determine the conditions under which a national identification number or any other identifier of general application may be processed.

ARTICLE 9: PROCESSING OF PERSONAL DATA AND FREEDOM OF EXPRESSION

Member States shall provide for exemptions or derogations from the provisions of this Chapter, Chapter IV and Chapter VI for the processing of personal data carried out solely for journalistic purposes or the purpose of artistic or literary expression only if they are necessary to reconcile the right to privacy with the rules governing freedom of expression.

 NOTES AND QUESTIONS

1   The wording of Article 8 is very clear and deliberately strict. Why would Europeans be concerned about protection for these specific types of information? Do other polities share this concern? Do you consider that the safeguards attached to the special processing of data are adequate to protect the interests of the data subject?

2   Article 9 articulates the dichotomy between the right to privacy and the right to free expression. The right to privacy did not always occupy a central place in the public conscience. In fact, in the past, when 'community' meant villages and towns (as opposed to today's global community) considerable importance was placed on the free flow of private information throughout a society. This flow acted as the regulator of social behaviour, the keeper of the *nomos*, in a society without the central institutions we rely upon today. To hide from one's neighbours was to hide from society, to remove oneself. In order to participate in society, these conventions meant scrutiny through knowledge of others and access to information which we, today, would consider private.

Section IV: Information to be Given to the Data Subject

ARTICLE 10: INFORMATION IN CASES OF COLLECTION OF DATA FROM THE DATA SUBJECT

Member States shall provide that the controller or his representative must provide a data subject from whom data relating to himself are collected with at least the following information, except where he already has it:

(a) the identity of the controller and of his representative, if any;
(b) the purposes of the processing for which the data are intended;
(c) any further information such as

- the recipients or categories of recipients of the data,
- whether replies to the questions are obligatory or voluntary, as well as the possible consequences of failure to reply,

- the existence of the right of access to and the right to rectify the data concerning him
- in so far as such further information is necessary, having regard to the specific circumstances in which the data are collected, to guarantee fair processing in respect of the data subject.

ARTICLE 11

INFORMATION WHERE THE DATA HAVE NOT BEEN OBTAINED FROM THE DATA SUBJECT

1   Where the data have not been obtained from the data subject, Member States shall provide that the controller or his representative must at the time of undertaking the recording of personal data or if a disclosure to a third party is envisaged, no later than the time when the data is first disclosed provide the data subject with at least the following information, except where he already has it:

(a) the identity of the controller and of his representative, if any;
(b) the purposes of the processing;
(c) any further information such as
   - the categories of data concerned,
   - the recipients or categories of recipients,
   - the existence of the right of access to and the right to rectify the data concerning him

in so far as such further information is necessary, having regard to the specific circumstances in which the data are processed, to guarantee fair processing in respect of the data subject.

2   Paragraph 1 shall not apply where, in particular for processing for statistical purposes or for the purposes of historical or scientific research, the provision of such information proves impossible or would involve a disproportionate effort or if recording or disclosure is expressly laid down by law. In these cases Member States shall provide appropriate safeguards.

Section V: The Data Subject's Right of Access to Data

ARTICLE 12: RIGHT OF ACCESS

Member States shall guarantee every data subject the right to obtain from the controller:
(a) without constraint at reasonable intervals and without excessive delay or expense:

- confirmation as to whether or not data relating to him are being processed and information at least as to the purposes of the processing, the categories of data concerned, and the recipients or categories of recipients to whom the data are disclosed,
- communication to him in an intelligible form of the data undergoing processing and of any available information as to their source,
- knowledge of the logic involved in any automatic processing of data concerning him at least in the case of the automated decisions referred to in Article 15(1);

(b) as appropriate the rectification, erasure or blocking of data the processing of which does not comply with the provisions of this Directive, in particular because of the incomplete or inaccurate nature of the data;

(c) notification to third parties to whom the data have been disclosed of any rectification, erasure or blocking carried out in compliance with (b), unless this proves impossible or involves a disproportionate effort.

Section VI: Exemptions and Restrictions

ARTICLE 13: EXEMPTIONS AND RESTRICTIONS

1 Member States may adopt legislative measures to restrict the scope of the obligations and rights provided for in Articles 6(1), 10, 11(1), 12 and 21 when such a restriction constitutes necessary measures to safeguard:

(a) national security;

(b) defence;

(c) public security;

(d) the prevention, investigation, detection and prosecution of criminal offences, or of breaches of ethics for regulated professions;

(e) an important economic or financial interest of a Member State or of the European Union, including monetary, budgetary and taxation matters;

(f) a monitoring, inspection or regulatory function connected, even occasionally, with the exercise of official authority in cases referred to in (c), (d) and (e);

(g) the protection of the data subject or of the rights and freedoms of others.

2 Subject to adequate legal safeguards, in particular that the data are not used for taking measures or decisions regarding any particular individual, Member States may, where there is clearly no risk of breaching the privacy of the data subject, restrict by a legislative measure the rights provided for in Article 12 when data are processed solely for purposes of scientific research or are kept in personal form for a period which does not exceed the period necessary for the sole purpose of creating statistics.

 NOTES AND QUESTIONS

1 Consider articles 10 and 12 in light of what you know about cookies. Do cookies contravene these articles?

2 Article 13 articulates the very essence of the public interest–privacy dichotomy. It clearly sets out the aspects of societal relations and operations that the EU considers to be more important than personal privacy. Critically examine the list of exceptions and consider what assumptions underlie these public interest concerns.

3 What do you think is meant by 'protection of the data subject or of the rights and freedoms of others' in 1(g)? Why might this provision have been included in the list?

Section VII: The Data Subject's Right to Object

ARTICLE 14: THE DATA SUBJECT'S RIGHT TO OBJECT

Member States shall grant the data subject the right:

(a) at least in the cases referred to in Article 7 (e) and (f), to object at any time on compelling legitimate grounds relating to his particular situation to the processing of data relating to him, save where otherwise provided by national legislation. Where there is a justified objection, the processing instigated by the controller may no longer involve those data;

(b) to object, on request and free of charge, to the processing of personal data relating to him which the controller anticipates being processed for the purposes of direct marketing, or to be informed before personal data are disclosed for the first time to third parties or used on their behalf for the purposes of direct marketing, and to be expressly offered the right to object free of charge to such disclosures or uses.

Member States shall take the necessary measures to ensure that data subjects are aware of the existence of the right referred to in the subparagraph of (b).

ARTICLE 15: AUTOMATED INDIVIDUAL DECISIONS

1   Member States shall grant the right to every person not to be subject to a decision which produces legal effects concerning him or significantly affects him and which is based solely on automated processing of data intended to evaluate certain personal aspects relating to him, such as his performance at work, creditworthiness, reliability, conduct, etc.

2   Subject to the other Articles of this Directive, Member States shall provide that a person may be subjected to a decision of the kind referred to in paragraph 1 if that decision:

(a) is taken in the course of the entering into or performance of a contract, provided the request for the entering into or the performance of the contract, lodged by the data subject, has been satisfied or that there are suitable measures to safeguard his legitimate interests, such as arrangements allowing him to put his point of view; or

(b) is authorized by a law which also lays down measures to safeguard the data subject's legitimate interests.

Section VIII: Confidentiality and Security of Processing

ARTICLE 16: CONFIDENTIALITY OF PROCESSING

Any person acting under the authority of the controller or of the processor, including the processor himself, who has access to personal data must not process them except on instructions from the controller, unless he is required to do so by law.

ARTICLE 17: SECURITY OF PROCESSING

1   Member States shall provide that the controller must implement appropriate technical and organizational measures to protect personal data against accidental or unlawful

destruction or accidental loss, alteration, unauthorized disclosure or access, in particular where the processing involves the transmission of data over a network, and against all other unlawful forms of processing.

Having regard to the state of the art and the cost of their implementation, such measures shall ensure a level of security appropriate to the risks represented by the processing and the nature of the data to be protected.

2 The Member States shall provide that the controller must, where processing is carried out on his behalf, choose a processor providing sufficient guarantees in respect of the technical security measures and organizational measures governing the processing to be carried out, and must ensure compliance with those measures.

3 The carrying out of processing by way of a processor must be governed by a contract or legal act binding the processor to the controller and stipulating in particular that:

- the processor shall act only on instructions from the controller,
- the obligations set out in paragraph 1, as defined by the law of the Member State in which the processor is established, shall also be incumbent on the processor.

4 For the purposes of keeping proof, the parts of the contract or the legal act relating to data protection and the requirements relating to the measures referred to in paragraph 1 shall be in writing or in another equivalent form.

 NOTES AND QUESTIONS

1 Under Article 14, the data subject has the right to object to the use of his or her personal data. This right, however, must be a 'justified objection' based upon 'compelling legitimate grounds'. Critically examine this provision. What does it imply for the data subject?

2 Direct marketing, so often regarded as the scourge of the Internet, has generated a separate provision enabling recipients to object. Carefully examine the wording of Article 14(a). Do these requirements adequately protect the interests of consumers? If so, why? If not, how would you alter the provisions and what other measures, if any, would you take to provide this protection?

3 In Article 17, do you consider the phrase 'a level of security appropriate to the risks' to be sufficiently rigorous to ensure that information does not get into the wrong hands?

Section IX: Notification

ARTICLE 18: OBLIGATION TO NOTIFY THE SUPERVISORY AUTHORITY

1 Member States shall provide that the controller or his representative, if any, must notify the supervisory authority referred to in Article 28 before carrying out any wholly or partly automatic processing operation or set of such operations intended to serve a single purpose or several related purposes.

2 Member States may provide for the simplification of or exemption from notification only in the following cases and under the following conditions:

- where, for categories of processing operations which are unlikely, taking account of the data to be processed, to affect adversely the rights and freedoms of data subjects, they specify the purposes of the processing, the data or categories of data undergoing processing, the category or categories of data subject, the recipients or categories of recipient to whom the data are to be disclosed and the length of time the data are to be stored, and/or
- where the controller, in compliance with the national law which governs him, appoints a personal data protection official, responsible in particular:
  ○ for ensuring in an independent manner the internal application of the national provisions taken pursuant to this Directive
  ○ for keeping the register of processing operations carried out by the controller, containing the items of information referred to in Article 21(2), thereby ensuring that the rights and freedoms of the data subjects are unlikely to be adversely affected by the processing operations.

3   Member States may provide that paragraph 1 does not apply to processing whose sole purpose is the keeping of a register which according to laws or regulations is intended to provide information to the public and which is open to consultation either by the public in general or by any person demonstrating a legitimate interest.

4   Member States may provide for an exemption from the obligation to notify or a simplification of the notification in the case of processing operations referred to in Article 8(2)(d).

5   Member States may stipulate that certain or all non-automatic processing operations involving personal data shall be notified, or provide for these processing operations to be subject to simplified notification.

ARTICLE 19: CONTENTS OF NOTIFICATION

1   Member States shall specify the information to be given in the notification. It shall include at least:

(a) the name and address of the controller and of his representative, if any;
(b) the purpose or purposes of the processing;
(c) a description of the category or categories of data subject and of the data or categories of data relating to them;
(d) the recipients or categories of recipient to whom the data might be disclosed;
(e) proposed transfers of data to third countries;
(f) a general description allowing a preliminary assessment to be made of the appropriateness of the measures taken pursuant to Article 17 to ensure security of processing.

2   Member States shall specify the procedures under which any change affecting the information referred to in paragraph 1 must be notified to the supervisory authority.

ARTICLE 20: PRIOR CHECKING

1   Member States shall determine the processing operations likely to present specific risks to the rights and freedoms of data subjects and shall check that these processing operations are examined prior to the start thereof.

2   Such prior checks shall be carried out by the supervisory authority following receipt of a notification from the controller or by the data protection official, who, in cases of doubt, must consult the supervisory authority.

3   Member States may also carry out such checks in the context of preparation either of a measure of the national parliament or of a measure based on such a legislative measure, which define the nature of the processing and lay down appropriate safeguards.

ARTICLE 21: PUBLICIZING OF PROCESSING OPERATIONS

1   Member States shall take measures to ensure that processing operations are publicized.

2   Member States shall provide that a register of processing operations notified in accordance with Article 18 shall be kept by the supervisory authority.

The register shall contain at least the information listed in Article 19(1)(a) to (e). The register may be inspected by any person.

3   Member States shall provide, in relation to processing operations not subject to notification, that controllers or another body appointed by the Member States make available at least the information referred to in Article 19(1)(a) to (e) in an appropriate form to any person on request.

Member States may provide that this provision does not apply to processing whose sole purpose is the keeping of a register which according to laws or regulations is intended to provide information to the public and which is open to consultation either by the public in general or by any person who can provide proof of a legitimate interest.

 NOTES AND QUESTIONS

1   Article 19 contains an extensive list of information to be provided to the supervisory authority. Why is this information important? Why is it so explicitly listed?

2   Article 19(1)(e) is particularly important in relation to the Safe Harbor Principles discussed below. You should keep this section in mind as you read the material below.

3   Examine Article 20. Are you confident that the Member States, and their individual supervisory authorities, will have the energy and resources to maintain the constant monitoring and supervision required by this section? Is this issue resolved by the obligation to notify contained in Article 18?

Directive 95/46/EC of the European Parliament and of the Council of 24 October 1995 on the Protection of Individuals with regard to the Processing of Personal Data and on the Free Movement of Such Data

Available at <http://europa.eu.int/eur-lex/en/lif/dat/1995/en_395L0046.html>
10 September 2001

Chapter III: Judicial Remedies, Liability and Sanctions

ARTICLE 22: REMEDIES

Without prejudice to any administrative remedy for which provision may be made, inter alia before the supervisory authority referred to in Article 28, prior to referral to the judicial authority, Member States shall provide for the right of every person to a judicial remedy for any breach of the rights guaranteed him by the national law applicable to the processing in question.

ARTICLE 23: LIABILITY

1   Member States shall provide that any person who has suffered damage as a result of an unlawful processing operation or of any act incompatible with the national provisions adopted pursuant to this Directive is entitled to receive compensation from the controller for the damage suffered.
2   The controller may be exempted from this liability, in whole or in part, if he proves that he is not responsible for the event giving rise to the damage.

ARTICLE 24: SANCTIONS

The Member States shall adopt suitable measures to ensure the full implementation of the provisions of this Directive and shall in particular lay down the sanctions to be imposed in case of infringement of the provisions adopted pursuant to this Directive.

 NOTES AND QUESTIONS

1   Compare the three provisions above with the compliance mechanisms in the Safe Harbor Principles below.
2   The question of enforcement is the unavoidable stumbling block for the Directive. The institutions required to give effect to the Directive would need to be very large and very vigilant to be effective. How significant is the inclusion of a requirement for a judicial remedy to be provided in the event of a breach of the safeguards of the Directive?

Directive 95/46/EC of the European Parliament and of the Council of 24 October 1995 on the Protection of Individuals with regard to the Processing of Personal Data and on the Free Movement of Such Data

Available at <http://europa.eu.int/eur-lex/en/lif/dat/1995/en_395L0046.html>

10 September 2001

Chapter IV: Transfer of Personal Data to Third Countries

ARTICLE 25: PRINCIPLES

1   The Member States shall provide that the transfer to a third country of personal data which are undergoing processing or are intended for processing after transfer may take place only if, without prejudice to compliance with the national provisions adopted pursuant to the other provisions of this Directive, the third country in question ensures an adequate level of protection.

2   The adequacy of the level of protection afforded by a third country shall be assessed in the light of all the circumstances surrounding a data transfer operation or set of data transfer operations; particular consideration shall be given to the nature of the data, the purpose and duration of the proposed processing operation or operations, the country of origin and country of final destination, the rules of law, both general and sectoral, in force in the third country in question and the professional rules and security measures which are complied with in that country.

3   The Member States and the Commission shall inform each other of cases where they consider that a third country does not ensure an adequate level of protection within the meaning of paragraph 2.

4   Where the Commission finds, under the procedure provided for in Article 31(2), that a third country does not ensure an adequate level of protection within the meaning of paragraph 2 of this Article, Member States shall take the measures necessary to prevent any transfer of data of the same type to the third country in question.

5   At the appropriate time, the Commission shall enter into negotiations with a view to remedying the situation resulting from the finding made pursuant to paragraph 4.

6   The Commission may find, in accordance with the procedure referred to in Article 31(2), that a third country ensures an adequate level of protection within the meaning of paragraph 2 of this Article, by reason of its domestic law or of the international commitments it has entered into, particularly upon conclusion of the negotiations referred to in paragraph 5, for the protection of the private lives and basic freedoms and rights of individuals.

Member States shall take the measures necessary to comply with the Commission's decision.

ARTICLE 26: DEROGATIONS

1   By way of derogation from Article 25 and save where otherwise provided by domestic law governing particular cases, Member States shall provide that a transfer or a set of transfers of personal data to a third country which does not ensure an adequate level of protection within the meaning of Article 25(2) may take place on condition that:

(a) the data subject has given his consent unambiguously to the proposed transfer; or

(b) the transfer is necessary for the performance of a contract between the data subject and the controller or the implementation of pre-contractual measures taken in response to the data subject's request; or

(c)   the transfer is necessary for the conclusion or performance of a contract concluded in the interest of the data subject between the controller and a third party; or

(d)   the transfer is necessary or legally required on important public interest grounds, or for the establishment, exercise or defence of legal claims; or

(e)   the transfer is necessary in order to protect the vital interests of the data subject; or

(f)   the transfer is made from a register which according to laws or regulations is intended to provide information to the public and which is open to consultation either by the public in general or by any person who can demonstrate legitimate interest, to the extent that the conditions laid down in law for consultation are fulfilled in the particular case.

2   Without prejudice to paragraph 1, a Member State may authorize a transfer or a set of transfers of personal data to a third country which does not ensure an adequate level of protection within the meaning of Article 25(2), where the controller adduces adequate safeguards with respect to the protection of the privacy and fundamental rights and freedoms of individuals and as regards the exercise of the corresponding rights; such safeguards may in particular result from appropriate contractual clauses.

3   The Member State shall inform the Commission and the other Member States of the authorizations it grants pursuant to paragraph 2.

If a Member State or the Commission objects on justified grounds involving the protection of the privacy and fundamental rights and freedoms of individuals, the Commission shall take appropriate measures in accordance with the procedure laid down in Article 31(2).

Member States shall take the necessary measures to comply with the Commission's decision.

4   Where the Commission decides, in accordance with the procedure referred to in Article 31(2), that certain standard contractual clauses offer sufficient safeguards as required by paragraph 2, Member States shall take the necessary measures to comply with the Commission's decision.

 ## NOTES AND QUESTIONS

1   Articles 25 and 26 are the most important articles of the Directive with respect to the Internet. Outline the implications of these Articles for on-line data transfers and, more importantly, for data usage by companies. Such usage might include activities such as the amalgamation of existing marketing data following a merger.

2   The provisions could make personalisation of sites difficult where individuals in the EU are accessing non-EU and non-protecting countries' sites. It might also have implications for individually targeted webvertisements.

3   It is important that the significance of these provisions is understood. Their operation has created widespread implications for on-line privacy, not least in the USA. The material discussing the Safe Harbor Principles (below) is directly related to the above articles.

Directive 95/46/EC of the European Parliament and of the Council of 24 October 1995 on the Protection of Individuals with regard to the Processing of Personal Data and on the Free Movement of Such Data

Available at <http://europa.eu.int/eur-lex/en/lif/dat/1995/en_395L0046.html>
10 September 2001

Chapter V: Codes of Conduct

ARTICLE 27

1   The Member States and the Commission shall encourage the drawing up of codes of conduct intended to contribute to the proper implementation of the national provisions adopted by the Member States pursuant to this Directive, taking account of the specific features of the various sectors.

2   Member States shall make provision for trade associations and other bodies representing other categories of controllers which have drawn up draft national codes or which have the intention of amending or extending existing national codes to be able to submit them to the opinion of the national authority. Member States shall make provision for this authority to ascertain, among other things, whether the drafts submitted to it are in accordance with the national provisions adopted pursuant to this Directive. If it sees fit, the authority shall seek the views of data subjects or their representatives.

3   Draft Community codes, and amendments or extensions to existing Community codes, may be submitted to the Working Party referred to in Article 29. This Working Party shall determine, among other things, whether the drafts submitted to it are in accordance with the national provisions adopted pursuant to this Directive. If it sees fit, the authority shall seek the views of data subjects or their representatives. The Commission may ensure appropriate publicity for the codes which have been approved by the Working Party.

Chapter VI: Supervisory Authority and Working Party on the Protection of Individuals with regard to the Processing of Personal Data

ARTICLE 28: SUPERVISORY AUTHORITY

1   Each Member State shall provide that one or more public authorities are responsible for monitoring the application within its territory of the provisions adopted by the Member States pursuant to this Directive. These authorities shall act with complete independence in exercising the functions entrusted to them.

2   Each Member State shall provide that the supervisory authorities are consulted when drawing up administrative measures or regulations relating to the protection of individuals' rights and freedoms with regard to the processing of personal data.

3   Each authority shall in particular be endowed with:

- investigative powers, such as powers of access to data forming the subject-matter of processing operations and powers to collect all the information necessary for the performance of its supervisory duties,
- effective powers of intervention, such as, for example, that of delivering opinions before processing operations are carried out, in accordance with Article 20, and ensuring appropriate publication of such opinions, of ordering the blocking, erasure or destruction of data, of imposing a temporary or definitive ban on processing, of warning or admonishing the controller, or that of referring the matter to national parliaments or other political institutions,

- the power to engage in legal proceedings where the national provisions adopted pursuant to this Directive have been violated or to bring these violations to the attention of the judicial authorities.
- Decisions by the supervisory authority which give rise to complaints may be appealed against through the courts.

4   Each supervisory authority shall hear claims lodged by any person, or by an association representing that person, concerning the protection of his rights and freedoms in regard to the processing of personal data. The person concerned shall be informed of the outcome of the claim. Each supervisory authority shall, in particular, hear claims for checks on the lawfulness of data processing lodged by any person when the national provisions adopted pursuant to Article 13 of this Directive apply. The person shall at any rate be informed that a check has taken place.

5   Each supervisory authority shall draw up a report on its activities at regular intervals. The report shall be made public.

6   Each supervisory authority is competent, whatever the national law applicable to the processing in question, to exercise, on the territory of its own Member State, the powers conferred on it in accordance with paragraph 3.

   Each authority may be requested to exercise its powers by an authority of another Member State. The supervisory authorities shall cooperate with one another to the extent necessary for the performance of their duties, in particular by exchanging all useful information.

7   Member States shall provide that the members and staff of the supervisory authority, even after their employment has ended, are to be subject to a duty of professional secrecy with regard to confidential information to which they have access.

 NOTES AND QUESTIONS

1   How onerous is the task of the supervisory authority? Is it a job that could easily be accommodated within an existing agency?

2   What does the explicit requirement for such an agency suggest about the European approach to government? How does this approach differ from others you have experienced or studied?

3   To what extent does the European emphasis on state-based protection discourage community vigilance? How would you respond to criticisms that argue a citizenry

should be responsible for its own affairs and not look to a paternal state to assist with such matters in every respect? Consider these ideas as you read through the US reactions to the Directive.

4   How significant is the Directive's similarity to legislation? Does this indicate the depth of resolve of the EU in the matter, or is it a case of misleading first impressions? Compare this impression with the following materials. Compare also the actual final effect of both sets of provisions. The crucial issue to consider is whether, after all the analyses, there is a significant difference between the outcomes produced using the system outlined by the Directive, and those produced using the system chosen by the USA.

(b)   The Directive and the Internet

The relevance of the EU Directive becomes apparent as we step back and consider its effects on non-EU countries. In privacy agendas the EU Directive has set off a chain reaction across countries. In Australia, for example, the EU Directive was one of the crucial factors in the development of the most recent privacy legislation. It is clear that problems of harmonisation are not necessarily insurmountable.

When we consider the adequacy of protection in the transfer of personal data and compliance with the EU Directive, there are two criteria by which we judge whether the protection given by a country's laws are adequate:

- the substantive rules that will apply to the data, and
- the methods of enforcement available to ensure that compliance is realistic.

The first criterion looks at whether the rules, despite their differences, achieve the same or similar protective outcomes as those rules contained within the Directive. There are a number of ways that this might be satisfied: legislation, codes of conduct at industry or sector level, specific contractual agreements, or any combination of these.

The second objective might be somewhat more difficult to achieve, particularly if the EU demands complete accordance with the provision. It is difficult to see how private rights might be enforced against a non-EU infringer if there is no applicable legislative regime. This problem highlights the final stumbling block on the road to harmonisation and is a recurring theme throughout this book. Even if the text of the laws is harmonised across jurisdictions—a task of considerable complexity—there is absolutely no guarantee that any of these laws will be enforced at all, or enforced in the same manner. These themes will be further explored in the context of the US response to the EU Directive.

(c)   The reverse jigsaw of US privacy policy

The US approach to the protection of privacy is very different from that of the EU, and is more complex. Despite the lack of a constitutional basis for the right to privacy in the US Constitution, this right, generally interpreted as the 'right to be let alone', has been accepted, at least theoretically, for a long time in the US legal system. However, the problem is that the issues addressed by this 'right to be let alone' and by the consequent legislative gestures, have tended to revolve around physical privacy rather than informational privacy. For example, where there is a reasonable expectation of personal privacy there has been found a right to be free from government surveillance. There has also been a reclassification of a woman's right to have or not have an abortion into one of 'decisional privacy'.

Where the Constitution has been held to contain positive privacy rights, it has always been against either a state or the federal government. This can be directly linked to the history of the American psyche, which has always included a mistrust of 'big government'. Therefore, laws are not intended to protect the privacy of a citizen against a third party, but to protect the citizen from the encroachment of the government on the citizen's personal, positive freedoms. There are occasional specific legislative provisions setting out third parties' obligations in dealing with the privacy of individuals, such as those dealing with credit details, but even these may be subject to constitutionality doubts.

This is not to say that the USA has no protection for the privacy of personal data, outside of the constitution, or against third parties. It is probably more accurate to say that the USA lacks focused data privacy laws. The main problem is that there are too many and they are too scattered. In 1999 there were 14 federal laws with some sort of personal data privacy provisions within their scope, and, at this stage, state laws have several hundred similar provisions.[15] The US privacy laws have arisen out of an effort to fill various legal holes rather than any attempt at a coherent privacy regime. The consequence of this approach is that there is no overall policy of privacy.

In the USA, the most heavily regulated sector is the government and its numerous agencies and departments, as opposed to private citizens. There are important constitutional and legislative controls on the uses agencies can make of information. In fact, there are striking similarities between the EU and US approaches. In particular, the federal *Privacy Act 1974* provides a regime for the public sector very similar to the EU Directive, although there is no body to monitor compliance or enforce this regime. The Act has been criticised for producing overly generous administrative interpretations of the provisions.

The federal scheme resembles a jigsaw puzzle in which the pieces simply do not fit together. It could be characterised as a *reverse* jigsaw puzzle. Rather than taking a survey of the problem and dividing up the government response according to the skills, abilities, and jurisdictions of various government bodies, the US approach has been to create specific institutional responses to fill specific lacunae, *post hoc*. However, this response is often inadequate or misconceived, or simply creates other holes, or results in a response that is incompatible with the other arms of government.

Two examples illustrate the reverse jigsaw:

- The example raised earlier in this chapter of Robert Bork, the Supreme Court nominee whose video records were accessed, is again relevant. As a result of this incident, Congress introduced a *Video Privacy Protection Act* of 1988 designed only, and specifically, to prevent such conduct in the future.

---

15   M Rotenberg (ed), *The Privacy Law Sourcebook 1999*, EPIC, Washington DC, 1999.

- The *Driver's Privacy Protection Act* of 1994 was enacted following the murder of an actor, Rebecca Schaefer, who was killed after a fan hired a private investigator to obtain her address from the motor registry. This Act was designed to restrict access to the residential details of drivers. However, an exception was included permitting personal details to be given to a private investigator.[16] This is a perfect, and somewhat sad, example of the failure of the US legislative process.

A further example of this patchwork approach can be seen by the fact that there is a separate legislative framework covering children's privacy, the *Children's Online Privacy Protection Act* of 1998. The FTC has provided an extensive Frequently Asked Questions document, of which a portion is extracted below to demonstrate the motivation for, and operation of, the Act.

The Federal Trade Commission, Frequently Asked Questions about the Children's Online Privacy Protection Rule

Available at <http://www.ftc.gov/privacy/coppafaqs.htm> 17 August 2006

The following FAQs are intended to supplement the compliance materials available on the FTC's web site.

General Questions

1 WHAT IS THE CHILDREN'S ONLINE PRIVACY PROTECTION RULE?

The *Children's Online Privacy Protection Act* (COPPA) was passed by Congress in October 1998, with a requirement that the Federal Trade Commission (FTC) issue and enforce rules concerning children's online privacy. The primary goal of the Act and the Rule is to place parents in control over what information is collected from their children online. The Rule was designed to be strong, yet flexible, to protect children while recognizing the dynamic nature of the Internet.

The COPPA Rule applies to operators of commercial web sites and online services directed to children under 13 that collect personal information from children, and operators of general audience sites with actual knowledge that they are collecting information from children under 13.

Those operators must:

(1) post clear and comprehensive Privacy Policies on the web site describing their information practices for children's personal information;
(2) provide notice to parents, and with limited exceptions, obtain verifiable parental consent before collecting personal information from children;
(3) give parents the choice to consent to the operator's collection and use of a child's information while prohibiting the operator from disclosing that information to third parties;

---

16   F H Cate, *Privacy in the Information Age*, Brookings Institution Press, Washington DC, 1997, p 79.

(4) provide parents access to their child's personal information to review and/or have it deleted;

(5) give parents the opportunity to prevent further collection or use of the information;

(6) maintain the confidentiality, security, and integrity of information they collect from children.

In addition, the Rule prohibits operators from conditioning a child's participation in an online activity on the child's providing more information than is reasonably necessary to participate in that activity ...

5 COPPA APPLIES TO 'WEB SITES DIRECTED TO CHILDREN'. WHAT DETERMINES WHETHER OR NOT A WEB SITE IS TARGETED TO CHILDREN?

The Rule sets out a number of factors in determining whether a web site is targeted to children, such as its subject matter, language, whether it uses animated characters, and whether advertising appearing on the site is directed to children. The Commission will also consider empirical evidence regarding the ages of the site's visitors. These standards are very similar to those previously established for TV, radio, and print advertising.

6 DOES COPPA APPLY TO INFORMATION ABOUT CHILDREN COLLECTED FROM PARENTS OR OTHER ADULTS?

No. COPPA and the Rule only apply to personal information collected from children, not their parents or other adults. The Rule's Statement of Basis and Purpose, however, notes that the Commission expects that operators will keep confidential any information obtained from parents in the course of obtaining parental consent or providing for parental access pursuant to COPPA. See Rule n 213.

7 WHY DOES COPPA APPLY ONLY TO CHILDREN UNDER 13? WHAT ABOUT PROTECTING THE ONLINE PRIVACY OF TEENS?

Young children may not understand the safety and privacy issues created by the online collection of personal information, and are therefore particularly vulnerable. 'Children under 13' has often been the standard for distinguishing adolescents from young children who may need special protections. As a general matter, however, the FTC encourages operators to afford teens privacy protections, given the risks inherent in the disclosure of personal information for all ages. The FTC has recommended that Congress pass legislation to ensure the fair information principles be implemented for all consumers. In the interim, web sites' information practices are still subject to Section 5 of the FTC Act, which prohibits deceptive or unfair trade practices.

10 I KNOW THE RULE IS TRIGGERED BY THE COLLECTION OF PERSONAL INFORMATION FROM CHILDREN, BUT THE INFORMATION I COLLECT AT MY SITE IS VOLUNTARY AND NOT MANDATORY. DOES THE RULE STILL APPLY?

Yes. Whether your information collection is voluntary or mandatory, it still constitutes collection and triggers the Rule.

COPPA Enforcement

13 HOW WILL THE FTC ENFORCE THE RULE?

The FTC will monitor the Internet for compliance with the Rule and bring law enforcement actions where appropriate to deter violations. Parents and others can submit complaints to the FTC through our web site www.ftc.gov and our toll-free number (877) FTC-HELP. We will also investigate referrals from consumer groups, industry, and approved safe harbor programs, as appropriate.

14 WHAT ARE THE PENALTIES FOR VIOLATING THE RULE?

Web site operators who violate the Rule could be liable for civil penalties of up to $11,000 per violation. The level of penalties assessed may turn on a number of factors including egregiousness of the violation, eg, the number of children involved, the amount and type of personal information collected, how the information was used, whether it was shared with third parties and the size of the company.

15 DO THE STATES OR OTHER GOVERNMENT AGENCIES HAVE JURISDICTION OVER THIS ISSUE?

Yes. COPPA also gives states and certain federal agencies authority to enforce compliance with the Act with respect to entities in their jurisdiction. For example, the Office of the Comptroller of the Currency will handle compliance by national banks and the Department of Transportation will handle air carriers.

 NOTES AND QUESTIONS

1   Look again at question 15. Do you think this is an effective framework for the implementation and enforcement of the privacy principles?
2   Consider question 7. Do you find the explanations provided here to be coherent? For a critique of COPPA, see K Howard & Y F Lim, 'Protection of Children in the Virtual World' (2005) 2(2) *Privacy Law Bulletin* 17.
3   What conclusions do you draw for the American legislative quilt given this brief snapshot of a single patch? Does this approach to privacy seem to be the most effective way to protect the interests of those for whom it is supposedly operating?

(d)   The Safe Harbor

In the USA, the Safe Harbor Principles were designed to protect personal data privacy so as to satisfy the requirements of the EU Directive. The EU's Directive on Data Protection became effective in October 1998, and with the provision permitting the transfer of personal data to a non-EU country only if that country 'ensures an adequate level of protection', the USA had no choice but to take some form of action. Thus the Directive has the effect of forcing any country that wishes to engage in transferring personal data from European countries to bring its privacy laws in line with the EU Directive. The USA clearly did not satisfy these requirements, as it had no uniform private sector legislation.

Under the Directive, the adequacy of the level of protection afforded by a third country is assessed in the light of all the circumstances surrounding a data transfer operation or set of data transfer operations. Particular consideration shall be given to the nature of the data, the purpose and duration of the proposed processing operation or operations, the country of origin and country of final destination, the rules of law (both general and sectoral) in force in the third country in question, and the professional rules and security measures in force in that country.[17] The result was a set of 'safe harbor' principles; US companies choosing to adopt them would be able to continue with self-regulation regarding their privacy policies.

A presumption of adequacy would apply to organisations within the Safe Harbor and all the EU member states would be bound by this. US organisations that receive personal data from the EU may choose to qualify for the Safe Harbor and its presumption of adequacy. Organisations may either adhere to the Principles and join a self-regulatory privacy program, such as TRUSTe or BBBOnLine, or choose to develop their own privacy policy in accordance with the Principles. An organisation is only obligated under the Safe Harbor to apply the Principles to personal data and personal information received from an EU country. It does not have to apply the Principles to information from any other country. This is another example of the USA's desire to maintain its own national views on privacy—but in doing so, it again endorses piecemeal privacy solutions, this time to appease trade and commercial interests in the EU.

Both the EU Directive and the Safe Harbor Principles consider certain information more sensitive and worthy of protection than others. It is, however, unsurprising that the US categories of protection are somewhat more arbitrary than those of the EU Directive. After all, the laws and regulations in Europe are far more extensive than those in the USA with respect to the protection of personal data. The term 'data protection' is a well-known and well-defined term familiar to the average European. In both approaches it is deemed necessary to demand minimum standards of personal data privacy in both commercial and private sectors. Therefore it becomes increasingly apparent that the difference is only in the mechanics of the concept of privacy itself. The EU Directive provides for a privacy regime that is backed by legislation, applicable to both public and private sectors and overseen by a regulatory authority, and that provides remedies. What we must examine is whether or not there is a clash of approaches between EU and the USA.

In general, there is surprisingly little difference between the two models. In the public sector, there is a perceived lack of a vigorous monitoring and enforcement agency, but this is not insurmountable. This appears to leave the US treatment of the private sector as the last stumbling block to achieving a convergence of US and EU privacy law. And the prevailing mood appears to weigh against the introduction of such a regime in the USA.

---

17   EU Directive, art 25(2).

An alternative approach that potentially meets the EU requirements is a technical solution. The Platform for Privacy Preferences Project (P3P) is an emerging industry standard that enables websites to express their privacy practices in a standardised format that can be automatically retrieved and interpreted by user agents such as web browsers. Users can be informed about website practices by simplifying the process of reading privacy policies. With P3P, users need not read the privacy policies at every site they visit, as information about what data is collected by a website can be automatically conveyed to a user and discrepancies between a site's practices and the user's preferences can be automatically flagged for the user to accept or reject.[18] As promising as this sounds, the method has yet to be thoroughly tested. Even if it does become a success, it only resolves the collection problems; the use problems remain.

United States Department of Commerce, *Safe Harbor Privacy Principles*, 21 July 2000

Available at <http://www.export.gov/safeharbor/SHPRINCIPLESFINAL.htm>
10 September 2001

The European Union's comprehensive privacy legislation, the Directive on Data Protection (the Directive), became effective on 25 October 1998. It requires that transfers of personal data take place only to non-EU countries that provide an 'adequate' level of privacy protection. While the United States and the European Union share the goal of enhancing privacy protection for their citizens, the United States takes a different approach to privacy from that taken by the European Union. The United States uses a sectoral approach that relies on a mix of legislation, regulation, and self-regulation. Given those differences, many US organizations have expressed uncertainty about the impact of the EU-required 'adequacy standard' on personal data transfers from the European Union to the United States.

To diminish this uncertainty and provide a more predictable framework for such data transfers, the Department of Commerce is issuing this document and Frequently Asked Questions ('the Principles') under its statutory authority to foster, promote, and develop international commerce. The Principles were developed in consultation with industry and the general public to facilitate trade and commerce between the United States and the European Union. They are intended for use solely by US organizations receiving personal data from the European Union for the purpose of qualifying for the safe harbor and the presumption of 'adequacy' it creates. Because the Principles were solely designed to serve this specific purpose, their adoption for other purposes may be inappropriate. The Principles cannot be used as a substitute for national provisions implementing the Directive that apply to the processing of personal data in the Member States.

Decisions by organizations to qualify for the safe harbor are entirely voluntary, and organizations may qualify for the safe harbor in different ways. Organizations that decide to adhere to the Principles must comply with the Principles in order to obtain and retain the benefits of the safe harbor and publicly declare that they do so. For example, if an organization joins a self-regulatory privacy program that adheres to the Principles, it qualifies for the safe

---

18   See their web site at <http://www.w3.org/P3P/> 26 September 2001.

harbor. Organizations may also qualify by developing their own self-regulatory privacy policies provided that they conform with the Principles. Where in complying with the Principles, an organization relies in whole or in part on self-regulation, its failure to comply with such self-regulation must also be actionable under Section 5 of the *Federal Trade Commission Act* prohibiting unfair and deceptive acts or another law or regulation prohibiting such acts. In addition, organizations subject to a statutory, regulatory, administrative or other body of law (or of rules) that effectively protects personal privacy may also qualify for safe harbor benefits. In all instances, safe harbor benefits are assured from the date on which each organization wishing to qualify for the safe harbor self-certifies to the Department of Commerce (or its designee) its adherence to the Principles in accordance with the guidance set forth in the Frequently Asked Questions on Self-Certification.

Adherence to these Principles may be limited: (a) to the extent necessary to meet national security, public interest, or law enforcement requirements; (b) by statute, government regulation, or case law that create conflicting obligations or explicit authorizations, provided that, in exercising any such authorization, an organization can demonstrate that its non-compliance with the Principles is limited to the extent necessary to meet the overriding legitimate interests furthered by such authorization; or (c) if the effect of the Directive or Member State law is to allow exceptions or derogations, provided such exceptions or derogations are applied in comparable contexts. Consistent with the goal of enhancing privacy protection, organizations should strive to implement these Principles fully and transparently, including indicating in their privacy policies where exceptions to the Principles permitted by (b) above will apply on a regular basis. For the same reason, where the option is allowable under the Principles and/or US law, organizations are expected to opt for the higher protection where possible.

Organizations may wish for practical or other reasons to apply the Principles to all their data processing operations, but they are only obligated to apply them to data transferred after they enter the safe harbor. To qualify for the safe harbor, organizations are not obligated to apply these Principles to personal information in manually processed filing systems. Organizations wishing to benefit from the safe harbor for receiving information in manually processed filing systems from the EU must apply the Principles to any such information transferred after they enter the safe harbor.

An organization that wishes to extend safe harbor benefits to human resources personal information transferred from the EU for use in the context of an employment relationship must indicate this when it self-certifies to the Department of Commerce (or its designee) and conform to the requirements set forth in the Frequently Asked Questions on Self-Certification. Organizations will also be able to provide the safeguards necessary under Article 26 of the Directive if they include the Principles in written agreements with parties transferring data from the EU for the substantive privacy provisions, once the other provisions for such model contracts are authorized by the Commission and the Member States.

US law will apply to questions of interpretation and compliance with the Safe Harbor Principles (including the Frequently Asked Questions) and relevant privacy policies by safe harbor organizations, except where organizations have committed to cooperate with European Data Protection Authorities. Unless otherwise stated, all provisions of the Safe Harbor Principles and Frequently Asked Questions apply where they are relevant.

'Personal data' and 'personal information' are data about an identified or identifiable individual that are within the scope of the Directive, received by a US organization from the European Union, and recorded in any form.

Notice

An organization must inform individuals about the purposes for which it collects and uses information about them, how to contact the organization with any inquiries or complaints, the types of third parties to which it discloses the information, and the choices and means the organization offers individuals for limiting its use and disclosure. This notice must be provided in clear and conspicuous language when individuals are first asked to provide personal information to the organization or as soon thereafter as is practicable, but in any event before the organization uses such information for a purpose other than that for which it was originally collected or processed by the transferring organization or discloses it for the first time to a third party.

Choice

An organization must offer individuals the opportunity to choose (opt out) whether their personal information is (a) to be disclosed to a third party or (b) to be used for a purpose that is incompatible with the purpose(s) for which it was originally collected or subsequently authorized by the individual. Individuals must be provided with clear and conspicuous, readily available, and affordable mechanisms to exercise choice.

For sensitive information (ie personal information specifying medical or health conditions, racial or ethnic origin, political opinions, religious or philosophical beliefs, trade union membership, or information specifying the sex life of the individual), they must be given affirmative or explicit (opt in) choice if the information is to be disclosed to a third party or used for a purpose other than those for which it was originally collected or subsequently authorized by the individual through the exercise of opt in choice. In any case, an organization should treat as sensitive any information received from a third party where the third party treats and identifies it as sensitive.

Onward transfer

To disclose information to a third party, organizations must apply the Notice and Choice Principles. Where an organization wishes to transfer information to a third party that is acting as an agent, as described in the endnote, it may do so if it first either ascertains that the third party subscribes to the Principles or is subject to the Directive or another adequacy finding or enters into a written agreement with such third party requiring that the third party provide at least the same level of privacy protection as is required by the relevant Principles. If the organization complies with these requirements, it shall not be held responsible (unless the organization agrees otherwise) when a third party to which it transfers such information processes it in a way contrary to any restrictions or representations, unless the organization knew or should have known the third party would process it in such a contrary way and the organization has not taken reasonable steps to prevent or stop such processing.

Security

Organizations creating, maintaining, using or disseminating personal information must take reasonable precautions to protect it from loss, misuse and unauthorized access, disclosure, alteration and destruction.

Data integrity

Consistent with the Principles, personal information must be relevant for the purposes for which it is to be used. An organization may not process personal information in a way that is incompatible with the purposes for which it has been collected or subsequently authorized by the individual. To the extent necessary for those purposes, an organization should take reasonable steps to ensure that data is reliable for its intended use, accurate, complete, and current.

Access

Individuals must have access to personal information about them that an organization holds and be able to correct, amend, or delete that information where it is inaccurate, except where the burden or expense of providing access would be disproportionate to the risks to the individual's privacy in the case in question, or where the rights of persons other than the individual would be violated.

Enforcement

Effective privacy protection must include mechanisms for assuring compliance with the Principles, recourse for individuals to whom the data relate affected by non-compliance with the Principles, and consequences for the organization when the Principles are not followed. At a minimum, such mechanisms must include (a) readily available and affordable independent recourse mechanisms by which each individual's complaints and disputes are investigated and resolved by reference to the Principles and damages awarded where the applicable law or private sector initiatives so provide; (b) follow-up procedures for verifying that the attestations and assertions businesses make about their privacy practices are true and that privacy practices have been implemented as presented; and (c) obligations to remedy problems arising out of failure to comply with the Principles by organizations announcing their adherence to them and consequences for such organizations. Sanctions must be sufficiently rigorous to ensure compliance by organizations.

 NOTES AND QUESTIONS

1   The section on Notice of the Safe Harbor principles contains the following note:

> It is not necessary to provide notice or choice when disclosure is made to a third party that is acting as an agent to perform task(s) on behalf of and under the instructions of the organization. The Onward Transfer Principle, on the other hand, does apply to such disclosures.

2 Compare the historical reactions to government in Europe and the USA. How have they differed? Is government viewed differently in Europe? In what ways? How important is the American national identity in the formulation of an institutional reaction to privacy concerns?

3 Does Australia have a similarly identifiable collective understanding of the relationship between government and citizen, and the role of the former in the relationships of the latter? If so, what is it, and how might it shape our privacy discourse in Australia? If not, are the legislative gestures relating to privacy simply that, or do they represent a sincere concern for the interests of the Australian citizen?

4 Examine the final provision of the Safe Harbor principles. Is the wording of this provision sufficiently rigorous to provide meaningful protection of personal privacy data?

5 The Safe Harbor concept was never going to be easily realised. When the initial principles came out in late 1998, they were heavily criticised and satisfied neither the USA nor the EU. They were then amended and reissued in April 1999. The EU was still not satisfied, and cited enforcement and implementation issues as the main problems. The third draft, which appeared in November 1999, was more acceptable to the EU. After further, extended discussions, on 13 July 2000 the EU accepted the agreements that the USA had proposed. In some respects they do not meet the EU requirements. However, the EU has accepted them subject to the need to renegotiate with individual companies as the need arises.

6 Compare the details of the Directive with the language of the Safe Harbor principles. How closely do they match? Has the USA acted in the spirit of the Directive, or simply avoided it?

7 Do you consider that it is appropriate to have the Federal Trade Commission as the agency responsible for protecting consumers under the Safe Harbor? While it is undeniable that the Safe Harbor Principles were born out of trade-related concerns, what does the continued FTC role suggest about the agenda of the USA in relation to Internet privacy concerns?

---

6   Privacy and Australia

Australia acceded to the OECD Guidelines in 1984, but legislation was passed only in 1988, and even then, only as a by-product of a failed attempt to implement a national identification scheme (the Australia Card). The *Privacy Act 1988* (prior to the 2001 amendments) applied only to the public sector. The legislation represented the federal government's recognition of the need for limited data protection measures. The Act regulated Commonwealth agencies in their processing of personal data. It did not regulate the private sector, except for their handling of tax file numbers and consumer credit information. This effectively meant that private companies had no legislative restrictions, or even guidelines, in their use of personal data.

(a)   The Information Privacy Principles

The *Privacy Act 1988* contains eleven Information Privacy Principles (IPPs). These principles are set out within the body of the Act and apply only to the public sector.

Privacy Act 1988 (Cth)

Available at < http://www.privacy.gov.au/publications/> 17 August 2006

Division 2: Information Privacy Principles

14. INFORMATION PRIVACY PRINCIPLES
The Information Privacy Principles are as follows:

PRINCIPLE 1

MANNER AND PURPOSE OF COLLECTION OF PERSONAL INFORMATION
1.   Personal information shall not be collected by a collector for inclusion in a record or in a generally available publication unless:

  (a) the information is collected for a purpose that is a lawful purpose directly related to a function or activity of the collector; and
  (b) the collection of the information is necessary for or directly related to that purpose.

2.   Personal information shall not be collected by a collector by unlawful or unfair means.

PRINCIPLE 2

SOLICITATION OF PERSONAL INFORMATION FROM INDIVIDUAL CONCERNED
Where:

(a) a collector collects personal information for inclusion in a record or in a generally available publication; and
(b) the information is solicited by the collector from the individual concerned;

the collector shall take such steps (if any) as are, in the circumstances, reasonable to ensure that, before the information is collected or, if that is not practicable, as soon as practicable after the information is collected, the individual concerned is generally aware of:

(c) the purpose for which the information is being collected;
(d) if the collection of the information is authorised or required by or under law—the fact that the collection of the information is so authorised or required; and
(e) any person to whom, or any body or agency to which, it is the collector's usual practice to disclose personal information of the kind so collected, and (if known by the collector) any person to whom, or any body or agency to which, it is the usual practice of that first-mentioned person, body or agency to pass on that information.

PRINCIPLE 3

SOLICITATION OF PERSONAL INFORMATION GENERALLY
Where:

(a) a collector collects personal information for inclusion in a record or in a generally available publication; and
(b) the information is solicited by the collector;

the collector shall take such steps (if any) as are, in the circumstances, reasonable to ensure that, having regard to the purpose for which the information is collected:

(c) the information collected is relevant to that purpose and is up to date and complete; and
(d) the collection of the information does not intrude to an unreasonable extent upon the personal affairs of the individual concerned.

PRINCIPLE 4

STORAGE AND SECURITY OF PERSONAL INFORMATION
A record-keeper who has possession or control of a record that contains personal information shall ensure:

(a) that the record is protected, by such security safeguards as it is reasonable in the circumstances to take, against loss, against unauthorised access, use, modification or disclosure, and against other misuse; and
(b) that if it is necessary for the record to be given to a person in connection with the provision of a service to the record-keeper, everything reasonably within the power of the record-keeper is done to prevent unauthorised use or disclosure of information contained in the record.

PRINCIPLE 5

INFORMATION RELATING TO RECORDS KEPT BY RECORD-KEEPER

1. A record-keeper who has possession or control of records that contain personal information shall, subject to clause 2 of this Principle, take such steps as are, in the circumstances, reasonable to enable any person to ascertain:

   (a) whether the record-keeper has possession or control of any records that contain personal information; and
   (b) if the record-keeper has possession or control of a record that contains such information:
       (i) the nature of that information;
       (ii) the main purposes for which that information is used; and
       (iii) the steps that the person should take if the person wishes to obtain access to the record.

2. A record-keeper is not required under clause 1 of this Principle to give a person information if the record-keeper is required or authorised to refuse to give that information to the

person under the applicable provisions of any law of the Commonwealth that provides for access by persons to documents.

3. A record-keeper shall maintain a record setting out:

    (a) the nature of the records of personal information kept by or on behalf of the record-keeper;
    (b) the purpose for which each type of record is kept;
    (c) the classes of individuals about whom records are kept;
    (d) the period for which each type of record is kept;
    (e) the persons who are entitled to have access to personal information contained in the records and the conditions under which they are entitled to have that access; and
    (f) the steps that should be taken by persons wishing to obtain access to that information.

4. A record-keeper shall:

    (a) make the record maintained under clause 3 of this Principle available for inspection by members of the public; and
    (b) give the Commissioner, in the month of June in each year, a copy of the record so maintained.

PRINCIPLE 6

ACCESS TO RECORDS CONTAINING PERSONAL INFORMATION

Where a record-keeper has possession or control of a record that contains personal information, the individual concerned shall be entitled to have access to that record, except to the extent that the record-keeper is required or authorised to refuse to provide the individual with access to that record under the applicable provisions of any law of the Commonwealth that provides for access by persons to documents.

PRINCIPLE 7

ALTERATION OF RECORDS CONTAINING PERSONAL INFORMATION

1. A record-keeper who has possession or control of a record that contains personal information shall take such steps (if any), by way of making appropriate corrections, deletions and additions as are, in the circumstances, reasonable to ensure that the record:

    (a) is accurate; and
    (b) is, having regard to the purpose for which the information was collected or is to be used and to any purpose that is directly related to that purpose, relevant, up to date, complete and not misleading.

2. The obligation imposed on a record-keeper by clause 1 is subject to any applicable limitation in a law of the Commonwealth that provides a right to require the correction or amendment of documents.

3. Where:

   (a) the record-keeper of a record containing personal information is not willing to amend that record, by making a correction, deletion or addition, in accordance with a request by the individual concerned; and

   (b) no decision or recommendation to the effect that the record should be amended wholly or partly in accordance with that request has been made under the applicable provisions of a law of the Commonwealth;

   the record-keeper shall, if so requested by the individual concerned, take such steps (if any) as are reasonable in the circumstances to attach to the record any statement provided by that individual of the correction, deletion or addition sought.

PRINCIPLE 8

RECORD-KEEPER TO CHECK ACCURACY ETC OF PERSONAL INFORMATION
BEFORE USE
A record-keeper who has possession or control of a record that contains personal information shall not use that information without taking such steps (if any) as are, in the circumstances, reasonable to ensure that, having regard to the purpose for which the information is proposed to be used, the information is accurate, up to date and complete.

PRINCIPLE 9

PERSONAL INFORMATION TO BE USED ONLY FOR RELEVANT PURPOSES
A record-keeper who has possession or control of a record that contains personal information shall not use the information except for a purpose to which the information is relevant.

PRINCIPLE 10

LIMITS ON USE OF PERSONAL INFORMATION
1. A record-keeper who has possession or control of a record that contains personal information that was obtained for a particular purpose shall not use the information for any other purpose unless:

   (a) the individual concerned has consented to use of the information for that other purpose;

   (b) the record-keeper believes on reasonable grounds that use of the information for that other purpose is necessary to prevent or lessen a serious and imminent threat to the life or health of the individual concerned or another person;

   (c) use of the information for that other purpose is required or authorised by or under law;

   (d) use of the information for that other purpose is reasonably necessary for enforcement of the criminal law or of a law imposing a pecuniary penalty, or for the protection of the public revenue; or

   (e) the purpose for which the information is used is directly related to the purpose for which the information was obtained.

2. Where personal information is used for enforcement of the criminal law or of a law imposing a pecuniary penalty, or for the protection of the public revenue, the record-keeper shall include in the record containing that information a note of that use.

PRINCIPLE 11

LIMITS ON DISCLOSURE OF PERSONAL INFORMATION

1. A record-keeper who has possession or control of a record that contains personal information shall not disclose the information to a person, body or agency (other than the individual concerned) unless:

    (a) the individual concerned is reasonably likely to have been aware, or made aware under Principle 2, that information of that kind is usually passed to that person, body or agency;

    (b) the individual concerned has consented to the disclosure;

    (c) the record-keeper believes on reasonable grounds that the disclosure is necessary to prevent or lessen a serious and imminent threat to the life or health of the individual concerned or of another person;

    (d) the disclosure is required or authorised by or under law; or

    (e) the disclosure is reasonably necessary for the enforcement of the criminal law or of a law imposing a pecuniary penalty, or for the protection of the public revenue.

2. Where personal information is disclosed for the purposes of enforcement of the criminal law or of a law imposing a pecuniary penalty, or for the purpose of the protection of the public revenue, the record-keeper shall include in the record containing that information a note of the disclosure.

3. A person, body or agency to whom personal information is disclosed under clause 1 of this Principle shall not use or disclose the information for a purpose other than the purpose for which the information was given to the person, body or agency.

 NOTES AND QUESTIONS

1   The IPPs are drafted in general language using words and phrases such as 'unreasonable', 'practicable', 'generally aware', 'as soon as practicable', etc. In particular, examine Principle 2. The following phrase is included therein: 'such steps (if any) as are, in the circumstances, reasonable'. Why do you think it was drafted in this way?

2   'Vague language reduces the enforceability of the principles and weakens the instrument to the point of inoperability. Drafting of the Principles in this manner indicates a deliberate ploy by the Federal Government to abide by their international responsibilities, as they had indicated they would, without actually providing any substantial practical protections or guarantees.' Discuss, with detailed reference to the Information Privacy Principles.

3   The IPPs do not contain explicit exceptions for national security, etc, to the same extent as the European Directive. The IPPs were formulated prior to the Directive. Why might this exception not have been included?

(b) The National Privacy Principles

In 1996, the Liberal–National Coalition promised as part of its election policy to reform Australian privacy law using a co-regulatory approach. Later in the same year, the Attorney-General published a discussion paper proposing a legislative framework for such laws. In March 1997, the government abandoned general privacy laws for the private sector, instead offering the services of the Federal Privacy Commissioner to assist business in the development of voluntary codes of conduct and to meet privacy standards.[19] In February 1998, the Australian Privacy Commissioner issued *National Principles for the Fair Handling of Personal Information* (NPPs). This is a set of ten principles based on the OECD Guidelines. However, they largely reflect the 1980s approach to information privacy. This suggests that they were designed more to demonstrate Australia's acceptance of European principles, agreed upon by other countries years earlier, than directly to resolve the privacy concerns of Australian citizens.

The new NPPs say little about the privacy challenges of a world based around electronic commerce and pervasive telecommunications. It must also be noted that the 'consensus-seeking' process, out of which the Principles arose, had to accommodate the resistance of some business organisations to basic privacy principles, including important matters such as enforcement issues.

In December 1998, the federal government announced their intention to legislate to support and strengthen self-regulatory privacy protection in the private sector, by way of a 'light-touch' legislative regime based on the NPPs. These NPPs were revised in January 1999, and by September that year, the Attorney-General's Department released the information paper on the matter entitled 'The Government's proposed legislation for the protection of privacy in the private sector'.

The paper led to the *Privacy Amendment (Private Sector) Act 2000* (Cth), which established a national scheme for the handling of personal information by private sector organisations. This legislation, which amends the *Privacy Act 1988*, is regarded as the most significant Australian development in the area of privacy law since the passage of the *Privacy Act* in 1988. It was given Royal Assent in December 2000, to take effect on 21 December 2001. It establishes a co-regulatory approach in relation to the private sector. As an amending piece of legislation, it must be read in conjunction with the *Privacy Act*. Many of the sections in the new legislation rely on existing definitions in the *Privacy Act* such as 'personal information' and 'individual'.

The Act implements the National Privacy Principles as a legislative benchmark, and allows organisations to develop privacy codes approved by the Privacy Commissioner. Organisations will have the option of adhering to the NPPs set out in the Act, or developing their own privacy codes. If businesses choose the latter option, the Act specifies that privacy codes must be approved by the Privacy Commissioner and must meet or exceed the standards set by the NPPs .The NPPs will apply as a default standard where there is any shortfall. Code adjudicators will need to report annually to the Privacy Commissioner in relation to the operation of the code, including details of complaints made and the results. The Privacy Commissioner may also decide independently to review the operation of a code.

---

19   See further G Greenleaf, 'Commonwealth abandons privacy for now' (1997) 4 *Privacy Law & Policy Reporter* 1.

The NPPs apply to 'personal information' as well as a class of personal information referred to as 'sensitive information'. Personal information means information about an individual whose identity is apparent, or can reasonably be ascertained from the information. Data that is depersonalised or aggregated or in some way masks the identity of an individual is not 'personal information'. Additional restrictions are placed on the handling of 'sensitive information', which includes information about a person's racial or ethnic origin, political or religious beliefs, or sexual practices, to name a few examples.

National Privacy Principles for the Fair Handling of Personal Information set out in *Privacy Act 1988* (Cth) as Amended, Schedule 3

Available at <http://www.privacy.gov.au/publications/npps01.html> 17 August 2006

1. Collection

1.1 An organisation must not collect personal information unless the information is necessary for one or more of its functions or activities.

1.2 An organisation must collect personal information only by lawful and fair means and not in an unreasonably intrusive way.

1.3 At or before the time (or, if that is not practicable, as soon as practicable after) an organisation collects personal information about an individual from the individual, the organisation must take reasonable steps to ensure that the individual is aware of:

(a) the identity of the organisation and how to contact it; and

(b) the fact that he or she is able to gain access to the information; and

(c) the purposes for which the information is collected; and

(d) the organisations (or the types of organisations) to which the organisation usually discloses information of that kind; and

(e) any law that requires the particular information to be collected; and

(f) the main consequences (if any) for the individual if all or part of the information is not provided.

1.4 If it is reasonable and practicable to do so, an organisation must collect personal information about an individual only from that individual.

1.5 If an organisation collects personal information about an individual from someone else, it must take reasonable steps to ensure that the individual is or has been made aware of the matters listed in subclause 1.3 except to the extent that making the individual aware of the matters would pose a serious threat to the life or health of any individual.

2. Use and disclosure

2.1 An organisation must not use or disclose personal information about an individual for a purpose (*the secondary purpose*) other than the primary purpose of collection unless:

(a) both of the following apply:
  (i) the secondary purpose is related to the primary purpose of collection and, if the personal information is sensitive information, directly related to the primary purpose of collection;
  (ii) the individual would reasonably expect the organisation to use or disclose the information for the secondary purpose; or
(b) the individual has consented to the use or disclosure; or
(c) if the information is not sensitive information and the use of the information is for the secondary purpose of direct marketing:
  (i) it is impracticable for the organisation to seek the individual's consent before that particular use; and
  (ii) the organisation will not charge the individual for giving effect to a request by the individual to the organisation not to receive direct marketing communications; and
  (iii) the individual has not made a request to the organisation not to receive direct marketing communications; and
  (iv) in each direct marketing communication with the individual, the organisation draws to the individual's attention, or prominently displays a notice, that he or she may express a wish not to receive any further direct marketing communications; and
  (v) each written direct marketing communication by the organisation with the individual (up to and including the communication that involves the use) sets out the organisation's business address and telephone number and, if the communication with the individual is made by fax, telex or other electronic means, a number or address at which the organisation can be directly contacted electronically; or
(d) if the information is health information and the use or disclosure is necessary for research, or the compilation or analysis of statistics, relevant to public health or public safety:
  (i) it is impracticable for the organisation to seek the individual's consent before the use or disclosure; and
  (ii) the use or disclosure is conducted in accordance with guidelines approved by the Commissioner under section 95A for the purposes of this subparagraph; and
  (iii) in the case of disclosure—the organisation reasonably believes that the recipient of the health information will not disclose the health information, or personal information derived from the health information; or
(e) the organisation reasonably believes that the use or disclosure is necessary to lessen or prevent:
  (i) a serious and imminent threat to an individual's life, health or safety; or
  (ii) a serious threat to public health or public safety; or
(f) the organisation has reason to suspect that unlawful activity has been, is being or may be engaged in, and uses or discloses the personal information as a necessary part of its investigation of the matter or in reporting its concerns to relevant persons or authorities; or

(g) the use or disclosure is required or authorised by or under law; or

(h) the organisation reasonably believes that the use or disclosure is reasonably necessary for one or more of the following by or on behalf of an enforcement body:

    (i) the prevention, detection, investigation, prosecution or punishment of criminal offences, breaches of a law imposing a penalty or sanction or breaches of a prescribed law;

    (ii) the enforcement of laws relating to the confiscation of the proceeds of crime;

    (iii) the protection of the public revenue;

    (iv) the prevention, detection, investigation or remedying of seriously improper conduct or prescribed conduct;

    (v) the preparation for, or conduct of, proceedings before any court or tribunal, or implementation of the orders of a court or tribunal.

Note 1: It is not intended to deter organisations from lawfully cooperating with agencies performing law enforcement functions in the performance of their functions.

Note 2: Subclause 2.1 does not override any existing legal obligations not to disclose personal information. Nothing in subclause 2.1 requires an organisation to disclose personal information; an organisation is always entitled not to disclose personal information in the absence of a legal obligation to disclose it.

Note 3: An organisation is also subject to the requirements of National Privacy Principle 9 if it transfers personal information to a person in a foreign country.

2.2 If an organisation uses or discloses personal information under paragraph 2.1(h), it must make a written note of the use or disclosure.

2.3 Subclause 2.1 operates in relation to personal information that an organisation that is a body corporate has collected from a related body corporate as if the organisation's primary purpose of collection of the information were the primary purpose for which the related body corporate collected the information.

2.4 Despite subclause 2.1, an organisation that provides a health service to an individual may disclose health information about the individual to a person who is responsible for the individual if:

(a) the individual:

    (i) is physically or legally incapable of giving consent to the disclosure; or

    (ii) physically cannot communicate consent to the disclosure; and

(b) a natural person (the *carer*) providing the health service for the organisation is satisfied that either:

    (i) the disclosure is necessary to provide appropriate care or treatment of the individual; or

    (ii) the disclosure is made for compassionate reasons; and

(c) the disclosure is not contrary to any wish:

    (i) expressed by the individual before the individual became unable to give or communicate consent; and

    (ii) of which the carer is aware, or of which the carer could reasonably be expected to be aware; and

(d) the disclosure is limited to the extent reasonable and necessary for a purpose mentioned in paragraph (b).

2.5 For the purposes of subclause 2.4, a person is *responsible* for an individual if the person is:

(a) a parent of the individual; or

(b) a child or sibling of the individual and at least 18 years old; or

(c) a spouse or de facto spouse of the individual; or

(d) a relative of the individual, at least 18 years old and a member of the individual's household; or

(e) a guardian of the individual; or

(f) exercising an enduring power of attorney granted by the individual that is exercisable in relation to decisions about the individual's health; or

(g) a person who has an intimate personal relationship with the individual; or

(h) a person nominated by the individual to be contacted in case of emergency.

2.6 In subclause 2.5:

- *child* of an individual includes an adopted child, a step-child and a foster-child, of the individual.
- *parent* of an individual includes a step-parent, adoptive parent and a foster-parent, of the individual.
- *relative* of an individual means a grandparent, grandchild, uncle, aunt, nephew or niece, of the individual.
- *sibling* of an individual includes a half-brother, half-sister, adoptive brother, adoptive sister, step-brother, step-sister, foster-brother and foster-sister, of the individual.

 NOTES AND QUESTIONS

1   Critically examine Principle 1.1. Are there any realistic limitations on when an organisation can collect information if the only requirements are that the information is necessary for one of its functions or activities?

2   What do you consider to be unreasonably intrusive (Principle 1.2)? Some people regard telephone surveys as unreasonably intrusive. How would a provision of law relying on such a standard be enforced?

3   The Direct Marketing Exception is the most controversial clause in the NPPs. It has been widely criticised. This exception is discussed below, in isolation, to allow more detailed analysis. The reader is directed to the section below on direct marketing for this discussion.

National Privacy Principles for the Fair Handling of Personal Information set out in *Privacy Act 1988* (Cth) as Amended, Schedule 3

Available at <http://www.privacy.gov.au/publications/npps01.html> 17 August 2006

3. Data quality

An organisation must take reasonable steps to make sure that the personal information it collects, uses or discloses is accurate, complete and up-to-date.

4. Data security

4.1 An organisation must take reasonable steps to protect the personal information it holds from misuse and loss and from unauthorised access, modification or disclosure.

4.2 An organisation must take reasonable steps to destroy or permanently de-identify personal information if it is no longer needed for any purpose for which the information may be used or disclosed under National Privacy Principle 2.

5. Openness

5.1 An organisation must set out in a document clearly expressed policies on its management of personal information. The organisation must make the document available to anyone who asks for it.

5.2 On request by a person, an organisation must take reasonable steps to let the person know, generally, what sort of personal information it holds, for what purposes, and how it collects, holds, uses and discloses that information.

6. Access and correction

6.1 If an organisation holds personal information about an individual, it must provide the individual with access to the information on request by the individual, except to the extent that:

(a) in the case of personal information other than health information—providing access would pose a serious and imminent threat to the life or health of any individual; or

(b) in the case of health information—providing access would pose a serious threat to the life or health of any individual; or

(c) providing access would have an unreasonable impact upon the privacy of other individuals; or

(d) the request for access is frivolous or vexatious; or

(e) the information relates to existing or anticipated legal proceedings between the organisation and the individual, and the information would not be accessible by the process of discovery in those proceedings; or

(f) providing access would reveal the intentions of the organisation in relation to negotiations with the individual in such a way as to prejudice those negotiations; or

(g) providing access would be unlawful; or

(h) denying access is required or authorised by or under law; or

(i) providing access would be likely to prejudice an investigation of possible unlawful activity; or

(j) providing access would be likely to prejudice:

(i) the prevention, detection, investigation, prosecution or punishment of criminal offences, breaches of a law imposing a penalty or sanction or breaches of a prescribed law; or

(ii) the enforcement of laws relating to the confiscation of the proceeds of crime; or

(iii) the protection of the public revenue; or

(iv) the prevention, detection, investigation or remedying of seriously improper conduct or prescribed conduct; or

(v) the preparation for,· or conduct of, proceedings before any court or tribunal, or implementation of its orders;

by or on behalf of an enforcement body; or

(k) an enforcement body performing a lawful security function asks the organisation not to provide access to the information on the basis that providing access would be likely to cause damage to the security of Australia.

6.2 However, where providing access would reveal evaluative information generated within the organisation in connection with a commercially sensitive decision-making process, the organisation may give the individual an explanation for the commercially sensitive decision rather than direct access to the information.

Note: An organisation breaches subclause 6.1 if it relies on subclause 6.2 to give an individual an explanation for a commercially sensitive decision in circumstances where subclause 6.2 does not apply.

6.3 If the organisation is not required to provide the individual with access to the information because of one or more of paragraphs 6.1(a) to (k) (inclusive), the organisation must, if reasonable, consider whether the use of mutually agreed intermediaries would allow sufficient access to meet the needs of both parties.

6.4 If an organisation charges for providing access to personal information, those charges:

(a) must not be excessive; and

(b) must not apply to lodging a request for access.

6.5 If an organisation holds personal information about an individual and the individual is able to establish that the information is not accurate, complete and up-to-date, the organisation must take reasonable steps to correct the information so that it is accurate, complete and up-to-date.

6.6 If the individual and the organisation disagree about whether the information is accurate, complete and up-to-date, and the individual asks the organisation to associate with the information a statement claiming that the information is not accurate, complete or up-to-date, the organisation must take reasonable steps to do so.

6.7 An organisation must provide reasons for denial of access or a refusal to correct personal information.

NOTES AND QUESTIONS

1   Principle 6 is extremely detailed. Critically examine the provisions it sets out and determine whether they provide sufficient substantive guarantees for the right to access and correct information.

2   Like the IPPs, the NPPs do not focus on the competing demands of national security or crime prevention as explicitly as the Directive. Principle 6.1(k) outlines a circumstance where these considerations were deemed relevant; however, there is a distinctly diminished emphasis on these matters in the Australian instruments. Why do you think this might be?

3   One of the significant problems raised in the introduction to this chapter was the fact that the Internet has created information flows which are nearly impossible to correct if they contain inaccurate data. Are the provisions in Principle 6 sufficient to alleviate this problem? Or, alternatively, is the problem simply a feature of the Internet that we must learn to accept?

National Privacy Principles for the Fair Handling of Personal Information set out in *Privacy Act 1988* (Cth) as Amended, Schedule 3

Available at <http://www.privacy.gov.au/publications/npps01.html> 16 August 2006

7. Identifiers

7.1. An organisation must not adopt as its own identifier of an individual an identifier of the individual that has been assigned by:

(a) an agency; or

(b) an agent of an agency acting in its capacity as agent; or

(c) a contracted service provider for a Commonwealth contract acting in its capacity as contracted service provider for that contract.

7.2. An organisation must not use or disclose an identifier assigned to an individual by an agency, or by an agent or contracted service provider mentioned in subclause 7.1, unless:

(a) the use or disclosure is necessary for the organisation to fulfil its obligations to the agency; or

(b) one or more of paragraphs 2.1(e) to 2.1(h) (inclusive) apply to the use or disclosure; or

(c) the use or disclosure is by a prescribed organisation of a prescribed identifier in prescribed circumstances.

7.3. In this clause:

identifier includes a number assigned by an organisation to an individual to identify uniquely the individual for the purposes of the organisation's operations. However, an individual's name or ABN (as defined in the *A New Tax System (Australian Business Number) Act 1999*) is not an *identifier*.

8. Anonymity

Wherever it is lawful and practicable, individuals must have the option of not identifying themselves when entering transactions with an organisation.

9. Transborder data flows

An organisation in Australia or an external Territory may transfer personal information about an individual to someone (other than the organisation or the individual) who is in a foreign country only if:

(a) the organisation reasonably believes that the recipient of the information is subject to a law, binding scheme or contract which effectively upholds principles for fair handling of the information that are substantially similar to the National Privacy Principles; or

(b) the individual consents to the transfer; or

(c) the transfer is necessary for the performance of a contract between the individual and the organisation, or for the implementation of pre-contractual measures taken in response to the individual's request; or

(d) the transfer is necessary for the conclusion or performance of a contract concluded in the interest of the individual between the organisation and a third party; or

(e) all of the following apply:

(i) the transfer is for the benefit of the individual;

(ii) it is impracticable to obtain the consent of the individual to that transfer;

(iii) if it were practicable to obtain such consent, the individual would be likely to give it; or

(f) the organisation has taken reasonable steps to ensure that the information which it has transferred will not be held, used or disclosed by the recipient of the information inconsistently with the National Privacy Principles.

 ## NOTES AND QUESTIONS

1 This provision is explicitly designed to reflect the concerns in articles 25 and 26 of the European Directive. Compare the two instruments. Critically analyse their operation and outline any differences, and give an indication as to which of the two instruments achieves its objectives most effectively, in your opinion.

2 As we have seen, the concept of 'transborder', in the broad sense of activities spanning jurisdictional boundaries, immediately conjures up issues of enforcement (within the larger picture of jurisdiction). There is no question that the organisations under the *Privacy Act* will incur personal jurisdiction. But how will a court decide whether a belief about a foreign jurisdiction's privacy protection standards is legitimate or reasonable?

National Privacy Principles for the Fair Handling of Personal Information set out in *Privacy Act 1988* (Cth) as Amended, Schedule 3

Available at <http://www.privacy.gov.au/publications/npps01.html> 17 August 2006

10. Sensitive information

10.1. An organisation must not collect sensitive information about an individual unless:

(a) the individual has consented; or

(b) the collection is required by law; or

(c) the collection is necessary to prevent or lessen a serious and imminent threat to the life or health of any individual, where the individual whom the information concerns:

(i) is physically or legally incapable of giving consent to the collection; or

(ii) physically cannot communicate consent to the collection; or

(d) if the information is collected in the course of the activities of a non-profit organisation—the following conditions are satisfied:

(i) the information relates solely to the members of the organisation or to individuals who have regular contact with it in connection with its activities;

(ii) at or before the time of collecting the information, the organisation undertakes to the individual whom the information concerns that the organisation will not disclose the information without the individual's consent; or

(e) the collection is necessary for the establishment, exercise or defence of a legal or equitable claim.

10.2. Despite subclause 10.1, an organisation may collect health information about an individual if:

(a) the information is necessary to provide a health service to the individual; and

(b) the information is collected:

(i) as required by law (other than this Act); or

(ii) in accordance with rules established by competent health or medical bodies that deal with obligations of professional confidentiality which bind the organisation.

10.3. Despite subclause 10.1, an organisation may collect health information about an individual if:

(a) the collection is necessary for any of the following purposes:

(i) research relevant to public health or public safety;

(ii) the compilation or analysis of statistics relevant to public health or public safety;

(iii) the management, funding or monitoring of a health service; and

(b) that purpose cannot be served by the collection of information that does not identify the individual or from which the individual's identity cannot reasonably be ascertained; and

(c) it is impracticable for the organisation to seek the individual's consent to the collection; and

(d) the information is collected:

    (i) as required by law (other than this Act); or

    (ii) in accordance with rules established by competent health or medical bodies that deal with obligations of professional confidentiality which bind the organisation; or

    (iii) in accordance with guidelines approved by the Commissioner under section 95A for the purposes of this subparagraph.

10.4. If an organisation collects health information about an individual in accordance with subclause 10.3, the organisation must take reasonable steps to permanently de-identify the information before the organisation discloses it.

10.5. In this clause:

non-profit organisation means a non-profit organisation that has only racial, ethnic, political, religious, philosophical, professional, trade, or trade union aims.

 NOTES AND QUESTIONS

1   What sort of information would you regard as sensitive? Do you think the safeguards here are adequate? Give reasons for your answer.

2   Having read both sets of principles, what justifications, if any, can you see for maintaining separate regimes for the public and private sectors? Are there significant differences between the two sets of principles? What are these differences? Are they such that the principles cannot be combined?

3   The reader is advised to consider the *Guidelines to the National Privacy Principles*, available at <http://www.privacy.gov.au/business/index.html> 17 August 2006. This document was one of an array of support publications offered by the federal government in 2001, specifically through the Privacy Commissioner's website at <http://www.privacy.gov.au/>, in preparation for the new regime. The government was clearly interested in promoting both awareness and understanding of the new regime and in ensuring that the protections offered in the statute generated substantive practical results. Do you think this hope for an effective institutional structure has been achieved?

4   The most significant criticisms of the NPPs have been targeted not at the drafting of the principles themselves, or at the commitment of the government to their effective implementation, but at the numerous exceptions which exempt a large number of organisations and activities. These exceptions are considered below.

(c)   Exemptions from coverage

The new NPPs apply to the activities of all organisations as defined under the Act. However, there are a number of exemptions from coverage by the legislation. These exemptions are the result of balancing many issues and interests. Some of the exemptions cover particular organisations; others cover particular activities. The exemptions have been controversial, particularly because of the breadth of their application. It has been suggested that the exemptions take so many potential 'organisations' out of the purview of the Act that the remaining sections are rendered meaningless.

Privacy Act 1988 (Cth) as Amended

6C. ORGANISATIONS
What is an organisation?

(1) In this Act:
organisation means:

    (a) an individual; or
    (b) a body corporate; or
    (c) a partnership; or
    (d) any other unincorporated association; or
    (e) a trust;

that is not a small business operator, a registered political party, an agency, a State or Territory authority or a prescribed instrumentality of a State or Territory.

 NOTES AND QUESTIONS

As you read these provisions, consider their applicability to the collection of data on-line through the mechanisms discussed in the opening sections of the chapter. Consider whether the challenges posed by the mechanisms discussed here are adequately met by this legislation.

Application to small business

Privacy Act 1988 (Cth) as Amended

6D. SMALL BUSINESS AND SMALL BUSINESS OPERATORS
Entities that are not small business operators

(4) However, an individual, body corporate, partnership, unincorporated association or trust is not a small business operator if he, she or it:

    (a) carries on a business that has had an annual turnover of more than $3,000,000 for a financial year that has ended after the later of the following:
        (i) the time he, she or it started to carry on the business;
        (ii) the commencement of this section; or
    (b) provides a health service to another individual and holds any health information except in an employee record; or

(c) discloses personal information about another individual to anyone else for a benefit, service or advantage; or

(d) provides a benefit, service or advantage to collect personal information about another individual from anyone else; or

(e) is a contracted service provider for a Commonwealth contract (whether or not a party to the contract).

 NOTES AND QUESTIONS

1   This exemption is designed to accord with the Government's policy of minimising regulatory burdens on small business. A small business is defined in s 6D as a business with an annual turnover of $3 million or less. In general, annual turnover will equate to the total of the instalment income the business notifies to the Commissioner of Taxation on its Business Activity Statement over the course of a financial year.

2   Outline some examples of when a small business will be exempt from the operation of the legislation. When will it not be exempt? Do you think these exemptions are justified?

3   Examine ss 6D(4)(c) and (d), which outline when a business will not be regarded as a small business. Activities such as dealing with the collection and dissemination of personal information will disqualify an organisation from the small business exception. How significant is this exemption in light of personal data privacy concerns? Does it effectively bring small businesses under the Act whenever they deal with collection of personal information? Combine this provision with the direct marketing exemption outlined below. What is the combined effect of these provisions?

4   Section 6EA includes a mechanism that will allow otherwise exempt small businesses to choose to be covered by the legislation, making them subject to the jurisdiction of the Privacy Commissioner or an approved code adjudicator. As the mechanism is based on the small business choosing, rather than the government requiring, compliance with the scheme, the mechanism will enable a small business subsequently to opt out of the scheme.

Application to states and territories and interaction with state and territory legislation

---

Privacy Act 1988 (Cth) as Amended

6F. STATE INSTRUMENTALITIES ETC TREATED AS ORGANISATIONS
Regulations treating a State instrumentality etc as an organisation

(1) This Act applies, with the prescribed modifications (if any), in relation to a prescribed State or Territory authority or a prescribed instrumentality of a State or Territory (except an instrumentality that is an organisation because of section 6C) as if the authority or instrumentality were an organisation.

Note 1: The regulations may prescribe different modifications of the Act for different authorities or instrumentalities. See subsection 33(3A) of the *Acts Interpretation Act 1901*.

Note 2: Regulations may prescribe an authority or instrumentality by reference to one or more classes of authority or instrumentality. See subsection 46(2) of the *Acts Interpretation Act 1901*.

 NOTES AND QUESTIONS

1   The private sector legislation is intended to establish a comprehensive national scheme providing for the appropriate collection, holding, use, correction, disclosure, and transfer of personal information by organisations in the private sector. However, it acknowledges Australia's federal system of government. The legislation does not regulate the state and territory public sectors or state and territory Government Business Enterprises (GBEs) that perform substantially core government functions. State and territory laws that make provision for the collection, holding, use, correction, disclosure, or transfer of personal information will continue to operate to the extent that they are not inconsistent with the Commonwealth legislation. Do you foresee complications arising from these arrangements?

2   In 1995 the uniform *Evidence Acts* were passed in all jurisdictions in Australia. Do you think it is feasible to implement a uniform regime with respect to privacy? What are the implications for the flow of information if there are separate regimes and separate approaches to privacy across Australia?

Application to political parties and political representatives

---

Privacy Act 1988 (Cth) as Amended

7C. POLITICAL ACTS AND PRACTICES ARE EXEMPT
Members of a Parliament etc
(1) An act done, or practice engaged in, by an organisation (the *political representative*) consisting of a member of a Parliament, or a councillor (however described) of a local government authority, is *exempt* for the purposes of paragraph 7(1)(ee) if the act is done, or the practice is engaged in, for any purpose in connection with:

   (a) an election under an electoral law; or
   (b) a referendum under a law of the Commonwealth or a law of a State or Territory; or
       the participation by the political representative in another aspect of the political process.

NOTES AND QUESTIONS

1   The government argued that as freedom of political communication is vitally important to the democratic process in Australia, political parties registered under Part XI of the *Commonwealth Electoral Act 1918* should be exempt from the operation of the legislation under the new regime. Acts and practices of political representatives such as Members of Parliament and local government councillors will also be exempt from the legislation provided their acts and practices relate to an election, a referendum, or other participation in the political process.

The acts and practices of contractors (and their subcontractors) of registered political parties and political representatives will be exempt provided the acts done or practices engaged in relate to an election or a referendum, or to the participation of a registered political party or a political representative in the political process. Acts done or practices engaged in by volunteers on behalf of and with the authority of a registered political party will also be exempt from the operation of the legislation.

2   Is the political exemption too wide? How much credence do you give these arguments? Might there be another reason, or reasons, that explain the inclusion of these sweeping exemptions?

3   Can you explain how this exemption will enhance the working of the Australian polity?

Application to the media

Privacy Act 1988 (Cth) as Amended

7B. EXEMPT ACTS AND EXEMPT PRACTICES OF ORGANISATIONS

JOURNALISM

(4) An act done, or practice engaged in, by a media organisation is exempt for the purposes of paragraph 7(1)(ee) if the act is done, or the practice is engaged in:

(a) by the organisation in the course of journalism; and
(b) at a time when the organisation is publicly committed to observe standards that:
   (i)   deal with privacy in the context of the activities of a media organisation (whether or not the standards also deal with other matters); and
   (ii) have been published in writing by the organisation or a person or body representing a class of media organisations.

NOTES AND QUESTIONS

1   This exception is as curious as those applying to political parties and related bodies. The term 'journalism' is not defined in the legislation—it is intended to have its everyday meaning and to apply in a technology-neutral way. In order to take advantage of the exemption, a media organisation must be able to show that it has publicly committed itself to observing published standards that deal with privacy.

    This exemption seeks to balance the public interest in providing adequate safeguards for the handling of personal information and the public interest in allowing a free flow of information to the public through the media. The objects clause in the legislation also highlights this need for a balanced approach.

2   Do you agree with the implicit idea that the media play a role in the protection of the public good through the provision of a service monitoring the activities of our government?

3   In the light of the Internet, how significant is the fact that 'journalism' is not defined? Does this leave the exemption open to exploitation?

4   In addition, s 66 provides that a journalist is not required to give information, answer a question, or produce a document or record where this would tend to reveal the identity of a person who gave information to the journalist in confidence. This is a significant provision codifying a principle that has long been misunderstood. Despite the romance surrounding the journalistic protection of sources in the interests of democracy, journalists have previously been jailed for contempt after refusing to reveal the names of sources.

Direct marketing

Direct mail, junk mail, spam. These features of the Internet incur the wrath of many a user, not only because of the inconvenience, but because they usually mean that someone has obtained the recipient's e-mail address without the permission of the recipient.

Information can be collected without the knowledge or consent of an Internet user and combined with other information. It is entirely possible to create databases including a range of information including e-mail addresses and a sample of personal preferences as garnered from Internet activity. Once this information is processed and obtained by an advertising or marketing company, a steady stream of unsolicited mail can result.

Despite this, a direct marketing exception exists within the Australian *Privacy Act*. Collecting information for the purposes of direct marketing is not prohibited, depending on the content of the direct mail generated by the information. Therefore, absurdly, the legality of the prior collection is determined by the subsequent use.

The Guidelines to the NPPs[20] contain the following advice on the meaning of 'impracticable to obtain consent'.

---

20   <http://www.privacy.gov.au/publications/nppgl_01.doc> 20 September 2001.

Considering whether it is impracticable to seek the individual's consent involves balancing a number of factors that could include:

- how often the organisation is in contact with an individual;
- the way an organisation communicates with an individual;
- the consequences for the individual of receiving the information without having consented; and
- the cost to the organisation of seeking consent.

The question of impracticability would generally be considered at the time of the proposed use of the personal information for direct marketing—not the time the personal information was collected.

As the cost of e-mail is negligible, ordinarily it will not be 'impracticable' to seek consent where an organisation chooses on-line methods of contact or communication.

Privacy Act 1988 (Cth) as Amended

Schedule 3. National Privacy Principles

2. USE AND DISCLOSURE

2.1. An organisation must not use or disclose personal information about an individual for a purpose (the *secondary purpose*) other than the primary purpose of collection unless ...

(c) if the information is not sensitive information and the use of the information is for the secondary purpose of direct marketing:

(i) it is impracticable for the organisation to seek the individual's consent before that particular use; and

(ii) the organisation will not charge the individual for giving effect to a request by the individual to the organisation not to receive direct marketing communications; and

(iii) the individual has not made a request to the organisation not to receive direct marketing communications; and

(iv) in each direct marketing communication with the individual, the organisation draws to the individual's attention, or prominently displays a notice, that he or she may express a wish not to receive any further direct marketing communications; and

(v) each written direct marketing communication by the organisation with the individual (up to and including the communication that involves the use) sets out the organisation's business address and telephone number and, if the communication with the individual is made by fax, telex or other electronic means, a number or address at which the organisation can be directly contacted electronically; or ...

NOTES AND QUESTIONS

1   The emphasis in the Guidelines indicates that the government is relying on the consent of the data subject to overcome concerns over direct marketing. Are you convinced that requiring consent, where 'practicable', is sufficient protection?

2   Critically analyse the provisions of the NPPs, extracted above. In doing so, compare them with the EU Directive and with the US Safe Harbor Principles. What justification can you suggest for including this exemption in the Australian regime?

3   The above provision applies where information is collected for the secondary purpose of direct mail. What is the position on information collected where direct mail is the primary purpose of collection? Why is there a distinction between this secondary purpose and others?

(d)   Co-regulation

The key to the private sector amendments is the relationship between the privacy principles, particularly the NPPs, and the industry or sectorial privacy codes. These codes can be developed and applied using the principles as a foundation and benchmark. The development of a privacy code is discretionary; however, to ensure consistency, each privacy code must be approved by the Privacy Commissioner. The standards in approved privacy codes operate in place of the standards in the legislation. However, to be approved, a code must provide at least the same standard of privacy protection as the legislated NPPs. Part IIIAA of the legislation sets out the matters that the Privacy Commissioner must take into account when deciding whether or not to approve a privacy code (ss 18BA–BG).

If an individual has a grievance over a possible invasion of his or her privacy, the first step is to approach the organisation. If the organisation has a Privacy Code, the matter will most likely proceed to an independent investigator and adjudicator. If the complainant is unsatisfied with the results here, there is a further recourse to the Privacy Commissioner who has the power to examine the claim and order redress if necessary. Although, on the surface, it may seem as though these provisions are stronger than the equivalent US provisions, an examination of the Act reveals otherwise.

A privacy code can include a procedure for lodging and dealing with complaints, and for the designation of an adjudicator to resolve disputes (a 'code adjudicator'). Under s 18BI, decisions made by a code adjudicator may be reviewed by the Privacy Commissioner. Section 18BB(3) states that where a code does contain a complaint resolution process, the Privacy Commissioner must consider a range of matters, including whether the process meets prescribed standards. Where a code does not cover the handling of complaints, the investigation and complaint provisions of the *Privacy Act* (Part V) will apply. The operation of privacy codes may be reviewed by the Privacy Commissioner under s 18BH.

When these provisions are compared with the enforcement provision of the Safe Harbour principles, the Australian framework appears quite rigorous. However, this rigour is eroded when we take into account the Act's numerous exemptions, for both organisations and activities, and the debatable success of self-regulation in other countries. In any case, the EU's attitude towards the new regime is that it does not completely comply with the EU Directive. The new laws fall short of the stringent requirements in EU countries. For example, the direct marketing exception is not present in EU countries and consumers there have to grant permission to companies before they can be sent marketing material. Intergovernmental negotiations were continuing even at the commencement date of the new privacy laws to avoid disruptions to trade with EU companies. The Internet Industry Association has been developing its own Privacy Code, which is more stringent than the requirements of the legislation, and it is hoped that the code will meet with the EU's approval.

 NOTES AND QUESTIONS

1   The definition of personal information means the restrictions apply only to information that can be tied to an individual. The nature of the Internet means that most information cannot be tied to an individual unless a specific identifying piece of information can be added to the data. Problems are possible if a large amount of data is collected with seeming anonymity, but subsequently linked with personal information obtained from elsewhere.

2   'The *Privacy Act* is purely a weapon of intimidation rather than application. That is, privacy can only be protected by brandishing the Act in the face of recalcitrant organisations, rather than by enforcing the rights and obligations it contains.' Do you agree?

3   The small business exception has been widely criticised. The criticisms are augmented when it is considered that ss 6(1) and 7B(3) include an exception for employee records. Neither of these exceptions is justified by the OECD Guidelines or the EU Directive. List the effects these exceptions might have on the flow of personal data within and to Australia. Consider in particular the issue of harmonisation.

4   Further to the harmonisation issue, conduct your own research to determine which of the Australian states have enacted parallel legislation. Section 6F provides for state instrumentalities and authorities to be treated as organisations for the purposes of the Act. What other peculiarities might arise out of Australia's federal system of government?

5   The new s 5B makes the legislation apply to certain acts and practices of organisations that occur outside Australia. This is to ensure that, as far as practicable, the legislation will apply in an environment where organisations operate across national boundaries and may move information overseas to use and process it. This is also intended to ensure that the provisions of the legislation are not avoided simply by moving personal information overseas. The

efficacy of this provision remains to be seen, however. It is one thing to legislate a provision with extraterritorial application; it is another altogether to bring its weight to bear on acts or persons outside Australia. Amendments to the legislation in April 2004 inserted a new s 5B(1A), which clarified the protection provided by NPP 9, which regulates transborder data flows; that protection applies equally to the personal information of individuals who are Australian and of those who are not. The nationality and residency limitations on the power of the Privacy Commissioner to investigate complaints relating to the correction of personal information has been removed.

6   Other amendments in 2004 also gave businesses and industries more flexibility in developing privacy codes by allowing the codes to cover, where there is a desire to do so, otherwise exempt acts and practices. See s 18BAA.

7   How do these exemptions, and their individual complexities, apply to the Internet? In theory, the new privacy legislation is designed to regulate the flow of personal data information. It applies to large corporations who collect and distribute data, it applies to a variety of information, and it places stricter controls on details such as health or medical records. However, the proof will come in the enforcement. Do you agree with criticisms that suggest there are more exemptions than rules? Do you think the exemptions should be restricted in any way?

8   The Act contains numerous exceptions both for organisations and for activities. The co-regulatory system adds multiple layers of complexity to the complaint procedure through the codes. Do you agree with the contention that the Act is designed to demonstrate Australia's compliance with the EU directive and OECD Guidelines, rather than to provide meaningful protection to the privacy of Australians' personal data?

9   Ross Pty Ltd runs a website that carries a weekly footy tipping competition, with a weekly prize for the winner. Participation in the tipping is free, but users must become a registered member of the site to join in. Rachel Smith wants to join the tipping, as she is sure she will win the weekly prize, but she is concerned about registering with the site because it requires her to enter personal information and her e-mail address. Rachel registers anyway because there was a small note on the bottom of the site that says information will be dealt with in confidence, and at any rate she enters a fake name, 'Rachel Evans'.

On Ross Pty Ltd's site, there is a link to Monster Ads Pty Ltd's site which gives, among other things, commentary on all of the details relevant to the week's football matches. Monster Ads Pty Ltd has struck a deal with Ross Pty Ltd to match Monster Ads' information, from the cookies, with the data Ross Pty Ltd has gathered from the registrations on Ross Pty Ltd's site. This means that Monster Ads Pty Ltd and Ross Pty Ltd both now have mailing lists, complete with personal details, which they can use for direct marketing. They also have information on sites visited by the users. Rachel visits Monster Ads Pty Ltd's site, and unbeknown to her, receives cookies from the site. (Rachel did not have cookies disabled on her browser.)

Joey, an employee of Rachel's ISP, contacts Rachel to let her know that he has been monitoring her in-box, and has noticed she has had a huge influx of e-mail. Some of this mail is from Ross Pty Ltd advertising new football sites, but the majority of the messages are in fact advertisements, addressed to 'Rachel Evans'. Advise Rachel.

(e)   Workplace privacy

Many jurisdictions in Australia have some form of legislation on surveillance devices which cover to some extent surveillance in the workplace (see for example Western Australia's *Surveillance Devices Act 1998* and Victoria's *Surveillance Devices Act 1999*). New South Wales is the first to pass legislation specifically dealing with computer surveillance in the workplace. The *Workplace Surveillance Act 2005* (NSW) repeals the *Workplace Video Surveillance Act 1998* and significantly restricts surveillance of employees and for the first time, regulates email and Internet monitoring, among other things.

The NSW Act prohibits surveillance by employers of their employees at work unless the employees have been given notice, or the surveillance is carried out under the authority of a covert surveillance authority issued by a magistrate for the purpose of establishing whether or not an employee is involved in any unlawful activity at work. The Act also limits an employer's ability to monitor or block employees' emails or restrict access to the Internet unless it is acting in accordance with a policy that has been notified to employees. There are also now new restrictions on the use and disclosure of surveillance records. Failure to comply with the Act may amount to a criminal offence and expose employers to fines. Worth noting is s 43 which provides that if a corporation contravenes any provision of the Act, a director or manager of the corporation may also be taken to have contravened the same provision if the director or manager knowingly authorised or permitted the contravention.

As a general rule, the Act requires that an employer must notify employees before surveillance can be carried out. Section 10 specifies that the notification must be in writing or by email and generally at least 14 days in advance of the commencement of the surveillance. The notice must contain certain information such as the kind of surveillance to be carried out, how the surveillance will be carried out, when it will commence.

Section 3 defines computer surveillance as 'surveillance by means of software or other equipment that monitors or records the information input or output, or other use, of a computer (including, but not limited to, the sending and receipt of emails and the accessing of Internet websites)'. The key provision on restricting employee access to emails or the Internet is s 17 reproduced below. How strong is the protection for employees? What is the purpose of the provision?

Workplace Surveillance Act 2005 (NSW) as Amended

17. RESTRICTIONS ON BLOCKING EMAILS OR INTERNET ACCESS

(1) An employer must not prevent, or cause to be prevented, delivery of an email sent to or by, or access to an Internet website by, an employee of the employer unless:

(a) the employer is acting in accordance with a policy on email and Internet access that has been notified in advance to the employee in such a way that it is reasonable to assume that the employee is aware of and understands the policy, and

(b) in addition, in the case of the preventing of delivery of an email, the employee is given notice (a 'prevented delivery notice') as soon as practicable by the employer, by email or otherwise, that delivery of the email has been prevented, unless this section provides that a prevented delivery notice is not required. Maximum penalty: 50 penalty units.

(2) An employee is not required to be given a prevented delivery notice for an email if delivery of the email was prevented in the belief that, or by the operation of a program intended to prevent the delivery of an email on the basis that:

(a) the email was a commercial electronic message within the meaning of the *Spam Act 2003* of the Commonwealth, or

(b) the content of the email or any attachment to the email would or might have resulted in an unauthorised interference with, damage to or operation of a computer or computer network operated by the employer or of any program run by or data stored on such a computer or computer network, or

(c) the email or any attachment to the email would be regarded by reasonable persons as being, in all the circumstances, menacing, harassing or offensive.

(3) An employee is not required to be given a prevented delivery notice for an email sent by the employee if the employer was not aware (and could not reasonably be expected to be aware) of the identity of the employee who sent the email or that the email was sent by an employee.

(4) An employer's policy on email and Internet access cannot provide for preventing delivery of an email or access to a website merely because:

(a) the email was sent by or on behalf of an industrial organisation of employees or an officer of such an organisation, or

(b) the website or email contains information relating to industrial matters (within the meaning of the *Industrial Relations Act 1996*).

----

7   The EU: Round 2

Frederic Debussere, 'The EU E-Privacy Directive: A Monstrous Attempt to Starve the Cookie Monster?'

(2005) 13 International Journal of Law and Information Technology 70

... on 12 July 2002, the European Parliament and the Council of the European Union ('EU') adopted Directive 2002/58/EC concerning the processing of personal data and the protection of privacy in the electronic communications sector ('Directive 2002/58'). This Directive is part of a package of five new Directives that aim to reform the legal and regulatory framework of electronic communications services in the EU, and it repealed and replaced Directive 97/66/EC of the European Parliament and of the Council of 15 December 1997 concerning the processing of personal data and the protection of privacy in the telecommunications sector ('Directive 97/66'). The latter Directive aimed to translate the general personal data protection principles laid down in Directive 95/46/EC of the European Parliament and of the Council of 24 October 1995 on the protection of individuals with regard to the processing of personal data and on the free movement of such data ('Directive 95/46'), into specific rules for the telecommunications sector. However, Directive 97/66 was already outdated at the moment of its adoption in 1997: it had been drawn up in the first half of the nineties and-as its title and terminology suggest—it applied only to the 'telecommunications' sector, whereas by 1997, the Internet and electronic communications had already begun to be used with regular frequency. Although the EU Article 29 Data Protection Working Party was of the opinion that this Directive also applied to the Internet and e-mails, it was still uncertain whether this was indeed the case, and the EU wanted to remove this uncertainty by adopting a new Directive.

Directive 2002/58 had to be implemented in national law by the EU Member States by 31 October 2003. However, nine Member States—Belgium, Germany, Greece, Finland, France, Luxembourg, the Netherlands, Portugal and Sweden—failed to do so, and in the beginning of December 2003, the European Commission opened infringement proceedings against them.

One of the innovative provisions of Directive 2002/58 is Article 5(3), as clarified by Recitals 24 and 25, which sets out a legal framework for the use of devices for storing or retrieving information, such as cookies.

This article aims to analyse this new EU legal framework for the use of cookies ... it is explained why their use can be problematic in the light of privacy and personal data protection. Third, a critical analysis is made of the new European rules for the use of cookies ....

4. The EU Legal Framework for the Use of Cookies

The new EU legal framework for the use of cookies is laid down in Article 5(3) of Directive 2002/58, which provides the following: 'Member States shall ensure that the use of electronic communications networks to store information or to gain access to information stored in the terminal equipment of a subscriber or user is only allowed on condition that the subscriber or user concerned is provided with clear and comprehensive information in accordance with Directive 95/46/EC, inter alia about the purposes of the processing, and is offered the right to refuse such processing by the data controller. This shall not prevent any technical storage or access for the sole purpose of carrying out or facilitating the transmission of a communication over an electronic communications network, or as strictly necessary in order to provide an information society service explicitly requested by the subscriber or user.' Article 5(3) is further clarified by Recitals 24 and 25 of the Directive.

This new legal framework was not included in the European Commission's initial proposal, but has been introduced by the European Parliament's amendments to the proposal, which were later modified by the Council of the EU. The European Parliament's intention was to prohibit the use of cookies without the Internet users' prior, explicit consent. It proposed the following provision: 'Member States shall prohibit the use of electronic communications networks to store information or to gain access to information stored in the terminal equipment of a subscriber or user without the prior, explicit consent of the subscriber or user concerned. This shall not prevent any technical storage or access for the sole purpose of carrying out or facilitating the transmission of a communication over an electronic communications network.' However, as will be explained below, the Council later replaced the Parliament's intended prohibition to use cookies unless prior, explicit consent by a permission to use cookies on the condition that information and a right to refuse the cookie are provided.

Before analysing Article 5(3) and its related Recitals, it is necessary to examine the legal framework's material and territorial scope.

4.1. Assessment of the Scope

4.1.1. INTERACTION BETWEEN DIRECTIVES 95/46 AND 2002/58: TWO INTERPRETATIONS

The interaction between Directive 95/46 and Directive 2002/58 is important for determining the exact scope of Directive 2002/58 and its provision about cookies. One is spontaneously inclined to think that, since Directive 2002/58 is intended to be a lex specialis vis-a-vis Directive 95/46, the former prevails over the latter in case of a conflict between provisions, so that an examination of their interaction seems superfluous. However, the provisions of Directive 2002/58 that set out its scope are written in an enigmatic way so that the interaction between both Directives is rather unclear. For instance, whereas Article 1 of Directive 2002/58 provides that the provisions of Directive 2002/58 'particularise and complement' those of Directive 95/46, Directive 2002/58 seems to retain different criteria as regards its territorial scope, laid down in Article 3: Although Directive 95/46's main criterion for determining its territorial application is the location of the controller of the processing of personal data, this location criterion is not taken into account in Article 3 of Directive 2002/58.

The text of Directive 2002/58 not being clear, there are two possible interpretations of the interaction between both Directives.

The first possible interpretation is based on the purpose of Directive 2002/58, set forth in Article 1(2) and clarified by Recital 10, and the opinion of the Article 29 Data Protection Working Party. Article 1(2) provides that '[t]he provisions of this Directive particularise and complement Directive 95/46/EC for the purposes mentioned in paragraph 1.' Recital 10 provides that '[i]n the electronic communications sector, Directive 95/46/EC applies in particular to all matters concerning protection of fundamental rights and freedoms, which are not specifically covered by the provisions of this Directive, including the obligations on the controller and the rights of individuals. Directive 95/46/EC applies to non-public communications services.' In 2000, the Article 29 Data Protection Working Party issued an opinion on the repealed Directive 97/66, in which it said that, '[i]t should [...] not be forgotten that the specific directive 97/66/EC only complements the general directive 95/46/EC by establishing specific legal and technical provisions. When revising the specific directive, it will be necessary to take into account, respect and be coherent with the provisions of the general data protection directive 95/46/EC, that applies to any processing of personal data falling under its scope, irrespective of the technical means used.' These provisions and the Working Party's opinion imply that both Directives apply cumulatively: Directive 95/46, being neutral with regard to its material scope, is the lex generalis for the processing of personal data, and Directive 2002/58, the material scope of which is specific for the electronic communications sector, is the lex specialis for the processing of personal data in the context of electronic communications, and both Directives interact according to the principle lex specialis derogat legi generali. There would, however, be one exception to this cumulative application: Directive 95/46 applies to natural persons only, whereas Article 1(2)—as explained by Recital 12—of Directive 2002/58 provides that this Directive also protects 'the legitimate interests of subscribers who are legal persons'.

Consequently, under this interpretation, except for the provisions with respect to legal persons, the scope of Directive 2002/58 is determined by the same criteria as those that determine the scope of Directive 95/46.

The second possible interpretation is based on the terminology used in Directive 2002/58 and the fact that it is not explicitly provided in Directive 2002/58 that its scope is determined by the same criteria as that of Directive 95/46. For instance, Article 3 of Directive 2002/58 does not seem to rely on the same criterion of territorial attachment as that of Directive 95/46 (see infra). In addition, some provisions do not seem to exclusively deal with the processing of personal data, for instance Article 5(3) about cookies (see infra). One could thus infer from this that Directive 2002/58, of course, deals with the processing of personal data in the framework of network and electronic communications services, but that it nevertheless does not have the same scope of territorial application as Directive 95/46 or even that it does not exclusively deal with the processing of personal data as is the case with Directive 95/46.

Below, it will be demonstrated that following the first or the second interpretation directly influences the determination of the precise scope of Directive 2002/58.

4.1.2. MATERIAL SCOPE: COOKIES AND OTHER LITTLE BROTHERS

Article 5(3) of Directive 2002/58 is vague as regards its material scope. It aims at regulating the use of electronic communications networks to store information or to gain access to information stored in the terminal equipment of a subscriber or user, but it neither refers to any specific technologies nor to any types of information that it covers.

As regards the technologies, this vagueness undoubtedly corresponds to the intention to remain as technology-neutral as possible. One source of interpretation is Recital 24, which provides some examples of technologies other than cookies that are covered: 'spyware, web bugs, hidden identifiers or other similar devices [that] can enter the user's terminal equipment without their knowledge in order to gain access to information, to store hidden information or to trace the activities of the user.'

The absence of an explanation of the term 'information' can lead to two possible interpretations of the types of information that are covered, depending on whether one sticks to the purpose of Directive 2002/58—which is to regulate the processing of personal data—or whether one thinks that the terminology used in Article 5(3) is aimed to be more neutral and silently departs from the Directive's purpose. If one emphasises the purpose of Directive 2002/58, which is, according to Article 1(1), to 'ensure an equivalent level of protection of fundamental rights and freedoms, and in particular the right to privacy, with respect to the processing of personal data in the electronic communication sector', then the information covered is limited to 'personal data' within the meaning of Article 2(a) of Directive 95/46. Consequently, under this interpretation, Article 5(3) only applies to cookies that store or gain access to data that is related to a natural person who is or can be identified. If, however, one stresses the difference in terminology between both Directives, ie the use of the term 'personal data' in Directive 95/46 and the use of the term 'information' in Directive 2002/58, then Article 5(3) applies to any information stored in the terminal equipment of a subscriber or user, whether or not this information consists of 'personal data'. It is clear that the scope under this interpretation is tremendously broader. One can find some support for this second interpretation in Recital 24 of Directive 2002/58, which provides that '[t]erminal equipment of users of electronic communications networks and any information stored on such computer equipment are part of the private sphere of the users requiring protection under the European Convention for the Protection of Human Rights and Fundamental Freedoms.' This Recital thus clearly says that information stored on terminal computer equipment is by definition part of the private sphere and seems to imply that Directive 2002/58 applies to such information and not only to information that is 'personal data' as defined in Directive 95/46. This interpretation is followed by the United Kingdom ('UK') Information Commissioner, who has explicitly stated that the UK Regulations (that implement Directive 2002/58) 'apply to all uses of such devices, *not just those involving the processing of personal data*' (emphasis added).

It has to be pointed out that Article 5(3) does not pay any attention to the purpose of the intrusion. It can be inferred from this that it applies no matter what the purpose is of the person or company that stores or accesses information.

4.1.3. TERRITORIAL SCOPE: WORLD-WIDE APPLICATION

One of the most relevant issues in practice is the question of when installing a cookie is subject to the rules set forth in Directive 2002/58. For instance, does the Directive apply to the situation in which a cookie is installed on an individual's hard drive which is located in the EU by an individual or a company located outside the Union, for instance in the US? Since the territorial scope of legal rules in the context of communications networks is usually complex, it is surprising that it can be inferred from the preparatory documents of Directive 2002/58 that its territorial scope was never discussed in any significant way during the drafting process.

The territorial scope of Directive 2002/58 is laid down in Articles 1(1) and 3(1). Article 1(1) provides that '[t]his Directive harmonises the provisions of the Member States required to ensure an equivalent level of protection of fundamental rights and freedoms, and in particular the right to privacy, with respect to the processing of personal data in the electronic communication sector and to ensure the free movement of such data and of electronic communication equipment and services *in the Community*.' (emphasis added). Article 3(1) provides that '[t]his Directive shall apply to the processing of personal data in connection with the provision of publicly available electronic communications services in public communication networks *in the Community*.' (emphasis added). According to these provisions, the criterion for determining whether the Directive territorially applies seems to be the fact that the personal data are processed in the framework of electronic communications services provided in public communications networks in the Community. The wording 'in the Community' does not only refer to 'public communications networks' but also to 'services', since a communication service is necessarily linked to a communications network; in addition, the European legislature confirms in Article 1(1) that it intends to regulate 'electronic communication services in the Community'. As a result, Directive 2002/58 would thus apply to a service provider established outside the EU offering electronic communication services to individuals situated in the EU.

At first sight, this constitutes a different scope from that of Directive 95/46, for the latter Directive's territorial point of attachment, set forth in its Article 4(1), is the establishment of the controller of the processing of personal data on the territory of an EU Member State, or, in the absence of such an establishment, the use of equipment, automated or otherwise, situated in an EU Member State. It thus seems that the territorial scope of Directive 2002/58, which follows the 'country of destination' principle, is much wider than that of Directive 95/46, which in principle does not apply to the processing of personal data conducted by a controller established outside the EU. This difference would be contrary to Article 1(2) of Directive 2002/58, which provides that this Directive 'particularises and complements' Directive 95/46 and can thus not have a wider territorial scope than the latter Directive.

However, it seems that, with regard to cookies, relying on the territorial point of attachment of Directive 95/46 does in fact not lead to a solution different from that resulting from Directive 95/46. The Article 29 Data Protection Working Party has indicated that, under its Article 4(1)(c), Directive 95/46 territorially applies if the controller of the processing (1) uses equipment over which he exercises at least partial control, and (2) has the intention to process personal data. In other words, the service provider thus has to have the intention to process personal data by means of the equipment, situated in an EU Member State, that is at its disposal. Accordingly, the simple act of using a publicly available communication network on the territory of the EU without the said intention does not suffice to justify the application of Directive 95/46. Applying this reasoning to cookies, the Working Party is of the opinion that Directive 95/46 applies to the installation of cookies on a computer located on the territory of the EU from outside the EU, since (1) a user's computer can be viewed as 'equipment' within the meaning of Article 4(1)(c) of Directive 95/46, (2) the installer of the cookie 'makes use' of that equipment when installing a cookie, and (3) 'the controller decided to use this equipment for the purposes of processing personal data and [...] several technical operations take place without the control of the data subject. The controller disposes over the user's equipment and this equipment is not used only for purposes of transit through Community territory.' The Working Party has consequently stated that the national law of the Member State where the user's computer is located applies to the question under what conditions his personal data may be collected by placing cookies on his hard drive.

Since the EU Member States' legislation implementing Directive 95/46 and Directive 2002/58 thus applies to persons and legal entities outside the Union (for instance those located in the US) installing cookies on a computer located on an EU Member State's territory, the European legal framework for the use of cookies has a tremendous extra-territorial application.

4.2. Assessment of the Legal Rules

The new legal framework for the use of cookies, laid down in Article 5(3) of Directive 2002/58, consists of two parts: (1) two substantive obligations, and (2) two exceptions to these obligations. It must be pointed out, however, that one must also comply with the rights and obligations set forth in Directive 95/46.

4.2.1. TWO SUBSTANTIVE OBLIGATIONS

Article 5(3) allows the use of electronic communications networks to store information or to gain access to information stored in the terminal equipment of a subscriber or user on the condition that the subscriber or the user (1) is provided with clear and comprehensive information in accordance with Directive 95/46, inter alia about the purposes of the processing, and (2) is offered the right to refuse such processing by the data controller. In other words, installing a cookie is subject to (a) an obligation to provide information, and (b) an obligation to offer a right to refuse.

OBLIGATION TO PROVIDE INFORMATION

The first condition set forth in Article 5(3) is that the user or subscriber is provided with clear and comprehensive information in accordance with Directive 95/46, inter alia about the purposes of the processing. The fact that Article 5(3) provides that information has to be provided 'in accordance with Directive 95/46' implies that the person placing the cookie must comply with the obligation to inform laid down in Article 10 of Directive 95/46. This information includes (1) the identity of the controller of the processing and of its representative, if any, (2) the purposes of the processing for which the personal data are intended, and (3) any further information such as (a) the recipients or categories of recipients of the personal data, (b) whether replies to the questions are obligatory or voluntary, as well as the possible consequences of failure to reply, and (c) the existence of the right of access to and the right to rectify the personal data. In all probability, the information about whether replies to the questions are obligatory or voluntary and about the consequences of failure to reply can be transposed to the cookie context into information about whether allowing a cookie to be placed is required or not to visit the website or make use of its service and about the consequences of not allowing a cookie to be placed. In this respect, Recital 25 of Directive 2002/58 provides that '[a]ccess to specific website content may still be made conditional on the well-informed acceptance of a cookie or similar device, if it is used for a legitimate purpose.' In other words, a legitimate consequence of not allowing a cookie may be that the individual cannot visit the website or make use of certain services.

It thus seems that Directive 2002/58 does not entail a new obligation to inform that is different from that set forth in Directive 95/46. Consequently, the question arises as to what the added value is of repeating the obligation to inform; the obligation to inform under Directive 95/46 applies anyway, since Recital 10 of Directive 2002/58 provides that '[i]n the electronic communications sector, Directive 95/46/EC applies in particular to all matters concerning protection of fundamental rights and freedoms, which are not specifically covered by the provisions of this Directive, including the obligations on the controller and the rights of individuals' (emphasis added).

A possible interpretation is that repeating the obligation to inform in Directive 2002/58 aims to—in the context of cookies—no longer distinguish between data of natural persons and data of legal persons. It could be argued that, since Article 1(2) of Directive 2002/58 provides that its provisions 'provide for protection of the legitimate interests of subscribers who are legal persons', the purpose of repeating the obligation to inform is that also subscribers who are legal persons have to be informed, and this in contrast with Directive 95/46, under which only natural persons have to be informed (since this Directive does not apply to data of legal persons). However, this interpretation would run counter to Recital 12 of Directive 2002/58, which provides that '[t]his Directive does not entail an obligation for Member States to extend the application of Directive 95/46 to the protection of the legitimate interests of legal persons'. It is unclear whether this then implies that there is no obligation to inform if the subscriber is a legal person.

Another—and the most plausible—interpretation is that repeating the obligation to inform in Directive 2002/58 aims to—in the context of cookies—no longer distinguish between 'personal data' (as defined in Article 2(a) of Directive 95/46) and 'non-personal data'. It could be argued that a person installing a cookie still has to provide information, even if that cookie processes data that do not identify a natural person or allow such person to be identified. This interpretation is in accordance with our assessment of the material scope of Article 5(3).

A consequence of explicitly referring to the obligation to inform about the purposes of the processing in accordance with Directive 95/46 is that Article 5(3) imposes another obligation, ie the obligation to comply with the requirement that the purposes of the processing be legitimate, as set forth in Articles 6 and 7 of Directive 95/46. This requirement is confirmed in Recital 24 of Directive 2002/58, which provides that '[t]he use of such devices should be allowed only for legitimate purposes, with the knowledge of the users concerned.' In this context, Recital 25 of Directive 2002/58 provides that 'such devices, for instance so-called 'cookies' can be a legitimate and useful tool, for example, in analysing the effectiveness of website design and advertising, and in verifying the identity of users engaged in on-line transactions.' It has to be pointed out that this again raises the question of whether or not this requirement applies with regard to data about legal persons.

OBLIGATION TO OFFER A RIGHT TO REFUSE

The second condition set forth in Article 5(3) of Directive 2002/58 is the offering of a 'right to refuse' the cookies. This terminology seems rather inappropriate, since the notion of refusal comes close to the notion of consent, which implies that the user would have only one single opportunity to deal with the cookie: If he does not refuse it the first time, then he can no longer withdraw his consent, for—according to Recital 25 (see infra)—the right to refuse can be offered once and cover any future use of the cookie during subsequent connections, which would thus deprive the user of any remedy during subsequent connections. It would undoubtedly have been better to use the term 'right to object', which is used in Directive 95/46 with regard to the processing of personal data for direct marketing purposes. The right to object can be exercised at any time, also during subsequent connections. In this respect, it has to be pointed out that, as mentioned above, technical solutions make it possible to suppress cookies at any time. The use of the right to object would have overcome the problem of multiple users of one terminal equipment, a problem which is explicitly addressed in Recital 25: 'Users should have the opportunity to refuse to have a cookies or similar device stored on their terminal equipment. This is particularly important where users other than the original user have access to the terminal equipment and thereby to any data containing privacysensitive information stored on such equipment.'An odd, circular problem of the rule that the offering of a right to refuse can cover subsequent connections is that, if the user or subscriber refuses the cookie, it is not clear how the service provider will be able to 'remember' this, since the provider is not allowed to install a cookie that contains the information that the user exercised his right to refuse. Maybe this may qualify as an example of the first exception to the obligation to provide information and a right to refuse (see infra).

Although the user or subscriber has a right to refuse cookies, he nevertheless has to bear the consequences of his refusal for further visiting the website or using a service, for—as already mentioned above in the context of the obligation to inform—Recital 25 of Directive 2002/58 provides that '[a]ccess to specific website content may still be made conditional on the wellinformed acceptance of a cookie or similar device, if it is used for a legitimate purpose.' This seems to imply that a service provider can refuse to give access to a service although the cookie installed on the computer is not necessary for the supply of the service. The existence of a legitimate purpose that justifies the use of a cookie suffices to permit the service provider to make the service conditional on the acceptance of the cookie.

WHO HAS TO COMPLY WITH THE OBLIGATIONS?

Article 5(1) of Directive 2002/58 does not specify who has to comply with the obligations to provide information and to offer the right to refuse, which seems to imply that it is the person or company that uses the cookie concerned. It is worth noting that Recital 25 of the Common Position No 26/2002 on Directive 2002/58 provided that these obligations had to be complied with by 'the operator of a website sending such devices or allowing third parties to send them via his website'. It is not clear why the latter wording has been deleted in the final version of the Directive, since it is an appropriate point of view. The UK Information Commissioner's point of view on this issue seems to be based on the Common Position's wording: 'The Regulations [ie the UK legislation implementing Directive 2002/58] do not define who should be responsible for providing the information outlined in Regulation 6(2). Where a person operates an on-line service and any use of a cookie type device will be for their purposes only, it is clear that that person will be responsible for providing the information in question. We recognise that it is possible for organisations to use cookie type devices on websites seemingly within the control of another organisation, for example through a third party advertisement on a website. In such cases the organisation to whom the site primarily refers will be obliged to alert users to the fact that a third party advertiser operates cookies. It will not be sufficient for that organisation to provide a statement to the effect that they cannot be held responsible for any use of such devices employed by other persons they allow to place content on their websites. In addition, the third party would also have a responsibility to provide the user with the relevant information.'

WHEN AND HOW MUST THE OBLIGATIONS BE COMPLIED WITH?

Recital 25 of Directive 2002/58 provides more guidelines as regards when and how the obligations to provide information and to offer a right to refuse must be complied with: 'Information and the right to refuse may be offered once for the use of various devices to be installed on the user's terminal equipment during the same connection and also covering any further use that may be made of those devices during subsequent connections. The methods for giving information, offering a right to refuse or requesting consent should be made as userfriendly as possible.'

As regards the moment to comply with the obligations, this provision seems to require a website to provide information and offer the right to refuse at the moment that the connection is made.

It is, however, not clear how the obligations have to be complied with. The text of Article 5(3) of Directive 2002/58 provides that the subscriber or user has to be 'provided with' the information and must be 'offered' a right to refuse. Similarly, Recital 25 merely provides that users 'should *have the opportunity* to refuse' (emphasis added). It is not clear whether or not this means that the information and the right to refuse expressly have to be brought to the individual's attention by means of an actively directed communication, for instance in the form of a pop-up window. Recital 25 does not explicitly prescribe that a pop-up window be used, but specifies that '[t]he methods for giving information, offering a right to refuse or requesting consent should be made as user-friendly as possible.' This terminology seems to imply that there has to be a specific communication addressed to the user or subscriber and that it does not suffice for the person who has to comply with the obligations to have recourse to a simple technical 'possibility' for the subscriber or user to access the information and exercise the right to refuse the cookies. This interpretation finds support in Recital 25, which provides that the information and the right to refuse may be offered once covering any further use that may be made of cookies during subsequent connections; if the information only has to be accessible to the user, then this concession would be of no practical interest.

The UK Information Commissioner seems to share this opinion, by saying that '[t]he requirement that the user or subscriber should be 'given the opportunity to refuse' the use of the cookie type device may be subject to differing interpretation. At the very least, however, the user or subscriber should be given a clear choice as to whether or not they wish to allow a service provider to engage in the continued storage of information on the terminal in question … *The fact that an 'opportunity to refuse' such storage or access must be provided imposes a greater obligation on the relevant party than that they should simply make such a refusal a possibility.'* (emphasis added). In translating this into practice, however, the Commissioner takes a rather pragmatic view: 'The mechanism by which a subscriber or user may exercise their right to refuse continued storage should, therefore, be prominent, intelligible and readily available to all, not just the most literate or technically aware. Where the relevant information is to be included in a privacy policy, for example, the policy should be clearly signposted at least on those pages where a user may enter a website. The relevant information should appear in the policy in a way that is suitably prominent and accessible and it should be worded so that all users and subscribers are capable of understanding and acting upon it, without difficulty. [...] Although a standard approach would be beneficial, whether service providers choose to make their own switch off facilities available or else explain to the user or subscriber how they can use the facilities specific to their browser type is less important than that the mechanism is uncomplicated, easy to understand and accessible to all. There is, in addition, nothing to prevent service providers from requiring users to 'opt in' to receipt of the cookie as opposed to providing them with the opportunity to 'opt out'.' The Information Commissioner thus seems to be of the opinion that it might suffice to provide the information and offer the right to refuse in a privacy policy visibly posted on the website.

As regards the obligation to offer a right to refuse, this opinion would then boil down to explaining in the privacy policy how the webbrowser can be used to refuse cookies. However, as regards the right to refuse, the Commissioner's statements seems to be inherently contradictory, since it is not clear what the difference is between simply making a refusal a possibility (which the Commissioner says is insufficient) and merely explaining in a privacy policy how a webbrowser can be used to refuse cookies (which the Commissioner says is sufficient). In any event, it would be logical that, unless an exception applies (see infra), a cookie may not be installed at the moment itself that an individual visits a website, since he then would not have had the opportunity to refuse the cookie.

As regards the obligation to inform, it is worth mentioning in this respect that in the Common Position version of Directive 2002/58, Article 5(3) provided that the user had to 'receive in advance' the information, and Recital 25 provided that 'clear and precise prior information' had to be provided (emphasis added). The fact that in the Directive's final version the wording 'in advance' in Article 5(3) and 'prior' in Recital 25 has been deleted and that the term 'receive' in Article 5(3) has been replaced by 'provide with', may be an argument for contending that providing information in a privacy policy (which is, as opposed to a pop-up window, a 'passive' way of communicating) is sufficient. However, this argument is not valid for offering the right to refuse.

4.2.2. TWO EXCEPTIONS

The second sentence of Article 5(3) of Directive 2002/58 contains a—rather enigmatic—exception to this general regime: 'This shall not prevent any technical storage or access for the sole purpose of carrying out or facilitating the transmission of a communication over an electronic communications network, or as strictly necessary in order to provide an information society service explicitly requested by the subscriber or user.'

The use of the wording 'this shall not prevent' does not make it easy to assess the exact scope of this exception. Does it aim to waive the obligation to provide information and/or to offer a right to refuse? Or does it allow the person or company that has to comply with the obligations to inform and offer the right to refuse to ignore the user's refusal? The Recitals do not provide any guidelines for answering this question. It may be useful to examine whether the national laws implementing Directive 2002/58 shed light on this matter. In the UK, for instance, Article 6(1) of the implementing Regulations provides that '[s]ubject to paragraph (4), a person shall not use an electronic communications network to store information, or to gain access to information stored, in the terminal equipment of a subscriber or user unless the requirements of paragraph (2) are met.' Paragraph 2 contains the obligations to inform and offer the opportunity to refuse. Paragraph 4 then provides that '[p]aragraph (1) shall not apply to the technical storage of, or access to, information for [...] the above-mentioned exceptions' (emphasis added). The wording 'shall not apply' seems to imply that, in such cases, the service provider does not have the obligation to provide information and offer a right to refuse.

The Directive's exception regime applies only in the event of a 'technical storage or access' for one or two possible purposes. It is not clear what such 'technical storage or access' exactly means. A plausible interpretation may be that the required 'technical' nature of the storage or access implies that there may not be any processing of personal data for the exception regime to apply.

A first situation in which a technical storage or access qualifies as an exception is if it is 'for the sole purpose of carrying out or facilitating the transmission of a communication over an electronic communications network'. It is not really clear what this exception exactly means, but it seems to intend to allow the use of mere session cookies. This interpretation is based on the Recital that the European Parliament proposed when it amended the European Commission's initial proposal with a provision about cookies. This proposed Recital referred to session cookies in general terms: 'The prohibition of storage of communications [...] by persons other than the users without the users' consent is not intended to prohibit any *automatic, intermediate and transient storage* of this information in so far as this takes place for the sole purpose of carrying out the transmission in the electronic communications network and provided that the information is not stored for any period longer than is necessary for the transmission [...]' (emphasis added). Although the European Parliament's proposal for a prohibition of cookies was replaced by a permission to install cookies in combination with an obligation to provide information and to offer a right to refuse, this first exception (although slightly reworded) was maintained in the Directive's final version, so that the Parliament's proposal is a solid basis for interpretation.

In any event, it is clear that the purpose of carrying out or facilitating the transmission of a communication has to be the sole purpose; if there is another, concurrent purpose, then the exception does not apply.

A second situation in which a technical storage or access qualifies as an exception is if it is 'as strictly necessary in order to provide an information society service explicitly requested by the subscriber or user'. The term 'information society services' is not defined in Directive 2002/58 but in Article 1(a) of Directive 98/34/EC of 22 June 1998 laying down a procedure for the provision of information in the field of technical standards and regulations, as explicitly referred to by Article 2(a) of the EU E-Commerce Directive. It means 'any service normally provided for remuneration, at a distance, by electronic means and at the individual request of a recipient of services'. Directive 98/34 does not explicitly explain what 'normally provided for remuneration' exactly means, but it is generally accepted that this means that the service has to be an economic activity. According to the case law of the European Court of Justice, an economic activity does not necessarily require that the beneficiary of the service pays for the service; the fact that a third party pays the provider of the service is sufficient (for instance a service provider which offers certain on-line services for free, which is made possible by revenue coming from advertisement fees paid by third parties).

Does this second exception imply that, if an individual has requested an information society service that involves collecting information regarding usage, it follows that he does not have to be informed and does not have a right to refuse the cookies concerned? It is hard to answer this question in abstracto; it will depend on whether the use of the cookie corresponds to a 'technical storage or access' (as mentioned above, it is not clear what this exactly means) and whether the cookie is 'strictly necessary'. The Directive does not give any information about how the wording 'as strictly necessary' should be interpreted. Something to hold on to can be found in the UK Information Commissioner's Guidelines, which provide that '[t]he term 'strictly necessary' means that such storage of or access to information should be essential, as opposed to reasonably necessary, for this exemption to apply. It will also, however, be restricted to what is essential for the provision of the service requested by the user, rather than what might be essential for any other uses the service provider might wish to make of that data. It will also include what is required for compliance with any other legislation to which the service provider might be subject, for example, the security requirements of the seventh data protection principle [...]. Where the use of a cookie type device is deemed 'important' as opposed to 'strictly necessary' the user of the device is still obliged to provide information about the device to the potential service recipient so that they can decide whether or not they wish to proceed. The information provided to the user about the uses the collector intends to make of that data should be of sufficient clarity to enable the user to make a truly informed decision.'

4.2.3. OTHER OBLIGATIONS UNDER DIRECTIVE 95/46 REMAIN APPLICABLE

Since Recital 10 of Directive 2002/58 provides that Directive 95/46 applies to all matters which are not specifically covered by the provisions of Directive 2002/58, including the obligations on the controller and the rights of individuals, persons and companies that place cookies have to comply with all provisions of Directive 95/46, such as the obligation to notify the national supervisory authority (provided in its Article 18) or the data subject's right of access to the personal data (provided in its Article 12), but only on the condition that the application criteria of Directive 95/46 are met. Amongst other things, this means that other obligations under Directive 95/46 apply only in the event that via the cookie 'personal data', as defined in its Article 2(a), are processed; these obligations do not apply if data related to legal persons or 'non-personal data' related to natural persons (for instance, data that do not identify or allow to identify a natural person) are processed.

The UK Information Commissioner is of the same opinion, saying that '[w]here the use of a cookie type device does involve the processing of personal data, service providers will·be required to ensure that they comply with the additional requirements of the *Data Protection Act 1988* [which implemented Directive 95/46]. This includes the requirements of the third data protection principle which states that data controllers shall not process personal data that is excessive [...]. Where personal data is collected, the data controller should consider the extent to which that data can be effectively processed anonymously. This is likely to be of particular relevance where the data is to be processed for a purpose other than the provision of the service directly requested by the user, for example the counting of visitors to a website.'

A provision of Directive 95/46 that does not apply is Article 7. This Article, which enumerates the few situations in which personal data may be processed, is overridden by Article 5(3) of Directive 2002/46: One is allowed to process personal data via cookies in any situation, also situations that are not enumerated in Article 7, provided that the obligations to provide information and offer a right to refuse are complied with.

One of the far-reaching consequences of the extra-territorial application of Directives 95/46 and 2002/58 to service providers established outside the EU placing cookies on hard drives of computers situated in the EU, is that these service providers, when processing personal data via such cookies, have to comply with Article 18 of Directive 95/46, which provides that they have to notify the supervisory authority of the EU Member States before placing any such cookie. An important issue in this respect is that Member States are allowed to provide certain exemptions from notification, which implies that a service provider placing such cookies may have to be obliged to notify the supervisory authority of one Member State while it may be exempted from notification in another Member State.

Such 'foreign' service providers also have to comply with Article 25 of Directive 95/46, which provides that the transfer of personal data from an EU Member State to a country outside the EU is allowed only if that country has an adequate level of protection of personal data. Article 25 applies since personal data are collected on the territory of an EU Member State, ie on the hard drives of computers located on that territory, and are subsequently electronically transferred outside the EU.

If a country has an adequate level of protection, then such transfer is allowed. As regards a service provider established in the US, this means that it is allowed to perform such transfers via cookies if it has adhered to the US Safe Harbor Principles.

According to Article 26 of Directive 95/46, other relevant grounds on which such transfers are allowed—even if the country to which the personal data are transferred does not have an adequate level of protection—are (1) the fact that the data subject has given his unambiguous consent to the transfer, (2) the transfer is necessary for the performance of a contract between the data subject and the controller or the implementation of precontractual measures taken in response to the data subject's request (for instance, in the context of electronic commerce), and (3) the transfer is necessary for the conclusion or performance of a contract concluded in the interest of the data subject between the controller and a third party.

If, however, the service provider is established in a country that has no adequate level of protection (for instance, an American company that has not adhered to the US Safe Harbor Principles) or cannot rely on one of the situations set forth in Article 26, then it is not allowed to transfer personal data via cookies outside the EU. This is again an example of the far-reaching consequences of the extra-territorial application of Directive 2002/58 ...

[Footnotes omitted]

 NOTES AND QUESTIONS

1   Directive 2002/58 is probably the first statutory legal framework in the world that specifically deals with the use of cookies. But how clear is the Directive? What is the exact interaction between Directive 2002/58 and its mother Directive 95/46?

2   What is the relationship between the introduction of the new concept of the right to 'refuse' and the right to 'object' used in Directive 95/46?

3   How are the obligations to provide information and offer a right to refuse to be complied with?

8   Data protection in Singapore

In 2002, the Model Data Protection Code was developed for the private sector in Singapore. This Model Code is a comprehensive, voluntary code modelled on internationally recognised minimum standards for electronic data protection. This Model Code is now in use in a voluntary co-regulation data protection scheme. A large majority of the sections in the Model Code were developed from the Canadian Standards Association's Model Code for the Protection of Personal Information adopted in 1996.

The Model Code by and large would satisfy the EU adequacy requirements. It applies to all data subjects regardless of nationality. However, as personal data is defined as being in electronic form, it would appear that the Model Code differs from the EU *Data Protection Directive* in that it does not apply to manual filing systems. The Model Code is designed to apply to all processing of personal data regardless of purpose, subject to a number of exceptions. The exceptions are fairly uncontroversial and they concern personal use, journalistic, artistic and literary purposes, research and statistical purposes, national security and law enforcement. It should be noted that the Model Code does not allow for loose secondary purposes permitted under the Australian legislation. There is no direct marketing exception. However, it must be remembered that the Model Code is not a statute and its development did not suffer from the intense industry pressures the Australian legislature was subjected to.

----

9   The Internet and privacy

Computers are designed to capture, store and manipulate data. No other machine in history has been better at this task than the computer. With the advent of the Internet, the power of the computer to collect and manipulate data grew exponentially. Whenever one uses the Internet, one leaves a trail, which provides information on where you were, what you saw, and what you did there. Electronic footprints left behind are everlasting.

Privacy issues have only been addressed at the international level in recent years, and concerted international effort to protect individual privacy has only just begun. For some countries, the concept of protecting privacy is still a novel one. While the Internet has been the impetus for instruments such as the European Union Data Protection Directive, countries such as Australia are still grappling with the basic concept of privacy and have barely touched upon the implications of the Internet on privacy specifically. We will see, in coming years, a growing awareness both internationally and domestically of the issues. It is only then that privacy problems peculiar to the Internet, such as e-mail privacy in the workplace, will be able to be tackled, either legally or technologically.

Encryption

- -

1   Introduction

We saw in Chapter 4 the importance of privacy to e-commerce and other transactions on the Internet. In this chapter, we look at encryption, which can simply be described as a tool to achieve privacy on the Internet. Encryption also plays a significant role in relation to authentication. As a general tool for privacy, it too is relevant to both e-commerce and non-e-commerce activity. Encryption, however, has been particularly prevalent in e-commerce for the obvious reason of necessity. Its use, however, is subject to legal concerns beyond privacy and in this chapter, we will examine the legal issues raised by encryption technologies.

Cryptography is the art of using mathematical codes and algorithms to scramble text so that it appears random to all statistical tests and can, therefore, only be read by specified individuals. While it is not a recent science, the need for cryptography has increased markedly since the arrival of widespread, near instantaneous, global communications. The peculiar demands of the Internet have brought cryptography, and encryption, to the attention of many who might previously have thought it irrelevant. Previously, cryptography was almost entirely the domain of government experts seeking to protect national security and defence information. Increasingly, private enterprise has found the need to protect the security of its own information in the corporate world.

We have always sought to secure both our means of communication and our communiqués. Before electronic communication, solutions were found in envelopes, bank vaults, certified couriers, locked filing cabinets, and alarms. On the Internet, there are no locks, no doors, and no security guards to secure information physically. Instead, encryption has become the electronic adaptation of these age-old techniques.

Encryption at its simplest can be explained as a process, or a series of steps.

1   A message is written.
2   The message is encoded using a key and a complex mathematical algorithm.
3   The message is sent.
4   The message is received and a key, related to the original algorithm, is used to decode the message.
5   The message is then read.

Why do we need encryption?

Why do we need encryption? Before a brief explanation of how encryption works, this simple question must first be answered. We need encryption because of the mechanics of the Internet. When information is communicated on the Internet, in forms such as a web page, an e-mail, or a search term, it moves through innumerable separate computers called routers. This journey is never preordained and is decided according to traffic flows of information across the Internet. Because information flows randomly and across numerous computers, it is possible to create software which screens information running through a certain point. This software can monitor all the information and sift out sections according to pointers, such as keywords, which might have been selected by the programmer. Therefore, in theory, anything that moves through the infrastructure of the Internet can be intercepted and read by third parties for whom it was not intended. This is why we need encryption.

----

2   Encryption explained

There are two basic types of cryptographic system. Symmetric key ciphers, where both sides use the same key, were the earliest forms of encryption technique, and asymmetric systems that utilise a key pair. The Data Encryption Standard (DES) and the Improved Data Encryption Algorithm (IDEA) are two of the more widely used symmetric key ciphers. In fact, DES has been used in the banking and finance sectors for decades. More recently, the Advanced Encryption Standard (AES) has been developed to meet the needs of the new millennium and the US government has adopted Rijndael as the AES algorithm.[1] The method is simple. Write a message, encode it with a key, and send it to someone who holds the same key. The recipient then simply decodes the message. The key can be as long or short as required. The longer the key, the more secure the message. The difficulty with symmetric key cryptography, however, relates to the security of the key. The system requires two identical keys and can therefore only be as secure as the method of transporting the keys. If a key is lost, stolen, or otherwise revealed, the system is compromised. One solution to the problem of key management and transportation lies in the second main type of system, public-key cryptography.

Public-key cryptography is an example of an asymmetric system, of which the most utilised example is RSA, named for the cryptographers who created it, and it uses two different, but mathematically related, keys. Using the RSA software a person can create two keys, known as a 'key pair'. One key is used to encode, the other to decode. One of these keys is called the public key, the other is the private key, both of which can encode and decode. The public key is a unique, individual key but it is designed to be freely distributed to anyone who requires it. The associated private key is kept by the individual. When a third party wants to send a message to our key holder, they encode it using the freely available public key. Once it is encoded with a particular public key, only the associated private key can decode the message. Therefore, the message can be sent through standard channels by anyone who has the public key, but can only be read by the intended recipient, the holder of the private key. Alternatively, a person can encode a message using a private key. This can then only be decoded using the associated public key. But the public key is freely available. Consequently, this use does not prevent the content of the mail being viewed; instead, using the system in this fashion acts as a guarantee of authenticity—a signature, if you will.

One-way-hash functions are a feature of cryptography which have a particular use in digital signatures. A one-way-hash function is an algorithm which, unlike a key, has no relation to any other algorithm and which is freely available. When the hash function is applied to simple text (a process called the 'crunch'), a number, known as a hash, is produced. The number is of a determined bit length depending on the size of the function—for example a 128-bit hash—and the longer the hash, the more secure the algorithm. The algorithm cannot be reversed, unlike key cryptography. Therefore, if a person is presented only with a 128-bit hash it is effectively useless; there is no way of knowing what the simple text is.

A one-way-hash function alone makes a perverse tool of encryption because it is impossible to reproduce the original simple text once a hash is created. Fortunately, this is not its purpose. A hash is usually included at the end of the simple text message that was the basis for its creation. Therefore, the recipient can verify a message by using the same simple text and the same one-way-hash function. If the new hash matches the hash in the message, it is guaranteed that the simple text sent with the hash has not been altered.

---

1   See the NIST home page at <http://www.nist.gov/aes/> 5 June 2002 for up-to-date information.

The final significant component of encryption is the phenomenon known as public-key infrastructure (PKI). Glenn Pure and Greg Taylor provide the following explanation of PKI:

> … In short, the purpose of a PKI is to provide a place for people to post their public keys. The PKI would normally be used for the public-key pair used for message signature. Most users also possess a second public-key pair used solely for encryption. Current trends are not to lodge the encryption public key with a PKI.
>
> PKIs are more than just simple 'notice boards' for public keys. They must do a host of other things before they are of much use including:
>
> • They must have a means for providing confidence that a particular public key belongs to a particular user. The way this is usually done is for the person who wants to lodge their key to show up in person at an office of the PKI and produce proof of their identity. The PKI will then take their public key and digitally sign it with the PKI's own key (in a tamper-proof way) to prove that the PKI has verified the key belongs to its correct owner.
>
> • PKIs must have a way of revoking keys if a user happens to lose or compromise their private key (just as a credit card owner who loses their card needs to cancel it as quickly as possible).
>
> • They must store old public keys so that for example, in the event of a dispute at some time in the future, the old public key can be retrieved and used to settle the dispute.
>
> The development of PKIs around the world is in its infancy and a number of different models are being used. Some models are relatively simple and require the key owner to take responsibility for key revocation and key archiving. Other systems, like that proposed for Australia, would provide a full range of services to users.[2]

In practice the public-key system is heavy on processing. It takes large amounts of computing power to encode and decode entire messages using this process. This means that it is only really practical to send short messages, such as signatures, using this system. Which brings us full-circle. Public-key cryptography is often used to encode a message which includes a symmetrical key. This way the transport of the symmetrical key is secure, and the subsequent messages, which are too long for the public-key cryptography, can be easily coded and decoded.

Peter D Junger v William Daley, United States Secretary of Commerce, et al

United States Court of Appeals for the Sixth Circuit, 4 April 2000, 2000 FED App 0117P (6th Cir)

Available at <http://www.cdt.org/crypto/litigation/000404junger.shtml> 17 August 2006

---

2   <http://www.efa.org.au/Issues/Crypto/cryptfaq.html> 17 September 2001.

Martin, Chief Judge; Clay, Circuit Judge; Weber, District Judge:

Encryption is the process of converting a message from its original form ('plaintext') into a scrambled form ('ciphertext'). Most encryption today uses an algorithm, a mathematical transformation from plaintext to ciphertext, and a key that acts as a password. Generally, the security of the message depends on the strength of both the algorithm and the key.

Encryption has long been a tool in the conduct of military and foreign affairs. Encryption has many civil applications, including protecting communication and data sent over the Internet. As technology has progressed, the methods of encryption have changed from purely mechanical processes, such as the Enigma machines of Nazi Germany, to modern electronic processes. Today, messages can be encrypted through dedicated electronic hardware and also through general-purpose computers with the aid of encryption software.

For a general-purpose computer to encrypt data, it must use encryption software that instructs the computer's circuitry to execute the encoding process. Encryption software, like all computer software, can be in one of two forms: object code or source code. Object code represents computer instructions as a sequence of binary digits (0s and 1s) that can be directly executed by a computer's microprocessor. Source code represents the same instructions in a specialized programming language, such as BASIC, C, or Java. Individuals familiar with a particular computer programming language can read and understand source code. Source code, however, must be converted into object code before a computer will execute the software's instructions. This conversion is conducted by compiler software. Although compiler software is typically readily available, some source code may have no compatible compiler.

NOTES AND QUESTIONS

1 The distinction between object code and source code, discussed by the judges in *Junger*, was relevant to the question before the court. The case is extracted further below.

2 Were you aware of the possibilities for interception before you began to study the Internet? Do you think the majority of Internet users are aware of the potential for surveillance?

3 What steps do you take to guard the integrity of your file system or your communications? What steps can you take?

4 Explain the operation of public-key cryptography in your own words. Are you satisfied that this method is the most secure method for encoding communications?

5 What is the weakest link in the encryption chain?

----

3   The encryption controversies

The need for the protection of information in the private sector becomes apparent as soon as we realise just how much information now exists as bytes on a computer: banking details, medical records, national accounts information, air traffic information, commercially valuable information of all varieties, politically sensitive material, and of course military and defence information. Increasing corporate reliance upon electronic mechanisms (not only the Internet, but a wide range of technologies) means that the continued growth of commerce depends to some extent on the degree to which the security of valuable information and communications can be guaranteed. Encryption has been used in particular industries for specific purposes for many decades. It seems logical that it should extend into standard business practice, and into everyday usage. However, there are complications.

It was not by accident that cryptography was the almost exclusive domain of government experts for most of the postwar years. Until very recently, it was felt by Western nations that national security interests would be threatened by an unfettered distribution of encryption throughout the private sector and foreign, non-allied countries. Various restrictions were placed on encryption technologies due to fears, first, about the consequences of these falling into the hands of uncooperative states, and second, that it would make it more difficult to monitor criminal activity. In the USA in particular, these restrictions led to a number of cases which centred on their constitutionality in the light of the First Amendment.

(a)   Encryption and the US Constitution

Peter D Junger v William Daley, United States Secretary of Commerce, et al

United States Court of Appeals for the Sixth Circuit, 4 April 2000, 2000 FED App 0117P
(6th Cir)

Available at <http://www.cdt.org/crypto/litigation/000404junger.shtml> 17 August 2006

Martin, Chief Judge; Clay, Circuit Judge; Weber, District Judge:
... Junger filed this action to make a facial challenge to the Regulations on First Amendment grounds, seeking declaratory and injunctive relief that would permit him to engage in the unrestricted distribution of encryption software through his web site. Junger claims that encryption source code is protected speech. The district court granted summary judgment in favor of the defendants, holding that encryption source code is not protected under the First Amendment, that the Regulations are permissible content-neutral regulations, and that the Regulations are not subject to facial challenge on prior restraint grounds.

We review the grant of summary judgment de novo. *See Smith v Wal-Mart Stores, Inc*, 167 F 3d 286 at 289 (6th Cir 1999).

The issue of whether or not the First Amendment protects encryption source code is a difficult one because source code has both an expressive feature and a functional feature. The United States does not dispute that it is possible to use encryption source code to represent and convey information and ideas about cryptography and that encryption source code can be used by programmers and scholars for such informational purposes. Much like a mathematical or scientific formula, one can describe the function and design of encryption software by a prose explanation; however, for individuals fluent in a computer programming language, source code is the most efficient and precise means by which to communicate ideas about cryptography.

The district court concluded that the functional characteristics of source code overshadow its simultaneously expressive nature. The fact that a medium of expression has a functional capacity should not preclude constitutional protection. Rather, the appropriate consideration of the medium's functional capacity is in the analysis of permitted government regulation.

The Supreme Court has explained that 'all ideas having even the slightest redeeming social importance', including those concerning 'the advancement of truth, science, morality, and arts' have the full protection of the First Amendment (*Roth v United States*, 354 US 476 at 484 (1957), quoting 1 J*ournals of the Continental Congress* 108 (1774)). This protection is not reserved for purely expressive communication. The Supreme Court has recognized First Amendment protection for symbolic conduct, such as draft-card burning, that has both functional and expressive features. *See United States v O'Brien*, 391 US 367 (1968).

The Supreme Court has expressed the versatile scope of the First Amendment by labeling as 'unquestionably shielded' the artwork of Jackson Pollock, the music of Arnold Schönberg, or the Jabberwocky verse of Lewis Carroll (*Hurly v Irish-American Gay, Lesbian and Bisexual Group*, 515 US 557 at 569 (1995)). Though unquestionably expressive, these things identified by the Court are not traditional speech. Particularly, a musical score cannot be read by the majority of the public but can be used as a means of communication among musicians. Likewise, computer source code, though unintelligible to many, is the preferred method of communication among computer programmers.

Because computer source code is an expressive means for the exchange of information and ideas about computer programming, we hold that it is protected by the First Amendment.

The functional capabilities of source code, and particularly those of encryption source code, should be considered when analyzing the governmental interest in regulating the exchange of this form of speech. Under intermediate scrutiny, the regulation of speech is valid, in part, if 'it furthers an important or substantial governmental interest' (O'Brien, 391 US at 377). In *Turner Broadcasting System v FCC*, 512 US 622 at 664 (1994), the Supreme Court noted that although an asserted governmental interest may be important, when the government defends restrictions on speech 'it must do more than simply "posit the existence of the disease sought to be cured" ' (*id*, quoting *Quincy Cable TV, Inc v FCC*, 768 F 2d 1434 at 1455 (DC Cir 1985)). The government 'must demonstrate that the recited harms are real, not merely conjectural, and that the regulation will in fact alleviate these harms in a direct and material way' (id). We recognize that national security interests can outweigh the interests of protected speech and require the regulation of speech. In the present case, the record does not resolve whether the exercise of presidential power in furtherance of national security interests should overrule the interests in allowing the free exchange of encryption source code.

Before any level of judicial scrutiny can be applied to the Regulations, Junger must be in a position to bring a facial challenge to these regulations. In light of the recent amendments to the Export Administration Regulations, the district court should examine the new regulations to determine if Junger can bring a facial challenge.

For the foregoing reasons, we reverse the district court and remand the case to the district court for consideration of Junger's constitutional challenge to the amended regulations.

Daniel J Bernstein v United States Department of Justice, et al

United States Court of Appeals for the Ninth Circuit, No 97-16686, DC No CV-97-00582, 6 May 1999, at pp 4234–5

Available at <http://www.cdt.org/crypto/litigation/bernstein4.html> 17 August 2006

Judge B Fletcher:

[6] ... The government, in fact, does not seriously dispute that source code is used by cryptographers for expressive purposes. Rather, the government maintains that source code is different from other forms of expression (such as blueprints, recipes, and 'how-to' manuals) because it can be used to control directly the operation of a computer without conveying information to the user. In the government's view, by targeting this unique functional aspect of source code, rather than the content of the ideas that may be expressed therein, the export regulations manage to skirt entirely the concerns of the First Amendment. This argument is flawed for at least two reasons.

[7] First, it is not at all obvious that the government's view reflects a proper understanding of source code. As noted earlier, the distinguishing feature of source code is that it is meant to be read and understood by humans, and that it cannot be used to control directly the functioning of a computer. While source code, when properly prepared, can be easily compiled into object code by a user, ignoring the distinction between source and object code obscures the important fact that source code is not meant solely for the computer, but is rather written in a language intended also for human analysis and understanding.

[8] Second, and more importantly, the government's argument, distilled to its essence, suggests that even one drop of 'direct functionality' overwhelms any constitutional protections that expression might otherwise enjoy. This cannot be so. The distinction urged on us by the government would prove too much in this era of rapidly evolving computer capabilities. The fact that computers will soon be able to respond directly to spoken commands, for example, should not confer on the government the unfettered power to impose prior restraints on speech in an effort to control its 'functional' aspects. The First Amendment is concerned with expression, and we reject the notion that the admixture of functionality necessarily puts expression beyond the protections of the Constitution.

 NOTES AND QUESTIONS

1   How significant is the US Constitution in the jurisprudence of the Internet? To what extent does the Bill of Rights, particularly the First Amendment, regulate the behaviour of all Internet users?

2   Do you agree that source code is a form of expression or do you consider it to be merely a functional instruction set?

(b)   Encryption and the politics of trade

Restrictions on the trade in cryptography are internationally codified in the *Wassenaar Arrangement on Export Controls for Conventional Arms and Dual-Use Goods and Technologies*.[3] The Wassenaar Arrangement controls the export of weapons and of dual-use goods, that is, goods that can be used both for a military and for a civil purpose. Cryptography is such a dual-use good. In 1995, 28 countries decided to re-group to follow-up the work of COCOM (Coordinating Committee for Multilateral Export Controls).

The Wassenaar Arrangement was finalised in July 1996 and the agreement was signed by 31 countries. The initial provisions were largely the same as old COCOM regulations. The General Software Note (GSN), applicable until the December 1998 revision, excluded mass market and public-domain crypto software from the controls. Australia, France, New Zealand, Russia, and the US deviated from the GSN and controlled the export of mass market and public domain crypto software. There is however a personal use exemption, allowing export of products accompanying their user for the user's personal use for example on a computer notebook.

The Wassenaar Arrangement was revised in December 1998 and 2000 so that currently, all symmetric crypto products of up to 56 bits, all asymmetric crypto products of up to 512 bits, and all subgroup-based crypto products (including elliptic curve) of up to 112 bits can be freely exported. Mass market symmetric crypto software and hardware can also be freely exported. There has been no change in the provisions on public domain cryptography, hence all public domain cryptography software is still free for export.

The question of course remains whether technically, any transfer through the Internet can be classed as export.

The OECD announced, in its 1997 *Cryptography Policy Guidelines*,[4] that it supported the relaxation of the majority of restrictions on cryptography.

In accordance with the Wassenaar Arrangement, Australia provides strict controls for the export of cryptographic products under the *Customs Act 1901*, in particular the *Customs (Prohibited Exports) Regulations*—Schedule 13E and the *Customs Act 1901* section 112 (*Prohibited Exports*). A review of cryptography in Australia, entitled *Review of Policy Relating to Encryption Technologies*,[5] was recently conducted. The Walsh Report, as it is known, had an uncertain future due to controversy surrounding its release.

The United Kingdom has been the most vehement supporter of controls on cryptography. Policy documents on the future direction of encryption controls, released in the same year as the OECD Guidelines, took a line of reasoning that was the Guidelines' polar opposite. However, subsequently there was a relaxation in the British stance, bringing it closer to the OECD position.

The OECD, the EU, and the US judiciary put pressure on the US Government. Eventually, in 2000, the restrictions on export of encryption technology were relaxed for certain, mostly Western, countries. There was further relaxation on the restrictions in

---

3   See further the web site <http://www.wassenaar.org>.
4   <http://www.oecd.org/dsti/iccp/crypto_e.html> 12 September 2001.
5   <http://www.efa.org.au/Issues/Crypto/Walsh/walsh.htm> 12 September 2001.

June 2002 (see <http://www.bis.doc.gov/Encryption/EncFactSheet6_17_02.html>) and December 2004 (http://www.bis.doc.gov/Encryption/). Restrictions remain on exports to so-called 'terrorist supporting' countries.

Department of Commerce Bureau of Export Administration, 15 CFR Parts 732, 734, 740, 742, 744, 748, 770, 772, and 774 [Docket No 001006282–0282–01] RIN 0694–AC32, *Revisions to Encryption Items*

Federal Register/Vol 65, No 203/Thursday, 19 October 2000/Rules and Regulations p 62600

Available at <http://www.bxa.doc.gov/Encryption/pdfs/EncryptionRuleOct2K.pdf>
12 September 2001

Agency: Bureau of Export Administration, Commerce

Action: Final rule.

Summary: This rule amends the Export Administration Regulations (EAR) and implements the July 17 White House announcement to streamline the export and re-export of encryption items to European Union (EU) member states, Australia, Czech Republic, Hungary, Japan, New Zealand, Norway, Poland, and Switzerland under License Exception ENC. The 30-day waiting period and the previous distinction between government and non-government end-users are removed by this rule for these destinations. This rule makes further revisions and clarifications to the rule published on 14 January 2000 including changes in the treatment of products incorporating short-range wireless technologies, open cryptographic interfaces, beta test software, encryption source code, and US content (de minimis) requirements. This rule also allows, for the first time, exporters to self-classify unilateral controlled encryption products (that fall under Export Control Classification Numbers (ECCNs) 5A992, 5D992, and 5E992) upon notification to the Bureau of Export Administration (BXA). Restrictions on exports by US persons to terrorist-supporting states (Cuba, Iran, Iraq, Libya, North Korea, Sudan, or Syria), their nationals and other sanctioned entities are not changed by this rule.

Dates: This rule is effective 19 October 2000.

 NOTES AND QUESTIONS

1 In light of the cases extracted above, was it inevitable that the US government relaxed the restrictions on exports?

2 Why would the US government want to restrict trade in encryption products? Outline the arguments for and against such restrictions.

3 What are the main drives behind the shift in policy? Can you identify the operation of an economic imperative in these decisions?

4 As you read the materials below, consider the various pressures operating in a society that might direct a policy stance on encryption. Which of these pressures would you consider the most important? Consider whether this preference is shared by decision-makers and policy-makers.

(c) The concerns of the US government

William Cohen, Janet Reno, Jacob J Lew, and William Daley, *Preserving America's Privacy and Security in the Next Century: A Strategy for America in Cyberspace:* A Report to the President of the United States, 16 September 1999

Available at <http://www.cdt.org/crypto/CESA/CESAwhitepaper.shtml> 17 August 2006

A new paradigm to protect prosperity, privacy and security

To support America's prosperity and protect her security and safety, we propose a new paradigm to advance our national interests. The new paradigm should be comprised of three pillars—information security and privacy, a new framework for export controls, and updated tools for law enforcement. We discuss each in turn.

Information security and privacy

As a nation, we have become increasingly dependent on computers and telecommunications. These new technologies create vast opportunities for personal expression and electronic commerce, while also creating new risks to public safety and national security. Computers and telecommunications rely on open protocols and ultra-accessibility, thus making individuals' and organizations' words and actions vulnerable to outsiders in new and potentially frightening ways. A first pillar of our new paradigm must be to promote information security and privacy, to assure the security and privacy of stored and transmitted data from unauthorized and unlawful access.

The President has recognized the challenge of updating privacy for new technologies:

> We've been at this experiment in Government for 223 years now. We started with a Constitution that was rooted in certain basic values and written by some incredibly brilliant people who understood that times would change, and that definitions of fundamental things like liberty and privacy would change, and that circumstances would require people to rise to the challenges of each new era by applying old values in practical ways.

In updating enduring constitutional values for the computer age, we need to assure that our citizens' personal data and communications are appropriately protected. Businesses need to privately communicate with their employees and manufacturing partners without risk that their proprietary information will be compromised through unauthorized access. Encryption is one of the necessary tools that can be used in this technological environment to secure information. Therefore, we encourage the use of strong encryption by American citizens and businesses to protect their personal and commercial information from unauthorized and unlawful access ...

The government's requirement to protect its own sensitive and privacy information is matched by individuals' and the private sector's own interests in proper handling of sensitive information. Many in industry and elsewhere are already developing and using sophisticated security and privacy products and processes. Government should act as a facilitator and catalyst and help stimulate the development of commercial products that will help all Americans protect their sensitive information.

In sum, the first pillar of the new paradigm calls on the Federal government, the Congress and all others to partner in promoting ways to bring information security and privacy to the Information age. Working together, we can develop tools and procedures for safe operation in cyberspace, applying enduring constitutional values to our new circumstances.

Encryption export controls for the new millennium

At the dawn of the new millennium, technology is advancing at such a rapid pace that attempts to control its global spread under the existing export control regime need to be regularly reevaluated. Encryption will continue to enable new economic realities that must be considered in a balanced approach to export controls.

Encryption products and services are needed around the world to provide confidence and security for electronic commerce and business. With the growing demand for security, encryption products are increasingly sold on the commodity market, and encryption features are being embedded into everyday operating systems, spreadsheets, word processors, and cell phones. Encryption has become a vital component of the emerging global information infrastructure and digital economy. In this new economy, innovation and imagination are the engines, and it is economic achievement that underpins America's status in the world and provides the foundation of our national security. We recognize that US information technology companies lead the world in product quality and innovation, and it is an integral part of the Administration's policy of balance to see that they retain their competitive edge in the international market place.

We as a nation must balance our desire and the need to assist industry with a prudent, objective and steady judgment about how to protect national security; a judgment that acknowledges that technological advantages may add new dimensions to an already complicated problem set. We must ensure that the advantages this technology affords us are not extended to those who wish us ill or who harbor criminal intent. This judgment must be informed by both foreign and domestic realities.

While the US is a huge market for telecommunications goods and services, the other nations of the globe present markets much larger than our domestic demand. Our networks are inextricably bound to those of our allies and adversaries alike. Likewise, America's interests do not end at our borders. American diplomats, service men and women, as well as countless business people work and live around the globe. America's interests are served by the ability to send and receive proprietary, personal and classified information to exactly where it is needed around the world. Likewise, America's interests are served daily by shared actions with our allies, which require accurate and authentic information be exchanged. Our policy must acknowledge these vital interests.

But even as we do, it is imperative that we uphold international understandings, and strive with other nations to prevent the acquisition of encryption technology to sponsors of terrorism, international criminal syndicates or those attempting to increase the availability of weapons of mass destruction. We must also meet our responsibilities to support our national decision makers and our military war fighters with intelligence information in time to make a difference.

Accordingly, the Administration has revised its approach to encryption export controls by emphasizing three simple principles that protect important national security interests:

- a meaningful technical review of encryption products in advance of sale,
- a streamlined post-export reporting system that provides us an understanding of where encryption is being exported but is aligned with industry's business and distribution models, and
- a license process that preserves the right of government to review and, if necessary, deny the sale of strong encryption products to foreign government and military organizations and to nations of concern.

With these three principles in place, the Federal Government would remove almost all export restrictions on encryption products. This approach will provide a stable framework that also will allow US industry to participate in constructing and securing the global networked environment. This approach also maintains reasonable national security safeguards by monitoring the availability of encryption products and limiting their use in appropriate situations.

The Administration intends to codify this new policy in export regulations by 15 December 1999, following consultations on details with affected industries and other private sector organizations.

However, with this new framework for export controls, the national security organizations will need to develop new technical tools and capabilities to deal with the rapid expansion of encrypted communications in support of its mission responsibilities. The Congress will need to support such new tools and technical capabilities through necessary appropriations.

Updated tools for law enforcement

Because of the need for and use of strong encryption globally, governments need to develop new tools to deal with the rapid expansion of encrypted communications. Updated tools for law enforcement that specifically address the challenges of encryption constitute the third pillar of the new strategy. We cannot ignore the fact that encryption will be used in harmful ways—by child pornographers seeking to hide pictures of exploited children, or commercial spies stealing trade secrets from American corporations, or terrorists communicating plans to destroy property and kill innocent civilians. Even more significant, because cyberspace knows no boundaries and because it is not immediately clear if a cyberattack involves Americans or foreigners, America's national security will increasingly depend on strong and capable law enforcement organizations. This is because the United States military and intelligence agencies have long been restricted by law from undertaking operations inside the United States against American citizens. Accordingly, America's national defense is now increasingly reliant on ensuring that our law enforcement community is capable of protecting America in cyberspace.

Under existing law and judicial supervision, law enforcement agents are provided with a variety of legal tools to collect evidence of illegal activity. With appropriate court orders, law enforcement may conduct electronic surveillance or search for and seize evidence. In an encrypted world, law enforcement may obtain the legal authority to access a suspect's communications or data, but the communications or data are rendered worthless, because they cannot be understood and cannot be decoded by law enforcement in a timely manner. Stopping a terrorist attack or seeking to recover a kidnapped child may require timely access to plaintext, and such access may be defeated by encryption. Hence, law enforcement's legal tools should be updated, consistent with constitutional principles, so that when law enforcement obtains legal authority to access a suspect's data or communications, law enforcement will also be able to read it.

Quite simply, even in a world of ubiquitous encryption, law enforcement with court approval must be able to obtain plaintext so that it can protect public safety and national security. Therefore, we must undertake several important and balanced initiatives.

First, we need to ensure that law enforcement maintains its ability to access decryption information stored with third parties, but only pursuant to rules that ensure appropriate privacy protections are in place. To ensure this result, the Administration and the Congress must develop legislation to create a legal framework that enhances privacy over current law and permits decryption information to be safely stored with third parties (by prohibiting, for example, third-party disclosure of decryption information), but allows for law enforcement access when permitted by court order or some other appropriate legal authority.

Second, since criminals will not always store keys with third-party recovery agents, we must ensure that law enforcement has the personnel, equipment, and tools necessary to investigate crime in an encrypted world. This requires that the Congress fund the Technical Support Center as proposed by the Administration, and work with the Administration to ensure that the confidentiality of the sources and methods developed by the Technical Support Center can be maintained.

Third, it is well recognized that industry is designing, deploying and maintaining the information infrastructure, as well as providing encryption products for general use. Industry has always expressed support, both in word and in action, for law enforcement, and has itself worked hard to ensure the safety of the public. Clearly, industry must continue to do so, and firms must be in a position to share proprietary information with government without fear of that information's disclosure or that they will be subject to liability. Therefore, the law must provide protection for industry and its trade secrets as it works with law enforcement to support public safety and national security. The law must also assure that sensitive investigative techniques remain useful in current and future investigations by protecting them from unnecessary disclosure in litigation. These protections must be consistent with fully protecting defendants' rights to a fair trial under the Constitution's Due Process clause and the Sixth Amendment.

The Administration and the Congress need to work jointly to pass legislation that provides these updated authorities. The Administration is in the final stages of drafting legislation and will shortly submit it to the Congress for consideration.

It is imperative to emphasize that the malicious use of encryption is not just a law enforcement issue—it is also a national security issue. The new framework for export controls must be complemented by providing updated, but limited authorities to law enforcement.

 ## NOTES AND QUESTIONS

1   Should we assume that governments have a right to monitor their citizens? Consider the following comments from Judge Fletcher in *Bernstein*, available at <http://www.cdt.org/crypto/litigation/bernstein4.html> 13 September 2001:

Whether we are surveilled by our government, by criminals, or by our neighbors, it is fair to say that never has our ability to shield our affairs from prying eyes been at such a low ebb. The availability and use of secure encryption may offer an opportunity to reclaim some portion of the privacy we have lost. Government efforts to control encryption thus may well implicate not only the First Amendment rights of cryptographers intent on pushing the boundaries of their science, but also the constitutional rights of each of us as potential recipients of encryption's bounty. Viewed from this perspective, the government's efforts to retard progress in cryptography may implicate the Fourth Amendment, as well as the right to speak anonymously.

This passage suggests not only that surveillance might not be as objectively necessary as we assume, but further, that encryption should be widely used to prevent the government from monitoring its citizens. What do you think of this position? How does it alter the landscape of the encryption debate?

2   The following extract also takes up the argument in favour of privacy protections; however, it looks to the government to improve privacy standards, rather than to the citizen to improve privacy fortifications.

Centre for Democracy and Technology, Initial CDT Analysis of the Clinton Administration's Proposed Cyberspace Electronic Security Act (CESA): Standards for Government Access to Decryption Keys, 23 September 1999

Available at <http://www.cdt.org/crypto/CESA/cdtcesaanalysis.shtml> 17 August 2006

As part of its package of encryption policy reforms announced on 16 September, the Clinton Administration is transmitting to Congress draft legislation entitled the Cyberspace Electronic Security Act ('CESA'). The proposal raises important issues concerning the application of Fourth Amendment search and seizure standards to the digital age. However, critical details of the draft are ambiguous or objectionable:

- The standard proposed by the Administration for government access to decryption keys falls far short of Fourth Amendment privacy protections.
- A provision for foreign governments to access passwords and keys of US citizens or foreigners using US recovery agents raises a host of questions.
- Another provision allowing courts to cast a cloak of secrecy over government decryption methods and product vulnerabilities raises due process concerns, implicating the Sixth Amendment right of defendants to cross-examine government witnesses.
- Finally, by narrowly focusing only on access to keys and passwords, the legislation fails to address the much larger question of privacy for documents and information stored in the emerging networked environment.

The proposal does not include the highly objectionable secret search provision previously circulated within the Administration.

Summary

This is our initial analysis of the proposed access provisions. We conclude that CESA does not set adequate privacy standards. The difficult issues it raises require hearings and deliberate consideration. The basic laws governing privacy in cyberspace have not been updated since 1986—well before the full emergence of the Internet. Last year, CDT convened a consultation with civil liberties groups, industry, and government officials to begin exploring privacy standards for decryption keys and networked information. CDT will be working to learn more about CESA and to promote through the Digital Privacy and Security Working Group a dialogue among policymakers and all interested parties aimed at developing a consensus on better privacy protections.

CESA has four primary components, which would:

- prohibit 'recovery agents' (those who hold keys, passwords or other decryption information for others under a confidentiality arrangement) from disclosing recovery information without a court order;
- establish standards for courts to issue orders for government access to escrowed keys or passwords;
- authorize courts to issue protective orders to block disclosure of trade secrets and government information about decryption techniques;
- authorize funds for the FBI Tech Center, to assist the FBI in building up a decryption capability.

CESA would establish a statutory standard for law enforcement access to decryption information held by third parties: courts would issue orders compelling disclosure of decryption information

> upon a finding, based on specific and articulable facts, that—(1) the use of the stored recovery information is reasonably necessary to allow access to the plaintext of data or communications … and (4) there is no constitutionally protected expectation of privacy in such plaintext, or the privacy interest created by such expectation has been overcome by consent, warrant, order, or other authority.

The draft also would prohibit immediate notice to the person whose decryption information is being given to the government.

This standard falls far short of the standard in the Constitution for government access to keys held by encryption users—probable cause to believe that a crime is being committed and notice at the time of the seizure. The CESA standard is not found in any other statute. It was apparently created solely for CESA. The section by section analysis of the Justice Department does not cite any judicial precedent for it. It requires a magistrate or trial court judge, based on the unchallenged presentation of the government, to determine whether there is a 'constitutionally' protected privacy interest in certain plaintext. This means that any statutory privacy interest in the plaintext is irrelevant.

NOTES AND QUESTIONS

1   The rhetoric of the above two extracts clearly embodies the concerns, values, debates, and discourse of American society. However, this does not exclude their content from relevance to all Internet users. The vast majority of Internet users are in the USA. American agendas on on-line issues are central to global debate. It is important to understand the US position, because of its potential to influence the shape of global policy regarding the Internet.

2   Further to the above policy announcement, *The Electronic Frontier: The Challenge of Unlawful Conduct Involving the Use of the Internet*, a report of the President's Working Group on Unlawful Conduct on the Internet, was released in March 2000.[6] The document represents a continuation of the policies announced in the above extract:

> Consistent with the Administration's overall policy, the Working Group recommends a 3-part approach for addressing unlawful conduct on the Internet:
>
> First, any regulation of unlawful conduct involving the use of the Internet should be analysed through a policy framework that ensures that online conduct is treated in a manner consistent with the way offline conduct is treated, in a technology-neutral manner, and in a manner that accounts for other important societal interests such as privacy and protection of civil liberties;
>
> Second, law enforcement needs and challenges posed by the Internet should be recognized as significant, particularly in the areas of resources, training, and the need for new investigative tools and capabilities, coordination with and among federal, state, and local law enforcement agencies, and coordination with and among our international counterparts; and
>
> Third, there should be continued support for private sector leadership and the development of methods—such as 'cyberethics' curricula, appropriate technological tools, and media and other outreach efforts—that educate and empower Internet users to prevent and minimize the risks of unlawful activity.

3   Do you think it is possible to balance all of the interests identified by the US government? If not, which set of interests do you think will prevail?

4   Why do the export policies of the US influence the global market? What significance might the events of September 11 have had on the encryption policy in the US?

---

6   <http://www.usdoj.gov/criminal/cybercrime/unlawful.htm> 14 September 2001.

4   Encryption: Australia

(a)   Australia: Export

The Australian position on regulating the flow of cryptography is much the same as that of our major allies, the USA and the United Kingdom. However, recent changes in the positions of these countries have not been reflected in changes in Australian policy. The exact position of the Australian government is unclear at present.

The regulation of cryptography is locked in a maze of legislation and executive orders. However, the system prior to 1996 was practically incomprehensible, with six relevant regulations and eight different control lists. What follows are four short extracts which set out the legal framework of control, leading from legislation to regulation, to definition, to export control list. The government prefers to view its policy as one of control rather than restriction, arguing that it seeks not the prohibition of exports, but the guarantee that exports accord with the national interest.

Customs Act 1901 (Cth)

Available at <http://www.austlii.edu.au/au/legis/cth/consol_act/ca1901124/s112.html>
17 August 2006

112. PROHIBITED EXPORTS

(1) The Governor-General may, by regulation, prohibit the exportation of goods from Australia.

(2) The power conferred by subsection (1) may be exercised:

   (a) by prohibiting the exportation of goods absolutely;
   (aa) by prohibiting the exportation of goods in specified circumstances;
   (b) by prohibiting the exportation of goods to a specified place; or
   (c) by prohibiting the exportation of goods unless specified conditions or restrictions are complied with.

(2A) Without limiting the generality of paragraph (2)(c), the regulations:

   (aa) may identify the goods to which the regulations relate by reference to their inclusion:
      (i) in a list or other document formulated by a Minister and published in the Gazette or otherwise; or
      (ii) in that list or other document as amended by the Minister and in force from time to time; and ...

Customs (Prohibited Exports) Regulations 1958 (Cth)

Available at <http://www.austlii.edu.au/au/legis/cth/consol_reg/cer1958439/s13e.html>
17 August 2006

13E. EXPORTATION OF CERTAIN GOODS

(1) In this regulation: ...
Defence and strategic goods list means the document:

    (a) formulated and published under paragraph 112(2A)(aa) of the Act by the Minister for Defence; and

    (b) titled 'The Defence and Strategic Goods List' in the publication 'Australian Controls on the Export of Defence and Strategic Goods'; and

    (c) dated November 1996; ...

(2) The exportation from Australia of goods specified in the defence and strategic goods list is prohibited unless:

    (a) a licence in writing to export such of those goods as are specified in the licence has been granted by the Minister for Defence or by an authorised person, and the licence is produced to a Collector; or

    (b) a permission in writing to export such of those goods as are specified in the permission has been granted by the Minister for Defence or by an authorised person, and the permission is produced to a Collector; or ...

Australian Controls on the Export of Defence and Strategic Goods, Defence and Strategic Goods List— Amendment No 1 of 1999 dated 23 June 1999

Available at <http://www.dmo.defence.gov.au/id/export/dsec/Changes.doc> 21 September 2001

'Asymmetric algorithm' means a cryptographic algorithm using different, mathematically-related keys for encryption and decryption.
NB: A common use of 'asymmetric algorithms' is key management.
'Symmetric algorithm' means a cryptographic algorithm using an identical key for both encryption and decryption.
NB: A common use of 'symmetric algorithms' is confidentiality of data.

Australian Controls on the Export of Defence and Strategic Goods, Defence and Strategic Goods List

Available at <http://www.defence.gov.au/strategy/dtcc/publications/PG14.pdf > 17 August 2006

Part Three: Dual Use Goods

CATEGORY 5—TELECOMMUNICATIONS AND 'INFORMATION SECURITY'

5A2 SYSTEMS, EQUIPMENT AND COMPONENTS

5A002

a   Systems, equipment, application-specific 'electronic assemblies', modules and integrated circuits for 'information security', as follows, and other specially designed components there for:

    1   Designed or modified to use 'cryptography' employing digital techniques performing any cryptographic function other than authentication or digital signature having any of the following:

        a   A 'symmetric algorithm' employing a key length in excess of 56 bits; or

        b   An 'asymmetric algorithm' where the security of the algorithm is based on any of the following:

            1   Factorisation of integers in excess of 512 bits (eg RSA);

            2   Computation of discrete logarithms in a multiplicative group of a finite field of size greater than 512 bits (eg Diffie-Hellman over Z/pZ); or

            3   Discrete logarithms in a group other than mentioned in 5A002.a.1.b.2. in excess of 112 bits (eg Diffie-Hellman over an elliptic curve); ...

[Notes omitted]

 NOTES AND QUESTIONS

1   Regardless of whether the revised system in the regulations is simpler, without a clear policy framework within which to operate the regulations are of limited use. Having read the above law, regulation and export control list, consider the following extract, which explains the limited policy framework in existence. More important than knowing the minutiae of the laws is understanding their role and operation, both in Australian and in international cryptography policy.

2   As you read, consider whether there is any significance in the fact that the Australian government has not publicised a shift in its thinking on encryption in the wake of global policy change. Consider whether this is likely to be deleterious for Australian industry.

(b)   Australia: Other issues

While there are restrictions on the export of cryptography from Australia, its importation and use within Australia is not the subject of direct controls. Under s 3LA of the *Crimes Act 1914* (Cth), however, an order may be obtained from a magistrate requiring release of encryption keys or decryption of encrypted data. The order may be granted if there are reasonable grounds for suspecting evidential material is held in or accessible from a computer, and the specified person is a suspect or (an employee of) the owner or lessee of the computer, who has relevant knowledge of the encryption. Failure to comply with the order attracts the penalty of up to six months' imprisonment. It should be noted that s 201A of the *Customs Act 1901* is similarly worded.

(c) Singapore

The situation in Singapore is one that adheres to the Wassenaar controls. The relevant legislation is the *Strategic Goods (Control) Act 2002*, revised in 2003 (see DL05, Category 5), and the *Strategic Goods (Control) Regulations* 2004, gazetted on 5 January 2004. The regulations contain provisions on electronic transmission of technology. There are currently no import restrictions. See generally the Singapore Strategic Goods Control website <http://www.stgc.gov.sg/stgc/index.jsp>. There are no domestic controls on crypto use.

----

5 Keystroke monitoring

The case of *United States v Nicodemo S Scarfo et al*,[7] before the US Federal District Court in the district of New Jersey, has raised a comprehensive collection of encryption-related issues for judicial consideration. The facts of the case present almost all of the issues discussed in this chapter.

After obtaining a warrant, the FBI placed a program, called a keystroke monitor, on the defendant's computer. This program, as its name suggests, recorded the keystrokes of the defendant and, as such, revealed the key ID and pass-phrase used in the defendant's private key. With this information the FBI was able to access encrypted communications. These communications form the backbone of the government's case involving loan sharking and gambling.

The defence sought discovery of the operation of the keystroke monitoring program. The government objected on the grounds of national security, stating that all of the functional components within the discovery request (that is, the program code) were classified in 1997 under the *Controlled Information Protection Act* (CIPA). The defence objected to the invocation of this classification. The judge was forced to determine whether the information should be disclosed to the defence, or disclosed only to the judge, who would then provide a summary to the defence omitting classified material concerning the program's functional components.

The US District Court Judge had initially ordered that the FBI reveal the functional components of the program in its entirety to the defence, holding that 'the Court cannot make a determination as to the lawfulness of the Government's search in this matter without knowing specifically how the search was effectuated'.[8] However, the government requested the order be modified pursuant to the CIPA and provided the defence with

---

7   Crim No 00-404. See further the documents at <http://www.epic.org/crypto/scarfo.html> 18 September 2001.
8   <http://www2.epic.org/crypto/scarfo/order_8_7_01.pdf> 19 September 2001.

only an unclassified summary of the report. In October, the Court denied discovery of the classified information. In December 2002, the Court upheld the legality of the FBI's use of the key logger program.

In any event, the value of the case is only partially in its outcome. Value is also to be found in the interrelationship between many fundamental technical, legal, and political encryption issues.

The technical issues fall into two categories. The threshold technical issue involves the problem of key security. It was stated in the introductory explanation earlier in this chapter that an encryption system using keys is only as secure as the protections on the keys. Lax key security makes for lax encryption, regardless of the strength of the algorithm. This has been clearly demonstrated here. Poignantly, the breach of security was the result of the deliberate actions of the government, rather than any omissions on the part of the defendant.

The second technical issue concerns the specific apparatus used to breach the security of the key protection, and hence to access the cipher. The keystroke monitoring program offers significant opportunity to bypass the need to utilise the brute force method of code-breaking. If you know the code, you don't need to break it! If the government can access the pass-phrases of its citizens without their knowledge (even without considering suggestions such as key banks), the potential for surveillance increases markedly. This leads to the legal and political questions.

The legal issues in this controversial area are inextricably linked with the political. However, of interest here is the extent of the legal protections seemingly afforded to the surveillance activities of the FBI. Through the use of executive orders, the government has attempted to frustrate all attempts to reveal the methods used for surveillance.

The second legal issue pertains to the adequacy of the information provided to the judge who granted the initial warrant permitting the placement of the program. There is widespread concern that the information provided was so inadequate as to render any real understanding of what was involved impossible. The argument here is that if the process requiring the warrant is not disclosed and not understood the warrant cannot, in good conscience, be approved for use.

The final legal issue is whether or not the activities of the government constituted the monitoring of communications, or merely the accessing of electronic documents. This raises issues peculiar to US law which need not be pursued at length here.

Third, and perhaps most significantly, there are political issues. The US Government has always argued for the maintenance of its legally enshrined right to monitor certain communications that flow through society. This argument is made by many, if not all, Western governments. We have shown in this chapter how this right is threatened by the increasing ability to conceal communications transmitted in code. The present case demonstrates the lengths to which the US government will go to infiltrate the communications of its citizens. Furthermore, it presents a challenge to the American polity. It illuminates the government's methods and demands a reaction. The case has been the subject of numerous newspaper editorials with varying perspectives. In essence, the political issues encapsulated in this case are emblematic of the entire encryption debate: namely, how far can the government legitimately go in its invasion of the privacy of its citizens in order to protect them, and to what extent do the interests of government and citizen coincide? Where they differ, the question becomes: is the government protecting its citizens' interests, or its own?

- -

6   Encryption and the global society

The relationships between encryption, privacy, crime, and the public interest are clearly apparent. It is broadly true to say that privacy concerns can be overcome by access to secure encryption methods. However, it is equally true to say that, regardless of the concerns to protect personal privacy, our society depends on the ability to invade the privacy of those we believe or suspect to be acting contrary to the public good.

The privacy we speak of in this context is slightly different from the notion of privacy discussed in the previous chapter. There, the focus was any information, especially personal information, which might be collected, collated, and used, and the regulation of these activities. The focus here is a subset of these—that is, the privacy of communications. Although encryption technologies protect and provide privacy, the protection afforded has no analogy in real space. In the real world, we expect certain information and communications to be private and confidential, and desire this to be so for the common good, but acknowledge the possibility that they might not be. The same cannot be said of cyberspace. It is now possible to remove the opportunity to monitor cyberspace communications. It is no longer always possible to access the communications of those who are or may be acting against the common good. This, in a nutshell, is what concerns the US government. Indeed, the recent terrorist attacks in New York and Washington, DC have sparked heated debates about the role of encryption in such attacks. Many have suggested that it is the use of encryption technology that has enabled the planning of such attacks to completely elude US intelligence. Others have acknowledged that while this may be the case, it would be an admission of defeat if the use of encryption technology was banned, as this would fatally endanger individual freedom.[9]

And so the question concerns not only the right to privacy through encryption, but also the need to protect a society. Encrypted communications unfortunately also allow all manner of subversive activity to be organised without the possibility of detection; the same tensions emerge here as in the privacy debate of the last chapter. How do we strike a balance between the public interest in the ability to monitor illegal behaviour and the private interest in secure communications? There are legitimate concerns on all sides of the debate. There are no perfect solutions. Encryption poses serious challenges to both the philosophical foundation and the operation of all western democracies. We will see in Chapter 7 that Internet crime is no small issue. Encryption technology, while it does not belong to the category of Internet crime, presents itself as a way of facilitating crime using the Internet.

---

9   S Shane, 'Bin Laden, Associates elude spy agency's eavesdropping: Encrypted calls may keep NSA off track', the *Baltimore Sun*, 15 Sept 2001, available at <http://www.sunspot.net/news/custom/attack/bal-intel15.story> 26 September 2001.

6 Electronic Signatures

1 Introduction

Electronic signatures are a vital ingredient in the success of electronic commerce. Without them, it is questionable whether commerce can be effectively carried out on the Internet. While they have many uses in non-commercial transactions, it is their utility in commerce that has brought them the international attention they currently have. In many respects, they have a close relationship with encryption technology, and electronic signatures are simply an electronic confirmation of authenticity. This definition is deliberately broad enough to encompass all forms of electronic identification, from the very informal (and insecure), such as initials at the end of an e-mail, to the very formal (and highly secure), such as iris scans. Digital signatures are a particular subset of electronic signatures.

Digital signatures explained

A digital signature uses encryption, specifically public-key encryption, and a one-way-hash function, as explained in the previous chapter, to guarantee authenticity. Using two methods, a user can create a unique, verifiable mark of authenticity.

Using public-key encryption, a signature is produced through a series of steps.[1]

1   The sender writes a message.
2   The sender then uses her own private key to encrypt the message.

If the intended recipient were to receive this message, he could be reassured of the integrity of content and authenticity of sender. However, anyone with access to the public key could read it. Therefore, to ensure confidentiality, further steps need to be taken.

3   The sender could then add a second layer of encryption using the public key of the recipient.
4   The message is sent.
5   The recipient decodes the message using the private key of the recipient.
6   The recipient then decodes the final layer using the public key of the sender.

The sender's private key guarantees the content and authenticity of the message; the recipient's public key guarantees that only the recipient can read the message. However, this is a very cumbersome process. As was highlighted in Chapter 5, public-key cryptography requires a significant amount of processing and a double layer of encryption, and therefore can be quite impractical. Instead, the one-way-hash function can be used to obviate this difficulty.

1   The sender writes a message.
2   The sender uses a one-way-hash function to 'crunch' the simple text and produce the hash.
3   The hash is then encrypted with the sender's private key.

At this point, the sender has done little more than the first two steps above. If the message is sent now, the contents will be secure and it will certainly be verified as having come from the sender, but anyone with the public key can decrypt the hash, and anyone at all can read the simple text. The private key guarantees that the message has come from the intended person and the encrypted hash guarantees that the message arrived in exactly the same form as when it was sent. This is a digital signature. However, in the interests of confidentiality:

---

1   See further <http://www.viacorp.com/crypto.html> 24 September 2001 and <http://www.cs.umbc. edu/~wyvern/ta/msginteg.html> 24 September 2001.

4   The sender encrypts both the simple text and the private-key-encrypted hash, with the recipient's public key.

5   The message is sent.

6   The recipient decrypts the entire encrypted message, that is, both the simple text and the hash, using his private key.

7   The recipient then decrypts the hash using the sender's public key.

8   The private key holder runs the simple text through the same one-way-hash function.

9   The recipient compares the hash produced at his end with the hash produced by the sender.

10 If the hash produced is identical to the one included in the message, the message is authentic.

Therefore, to produce a signature, in theory, steps one and two would be sufficient in the first process, and steps one, two, and three would be sufficient in the second process. The recipient's public key ensures that none other than the intended recipient can read it. This confidentiality feature is not technically part of the signature, but is generally included in most explanations of signatures. See also Y F Lim, 'Digital Signature, Certification Authorities and the Law' *E Law* Vol 9 no 3 (September 2002).

Authenticity, integrity, and confidentiality are the three key components of effective and useful digital signatures. The one-way-hash method most efficiently ensures confidentiality because the hash is a relatively small number, and therefore easier to encrypt. Both methods are effective. One is mathematically more practical than the other.

No one can describe exactly how she produces a written signature because it is an infinitely individual product of mind, brain, and body. It is of course possible to duplicate the signature itself, but not the actual method for producing it, and these duplicates are difficult to produce and difficult to guarantee. Digital signatures, on the other hand, cannot be copied once produced; however, they are produced through a mathematical process which is easily describable and useful to anyone who knows it. Signatures rely on the secrecy of the keys used in their production. In paper signatures the keys, or processes, cannot be known by another, but digital signatures are a different story. The standard for the security of electronic signatures must be the standard for the measures taken to keep the keys secret.

 NOTES AND QUESTIONS

1   Are electronic signatures, or digital signatures, directly analogous to paper-based authentications, particularly a handwritten signature? Can you suggest any other analogies to real-world tools? In doing so you might consider how the three important features of electronic signatures are produced in real space.

2   Is it useful to insist on defining the features of cyberspace with reference to real space analogies, or does this merely perpetuate a misunderstanding as to the uniqueness of the Internet?

3   Write a short paragraph explaining the mechanics of the digital signatures procedures. If you had a choice, which of the two methods would you use, and why?

4   Do you think digital signatures will solve the problems of electronic commerce? Consider for a moment the standard of security in most workplaces. Consider the very few people who employ even elementary file security. Consider also the standard employee who is attempting to handle three jobs at once: an encryption system is only as secure as the keys.

5   The key to the effectiveness of our personal written signature is that we do not have to guard them. They are ours by virtue of our individuality. They are not a mechanical mathematical construct. The material in this chapter will demonstrate a willingness of government as well as private sector bodies to encourage and facilitate the increased use of digital signatures. As you examine these attempts, consider whether digital signatures are in fact the panacea we have been led to believe.

----

2   The legal challenges of digital signatures

(a)   Definition and recognition

The key to a coordinated legal response to the challenges of signatures lies in a workable, acceptable, and practical definition that will be recognised in all courts of law. Currently, no definition of digital signatures has been internationally agreed upon. Definitions range in rigour from the very loose to the very strict. This issue is patently of international significance because without common, or similar, definitional frameworks, there can be little progress in developing the legal institutions necessary for the conduct of international electronic commerce.

The first step is to examine what it is about standard, paper-based signatures that makes them legal. The Statute of Frauds makes writing a requirement of signature recognition but defines this requirement very broadly. This is aptly summed up in the 1869 case of *Howley v Whipple*:[2]

> It makes no difference whether that operator writes the offer or the acceptance ... with a steel pen an inch long attached to an ordinary penholder, or whether his pen be a copper wire a thousand miles long. In either case the thought is communicated to the paper by use of the finger resting upon the pen; nor does it make any difference that in one case common record ink is used, while in the other case a more subtle fluid, known as electricity, performs the same office.

This requirement encapsulates an awareness of the terms above the signature, agreement to be bound by those same terms, knowledge of consequence of breach,

---

2   48 NH 487 (1869).

awareness that the signature is non-repudiable as a sign of intent, and providing an unalterable permanent record of event.

The question 'What is a digital signature?' is not answered by merely pointing to the electronic equivalent of writing. The following extract outlines the various legislative approaches to defining and recognising signatures and highlights the difficulties for business which arise.

Thomas J Smedinghoff and Ruth Hill Bro, 'Moving with Change: Electronic signature legislation as a vehicle for advancing e-commerce'

(1999) 17 *John Marshall Journal of Computer and Information Law* 723

Smedinghoff is now a partner with Wildman Harrold (smedinghoff@wildmanharrold.com); Bro is now a partner at Baker & McKenzie LLP (bro@bakernet.com)

What qualifies as a signature?

Perhaps the biggest issue that arises in legislation devoted to removing barriers to e-commerce is the question of what type of electronic signature qualifies as a signature (ie, meets statutory and regulatory signature requirements). Unfortunately, there is no uniform answer to this question. Typically, legislation has taken one of three apparently inconsistent approaches: (1) all electronic signatures satisfy legal signature requirements; (2) electronic signatures satisfy legal signature requirements only when they possess certain security attributes; or (3) digital signatures satisfy legal signature requirements.

Moreover, not only is legislation inconsistent from state to state, but in some cases inconsistent approaches have been enacted within the same state.

In the paper world, at least in the United States, anything can qualify as a signature. The current definition of signature in the Uniform Commercial Code (UCC) includes '*any symbol made with an intent to authenticate*'. Because there is no requirement as to the nature of the mark that qualifies, courts have found that, in addition to the traditional handwritten signature, a wide variety of marks (including a simple 'X') will qualify. Several states have taken the same approach with electronic signatures—that is, any form of electronic 'symbol' on a message can qualify as a signature. All such statutes take a technology-neutral approach to the means by which such signatures are created (ie, they do not specify the technology that must be used, only the result that must be achieved). The only requirements are, quite simply, the existence of a symbol or security procedure, and an intent to authenticate on the part of the signer. The proposed *Uniform Electronic Transactions Act* also takes this approach.

A second category of statutes, however, requires that electronic signatures possess certain attributes or meet certain requirements before they will be considered legally enforceable. Virtually all of these statutes take a technology-neutral approach to these requirements.

Perhaps the most common requirements imposed by this second category of statutes derive from a decision of the US Comptroller General that was first included in the California legislation enacted in late 1995. Under statutes adopting this approach, an electronic signature is legally effective as a signature only if it is:

1 unique to the person using it;
2 capable of verification;
3 under the sole control of the person using it; and
4 linked to the data in such a manner that if the data is changed, the signature is invalidated.

Some statutes have varied this approach by including these four requirements in the definition of an electronic signature (ie, it's not an electronic signature if it doesn't possess those four attributes) but also specifying that only electronic signatures are legally effective as signatures. In either case, however, this approach requires attributes of security as a precondition to the validity of the signature itself, something not required for paper-based signatures. Statutes in nearly a third of the states have adopted this approach. The draft European Directive takes a similar approach. Unfortunately, the meaning of these four requirements is not entirely clear, and such requirements may create significant and unnecessary hurdles.

A different set of legal signature requirements is imposed by the UNCITRAL Model Law. Specifically, the UNCITRAL Model Law requires that:

1 an electronic signature must include a method to identify the signer,
2 an electronic signature must include a method to indicate the signer's approval of the information contained in the message, and
3 the method used must be as reliable as was appropriate for the purpose for which the message was generated or communicated.

A third category of legislation focuses not on the attributes an electronic signature must possess in order to be enforceable as a signature, but rather on the technology used to create the signature itself. Statutes falling within this third category authorize the use of only a specific type of electronic signature (ie, a digital signature) and ignore the general category of electronic signatures. Such legislation has been enacted in five states: Minnesota, Missouri, New Hampshire, Utah, and Washington.

Yet a fourth category of enacted legislation says nothing whatsoever about what constitutes a valid electronic signature.

These inconsistent approaches create a certain level of uncertainty for businesses trying to do e-commerce in multiple jurisdictions, especially if such businesses do not use electronic signatures that comply with requirements in all jurisdictions.

What types of transactions are covered?

Electronic signature legislation has also taken a variety of approaches regarding the types of transactions for which the use of electronic signatures is authorized. Nearly 40% of the states expressly authorize the use of electronic signatures for virtually all transactions. Other states have statutes that authorize the use of electronic signatures only for certain categories of transactions, such as UCC filings, medical records, or motor vehicle records.

Some states, however, condition the authorization to use electronic signatures on the type of party involved in the transaction. For example, some statutes authorize the use of electronic signatures only where both parties are government agencies, while other statutes require at least one of the parties to be a government entity. In yet other states, statutes authorize the use of electronic signatures only for transactions involving a specific private entity, such as a financial institution.

[Footnotes omitted]

 ## NOTES AND QUESTIONS

1   The issue of definition is closely linked to that of recognition. Definition of signatures can be regarded as a necessary but insufficient condition for recognition. Throughout the above extract the two issues are ostensibly fused.

2   The nature of the definition adopted within a jurisdiction is likely to signify the nature of the legislative approach. That is, jurisdictions with a minimalist signatures definition tend to encapsulate it within a relatively hands-off, choice-based system, while jurisdictions that outline detailed definitional criteria enact legislation with the purpose of overseeing the development of effective electronic commerce.

(b)   Deniability and non-repudiation

One correlative of recognition is the requirement that, once a signature is recognised in a court of law, the person to whom that signature is attributed cannot deny the authenticity of the document to which it is attached. This idea is central to the way many people do business and demonstrates the need for trust within all transactions. It is expected that a contractor will be legally bound by a signed agreement, even if she later changes her mind. If a signature cannot be proven to be technically authentic—that is, if it cannot be proven to be the sender's electronic signature—the legal questions become moot. However, in the case of repudiation of a *prima facie* valid signature, the legal question is at the forefront of concern.

Thomas J Smedinghoff and Ruth Hill Bro, 'Moving With Change: Electronic Signature Legislation as a Vehicle for Advancing E-Commerce'

(1999) 17 *John Marshall Journal of Computer and Information Law* 723

Available at < http://www.bakernet.com/ecommerce/articles-t.htm> 17 August 2006

Authenticity

Authenticity is concerned with the source or origin of a communication. Who sent the message? Is it genuine or a forgery?

A party entering into an online transaction in reliance on an electronic message must be confident of that message. For example, when a bank receives an electronic payment order from a customer directing that money be paid to a third party, the bank must be able to verify the source of the request and ensure that it is not dealing with an impostor.

Likewise, a party must also be able to establish the authenticity of its electronic transactions should a dispute arise. That party must retain records of all relevant communications pertaining to the transaction and keep those records in such a way that the party can show that the records are authentic. For example, if one party to a contract later disputes the nature of its obligations, the other party may need to prove the terms of the contract to a court. A court, however, will first require that the party establish the authenticity of the record that the party retained of that communication before the court will consider it as evidence.

Integrity

Integrity is concerned with the accuracy and completeness of the communication. Is the document the recipient received the same as the document that the sender sent? Is it complete? Has the document been altered either in transmission or storage?

The recipient of an electronic message must be confident of a communication's integrity before the recipient relies and acts on the message. Integrity is critical to e-commerce when it comes to the negotiation and formation of contracts online, the licensing of digital content, and the making of electronic payments, as well as to proving these transactions using electronic records at a later date. For example, consider the case of a building contractor who wants to solicit bids from subcontractors and submit its proposal to the government online. The building contractor must be able to verify that the messages containing the bids upon which it will rely in formulating its proposal have not been altered. Likewise, if the contractor ever needs to prove the amount of the subcontractor's bid, a court will first require that the contractor establish the integrity of the record he retained of that communication before the court will consider it as evidence in the case.

Nonrepudiation

Nonrepudiation is the ability to hold the sender to his communication in the event of a dispute. A party's willingness to rely on a communication, contract, or funds transfer request is contingent upon having some level of comfort that the party can prevent the sender from denying that he sent the communication (if, in fact, he did send it), or claim that the contents of the communication as received are not the same as what the sender sent (if, in fact, they are what was sent). For example, a stockbroker who accepts buy/sell orders over the Internet would not want his client to be able to place an order for a volatile commodity, such as a pork bellies futures contract, and then be able to confirm the order if the market goes up and repudiate the order if the market goes south.

With paper-based transactions, a party can rely on numerous indicators of trust to determine whether the signature is authentic and the document has not been altered. These include using paper (sometimes with watermarks, colored backgrounds, or other indicia of reliability) to which the message is affixed and not easily altered, letterhead, handwritten ink signatures, sealed envelopes for delivery via a trusted third party (such as the US Postal Service), personal contact between the parties, and the like. With electronic communications, however, none of these indicators of trust are present. All that can be communicated are bits (0s and 1s) that are in all respects identical and can be easily copied and modified.

This has two important consequences. First, it often becomes extremely difficult to know when one can rely on the integrity and authenticity of an electronic message. This, of course, makes difficult those decisions that involve entering into contracts, shipping products, making payments, or otherwise changing one's position in reliance on an electronic message. Second, this lack of reliability makes proving one's case in court virtually impossible. For example, while a typewritten name appended at the end of an e-mail message may qualify as a signature under applicable law, that name could have been typed by anyone, and if the defendant denies the 'signature' in a lawsuit, it may be virtually impossible for the plaintiff to prove the authenticity of that signature. As a result, nonrepudiation is by no means assured in such a case, and parties thus may choose to forgo e-commerce where the risk of repudiation is too great.

In many respects, trust is a key element of the measurement of risk. And the need for trust can vary significantly, depending on the risk involved. Selling books on the Internet, for example, may not require a high level of trust in each transaction, especially where a credit card number is provided and the risk of loss from fraud is relatively low (eg, a $20 book). On the other hand, entering into long-term, high-dollar value contracts electronically may require a much higher level of trust. At a minimum, the risk of a fraudulent message must be acceptable given the nature and size of the transaction.

Thus, where the amount at issue is relatively small or the risk is otherwise low, trust in an electronic message's authenticity and integrity may not be a critical issue. If e-commerce is to reach its full potential, however, parties must be able to trust electronic communications for a wide range of transactions, particularly ones where the size of the transaction is substantial or the nature of the transaction is of higher risk. In such cases, a party relying on an electronic communication will need to know, at the time of reliance, whether the message is authentic, whether the integrity of its contents is intact, and, equally important, whether the relying party can establish both of those facts in court if a dispute arises (ie, nonrepudiation).

[Footnotes omitted]

 NOTES AND QUESTIONS

When you receive e-mail from an address you recognise, how do you know it was sent by the person you associate with that address? Do you simply assume so, based upon the content of the message? Would you make the same assumption if the message concerned a valuable commercial contract?

(c) Public key infrastructure

If businesses and consumers cannot be assured of the authenticity and impenetrability of the signature systems they use, there is little likelihood of e-business becoming the benchmark for global commerce. Chapter 5 provided a brief outline of a developing institution known as public-key infrastructure. Emphasis was placed on the role of PKI in disseminating public keys for use in communication. But there is another important aspect of PKI.

Public-key infrastructure is a matrix of non-governmental certification bodies that have developed a system of cross-verification. This system produces authenticity by assuming that each authority wishes to protect and enhance its reputation. This assumption is then tested as each authority checks the security of another authority's system. In this way, one authority often carries the seals of numerous others, as testimony to its own reliability. In return, that authority will test and seal numerous others.

The question for users is one of information. Without certification, it would be impossible to tell whether the public key to be used in a transaction was either legitimately attached to the person you were led to believe it was, or as secure as you were led to believe. If the non-governmental authorities are relatively unknown in the sender's jurisdiction the problem is only slightly alleviated, because while there may be a seal, the consumer may have little knowledge of the authority behind it. The challenge for international policy-makers is to establish a system that clearly articulates the status of non-government certification bodies across jurisdictions. The PKI system is a non-governmental response to this dilemma but relies heavily upon quasi-customary notions of reputation and mutual trust.

The development of PKI is still in its infancy. The infrastructure is in the early stages of development and most of the progress thus far is a result of industry cooperation rather than legislative codification.[3]

The trends in PKI systems indicate the widespread use of two key pairs: one for use in signatures, the other for use in general communication. As noted in the previous chapter, there are indications of widespread use of PKI databases to lodge signature-only public keys. Access to standard encryption keys remains restricted in order to manage the flow of encrypted communication effectively.

(d) Liability for certification authorities?

In relation to public-key infrastructure, what are the procedures in the event of the failure of a certified signature? This is a vexed question for national legislators and has produced, unfortunately, a variety of responses. In some jurisdictions there is neither statute nor regulation covering certification authority liability. The EU Directive on a Community Framework for Electronic Signatures[4] requires that EU member states legislate liability of certification authorities. This would extend to damage caused to any entity that reasonably relies on a certificate, with the qualification that liability will be avoided if the certification authority can prove that it has not acted negligently. In any

---

3   There are still many legal issues that require resolution; see, for example, the consultation paper re-leased in June 2001 by the Australian Privacy Commissioner, *Privacy Issues in the Use of Public Key Infrastructure for Individuals*, available at <http://www.privacy.gov.au/publications/dpki.html> 26 September 2001.

4   Directive 1999/93/EC, available at <http://europa.eu.int/comm./dg15/en/media/sign/Dir99-93-ec%20EN.pdf> 8 April 2001.

case, the Directive would only extend to European nations, and then only if complying legislation is enacted. See further Y F Lim, 'Digital Signatures, Certification Authorities: Certainty in the Allocation of Liability' (2003) 7 *Singapore Journal of International & Comparative Law* 183.

 NOTES AND QUESTIONS

1   Signatures are distinguished from autographs by the intention we attach to them. When we sign something, we intend to authenticate its contents—or, at the very least, we are deemed to have so intended. However, the nature of the intent will vary according to the transaction. Often, the specific intention can only be determined by examining the circumstances in which the signature was made. What problems does this intricate process of interpretation cause in the electronic context?

2   Briefly outline the legal challenges posed by electronic and digital signatures. Which of these challenges do you think is the most important?

3   Is it possible to understand the legal ramifications of this area without grasping the technical foundations of the subject matter? Do you think the technicalities might prove to be a problem when a court of law is forced to examine this area?

4   'Gatekeeper' is the Australian Commonwealth Government's strategy for the use of PKI and a key enabler for the delivery of Government Online and e-commerce. It represents one example of a public sector section of the PKI matrix.

5   How would you react to the suggestion that Internet users, particularly companies or individuals using the Internet for business, utilise two different key pairs? How does this affect your answer to the question posed above regarding key security?

6   An important consideration is the nature of the transaction the signature seeks to enforce. If it is a contract for the sale of land, for example, recent legislative action at the State level in electronic commerce denies validity to such dealings if conducted electronically, thus perpetuating the attachment to tangible writing and signature in some contexts.

7   The issue of liability of certification authorities is as much technical as it is legal. It is tied in with the authentication and verification requirements of a standard handwritten signature. If a traditional signature is disputed, we may rely on handwriting experts. Whether we will see experts wrangling over disputed electronic signatures depends on whether a satisfactory legal solution can be found in the meantime.

8   There are more questions than answers at this stage. Students are encouraged to read further in this area. Developments occur almost daily and this area makes a fascinating and innovative topic for further research.

---

3 International responses to digital signatures

(a) UNCITRAL Model Laws

In 1996 UNCITRAL decided to place the issues of digital signatures and certification authorities on its agenda. The Working Group on Electronic Commerce, having considered the matter, concluded that the uniform rules should deal with such issues as:

- the legal basis supporting certification processes, including emerging digital authentication and certification technology;
- the applicability of the certification process; the allocation of risk and liabilities of users, providers and third parties in the context of the use of certification techniques;
- the specific issues of certification through the use of registries; and
- incorporation by reference.

The text of the *UNCITRAL Model Law on Electronic Signatures* was adopted on 5 July 2001 in New York. The rules are designed to facilitate the increased use of electronic signatures in international business transactions.

UNCITRAL Model Law on Electronic Signatures (2001)

Available at
<http://www.uncitral.org/english/texts/electcom/ml-elecsig-e.pdf> 19 September 2001

ARTICLE 1: SPHERE OF APPLICATION

This Law applies where electronic signatures are used in the context of commercial activities. It does not override any rule of law intended for the protection of consumers.

ARTICLE 2: DEFINITIONS

For the purposes of this Law:

(a) 'Electronic signature' means data in electronic form in, affixed to or logically associated with, a data message, which may be used to identify the signatory in relation to the data message and to indicate the signatory's approval of the information contained in the data message;

(b) 'Certificate' means a data message or other record confirming the link between a signatory and signature creation data;

(c) 'Data message' means information generated, sent, received or stored by electronic, optical or similar means including, but not limited to, electronic data interchange (EDI), electronic mail, telegram, telex or telecopy;

(d) 'Signatory' means a person that holds signature creation data and acts either on its own behalf or on behalf of the person it represents;

(e) 'Certification service provider' means a person that issues certificates and may provide other services related to electronic signatures;

(f) 'Relying party' means a person that may act on the basis of a certificate or an electronic signature.

ARTICLE 3: EQUAL TREATMENT OF SIGNATURE TECHNOLOGIES

Nothing in this Law, except article 5, shall be applied so as to exclude, restrict or deprive of legal effect any method of creating an electronic signature that satisfies the requirements referred to in article 6, paragraph 1, or otherwise meets the requirements of applicable law.

ARTICLE 4: INTERPRETATION

1   In the interpretation of this Law, regard is to be had to its international origin and to the need to promote uniformity in its application and the observance of good faith.

2   Questions concerning matters governed by this Law which are not expressly settled in it are to be settled in conformity with the general principles on which this Law is based.

ARTICLE 5: VARIATION BY AGREEMENT

The provisions of this Law may be derogated from or their effect may be varied by agreement, unless that agreement would not be valid or effective under applicable law.

ARTICLE 6: COMPLIANCE WITH A REQUIREMENT FOR A SIGNATURE

1   Where the law requires a signature of a person, that requirement is met in relation to a data message if an electronic signature is used that is as reliable as was appropriate for the purpose for which the data message was generated or communicated, in the light of all the circumstances, including any relevant agreement.

2   Paragraph 1 applies whether the requirement referred to therein is in the form of an obligation or whether the law simply provides consequences for the absence of a signature.

3   An electronic signature is considered to be reliable for the purpose of satisfying the requirement referred to in paragraph 1 if:

(a) The signature creation data are, within the context in which they are used, linked to the signatory and to no other person;

(b) The signature creation data were, at the time of signing, under the control of the signatory and of no other person;

(c) Any alteration to the electronic signature, made after the time of signing, is detectable; and

(d) Where a purpose of the legal requirement for a signature is to provide assurance as to the integrity of the information to which it relates, any alteration made to that information after the time of signing is detectable.

4   Paragraph 3 does not limit the ability of any person:

(a) To establish in any other way, for the purpose of satisfying the requirement referred to in paragraph 1, the reliability of an electronic signature; or
(b) To adduce evidence of the non-reliability of an electronic signature.

5   The provisions of this article do not apply to the following: [...].

ARTICLE 7: SATISFACTION OF ARTICLE 6

1   [Any person, organ or authority, whether public or private, specified by the enacting State as competent] may determine which electronic signatures satisfy the provisions of article 6 of this Law.
2   Any determination made under paragraph 1 shall be consistent with recognized international standards.
3   Nothing in this article affects the operation of the rules of private international law.

ARTICLE 8: CONDUCT OF THE SIGNATORY

1   Where signature creation data can be used to create a signature that has legal effect, each signatory shall:

(a) Exercise reasonable care to avoid unauthorized use of its signature creation data;
(b) Without undue delay, utilize means made available by the certification service provider pursuant to article 9 of this Law, or otherwise use reasonable efforts, to notify any person that may reasonably be expected by the signatory to rely on or to provide services in support of the electronic signature if:
    (i) The signatory knows that the signature creation data have been compromised; or
    (ii) The circumstances known to the signatory give rise to a substantial risk that the signature creation data may have been compromised;
(c) Where a certificate is used to support the electronic signature, exercise reasonable care to ensure the accuracy and completeness of all material representations made by the signatory that are relevant to the certificate throughout its life cycle or that are to be included in the certificate.

2   A signatory shall bear the legal consequences of its failure to satisfy the requirements of paragraph 1.

ARTICLE 9: CONDUCT OF THE CERTIFICATION SERVICE PROVIDER

1   Where a certification service provider provides services to support an electronic signature that may be used for legal effect as a signature, that certification service provider shall:

(a) Act in accordance with representations made by it with respect to its policies and practices;

    (b) Exercise reasonable care to ensure the accuracy and completeness of all material representations made by it that are relevant to the certificate throughout its life cycle or that are included in the certificate;

    (c) Provide reasonably accessible means that enable a relying party to ascertain from the certificate:

      (i) The identity of the certification service provider;

      (ii) That the signatory that is identified in the certificate had control of the signature creation data at the time when the certificate was issued;

      (iii) That signature creation data were valid at or before the time when the certificate was issued;

    (d) Provide reasonably accessible means that enable a relying party to ascertain, where relevant, from the certificate or otherwise:

      (i) The method used to identify the signatory;

      (ii) Any limitation on the purpose or value for which the signature creation data or the certificate may be used;

      (iii) That the signature creation data are valid and have not been compromised;

      (iv) Any limitation on the scope or extent of liability stipulated by the certification service provider;

      (v) Whether means exist for the signatory to give notice pursuant to article 8, paragraph 1(b), of this Law;

      (vi) Whether a timely revocation service is offered;

    (e) Where services under subparagraph (d)(v) are offered, provide a means for a signatory to give notice pursuant to article 8, paragraph 1(b), of this Law and, where services under subparagraph (d)(vi) are offered, ensure the availability of a timely revocation service;

    (f) Utilize trustworthy systems, procedures and human resources in performing its services.

2   A certification service provider shall bear the legal consequences of its failure to satisfy the requirements of paragraph 1.

ARTICLE 10: TRUSTWORTHINESS

For the purposes of article 9, paragraph 1(f), of this Law in determining whether, or to what extent, any systems, procedures and human resources utilized by a certification service provider are trustworthy, regard may be had to the following factors:

(a) Financial and human resources, including existence of assets;

(b) Quality of hardware and software systems;

(c) Procedures for processing of certificates and applications for certificates and retention of records;

(d) Availability of information to signatories identified in certificates and to potential relying parties;

(e) Regularity and extent of audit by an independent body;

(f) The existence of a declaration by the State, an accreditation body or the certification service provider regarding compliance with or existence of the foregoing; or

(g) Any other relevant factor.

ARTICLE 11: CONDUCT OF THE RELYING PARTY

A relying party shall bear the legal consequences of its failure:

(a) To take reasonable steps to verify the reliability of an electronic signature; or

(b) Where an electronic signature is supported by a certificate, to take reasonable steps:

    (i) To verify the validity, suspension or revocation of the certificate; and

    (ii) To observe any limitation with respect to the certificate.

ARTICLE 12: RECOGNITION OF FOREIGN CERTIFICATES AND ELECTRONIC SIGNATURES

1   In determining whether, or to what extent, a certificate or an electronic signature is legally effective, no regard shall be had:

    (a) To the geographic location where the certificate is issued or the electronic signature created or used; or

    (b) To the geographic location of the place of business of the issuer or signatory.

2   A certificate issued outside [*the enacting State*] shall have the same legal effect in [*the enacting State*] as a certificate issued in [*the enacting State*] if it offers a substantially equivalent level of reliability.

3   An electronic signature created or used outside [*the enacting State*] shall have the same legal effect in [*the enacting State*] as an electronic signature created or used in [*the enacting State*] if it offers a substantially equivalent level of reliability.

4   In determining whether a certificate or an electronic signature offers a substantially equivalent level of reliability for the purposes of paragraph 2 or 3, regard shall be had to recognized international standards and to any other relevant factors.

5   Where, notwithstanding paragraphs 2, 3 and 4, parties agree, as between themselves, to the use of certain types of electronic signatures or certificates, that agreement shall be recognized as sufficient for the purposes of cross-border recognition, unless that agreement would not be valid or effective under applicable law.

 # NOTES AND QUESTIONS

1   The following Notes are attached to Article 1 of the Model Law on Signatures.

> * The Commission suggests the following text for States that might wish to extend the applicability of this Law: 'This Law applies where electronic signatures are used, except in the following situations: [...].'

> ** The term 'commercial' should be given a wide interpretation so as to cover matters arising from all relationships of a commercial nature, whether contractual or not. Relationships of a commercial nature include, but are not limited, to the following transactions: any trade transaction for the supply or exchange of goods or services; distribution agreement; commercial representation or agency; factoring; leasing; construction of works; consulting; engineering; licensing; investment; financing; banking; insurance; exploitation

agreement or concession; joint venture and other forms of industrial or business cooperation; carriage of goods or passengers by air, sea, rail or road.

What situations can you think of where electronic signatures are used but the provisions of this Model Law should not apply? Why? Do your reasons take into account the subject matter to which the electronic signatures should not apply, or the security (or lack thereof) of electronic signatures?

2   In Chapter 3, the UNCITRAL Model Law on Electronic Commerce is excerpted at considerable length. Within this model law, Article 7 states:

> Article 7: Signature
>
> (1) Where the law requires a signature of a person, that requirement is met in relation to a data message if:
>
> > (a) a method is used to identify that person and to indicate that person's approval of the information contained in the data message; and
> >
> > (b) that method is as reliable as was appropriate for the purpose for which the data message was generated or communicated, in the light of all the circumstances, including any relevant agreement.
>
> (2) Paragraph (1) applies whether the requirement therein is in the form of an obligation or whether the law simply provides consequences for the absence of a signature.
>
> (3) The provisions of this article do not apply to the following: [...].

In light of this, there was potential for confusion once UNCITRAL embarked upon drafting an instrument devoted to signatures alone. It was acknowledged that the relationship between the two documents needed to be clearly outlined so as to avoid this confusion. Consequently, the following paragraph was included in the *Draft Guidelines for Enactment of the Model Law on Electronic Signatures*:

> 3. Relationship with article 7 of the UNCITRAL Model Law on Electronic Commerce
>
> In the preparation of the new Model Law, the view was expressed that the reference to article 7 of the UNCITRAL Model Law on Electronic Commerce in the text of article 6 of the new Model Law was to be interpreted as limiting the scope of the new Model Law to situations where an electronic signature was used to meet a mandatory requirement of law that certain documents had to be signed for validity purposes. Under that view, since the law of most nations contained very few such requirements with respect to documents used for commercial transactions, the scope of the new Model Law was very narrow. It was generally agreed, in response, that such interpretation of article 6 (and of article 7 of the UNCITRAL Model Law on Electronic Commerce) was inconsistent with the interpretation of the words 'the law' adopted by the Commission in paragraph 68 of the Guide to Enactment of the UNCITRAL

Model Law on Electronic Commerce, under which 'the words "the law" are to be understood as encompassing not only statutory or regulatory law but also judicially created law and other procedural law'. In fact, the scope both of article 7 of the UNCITRAL Model Law on Electronic Commerce and of article 6 of the new Model Law is particularly broad, since most documents used in the context of commercial transactions are likely to be faced, in practice, with the requirements of the law of evidence regarding proof in writing.[5]

3   Analyse the above paragraph and the two model laws. Do you believe they can operate together?

4   The professed goal of these documents is to facilitate use of the technology by legislating wide, flexible definitions. In your experience, will courts interpret flexible provisions consistently throughout a legal system? Can we be sure that courts all over the world will interpret the flexible provisions consistently— especially given the reliance on the laws of evidence, which differ widely from state to state?

5   Critically analyse both the UNCITRAL document and the European Directive on a Community Framework for Electronic Signatures, which is extracted below. Carefully examine the provisions of each of these documents. Are there significant differences?

(b)   OECD

The OECD has not produced a policy document specifically on electronic signatures as yet. Nevertheless, the organisation has been active in the development of ideas and the facilitation of discussion in this area. For example, in June 1999 it presented the *Joint OECD–Private Sector Workshop on Electronic Authentication*, at Stanford and Menlo Park, California, in cooperation with Stanford Law School. This workshop produced a number of discussion papers and materials, all designed to enhance commercial and legal understanding of the technology and its implications.[6] As such, the OECD has played the role of facilitator for business organisations and NGOs, rather than operating solely as a policy-maker.

(c)   European Union

In contrast to the OECD, the EU has been very active in the development of policy in this area of electronic commerce. On 13 May 1998, the European Commission presented a Proposal for a directive aimed at establishing a legal framework for electronic signatures and certification authorities in Europe. The Directive came into operation in January 2000. It takes a technology-neutral approach to signatures, which does not hinder the use or development of new authentication technologies. This approach is flexible enough to

---

5   Available at <http://www.uncitral.org/english/workinggroups/wg_ec/wp-88e.pdf> 19 September 2001.
6   Joint OECD–Private Sector Workshop on Electronic Authentication, available at <http://www1.oecd.org/dsti/sti/it/secur/act/wksp-auth.htm> 24 September 2001.

permit experimentation, which is essential for an area of business still in its infancy. The Directive leaves room for party autonomy and for the exclusion of closed groups, for example a local area network, from the Proposal's sphere of application. The Directive employs a voluntary accreditation scheme, which is a non-discriminatory approach that embodies the ethos of much of modern corporate regulation. Significantly, the proposal includes strict-liability rules for certain obligations concerning the issue of the certificates.

The European Union Directive on a Community Framework for Electronic Signatures (1999/93/EC) grants legal recognition to e-signatures. The Directive establishes a rebuttable presumption that, as long as the e-signature meets specific requirements laid down in legislation, it is as legally valid as a handwritten signature. Member States had until July 2001 to enact conforming national legislation. For a detailed study on the legal and practical issues concerning the implementation of the EU Directive, see Interdisciplinary Centre for Law & Information Technology et al, *The Legal and Market Aspects of Electronic Signatures* (2003).

Further, the Directive prohibits mandatory prior authorisation of certification schemes. However, it permits member states to set up voluntary accreditation schemes for certification authorities. Implementation of this provision would result in the creation of a state-endorsed layer, interconnected with the non-governmental accreditation matrix. In the United Kingdom, the *Electronic Communications Act 2000* provides for the creation of a voluntary accreditation scheme for certification authorities that meet the relevant standards. The theory here is simply to add a codified guarantee of legitimacy, underwritten by the apparatus of the state, on top of a technical legitimacy which might, perhaps arguably, already exist.

Directive 1999/93/EC of the European Parliament and of the Council of 13 December 1999 on a Community Framework for Electronic Signatures

Available at
<http://europa.eu.int/eur-lex/en/lif/dat/1999/en_399L0093.html> 19 September 2001

ARTICLE 1: SCOPE

The purpose of this Directive is to facilitate the use of electronic signatures and to contribute to their legal recognition. It establishes a legal framework for electronic signatures and certain certification services in order to ensure the proper functioning of the internal market. It does not cover aspects related to the conclusion and validity of contracts or other legal obligations where there are requirements as regards form prescribed by national or Community law nor does it affect rules and limits, contained in national or Community law, governing the use of documents.

ARTICLE 2: DEFINITIONS

For the purpose of this Directive:

1 'electronic signature' means data in electronic form which are attached to or logically associated with other electronic data and which serve as a method of authentication;

2 'advanced electronic signature' means an electronic signature which meets the following requirements:

   (a) it is uniquely linked to the signatory;
   (b) it is capable of identifying the signatory;
   (c) it is created using means that the signatory can maintain under his sole control; and
   (d) it is linked to the data to which it relates in such a manner that any subsequent change of the data is detectable;

3 'signatory' means a person who holds a signature-creation device and acts either on his own behalf or on behalf of the natural or legal person or entity he represents;

4 'signature-creation data' means unique data, such as codes or private cryptographic keys, which are used by the signatory to create an electronic signature;

5 'signature-creation device' means configured software or hardware used to implement the signature-creation data;

6 'secure-signature-creation device' means a signature-creation device which meets the requirements laid down in Annex III;

7 'signature-verification-data' means data, such as codes or public cryptographic keys, which are used for the purpose of verifying an electronic signature;

8 'signature-verification device' means configured software or hardware used to implement the signature-verification-data;

9 'certificate' means an electronic attestation which links signature-verification data to a person and confirms the identity of that person;

10 'qualified certificate' means a certificate which meets the requirements laid down in Annex I and is provided by a certification-service-provider who fulfils the requirements laid down in Annex II;

11 'certification-service-provider' means an entity or a legal or natural person who issues certificates or provides other services related to electronic signatures;

12 'electronic-signature product' means hardware or software, or relevant components thereof, which are intended to be used by a certification-service-provider for the provision of electronic-signature services or are intended to be used for the creation or verification of electronic signatures;

13 'voluntary accreditation' means any permission, setting out rights and obligations specific to the provision of certification services, to be granted upon request by the certification-service-provider concerned, by the public or private body charged with the elaboration of, and supervision of compliance with, such rights and obligations, where the certification-service-provider is not entitled to exercise the rights stemming from the permission until it has received the decision by the body.

ARTICLE 3: MARKET ACCESS

1   Member States shall not make the provision of certification services subject to prior authorisation.

2   Without prejudice to the provisions of paragraph 1, Member States may introduce or maintain voluntary accreditation schemes aiming at enhanced levels of certification-service provision. All conditions related to such schemes must be objective, transparent, proportionate and non-discriminatory. Member States may not limit the number of accredited certification-service-providers for reasons which fall within the scope of this Directive.

3   Each Member State shall ensure the establishment of an appropriate system that allows for supervision of certification-service-providers which are established on its territory and issue qualified certificates to the public.

4   The conformity of secure signature-creation-devices with the requirements laid down in Annex III shall be determined by appropriate public or private bodies designated by Member States. The Commission shall, pursuant to the procedure laid down in Article 9, establish criteria for Member States to determine whether a body should be designated. A determination of conformity with the requirements laid down in Annex III made by the bodies referred to in the first subparagraph shall be recognised by all Member States.

5   The Commission may, in accordance with the procedure laid down in Article 9, establish and publish reference numbers of generally recognised standards for electronic-signature products in the Official Journal of the European Communities. Member States shall presume that there is compliance with the requirements laid down in Annex II, point (f), and Annex III when an electronic signature product meets those standards.

6   Member States and the Commission shall work together to promote the development and use of signature-verification devices in the light of the recommendations for secure signature-verification laid down in Annex IV and in the interests of the consumer.

7   Member States may make the use of electronic signatures in the public sector subject to possible additional requirements. Such requirements shall be objective, transparent, proportionate and non-discriminatory and shall relate only to the specific characteristics of the application concerned. Such requirements may not constitute an obstacle to cross-border services for citizens.

ARTICLE 4: INTERNAL MARKET PRINCIPLES

1   Each Member State shall apply the national provisions which it adopts pursuant to this Directive to certification-service-providers established on its territory and to the services which they provide. Member States may not restrict the provision of certification-services originating in another Member State in the fields covered by this Directive.

2   Member States shall ensure that electronic-signature products which comply with this Directive are permitted to circulate freely in the internal market.

ARTICLE 5: LEGAL EFFECTS OF ELECTRONIC SIGNATURES

1   Member States shall ensure that advanced electronic signatures which are based on a qualified certificate and which are created by a secure-signature-creation device:

(a) satisfy the legal requirements of a signature in relation to data in electronic form in the same manner as a handwritten signature satisfies those requirements in relation to paper-based data; and

(b) are admissible as evidence in legal proceedings.

2 Member States shall ensure that an electronic signature is not denied legal effectiveness and admissibility as evidence in legal proceedings solely on the grounds that it is:

- in electronic form, or
- not based upon a qualified certificate, or
- not based upon a qualified certificate issued by an accredited certification-service-provider, or
- not created by a secure signature-creation device.

ARTICLE 6: LIABILITY

1 As a minimum, Member States shall ensure that by issuing a certificate as a qualified certificate to the public or by guaranteeing such a certificate to the public a certification-service-provider is liable for damage caused to any entity or legal or natural person who reasonably relies on that certificate:

(a) as regards the accuracy at the time of issuance of all information contained in the qualified certificate and as regards the fact that the certificate contains all the details prescribed for a qualified certificate;

(b) for assurance that at the time of the issuance of the certificate, the signatory identified in the qualified certificate held the signature-creation data corresponding to the signature-verification data given or identified in the certificate;

(c) for assurance that the signature-creation data and the signature-verification data can be used in a complementary manner in cases where the certification-service-provider generates them both;

unless the certification-service-provider proves that he has not acted negligently.

2 As a minimum Member States shall ensure that a certification-service-provider who has issued a certificate as a qualified certificate to the public is liable for damage caused to any entity or legal or natural person who reasonably relies on the certificate for failure to register revocation of the certificate unless the certification-service-provider proves that he has not acted negligently.

3 Member States shall ensure that a certification-service-provider may indicate in a qualified certificate limitations on the use of that certificate, provided that the limitations are recognisable to third parties. The certification-service-provider shall not be liable for damage arising from use of a qualified certificate which exceeds the limitations placed on it.

4 Member States shall ensure that a certification-service-provider may indicate in the qualified certificate a limit on the value of transactions for which the certificate can be used, provided that the limit is recognisable to third parties. The certification-service-provider shall not be liable for damage resulting from this maximum limit being exceeded.

5   The provisions of paragraphs 1 to 4 shall be without prejudice to Council Directive 93/13/EEC of 5 April 1993 on unfair terms in consumer contracts.

ARTICLE 7: INTERNATIONAL ASPECTS

1   Member States shall ensure that certificates which are issued as qualified certificates to the public by a certification-service-provider established in a third country are recognised as legally equivalent to certificates issued by a certification-service-provider established within the Community if:

   (a) the certification-service-provider fulfils the requirements laid down in this Directive and has been accredited under a voluntary accreditation scheme established in a Member State; or

   (b) a certification-service-provider established within the Community which fulfils the requirements laid down in this Directive guarantees the certificate; or

   (c) the certificate or the certification-service-provider is recognised under a bilateral or multilateral agreement between the Community and third countries or international organisations.

2   In order to facilitate cross-border certification services with third countries and legal recognition of advanced electronic signatures originating in third countries, the Commission shall make proposals, where appropriate, to achieve the effective implementation of standards and international agreements applicable to certification services. In particular, and where necessary, it shall submit proposals to the Council for appropriate mandates for the negotiation of bilateral and multilateral agreements with third countries and international organisations. The Council shall decide by qualified majority.

3   Whenever the Commission is informed of any difficulties encountered by Community undertakings with respect to market access in third countries, it may, if necessary, submit proposals to the Council for an appropriate mandate for the negotiation of comparable rights for Community undertakings in these third countries. The Council shall decide by qualified majority. Measures taken pursuant to this paragraph shall be without prejudice to the obligations of the Community and of the Member States under relevant international agreements.

ARTICLE 8: DATA PROTECTION

1   Member States shall ensure that certification-service-providers and national bodies responsible for accreditation or supervision comply with the requirements laid down in Directive 95/46/EC of the European Parliament and of the Council of 24 October 1995 on file protection of individuals with regard to the processing of personal data and on the free movement of such data.

2   Member States shall ensure that a certification-service-provider which issues certificates to the public may collect personal data only directly from the data subject, or after the explicit consent of the data subject, and only insofar as it is necessary for the purposes of issuing and maintaining the certificate. The data may not be collected or processed for any other purposes without the explicit consent of the data subject.

3   Without prejudice to the legal effect given to pseudonyms under national law, Member States shall not prevent certification service providers from indicating in the certificate a pseudonym instead of the signatory's name.

ARTICLE 11: NOTIFICATION

1 Member States shall notify to the Commission and the other Member States the following:

   (a) information on national voluntary accreditation schemes, including any additional requirements pursuant to Article 3(7);
   (b) the names and addresses of the national bodies responsible for accreditation and supervision as well as of the bodies referred to in Article 3(4);
   (c) the names and addresses of all accredited national certification service providers.

2 Any information supplied under paragraph 1 and changes in respect of that information shall be notified by the Member States as soon as possible.

 N O T E S   A N D   Q U E S T I O N S

1 Consider Article 2. Why do you think separate definitions of 'electronic signature' and 'advanced electronic signature' are necessary?

2 Consider Article 3 and discuss the following statement: 'The accreditation schemes create a "pyramid" regime which will become unworkable and prone to corruption'.

3 What is the effect of Article 5? Is it too early for such a recognition?

4 Article 6 is by far one of the most significant articles. Critically analyse the effect of this article on the operation of electronic signatures.

5 Note the presence of Article 8 in this directive. What does this indicate about the EU's drive for a coherent system? What is the effect on harmonisation?

6 In addition to the three discussed above, what other relevant international bodies are contributing to the debate on regulation? What role do these organisations play?

7 Do you think this array of international organisations assists in the harmonisation of the law in this area? How might they hamper each other's goals?

8 Do you consider that the UNCITRAL Model Law or the Directive is enough to produce effective legal institutions in this area? If not, what strategies would you employ to bring about these institutions?

9 Is it simply too early to begin to regulate this area? Has technology too far to go before it settles into a form that can be regulated? If the law must wait for technology to settle, will there ever be a 'right time' to regulate? What options could be considered in the face of these possibilities?

(d)   UN convention (2005)

The United Nations *Convention on the Use of Electronic Comunications in International Contracts* (23 Nov 2005) has already been referred to in Chapter 3. Importantly, Article 2 excludes consumer transactions from its scope. The Convention does not define the term 'electronic signature' but Article 9(3) represents a compromise on the position of electronic signatures. It requires that a method is used to identify the signer and a method is used to indicate the signer's intention in respect of the information contained in the electronic communication. The method used must be as reliable as appropriate for the purpose in light of all the relevant circumstances, or alternatively, is proven in fact to have fulfilled the functions described above, by itself or together with further evidence. The Convention, while maintaining a technology neutral stance makes an oblique reference to technology when it permits the stated functions to be met independently.

----

4   National responses to digital signatures

(a)   Australia

Developments regarding electronic signatures in Australia have been slow since the adoption of the *Electronic Transactions Act*, under the UNCITRAL Model Law for Electronic Commerce. There have been a number of private sector moves, such as the establishment of a public-key infrastructure project for those in the medical profession known as the Health eSignature Authority. This will allow doctors and hospitals to register and obtain a digital certificate to transmit patient records securely over the Internet.[7]

Significantly, the Australian Commonwealth Government has established its own public-key infrastructure framework for the public sector, known as Gatekeeper. This PKI is designed to facilitate the production of government services on-line and grew out of the *Investing for Growth* industry statement of 1996.[8]

The present Federal Government believes that the development of the information economy in Australia should be market-led, rather than government-led. As such, the development and use of appropriate forms of authentication technology is to be left to industry.

Thus far, the only legislative guidance on electronic signatures is to be found in the *Electronic Transactions Act 1999*. The government describes its position as a 'principled technology-neutral approach' to the electronic authentication techniques set out in the *Electronic Transactions Act 1999*.

Section 10 of the *Electronic Transactions Act*, extracted below, is based on Article 7 of the UNCITRAL Model Law on Electronic Commerce. The Model Law provides that if a method of sending a data message identifies the sender and indicates his or her approval of the information contained in the data message, and if the method used was as reliable as was appropriate for the purposes for which the data message was communicated, a signature will be legally recognised as equivalent to a handwritten signature. In reality, however, the phrase 'as reliable as was appropriate' stands in stark contrast to the detail and specificity (regardless of its neutrality with respect to technology) of the new

----

7   Concerns have been raised about the security of this project; see M Spencer, 'PKI "dangerous" for health sector', *The Australian (IT)* 20 March 2001, available at <http://australianit.news.com.au/ common/ storyPage/0,3811,1815922^442,00.html> 26 September 2001.

8   See further AGIMO's web site <http://www.gatekeeper.gov.au/>.

UNCITRAL Model Law on Electronic Signatures. The government has acknowledged the potential for specific legislation in the future, particularly as the use of electronic authentication techniques develops.

Electronic Transactions Act 1999 (Cth)

10. SIGNATURE

REQUIREMENT FOR SIGNATURE

(1) If, under a law of the Commonwealth, the signature of a person is required, that requirement is taken to have been met in relation to an electronic communication if:

   (a) in all cases—a method is used to identify the person and to indicate the person's approval of the information communicated; and

   (b) in all cases—having regard to all the relevant circumstances at the time the method was used, the method was as reliable as was appropriate for the purposes for which the information was communicated; and

   (c) if the signature is required to be given to a Commonwealth entity, or to a person acting on behalf of a Commonwealth entity, and the entity requires that the method used as mentioned in paragraph (a) be in accordance with particular information technology requirements—the entity's requirement has been met; and

   (d) if the signature is required to be given to a person who is neither a Commonwealth entity nor a person acting on behalf of a Commonwealth entity—the person to whom the signature is required to be given consents to that requirement being met by way of the use of the method mentioned in paragraph (a).

CERTAIN OTHER LAWS NOT AFFECTED

(2) This section does not affect the operation of any other law of the Commonwealth that makes provision for or in relation to requiring:

   (a) an electronic communication to contain an electronic signature (however described); or

   (b) an electronic communication to contain a unique identification in an electronic form; or

   (c) a particular method to be used in relation to an electronic communication to identify the originator of the communication and to indicate the originator's approval of the information communicated.

 NOTES AND QUESTIONS

The Australian Government's strategy could be described as a hands-off approach to digital and electronic signatures. Do you think this is the most appropriate approach? Consider this question as you read the material below, which is intended to provide some comparison between approaches across jurisdictions.

(b) Singapore

In contrast to Australia, Singapore has produced a comprehensive legislative framework for the regulation of signatures. In accordance with its drive to be at the forefront of the information economy, Singapore has enacted a number of detailed statutes and regulations. These include the *Electronic Transactions Act 1998*, the *Electronic Transactions (Certification Authority) Regulations* 1999, the Security Guidelines for Certification Authorities, and the Information Technology Security Guidelines. The *Electronic Transactions Act 1998* is at the apex of the regulatory structure.

The certification authority regulations govern the application procedures, including fees and financial criteria, as well as the renewal and duration of an authority's licence. Certification authorities must also undergo a compliance audit and maintain logs of their transactions. The regulations outline the types of certificates that can be awarded and set out requirements for their issuance, renewal, suspension and revocation. Key repositories are recognised under the regulations and come under their control, as do the legal requirements for secure digital signatures and the formation of an electronic contract.

The *Electronic Transactions Act 1998* includes the authority for the regulations discussed above and contains detailed definitions and provisions. It was noted above that providing satisfactory definitions is crucial for the operation of a legal system. The following definition of digital signature is included in the Singapore Act:

> an electronic signature consisting of a transformation of an electronic record using an asymmetric cryptosystem and a hash function such that a person having the initial untransformed electronic record and the signer's public key can accurately determine: (a) whether the transformation was created using the private key that corresponds to the signer's public key; and (b) whether the initial electronic record has been altered since the transformation was made.

The Singapore regime is certainly one of the more detailed approaches to electronic and digital signatures. The regulatory culture of Singapore contrasts significantly with that of, for example, the USA, which prefers a more 'hands off' approach. For a detailed analysis, see Y F Lim, 'Digital Signatures, Certification Authorities: Certainty in the Allocation of Liability' (2003) 7 *Singapore Journal of International & Comparative Law* 183.

Electronic Transactions Act 1998 (Singapore)

8. ELECTRONIC SIGNATURES

(1) Where a rule of law requires a signature, or provides for certain consequences if a document is not signed, an electronic signature satisfies that rule of law.

(2) An electronic signature may be proved in any manner, including by showing that a procedure existed by which it is necessary for a party, in order to proceed further with a transaction, to have executed a symbol or security procedure for the purpose of verifying that an electronic record is that of such party.

NOTES AND QUESTIONS

1   Compare the Singapore definition of signatures to that included in the South Korean *Basic Law on Electronic Commerce*:

> A 'Digital Signature' shall mean 'a seal affixed in a digital form which is to identify the originator of an electronic message, and to indicate that the electronic message was generated by the originator'.

Which do you consider to be more useful? Why? If you were faced with a choice, would the difference between these provisions influence a business decision in relation to either of these countries?

2   Do you believe that a closely defined and controlled regulatory framework is the most effective structure for Internet regulation?

(c)   United Kingdom

In 2000 the United Kingdom government introduced the *Electronic Communications Act* in fulfilment of part of its obligations under the EU Directive. For our purposes, the focus will be on the PKI system in place. In the United Kingdom, the development of a voluntary accreditation scheme *'tScheme'* has eliminated the need for the government, at least at this point, to adopt a statutory voluntary accreditation scheme. Part I of the UK Act deals solely with cryptography service providers. Section 1(1) states that it is the duty of the Secretary of State to establish and maintain a register of approved providers of cryptography support services. Section 2(1) provides that it will be the duty of the Secretary of State to secure arrangements in force for granting approvals to persons who either provide or propose to provide cryptography services in the United Kingdom and are seeking approval with respect to the services they are providing. Section 2(3) dictates the conditions that must be fulfilled before an approval will be granted, including: compliance with technical requirements; continued compliance with any requirements; and being a fit and proper person to be approved in respect of those services.

Further, subsection 16(2) provides that Part I will only come into force when the Secretary of State makes an order by statutory instrument. What is unusual about Part I, however, is the inclusion in the *Electronic Communications Act* of Part III, subsection 16(4), of a 'sunset' clause, which states:

> If no order for bringing Part I of this Act into force has been made under subsection (2) by the end of the period of five years, beginning with the day on which this Act is passed, that Part shall, by virtue of this subsection, be repealed at the end of that period.

Subsection 16(4) also provided a date—25 May 2005, which was five years after the *Electronic Communications Act* came into force—by which the government had to enact a statutory voluntary accreditation scheme, or the provisions would be repealed. The government failed to enact a scheme and the subsection was repealed.

There appear to be two reasons for this failure to exercise the option of a voluntary accreditation scheme for certification authorities. First, it is is reflective of the government's minimalist, 'hands off' approach to the regulation of electronic and digital signatures. This is interesting, considering that at the time of its enactment, the UK government was accused of wanting to regulate suppliers of encryption keys and the lapsing of Part I of the Act was seen as a 'victory in the United Kingdom's crypto wars.'[9] It is also interesting considering that the EU Directive prohibits mandatory licensing of certification authorities and merely gives Members States the option of having a voluntary scheme.

Second, the evolution and success of *tScheme*, a voluntary accreditation scheme, appears to have saved the government from having to develop a statutory scheme. It was incorporated in May 2000 and is administered by a non-profit organisation, funded by its members, which include Microsoft, IBM, Vodafone, Royal Mail, BT Ignite, and the British Chambers of Commerce. It was formed with the primary aim of industry regulation, rather than government intervention, fulfilling Part I of the *Electronic Communications Act 2000*. The strength of *tScheme* lies in its Approvals Profiles. Trust Service Providers are independently assessed for each of the trust services to be provided to their clients. There are numerous Approval Profiles, and a provider is first evaluated against the *tScheme* Base Approvals Profile to establish its general integrity. That profile looks at management competence, security policy and procedures and the suitability of personnel.[10]

The first step for a service seeking accreditation is to apply to *tScheme* for Registered Applicant Status, indicating commitment to the process. An audit of the Trust Service Provider is then undertaken by an independent assessor, who evaluates the services of the provider against the appropriate Approval Profile. The assessor completes an assessment report that the Trust Service Provider must submit to *tScheme* as certification of compliance with the profile. If satisfied, *tScheme* will invite the Trust Service Provider to sign a contract, a fee is paid and the name of the provider is added to the *tScheme* web directory of approved services, indicating that the provider conforms to standards deserving of trust.[11] Many of the *tScheme*-approved service providers use qualified certificates—the basis of an Advanced Electronic Signature pursuant to the *Electronic Signatures Regulations 2002* (UK)—as these provide additional legal benefits.[12]

As *tScheme* is a voluntary accreditation scheme, there is no specific need for a Trust Service Provider to undergo the approval process. If a provider is approved by *tScheme*, the provider earns the right to display the *tScheme* trade mark in relation to its services: an advantage in the competitive digital signature market. Further, consumers derive a benefit from knowing that the cryptographic services they have chosen are secure and have been evaluated against high, independently assessed standards. While *tScheme* has no powers to 'punish' errant providers, the approval contract between *tScheme* and the Trust Service Provider is binding and sanctions may be imposed should a justifiable complaint or failure be established against Trust Service Provider. Penalties for a complaint or failure

9   Ross Anderson in SA Mathieson, 'UK Crypto Regulation Option Dies', *InfoSecurity Magazine*, 25 May 2005.
10   See Jamie Murray, 'Public Key Infrastructure Digital Signatures and Systematic Risk' (2003) 1 *The Journal of Information, Law and Technology (JILT)* <http://elj.warwick.ac.uk/jilt/03-1/murray.html>.
11   For more information, see <http://www.tscheme.org>.
12   See Schedule 1, *Requirements for Qualified Certificates, Electronic Signatures Regulations 2002* (UK). Schedule 1 of the Regulations is the equivalent of Annex I to Directive 1999/93/EC.

include compensation and termination of approval rights. The contract, however, also provides the Trust Service Provider a right of appeal.

While it is generally claimed that *tScheme* was an industry-led and funded development, the UK government has made it clear that, at least according to its view, *tScheme* is a form of co-regulation of certification authorities.[13] The fact that the government did not choose to establish the statutory scheme indicates that, at least for now, *tScheme* is fulfilling its objectives.[14] The UK experience thus provides an interesting approach to accreditation schemes for certification authorities: a hands-off approach where a government originally accused of wanting to regulate encryption has essentially allowed self-regulation.

It may seem, however, that despite the legislative activity in establishing a framework for digital signatures, the average person is still utilising methods of signing more commonly found in everyday usage of the Internet. In the decision of *Metha v J Pereira Fernandes* [2006] EWHC 813 (Ch) 07 April 2006, the High Court of the United Kingdom had to consider whether an email address included (automatically) at the top of a message constituted a signature. It held that it did not constitute a signature under s 4 of the Statute of Frauds 1677 because it had not been inserted to give authenticity.

(d) The USA

In 1999, faced with a plethora of diverse, inconsistent state legislation, the US National Conference of Commissioners on Uniform State Law agreed upon the *Uniform Electronic Transactions Act 1999*. UETA is an interesting piece of legislation in that it rejects the technology-specific approach already adopted by many of the US states[15] in favour of the UNCITRAL Model Law technology-neutral approach. The UETA has been adopted in almost all US jurisdictions, either in its original form or with amendments.[16]

The UETA applies when the *Uniform Commercial Code* is not applicable in transactions related to business; commercial transactions including consumer transactions; and governmental matters.[17] Like the EU Directives, UETA is procedural and does not affect the substantive law of contracts.

An 'electronic signature' is defined in the Act as an electronic sound, symbol, or process associated with a record and executed or adopted by a person with the intent to sign the record.[18] The reference to 'process' would include clicking buttons on web pages as electronic signatures if the other applicable requirements are also present. It is also immediately apparent that the focus on UETA is not necessarily on the 'signature'

---

13   Ibid.
14   Phillip Rees, 'Electronic Signatures—Not Worth The Paper They're Written On?' *International Journal of Electronic Commerce Law and Practice*, 12 September 2002, ECom 2.1(25).
15   See, for example, the *Illinois Electronic Commerce Security Act 1998* (HB. 3180), which focused on digital signature technology.
16   Christopher William Pappas, *Comparative US & EU Approaches to E-Commerce Regulation: Jurisdiction, Electronic Contracts, Electronic Signatures and Taxation* (2002) 31 Denv J Intl L & Policy 325 at 341.
17   UETA s 3; *Uniform Commercial Code* Article 2 applies to transactions in goods. UCC 2-107. Benjamin A Pearlman, 'Finding An Appropriate Global Legal Paradigm for the Internet: United States and International Responses' (2001) 29 *Ga J Int'l & Comp L* 597 at 615.
18   Section 2(8) *Uniform Electronic Transactions Act 1999*.

itself but whether the person intended to 'sign' that record or contract. Such an approach is consistent with the remainder of the Act. UETA does not require a signature in electronic form to be used or created[19] and it only applies to transactions where both parties agreed to transact through electronic means.[20] Further, whether an electronic signature carries any legal consequences is determined not just by the UETA but also by other applicable laws.[21]

UETA does provide, however, that an electronic signature cannot be denied legal effect or enforceability solely because it is in electronic form,[22] and that if a law requires a signature, an electronic signature satisfies that law.[23] These provisions reflect Articles 5, 6 and 7 of the UNCITRAL *Model Law on Electronic Commerce*.[24] UETA further deals with the attribution and effect of electronic signatures. An electronic signature is attributable to a person if it was the act of the person, and this may be shown in any manner, including a demonstration of the efficacy of any security procedure applied to determine the person to which the electronic signature was attributable.[25] The effect of a signature attributed to a person will be determined by the context and circumstances of the signature and as otherwise provided by law.[26] Finally, UETA establishes that in legal proceedings, evidence of a signature may not be excluded solely because it is in electronic form.[27] This mirrors Article 9 of the UNCITRAL *Model Law on Electronic Commerce*.[28]

The reference in the UETA to intent is noteworthy. The nature of the intent of a signer will vary with the transaction, and in many cases requires examination of the circumstances in which the signature was made. Under the UETA, it is important that the process by which an electronic signature is applied is established in a manner designed to ensure that the application of the signature evidences the intent of the signer to sign or otherwise be bound by the document. This is usually accomplished by the context in which the signature is applied.[29]

In 2000, President Clinton signed into law the *Electronic Signatures in Global and National Commerce Act*. E-SIGN was a federal reaction to the fact that by mid-2000, only 18 states had adopted UETA, with many choosing to retain their individual legislation.[30] The US Congress thus enacted a technology-neutral law, focusing on the intent of the party rather than the technology used, and specifically designed to pre-empt any

---

19   See s 5(a).
20   See s 5(b).
21   Section 5(e).
22   Section 7(a).
23   Section 7(d).
24   See *Uniform Electronic Transactions Act*, with Prefatory Note and Comments, at 27, accessed at www. law.upenn.edu/bll/ulc/fnact99/1990s/ueta99.htm on 6/12/05.
25   Section 9(a).
26   Section 9(b).
27   Section 13.
28   See *Uniform Electronic Transactions Act*, with Prefatory Note and Comments, at 42, accessed at www. law.upenn.edu/bll/ulc/fnact99/1990s/ueta99.htm on 6/12/05.
29   Thomas J Smedinghoff, *Seven Key Legal Requirements for Creating Enforceable Electronic Transactions*, available online at <http://www.bakernet.com/ecommerce/7-etran-req.pdf>.
30   Jonathan E Stern, 'The Electronic Signatures in Global and National Commerce Act' (2001) 16 *Berkeley Technology Law Journal* 391 at 399.

inconsistent state laws. E-SIGN reflects the core principles of UETA while imposing additional requirements for the protection of consumers in electronic transactions. The definition of an electronic signature is the same as the definition contained in UETA: a signature can be a sound, process, or symbol and must have been executed or adopted by a person who intended to sign a record or contract.[31] This broad definition was designed to encompass everything from the creation of a binding electronic signature by clicking 'yes' on a website to creating a signature using a more complex method—for example, biometric authentication.[32]

E-SIGN is divided into four titles. Titles I and III apply to electronic signatures. The first section of Title I establishes the general rule of validity for electronic signatures. A signature cannot be denied legal effect solely because it is in electronic form.[33] The Act then establishes that Title I does not affect any requirement imposed by another statute, regulation, or rule of law relating to the rights and obligations of parties, other than any statute stating that contracts must be signed in a non-electronic form.[34] Further, the Act does not require any person to use electronic signatures, other than a governmental agency, whose responsibilities are later defined.[35] Title I then deals with consumer protection, requiring the consent of a person when using electronic records[36] and allowing an electronic signature to be used for notarisation purposes.[37]

The second section states that E-SIGN pre-empts any inconsistent state law. While a state statute may modify, limit or supersede the first section of E-SIGN, the statute may only do this in certain circumstances. First, a state statute will not be pre-empted if it constitutes an adoption of UETA.[38] Second, the statute will not be pre-empted if the alternative procedures or requirements that it imposes are consistent with Titles I and II of the Act.[39] These alternative requirements must not require or accord greater legal status to a specific technology for, among other things, performing, creating, or authenticating electronic signatures—and, if enacted after E-SIGN, the statute must refer to the Act.[40] The effect of these provisions is to remove all remaining inconsistent legislation. E-SIGN therefore 'immediately provides nationwide uniformity regarding the legal validity of an electronic contract.'[41]

E-SIGN also includes specific exceptions to the application of the electronic signature provisions, including wills or testamentary trusts[42] and adoption, divorce or family law

---

31   See *Electronic Signatures in Global and National Commerce Act* 15 USC § 7006(5).
32   Jonathan E Stern, 'The Electronic Signatures in Global and National Commerce Act' (2001) 16 *Berkeley Technology Law Journal* 391 at 395.
33   *Electronic Signatures in Global and National Commerce Act* 15 USC § 7001 (a)(1) (2000).
34   *Electronic Signatures in Global and National Commerce Act* 15 USC § 7001 (b)(1) (2000).
35   *Electronic Signatures in Global and National Commerce Act* 15 USC § 7001 (b)(2) (2000).
36   *Electronic Signatures in Global and National Commerce Act* 15 USC § 7001 (c)(1) (2000).
37   *Electronic Signatures in Global and National Commerce Act* 15 USC § 7001 (g) (2000).
38   *Electronic Signatures in Global and National Commerce Act* 15 USC § 7002 (a)(1) (2000).
39   *Electronic Signatures in Global and National Commerce Act* 15 USC § 7002 (a)(2)(A) (2000).
40   *Electronic Signatures in Global and National Commerce Act* 15 USC § 7002 (a)(2)(A)(ii) and (B) (2000).
41   Jonathan E Stern, 'The Electronic Signatures in Global and National Commerce Act' (2001) 16 *Berkeley Technology Law Journal* 391 at 399.
42   *Electronic Signatures in Global and National Commerce Act* 15 USC § 7003(a)(1) (2000).

papers.[43] Additional exceptions include court orders or notices, the termination of utility services and product recalls.[44] The Act then deals with its application to Federal and State governments.[45]

Title III of E-SIGN, 'Promotion of International Electronic Commerce', requires the Secretary of Commerce to promote the acceptance of electronic signatures internationally, in order to reduce any impediments to their use.[46] The Secretary of Commerce must do so in accordance with a number of principles specified in the Act—which include the removal of paper-based obstacles to electronic transactions—through the adoption of the relevant principles of the UNCITRAL 1996 Model Law on Electronic Commerce, which allows parties to determine the appropriate electronic signature authentication technologies.[47]

E-SIGN is arguably most interesting for its firm rejection of any law preferring or dictating one technology over another. The Act explicitly disallows states from enacting legislation conferring any additional benefits on a particular technology. This rejection makes a useful introduction to the arguments on the technology-neutral aspect of the debate. It is argued that legislation that does not prescribe a specific technology allows for the use of a variety of technologies to create contracts and reflects the changing state of electronic signature technology as well as using appropriate technology on a case-by-case basis.[48] Such an approach promotes freedom of contract and allows parties the freedom to decide what technologies will authenticate their signatures.[49] This freedom 'is a position that most businesses gladly embrace' as an individual business can now choose how to transact with its customers.[50] However, the argument against allowing parties such freedom is that consumers may not want such freedom and that it may confuse and reduce trust among them. New technologies create further uncertainties and possibly additional legal issues, for example, fraud.[51]

Further, while there are substantial similarities between UETA and E-SIGN, there is also an interesting difference. E-SIGN does not state 'any standards for attributing responsibility in the event that an electronic signature is forged or stolen.'[52] It is 'presumed' that existing laws would apply.[53] UETA, however, 'creates a framework for attributing an electronic signature.'[54] This framework appears in Section 9, which states an 'electronic

43   *Electronic Signatures in Global and National Commerce Act* 15 USC § 7003(a)(2).
44   *Electronic Signatures in Global and National Commerce Act* 15 USC § 700 (b).
45   See generally *Electronic Signatures in Global and National Commerce Act* 15 USC § 7004.
46   *Electronic Signatures in Global and National Commerce Act* 15 USC § 7031(a)(1).
47   *Electronic Signatures in Global and National Commerce Act* 15 USC § 7031(a)(2)(A) and (B).
48   Anda Lincoln, 'Electronic Signature Laws and the Need for Uniformity in the Global Market' (2004) 8 *Journal of Small and Emerging Business Law* 67 at 78.
49   Jonathon E Stern in Anda Lincoln, 'Electronic Signature Laws and the Need for Uniformity in the Global Market' (2004) 8 *Journal of Small and Emerging Business Law* 67 at 78.
50   Jonathan E Stern, 'The Electronic Signatures in Global and National Commerce Act' (2001) 16 *Berkeley Technology Law Journal* 391 at 402-3.
51   Anda Lincoln, 'Electronic Signature Laws and the Need for Uniformity in the Global Market' (2004) 8 *Journal of Small and Emerging Business Law* 67 at 78.
52   Jonathan E Stern, 'The Electronic Signatures in Global and National Commerce Act' (2001) 16 *Berkeley Technology Law Journal* 391 at 403.
53   Ibid.
54   Ibid.

signature is attributable to a person if it was the act of the person' and directs attention to a number of factors that may be considered when determining whether a signature was the act of the person.[55]

It is also worth noting that E-SIGN is unique in that it explicitly concerns itself with consumer protection.[56] Other laws, for example, the UNCITRAL Model Law on Electronic Commerce, state that their provisions do not override any pre-existing consumer protection laws.[57] It is obvious, however, that the Model Law is simply intended to give guidance.

E-SIGN provides a special information disclosure and corresponding consent requirement for certain consumer transactions, namely where a law requires that information relating to the transaction be provided to the consumer in writing, and that the vendor desires to deliver that information to the consumer electronically.[58] The vendor must first obtain the consumer's affirmative consent. Further, prior to obtaining the consumer's consent, the consumer must be provided with a clear and conspicuous notice that informs the consumer of numerous matters.[59]

 ## NOTES AND QUESTIONS

1   As a basic premise, parties must agree to conduct their dealings electronically before E-SIGN applies. Therefore, there is no requirement to accept an electronic signature if it is received without notification and prior agreement. Is this a satisfactory approach to electronic signatures? Does it place them on an equal footing with handwritten signatures? Is there another option?

2   One of the most important aspects of the federal E-SIGN legislation is its relationship with other state-enacted electronic commerce laws. How significant are the problems of enacting uniform legislation in a federation? Do you foresee similar problems in Australia? Consider the Australian *Electronic Transactions Act* in your answer.

3   How important is it that the US federal legislation defines 'transaction' to mean international commercial interaction, as well as intra-national?

4   Is international harmonisation a realistic goal? If not, what are the alternatives to harmonisation? Is it possible that institutions such as PKI that operate independently of sovereign states might be more effective because they provide customary regulatory structures rather than coercive formal structures in the realm of electronic signatures?

---

55   See s 9(a), *Uniform Electronic Transactions Act 1999*.

56   See *Electronic Signatures in Global and National Commerce Act* 15 USC § 7001(c).

57   See Footnote 3 to Article 1, UNCITRAL Model Law on Electronic Commerce 1996, GA Res 51/162 UN GAOR, 51st sess, 85th plen mtg, UN Doc A/RES/51/162 (1996), accessed on the UNCITRAL website, <http://www.uncitral.org/uncitral/en/uncitral_texts/electronic_commerce/1996Model.html> on 6/12/05. Article 1 of the UNCITRAL Model Law on Electronic Signatures 2001 also explicitly states that it does not override any consumer protection law.

58   See *Electronic Signatures in Global and National Commerce Act* 15 USC § 7001(c).

59   See *Electronic Signatures in Global and National Commerce Act* 15 USC § 7001(c)(1)(B).

7   Internet Crime

----

1   Introduction

The Internet brings with it unprecedented potential for the positive development of our society. The ability to disseminate information and to communicate almost instantaneously has already revolutionised numerous facets of our lives and will continue to do so. Simultaneously, the Internet provides extremely effective tools and mechanisms for individuals and groups who seek to conduct unlawful activity. Throughout history, each advance in technology has brought new means by which traditional crimes could be committed. So it is with the Internet. With this new tool for mass communication comes the ability to commit crimes inexpensively, quickly, and across an enormous geographical space (in theory, across the entire planet!).

In keeping with the historical trend, the Internet also provides new means for combating this innovative illegality, and raises the question: how should our society, and our government, respond to this new challenge? And what means allow us the capability of doing so? Legal systems have evolved to enforce continuing legal norms in unfamiliar contexts to meet the demands of developing technology. As always, this requires balancing competing interests in a society.

In 1999, in the USA, the President and Vice President established an inter-agency Working Group on Unlawful Conduct on the Internet, chaired by the Attorney General. This working group was to provide an initial analysis of legal and policy issues surrounding the use of the Internet to commit unlawful acts.

(a)   A policy framework and legal analysis

The President's Working Group on Unlawful Conduct on the Internet, The Electronic Frontier: The Challenge of Unlawful Conduct Involving the Use of the Internet, March 2000

Available at <http://www.cybercrime.gov/unlawful.htm> 17 August 2006

A. Understanding the nature of unlawful conduct involving computers

Although definitions of computer crime may differ, not every crime committed with a computer is a computer crime. For example, if someone steals a telephone access code and makes a long distance call, the code they have stolen is checked by a computer before the call is processed. Even so, such a case is more appropriately treated as 'toll fraud', not computer crime. Although this example may seem straightforward, many cases cannot be so neatly categorized. For example, a bank teller who steals a $10 bill from a cash drawer is embezzling. A bank teller who writes a computer program to steal pennies from many accounts (at random) and to funnel that money into another bank through the electronic funds transfer system may also be embezzling, but both committing and prosecuting this offense may require a working knowledge of the bank's computer system. Thus, such a crime may reasonably be characterized as a computer offense.

Broadly speaking, computers can play three distinct roles in a criminal case. First, a computer can be the target of an offense. This occurs when conduct is designed to take information without authorization from, or cause damage to, a computer or computer network. The 'Melissa' and 'Explore.Zip.Worm' viruses, along with 'hacks' into the White House and other web sites, are examples of this type of offense. Second, a computer can be incidental to an offense, but still significant for law enforcement purposes. For example, drug traffickers may store transactional data (such as names, dates, and amounts) on computers, rather than in paper form. Third, computers can be a tool for committing an offense, such as fraud or the unlawful sale of prescription drugs over the Internet. Each of these three roles can be and often are present in a single criminal case. Although this report focuses primarily on this third category of computer crime, it is important to understand the range of unlawful conduct that involves computers to appreciate the context of law enforcement needs and challenges relating to such conduct.

...

B. A framework for evaluating unlawful conduct on the Internet

In its assessment of the extent to which existing federal laws are sufficient to address unlawful conduct involving the use of the Internet, the Working Group developed four general principles to guide its analysis ...

1. ONLINE–OFFLINE CONSISTENCY

First, substantive regulation of unlawful conduct (eg, legislation providing for civil or criminal penalties for given conduct) should, as a rule, apply in the same way to conduct in the cyberworld as it does to conduct in the physical world. If an activity is prohibited in the physical world but not on the Internet, then the Internet becomes a safe haven for that unlawful activity. Similarly, conduct that is not prohibited in the physical world should not be subject to prohibition merely because it is carried out in cyberspace.

Thus, the first step in any analysis of unlawful conduct involving the use of the Internet is to examine how the law treats the same conduct in the offline world. That is, unlawful conduct involving the use of the Internet should not be treated as a special form of conduct outside the scope of existing laws. For example, fraud that is perpetrated through the use of the Internet should not be treated any differently, as a matter of substantive criminal law, from fraud that is perpetrated through the use of the telephone or the mail. To the extent existing laws treat online and offline conduct inconsistently, they should be amended to remove inconsistencies. As the discussion below and the detailed analyses of several examples in the appendices to this report illustrate, however, existing substantive law is generally sufficient to cover unlawful conduct involving the use of the Internet.

2. APPROPRIATE INVESTIGATORY TOOLS

Second, to enforce substantive laws that apply to online conduct, law enforcement authorities need appropriate tools for detecting and investigating unlawful conduct involving the Internet. For example, as discussed in greater detail below, to the extent existing investigative authority is tied to a particular technology, it may need to be modified or clarified so that it also applies to the Internet.

Indeed, new technologies may justify new forms of investigative authority. Before the invention of the telephone, for example, law enforcement had no need for wiretaps, but once it was clear that the telephone was being used to facilitate illegal activity, that new authority—circumscribed with protections for civil liberties and other societal interests— became necessary and appropriate. Similarly, features of the Internet that make it different from prior technologies may justify the need for changes in laws and procedures that govern the detection and investigation of computer crimes. These features, highlighted here in summary form, are discussed in greater detail below:

- *The global and boundaryless nature of the Internet* means that different law enforcement agencies in different jurisdictions will have to cooperate and coordinate their activities in ways that they have probably never before done.
- *Anonymity* on the Internet can provide social benefits, but misrepresentation of identity can also facilitate fraud and deception. Misrepresentation of identity can also result in access by children to inappropriate material and can create law enforcement investigatory challenges, especially if perpetrated by sophisticated computer users, for it can make criminal activity on the Internet more difficult to detect and prove.
- *The potential to reach vast audiences easily* means that the scale of unlawful conduct involving the use of the Internet is often much wider than the same conduct in the offline world. To borrow a military analogy, use of the Internet can be a 'force multiplier'.
- *The routine storage of information that can be linked to an individual* can often provide more information to law enforcement (where an individual has been identified or a computer lawfully seized) than may be available in the offline world, but only if the electronic information is handled properly by a trained investigator and if the information obtained is ultimately available in usable form.

Thus, apart from ensuring that online and offline behavior is treated consistently as a matter of substantive law, legislators and policy-makers should examine whether law enforcement agencies have appropriate tools to detect and investigate unlawful conduct involving the Internet …

3. TECHNOLOGY-NEUTRALITY

Third, to the extent that specific regulation of online activity may be necessary (in view of the consistency principle noted above), any such regulation should be drafted in a technology-neutral way. Regulation tied to a particular technology may quickly become obsolete and require further amendment. In particular, laws written before the widespread use of the Internet may be based on assumptions regarding then-current technologies and thus may need to be clarified or updated to reflect new technological capabilities or realities. For example, regulation of 'wire communications' may not account for the fact that communications may now occur through wireless means or by satellite …

4. CONSIDERATION OF OTHER SOCIETAL INTERESTS

Fourth, any government regulation of conduct involving the use of the Internet requires a careful consideration of different societal interests. In addition to society's strong interests in investigating and prosecuting unlawful conduct, society also has strong interests in promoting free speech, protecting children, protecting reasonable expectations of privacy, providing broad access to public information, and supporting legitimate commerce.

As applied to the Internet, consideration of other societal interests can present difficult issues, in part because the Internet is different in important ways from existing, 'traditional' modes of communication. For example, the Internet is a multi-faceted communications medium that allows not only point-to-point transmission between two parties (like the telephone), but also the widespread dissemination of information to a vast audience (like a newspaper). Internet-specific laws and policies that operate by analogy to those designed for telephone communications or the press may not fit the new medium. The Internet also presents new issues relating to online expectations of privacy and confidentiality that may or may not have analogues in the offline world. Accordingly, rules and regulations designed to protect the safety and security of Internet users should be carefully tailored to accomplish their objectives without unintended consequences, such as stifling the growth of the Internet or chilling its use as a free and open communication medium.

Another aspect of the need to consider different societal interests is to appreciate the need for an appropriate balance among the roles of the government (whether federal, state, local, or other) and the role of the private sector in formulating solutions to Internet policy issues. For example, because regulation of the practices of medicine and pharmacy has traditionally been the province of the states, regulation of online pharmacies presents difficult federal–state jurisdictional and coordination issues. And, as discussed in the next section, given the Administration's support for private-sector leadership and market-based self-regulation regarding e-commerce, there must be ongoing and regular dialogue with interested parties and groups to ensure that government policies do not have unintended consequences.

C. Promoting private sector leadership

Consistent with the Administration's overall e-commerce policy, the private sector has a critical role to play in ensuring a safe and secure online environment. The distributed, networked, and decentralized nature of the Internet now means that the 'rules of the road' must be global, flexible, effective, and readily adaptable to technological change. In particular, the private sector must take the lead in areas such as the design of new technologies to protect children online, self-regulatory consumer protection initiatives, and coordination and cooperation with law enforcement authorities.

In response to the marketplace, for example, there are now many technological options for shielding children from inappropriate content ... [T]hese technological developments include filtering and blocking software, outgoing information blocks, filtered Internet browsers and search engines, filtered Internet service providers, time blocking mechanisms and monitoring tools. Similarly, child-friendly web sites are now widespread on the Internet...

In addition, in response to challenges issued by Commerce Secretary Daley, industry has worked with consumer representatives to develop consumer protection practices, codes of conduct for business-to-consumer e-commerce, and alternative, easy-to-use mechanisms for consumer resolution, redress, and enforcement.

- For example, the Better Business Bureau's online division, BBBOnLine, is working with industry, consumer, and government representatives to develop a voluntary code to provide online merchants with guidelines to implement consumer protections. The code includes guidance on key consumer protections such as disclosure of sale terms, data privacy, dispute resolution mechanisms, and non-deceptive advertising.
- Another group, the Electronic Commerce and Consumer Protection Group, whose members include America Online, American Express, AT&T, Dell, IBM, Microsoft, Time Warner, Inc, and Visa, is working with consumer leaders to develop an innovative approach to jurisdiction as it applies to consumer protection in a global electronic marketplace. This group is also developing a voluntary code of conduct. The goal of the group is to formulate concrete approaches to protect consumers and facilitate e-commerce.

These creative efforts are important to developing effective consumer protection in e-commerce, because as e-commerce expands to encompass more international business-to-consumer transactions, the traditional means of protecting consumers solely through national laws will become more difficult.

In addition to specific consumer protection initiatives, the private sector's dedication and support for a secure Internet system are crucial to curbing unlawful conduct on the Internet. Not only must industry continue to develop security policies and safeguards for their networks and systems, but it should also continue its efforts to identify security flaws that threaten the Internet ...

The private sector also has a key role to play in continuing to coordinate and cooperate with law enforcement authorities as appropriate. Industry trade groups, such as the Internet Alliance and the Information Technology Association of America ('ITAA'), have been working to develop public–private cooperative efforts that will mutually benefit law enforcement, industry, and consumers. The Internet Alliance's Law Enforcement and Security Council has been developing parental control software and educational campaigns, opening channels of communication between industry and law enforcement representatives, and creating training programs for law enforcement and industry on issues of mutual interest. ITAA, through its Cybercitizen Project, is working with the Department of Justice to develop education campaigns, personnel exchange programs, and a directory of industry contacts.

Although the private sector has taken important steps in the areas of prevention and online security, there is still much that industry can do to ensure that the Internet is a safe and secure environment. For example:

- Industry should continue to develop and embrace initiatives to protect consumers and children online. These may include technological tools (eg, more sophisticated blocking, filtering, and parental control software) as well as non-technological tools (eg, educational campaigns). In particular, industry should continue to be involved in education programs that teach younger Internet users about online responsibilities and online citizenship.
- Industry should continue to cooperate with law enforcement agencies as appropriate. This does not mean that industry ought to be a 'co-regulator' with government or that industry needs to be an online police officer. But it does mean that industry should be a voluntary, responsible partner in society's fight against crime, educating its employees

on how to recognize unlawful conduct on the Internet and what to do if they discover such conduct. It means working with law enforcement agencies to develop reliable and efficient procedures and channels of communication and cooperation for processing law enforcement requests and investigative information. As the 'Melissa' virus case demonstrates, industry's involvement and reporting of information is often crucial to the investigation and prosecution of online offenders.

• Industry should carefully balance reasonable expectations of customer privacy with the need to ensure a safe and secure online environment. For example, some industry members may not retain certain system data long enough to permit law enforcement to identify online offenders. This does not mean that data retention policies need to be uniform or mandatory. To the contrary, in evaluating the costs and benefits of data retention—which include a wide variety of considerations, including market needs, protection of consumer privacy, and public safety—industry should simply give appropriate weight to the wider value to itself and to society of retaining certain information that, among other things, may be essential to apprehending a lawbreaker.

• Industry should be encouraged to recognize that meaningful self-regulation is in its interest as well as in the interests of its customers. Information technology security programs (that teach employees about computer ethics, responsible online practices, and security policies), for instance, help protect computer systems from intruders as well as online offenders. Indeed, as we noted at the outset of this report, law enforcement and industry share a common mission in reducing unlawful online conduct, for a safe and secure online environment is essential to consumer confidence, which is in turn essential to ensuring that the Internet continues to grow as a medium for communications and commerce.

The Working Group looks forward to continuing to work with the private sector and other interested parties and groups in partnership on these important issues.

D. Sufficiency of existing federal laws

Private sector leadership is, of course, necessary but not sufficient to address unlawful conduct involving the use of the Internet. Substantive criminal laws represent a societal determination, expressed through our democratic institutions of government, that certain conduct is so harmful or morally unacceptable that reliance on self-regulation or the market to regulate the conduct is inappropriate. There is thus a need to evaluate whether existing substantive laws apply to unlawful conduct that is committed through the use of the Internet ...

1. ANALYSIS OF SUBSTANTIVE LAWS

The Working Group's analysis reveals that existing substantive federal laws appear to be generally adequate to protect users from unlawful conduct on the Internet ...

For example, laws governing fraud—such as credit card fraud, identity theft, securities fraud, and unfair and deceptive trade acts or practices—apply with equal force to online as well as offline conduct. Laws prohibiting the distribution and possession of child pornography and the luring of minors across state lines for unlawful sexual activity have been used with success to prosecute and convict those who use the Internet to distribute such material or to communicate with child victims in violation of statutory prohibitions ...

Laws in other areas—the sale of firearms; interstate transmission of gambling information; sale of alcohol; securities fraud; and theft of intellectual property—also generally apply to online conduct as well as offline conduct. ...

2. NEW INVESTIGATORY CHALLENGES

As law enforcement agencies adapt to a more technology-based society, they need to be aware of the challenges, as well as the benefits, of online investigations. In certain circumstances, law enforcement agencies have available to them tools and capabilities created by the Internet and computers that can assist them in their fight against computer-facilitated unlawful conduct. For example, just as advances in telephone technology gave law enforcement agents the ability to determine the origin of fraudulent or threatening calls, the Internet has given law enforcement agencies the ability to find unsophisticated offenders who leave the equivalent of 'fingerprints' as they commit unlawful acts. Indeed, someone who makes a threat in an Internet chat room to set off a bomb at a school and who makes little or no effort to hide his or her identity (eg, where accurate identifying information exists for a particular 'screen name') can often be traced and found with relative ease ...

At the same time, law enforcement agencies must also acknowledge the growing sophistication of other computer users, who wear the equivalent of Internet gloves that may hide their fingerprints and their identity. The following is an overview of investigatory challenges—taken from actual experiences involving online investigations and discussed in greater detail in the appendices for each example of Internet-facilitated unlawful conduct—that law enforcement agencies must consider as they become more proficient with such investigations ...

(A) JURISDICTION

In the physical world, one cannot visit a place without some sense of its geographic location. Whether visiting a particular street address or an area of the world, human travel is spatially based. By contrast, because one can access a computer remotely without knowing where, in physical space, that computer is located, many people have come to think of the collection of worldwide computer linkages as 'cyberspace' (a term coined by science fiction writer William Gibson). In short, cybercriminals are no longer hampered by the existence of national or international boundaries, because information and property can be easily transmitted through communications and data networks.

As a result, a criminal no longer needs to be at the actual scene of the crime (or within 1000 miles, for that matter) to prey on his or her victims. Just as telephones were (and still are) used by traditional boiler-room operators to defraud victims from a distance, a computer server running a web page designed to defraud senior citizens might be located in Thailand, and victims of the scam could be scattered throughout numerous different countries. A child pornographer may distribute photographs or videos via e-mail running through the communications networks of several countries before reaching the intended recipients. Likewise, evidence of a crime can be stored at a remote location, either for the purpose of concealing the crime from law enforcement and others, or simply because of the design of the network. To be sure, the Internet increases the ability of law enforcement officials and others to detect and gather evidence from a distance. For example, a web site used in a fraud scheme can be spotted from an agent's office, whereas detecting a fraudulent telemarketing or mail-fraud scheme might well require extensive field work. Long-distance detection, however, may take the investigation and prosecution of these crimes out of the exclusive purview of any single jurisdiction, thereby creating yet other challenges and obstacles to crime-solving.

For example, a cyberstalker in Brooklyn, New York may send a threatening e-mail message to a person in Manhattan. If the stalker routes his communication through Argentina, France, and Norway before reaching his victim, the New York Police Department may have to get assistance from the Office of International Affairs at the Department of Justice in Washington, DC which, in turn, may have to get assistance from law enforcement in (say) Buenos Aires, Paris, and Oslo just to learn that the suspect is in New York. In this example, the perpetrator needs no passport and passes through no checkpoints as he commits his crime, while law enforcement agencies are burdened with cumbersome mechanisms for international cooperation, mechanisms that often derail or slow investigations. With scores of Internet-connected countries around the world, the coordination challenges facing law enforcement are tremendous. And any delay in an investigation is critical, as a criminal's trail often ends as soon as he or she disconnects from the Internet.

This does not mean that traditional legal structures cannot be meaningfully applied to the Internet. Even though connections may be of short duration, computers are still physically located in particular places. The challenge to law enforcement is identifying that location and deciding which laws apply to what conduct. The question is how sovereign nations can meaningfully enforce national laws and procedures on a global Internet.

Inconsistent substantive criminal laws are only part of the problem, for investigative techniques are also controlled by national (or local) law. For example, law enforcement agencies must consider such issues as transborder execution of search warrants. If law enforcement agents in the United States access a computer and seize data from a computer, the fact that they have a search warrant makes that action lawful. If, with that same search warrant, they remotely access a Canadian computer (from the United States), might this constitute a criminal act under Canadian law notwithstanding the existence of the US warrant? To the extent that agents know nothing more than an Internet protocol address (essentially, a series of numbers that identify a particular machine), the physical location of the computer to be searched may not be accurately known. Yet ignorance of physical location may not excuse a transborder search; consider how we would react to a foreign country's 'search' of our defense-related computer systems based upon a warrant from that country's courts.

This transborder issue may raise domestic issues as well. Gambling and obscenity laws provide criminal sanctions for individuals based, in part, upon their location. One federal law prohibits transmitting information assisting in the placing of bets or wagers on sporting events or contests unless both the sender and receiver are in states or foreign countries where gambling is legal: see 18 USC s 1084. Obscenity laws are also typically interpreted in light of local community standards: cf *Miller v California*, 413 US 15 (1973). Even the search warrant provision in the federal rules requires that agents seek a warrant in the district where the property to be seized is located: see Fed R Crim P 41(a). To the extent the location of the sender, recipient, or data is unknown and perhaps unknowable, it may be difficult for law enforcement to investigate and prosecute online offenders.

(B) IDENTIFICATION

Another thorny issue stems from the lack of identification mechanisms on global networks, and the fact that individuals can be anonymous or take on masked identities (ie, adopt false personas by providing inaccurate biographical information and misleading screen names). Simply stated, given the current state of technology, it can be difficult to accurately identify an individual (especially sophisticated users who take affirmative steps to hide their identity) on the Internet ... [T]here are cases ... where law enforcement agencies have been able to track down online criminals who leave evidence of their unlawful conduct. Over time, the ability of criminals to use technology to evade identification and the ability of law enforcement to use technology to overcome such evasion will continue to evolve. Some of the challenges of identifying perpetrators of unlawful conduct on the Internet, as well as measures taken by law enforcement and the private sector to respond to such challenges, are discussed below ...

(C) EVIDENTIARY ISSUES

Electronic data generated by computers and networked communications such as the Internet can be easily destroyed, deleted, or modified. Digital photographs are but one example of digital information that can be altered in ways that may be difficult to detect. As a result, law enforcement officials must be cognizant of how to gather, preserve, and authenticate electronic evidence. This will not only require substantial training of law enforcement personnel, but also sufficient experience with such evidence by investigators, prosecutors, defense counsel, courts, and others until clear rules and standards are established. The volume of electronic evidence that requires forensic analysis is also increasing substantially. The increasing use of computers and the Internet, of course, often means that information or records of communications that were previously never retained or routinely destroyed can (in some instances) now be recovered, but such recovery may still require sophisticated computer forensics ...

(D) INFRASTRUCTURE PROTECTION

Protecting our information infrastructure is imperative but difficult for a host of reasons: the number of different systems involved, the interdependency of these systems, the varied nature of the threats (physical and cyber, military, intelligence, criminal, natural), and the fact that many of these infrastructures are maintained primarily by the commercial sector. Addressing cyberthreats to our infrastructure is particularly difficult, because of differing views regarding our vulnerabilities; the need to balance interests relating to privacy, economic competitiveness, commercial risk, national security, and law enforcement; and the overlapping authorities within the federal government for dealing with information infrastructure issues. Although such issues are beyond the scope of this report, see National Plan for Information Systems Protection (released 7 January 2000), appreciating the importance and complexity of infrastructure protection is key to understanding the needs of law enforcement in countering unlawful conduct involving the Internet.

(E) COMMINGLING

The ability of an individual to use one computer to conduct both lawful and unlawful activities or to store both contraband and legally possessed material presents another significant issue. Such commingling defies simple solutions. The fact is, one computer can be used simultaneously as a storage device, a communications device (eg, to send, store, or retrieve e-mail), and a publishing device. Moreover, that same computer can be used simultaneously for both lawful and unlawful ventures, and the problem becomes more complex when a single machine is shared by many users.

For example, individuals who distribute child pornography or copyrighted software using their home computers may also publish a legitimate newsletter on stamp collecting or use an e-mail service with that same computer. By seizing the computer, law enforcement agencies can stop the illegal distribution of contraband, but may, at the same time, interfere with the legitimate publication of the newsletter and the delivery of e-mail, some of which may be between users who have no connection with the illegal activity. Similarly, a doctor who is illegally prescribing drugs over the Internet may not only have on her computer evidence relating to the illegal prescriptions, but files related to her lawfully treated patients. Likewise, an attorney accused of operating an Internet sportsbook may keep in the same folder on his computer materials relating to his gambling business and documents subject to the attorney–client privilege. Seizure of the doctor's or the lawyer's files in such circumstances could result in the seizure of legally privileged material.

 NOTES AND QUESTIONS

1 What are the three main roles computers can play in a criminal act? Give examples of each.

2 What are the standards by which we might judge the effect of our legal system in combating computer crime?

3 'If you aim to please everyone, you will end up pleasing no one.' Discuss this quote, with particular emphasis on the attempt to consider a range of societal interests as we seek to combat crime on the Internet.

4 The Working Group gave considerable emphasis to the private sector. Do you think this is a result of a genuine need for its inclusion in the regulatory process, or simply a manifestation of the American fear of big government?

5 For law enforcement agencies, what are the new challenges currently not faced by them in the real world?

(b) Law enforcement needs and challenges

The President's Working Group on Unlawful Conduct on the Internet, The Electronic Frontier: The Challenge of Unlawful Conduct Involving the Use of the Internet, March 2000

Available at <http://www.cybercrime.gov/unlawful.htm> 17 August 2006

As the examples of Internet-facilitated unlawful conduct discussed above and in the appendices illustrate, the increasing sophistication and global reach of such conduct make it all the more important to adequately equip law enforcement agencies at all levels.

The following are some of the principal issues that should be considered when evaluating how to better equip federal, state, and local law enforcement agencies to ensure the safety and security of Internet users. We urge further analysis ... to determine the most appropriate ways to promote private sector leadership in this area and to empower law enforcement—at all levels—with the needed tools, capabilities, and legal authorities to curb unlawful conduct on the Internet while protecting privacy and supporting the growth of the electronic marketplace.

A. *Protecting computers and networks*

In assessing the tools, capabilities, and legal authorities needed by law enforcement to address unlawful conduct on the Internet, we must consider the larger context of how to protect the systems and networks of this nation that make our businesses run and operate our nation's defenses and infrastructure. As we have become more dependent on technology, our energy production and distribution channels, our transportation networks, and our telecommunication systems have become increasingly reliant on a computer-based infrastructure.

Without a protected infrastructure, there could be no conduct, lawful or unlawful, on the Internet. Electronic commerce and the marketplace cannot thrive without a strong infrastructure that the public can trust and rely upon. Consequently, proposals relating to law enforcement challenges in this area (eg, new investigative tools, capabilities, or legal authorities) need to be assessed in light of the broader need to protect the vital infrastructure, because cyberattacks on infrastructures and other cybercrimes can lead to telecommunications breakdowns that disable electronic commerce and destroy our citizens' confidence in the Internet and computer networks.

The protection of this country's computers and networks requires everyone's cooperation. It demands a partnership among all federal agencies with responsibilities for certain special functions, such as law enforcement, intelligence, and defense ... Most important, because the overwhelming majority of the nation's infrastructure is in private hands, the private sector must take the steps necessary to prevent attacks against its systems ...

B. *Federal tools and capabilities*

1. PERSONNEL, EQUIPMENT, AND TRAINING

In 1986, an astronomer-turned-systems-manager at the University of California at Berkeley found a 75-cent accounting error in a computer's billing program, which led to the discovery that an unauthorized user had penetrated Berkeley's computer system. When the astronomer, Clifford Stoll, began to investigate further, he discovered that a hacker identified as 'Hunter' was using Berkeley's computer system as a conduit to break into US government systems and steal sensitive military information. The hacker's objective seemed to be to attain US anti-ballistic missile technology.

As he began to pursue the hacker, Stoll encountered serious problems. To begin with, Stoll was unable to find computer-literate law enforcement personnel with an appreciation of the technical nature of the criminal activity. Local and federal agencies that Stoll contacted, including the FBI and CIA, initially expressed little interest in pursuing what at first looked like a computer prank. (Moreover, until government investigators learned of the potential threat to national security, they had no interest in pursuing a case which appeared to have damages valued at less than one dollar.) Because Hunter's trail vanished each time he ended a communication, he could only be traced when he was online. But because it was often after business hours (and, indeed, sometimes in the middle of the night) when Hunter attacked, there were few (if any) law enforcement personnel available during those sessions. The call was eventually traced to Germany, but adding an international element to the case now meant that it was usually after business hours in at least one time zone where the communication was passing through. Stoll cleverly resorted to generating phony official-looking data to keep the hacker interested and online long enough for the trace to be completed. Eventually, the source of the attacks was identified as a German hacker, and he was successfully prosecuted there.

Ironically, one reason this investigation was successful is that Stoll did not rely solely on law enforcement, but instead was able to work directly with telephone company personnel, who in turn worked with other telecommunications providers. His investigation brought to light a number of interdependent personnel and resource requirements that, unless fulfilled, will impede the success of law enforcement in this area. Despite significant progress since the time of this example, it remains a useful illustration of some of the fundamental issues that continue to need further attention at the domestic and international level to eliminate weak links in the chain of an investigation.

(A) EXPERTS DEDICATED TO HIGH-TECH CRIME

The complex technical and legal issues raised by computer-related crime require that each jurisdiction have individuals who are dedicated to high-tech crime and who have a firm understanding of computers and telecommunications. The complexity of these technologies, and their constant and rapid change, mean that investigating and prosecuting offices must designate investigators and prosecutors to work these cases on a full-time basis, immersing themselves in computer-related investigations and prosecutions ...

(B) EXPERTS AVAILABLE ON A 24-HOUR BASIS

A unique feature of high-tech and computer-related crime is that it often requires immediate action to locate and identify criminals. The trail of a criminal may be impossible to trace once a communication link is terminated, because the carrier may not keep (or is not required by law to keep) records concerning each individual communication. This lack of information is due, in part, to the fact that there often is no longer a revenue-related reason for recording transmission information (ie, connection times or source and destination) for individual connections. For example, many businesses no longer bill their customers by individual telephone call or Internet connection but, instead, by bulk billing (eg, a single rate for one month of usage). When a carrier does not collect traffic data, a suspect's trail may evaporate as soon as the communication terminates.

Therefore, investigators and prosecutors with expertise in this field must be available 24 hours a day so that appropriate steps can be taken in a fast-breaking high-tech case. For example, the National Infrastructure Protection Center operates a 24-hour/seven-day-a-week command post for around-the-clock coverage of computer intrusion matters. And, Attorney General Reno recently challenged the National Association of Attorneys General to work with the Department of Justice and other appropriate organizations (among other things) to create a '24/7' network of computer crime enforcement personnel in every state.

(C) REGULAR AND FREQUENT TRAINING

Because of the speed at which communications technologies and computers evolve, and because criminal methods in these areas generally change more rapidly than those in more traditional areas of crime, experts must receive regular and frequent training in the investigation and prosecution of high-tech cases. Programs such as those offered by the FBI at its Quantico facility and elsewhere and under the National Cybercrime Training Partnership provide such training to federal, state, and local law enforcement personnel, but more is needed ...

In addition to domestic training, countries should participate in coordinated training with other countries, so transnational cases can be pursued quickly and seamlessly. By way of example, in the US, high-tech prosecutors at the federal level attend a one-week training course every year, with training provided by both government and private sector personnel. Likewise, in 1998, the G-8 countries held an international high-tech training conference for its countries' law enforcement personnel.

(D) UP-TO-DATE EQUIPMENT

In the past, a police officer would be given a gun, a flashlight, and a notepad when he or she was hired. Twenty years later, the three items would be returned to the police department when the officer retired, and the only intervening equipment expenses would have had to do with replacement bullets, batteries, and note paper. Today, keeping pace with computer criminals means that law enforcement experts in this field must be properly equipped with the latest hardware and software. Providing proper equipment, however, can be one of the more difficult challenges, because the cost of purchasing and upgrading sophisticated equipment and software places considerable burdens on the budget process.

Ultimately, personnel, training, and equipment needs require the direct involvement of senior officials, such as the Attorney General and FBI Director, because of the budget-request and budget-allocation processes that are involved with such expenditures. Moreover, in many jurisdictions, senior policy-makers may not be as familiar with new computer and telecommunications technologies and with threats posed by cybercriminals. If senior government officials in those jurisdictions are unfamiliar with the technologies at issue or the new threats and challenges they pose, they may be hesitant to support law enforcement by seeking appropriate legislative and budgetary changes. The need for adequate personnel, resources, and training is thus a critical issue in this increasingly important area of law enforcement.

2. LOCATING AND IDENTIFYING CYBERCRIMINALS

When a hacker disrupts air traffic control at a local airport, when a cyberstalker sends a threatening e-mail to a public school or a local church, or when credit card numbers are stolen from a company engaged in e-commerce, investigators must locate the source of the communication. To accomplish this, they must trace the 'electronic trail' leading from the victim back to the perpetrator. But the realities for law enforcement engaged in such a pursuit are very different from those of just a few years ago. Consequently, society faces significant challenges in the coming years as online criminals become more sophisticated and as technology may make anonymity more easily available. The following are some of the challenges facing both industry and law enforcement.

Divested and diverse environment. In today's communications environment, where telecommunication services are no longer provided by a monopoly carrier, a single end-to-end transmission is often carried by more than one carrier. As a result, the communications of a hacker or other criminal may pass through as many as a dozen (or more) different types of carriers, each with different technologies (eg, local telephone companies, long-distance carriers, Internet service providers ('ISPs'), and wireless and satellite networks). The communication may also pass through carriers in a number of different countries, each in different time zones and subject to different legal systems. Indeed, each of these complications may exist within a single transmission. This phenomenon makes it more difficult (and sometimes impossible) to track criminals who are technologically savvy enough to hide their location and identity.

Wireless and satellite communications. Cellular and satellite-based telephone networks allow users to roam almost anywhere in the world using the same telephone. Although the social and commercial benefits of such networks are obvious, these networks can also provide a valuable communication tool for criminal use. Although sophisticated technology may allow law enforcement, under certain circumstances, to identify the general geographic region from which a wireless call is originating or terminating, the use of such technology raises profound and difficult issues at the intersection of privacy and law enforcement policies ...

Real-time tracing. Tracing a communication from victim back to attacker may be possible only when the attacker actually is online. Sophisticated criminals can alter data concerning the source and destination of their communications, or they may use the Internet account of another. In addition, transmission information may not be retained or recorded by communications providers or may not be captured at all or held for only a short period of time. Even if it is generated and retained, it might be deleted by a skilled intruder to hide his identity.

Consequently, when law enforcement officials have information that a crime is being committed online, they often must attempt to trace a communication as it occurs. To do so, a law enforcement agency must know which computer crime expert to call in which jurisdiction, be able to contact the relevant individuals at various ISPs and carriers, and secure appropriate legal orders in each jurisdiction where a relevant carrier or ISP is located. (Notably, many ISPs already coordinate and cooperate with law enforcement agencies in this respect, and industry groups are developing 'best practices' to encourage others to do the same.) Critical personnel must also be available when network-facilitated crimes occur after business hours. When these crimes occur across borders, real-time investigations must be able to proceed on an international scale.

Technical infrastructure and data retention. If the communications network and the computers and software that run it have not been designed and configured to generate and preserve critical traffic data, information relating to the source and destination of a cyber-attack will likely not exist. Consider, for example, the use by many ISPs of modem banks to provide Internet access to incoming callers. An ISP may have two million customers, but maintain only 100,000 phone lines, based on an expectation that no more than 100,000 customers will ever dial in at any given time. The ISP may give only one access number to its customers and dynamically assign each incoming call to the next available line. Without a revenue-related reason for knowing the specific line used for each connection, the ISP's network may not be designed to generate the data necessary to link a customer with a specific incoming line. This, in turn, may make it impossible to trace the origin of the telephone call into the ISP's network. Such a network design can make it difficult to obtain traffic data critical to an investigation.

Even if a particular piece of the technical infrastructure is capable of generating and preserving needed data, such data are not useful if carriers do not collect and retain such records. Issues concerning whether, to what extent, and for how long critical data are retained are decided both by national laws (or the lack thereof) and by industry practices, which generally reflect market preferences and other revenue-related needs. In examining data retention practices and laws, careful consideration must be given to privacy concerns, market realities, and public safety needs.

US law enforcement may be significantly affected by the 1995 and 1997 directives of the European Union ('EU') concerning the processing of personal data, including the deletion of traffic data. EU Member States are in the process of developing implementing legislation. As the directives are implemented into national legislation throughout the EU, it is vital that public safety be considered, along with the privacy and market force elements.

Anonymity. Anonymous e-mail accounts, which are e-mail accounts where subscriber information is not requested or verified, are the proverbial double-edged sword. Such anonymous accounts can protect privacy, but they add new complexities to identifying online lawbreakers, such as individuals who send child pornography, death threats, computer viruses, or copyright-protected works by e-mail.

Similarly, 'anonymous re-mailer services, which are e-mail services that strip the source address information from e-mail messages before passing them along to their intended recipients, raise difficult privacy and law enforcement policy issues. On the one hand, anonymous re-mailer services provide privacy and encourage freedom of expression ... On the other hand, such services can plainly frustrate legitimate law enforcement efforts ...

To be sure, individuals can generally engage in many 'real world' activities relatively anonymously, such as making small cash payments and attending public events. But they cannot remain anonymous in other contexts, such as opening a bank account or registering a car. Indeed, many financial institutions have substantial customer identification requirements. As discussed in Part II.B above, Internet-based activities should be treated consistently with physical world activities and in a technology-neutral way to further important societal goals (such as the deterrence and punishment of those who commit money laundering). National policies concerning anonymity and accountability on the Internet thus need to be developed in a way that takes account of privacy, authentication, and public safety concerns.

3. COLLECTING EVIDENCE

When computers are used to store information, law enforcement agents generally can, upon securing a warrant, search the computer in the same way that they would a briefcase or file cabinet. The difference, of course, is that a computer can store a tremendous amount of information, including evidence that might not be known to the computer's owner. This feature of computer information can, of course, be both a benefit to and a challenge for law enforcement. It can benefit law enforcement by providing information (sometimes in a readily searchable way) that might not have existed in the non-computer world. But it can obviously present law enforcement challenges by highlighting the need for training and expertise (and time) for the information to be recovered. For example, one computer with three gigabytes of memory can contain the equivalent of one million pages of information. 'Keyword' searches can miss relevant information, and the difficulty of the search and recovery of information may depend on how familiar the forensic expert is with the particular hardware and software configuration of the computer at issue. Moreover, if information on the computer is encrypted, it may be completely inaccessible to law enforcement and contribute little to solving the crime at issue.

C. State and local tools and capabilities

State and local law enforcement agencies play a significant role in addressing unlawful conduct on the Internet. These agencies have been crucial in combating online child pornography, prescription drug sales, gambling, and fraud. Consequently, any initiatives by the federal government to address unlawful conduct on the Internet must account for the important role state and local governments play in online investigations and prosecutions and should address the following three areas of fundamental concern to these state and local law enforcement authorities: (1) jurisdiction; (2) cooperation and coordination; and (3) resources ...

1. JURISDICTION

In responding to the challenge of law enforcement on the Internet, one of the problems that state and local governments face is that, although the crimes and schemes on the Internet may victimize local populations, the medium over which these crimes are committed permits a defendant to be located anywhere in the world. The traditional investigative tools available to the state—interviews, physical or electronic surveillance, and service of subpoenas for the production of documents or for testimony—are not necessarily adequate to compel information from a wrongdoer who is located out of state ...

2. INTERSTATE AND FEDERAL–STATE COOPERATION

Because the gathering of information in other jurisdictions and internationally will be crucial to investigating and prosecuting cybercrimes, all levels of government will need to develop concrete and reliable mechanisms for cooperating with each other. The very nature of the Internet—its potential for anonymity and its vast scope—may cause one law enforcement agency to investigate, inadvertently, the activities of another agency that is conducting an undercover operation. Likewise, the law enforcement agency of one state may require the assistance of another for capturing and extraditing a criminal to its state for prosecution. In other words, crimes that were once planned and executed in a single jurisdiction are now planned in one jurisdiction and executed in another, with victims throughout the United States and the world.

In January 2000, Attorney General Reno challenged the National Association of Attorneys General and other state and local law enforcement groups to make it a priority to respond to these significant needs. Among other things, she specifically urged the groups to:

- Create a 24-hour cybercrime point of contact network, where each participating federal, state, and local law enforcement agency would provide a designated contact who is available 24 hours per day, seven days per week to assist with cybercrime issues. This contact could be available via a pager system or coordinated through a centralized 'command center'.
- Create an online clearinghouse for sharing information to avoid duplication of effort and multiple investigations of the same unlawful conduct. Existing mechanisms, such as XSP, LEO, or Consumer Sentinel, may either serve this function or serve as building blocks for such a service.
- Develop conferences for all state and local Internet investigators and prosecutors, yearly or biannually, at which recent developments are discussed, case progress shared, and networks reinforced that will facilitate state, federal, and local cooperation.
- Develop additional policies and mechanisms to enhance cooperative interstate investigative and prosecutorial capacities and encourage coordination among their constituents.

3. RESOURCES

Although state and local law enforcement organizations are responsible for investigating and prosecuting most forms of unlawful conduct involving the use of the Internet, they have limited resources with which to pay the substantial costs of developing the technical, investigative, and prosecutorial expertise and acquiring the new and often expensive technology necessary to address these crimes. Personnel, equipment, and training must be funded not only once but on a recurring basis. In addition, the structure of state and local law enforcement agencies is different from state to state and even county to county within a state. Resources must not be so restricted as to prohibit a state or local government from tailoring programs and initiatives within their current structures.

Federal funding can be useful in supplementing state and local spending on the necessary personnel, training, and equipment to properly investigate and prosecute high technology crime cases. To the extent that federal funds are expended on enhancing federal law enforcement's forensic capabilities, these projects should be structured in a way that allows state and local law enforcement to use these forensic resources. Regional computer forensic laboratories, such as the new laboratory in San Diego, have been successful and may be a model for other such facilities ...

E. Challenges for international cooperation

1. SUBSTANTIVE INTERNATIONAL CRIMINAL LAW

When one country's laws criminalize high-tech and computer-related crime and another country's laws do not, cooperation to solve a crime, as well as the possibility of extraditing the criminal to stand trial, may not be possible. Inadequate regimes for international legal assistance and extradition can therefore, in effect, shield criminals from law enforcement:

criminals can go unpunished in one country, while they thwart the efforts of other countries to protect their citizens.

International legal assistance can be requested and provided through several means. The United States is party to over 20 bilateral mutual legal assistance treaties ('MLATs'). Where there is no MLAT in force, international legal assistance is governed by domestic mutual legal assistance laws and practices, which include the letters rogatory process. (A letter rogatory is a letter request for assistance from one country's judicial authority—eg, a US District Court—to that of another country. See, eg, 28 USC s 1782.) MLATs and domestic laws vary with regard to the requirements relating to a request for assistance. To issue subpoenas, interview witnesses, or produce documents, some MLATs and some laws permit assistance as long as the conduct under investigation is a crime in the requesting state, even where it is not also a crime in the requested state.

In the more sensitive area of searches and seizures, however, dual criminality (ie, that the conduct under investigation is a crime in both the requesting and requested countries and is punishable by at least one year in prison) is often required (eg, US–Netherlands MLAT). In other circumstances, a country can refuse a request if the request 'relates to conduct in respect of which powers of search and seizure would not be exercisable in the territory of the Requested Party in similar circumstances' (eg, US–UK MLAT). Finally, some MLATs and domestic laws permit assistance only if dual criminality exists and if the offense is extraditable (eg, mutual assistance laws of Germany). With regard to extradition, the United States has entered into bilateral treaties with over 100 countries. These treaties are either 'list treaties', containing a list of offenses for which extradition is available, or they require dual criminality and that the offense be punishable by a specified minimum period. Therefore, if one country does not criminalize computer misuse (or provide for sufficient punishment), extradition may be prohibited.

The issue of dual criminality is not an academic or theoretical matter. In 1992, for example, hackers from Switzerland attacked the San Diego Supercomputer Center. The US sought help from the Swiss, but the investigation was stymied due to lack of dual criminality (ie, the two nations did not have similar laws banning the conduct), which in turn impeded official cooperation. Before long, the hacking stopped, the trail went cold, and the case had to be closed.

The solution to the problems stemming from inadequate laws is simple to state, but not as easy to implement: countries need to reach a consensus as to which computer and technology-related activities should be criminalized, and then commit to taking appropriate domestic actions. Unfortunately, a true international 'consensus' concerning the activities that universally should be criminalized is likely to take time to develop. Even after a consensus is reached, individual countries that lack appropriate legislation will each have to pass new laws, an often time-consuming and iterative process.

2. MULTILATERAL EFFORTS

Although bilateral cooperation is important in pursuing investigations concerning unlawful conduct involving the use of the Internet, multilateral efforts are a more effective way to develop international policy and cooperation in this area. The reason for this stems from the nature of the Internet itself. Because Internet access is available in over 200 countries, and because criminals can route their communications through any of these countries, law enforcement challenges must be addressed on as broad a basis as possible, because law enforcement assistance may be required from any Internet-connected country. That is, even if two countries were able to resolve all the high-tech crime issues they faced, they would still (presumably) only be able to solve those crimes that involved their two countries. Multilateral fora allow many countries to seek solutions that will be compatible to the greatest extent with each country's domestic laws.

Several multilateral groups currently are addressing high-tech and computer-related crime. Of these groups, the Council of Europe ('COE'), and the Group of Eight ('G-8') countries are the most active. To begin to address the need to harmonize countries' computer crime laws, the COE is drafting a Cybercrime Convention, which will define cybercrime offenses and address such topics as jurisdiction, international cooperation, and search and seizure. The Convention may be completed as soon as December 2000. After approval by a high-level committee, the Convention will be open for signature by COE members and non-member states which participated in the drafting. The G-8 Subgroup on High-tech Crime has been focusing on ways to enhance the abilities of law enforcement agencies to investigate and to prosecute computer- and Internet-facilitated crimes, such as establishing a global network of high-tech crime experts and developing capabilities to locate and identify those who use the Internet to commit crimes. In May 1998, President Clinton and his G-8 counterparts adopted a set of principles and an action plan, developed by the Subgroup, for fighting computer crime. The COE and G-8 efforts, as well as other international efforts, are described in more detail in Appendix J to this report.

3. CONTINUING NEED FOR INTERNATIONAL COOPERATION

As these multilateral efforts progress and as more formal mechanisms for cooperation are developed, law enforcement agencies in the US and other countries are cooperating informally and have undertaken joint initiatives to achieve their goals. For example, the Customs Service has been involved in joint cyber-investigations with the German Federal police. These joint investigations have resulted in 24 referrals from Customs' Cybersmuggling Center to field offices during the last three months. In most instances, these referrals have led to the issuance of federal or state search warrants. Customs is also involved in joint efforts on Internet-related investigations involving money laundering and child pornography distribution with officials in countries such as Indonesia, Italy, Honduras, Thailand, and Russia.

As international issues become more prevalent in investigations of Internet-facilitated offenses, US law enforcement agencies must continue to develop cooperative working relationships with their foreign counterparts. The 24/7 high-tech point-of-contact network established among the G-8 countries and others must continue to be developed and expanded to include more countries. In addition, the US should continue to work with other countries, international groups, and industry to develop comprehensive and global plans for addressing the complex and challenging legal and policy issues surrounding jurisdiction raised by unlawful conduct on the Internet.

NOTES AND QUESTIONS

1   Explain some ways in which law enforcement agencies must evolve to meet the challenges of crime on the Internet. Do you think these requirements can be met?

2   'The Internet will revolutionise the way police fight crime because it will revolutionise the crimes committed. However, in this new revolution, the criminals will always be one step ahead and therefore all attempts at regulation are useless because they will be obsolete and inappropriate before they become law.' Discuss.

3   The working group identifies three requirements for effective state and local government participation in the new fight. What are they? Are these requirements also relevant on the international level of cooperation? Outline the other factors in the development of international networks designed to combat criminal activities.

4   'Cooperation, as understood by the USA, simply means letting American agencies operate at will across national boundaries in the protection of US interests. It does not mean, in any substantive sense, a shared, cooperative, or mutual approach to the global problem of Internet crime.' Discuss.

(c)   The role of public education and empowerment

The President's Working Group on Unlawful Conduct on the Internet, The Electronic Frontier: The Challenge of Unlawful Conduct Involving the Use of the Internet, March 2000

Available at <http://www.cybercrime.gov/unlawful.htm> 17 August 2006

The third component of the Working Group's three-part strategy for responding to unlawful conduct involving the use of the Internet is to implement aggressive efforts to educate and empower the public to minimize risks associated with the Internet and to use the Internet responsibly through technological and non-technological tools. Although both types of tools can be extremely useful when used appropriately, 'one size does not fit all'. One must weigh the advantages and disadvantages in determining which set of tools will work best for an individual's particular situation.

   This part of the report therefore discusses existing and potential new tools and resources that can be used to educate and empower parents, teachers, and others to prevent or minimize the risks from unlawful conduct involving use of the Internet. First, we review the technological and non-technological tools that are available for parents and teachers to use to help ensure that children have a safe and rewarding experience online. Next, we discuss how consumers can educate themselves in order to avoid fraudulent and deceptive practices on the Internet. In particular, this part highlights how several federal agencies are using technology to educate consumers and how they are working with the private sector to develop effective consumer protection practices. Many other agencies are undertaking similar efforts. Last, we discuss government-industry cooperation efforts to educate the public on the importance of being good 'cybercitizens'.

A. Educating and empowering parents, teachers, and children

With the growing number of US classrooms connected to the Internet and the rising number of personal computers used in the home, more and more children are now able to access the Internet. Almost 90 percent of public schools—including over 1 million classrooms—in the US are connected to the Internet. Over 40 percent of American households own computers and one-quarter of all households have Internet access.

One of the greatest benefits of the Internet is the access it provides children to such things as educational materials, subject matter experts, online friendships, and penpals. Nevertheless, like many other pursuits that children engage in without adequate parental supervision, the Internet should also be approached with careful consideration of risks and benefits. One concern of course is that the Internet may allow children unrestricted access to inappropriate materials. Such materials may contain sexually explicit images or descriptions, advocate hate or bigotry, contain graphic violence, or promote drug use or other illegal activities. In the worst instances, children have become victims of physical molestation and harassment by providing personal information about themselves over the Internet and making contact with strangers ...

B. Educating and empowering consumers

The electronic marketplace offers consumers unprecedented choice and around-the-clock accessibility and convenience. It gives established marketers and new entrepreneurs low-cost access to a virtually unlimited customer base. With these benefits, however, comes the challenge of ensuring that the virtual marketplace is a safe and secure place to purchase goods, services, and digitized information. Consumers must be confident that the goods and services offered online are fairly represented and the merchants with whom they are dealing—many of whom may be located in another part of the world—deliver their goods in a timely manner and are not engaged in illegal business practices like fraud or deception. Consumer confidence also requires that consumers have access to fair and effective redress if they are not satisfied with some aspect of the transaction.

This section highlights some of the Federal Trade Commission's initiatives to educate consumers through technology; the Department of Commerce's coordination efforts with the private sector to develop effective consumer protection practices; and the Food and Drug Administration's outreach campaign regarding medical products on the Internet. As described more fully below, the FTC has made innovative use of the Internet to educate and alert consumers about fraud and deceptive practices online, to disseminate its publications, to investigate potential violations, and to receive and respond to consumer complaints. The Department of Commerce has also worked with consumer and business representatives to develop codes of conduct for electronic commerce and mechanisms for consumer dispute resolution, redress, and enforcement. In addition, the FDA has used the Internet to educate consumers and health professionals about the possible risks of ordering prescription medications and other medical products on the Internet, and the Securities and Exchange Commission ('SEC') has likewise used the Internet to help investors avoid online securities fraud. The Postal Inspection Service posts consumer fraud prevention 'tip sheets' and other fraud prevention information on its web site (www.usps.gov/postalinspectors). And, as part of its Internet Fraud Initiative, the Department of Justice has been active in public education and outreach efforts to prevent online fraud (eg, establishing a web site on identity theft and fraud (www.usdoj.gov/criminal/fraud/idtheft)), and the FBI has prepared an online Parent's Guide to Internet Safety (www.fbi.gov) ...

C. Developing cybercitizens

Children and young adults are the fastest growing group using the Internet. Helping children draw conclusions about behavior and its consequences in cyberspace is an important part of educating responsible (future) online users. Although most children are taught at an early age that it is wrong to break into a neighbor's house or read their best friend's diaries, we must also emphasize that it is equally wrong, and potentially more damaging, to break into their neighbor's computers and snoop through their computer files. Computer hacking 'for fun' is a very serious problem, not only for the targets of the attacks, but also for law enforcement personnel who often have no way to determine the motivation for and the identity of the person behind the intrusion.

Educating children (and adults) about acceptable online behavior is crucial for the Internet to continue to grow as a safe and useful medium. Likewise, there is a need to educate the public on the dangers posed by cybercrimes and how harm can be reduced if people use technology responsibly. As the proliferation of low-cost computers and networks has spread information technology to every corner of society, people of all ages who use this technology must understand that along with the obvious benefits of technology comes a set of corresponding responsibilities. To this end, the Attorney General announced in April 1999 that the Department of Justice had joined with the Information Technology Association of America ('ITAA') for a partnership on a national campaign to educate and raise awareness of computer responsibility and to provide resources to empower concerned citizens.

The Cybercitizen Awareness Program seeks to engage children, young adults, and others on the basics of critical information protection and security and on the limits of acceptable online behavior. The objectives of the program are to give children:

- An understanding of cyberspace benefits and responsibilities;
- An awareness of potential negative consequences resulting from the misuse of the medium;
- An understanding of the personal dangers that exist on the Internet and techniques to avoid being harmed; and
- An ability to commit to adhere to these principles as they mature.

Thus far, the campaign has received $300,000 in grants from the Department of Justice's Office of Justice Programs. The partnership awarded a contract to a public relations firm in December 1999 to implement the objectives of the campaign. The Department of Justice and ITAA believe that the program will play a significant role in deterring potential hacking, educating the public about the potential dangers of the Internet, raising awareness about the potential consequences of online activities, reducing the threat to the nation's critical infrastructure, increasing online security in the United States, and providing savings to information technology resources owners and users who suffer economic losses as a result of computer crimes.

In addition to the awareness program detailed above, the Cybercitizen Partnership also has initiated a personnel exchange program between private business and federal agencies that is designed to educate both groups about how the other responds to threats and crimes over the Internet. This initiative will allow companies to find out how best to help law-enforcement agencies, and government officials will learn what business interests and influences drive industry decisions. The exchange program will be coordinated by the ITAA, which intends to detail personnel from the private sector to the FBI's National Infrastructure Protection Center. The partnership also expects to create a directory of computer experts and computer security resources so that law enforcement will know where to turn when they need assistance from industry ...

 NOTES AND QUESTIONS

1   Why is it important to educate parents about the realities and dangers of the Internet? What might be the consequences of failing to persuade older generations of the necessity of this?

2   What do you understand by the term 'cybercitizen'? Is this a meaningful and realistic goal of public policy or is it simply an advertising slogan designed to appease certain interest groups?

3   Do you think that most people are ignorant of the perils that exist within the Internet? If so, what implications might this ignorance have for the proliferation of illegal activity on the Internet?

(d)   Recommendations

The President's Working Group on Unlawful Conduct on the Internet, The Electronic Frontier: The Challenge of Unlawful Conduct Involving the Use of the Internet, March 2000

Available at <http://www.cybercrime.gov/unlawful.htm> 17 August 2006

Ensuring the safety and security of those who use the Internet is a critical element of the Administration's overall policy regarding the Internet and electronic commerce, a policy that seeks to promote private sector leadership, technology-neutral laws and regulation, and an appreciation of the Internet as an important medium for commerce and communication both domestically and internationally.

Consistent with the Administration's overall policy, the Working Group recommends a three-part approach for addressing unlawful conduct on the Internet:

- First, any regulation of unlawful conduct involving the use of the Internet should be analyzed through a policy framework that ensures that online conduct is treated in a manner consistent with the way offline conduct is treated, in a technology-neutral manner, and in a manner that accounts for other important societal interests such as privacy and protection of civil liberties;
- Second, law enforcement needs and challenges posed by the Internet should be recognized as significant, particularly in the areas of resources, training, and the need for new investigative tools and capabilities, coordination with and among federal, state, and local law enforcement agencies, and coordination with and among our international counterparts; and
- Third, there should be continued support for private sector leadership and the development of methods—such as 'cyberethics' curricula, appropriate technological tools, and media and other outreach efforts—that educate and empower Internet users to prevent and minimize the risks of unlawful activity.

The challenges to the federal government of unlawful conduct involving the use of the Internet are many. On one hand, the Internet offers unparalleled opportunities for socially beneficial endeavors. At the same time, individuals who wish to use a computer as a tool to facilitate unlawful activity may find that the Internet provides a vast, inexpensive, and potentially anonymous way to commit unlawful acts, such as fraud, the sale or distribution of child pornography, the sale of guns or drugs or other regulated substances without regulatory protections, and the unlawful distribution of computer software or other creative material protected by intellectual property rights.

In its analysis of existing federal laws, the Working Group finds that existing substantive federal laws generally do not distinguish between unlawful conduct committed through the use of the Internet and the same conduct committed through the use of other, more traditional means of communication. To the extent these existing laws adequately address unlawful conduct in the offline world, they should, for the most part, adequately cover unlawful conduct on the Internet. There may be a few instances, however, where relevant federal laws need to be amended to better reflect the realities of new technologies, such as the Internet.

Despite the general adequacy of laws that define the substance of criminal and other offenses, however, the Working Group finds that the Internet presents new and significant investigatory challenges for law enforcement at all levels. These challenges include the need for real-time tracing of Internet communications across traditional jurisdictional boundaries, both domestically and internationally; the need to track down sophisticated users who commit unlawful acts on the Internet while hiding their identities; the need for hand-in-glove coordination among various law enforcement agencies; and the need for trained and well-equipped personnel—at federal, state, local, and international levels—to gather evidence, investigate, and prosecute these cases. In some instances, federal procedural and evidentiary laws may need to be amended to better enable law enforcement to meet these challenges.

Indeed, the Working Group concludes that the federal government must continue to devote further attention to these important challenges. The report contains specific suggestions on areas on which additional resources and further evaluation are needed. These recommendations recognize that there are no easy answers to the challenges posed by unlawful conduct on the Internet. At the very least, however, significant attention should be given to the issues, and open dialogue and partnerships among law enforcement agencies, industry, and the public must continue.

In light of its mandate, the Working Group confined its analysis to existing federal laws. A logical next step would be an expanded analysis of state (and, to the extent relevant, local) laws that focuses on whether those laws are adequate to investigate and prosecute unlawful conduct on the Internet. Because coordination and cooperation among federal, state, and local law enforcement agencies are key to our efforts to prevent, deter, investigate, and prosecute such unlawful conduct, such an analysis would provide states and others with a blueprint for translating the conclusions in this report into a more comprehensive approach to meeting the substantial challenges presented.

Finally, an essential component of the Working Group's strategy is continued support for private sector leadership, industry self-regulation, and the development of methods—such as 'cyberethics' curricula, appropriate technological tools, and media and other outreach efforts—that educate and empower Internet users so as to prevent and minimize the risks of unlawful activity. This Administration has already initiated numerous efforts to educate consumers, parents, teachers, and children about ways to ensure safe and enjoyable Internet experiences, and those efforts should continue. The private sector has also undertaken substantial self-regulatory efforts—such as voluntary codes of conduct and appropriate cooperation with law enforcement—that show responsible leadership in preventing and minimizing the risks of unlawful conduct on the Internet. Those efforts must also continue to grow. Working together, we can ensure that the Internet and its benefits will continue to grow and flourish in the years and decades to come.

 NOTES AND QUESTIONS

> Outline the three steps the Working Group has identified for addressing unlawful conduct on the Internet. In light of this introductory material, critically analyse the recommendations for the road ahead. Do you consider the goals to be realistic?

---

2   Specific examples of Internet crime

Many people associate Internet crime with hacking and the like. This section will introduce a variety of other Internet crimes that might not come immediately to mind. The aim here is not to present a comprehensive picture of the law on the matter, but to suggest the scope of what could be included under the umbrella of Internet crime.

(a) Paedophilia

The President's Working Group on Unlawful Conduct on the Internet, Appendix to The Electronic Frontier: The Challenge of Unlawful Conduct Involving the Use of the Internet, March 2000

Available at <http://www.cybercrime.gov/append.htm> 17 August 2006

Appendix C: Online Child Pornography, Child Luring, and Related Offenses

2. NATURE OF THE POTENTIALLY UNLAWFUL CONDUCT

The Internet, despite its many benefits, has unfortunately provided paedophiles with a new tool. Offering relative anonymity for sophisticated users and continuous access, the Internet has made it easy for child pornographers to distribute their materials and for paedophiles to lure and prey on children. As a result, child pornography is traded 24 hours a day in online chat rooms and in Internet Relay Chat channels, and thousands of images of child sex abuse are available in easily accessible newsgroups. In addition, paedophiles can lurk around chat channels and rooms and message boards and use e-mail to lure children for sex.

The prosecution of Internet-related child pornography and luring cases is increasing. The Department of Justice has found that prosecution of these cases has increased by 10 percent every year since 1995. Last year, the Department of Justice expects to have prosecuted over 400 such cases. Many of these cases are international in scope. For example, Operation Cheshire Cat, a joint investigation between the Customs Service and the English National Crime Squad, involved over 100 members of a major pedophile ring that operated in 21 countries ...

4. SPECIFIC FEDERAL INITIATIVES

Federal, state, and local law enforcement agencies have all responded vigorously to child pornography and sexual exploitation on the Internet. In particular, the FBI, the Customs Service, the Postal Inspection Service, the Department of Justice's Child Exploitation and Obscenity Section ('CEOS'), and the National Center for Missing and Exploited Children ('NCMEC') have developed extensive programs and investigative and prosecutorial tools in response to child pornography and sexual exploitation on the Internet. In addition, the Department of Justice's Office of Juvenile Justice and Delinquency Prevention ('OJJDP') has played a leading role in coordinating cooperative efforts between federal, state, and local officials.

- **FBI's Innocent Images Initiative:** The FBI began the Innocent Images National Initiative in 1995 to address the problem of child pornography and child sexual exploitation facilitated through the use of the Internet and online services. Innocent Images is a proactive, intelligence-driven, multiagency investigative initiative. It is the central operation and case management system for all FBI investigations involving online child pornography and child sexual exploitation. The initiative focuses on individuals who indicate a willingness to travel for the purpose of engaging in sexual activity with a minor and those who produce or distribute child pornography. Cases evolving from the Innocent Images initiative have resulted in 358 convictions as of December 1999.

- **Customs' CyberSmuggling Center:** In August 1997, the Customs Service formed the CyberSmuggling Center, which (among other things) develops leads, tips, and complaints of child pornography and luring and forwards them to area offices for further investigation and case development. Some of these leads come from the Center's web site, which received almost 6000 tips between November 1997 and November 1998. The Center also conducts undercover operations to identify child pornography producers and distributors at the international level. These undercover operations have investigated operations on the World Wide Web, in newsgroups, in IRCs, in bulletin board services, and in commercial online services. Between November 1998 and September 1999, the Customs Service's child pornography investigations have resulted in 436 convictions.

- **Postal Inspection Service:** Since the enactment of the Federal *Child Protection Act* of 1984, Pub L 98-292 (codified as 18 USC s 2251 note), the Postal Inspection Service has conducted more than 3500 child exploitation investigations, resulting in the arrest and conviction of over 2900 child molesters and pornographers. The Service increasingly is discovering that child molesters and pornographers are using computers, along with the mail, to find potential victims, to communicate with other criminals, and to locate sources of child pornography. In Fiscal Year 1998, nearly half of the Service's child exploitation cases involved computers. Among the Service's undercover operations are the placement of contact advertisements in sexually oriented publications, written contact and correspondence with subjects of investigations, development of confidential sources, and more recently, undercover contact with suspects via the Internet.

- **Child Exploitation and Obscenity Section, Department of Justice:** CEOS has taken an active role in training federal prosecutors to handle child crime cases that were once mainly handled by local jurisdictions. The Section has sponsored several training seminars for federal prosecutors on the issues of child pornography and child exploitations. These training sessions have taught prosecutors and federal law enforcement agents the mechanics of computer hardware and software, the Internet, online investigative tools and techniques, and child exploitation laws. CEOS also offers US Attorneys' offices litigation support through investigative advice, computer search warrant and indictment reviews, and joint prosecution of cases.

- **CyberTipline:** NCMEC launched the CyberTipline in March 1998 to serve as a national online clearinghouse for tips and leads about child sexual exploitation (www.cybertipline.com). Mandated by Congress, the CyberTipline allows individuals to report online (and via a toll-free number) incidents of child luring, molestation, pornography, sex tourism, and prostitution. Since March 1998, the CyberTipline has received over 8000 reports of child pornography alone.

- **Office of Juvenile Justice and Delinquency Prevention, Department of Justice:** Pursuant to direct Congressional appropriations, OJJDP administers the Internet Crimes Against Children ('ICAC') Task Force Program to help state and local law enforcement agencies respond to computer-facilitated child sexual exploitation offenses by creating regional clusters of forensic and investigative expertise. Currently, ten agencies (covering 12 states) are operating, with an additional 16 sites slated to start online operations by April 2000.

5. INVESTIGATORY CHALLENGES

Despite the general sufficiency of existing federal laws to combat child pornography and luring, and despite the extent to which law enforcement has gained effective new tools from the Internet and related technologies (such as CyberTipline noted above and the 'investigative interests' database discussed below), law enforcement continues to face daunting challenges in its fight against online child pornography and paedophiles.

The ease with which sophisticated users can be anonymous on the Internet, the use of sophisticated encryption to conceal evidence of unlawful conduct on the Internet, and the need to coordinate international investigations and prosecutions, all hinder law enforcement agencies' ability to fight these types of crimes. In addition, ISPs may not generate records and data or retain them for a sufficient length of time to permit law enforcement agencies to respond to child pornography traffickers and predators. These challenges create barriers to the identification of perpetrators and to the gathering of other data and evidence for their prosecution.

One area in which law enforcement is having some success in responding to investigatory challenges posed by the Internet is the area of interagency coordination. Because the Internet renders conventional law enforcement boundaries virtually meaningless, one of the most important issues in general, but particularly in the area of child pornography and sexual exploitation investigations, is the effective coordination of interagency referrals and cases. Absent meaningful case coordination, law enforcement agencies are likely to conduct redundant investigations or disrupt undercover operations of other agencies. Consider the following examples:

- To avoid entrapment and to establish a suspect's predilection for sex with minors, a federal agent posing as a 13-year-old girl develops a chat-room relationship with a middle-aged male. The agent becomes alarmed when the suspect postpones a meeting, citing weekend travel plans to meet another underage girl. Concerned for the potential victim's safety, the agent requests an arrest warrant for a lesser charge of conspiracy, while other agents attempt to identify the victim. One day later, the agent discovers that the 'victim' was an undercover officer from another state.
- In another case, three federal agencies and one local law enforcement organization conduct parallel undercover operations targeting the same corporation. The independent investigations, aside from being redundant and a waste of resources, nearly result in the corporation learning prematurely of its target status and providing it an opportunity to destroy evidence or alter operating procedures.

OJJDP is addressing communication and coordination concerns by requiring ICAC Task Force agencies to register 'investigative interests' in a common database. Before conducting a full-blown investigation, ICAC Task Forces check this database to determine if a screen name or other potentially identifiable entity is targeted by another agency. If so, that agency is contacted to discuss the investigation and provided the additional information. If not, the inquiring agency registers its interest and proceeds with the investigation.

Nearly all ICAC Task Force investigations involve more than one jurisdiction and routinely require an extraordinary degree of multiagency collaboration. In anticipation of increased interagency referrals, federal, state, and local law enforcement agencies have expressed some concern about investigations that are initiated on the basis of information that may have been gathered through inappropriate investigative conduct or techniques by officers of another agency. In response to these concerns, OJJDP, with the input from the 10 original ICAC Task Force organizations and federal prosecutorial and law enforcement agencies, established ICAC Task Force operational and investigative standards. These standards address issues of information sharing, case coordination, undercover officer conduct, evidence collection, target selection, media relations, and supervision practices.

6. CONCLUSIONS

Many federal laws that have traditionally protected children—such as those used to combat child pornography and luring—also apply when individuals use the Internet to commit those offenses. Other laws have specifically been designed to deal with online child pornography and related crimes. Federal agencies, including the Customs Service and the Department of Justice, have developed numerous programs to protect children on the Internet. These have, for the most part, been successful. Despite the successes, law enforcement agencies still face numerous challenges in combating online child pornography and related crimes. The most daunting of these challenges are the anonymous nature of the Internet and the need for extensive coordination and communication between federal, state, and local law enforcement agencies.

Protecting children

A Report from the Attorney General to the Vice President August 1999, Report on Cyberstalking: A New Challenge for Law Enforcement and Industry

Available at <http://www.cybercrime.gov/cyberstalking.htm> 17 August 2006

Protecting children from online dangers

Although the Internet and other forms of electronic communication offer new and exciting opportunities for children, they also expose children to new threats. For example, federal law enforcement agencies have encountered numerous instances in which adult pedophiles have made contact with minors through online chat rooms, established a relationship with the child, and later made contact for the purpose of engaging in criminal sexual activities.

Federal, state, and local law enforcement agencies have responded aggressively to protect children from online sexual predators. For example, in 1995, the Federal Bureau of Investigation launched an undercover initiative, dubbed Innocent Images, to combat the exploitation of children via commercial online services. Based in Calverton, Maryland, 'Innocent Images' is the central operation and case management system for all FBI undercover online child pornography and child sexual exploitation investigations. As of 31 December

1998, the initiative has resulted in 232 convictions. Similarly, the US Customs Service's CyberSmuggling Center, based in Sterling, Virginia, plays an important role in combating sexual exploitation of children via the Internet and other online communications media. The Center develops leads and tips for law enforcement investigation, receives complaints via the US Customs Service web site, and coordinates undercover operations against international child pornography and child sexual exploitation rings. The National Center for Missing and Exploited Children unveiled a new CyberTipline in March 1998 to serve as a national online clearinghouse for tips and leads about child sexual exploitation (www.cybertipline.com).

The Department of Justice, through the Office of Juvenile Justice and Delinquency Prevention's Missing and Exploited Children Program (MECP), provides funding to state and local law enforcement agencies to create multijurisdictional responses to prevent and combat Internet crimes against children. In 1998, ten state and local agencies received grants under MECP; an additional eight task forces will be funded in 1999.

There are steps parents and others can take to protect children from online dangers. Parents should teach their children to follow the common-sense 'rules of the road' for the Internet, including the need to protect their privacy in the online world. The FBI, for example, has prepared an online 'Parent's Guide to Internet Safety' (www.fbi.gov). Moreover, individuals should report inappropriate behavior to their Internet Service Provider (ISP) or, if it involves potentially illegal conduct, to appropriate law enforcement agencies. Law enforcement agencies need to establish and/or improve programs that train their personnel to recognize the seriousness of online child sexual exploitation and how to investigate this new form of criminal conduct. They also need to work closely with ISPs and others to facilitate communication and cooperation. Finally, private companies, including ISPs, need to provide parents and children with effective tools to protect children from online exploitation, including filtering technology, parental controls, and other efforts. ISPs also need to establish clear policies that prohibit online solicitation or exploitation of children and to take appropriate action when such incidents come to their attention, as is now required under federal law (see USC 13032).

 NOTES AND QUESTIONS

1   In September 1999, the International Child Pornography Conference was held in Vienna, Austria. The conference targeted child pornography and exploitation on the Internet, using pre-existing international obligations and commitments designed to protect children, such as the Convention on the Rights of the Child. Prior to this, the Stockholm World Congress against the Commercial Sexual Exploitation of Children was held in 1996. The 1999 conference sought to build and act upon commitments undertaken in 1996 as well as to foster ongoing initiatives in many countries and regions. International efforts have recently been encapsulated in the Council of Europe's Convention on Cybercrime.

2   Child pornography is possibly the most insidious of all crimes. Nevertheless, is a legal approach the best means to eliminate it? Describe some of the initiatives outlined above for the development of an active citizenry. Discuss the need for an effective combination of codified hard law and soft law preventive initiatives.

3 There is a fine line between active citizens and vigilantes. Is it possible that attempts to empower citizens might lead only to more violence and conflict in society, without producing any tangible results for children?

4 How has the Internet changed the way paedophiles operate? Do you think this has made their activities more open and consequently easier to enforce laws against them? Many countries have now established initiatives to combat Internet child pornography. This will be discussed further below.

(b) Fraud

The President's Working Group on Unlawful Conduct on the Internet, The Electronic Frontier: The Challenge of Unlawful Conduct Involving the Use of the Internet, March 2000

Available at <http://www.cybercrime.gov/append.htm> 17 August 2006

Appendix B: Internet Fraud

1. NATURE OF THE POTENTIALLY UNLAWFUL CONDUCT

The electronic marketplace offers consumers unprecedented choice and convenience, and it gives businesses of all kinds low-cost access to a global consumer base. With these benefits, however, comes the challenge of ensuring that the virtual marketplace is a safe and secure place to purchase goods, services, and digitized information.

As commerce on the Internet grows, law enforcement agencies are observing a growing variety of fraudulent schemes that use the Internet, either to communicate false or fraudulent representations to prospective victims or to obtain valuable information or resources necessary for the success of the schemes. In 1998, for example, roughly 8000 Internet-related complaints were entered into Consumer Sentinel, a consumer fraud database administered by the Federal Trade Commission ('FTC') and used by over 220 law enforcement agencies across the United States and Canada. In 1999, Consumer Sentinel received over 18,600 Internet-related complaints, more than double the prior year's number.

One form of Internet fraud that is of particular concern is that of 'identity theft', which generally involves obtaining data from individual consumers' financial transactions on the Internet or elsewhere, and either billing the consumers' credit cards for nonexistent transactions or services or using consumers' personal data to conduct actual transactions that are billed to the consumers. Other Internet fraud schemes include so-called 'pyramid schemes'; entities that purport to be Internet banks that offer above-market rates for deposits; companies that promise to repair consumers' credit, but that do nothing after taking consumers' money; companies that purport to offer investments in nonexistent items, such as 'prime bank' securities or software to solve the Y2K problem; companies that are thinly traded on securities markets or in fact are merely shell companies; and companies that fraudulently offer to sell Internet-related goods and services, or collectible goods through online auctions. Finally, some fraud schemes combine use of Internet web sites with telemarketing 'boiler rooms' to enhance direct contact with prospective victims.

2. ANALYSIS OF EXISTING LAW

Each of the Internet fraud schemes described above may violate one or more of the general federal criminal statutes dealing with fraud—such as credit card fraud (see 15 USC s 1644, 18 USC s 1029); financial institution fraud (see 18 USC s 1344); mail fraud (see *id* s 1341); and wire fraud (see *id* s 1343)—as well as specialized federal criminal statutes that prohibit money laundering (see *id* s 1956), and identity theft (see *id* s 1028). The FBI has jurisdiction to investigate violations of each of these statutes, and the Postal Inspection Service has jurisdiction to investigate most of these violations as they relate to mail fraud schemes. In addition, the Secret Service has jurisdiction to investigate credit card fraud and identity theft, and the Internal Revenue Service has jurisdiction to investigate money laundering. The Customs Service and Secret Service also have jurisdiction over some of the predicate offenses related to money laundering. (As discussed in Appendix H below, the Securities and Exchange Commission has jurisdiction to investigate violations of the federal securities laws.) And, the Department of Justice, through its Criminal and Civil Divisions and local US Attorneys' Offices, conducts criminal prosecutions of these fraud schemes and may seek civil injunctive relief under 18 USC s 1345.

In addition, the FTC has authority to bring civil actions against fraudulent Internet schemes under the FTC Act, which prohibits unfair and deceptive acts or practices (15 USC s 45(a)). The FTC is also authorized to seek injunctions and other equitable relief in federal court (*id* s 53(b)), and may obtain a temporary restraining order that freezes a defendant's assets and results in the appointment of a temporary receiver.

Because these federal criminal and civil laws make no distinction between fraudulent representations over a telephone or fax machine and fraudulent representations posted on an online bulletin board or web site, federal substantive law appears generally adequate to address Internet fraud. Since 1995, for example, the FTC has brought over 100 Internet-related cases, obtained permanent injunctions against dozens of Internet-related schemes, collected over $20 million in redress for victims of online fraud, and frozen another $65 million in cases currently in litigation. An Illinois man was recently sentenced to six months home confinement and probation for three years for conducting a million-dollar mail-fraud scheme that involved the use of a web site to solicit investors in oil and gas drilling ventures. And five individuals were recently convicted in an online scam in which the perpetrators stole the identities of legitimate vendors and advertised and sold non-existent products to their victims, resulting in losses to the victims of over $50,000.

3. SPECIFIC FEDERAL INITIATIVES

- **Project SafeBid:** Online auction fraud is the most common Internet-related problem reported by consumers. Thousands of individuals have been 'winning bidders' on an Internet auction, sent money to the seller, but never received their goods. To address this problem, the FTC initiated Project SafeBid, disseminating educational materials to consumers, encouraging fraud prevention by Internet auction sites, and providing training and support to law enforcement agencies around the country in their efforts to stop Internet auction fraud artists. Project SafeBid has also generated over 40 case referrals, resulting in eight criminal or civil actions to date.

- **Operation Cure.All:** In 1997 and 1998, the FTC led two 'surf days' to target 'miracle cures' for serious illnesses. After these surfs, the FTC and the FDA brought several cases against marketers of products such as magnetic therapy devices and shark cartilage for claims that these products could cure cancer, HIV/AIDS, multiple sclerosis, arthritis, or other diseases.

- **Website 'Cramming' Sweep:** The FTC has brought five federal court cases against 20 defendants, alleging that they placed unauthorized charges on small businesses' telephone bills for web site services that the defendants promoted as 'free'. The defendants collectively solicited over one million small businesses nationwide. The FTC's Small Business Alliance for Fraud Education ('SAFE') also helped disseminate fraud warnings to the business community.

- **FTC's Internet Lab:** In September 1999, the FTC unveiled a new Internet Lab with high-technology tools to investigate high-technology consumer problems. The lab allows investigators to search for fraud and deception on the Internet in a secure environment and provides staff with the necessary equipment to preserve evidence for presentation in court. The lab also provides a means to train FTC staff and other law enforcement agents on new investigative techniques. The FTC's Internet Lab was instrumental in a recent 'page-jacking' case … that halted a global scheme in which millions of webpages were manipulated and unsuspecting consumers were driven to unwanted adult web sites.

The Department of Justice, in coordination with the FTC, the FBI, and other agencies, is also actively pursuing online fraud as part of its Internet Fraud Initiative, announced by the Attorney General in February 1999. These efforts include prosecuting Internet-related fraud schemes such as securities and investment schemes, online auction schemes, and bank fraud; training prosecutors and agents on online fraud; developing online investigative and analytical resources; providing interagency coordination on online fraud prosecutions; and conducting public education and prevention efforts (eg, a web site on identity theft and fraud <www.usdoj.gov/criminal/fraud/idtheft>).

In addition, because most Internet fraud schemes (and, for that matter, non-Internet fraud schemes) rely on the use by victims of the US mails or private couriers to make payments, the Postal Inspection Service is working with international postal administrators—most notably in Canada, Nigeria, and Ghana—to identify and to intercept victims' payments that are destined for addresses identified with fraud promotions. In addition to such cooperative administrative efforts, law enforcement agencies can combat fraud through the use of civil injunctive powers, such as temporary restraining orders on mail, false representation orders, and injunctions against fraud.

The Consumer Product Safety Commission ('CPSC') has stepped up its role in an area that complements the battle against online fraud: the need to ensure that products sold over the Internet (like other products sold) are safe. Products sold online must meet the same safety standards as products sold in brick-and-mortar stores (cf 15 USC ss 1192,

1263, 2068). As a result, the CPSC recently launched Operation Safe Online Shopping, in which CPSC staff search online for products that violate federal safety standards or that are otherwise dangerous. Among the unsafe products it has found are flammable children's sleepwear that violate flammability standards, toys that violate safety standards, novelty lighters that are not child-resistant in violation of CPSC regulations, and children's jackets with drawstrings that can catch and strangle a child.

Finally ... educational efforts are a critical part of any comprehensive strategy to protect consumers from online fraud. For instance, efforts to improve the reporting of complaints about Internet fraud, such as the Internet Fraud Complaint Center and the FTC's Consumer Sentinel web site, can significantly enhance the ability of law enforcement and regulatory agencies to take effective action against Internet fraud schemes. The FTC and the Postal Inspection Service are working together to improve the sharing of complaint information to enable their investigators to respond to schemes while they are still in progress. The Postal Inspection Service has also modified its Fraud Complaint System and web site to accept complaints filed via the Internet. And a major recent multi-agency fraud prevention campaign—Project 'Know Fraud', which included mass mailings to consumers, a toll-free telephone number, videos, and a webpage (www. consumer.gov/knowfraud)—serves as an excellent example of how law enforcement agencies and the private sector can combine their capabilities and resources to educate consumers and prevent fraud.

4. INVESTIGATORY CHALLENGES

Although existing substantive federal laws may generally be adequate to protect consumers against Internet fraud, certain aspects of the Internet may make certain fraud schemes more efficient in contacting victims in multiple jurisdictions or more effective in evading prompt detection and investigation by law enforcement.

The fact that the Internet transcends traditional jurisdictional boundaries, for example, presents special challenges in Internet fraud investigations:

- In 1996, Fortuna Alliance, a business headquartered in the United States, advertised on the Internet an investment opportunity, in which investors could earn as much as $5000 per month, in perpetuity, after recruiting 300 new investors. After the Federal Trade Commission ('FTC') brought enforcement action against Fortuna Alliance and its principals, the head of the company left the country and transferred nearly $3 million of Fortuna's receipts to offshore bank accounts. Ultimately, the FTC returned $5.5 million from other Fortuna assets to 15,625 victims in 71 countries.

- In 1999, an individual in a Western European country accessed an online web site based in Chicago, Illinois to purchase stereo speakers costing over $2000. When the web site merchant ran the individual's credit card through, it received authorization for the transaction and shipped the speakers. Subsequently, the true owner of the credit card disputed the charge, and the merchant had the full amount of the charge deducted from his merchant account. The merchant had no success in contacting the buyer abroad. Even if the buyer were identified and apprehended, prosecution of the perpetrator abroad would most likely not have been worth the expense of trial, particularly if witnesses had to be flown from the US, given the relatively low (though significant to the merchant) monetary loss.

To investigate these types of Internet-facilitated schemes, law enforcement agents must deal with many of the same issues they would encounter in any international fraud investigation. These include the need to determine the validity of foreign addresses, the true identities of participants in the scheme, the location and content of banking information, and the location of suspects' assets.

The Internet, however, allows operators of an online fraud scheme to initiate, conduct, and terminate the scheme in a matter of hours, days, or weeks, in virtual anonymity, and operating rapidly across international boundaries, before traditional mechanisms such as mutual legal assistance treaties or letters rogatory (a letter request for assistance from one country's judicial authority to that of another country: see, eg, 28 USC s 1782) can be effectively employed to gather investigative information. The international reach of these schemes also increases the difficulty of carrying out restitution to victims of the schemes.

The global scope and impact of the problem therefore means that enforcement against all major forms of Internet fraud both domestically and internationally must be coordinated and effective. Through various international fora such as the G-8 and the International Marketing Supervision Network, as well as the Internet Fraud Initiative, federal law enforcement officials are moving to address several aspects of enforcement that warrant improvement.

A particular set of Internet-specific law enforcement challenges arises from the ability of criminals and hackers to obtain online and then use certain computer programs, such as Credit Master and Credit Wizard, that generate large volumes of credit card numbers. The sole purpose of these credit-card generator programs is to aid in finding particular credit card numbers that the program's user is not authorized to use, but that online merchants will accept. By generating a large enough group of card numbers that merchants will accept, participants in an online fraud scheme can make substantial fraudulent purchases of goods or services, or cause fraudulent billings for nonexistent goods or services, at the expense of the credit card company or the customers to whom the valid credit card numbers have been assigned. Although the use of such computer programs to further a fraud scheme would constitute credit card fraud in violation of 15 USC s 1644 and 18 USC s 1029, the relative ease with which such programs can be obtained increases the likelihood of such schemes being perpetrated.

In sum, law enforcement and regulatory authorities face significant challenges in investigating and prosecuting individuals responsible for Internet fraud schemes. The ability to gather and access evidence in a timely manner, for example, is crucial to the success of any investigation. There is little question that existing investigatory capabilities—including legal processes such as subpoenas, wiretaps, warrants, orders, and data-preservation letters (pursuant to 18 USC s 2703(f))—are important tools in that effort. These legal authorities, however, can be of limited value to the extent some of them need to be updated to better reflect the realities of the online world.

In addition, to protect consumers online and prevent online fraud, cooperation and coordination with foreign law enforcement counterparts and industry must play an essential role. In particular, efforts to improve assistance mechanisms internationally must continue to be developed. The private sector must also continue to take responsibility and show leadership in efforts to address fraud on the Internet and to prevent offenders from evading law enforcement detection. For example, representatives of industry should consider evaluating their data retention policies so as to balance reasonable expectations of privacy with the need to protect consumers and merchants from perpetrators of fraud and other unlawful acts. Efforts to improve the reporting of complaints about Internet fraud, such as the FTC's Consumer Sentinel and the Internet Fraud Complaint Center (see above), can also significantly enhance the ability of law enforcement and regulatory agencies to prevent and to take effective action against Internet fraud schemes.

Case study in cyber fraud

US Department of Justice, United States Attorney, Central District of California, Thom Mrozek, 'Five charged In Los Angeles with fraud in Internet auctions'

Available at <http://www.cybercrime.gov/mcclain.htm> 17 August 2006

Five defendants, including a former professional football player, have been charged with federal fraud charges for allegedly offering items for sale on Internet auction services and failing to provide merchandise promised to those who paid for various goods.

Federal officials in Los Angeles today announced the filing of three criminal cases, involving a total of five Southland defendants, who are accused of taking money from unsuspecting victims who thought they would receive various items for being the highest bidder in a particular auction.

'These cases demonstrate that shoppers on the Internet must be careful,' said Acting United States Attorney Consuelo S Woodhead. 'Those purchasing goods on the Internet should have a complete understanding of the terms of the sale, and those who are suspicious should consider using an escrow service.'

Those who believe they are victims of Internet fraud can file complaints with the government at http://www.ifccfbi.gov, which is a joint effort between the Federal Bureau of Investigation and the National White Collar Crime Center.

Today's announcement was triggered by the indictment this morning of Kevin McLain, 47, of Newport Beach, who was a linebacker with the Los Angeles Rams from 1976 to 1979. A federal grand jury in Los Angeles charged McLain with eight counts of mail fraud.

In 1998, McLain became a registered user of eBay.com, the online auction site, and posted and sold various items. At first, McLain posted low-priced collectibles and delivered them to the highest bidder, which caused eBay users to post favorable reviews about him as a seller. Once he had those favorable reviews, McLain then turned to posting expensive equipment, such as laptop computers and digital cameras. McLain allegedly accepted payment but never delivered the goods.

McLain is alleged to have defrauded more than 30 victims out of at least $36,000. McLain is currently being held in San Diego by state authorities on unrelated charges. If he is convicted of all eight counts in the federal indictment, McLain faces a maximum penalty of 40 years in federal prison.

In the second case announced today, John Allen Nobles Jr, 31, of Whittier, was indicted last Friday on charges of defrauding more than 130 victims who were users of eBay. A federal grand jury in Los Angeles charged Nobles with nine counts of mail fraud in a case that allegedly resulted in losses of more than $10,000.

According to the indictment, from March 1999 through December 1999, Nobles used false names to register with eBay, and then he posted fraudulent auction listings in which he offered to sell golf clubs, beanie babies, Pokemon paraphernalia and other products. After the auctions closed, Nobles contacted the winning bidders via e-mail and instructed them to mail a check or money order for the amount of their bid, sometimes charging additional money for 'shipping and handling'. Victims were instructed to mail payment to 'mail drops' that he rented.

Nobles cashed the checks and money orders sent by the winning bidders, but either never delivered the merchandise promised or delivered merchandise that was materially different from what had been ordered.

In addition to the more than $10,000 he fraudulently obtained from individual bidders, Nobles is accused of failing to pay eBay over $60,000 he owed in auction fees and expenses. If convicted of all nine counts in the indictment, Nobles faces a maximum possible penalty of 45 years in federal prison. (Contact Assistant United States Attorney Jackie Chooljian, 213-894-5615.)

The third case involves three defendants who advertised high-end electronics and consumer goods for sale on Yahoo!Auctions. The trio offered Rolex watches, BOSE speaker systems, and Sony VAIO laptop computers to victims who were told to send their money to a 'penthouse' suite on Valley Boulevard in Alhambra. The penthouse was in fact a 'Ship and Mail' center.

The three indicted by a federal grand jury last Thursday are Amy Liang, 22; her brother, Alan Liang, 21; and Benson Ip, 21. The Liangs were residents of Arcadia, but they are currently fugitives being sought by federal authorities. Ip also lives in Arcadia and was a student at Pasadena City College at the time of the alleged criminal conduct.

All three defendants in this case are charged with five counts of mail fraud and eight counts of wire fraud.

The Liangs and Ip convinced about 20 people to send approximately $65,000. The victims included people from as far away as England and the Palestinian Authority. After receiving the money, the defendants generally sent nothing, although some victims did receive a box of Godiva chocolates.

Ip will be summoned by the court to appear for an arraignment at a future date. The 13 charges in the indictment carry a potential penalty of 65 years in prison.

 NOTES AND QUESTIONS

1 Carefully examine the charges brought against the accused persons in the above cases. How would you categorise the majority of them? Are the charges specifically Internet- or computer-related, or have the illegal activities been cast into the mould of pre-existing real world offences? Why would the offences be labelled mail fraud, or wire fraud, as opposed to Internet fraud? Is there a need for a category called Internet fraud?

2 What are the challenges of investigating on-line computer fraud?

3 The concept of trust is a central component of an effective commercial system. Trust was discussed in terms of the commercial implications of encryption and is obviously relevant here. Examine the materials above and outline how consumers

might go about their activities on the Internet while maintaining their trust in its efficacy as a commercially legitimate framework for commerce. How important is consumer confidence in this context?

(c) Stalking

A Report from the Attorney General to the Vice President August 1999, Report on Cyberstalking: A New Challenge for Law Enforcement and Industry

Available at <http://www.cybercrime.gov/cyberstalking.htm> 17 August 2006

What is cyberstalking?

Although there is no universally accepted definition of cyberstalking, the term is used in this report to refer to the use of the Internet, e-mail, or other electronic communications devices to stalk another person. Stalking generally involves harassing or threatening behavior that an individual engages in repeatedly, such as following a person, appearing at a person's home or place of business, making harassing phone calls, leaving written messages or objects, or vandalizing a person's property. Most stalking laws require that the perpetrator make a credible threat of violence against the victim; others include threats against the victim's immediate family; and still others require only that the alleged stalker's course of conduct constitute an implied threat. While some conduct involving annoying or menacing behavior might fall short of illegal stalking, such behavior may be a prelude to stalking and violence and should be treated seriously ...

Nature and extent of cyberstalking

AN EXISTING PROBLEM AGGRAVATED BY NEW TECHNOLOGY

Although online harassment and threats can take many forms, cyberstalking shares important characteristics with offline stalking. Many stalkers—online or off—are motivated by a desire to exert control over their victims and engage in similar types of behavior to accomplish this end. As with offline stalking, the available evidence (which is largely anecdotal) suggests that the majority of cyberstalkers are men and the majority of their victims are women, although there have been reported cases of women cyberstalking men and of same-sex cyberstalking. In many cases, the cyberstalker and the victim had a prior relationship, and the cyberstalking begins when the victim attempts to break off the relationship. However, there also have been many instances of cyberstalking by strangers. Given the enormous amount of personal information available through the Internet, a cyberstalker can easily locate private information about a potential victim with a few mouse clicks or key strokes.

The fact that cyberstalking does not involve physical contact may create the misperception that it is more benign than physical stalking. This is not necessarily true. As the Internet becomes an ever more integral part of our personal and professional lives, stalkers can take advantage of the ease of communications as well as increased access to personal information. In addition, the ease of use and non-confrontational, impersonal, and sometimes anonymous nature of Internet communications may remove disincentives to cyberstalking. Put another way, whereas a potential stalker may be unwilling or unable to confront a victim in person or on the telephone, he or she may have little hesitation sending harassing or threatening electronic communications to a victim. Finally, as with physical stalking, online harassment and threats may be a prelude to more serious behavior, including physical violence.

Offline vs online stalking: a comparison

MAJOR SIMILARITIES

- Majority of cases involve stalking by former intimates, although stranger stalking occurs in the real world and in cyberspace.
- Most victims are women; most stalkers are men.
- Stalkers are generally motivated by the desire to control the victim.

MAJOR DIFFERENCES

- Offline stalking generally requires the perpetrator and the victim to be located in the same geographic area; cyberstalkers may be located across the street or across the country.
- Electronic communications technologies make it much easier for a cyberstalker to encourage third parties to harass and/or threaten a victim (eg, impersonating the victim and posting inflammatory messages to bulletin boards and in chat rooms, causing viewers of that message to send threatening messages back to the victim 'author'.)
- Electronic communications technologies also lower the barriers to harassment and threats; a cyberstalker does not need to physically confront the victim
- While there are many similarities between offline and online stalking, the Internet and other communications technologies provide new avenues for stalkers to pursue their victims.

A cyberstalker may send repeated, threatening, or harassing messages by the simple push of a button; more sophisticated cyberstalkers use programs to send messages at regular or random intervals without being physically present at the computer terminal. California law enforcement authorities say they have encountered situations where a victim repeatedly receives the message '187' on his or her pager—the section of the California Penal Code for murder. In addition, a cyberstalker can dupe other Internet users into harassing or threatening a victim by utilizing Internet bulletin boards or chat rooms. For example, a stalker may post a controversial or enticing message on the board under the name, phone number, or e-mail address of the victim, resulting in subsequent responses being sent to the victim. Each message—whether from the actual cyberstalker or others—will have the intended effect on the victim, but the cyberstalker's effort is minimal and the lack of direct contact between the cyberstalker and the victim can make it difficult for law enforcement to identify, locate, and arrest the offender ...

The anonymity of the Internet also provides new opportunities for would-be cyberstalkers. A cyberstalker's true identity can be concealed by using different ISPs and/or by adopting different screen names. More experienced stalkers can use anonymous re-mailers that make it all but impossible to determine the true identity of the source of an e-mail or other electronic communication. A number of law enforcement agencies report they currently are confronting cyberstalking cases involving the use of anonymous re-mailers.

Anonymity leaves the cyberstalker in an advantageous position. Unbeknownst to the target, the perpetrator could be in another state, around the corner, or in the next cubicle at work. The perpetrator could be a former friend or lover, a total stranger met in a chat room, or simply a teenager playing a practical joke. The inability to identify the source of the harassment or threats could be particularly ominous to a cyberstalking victim, and the veil of anonymity might encourage the perpetrator to continue these acts. In addition, some perpetrators, armed with the knowledge that their identity is unknown, might be more willing to pursue the victim at work or home, and the Internet can provide substantial information to this end. Numerous web sites will provide personal information, including unlisted telephone numbers and detailed directions to a home or office. For a fee, other web sites promise to provide social security numbers, financial data, and other personal information.

EVIDENCE SUGGESTS CYBERSTALKING IS A GROWING PROBLEM

Although there is no comprehensive, nationwide data on the extent of cyberstalking in the United States, some ISPs compile statistics on the number and types of complaints of harassment and/or threats involving their subscribers, and individual law enforcement agencies have compiled helpful statistics. There is, moreover, a growing amount of anecdotal and informal evidence on the nature and extent of cyberstalking.

First, data on offline stalking may provide some insight into the scope of the cyberstalking problem. According to the most recent National Violence Against Women Survey, which defines stalking as referring to instances where the victim felt a high level of fear:

* In the United States, one out of every 12 women (8.2 million) and one out of every 45 men (2 million) have been stalked at some time in their lives.
* One percent of all women and 0.4 percent of all men were stalked during the preceding 12 months.
* Women are far more likely to be the victims of stalking than men—nearly four out of five stalking victims are women. Men are far more likely to be stalkers—87 percent of the stalkers identified by victims in the survey were men.
* Women are twice as likely as men to be victims of stalking by strangers and eight times as likely to be victims of stalking by intimates.

In the United States, there are currently more than 80 million adults and 10 million children with access to the Internet. Assuming the proportion of cyberstalking victims is even a fraction of the proportion of persons who have been the victims of offline stalking within the preceding 12 months, there may be potentially tens or even hundreds of thousands of victims of recent cyberstalking incidents in the United States. Although such a 'back of the envelope' calculation is inherently uncertain and speculative (given that it rests on an assumption about very different populations), it does give a rough sense of the potential magnitude of the problem.

Second, anecdotal evidence from law enforcement agencies indicates that cyberstalking is a serious—and growing—problem. At the federal level, several dozen matters have been referred (usually by the FBI) to US Attorney's Offices for possible action. A number of these cases have been referred to state and local law enforcement agencies because the conduct does not appear to violate federal law.

In addition, some local law enforcement agencies are beginning to see cases of cyberstalking. For example, the Los Angeles District Attorney's Office estimates that e-mail or other electronic communications were a factor in approximately 20 percent of the roughly 600 cases handled by its Stalking and Threat Assessment Unit. The chief of the Sex Crimes Unit in the Manhattan District Attorney's Office also estimates that about 20 percent of the cases handled by the unit involve cyberstalking. The Computer Investigations and Technology Unit of the New York City Police Department estimates that almost 40 percent of the caseload in the unit involves electronic threats and harassment—and virtually all of these have occurred in the past three or four years.

Third, ISPs also are receiving a growing number of complaints about harassing and threatening behavior online. One major ISP receives approximately 15 complaints per month of cyberstalking, in comparison to virtually no complaints of cyberstalking just one or two years ago.

Finally, as part of a large study on sexual victimization of college women, researchers at the University of Cincinnati conducted a national telephone survey of 4446 randomly selected women attending two- and four-year institutions of higher education. The survey was conducted during the 1996–97 academic year. In this survey, a stalking incident was defined as a case in which a respondent answered positively when asked if someone had 'repeatedly followed you, watched you, phoned, written, e-mailed, or communicated with you in other ways that seemed obsessive and made you afraid or concerned for your safety'. The study found that 581 women (13.1 percent) were stalked and reported a total of 696 stalking incidents; the latter figure exceeds the number of victims because 15 percent of the women experienced more than one case of stalking during the survey period. Of these 696 stalking incidents, 166 (24.7 percent) involved e-mail. Thus, 25 percent of stalking incidents among college women could be classified as involving cyberstalking.

Current efforts to address cyberstalking

THE LAW ENFORCEMENT RESPONSE

Cyberstalking is a relatively new challenge for most law enforcement agencies. The first traditional stalking law was enacted by the state of California in 1990 ... Since that time, some law enforcement agencies have trained their personnel on stalking and/or established specialized units to handle stalking cases. Nonetheless, many agencies are still developing the expertise and resources to investigate and prosecute traditional stalking cases; only a handful of agencies throughout the country have focused attention or resources specifically on the cyberstalking problem ...

LAW ENFORCEMENT RESPONSE: AWARENESS AND TRAINING ARE KEY FACTORS

Based on recent informal surveys of law enforcement agencies, it appears that the majority of agencies have not investigated or prosecuted any cyberstalking cases. However, some agencies—particularly those with units dedicated to stalking or computer crime offenses—have large cyberstalking caseloads. As noted above, the New York Police Department's Computer Investigation and Technology Unit and the Los Angeles District Attorney's Stalking and Threat Assessment Team estimate that 40 and 20 percent of their caseloads, respectively, involve cyberstalking-type cases ...

The disparity in the activity level among law enforcement agencies can be attributed to a number of factors. First, it appears that the majority of cyberstalking victims do not report the conduct to law enforcement, either because they feel that the conduct has not reached the point of being a criminal offense or that law enforcement will not take them seriously. Second, most law enforcement agencies have not had the training to recognize the serious nature of cyberstalking and to investigate such offenses. Unfortunately, some victims have reported that rather than open an investigation, a law enforcement agency has advised them to come back if the cyberstalkers confront or threaten them offline. In several instances, victims have been told by law enforcement simply to turn off their computers ...

Another indication that many law enforcement agencies underestimate the magnitude of the cyberstalking problem is the wide disparity in reported cases in different jurisdictions across the country. For example, one state attorney general's office in a midwestern state indicated that it received approximately one inquiry a week regarding cyberstalking cases and that it is aware of approximately a dozen prosecutions last year alone. In contrast, the state attorney general's offices in neighboring states indicated they have never received an inquiry into this type of behavior. Although one would generally expect some disparity in differing jurisdictions, the size of the disparity suggests that some law enforcement agencies do not have the training or expertise to recognize the magnitude of the problem in their jurisdictions.

JURISDICTIONAL AND STATUTORY LIMITATIONS MAY FRUSTRATE SOME AGENCIES

Some state and local law enforcement agencies also have been frustrated by jurisdictional limitations. In many instances, the cyberstalker may be located in a different city or state from the victim, making it more difficult (and, in some cases, all but impossible) for the local authority to investigate the incident. Even if a law enforcement agency is willing to pursue a case across state lines, it may be difficult to obtain assistance from out-of-state agencies when the conduct is limited to harassing e-mail messages and no actual violence has occurred. A number of matters have been referred to the FBI and/or US Attorney's offices because the victim and suspect were located in different states and the local agency was not able to pursue the investigation.

The lack of adequate statutory authority also can limit law enforcement's response to cyberstalking incidents. At least 16 states have stalking statutes that explicitly cover electronic communications, and cyberstalking may be covered under general stalking statutes in other states. It may not, however, meet the statutory definition of stalking in the remainder. In many cases, cyberstalking will involve threats to kill, kidnap, or injure the person, reputation, or property of another, either on or offline and, as such, may be prosecuted under other federal or state laws that do not relate directly to stalking.

Finally, federal law may limit the ability of law enforcement agencies to track down stalkers and other criminals in cyberspace. In particular, the *Cable Communications Policy Act* of 1984 (CCPA) prohibits the disclosure of cable subscriber records to law enforcement agencies without a court order and advance notice to the subscriber (see 47 USC 551(c), (h)). As more and more individuals turn to cable companies as their ISPs, the CCPA is posing a significant obstacle to the investigation of cybercrimes, including cyberstalking. For example, under the CCPA, a law enforcement agency investigating a cyberstalker who uses a cable company for Internet access would have to provide the individual notice that the agency has requested his/her subscriber records, thereby jeopardizing the criminal investigation. While it is appropriate to prohibit the indiscriminate disclosure of cable records to law enforcement agencies, the better approach would be to harmonize federal law by providing law enforcement access to cable subscriber records under the same privacy safeguards that currently govern law enforcement access to records of electronic mail subscribers under 18 USC 2703. Moreover, special provisions could be drafted to protect against the inappropriate disclosure of records that would reveal a customer's viewing habits.

THE CHALLENGE OF ANONYMITY

Another complication for law enforcement is the presence of services that provide anonymous communications over the Internet. To be sure, anonymity provides important benefits, including protecting the privacy of Internet users. Unfortunately, cyberstalkers and other cybercriminals can exploit the anonymity available on the Internet to avoid accountability for their conduct.

Anonymous services on the Internet come in one of two forms: the first allows individuals to create a free electronic mailbox through a web site. While most entities that provide this service request identifying information from users, such services almost never authenticate or otherwise confirm this information. For these services, payment is typically made in advance through the use of a money order or other non-traceable form of payment. As long as payment is received in advance by the ISP, the service is provided to the unknown account holder. The second form comprises mail servers that purposely strip identifying information and transport headers from electronic mail. By forwarding e-mail through several of these services serially, a stalker can nearly perfectly anonymize the message. The presence of both such services makes it relatively simple to send anonymous communications, while making it difficult for victims, providers, and law enforcement to identify the person or persons responsible for transmitting harassing or threatening communications over the Internet.

SPECIALIZED UNITS SHOW PROMISE IN COMBATING CYBERSTALKING

A growing number of law enforcement agencies are recognizing the serious nature and extent of cyberstalking and taking aggressive action to respond. Some larger metropolitan areas, such as Los Angeles and New York, have seen numerous incidents of cyberstalking and have specialized units available to investigate and prosecute these cases. For example, Los Angeles has developed the Stalking and Threat Assessment Team. This team combines special sections of the police department and district attorney's office to ensure properly trained investigators and prosecutors are available when cyberstalking cases arise. In addition, this specialized unit is given proper resources, such as adequate computer hardware and advanced training, which is essential in investigating and prosecuting these technical cases. Similarly, the New York City Police Department created the Computer Investigation and Technology Unit. This unit provides regular training for police officers and prosecutors regarding the intricacies of cyberstalking investigations and prosecutions. The training includes understanding how chat rooms operate, how to obtain and preserve electronic evidence, and how to draft search warrants and subpoenas.

The programs in New York and Los Angeles both ensure that enforcement personnel receive proper training and have adequate resources to combat cyberstalking. Other jurisdictions are also taking steps to combat cyberstalking. One of the critical steps is learning how to trace communications sent over computers and the Internet. Traditional law enforcement techniques for surveillance, investigation, and evidence gathering require modification for use on computer networks and often require the use of unfamiliar legal processes. Law enforcement at all levels must be properly trained to use network investigative techniques and legal process while protecting the privacy of legitimate users of the Internet. These techniques are similar to those used in investigating other types of computer crime. Just as a burglar might leave fingerprints at the scene of a crime, a cyberstalker can leave an 'electronic trail' on the web that properly trained law enforcement can follow back to the source. Thus, technological proficiency among both investigators and prosecutors is essential.

At present, there are numerous efforts at the federal and state levels that focus solely on high technology crimes. These units do not focus on cyberstalking alone, but they have the necessary expertise in computers and the Internet to assist in the investigation of cyberstalking when it arises. For example, the Federal Bureau of Investigation (FBI) has Computer Crime Squads throughout the country, as well as the National Infrastructure Protection Center in Washington, to ensure cybercrimes are properly investigated. Additionally, they have Computer Analysis and Response Teams to conduct forensics examinations on seized magnetic media. Similarly, in 1996 the Justice Department established the Computer Crime and Intellectual Property Section within the Criminal Division. These units have highly trained personnel who remain on the cutting edge of new technology and investigative techniques. In addition, each US Attorney's office contains experienced computer crime prosecutors. These individuals—Computer and Telecommunications Coordinators—assist in the investigation and prosecution of a wide variety of computer crimes, including cyberstalking. In addition, at the state level, several attorneys general have established special divisions that focus on computer crimes.

Although high-tech expertise is essential, police and prosecutors have developed other strategies for helping victims of cyberstalking. An Assistant US Attorney reported that in two recent cases of e-mail harassment, he asked an FBI agent to confront the would-be harasser. The agent advised that such behavior might constitute a criminal offense. In both instances, the harassment stopped. Such strategies, however, are no substitute for prosecution under federal or state law in the appropriate circumstances.

A critical step in combating cyberstalking is understanding stalking in general. In many instances, cyberstalking is simply another phase in an overall stalking pattern, or it is regular stalking behavior using new, high-technology tools. Thus, strategies and techniques that have been developed to combat stalking in general often can be adapted to cyberstalking situations. Fortunately, many state and local law enforcement agencies have begun to focus on stalking, and some have developed special task forces to deal with this problem. In addition, the Attorney General submits an annual report to Congress entitled 'Stalking and Domestic Violence'. This report compiles valuable information about what the Department of Justice has learned about stalking and stalkers and is a valuable resource for law enforcement agencies and others.

Cyberstalking is expected to increase as computers and the Internet become more popular. Accordingly, law enforcement at all levels must become more sensitive to cyberstalking complaints and devote the necessary training and resources to allow proper investigation and prosecution. By becoming technologically proficient and understanding stalking in general, agencies will be better prepared to respond to cyberstalking incidents in their jurisdictions. In addition, state and local agencies can turn to their local FBI or US Attorney's office for additional technical assistance. Also, computer crime units and domestic violence units should share information and expertise, since many cyberstalking cases will include elements of both computer crime and domestic violence. Finally, law enforcement must become more sensitive to the fear and frustration experienced by cyberstalking victims. Proper training should help in this regard, but law enforcement at all levels should take the next step and place special emphasis on this problem. Computers and the Internet are becoming indispensable parts of America's culture, and cyberstalking is a growing threat. Responding to a victim's complaint by saying 'just turn off your computer' is not acceptable.

INDUSTRY EFFORTS

Although the Internet industry has tried to combat abusive electronic communications overall, the industry as a whole has not addressed cyberstalking in particular. According to a review conducted as part of the preparation of the report, most major ISPs have established an address to which complaints of abusive or harassing electronic mail can be sent (generally, this address is 'abuse@[the ISP's domain]'—for example, 'abuse@aol.com'). In addition, these providers almost uniformly have provisions in their online agreements specifically prohibiting abusive or harassing conduct through their service and providing that violations of the policy will result in termination of the account.

In practice, however, ISPs have focused more on assisting their customers in avoiding annoying online behavior, such as receiving unsolicited commercial electronic mail ('spamming') or large amounts of electronic mail intentionally sent to an individual ('mail-bombing'); relatively less attention has been paid to helping victims of cyberstalking or other electronic threats. For some ISPs, the procedures for lodging complaints of online harassment or threats were difficult to locate, and their policies about what does or does not constitute a violation of service agreements were generally unhelpful. In addition, many ISPs do not inform their customers about what steps, if any, the ISP has taken to follow up on their customer's complaint. These problems—hard-to-locate complaint procedures, vague policies about what does and does not constitute prohibited harassment, and inadequate follow-up on complaints—may pose serious obstacles to cyberstalking victims who need help.

Online industry associations respond that providing such protection to their customers is costly and difficult. Although they recognize that larger ISPs have begun to commit resources to dealing with harassment online, they caution that the costs of imposing additional reporting or response obligations upon ISPs may make it difficult for small or entrepreneurial ISPs to continue providing service at competitive rates. For example, the Commercial Internet Exchange, whose members carry approximately 75 percent of US backbone traffic, cautions that no attempt to impose reporting requirements should be made unless fully justified by the record. However, according to the same group, the decentralized nature of the Internet would make it difficult for providers to collect and submit such data. Accordingly, the evidence of the scope of the cyberstalking problem is likely to remain for the foreseeable future defined primarily by anecdotal evidence, with no basis to determine whether the phenomenon is growing, static, or declining.

EDUCATING AND PROTECTING CONSUMERS

Despite the difficulty in fully defining the scope of the cyberstalking problem, however, industry has made notable efforts to inform consumers about ways to protect themselves online. Such information is principally focused on protecting children and consumers on the Internet. For example, since 1996, the Internet Alliance, one of the key Internet industry groups, has worked with the Federal Trade Commission and government agencies on Project OPEN (Online Public Education Network). Project OPEN provides information about fraud, parental controls, and protecting privacy. Although this information is not specifically relevant to cyberstalking, much of the advice about protecting children and safeguarding privacy while online may be of assistance to individuals who want to use the Internet while protecting against potential cyberstalkers. More recently, a number of industry organizations have joined together to develop GetNetWise.Com—a single, comprehensive online resource to help parents and children use the Internet in a safe and educational manner.

Other similar industry efforts have recently been announced to address other aspects of computer-related crime. For example, the Department of Justice and the Information Technology Association of America (ITAA) announced the Cybercitizen Partnership in March 1999. This partnership is intended to boost cooperation between industry and government, expand public awareness of computer crime issues among children and adolescents, and provide resources for government to draw upon in addressing computer crime. The industry has also responded to the complaints of parents who are worried about the content available to their children over the Internet by announcing the 'One Click Away' initiative to give parents important information about protecting their children in a central location. Similar education and outreach efforts, approached through cooperation between industry and government, may educate individuals concerned about these issues and therefore mitigate some of the dangers of cyberstalking.

In addition, other Internet industry sectors have begun to address aspects of the cyberstalking problem. Many of these solutions focus on the ability of individuals to protect themselves against unwanted communications. For example, most Internet 'chat' facilities offer users the ability to block, squelch, or ignore chat messages or 'paging' from individuals who are attempting to annoy or threaten them. Similarly, many e-mail users have tools which allow the users to block e-mail from individuals who are attempting to harass or annoy them. Such a solution may be useful in situations where the communications are merely annoying. Unfortunately, such a solution is less appropriate when threatening communications are received, because a victim who never 'receives' the threat may not know that he or she is being stalked, and may be alerted, for the first time, when the stalker shows up to act on the threat.

In another type of response, providers have begun to set up 'gated communities' for individuals, families, and children. The techniques used by such communities are still in developmental stages, but they range from specialized servers, which allow potentially objectionable content to be filtered at the server, to designated areas for children and teens, which place restrictions on the amount or types of personal information that will be provided to others. Individuals who are concerned about being stalked may find refuge in such communities.

While these efforts all reflect important initiatives for self-protection, both industry and government representatives agree that a key component of addressing the cyberstalking problem is education and empowerment: If individuals are given clear direction about how to protect themselves against threatening or harassing communications, and how to report incidents when they do occur, both industry and law enforcement will be in a position to cooperate to conduct investigations.

COOPERATION WITH LAW ENFORCEMENT

Both industry and law enforcement benefit when crime over the Internet is reduced. In particular, the Internet industry benefits significantly whenever citizen and consumer confidence and trust in the Internet is increased. Accordingly, both industry and law enforcement recognize the need to cooperate more fully with one another in this area. Industry representatives have noted that contact between industry and law enforcement—particularly in the area of harassment—is sporadic and episodic. Industry representatives, who were consulted as part of the preparation of this report, indicated their willingness to participate in training efforts for law enforcement. Law enforcement—particularly on the state and local level, who will often be first responders to cyberstalking complaints—should be willing to engage industry in dialogue and take advantage of the expertise offered by industry in designing training programs. Moreover, closer cooperation between law enforcement and industry will help to ensure that law enforcement officers know who at the ISPs to call and how to proceed when they receive a complaint, and ISPs have a contact in law enforcement when they receive a complaint that warrants intervention by law enforcement.

VICTIMS AND SUPPORT ORGANIZATIONS

Because cyberstalking is a relatively new criminal phenomenon, very little public attention and resources have been committed to addressing this crime. Consequently, victims of online harassment and threats, often in collaboration with victim service providers and advocates, have had to step in to fill the void by developing their own informal support networks and informational web sites to exchange information about how to respond to these crimes effectively.

Victim service providers report that the Internet is rapidly becoming another weapon used by batterers against their victims. Just as in real life, abused women can be followed in cyberspace by their batterers, who may surreptitiously place their target under surveillance without her knowledge and use the information to threaten her or discredit her by putting misinformation on the Internet. Victim service providers recommend that victims make copies of all e-mail messages sent by the batterer as evidence of his stalking and advise a victim to let the stalker know that she does not want to have any further contact with him. SAFE House, a domestic violence victim service provider in Michigan, suggests that victims change their passwords often; refrain from telling anyone what the password is; do not use a password or other identifying information that the batterer/stalker can guess; set up a program that requires a password even to get on the computer; be sure to clear out the history information if programs such as ICQ, AOL Communicator, and Excite PAL, are used; remember that many chat rooms have archives that can be accessed later on by anyone; be careful about what is said in chat rooms and use an alias that is only known to good friends; be aware that if the screen name of the assailant is known, he can be blocked from tracking victims through a buddy list on AOL; and, consult the ISP about the best way to secure their account.

Case studies in cyberstalking

A Report from the Attorney General to the Vice President August 1999, Report on Cyberstalking: A New Challenge for Law Enforcement and Industry

Available at <http://www.cybercrime.gov/cyberstalking.htm> 17 August 2006

In the first successful prosecution under California's new cyberstalking law, prosecutors in the Los Angeles District Attorney's Office obtained a guilty plea from a 50-year-old former security guard who used the Internet to solicit the rape of a woman who rejected his romantic advances. The defendant terrorized his 28-year-old victim by impersonating her in various Internet chat rooms and online bulletin boards, where he posted, along with her telephone number and address, messages that she fantasized of being raped. On at least six occasions, sometimes in the middle of the night, men knocked on the woman's door saying they wanted to rape her. The former security guard pleaded guilty in April 1999 to one count of stalking and three counts of solicitation of sexual assault. He faces up to six years in prison.

A local prosecutor's office in Massachusetts charged a man who, utilizing anonymous re-mailers, allegedly engaged in a systematic pattern of harassment of a co-worker, which culminated in an attempt to extort sexual favors from the victim under threat of disclosing past sexual activities to the victim's new husband.

An honors graduate from the University of San Diego terrorized five female university students over the Internet for more than a year. The victims received hundreds of violent and threatening e-mail messages, sometimes receiving four or five messages a day. The graduate student, who has entered a guilty plea and faces up to six years in prison, told police he committed the crimes because he thought the women were laughing at him and causing others to ridicule him. In fact, the victims had never met him.

 NOTES AND QUESTIONS

1   Outline some of the techniques used to stalk a person over the Internet.
2   What protections can people install in order to avoid such dangers?
3   The Supreme Court of Victoria, Australia, in 2001 ruled that if the law protecting women against stalking could not apply to activities that caused harm overseas,

it would be rendered unworkable.[1] A lower court had decided that it did not have jurisdiction because the effects of the crime were felt in another territory. The Supreme Court reversed the decision, ruling that the charge, brought by a Canadian woman against an Australian man, could be tried in Australia. Is this case emblematic of a paradigm shift in jurisprudence when faced with the challenges of the Internet? Do you think the court would have reached the same conclusions had the stalking been conducted through traditional means?

4   How prevalent is stalking on the Internet? Are there parallels between rates of stalking on-line and off-line? Are you surprised by the figures for stalking on the Internet presented by the above extract?

5   'People who complain about cyberstalking should spend less time on their computers and more time in the real world, and besides, you cannot actually get hurt on the Internet because it's not real, so there is no real problem anyway.' Is this a realistic perception of the perils of the Internet?

6   Critically evaluate the strategies outlined above to combat stalking on the Internet. Do you believe that the programs and proposals will be effective? Can you suggest any further options for the further protection of Internet users?

(d)   Gambling

The President's Working Group on Unlawful Conduct on the Internet, The Electronic Frontier: The Challenge of Unlawful Conduct Involving the Use of the Internet, March 2000

Available at <http://www.cybercrime.gov/append.htm> 17 August 2006

Appendix F: Internet gambling

1. NATURE OF THE POTENTIALLY UNLAWFUL CONDUCT
The growing availability of the Internet and other emerging technologies has had a dramatic impact on gambling businesses. Studies estimate that between 1997 and 1998, Internet gambling more than doubled, from 6.9 million to 14.5 million gamblers, with revenues more than doubling from $300 million to $651 million. A recent estimate reported 300 Internet gambling sites in operation. This rapid rate in the growth of Internet gambling is alarming and has caused several problems for federal, state, tribal, and local governments in the enforcement of their gambling laws.

First, the Internet is attractive to organized crime groups that operate gambling businesses, because it allows virtually instantaneous and anonymous communication that can be difficult to trace to any particular individual or organization. There is also the possibility of abuse by

---

1   The report is available at <http://www.bmck.com/ecommerce/whatsnew-cybercrime.htm> 29 September 2001.

unscrupulous gambling operators. The ability for operators to alter, move, or entirely remove sites from the Internet within minutes makes it possible for dishonest operators to take credit card numbers and money from deposited accounts and close down. Operators may tamper with gambling software to manipulate games to their benefit. Unlike the highly-regulated physical world casinos, assessing the integrity of Internet operations is difficult. Gambling on the Internet also may provide an easy means for money laundering, as it provides criminal anonymity, remote access, and access to encrypted data.

Second, the anonymous nature of the Internet also creates the danger that access to Internet gambling will be abused by underage gamblers. Gambling businesses have no surefire way of confirming that gamblers are not minors who have gained access to a credit card and are gambling on their web sites. The government has received numerous complaints from concerned and affected citizens regarding this problem.

Third, because the Internet provides people with the opportunity to gamble at any time and from any place, Internet gambling presents a greater danger for compulsive gamblers and may cause severe financial consequences for the player and those dependent on the player's resources (eg dependent children).

As the National Gambling Impact Study Commission recently found:

> Internet gambling is raising issues never previously addressed and exacerbating concerns associated with traditional forms of gambling. While preventing underage gambling and reducing problems associated with problem and pathological gambling are concerns for all forms of gambling, reducing these concerns is particularly challenging for Internet gambling. The Internet provides the highest level of anonymity for conducting gambling to date … Screening clients to determine age or if they have a history of gambling problems is difficult at best.

These problems are exacerbated by the international scope of the Internet. Although the United States has determined that there is a strong law enforcement priority to prohibit Internet gambling, other countries have chosen to allow unrestricted Internet gambling (as certain countries in the Caribbean have done) or, in the alternative, to regulate betting and wagering on the Internet. The United States government, in its assessment of existing and needed laws, must adopt solutions that do not interfere with the operation of these lawful foreign gambling operations, while protecting its citizens from the transmission of bets or wagers into or from the United States. …

3. INVESTIGATORY CHALLENGES

On the one hand, as noted above, existing laws have provided the basis for successful prosecutions against Internet gambling. The use of credit cards for the bulk of gambling over the Internet also means that detailed records of such transactions are likely to exist. These records may be used as evidence of criminal conduct once alleged gambling operations have been identified. Indeed, the existence of such records may well have reduced the level of illegal, online casino gambling that is conducted from US-based web site operators. On the other hand, however, online casino gambling has largely shifted to offshore locations, where it may be difficult for US law enforcement agencies to gain access to relevant records. In addition, the use of fraudulently obtained credit card numbers can limit the usefulness of transaction records generated by the use of such cards.

Some legal changes are also needed. Although existing federal laws provide an adequate basis for prosecuting traditional forms of gambling on the Internet, new telecommunications technology has brought about entirely new types of electronic gambling, such as interactive Internet poker and blackjack, that some gambling operations claim are not prohibited by section 1084 as it currently exists. As a result, section 1084 needs to be amended to clarify the law and to remove any doubt as to whether new types of gambling activities made possible by emerging technologies are prohibited.

The Department of Justice, working with the Departments of Commerce and Treasury and the Office of the US Trade Representative, has drafted amendments that would ensure that individuals in the business of betting and wagering do not use communications facilities to transmit bets or wagers in interstate or foreign commerce, within the special maritime and territorial jurisdiction of the United States, or to or from any place outside the jurisdiction of any nation with respect to any transmission to or from the United States. Specifically, these amendments would, among other things:

- clarify that section 1084 applies to all betting or wagering (not merely betting or wagering on sports events) and includes the transmission of bets and wagers over any communication facilities;
- require any person, not just a common carrier, that provides a communications facility to an individual in the business of betting and wagering to cooperate with law enforcement agencies;
- apply section 1084 to those engaged in the business of betting or wagering who are located outside the territorial jurisdiction of the United States, when those individuals knowingly facilitate or aid in unlawful betting and wagering by transmitting a bet or wager, or information assisting in the placing of a bet or wager, to or from an individual located within the United States;
- clarify that section 1084 does not prohibit the lawful use of communication facilities in the operation of state lotteries; and
- clarify that section 1084 does not amend or repeal the *Indian Gaming Regulatory Act*.

Last year, both the House and the Senate introduced the *Internet Gambling Prohibition Act* of 1999 (HR 3125 and S 692); the Senate version passed in November 1999. This proposed legislation, however, would leave traditional gambling statutes in effect for non-Internet media, while creating special rules for Internet gambling. This non-technology-neutral approach would create overlapping and inconsistent federal gambling laws. In addition, these legislative proposals contain a number of broad exemptions from its general prohibition on Internet gambling. Such exemptions are not only questionable as a matter of policy, but, because they would apply only to Internet gambling, they would exacerbate the problems created by the existence of a separate legal framework for Internet gambling.

CONCLUSIONS

Existing federal laws generally prohibit individuals from transmitting bets or wagers (using a 'wire communication facility', which includes the Internet) on sporting events or contests in the US. The advances of the Internet, however, have made it necessary to update existing federal laws to ensure that they are technology-neutral and prohibit new as well as traditional forms of online gambling activities. Law enforcement also needs better mechanisms by which to track and identify online gambling businesses. The anonymous nature of the Internet complicates the ability of law enforcement to successfully track online gambling operators.

 NOTES AND QUESTIONS

1   To what extent is gambling a social problem, as opposed to a legal problem? Carefully consider the relationship between objectionable Internet content and Internet crime. Do you think making a criminal offence of this type of activity will help solve the social problems gambling can cause?

2   'Laws against gambling on the Internet exist not because governments object to gambling, but because governments object to not being able to tax gambling. If they cannot tax it, they will criminalise it. This is the real motive behind regulation of Internet gambling.' Discuss.

3   Does the extent of on-line gambling surprise you? In your answer, consider what you have read above regarding the importance of trust, in commerce generally and specifically on the Internet.

4   The Australian Federal *Interactive Gambling Act 2001* received Royal Assent on 11 July 2001. The Act makes it an offence to provide an interactive gambling service to a person in Australia, and bans the advertising of interactive gambling in Australia. The Act targets the providers of interactive gambling services, not their potential or actual customers. The Act makes it an offence to provide interactive gambling services to a customer physically present in Australia and this applies to all interactive gambling service providers, whether based in Australia or offshore, whether Australian or foreign-owned.[2] Interestingly enough, there is a 'reasonable diligence' clause in the Act whereby the operator of the service can escape liability if reasonable diligence is established. It remains to be seen how this will be interpreted by the courts. A review of the *Interactive Gambling Act 2001* was concluded in 2004 and the Federal government decided not to take any specific regulatory action. Instead, the Federal government called on the State and Territories governments to take the responsible lead in strengthening the licensing regimes.

(e)   Alcohol

The President's Working Group on Unlawful Conduct on the Internet, The Electronic Frontier: The Challenge of Unlawful Conduct Involving the Use of the Internet, March 2000

Available at <http://www.cybercrime.gov/append.htm> 17 August 2006

---

2   See s 15, *Interactive Gambling Act 2001* (Cth).

Appendix G: Internet sale of alcohol

1. NATURE OF THE POTENTIALLY UNLAWFUL CONDUCT
Internet sales of alcohol beverages have caused direct shipments of such beverages to consumers to proliferate. Selling over the Internet allows small alcohol producers to reach consumers well beyond their immediate area. These Internet sales of alcohol beverages enable adults—and, potentially, minors—to receive products that are not ordinarily available through traditional distribution channels.

Fifteen states have established reciprocal arrangements that permit the shipment of wine (but not beer or distilled spirits) into their jurisdictions from one reciprocal state to another. Sales by alcohol marketers are not, however, limited to consumers in other reciprocal states. In many cases, these marketers may ship to consumers in other states, a practice that may violate state alcohol control laws. Even if federal excise taxes are paid on these products, direct shipments to consumers across state lines causes a loss of state tax revenue and may result in federal and state regulatory violations. Such regulatory violations may include deliveries to underage persons and the sale of unregistered brands in a state. The sale of unregistered brands results in a loss of state registration fees, state excise tax revenues, and local sales tax revenues.

2. ANALYSIS OF EXISTING LAW
Under the *Federal Alcohol Administration Act*, the Bureau of Alcohol, Tobacco and Firearms ('ATF') issues 'basic permits' to importers, producers (except brewers), and wholesalers of alcohol beverages (see 27 USC s 204). Retailer sellers of alcohol beverages are not required to have a federal permit. The Webb-Kenyon Act, 27 USC s 122, prohibits the shipment of alcohol beverages into a state in violation of state law. Although the Webb-Kenyon Act has no separate penalty provisions, basic permits are conditioned on compliance with that statute.

As a result, ATF may, depending on the circumstances, take administrative action against a permittee that ships alcohol beverages into a state in violation of that state's law. ATF may also intervene if there is a continuing material adverse impact upon a state by an out-of-state permittee. Many of the entities selling on the Internet are, however, state-licensed retailers that do not hold federal basic permits and, therefore, are not subject to ATF's administrative sanctions against permittees.

Also relevant are the liquor traffic provisions of 18 USC ch 59, which require any shipment of alcohol beverages in interstate commerce to have a bill of lading that identifies its contents, and which require deliveries to be restricted to the consignee. Some state laws allow limited quantities of alcohol beverages to be shipped directly to consumers, although in some instances notifications to state alcohol agencies may be required.

3. INVESTIGATORY CHALLENGES
The primary issue concerning the sale of alcohol beverages over the Internet is the difficulty sellers have in determining whether a purchaser is underage. Some minors could conceivably seek to use credit cards, legitimately or not, to place an order through the Internet and have alcohol beverages delivered through a shipping company. Several web sites require purchasers

to 'certify' that they are of legal age either by clicking on part of the web page or by faxing a copy of a driver's license. Restricting the delivery of alcohol beverage to situations where proof of age is obtained and recorded would assist in preventing access to alcohol beverages by underage persons. Currently, however, there is a significant potential for abuse in the sale of alcohol to minors.

A second investigatory issue relates to the broader issue of jurisdiction. An out-of-state seller that sells alcohol beverages through a web site is not generally licensed by the state, and state courts often have difficulty establishing jurisdiction over such sellers. Under certain circumstances, as noted above, ATF may take administrative action against a permittee that ships alcohol beverages into a state in violation of the laws of that state. This authority would not reach situations where a retailer in one state ships to a purchaser in another state, because retailers are not required to have basic permits. But if the in-state purchaser resells the alcohol beverages, the out-of-state retailer then becomes a wholesale agent, against whom ATF may take enforcement action.

4. SPECIFIC FEDERAL LEGISLATIVE INITIATIVES

The *Violent and Repeat Juvenile Offender Accountability and Rehabilitation Act* of 1999 (HR 1501 and S 254, 106th Congress), as passed by the Senate last year, contained two provisions related to Internet sales of alcohol beverages. Although these proposals were not ultimately passed, they are likely to be advanced again:

The first provision, sponsored by Senators Byrd and Hatch and Representative Ehrlich, would amend the Webb-Kenyon Act, 27 USC s 122, to allow state Attorneys General to obtain preliminary and permanent injunctions in federal court against persons who engage in any act that constitutes a violation of state law regulating the importation or transportation of alcohol beverages.

The second provision, sponsored by Senator Feinstein, would amend the liquor trafficking prohibitions (see 18 USC ch 59), to require persons who ship alcohol beverages in interstate commerce to label the packages as containing alcohol beverages and to require shipping companies to obtain the signature of the person receiving delivery and to verify that that person is of legal age for the purchase of alcohol beverages within the receiving state.

In addition, in August 1999, the House of Representatives passed the *Twenty-First Amendment Enforcement Act*, HR 2031, which would amend the Webb-Kenyon Act to permit state Attorneys General to obtain injunctions in federal court (an approach similar to the first provision in the juvenile crime bill noted above). The Bill provides that nothing in it permits state regulation or taxation of Internet services or authorizes injunctions against interactive computer services or electronic communications services.

5. CONCLUSIONS

As existing laws address the legality of shipping and selling alcohol beverages in interstate commerce, the primary issue concerning the sale of alcohol over the Internet is the potential anonymity of the buyer. The anonymous nature of the Internet makes it difficult, using current technology, for a seller to verify at the time of sale whether a prospective purchaser is of legal drinking age. In addition, the Internet facilitates direct shipments of alcohol beverages to consumers across state lines, resulting in a loss of state registration fees and state excise and local sales tax revenues and possibly resulting in federal or state regulatory violations.

NOTES AND QUESTIONS

1 Illegal sale of alcohol is one example that might not spring instantly to mind when considering the varieties of Internet crime. What does this suggest about the possibilities for other types of crime?

2 How significant do you think a problem such as this might be in your own jurisdiction? Are there other restricted or prohibited substances which could be distributed on the Internet?

3 What is the primary concern of legislatures in this area? What does this say about the motivation for Internet regulation more generally?

(f)   Securities fraud

The President's Working Group on Unlawful Conduct on the Internet, The Electronic Frontier: The Challenge of Unlawful Conduct Involving the Use of the Internet, March 2000

Available at <http://www.cybercrime.gov/append.htm> 17 August 2006

Appendix H: Online securities fraud

1. NATURE OF THE POTENTIALLY UNLAWFUL CONDUCT

The Internet has had a profound effect on how investors research and trade securities. Millions of investors are signing on to the Internet to obtain investment information and to execute trades. Recent estimates are that close to 16 percent of all equity trades are conducted online. The number of online accounts open as of the second quarter of 1999 (nearly 10 million) is nearly triple the number open as recently as 1997. The Internet has brought significant benefits to investors, including enhanced access to information (both in speed and quantity) and lower costs to execute trades.

Unfortunately, the Internet also has opened new avenues for fraud artists to attempt to swindle the investing public. This is because the Internet offers perpetrators of securities fraud a medium to commit their crimes that is speedy, cheap, easy to use, and relatively anonymous. For the most part, there are three categories of securities frauds that have been encountered online by law enforcement.

Market Manipulation: This category of fraud most often involves attempts to artificially inflate a stock's price by creating demand for thinly traded lower-priced securities. The manipulators create the demand through the dissemination of false and misleading information, such as phony announcements pertaining to strategic alliances, future earnings, mergers, or other important corporate developments. The Internet has proven to be fertile ground for such manipulations, because information can be disseminated with the simple click of a mouse to millions of users via web sites, newsletters, spam, message boards, and other Internet media. The manipulator normally owns shares in the company's stock and sells during the run-up that the manipulator creates. This fraud is commonly known as a 'pump-and-dump' scheme. The PairGain case discussed at the beginning of this report is an example of a market manipulation case.

Offering Frauds: These cases generally involve either false or misleading offerings of securities. Falling into this category of cases are pyramid and Ponzi schemes, and affinity frauds targeted at specific racial, ethnic, or religious groups. In addition, there have been numerous fraudulent offerings of non-traditional securities over the Internet, such as offerings for 'prime bank' programs and other esoteric securities, including interests in eel farms, coconut plantations, and fictional countries. Persons offering these securities often violate the law by failing to register as broker-dealers. The SEC has successfully tracked many of these offerings and conducted a May 1998 'sweep', in which it charged 26 individuals and companies for engaging in bogus securities offerings on the Internet.

Illegal Touting: This type of securities fraud takes place when persons are paid to hype a company's stock without making legally required disclosure of the nature, source, and amount of their compensation. This disclosure is necessary because investors have a right to know whether information they are receiving is objective or 'bought and paid for'. The SEC has brought two Internet touting 'sweeps' charging a total of 57 individuals and companies.

These three categories are not exhaustive. There are other securities law violations taking place on the Internet, including unregistered offerings of securities as well as broker-dealer registration violations. For example, in July 1999, the SEC coordinated the filing of four so-called 'free stock' actions charging those who offered securities over the Internet with having failed to register those offerings. Two of those actions also alleged fraud.

2. ANALYSIS OF EXISTING LAW

The existing statutory framework provided by the federal securities laws has generally been adequate in the federal government's efforts to fight online securities fraud. As with the other examples of Internet-facilitated unlawful conduct discussed in this report, however, as our experience fighting such conduct continues to evolve, it may be necessary to revisit whether any new legislation or rule-making is needed.

Section 10(b) of the *Securities Exchange Act* of 1934, 15 USC s 78j(b), and Rule 10b-5 thereunder, 17 CFR s 240.10b-5, are the primary authorities used by the SEC to combat market manipulation and other frauds in the securities market. These provisions make it unlawful to use a fraudulent scheme or to make material misrepresentations and omissions in connection with the purchase or sale of any security. Both section 10(b) and Rule 10b-5 were drafted broadly to capture new and unforeseen frauds. Most of the cases brought by the SEC have charged defendants with violating section 10(b).

Unlawful touting is covered by section 17(b) of the *Securities Act* of 1933, 15 USC s 77q(b), which makes it unlawful to use interstate facilities to fraudulently offer or sell securities. Specifically, this statute deems it unlawful for any person to give publicity to, or otherwise tout, a security in exchange for compensation without full disclosure of the fee arrangement. It applies to information spread in cyberspace just as it does to information spread by newsletters, radio, or any other traditional media.

Individuals engaged in unregistered offerings of securities on the Internet may be liable under section 5 of the Securities Act, 15 USC s 78e, unless the offering qualifies for one of certain exemptions. This law is designed to assure that investors have adequate information upon which to base their investment decisions. The SEC has brought several cases charging violations of this statute in connection with Internet offerings, including four cases brought in July 1999 against issuers of so-called 'free' stock. The SEC has also brought cases charging unlawful offerings of securities on an Internet auction site.

The federal securities laws also impose registration requirements upon anyone acting as a broker or dealer and upon large investment advisers. Those persons acting in these capacities by virtue of conduct on the Internet are required to register with the SEC to the same extent as those acting in the offline world are.

3. SPECIFIC FEDERAL INITIATIVES

The SEC has devoted substantial resources to policing the Internet, including creating the Office of Internet Enforcement ('OIE') in July 1998. OIE, currently staffed with ten attorneys, regularly conducts investigations on the Internet, referring matters to other SEC staff, as well as to other agencies and the self-regulatory organizations, when appropriate. OIE also conducts national law enforcement training. For example, in November 1999, OIE hosted the first-ever Internet securities fraud training program, attended by more than 300 law enforcement personnel nationwide. OIE also oversees the Commission's 'cyber-force', a group of approximately 240 SEC staff members who use the Internet as part of their investigations.

As a result of these and other efforts, the SEC has brought approximately 110 Internet-related enforcement actions since 1995, with the vast majority coming in the past two years as the use of the Internet by prospective investors has surged. The SEC has articulated a 5-pronged approach to counteracting Internet fraud: (a) vigilant and flexible surveillance; (b) aggressive prosecution; (c) coordinated liaison work with other agencies, criminal prosecutors, and self-regulatory organizations; (d) investor education; and (e) the fostering of self-policing and encouraging members of the public to provide the agency with tips and complaints.

4. INVESTIGATORY CHALLENGES

The shift of securities fraud from traditional media, such as 'boiler room' telephone banks, to the Internet certainly poses new challenges for regulators. The SEC's greatest challenge to date has been one of resources. As the SEC's Director of Enforcement stated in testimony before the Senate Permanent Subcommittee on Investigations in March 1999, 'Our greatest problem will likely be one of resources, as the size of our staff has remained relatively constant while the Internet has grown by leaps and bounds.' The vastness of the Internet requires significant resources for appropriate surveillance coupled with timely investigation and prosecution of violations.

The resource issue is particularly acute with respect to the investigation and prosecution of illegal conduct. Experience shows that securities fraud artists operating on the Internet typically do not hide; rather, they operate in plain view in an attempt to reach as many potential investors as possible. The Internet offers investigators in the SEC an important window through which to observe developing frauds, and, in certain cases, to halt them before they reach investors' pockets. For example, in several of the actions comprising the SEC's May 1999 fraudulent offering sweep, the SEC stopped the fraud before investors lost a penny.

The Internet also poses the challenge of requiring the SEC to stay abreast of new variants of fraud and manipulation. Fraud artists often design new forms of fraud to exploit opportunities offered by the Internet. For example, the SEC's Division of Enforcement is investigating a number of web sites that offer daily or periodic stock recommendations designed to generate trading momentum and an accompanying rise in the price of the underlying security. Those involved in such activities then profit by selling the security at the artificially inflated price.

An additional challenge posed by the Internet is the ability to investigate, in a timely manner, fraud artists who operate without regard to territorial borders. An individual virtually anywhere in the world, for example, can target US investors without stepping foot in this country. Sophisticated scam artists also seem to think that they have a better chance of escaping detection, hiding funds, or dodging regulators if they shift operations and funds from one country to another. Accordingly, we need to ensure that our foreign counterparts also have the technical expertise needed to track Internet fraud artists. To that end, the SEC recently hosted an international symposium focused on Internet securities fraud, so that international regulatory authorities might share investigative techniques, enhance communication, and increasingly cooperate in combating cross-border securities fraud.

5. CONCLUSIONS

The federal securities law provides flexible but extensive mechanisms by which securities offenses can be prosecuted. Although the substantive laws may be adequate, law enforcement agencies still need adequate resources to counter online securities fraud. As with other types of unlawful conduct on the Internet, the interstate and foreign nature of the Internet hinders the ability of law enforcement to investigate and prosecute online criminals.

 NOTES AND QUESTIONS

1 Outline the methods for conducting securities fraud over the Internet.
2 How is securities fraud distinguished from other types of fraud? Is this particular type of fraud more dangerous? Why, or why not?
3 Read the last sentence in the above extract again (the one commencing: 'As with other types of unlawful conduct ...'). Does a statement such as that, placed as it was at the very end of an analysis, understate the size and importance of Internet securities fraud?

(g) Page-jacking

The President's Working Group on Unlawful Conduct on the Internet, The Electronic Frontier: The Challenge of Unlawful Conduct Involving the Use of the Internet, March 2000

Available at <http://www.cybercrime.gov/append.htm> 17 August 2006

Page-jacking: a new type of computer crime?

Page-jacking involves the appropriation of web site descriptions, key words, or meta-tags from other sites. The page-jacker inserts these items into his own site, seeking to draw consumers to a particular site. This is because the descriptions, key words, and meta-tags are used by search engines when sorting and displaying sites on a particular topic requested by an individual. When the sites for a particular topic appear, an individual might see two or three descriptions for what appear to be the same site. If a person happens to click on one of the duplicated descriptions, he or she will be directed to the 'fake site', which often is a pornographic site. Complicating matters even further is that page-jackers often 'mouse-trap' a user's browser so that attempts to close the browser's windows or to use the 'back' or 'forward' button will simply direct the user to another pornographic site.

The FTC has taken the lead in addressing page-jacking. In September 1999, the FTC announced that it had obtained temporary restraining orders in federal district court against several web site owners for page-jacking. The FTC alleged that the web site owners engaged in deceptive and unfair trade practices in violation of the FTC Act, 15 USC s 45(a). Page-jacking could also potentially violate federal intellectual property laws. That is, if a page-jacker copies substantial portions of the imitated sites, then he might be criminally liable for copyright infringement. In addition, if a page-jacker hacks into a domain name server and changes the data to redirect visitors to the hacker's site, that person could also be in violation of federal computer crime statutes, such as 18 USC s 1030, which protect the integrity of computer systems against hackers.

 NOTES AND QUESTIONS

1   The above example, although short, combines a number of the threads that run through the legal issues of the Internet. It raises issues regarding personal data privacy and privacy of conduct while on-line. It highlights the potential for the creation of an Internet class structure whereby those skilled in the mechanics of the Internet are able to manipulate it to their own benefit. In the meantime, those who simply use the Internet without understanding it are left at the mercy of the powerful minority.

2   In one of the first global cooperations to break a global page-jacking and mouse-trapping Internet scam, the law enforcement bodies in Australia and the USA worked together to successfully to stop the perpetrators in the their tracks. In

FTC v Carlos Periera d/b/a atariz.com, No 99-1367-A (ED Va, filed 14 September 1999) defendants in Portugal and Australia allegedly captured unauthorised copies of US-based websites such as *The Harvard Law Review*, totalling 25 million web pages, and produced look-alike versions that were indexed by major search engines. The defendants then diverted unsuspecting consumers to a sequence of pornography sites from which they could not exit. The FTC obtained a permanent injunction (28 February 2000) stopping the scheme and suspending the defendants' website registrations. See the pleadings, available at <http://www.ftc.gov/os/1999/9909/index.htm#22> 26 September2001, and press release, available at <http://www.ftc.gov/opa/1999/9909/atariz.htm> 26 September 2001.

3   The above examples of Internet-related crime must be considered in conjunction with numerous other Internet issues. Perhaps the most significant issue that overlaps with Internet crime is Internet content, which will be examined in detail in Chapter 8. Put simply, objectionable content is often responded to by criminalising a particular target of objection. This might seem somewhat reactionary; however, it has been the tactic of legislatures in the offline world for centuries. In examining this process it is important to understand the motives for this regulation. That is, it is important to realise that governments do not criminalise an activity only because we think it is criminal.

Examination of on-line and offline content confronts the non-legal foundations of our values and forces their re-examination. Some reactions to content, such as the criminalisation of on-line child pornography, are almost unanimously supported in communities. Some, however, such as the criminalisation of adult content, or of on-line gambling, have been widely criticised. In light of this, the reader should be constantly aware of the multi-layered debates which colour all of the materials in this chapter. There are textures and subtleties in the discourse of Internet crime that reveal much more about our legal system and our society than merely our penchant for regulation.

----

3   Council of Europe Convention on Cybercrime

The Council of Europe has been active for more than ten years in addressing international concerns about hacking and computer-related crime. Throughout the 1990s the Council studied the effects of computer crime and potential options for international cooperation in the implementation and enforcement of laws on the subject.

The Council of Europe's *Convention on Cybercrime 2001* is the first attempt at an international instrument to address substantive as well as procedural aspects of offending behaviour directed against computer systems, networks, or data, as well as other abuses.

It aims to harmonise national legislation in this field, to facilitate investigations and to encourage efficient cooperation between the authorities of different nation states.[3]

In June 2001, the European Committee on Crime Problems (CDPC)—an intergovernmental expert body reporting to the Council of Europe's Committee of Ministers—approved the final draft of the Convention, and it was adopted on 23 November 2001.

The treaty creates nine areas of criminal offences:

- illegal access;
- illegal interception;
- data interference;
- system interference;
- misuse of devices;
- computer-related forgery;
- computer-related fraud;
- on-line child pornography; and
- offences related to copyright and neighbouring rights.

In conjunction with these codified offences, the treaty sets legal rules and guidelines for a variety of state actions, such as obtaining information from Internet service providers (ISPs), tapping and collecting traffic data and content data, extradition of cyber-criminals, and international cooperation among authorities.

During the drafting process there was at least some attempt to balance the competing interests that arise in this area. This is indicated by the collaboration between the Council of Europe and Internet access providers, civil liberties organisations, academics and independent experts. Despite these attempts there remain strong criticisms that the convention represents the interests of law enforcement agencies, lacks accountability, and ignores civil liberties.[4] It seems that despite consultative appearances, the Council of Europe succeeded in entrenching the powers of law enforcement agencies. The inclusion of safeguards does not appease detractors, who argue that they simply do not extend far enough to compensate for the powers granted by the convention. For example, Article 14 (Search and Seizure of Stored Computer Data) requires countries to enact legislation compelling individuals to disclose their decryption keys in order to allow law enforcement access to computer data. This would be contrary to the right against self-incrimination that exists in many jurisdictions. Further, the disclosure of these keys can drastically reduce the security of a wide range of computer systems.

---

3   The text of the convention is available at <http://conventions.coe.int/Treaty/EN/projets/FinalCyber-crime.htm>. See also <http://www.usdoj.gov/criminal/cybercrime/COEFAQs.htm>, <http://www.po-litechbot.com/docs/treaty.html>, <http://www.guardian.co.uk/internetnews/story/0,7369,503987,00.html>, and <http://press.coe.int/cp/2001/456a(2001).htm> 25 September 2001.

4   See Global Internet Liberty Campaign, *Letter on Council of Europe Convention on Cyber-Crime Version 24.2* at <http://www.dfn.org/voices/intl/coeletter-1200.htm> 25 September 2001.

Although more than eighty countries signed the convention, only a small number have ratified the Convention. The US signed the Convention but at the time of writing, in early 2006, the USA has not ratified the Convention and there is strong opposition within the US against ratification.

----

4   National cybercrime laws: Australia

(a)   The Federal System of Government

There are literally hundreds of laws, spread throughout the jurisdictions of Australia, which could potentially apply to criminal activity that targets or utilises the Internet, computers, and information networks. It is therefore not feasible to consider them all in this context. The focus here will be the main provisions enacted by the federal and state governments.

Under Australia's federal system of government, all states and territories have the constitutional power to enact legislation with respect to crime. Federally, the government is limited to enacting laws with respect to one of its enumerated heads of power. Specifically, the power with respect to 'telephonic, telegraphic and other like services' provides jurisdiction over the Internet and therefore over Internet-related crime.

(b)   New South Wales

The NSW legislation in force prior to the 2001 amendments contained general computer crime provisions that could also be used to cover Internet crime (the old sections 307–310). In June 2001 an amendment to the *Crimes Act 1900* was enacted through the *Crimes Amendment (Computer Offences) Act 2001*. This amending Act was designed to tighten penalties for prohibited acts relating to computers and to introduce specific provisions covering viruses and hacking. Prior to the amendments, the provisions in the Act relating to computer crime had not been drafted specifically to cover the Internet. The new Act addresses this by altering the terminology of the *Crimes Act* and outlining a number of new offences and penalties. This approach seeks to avoid accusations that the legislation is over-broad, and to ensure that standard practices of Internet-based industries and individuals are not inadvertently prohibited. The new provisions were based on the *Model Criminal Code* recommendations; they introduced a new Part 6 into the Act that mirrored the provisions of the Commonwealth *Cybercrime Act 2001*. The NSW provisions were passed by the NSW Parliament in April 2001, some five months before the passage of the Commonwealth provisions in September 2001 (see below). For this reason, it is instructive to consider the NSW provisions before the Commonwealth provisions.

Crimes Act 1900 (NSW) as Amended

308. GENERAL DEFINITIONS
In this Part:
data includes:

(a) information in any form, or

(b) any program (or part of a program).

data held in a computer includes:

(a) data entered or copied into the computer, or

(b) data held in any removable data storage device for the time being in the computer, or

(c) data held in a data storage device on a computer network of which the computer forms part.

data storage device means any thing (for example a disk or file server) containing or designed to contain data for use by a computer.

electronic communication means a communication of information in any form by means of guided or unguided electromagnetic energy.

serious computer offence means:

(a) an offence against section 308C, 308D or 308E, or

(b) conduct in another jurisdiction that is an offence in that jurisdiction and that would constitute an offence against section 308C, 308D or 308E if the conduct occurred in this jurisdiction.

308A. MEANING OF ACCESS TO DATA, MODIFICATION OF DATA AND IMPAIRMENT OF ELECTRONIC COMMUNICATION

(1) In this Part, access to data held in a computer means:

   (a) the display of the data by the computer or any other output of the data from the computer, or

   (b) the copying or moving of the data to any other place in the computer or to a data storage device, or

   (c) in the case of a program the execution of the program.

(2) In this Part, modification of data held in a computer means:

   (a) the alteration or removal of the data, or

   (b) an addition to the data.

(3) In this Part, impairment of electronic communication to or from a computer includes:

   (a) the prevention of any such communication, or

(b) the impairment of any such communication on an electronic link or network used by the computer,

but does not include a mere interception of any such communication.

(4) A reference in this Part to any such access, modification or impairment is limited to access, modification or impairment caused (whether directly or indirectly) by the execution of a function of a computer.

308B. MEANING OF UNAUTHORISED ACCESS, MODIFICATION OR IMPAIRMENT

(1) For the purposes of this Part, access to or modification of data, or impairment of electronic communication, by a person is unauthorised if the person is not entitled to cause that access, modification or impairment.

(2) Any such access, modification or impairment is not unauthorised merely because the person has an ulterior purpose for that action.

(3) For the purposes of an offence under this Part, a person causes any such unauthorised access, modification or impairment if the person's conduct substantially contributes to the unauthorised access, modification or impairment.

308C. UNAUTHORISED ACCESS, MODIFICATION OR IMPAIRMENT WITH INTENT TO COMMIT SERIOUS INDICTABLE OFFENCE

(1) A person who causes any unauthorised computer function:

(a) knowing it is unauthorised, and

(b) with the intention of committing a serious indictable offence, or facilitating the commission of a serious indictable offence (whether by the person or by another person),

is guilty of an offence.

Maximum penalty: The maximum penalty applicable if the person had committed, or facilitated the commission of, the serious indictable offence in this jurisdiction.

(2) For the purposes of this section, an unauthorised computer function is:

(a) any unauthorised access to data held in any computer, or

(b) any unauthorised modification of data held in any computer, or

(c) any unauthorised impairment of electronic communication to or from any computer.

(3) For the purposes of this section, a serious indictable offence includes an offence in any other jurisdiction that would be a serious indictable offence if committed in this jurisdiction.

(4) A person may be found guilty of an offence against this section:

(a) even if committing the serious indictable offence concerned is impossible, or

(b) whether the serious indictable offence is to be committed at the time of the unauthorised conduct or at a later time.

(5) It is not an offence to attempt to commit an offence against this section.

NOTES AND QUESTIONS

1. What kinds of activities are covered by s 308A?

2. Examine s 308B(3). This requires a substantial contribution to an unauthorised access. The provision indicates that the laws apply to those who supply, but do not actually use, viruses and similar disabling mechanisms. How important is this provision in the overall problem of computer and Internet crime?

3. Section 308C(2)(c) is a new provision designed to penalise the spreading of computer viruses using the e-mail communication function in unsuspecting users' computers. Does it also cover viruses that destroy data on a user's computer? Is this covered by any other section?

4. Some computer crimes are ends in themselves, others are merely means to larger ends. Section 308C(4)(a) states that the section may be breached even if the serious indictable offence (the end) is impossible. This has the effect of criminalising unauthorised access that is a means to a criminal end even when the ultimate goal will not be achieved. Therefore, unauthorised access that produces an attempt to commit a serious indictable offence is also prohibited.

5. In contrast to section 308C(4)(a), under subsection (5) of the same section, an attempt to gain unauthorised access is not an offence. Critically analyse the relationship between these two provisions with particular emphasis on the policy choices that lie beneath the legislation.

6. Examine the sections above that define the terms in the Part. Why is it so important to carefully define the terms used in an Act such as this?

Crimes Act 1900 (NSW) as Amended

308D. UNAUTHORISED MODIFICATION OF DATA WITH INTENT TO CAUSE IMPAIRMENT

(1) A person who:

(a) causes any unauthorised modification of data held in a computer, and

(b) knows that the modification is unauthorised, and

(c) intends by the modification to impair access to, or to impair the reliability, security or operation of, any data held in a computer, or who is reckless as to any such impairment,

is guilty of an offence.
Maximum penalty: Imprisonment for 10 years.

(2) A conviction for an offence against this section is an alternative verdict to a charge for:

(a) an offence against section 195 (Maliciously destroying or damaging property), or

(b) an offence against section 308E (Unauthorised impairment of electronic communication).

308E. UNAUTHORISED IMPAIRMENT OF ELECTRONIC COMMUNICATION

(1) A person who:

(a) causes any unauthorised impairment of electronic communication to or from a computer, and

(b) knows that the impairment is unauthorised, and

(c) intends to impair electronic communication to or from the computer, or who is reckless as to any such impairment,

is guilty of an offence.

Maximum penalty: Imprisonment for 10 years.

(2) A conviction for an offence against this section is an alternative verdict to a charge for:

(a) an offence against section 195 (Maliciously destroying or damaging property), or

(b) an offence against section 308D (Unauthorised modification of data with intent to cause impairment).

308F. POSSESSION OF DATA WITH INTENT TO COMMIT SERIOUS COMPUTER OFFENCE

(1) A person who is in possession or control of data:

(a) with the intention of committing a serious computer offence, or

(b) with the intention of facilitating the commission of a serious computer offence (whether by the person or by another person),

is guilty of an offence.

Maximum penalty: Imprisonment for 3 years.

(2) For the purposes of this section, possession or control of data includes:

(a) possession of a computer or data storage device holding or containing the data or of a document in which the data is recorded, and

(b) control of data held in a computer that is in the possession of another person (whether the computer is in this jurisdiction or outside this jurisdiction).

(3) A person may be found guilty of an offence against this section even if the serious computer offence concerned is impossible.

(4) It is not an offence to attempt to commit an offence against this section.

308G. PRODUCING, SUPPLYING OR OBTAINING DATA WITH INTENT TO COMMIT SERIOUS COMPUTER OFFENCE

(1) A person who produces, supplies or obtains data:

(a) with the intention of committing a serious computer offence, or

(b) with the intention of facilitating the commission of a serious computer offence (whether by the person or by another person),

is guilty of an offence.

Maximum penalty: Imprisonment for 3 years.

(2) For the purposes of this section, 'produce', 'supply or obtain data' includes:

    (a) produce, supply or obtain data held or contained in a computer or data storage device, or

    (b) produce, supply or obtain a document in which the data is recorded.

(3) A person may be found guilty of an offence against this section even if committing the serious computer offence concerned is impossible ...

308H. UNAUTHORISED ACCESS TO OR MODIFICATION OF RESTRICTED DATA HELD IN COMPUTER (SUMMARY OFFENCE)

(1) A person:

    (a) who causes any unauthorised access to or modification of restricted data held in a computer, and

    (b) who knows that the access or modification is unauthorised, and

    (c) who intends to cause that access or modification,

is guilty of an offence.

Maximum penalty: Imprisonment for 2 years.

(2) An offence against this section is a summary offence.

(3) In this section: 'restricted data' means data held in a computer to which access is restricted by an access control system associated with a function of the computer.

308I. UNAUTHORISED IMPAIRMENT OF DATA HELD IN COMPUTER DISK, CREDIT CARD OR OTHER DEVICE (SUMMARY OFFENCE)

(1) A person:

    (a) who causes any unauthorised impairment of the reliability, security or operation of any data held on a computer disk, credit card or other device used to store data by electronic means, and

    (b) who knows that the impairment is unauthorised, and

    (c) who intends to cause that impairment,

is guilty of an offence.

Maximum penalty: Imprisonment for 2 years.

(2) An offence against this section is a summary offence.

(3) For the purposes of this section, impairment of the reliability, security or operation of data is unauthorised if the person is not entitled to cause that impairment.

 NOTES AND QUESTIONS

    1   This Act clearly distinguishes between hacking as a means to an end, hacking as an end in itself designed to cause damage, and hacking that is an end in itself but which neither causes nor is intended to cause damage. Do you agree that the offences should be separated in this manner?

2 The new Act will only cover acts inside the jurisdiction of New South Wales. It is, therefore, unlikely to have a substantial role in preventing any actual incidents of Internet crime involving viruses. Given that this is so, how important is it to have such a law on the books? Why?

3 Which level of Australian government do you consider to be the most effectively equipped to deal with Internet-related crime? Why?

(c) Commonwealth: pre-2001

The Commonwealth *Crimes Act 1914* is not a broad-based, sweeping piece of legislation. Instead, in order to bring the law within the Constitution, it targets particular types and elements of crimes. For example, the crimes relating to computers are targeted at offences involving computers owned or leased by the Commonwealth, and offences involving a telecommunications carriage service. The following case was prosecuted under the Commonwealth law in 1999. As such, it provides a useful discussion of the application of the old provisions, which were adequate and effective in combating many of the Internet related crimes. These provisions were repealed by the *Cybercrime Act 2001* (Cth). The *Cybercrime Act 2001* also amended the *Criminal Code Act 1995* (Cth) by adding a new Part 10.7. These provisions will be discussed further below.

R v Stevens

[1999] NSWCCA 69 (15 April 1999)

NSW Court of Criminal Appeal

Available at <http://www.austlii.edu.au//cgi-bin/disp.pl/au/cases/nsw/NSWCCA/1999/69.html>
17 August 2006

Studdert J:

3 This is an application for leave to appeal against a sentence imposed in the District Court on 27 March 1998.

4 The applicant, Skeeve Stevens, pleaded guilty to a charge concerning computer abuse and a number of further offences were brought into account pursuant to s 16BA of the Commonwealth *Crimes Act*. Her Honour Judge Backhouse QC sentenced the applicant to a total term of imprisonment of three years but directed his release on recognizance for a term of eighteen months at the expiration of eighteen months in custody, which period in custody was to commence on 27 March 1998 and to expire on 26 September 1999.

5 The indictment presented and in respect of which the applicant made his plea charged the applicant with an offence under s 76E(a) of the Commonwealth *Crimes Act* which, so far as is relevant, provides:

> A person who, by means of a facility operated or provided by the Commonwealth or by a carrier, intentionally and without authority or lawful excuse:

(a) ... inserts data into a computer... is guilty of an offence.

Penalty: Imprisonment for 10 years.

6. The indictment charged the applicant with having:

On 17 April 1995 at Waverley in the State of New South Wales intentionally, by means of a facility provided by a carrier, namely Telstra Corporation, insert[ed] data into a computer, namely a computer described as 'sydney2.world.net' owned and operated by AUSNet Services Pty Limited.

7. Her Honour found that the applicant regarded himself at relevant times as an Internet consultant. AUSNet Services Pty Limited conducted a business for which it had a computer network with computer sites in Sydney and Melbourne, and its technical director, who gave evidence before her Honour, was Mr Ernst Van Oeveren.

8. A statement of facts was tendered before her Honour without objection and the judge drew on this in reciting the relevant facts in her remarks on sentence. It suffices for present purposes that I refer to the judgment to record the objective facts.

9. On 17 April 1995 the applicant utilised Mr Van Oeveren's user account and password details to gain access to the file that controlled the appearance and content of AUSNet's home page on the World Wide Web. He proceeded then to alter the information on that file to display in a permanent fashion the following message:

> Did you know that AUSNETS clients credit cards details are all sitting readable on their system?!?!?! We have the file of card numbers, and it has already been distributed to many hackers and carders around the world. So don't be surprised if all you cards have millions of dollars of shit on them AUSNET is a disgusting network ... and should be shut down and sued by all their users! hehe REMEMBER ... TOO MANY SECRETS!!!!!!!!!!

The additional offences

10. The offences taken into account pursuant to s 16BA (and I shall describe these as the 'additional offences') also related to the applicant's computer activities. These offences comprised two offences under s 76D(2)(b)(viii), and six offences under s 76D(1) of the Commonwealth *Crimes Act*. Section 76D, so far as is relevant, provides as follows:

76D

(1) A person who, by means of a facility operated or provided by the Commonwealth or by a carrier, intentionally and without authority obtains access to data stored in a computer, is guilty of an offence.

Penalty: Imprisonment for 6 months.

(2) A person who ...

    (b) by means of such facility, intentionally and without authority obtains access to data stored in a computer, being data that the person knows or ought reasonably to know relates to ...

        (viii)   commercial information the disclosure of which could cause advantage or disadvantage to any person;

    is guilty of an offence.

Penalty: Imprisonment for 2 years.

11. The additional offences described in the Schedule and a short statement of the relevant facts I now record.

12. Additional Offence 1:

    Between 6 April 1995 and 11 April 1995 by means of a facility provided by a carrier, namely Telstra Corporation, intentionally and without authority obtain access to data namely the computer files 'cisco-cs' and 'newuser.wc.log', stored in a computer namely the computer described as 'sydney2.world.net' owned and operated by AUSNet Services Pty Ltd, being data which he knew related to commercial information the disclosure of which could cause advantage or disadvantage to a person (s 76D(2)(b)(viii) *Crimes Act 1914*).

13. Additional Offence 5:

    On 8 April 1995 by means of a facility provided by a carrier namely Telstra Corporation, intentionally and without authority obtain access to data namely the user account 'mitnick' stored in a computer namely the computer described as 'sydney2.world.net' owned and operated by AUSNet Services Pty Ltd (s 76D(1) *Crimes Act 1914*).

14. Her Honour recorded these facts in relation to additional offences 1 and 5 which it is convenient to address together:

    On 8 April 1995 at around midnight, the [applicant] used the 'admin' user account and connected on to the Melbourne site ('melb.world.net'). Using Van Oeveren's user account and user password, he proceeded to 'download' or transfer on to his own equipment the files 'newuserwc-log' and 'cisco-cs'. Coincidentally at around that time Van Oeveren happened to connect to AUSNet from a computer terminal at his home and came across the 'admin' user account accessing 'melb.world.net'. Van Oeveren confirmed that it was not Ferrett accessing the site and terminated the connection. Van Oeveren observed that the connection had come without authority through the AUSNet computer known as 'syd.sc1'. Van Oeveren proceeded to cancel the 'admin' user account and removed the password files which had allowed 'admin' to access the 'melb.world.net'. As Van Oeveren was unaware that his user name and password had been obtained, he believed that once he had terminated the 'admin' account, the Melbourne site remained secure and that any unauthorised person could no longer access the site again.

    On about 10 April 1995 the [applicant] contacted Anthony Healey, Managing Director of Healey Communications, via the Internet and proceeded to have an 'IRC' or 'Internet Relay Chat' conversation. ... [T]his novel medium permits users connected via the Internet to communicate or 'chat' in real time with each other via their computer terminals by typing messages via the keyboard, not unlike using a CB radio. During this conversation the [applicant] told him that he was 'playing around via a hacked account at Monash' and had stolen information such as credit card details and passwords from AUSNet. The [applicant] added, 'This information will seriously nearly put them out of business (and) most likely make front page of the newspapers.'

    On 11 April 1995, the [applicant] had a telephone conversation with Tony Sarno, a journalist from the *Sydney Morning Herald*. The [applicant] offered Sarno a story relating to security holes in Internet Service Providers.

    On 15 April 1995 the [applicant] contacted Steven Harrison and offered him the credit card details he obtained from the AUSNet 'newuserwc-log' file. Harrison declined the information.

15. Additional Offence 2:

On 15 April 1995 by means of a facility provided by a carrier namely Telstra Corporation, intentionally and without authority obtain access to data namely the computer files 'cisco-cs' and 'newuser.wc.log', stored in a computer namely the computer described as 'sydney2.world.net' owned and operated by AUSNet Services Pty Ltd, being data which he knew related to commercial information the disclosure of which could cause advantage or disadvantage to a person (s 76D(2)(b)(viii) *Crimes Act 1914*).

16. The facts relating to this offence her Honour expressed as follows:

On 15 April 1995, Sarno met the [applicant] at his office located in the Fairfax Building, 210 Sussex Street, Sydney. During this meeting the [applicant] provided a detailed description of how it was possible to break into the AUSNet computer system and to obtain customer credit card details. The [applicant] produced a floppy diskette and, using Sarno's computer terminal, demonstrated this. The [applicant] told Sarno he was 'using the technical director's password.' Sarno then watched as the [applicant] retrieved credit card information which appeared on his terminal screen. At the time Sarno was unsure if the [applicant] had actually accessed the AUSNet site.

17. Additional Offence 3:

Between 1 March 1995 and 24 April 1995 by means of a facility provided by a carrier namely Telstra Corporation, intentionally and without authority obtain access to data namely the user account 'tgl', stored in a computer namely the computer described as 'ozemail.com.au' owned and operated by OzEmail Pty Ltd (s 76D(1) *Crimes Act 1914*).

18. Her Honour recorded these facts in relation to this offence:

In the presence of Sarno, the [applicant] accessed the AUSNet computer network using Internet account 'tgl@ozemail.com.au'. This is an account with the Internet Service Operator, OzEmail. The [applicant] described to Sarno that this was a 'hacked' OzEmail account which belonged to Thomas Liddle, a journalist then employed by Australian Consolidated Press Pty Ltd. [The applicant] had obtained Liddle's account and password in July 1994 in an unrelated incident solely for the purposes of the [applicant] installing software for Liddle. Liddle did not provide his account and password details to anyone else. Liddle would later identify, from his account records, that there were approximately 36 unauthorised connections between 1 March 1995 to 24 April 1995.

19. Additional Offence 4:

Between 1 April 1995 and 3 April 1995 by means of a facility provided by a carrier namely Telstra Corporation, intentionally and without authority obtain access to data namely the user account 'admin' stored in a computer namely the computer described as 'melbourne.world.net' owned and operated by AUSNet Services Pty Ltd (s 76(1) *Crimes Act 1914*).

20. The relevant facts expressed in the remarks on sentence were these:

On 23 March the [applicant] accessed the Internet and proceeded to 'hack' (or improperly access without authority) into AUSNet's Sydney site at 'sydney2.world.net', its security having been weakened from Van Oeveren's previous maintenance. The [applicant] proceeded to create an online AUSNet user account on this site which he entitled 'admin'. He provided fictitious customer and credit card details in order to register 'admin' as an active account. The [applicant] would later provide the 'admin' user account details to two other Internet users, Kimberley Cunningham and Stephen Harrison.

In the course of the next four weeks the [applicant] used the 'admin' user account to access the Sydney site ('sydney2.world.net'). He discovered he was able to gain unauthorised access to the Melbourne site ('melb.world.net') and the files contained therein. The [applicant] accessed these sites from computer terminals from his home and at Monash University, the latter he used during a trip to Melbourne in March/April 1995 when he utilised his student's user account name and password which he had previously obtained.

After having 'hacked' into the system, the [applicant] discovered Van Oeveren's user name and password from the file titled 'web-reg-wc.log'. By using passwords he had obtained from the 'cisco-cs' file he was able to avoid leaving a traceable trail of his hacking activities. Unless AUSNet staff happened upon the connection when the hacker was actually connected to the Melbourne site, it was conceivable that he would remain undetected.

On or about 4 April the [applicant] spoke with a Monash University student, Thea Baker, while at Monash University. The [applicant] informed Baker that he had broken into the AUSNet computer system and was in possession of AUSNet's customer credit card details. The [applicant] told Baker that he was going to do something that would ensure AUSNet did not keep their clients.

21. Additional Offence 6:

Between 15 April 1995 and 17 April 1995 by means of a facility provided by a carrier namely Telstra Corporation, intentionally and without any authority obtain access to data namely the user account 'mitnick' stored in a computer namely the computer described as 'sydney2.world.net' owned and operated by AUSNet Services Pty Ltd (s 76D(1) *Crimes Act 1914*).

22. After the events outlined in paragraph 13 in relation to the second additional offence, the applicant then demonstrated to Sarno how he created a false Internet user account by utilising a fake credit card generating program. Her Honour recorded these facts:

The [applicant] connected onto the AUSNet computer network. Sarno watched as he completed the on-line registration form and used the name 'Kevin Mitnick' and used a false billing address and bogus credit card number. The [applicant] recorded the password, 'tomanysecrets'. It was later confirmed by AUSNet that this account was created on 15 April 1995, and used on 16 and 17 April 1995 for a total of 133 minutes. The bill for this usage remains unpaid.

23. Additional Offence 7:

On 18 April 1995 by means of a facility provided by a carrier namely Telstra Corporation, intentionally and without authority obtain access to data stored in a computer namely the computer described as 'sydney2.world.net' owned and operated by AUSNet Services Pty Ltd (s 76D(1) *Crimes Act 1914*).

24. Additional Offence 8:

On 18 April 1995 by means of a facility provided by a carrier namely Telstra Corporation, intentionally and without authority obtain access to data namely the user account 'optik' stored in a computer namely the computer described as 'ozemail.com.au' owned and operated by OzEmail Pty Ltd (s 76D(1) *Crimes Act 1914*).

25. The facts as recorded by her Honour in relation to these two additional offences I now set out:

... the [applicant] posted an electronic mail message using the pseudonym 'Optik Surfer' from Van Oeveren's user account. The message was addressed to other Australian Internet Service Providers, journalists (Tony Sarno from the *Sydney Morning Herald* and Thomas Liddle from the Australian Consolidated Press) and to himself. The message appeared in the following terms (reproduced verbatim):

The mail you are now reading is an account from AUSNet, that has been hacked.

This mail contains details of Ausnets lack security, and the way they left the credit card details of all their users, out on the open which anyone could have picked up.

This is the stages of the Ausnet hack.

- registered a fake account at Ausnet
- logged into melbourne.world.net shell server
- sydney2.world net (main fileserver) was mounted on the melbourne machine for complete access to any user.
- the 'newuser' account which was used to register the credit details and make peoples accounts, was wide open. In that directory contained a number of files which contained the credit card details of all 1 thousand or more clients of Ausnet.
- this file has been accessed, and distributed by hackers, and Ccers all over the world.
- in an attempt to alert people to this crime of stupidity by Ausnet I contacted some people that may be able to assist in getting publicized, and Ausnet brought to be responsible for their screw up.
- I let a journalist film my access into Ausnet and some other sites, to prove it, incase, like many other times, the company has denied it. I will leave it up to the journalist concerned to decide what he will do with that film.
- The afternoon of the easter monday, I hacked Ausnets web server, in an attempt to alert their clients myself..., it seems thou they were quick to find and fix the situation.
- Below is an extract of the Credit card log on Ausnet.

Personal information of 26 customers were then listed, including the AUSNet customer's name, address, telephone number, credit card number and credit card expiry date. The message then continued:

> well thats a sample. There is 1 thousand or more details, and almost all of those will be used for carding. Ausnet has a lot to answer for. I cannot be contacted for further information about this, I hope you will make proper use of this information. If more information is needed ... please post a message to the aus.org.efa newgroup with the subject 'Help needed' and no body. And if I think it is worth it, I will contact the author. Remember—Too many Secrets. for the sake of it you can refer to me as 'Optik Surfer' bye for now.

On 19 April 1995, the [applicant] used the 'optik' user account and published five of the credit card numbers and other AUSNet customer details which he had obtained from the 'newuserwc-log' files on the Internet in an Internet Relay Chat (IRC) session.

26. Her Honour found that there was considerable harm done to the business of AUSNet by reason of the applicant's unlawful activities, basing those findings upon the statements tendered in evidence. Those statements came from the former general manager of AUSNet Services Pty Ltd, Amanda Wilson, and from the former managing director of

that company, Tom Koltai. It will be necessary to make some closer reference to this finding and the evidence on which it was based in considering one of the challenges to the approach to sentence taken by the judge.

27. The applicant was born on 12 December 1971 so that he was twenty-six years of age at the time he was sentenced. He is a married man. Evidence was presented in the form of reports from a psychologist, Ms Devlin, and from a psychiatrist, Dr Blows. Her Honour addressed the detail of that evidence at considerable length. It appears that the applicant has a personality disorder which called for supportive psychotherapy.

28. The applicant had an earlier conviction for a computer offence. This related to obtaining access to a Commonwealth computer which the applicant broke into at the Australian National University. The applicant was convicted for that offence in 1993 and was punished by way of fine ...

55. I am not persuaded that error has been demonstrated in the sentence which was fixed by the judge in this case. Having regard to all the circumstances both objective and subjective, it has not been established that this sentence was manifestly excessive.

56. I would propose that leave to appeal be granted but that the appeal be dismissed.

 NOTES AND QUESTIONS

1 Stevens was charged under the Commonwealth *Crimes Act* because of the use of the Telstra communications infrastructure. The matter could just as easily have been heard under the *Crimes Act* of New South Wales, which contained similar provisions. This case illustrates the extent to which Commonwealth Government powers can reach in relation to Internet crime. Under normal circumstances, the states' crimes legislation is regarded as the 'catch-all' legislation, while the Commonwealth is left with specific crimes that fall under an enumerated head of power. However, it is practically impossible to use the Internet in Australia without utilising some of Telstra's infrastructure. Therefore, it is difficult to see how the Commonwealth Government could not exercise jurisdiction over crimes relating to the Internet.

2 Would Stevens have been prosecuted if he had been unwilling to reveal his identity? What is the likelihood of the above legislation resulting in conviction of a person who conceals his or her identity?

(d) Commonwealth: 2001

The *Cybercrime Act 2001* was passed by Parliament on 27 September 2001 and given royal assent on 1 October 2001.[5] The Act inserted a number of new offences into the *Criminal Code Act 1995* and repealed existing computer offence provisions from the existing Federal criminal legislation. It also amended existing Federal legislation including the *Crimes Act 1914* (Cth) and the *Customs Act 1901* (Cth). It has been suggested that

5   The Act is available at <http://scaleplus.law.gov.au/html/pasteact/3/3486/top.htm>.

the implementation of these new provisions was essentially symbolic, aimed at 'painting cyberspace as a more regulated and safer place to inhabit.'[6] Further, there have also been fears that the *Cybercrime Act* over-criminalises certain computer behaviour, particularly given the new powers of investigation it provides for and the scope of jurisdiction.[7]

Many of the new offences are based on the Council of Europe Draft Convention on Crime—the twenty-fifth draft, as it was at December 2000. However, the Final Draft was the twenty-eighth, agreed on 23 November 2001. The result is that the new offences are based on provisions considered unsatisfactory by the Council of Europe and subsequently changed.

The *Cybercrime Act* implements changes to the *Criminal Code Act 1995* and replaces existing computer offences in the *Crimes Act*. There are two main areas of amendment. One focuses on prohibiting certain acts against or using computers, the other on the powers of law enforcement and security agencies to compel revelation of encryption keys or otherwise to access data on personal computers.[8]

The *Cybercrime Act* inserted a new Part 10.7 into the *Criminal Code*, entitled 'Computer Offences'. Division 476 of Part 10.7 is divided into several sections. Section 476.1 contains a number of definitions, including what constitutes data held in a computer, access to data held in a computer, impairment of an electronic communication and modification.[9] Section 476.2(1) deals with the meaning of unauthorised access to, modification or impairment of data. These actions are defined to be 'unauthorised' if the person is not entitled to cause that access, modification or impairment.[10] Such a definition is essentially straightforward, although the section becomes more complex when considered in the context of subsection (2), which states any such access, modification or impairment caused by the person is not unauthorised merely because he or she has an ulterior purpose for causing it.[11] Thus, it appears, for example, if Jane, an employee with full access privileges to her employer's computer and the right to view any data, accesses this computer after an argument with her boss and with intent to view her employer's confidential information, this ulterior purpose will not deem her conduct to be 'unauthorised'. The section is further expanded in subsection (3), which states that a person causes unauthorised access, modification, or impairment if the person's conduct 'substantially contributes to it'.[12] There is no guidance as to when a person's action would satisfy this requirement.

---

6   Robert Chalmers, 'Regulating the Net in Australia: Firing Blanks or Silver Bullets?' (2002) 9(3) *E-law Murdoch University Electronic Journal of Law*, accessible at the E-Law Murdoch University *Electronic Journal of Law* web site, <http://www.murdoch.edu.au/elaw/issues/v9n3/chalmers93.html>, last accessed 08/02/06.

7   Simon Bronitt and Miriam Gani, 'Shifting Boundaries of Cybercrime: From Computer Hacking to Cyber-terrorism' (2003) 27 *Criminal Law Journal* 303 at 304.

8   See also <http://www.efa.org.au/Campaigns/cybercrime.html>, <http://www.efa.org.au/Analysis/cyber crime_bill.htm>, <http://www.idg.net.nz/webhome.nsf/UNID/AB52F62A2C9AA8F6CC256A8 0001760B2!opendocument>, and <http://www.claytonutz.com.au/issalert/010717.htm> 29 August 2001.

9   Section 476.1 *Criminal Code Act 1995* (Cth).

10   Section 476.2(1) *Criminal Code Act 1995* (Cth).

11   Section 476.2(2) *Criminal Code Act 1995* (Cth).

12   Section 476.2(3) *Criminal Code Act 1995* (Cth).

Further, before detailing the specific offences, the Act states its geographical jurisdiction. Section 476.3 states that s 15.1 (extended geographical jurisdiction—Category A) applies to all offences under this Part. Given this statement of jurisdiction, the provisions of the *Cybercrime Act* have the potential to a have a far-reaching effect.

The Act also saves other Commonwealth, State, and Territory laws,[13] and exempts criminal or civil liability for any act done by a staff member or agent of the Australian Secret Intelligence Service or the Department of Defence, provided certain criteria are met.[14]

The *Cybercrime Act* introduced several new offences carrying jail terms of up to 10 years. Some of the more controversial offences (similar to those already looked at in the New South Wales legislation) include:

- unauthorised access, impairment or impairment with intent to commit a serious offence (s 477.1);
- unauthorised modification of data to cause impairment (s 477.2);
- unauthorised impairment of electronic communication (s 477.3);
- unauthorised access to, or modification of, restricted data (s 478.1);
- possession or control of data with intent to commit a computer offence (s 478.3); and
- failure to comply with an assistance order (Schedule 2—Law Enforcement powers relating to electronically stored data, amending section 201A of the *Customs Act* and section 3LA of the *Crimes Act*).

Of particular concern is the inclusion of an absolute liability standard in several of the above sections. Absolute liability removes the mistake of fact defence and as such is the highest possible standard for liability under common law.

The legislation has also been criticised for being too broadly drawn. For example, s 478.1 is drafted such that access to a private network causing no damage and with no criminal intent would still attract a penalty. The nature of computers and the Internet requires the utmost care from legislators in their regulatory attempts. Otherwise, the community is faced with ambiguous provisions that may be unenforceable when applied to technical realities.

Section 478.3 is based on an analogy with burglary in the real world. This analogy may not be appropriate for a number of reasons. It is entirely possible to possess a program which is capable of use in a computer offence; however, the problem arises in inferring intent. Unlike burglary, there is no physical proximity to rely upon, and the Act does not explicitly recognise that some potentially harmful programs may also have entirely legitimate purposes.

The last item of the above list—failure to comply with an assistance order—is of particular interest. The *Cybercrime Act* includes amendments to both the federal *Crimes Act 1914* and the *Customs Act 1901*. These amendments require compliance with a court-endorsed assistance order. The assistance order can be used to request access to

---

13　See s 476.4 *Criminal Code Act 1995* (Cth).
14　See generally s 476.5, *Criminal Code Act 1995* (Cth).

an individual's private key. In these provisions, we see the enactment of legislation in an area of enormous debate overseas, particularly in the USA. In Chapter 5, we saw that there has been considerable controversy surrounding access to keys and the implications for citizen and corporate privacy. There appear to be few limitations on the scope of possible assistance orders. Further, there is no flexibility regarding the circumstance where the private key has been lost.

Finally, a general concern surrounding the legislation is that it is reactionary in its extreme breadth. The technical and legal problems should be analysed separately, then, when treated together, handled with great care to ensure that neither is compromised. Instead, the government has attempted to draft a legislative drift-net, with provisions so broad that all manner of activity are caught within its purview. This may result in the law being unenforceable, because the scope of coverage allows too much room for lawyers to manoeuvre.

In the USA, the *Providing Appropriate Tools Required to Intercept and Obstruct Terrorism (PATRIOT) Act 2001* became law on 26 October 2001. The Act gives the US government the ability to treat offences committed with computers as terrorist acts if they were intended to intimidate government officials, or to retaliate in some way against the government. The Act was a direct result of the 11 September 2001 terrorist attacks in the USA. In Australia, the Federal government has enacted a series of laws intended to combat terrorism. These will now be considered.

(e)   Commonwealth: Cyberterrorism

Peter Coroneos, Chief Executive of the Internet Industry Association, has chillingly noted that it is 'safer and more convenient to conduct disruptive activities from a remote location over the Internet than it is driving planes into buildings'.[15]

Terrorism is not a new phenomenon or a new crime, but the development of new technologies have facilitated these types of attacks and provided a new medium in which attacks can occur. It is hardly necessary to point out that a person sitting in America could attack Australian computers through the use of a computer and the Internet. Even prior to the September 11 attacks, these fears were already developing.[16] Individuals have already managed to show—through hacking and the release of viruses—that systems can be penetrated via a simple notebook computer. In 2002 an individual was responsible for hacking into the waste management system of Maroochy Shire in Queensland and causing the release of millions of litres of sewage into parks and rivers.[17]

This new phenomenon has been dubbed 'cyberterrorism' and is defined as 'unlawful attacks against computers, networks and the information stored therein when done to intimidate or coerce a government or its people in furtherance of political or social objectives'.[18] Not all Internet crimes against government will satisfy this definition. For example, harassing or annoying a government department or hijacking its website over

---

15   Peter Coroneos in James Elder, 'Cyber Terrorism' (2001/2002) 9 *E Law Practice* 24.
16   Gregor Urbas, 'Cyber Terrorism and Australian Law' (2005) 8(1) *Internet Law Bulletin* 5 at 6.
17   Peter Grabosky and Michael Stohl, 'Cyberterrorism' (2003) 82 *Reform* 8 at 10.
18   Dorothy Denning in Peter Grabosky and Michael Stohl, 'Cyberterrorism' (2003) 82 *Reform* 8.

the Internet does not constitute a 'terrorist attack' unless the elements of 'coercion' and 'intimidation' are present.[19] It is believed that, should a cyberterrorist attack occur, such an attack would be aimed towards Australia's critical national infrastructure.[20] This infrastructure includes publicly and privately owned utilities, including water, electricity and gas supplies; air-traffic control systems; banking and finance; telecommunications; and transport systems.[21] Most of these systems are computer-operated, thus increasing their vulnerability to an Internet-based attack.[22]

Following the September 11 attacks, the *Cybercrime Act* was praised as being 'almost prophetic'[23] as its broadly worded provisions could be used in the prosecution of those responsible for these cyberterrorist attacks. These provisions had the potential not only to catch 'ordinary cyber-criminality … (but also) the more serious manifestations of crime that might attract the label of cyberterrorism'.[24] Further, Section 15.1 of the *Criminal Code* will extend Commonwealth jurisdiction to cover situations where either criminal conduct occurs in Australia, or the result of the conduct occurs in Australia.[25]

In 2002, the Federal government introduced a package of laws specifically aimed at legislatively protecting Australia from terrorist attacks. These laws included, among others, the *Suppression of the Financing of Terrorism Act 2002*, the *Criminal Code Amendment (Suppression of Terrorist Bombings) Act 2002*, the *Telecommunications Interception Legislation Amendment Act 2002*, and the Act under consideration here, the *Security Legislation Amendment (Terrorism) Act 2002*. While this Act does not specifically deal with 'Internet crime'—and to date Australia does not have a 'single cyberterrorism offence'[26]—it does deal with occurrence of this age-old crime via this thoroughly modern medium.

While this Federal legislation does not specifically deal with Internet crime, it does deal with what is in reality a long-established crime through a modern medium. Schedule 1 of the *Security Legislation Amendment (Terrorism) Act* inserted a new Part 5.3 into the *Criminal Code Act*, entitled 'Terrorism'. Section 100.1(1) defines the term 'terrorist act' to mean action falling within s 100.1(2).[27] Action falls within that section if it:

> (e)   seriously interferes with, seriously disrupts, or destroys an electronic system including, but not limited to:
>
> > (i)   an information system; or
> >
> > (ii)   a telecommunications system; or
> >
> > (iii)   a financial system; or

19   Peter Grabosky and Michael Stohl, 'Cyberterrorism' (2003) 82 *Reform* 8 at 9.
20   Peter Grabosky and Michael Stohl, Ibid.
21   Parliamentary Joint Committee on the Australian Crime Commission, Parliament of Australia, *Cybercrime* (2004) [5.1].
22   Peter Grabosky and Michael Stohl, 'Cyberterrorism' (2003) 82 *Reform* 8 at 9; see also Parliamentary Joint Committee on the Australian Crime Commission, Parliament of Australia, *Cybercrime* (2004) [5.3].
23   Peter Coroneos in James Elder, 'Cyber Terrorism' (2001/2002) 9 *E Law Practice* 24.
24   Peter Grabosky and Michael Stohl, 'Cyberterrorism' (2003) 82 *Reform* 8 at 12.
25   See generally s 15.1 *Criminal Code Act 1995* (Cth); Peter Grabosky and Michael Stohl, 'Cyberterrorism' (2003) 82 *Reform* 8 at 12.
26   Gregor Urbas, 'Cyber Terrorism and Australian Law' (2005) 8(1) *Internet Law Bulletin* 5.
27   Section 100.1(1) *Criminal Code Act* (Cth).

(iv)   a system used for the delivery of essential government services; or

(v)   a system used for, or by, an essential public utility; or

(vi)   a system used for, or by, a transport system.[28]

Section 100.2(1) states the constitutional basis for offences: Part 5.3 applies to a terrorist act constituted by an action in relation to which Parliament has power to legislate.[29] Section 100.2(2) states Part 5.3 applies to a terrorist act constituted by an action, or threat of action if, among other things:

(h) the action involves, or if carried out would involve, the use of an electronic communication; or

(i) the threat is made using an electronic communication.[30]

The inclusion in the amendments of the term 'electronic communication' indicates a recognition by the government of the increasing use of computers to facilitate attacks of terrorism and provides a constitutional basis for its regulation of this area.

Pursuant to s 101.1(1), entitled 'Terrorist Acts', a person commits an offence if the person engages in a terrorist act, with the penalty for such an offence being imprisonment for life.[31] Of all the crimes that can be committed via the Internet in Australia, this is the one that carries the most severe penalty.

While the purpose of the *Security Legislation Amendment (Terrorism) Act 2002* was to amend the *Criminal Code*, the provisions have been further amended. The *Criminal Code Amendment (Terrorism) Act 2003* changed the terrorism provisions in the *Criminal Code* and the newer provisions, while including the electronic medium provisions already discussed, reflect the increasing regulation of this crime. Section 100.1(2) remains fundamentally the same, including in its definition of a 'terrorist act' conduct against an information system or telecommunications system.[32] Section 100.2 no longer contains the constitutional bases for the provisions but instead deals with 'referring states';[33] s 100.3, while entitled 'Constitutional Bases', also deals with referring states and does not mention the 'electronic communications' aspects contained in the *Security Legislation Amendment (Terrorism) Act 2002*.[34] Section 100.4 deals with the applications of the provisions and subsections 100.4(5)(h) and (i) include attacks via electronic media.[35]

There will undoubtedly be more legislative changes in this area should the threat of cyberterrorism become more serious. As noted by Urbas, 'cyberterrorism has increasingly been identified as a threat by academics, security analysts and governments' although 'there is little in the way of empirical data that would clarify the magnitude of current or potential cyberterrorism activity'.[36]

---

28   Section 100.1(2)(e) *Criminal Code Act* (Cth).
29   Section 100.2(1) *Criminal Code Act* (Cth).
30   Subsections 100.2(2)(h) and (i) *Criminal Code Act* (Cth).
31   Section 101.1(1) *Criminal Code Act* (Cth).
32   Section 100.1(2) *Criminal Code Act* (Cth).
33   Section 100.2 *Criminal Code Act* (Cth).
34   See generally s 100.3 *Criminal Code Act* (Cth).
35   See generally s 100.4 *Criminal Code Act* (Cth).
36   Gregor Urbas, 'Cyber Terrorism and Australian Law' (2005) 8(1) *Internet Law Bulletin* 5.

(f) Commonwealth: 2004 (general and sexual offences)

The *Crimes Legislation Amendment (Telecommunications Offences and Other Measures) Act (No 2) 2004* is by far the most detailed Internet crime legislation to be introduced by any Australian government. It is not an understatement to say that this Act was rushed through the Parliament, nor to suggest that further consideration and the gathering of submissions from interested parties may have aided its development. The Senate and Legal Constitutional Committee was given a week in which to conduct its inquiry into the proposed provisions of the *Crimes Legislation Amendment (Telecommunications Offences and Other Measures) Bill 2004*.[37] Interested parties were given only one day in which to prepare and submit responses to the inquiry into the Bill. Some parties, including the Australian Federal Police and Electronic Frontiers Australia, did respond. Both, however, noted in their submissions the difficulties in having to work within such a limited timeframe. Electronic Frontiers stated that giving the Senate Committee only one week to consider the proposed legislation 'is not enough to enable the public to have faith in the Committee system and processes'.[38] Other parties simply refused to make a submission. The Law Council of Australia, for example, stated that the 'timelines imposed by the Senate in this instance are not only unreasonable, they (also) undermine the integrity of the Senate inquiry process'.[39] The Bill was passed on August 31 2004.

The Act introduced amendments to the *Criminal Code*, including changes to those created in the Code by the *Cybercrime Act*. The application of the amendments were not limited solely to the Internet; 'carriage service', defined in s 7 of the *Telecommunications Act 1997*, 'means a service for carrying communications by means of guided and/or unguided electromagnetic energy'.[40] This definition encompasses the Internet, television, and radio. However, from the definitions contained at the start of the amendments and the nature of many of the provisions, it is clear that the Internet is the main focus. Rather than target crimes that occur only via computers and the Internet—for example, computer access, modification and impairment crimes, as covered by the *Cybercrime Act*—it introduces offences involving traditional crimes that can now be committed on the Internet, including threats, hoaxes and the distribution of child pornography.

Part 1 of Schedule 1 to the Act repeals Part 10.6 of the *Criminal Code* and substitutes a new Part 10.6 in its place, entitled 'Telecommunications Services'. Section 473.1 contains several important definitions including definitions of 'child abuse material', 'child pornography material', 'communication in the course of telecommunications

---

37   Senate Legal and Constitutional Legislation Committee, Parliament of Australia, *Provisions of the Crimes Legislation Amendment (Telecommunications Offences and Other Measures Bill No 2 2004* (2004) [1.1].

38   See Electronic Frontiers Australia, 'Submission to Senate Legal and Constitutional Legislation Committee Re:*Crimes Legislation Amendment (Telecommunications Offences and Other Measures) Bill (No 2) 2004*', 6 August 2004, accessible at the Senate Legal and Constitutional Legislation Committee website, <http://www.aph.gov.au/senate/committee/legcon_ctte/completed_inquiries/2002-04/cyberporn/submissions/sublist.htm>, last accessed 23/01/06.

39   See Law Council of Australia, 'Submission to Senate Legal and Constitutional Legislation Committee', accessible at the Senate Legal and Constitutional Legislation Committee website, <http://www.aph.gov.au/senate/committee/legcon_ctte/completed_inquiries/2002-04/cyberporn/submissions/sublist.htm>, last accessed 23/01/06.

40   Section 7 *Telecommunications Act 1997* (Cth).

carriage', 'Internet content host' and 'Internet service provider', 'serious offence against a foreign law' and 'serious offence against a law of the Commonwealth, a State or a Territory'.[41] Several definitions from other Acts are also imported. 'Carriage service provider' is defined in s 87 of the *Telecommunications Act 1997*. If a person supplies, or proposes to supply, a listed carriage service to the public using either a network unit owned by one or more carriers or a network unit in relation to which a nominated carrier declaration is in force, that person is a carriage service provider.[42] 'Internet content host' and 'Internet service provider' are to be given the same meaning as in Schedule 5 of the *Broadcasting Services Act 1992* (Cth). Clause 3 of Schedule 5 to this Act defines 'Internet content host' as a person who hosts content in Australia, or who proposes to host content in Australia.[43] Clause 8(1) of Schedule 5 defines an 'Internet service provider' to be a person who supplies, or proposes to supply, an Internet carriage service to the public. Sections 473.2 and 473.3 provide further relevant definitions, stating the non-exhaustive meanings of possession or control of data[44] and producing, supplying, or obtaining data respectively.[45]

Division 474 is entitled 'Telecommunications Offences' and is divided into three subdivisions. Subdivision A of Division 474 contains only two provisions: s 474.1, which states a general definition of dishonesty and provides that whether dishonesty has occurred is a matter for the trier of fact;[46] and s 474.2, entitled 'General dishonesty with respect to a carriage service provider' (CSP). This section deals with three offences. First, a person is guilty if the person does anything with the intention of dishonestly obtaining a gain from a CSP by way of the supply of a carriage service.[47] Second, a person is guilty of an offence if the person does anything with the intention of dishonestly causing a loss to a CSP in connection with the supply of a carriage service.[48] Third, a person commits an offence if the person dishonestly causes a loss, or a risk of loss, to a CSP and the person knows the loss will occur, or there is a substantial risk of the loss occurring.[49] In all three offences, the applicable penalty is 5 years' imprisonment.[50]

Subdivision B of Division 474 is entitled 'Interference with telecommunications'. The Subdivision contains ten provisions; some apply solely to the Internet, a number apply both to the Internet and to other carriage services, and others do not deal with the Internet at all. The arrangement of the Subdivision, and the language used, does not make for a coherent legislative position on the specific offences the subdivision purports to regulate. Section 474.3 defines, in general terms, who constitutes a person acting for a carrier or carriage service provider. This definition becomes important when considering s 474.4, which deals with offences involving interception devices. Section

---

41   See generally s 473.1 *Criminal Code Act* (Cth).
42   See generally s 87 *Telecommunications Act 1997* (Cth).
43   See Schedule 5, Clause 3, *Broadcasting Services Act 1992* (Cth).
44   See generally s 473.2 *Criminal Code Act* (Cth).
45   See generally s 473.3 *Criminal Code Act* (Cth).
46   See generally s 474.1 *Criminal Code Act* (Cth).
47   See s 474.2(1) *Criminal Code Act* (Cth).
48   See s 474.2(2) *Criminal Code Act* (Cth).
49   See s 474.2(3) *Criminal Code Act* (Cth).
50   See generally s 474.2 *Criminal Code Act* (Cth).

474.4 states that it is an offence for a person to manufacture, advertise, display, offer for sale, sell, or possess an apparatus or device where that apparatus or device is an interception device.[51] 'Interception device' is defined in s 473.1 to mean an apparatus or device that is capable of being used to enable a person to intercept a communication passing over a telecommunications system and could reasonably be regarded as having been designed for the purpose of interception of communications.[52] While both s 474.4 and this definition contain a number of technical concepts, the purpose of the section is clear. It is an offence to possess, manufacture or sell any type of device that can be used to intercept communications over the Internet. Section 474.4 also provides two exclusions to criminal liability, including one that would exclude police from criminal responsibility under this section.[53]

Section 474.5 deals with Internet communications. Specifically, it is an offence if a person causes a communication to be received by a person or carriage service other than the person or service to whom it is directed.[54] A penalty of imprisonment for 1 year is imposed.[55] A person will not have committed this offence where the person has obtained consent or authorisation from the person who is the recipient or from the CSP of the communication.[56]

In its submission to the Senate and Legal Constitutional Committee Inquiry, Electronic Frontiers Australia highlighted that this provision had the potential to criminalise conduct that should not incur any type of sanction.[57] EFA noted that if an employer redirected email sent to the email address of an ex-employee to the email address of a current employee without seeking permission from the ex-employee, this conduct would be caught by s 474.5(1).[58] Given that this can be viewed as a perfectly acceptable commercial practice, such conduct should not be criminalised. Further, the fact this type of action could be included does nothing to quell fears from commentators that the government has over-zealously criminalised certain types of Internet conduct.

Section 474.6 deals generally with interference of facilities. Section 474.6(1) states that it is an offence for a person to tamper or interfere with a facility owned or operated by a carrier, carriage service provider or a nominated carrier, with a penalty of 1 year imprisonment.[59] Section 474.6(3) states that it is an offence if a person tampers with, or interferes with, a carriage service provider and the conduct results in hindering the

---

51   Section 474.4(1) *Criminal Code Act* (Cth).
52   Section 473.1 *Criminal Code Act* (Cth).
53   See sections 474.4(2) and (3) *Criminal Code Act* (Cth).
54   See generally s 474.5 *Criminal Code Act* (Cth).
55   See s 474.5(1) *Criminal Code Act* (Cth).
56   Section 474.5(2) *Criminal Code Act* (Cth).
57   Electronic Frontiers Australia, 'Submission to Senate Legal and Constitutional Legislation Committee Re: *Crimes Legislation Amendment (Telecommunications Offences and Other Measures) Bill (no 2) 2004'*, 6 August 2004, accessible at the Senate Legal and Constitutional Legislation Committee website, <http://www.aph.gov.au/senate/committee/legcon_ctte/completed_inquiries/2002-04/cyberporn/sub-missions/sublist.htm>, last accessed 23/01/06, at 5.
58   Electronic Frontiers Australia, 'Submission to Senate Legal and Constitutional Legislation Committee Re:*Crimes Legislation Amendment (Telecommunications Offences and Other Measures) Bill (no 2) 2004'*, 6 August 2004, accessible at the Senate Legal and Constitutional Legislation Committee website, <http://www.aph.gov.au/senate/committee/legcon_ctte/completed_inquiries/2002-04/cyberporn/sub-missions/sublist.htm>, last accessed 23/01/06, at 5.
59   Section 474.6(1) *Criminal Code Act* (Cth).

normal operation of a carriage service supplied by the carriage service provider.[60] The applicable penalty is 2 years' imprisonment. Section 474.6(5) states that it is an offence if a person uses or operates any apparatus or device and this conduct results in the hindering of a carriage service supplied by a carriage service provider.[61] The applicable penalty is again 2 years' imprisonment.

Subdivision C deals generally with offences related to the use of telecommunications. This subdivision contains offences relating to Internet crimes and the applicable penalties. The offences can be divided into two main categories: using a carriage service generally to do some act and using a carriage service for child pornography or child abuse material purposes. It contains 18 provisions but they do not apply to just the Internet. Section 474.13 defines what does *not* constitute 'use of a carriage service'; this definition includes persons engaging in activities solely in their capacity as a carrier, carriage service, Internet service provider, or Internet content host.[62]

Sections 474.15 through 474.17 criminalise several similar types of action. Section 474.15, entitled 'using a carriage service to make a threat', covers two offences. The first involves using a carriage service to make a threat to kill;[63] this offence is satisfied if the person making the threat intends the recipient to fear that the threat will be carried out.[64] The offence carries a 10-year jail term. The second offence involves using a carriage service to make a threat to cause serious harm; again, this offence is satisfied if the person making the threat intends the second person (the recipient) to fear that the threat will be carried out.[65] The second offence carries a term of 7 years' imprisonment.[66] It is not necessary for the prosecution to prove the person receiving the threat actually feared it would be carried out.[67] These provisions are extremely useful in combating 'remotely communicated threats of violence'.[68] Their introduction makes it easier to catch offenders who use the Internet to make such threats. As Gregor and Urbas have noted:

> Traditional offences against the person such as homicide or inflicting bodily harm, if committed by computer assisted means such as hacking into a hospital system and altering a patient's prescribed medication to a lethal dosage, could be adequately prosecuted under existing criminal laws. However, remotely communicated threats of violence may be difficult to prosecute as common assault due to the requirement of an apprehension of both immediate bodily harm on the part of the victim. On the other hand, they may also fall outside the scope of provisions dealing with 'documents' containing threats.[69] (citations omitted)

---

60   Section 474.6(3) *Criminal Code Act* (Cth).
61   Section 474.6(5) *Criminal Code Act* (Cth).
62   See s 474.13(a)-(d) *Criminal Code Act* (Cth) respectively.
63   See generally s 474.15(1) *Criminal Code Act* (Cth).
64   See generally s 474.15(1)(b) *Criminal Code Act* (Cth).
65   See generally s 474.15(2) *Criminal Code Act* (Cth).
66   See generally s 474.15(2) *Criminal Code Act* (Cth).
67   Section 474.15(3) *Criminal Code Act* (Cth).
68   Gregor F Urbas and Russell G Smith, 'Computer Crime Legislation in Australia' (2004) 7(2) *Internet Law Bulletin* 21.
69   Gregor F Urbas and Russell G Smith, 'Computer Crime Legislation in Australia' (2004) 7(2) *Internet Law Bulletin* 21.

Section 474.16 makes it an offence to use a carriage service to send a communication where the person does this with the intention of inducing a false belief that an explosive, among other things, has been or will be left in any place.[70] Such a section reflects modern times. Persons making hoax threats no longer need to telephone a hoax bomb threat.

Section 474.17 deals with using a carriage service to menace, harass or cause offence. Generally, a person is guilty of an offence if the person uses a carriage service and the person does so in a way that reasonable persons would regard as being, in all the circumstances, menacing, harassing or offensive.[71] Section 474.17(2) states that, without limiting subsection (1), that subsection applies to menacing, offending or harassing a range of government employees and, emergency call persons.[72] The use of the term 'carriage service' indicates that this offence is not applicable solely to the Internet. For example, a person could use a telephone to verbally menace, harass or offend the recipient. However, the use of the term 'carriage service' also serves to include a lot of different Internet activities. For example, menacing, harassing or offensive communications via email, websites, message boards or chat-rooms would all be included.

This section was both based on and replaced the existing s 85ZE of the *Crimes Act 1914*.[73] The newer provision is intended, among other things, to deal with on-line harassment and stalking.[74] This provision would cover the practice of 'cyberstalking', a term increasingly used to cover three types of situations:[75]

> *Email stalking* involving direct communications designed to intimidate the recipient; *internet stalking* involving the posting of slanderous or threatening material on publicly accessible websites; and *computer stalking*, in which the computer of the targeted victim is taken over.[76] (citations omitted)

On its face, s 474.17 appears to be extremely useful. It is broad enough to catch Internet crimes ranging from cyberstalking, where communications could be seen as menacing and harassing, to offensive content on Internet chat rooms or message boards. The problem with this provision, however, is that it does not require a specific person to be menaced, harassed or offended. Careful consideration of the provision shows that a person is guilty of an offence if the person uses a carriage service and does so in a way that reasonable persons would regard as being menacing, harassing or offensive. Electronic Frontiers Australia was particularly concerned about this problem in its submission to

---

70   See s 474.16 *Criminal Code Act* (Cth).

71   See s 474.17(1) *Criminal Code Act* (Cth).

72   See s 474.17(2) *Criminal Code Act* (Cth).

73   Electronic Frontiers Australia, 'Submission to Senate Legal and Constitutional Legislation Commit-tee Re:*Crimes Legislation Amendment (Telecommunications Offences and Other Measures) Bill (no 2) 2004*', 6 August 2004, accessible at the Senate Legal and Constitutional Legislation Committee website, <http://www.aph.gov.au/senate/committee/legcon_ctte/completed_inquiries/2002-04/cyberporn/sub-missions/sublist.htm>, last accessed 23/01/06, at 3.

74   Gregor F Urbas and Russell G Smith, 'Computer Crime Legislation in Australia' (2004) 7(2) *Internet Law Bulletin* 21 at 22.

75   Ibid.

76   Ibid.

the Senate Legal and Constitutional Committee Inquiry.[77] The Australian Democrats also noted this concern.[78]

As it has been seen, s 474.17(2) states that, without limiting subsection (1), that subsection applies to menacing, harassing or causing offence to, for example, an emergency call person. Therefore, if the provision does not apply to the general public it is too limited in its scope; if it does apply to the general public, then a person could be imprisoned for three years even if no person actually was menaced, harassed, or offended.

Section 474.19 is the first of eleven provisions concerning child abuse and child pornography material on the Internet. These are crimes that Urbas and Smith have dubbed 'crimes against morality' that can occur via an electronic medium.[79] According to Australian law enforcement authorities, 80 per cent of all child pornography comes from the Internet.[80]

As the Australian Federal Police noted in its submission to the Senate Legal and Constitutional Committee, the Internet provides child sex offenders with a new medium in which to offend.[81] Pictures of children who have already suffered harm at the hands of offenders can be easily distributed; offenders can meet children in chat-rooms and identify potential victims; and offenders can form support groups and networks that remain unseen and undetectable.[82] In early cases, courts encountered difficulties in ruling on whether persons accused of posting indecent images of children on the Internet could properly be convicted of 'publishing' the material.[83] Similar difficulties occurred in terms of 'possession' of such material, where the accused has downloaded material but denied doing so consciously and voluntarily, or with knowledge of its offensive content.[84]

---

77   Electronic Frontiers Australia, 'Submission to Senate Legal and Constitutional Legislation Committee Re:*Crimes Legislation Amendment (Telecommunications Offences and Other Measures) Bill (No 2) 2004'*, 6 August 2004, accessible at the Senate Legal and Constitutional Legislation Committee website, <http://www.aph.gov.au/senate/committee/legcon_ctte/completed_inquiries/2002-04/cyberporn/submissions/sublist.htm>, last accessed 23/01/06, at 6.

78   Senator Brian Greig, 'Additional Comments by the Australian Democrats', Senate Legal and Constitutional Legislation Committee, Parliament of Australia, *Provisions of the Crimes Legislation Amendment (Telecommunications Offences and Other Measures Bill No 2 2004* (2004) [1.1](a).

79   Gregor F Urbas and Russell G Smith, 'Computer Crime Legislation in Australia' (2004) 7(2) *Internet Law Bulletin* 21 at 22.

80   Edwin Wong, 'Tough New Laws For Child Pornography and Other Internet Offences' (2004) 7(7) *Internet Law Bulletin* 89.

81   Australian Federal Police 'Submission to Senate Legal and Constitutional Legislation Committee Inquiry Into the Provisions of the *Crimes Legislation Amendment (Telecommunications Offences and Other Measures Bill 2004*', accessible at the Senate Legal and Constitutional Legislation Committee website, <http://www.aph.gov.au/senate/committee/legcon_ctte/completed_inquiries/2002-04/cyberporn/submissions/sublist.htm>,last accessed 23/01/06, at 2.

82   Australian Federal Police 'Submission to Senate Legal and Constitutional Legislation Committee Inquiry Into the Provisions of the *Crimes Legislation Amendment (Telecommunications Offences and Other Measures Bill 2004*', accessible at the Senate Legal and Constitutional Legislation Committee website, <http://www.aph.gov.au/senate/committee/legcon_ctte/completed_inquiries/2002-04/cyberporn/submissions/sublist.htm>,last accessed 23/01/06, at 2.

83   Gregor F Urbas and Russell G Smith, 'Computer Crime Legislation in Australia' (2004) 7(2) *Internet Law Bulletin* 21 at 23.

84   Gregor F Urbas and Russell G Smith, 'Computer Crime Legislation in Australia' (2004) 7(2) *Internet Law Bulletin* 21 at 23.

Section 474.19 states it is an offence for a person to use a carriage service to either access material, cause material to be transmitted to the person, transmit material, make material available or publish or otherwise distribute material where the material is child pornography.[85] The penalty is imprisonment for 10 years.[86] 'Child pornography material' is defined earlier, and quite extensively, in s 473.1. It essentially has four meanings; in all cases, there is a recurring theme that the material is of a sexual and offensive nature, involving persons under the age of 18 years.[87]

Section 474.20 further provides that it is an offence to possess, control, produce, supply or obtain child pornography material for use through a carriage service. A person commits an offence if the person possesses, controls, or produces, supplies or obtains child pornography material and the person intends the material be used in committing an offence against s 474.19.[88] What this section essentially provides is that it is an offence if a person has in their possession child pornography material with the intent that this material be placed—either by themselves or by another person—on the Internet.[89] Interestingly, the person can be found guilty of an offence against s 474.20 even if the offence against s 474.19 is impossible,[90] although it is not an offence to attempt to commit an offence against s 474.20(1).[91] Section 474.21 then lists a number of available defences to offences against sections 474.19 and 474.20, including a public benefit defence.[92]

When dealing with crimes that occur on the Internet, one of the most important goals of any legislation implemented to combat such crimes is that the law be consistent with other jurisdictions. Prior to the enactment of this legislation, one of the major criticisms of existing child pornography material offences was the inconsistency between the applicable laws at the Federal and State and Territory levels.[93] These inconsistencies were highlighted by 'Operation Auxin', a national investigation into child pornography material offences that was 'sparked by information from US authorities regarding the use of credit cards to access child pornography from European Internet sites'. More than 200 arrests were eventually made.[94] However, as Penfold has noted, the charges that were laid against these alleged offenders, the defences that were available, and the applicable penalties, varied greatly between the Australian states.[95] At the time, due to Australia's legislative structure these alleged offenders could not be charged under any Federal law,[96] and the amendments discussed had been introduced but were not yet in force.[97]

---

85 See generally s 474.19(1) *Criminal Code Act* (Cth).
86 Section 474.19(1) *Criminal Code Act* (Cth).
87 See s 473.1 *Criminal Code Act* (Cth).
88 Section 474.20 *Criminal Code Act* (Cth).
89 Section 474.20(1) *Criminal Code Act* (Cth).
90 See s 474.20(2) *Criminal Code Act* (Cth).
91 See s 474.20(3) *Criminal Code Act* (Cth).
92 See ss 474.21(1) and (2), *Criminal Code Act* (Cth).
93 See generally Carolyn Penfold, 'Child Pornography Laws: The Luck of the Locale' (2005) 30(3) *Alternative Law Journal* 123.
94 Edwin Wong, 'Tough New Laws for Child Pornography and Other Internet Offences' (2004) 7(7) *Internet Law Bulletin* 89.
95 Carolyn Penfold, 'Child Pornography Laws: The Luck of the Locale' (2005) 30(3) *Alternative Law Journal* 123.
96 Ibid.
97 Ibid at 125.

The provisions are a solid attempt at rectifying any inconsistencies and 'federally' catching this type of crime. However, Penfold has argued that these laws are still unsatisfactory because while a person may be charged under a Federal law with accessing such material, this Federal legislation does not do the same for possessing child pornography material.[98] This is true: s 474.20 only goes so far as to criminalise the possession of child pornography material for use through a carriage service.[99] However, it is important not to be over-critical of these provisions. The Federal legislation goes as far as it can and covers as much criminal activity as it is allowed to, with the States and Territories remaining responsible for any conduct that falls within their legislative arena.

Section 474.22 deals with using a carriage service for child abuse material. It is similar to s 474.19. Section 474.23 is also similar to s 474.20, in relation to possessing, controlling, producing, supplying or obtaining child abuse material for use through a carriage service. Lastly, s 474.24 deals with defences in respect of child abuse material.

Section 474.25 is an interesting, albeit peculiarly placed, provision and it deals with obligations of Internet service providers and Internet content hosts. This section will be considered in the next chapter on content regulation.

Sections 474.26 and 474.27 reflect two very modern Internet crimes. Section 474.26, is entitled, 'Using a carriage service to procure persons under 16 years of age' and deals with three offences. In all three cases, one of the requirements for the offence is for a person (the sender) to use a carriage service to transmit a communication to another person (the recipient).[100] The sender must be at least 18 years of age and must believe the recipient is under 16 years of age.[101] The intention of the sender is similar for each offence; in all three cases, the sender intends to procure the recipient to engage in sexual conduct, whether it be with the sender,[102] with another person,[103] or in the presence of the sender or another person.[104] 'Procure' is defined to include encouraging, enticing, recruiting or inducing the person to engage in this type of activity.[105]

In all three cases, the punishment is imprisonment for 15 years. These provisions are aimed at decreasing the vulnerability of children on the Internet, particularly in email and chat-rooms. Adults posing as children in chat-rooms and encouraging meetings have become a modern nightmare for parents. This provision is a strong reaction to this type of conduct.

Section 474.27 deals with using a carriage service to 'groom' persons under 16 years of age. The Parliamentary Joint Committee on the Australian Crime Commission in its *Cybercrime* inquiry recommended that the government introduced this new offence relating to the luring and grooming of children for sexual purposes.[106] The term 'groom'

---

98   Ibid.
99   See s 474.20(1) *Criminal Code Act* (Cth).
100   See ss 474.26(1)(a), 474.26(2)(a) and 474.3(a) *Criminal Code Act* (Cth).
101   See ss 474.26(1)(c), 474.26(2)(c), 474.26(3)(c) *Criminal Code Act* (Cth).
102   See s 474.26(1)(b) *Criminal Code Act* (Cth).
103   See s 474.26(2)(b) *Criminal Code Act* (Cth).
104   See s 474.26(3)(b) and (e) *Criminal Code Act* (Cth).
105   Section 474.28(11) *Criminal Code Act* (Cth).
106   See Parliamentary Joint Committee on the Australian Crime Commission, Parliament of Australia, *Cybercrime* (2004), Recommendation 4.

is not defined in the amendments but the three offences in s 474.27 give an indication of its meaning. In all three offences, a person (the sender) commits an offence if the sender, who is at least 18 years old, sends a communication to a recipient, who is either under 16 years of age or whom the sender believes to be under 16.[107] The sender must intend for the material to either make it easier to procure the recipient to engage in sexual activity either with the sender,[108] with another person,[109] or in the presence of the sender or another person aged over 18 years.[110] In the first two offences, the punishment is imprisonment for 12 years. In the third type of offence, where the sexual activity will take place in either the presence of the sender or another person, punishment is 15 years' imprisonment.[111]

The first conviction under these provisions occurred in July 2006, when a 55-year-old Melbourne man was convicted and jailed for three months, with a further 21 months suspended, for using Internet chat-rooms and mobile phone text messages in an attempt to procure underage sex with a 14-year-old Canberra girl after she had accidentally left a message on his mobile phone. He pretended to be in love with her and used coded messages in an 'elaborate plan' to arrange a meeting outside her school.[112]

Section 474.28 is a lengthy provision that essentially fills in any gaps left by sections 474.26 and 474.27. For our purposes, one subsection is of particular interest. Subsection (9) states that it does not matter that the recipient to whom the sender sends the communication does not exist and is merely represented to the sender as a real person.[113] At first glance, this provision may seem inconsequential, but on more careful consideration it is obviously included as a means of validating a common method police use to combat this type of crime: posing as children in chat rooms and 'waiting for the predators to come to them.'[114] Finally, s 474.29 provides defences against ss 474.26 and 474.27.

(g) Commonwealth: 2004 (financial information offences)

The implementation of Internet and phone banking has undoubtedly enabled people to maintain greater access and control over their bank accounts and financial information. However, with these new technological developments have come a number of insidious threats aimed at stealing funds and other financial information. According to the 2005 Australian Computer Crime and Security Survey, all of Australia's five major banks have

---

107   See generally, s 474.27(1), 474.27(2), 474.27(3) *Criminal Code Act* (Cth).
108   Section 474.27(1)(c) *Criminal Code Act* (Cth).
109   Section 474.27(2)(c) *Criminal Code Act* (Cth).
110   Section 474.27(3)(f) *Criminal Code Act* (Cth).
111   Section 474.27(3) *Criminal Code Act* (Cth).
112   Daniel Hoare, 'Internet Predator Jailed Under New Laws' *PM*, ABC Radio National 21 July 2006 18:34:00, <http://www.abc.net.au/pm/content/2006/s1693718.htm> last accessed 16/08/06.
113   Section 474.28(9) *Criminal Code Act* (Cth).
114   Tony Krone, 'Queensland Police Stings In Online Chat Rooms' (2005) 301 *Trends and Issues In Crime and Criminal Justice* 1, accessible the Australian Institute of Criminology website, <www.aic.gov.au/publications/tandi2/tandi.html> , last accessed 08/02/06.

experienced unauthorised Internet banking transactions.[115] On its NetBank website, the Commonwealth Bank of Australia warns customers of four types of threats to their accounts when banking on-line: hoax emails (also known as 'phishing'); keyloggers; email employment scams; and identity theft.[116] Phishing, keylogging and identity theft are the most commonly identified in law enforcement circles, although phishing is often categorised as identity crime.

Krone has stated, with regards to phishing, that the term 'connotes the speculative baiting of victims in order to get them to reveal details of their online identity.'[117] More often that not, an offender will phish by sending an email to a person purporting to be from his or her financial institution. The email will request the person to click on a weblink contained in the email that will lead the person to a fake Internet banking site to input his or her on-line banking information. The offender will often then use this information to steal the victim's funds. Keylogging is slightly different in that it may involve no direct contact with the victim: his or her computer may be infected over the Internet with 'Trojan Horse' or other software in order to capture and relay the keystrokes of the victim to the hacker's computer. Both 'phishing' and 'keylogging' are often the prelude to 'identity theft' and 'identity crime'. These can occur in two ways: the perpetrator will either use the identity of another person to open bank accounts or obtain loans, or will use the identity of another to commit a criminal offence.[118] Those victimised by such activity include consumers, credit card companies, government agencies, businesses and entire nations.

Schedule 3 of the Act introduces a new Part 10.8 to the end of Chapter 10 of the *Criminal Code.* The new section 480.4 makes it is an offence for a person to dishonestly obtain or deal in personal financial information without the consent of the person to whom the financial information relates, with an applicable penalty of 5 years' imprisonment. 'Personal financial information' is defined in s 480.1 to mean information that may be used to access funds, credit or other financial benefits. 'Dishonest' is defined by s 480.2 to mean dishonest according to the standards of ordinary people and known by the defendant to be dishonest according to the standards of ordinary people. Finally, and arguably most interestingly, the definition of 'obtaining personal financial information' given in s 480.1 includes possessing or making personal financial information.

Section 480.5(1) states that a person is guilty of an offence if the person has possession or control of anything with the intention that the thing be used by the person or another person to commit an offence against s 480.4. The penalty is 3 years' imprisonment. A person may be guilty under s 480.5 even if the offence to be committed against s 480.4

---

115 AusCERT, AFP, AHTCC, NSW Police, NT Police, Queensland Police, SA Police, Tasmania Police, WA Police, Victoria Police, 2005 Australian Computer Crime and Security Survey, accessible at the Australian Crime Commission website, <http://www.aic.gov.au/topics/cybercrime/stats/> last accessed 23/01/06, at 36.

116 See the Commonwealth Bank of Australia 'Online Fraud' website, accessible at <http://www.commbank.com.au/NetBank/onlinefraud.asp>, last accessed 05/02/2006.

117 See Tony Krone, 'Phishing' (2005) 9 *High Tech Crime Brief* 1, accessible at the Australian Institute of Criminology website, <http://www.aic.gov.au/publications/htcb/htcb009.html>, last accessed 08/02/06.

118 See Henry Pontell, 'Pleased to Meet You ... Won't You Guess My Name? Identity Fraud, Cyber-Crime and White-Collar Delinquency' (2002) 23 *Adelaide Law Review* 305 at 306.

is impossible[119] and again, interestingly, it is not an offence to attempt to commit an offence against s 480.5(1).[120] The final section of Schedule 3, s 480.6, provides that it is an offence for a person to import a thing into Australia with the intention that the thing be used by the person, or another person, to commit an offence against s 480.4, with an applicable penalty of 3 years' imprisonment.

(h)   Commonwealth: 2005 (suicide-related material)

The *Criminal Code Amendment (Suicide Related Material Offences) Act 2005* inserted two new sections into the *Criminal Code*. These create offences for certain materials related to suicide. While these are criminal offences, they also overlap with content regulation. They will be considered in more detail in the next chapter.

 NOTES AND QUESTIONS

1   Can you think of any justifications for including an absolute liability standard in the new Act? Would you, as a citizen, be reassured by such a provision?

2   Compare the materials in this chapter with what you already know about the difficulties in applying an effective nation-based regulatory regime to the Internet. Do you think that the general difficulties of Internet regulation, as opposed to the specific difficulties of criminal investigations, have been overlooked in some quarters?

3   Do you believe that governments understate or overstate the extent of Internet crime? Do governments have an interest in understating the difficulties of addressing on-line crime? Whose interests do they ultimately serve in promoting such a perception?

----

5   National cybercrime laws: Singapore

Singapore's *Computer Misuse Act 1993* was first introduced in 1993 and has been amended several times since to take into account the new types of computer illegalities. It is a relative short piece of legislation compared with the Australian provisions but it nevertheless captures a large number of different types of possible computer misuses.

The offences are set out in Part II of the Act and in some respects they are similar to the Australian computer crime provisions prior to the amendments in 2001. Section 3 provides that it is an offence to access any program or data held in a computer. The maximum penalty is a fine of $2000 or imprisonment for up to 2 years or both. The penalties increase for repeat offenders. Subsection 3(2) provides that if there was damage as a result of the access, then the maximum penalty increases to a maximum fine of $50,000 or 7 years' imprisonment or both.

---

119   Section 480.5(2) *Criminal Code Act* (Cth).
120   Section 480.5(3) *Criminal Code Act* (Cth).

Section 4 builds on s 3 and provides that it is an offence if a person accesses a computer with the intention of committing an offence involving property, fraud, dishonesty, or which causes bodily harm; it carries a penalty of 2 years or more. Under subsection (4), it is immaterial if the access was authorised or unauthorised. This would in effect catch situations where a person such as an employee is authorised to access the computer; the authorisation would obviously not be authorisation to commit offences involving dishonesty. Section 4 would arguably deal with many of the specific offences caught by the changes to the Australian *Criminal Code* introduced in 2004 discussed above. The Singaporean provision is in effect neater and requires less updating than the Australian provisions, which are more specific and therefore vulnerable to changing conditions.

Section 5 of the Act is similar to s 3; it provides that it is an offence to cause an unauthorised modification of the contents of any computer. Section 6 provides for broad offences involving unauthorised use of any computer service and unauthorised interception of any function of a computer. The reference to the interception of any function of a computer would arguably catch those who knowingly utilise key-logger programs, viruses and worms as well as the more traditional hacking activities. The knowing release of viruses and worms would also be caught by s 7, which provides offences involving unauthorised interference, interruption, and obstruction of the lawful use of and access to a computer. Section 7 is obviously also wide enough to catch denial of service attacks.

Section 8 is unusual: it introduces a duty not to disclose access codes without authorisation, and provides that it is an offence to knowingly and without authority disclose a password or any other means of accessing any program or data held in a computer. Under s 10, abetments and attempts are also punishable as offences under the Act.

Section 2 defines many of the terms use in the legislation and the terms are generally very broadly defined. All the offences carry fines and imprisonment penalties. Section 9 provides for 'enhanced' penalties for offences involving 'protected computers', which include computers providing services directly related to communications infrastructure, banking and financial services, public utilities, public transportation and public-key infrastructure, as well as the usual security, defence, law enforcement, and medical computers.

In 2003, a new s 15A was introduced into the Act to empower security agencies to take pre-emptive steps to prevent a cyber attack. Previously, authorities could only act after a crime had been committed.

Computer Misuse Act 1993 (Singapore) as Amended

15A. PREVENTING OR COUNTERING THREATS TO NATIONAL SECURITY, ETC

(1) Where the Minister is satisfied that it is necessary for the purposes of preventing or countering any threat to the national security, essential services, defence or foreign relations of Singapore, the Minister may, by a certificate under his hand, authorise any

person or organisation specified in the certificate to take such measures as may be necessary to prevent or counter any threat to a computer or computer service or any class of computers or computer services.

(2) The measures referred to in subsection (1) may include, without limitation, the exercise by the authorised person or organisation of the powers referred to in sections 125A and 125B of the Criminal Procedure Code (Cap 68).

(3) Where an offence is disclosed in the course of or pursuant to the exercise of any power under this section —

    (a) no information for that offence shall be admitted in evidence in any civil or criminal proceedings; and

    (b) no witness in any civil or criminal proceedings shall be obliged —

        (i) to disclose the name, address or other particulars of any informer who has given information with respect to that offence; or

        (ii) to answer any question if the answer would lead, or would tend to lead, to the discovery of the name, address or other particulars of the informer.

(4) If any book, document, data or computer output which is admitted in evidence or liable to inspection in any civil or criminal proceedings contain any entry in which any informer is named or described or which may lead to his discovery, the court shall cause those entries to be concealed from view or to be obliterated so far as may be necessary to protect the informer from discovery.

(5) In subsection (1), 'essential services' means —

    (a) services directly related to communications infrastructure, banking and finance, public utilities, public transportation or public key infrastructure; and

    (b) emergency services such as police, civil defence or medical services.

 NOTES AND QUESTIONS

1   The new section 15A would be invoked to deal with situations of an outright cyber attack or where specific intelligence is received of an imminent cyber attack against Singapore's critical infrastructure, such as power stations or water filtration plants. Concerns have been raised that the section gives authorities too much power and could be open to abuse. The new laws do not specify what measures the government could take to find and act against potential wrongdoers.

2   Does s 15A give the government sweeping powers to monitor all computer activity in the city-state and act against anyone it believes could use computers to threaten national security? Does it allow for pre-emptive scanning of electronic networks to detect possible threats? What are the privacy concerns raised by s 15A?

6   Conclusion

We have in this chapter examined the vast range of possible illegalities involving computers. The precise acts involving computers and computer networks that are prohibited will differ from jurisdiction to jurisdiction. Some jurisdictions—such as Australia and the USA—prohibit individual activities in specifically worded provisions, while other jurisdictions—such as Singapore—prohibit activities in generally worded legislation. The objective in both approaches is the same: to prohibit, in the on-line world, activities considered to be criminal in the real world. Whether the illegality involves dishonesty or fraud, or preventing damage to property, it is no less reprehensible because it occurs on-line.

Jurisdictions such as Australia have placed certain activities involving computers and computer networks that have social morality elements under the umbrella of criminal law. While these activities have been criminalised, they also raise overlapping issues with content regulation, the subject-matter of the next chapter. The reader should carefully consider the interrelationship between criminalising certain activities which may not necessarily cause immediate or direct harm and regulating such activity without attaching criminal sanctions to it.

8 Internet Content Regulation

----

1   Introduction

The term 'Internet content' covers everything from pornography to defamation, gambling, racism, copyright, obscenity, discrimination, and much more. Put simply, regulating Internet content involves examining what is on the Internet, then deciding whether we, as a society, want it to be there. As you might imagine, this is no simple task.

In the traditional context, 'content' issues are essentially questions for social, cultural, moral, religious or political consideration. 'Content' can mean everything in the traditional context that it can in the cyber context: content of literature, of speech, of activity, of art, or of music. Controversial content questions our collective priorities, our values. Yet, despite the largely non-legal nature of content, it is often discussed in purely legal terms. When faced with a content problem, a legal solution is often the only option considered, perhaps because it is regarded as the simplest option. However, whenever we attempt to solve non-legal issues with legal solutions, problems abound.

Internet content challenges the fabric of a society by questioning its values. Issues as basic as speech and the right to free expression, or to gambling or explicit sexual material, have rarely been collectively presented for extensive public discourse. Once these issues enter public debate they inevitably challenge society's legal norms. Changing laws grounded so firmly in the social fabric requires either a fundamental re-evaluation of this non-legal foundation, or the removal of the interrelation between a society and its law, which we so clearly demand. Content laws differ internationally simply because nations have different value systems.

In the cyber context, the core concern is not what the content should be, but whether and how we can regulate it. The regulation dilemma is so crucial to the Internet that it shapes its structure and its very existence. Should we seek a legal solution to the Internet's challenge, we must confront jurisdiction.

In theory, effective regulation of the Internet requires identical laws across all jurisdictions and universal enforcement. Jurisdiction is the main obstacle in the path of Internet regulation. Faced with inconsistent national laws, each jurisdiction must decide how far its laws may legitimately extend. Chapter 2 outlined the complexities of jurisdiction. This chapter will examine these complexities in a specific context: Internet content.

The problem of regulating content on the Internet, therefore, raises a dual dilemma. Is it possible to harmonise laws that differ simply because societies differ? For example, how do we create institutions accommodating the legal norms embodied in the First Amendment to the American Constitution, without disregarding those norms embodied in the German prohibitions on holocaust denial? Each of these laws has its basis in the historical, cultural, and societal understanding of their respective societies. Each is now part of the national psyche. Each is an entirely legitimate and accepted institution. Yet they cannot coexist—or can they?

Exploration of these issues requires more than can be provided in this introductory publication. This chapter will consider only one of the many controversial aspects of Internet content.

The focus in this chapter will be Internet pornography. This is possibly the most publicised controversy generated by the Internet. Most of the issues discussed in this chapter are relevant to each of the subject areas mentioned above. As you read this chapter it is recommended that you consider how the points made in relation to pornography translate into the other realms of Internet content.

Gavin Sutter, '"Nothing new under the Sun": Old Fears and New Media'

(2000) 8 *International Journal of Law and Information Technology* 338

1. Introduction

The Internet, about which so much has been written and said in the late 1990s, perhaps represents the greatest revolution in communications technology since the television ...

The Internet, it is submitted, is in many ways a paragon of democratic media, allowing anyone their say. For instance, with a little technical capability anyone with occasional access can easily acquire free Web space and publish a home page, allowing them a voice in a forum with a potential audience of millions. Usenet and web-based, real-time chat rooms allow great potential for enriching communications across cultural boundaries between users in different countries or even continents. As Basque has noted, '[t]he Internet's most important long-term effect ... is that it brings people together and facilitates discussion on many different sorts of subjects which it would not have been possible to address with traditional means of communication.'

In spite of the best efforts of certain governments, the Internet remains for all practical purposes an open forum with few limitations upon freedom of expression. The G7 Ministerial Conference on the Information Society at Brussels in July 1994 considered that, '[f]or those able to exploit it, the information society is already a liberating experience which widens individual choice, releases new creative and commercial energies, offers cultural enrichment and brings greater flexibility to the management of working and leisure time.'

However, there are those who are firmly of the opinion that 'information technology, like other human creations, is not an unqualified good.' The Internet, it is argued, is a state of virtual anarchy to which none of the current regulations placed upon other media—telephone, television and radio, cinema, video, computer games, magazines or advertising—are 'directly transferable'. Those who would wish to 'rectify' this situation argue that children are only ever a few mouse clicks away from all kinds of undesirable material, whether racist propaganda, bomb-making recipes, or pornography. There is a need to enact specific legislation in order to protect children from exposure to such material. On the other hand, those opposing the introduction of new regulations for the Internet regard censorship as an unwarranted and undemocratic limitation upon fundamental civil liberties of freedom of expression and discussion. This debate has, within the last four years, come to centre on the issue of pornography on the web and Usenet. There are two main areas of concern: child pornography, that is pornographic images involving children, and other pornography to which children may be able to gain access on the Internet. This paper seeks to consider the issues raised, both explicitly and implicitly, in this debate, and to suggest some answers for these important questions:

- Where did it arise from?
- Is it all just a moral panic, or is there a genuine problem which requires specific legal action?

2. Nothing new

'There is nothing new under the sun.'

Loud demands for censorship in order to protect children are nothing new. Indeed, '[s]ince the Greek philosopher Plato first expressed concern about the influence of the dramatic poets on the "impressionable minds" of young people, a succession of new media—the novel, music hall, the cinema, comics, television, video and computer games—have each in turn become the focus of recurrent waves of public anxiety.'

In the nineteenth century, 'penny dreadfuls'—cheap, sensationalist literature—were regarded as a source of corruption of children; by the 1910s *The Times* was proclaiming that 'all who care for the moral well being and education of the child will set their faces like flint against this new form of excitement [the early cinema].'

In the 1950s it was the turn of horror comics to be vilified as poisoners of children's minds; in the 1980s, the video nasty. It was assumed that not only must their innocence be protected, but also that children will copy what they see on screen: movie violence breeds actual violence in the minds and actions of its young viewers.

Concerns about the amount of screen violence to which young children are exposed came to a head in the moral panic which followed in the wake of the murder of two-year-old Jamie Bulger on a railway line in Bootle in February 1993. This moral panic was given impetus by the media reaction, largely tabloid-led, to a passing remark made by Morland J in his summing up in the Bulger case. He suggested that 'exposure to violent video films' may partly explain the brutal actions of the child killers. Although the issue had not been mentioned at trial, when it was revealed that the father of one of the killers, with whom the child was not living at that time, had recently hired a copy of the video *Child's Play III*—scenes which, it was alleged, bore striking similarities to the manner of Jamie Bulger's murder—the moral panic truly began.

Throughout the latter half of 1993, popular debate on censorship issues came increasingly to be dominated by the issue of media depictions of violence and its effects on children ...

By 1997, mainstream arguments for censorship had, by and large, come to be dominated by the contention that children are negatively affected by the depiction of violence. But does the depiction of violent acts on screen *really* have a perceptible effect on children? Contrary to the claims made by Professor Newson in her report, this has never been proven. Indeed, the report itself was highly questionable. '[I]ts primary source [wa]s ... Medved's populist tract on screen violence, *Hollywood Versus America*. Michael Medved, it should be noted, unquestioningly upheld claims that 'without TV there would be 10,000 fewer murders per year in the United States, 70,000 fewer rapes and 700,000 fewer assaults'. Further, neither Newson herself nor any of the twenty-five doctors and academics who sponsored her paper had completed any research into screen violence. In the Bulger case itself, after thorough consideration of all the evidence, Albert Kirby, the chief investigating officer, insisted that 'the police could make no connection between the killing and the viewing of videos'. Indeed, the supposed link between violent images on screen and violent behaviour has never been proven.

The Bulger case is perhaps the best example in recent history of how a moral panic can develop momentum to the point where a change in the law is perceived to be necessary, and new censorship is introduced. Such moral panics have surrounded calls for and enactment of censorship of mass media for hundreds of years, For example, under UK law the theatre is no longer regulated. Theatre censorship did, however, exist for a very long time, having its origins with the Master of the Revels, an officer of the Royal Court first appointed by Henry VIII to work under the Lord Chamberlain, supervising the various entertainers who performed before the King. By 1551 a Royal Proclamation deemed that no play could be performed unless licensed by the Master of the Revels. This early censorship regime was, it should be noted, concerned entirely with the presentation of material subversive of the monarchy, the state and/or the established church. The issue of 'protection of public morals' did not arise until the eighteenth century, in the form of the 1737 *Stage Licensing Act*, under which all new plays, as well as any additions to old plays, were required to be submitted to the office of the Lord Chamberlain for licensing prior to public performance. Powers of refusal of a whole work or specific parts of a work were granted to the Lord Chamberlain, whose decision was final and who was under no obligation to give reasons for it. This direct political censorship was justified on the basis of the preservation of public morals. The Lord Chancellor's brief encompassed the control of theatre presentation of sex, religion, and especially the depiction of crime, and here lie the roots of the 'modern' debate regarding the effects of film and television.

The *Stage Licensing Act* was not without its critics; however, until 1968 their words were to fall on deaf ears. When the Select Committee on Dramatic literature met in 1832, the critics were in the minority: generally those witnesses called agreed that the system put in place by the 1737 legislation should continue, a view accepted by the Committee, and the subsequent 1843 *Theatres Act* merely consolidated the Lord Chancellor's powers and role as protector of the status quo and controller of popular culture.

By the mid 1960s, change was afoot. The 1966 Joint Committee on Theatre Censorship recommended the repeal of the 1843 Act; the *Theatre Act 1968* repealed the 1843 legislation in its entirety and abolished the powers of the Lord Chamberlain. Theatre in the future was to be subject only to the regular common and statutory law as regards, for example, defamation or obscenity. Any return to a system of pre-censorship is unlikely, at least while theatre remains divorced from mass entertainment.

The first public screening of a film was in 1895; one year later the first pornographic film (*Bedtime for the Bride*) appeared. The growth in popularity of the cinema was rapid: Britain's first purpose-built cinema opened in 1906. It has been estimated that by the middle of the First World War the weekly attendance figure for British cinemas was in the region of 20 million. The first legislative controls placed on film were contained in the 1909 *Cinematograph Act*, which gave powers to local authorities to license premises for the presentation of films and to censor films. Those powers are now encompassed by the 1985 *Cinemas Act*. The film industry was (understandably) concerned that different policies towards what would or would not be permitted were likely to be adopted in different parts of the country, potentially damaging their economic interest; further it feared state censorship in the form of a governmental regulatory body. With this in mind representatives of the film industry approached the government and presented plans for a self-censorship body, and thus the British Board of Film Censorship (later 'Classification') was established in 1913. Local authorities retained the power to reject a film passed by the BBFC—or to allow an unclassified film to be shown. However, in practice a film, once classified, would be exempt from any possible legal proceedings. Between 1913 and the early 1970s, some 500 films were banned outright, including many now regarded as classics of their genre.

In 1950, the advent of television moved the goalposts somewhat. Prior to this date, cinemas had attracted large, family audiences on a weekly, if not nightly, basis. However, as more and more households possessed a television, cinema audiences declined in direct proportion to the growth in popularity of the new medium. The film industry began to attempt to offset the decline by exploiting the allure of stronger, 'adult' material: certificate 'X' arrived in 1951. The *Report of the Williams Committee on Obscenity and Film Censorship*, arriving in the new age of *Dirty Harry* and graphic violence, considered cinema a '... uniquely powerful medium, the close-up fast cutting, the sophistication of modern make-up and special effects and music all combine on the large screen to produce an impact, which no other medium can create'; thus heavy censorship of film was justified. The general public, however, remained largely indifferent until the early 1980s. The introduction of home video in the early part of the last decade brought with it a seemingly limitless flow of video films not subject to any legal constraint. Tabloid (particularly the *Daily Mail*) identification of the 'video nasty' genre of graphic violence and bloodshed, which included titles such as *I Spit On Your Grave*, *The Evil Dead*, and *Driller Killer*, sparked off what Buckingham has identified as a 'moral panic'. Concerns that children could gain access to such material in the home (as opposed to cinemas where strict door policies regarding age limitations are enforced) and that video allowed such material to be watched over and over were raised, and the ensuing hysteria blew the problem out of all proportion.

The 1984 *Video Recordings Act* was based on a Private Member's Bill which gained much support in the wake of a (later discredited) report which claimed that a large proportion of children had seen a video nasty, and a majority had seen an '18' certificate film. It required videos to be separately certified under the criminal law 'and not simply, as was still the case with cinema films, by private agreement with the trade'. The controversy over home video and the effect particularly of violence on viewers did not end with this Act: events such as the 1987 Hungerford Massacre kept that spectre alive as (false) claims abounded that Michael Ryan had been motivated by *Rambo*. Again matters came to a head in the early 1990s in the wake of the Bulger panic and the ensuing rush to censor material such as *Child's Play III*.

In spite of more reliable investigations which tended to disprove the existence of any link between delinquent behaviour and film, the moral panic surrounding film—both cinema and video—was fuelled and largely dominated the censorship debate in the mid 1990s by various 'notorious' films such as *Reservoir Dogs*, released in the cinema in 1992 but not on video until 1996, and *Natural Born Killers*, released—controversially—with an '18' certificate in 1995 but by mid 2000 still not yet passed for video release ...

Statutory regulation of television is now contained within the *Broadcasting Act* of 1990. This Act established the Broadcasting Standards Council, a regulatory body with various responsibilities including the monitoring of both television programs and attitudes towards them, and receiving and investigating complaints from the public with regard to specific programs. The BSC may commission research into the effects of and attitudes towards television; it is also responsible for drawing up a Code of Practice to provide guidelines for the portrayal of violence, sexual conduct, and standards of taste and decency. Further, the Act amends the *Obscene Publications Act* in order, *inter alia*, to bring television under that Act's jurisdiction, while certain programs or material are prohibited: neither 'racially inflammatory' material nor 'material likely to stir up hatred or arouse fear' is allowed to be shown. The scope of liability is further widened by a provision that television broadcasts may be treated as publications for purposes of libel or slander. Both the BBC and ITV/Channel 4/Channel 5 operate under the 1990 Act, while the BBC also retains its Royal Charter. Ostensibly this charter gives the BBC greater autonomy, not being dependent on advertising revenue; however, in practice it is somewhat more restrictive: the Royal Charter could be removed, while (as the Corporation itself has put it) the 'unique way the BBC is funded by you, the viewer' places certain standards and expectations over and above simple ratings upon those responsible for its programming. In contrast, ITV functions under the Independent Television Commission, previously legally accountable as the broadcaster; however, since

1993 it has delegated broadcasting responsibility to the licensee independent television companies. The ITC's role now is to adduce annual performance appraisals and, when felt to be necessary, to issue warnings to television companies with the ultimate threat of revocation or non-renewal of their licences.

So, in the modern law of the UK, theatre is not subject to any direct form of censorship—nor, for that matter, is literature. Both film and television, on the other hand, are extensively regulated. Why is this the case? It is sometimes claimed that the theatre has less of a capacity to shock, lacking, as it does, the same scope for effects. A stage production cannot be halted while an actor who is, say, to be shot, spends considerable time in make-up, or use slow motion or close-ups, or any one or several of a host of tricks available to a film director. Yet some of the most profoundly disturbing and/or violent images in cinematic history are never actually seen but rather imagined by the viewer: the stabbing in the shower in *Psycho*, the ear-severing in *Reservoir Dogs*, the brutal murders in *Seven*. Such powers of suggestion can be used to equal effect on stage—the infamous ear scene in Tarantino's finest work is strongly reminiscent of the eye-gouging ('Out, out vile jelly!') in *King Lear*. Conversely, it might be noted that the 'video nasties' which caused such consternation in the 1980s were invariably very low-budget affairs, far removed from convincing and realistic special effects. In any case, violence—as other activities such as sex, profanity, blasphemy—has a much greater capacity to shock or disturb (and corrupt?) in the much more immediate medium of theatre. It is the case, then, that theatre can be equally as shocking as, if not more so than, either film or television. This being so, why is modern theatre not directly censored in the same way as either film or television? By the late 1960s, theatre was no longer a medium of mass entertainment, having been superseded in the twentieth century first by cinema and then by television. Theatre drew only a small, mostly middle-class audience and was no longer regarded as a threat: the powers of the Lord Chamberlain came to be regarded as 'anachronistic'. This had not always been the case, however. After its earliest origins as a method of political control, in the eighteenth century the censorship of theatre began to take on a more self-righteous tone as a protector of public morals. The tone of the debate surrounding the alleged 'copycat' phenomenon with respect to screen violence is nothing new—such fears were expressed relating to the stage too and date back even further: Plato is known to have expressed concerns about the influence of the dramatic poets on the 'impressionable minds' of young people.

So, then, the underlying reason behind the lack of direct censorship of the modern theatre is that the context of the debate has moved on. Theatre is no longer a source of concern due to its decline as a medium of mass entertainment, and modern moral panics surround newer media including film (cinema and video), television, and now the Internet. However, societal reaction has remained the same: waves of public hysteria, enhanced by the (tabloid) press, resulting in new censorship provisions being passed by politicians either in a misguided belief that there does exist a new moral crisis or with the calculated aim of 'scoring points' over the 'other side', one of the many dangers of the adversarial model of government. The paramount examples of recent times remain the Bulger murder, the still unproven claims that the video film *Child's Play III* motivated the killers, the fundamentally flawed Newson report, and the resulting Alton amendment to the 1994 *Criminal Justice and Public Order Act*.

When theatre censorship was at its peak, matters sexual were of most concern. By the early-mid 1990s, the emphasis had shifted to screen violence. As the debate lurched on to the Internet, incitement of violence has remained an issue. When, in April 1999, Eric Harris (18) and Dylan Klebold (17), carried out a murderous attack on fellow pupils and staff at Columbine High School in Denver, Colorado, much was made in the tabloid press of the claimed influence of rock musician Marilyn Manson, as well as of the fact that the pair shared extreme right-wing political views, including a strong admiration of Hitler (the massacre was timed to coincide with his birth date): views which, crucially, they had espoused on their own web site. There were rumblings in certain quarters as to how far they had used the Web to express these views, and how far it was the source of them. During the same month, in the UK, 22-year-old David Copeland, a self-confessed homophobic racist, carried out a series of brutal bombing attacks across London, climaxing in the deaths of three people in the Admiral Duncan, a well-known gay venue in Soho. Upon his conviction for the attacks and murders, much was made in the press of the Internet as his source of bomb-making knowledge. Both the London City Riots of June 1999 and the May Day Riots in 2000 were much touted as having been orchestrated via the Internet. Even the murder of television celebrity Jill Dando apparently had an Internet element: '[a]n obsessed fan used the Internet to track down [her] address ... before she was murdered'. However, while from time to time the tabloid press still gets in a froth about Internet violence, by far the majority of negative press the web receives is to do with pornography, for instance, the *Metro* report which claimed that '[s]even in ten sales on the Internet are X-rated ... Of the £875 million spent on products on the World Wide Web, £603 million went on adult-only material'. Not to mention the acres of media coverage given the Duke of Edinburgh's attack on Internet pornographers during a UK–Korean business conference in Seoul in April 1999, and many, many other stories either implicitly or explicitly linking the Internet and online pornography with negative social trends.

This swing would seem to reflect changing social conditions. The 1980s and early to mid 1990s censorship debate took place against the backdrop of such atrocities as Hungerford, Dunblane, and the Bulger murder, and was characterised by the seeming compulsion to displace societal or (particularly in the case of child perpetrators) individual responsibility for such heinous acts. For example, it was widely accepted that the Bulger killers were motivated by *Child's Play III*; the break-up of the family was rarely (if ever) mentioned in the popular press, and certainly no real significance was placed upon it. Yet

> Bobby Thompson [one of James Bulger's murderers] came from a family with a history of abuse and hardship, and although his older brothers had voluntarily put themselves into local authority care, it is not clear whether he had been abused himself. Jon Venables' [the other murderer] brother and sister had learning difficulties, and his parents were separated, and it is likely that he felt rejected as a result.

To argue that it was a video that killed James Bulger is precisely to avoid the uncomfortable questions that such cases are bound to raise. As the 1990s draw to a close, the popular media is rife with reports of the premature sexualisation of children: 'Sex at Eleven, Baby at Twelve' screamed one *Sun* headline, typical of the kind of tabloid stories claiming that younger and younger children are indulging in sexual behaviour. News items regarding the exploitation of children by child pornographers are commonplace. Once again there is a societal need for a scapegoat, and this, coupled with traditional suspicion of new media (and a desire to regulate the mass media), has done much to put the issue of pornography on the Internet at the forefront of calls for censorship.

Shallit proposes 'Three Laws of New Media':

(1) Every new medium of expression will be used for sex.
(2) Every new medium of expression will come under attack, usually because of Shallit's First Law.
(3) Protection afforded for democratic rights and freedoms in traditional media will merely be understood to apply to new media ... the fallacy of focusing on the medium and not the message.

Certainly these would seem broadly consistent with the development of theatre and film; for example: most new media (the exception, perhaps, being radio) have indeed been 'used for sex' and come under attack for the same, although the depiction of violence was a more prominent issue in recent years. Shallit's Third Law is of most interest here: as noted above, each new medium has found itself under fire for the dissemination of material quite readily available elsewhere, but there is a perceived need to control content in the mass media rather than less popular forms.

2.1. PORNOGRAPHY

Stems from the Greek words, porno, meaning prostitutes and graphos, meaning writing. ... [it] include[s] the depiction of actual sexual content ... and depiction of ... nudity or lascivious exhibition.

It is indeed available on the Internet in several formats.

These range from pictures, short animated movies, to sound files and stories [via both web and Usenet]. It is also possible to see live sex shows by connecting to some World Wide Web ... sites by using special software [downloadable from the Web].

The moral panic surrounding such availability began in earnest in the USA during 1995. On 3 July that year, *Time* magazine ran an article by Philip Elmer-Dewitt as its cover story. Entitled 'On a screen near you: Cyberporn', this article gave the casual reader otherwise uninformed about the issue the impression that the Internet is rife with pornography. Just as the Alton lobby and other similar groups' claims of a relationship between screen and actual violence had been given a veneer of scientific respectability by the deeply flawed Newson Report, so too the *Time* story had its study. In this case the report relied upon was a research paper written by Marty Rimm at Carnegie–Mellon University in Pittsburgh, Pennsylvania. Rimm claimed that '[p]edophilic [*sic*] and paraphilic [including urination, voyeurism, transgenderism, S&M and bestiality] pornography are widely available [on] ... Usenet, World Wide Web, and commercial 'adult' BBS [bulletin board services]'. Such images were said to be in greater demand than supply, and accounted for half of those downloaded from private adult BBSs.

The Elmer-Dewitt article caused some outrage and much concern, especially among parents, throughout the USA, yet it was not completely factual. Elmer-Dewitt claimed that the Rimm study showed that 'on those Usenet newsgroups where digitised images are stored, 83.5% of the pictures were pornographic'. This claim can also be found in Rimm's 'Summary of Significant Results of the Carnegie Mellon Study'. In fact the correct conclusion based on Rimm's results is that 83.5% of images posted to the alt.binaries newsgroups—a *subset* of newsgroups within Usenet—contained images classifiable as pornography. By Rimm's own figures 'fewer than one half of 1% of the messages on the Internet (3% of 11.5%) [ie 3% of messages posted to Usenet, which itself constitutes only 11.5% of traffic on the Internet] are 'associated with' newsgroups that contain pornographic imagery; since some (many? most?) of those messages are, presumably, not themselves pornographic, the actual proportion of pornographic messages is even smaller than that'. To put it another way, 'while there are 917,410 pornographic files, the majority of these were found on adult BBSs [places into which children cannot link]; only 2830 potentially pornographic messages were found over a four-month period on the Usenet'. These figures are not highlighted in Rimm's 'Summary of Significant Results'. Rimm also claimed that, while only one of the worldwide top forty newsgroups—alt.binaries.pictures.erotica—contained pornographic *images,* 'three of the five most popular newsgroups are pornographic. Moreover, of the 101,211 monthly Usenet posts in the top forty newsgroups, 20.4% are pornographic'. However, no data which might substantiate such a claim are provided by Rimm. 'Nor is it clear whether Rimm, as he appears to claim, actually looked at 101,211 Usenet posts in the top forty newsgroups in order to determine that 20.4% of the postings 'are pornographic'. Beyond such statistics, it would seem that the Rimm study is fundamentally flawed. It is proclaimed throughout as the fruits of the labour of a research team at Carnegie–Mellon University; however, Rimm—described variously as 'Researcher' and 'Principal Investigator'—was, in fact, an undergraduate student reading electrical engineering when this study was performed. Rimm wrote the published paper alone: '[g]iven established standards of authorship as ownership of intellectual property in the academic and scientific community, one can only infer from this that no one on the research team felt their contributions merited the significance of shared authorship.' The pornographic images which the study referred to were found on selected 'adult' subscriber-only BBSs in the USA. Rimm attempted to generalise beyond these to the Internet generally, but no such generalisation is possible. Rimm's juxtaposition of unrelated analyses of adult BBSs and Usenet newsgroups may create in the casual reader's mind the impression that what is stated about adult BBSs is also true of the [Internet] as a whole.

The World Wide Web is, in the late 1990s, increasingly the dominant element of the Internet, and thus is a highly important factor. Rimm, in his 'Summary of Significant Results', insists that' [p]edophilic [*sic*] and paraphilic pornography are widely available through various computer networks and protocols such as the World Wide Web'. Yet '[n]o evidence is presented to demonstrate that such material is available anywhere on the Web'. In Appendix C, in which the results of a Web Survey undertaken during March 1995 are discussed, Rimm notes that only 123 web sites which contained any 'sexually explicit imagery or materials' were located—just nine of these contained pornographic material. No evidence is presented that any of these sites—less than 0.1% of all World Wide Web sites—contained paedophilic or paraphilic material. Rimm's paper was

> rife with methodological flaws ... Much greater attention [was] paid to sensationalistic and inflammatory descriptions of image files, for example, than accurate descriptions of the survey methodology. In fact, in many cases important aspects of the methodology are simply not described at all.

Further, the paper is confusingly structured, the results are not clearly described, and the whole is overlong.

Significantly, there was no peer review of the Rimm paper. Hoffman and Novak, two of Rimm's strongest critics, in light of the fact that Rimm's study 'was submitted to a law journal which is not peer-reviewed, despite the fact that it probably would be more appropriate in a behavioural science or public policy journal (most of which are peer-reviewed)', pose the question: 'Did Rimm place his article somewhere where it would appear credible and go unchallenged?'

Time came under fire from Hoffman and Novak for rushing to publish its exclusive without first attempting to validate Rimm's claims by way of '[seeking] its own panel of objective experts for a "private" peer review'. Instead of doing so, *Time* printed an uncritical feature based on the Rimm study, both granting it an undeserved 'instant credibility' and—much like the Newson Report before it—adding fuel to the pro-censorship lobby.

A careful, objective reading of the *Time* story, it is submitted, would reveal that it is not entirely caught up in pro-censorship hysteria. However, what really sticks in the mind are the claims made about the availability and popularity of 'cyberporn'—'popular, pervasive, and surprisingly perverse'—based on the supposed evidence of the Rimm paper. The article may present anecdotal comments from users on both sides of the debate, but it is phrases such as

> When the kids are plugged in, will they be exposed to the seamiest sides of human sexuality?
>
> Will they fall prey to child molesters hanging out in electronic chat rooms?

which are most memorable.

Around this time a number of organisations began lobbying the US Congress, demanding that legislation which would protect children from adult Internet content be enacted, over and above already existing laws which include the Internet in their scope.

Concurrently with *Time* going to press with the cyberporn cover story, a Senate anti-Internet porn bill was being debated. The bill proposed to outlaw obscene material and impose fines of up to $100,000 and prison terms of up to two years on anyone who knowingly makes 'indecent' material available to children under 18. The *Communications Decency Act*, as first proposed, however, was too draconian to gain much support. The Bill was revised, removing the imposition of criminal liability upon Internet service providers for any obscene material which passed through their systems. It was written off by many as unconstitutional and unlikely to be upheld by the courts; however, they did not allow for the strength of the effects of the moral panic on public opinion. During a televised Senate debate, Senator Exon produced a file of printouts of the more extreme adult images available online, material which he claimed 'made *Playboy* and *Hustler* look like Sunday-school stuff'. Following the debate, which was broadcast live nationally, a large majority—84 to 16—voted in its favour: few were prepared to so publicly cast a vote which may retrospectively have been interpreted as pro-porn. The crux of the debate lay in how the Internet should be classified: as a broadcast medium, like television, and therefore subject to all manner of regulation, or as a print medium with the attendant free speech protections. The Bill was indeed the subject of some controversy in Congress, opinions both for and against being argued vociferously, adult rights to free speech being pitted against protection of minors. Ultimately, however, the moral panic instigated by the *Time* story and other sensationalist articles won out. The CDA was passed and signed into law by President Clinton on 8 February 1996.

Opposition to the CDA came from a diverse group of organisations and bodies supportive of the right to free speech, organised under the umbrella Citizens Internet Empowerment Coalition ('CIEC'). Lawyers representing this group prepared a 17,000-word complaint, outlining their reasons for opposing the CDA. The complaint was submitted to a federal court in Philadelphia on 27 February 1996. The American Civil Liberties Union had already entered a similar complaint on 8 February, and the two actions were later joined. This opposition concentrated on the two key prohibitions within the CDA. Firstly, the Act provided that:

(a) Whoever—
   (1) in interstate or foreign communications ...
   (B) by means of a telecommunications device knowingly—
       (i)   makes, creates, or solicits, and
       (ii)   initiates the transmission of,
   any comment, request, suggestion, proposal, image, or other communication which is obscene or indecent, knowing that the recipient of the communication is under 18 years of age, regardless of whether the maker of such communication placed the call or initiated the communication; ...
   (2) ... shall be fined ... or imprisoned for not more than two years, or both.

In other words, this section imposed criminal liability upon anyone knowingly sending to a minor material which is legally 'obscene' or 'indecent'. Only the definition of 'indecent' was a live issue so far as the CIEC case was concerned, the Supreme Court of the United States having already drawn a legal distinction between obscenity and 'indecent' speech. Obscenity—like child pornography—falls outside the scope of First Amendment protection. Under US federal law, the national or international transportation of 'any obscene, lewd, lascivious, or filthy book, pamphlet, picture, film, paper, letter, writing, print, silhouette, drawing, figure, image, cast, phonograph recording, electrical transcription or other article capable of producing sound or any other matter of indecent or immoral character' is an offence punishable by fines and imprisonment for up to five years.

The second key prohibition in the CDA is as follows. Whoever:

(2) knowingly permits any telecommunications facility under such person's control to be used for an activity prohibited by paragraph (1) with the intent that it be used for such activity, shall be fined ... or imprisoned not more than two years, or both.

In effect this 'prohibits the knowing sending or displaying of patently offensive messages in a manner that is available to a person under 18 years of age'. In defining 'patently offensive', the statute used part of the *Miller v California* obscenity test, which considers:

(a) whether the average person, applying contemporary standards, would find the work taken as a whole appeals to the prurient interest
(b) whether the work depicts or describes, in a patently offensive way, sexual conduct specifically defined by the applicable state law; and
(c) whether the work, taken as a whole, lacks serious literary, artistic, political or scientific value.

However, while this test was adapted to the CDA in order to identify what is 'patently offensive' by accessing the material in question against community standards, criteria for distinction between material which is harmless and that which is to be considered harmful remained unclear, as did any indication as to whose community standards were to be upheld.

The CDA did also provide 'several affirmative defenses [sic] for content creators and Internet service providers'. One key defence entailed the use of blocking software. It was a valid defence to show that a defendant had taken

> good faith, reasonable, effective and appropriate actions under the circumstances to restrict or prevent access by minors ... including any method which is feasible under available technology.

Internet service providers were also granted a defence against liability for information which originated with a third-party service user:

> No provider or user of an interactive computer service shall be treated as the publisher or speaker of any information provided by another information content provider.

Such defences, however, were not enough for the CDA's opponents, who argued that it violated the First Amendment—the constitutional right to Free Speech. A three-judge panel in the United States District Court for the Eastern District of Pennsylvania found in favour of the ACLU's claim that the CDA effectively criminalised protected adult speech. US Attorney General Reno contended that the CDA was not in contravention of the US Constitution, merely furthering the state's interest in the protection of minors' well-being and providing adequate safeguards to ensure that 'innocent users' were not open to prosecution. The court rejected such argument, instead '[f]inding that the law was a content-based restriction of speech in a unique medium of communication deserving full First Amendment protection'. The CDA was found unconstitutional on grounds that it was, *inter alia,* overly broad, banning, as it did, adult speech which despite being indecent was constitutionally protected. This was held too intrusive to be justifiable under any state interest in the protection of the well-being of minors which the Attorney General asserted. 'The scope of the CDA,' the court held, 'is not confined to material that has a prurient interest or appeal, one of the hallmarks of obscenity, because Congress sought to reach farther.' It followed that the ACLU's request for an injunction was granted.

The Attorney General appealed to the Supreme Court which, by a 7:2 majority, upheld the Philadelphia District Court ruling. The specific provisions of the 1996 CDA were found to be in breach of the First Amendment, therefore unconstitutional, and were struck out. The judgment of the Supreme Court, delivered by Justice Stevens, recognised that there is a 'governmental interest in protecting children from harmful materials ... [b]ut that interest does not justify an unnecessarily broad suppression of speech addressed to adults'. In drawing this conclusion, the Court made reference to earlier cases in which it had held, the issues being similar, that the Government may not 'reduc[e] the adult population ... to ... only what is fit for children'. The earlier case of *Sable*, the Court stated, 'made clear that the mere fact that a statutory regulation of speech was enacted for the important purpose of protecting children from exposure to sexually explicit material does not foreclose enquiry into its validity'. Essentially the Supreme Court recognised that it had to perform a balancing act between the protection of children from potentially harmful material and the constitutional right to free speech; its ruling reflected the view that the CDA went too far, tipping the balance unduly against adult free speech.

The Supreme Court also remarked that:

> [t]he breadth of the CDA's coverage is wholly unprecedented … Its open-ended prohibitions embrace all non-profit entities and individuals posting indecent messages or displaying them on their own computers in the presence of minors. The general, undefined terms 'indecent' and 'patently offensive' cover large amounts of non-pornographic material with serious educational or other value. However, the 'community standards' criterion as applied to the Internet means that any communication available to a nationwide audience will be judged by the standard of the community most likely to be offended by the message.

The Attorney General failed 'to explain why a less restrictive provision would not be as effective as the CDA'. As passed by Congress and signed by Clinton, the CDA—in light of the above and also the fact that it 'was a criminal statute which, in addition to potentially stigmatising violators of the Act with a criminal conviction, threatened to silence speakers by issuing severe sanctions for noncompliance'—was thus held to be unconstitutional, as it was likely to inhibit the free flow of expression and ideas, and was struck out.

Taken together with the *Reno* judgment, other cases in Federal District Courts surrounding state laws which sought to censor Internet content, make it clear that in order to be constitutionally valid US laws attempting to regulate Internet content must be very narrowly drafted and highly specific so as to maintain the delicate balance between the protection of children and freedom of speech and expression. However, as Ann Beeson, ACLU lawyer representing the plaintiffs in *ALA v Pataki,* has noted, 'a Supreme Court opinion striking down the CDA will not prevent state legislators from passing unconstitutional statutes'. Indeed, the Supreme Court may have made an important step in blocking unwise legislation arising out of a moral panic; however, moves were soon afoot to create similar acts, narrow enough to pass constitutional muster …

In early 1998, a collective including the ACLU, *Oasis Magazine* (an online gay rights and information journal), and the Association of American Publishers mounted a legal action against the State of New Mexico. 'The suit challenge[d] a newly enacted statute that prohibit[ed] computer dissemination of materials involving "sexual conduct" or "nudity" to persons under 18.' The plaintiffs alleged, *inter alia,* that this law was too broad and would be interpreted as to include, for example, 'Michelangelo's David or a description of prisoner rape in a human rights document'. Following a two-day trial in New Mexico Federal Court, Judge C LeRoy Hansen granted a preliminary injunction against the law coming into force on 1 July as planned. No final judgment has yet appeared: presumably the case is still entangled in the matrix that is the US appeals system. However, the plaintiffs are likely to succeed in light of similarities on the facts to aspects of both *Reno v ACLU* cases. Attempts to introduce legislation to censor the Internet in the US continue, prompted by a mix of parental concern—as demonstrated in the much publicised recent descent of 'anti-porn activists' upon Washington DC—and political activity (if not opportunism); Senator McCain may have dropped out of the presidential race, paving the way for George Bush Jr to stand as the Republican candidate … however, his profile can only have been raised by this exposure and it is unlikely that his public opposition to 'cyberporn' will diminish. High-profile cases such as the October 1999 arrest of Patrick Naughton, a former Infoseek

Corporation executive vice president, for allegedly attempting to use the Internet to arrange sex with a thirteen-year-old girl, certainly only help to fuel fears that the Internet presents a very real danger to children.

Of course, while specific legislation aimed at censoring the content of the Internet may be unlikely to pass constitutional muster in the USA, except where very narrowly drafted, this does not mean that cyberporn goes unrestricted. Federal pornography laws—focusing mainly on child pornography—do exist. Any person who 'knowingly makes, prints, or publishes, or causes to be made, printed or published advertisements soliciting receipt, exchange, buying, production, display, distribution or reproduction of any visual depiction of sexually explicit behaviour which involves a minor may be imprisoned for up to ten years'. Appropriate *mens rea* for this offence is knowing or having reason to know that the advertisement will be transported in foreign or interstate conference 'by any means including by computer'. For example, in *United States v Maxwell*, the court martial conviction of an Air Force officer for exchanging child pornography via America Online, in violation of 18 USC s 2252, was upheld. Significantly, the language of the statute—'causes to be made, printed or published'—'is broad enough to include establishing a pointer on another server'. The related 18 USC s 2251 renders the advertising of child pornography illegal. Such federal provision is reflected in many state statutes, some being much broader.

On this side of the Atlantic, the issue of computer pornography first came to light as long ago as the early part of 1993, when John Major, the Conservative Prime Minister, issued instructions to the Home Office to the effect that the 'young and vulnerable'—particularly children—required protection from the looming threat of computer porn. Conservative Home Secretary Michael Howard included measures in his Criminal Justice and Public Order Bill which reflected Major's call. During the first quarter of 1994, the parliamentary select committee for Home Affairs published a report which argued that new legislation specifically tailored to deal with computer pornography was necessary. Meanwhile, James Ferman, the director of the BBFC, drew comparison between computer pornography and 'the international trade in drugs'; opposition MP Frank Cook (Labour) even went so far as to claim that 'computer pornography is tantamount to the injection of heroin into a child's school milk' ...

As in the USA, the pro-censorship lobby proclaimed that an epidemic of Internet pornography was upon the UK, and restrictive censorship laws were required to counteract it ...

Various claims were made as to the spread of computer disks containing pornographic materials in schools throughout the UK—these too remain uncorroborated by hard evidence. Also seized upon by journalists and politicians as evidence of a computer porn epidemic were statements made to the committee by one Vicki Merchant, harassment officer at the University of Central Lancashire, who, among other things, was collator of the first survey of computer pornography in schools in the UK. Yet Merchant's own preliminary findings proved only that rumours of cyberporn—gossip—had spread rapidly from school to school. However, no less than the *Sunday Times* reported this as fact, claiming 'explicit computer porn plagues 50 per cent of schools'. Parallels between such responses to a supposed but unproven threat and the press reaction to the most tenuous of links between *Child's Play III* and the murder of James Bulger are strong. Of course, it is likely that some genuine cases of computer disks containing pornographic material did find their way into UK schools;

however, it is submitted that pornographic images have been accessed to a limited degree by schoolchildren—specifically adolescent boys—for many years, ranging in format from a tabloid 'Page 3' photograph to an illicit copy of *Playboy* or similar such publication. With the growth in popularity of powerful home computers with CD-ROM drives and high-resolution graphics, it is no surprise that similar images may find their way on to this new format. Such disks are to be distinguished from the Internet *per se*; however, the moral panic generated around them by the media and pro-censorship lobbyists only served to enhance a certain negative public view of such new technology, including the 'net'.

> The Home Affairs select committee expressed concerns that minors are able to freely access
> pornographic material from specialised electronic bulletin boards accessible via the Internet;
> however, memoranda sent to the committee suggesting that this only happened very rarely,
> if at all, went unpublished.

Other submissions to the committee were equally sceptical. The University of Greenwich pointed out that 'the main entry point into the UK for Usenet messages is the University of Kent at Canterbury, whose policy is not to pass on messages in conferences that are overly pornographic'. Feminists Against Censorship decried the Cook Report for having created a false impression that pornographic bulletin boards based outside the UK were easily accessible by children. One bulletin board operator, remarking on the approach of the tabloid press, opined that '[i]n the sixties it was motorcyclists, and, more recently, football fans who received the journalists' vitriol. Now they have found a new target.' Significantly, of these only the comments of the University of Greenwich were published in the report.

The foundations of the UK's laws on all shades of pornography lie in the *Obscene Publications Acts* of 1959 and 1964. Under Section 1(1) of the 1959 Act:

> an article shall be deemed to be obscene if its effect or the effect of any one of its terms
> is, if taken as a whole, such as to tend to deprave and corrupt persons who are likely,
> having regard to all relevant circumstances, to read, see or hear the matter contained or
> embodied in it.

This legal definition of 'obscenity' is narrower than its normal dictionary meaning of 'repulsive, filthy, loathsome … greedy, indecent, lewd'.

Section 2(1) renders it an offence to publish an article which is obscene or to have an obscene article for publication for gain. Prior to 1994, a potential loophole lay in the definition given 'articles' by section 1(3) of the 1959 Act. This made it clear that computer disks were included. However, Internet pornography is transmitted electronically between computers via modems and telephone lines; the original images may be stored on some remote server, but in the ether of the Internet they are not transferred via any tangible medium. The problem was rectified by the 1994 *Criminal Justice and Public Order Act*, which amended the meaning of 'publication' in section 1(3) of the 1959 Act so as to include the electronic transmission—via e-mail, for instance—of pornographic material.

The ownership, possession or control of an obscene article with a view to publication for gain is an offence under section 1(2) of the 1964 *Obscene Publications Act*. As amended by the *Criminal Justice and Public Order Act 1994*, a section 1(2) offence can be committed simply by the act of making pornographic material available for electronic transfer or downloading by another party who is thus enabled to access and copy that material. Under this a commercial ISP may be liable as host of the offending material if it receives a subscription fee and by return provides access to, *inter alia*, material it has stored on its disks and has that material for possession for gain. If, however, the ISP is a 'pass-through' access provider, not hosting the obscene material itself, it should have a valid defence to such charges.

Transmission of obscene material via the Internet can also amount to an offence under the 1990 *Broadcasting Act*. This Act amends the 1959 *Obscene Publications Act* in order to extend its remit to include both live and pre-recorded 'program services'. Per section 201 of the *Broadcasting Act*, a 'program service' includes

> ... any other service which consists in the sending, by means of a telecommunications system, of sounds or visual images or both ... for reception at two or more places in the United Kingdom (whether they are so sent for simultaneous reception or at different times in response to requests made by different users of the service).

Among other things, the Act does not apply to a local delivery service or a two-way service (both as defined by the 1990 Act).

The provisions would appear to apply to activities on the Internet. Section 1(4) of the 1959 Act, as amended, provides that a person publishes an article to the extent that any matter recorded on it is included by him in a program service. A program includes any item included in that service. Section 1(5) contains provisions applying the Act to live as well as recorded material.

As regards possession offences, Schedule 15, paragraph 3 of the 1990 *Broadcasting Act* is significant. These provisions state that an obscene article in the possession, ownership or control of a person who intends to include the matter recorded on it in a relevant program is to be regarded as an obscene article had or kept by that person for publication for gain.

For both possession and publication offences it is a valid defence for the defendant to show that he had not examined the article and had no reasonable grounds for suspicion that either publication of that article or his possession of it amount to an offence under the *Obscene Publications Act*.

For inclusion in a program, the defendant must show that he did not know and had no reason to suspect that the program would include matter rendering him liable to be convicted.

Both elements must be proven for any of these defences to be valid, thus an Internet service provider (ISP) cannot just maintain a policy of non-enquiry into the content of material which it stores and transmits for its clients. Rather, the ISP must have no reasonable grounds for suspicion that that material is legally obscene. An ISP may face criminal liability under the Obscene Publications legislation for a number of reasons. For instance, liability may arise from a web site held for a specific client: if the ISP is aware of facts which should have prompted it to question the nature of material to be posted on the site. Whether an ISP may be liable for obscene material posted to a Usenet newsgroup is a matter of some debate. The issue will hinge on whether the 'explicit names' and/or reputation of a newsgroup is enough to indicate to the Usenet host the likely nature of the material posted to it. It is also conceivable that an ISP may, under certain conditions, be liable for the publication of obscene material which it does not host. For example, if an ISP provides a known publisher of obscene materials with an Internet link which (he or she then uses to make such material available via a self-hosted web site), the ISP is potentially liable for that publication. However, as Smith notes, it will be much harder for the prosecuting authority to defeat the ISP's 'innocence' defence in such a case.

Far from being the anarchic den of iniquity where pornography is uncontrolled, as the self-appointed moral guardians paint it, then, the Internet is, in fact, subject to the plethora of laws passed by the UK parliament for the control of pornography whatever the medium.

If the moral panic surrounding easy access by children to pornography was beginning to gain pace by the early to mid 1990s, the fear of the Internet as an enhanced breeding ground for paedophilic material and the associated sexual exploitation and abuse of children gave it an added impetus. Again, however, there are general statutes, updated to encompass new technologies, which prohibit such obscene material. The *Protection of Children Act* of 1978 was, at the time it was passed, a response to the growing problem of paedophilic pornography, its key aim being to eliminate loopholes in the measures available to the police and CPS. In 1994 a new loophole—the result of advanced computer technology—was plugged when the *Criminal Justice and Public Order Act* introduced the concept of a 'pseudo-photograph' to the *Protection of Children Act*. A 'pseudo-photograph' is *technically* a photograph; however, it is created by means of utilising specialist computer software to paste together an image from elements of two or more pre-existing photographs. A pornographic image of what seems to be a child may thus be artificially created without the involvement of a real child. For instance, a child's head can be superimposed onto a (naked) adult body, and body characteristics may be altered—breasts reduced, pubic hair removed—in order to render the whole more childlike. Prior to 1994, pseudo-photographs fell outside section 1 of the 1978 Act; however, as amended by the 1994 Act, the new section fills that lacuna. In *R v Bowden*, the Court of Appeal was asked to consider the limits of this amended section. The Appellant had downloaded paedophilic pictures from the Internet featuring young boys, and either printed them out or stored them on disks. One of the pictures existed only as data; all were intended solely for the appellant's own use. The Court of Appeal held that to download or print out images from the Internet was sufficient 'to make' the images, as required by the legislation; downloading or printing the images within the jurisdiction is creating new material.

Per section 160 of the 1988 *Criminal Justice Act*, the possession of an indecent photograph or pseudo-photograph of a child is a serious arrestable offence punishable by imprisonment for a maximum term not exceeding six months. This amended provision has been successfully used in several recent prosecutions for possession of child pornography.

A number of other statutes may also be utilised against Internet pornography, both child pornography and the 'normal', legal variety. The 1994 *Telecommunications Act* renders it an offence to send any grossly offensive, indecent, obscene or menacing message originating in the UK via telephone. This section encompasses data sent via telephone lines, thus including the Internet in its remit. The Act's real targets, however, are the originators of such material, and it is they rather than the ISPs who will be caught by its provision.

Per section 1(1) of the *Indecent Displays (Control) Act 1981*, it is an offence to publicly display indecent matter. As with the 1984 Act, those caught by this section are the originators—ie those making the display—and not those who cause or merely print it. The 1981 Act is primarily targeted at the control of displays in public places which persons can physically enter. By section 1(2), any matter which is displayed in public or in a manner which permits it to be visible from any public place is to be regarded as being publicly displayed. Computer terminals with Internet access in public libraries or in cybercafés could be included here. Section 1(3) allows for exemption from classification as a public place for the purposes of section 1(2) if a fee, to include payment for the display, is charged and on strict condition that persons under 18 are barred. The general provisions under section 1(1), however, are not restricted by any such qualifications. As Smith notes, section 1(1) 'could possibly apply directly to the provider of a web site accessible to the public, as opposed to a person locating the screen in public places'.

In spite of such comprehensive coverage of the Internet by both general obscenity and child protection statutes, the moral panic, boosted by such stories as '[t]he launch of the first 'cyber-brothel'' in December 1994, continued to grow. A 1995 report by the CCTA reported the views of the CCTA Open Group on Ethical Issues ('Ethics COG'). By and large these were on the libertarian side in 'the Freedom of speech versus Protection/Censorship debate'. Those who drafted the Interim Report of the Ethics COG for inclusion as Annex B5 to the CCTA report felt the need to point out that

> [t]he principal difficulty with Ethics COG at present is that it is not necessarily representative of all interested parties. Most members of the group are liberal-minded members of academic institutions ...

During July 1995, the British police force was involved in an international investigation into the activities of a paedophile ring which was utilising the Internet as a distribution medium for graphic pictures involving its preferred brand of porn. Operation Starburst identified 37 men globally and arrests were made in America, South America, the Far East, and Europe (including nine British men). Many prosecutions for simple possession offences were made in the light of information gathered during that investigation. Operation Starburst also resulted in prosecutions for a number of distribution offences, most particularly the case of *Fellows and Arnold*. Charges arising out of their involvement in an online database of paedophilic images, eighteen in total, were brought against these men under the 1978 *Protection of Children Act*, 1959 *Obscene Publications Act*, and the 1994 *Criminal Justice and Public Order Act*. Owen J, setting a legal precedent, ruled that a pornographic computer image is a photograph for the law's purposes. This ruling was upheld in the Court of Appeal by Evans LJ. Further, Evans LJ reconsidered the 1978 *Protection of Children Act*, finding that while images stored on a computer disk could not be said to constitute photographs for the purposes of that Act, any such image is 'a copy of an indecent photograph'.

Almost simultaneously with the publication of the Court of Appeal's judgment in *R v Fellows, R v Arnold,* the *Sexual Offences (Conspiracy and Incitement) Act* entered into force as of 1 October 1996. While its primary aim was to make triable in England and Wales certain offences committed abroad—specifically child sex tourism—it is also of relevance to the Internet. Per section 2(3) of that Act, any act of incitement to commit the relevant offences by means of a message—whatever the media with which it is committed—is to be regarded in law as if it had been done in England and Wales if the message has been sent from or received in that jurisdiction. '[This] should ... cover advertising on web sites, whose contents can easily be characterised as messages received by the viewers of the site.'

Rather than help to alleviate fears of an epidemic of cyber-filth, however, cases such as *Fellows and Arnold*, as well as television news coverage of Operation Starburst and other police swoops showing pictures of police retaining large quantities of computer disks and equipment, served only to widen the moral panic. In August 1996, Chief Inspector Stephen French, of the Clubs and Vice Unit of the Metropolitan Police, sent an open letter to the Internet Service

Providers Association ('ISPA'), requesting that they ban access to 134 Usenet newsgroups, 'many of which [were] deemed to contain pornographic images or explicit text'.

Approximately 55% of the newsgroups which the Clubs and Vice Unit sought to ban were primarily sites for the distribution and exchange of pictures. This police action came in the wake of a statement issued by one Mr Ian Taylor of the Department of Trade and Industry. Presumably recognising the strength of feeling against strong censorship in the Internet community with the CIEC court action against the CDA in America and growing 'Blue Ribbon' campaign, Taylor expressed an official reluctance to follow the legislative route. Referring to the embarrassing situation President Clinton found himself in over the CDA debacle (which would ultimately result in legislation which he had publicly supported being ruled unconstitutional), Taylor's statement made clear that the British government were in favour of a self-regulatory approach by the ISPs.

Following the Metropolitan Police's letter, on 25 August a tabloid style 'shock-horror' exposé of ISP company Demon Internet appeared in the *Observer*. The same paper published a self-congratulatory follow-up story in which it claimed to have prompted a Demon policy change involving the adoption of a system permitting parental control over Internet content accessed. Demon countered this article saying that it had announced this 'porn policy' as early as 20 August. Whatever the rights and wrongs of the case, such news stories served only to further entrench the (erroneous) image of the Internet as being rife with all sorts of hardcore pornography.

On 23 September 1996, the *Daily Telegraph* reported official plans for a system it dubbed 'Safety Net', to be operational as of October 1996. Designed by Peter Dawe, the co-founder and former head of the UK's first commercial ISP, Pipex, Safety Net was a response to governmental pressure upon the Internet industry to establish some form of self-regulation or be liable to be prosecuted for the distribution of illegal pornographic material. The Safety Net initiative was backed by the Home Office, the DTI, Scotland Yard, as well as the ISPA and London Internet Exchange (another representative body for the interests of ISPs). In essence, the Safety Net, now known as the Internet Watch Foundation, is based on a hotline via which commercial organisations and members of the public can report any obscene or otherwise illegal material which they encounter on the Internet. Such complaints will be verified and then brought to the attention of all UK ISPs, whose responsibility it will be to remove offending material from their pages. Removal can, at the ISP's request, be effected by an IWF 'cancelbot' which will trace the material to its source and delete it.

The Internet Watch Foundation states explicitly on its web site: 'Our first priority is child pornography.' Judging from this statement and other information given, the IWF has clearly been influenced by the concentration of the Internet censorship debate and the moral panic at its root on pornography as the chief problem online. Its policy does, however, reflect the distinction drawn by the Home Office between the illegal and the merely offensive. This is consistent with much of the argument from the freedom of speech lobby who by and large accept that certain material should be 'censored' on the basis that it is already illegal, but that the right to use 'offensive' speech must be recognised.

One advantage of the IWF scheme is that it at least begins to offer the basis of a compromise between ISPs and the police. ISPs see themselves as being akin to a postal service, merely providing a service by passing on material, remaining ignorant of its contents. The police, on the other hand, prefer to view ISPs as being more akin to publishers, irrespective of the medium, distributing material, the details of which they should be aware—'the titles of newsgroups such as alt.sex.lolita, alt.sex.babies and alt.sex.bestiality.pictures make their contents quite clear.' With the IWF, ISPs have offending material explicitly drawn to their attention, at which stage they can take appropriate measures to remove it from their networks. Through this system, then, they can begin to take the responsibility for material on their systems for which the police have argued, but without the immense burden of trying to sift through every single page submitted by its clients. There are, however, still causes of conflict if, rather than accepting this self-regulatory approach encouraged by the UK government and accepted by the ISPs, the police instead choose to pursue a more pro-active regulatory role as they did in their August 1996 request that certain newsgroups be banned.

In January 1997 the IWF was beginning to show some initial signs of success. '[A] relatively small amount' of child pornography, all of which originated without the UK, had been removed by ISPs as a result of reports from Internet users. A number of web sites with potentially illegal content, based on Japanese, Dutch and Swedish servers, were reported; police passed this information on to their counterparts in those jurisdictions. In its most recent annual report, the IWF notes its own success:

> The volume of reports received by IWF continued to increase significantly during 1999, with the total number of reports standing at over double the figure for 1998, which in turn was more than 2 1/2 times the number received in our first year of operation. 4889 reports have been processed relating to nearly 20,000 items (a single report often includes many individual items to consider).
>
> Our analysis would suggest that this increase can be attributed to growing awareness of the existence and role of the IWF as well as the general increase in the number of people online in the UK, rather than to a rise in the population of illegal material on the Internet. This remains only a tiny proportion of the vast volume of material available. For example, we now regularly monitor fewer than 20 Usenet newsgroups out of a total of more than 40,000 available.

Those Internet users who do report online material to the IWF would indeed seem to be mainly concerned with child pornography, which accounts for '[o]ver 99% of actioned reports'. Significantly, in spite of the public fears surrounding the Web, less than two per cent of actionable items concern web sites, the vast majority being found in the arcane world of Usenet newsgroups—not much frequented by children. Also worthy of note is the fact that:

> [t]he proportion of actioned items appearing to originate in the UK has decreased from about 6% in 1998 to 4% in 1999 ... most of this material appears to come from overseas: USA, 77%; Japan, 2%; Europe, 3%; other, 7%; unidentified, 7%.

A successful self-regulatory body, however, has not stemmed the moral panic surrounding cyber-pornography; if anything the panic has worsened. Since the Bulger murder and ensuing tabloid witch hunt surrounding *Child's Play III*, which spilled over into a moral panic about screen violence in general, that had been the issue at the forefront of the mainstream censorship debate. During the summer of 1996 it appeared almost mandatory that every serious investigative, news-based, documentary-type program, talk or panel discussion show on radio and television dedicate at least one edition to the debate on whether screen violence causes actual violence. Comedian Ben Elton published a novel based on the debate, echoing elements of the alleged *Natural Born Killers* 'copycat' cases, and became a ubiquitous media figure, offering his analysis on television, radio, and even in the *Sunday Times.* Eventually, however, media interest began to wane, and as the moral panic over screen violence lost its impetus, that over cyberporn was beginning to rise. In November 1997, Gary Glitter was arrested and later (5 May 1998) charged under the amended 1978 *Protection of Children Act* with 50 counts of 'making indecent pseudo-photographs' and 50 alternative offences in respect of the possession of indecent photographs of children under the age of 16. This story generated much press coverage, especially in the tabloids. Much was made of the pictures' origins, presumed to be from the Internet. This coincided with other well-covered police seizures of illegal pornographic material, mostly child pornography. Much of this was not of Internet origin, black market videocassettes smuggled through customs from countries in the Far East and Holland being among the most common. A stream of 'paedophile-priest' cases in Ireland and the UK, among others, represented a significant proportion of cases reported on. Through news reportage, especially that of the tabloid outrage variety, an impression was created in the public mind that the spread of computerised pornography, especially child pornography, was easily available to children and reaching epidemic proportions. The Internet, as the newest mass media, seemingly an unregulated information anarchy and already the subject of growing concern, bore the brunt of these 'exposés' and both sides of the mainstream of the censorship debate in the UK, already moving away from the no longer 'media sexy' screen violence issue, jumped on the bandwagon.

In late February 1998 it was announced that the UK police were considering attempting to prosecute under existing legislation ISPs who fail to block access to illegal pornographic material on the Internet. And still the shock stories continued: the Tory councillor 'sacked from positions of responsibility after admitting looking at Internet pictures of "busty women" on a council computer'; the 'convicted British child molester ... jailed after flying to the United States to meet a 15-year-old girl he had met over the Internet'; the former Tory mayor convicted of possession of paedophilic images; the 'UK Internet porn king ... [whose] sites featured extreme pornography, including bestiality and torture ... [one of which] took in up to £30,000 a week'; a computer game designer, '[o]ne of the masterminds behind sexy ... heroine Lara Croft', who was 'charged with trying to procure a nine-year-old girl for sex'. Not to mention the slew of lurid tabloid stories which once more raked over the sordid details of the Gary Glitter case upon his conviction in November 1999, his early release from prison in January 2000, when he apparently left Britain to 'begin a new life in Cuba', and his return to the UK, when '[a] mob of vigilantes threatened to attack [him]'. Never far from the headlines was a reminder that the supposed source of the paedophilic images in respect of which the former celebrity was convicted was the Internet. Many other stories, such as 'Fears for youngsters who are too trusting on Net', or 'Prostitutes target Internet lonely hearts', or 'Sex via the Net', continue to portray the Web in a negative light: it would seem that the Internet will continue to be surrounded by moral panic—at least until the next new medium arrives.

The UK government's position under both Major and Blair administrations has been characterised by seeking to police the Internet by means of a mix of self-regulation and application of the existing law to the new medium. Significantly, while, as discussed, elements of broadcasting law may be relevant to illegal pornographic Internet content, the official UK prosecution strategy has been to bring charges under the Obscene Publications legislation, as well as the 1978 *Protection of Children Act*. The OPAs of 1959 and 1965 were specifically aimed at regulating *printed* material: in adopting this approach in favour of more restrictive broadcasting controls, the CPS is following a similar path to that taken by the US Supreme Court in its ruling in *Reno*.

The UK government's approach, perhaps unusually, appears to be largely in harmony with that encouraged by the European Union. In response to calls for Internet regulation coming from within the EU in early 1996, October of that year saw the launch of a European Commission Communication Paper on 'Illegal and Harmful Content' and alongside it a Green Paper on 'the Protection of Minors and Human Dignity in Audio-visual and Information Services' in October 1996. These documents followed on the heels of a September 1996 adoption by the Telecommunications Council of Ministers of a resolution concerning dissemination of illegal material—particularly child pornography—over the Internet. The Communication laid out policy options for immediate action to be taken, while the Green Paper concerned itself with an examination of 'the challenge that society faces in ensuring that these issues of over-riding public interest are adequately taken into account in the rapidly evolving world of audio-visual and information services'. In November 1996 all of these European initiatives were adopted by a Resolution of the Telecommunications Council.

As have many governments, the EC has recognised the significance of the ISPs when it comes to regulating content of the Internet. Users cannot gain access except via an ISP—target the ISPs, then, and there is an improved chance of controlling the Internet. The Commission, however, in its communication paper, made strong criticisms of any system of regulation aimed at the level of ISPs. Such a system not only restricts access to much material which does not fall into the narrow bandwidth illegality, it also runs contrary to notions of individual freedom and other similar traditions in EC politics.

The European Scrutiny Committee's 'Child Pornography on the Internet' Second Report made further provisions in this direction. For example, Article 1 asks that EU member states encourage Internet users to report instances of child pornography, and to enable them to make such reports. It is also requested that member states ensure that law enforcement agencies react quickly to such reports; where necessary, it is suggested, specialised units within law enforcement bodies should be established in order to deal with child pornography. Article 2 makes it a requirement that member states cooperate fully with each other in the facilitation of investigations and prosecutions, including via existing channels such as Interpol, while Article 3 requires that member states, in conjunction with industry, look at both binding and voluntary measures for removing child pornography from the Internet. This document has been endorsed by the UK government.

The UK is evolving a specific strategy for dealing with illegal—mainly illegal *pornographic*—content on the Internet, but the debate is far from over. There remains a question mark over the position of ISPs, currently walking a fine line between potential statutory liability for content carried—a possibility as yet untested in UK courts—and leaving themselves open to attack from users accusing them of imposing censorship. There is a need for clarification of the law in this area, particularly in light of the fears raised by *Godfrey v Demon*. Further, there are still those who loudly demand that the government move to create new laws specifically designed to allow tight control over the medium. There are also those who refuse to countenance any form of censorship whatever. The moral panic may surround a different medium, but the essence of the debate remains unchanged.

[Footnotes omitted]

NOTES AND QUESTIONS

1 Give examples of a moral panic in your own society. Can you think of any local moral panics that have sprung from the Internet?

2 Do you think that, despite the difficulties that are obviously encountered, regulation of Internet content is essential? Provide a detailed explanation of why you consider it to be essential.

3 What is the role of outrage in legislation? Is this a positive force at work in our governments? What measures could be used to produce more considered outcomes?

4 What is your reaction to the supposed correlation between film violence and criminal violence in society? Do you think there is a danger in propagating images of violence without consequence?

5 The *Reno* decision in the USA is a watershed for Internet regulation of content across all areas. Critically analyse the influence that the US Supreme Court can exert over the shape of Internet content regulation. Why is this influence possible and why is it important? To what extent does the US Supreme Court operate as the de facto cyber court?

----

2 Reactions to Internet pornography

(a) Regulation

In order to discuss pornography we must define exactly what it is. Pornography can generally be divided into two separate categories. First, there is material aimed at adults that is illegal for adults to read or view according to the rules of a particular legal system. Second, there is material aimed at adults that is not illegal for adults to view under the legal system, but which might be harmful or disturbing for children to see, according to a society's normative values. The simplest example of the first category is child pornography. The second category is characterised by magazines such as *Playboy* and so on.

It is very difficult to guarantee that children cannot access Internet content in this second category. This is achieved in the physical world by enacting restrictions on the sale of pornography to minors. These restrictions are simply made redundant by the Internet. The question, then, is whether we regulate the content according to what is illegal for all to see—that is, child pornography and the like—or regulate all content according to what it is illegal for minors to access—that is, adult content. The corollary of the second option is that, if we restrict only material that is generally illegal, there can be no guarantee that materials deemed to have adult content will be available only to adults.

Realistically, it is almost impossible to gauge the amount of pornography that exists on the Internet. The nature of the medium makes it extremely difficult to keep an accurate record of the types of data made available.

It is generally agreed that popular perceptions of the Internet as an enormous pornographic free-for-all are quite misguided. The percentage of freely available pornographic material is actually very small. Civil libertarians then take this information and add the argument that, of this small percentage, due to the profit motives of Internet pornographers, almost all of it requires some sort of payment or password. Opponents of Internet porn take the alternative stance, arguing that access to pornographic material, on the other hand, is disproportionately high and pointing to these figures in support of greater regulation. Whatever the true state of affairs, the author used a number of search engines such as 'Yahoo' and 'Excite', entered the search term 'sex', and obtained quite a comprehensive range of pornography sites with fairly explicit nudity. Some subscriber sites even offered free access for three days.

If we assume that our society demands at least some degree of regulation of the Internet, we must next decide who is to enforce the standards we seek to apply to this new medium and who is to be penalised for a breach.

The first possibility for enforcement is to employ the apparatus of the nation state. Each nation would establish its own standards and enforce them within its own boundaries, and conceivably beyond to the extent deemed to be its legitimate scope. The difficulties in measuring Internet content create difficulties in determining the effectiveness of national regulation in controlling that same content. However, contemporary politics compel governments to perpetuate the notion that they are able to assert a degree of control over Internet content.

Whether or not national laws regulating content are actually enforceable across international borders is a difficult question. One of the most traditional responses to national regulation is that such regulation represents an attempt to force the particular standards of a regulating nation state upon the entire global community. Nevertheless, it is theoretically possible, depending on the drafting of national laws, to prosecute and punish breaches of content laws across national boundaries. However, content providers can avoid liability by carefully placing their servers within particular nations. The final answer to the question of enforcement is that it simply depends on the particular circumstances of each case. There is no guarantee that national standards can be enforced across the expanse of the Internet.

The second option for enforcement is to educate individuals, particularly parents, and corporations, particularly the ISPs, to develop an active citizenry willing to enforce the normative standards of each society. The goal here would be to protect society's vulnerable: children. The difficulties with this option are simply that, with the increasing numbers of computers throughout society, it is not possible to supervise the Internet activities of children at all times. This is particularly so in the USA, where there exist free ISPs with toll-free connection phone numbers. This means that children need not pay for their access, and therefore do not need an income to use the Internet.

There are three distinct targets for penalty when prohibiting certain Internet content:

- the originator of the content;
- the users who access the content; and
- the Internet service provider.

Measures taken against an ISP are the most controversial, especially with respect to freedom of expression. As a carrier, and a quasi-publisher, an ISP could potentially be held liable for the materials that sit on its server. ISPs are technically just gatekeepers. If they are to be held responsible for the material they let through their gates, the logical response would be to limit their exposure to risk by withdrawing any materials that might subject them to liability. This is obviously anathema to cyber libertarians, who argue that the content of the Internet should be determined by users, who in turn should be responsible for that content. To leave these decisions in the hands of ISPs is to create an undemocratic censorship regime. Legislation drafted to apply to end users and content producers may still offend principles of free speech, but at the very least this approach makes those responsible for the content liable for its illegality.

The question raised by these considerations is whether the peculiar nature of the Internet justifies new, or more intensive, regulation of Internet content than would otherwise be accepted in the material world. If the Internet presents a novel risk, then it would be reasonable to expect novel regulation. There are a number of aspects in which Internet pornography differs from the traditional kind:

- It can be infinitely copied and distributed at minimal cost.
- The quality of image does not degrade on copying.
- It is difficult for law enforcement to detect due to the size and structure of the Internet and the availability of encryption.
- It cannot be seized, in the normal sense of the term, once it has been deemed illegal because it is very easy to re-stock after a confiscation.

The present state of Internet content regulation sees numerous disparate national regulatory responses to the issues outlined herein, each operating with various successes and each with its own objectors. The materials below examine some of these national responses.

(b) A comparative analysis: USA and Singapore

Throughout this chapter it is hoped that the reader will be stimulated to look beyond the mere content of the Internet and its attendant national laws, into the substrata of values which underpin both of these things. It is by examining the various societal frameworks that we can ultimately explain the various national approaches to content. In this section we will compare the USA and Singapore, whose belief systems are quite different. In Singapore, a culture based upon the ideals of Confucianism, there is a strong emphasis on the importance of society over the individual. Sacrifices are expected for the common good and this is achieved, in part, through discipline and reverence for authority. In contrast, the USA is founded upon the ideal of rugged individualism, where if one is granted some basic but essential protections and freedoms, one can strive among equals to achieve prosperity in life. In the extract below we see two vastly different reactions to Internet content.

Joseph C Rodriguez, 'A Comparative Study of Internet Content Regulations in the United States and Singapore: The Invincibility of Cyberporn'

1. *Asian-Pacific Law and Policy Journal* 9:1

Available at <http://www.hawaii.edu/aplpj/> 17 August 2006

III. Singapore

E. SINGAPORE INTERNET POLICY AND REGULATORY FRAMEWORK

In developing Internet content regulations, Singapore had to resolve the obvious tension between its aggressive IT growth strategies that allowed colossal amounts of uncensored information into the country via the Internet and the government's traditional restrictions on media. In 1996, Singapore took an initial step by indicating it would make no legal distinction between the Internet and other types of media by shifting the responsibility for regulating the Internet from the Telecommunication Authority of Singapore to the Singapore Broadcasting Authority (SBA).

The SBA adopted the following three-pronged approach to encourage Internet development:

(a) promoting the public awareness of positive aspects and hazards of using the Internet through public education;
(b) encouraging the industry to set its own standards through industry self-regulation; and
(c) instituting a light-touch policy framework in regulating content which is regularly fine-tuned based on consultation.

Pursuant to this policy, the SBA instituted a 'light-touch policy framework' in July 1996 by establishing a Class Licensing Scheme ('licensing') and Internet Code of Practice ('Code').

Procedurally, the SBA licensing—an administrative law technique commonly utilized to regulate the media in Singapore—acts as 'an automatic licensing scheme and there is no need to obtain prior approval from the SBA'. Licensing focuses on eliminating objectionable content and targets ISPs and Internet Content Providers (ICPs). Licensing achieves control over ISPs and ICPs by establishing situations in which both must register with the SBA and by establishing content restrictions that require both to comply. The SBA content restrictions have pornography as a primary concern and also 'focus on content which may undermine public morals, political stability and religious harmony in Singapore'.

The Code provides clearer guidelines as to what is objectionable content. Also, due to a recommendation by the National Internet Advisory Committee ('NIAC'), the SBA amended the Code to provide clearer guidelines as to what is 'prohibited material'. The 1997 Amendment to the Internet Code of Practice provides:

4.

(1) Prohibited material is material that is objectionable on the grounds of public interest, public morality, public order, public security, national harmony, or is otherwise prohibited by applicable Singapore laws.

(2) In considering what is prohibited material, the following factors should be taken into account:

    (a) whether the material depicts nudity or genitalia in a manner calculated to titillate;

    (b) whether the material promotes sexual violence or sexual activity involving coercion or non-consent of any kind;

    (c) whether the material depicts a person or persons clearly engaged in explicit sexual activity;

    (d) whether the material depicts a person who is, or appears to be, under 16 years of age in sexual activity, in a sexually provocative manner or in any other offensive manner;

    (e) whether the material advocates homosexuality or lesbianism, or depicts or promotes incest, paedophilia, bestiality and necrophilia;

    (f) whether the material depicts detailed or relished acts of extreme violence or cruelty;

    (g) whether the material glorifies, incites or endorses ethnic, racial or religious hatred, strife or intolerance.

(3) A further consideration is whether the material has intrinsic medical, scientific, artistic or educational value.

(4) A licensee who is in doubt as to whether any content would be considered prohibited may refer such content to the Authority for its decision.

Notably, the Amendment specifically directs that current laws shall extend to the Internet, and the SBA has stated that '[b]y licensing content powers, SBA also reinforces the message that the laws of Singapore such as the Penal Code, *Defamation Act*, *Sedition Act* and *Maintenance of Religious Harmony Act* apply as much to communications on the Internet as they do to traditional print and broadcasting media.'

To enforce the Code, the SBA licensing framework requires that licensees, ISPs, and ICPs must use their 'best efforts' to comply with the Code and must act to ensure that nothing is included in any broadcasting service that is against 'public interest, public order or national harmony … or [which] offends against good taste or decency'.

To clarify the meaning of 'best efforts', the SBA set forth further guidelines in an attempt to clarify ambiguities surrounding the obligations and responsibilities of ISPs and ICPs. The SBA stated that ISPs are 'not required to monitor the Internet or its users. They will, however, need to limit access to only 100 high impact pornographic sites, as identified by SBA, as a statement of societal values.' Additionally, ISPs are encouraged to take their own initiative against offensive content through their own 'Acceptable Use Policies' and are encouraged to exercise judgment in which newsgroups to subscribe to and make available to their users. The Code also requires ISPs to deny access to sites that have been identified by the SBA as possessing prohibited material. Moreover, licensing requires that an ISP 'faithfully and truthfully furnish such information, and furnish such undertakings, as the [SBA] may require'.

As opposed to individuals or entities that merely act as a gateway for content, the Code is more clearly applicable to individuals or entities that produce content. Consequently, ICPs, particularly Web authors, must observe the Code. Additionally, although the SBA does not require prior approval for content, licensees are advised to consult with the SBA if they are unsure whether their content would be prohibited. Further, 'best efforts' do not require an ICP, such as a Web publisher or server administrator, to monitor the Internet or to pre-censor content, but an ICP is required to bar access to prohibited materials when directed by the SBA. If an ICP is responsible for discussions on Websites with public access, the ICP is advised to choose themes according to the Code and exercise editorial judgment accordingly.

Individuals are exempted from licensing, unless their Web pages are for commercial purposes, or to promote political or religious causes. The licensing exemption for individuals reflects the SBA's attempt to limit licensing in deference to individual privacy. To provide reassurance to the public, the SBA stated:

> SBA's purview only covers the provision of material to the public. It is not concerned with what individuals receive, whether in the privacy of their own home or at their workplace. Corporate Internet access for business use is also outside the scope of the regulations, as is private communications eg electronic mail and Internet Relay Chat (IRC).

The SBA has also announced that its Internet administrative law framework 'emphasises public education, industry self-regulation, the promotion of positive sites and minimum regulation'.

In contrast to SBA rhetoric, former Prime Minister Lee, in a brutal assessment of the Singapore population's ability to handle the free flow of information on the Internet, contended, 'The top 3 to 5 percent of a society can handle this free-for-all, this clash of ideas.' Therefore, in Lee's view, Internet censorship is required to prevent the Internet's destabilizing social and political effects.

F. IMPLEMENTATION AND ENFORCEMENT

Despite Singapore's technological prowess and the relatively small number of users and content it must regulate, censoring the Internet has proved virtually impossible for the SBA. Singapore has realized that it is unfeasible to censor the Internet in the same manner as other types of media. In recognition that 'there is a limit to what domestic legislation can achieve in the face of a global and borderless medium like the Internet', the SBA chief stated 'that it was impossible to fully regulate the Internet'.

Censoring the Internet has proved difficult despite assistance from ISPs within Singapore. The three major ISPs within Singapore, being either partially government-owned or linked to government companies, evince the SBA's considerable influence in the domestic Internet industry. These three ISPs utilize proxy servers to regulate all incoming Internet traffic and to implement the SBA's policies. The proxy servers act as filters and block access to sites the government deems objectionable. However, the effectiveness of the SBA content restrictions must be questioned when the SBA has announced it would block access to only one hundred high-impact pornographic sites, and over 28,000 cyberporn web sites existed as of 1998.

Moreover, the explosive growth of new cyberporn sites would seemingly circumvent any SBA attempts to block identifiable cyberporn sites.

The SBA has also directed the three ISPs to provide an optional Family Access Network ('FAN') to which parents can subscribe for their children. The FANs essentially empower the parents, who are unfamiliar with other methods of protection, such as filtering software, to manage how their children access the Internet. However, the effectiveness of the FANs must also be questioned when considering the difficulties in censoring the Internet via proxy servers. Moreover, by simply downloading bypass programs that are readily available on the Internet, other methods of protection such as software filters can be circumvented.

The difficulties in regulating the Internet are further compounded by the ambiguities that exist in applying the current laws and the SBA licensing to the Internet. For example, if an individual posts a libelous message against the PAP, the question remains whether both the ISP and ICP are liable. Due to these ambiguities and the Internet's young and evolving condition, the SBA and other enforcement agencies have implemented a 'light-touch approach' in enforcing current laws on the Internet and to the enforcement of its Internet regulatory framework. This means that an offender will be given a chance to rectify the violation before the SBA takes action. However, it is still unclear whether a violation of an existing law will be forgiven upon rectifying the violation. If a violation of an Internet regulation persists, the SBA has discretionary authority on how much to fine the offender and whether to revoke his license. The SBA web site proclaims that '[t]o date, SBA has not taken action against anyone for objectionable content on the Internet, as service and content providers have generally abided by the guidelines.'

Although the SBA may not have acted, Singapore Telecom reportedly shut down the web page of a seventeen-year-old who was disseminating racist jokes about Malays. Also, in a high-profile case, Singaporean Lai Chee Chuen faced seventy-seven charges of possessing obscene films, including material from the Internet. Authorities emphasized that Lai's arrest followed a tip from Interpol, which had been monitoring child pornography rings via the Internet. Regardless, individuals remain concerned about personal privacy especially when licensing specifically obligates ISPs to cooperate with authorities in any manner necessary.

Supposedly, individuals who limit their Internet activities to engaging in private communications and to receiving information, such as downloading pornographic images, are outside of the SBA's purview. However, in 1994, Singapore authorities searched public Internet accounts for graphics files usually associated with pornographic images. Of the 80,000 image files found, only five were considered pornographic by authorities ...

IV. United States

E. US INTERNET POLICY AND REGULATORY EFFORTS

In July 1997, the US government released its policy towards the Internet in a report entitled *A Framework for Global Electronic Commerce*. In establishing a 'hands-off' policy, the report emphasized that

> [t]he US government supports the broadest possible flow of information across international borders. In contrast to traditional broadcast media, the Internet promises users greater opportunity to shield themselves and their children from content they deem offensive or

inappropriate. To the extent, then, that effective filtering technology becomes available, content regulations traditionally imposed on radio and television would not need to be applied to the Internet. In fact, unnecessary regulation could cripple the growth and diversity of the Internet.

The report further explained that the US government supports industry self-regulation such as the adoption of competing ratings systems and the development of easy-to-use technical solutions, including filtering technologies and age verification systems.

Despite this 'hands-off' policy, lawmakers grew weary of waiting for the Internet industry to develop acceptable standards and introduced a flurry of new Internet-related legislation during the legislative sessions of the 105th Congress in 1998. Much of the new legislation focused on protecting children. Although existing laws, such as those dealing with child pornography and obscenity, are applicable to the Internet, the new legislation appears better suited to policing the Internet.

For example, the *Children's Online Privacy Protection Act* regulates the collection, use, and distribution of information obtained online from children under the age of thirteen. This Act prohibits the collection and dissemination of individually identifying information via notice and parental consent. Another example, the *Protection of Children from Sexual Predators Act*, adapts and strengthens existing laws protecting children from sexual predators on the Internet. Although this Act largely targets serious criminals, a significant aspect of the Act is that it makes ISPs liable as well. The Act also requires ISPs to report apparent exploitation of children involving child pornography that occurs via the ISP's servers, and prohibits ISPs from knowingly transferring obscene material to individuals who are known to be under the age of sixteen. ISPs are not required to monitor their users' content and are protected from civil liability if they act in good faith to comply with the Act.

Another Act establishing potential ISP liability is the *Digital Millennium Copyright Act*. This Act governs the liability of Internet sites and ISPs for the copyright infringement of its users. It provides a mechanism for copyright owners to force site owners and ISPs to remove infringing material. Therefore, the *Digital Millennium Copyright Act* may have a considerable, and perhaps unintended, impact on Internet pornography, as a large percentage of Internet pornography consists of images that are being sold and transferred in violation of the original copyright.

Much of the new legislation came in response to the US Supreme Court decision in *Reno v ACLU* ('*ACLU I*') that declared certain provisions of the Communications Decency Act ('CDA I') of 1996 unconstitutional. The provisions in question attempted to prohibit transmissions of 'obscene', 'indecent', or 'patently offensive' communications by means of telecommunications devices to persons under the age of eighteen by threatening civil and criminal penalties. Considering the constitutional guarantee of freedom of expression, the Supreme Court in a unanimous decision agreed with the lower court's conclusion that the statute 'sweeps more broadly than necessary and thereby chills the expression of adults' and that the terms 'patently offensive' and 'indecent' were 'inherently vague.' Therefore, although the Court found the well-being of the nation's youth important, it did not justify a content-based blanket restriction on speech and did not outweigh the importance of freedom of expression.

In the 105th Congress, legislators responded to the defeat in *ACLU I* with the *Communications Decency Act II* or *Child Online Protection Act* ('COPA'). Legislators tailored COPA to address weaknesses in CDA I. For instance, legislators 'modifie[d] the "patently offensive" language by explicitly describing the material that [wa]s harmful to minors'. Legislators also reduced the scope of COPA to cover only materials posted on the World Wide Web. Legislators further restricted COPA's scope to commercial transactions in response to another major flaw in CDA I, the mandate to use age-verification systems to prevent minors from accessing pornography.

Despite legislative efforts to tailor COPA narrowly to pass judicial scrutiny, COPA has received similar constitutional challenges from the same interest groups that challenged CDA I. As of April 1999, a US federal district court has issued a preliminary injunction that protects web site operators from prosecution in anticipation of a full trial.

The House Commerce Committee's Subcommittee on Telecommunications, Trade and Consumer Protection is also considering several other Internet Bills. Two similar Bills, the *Family Friendly Access Act* of 1997 and the *Internet Freedom and Child Protection Act* of 1997, would require ISPs to provide customers with filtering software. The *Communications Privacy and Consumer Empowerment Act* would require ISPs to provide 'parental empowerment through marketplace solutions'. The *E-Rate Policy and Child Protection Act* would require that public schools and libraries that receive federal funds for Internet services 'establish a policy with respect to access to material that is inappropriate for children'. Finally, the *Safe Schools Internet Act* of 1998 would require that public schools and libraries that receive federal funds for Internet services install blocking software.

F. IMPLEMENTATION AND ENFORCEMENT

As demonstrated by the litigation surrounding CDA I and II, enforcement of Internet regulation is being fiercely challenged on a constitutional basis. For instance, the *Child Pornography Prevention Act* ('CPPA') of 1996 has withstood a constitutional challenge in the First Circuit case of *US v Hilton*. *Hilton* involved the criminal prosecution of electronic technician David Hilton, who was charged under CPPA for allegedly possessing child pornography sent to him via the Internet. In response to Hilton's argument that CPPA was both unconstitutionally overbroad and vague, the First Circuit said that even though the Act was a content-based restriction, it was constitutional because it targeted child pornography, a category of speech not entitled to First Amendment protection. Therefore, *Hilton* illustrates that child pornography does not enjoy the constitutional protections given to the freedom of expression.

Aside from regulations protecting children, the Internet has been left largely unregulated by the US. Additionally, as the Internet is not supervised by any specific federal agency and the government has adopted a 'hands-off' policy, only the threat of future regulations by lawmakers encourages the development of self-regulation. Therefore, being unable to develop acceptable content restrictions, the government must wait for industry to suggest legislative proposals on how to address the difficult issue of regulating the Internet ...

V. Analysis

A. DIFFERENCES IN THE INTERNET CONTENT REGULATIONS IN THE US AND SINGAPORE ILLUSTRATE A FUNDAMENTAL DIFFERENCE IN THE ROLE OF THE INDIVIDUAL IN THE TWO NATIONS

The differences between the US and Singapore Internet content regulations demonstrate that the individual plays a more subordinate role in Singapore society than in US society.

That is, individual rights are more subordinate to government interests in Singapore than in the US. Analytically, this lower regard for individual rights becomes apparent when examining the type of treatment given to individual rights in relation to community interests, the type of constitutional rights granted to individuals, and the type of protection given to an individual's constitutional rights. Moreover, by considering differences in the ideology and in the socioeconomic and political conditions influencing the development of the role of the individual in the US and Singapore, one gains a better understanding of the differences between the two nations' Internet content regulations.

For example, the different treatment given to individual rights in relation to community interests can be traced to the conflicting ideologies of the two societies: a classic confrontation between the values espoused by Confucianism and by Western liberal democracy. In the US, the individual is seen as the cornerstone of society. In the US capitalist system, the individual is not only allowed but also encouraged to pursue her interests in the free market. Moreover, US liberalism emphasizes a limited government that frees individuals to pursue their interests. Accordingly, the importance given to the preservation of individual rights limits the government's authority in US society.

In stark contrast, individual rights did not even exist in Confucianism. Individual rights were immaterial since Confucianism assumed a harmony of interests between the community and the individual. However, because of the development of individual rights in modern Singapore, the difference in treatment of individual rights in the US and Singapore is no longer as distinct and is now one of degree. That is, if a conflict existed between community interests and the exercise of an individual's rights, Singapore would be more likely to subvert the individual's rights because of Singapore's greater emphasis on social harmony and group interests.

This different treatment of individual rights in the US and Singapore led to the development of different constitutional rights in the respective nations. In each nation, its constitution explicitly protects the freedom of speech, assembly, and religion. Additionally, although not explicit in the US constitution, both nations also protect the freedom of expression and of association. However, because of the perceived role of the press in aggravating social tensions, Singapore excluded the freedom of the press from its Constitution. In contrast, the US constitutional grant of freedom of the press acts as a crucial safeguard against the US government, making the government accountable to the people.

The different treatment of individual rights also affects the type of protection given to an individual's constitutional rights, explaining how these nearly identical sets of core constitutional rights can offer different protections in the two nations. Moreover, the different constitutional protections also explain some of the differences in the two nations' Internet content regulations.

The regulation of pornographic content in the respective nations offers a prime example of the effect of different constitutional protections on Internet content regulations. In the US, the concept of checks and balances acts in accordance with the Bill of Rights to protect individual interests, while 'government in the Confucian tradition "was established on trust and not distrust, on ethical foundations and not checks and balances." ' The importance of this difference is illustrated by the US Supreme Court's display of its powers of judicial review in *ACLU I*, demonstrating the US legislature's accountability to the judiciary branch when violating individual interests. In voiding the statute on a constitutional basis, the Court concluded that the statute was too vague to regulate the content of speech.

Unlike the US, Singapore's rather broad and vague definitions of pornography remain intact. Even though an avenue exists for constitutional challenges in Singapore, Chinese traditionally disfavor litigation, especially litigation involving authority figures. Thus, individuals or groups are unlikely to challenge governmental policies or regulations. Even if one overcomes the traditional deference to authority, Singapore's self-restrained judiciary seems unwilling to play the role of protector of individual interests. Moreover, Singapore's history indicates that criticizing or challenging the supreme legislative power of the Singapore Parliament is unwise. Consequently, Singaporeans have essentially no realistic method of preventing the government from interfering with their constitutional rights.

The lack of effective safeguards for constitutional rights in Singapore has not only allowed the censoring of pornographic content but has also allowed the censoring of a broad range of content. Moreover, if one accepts the premise that the Constitution of Singapore only subordinates individual rights if community interests are involved, the justification for the wide array of content regulations can be discovered in the underlying socioeconomic and political factors influencing Singaporean society.

A primary influence on the social harmony of the Singapore community is the bloody ethnic violence and social tensions that Singapore has experienced since its independence in 1959. Even today, disruptive socioeconomic conditions exist because of differences in language, color, religion, and culture. These largely ethnic and religious tensions exist internally, in Singapore's diverse community, and externally, with Singapore's Malay-Muslim neighbors.

Because of these tensions, Singapore prohibits Internet content that incites ethnic, racial, or religious strife. Religious content is closely monitored as groups or individuals that want to promote religious causes or that want to discuss religion online must register with the SBA. Further, ICPs are strongly advised to choose discussion themes that do not cause ethnic, racial, or religious upheaval and to exercise editorial judgment accordingly.

In the US, the importance of individual rights has translated into more stringent constitutional protections, preventing the censoring of ethnic, religious, or racial content. Moreover, the freedom of expression has protected almost all types of Internet content from censorship in the US, a nation not unfamiliar with ethnic, racial, or religious conflict itself. Only child pornography has overcome the constitutional protections so far, and the failed attempts at censoring other types of content on the Internet emphasize the difficulty in interfering with an individual's freedom of expression in the US

Unlike the US, Singapore's lesser constitutional protections have allowed considerable interference with Singaporeans' freedom of expression on the Internet. These lesser constitutional protections have allowed the development of a massive administrative law framework that uses broad definitions of 'prohibited material' to censor the Internet. Thus, in contrast to US censorship in the one narrowly defined area of child pornography, Singapore's broad definitions serve to inhibit individuals in virtually all areas of content development. This is a classic illustration of the difference in Internet content regulations caused by the different role of the individual in the US and Singapore.

B. DIFFERENCES IN THE INTERNET CONTENT REGULATIONS ILLUSTRATE A FUNDAMENTAL DIFFERENCE IN THE ROLE OF LAW IN THE US AND SINGAPORE

The differences between the Internet content regulations of Singapore and those of the US also demonstrate that Singapore takes a more instrumentalist approach to the role of law than the US. That is, in relation to the US, Singapore uses law more to protect and serve government interests than to protect individual interests. These differences in the role of law can also be traced to differences in ideology and in political structure of the two nations.

In Singapore, the 'rule by law' approach is rooted in classical Chinese philosophy. In addition to a strong ideological basis, the super-parliamentary structure and lack of effective constitutional protections further contribute to creating an environment conducive to law being used in an instrumentalist fashion. Accordingly, a long history of the government's use of various laws as a means of social control, such as subduing the political opposition and employing social engineering, exists in Singapore. Moreover, a long history of social control via censorship of all types of media exists. Therefore, the existence of a broad administrative law framework to censor the Internet is but another example of Singapore taking an instrumentalist approach to the role of law.

In contrast, individualism and liberalism heavily influenced the US, explaining the distinctive role of law in the US, ie, the protection of individual interests. With such a focus on protecting the individual, the protection of children and the prevention of child pornography on the Internet can be expected. However, when adults are concerned, the importance of maintaining a free exchange of ideas outweighs the ill effects of pornography. Moreover, unlike Singapore, the US distinguishes the Internet from other forms of media, taking into consideration that the Internet offers users greater opportunity to shield themselves from content they find offensive or inappropriate. Consequently, the US 'hands-off' policy merely reflects an ideology where individuals are free to pursue their own interests in a society with minimal government intervention.

The differences in the role of law in the two nations are further demonstrated by the censoring of political content by Singapore. Administrative law has traditionally been used as a tool to subdue the PAP's political opposition in Singapore. Accordingly, the presence of regulations targeting political discussion on the Internet is a clear example of Singapore's 'rule by law' approach in its Internet regulations.

In the US, the guarantee of freedom of speech prevents government interference with an individual's right to engage in political debate on the Internet. The traditional Western democracy embraces 'ideologies of oppositions', such as opposition politics and the value of protest. Therefore, political pluralism, the voicing of different viewpoints and opinions from different political groups, is encouraged and accepted as part of the policy-making process. Accordingly, the role of political pluralism is illustrated by the uniting of several Internet interest groups who combat government regulations and who, so far, have been successful in doing so. Consequently, the absence of any US legislation regulating political content on the Internet is indicative of the US ideology of opposition, another example of the difference in Internet content regulations due to the different role of law in the US and Singapore.

VI. Conclusion

In attempting to predict the future of Internet regulation, two important considerations contribute to the fact that the US is unlikely to relinquish dominion over the Internet: the US's dominant Internet presence and the US government's continued investment in the Internet. Therefore, although the Internet is purportedly universal, the US will foreseeably be the dominant content provider. Thus, any content regulation necessitates the cooperation of the US government and the US Internet industry.

Consequently, only two realistic options remain for Internet regulation: (1) acceptance of US Internet policy or (2) rejection of US Internet policy. Admittedly, this dichotomy is overly simplistic and the majority of nations will choose the latter category and attempt to enact their own brand of Internet regulation. However, as Singapore's efforts have demonstrated, one country cannot effectively censor the Internet—no matter how technologically advanced. Nevertheless, national Internet regulation would entail (1) the regulation of ISPs and ICPs within the nation's jurisdiction and (2) the use of technology to filter the Internet. As policing the nation's ISPs and ICPs is an ineffective way of controlling content because of the dominance of the US Internet industry as well as the content produced by other foreign nations, the role of new technologies is increasingly important.

Unfortunately, for those countries seeking to enact their own brand of regulation, Singapore's attempt at regulation demonstrates that the technology does not yet exist, and it is impossible to filter the Internet. The task of filtering is made more difficult by evolving technology that circumvents filters and by increasing bandwidth that allows greater flows of information. Therefore, unless a nation takes the drastic step of blocking all foreign Websites and essentially creating a national Intranet, a grudging acceptance of US Internet policy is in order.

For US Internet policy, the legislative trend indicates that US ISPs will be gaining more responsibility and legal liability. As in Singapore, the protection of children is an area where US legislation is placing more responsibility on ISPs. The current and pending legislation in the US appears focused on providing some layer of protection for the child such as filtering software or other blocking technologies. The Singapore equivalent would be the Family Access Networks that utilize proxy servers to ban objectionable content. Therefore, although Singapore will likely prohibit a broader range of material from reaching the child's viewing screen, a clear trend is emerging wherein ISPs will, at the minimum, be required to make available some form of filtering or blocking technology to the parent. For us adults, we must bear the task of choosing what content we can and cannot tolerate.

[Footnotes omitted]

 # NOTES AND QUESTIONS

1   Critically analyse the arguments for and against the regulation of Internet content. Examine the pros and cons of both sides. Is one argument stronger than the other? Consider all the materials in this chapter, above and below, in your answer.

2   The Singapore Broadcasting Authority was merged with the Films and Publications Department, and the Singapore Film Commission (SFC) on 1 January 2003 to

form the Media Development Authority. This was in response to the convergence of different media that required a consistent approach in developing and managing the different forms of media. What physical advantages does Singapore hold in its attempts to control Internet content? How successful have its regulatory attempts been thus far?

3 To what extent is the rhetoric of child protection used to cloak general moral conservatism?

4 Question 5 at the end of Section 1 (above) posed a question regarding the place of the US Supreme Court in Internet regulation. Reconsider your answer to that question in light of the conclusions reached by Rodriguez above. Is there a danger of intellectual and cultural imperialism stemming from American domination of the Internet and its content? Is there an alternative to this situation?

5 The saga of Nazi memorabilia being auctioned on Yahoo! sites mentioned in Chapter 2 is a classic example of local sensitivities extending into the global Internet. Jurisdictional issues aside, should one nation regulate content originating from it that offends another nation?

----

3   Regulation in Australia

(a)   *Broadcasting Services Act* provisions

Australia has taken a different regulatory approach. At the Commonwealth level, the government has enacted the *Broadcasting Services Amendment (Online Services) Act 1999*. This Act has generated a huge amount of criticism, especially regarding its restrictive effect on freedom of speech. The provisions of the amendment Act are now incorporated into Schedule 5 of the *Broadcasting Services Act 1992* (Cth).

According to subsection 3(1)(k),(l), and (m), the amendments were intended

> to provide a means for addressing complaints about certain Internet content; and to restrict access to certain Internet content that is likely to cause offence to a reasonable adult; and to protect children from exposure to Internet content that is unsuitable for children.

In Australia, the content of many publications has long been restricted, and although this occasionally leads to objections to the classification or restriction of access to a particular piece of work, protest over the censorship regime generally is quite unusual. By contrast, the topic of net censorship has often generated a huge outcry.

The stated intent of the amendments is to only censor on-line what would be subject to censorship off-line, and in a method commensurate with the regulation of other media. Nevertheless, many believe that the effect of the Act is potentially much more damaging than this. It has been argued that provisions will:

1 stifle Internet development;
2 introduce anti-information politics to the currently anarchic Internet;

3   not work for technical reasons;

4   hinder the exploitation of commercial opportunities;

5   introduce political censorship through the introduction of politicised filtering software;

6   breach privacy principles;

7   lead to an unacceptable degree of censorship or to collateral damage;

8   put Australia out of step with the global information community.

Prior to the commencement of the provisions, some critics accused the government of lacking any appreciation of the social value of the Internet. They condemned the legislation as destroying the Internet's anarchic and non-hierarchical nature and preventing it from being the information-rich resource it is.

The Act is intended to operate through a system of co-regulation, whereby the Australian Communications and Media Authority (ACMA), formerly the Australian Broadcasting Authority investigates and makes decisions about Internet content, and industry bodies develop codes or standards which specify the technical aspects of how those decisions are to be applied.

Broadcasting Services Act 1992 (Cth) as Amended

Schedule 5: Online services

13. CLASSIFICATION OF INTERNET CONTENT THAT DOES NOT CONSIST OF A FILM OR A COMPUTER GAME

If Internet content does not consist of:

(a) the entire unmodified contents of a film; or

(b) a computer game;

the Classification Board is to classify the Internet content under this Schedule in a corresponding way to the way in which a film would be classified under the *Classification (Publications, Films and Computer Games) Act 1995*.

Division 1: Making of complaints to the ACMA

22. COMPLAINTS ABOUT PROHIBITED CONTENT OR POTENTIAL PROHIBITED CONTENT

COMPLAINTS ABOUT ACCESS TO PROHIBITED CONTENT OR POTENTIAL PROHIBITED CONTENT

(1) If a person has reason to believe that end-users in Australia can access prohibited content or potential prohibited content using an Internet carriage service, the person may make a complaint to the ACMA about the matter.

COMPLAINTS RELATING TO INTERNET CONTENT HOSTS

(2) If a person has reason to believe that an Internet content host is:

    (a) hosting prohibited content in Australia; or

    (b) hosting potential prohibited content in Australia;

       the person may make a complaint to the ACMA about the matter ...

26. INVESTIGATION OF COMPLAINTS BY THE ACMA

(1) The ACMA must investigate a complaint under Division 1.

(2) However, the ACMA need not investigate the complaint if:

    (a) the ACMA is satisfied that the complaint is:

       (i) frivolous; or

       (ii) vexatious; or

       (iii) not made in good faith; or

    (b) the ACMA has reason to believe that the complaint was made for the purpose, or for purposes that include the purpose, of frustrating or undermining the effective administration of this Schedule.

(3) The ACMA must notify the complainant of the results of such an investigation.

(4) The ACMA may terminate such an investigation if it is of the opinion that it does not have sufficient information to conclude the investigation.

 NOTES AND QUESTIONS

1   The complaints mechanism outlined in section 26 is the backbone of the regulatory regime. It provides the system with the apparatus to investigate and act upon complaints from any sector of the community. Under s 27, the ACMA may also investigate material of its own volition. What does this indicate to you about the role of the ACMA?

2   Read s 22 carefully. At whom is the regulation targeted? Why? Is that appropriate?

3   'Internet content' is defined as information that is accessed or available for access over the Internet but excludes 'ordinary electronic mail'. The Act does not provide much guidance on what 'ordinary electronic mail' is, apart from saying that it does not include a posting to a newsgroup. What is the significance of this?

Where the ACMA identifies Internet material which is, or would likely be classified R, X, or RC, the action to be taken by the ACMA depends on whether the material is hosted in Australia or is hosted overseas.

Broadcasting Services Act 1992 (Cth) as Amended, Schedule 5: Online Services

Division 3: Action to be taken in relation to a complaint about prohibited content hosted in Australia

30. ACTION TO BE TAKEN IN RELATION TO A COMPLAINT ABOUT PROHIBITED CONTENT HOSTED IN AUSTRALIA

PROHIBITED CONTENT

(1) If, in the course of an investigation under Division 2, the ACMA is satisfied that Internet content hosted in Australia is prohibited content, the ACMA must give the relevant Internet content host a written notice (a *final take-down notice*) directing the Internet content host not to host the prohibited content.

POTENTIAL PROHIBITED CONTENT

(2) The following provisions have effect if, in the course of an investigation under Division 2, the ACMA is satisfied that Internet content hosted in Australia is potential prohibited content:

   (a) if the ACMA is satisfied that, if the Internet content were to be classified by the Classification Board, there is a substantial likelihood that the Internet content would be classified RC or X 18+—the ACMA must:
       (i)   give the relevant Internet content host a written notice (an *interim take-down notice*) directing the Internet content host not to host the Internet content until the ACMA notifies the host under subclause (4) of the Classification Board's classification of the Internet content; and
       (ii) request the Classification Board to classify the Internet content;
   (b) if the ACMA is satisfied that, if the Internet content were to be classified by the Classification Board, there is a substantial likelihood that the Internet content would be classified R 18+— the ACMA must request the Classification Board to classify the Internet content.

(3) If the Classification Board receives a request under paragraph (2)(a) or (b) to classify particular Internet content, the Classification Board must:

   (a) classify the content; and
   (b) inform the ACMA, in writing, of its classification.

(4) If the ACMA is informed under paragraph (3)(b) of the classification of particular Internet content, the ACMA must:

   (a) give the relevant Internet content host a written notice setting out the classification; and

(b) in a case where the effect of the classification is that the Internet content is prohibited content—give the Internet content host a written notice (a *final take-down notice*) directing the host not to host the prohibited content.

(5) If the ACMA requests the Classification Board to classify particular Internet content:

(a) the ACMA must give the Classification Board:
   (i) sufficient information about the content to enable the Classification Board to access the content; or
   (ii) a copy of the content; and
(b) the ACMA must give the Classification Board sufficient information about the content to enable the Classification Board to classify the content; and
(c) the ACMA may, at the request of the Classification Board or on its own initiative, give the Classification Board additional information about the content if the ACMA is of the opinion that the additional information would be likely to facilitate the classification of the content.

(6) If the ACMA makes a decision under paragraph (2)(b) to request the Classification Board to classify Internet content, the ACMA must give the relevant Internet content host a written notice setting out the decision.

Division 4: Action to be taken in relation to a complaint about prohibited content hosted outside Australia

40. ACTION TO BE TAKEN IN RELATION TO A COMPLAINT ABOUT PROHIBITED CONTENT HOSTED OUTSIDE AUSTRALIA

(1) If, in the course of an investigation under Division 2, the ACMA is satisfied that Internet content hosted outside Australia is prohibited content or potential prohibited content, the ACMA must:

(a) if the ACMA considers the content is of a sufficiently serious nature to warrant referral to a law enforcement agency (whether in or outside Australia)—notify the content to:
   (i) a member of an Australian police force; or
   (ii) if there is an arrangement between the ACMA and the chief (however described) of an Australian police force under which the ACMA is authorised to notify the content to another person or body (whether in or outside Australia)—that other person or body; and
(b) if a code registered, or standard determined, under Part 5 of this Schedule deals with the matters referred to in subclause 60(2)—notify the content to Internet service providers under the designated notification scheme set out in the code or standard, as the case may be; and
(c) if paragraph (b) does not apply—give each Internet service provider known to the ACMA a written notice (a standard access-prevention notice) directing the provider to take all reasonable steps to prevent end-users from accessing the content.

(2) For the purposes of paragraph (1)(c), in determining whether particular steps are reasonable, regard must be had to:

(a) the technical and commercial feasibility of taking the steps; and

(b) the matters set out in subsection 4(3).

(3) Subclause (2) does not, by implication, limit the matters to which regard must be had.

RECOGNISED ALTERNATIVE ACCESS-PREVENTION ARRANGEMENTS

(4) An Internet service provider is not required to comply with a standard access-prevention notice in relation to a particular end-user if access by the end-user is subject to a recognised alternative access-prevention arrangement (as defined by subclause (5)) that is applicable to the end-user.

(5) The ACMA may, by written instrument, declare that a specified arrangement is a recognised alternative access-prevention arrangement for the purposes of the application of this Division to one or more specified end-users if the ACMA is satisfied that the arrangement is likely to provide a reasonably effective means of preventing access by those end-users to prohibited content and potential prohibited content.

(6) The following are examples of arrangements that could be declared to be recognised alternative access-prevention arrangements under subclause (5):

(a) an arrangement that involves the use of regularly updated Internet content filtering software;

(b) an arrangement that involves the use of a 'family-friendly' filtered Internet carriage service.

(7) An instrument under subclause (5) is a disallowable instrument for the purposes of section 46A of the *Acts Interpretation Act 1901*.

REFERRAL TO LAW ENFORCEMENT AGENCY

(8) The manner in which Internet content may be notified under paragraph (1)(a) to a member of an Australian police force includes (but is not limited to) a manner ascertained in accordance with an arrangement between the ACMA and the chief (however described) of the police force concerned.

(9) If a member of an Australian police force is notified of particular Internet content under this clause, the member may notify the content to a member of another law enforcement agency (whether in or outside Australia).

(10) This clause does not, by implication, limit the ACMA's powers to refer other matters to a member of an Australian police force.

 NOTES AND QUESTIONS

1   What kinds of materials are not subject to interim take-down orders?

2   What is the procedure if content is rated X or RC and is hosted outside Australia? Since the legislation has been in force, an industry code has always been registered. See the Internet Industry Association's website for the most current code (<http://www.iia.net.au/).

3   Most of the Internet service provider obligations can be backed up by monetary fines under clause 83(4).

4   Under clause 80, the ACMA may make written determinations setting out rules that apply to Internet service providers and Internet content hosts. These determinations have the force of law of themselves, and any failure to comply with an on-line provider determination will be an offence.

5   The word 'host' is not defined in the legislation. Would it apply to materials 'hosted' in transit via a server for the purpose of enabling that transit? What about the creation of a cache?

6   A number of arguments against the technical feasibility of the measures prescribed by the Act were put to the government by stakeholders. However, the fundamental objection is simply that the Act is wrong in principle. Earlier in this chapter the three target options for content liability were outlined—content provider, content accessor, Internet service provider—and it was noted that the last of these was the most controversial. The Act imposes liability for content upon the carrier. Carrier liability introduces significant compliance costs at the wrong point in the distribution chain. Putting this into a real-world context highlights the problems. An analogy might be that the Post Office should be liable for policing access to inappropriate content sent through the post. First, the Post Office would need to inspect all articles passing through its system. To perform this function, it would need to acquire expertise irrelevant to its core function (the delivery of mail) and incur compliance costs in effecting the content review. This would have a detrimental impact on its ability to perform its core function efficiently. Costs would then rise and performance would drop. Businesses that used the Post Office would in turn become less efficient.

7   It is also not at all clear what relationship Internet content bears to broadcasting services, or to the *Broadcasting Services Act 1992* to which it has been added as an amendment. There are strong grounds for regarding broadcasting and the Internet as antonymous. Make a list of the characteristics of the broadcast media and of the Internet media. Are the infrastructures or the content selection procedures similar?

8   One of the major criticisms of the Act is that it restricts freedom of speech, and some American civil libertarians have criticised the Act's free speech implications. Unfortunately, however, many of those who criticise the legislation on these grounds have little appreciation of how different Australian law is from US law in terms of protection for freedom of speech. Australia has no explicitly guaranteed freedom of speech such as that enshrined in the US Constitution, although the High Court has indicated that there is implied protection for political communication in the Constitution—so these criticisms can only really apply to the extent that Internet content is political.

9   It was originally intended that each of the States and Territories would pass uniform legislation mirroring the Federal position. However, this has not occurred. Only New South Wales and South Australia have made any movements towards such model legislation. No doubt the resistance stems from the objections

raised by civil libertarian groups to the Federal scheme. The Electronic Frontiers Australia (EFA) has been very active in this area and their website provides a rich source of information and critique, see further <http://www.efa.org.au/Issues/Censor/cens1.html>. In March 2006, the Labor Party announced that a Labor Government would introduce a plan requiring mandatory Internet filtering; this too has been heavily criticised by the EFA.

10 There are numerous pieces of legislation in the various Australian jurisdictions that touch and concern Internet content regulation and some of these are embedded in general content regulation statutes. They include *Interactive Gambling (Moratorium) Act 2000* (Cth); *Crimes Legislation Amendment (Telecommunications Offences and Other Measures) Act (No 2) 2004* (Cth); *Adoption Act 2000* (NSW) s 179; *Classification (Publications, Films And Computer Games) Act 2001* (NSW) Part 5A; *Unlawful Gambling Act 1998* (NSW) s 8; *Classification (Publications, Films And Computer Games) Act 1995* (Vic) Part 6; *Classification (Publications, Films And Computer Games) Act 1995* (SA) Part 7A; *Betting Control Act 1954* (WA) s 27A.

11 It should be noted that while the focus in this chapter is on Internet content regulation, much content is accessible nowadays on mobile phones. Some of this content is available through the Internet technology available on the phones but the content can equally be available through SMS and MMS. Regardless, they raise the same content regulation issues as the Internet and other forms of media.

(b) Criminal law provisions

The material in the previous chapter on the criminal provisions concerning, *inter alia*, the use of a carriage service to access, transmit or publish child pornography, child abuse material or to procure or groom under-aged persons is also relevant to the issue of Internet content regulation. The legislature has made a decision to regulate objectionable content through criminalising the conduct. In addition to these, as already noted, there are provisions relating to Internet service providers and Internet content hosts as well as suicide related material that require discussion.

Section 474.25 of the *Criminal Code* is entitled 'Obligations of Internet service providers and Internet content hosts' (ISP and ICH) and, given this specificity, obviously deals solely with the Internet. The provision applies where a person is either an ISP or a ICH, is aware that the service provided can be used to access particular material, and has reasonable grounds to believe material provided is either child pornography or child abuse material. An ISP or ICH who does not provide details of the material to the Australian Federal Police within a reasonable period of time after becoming aware of its existence commits an offence. Punishment for a failure to report such material is 100 penalty units. This equates to approximately AUS$11,000.

It is certainly important that there be a burden on Internet service providers and content hosts to be on the alert for this type of material. However, it is arguable that too high a burden is placed on ISPs and ICHs. In its *Cybercrime* report, the Parliamentary Joint Committee on the Australian Crime Commission noted in several contexts the problems with placing the burden on Internet service providers and Internet content hosts. One of the major criticisms was that these service providers are not licensed, and any person can be established as an ISP.[1] Therefore, this provision can be seen as an attempt to expose ISPs and ICHs to potential criminal liability for at least one type of Internet crime. The fact that these types of materials have been criminalised implies that other types of material are not as offensive. Certainly, there is a difference, for example, between child pornography and general pornography involving persons of legal age. However, other material—even material that has a criminal connection—does not receive the same treatment as child pornography or child abuse material. For example, no similarly specific provision under the *Criminal Code Amendment (Suicide Related Material Offences) Act 2005* (Cth) places the same criminal liability on an ISP or ICH for being aware of suicide-related material that is accessible through their service or that they are hosting (see below). This is not to devalue the seriousness of child pornography or child abuse offences, but merely to highlight the peculiarity of criminalising one form of activity for ISPs and ICHs but not another. Arguably, however, an ISP or ICH may still be caught under a provision of Division 474 Subdivision C if the person is an ISP or ICH and the conduct in question does not relate solely to the person's capacity as an ISP or ICH.[2]

In the Second Reading Speech to the Criminal Code Amendment (Suicide Related Material Offences) Bill 2005, the Attorney General said:

> There is a real need to protect vulnerable individuals from people who use the Internet with destructive intent to counsel or incite others to take their own lives. The Internet contains readily accessible sites and chat rooms that positively advocate suicide and discourage individuals from seeking psychiatric or other help. Many of these sites also provide explicit instructions on methods of committing suicide. There have been instances where Internet chat rooms have been used by a person, or even a group of persons, to urge another to commit suicide. Recent studies have shown that in some cases such Internet chat room discussions have led to a person attempting suicide, and sometimes successfully.[3]

The provisions introduced by the *Criminal Code Amendment (Suicide Related Material Offences) Act 2005* were originally included in the *Crimes Legislation Amendment (Telecommunications) Bill*. However, the Federal Government instead chose to introduce these provisions separately. This Act amends the *Criminal Code* by introducing a number of new offences based on the use of a carriage service in order to counsel or incite suicide, or promote a particular method of suicide.

---

1   Parliamentary Joint Committee on the Australian Crime Commission, Parliament of Australia, *Cybercrime* (2004) [2.58].
2   Subsection 474.13(c) deals with Internet service providers; Subsection 474.13(d) deals with Internet content hosts.
3   The Hon Philip Ruddock MP, Attorney General in Senate Legal and Constitutional Legislation Committee, Parliament of Australia, *Provisions of the Crimes Legislation Amendment (Telecommunications Offences and Other Measures) Bill No 2 2004* (2004) [3.2].

The Act itself is relatively short and introduces into the *Criminal Code Act* two provisions: s 474.29A, entitled 'Using a carriage service for suicide related material', and s 474.29B, 'Possessing, controlling, producing, supplying or obtaining suicide related material for use through a carriage service.'

Section 474.29A sets out two main offences. Pursuant to s 474.29A(1), a person is guilty of an offence if the person uses a carriage service to access material, make material available, transmit, publish or otherwise distribute material, and the material counsels or incites committing or attempting to commit suicide, and the person intended that material to counsel or incite suicide. The penalty for such an offence is 1000 penalty units, equating to approximately $110,000 for an individual or $550,000 for a corporation. However, s 474.29A(3) explicitly provides that it is not an offence to use a carriage service to engage in discussion about euthanasia or suicide, or advocate law reform in these areas. This is providing the person does not intend the material concerned to either counsel or incite suicide or to be used by another person for those purposes.

Section 474.29A(2) states that it is an offence to use a carriage service to access material, transmit material, make material available, publish or otherwise distribute material if the material promotes a particular method of or provides instruction on a particular method of suicide and it was intended that material would have that effect. The penalty for this offence is again 1000 penalty units. Consider this example: Professor X, a well known scientific academic who advocates euthanasia and intends her materials to be used by those considering suicide, publishes a paper on an Internet site titled 'Euthanasia: Your Choice, Your Right' that discusses common medications and suicide. She includes in her paper a statistical graph that shows drug Y, an over-the-counter painkiller, to be the most effective medication for suicide. It is arguable, given the wording of s 474.29A(2), that this provision would be infringed, given she included that material and it indirectly promoted a particular method of suicide.

Further, s 474.29A(4) states, similar to s 474.29A(3), that it is not an offence to use a carriage service to engage in discussion about euthanasia, suicide or law reform providing the material concerned was not intended to promote a particular method or instruct on a method of suicide.

Section 474.29B deals with the possession and supplying suicide related material for use through a carriage service. Under Section 474.29B, it is an offence to possess, control, produce, supply or obtain material that counsels, incites, promotes a particular method of, or provides instruction in, committing or attempting to commit suicide, and there is the intent the material be used to commit an offence against s 474.29A. The penalty for this offence is again 1000 penalty units. Section 474.29B(2) provides subsection (1) will be infringed even if the offence against s 474.29A is impossible, while s 474.29B(3) provides it is not an offence to attempt to commit an offence against s 474.29B(1). As the sections sit within Part 10.6 of the *Criminal Code*, extended geographical jurisdiction applies to the provisions.

Although the term 'carriage service' encompasses a wide variety of technological mediums, it is undeniable that the provisions of this Act were crafted with the Internet in mind. As the Senate Legal and Constitutional Legislation Committee noted in its report on its inquiry into the Bill, the Act was 'more a reaction in part to perceived community concern over the risks posed by the Internet.'[4] However, as noted in a number of submissions to the Committee, 'the premise of the Bill in specifically targeting the Internet was incorrect as the rate of suicide in Australia has decreased since the Internet became publicly accessible in 1994.'[5] Electronic Frontiers Australia also argued that it is 'extremely unlikely that criminalising use of the Internet to access, and/or make available, the subject material will make the slightest difference to the incidence of suicide in Australia.'[6]

Further, there is also the issue, which the Committee noted, that the provisions would not and could not 'prevent Australians from accessing suicide related material or chat rooms on websites hosted outside Australia.'[7] As Irene Graham from Electronic Frontiers Australia noted, 'this bill will not stop the amount of information that is on the Internet on overseas sites. To the best of my knowledge, there is no way that any ISP can block access to material on international sites short of the development of the great Australian firewall.'[8]

----

4   Concluding remarks

In this chapter and the previous chapter, we have seen the legislative result when off-line standards and analogies are used to appease the moral panic of sections of a population. We have seen the development of schemes that are only mildly effective, and heavily criticised. It is evident that confusion still abounds in the minds of regulators as to the most effective method for regulating the Internet. Nevertheless, the body of regulation on the Internet continues to grow. Sadly, some of the regulation is finding place in the criminal law books.

---

4   Senate Legal and Constitutional Legislation Committee, Parliament of Australia, Provisions of the *Criminal Code Amendment (Suicide Related Material Offences) Bill 2005* (2005) [3.4].

5   Ibid [3.8].

6   Ibid.

7   Ibid [3.17].

8   Irene Graham in Senate Legal and Constitutional Legislation Committee, Parliament of Australia, Provisions of the *Criminal Code Amendment (Suicide Related Material Offences) Bill 2005* (2005) [3.17].

Copyright on the Internet

---

1 Introduction

The Internet presents enormous opportunities for artistic and literary creation and re-creation. The ease of transmission from creator to viewer, and on from viewer to viewer, makes the Internet an ideal medium for artists and authors to disseminate their work. Simultaneously, technology provides the potential for any of these viewers to quickly and easily edit, alter, distort, or redistribute an original work without an author's permission. This reality highlights the importance of both copyright and moral rights in Internet law.

There are numerous ways to misappropriate a creation on the Internet. It is possible to:

- copy a work without permission or licence;
- present the work of another as the work of oneself;
- produce an on-line parody or an on-line endorsement;
- reproduce the style of the original creation, deliberately leading others to believe that the work is that of the original creator;
- fail to give credit for a reproduction; or
- inaccurately attribute credit in the case of a distorted work.

The motivations for such acts are varied. Some work is appropriated to create new works of art, some for social commentary, some as a form of homage, and some in the pursuit of financial gain.

The problems inherent in protecting moral rights and copyright are not exclusive to the Internet. What is exclusive to the Internet is the ease with which an author's work can be compromised. Historically, to reproduce a work on a large scale required considerable investment of both time and money. With the advent of computers, and later of the Internet, the obstacles to reproduction have been considerably eroded.

It is possible to access vast amounts of published works that have been placed on the Internet although it is often difficult to determine whether the content has been uploaded with or without the permission of the author. It is possible to reproduce large quantities of this material with some basic clicks and keystrokes. Most importantly, it is possible to do all of this with very little capital outlay when compared to the demands of traditional methods of reproduction. Finally, the Internet is ubiquitous, so it is almost impossible to detect and penalise all but the most high-profile of breaches. An individual who happens across a work, then decides to alter or misappropriate it, might contravene both the moral rights of the author and the copyright of the copyright holder, but he or she will never be prosecuted.

These are the issues facing creators. In this chapter, we will consider a number of problems and issues of copyright that are particularly relevant to the Internet.

---

2 Moral rights

Moral rights are related to the author's creativity and personality and are separate from the economic rights conferred by copyright legislation. Moral rights are held by individuals and generally cannot be held by corporations. They can be waived, but generally cannot be transferred.

> Copyright is treated as personal property that can be bought and sold outright—that is, assigned—or at least licensed. Moral rights are treated as personal rights—like the right to be free of defamation or the right not to be assaulted—and cannot be transferred but can be waived. Moral rights last at least as long as the copyright, but states have some leeway in other respects in implementing them, mainly remedies.

Moral rights grew up in continental Europe during the 19th century and find their philosophical justification in the idea that an author's work is an extension of the author: any assault on the work is as much an attack on the author as a physical assault. Parting with the copyright does not lessen the author's personal attachment to the work. It follows that the author should have recourse against those who present the work differently from the way the author originally intended. That theory can lead, expansively, beyond mere rights to attribute and to prevent prejudicial changes, to include rights such as the right to decide when to first publish (to prevent excessive criticism of the work), and even to withdraw a work from circulation when it no longer represents the author's views.[1]

The continental understanding of the relationships between author and work did not survive the journey across the English Channel intact. Within the common law, moral rights are regarded, not as a nebulous manifestation of relationship, but as a bundle of relatively rigid, distinct, and somewhat disconnected rights.

In the light of the common law discourse, the materials in the following sections will introduce two of these general rights, respect and integrity. The intention is not to provide a comprehensive analysis of the issues at play here. Rather, it is hoped that the following materials will familiarise the reader with the relevant themes and debates and also with the institutional responses to the challenges posed by the Internet in this area.

(a) *Star Trek* fan fiction

Fan fiction, as its name suggests, is the work of fans who take existing characters and themes from their favourite programs or movies and adapt them to create new fiction. These episodes are then usually published and distributed through a posting on a website. The majority of fan fiction relates to science fiction and science fantasy programs, such as *The X-Files*, or *Star Trek*.[2] Lately, fan fiction has moved beyond the science fiction genre and has included even children's programs, such as *Harry Potter*.

Star Trek fan fiction writers, and their postings on the Internet, have existed since long before the creation of the official *Star Trek* website. There was even an organisation, called the Trek Writers Guild,[3] that assisted the amateur writers with plots and other related matters. However, the guild did advise that all writers use disclaimers in order to clearly distinguish the fan fiction from the Paramount Company productions. Paramount, at first, took little or no action against fan fiction, possibly because of the favourable publicity created by fan fiction postings.

In 1996 Paramount set up the *Star Trek* website. At this point it sent 'cease and desist' letters to the numerous fan fiction websites on the grounds of breach of copyright. As well as the obvious copyright issues, there are also important moral rights considerations within this dispute relating, in particular, to attribution and integrity. If Paramount's authors create certain characters with certain characteristics, which they deem to be

---

1   D Vaver, 'Moral Rights Yesterday, Today and Tomorrow' (2000) 7(3) *International Journal of Law and Information Technology* 2000 7(3) 270–1.

2   See further <http://www.wired.com/news/culture/0,1284,1076,00.html> 29 September 2001.

3   The Guild's web site address is <http://www.twguild.com/> 29 September 2001.

crucial to the artistic integrity of their work, and if these same characters are placed, by fan fiction writers, in plot scenarios which might alter the public's understanding of a character, there is a possibility that some readers might confuse the fan fiction characters with the originals. In this event, there are immediate attribution issues, as well as the claim of the author over the integrity of his or her original work, which could quite easily include characters and characteristics.[4]

Although some websites voluntarily shut down, some ISPs also monitored and filtered offending sites to avoid liability for contributory infringement of copyright. The matter has never been tested in court. Paramount insists that it has a duty to protect its authors, designers, and creative directors, and that, therefore, their actions were completely justified.

(b) Third Voice

Third Voice was annotation software that allowed web surfers to post public commentary on websites that could be seen by anyone else who had Third Voice installed. This browser utility could be attached to the web browser and it enabled users to publicly annotate web pages. It allowed users to say whatever they chose about anything on-line, be it political, sporting, artistic, or legal. The comments looked much like Post-it Notes. In cases where there were several annotations on a web page, the viewer would have to close each of the notes separately in order to see through to the content of the page itself. Significantly, the notes could be more than simple text messages. They could also contain hyperlinks. Therefore, it was entirely possible that a note on a children's website could contain a link to a pornography website. On the other hand, some notes contained genuine comments and the collection of notes on a page could amount to a critical dialogue at times. The creators of Third Voice referred to such dialogue as 'inline discussions'. On the whole, however, the majority of the postings were the Internet equivalent of scribbles on the walls of public toilets.

In theory, annotation programs are a great idea, and a useful tool, because they encourage communication and interaction on the Internet. The problems lie not in the theory, but in the implementation of the software concept. A number of concerns were raised about the Third Voice annotation program and the attacks on the respect for and integrity of both website owners and the note posters.

The first and most significant concern related to security. A number of security breaches accompanied each release of the software. Although most of these were rectified, the fact that so many problems found their way into the marketplace indicates a deficiency in the testing systems at Third Voice. An example of the types of problems encountered can be seen in the events of 9 July 1999 on the Bowers website. A note containing embedded java script was posted on the site. The java script then, either by design or by accident, broke into the source html of the site and altered the content of the site itself. The result was that the note was not merely placed on top of the unaltered, original website content; it changed the actual site content, as well as the registration

---

4   Paramount sent an open letter to fans explaining its actions, available at <http://www.paramount.com/openletter/> 1 April 2001.

and ownership details and other important information, with no corresponding change in domain name. This was a source of much concern among computing professionals.[5]

The second concern related to the privacy of the users who posted notes. The notes themselves gave away a lot of information about users, even if they did not post materials on that particular occasion. As soon as a Third Voice user logged on to the Internet, the program tracked his or her movements. This information can be, obviously, very valuable to companies seeking to build consumer profiles and target marketing databases. The Third Voice users were given no notification that their movements were tracked and as a result were given no means of opting out.

Third, critics have drawn direct parallels between Third Voice and graffiti. Graffiti are generally defined as inscriptions or drawings made on some public surface. The mechanics of Third Voice seem to fit with this definition quite neatly. Even more pejoratively, some have equated Third Voice with vandalism, defined as 'wilful malicious destruction or defacement of public or private property'. Such analogies demonstrate the consensus that the postings were generally used to deface, rather than debate, website content.

Fourth, there were concerns relating to the concept of exclusion. The program could only snap on to certain versions of certain software platforms. For example, Macintosh users who ran a website could not view the notes. This was of concern because some site owners could not view what had been posted, and therefore they had little chance to protect their rights to respect and integrity.

Fifth, the content of the notes could relate to anything at all. The problem with this is that visitors to a website may have interpreted notes as being endorsed by the website owner, for example, notes that included links to pornographic sites. This is particularly relevant if the viewer did not load Third Voice onto the computer he was using (such as in a public library or a university), and was, consequently, unaware of the program and its mechanisms.

Sixth, there was no choice involved in the process. Website owners could not opt out of having the notes on their websites. Therefore, even if site owners were aware of the notes on their site, they could not permanently remove them. Users who posted notes also were unable to remove the notes they themselves had posted. Only Third Voice had this capacity.

Lastly, there were copyright concerns. In newer versions, there was the facility for Third Voice users to highlight text within a website. The mechanism involved here involves taking the entire page, copying it, and storing it on the server of the Third Voice user. This can be regarded as a breach of copyright, however, and perhaps surprisingly, this point was never litigated.

The degree of concern regarding annotation programs varies considerably. Some authors regard them as little more than a nuisance with little consequence for their rights and the content of their work. Others have vehemently expressed their displeasure at what they perceive to be the threat to their ability to control the content of their website. This latter view saw the formation of several groups opposing the Third Voice program. These groups have sought both legal and technical solutions.

---

5   See further <www.saynotothirdvoice.com> 3 March 2001.

On the technical side, a program called No Third Voice was developed which claimed to either block Third Voice users from a website, re-direct them to another website, or demand that the Third Voice user sign a declaration that she would not annotate the protected site. However, the makers of this software refused to provide a warranty that it actually worked and this led others to consider any legal options that might provide some protection for concerned authors. However, these efforts did not have a chance to bear fruit.

In April 2001, Third Voice ceased to exist.[6] Although this indicates, *prima facie*, a victory for the opponents of Third Voice, the decision to close was in fact based purely on financial considerations. The creators of Third Voice had attempted to run it as a commercial enterprise; however, they could attract neither sufficient advertising revenue nor the customer or user base to support it in this form. In any case, the initial furore over the program had certainly petered out well before the closure of the business.

 NOTES AND QUESTIONS

1 Explain the differences between moral rights and copyright. Which has priority in common law countries? Why? Which has priority in civil law? Why?

2 Explain exactly how the Third Voice program facilitated the breach of authors' moral rights. Do you agree that the concept of annotation software is a potentially positive development for the Internet? Why do you think it degenerated into such an obviously detested phenomenon?

3 Do you think moral rights are more important in the context of the Internet than they otherwise would be in the world of tangible copyright? If so, what features peculiar to the Internet might make this so?

(c) The *Copyright Amendment (Moral Rights) Act*

The *Copyright Amendment (Moral Rights) Act*, passed by the Australian Commonwealth Government on 21 December 2000, may afford some assistance to website and content owners in relation to respect and integrity rights.

Prior to this Act, moral rights existed only theoretically within numerous other, unrelated rights. For example, protection for false attribution could be found in the law of passing off and the *Trade Practices Act* (Cth). Among these rights, there was no positive right of attribution. Following the introduction of the *Copyright Amendment (Moral Rights) Act* there are three categorical moral rights:

- the right of attribution;
- the right against false attribution; and
- the right of integrity.

---

6   More information is available at <http://www.wired.com/news/business/0,1367,42803,00.html> 1 October 2001.

The question to consider then is: Who is the author? The answer is simply the person, or persons, who create a piece of work. The author and the holder of copyright can be different. Copyright, as a form of property, can be assigned from one person to another, moral rights cannot. The application of moral rights now applies to all creations whether created before or after the commencement of the Act (with the exception of films and works to the extent that they are included in films).

Copyright Act 1968 (Cth) as Amended

193. AUTHOR'S RIGHT OF ATTRIBUTION OF AUTHORSHIP

(1) The author of a work has a right of attribution of authorship in respect of the work ...

195AC. AUTHOR'S RIGHT NOT TO HAVE AUTHORSHIP FALSELY ATTRIBUTED

(1) The author of a work has a right not to have authorship of the work falsely attributed.

(2) The author's right is the right not to have a person (the *attributor*) do, in respect of the work, any of the acts (the *acts of false attribution*) mentioned in the following provisions of this Division.

195AI. AUTHOR'S RIGHT OF INTEGRITY OF AUTHORSHIP

(1) The author of a work has a right of integrity of authorship in respect of the work.

(2) The author's right is the right not to have the work subjected to derogatory treatment.

195AJ. DEROGATORY TREATMENT OF LITERARY, DRAMATIC OR MUSICAL WORK

In this Part: *derogatory treatment*, in relation to a literary, dramatic or musical work, means:

(a) the doing, in relation to the work, of anything that results in a material distortion of, the mutilation of, or a material alteration to, the work that is prejudicial to the author's honour or reputation; or

(b) the doing of anything else in relation to the work that is prejudicial to the author's honour or reputation.

195AK. DEROGATORY TREATMENT OF ARTISTIC WORK

In this Part: *derogatory treatment*, in relation to an artistic work, means:

(a) the doing, in relation to the work, of anything that results in a material distortion of, the destruction or mutilation of, or a material alteration to, the work that is prejudicial to the author's honour or reputation; or

(b) an exhibition in public of the work that is prejudicial to the author's honour or reputation because of the manner or place in which the exhibition occurs; or

(c) the doing of anything else in relation to the work that is prejudicial to the author's honour or reputation ...

NOTES AND QUESTIONS

1   'Honour' and 'reputation' are not defined in the Act. There are, however, some specific types of derogatory treatment outlined in the Act, such as mutilation, material distortion, and alteration. The 'honour and reputation' clause is a product of the *Berne Convention for the Protection of Artistic and Literary Works* (Berne), and its meaning and application have been a source of considerable controversy since then.

2   How would you define honour and reputation? Do you think the definition has been deliberately avoided? Why or why not?

3   'It is truer to the spirit of these rights to leave the central normative principles free from legislative ossification. Such concepts can only operate as intended if they are left so.' Critically analyse this statement and compare the concepts of honour and reputation with the general civil law approach to authorial rights.

4   Is it necessary to have a right of attribution in addition to a right of false attribution? Why?

5   Does the Internet aid breaches of the rights extracted above to any significant extent? Or is it simply digital technology itself that has been the main culprit— enabling users to scan, edit, and morph images, as well as altering other types of copyright protect materials?

Copyright Act 1968 (Cth) as Amended

195AM. DURATION OF MORAL RIGHTS

(1)   An author's right of integrity of authorship in respect of a cinematograph film continues in force until the author dies.

(2)   An author's right of integrity of authorship in respect of a work other than a cinematograph film continues in force until copyright ceases to subsist in the work.

(3)   An author's moral rights (other than the right of integrity of authorship) in respect of a work continue in force until copyright ceases to subsist in the work.

195AN. EXERCISE OF MORAL RIGHTS

(1)   If the author of a work dies, the author's moral rights (other than the right of integrity of authorship in respect of a cinematograph film) in respect of the work may be exercised and enforced by his or her legal personal representative.

(2)   If the affairs of the author of a work are lawfully administered by another person (except under a law for the relief of bankrupt or insolvent debtors), the author's moral rights may be exercised and enforced by the person administering his or her affairs.

(3)   Subject to this section, a moral right in respect of a work is not transmissible by assignment, by will, or by devolution by operation of law ...

NOTES AND QUESTIONS

1   What is the point of extending the operation of moral rights beyond the death of the author? Construct an argument in favour of such a provision.
2   Give reasons why the duration of moral rights might differ depending on the type of work in question.
3   What is the significance of s 195AN(2)?

Copyright Act 1968 (Cth) as Amended

195AO. INFRINGEMENT OF RIGHT OF ATTRIBUTION OF AUTHORSHIP

Subject to this Division, a person infringes an author's right of attribution of authorship in respect of a work if the person does, or authorises the doing of, an attributable act in respect of the work without the identification of the author in accordance with Division 2 as the author of the work.

195AP. INFRINGEMENT OF RIGHT NOT TO HAVE AUTHORSHIP FALSELY ATTRIBUTED

Subject to this Division, a person infringes an author's right not to have authorship of a work falsely attributed if the person does an act of false attribution in respect of the work.

195AQ. INFRINGEMENT OF RIGHT OF INTEGRITY OF AUTHORSHIP

(1)   This section has effect subject to this Division.
(2)   A person infringes an author's right of integrity of authorship in respect of a work if the person subjects the work, or authorises the work to be subjected, to derogatory treatment
...

195AR. NO INFRINGEMENT OF RIGHT OF ATTRIBUTION OF AUTHORSHIP IF IT WAS REASONABLE NOT TO IDENTIFY THE AUTHOR

(1)   A person who does, or authorises the doing of, an attributable act in respect of a work does not, because the author of the work is not identified, infringe the author's right of attribution of authorship in respect of the work if the person establishes that it was reasonable in all the circumstances not to identify the author ...

195AS. NO INFRINGEMENT OF RIGHT OF INTEGRITY OF AUTHORSHIP IF DEROGATORY TREATMENT OR OTHER ACTION WAS REASONABLE

(1)   A person does not, by subjecting a work, or authorising a work to be subjected, to derogatory treatment, infringe the author's right of integrity of authorship in respect of the work if the person establishes that it was reasonable in all the circumstances to subject the work to the treatment.

(2) The matters to be taken into account in determining for the purposes of subsection (1) whether it was reasonable in particular circumstances to subject a literary, dramatic, musical or artistic work to derogatory treatment include the following:

    (a) the nature of the work;

    (b) the purpose for which the work is used;

    (c) the manner in which the work is used;

    (d) the context in which the work is used;

    (e) any practice, in the industry in which the work is used, that is relevant to the work or the use of the work;

    (f) any practice contained in a voluntary code of practice, in the industry in which the work is used, that is relevant to the work or the use of the work;

    (g) whether the work was made:

        (i) in the course of the author's employment; or

        (ii) under a contract for the performance by the author of services for another person;

    (h) whether the treatment was required by law or was otherwise necessary to avoid a breach of any law;

    (i) if the work has 2 or more authors—their views about the treatment.

(3) The matters to be taken into account in determining for the purposes of subsection (1) whether it was reasonable in particular circumstances to subject a cinematograph film to derogatory treatment include the following:

    (a) the nature of the film;

    (b) whether the primary purpose for which the film was made was for exhibition at cinemas, for broadcasting by television or for some other use;

    (c) the purpose for which the film is used;

    (d) the manner in which the film is used;

    (e) the context in which the film is used;

    (f) any practice, in the industry in which the film is used, that is relevant to the film or the use of the film;

    (g) any practice contained in a voluntary code of practice, in the industry in which the film is used, that is relevant to the film or the use of the film;

    (h) whether the film was made in the course of the employment of the director, producer or screenwriter who alleges that the treatment was derogatory;

    (i) whether the treatment was required by law or was otherwise necessary to avoid a breach of any law.

(4) A person who does any act referred to in subsection 195AQ(3), (4) or (5) in respect of a work that has been subjected to derogatory treatment of a kind mentioned in that subsection does not, by doing that act, infringe the author's right of integrity of authorship in respect of the work if the person establishes that it was reasonable in all the circumstances to do that act.

195AX. ACTS OR OMISSIONS OUTSIDE AUSTRALIA

It is not an infringement of an author's moral right in respect of a work to do, or omit to do, something outside Australia.

195AZ. ACTIONS FOR INFRINGEMENT OF MORAL RIGHTS

If a person infringes any of the moral rights of an author in respect of a work, the infringement is not an offence but the author or a person representing the author may bring an action in respect of the infringement, subject to any co-authorship agreement in force under section 195AN to which the author is a party.

195AZA. REMEDIES FOR INFRINGEMENTS OF MORAL RIGHTS

(1) Subject to section 203, the relief that a court may grant in an action for an infringement of any of an author's moral rights in respect of a work includes any one or more of the following:

   (a) an injunction (subject to any terms that the court thinks fit);
   (b) damages for loss resulting from the infringement;
   (c) a declaration that a moral right of the author has been infringed;
   (d) an order that the defendant make a public apology for the infringement;
   (e) an order that any false attribution of authorship, or derogatory treatment, of the work be removed or reversed ...

195AZE. PRESUMPTION AS TO SUBSISTENCE OF MORAL RIGHTS

In an action brought under this Part for an infringement of a moral right in respect of a work, if copyright is presumed or proved to have subsisted in the work when the infringement is alleged to have occurred, the moral right is presumed to have subsisted in the work at that time.

195AZI. WORKS OF JOINT AUTHORSHIP

(1) This section applies to a literary, dramatic, musical or artistic work that is a work of joint authorship.
(2) The right of attribution of authorship in respect of the work is a right of each joint author to be identified as a joint author.
(3) An act of false attribution in respect of the work infringes the right of each joint author not to have authorship of the work falsely attributed.
(4) The right of integrity of authorship in respect of the work is a right of each joint author.
(5) The consent of one joint author to any act or omission affecting his or her moral rights in respect of the work does not affect the moral rights of the other joint author or other joint authors in respect of the work.

NOTES AND QUESTIONS

1   Consider s 195AS. What are the circumstances where it might be 'reasonable' to infringe moral rights? Do these circumstances occur only on the Internet? Are materials on the Internet more susceptible to a finding of non-infringement of moral rights when they have been subjected to, say, derogatory treatment? Why are the considerations for films different?

2   The conclusion to be drawn from s 195AZI is that the moral rights are individual rights held by each separate author, not held jointly. Therefore, the process of obtaining permission is likely to be quite involved in respect of works which have multiple authors. What implications does this have for creative outputs on the Internet?

3   What is the effect of 195AX in the light of the Internet? Is it significant that 'outside Australia' is not defined?

4   'The moral rights amendments to the Australian *Copyright Act* will make absolutely no impact on the ability of authors to protect their works from misappropriation. The provisions are merely legislative window-dressing designed to appease supposed international obligations, rather than to assist authors.' Critically assess this proposition with regard both to the Australian legislation and to the civil law tradition.

(d)   A critique of moral rights

In this section, David Vaver critiques the approach to moral rights taken in the United Kingdom. The law in Australia, although it has been influenced to some degree by that of the United Kingdom, is not identical to it. As you read through the extract, consider how many of the critiques apply to the Australian Act.

David Vaver, 'Moral Rights Yesterday, Today and Tomorrow'

(2000) 7(3) *International Journal of Law and Information Technology* 271

II. Terminological and conceptual difficulties

The expression 'moral rights' is misleading. Shakespeare was wrong: a rose by any other name does not smell as sweet. Whoever first translated '*droit moral*' as 'moral right(s)' virtually made these rights perpetually suspect to English speakers. Since the word 'moral' is commonly contrasted with 'legal', one's first reaction to a 'moral right' is that it is something to which one has no legal entitlement—only a moral or (if one prefers polysyllables) deontological entitlement.

On the one hand, retaining *droit moral* is unsatisfactory. It emphasizes the foreignness of the whole concept and inhibits its easy integration into English law. Before the advent of the current fashion to de-Latinize legal language, one might have given the concept an instantly respectable pedigree and mystique by Latinizing it: perhaps *ius auctoris personalis* or *ius operis*. This route is, post-Woolf, *prima facie* closed.

On the other hand, there is no good English translation or shorthand for *droit moral*: 'personal rights' or 'intellectual rights' come within range but still are connotatively off-target.

Terminology and pedigree matter in law. A new right may be introduced and treated more sympathetically in a jurisdiction where it resembles existing rights, or flows logically from accepted principles, than where it is a completely new transplant onto inhospitable soil. Writers in both the US and the Commonwealth have therefore sought to demonstrate the presence of common law analogues to moral rights of attribution and integrity. Indeed, when moral rights were first introduced into the Berne Convention in 1928, some thought, or at least acted as if, Commonwealth countries already adequately protected moral rights through the common law and need do nothing more to comply with Berne. The United States took this stance in implementing Berne in 1989, while later backtracking to introduce some specific moral rights for visual artists.

III. The impoverished state of moral rights in the UK

Unfortunately, the UK is at the forefront of common law states that take a grudging attitude toward moral rights, at least if the expression given these rights in the CDP Act is any testament.

It is not as if article 6 *bis* of the Berne Convention is particularly opaque. It reads:

(1) Independently of the author's economic rights [ie, copyright], and even after the transfer of the said rights, the author shall have the right to claim authorship of the work and to object to any distortion, mutilation or other modification of, or other derogatory action in relation to, the said work, which would be prejudicial to his honour or reputation.

(3) The means of redress for safeguarding the rights granted by this Act shall be governed by the legislation of the country where protection is claimed.

This text is readily intelligible to those who are willing to understand. The rights of attribution and integrity of all 'authors' of all 'literary and artistic works'—in the Berne sense of those words—must be 'safeguarded'. Berne members have discretion over the 'means of redress'—ie, remedies—for safeguarding these rights, but these means must be effective as safeguards and should not merely be seen as going through the motions. The full force of *ubi ius ibi remedium* applies, subject of course to a rule of *de minimis*.

Judged by such standards, the CDP Act falls pitifully short. A few examples will suffice:

• The attribution right is not infringed unless it has first been 'asserted' in writing. This provision does not comply with the obligation under Berne article 5(1) that 'the enjoyment and exercise' of author's rights—both economic and moral—'shall not be subject to any formality'. Under Berne, the onus of satisfying oneself that attribution is unnecessary lies on the user, not the author.

- The attribution right does not apply to wide classes of work: computer programs, typeface designs, newspapers, magazines, encyclopaedias, dictionaries, yearbooks—and, perhaps most extraordinarily, virtually anything done by employees on the job. The CDP Act here was, and is, out of step with international practice, under which much of this work is in fact attributed on first publication, either voluntarily or under contract. Why later users should be better off than the initial publisher is not explained.
- Not only is the integrity right excluded from a wide range of publications—newspapers, magazines, encyclopaedias and the like, as for the attribution right—but it also is excluded from such things as botched translations or BBC program censorship on grounds of 'offend[ing] good taste'. An author's claim against a translator who produces a version that prejudices the author's reputation is therefore for defamation or breach of contract, not breach of moral rights. Why translation is treated better than other forms of adaptation is puzzling.
- At first sight, the requirement that waivers should be in writing seems to favour authors, but whether such a waiver is fairly extracted depends on the bargaining power of the author in the particular situation. In any event, other provisions chip away at the writing rule so as to leave little of it standing. Conduct, implied consent, or oral waivers for peppercorn consideration may all also effectively eliminate moral rights.

When the UK first introduced these moral rights provisions in 1988, some thought they were just a first step along the path to a stronger moral rights regime. Looked at from the perspective of a decade later, this optimism seems unjustified. While the digital revolution has caused economic rights to go forth, multiply and get harmonized, moral rights seem perpetually stuck in their old groove, even though the digital threat to moral rights is at least as great as for economic rights.

What little UK litigation there has been has also not been particularly encouraging to potential claimants. True, George Michael got a pre-trial injunction to stop snatches of his music being strung together in a record medley; but Bill Tidy failed to get even interim relief against the Natural History Museum for shrinking his large-scale dinosaur cartoons to fit into a book. Nor could a brochure designer stop bits of his work from being used without attribution in an updated brochure produced by someone else, since the revision was done competently and left his honour or reputation unsullied.

Such decisions, coupled with the high cost of litigating moral rights claims and the widespread use of written waivers, should give little comfort to those performers who are looking forward to the new moral rights regime that the UK is committed to introducing under the WIPO Performances and Phonograms Treaty 1996. Judging from the consultation paper the UK Patent Office issued on the subject earlier this year, the moral rights that performers will get will likely be as dilute as those granted to authors under the current regime. Indeed, improving the moral rights lot of performers, without correspondingly improving that of authors, would be difficult politically, and difficult politics in the intellectual property sphere does not presently seem to rate high on the government's reform agenda.

IV. Other common law countries

This common law antipathy to moral rights is not confined to the UK. The US shares it with a passion: the excision of moral rights from both TRIPs and the WIPO Copyright Treaty bears ample witnesses. Nor has the US enacted new law to comply with its obligations under the WIPO Performances and Phonograms Treaty to protect performers' moral rights, presumably on the same theory that led it to enact nothing to comply with Berne art 6 *bis*: moral rights are already adequately protected under existing laws. Australia has been batting the idea of enacting moral rights around for the last decade or so, so far with little result.

Folklore has it that Canada is an exception to this common law antipathy, since that country expressly incorporated Berne art 6 *bis* in its *Copyright Act* as long ago as 1931. But decisions speak louder than statutes. No Canadian case on the moral rights provision was reported for nearly half a century, and since then moral rights claims have been upheld only six times. But, on closer analysis, these apparently favourable decisions are more equivocal. Three cases were interlocutory; and, more importantly, of the three that went to trial, two resulted in no damages for the plaintiff because of a failure to prove any decline in honour or reputation as a result of the infringement. Modest damages—less than £1000—were awarded in the third case for infringement of a photographer's attribution right. Somewhat perversely, claimants have fared better relying on the common or civil law to vindicate moral rights interests. The overall record of Canadian courts to date has, with few exceptions, shown little inclination to press moral rights liability much beyond what the common law or the civil law would have imposed anyway. Claims relying purely on the [*Copyright Act*] may therefore be risky propositions unless strong common or civil law support is also available.

Judging from available data so far, the same comment may be made of the UK (of course, omitting any reference to the civil law).

V. Reorienting moral rights theory

Are moral rights really that alien to a common law system? Certainly, the theorizing of Kant and Hegel, emphasizing intellectual output as being an extension of the author's personality and hence inalienably linked to and under the control of the author, musters little enthusiasm among common lawyers, whose bent is more pragmatic than metaphysical. The theory recognizes the importance of the individual and individual rights, but does not suggest any broader public interest for a strong moral rights regime.

A public interest case can, however, be made along the following lines:

- *Truth-in-marketing.* Moral rights help assure the public that the works it has come to associate with a particular author are indeed that author's genuine product. A book labelled 'by Stephen King' is different from a book labelled 'by Enid Blyton'. Both labels tell the public a lot about the particular book. The attributions function like trade marks: they tell the public that each book has particular qualities that have come to be associated with each author's writing and that distinguish one book from the other, and indeed every (or at least many) others. Attribution and integrity rights therefore help to bring the author's name before the public and help to assure that the work is an authentic product, vouched for by the author.
- *Social reward.* Rights are often allocated by law to encourage and reward desirable social activity. Moral rights help authors to benefit from whatever reward (or lack of it) their work may bring. The reward should come from the work in the form and with the credit line that the author has approved, not through some other work that has later been changed by someone else, whether for better or worse.

- *Cultural preservation.* There is a public interest in having a continuous record of its culture. This interest could be pursued by those in government whose brief is the preservation of the country's cultural heritage; but, in an era devoted to less government, this goal may equally be pursued by giving authors and their estates some control over their works. The hope and expectation are that their exercise of private rights will ultimately be in the public interest.
- *Author empowerment.* Moral rights provide authors with a bargaining chip which, given the greater power generally wielded by entrepreneurs, allows authors some say over the manner in which their work is later exploited. Moral rights are therefore a force for equality in authors' dealings with media entrepreneurs and distributors.

VI. Conclusion

If this analysis is accepted, the logical consequence is that moral rights should be taken more seriously. They need to be more comprehensive, and waivers need to be more strictly controlled. The grant of blanket immunities to large classes of work, as now occurs under the CDP Act, should be recognized for what it is: the product of special pleading, rather than any coherent policy. The answer for those who do not wish to be bothered by moral rights is not a grant of statutory exemption but the right to seek waivers from authors. Holders of economic rights are familiar with that line of reasoning: they have used it to their advantage for the last three centuries to expand their rights and to narrow exceptions. Sauce for the copyright goose should also be sauce for the moral rights gander.

The justification suggested for moral rights also suggests that moral rights should not be generally waivable. This is the position in France, as *The Asphalt Jungle* colorization case in 1991 demonstrates. John Huston's heirs sued in France to stop the televising of a colorized version of *The Asphalt Jungle*. Huston had no moral rights in the US, the film's country of origin: under US law, the film was 'made for hire', so the commissioning movie studio was both copyright owner and author. The *Cour de Cassation* nevertheless held that, whatever the position in the US, in France Huston was the film's author and had moral rights that he and his estate could assert as a matter of *ordre public*. If a foreign statute cannot take away an author's moral rights, a mere contractual clause waiving them presumably can fare no better.

If this approach were thought too absolutist for the UK, a halfway house might be suggested: waivers could be subjected to a touchstone of reasonableness. For example, were the exceptions to moral rights removed from UK law, one would not want them simply supplanted by blanket waivers inserted routinely in every exploitation contract. On the other hand, not all waivers may be unreasonable. Ghost-writers may be willing to waive credit; novels that are made into films need changing to fit the exigencies of the different medium. Waivers should therefore be enforceable to the extent reasonably necessary in the circumstances. This approach builds on a scheme in the old *Copyright Act 1911* dealing with the compulsory licences for sound recordings. Under the 1911 Act, a cover record could be made of earlier released music, at a fixed royalty. The record could make alterations or omissions to the music, but only if such changes were 'reasonably necessary for the adaptation of the work'. This provision must have worked well enough in practice for no litigation on it is reported. Reasonableness is, after all, a requirement that discourages parties from taking extravagant stands and focuses them on how the work might best be exploited to their mutual advantage.

A moral rights regime that is 'sufficiently flexible to provide a fair and satisfactory balance between authors and owners of copyright' and performers seems a worthy goal. In the long run, solid legal protection for authors and performers is more likely to produce a beneficial creative climate than the current system, in which 'broad exceptions and qualifications and waiver provisions … totally undermine' the moral rights regime the UK has enacted.

 NOTES AND QUESTIONS

1 Can Vaver's criticisms be applied to the Australian legislation? If so, how might the legislation be amended to attain the coherence sought by Vaver? Is it possible to include the concept of moral rights, as Vaver would regard it, within the Western legal tradition?

2 The implication from the materials is that moral rights are not regarded highly enough by common law nations to bring about their effective enforcement. This results in situations such as the *Star Trek* fan fiction dispute, where Paramount did not contest its grievance in court, and instead resorted to force to protect its interests. Does it seem ironic that this corporation was so willing to protect rights which, by their definition, it could never hold? Or is it perhaps the case that economic interests were the core concern and were simply presented in the rhetoric of author protection?

3 What is the likelihood of the Internet witnessing an upswell of moral rights activism when the potential plaintiffs do not have the resources of a multinational to call upon?

---

3 Copyright

(a) The principles of copyright

While it is true that a great deal of material is placed on the Internet freely with the intention that it be accessed and reproduced without cost or licence, it is also true that a great deal of material is placed on the Internet without the permission of the copyright holder. Further, in some instances, copyright holders place works on the Internet but do not intend them to be reproduced and copied.

Before we can examine copyright as it relates to the Internet, we must first understand some basic intellectual property law issues, because it is these issues that define our point of departure.

Historically, copyright developed as a response to the growth of printing technology. The Gutenberg printing press facilitated rapid multiplication and distribution of copies. Owners of the works, generally publishers who had bought them from authors, demanded a right to control this new form of copying. Subsequently, almost all changes in the law of copyright have been driven by technological advances, such as photography, broadcasting, cable transmission, and computer programs.

There are two major conceptualisations of the function of copyright, one in the common law tradition, the other in the civil law tradition.

The common law tradition is mainly concerned with the economic role of copyright. Concern for the protection of copyrighted subject matter can be said to be incidental to concern for the protection of value and property rights. Without this latter protection, the theory goes, there is no incentive to produce new works. Without guaranteed rewards, there can be no innovation. The market alone cannot provide the rewards because of free riding often brought on by technology. Copyright is the legal response to a technologically induced market failure.

The civil law views copyright as an extension of the personality rights of the author. This can be seen by the title of this area of law in these jurisdictions—author law. The author law framework arises out of respect for the author, the integrity of the creation, and the relationship between the author and the creation. Whereas the common law seeks to separate the two, the notion of copyright, as we understand it, is almost indistinguishable from moral rights under civil law.

The distinction has therefore been drawn between the common law that protects the entrepreneur and the civil law system that protects the author. This distinction is demonstrated in various areas of the law, for example, the work of employees in the course of employment. The common law grants the first copyright to the employer; civil law grants the first copyright to the employee.

Despite the importance of recognising the difference between the two traditions, it is important to note that both conceptions are bases for the efficient function of market operations. The *Berne Convention for the Protection of Literary and Artistic Works 1928*, discussed below, sets minimum standards for copyright, and, despite the differences in interpretation, there are core standards and goals common to both systems. Examining the difference between the two systems helps to illuminate the true foundations and functions of the common law system. Through comparison comes clarity.

The Internet offers the law of copyright a chance to evolve still further, or to start from scratch. There are ongoing debates as to whether or not the simple accessing of material on the Internet actually qualifies as reproduction, for the purposes of copyright legislation. These debates recognise the fact that the Internet fits uneasily within the regulatory frameworks that were built before its conception.

There are a number of questions that relate to copyright and the Internet:

• Will perfect reproduction of materials sound the death knell for copyright as we know (or knew) it? Perfect reproduction arises when a digital product can be endlessly reproduced with no loss in quality, so that there is little or no distinction between that and the original.
• Will we have to reconsider the fundamentals of copyright law? Will concepts such as copying, fair use, public performance, and the very definition of literary work need to be redefined?

- What rights can authors and users hold on the Internet? Will they remain the same as they were prior to the Internet?
- Will there arise a marketplace where producers and consumers bargain directly over the price of access to a work? Will the Internet do away with the middle entity?
- Given the flow of materials across the Internet, do we need further harmonisation of copyright law?
- Can copyright survive this latest challenge to the versatility which has been maintained for over 100 years?

John Perry Barlow, 'The Economy of Ideas: Selling Wine Without Bottles on the Global Net'

Available at <http://homes.eff.org/~barlow/EconomyOfIdeas.html> 17 August 2006

Throughout the time I've been groping around Cyberspace, there has remained unsolved an immense conundrum that seems to be at the root of nearly every legal, ethical, governmental, and social vexation to be found in the Virtual World. I refer to the problem of digitized property.

The riddle is this: if our property can be infinitely reproduced and instantaneously distributed all over the planet without cost, without our knowledge, without its even leaving our possession, how can we protect it? How are we going to get paid for the work we do with our minds? And, if we can't get paid, what will assure the continued creation and distribution of such work?

Since we don't have a solution to what is a profoundly new kind of challenge, and are apparently unable to delay the galloping digitization of everything not obstinately physical, we are sailing into the future on a sinking ship.

This vessel, the accumulated canon of copyright and patent law, was developed to convey forms and methods of expression entirely different from the vaporous cargo it is now being asked to carry. It is leaking as much from within as without.

Legal efforts to keep the old boat floating are taking three forms: a frenzy of deck chair rearrangement, stern warnings to the passengers that if she goes down, they will face harsh criminal penalties, and serene, glassy-eyed denial.

Intellectual property law cannot be patched, retrofitted, or expanded to contain the gases of digitized expression any more than real estate law might be revised to cover the allocation of broadcasting spectrum. (Which, in fact, rather resembles what is being attempted here.) We will need to develop an entirely new set of methods as befits this entirely new set of circumstances.

Most of the people who actually create soft property—the programmers, hackers, and Net surfers—already know this. Unfortunately, neither the companies they work for nor the lawyers these companies hire have enough direct experience with immaterial goods to understand why they are so problematic. They are proceeding as though the old laws can somehow be made to work, either by grotesque expansion or by force. They are wrong.

The source of this conundrum is as simple as its solution is complex. Digital technology is detaching information from the physical plane, where property law of all sorts has always found definition.

Throughout the history of copyrights and patents, the proprietary assertions of thinkers have been focused not on their ideas but on the expression of those ideas. The ideas themselves, as well as facts about the phenomena of the world, were considered to be the collective property of humanity. One could claim franchise, in the case of copyright, on the precise turn of phrase used to convey a particular idea or the order in which facts were presented.

The point at which this franchise was imposed was that moment when the 'word became flesh' by departing the mind of its originator and entering some physical object, whether book or widget. The subsequent arrival of other commercial media besides books didn't alter the legal importance of this moment. Law protected expression and, with few (and recent) exceptions, to express was to make physical.

Protecting physical expression had the force of convenience on its side. Copyright worked well because, Gutenberg notwithstanding, it was hard to make a book. Furthermore, books froze their contents into a condition that was as challenging to alter as it was to reproduce. Counterfeiting or distributing counterfeit volumes were obvious and visible activities, easy enough to catch somebody in the act of doing. Finally, unlike unbounded words or images, books had material surfaces to which one could attach copyright notices, publishers' marques, and price tags.

Mental to physical conversion was even more central to patent. A patent, until recently, was either a description of the form into which materials were to be rendered in the service of some purpose or a description of the process by which rendition occurred. In either case, the conceptual heart of patent was the material result. If no purposeful object could be rendered due to some material limitation, the patent was rejected. Neither a Klein bottle nor a shovel made of silk could be patented. It had to be a thing and the thing had to work.

Thus the rights of invention and authorship adhered to activities in the physical world. One didn't get paid for ideas but for the ability to deliver them into reality. For all practical purposes, the value was in the conveyance and not the thought conveyed.

In other words, the bottle was protected, not the wine.

Now, as information enters Cyberspace, the native home of Mind, these bottles are vanishing. With the advent of digitization, it is now possible to replace all previous information storage forms with one meta-bottle: complex—and highly liquid—patterns of ones and zeros.

Even the physical/digital bottles to which we've become accustomed—floppy disks, CD-ROMs, and other discrete, shrink-wrappable bit-packages—will disappear as all computers jack in to the global Net. While the Internet may never include every single CPU on the planet, it is more than doubling every year and can be expected to become the principal medium of information conveyance if, eventually, the only one.

Once that has happened, all the goods of the Information Age—all expressions once contained in books or film strips or records or newsletters—will exist either as pure thought or something very much like thought: voltage conditions darting around the Net at the speed of light, in conditions which one might behold in effect, as glowing pixels or transmitted sounds, but never touch or claim to 'own' in the old sense of the word.

Some might argue that information will still require some physical manifestation, such as its magnetic existence on the titanic hard disks of distant servers, but these are bottles that have no macroscopically discrete or personally meaningful form.

Some will also argue that we have been dealing with unbottled expression since the advent of radio, and they would be right. But for most of the history of broadcast, there was no convenient way to capture soft goods from the electromagnetic ether and reproduce them in anything like the quality available in commercial packages. Only recently has this changed and little has been done legally or technically to address the change.

Generally, the issue of consumer payment for broadcast products was irrelevant. The consumers themselves were the product. Broadcast media were supported either by selling the attention of their audience to advertisers, using government to assess payment through taxes, or the whining mendicancy of annual donor drives.

All of broadcast support models are flawed. Support either by advertisers or government has almost invariably tainted the purity of the goods delivered. Besides, direct marketing is gradually killing the advertiser support model anyway.

Broadcast media gave us another payment method for a virtual product in the royalties which broadcasters pay songwriters through such organizations as ASCAP and BMI. But, as a member of ASCAP, I can assure you this is not a model that we should emulate. The monitoring methods are wildly approximate. There is no parallel system of accounting in the revenue stream. It doesn't really work. Honest.

In any case, without our old methods of physically defining the expression of ideas, and in the absence of successful new models for non-physical transaction, we simply don't know how to assure reliable payment for mental works. To make matters worse, this comes at a time when the human mind is replacing sunlight and mineral deposits as the principal source of new wealth.

Furthermore, the increasing difficulty of enforcing existing copyright and patent laws is already placing in peril the ultimate source of intellectual property, the free exchange of ideas.

That is, when the primary articles of commerce in a society look so much like speech as to be indistinguishable from it, and when the traditional methods of protecting their ownership have become ineffectual, attempting to fix the problem with broader and more vigorous enforcement will inevitably threaten freedom of speech.

The greatest constraint on your future liberties may come not from government but from corporate legal departments laboring to protect by force what can no longer be protected by practical efficiency or general social consent.

Furthermore, when Jefferson and his fellow creatures of The Enlightenment designed the system that became American copyright law, their primary objective was assuring the widespread distribution of thought, not profit. Profit was the fuel that would carry ideas into the libraries and minds of their new republic. Libraries would purchase books, thus rewarding the authors for their work in assembling ideas, which otherwise 'incapable of confinement' would then become freely available to the public. But what is the role of libraries if there are no books? How does society now pay for the distribution of ideas if not by charging for the ideas themselves?

Additionally complicating the matter is the fact that along with the physical bottles in which intellectual property protection has resided, digital technology is also erasing the legal jurisdictions of the physical world, and replacing them with the unbounded and perhaps permanently lawless seas of Cyberspace.

In Cyberspace, there are not only no national or local boundaries to contain the scene of a crime and determine the method of its prosecution, there are no clear cultural agreements on what a crime might be. Unresolved and basic differences between European and Asian cultural assumptions about intellectual property can only be exacerbated in a region where many transactions are taking place in both hemispheres and yet, somehow, in neither.

Even in the most local of digital conditions, jurisdiction and responsibility are hard to assess. A group of music publishers filed suit against Compuserve this fall for it having allowed its users to upload musical compositions into areas where other users might get them. But since Compuserve cannot practically exercise much control over the flood of bits that pass between its subscribers, it probably shouldn't be held responsible for unlawfully 'publishing' these works.

Notions of property, value, ownership, and the nature of wealth itself are changing more fundamentally than at any time since the Sumerians first poked cuneiform into wet clay and called it stored grain. Only a very few people are aware of the enormity of this shift and fewer of them are lawyers or public officials.

Those who do see these changes must prepare responses for the legal and social confusion that will erupt as efforts to protect new forms of property with old methods become more obviously futile, and, as a consequence, more adamant ...

From swords to writs to bits

... I sometimes give speeches on this subject, and I always ask how many people in the audience can honestly claim to have no unauthorized software on their hard disks. I've never seen more than ten percent of the hands go up.

Whenever there is such profound divergence between the law and social practice, it is not society that adapts. And, against the swift tide of custom, the Software Publishers' current practice of hanging a few visible scapegoats is so obviously capricious as to only further diminish respect for the law.

Part of the widespread popular disregard for commercial software copyrights stems from a legislative failure to understand the conditions into which it was inserted. To assume that systems of law based in the physical world will serve in an environment that is as fundamentally different as Cyberspace is a folly for which everyone doing business in the future will pay.

As I will discuss in the next segment, unbounded intellectual property is very different from physical property and can no longer be protected as though these differences did not exist. For example, if we continue to assume that value is based on scarcity, as it is with regard to physical objects, we will create laws that are precisely contrary to the nature of information, which may, in many cases, *increase* in value with distribution.

The large, legally risk-averse institutions most likely to play by the old rules will suffer for their compliance. The more lawyers, guns, and money they invest in either protecting their rights or subverting those of their opponents, the more commercial competition will resemble the Kwakiutl Potlatch Ceremony, in which adversaries competed by destroying their own possessions. Their ability to produce new technology will simply grind to a halt as every move they make drives them deeper into a tar pit of courtroom warfare.

Faith in law will not be an effective strategy for high tech companies. Law adapts by continuous increments and at a pace second only to geology in its stateliness. Technology advances in the lunging jerks, like the punctuation of biological evolution grotesquely accelerated. Real world conditions will continue to change at a blinding pace, and the law will get further behind, more profoundly confused. This mismatch is permanent.

Promising economies based on purely digital products will either be born in a state of paralysis, as appears to be the case with multimedia, or continue in a brave and willful refusal by their owners to play the ownership game at all ...

An economy of verbs

The future forms and protections of intellectual property are densely obscured from the entrance to the Virtual Age. Nevertheless, I can make (or reiterate) a few flat statements that I earnestly believe won't look too silly in fifty years.

- In the absence of the old containers, almost everything we think we know about intellectual property is wrong. We are going to have to unlearn it. We are going to have to look at information as though we'd never seen the stuff before.
- The protections that we will develop will rely far more on ethics and technology than on law.
- Encryption will be the technical basis for most intellectual property protection. (And should, for this and other reasons, be made more widely available.)
- The economy of the future will be based on relationship rather than possession. It will be continuous rather than sequential.

And finally, in the years to come, most human exchange will be virtual rather than physical, consisting not of stuff but the stuff of which dreams are made. Our future business will be conducted in a world made more of verbs than nouns.

 NOTES AND QUESTIONS

1   This opening of Barlow's article was written many years ago, during the infancy of the Internet. Do you think Barlow would amend any of his assertions in light of developments in the last five years? In your answer, take into account that the final section of the above extract was actually written much more recently and specifically designed to update his writing. Compare this final section with the tone of the rest of the essay. What lessons can be learned from the differences here?

2   It is easy to be seduced by the romance of Barlow's prose. Armed with this awareness, analyse his approach to the regulation of the Internet. If it is possible, your analysis would be greatly assisted by consideration of the entire piece, accessible at the reference above.

3   Barlow states:

> ... if we continue to assume that value is based on scarcity, as it is with regard to physical objects, we will create laws that are precisely contrary to the nature of information, which may, in many cases, *increase* in value with distribution.

What does he mean by 'increase in value with distribution'? Is he correct?

4   Taking Barlow's thesis as a premise, can you construct an alternative system of intellectual property rights and protections?

5   Regardless of your conclusions on the merits of Barlow's work, it is critical to keep such criticisms in mind as you read the materials throughout this chapter.

(b)   The copyright regime

Efforts at international harmonisation of intellectual property law began more than a century ago and have had considerable success. A rich political tapestry accompanies the development of the international copyright regime. The Berne Convention was concluded in 1886 and, shortly after, the Berne Union was formed to administer the international regime. The Berne Convention replaced a myriad of bilateral agreements between countries which were of little or no use in protecting copyright.

Despite the obvious common understandings and desire for harmony, the international copyright regime was in a constant state of flux for most of the last century. Since 1886, both the Berne Convention and the Berne Union have undergone substantial changes and revisions. The two most recent of these took place in 1967 in Stockholm and 1971 in Paris. Since 1967, the Berne Union has been administered by the International Bureau, the Secretariat of World Intellectual Property Organisation (WIPO), which itself became a specialist agency of the United Nations in 1974. There have also arisen a number of other international instruments designed to enhance copyright protection so that there are now three international instruments aimed at copyright protection:

- The Berne Convention, administered by the WIPO;
- The Universal Copyright Convention 1952, administered by UNESCO; and
- The Agreement on Trade-Related Aspects of Intellectual Property Rights (TRIPS), administered by the World Trade Organisation (WTO).

The entry of UNESCO into intellectual property initially led to considerable unease within the Berne Union. However, the two organisations have since developed a useful network of cooperation. In fact, in 1971, the Berne Convention revisions were mirrored by similar revisions in the Universal Copyright Convention, thereby creating parallel regimes.

The Berne Convention outlines three basic principles:

- *National treatment:* this essentially prevents any discrimination against foreigners in respect of copyright protection.

- *Automatic protection:* protection should not be made conditional upon compliance with any formality.
- *Independence of protection:* a work will be protected within a signatory state regardless of whether that work would receive protection within its country of origin.

The convention also stipulates minimum standards of protection relating to the works protected, the scope of the protection, and the duration of protection. However, the problem with this convention was that there were no effective enforcement mechanisms. This caused the USA to lobby for a major reinvention of the copyright protection regime.

These efforts culminated in 1994 with the conclusion of the Agreement on Trade-Related Aspects of Intellectual Property Rights (TRIPS) as an integral part of the Uruguay Round of negotiations on modifications and additions to the General Agreement on Tariffs and Trade (GATT). This was the most significant development in the international copyright landscape in decades. The TRIPS agreement embodies all of the substantive provisions of the Berne regime and includes them within the GATT, a new global trade regime. TRIPS is administered by the World Trade Organisation (WTO) and this regime adds a powerful, trade-focused element to the international copyright regulatory matrix.

The reason for the linking of intellectual property rights and trade is so that the WTO is empowered to apply trade sanctions to any member state that does not comply with the copyright provisions. Therefore, there are clear and substantial enforcement mechanisms. TRIPS actually extends further than Berne in some respects; for example, it includes provisions on producers' and performers' rights which cannot be found in the Berne Conventions.

In 1996 WIPO finalised two treaties of relevance here: the WIPO Copyright Treaty and the WIPO Performances and Phonograms Treaty, designed to update Berne to deal with digital technology and to bring Berne in line with TRIPS. These treaties will be examined below in the section on 'Communication right'.

The interoperation of these instruments results in protection for exported works being assured by any one of a number of international agreements, and protection for imported works being assured by legislation enacted according to principles embodied in these same agreements. As such, an examination of general copyright principles can be conducted by focusing on the laws of one jurisdiction to demonstrate the positions of many.

(c) The subject matter of copyright

It is important to delineate what copyright does and does not protect. It does not protect:

- mere ideas as distinguished from the expression of ideas;
- discoveries or principles;
- methods of operation and ways of doing things;
- mere information or facts;

- trivialities as defined by things such as slogans or titles; or
- anything that is not in material form.

An examination of what it actually does protect is more complicated. Article 1 of the Berne Convention states that the countries to which the convention applies constitute a union for the protection of the rights of authors over their literary and artistic works. The term 'literary and artistic works' is not exhaustively defined in the convention; however, Art 2(1) of the Paris Act provides that it includes every production in the literary, scientific, and artistic domain, whatever may be the mode or form of its expression. State parties must enact legislation protecting subject matter that falls within this broad definition although some flexibility is allowed for certain types of materials. In addition to these compulsory protections, the convention outlines certain subject matter, such as industrial designs, that may attract copyright protection subject to the discretion of State Parties.

In Australia, the *Copyright Act 1968* (Cth) distinguishes between two major categories of matter which attract copyright protection: original works, and subject matter other than works. Original works, often simply referred to as works, generally constitute the traditional subject matter of copyright as it was understood at the time of the British *Copyright Act 1911*. There are four types of works:

- literary;
- dramatic;
- musical; and
- artistic.

The category 'subject matter other than works' comprises the outcomes of new technological processes for which copyright protection is deemed suitable, for example:

- sound recordings;
- cinematograph films;
- television and sound broadcasts; and
- published editions of works.

For copyright to exist at all, there must be originality. It must not be copied. Some skill, labour, judgment, or analysis must be used in the creation of the item. Sometimes, it is a question of degree. The distinction between works and subject matter other than works does produce some differences in the application of the copyright protection afforded. For example, for works, the first copyright is vested in the author of the work, whereas for subject matter other than works, in many instances, the first copyright is usually held by those who invested money to produce the subject matter. In many jurisdictions, only works can attract moral rights.

Copyright and websites: Australia and the United States

In the following sections, we will consider the question of whether websites, as whole entities, can be copyrighted. In Australia, in order for websites to attract copyright protection, they must be brought within one of the categories of protected works, or protected subject matter other than works. Websites contain numerous components. Almost all contain a collection of text and/or images. Some contain music, some contain moving images. Theoretically, each individual component of the website is entitled to the protections of copyright, and the total protection afforded will be cumulative. However, the issue of increasing importance to website owners and designers is whether there exists a category appropriate to protect the totality from misappropriation by another. In *Sega v Galaxy Electronics*,[7] a 1997 case of the Federal Court of Australia, it was held that computer games could be protected under the head of films. A film is defined as something which can include sounds as well as moving images in s 10 of the *Copyright Act 1968* (Cth). Although some websites contain moving images and sounds, it would take a stretch of the imagination to regard all websites as films. The most likely head, then, for websites would appear to be compilations which fall under literary work in s 10 of the *Copyright Act*.

Compilations come under the definition of 'literary work' in s 10 of the *Copyright Act*. The most common issue that has arisen thus far regarding compilations is the element of originality. For a compilation to be protected by copyright, it must be regarded as 'original'. A compilation usually involves the putting together of materials that are generally available. So the question becomes, what degree of effort confers originality?

In *Macmillan v Cooper*,[8] it was held that if labour, sound judgment, and literary skill were used to create the compilation, then copyright would subsist. However, the precise amount of labour, judgment, or literary skill required to acquire copyright in a compilation cannot be defined in precise terms. Every case will depend on its special facts and must in each case be a question of degree. In *Cramp & Sons Ltd v Frank Smythson Ltd*,[9] a case dealing with several tables of information on the weather, sunrise and sunset times, and so on, it was held that minimal amounts of labour and judgment would be insufficient for the requirement of originality, as the court found that the tables were simply gobbets of information put together with very little labour, judgment, and skill.

The exact role of originality and the required proportions of the multiple components is unclear. What if there is an enormous amount of labour and a certain degree of judgment and not a lot of creativity? There is some authority in Australia from *Victoria Park Racing & Recreation Grounds Co Ltd v Taylor*[10] that a compilation must produce some original result. In the USA, however, the matter has been laid to rest in the case of *Feist Publications Inc v Rural Telephone Service Co Inc*.[11] The item at issue in this case was a white pages telephone directory listing that was organised alphabetically. The court held that some minimal degree of creativity was required and such an arrangement of data did not move beyond the mechanical or routine manner that could amount to creativity. The court was quite scathing when it said the directory at issue was devoid of the slightest trace of creativity.[12]

---

7   (1997) 37 IPR 462.
8   (1923) LJPC 113.
9   [1944] AC 329.
10   (1937) 58 CLR 479.
11   (1991) 20 IPR 129.
12   In effect, the US Supreme Court rejected the 'sweat of the brow' theory.

In Australia, the unanimous decision of the Full Federal Court in *Desktop Market Systems Pty Ltd v Telstra*[13] seems to suggest substantial labour and expense would be sufficient for copyright to subsist in a compilation. The case concerned Telstra's published white and yellow pages telephone directories and unpublished headings books. Like the US case, the data was arranged alphabetically. At first instance in *Telstra v Desktop Market Systems Pty Ltd*,[14] Finkelstein J stated at [64] that 'copyright will subsist if there has been sufficient intellectual effort in the selection or arrangement of the facts. It will also subsist if the author has engaged in sufficient work or incurred sufficient expense in gathering the facts. The cases have not defined with any precision what amount of intellectual effort, labour, etc, is required to justify copyright.' The Full Court approved this approach and held that originality may be found in industrious collections.

Relating these real-world principles to the Internet, the copyright status of a website will depend on whether the contents on the website, including their selection and arrangement, display a sufficient degree and proportion of originality, labour, skill, and judgment. Only if all of these elements are present to a sufficient degree will the site be protected as a compilation.

 NOTES AND QUESTIONS

1 Why would it be necessary to protect websites as a whole? Would not the protection of the individual parts—for example the text, images and so on—be sufficient?

2 What do you think is the copyright status of websites that contain lists of items arranged alphabetically, without any spark of creativity, but which also contain very original and creative artistic works surrounding the lists on the web pages?

Copyright and websites: the European Union

In the United Kingdom and other EU countries, protection for websites can now come under the category of databases as a result of Directive 96/9/EC of the European Parliament and of the Council of 11 March 1996 on the Legal Protection of Databases.

Directive 96/9/EC of the European Parliament and of the Council of 11 March 1996 on the legal protection of databases

Available at <http://europa.eu.int/eur-lex/en/lif/dat/1996/en_396L0009.html>
4 September 2001

---

13   [2002] FCAFC 112
14   [2001] FCA 612

Chapter I: Scope

ARTICLE 1: SCOPE

1   This Directive concerns the legal protection of databases in any form.
2   For the purposes of this Directive, 'database' shall mean a collection of independent works, data or other materials arranged in a systematic or methodical way and individually accessible by electronic or other means.
3   Protection under this Directive shall not apply to computer programs used in the making or operation of databases accessible by electronic means.

ARTICLE 2: LIMITATIONS ON THE SCOPE
This Directive shall apply without prejudice to Community provisions relating to:

(a) the legal protection of computer programs;
(b) rental right, lending right and certain rights related to copyright in the field of intellectual property;
(c) the term of protection of copyright and certain related rights.

Chapter II: Copyright

ARTICLE 3: OBJECT OF PROTECTION

1   In accordance with this Directive, databases which, by reason of the selection or arrangement of their contents, constitute the author's own intellectual creation shall be protected as such by copyright. No other criteria shall be applied to determine their eligibility for that protection.
2   The copyright protection of databases provided for by this Directive shall not extend to their contents and shall be without prejudice to any rights subsisting in those contents themselves.

ARTICLE 4: DATABASE AUTHORSHIP
1   The author of a database shall be the natural person or group of natural persons who created the base or, where the legislation of the Member States so permits, the legal person designated as the rightholder by that legislation.
2   Where collective works are recognized by the legislation of a Member State, the economic rights shall be owned by the person holding the copyright.
3   In respect of a database created by a group of natural persons jointly, the exclusive rights shall be owned jointly.

 NOTES AND QUESTIONS

1   The emphasis in these provisions is on the intellectual creation of the author as demonstrated through the collection of independent works, data or other materials arranged in a systematic or methodical way. From this, it follows that

the protection is offered to the selection and arrangement of the database, rather than to its contents as such. Of course, the contents may attract copyright—or several copyrights—in their own right.

2　The definition of databases also includes the provision that each component may be individually accessible by electronic or other means. Traditional compilations were grounded by an attachment to the literary form. The new database definition means that database protection is not confined to written collections, or collections based on written material, as distinct from other forms of expression such as graphical. Therefore, this definition can more readily extend to multimedia material that is so crucial to the Internet.

3　What does the use of the phrase 'intellectual creation' in Article 3 indicate about the requirement of originality?

4　This definition of a database seems to encompass websites very comfortably. Individual pages, as well as material included within them, could easily be independent works in their own right, because each element is intended to be and is indeed used on its own; there is no necessary interaction between them. The requirement that the works be individually accessible to the user through electronic means is clearly satisfied, as websites and web pages can be accessed by a computer link to the Internet. Finally, websites are very often constructed in such a way as to represent the intellectual creation of the designer, irrespective of the actual content within the site. The selection and arrangement of material for website presentation involves considerable skill and creativity, which, *prima facie*, satisfies this third requirement of the definition.

5　Consider the definition of databases. Does the directive also protect websites that are random storehouses of materials over which no control or personal selection has been exerted, or where the method of control used has been a standard or common one? Can you find any such websites on the Internet? An Australian example could arguably be AustLII's website at <www.austlii.edu.au>. Authors of such websites could seek protection from the additional *sui generis* database right also introduced under the Database Directive.

Directive 96/9/EC of the European Parliament and of the Council of 11 March 1996 on the legal protection of databases

Available at
<http://europa.eu.int/eur-lex/en/lif/dat/1996/en_396L0009.html> 4 September 2001

Chapter III: Sui Generis Right

ARTICLE 7: OBJECT OF PROTECTION

1　Member States shall provide for a right for the maker of a database which shows that there has been qualitatively and/or quantitatively a substantial investment in either the obtaining, verification or presentation of the contents to prevent extraction and/or re-utilization of the whole or of a substantial part, evaluated qualitatively and/or quantitatively, of the contents of that database.

2   For the purposes of this Chapter:

(a) 'extraction' shall mean the permanent or temporary transfer of all or a substantial part of the contents of a database to another medium by any means or in any form;

(b) 're-utilization' shall mean any form of making available to the public all or a substantial part of the contents of a database by the distribution of copies, by renting, by on-line or other forms of transmission. The first sale of a copy of a database within the Community by the rightholder or with his consent shall exhaust the right to control resale of that copy within the Community; Public lending is not an act of extraction or re-utilization.

3   The right referred to in paragraph 1 may be transferred, assigned or granted under contractual licence.

4   The right provided for in paragraph 1 shall apply irrespective of the eligibility of that database for protection by copyright or by other rights. Moreover, it shall apply irrespective of eligibility of the contents of that database for protection by copyright or by other rights. Protection of databases under the right provided for in paragraph 1 shall be without prejudice to rights existing in respect of their contents.

5   The repeated and systematic extraction and/or re-utilization of insubstantial parts of the contents of the database implying acts which conflict with a normal exploitation of that database or which unreasonably prejudice the legitimate interests of the maker of the database shall not be permitted.

 NOTES AND QUESTIONS

1   As there is no requirement of a personal intellectual creation, what are the requirements for protection in Article 7? What significance might this have for most Internet web pages?

2   What type of creativity or originality is required?

3   We see, therefore, that the EU has responded to intellectual property-based legal challenges with the active development of new legal doctrines. It remains to be seen how effective this doctrine will be in protecting the interests of Internet-based property holders, and whether the European response will be any more effective than the legal rules operating in Australia, and their relatives in the USA.

(d)   Exclusive rights of copyright owners

The goal of lawmakers is to protect authors against unauthorised reproduction, dissemination, or exploitation of their works. Simultaneously it seeks to ensure that the public is neither denied the opportunity to enjoy others' creative output nor unfairly burdened by a proliferation of exclusive rights and the consequent necessity to seek a large number of licences to use copyright material. To this end, the regime of copyright gives owners a set of exclusive rights. It is an infringing act for a person other than the copyright owner to do or authorise the doing of any of these acts without the licence of the copyright owner. Therefore, no person other than the copyright holder can use copyrighted material without the permission or licence of the owner. The copyright regime, in balancing the interests of the public against the interests of copyright owners, also gives users some rights, which we will consider later in this chapter.

Copyright Act 1968 (Cth) as Amended

31. NATURE OF COPYRIGHT IN ORIGINAL WORKS

(1) For the purposes of this Act, unless the contrary intention appears, copyright, in relation to a work, is the exclusive right:

(a) in the case of a literary, dramatic or musical work, to do all or any of the following acts:
   (i)   to reproduce the work in a material form;
   (ii) to publish the work;
   (iii) to perform the work in public;
   (iv) to communicate the work to the public;
   (vi) to make an adaptation of the work;
   (vii) to do, in relation to a work that is an adaptation of the first-mentioned work, any of the acts specified in relation to the first-mentioned work in subparagraphs (i) to (iv), inclusive; and

(b) in the case of an artistic work, to do all or any of the following acts:
   (i)   to reproduce the work in a material form;
   (ii) to publish the work;
   (iii) to communicate the work to the public; and

(c) in the case of a literary work (other than a computer program) or a musical or dramatic work, to enter into a commercial rental arrangement in respect of the work reproduced in a sound recording; and

(d) in the case of a computer program, to enter into a commercial rental arrangement in respect of the program.

 NOTES AND QUESTIONS

1   Are the acts in s 31(1)(a) mutually exclusive? Is it possible to be doing more than one of those acts at any one time? Consider the communication powers of the Internet.

2   What is the relevance of the inclusion of s 31(1)(a)(vi) as well as s 31(1)(a)(vii)? Of what relevance might the inclusion of both subsections be for materials on the Internet?

3   The above rights are the rights given to owners of works. There are similar rights given to owners of subject matter other than works contained in ss 85–88 inclusive.

Reproduction right

Only the author, or his or her licensees or successors in title, can make copies of the work. The 1968 Act states that the copying of works means the reproduction of the work in any material form. The term 'material form' is defined in s 10(1) as including any visible or non-visible form of storage from which the work can be reproduced. Copying then clearly applies to any form of reproduction, including transient and temporary copies. This has been interpreted in the USA[15] and in Australia[16] to apply to the process that occurs when a file is loaded into the Random Access Memory ('RAM') of a computer. For example, whenever Internet users load copyrighted documents onto their screens, they are technically in breach of copyright. Furthermore, as users browse the Internet, the website might be reproduced on a number of servers as it is transmitted from the original source to the user. This, too, would technically be a breach of copyright. This suggests that the entire architecture of the Internet offers users no choice but to breach copyright.

Organisations which employ proxy server caching, where they store a copy of web pages and even whole websites on their own server in order to make the information more readily accessible rather than congest the live site, would also be breaching copyright as they are clearly copying and storing by electronic means. For many of these activities, inherent to the use of the Internet but which seemingly also infringe copyright, the only hope is for an interpretation which brings the activities under the implied licence protection, or some statutorily permitted act.[17]

The extract from Litman, below, examines the position in the USA. At the time the article was published, the Internet as we know it today was only embryonic. Litman's reference throughout to the National Information Infrastructure ('NII') is the umbrella term used in the USA for the American Internet infrastructure. The article is in response to a report entitled *Intellectual Property and the National Information Infrastructure: A Preliminary Draft of the Report of the Working Group on Intellectual Property Rights*, which was released by the Information Infrastructure Task Force in July 1994.

Jessica Litman, 'The Exclusive Right to Read'

13 *Cardozo Arts and Entertainment Law Journal* 29 (1994)

Available at <http://www.law.wayne.edu/litman/papers/read.htm> 17 August 2006

... The Report takes the position that current law secures to the copyright owner control over virtually any reproduction, but finds the state of current law regarding transmission to be less than clear. It therefore recommends amending the law in several respects. First, the distribution right should be amended to 'reflect that copies of works can be distributed to the public by transmission, and such transmissions fall within the exclusive distribution right of the copyright owner.' Second, the Draft Report recommends expanding the current definition of 'transmit' in section 101, to encompass transmissions of reproductions as

---

15   *MAI Systems Corp v Peak Computer Inc* 991 F2d 511 (9th Cir 1993).
16   *Microsoft Corporation v Business Boost Pty Ltd* (2000) 49 IPR 573.
17   See discussion below.

well as transmissions of performances or displays, and to add a test distinguishing between transmissions of reproductions and transmissions of performances and displays based on 'the primary purpose and effect of the transmission'. Third, the Draft Report suggests an amendment making it clear that transmission of a work into the United States violates the copyright owner's exclusive importation rights. Fourth, the Report suggests that the first sale doctrine, which allows the owner of a lawfully made copy to sell, loan, rent or otherwise dispose of the possession of that copy, be repealed insofar as it might apply to transmissions. Finally, the Draft Report offers miscellaneous suggestions to forestall the emergence of other perceived threats to the copyright owners' bundle of rights.

By vesting copyright owners with control of any reproduction or transmission of their works, and then defining reproduction and transmission to include any appearance, even a fleeting one, of a protected work in any computer, and any transfer of that work to, from, or through any other computer, the Draft Report's recommendations would enhance the exclusive rights in the copyright bundle so far as to give the copyright owner the exclusive right to control reading, viewing or listening to any work in digitized form. The Draft Report comes down firmly on the side of increased rights for copyright owners and it endorses the goal of enhanced copyright protection without acknowledging any countervailing concerns. Because it is an advocacy document, it at times misrepresents the state of current law. It gives voice to only one side of complicated policy debates. In some cases, the Report identifies a particular alternative as more desirable because it gives copyright owners rights subject to fewer exceptions. The Report's drafters apparently did not perceive objectivity or balance to be their job.

Nor is anyone else clamoring to volunteer. The general public's interest in copyright legislation is diffuse; a grass-roots revolt of copyright users seems unlikely. Interest groups with copyright on their agendas have a long history of dropping their opposition to copyright amendments of general application in return for narrow provisions addressing their specific concerns. Congress, for its part, has, since the turn of the century, been delegating the policy choices involved in copyright matters to the industries affected by copyright. But, before we succumb to calls for further enhancement of the rights in the copyright bundle, we need to reexamine the intellectual property bargain from the vantage point of the public, on whose behalf, after all, the copyright deal is said to be struck in the first place. Does the shape of the law as it currently stands make sense? Do the changes that are being proposed cause it to make more sense, or less sense?

I.

At the turn of the century, US copyright law was technical, inconsistent, and difficult to understand, but it didn't apply to very many people or very many things. If one were an author or publisher of books, maps, charts, paintings, sculpture, photographs, or sheet music, a playwright or producer of plays, or a printer, the copyright law bore on one's business. Booksellers, piano-roll and phonograph record publishers, motion picture producers, musicians, scholars, members of Congress, and ordinary consumers could go about their business without ever encountering a copyright problem.

Ninety years later, the US copyright law is even more technical, inconsistent and difficult to understand; more importantly, it touches everyone and everything. In the intervening years, copyright has reached out to embrace much of the paraphernalia of modern society. The current copyright statute weighs in at 142 pages. Technology, heedless of law, has developed modes that insert multiple acts of reproduction and transmission—potentially actionable events under the copyright statute—into commonplace daily transactions. Most of us can no longer spend even an hour without colliding with the copyright law. Reading one's mail or picking up one's telephone messages these days requires many of us to commit acts that the government's Information Infrastructure Task Force now tells us ought to be viewed as unauthorized reproductions or transmissions.

What we know about the general public's impression of the shape of copyright law suggests that the public believes that the copyright statute confers on authors the exclusive right to profit commercially from their copyrighted works, but does not reach private or non-commercial conduct. The law in this country has never been that simple; the copyright statute has never expressly privileged private or non-commercial use. Until recently, however, the public's impression was not a bad approximation of the scope of copyright rights likely, in practice, to be enforced. If copyright owners insisted, as sometimes they did, that copyright gave them broad rights to control their works in any manner and in all forms, the practical costs of enforcing those rights against individual consumers dissuaded them from testing their claims in court. So long as nobody proposed to sue the nation's teenagers for copying music onto audio cassette tapes, or copying computer games onto floppy disks, what did it matter that some folks argued that if they chose to sue they could win?

Nonetheless, by asserting that what members of the public think of as ordinary use of copyrighted works was, in fact, flagrant piracy, and that, as such, it undermined the national economy, copyright owners may well have won a rhetorical battle the rest of the country never realized was being fought. As industries lobby, scholars analyze, and bureaucrats convene in too many meetings to consider the shape of the new-and-improved National Information Infrastructure, few people have seriously challenged copyright owners' claims to control all access to and use of the material they say they own. Arguments for universal access are, so far, cast in terms of good citizenship rather than entitlement. Even those who favor liberal subsidy of public access to the information highway seem to accept the contention that if copyright owners cannot maintain control of their asserted property, the wellspring of American creativity will dry up, our trade deficit will turn into a mushroom cloud, and our balance of payments will drop off and fall into the sea. Meanwhile, because the assumptions underlying copyright owners' claims to expansive control over the works they create and disseminate crept into our discourse without much examination at a time when the price of acknowledging them was only nominal, we have so far allowed important policy choices to be made without debate.

II.

Imagine that you have been retained as the public's copyright lawyer. One morning, your client, the public, walks into your office to consult you about a deal that it has been offered.

It seems that all of the industries with substantial economic stakes in copyright have gotten together and written up a proposal. Here it is: the current copyright statute. It's 142 pages long, and, frankly, it's a little hard to decipher. Your client stayed up all night to read it, and can't seem to make head or tail of it. In any event, your client drops this 142 page tome on your desk.

> Client: 'So, whaddya think? Should I sign it? Is it a good deal?'
>
> You (temporizing): 'It depends,' you say. 'What sort of a bargain do you want?'
>
> Client: 'Look; I'm not out to get something for nothing. I understand that authors won't write stuff if they can't get paid. I want them to make new works and I'm willing to pay them to do so. I want to encourage authors to write as many new works as they can. As for me, I want to be able to read, see, hear or download any work in captivity, and pay appropriate royalties for doing so. Will this proposal let me do that?'

Would you recommend that your client sign on the dotted line?

I would not. The text we're considering wasn't really written with your client's interests in mind. Most of it was drafted by the representatives of copyright-intensive businesses and institutions, who were chiefly concerned about their interaction with other copyright-intensive businesses and institutions. For that reason, there's lots of verbiage speaking to the behavior of a public television station or a cable system operator with respect to the programming it might transmit, but very few words addressing the behavior of a consumer with respect to the programming she might watch or record. You can find a fair amount of language relevant to the actions of a publisher bringing out an author's new novel, and the film producer that seeks to adapt the story for the screen, but not so much about the actions of the police officer who buys and reads the book, rents and sees the film, and wishes the producer had not cast Tom Cruise in the leading role. The law has a specific provision for retail stores who play the radio for their customers, but no language that seems to contemplate fraternities who play loud music for their neighbors. Thus, the statute fails to discuss your client's ability or obligation to pay appropriate royalties in return for access, and there is no provision securing your client's opportunity to read, see, hear, or download copyrighted works.

One can draw different conclusions from the paucity of language speaking to the behavior of individuals who are consuming rather than exploring copyrighted material. One conclusion that is commonly voiced is that the statute really doesn't address the legal obligations of individuals acting in their private capacities. An equally plausible interpretation, favored by copyright owners and copyright lawyers, is that the statute forbids private individuals, acting without permission, to invade the copyright owner's broad rights unless their behavior falls within an express statutory exception. In the words of the Draft Report: 'Users are not granted any affirmative "rights" under the *Copyright Act*; rather, copyright owners' rights are limited by certain exemptions from user liability.' There are not very many specific exceptions addressed to individuals' private actions, which means that individuals are routinely prohibited from doing the sorts of things that businesses have statutory exceptions for unless they first secure the copyright owner's permission.

Either way, though, it doesn't seem as if the agreement reflected in the 142 pages is yet in your client's interest as your client has expressed it. Perhaps the changes suggested by the Draft Report will help.

III.

The IITF Draft Report presents its task as the proposal of modest adjustments to repair the unintended damage that the passage of time and the growth of technology have had on the copyright law:

It is difficult for intellectual property laws to keep pace with technology. When technological advances cause ambiguity in the law, courts rely on the law's purposes to resolve that ambiguity. However, when technology gets too far ahead of the law, and it becomes difficult and awkward to apply the old principles, it is time for reevaluation and change. 'Even though the 1976 *Copyright Act* was carefully drafted to be flexible enough to be applied to future innovations, technology has a habit of outstripping even the most flexible statutes.'

The coat is getting a little tight. There is no need for a new one, but the old one needs a few alterations.

The Draft Report recapitulates oft-voiced complaints about the damage to the integrity of the rights in the copyright bundle caused by the unanticipated fallout from digital technology. The ease of digital copying is frequently said to pose a profound threat to copyright at its core. The same technological miracles that pose the threat, however, have served up some unanticipated windfalls for the copyright owner. The most crucial example is the evolution of the reproduction right into something more encompassing than envisioned in any copyright revision until now. United States copyright law has always given copyright owners some form of exclusive reproduction right. It has never before now given them an exclusive reading right, and it is hard to make a plausible argument that Congress would have enacted a law giving copyright owners control of reading. A handful of recent interpretations of the statute, however, insist that one reproduces a work every time one reads it into a computer's random access memory. For all works encoded in digital form, any act of reading or viewing the work would require the use of a computer, and would, under this interpretation, involve an actionable reproduction. One might therefore expect an analysis proposing modest alterations of the law (to fix unintended ambiguities) to suggest clarifying this point: amending the law to provide explicitly that an individual's ordinary reading, viewing, or listening to an authorized copy of a work does not invade the copyright owner's rights. Instead, debates on the intellectual property underpinnings of the proposed National Information Infrastructure have proceeded on the assumption that copyright does, and should, assure such rights to the copyright owner. The Draft Report adopts this view; it claims that 'it has long been clear that under US law the placement of a work into a computer's memory amounts to a reproduction of that work' and suggests that the expansiveness of the reproduction right should be exploited to ensure copyright owners' enhanced control of protected works.

In fact, the Draft Report's characterization of current law is dubious, and the Report does not cite authority to support it. There is support available: the Report could have mentioned three recent cases, a stray remark in the CONTU Report, and brief discussions in a couple of recent law review articles. This is some support, but it is hard to argue that the proposition 'has long been clear under US law'. The CONTU reference is ambiguous; the other sources are recent. Authority on the other side of the question includes the statutory language, and the following passage from the House Report accompanying the 1976 Act:

Reproduction under clause (1) of section 106 is to be distinguished from 'display' under clause (5). For a work to be 'reproduced', its fixation in tangible form must be 'sufficiently permanent or stable to permit it to be perceived, reproduced, or otherwise communicated for a period of more than transitory duration'. Thus, the showing of images on a screen or tube would not be a violation of clause (1), although it might come within the scope of clause (5).

I would argue that the better view of the law is that the act of reading a work into a computer's random access memory is too transitory to create a reproduction within the meaning of section 106(1).

In any event, even if the Draft Report's characterization of current law were not skewed, its endorsement of what it presents as well-settled law deserves examination. If a bargain between the public and the authors and producers of copyrighted works were negotiated (at arm's length) and drafted up today, it might include a reproduction right, but it surely wouldn't include a 'reading' right. It might include a performance right but not a 'listening' right; it might have a display right, but it wouldn't have a 'viewing' right. From the public's vantage point, the fact that copyright owners are now in a position to claim exclusive 'reading', 'listening', and 'viewing' rights is an accident of drafting: when Congress awarded authors an exclusive reproduction right, it did not mean what it may mean today.

The Draft Report's proposed resolution of the ambiguities introduced into the law by the passage of time and the invention of new media is not, from the public's point of view, an improvement. If you were the public's copyright lawyer, you would, in my view, be hard pressed to assure your client that the Draft Report's proposals for modest alterations were in fact a good deal.

IV.

The Draft Report argues that its proposed enhancement of copyright owners' rights is without question in the public interest, for it is a necessary first step in the creation of the information superhighway. This is the central justification for further enhancing the rights in the copyright bundle: without strong copyright protection, there will be no National Information Infrastructure. The public might believe that what it wants is unfettered access to copyrighted works in return for reasonable royalty payments to authors, but, if we let the public set the freight charges, we risk underproduction of freight. If authors and publishers cannot reliably control their works, they will decline to make them available at all. The Draft Report puts it this way:

The potential of the NII will not be realized if the information and entertainment products protectable by intellectual property laws are not protected effectively when disseminated via the NII. Owners of intellectual property rights will not be willing to put their interests at risk if appropriate systems—both in the US and internationally—are not in place to permit them to set and enforce the terms and conditions under which their works are made available in the NII environment. Likewise, the public will not use the services available on the NII and generate the market necessary for its success unless access to a wide variety of works is provided under equitable and reasonable terms and conditions, and the integrity of those works is assured. All the computers, telephones, fax machines, scanners, cameras, keyboards, televisions, monitors, printers, switches, routers, wires, cables, networks and satellites in the world will not create a successful NII, if there is not *content*. What will drive the NII is the content moving through it.

If the public wishes an NII, the argument goes, it must offer strong copyright protection as a bribe to those whom it hopes to persuade to create enough stuff to make an NII worthwhile. Relying on a hope that if the public only builds the infrastructure, the information to travel it will come is said to be naive; of course the owners of protectable works will refuse to permit those works to be exploited unless their ownership rights are secure.

It appears to follow from that analysis that my thought experiment is ill-considered. We should not pursue the public's hypothetical interest in paying reasonable fees in return for unfettered access to copyrighted works because the deal cannot be struck on those terms. If the public stops promising authors 'a reward in the form of control', we will soon run short of new copyrighted works to read, see, hear or download. Representatives of copyright owners have made this argument repeatedly in the context of the NII. They couldn't be bluffing about that, could they?

B.

The model suggesting that production and dissemination of valuable, protectable works is directly related to the degree of available intellectual property protection is much too simplistic. In fact, history teaches us a more equivocal lesson. Whenever we have discovered or enacted a copyright exception, an industry has grown up within its shelter. Player piano rolls became ubiquitous after courts ruled that they did not infringe the copyright in the underlying musical composition; phonograph records superseded both piano rolls and sheet music with the aid of the compulsory license for mechanical reproductions; the jukebox industry arose to take advantage of the copyright exemption accorded to 'the reproduction or rendition of a musical composition by or upon coin-operated machines'. Composers continued to write music, and found ways to exploit these new media for their works.

The videotape rental business swept the nation shielded from copyright liability by the first sale doctrine. The motion picture industry predicted that if Congress failed to rush in to correct the problems posed by the invention and marketing of the videocassette recorder, American television would slowly be destroyed, and American motion picture production would sustain grave injury. Howard Wayne Oliver, Executive Secretary of AFTRA (American Federation of Television and Radio Artists) told the House Subcommittee:

> Unless we do something to ensure that the creators of the material are not exploited by the electronics revolution, that same revolution which will make it possible for almost every household to have an audio and video recorder will surely undermine, cripple, and eventually wash away the very industries on which it feeds and which provide employment for thousands of our citizens.

Notwithstanding all of the gloom and doom, however, both the motion picture and television industries discovered that the videocassette recorder generated new markets for prerecorded versions of their material.

Cable television began spreading across America with the aid of a copyright exemption; it eclipsed broadcast television while sheltered by the cable compulsory license. Yet, there is no dearth of television programming, and the popular media image of the new information superhighway includes 500 television channels to accommodate it all.

Even an erroneous assumption of copyright immunity can stimulate a nascent industry. The commercial photocopy shop prospered in part because of the university coursepack business made possible by a supposed fair use privilege. Commercial and non-commercial subscriptions to services providing access to the Internet are increasing geometrically, and much of the activity on the net takes place on the mistaken assumption that any material on the Internet is free from copyright unless expressly declared to be otherwise. Nonetheless, there are scores of electronic magazines and news services developed specifically for electronic distribution, and many commercial publishers are currently releasing their works over the Internet despite the absence of effective coercive means of protection.

Of course, copyright owners would prefer to maximize their own control over the works they produce. Of course, if we ask them to come up with an optimal copyright law, they will draft one that meets that specification. If the general public had a lawyer to sit at the copyright negotiating table on its behalf, however, the law that emerged from the negotiating process might be a different one.

V.

... Our current copyright law is a descendant of the copyright laws in force at the turn of the century and before, which were designed to bring order to the interaction among affected industries. Because affected industries, and their lawyers, were invited to draft those rules themselves, the law became so technical, detailed, and counterintuitive that those industries now need to bring their copyright lawyers along to tell them how to play. If the law is intended to affect only the behavior of players with substantial economic stakes in copyright-affected matters, there is not much wrong with that degree of complexity. As soon, however, as the law is claimed to control the ordinary behavior of ordinary members of the public going about their ordinary daily business, then that species of law will no longer serve.

If we want ordinary people to look at unlicensed music, unlicensed software, and unlicensed digital reading material the same way they see stolen personal property, and to treat them accordingly, then we need to teach them the rules that govern intellectual property when we teach them the rules that govern other personal property, which is to say, in elementary school. That proposition should not be controversial; the Draft Report suggests that very thing. The problem, though, is that our current copyright statute could not be taught in elementary school, because elementary school students couldn't understand it. Indeed, their teachers couldn't understand it. Copyright lawyers don't understand it. If we are going to teach the copyright law to school children, then we need the law to be sensible, intuitive, and short enough that school children can hold its essential provisions in their heads. What we have now is not even close. We need, in other words, to abandon entirely the idea that we can make members of the public conduct their daily affairs under rules thought up by and for major players in copyright-affected industries. If the public is to play by copyright rules, then those rules must be designed with the public's interests in mind.

VI.

Imagine once again that the public has retained you as its copyright lawyer. Acting in your new role, you review the current statute, and the government's proposal for adjusting it, and you chat with your client about where to go from here:

> You: 'Look. I think the copyright concept is a good one, but I'm not happy with the details. There are a bunch of places where I think the language is unfortunate, and not in your long term best interest. Let me take it home and see if I can draft up a counterproposal that'll meet your needs, here.'
>
> Client: 'Gee. That's great; that's what I hoped you'd say. But look, this time, when you're writing it up, could you make it real short? I don't read so fast, and this is real important to me. I want to understand what it says.'

So, you have yourself a drafting project. Your job is to construct a copyright law that affords members of the public the opportunity to read, see, hear, and otherwise experience, download, buy, borrow and keep copies of all, or at least most, of the works that are out there, while according ample compensation to the authors and publishers of copyrighted works, and encouraging them to produce and disseminate as many copyrighted works as they are able to. The law should be about three pages long, should strike more folks than not as more fair than not, and should be sufficiently intuitive to appeal to school children. Let's say that you take about an hour, and come up with some language that meets spec. Your client approves it. You take it over to Congress. Or maybe you take it over to the Patent and Trademark Office at the US Commerce Department, home of the Information Infrastructure Task Force's Working Group on Intellectual Property Rights. Or, maybe, you sign on to the Internet and post it for all to read. You have only one final problem: Congress isn't going to enact it.

The only way that copyright laws get passed in this country is for all of the lawyers who represent the current stakeholders to get together and hash out all of the details among themselves. In the past, this process has produced laws that are unworkable from the vantage point of people who were not among the negotiating parties, and it won't generate any better results this time. The public needs to sit at the negotiating table and insist that any solution must seriously address its interests, as well as theirs.

What the public needs is a copyright lawyer of its own to represent it in the revision or replacement of the copyright law we now have, and the proposals for amending it that the National Information Infrastructure is inspiring. If you were unable to take the assignment yourself, where would you send your prospective client to find someone who would act as the copyright lawyer for the general public? Where would you send your prospective client to find someone who could do it well?

That is supposed to be Congress's job, of course. Congress is the public's copyright lawyer. The problem is that Congress is also the public's bankruptcy lawyer, and our trade lawyer, and our outer-space lawyer. Congress seems to lack the interest, expertise, and institutional memory to represent the public on this particular project; indeed, what Congress has done more often than not is delegate the job of coming up with legislation to interested private parties, which is how the statute got so long and convoluted in the first place.

But, Congress *has* a copyright lawyer of its own. That is the Copyright Office's job. The Copyright Office *does* have both the expertise and institutional memory; it has functioned as Congress's copyright lawyer and copyright expert for almost a century. The Office has, of course, some history of being 'captured' by industry for most of the usual reasons (limited budgets, revolving doors, and the growing perception that copyright owners were in fact the Office's real constituency), but the public badly needs a copyright lawyer. The Copyright Office is in the very best position to perform that function. Besides, the Draft Report issued by the Working Group headquartered in the Patent and Trademark Office indicates that the Patent Office has already managed to assume much of the job of serving the interests of industry. This may be an unusually good moment for the Copyright Office to think very hard about redefining its role.

The Copyright Office's enormous expertise could enable it not only to persuade all of us (that is, both stakeholders and individual members of the public) that the public's interests are compatible rather than adverse to the interests of copyright owners, but also to make it so. What it would require, though, is a different sort of legislative proposal than the ones we have gotten used to seeing over the years. The Copyright Office has focused much of its recent attention on the threats that technology might unbalance the copyright bargain to the detriment of copyright owners, and has failed to attend to the danger that the bargain might unbalance to the detriment of the public. All it would take would be for the Office to view the public as its copyright client. And somebody certainly should.

[Footnotes omitted]

 NOTES AND QUESTIONS

1   One of the intentions of the WIPO Copyright Treaty, discussed below, was to clarify whether temporary or incidental copying, as occurs in routine Internet activity, amounts to reproduction as prohibited by the current copyright regime. The USA had argued that this temporary copying should be viewed as a reproduction and that a new article be inserted to state that all reproduction whether direct or indirect, whether permanent or temporary, in any manner or form would amount to a reproduction. This is an extraordinarily broad provision which goes well beyond current provisions. As a counterweight, the USA suggested that the States Parties could then enact exceptions to this rule as they wished. This was a controversial suggestion, and it generated substantial criticisms aimed both at the breadth of the rule and the proposed freedom to enact exceptions. Therefore, this provision was not adopted. The conference did agree on an Agreed Statement providing that electronic storage was covered under the existing Article 9 of the Berne Convention. However, this statement only serves to raise more questions—such as the definition of electronic storage—while leaving the original question unanswered.

2   At the national level, in Australia, the 2000 amendments to the *Copyright Act* do include provisions that specifically refer to browsing. Section 43A(1) excludes temporary reproductions made in the course of the technical process of making or receiving electronic communications from the scope of the existing reproduction right. This is intended to include the browsing (or simply viewing) of copyright

material, including copyright material that involves the production of sound. As such, the position in Australia is considerably clearer than at the international level. Similarly, a new s 43B and s 111B were added in 2004 to clarify that a temporary copy of a non-infringing copy of the copyright material created in the RAM in the ordinary course of use would not be an infringement of copyright.

3   Litman's article is entitled 'The Exclusive Right to Read'. Does she present a compelling critique of the US position? What is her thesis?

4   Litman criticises the development of legislation through lobby groups. Are her criticisms valid? What alternatives are there for the development of new legal norms? Can you suggest an alternative model?

5   Compare and contrast the arguments of Litman and Barlow. Which, if either, do you find more compelling, and why? If you are equally unimpressed with both, explain why and outline some alternative propositions to rebut their assertions and conclusions.

6   The issues of linking and deep linking have also arisen in the context of breach of the reproduction right. See the section on this topic in Chapter 10, below.

Public performance right

The public performance right is enjoyed by literary, dramatic, and musical work copyright holders. It is particularly important for those involved in music and drama. Section 27(1)(a) of the *Copyright Act 1968* (Cth) defines performance as any mode of visual or aural presentation. This would mean that an unauthorised display of a literary work on a website could be regarded as a performance. If the presentation occurs in public, then it will infringe the right of public performance. For subject matter other than works, the equivalent right is the right to cause the recording or film to be heard or seen in public.

Most computer displays do not take place in public or for an assembled mass. However, there is technically nothing to prevent such a use of computers. A further possible interpretation of performing in public is whether the Internet itself could be considered a public place or in public. It is arguable that settings such as chat rooms on the Internet would be considered to be public, thus if a user were to post a literary work, for example to the chat room, it would indeed be an infringement of the public performance right. But where do websites stand on this? Would it be an infringement of the public performance right to show a film on a website? The film may or may not be viewed by audiences simultaneously, or by anyone at all. Would this be significant to the concept of 'in public'? There are currently no definitive legal answers to these questions.

 ## NOTES AND QUESTIONS

1   The relationship between the numerous exclusive rights can sometimes be quite complex. The publication right contained in s 29 of the *Copyright Act 1968* (Cth) provides for both the exclusive right of first publication and the right to distribute copies of previously published works. Section 29(1)(a) states that a

work is only published if reproductions of it have been supplied to the public by sale or otherwise. However, in relation to a work for which a sound recording has been made, it is not a publication of a work to supply records of it to the public. Nor is it a publication of a literary, dramatic or musical work to perform it. These acts are covered by the performance right.

2   Investigate the provisions of the Berne Convention relevant to the right to first publication. Are these rules drafted such that they will accommodate the demands of Internet publication? Are the Australian provisions so drafted?

3   List all of the exclusive rights held by copyright owners. For each right outline at least one point of overlap with another right. Does the overlap make for a more coherent matrix of protection, or does it merely serve to produce confusion in the minds of both authors and users of copyright material?

Communication right

The genealogy of the communication right is crucial to understanding its place in the copyright protection regime. Therefore, a brief digression is necessary to highlight the developments that have engineered it.

In 1996 the WIPO Diplomatic Conference on Certain Copyright and Neighbouring Rights Questions adopted two treaties: the *Treaty on Certain Questions Concerning the Protection of Literary and Artistic Works* (Copyright Treaty) and the *WIPO Performances and Phonograms Treaty*. The treaties are open for membership to any member state of WIPO and the European Community. The focus here will be on the former of these two enactments.

The treaties were an attempt to deal with the copyright challenges posed by digital technology, particularly the Internet, and the challenges to Berne posed by the recent TRIPS Agreement. The Copyright Treaty does not amend TRIPS. TRIPS operates under the WTO and as such, any amendments must be approved by all WTO member states. The signatories to TRIPS and Berne are not parallel, although they are related.

As stated in Article 1 of the Copyright Treaty, the treaty is actually a special agreement under the Berne Convention and has no connection to any other convention.

Treaty on Certain Questions Concerning the Protection of Literary and Artistic Works (The Copyright Treaty) 1996

Available at <http://arl.cni.org/info/frn/copy/copytreaty.html> 5 August 2001

ARTICLE 8: RIGHT OF COMMUNICATION TO THE PUBLIC

Without prejudice to the provisions of Articles 11(1)(ii), 11 *bis* (1)(i) and (ii), 11 *ter* (1)(ii), 14(1)(ii) and 14 *bis* (1) of the Berne Convention, authors of literary and artistic works shall enjoy the exclusive right of authorizing any communication to the public of their works, by wire or wireless means, including the making available to the public of their works in such a way that members of the public may access these works from a place and at a time individually chosen by them.

 NOTES AND QUESTIONS

1   To which particular area of Internet technology is the following targeted: '… may access these works from a place and at a time individually chosen by them'?

2   The inclusion of wire or wireless was intended to cover those links of the Internet via wireless means, such as satellite dishes, using mobile phones with laptop computers to connect to the Internet, and so on.

3   From your reading of Article 8, do you think it is intended to include the mere provision of physical facilities for enabling or making a communication? See the Agreed Statement concerning Article 8.

4   Who do you think is included in 'members of the public'? Does it include members of a private on-line chat group that limits its membership to, say, twenty users from around the world?

5   Although communication is closely related to transmission, the distinction is more than mere semantics. 'Communication' is an umbrella term which can cover transmission, along with a number of other actions. Put simply, transmission must occur before communication can take place, and the term 'transmission' carries an implication of an added technical requirement. Nevertheless, for the purposes of state parties, it was suggested that parallel legislation could use 'transmission' and 'communication' interchangeably.

6   The communication right was, of course, not the only new development within the copyright treaty. The treaty also consolidates, expands, or creates a number of other rights, including the distribution right and rental rights. The distribution right is specifically stated in the Agreed Statement concerning Article 6 to apply only to tangible items, and hence the distribution right would not be applicable to distribution over the Internet. The Treaty also requires states to prohibit circumvention of technological protection measures used to protect copyright, and to prohibit the removal or alteration of rights management information. These issues will be discussed later in this chapter.

In order to have any substantive effect, the new communication right must be embodied in national legislation. In Australia, this was implemented in the form of the *Copyright Amendment (Digital Agenda) Act 2000*. This Act stemmed from both the Copyright Treaty and a government white paper entitled *Copyright Reform and the Digital Agenda, 1997*. The original discussion paper attempted to split the communication right into two components: a one-way transmission right, and a right to control the process of making materials available for access via interactive servers. Subsequently, the Australian Act followed the WIPO Copyright Treaty very closely.

Copyright Amendment (Digital Agenda) Act 2000 (Cth)

3. OBJECT OF THE ACT

The object of this Act is to amend the *Copyright Act 1968* so as to:

(a) ensure the efficient operation of relevant industries in the online environment by:

  (i) promoting the creation of copyright material and the exploitation of new online technologies by allowing financial rewards for creators and investors; and

  (ii) providing a practical enforcement regime for copyright owners; and

  (iii) promoting access to copyright material online; and

(b) promote certainty for communication and information technology industries that are investing in and providing online access to copyright material; and

(c) provide reasonable access and certainty for end users of copyright material online; and

(d) ensure that cultural and educational institutions can access, and promote access to, copyright material in the online environment on reasonable terms, including having regard to the benefits of public access to the material and the provision of adequate remuneration to creators and investors; and

(e) ensure that the relevant global technical standards which form the basis of new communication and information technologies, such as the Internet, are not jeopardised.

 NOTES AND QUESTIONS

  1 The above section is the only stand-alone section of the Amendment Act. The provisions extracted below were inserted by the Amendment Act and now exist within the *Copyright Act* as amended.

  2 Consider the object of promoting access to copyright material on-line as you read the sections below. Critically evaluate whether this object is achieved.

Copyright Act 1968 (Cth) as Amended

10. INTERPRETATION

(1) In this Act, unless the contrary intention appears ...

broadcast means a communication to the public delivered by a broadcasting service within the meaning of the *Broadcasting Services Act 1992*.

communicate means make available online or electronically transmit (whether over a path, or a combination of paths, provided by a material substance or otherwise) a work or other subject-matter, including a performance, or live performance within the meaning of this Act.

85. NATURE OF COPYRIGHT IN SOUND RECORDINGS

(1) For the purposes of this Act, unless the contrary intention appears, copyright, in relation to a sound recording, is the exclusive right to do all or any of the following acts: ...

    (c) to communicate the recording to the public; ...

 NOTES AND QUESTIONS

1   This new right of communication is given to all works, sound recordings, films, and television and radio broadcasts. The only subject matter of copyright which does not receive this new right is the published edition.

2   Critically analyse the definition of 'communicate'. How significant is the fact that the definition is technology-neutral? Does the definition include one-to-one transmissions such as e-mail?

3   The new right of communication replaced and extended the technology-specific broadcasting right, which previously only applied to wireless broadcasts. The new right also replaced the right to transmit to subscribers of a diffusion service.

4   The term 'communicate' is limited to the making available of materials on-line or through electronic transmissions. It is not intended to cover the physical distribution of copyright material in a tangible form.

5   The communication right is a right of communication 'to the public'. Section 10(1) defines 'to the public' to mean 'to the public within or outside Australia'. What is the purpose of the reference to Australia in this definition? How useful is this definition to copyright holders?

6   In the High Court of Australia case of *Telstra Corp Ltd v Australasian Performing Right Assn Ltd*,[18] 'to the public' was considered in relation to music played to mobile phone users on hold. The Court found that the fact that at any one time the number of persons to whom the transmission is made may be small does not mean that the transmission is not made to the public. Nor does it matter that those persons in a position to receive the transmission form only a part of the public, though it is no doubt necessary that the facility be available to those members of the public who choose to avail themselves of it.[19]

7   Consider the communication right in the light of the arguments put forward by Litman above. To what extent can the criticisms of the US regulations be applied to the Australian attempts at control?

8   Consider all the exclusive rights given to copyright owners. Which other rights may overlap with the right of communication?

Protecting the new copyright: offences and remedies

The exclusive rights of copyright holders, particularly the most recently created rights, combined with the increasing sophistication of software demand a new set of offences

---

18   (1997) 38 IPR 294.
19   (1997) 38 IPR 294 at 303.

and remedies to help copyright owners protect and monitor their exclusive rights and to empower them generally with respect to those rights.

Section 116A prohibits the making, dealing in, or distribution of circumvention devices for technological protection measures as well as their importation for commercial purposes, by giving copyright holders civil remedies. The prohibition is not on the use of such devices. The section also contains a rebuttable presumption that the defendant knew, or ought reasonably to have known, that the device would be used to circumvent, or facilitate the circumvention of, technological protection measures. There are also exemptions from liability in instances where the device is supplied for 'permitted purposes', such as to make interoperable products or to correct program errors.

Copyright Act 1968 (Cth) as Amended

10. INTERPRETATION

'circumvention device' means a device (including a computer program) having only a limited commercially significant purpose or use, or no such purpose or use, other than the circumvention, or facilitating the circumvention, of an effective technological protection measure.

'technological protection measure' means a device or product, or a component incorporated into a process, that is designed, in the ordinary course of its operation, to prevent or inhibit the infringement of copyright in a work or other subject-matter by either or both of the following means:

(a) by ensuring that access to the work or other subject matter is available solely by use of an access code or process (including decryption, unscrambling or other transformation of the work or other subject-matter) with the authority of the owner or exclusive licensee of the copyright;

(b) through a copy control mechanism

 NOTES AND QUESTIONS

1   Apart from password protection, what else might be considered a technological protection measure?

2   Is the definition of circumvention device drawn tightly enough? Why, or why not?

3   Subsections 132(5A) and (5B) create criminal offences for, *inter alia*, providing, manufacturing and importing a circumvention device. Do you think the inclusion of criminal sanctions is excessive?

Copyright Act 1968 (Cth) As Amended

116B. REMOVAL OR ALTERATION OF ELECTRONIC RIGHTS MANAGEMENT INFORMATION

(1) This section applies if:

    (a) either:
        (i) a person removes, from a copy of a work or other subject-matter in which copyright subsists, any electronic rights management information that relates to the work or other subject-matter in which copyright subsists; or
        (ii) a person alters any electronic rights management information that relates to a work or other subject-matter in which copyright subsists; and
    (b) the person does so without the permission of the owner or exclusive licensee of the copyright; and
    (c) the person knew, or ought reasonably to have known, that the removal or alteration would induce, enable, facilitate or conceal an infringement of the copyright in the work or other subject-matter.

(2) If this section applies, the owner or exclusive licensee of the copyright may bring an action against the person.

(3) In an action under subsection (2), it must be presumed that the defendant knew, or ought reasonably to have known, that the removal or alteration to which the action relates would have the effect referred to in paragraph (1)(c) unless the defendant proves otherwise.

116C. COMMERCIAL DEALINGS ETC WITH WORKS WHOSE ELECTRONIC RIGHTS MANAGEMENT INFORMATION IS REMOVED OR ALTERED

(1) This section applies if:

    (a) a person does any of the following acts in relation to a work or other subject-matter in which copyright subsists without the permission of the owner or exclusive licensee of the copyright:
        (i) distributes a copy of the work or other subject-matter to the public;
        (ii) imports into Australia a copy of the work or other subject-matter for distribution to the public;
        (iii) communicates a copy of the work or other subject-matter to the public; and
    (b) either:
        (i) any electronic rights management information that relates to the work or other subject-matter has been removed from the copy of the work or subject-matter; or
        (ii) any electronic rights management information that relates to the work or other subject-matter has been altered; and

(c) the person knew that the electronic rights management information had been so removed or altered without the permission of the owner or exclusive licensee of the copyright; and

(d) the person knew, or ought reasonably to have known, that the act referred to in paragraph (a) that was done by the person would induce, enable, facilitate or conceal an infringement of the copyright in the work or other subject-matter.

(2) If this section applies, the owner or exclusive licensee of the copyright may bring an action against the person.

(3) In an action under subsection (2), it must be presumed that the defendant:

(a) had the knowledge referred to in paragraph (1)(c); and

(b) knew, or ought reasonably to have known, that the doing of the act to which the action relates would have the effect referred to in paragraph (1)(d);

unless the defendant proves otherwise.

10. INTERPRETATION

(1) In this Act, unless the contrary intention appears: ...

Electronic rights management information, in relation to a work or other subject-matter, means information that:

(a) is electronic; and

(b) either

(i) is or was attached to, or is or was embodied in, a copy of the work or subject-matter; or

(ii) appears or appeared in connection with a communication, or the making available, of the work or subject-matter; and

(c) either:

(i) identifies the work or subject-matter, and its author or copyright owner (including such information represented as numbers or codes); or

(ii) identifies or indicates some or all of the terms and conditions on which the work or subject-matter may be used, or indicates that the use of the work or subject-matter is subject to terms or conditions (including such information represented as numbers or codes).

 NOTES AND QUESTIONS

1 The definition of electronic rights management information is intended to be consistent with the WIPO Copyright Treaty and s 116C was designed to ensure compliance with Article 12 of the Treaty. However, these were amended as a result of the Australia-US Free Trade Agreement ('AUSFTA') to bring them in line with the US position.

2 Against whom is the s 116B action directed? What are the requirements of such an action?

3 What are the actions which s 116C attempts to prohibit? Read carefully s 116C(1)(a). Why is there a need for each of the three subsections? Prior to the AUSFTA, two of the three subsections referred to the purpose of trade but these

were dropped in the 2004 amendments. What do you think was the reason for this? What does this indicate about the scope of the action under this section?

4   In ss 116B and 116C, as in a number of other sections, the law presumes that the defendant has the requisite knowledge ('defendant knew, or ought reasonably to have known'). Why do you think the onus was placed on the defendant? Is this fair?

5   Section 116D provides that a court may grant an injunction and either damages or an account of profits for actions under ss 116A, 116B 116C and 116CA. Additional damages may also be awarded under s 116D(2).

6   Subsections 132(5C) and (5D) create criminal offences corresponding to the civil actions under sections 116B and 116C. See also ss 132(5A) and (5B).

7   Critically evaluate the effectiveness of the remedies and offences that have just been considered. How well do they arm the copyright holder to prevent copyright infringements?

8   The first dispute reaching the High Court of Australia to consider the anti-circumvention law introduced by the *Copyright Amendment (Digital Agenda Act) 2000* in s 116A of the *Copyright Act* was the case of *Stevens v Kabushiki Kaisha Sony Computer Entertainment* [2005] HCA 58. The dispute concerned the 'mod chip' which Stevens made and sold. The Sony PlayStation is coded so that it will only play games available in the region in which the PlayStation was sold. Regional Access Coding (RAC) contained within a track on each CD read by a chip known as a 'Boot ROM' located on the circuit board of the PlayStation console enabled this restriction to be implemented by Sony. This means that a game purchased in the USA or Japan cannot be played on a PlayStation purchased in Australia. Also, a copied, burnt or unauthorised version of a game will not play on the PlayStation, as the copying process does not embed the necessary coding in the copy. Stevens' 'mod chip' extended the functionality of the PlayStation allowing games from other regions as well as copied, unauthorised or burnt games to be played on the PlayStation.

Sony argued that Stevens had breached s 116A of the *Copyright Act 1968* in that he had sold or distributed a circumvention device, namely mod chips, which he knew or ought reasonably have known would be used as a circumvention device. A circumvention device as defined by the *Copyright Act*, is something that has little other purpose than to circumvent a technological protection measure (TPM). A TPM is something that is designed in the ordinary course of its operation, to prevent or inhibit the infringement of copyright. It must achieve this through either ensuring access to the work is available solely by use of an access code of process, or through a copy control mechanism. The Australian High Court held that the RAC and the components that enabled it did not constitute a TPM under the legislation and hence the mod chip was not a circumvention device. The Court held that the Boot Rom system did not prevent all copying, and although it did prevent the use of unauthorised copies, it did not do so through the means of an access code or process or through a copy control mechanism.

9 Article 17.4.7 of the Australia-US Free Trade Agreement would appear to place an obligation on Australia to amend the definition of a TPM. At the time of writing, no decision had been made in regards to the changes that would occur. See also House of Representatives Standing Committee on Legal and Constitutional Affairs, *Review of Technological Protection Measure Exceptions* (Canberra 2006).

10 The first criminal prosecution for Internet music copyright infringement in Australia involved three university students. In *Commonwealth Director of Public Prosecutions v Ng, Tran and Le* (Unreported, Sydney Central Local Court, Henson DCM, 18 November 2003), Peter Tran, Charles Ng and Tommy Le ran a website which essentially provided free MP3 music downloads to 390 commercially available CD albums. The site proved very popular and attracted more than 7 million hits during its operation. The Court found the three defendants guilty under s 132(2)(b) of the *Copyright Act 1968* (Cth) for knowingly distributing copyrighted work, to an extent that prejudicially affects the owner of copyright. Tran and Ng both received custodial sentences of 18 months but their sentences were suspended for three years on $1000 good behaviour bond because of their age and because they had not profited from the site. Le who had a lesser role in the operation of the site was sentenced to 200 hours of community service.

11 At the time of writing, Hew Raymond Griffiths is likely to become the first Australian to be extradited to the US for on-line copyright piracy. It is also the first time the USA has sought extradition of an individual solely on the alleged on-line violations of US copyright laws. In *Griffiths v United States of America* [2005] FCAFC 34, Griffiths lost an appeal in the Federal Court of Australia against his eligibility for surrender to the USA. Griffiths then sought special leave to appeal to the High Court of Australia but special leave was refused. It is alleged that Griffiths was involved in the DrinkOrDie piracy ring which distributed pirated software, music, and movies. Other members of the group have already been charged and convicted in their home countries including the United Kingdom, Finland and Norway. It is alleged that Griffiths was one of the ringleaders of the group. At the time of writing, the issue of whether Griffiths would be extradited to the USA remains in the hands of the Justice Minister, Chris Ellison.

(e) Intermediary or service provider liability

We have thus far looked at direct infringements of copyright. It is also possible to be liable for secondary or indirect copyright infringements, as the exclusive rights also include the exclusive right to authorise a person to do any of the exclusive acts. In Australia, this is contained in s 13(2) of the *Copyright Act* and the word 'authorise' has been held—in the seminal case of *University of New South Wales v Moorhouse* (1975) 133 CLR 1—to have its dictionary meaning of 'sanction, approve, countenance'. This head of liability has only very recently been utilised in Australia for cases concerning the Internet and they will be discussed below (see discussion on *Universal Music Australia*

Pty Ltd v Sharman License Holdings [2005] FCA 1242 and *Universal Music Australia Pty Ltd v Cooper* [2005] FCA 972). This is not the case in the USA, however, which has seen several high profile cases over the years. The following extract outlines the extent of legal doctrine dealing with indirect copyright infringement. The focus of the paper is the Information Infrastructure Task Force report, released in 1995, entitled *Intellectual Property and the National Information Infrastructure: The Report of the Working Group of Intellectual Property Rights* and the liability for indirect infringement that Internet service providers could potentially attract. It is important to note, however, that an action for indirect infringement is not limited to Internet service providers. The extract from the *Napster* decision, below, demonstrates how service providers other than Internet service providers can be subjected to an action for indirect infringement.

Yee Fen Lim, 'The Application of the Doctrines of Contributory Infringement and Vicarious Liability to Internet Service Providers'

3 *West Virginia Journal of Law and Technology* 2.3 (15 March 1999)

Available at <http://www.wvu.edu/~wvjolt/Arch/Lim/Lim.htm> 4 May 2001

I. Introduction

The Information Infrastructure Task Force suggested in the White Paper that the existing United States doctrines of contributory infringement and vicarious liability are useful and adequate to handle the issue of Internet service provider liability. This article will examine these two doctrines and analyze their application to Internet service providers. It will be argued that the doctrine of contributory infringement is currently very unclear and hence does not represent an ideal resolution of the problems presented by Internet service providers. The doctrine of vicarious liability offers a more workable solution than contributory infringement to the problems posed by the online world. However, it too fails to provide the perfect legal framework for resolving Internet service provider issues, as it does not sufficiently protect copyright owners. It must be pointed out at the outset that the two heads of liability have not always been clearly delineated by the United States courts. As the Supreme Court of the United States has acknowledged, confusion has reigned over the requirements of each.

1. THE DOCTRINE OF CONTRIBUTORY INFRINGEMENT

The dual system of copyright law in the United States ended in 1976 when Congress passed the *Copyright Act* of 1976. The copyright regime was not completely changed, as many of the common law doctrines survived. One such doctrine is the doctrine of contributory infringement. Although the *Copyright Act* of 1976 does not specifically refer to contributory infringement, the House and Senate Reports clearly indicate that Congress intended to retain the long-standing common law doctrine as a judicial doctrine. This was the reason for the introduction of the phrase 'to authorize' in s 106 of the 1976 *Copyright Act*. Despite judicial support, the question has been a long-standing issue and has been hotly debated.

No United States copyright legislation has ever contained express provisions for the doctrine of contributory infringement. Instead, the United States courts have imported the doctrine from decisions in patent law and tort law. One of the earliest cases where the contributory infringement doctrine was utilized for a copyright dispute was *Harper v Shoppell* in 1886. More recently, the United States Supreme Court in *Sony Corp of America v Universal City Studios, Inc* ('Sony') has cited the 'historic kinship between patent law and copyright law' to explain the application of the contributory infringement doctrine to copyright law.

The courts have employed the doctrine, as a form of third-party liability, to impose liability on those parties who play a significant role in copyright infringement even though their conduct is insufficient to attract liability as primary infringers. For a party to be held liable as a contributory infringer of copyright, a primary infringement must be first established. That is, there must be actual conduct by another which in itself constitutes an infringement. A direct or primary infringer is one who infringes any one of the exclusive rights of the copyright owner. The exclusive rights given to copyright owners are now set out in Title 17, s 106 of the United States Code. Section 501 further provides that anyone who violates any of the exclusive rights is an infringer of copyright. Hence, liability for direct infringement is imposed on a strict liability basis, although there are several defenses available.

Five factors are pivotal in determining the existence of contributory infringement. Samuel Oddi has identified these factors:

1) the standard for direct infringement, for without a direct infringement, there cannot be a contributory infringement;
2) the type of contributory conduct and the necessary fault standard;
3) whether the owner of the intellectual property has extended the monopoly granted beyond the scope of the grant;
4) the nature of the article being sold for use in direct infringement; and
5) whether the accused contributory infringer has a duty to the owner of the intellectual property.

Of these factors, contributory conduct, the necessary fault standard, and the nature of the article being sold are particularly relevant to Internet service providers.

A. CONTRIBUTORY CONDUCT

Contributory conduct can be of two types. It can be personal conduct that forms part of or furthers the infringement; conduct that 'induces, causes or materially contributes to the infringing conduct of another'. For example, A may actively assist B to copy a copyright item illegally. Conduct can also take the form of contribution of items or machinery that provide the means to infringe, and an example of this would be A giving to B a dubbing machine so that B can copy tapes, though A does not actually take part in the action of copying. A simple causal relationship is all that is required. Contributory infringement, in this respect, differs from vicarious liability. As will be discussed further below, vicarious liability requires a relationship of control and benefit between the primary actor and the vicarious infringer.

At least two courts have held that the services offered by Internet service providers are included in the second category of contributory conduct. Internet service providers, through the provision of online services, contribute to the infringing conduct of others by providing the means to infringe. Without access to online services, the illegal copying and mass distribution of copyrighted material through the use of the online services cannot take place.

B. FAULT STANDARD

Because contributory liability is a form of third-party liability, it is expected that the standard of liability for contributory infringement will not be strict liability but that a higher threshold for liability should apply. The rationale behind this principle is that the third-party infringer is further removed from the infringement than the primary infringer. The courts have held that a contributory infringer must have knowledge of the infringing activity. The crucial issue, however, is the level of knowledge that is required. Courts and commentators have disagreed on this over the years. In the area of patent law, from which the doctrine of contributory infringement evolved, the level of knowledge required was unsettled for many years. Although the knowledge requirement for contributory infringement in patent law has its roots in the knowledge requirement for contributing tortfeasors, the knowledge requirement was only unequivocally resolved by the United States Supreme Court in 1964 in *Aro Manufacturing Co v Convertible Top Replacement Co* ('Aro').

Aro involved fabric tops for convertible cars. The Convertible Top Replacement Company held patent rights for the convertible top structure and Aro Manufacturing Company produced fabric components designed to replace worn-out fabric tops for convertible cars. Convertible Top informed Aro Manufacturing of its patent but Aro Manufacturing continued to produce the fabric components, contrary to Convertible Top's patent. The Supreme Court found Aro Manufacturing liable for contributory infringement and held that the level of knowledge required for contributory infringement was actual knowledge. The current United States *Patent Act* of 1988 codifies this level of knowledge.

Only a few copyright cases have dealt directly with the question of the level of knowledge required for the application of the doctrine of contributory infringement. In many of these cases, actual knowledge has been present. However, proving the existence of actual knowledge is only one way of fulfilling the knowledge requirement. The cases that have squarely addressed the issue of knowledge indicate that showing constructive discharge is another way of fulfilling the knowledge requirement ...

Constructive knowledge can be imputed to a party if the circumstances surrounding an activity should have indicated to the party that the activity was illegal. A common situation where constructive knowledge could be imputed is when a defendant sells, manufactures, or provides access to equipment that facilitates infringement. In *RCA Records, Inc v All-Fast Systems, Inc*, a retail copy service provided access to a machine capable of making high-speed copies of cassette tapes. The copy service did not supply tapes for copying. Customers who wanted to have tapes duplicated had to supply the source tapes. Manufacturers of pre-recorded, copyrighted music cassettes sued the copy service, alleging copyright infringement. In addition to a finding of direct infringement, the court also found contributory infringement. The court suggested that by providing access to equipment capable of copyright infringement, the defendants were deemed to have constructive knowledge of the infringements.

It remains largely unresolved whether constructive knowledge can be generally imputed to sellers and manufacturers of devices that facilitate infringement. The Supreme Court in *Sony* referred to such a proposition but did not resolve the issue and based its decision on another ground. A recent District Court case, *Religious Technology Center v Netcom On-Line Communication Services, Inc* ('Netcom'), which dealt with the liability of Internet service providers, reaffirmed a constructive knowledge standard and stated that it was a question of fact whether constructive knowledge of infringements could be imputed to Internet service providers.

If constructive knowledge of infringements could be generally imputed to providers of equipment, then the proposition could also be applied to Internet service providers. Although it is unlikely that the average Internet service provider will have actual knowledge of the infringements that occur on its systems, it is not unlikely that the Internet service provider would have constructive knowledge of the infringements that may occur on the computer systems. The copyright problems associated with online systems should be well known to all Internet service providers. There have been so many outcries from copyright owners all over the world regarding the problems which online systems pose that many governments and organizations have commissioned reports on the situation. The issues concerning copyright law and online systems are raised in the media and in the popular press so often that it is difficult to be unaware of them. It is clear that Internet service providers should know that copyright infringements do occur on their systems.

Although the law is unclear as to whether constructive knowledge can be generally imputed to sellers, manufacturers, and providers of equipment that facilitate copyright infringement, this does not preclude constructive knowledge from being imputed in individual cases based on particular facts. This was the approach adopted in *Netcom*. The element of knowledge may or may not prove to be a problematic one for establishing contributory liability. However, the biggest stumbling block to holding Internet service providers liable for contributory infringement is the nature of the article being sold.

C. THE NATURE OF THE ARTICLE BEING SOLD

The main issue concerning the nature of the article being sold is whether or not the article is a staple article of commerce. If an article is a staple, there are presumably significant non-infringing uses to which it could be put. An example of a staple would be a photocopier which can be legitimately used to duplicate private documents, but can also be used to infringe the copyright in books and other copyright-protected items. Therefore, the sale of the article would not automatically support an inference that the vendor was causing another to infringe the intellectual property of others. If an article is a non-staple, it may not be capable of substantial non-infringing uses. In these circumstances, the sale of the item would give rise to an inference that the seller knew of and intended the infringement to take place. This element, initially adopted from patent law, has developed into a requirement that unless the sale of a non-staple article of commerce is involved, there is no copyright infringement ...

II. Sony Corp of America v Universal City Studios, Inc

The principal case incorporating the staple article of commerce rationale into copyright law is the United States Supreme Court decision in *Sony*. In this case, the plaintiffs, Universal City Studios, were the owners of copyright in certain television programs. Sony, the defendant, manufactured Betamax video tape recorders which enabled the recording of television programs. The plaintiffs sued Sony for contributory infringement, claiming that the purchasers of the video tape recorders used the devices to record unauthorized copies of copyrighted television programs.

The Supreme Court utilized the staple article of commerce doctrine to determine whether there was a primary or direct infringement. It did not utilize the staple article of commerce rationale to determine whether there is contributory infringement, as the doctrine has been applied in patent law. The court held that if an item was a staple and capable of non-infringing uses, then a user who uses that item cannot be held liable for infringement. Because there is no primary infringement, the manufacturer of the item cannot be held liable as a third party for contributory infringement. Oddi has criticized this approach on the basis that it is ineffectual and that it collapses the two elements of the tort of contributory infringement into one. One element of contributory infringement is that there must be a direct infringement. The second element of contributory infringement is that the product being sold must not be a staple. The second element should play no part in determining the existence of the first. However, the Supreme Court used the second element as a factor in its consideration of the first element, thereby collapsing the two elements into one.

Although the general thrust of the decision indicated that there would be no contributory infringement if the article is capable of non-infringing uses, the court formulated the copyright law version of the doctrine in three different ways. It first stated that there would be no contributory infringement if the item used in perpetrating the copyright infringement is widely used for legitimate, unobjectionable purposes. It then suggested that if the item is merely capable of substantial non-infringing uses, then no contributory infringement would arise. Finally, the court stated that if an item was capable of commercially significant non-infringing uses, then there would be no liability for contributory infringement.

The three formulations appear to set differing standards for liability. The first formulation concerns whether the item is widely used for legitimate purposes. However, because the focus is on the normal uses of the item, it may have nothing to do with the uses that the item is capable of. The second formulation is focused upon the capabilities of the item—whether the item is capable of substantial non-infringing uses. It is quite possible for an article to be merely capable of substantial non-infringing uses, satisfying the second formulation, yet users choose to use the article for infringing purposes, offending the first formulation. Similarly, it is also possible for an article to be capable of commercially significant non-infringing uses, satisfying the third formulation, but users may choose to use the article primarily for infringing purposes, offending the first formulation. The first formulation focuses on the manner in which users utilize the article, while the other two formulations focus on the uses to which the article can be put.

Of the three formulations advanced by the court, it is unclear which one represents the preferred test. The court merely stated that it was not necessary for it to explore all the different potential uses of the video tape recorders and to determine whether the uses would constitute infringement. The court also did not find it necessary to elaborate on how much use is commercially significant. This decision was based on one potential use of the machine. The court stated that the machines were capable of being used to time-shift. That is, the machines allowed users to choose the time at which they could view programs. This use, in private and non-commercial settings, would constitute a use sufficient to render the Betamax a staple article of commerce. Furthermore, the court also found that time-shifting is permissible under the fair use doctrine. Because the Betamax machine is a staple and its use fair, there was no contributory copyright infringement by Sony.

The manner in which the court applied the doctrine to the facts of the case reveals more about the doctrine than the formulations themselves. It seems that the primary concern of the court was with the effect of holding Sony liable for contributory copyright infringement.

The court was interested in preserving the monopoly rights given to copyright holders while simultaneously upholding the rights of others freely to engage in substantially unrelated areas of commerce. It was concerned that a finding of contributory infringement would 'block the wheels of commerce'. After all, if an item is capable of lawful uses, its capacity for infringing uses should play a secondary role, in light of the public policy to support free competition in staples that have the capability to be used in non-infringing ways.

It is uncertain whether the staple article of commerce doctrine can be applied to Internet service providers: Can Internet service providers be considered analogous to manufacturers such as Sony? Michael Dobbins has argued that Internet service providers are not analogous to manufacturers in that they do not sell products to consumers; the only thing Internet service providers sell is time to operate the central computers. Kelly Tickle, on the other hand, has argued that Internet service providers do in fact offer subscribers products by allowing access to the computer systems. At least one United States court has characterized the services of Internet service providers as 'products'. One fact all agree on is that Internet service providers retain slightly more control over how the computer systems are used than manufacturers do over their products after they are sold.

If the services offered by Internet service providers can be considered products, they would no doubt come within the scope of the definition of a staple article of commerce. The computer systems operated by Internet service providers can be used for many legitimate and non-infringing uses. Furthermore, there is evidence that they are widely used for these legitimate non-infringing uses. Thus, if the staple article of commerce doctrine is applicable to the services offered by Internet service providers, Internet service providers would be held not liable for contributory infringement of copyright ...

D. INTERNET SERVICE PROVIDERS AND CONTRIBUTORY INFRINGEMENT

Whether a claim for contributory copyright infringement will be successful depends on a number of factors. The factors most pertinent to Internet service providers have been discussed. Although Internet service providers have the constructive knowledge required for contributory infringement and the services they offer fall within the definition of a 'contribution' to infringement, the staple article of commerce doctrine may free Internet service providers from general liability for contributory copyright infringement.

If the staple article of commerce applies, the only circumstance where it will operate so as to impose contributory infringement liability on Internet service providers is when Internet service providers are solely in the business of profiting from infringing the copyright of others as was the case in *Sega*. On the other hand, the staple article of commerce doctrine may be inapplicable to Internet service providers, in which case other principles such as those advanced in *Netcom* may apply. These may well lead to Internet service providers being liable for contributory infringement in the large majority of cases where the other elements of the wrong (namely knowledge and a direct infringement) are also satisfied.

The legal concept of contributory copyright infringement as it currently stands is not clear. For this very reason, the concept cannot be applied with certainty. Because of this uncertainty, contributory copyright infringement is not useful for resolving the issue of Internet service provider liability.

2. THE DOCTRINE OF VICARIOUS LIABILITY

Vicarious liability, like contributory infringement, is not specifically provided for by the United States copyright statute. Like contributory infringement, its continued application as a principle of copyright law has been affirmed by the courts. Contributory infringement focuses on the causal relationship between the primary infringement and the secondary infringement; the conduct and state of mind of the secondary infringer is at issue. Vicarious liability, on the other hand, concerns the relationship between the direct and secondary infringers.

Vicarious liability, like contributory infringement, also has roots in tort law. Vicarious liability stems from the tort theory of *respondeat superior*. As with contributory infringement, there must first be a primary or direct infringement. To be successful in a claim for vicarious liability, the plaintiff must then show that the defendant not only had the right and ability to supervise or control the actions of the primary infringer, but also had a direct financial interest in the exploitation of the copyrighted material. These two elements form the cornerstones of vicarious liability. It has been said that the two elements show that the underlying rationale of vicarious liability is the master and servant theory. The master and servant theory aims to impose liability on those parties (the masters) who can best avoid risk at the least cost as compared to outsiders. It also aims to shift the burden of loss to those (again, the masters) who will benefit most from the success of an activity. Translating this into the two elements, the party that can avoid risk at the least cost would be the party with the right and ability to supervise and control. The party that stands to gain the most from the success of an activity is the party that gains a direct financial advantage from an activity. Since vicarious liability stipulates that both elements are essential, the vicarious infringer becomes the equivalent of the master in the master and servant theory.

Unlike contributory infringement, there is no requirement that the vicarious infringer have knowledge of the direct infringement. Although the most obvious instances giving rise to vicarious liability involve agents or employees of the defendant acting as the direct infringer, the cases have demonstrated that this relationship is not necessary if the two elements outlined above are otherwise established.

A. THE DEVELOPMENT OF VICARIOUS LIABILITY

Four distinct lines of cases have emerged over the years as the courts developed the requirements for vicarious liability in copyright law. These are the dance hall cases, the landlord and tenant cases, the broadcasting cases and the booth cases. These will now be considered within the context of the two requirements of control and financial interest ...

IV. The booth rental cases

A new category of cases, labeled the 'booth rental cases' by Edward Cavazos and and Chin Chao, deal with defendants who lease out booths at events such as exhibitions. In the booth rental cases, the booth renters committed copyright infringement by playing music without a license or by selling pirate copies of sound recordings. The plaintiffs in each case sued the organizers of the events for vicarious copyright infringement. The cases of *Polygram International Publishing v Nevada/TIG, Inc* ('*Nevada*') and *Artists Music, Inc v*

Reed Publishing, Inc ('*Artists Music*') both involved professional trade show and exhibition organizers. The case of *Fonovisa, Inc v Cherry Auction* ('*Fonovisa*'), on the other hand, dealt with a defendant who was a 'flea market' organizer. Although all three cases were decided at the district court level, *Fonovisa* was appealed ('*Fonovisa II*') making it the first case raising the issue of vicarious liability in the context of booth rental situations to reach a federal appeals court. These four decisions will now be examined to determine the importance of the two elements of vicarious liability.

A. CONTROL OR SUPERVISION

Each of the three District Court cases took different approaches with respect to the element of right and liability to control or supervise. The court in *Nevada* found that the organizers did possess the requisite control. This is in contrast to the earlier cases of *Fonovisa* and *Artists Music*, both of which found that the organizers did not have the requisite right and liability to control or supervise. It should be noted however that the District Court decision in *Fonovisa* was subsequently reversed by the Court of Appeals in *Fonovisa II*, which adopted much of the reasoning set out in *Nevada*. As a result of the successful appeal, *Artists Music* remains the only precedent for the proposition that the control element is not present in booth rental situations.

The District Court in *Fonovisa* based its decision largely on the types of power available to defendants of vicarious infringement claims. If the defendants have a general power to supervise or control the primary infringers in the general course of business, then the defendants possess an *a priori* supervisory power, which is the type of power necessary to ground a finding of vicarious infringement. The court found that this was in fact the type of power the defendants in *Shapiro* possessed. If the defendants only have the power to stop the primary infringer by not renting the booth to the primary infringer, then that is an *a posteriori* supervisory power and it is not sufficient to satisfy the control element. The court concluded that the type of power that the defendant in *Fonovisa* possessed was an *a posteriori* supervisory power and thus the first element of right and ability to control or supervise could not be met. Although the decision was couched in terms of the types of powers the defendants had, the decision was really based on the model of the landlord and tenant cases. The power that landlords generally have is of the *a posteriori* type and hence landlords are generally not liable for vicarious liability. When landlords have the general power to supervise and control the primary infringers as in *Shapiro*, then they are liable, as they have an *a priori* supervisory power.

Artists Music was decided by another District Court about the same time as *Fonovisa*. It found that the relationship between the organizer of the exhibition and the exhibitors was akin to the relationship between landlord and tenants. The court reached this decision despite the fact that the defendant issued a manual to all exhibitors, setting out the rules and regulations governing conduct of the booth renters. Additionally, the defendant instructed the booth renters through a flyer inserted into the manual, to contact the plaintiff to obtain licenses to perform copyrighted music at their booths. It is difficult to see how these defendants are similar to the absentee landlords when the rules and regulations governing conduct gave the defendants very broad powers of control over the booth renters.

One interesting point that was raised in both *Fonovisa* and *Artists Music* concerns the responsibility of the organizers to police the booth renters for conduct which infringed copyright. The court in *Fonovisa* rejected the existence of any such responsibility. The defendants in *Fonovisa* were well aware that some of the booth renters were selling bootleg recordings but they took no action to stop the infringing activity. The court found that the defendants were in the business of renting cheap booths to vendors and not in the business of overseeing the market or ensuring the integrity of the goods sold. Furthermore, the District Court also stated that the defendants were not in the best economic position to prevent the infringements from occurring because they would have had to hire people to patrol for infringing conduct. In addition, the court stated that the plaintiff was in a better position to identify infringing conduct due to familiarity with the copyright content. In contrast to the decision of *Fonovisa*, the court in *Artists Music* was not as lenient on the organizers of the trade shows. It stated that the organizers have a duty to police the booth renters for infringing conduct if it gained an obvious and direct financial benefit from the infringing conduct. Thus, if a relationship existed between the organizers and the booth renters which could trigger liability for vicarious infringement, then the organizers would have a duty to police the booth renters for copyright infringement, however costly it may be.

The final district court booth rental case is *Nevada*. The facts in this case are very similar to those in *Artists Music*. The defendants issued handbooks to booth renters that described the rules and regulations that the booth renters had to follow. Additionally, the defendants advised the booth renters to comply with copyright laws. The presiding judge, Judge Keeton, found that although many cases recited the element of right and ability to control or supervise, no case had actually defined the precise terms of the test to be applied in determining when there is a right and ability to control or supervise. He then took the opportunity to promulgate an interpretation of control drawn from examining the legislative history and case law and from the legislative record of amendments to the 1976 *Copyright Act*. Judge Keeton held that a party has control if it 'either actively operates or supervises the operation of the place wherein the performances occur or controls the content of the infringing program'.

This test for control is slightly more expansive than the interpretation advanced by the *Shapiro* court, due to the object of the control. Under the *Shapiro* test, the vicarious infringer must control the activities of the primary infringer. In the *Nevada* test, control over the operation of the place where the direct infringements take place is all that is required. However, *Nevada* test is more useful than the *Shapiro* interpretation because it takes the inquiry one step further. If a party is actively operating or supervising the operation of a place, then, more likely than not, that party has the right and ability to do so. Even if the party did not have the right or the ability to do so, the mere fact of the activity indicates an acceptance of the responsibilities that are attached to supervising and controlling.

Using its control test, the *Nevada* court found that the defendants did in fact have control. It based its finding on three grounds. First, the defendants admitted that employees had walked the aisles during the exhibition to ensure that the booth renters were complying with the rules and regulations set out in the handbook. These employees were also available to address the booth renters' needs and to respond to complaints. These complaints included complaints about exhibitors encroaching on other exhibitors' space or exhibitors blocking aisles. Despite the defendants' claim that the employees' job was not to police the exhibition for all rules violations, as that would have been impractical, the fact that there were employees walking the aisles was enough for the court to distinguish the defendants from absentee landlords and to conclude that the defendants did supervise the exhibition.

Second, the facts indicated that the rules and regulations manual gave the defendants extensive powers and hence control over the exhibitors. The court pointed out that the defendants had the right and power to restrict exhibits which became objectionable because of noise, method of operation, materials or any other reason. Additionally, the defendants had the broad power to prohibit or remove any exhibit which in their opinion detracted from the general character of the exhibition as a whole. Finally, the court pointed to the ability of the defendants to exercise control over details such as the distribution of food and drink from booths, the design and construction of booths, the use of video cameras and access to the exhibition by attendees. The court concluded that the defendants did in fact have the contractual right to control and supervise the exhibitors. More importantly, the court found that because the defendants had acted on those powers, they had actively operated and supervised the operation of the exhibition.

One interesting point that was raised by the court in *Nevada* concerns the advice and instruction by the defendants to the exhibitors to comply with copyright law. The court interpreted this as an attempt by the defendants to shift legal responsibility from themselves to others while still retaining and exercising control. Relying on the case of *Famous Music Corp v Bay State Harness Horse Racing*, the court stated that the defendants must shoulder the responsibility when their instructions are not followed. Therefore, it seems that the only way for a party, or at least a show organizer, to ensure that its instructions are followed and that it does not incur liability in the event of disobedience, is to include sanction clauses whereby the primary infringer contracts to accept strict liability when instructions are not followed.

The final booth rental decision that needs to be considered is *Fonovisa II*. The Ninth Circuit adopted much of Judge Keeton's reasoning in *Nevada*, including his interpretation of control. The Ninth Circuit's decision hinged on three facts that were overlooked by the lower court. First, the premises within which the booths were located were patrolled by the defendants. Second, the defendants controlled the access of customers to the entire premises. Third, the defendants had the right to terminate the booth rental of any renter for any reason whatsoever. Together, these factors were sufficient to show that the defendants did have control over the booth renters. The court's decision was based on the interpretation of control advanced by Judge Keeton in *Nevada* which only required that the defendants actively operate or supervise the operation of the premises. Under this interpretation, the defendants clearly had control because they had actively patrolled and controlled the premises.

Surprisingly, the Ninth Circuit found the level of control in this case to be 'strikingly similar' to that in *Shapiro*. The only reason the court gave for this similarity was the broad contract the defendants had with the renters. It is difficult to see how the level of control in the two cases can be equated. In *Shapiro*, the license agreement actually gave the defendants broad powers to promulgate particular rules and regulations. In *Fonovisa II*, the only broad power the defendants had was the power to stop renting the booths to the renters for any reason. The defendants did not have any powers to control the particular activities of the renters. It is for precisely this reason that the lower court in *Fonovisa* distinguished *Shapiro*.

In spite of the comparison to *Shapiro*, it is clear that its finding on the element of control was largely based on the interpretation of control proposed by the court in *Nevada*.

The analysis in the booth rental cases has shed some light on the element of control. First, *Fonovisa II* seems to uphold a control standard equivalent to that pronounced in the dance hall cases by finding that a party has control when it is able to prevent infringements by terminating its relationship with the direct infringer. Second, the *Nevada* court advanced a control test for determining when a right and ability to control or supervise exists. The court stated that a party has control if it actively operates or supervises the operation of the place where the infringement occurs. This test of control clarifies the requirements necessary for the control element and it has also been adopted by a court at the federal appeals level. Third, the *Nevada* court confirmed that any attempt to shift legal liability for specific acts while retaining and exercising general control would be unsuccessful. Thus it would seem that the only way for a party to successfully retain control and to shift liability for wrongful acts such as copyright infringement, is to contract with potential direct infringers for indemnity.

B. FINANCIAL BENEFIT

The second element relevant to the determination of vicarious liability is financial benefit. The court in *Shapiro* held that the financial benefit had to be direct and that indirect financial benefits from the infringing acts of another did not satisfy the element. This is in contrast to the dance hall cases where directness was not a necessary part of the financial benefit element.

The consideration of the financial benefit element in *Fonovisa* and in *Artists Music* focused on whether the financial benefits the defendants received were directly related to the infringing activities of the booth renters. Both courts found that the financial benefits the defendants gained were not directly related to infringing activities of the booth renters. In both cases, the decision turned on the fact that the defendants did not receive financial benefits in terms of percentages of the infringers' gross sales. Addressing, the argument that the infringements enhanced the number of attendees at the exhibition, and increased the defendants' revenues generated by the sale of admission tickets, the court in *Artists Music* stated that there was no evidence that so much as a single attendee came to the exhibition for the sake of the unauthorized music played by four out of 134 exhibitors.

The Court of Appeals in *Fonovisa II* and the court in *Nevada* dealt with the issue of financial benefits very differently from the court in *Artists Music* and the *Fonovisa* trial court. First, in *Nevada*, the court stated very clearly that there was no reason for 'direct' to be interpreted so narrowly as to only encompass percentages of profits, as was the case in *Shapiro*. The court cited a series of cases where there were held to be direct financial benefits but which would not be 'direct' when judged by the *Shapiro* standard. The court then explained the difficulty and impossibility, in many situations, of determining whether the benefit was direct. As an example, it cited the benefits of music to restaurant owners in creating moods for their restaurants. The court found that benefit of the music was immeasurable, and asked 'how many minutes of music per meal does it take to show that the financial benefit to a restaurant is "direct"?'

Finally, the court adopted the House Reports' interpretation of direct financial benefits and held that the phrase means 'expect commercial gain from the overall operation and either direct or indirect benefit from the infringement itself '. The court concluded that the defendants expected commercial gain from the exhibition and they did gain a gross revenue of $44 million. Additionally, that gain was an indirect result of the infringements by the booth renters as music played an important role in attracting attendees to such exhibitions.

The Ninth Circuit in *Fonovisa II* also adopted the liberal approach to determining whether the financial benefit was direct as advanced by *Nevada*. In reversing the lower court's decision and in finding that the financial benefits received by the defendants were direct, the court elaborated on all the substantial financial benefits that the defendants received. It stated that through the desire of customers to buy counterfeit recordings at bargain basement prices, the defendants reaped financial benefits not only from admission fees, but also from parking fees as well as profits from the sale of food and drinks. In contrast to the district court in *Artists Music*, the Ninth Circuit also found that the infringing recordings were in fact a 'draw' for customers. That is, without the infringements of the booth renters, the defendants' revenues would have been diminished.

In summary, two out of the four booth rental decisions have downplayed the direct financial benefit requirement. One of these was a decision from the Ninth Circuit. These two decisions provide a sound basis from which to approach the issue of direct financial benefit. They take the definition of the element back to the days of the dance hall cases where vicarious liability was first imposed for copyright infringement. This approach avoids *Shapiro*'s overly restrictive interpretation of 'direct' by allowing the financial benefit to be direct or indirect.

B. INTERNET SERVICE PROVIDERS AND VICARIOUS LIABILITY

Vicarious liability depends upon the relationship between the primary infringer and the secondary infringer. In order to determine the liability of Internet service providers for vicarious infringement, the relationship between Internet service providers and their users must first be examined. If the relationship fits into the mould of any of the earlier relationships where vicarious liability was found, then Internet service providers can expect to be held vicariously liable for the infringements of their users. The relationship that bears the closest resemblance to the relationship between Internet service providers and their users is that between exhibition organizers and the exhibitors who rent booths from them. Cavazos and Chao, the major scholars to discuss the tort of vicarious liability and Internet service providers in any detail, prefer this analogy.

Exhibition organizers rent out booth space to exhibitors. Internet service providers sell access to their computer systems. The access can be to particular areas on the systems, called hard disk space, or Internet service providers can give access to temporary areas of the systems (RAM), accessed when users are reading or downloading. Exhibition organizers do not generally know or control the activities of their booth renters. Internet service providers do not generally know or control the activities of their users. Exhibition organizers do concern themselves with the overall operation and success of the exhibitions and do take steps in running the exhibitions. Internet service providers must keep their systems operating and running smoothly to ensure that their online systems provide successful and satisfactory services. Thus the similarities between exhibition organizers and Internet service providers are plentiful.

I. Internet service providers: the element of control

Under the formulation enunciated in *Nevada* and approved in *Fonovisa II*, there is control by a party if the party either actively operates or supervises the operation of the place wherein the infringements occur. Internet service providers could satisfy this control test quite easily. Internet service providers sell access to the online computer system. The infringements occur on these systems. To keep their systems running, Internet service providers must actively operate, maintain and control their systems. It is essential that they continuously monitor and maintain supervision over their systems for technical faults and break-ins, perform routine general maintenance to avoid system crashes, and create backups to protect against data loss. It would be very difficult to argue that Internet service providers do not actively operate or supervise the operation of their computer systems. Hence, Internet service providers do have the requisite control.

In *Fonovisa II*, the Ninth Circuit reaffirmed the view that if a party can prevent infringements by terminating its relationship with the primary infringer, then that party is considered to have the requisite control. In that case, the event organizer was held to have the requisite control, as it could have prevented the infringements by not renting booths to the primary infringers. Similarly, Internet service providers can prevent copyright infringements performed by their users by not allowing those users who infringe copyright access to their systems. Therefore, Internet service providers would also have the requisite control.

Netcom, discussed above with respect to contributory infringement, also involved a claim for vicarious infringement. The court there applied the control element set out in *Shapiro* and found that the defendants who were Internet service providers did have the requisite right and ability to control their users. The court's decision was based largely on ample evidence of past instances where the defendants had exercised control over and policed the conduct of their users. In this case, the ability of the defendants to control their users stemmed from the terms and conditions that all subscribers agreed to. The facts in *Netcom* clearly demonstrated that the defendants had control over their users and that they exercised that control. The control element formulated in *Shapiro* may be more difficult to show in circumstances involving more apathetic Internet service providers.

II. Internet service providers: the element of direct financial benefit

Direct financial benefit exists if the party in question expects commercial gain from the overall operation and either directly or indirectly benefits from the infringement itself. This element will allow those Internet service providers who operate in a non-commercial and non-profit manner to escape vicarious liability. Most commercial and for-profit Internet service providers, however, will find it very difficult to escape liability on this basis. With respect to the first part of the test, it is obvious that commercial Internet service providers operate with an expectation of a commercial gain from running the online computer systems. The most apparent commercial gain Internet service providers receive would be subscription or access fees from users who use their systems.

With respect to the second part of the test, there must be direct or indirect benefit from the infringement itself. Showing that the availability of free copyrighted materials affects the number of users wanting to access the systems would establish liability. In the words of the court in *Fonovisa II*, the availability of the copyrighted materials for free and easy access must be shown to be a 'draw'. That is, it must be shown that the uploading, downloading, viewing of, or listening to copyrighted materials serves as an inducement to potential subscribers. If this can be demonstrated, then commercial Internet service providers can be said to gain direct financial benefits from the infringements. It is uncertain whether this can be proven easily. Some may try to argue that just as music is a 'draw' for restaurant patrons because music sets moods, the existence of free copyrighted materials is a 'draw' because of the greedy nature of people. On the other hand, it can also be argued that online services offer so many legitimate information sources and communication tools that the mere existence of free copyright materials is irrelevant to the motives of users. This in fact was the position of the *Netcom* court when it found no evidence that suggested the copyright infringements attracted new subscribers. It must be pointed out, however, that the plaintiffs in this case produced only one piece of tenuous evidence in support of this aspect of their claim. This deficiency was raised by the court. Had the defendants produced more evidence, the finding of the court on this matter may have been different. It must also be noted that because the court's decision was based on the trial court's opinion in *Fonovisa*, it was not convinced that even if the plaintiffs could show the existence of a 'draw', that would be sufficient to constitute a direct financial benefit. This doubt was later resolved by the Ninth Circuit in *Fonovisa II*. In this regard, mention must be made of the District Court case of *Marobie-FL, Inc v National Association of Fire Equipment Distributors & Northwest Nexus, Inc*. In *Marobie*, it was found that an Internet service provider was not vicariously liable for the infringements of one of its subscribers because the subscriber had paid a one-time-only set-up fee and a flat quarterly rate. The court concluded that the subscriber's infringements did not financially benefit the Internet service provider. It is submitted that *Marobie* was wrongly decided and the fact that a flat quarterly fee was payable does not immediately lead to the conclusion that there is no vicarious liability.

In summary, the relationship between commercial Internet service providers and their users is akin to the relationship between exhibition organizers and booth renters. All Internet service providers possess the right and ability to supervise and control their systems. However, the question of whether they receive direct financial benefits from the infringements is not as straightforward. Although non-commercial Internet service providers do not receive direct financial benefits from the infringements, it may be possible to show that commercial Internet service providers do receive such benefits. If it can be shown that commercial Internet service providers satisfy the direct financial benefit element, then they can be held vicariously liable for the infringing activities of their users.

It is useful to note here that, if Internet service providers attempted to shift legal liability for the infringing activities of their users, they would be unsuccessful: the court in *Nevada* observed that any attempt to shift legal liability for specific acts while retaining and exercising general control will be unsuccessful. Hence, if commercial Internet service providers wish to avoid liability, the only way they can achieve this is by entering into indemnity contracts with their users.

3. CONCLUSION
The two third-party heads of liability in the United States copyright law have been examined. Contributory infringement is presently an uncertain head of liability. An attempt to use

contributory infringement to fix liability on Internet service providers may yield unexpected results. Therefore, until contributory infringement is more clearly elucidated, it should not be relied upon to impose liability on Internet service providers.

Vicarious liability is a better defined head of liability than contributory infringement. Its application to Internet service providers may find most Internet service providers liable for the infringements of their users. The only instance where Internet service providers cannot be held vicariously liable is when Internet service providers are non-commercial entities.

In conclusion, when the United States doctrines of contributory infringement and vicarious liability are utilized together, they will impose liability on Internet service providers in a considerable number of circumstances. These two doctrines, however, will not find all Internet service providers liable for the infringements which occur on their computer systems.

[Footnotes omitted]

 ## NOTES AND QUESTIONS

1   Outline the requirements for liability under contributory infringement and vicarious liability. How do they differ?
2   Consider the concept of control. How relevant should control be in determining indirect liability?
3   In Australia, the 2000 amendments to the *Copyright Act* saw the insertion of s 36(1A), which qualifies the concept of authorisation to take into account a number of things, including the defendant's power to prevent the infringing act (see further below). These largely reflect the common law. Section 39B, however, was inserted to protect Internet service providers from liability for authorisation of copyright infringement.

In what has become one of the most high-profile cases relating to the Internet, the Federal District Court and later the Court of Appeals for the Ninth Circuit of the USA ruled against the Internet file-sharing service provider known as Napster. Napster, a software application that can be downloaded and used on the Internet, was created by a college student in the USA. As one might have guessed, file-sharing software enables users to share files across an electronic medium. In the case of Napster, the program enables users to share music files in MP3 format, a high-quality and highly compact file format for music, through a process commonly called 'peer-to-peer' (P2P) file sharing.

The Napster MusicShare software allows its users to:

• make MP3 music files stored on individual computer hard drives available for copying by other Napster users;
• search for MP3 music files stored on other users' computers; and
• transfer exact copies of the contents of other users' MP3 files from one computer to another via the Internet.

Napster provides technical support for the indexing and searching of MP3 files, as well as for other functions, which include a 'chat room' where users meet to discuss music, and a directory where participating artists can provide information about their music. Users can list, search for, and transfer MP3 files.

A complaint was lodged against Napster that alleged both contributory and vicarious copyright infringement. On 26 July 2000, the District Court granted the plaintiffs' motion for a preliminary injunction. This was slightly modified by written opinion on 10 August 2000 in the case *A&M Records, Inc v Napster, Inc.*[20] The court preliminarily enjoined Napster from engaging in the complained conduct until the matter could be heard in full.

A & M Records, Inc, et al, v Napster, Inc

United States Court of Appeals for the Ninth Circuit, No 00-16401 DC

Available at <http://laws.lp.findlaw.com/getcase/9th/case/0016401&exact=1> 17 August 2006

Beezer, Circuit Judge:

II

… We review a grant or denial of a preliminary injunction for abuse of discretion (*Gorbach v Reno*, 219 F3d 1087 at 1091 (9th Cir 2000) (*en banc*)). Application of erroneous legal principles represents an abuse of discretion by the district court. If the district court is claimed to have relied on an erroneous legal premise in reaching its decision to grant or deny a preliminary injunction, we will review the underlying issue of law de novo (*id* at 4, citing *Does 1-5 v Chandler*, 83 F3d 1150 at 1152 (9th Cir 1996)).

On review, we are required to determine 'whether the court employed the appropriate legal standards governing the issuance of a preliminary injunction and whether the district court correctly apprehended the law with respect to the underlying issues in the case' (*id*). 'As long as the district court got the law right, "it will not be reversed simply because the appellate court would have arrived at a different result if it had applied the law to the facts of the case" ' (*Gregorio T v Wilson*, 59 F 3d 1002 at 1004 (9th Cir 1995), quoting *Sports Form, Inc v United Press, Int'l*, 686 F 2d 750 at 752 (9th Cir 1982)).

[1] Preliminary injunctive relief is available to a party who demonstrates either: (1) a combination of probable success on the merits and the possibility of irreparable harm; or (2) that serious questions are raised and the balance of hardships tips in its favor (*Prudential Real Estate Affiliates, Inc v PPR Realty, Inc*, 204 F 3d 867 at 874 (9th Cir 2000)). 'These two formulations represent two points on a sliding scale in which the required degree of irreparable harm increases as the probability of success decreases' (*id*).

III

Plaintiffs claim Napster users are engaged in the wholesale reproduction and distribution of copyrighted works, all constituting direct infringement. The district court agreed. We note that the district court's conclusion that plaintiffs have presented a prima facie case of direct infringement by Napster users is not presently appealed by Napster. We only need briefly address the threshold requirements.

---

20   114 F Supp 2d 896 (ND Cal 2000); (2000) 50 IPR 232.

A. INFRINGEMENT

[2] Plaintiffs must satisfy two requirements to present a *prima facie* case of direct infringement: (1) they must show ownership of the allegedly infringed material and (2) they must demonstrate that the alleged infringers violate at least one exclusive right granted to copyright holders under 17 USC s 106. See 17 USC s 501(a) (infringement occurs when alleged infringer engages in activity listed in s 106); see also *Baxter v MCA, Inc*, 812 F 2d 421 at 423 (9th Cir 1987); see, eg, *SOS, Inc v Payday, Inc*, 886 F 2d 1081 at 1085 n3 (9th Cir 1989) ('The word "copying" is shorthand for the infringing of any of the copyright owner's five exclusive rights ...'). Plaintiffs have sufficiently demonstrated ownership. The record supports the district court's determination that 'as much as eighty-seven percent of the files available on Napster may be copyrighted and more than seventy percent may be owned or administered by plaintiffs' (*Napster*, 114 F Supp 2d at 911).

 [3] The district court further determined that plaintiffs' exclusive rights under s 106 were violated: 'here the evidence establishes that a majority of Napster users use the service to download and upload copyrighted music. ... And by doing that, it constitutes—the uses constitute direct infringement of plaintiffs' musical compositions, recordings' (*A&M Records, Inc v Napster, Inc*, Nos 99-5183, 00-0074, 2000 WL 1009483, at 1 (ND Cal 26 July 2000)) (transcript of proceedings). The district court also noted that 'it is pretty much acknowledged ... by Napster that this is infringement' (*id*). We agree that plaintiffs have shown that Napster users infringe at least two of the copyright holders' exclusive rights: the rights of reproduction, s 106(1); and distribution, s 106(3). Napster users who upload file names to the search index for others to copy violate plaintiffs' distribution rights.

 Napster users who download files containing copyrighted music violate plaintiffs' reproduction rights. Napster asserts an affirmative defense to the charge that its users directly infringe plaintiffs' copyrighted musical compositions and sound recordings ...

 ## NOTES AND QUESTIONS

> The court considered the questions of fair use and other matters as threshold matters to be decided prior to consideration of the complaint. The discussion of these issues has been excluded from this extract. Treatment of these aspects of copyright is contained in the section immediately following.

A & M Records, Inc, et al, v Napster, Inc

United States Court of Appeals for the Ninth Circuit, No 00-16401 D.C.

Available at <http://laws.lp.findlaw.com/getcase/9th/case/0016401&exact=1> 17 August 2006

Beezer, Circuit Judge:

... Accordingly, we next address whether Napster is secondarily liable for the direct infringement under two doctrines of copyright law: contributory copyright infringement and vicarious copyright infringement.

IV

[17] We first address plaintiffs' claim that Napster is liable for contributory copyright infringement. Traditionally, 'one who, with knowledge of the infringing activity, induces, causes or materially contributes to the infringing conduct of another, may be held liable as a "contributory" infringer' (*Gershwin Publishing Corp v Columbia Artists Management, Inc*, 443 F 2d 1159 at 1162 (2d Cir 1971); see also *Fonovisa, Inc v Cherry Auction, Inc*, 76 F 3d 259 at 264 (9th Cir 1996)). Put differently, liability exists if the defendant engages in 'personal conduct that encourages or assists the infringement' (*Matthew Bender & Co v West Publishing Co*, 158 F 3d 693 at 706 (2d Cir 1998)).

The district court determined that plaintiffs in all likelihood would establish Napster's liability as a contributory infringer. The district court did not err; Napster, by its conduct, knowingly encourages and assists the infringement of plaintiffs' copyrights.

A. KNOWLEDGE

Contributory liability requires that the secondary infringer 'know or have reason to know' of direct infringement (*Cable/Home Communication Corp Network Prods, Inc*, 902 F 2d 829 at 845 and 846 n29 (11th Cir 1990); *Religious Tech Ctr v Netcom On-Line Communication Services, Inc*, 907 F Supp 1361 at 1373–4 (ND Cal 1995) (framing issue as 'whether Netcom knew or should have known of' the infringing activities)). The district court found that Napster had both actual and constructive knowledge that its users exchanged copyrighted music. The district court also concluded that the law does not require knowledge of 'specific acts of infringement' and rejected Napster's contention that because the company cannot distinguish infringing from non-infringing files, it does not 'know' of the direct infringement (114 F Supp 2d at 917).

[18] It is apparent from the record that Napster has knowledge, both actual and constructive, of direct infringement. Napster claims that it is nevertheless protected from contributory liability by the teaching of *Sony Corp v Universal City Studios, Inc*, 464 US 417 (1984). We disagree. We observe that Napster's actual, specific knowledge of direct infringement renders *Sony*'s holding of limited assistance to Napster.

We are compelled to make a clear distinction between the architecture of the Napster system and Napster's conduct in relation to the operational capacity of the system.

The *Sony* Court refused to hold the manufacturer and retailers of video tape recorders liable for contributory infringement despite evidence that such machines could be and were used to infringe plaintiffs' copyrighted television shows. Sony stated that if liability 'is to be imposed on petitioners in this case, it must rest on the fact that they have sold equipment with constructive knowledge of the fact that their customers may use that equipment to make unauthorized copies of copyrighted material' (*id* at 439 … The *Sony* Court declined to impute the requisite level of knowledge where the defendants made and sold equipment capable of both infringing and 'substantial non-infringing uses' (*id* at 442 (adopting a modified 'staple article of commerce' doctrine from patent law)). See also *Universal City Studios, Inc v Sony Corp*, 480 F Supp 429 at 459 (CD Cal 1979) ('This court agrees with defendants that their knowledge was insufficient to make them contributory infringers'), rev'd, 659 F 2d 963 (9th Cir 1981), rev'd, 464 US 417 (1984); Alfred C Yen, 'Internet

Service Provider Liability for Subscriber Copyright Infringement, Enterprise Liability, and the First Amendment' (2000) 88 *Geo LJ* 1833 at 1874 and 1893 n 210 (suggesting that, after *Sony*, most Internet service providers lack 'the requisite level of knowledge' for the imposition of contributory liability).

[19] We are bound to follow *Sony*, and will not impute the requisite level of knowledge to Napster merely because peer-to-peer file sharing technology may be used to infringe plaintiffs' copyrights. See 464 US at 436 (rejecting argument that merely supplying the '"means" to accomplish an infringing activity' leads to imposition of liability). We depart from the reasoning of the district court that Napster failed to demonstrate that its system is capable of commercially significant non-infringing uses. See *Napster*, 114 F Supp 2d at 916, 917–18. The district court improperly confined the use analysis to current uses, ignoring the system's capabilities. See generally *Sony*, 464 US at 442–3 (framing inquiry as to whether the video tape recorder is 'capable of commercially significant non-infringing uses') ... Consequently, the district court placed undue weight on the proportion of current infringing use as compared to current and future non-infringing use. See generally *Vault Corp v Quaid Software Ltd*, 847 F 2d 255 at 264–7 (5th Cir 1997) (single non-infringing use implicated Sony). Nonetheless, whether we might arrive at a different result is not the issue here. See *Sports Form, Inc v United Press International, Inc*, 686 F 2d 750 at 752 (9th Cir 1982).

The instant appeal occurs at an early point in the proceedings and 'the fully developed factual record may be materially different from that initially before the district court. ...' (*id* at 753). Regardless of the number of Napster's infringing versus non-infringing uses, the evidentiary record here supported the district court's finding that plaintiffs would likely prevail in establishing that Napster knew or had reason to know of its users' infringement of plaintiffs' copyrights.

This analysis is similar to that of *Religious Technology Center v Netcom On-Line Communication Services, Inc*, which suggests that in an online context, evidence of actual knowledge of specific acts of infringement is required to hold a computer system operator liable for contributory copyright infringement (907 F Supp at 1371). *Netcom* considered the potential contributory copyright liability of a computer bulletin board operator whose system supported the posting of infringing material (*id* at 1374). The court, in denying Netcom's motion for summary judgment of noninfringement and plaintiff's motion for judgment on the pleadings, found that a disputed issue of fact existed as to whether the operator had sufficient knowledge of infringing activity (*id* at 1374–5).

The court determined that for the operator to have sufficient knowledge, the copyright holder must 'provide the necessary documentation to show there is likely infringement' (907 F Supp at 1374; *cf Cubby, Inc v Compuserve, Inc*, 776 F Supp 135 at 141 (SDNY 1991) (recognizing that the online service provider does not and cannot examine every hyperlink for potentially defamatory material)). If such documentation was provided, the court reasoned that Netcom would be liable for contributory infringement because its failure to remove the material 'and thereby stop an infringing copy from being distributed worldwide constitutes substantial participation' in distribution of copyrighted material (*id*).

[20] We agree that if a computer system operator learns of specific infringing material available on his system and fails to purge such material from the system, the operator knows

of and contributes to direct infringement. See *Netcom*, 907 F Supp at 1374. Conversely, absent any specific information which identifies infringing activity, a computer system operator cannot be liable for contributory infringement merely because the structure of the system allows for the exchange of copyrighted material. See *Sony*, 464 US at 436, 442–3. To enjoin simply because a computer network allows for infringing use would, in our opinion, violate *Sony* and potentially restrict activity unrelated to infringing use.

[21] We nevertheless conclude that sufficient knowledge exists to impose contributory liability when linked to demonstrated infringing use of the Napster system. See *Napster*, 114 F Supp 2d at 919 ('Religious Technology Center would not mandate a determination that Napster, Inc lacks the knowledge requisite to contributory infringement.'). The record supports the district court's finding that Napster has actual knowledge that specific infringing material is available using its system, that it could block access to the system by suppliers of the infringing material, and that it failed to remove the material. See *Napster*, 114 F Supp 2d at 918, 920–1.

B. MATERIAL CONTRIBUTION

[22] Under the facts as found by the district court, Napster materially contributes to the infringing activity. Relying on *Fonovisa*, the district court concluded that '[w]ithout the support services defendant provides, Napster users could not find and download the music they want with the ease of which defendant boasts' (*Napster*, 114 F Supp 2d at 919–20 ('Napster is an integrated service designed to enable users to locate and download MP3 music files')). We agree that Napster provides 'the site and facilities' for direct infringement. See *Fonovisa*, 76 F 3d at 264; *cf Netcom*, 907 F Supp at 1372 ('Netcom will be liable for contributory infringement since its failure to cancel [a user's] infringing message and thereby stop an infringing copy from being distributed world-wide constitutes substantial participation'). The district court correctly applied the reasoning in *Fonovisa*, and properly found that Napster materially contributes to direct infringement.

We affirm the district court's conclusion that plaintiffs have demonstrated a likelihood of success on the merits of the contributory copyright infringement claim. We will address the scope of the injunction in part VIII of this opinion.

V

[23] We turn to the question whether Napster engages in vicarious copyright infringement. Vicarious copyright liability is an 'outgrowth' of *respondeat superior* (*Fonovisa*, 76 F 3d at 262). In the context of copyright law, vicarious liability extends beyond an employer/ employee relationship to cases in which a defendant 'has the right and ability to supervise the infringing activity and also has a direct financial interest in such activities' (*id*, quoting Gershwin, 443 F 2d at 1162); see also *Polygram International Publishing, Inc v Nevada/TIG, Inc*, 855 F Supp 1314 at 1325–6 (D Mass 1994) (describing vicarious liability as a form of risk allocation).

Before moving into this discussion, we note that *Sony*'s 'staple article of commerce' analysis has no application to Napster's potential liability for vicarious copyright infringement. See *Sony*, 464 US at 434–5; see generally Melville B Nimmer and David Nimmer, *Nimmer On Copyright*, ss 12.04[A][2] and [A][2][b] (2000) (confining *Sony* to contributory infringement analysis: 'Contributory infringement itself is of two types—personal conduct that forms part of or furthers the infringement and contribution of machinery or goods that provide the means to infringe'), 617 PLI/Pat 455, 528 (2 September 2000) (indicating that the 'staple article of commerce' doctrine 'provides a defense only to contributory infringement, not to vicarious infringement'). The issues of Sony's liability under the 'doctrines of "direct infringement" and "vicarious liability"' were not before the Supreme Court, although the Court recognized that the 'lines between direct infringement, contributory infringement, and vicarious liability are not clearly drawn' (*id* at 435 n 17. Consequently, when the *Sony* Court used the term 'vicarious liability', it did so broadly and outside of a technical analysis of the doctrine of vicarious copyright infringement (*id* at 435: '[V]icarious liability is imposed in virtually all areas of the law, and the concept of contributory infringement is merely a species of the broader problem of identifying the circumstances in which it is just to hold one individual accountable for the actions of another'; see also *Black's Law Dictionary* 927 (7th ed 1999), defining 'vicarious liability' in a manner similar to the definition used in *Sony*).

A. FINANCIAL BENEFIT

[24] The district court determined that plaintiffs had demonstrated they would likely succeed in establishing that Napster has a direct financial interest in the infringing activity (*Napster*, 114 F Supp 2d at 921–2). We agree. Financial benefit exists where the availability of infringing material 'acts as a "draw" for customers' (*Fonovisa*, 76 F 3d at 263–4 (stating that financial benefit may be shown 'where infringing performances enhance the attractiveness of a venue')). Ample evidence supports the district court's finding that Napster's future revenue is directly dependent upon 'increases in userbase'. More users register with the Napster system as the 'quality and quantity of available music increases' (114 F Supp 2d at 902). We conclude that the district court did not err in determining that Napster financially benefits from the availability of protected works on its system.

B. SUPERVISION

The district court determined that Napster has the right and ability to supervise its users' conduct (*Napster*, 114 F Supp 2d at 920–1 (finding that Napster's representations to the court regarding 'its improved methods of blocking users about whom rights holders complain ... is tantamount to an admission that defendant can, and sometimes does, police its service')). We agree in part.

[25] The ability to block infringers' access to a particular environment for any reason whatsoever is evidence of the right and ability to supervise. See *Fonovisa*, 76 F 3d at 262 ('Cherry Auction had the right to terminate vendors for any reason whatsoever and through that right had the ability to control the activities of vendors on the premises'); cf *Netcom*, 907 F Supp at 1375–6 (indicating that plaintiff raised a genuine issue of fact regarding ability to supervise by presenting evidence that an electronic bulletin board service can suspend subscriber's accounts). Here, plaintiffs have demonstrated that Napster retains the right to control access to its system. Napster has an express reservation of rights policy, stating on its web site that it expressly reserves the 'right to refuse service and terminate accounts in [its] discretion, including, but not limited to, if Napster believes that user conduct violates applicable law ... or for any reason in Napster's sole discretion, with or without cause.'

[26] To escape imposition of vicarious liability, the reserved right to police must be exercised to its fullest extent. Turning a blind eye to detectable acts of infringement for the sake of profit gives rise to liability. See, eg, *Fonovisa*, 76 F 3d at 261 ('There is no dispute for the purposes of this appeal that Cherry Auction and its operators were aware that vendors in their swap meets were selling counterfeit recordings'); see also Gershwin, 443 F 2d at 1161–2 (citing *Shapiro, Bernstein & Co v H L Greene Co*, 316 F 2d 304 (2d Cir 1963), for the proposition that 'failure to police the conduct of the primary infringer' leads to imposition of vicarious liability for copyright infringement).

[27] The district court correctly determined that Napster had the right and ability to police its system and failed to exercise that right to prevent the exchange of copyrighted material. The district court, however, failed to recognize that the boundaries of the premises that Napster 'controls and patrols' are limited. See, eg, *Fonovisa*, 76 F 2d at 262–3 (in addition to having the right to exclude vendors, defendant 'controlled and patrolled' the premises); see also *Polygram*, 855 F Supp at 1328–9 (in addition to having the contractual right to remove exhibitors, trade show operator reserved the right to police during the show and had its 'employees walk the aisles to ensure "rules compliance" '). Put differently, Napster's reserved 'right and ability' to police is cabined by the system's current architecture. As shown by the record, the Napster system does not 'read' the content of indexed files, other than to check that they are in the proper MP3 format.

[28] Napster, however, has the ability to locate infringing material listed on its search indices, and the right to terminate users' access to the system. The file name indices, therefore, are within the 'premises' that Napster has the ability to police. We recognize that the files are user-named and may not match copyrighted material exactly (for example, the artist or song could be spelled wrong). For Napster to function effectively, however, file names must reasonably or roughly correspond to the material contained in the files, otherwise no user could ever locate any desired music. As a practical matter, Napster, its users and the record company plaintiffs have equal access to infringing material by employing Napster's 'search function'.

[29] Our review of the record requires us to accept the district court's conclusion that plaintiffs have demonstrated a likelihood of success on the merits of the vicarious copyright infringement claim. Napster's failure to police the system's 'premises', combined with a showing that Napster financially benefits from the continuing availability of infringing files on its system, leads to the imposition of vicarious liability ...

VIII

The district court correctly recognized that a preliminary injunction against Napster's participation in copyright infringement is not only warranted but required. We believe, however, that the scope of the injunction needs modification in light of our opinion. Specifically, we reiterate that contributory liability may potentially be imposed only to the extent that Napster:

(1) receives reasonable knowledge of specific infringing files with copyrighted musical compositions and sound recordings;

(2) knows or should know that such files are available on the Napster system; and

(3) fails to act to prevent viral distribution of the works. See *Netcom*, 907 F Supp at 1374–5.

The mere existence of the Napster system, absent actual notice and Napster's demonstrated failure to remove the offending material, is insufficient to impose contributory liability. See *Sony*, 464 US at 442–3.

Conversely, Napster may be vicariously liable when it fails to affirmatively use its ability to patrol its system and preclude access to potentially infringing files listed in its search index. Napster has both the ability to use its search function to identify infringing musical recordings and the right to bar participation of users who engage in the transmission of infringing files.

The preliminary injunction which we stayed is overbroad because it places on Napster the entire burden of ensuring that no 'copying, downloading, uploading, transmitting, or distributing' of plaintiffs' works occur on the system. As stated, we place the burden on plaintiffs to provide notice to Napster of copyrighted works and files containing such works available on the Napster system before Napster has the duty to disable access to the offending content. Napster, however, also bears the burden of policing the system within the limits of the system. Here, we recognize that this is not an exact science in that the files are user named. In crafting the injunction on remand, the district court should recognize that Napster's system does not currently appear to allow Napster access to users' MP3 files.

Based on our decision to remand, Napster's additional arguments on appeal going to the scope of the injunction need not be addressed. We, however, briefly address Napster's First Amendment argument so that it is not reasserted on remand. Napster contends that the present injunction violates the First Amendment because it is broader than necessary. The company asserts two distinct free speech rights: (1) its right to publish a 'directory' (here, the search index) and (2) its users' right to exchange information. We note that First Amendment concerns in copyright are allayed by the presence of the fair use doctrine. See 17 USC s 107; see generally *Nihon Keizai Shimbun v Comline Business Data, Inc* 166 F 3d 65 at 74 (2d Cir 1999); *Netcom*, 923 F Supp at 1258 (stating that the *Copyright Act* balances First Amendment concerns with the rights of copyright holders). There was a preliminary determination here that Napster users are not fair users. Uses of copyrighted material that are not fair uses are rightfully enjoined. See *Dr Seuss Enters v Penguin Books USA, Inc*, 109 F 3d 1394 at 1403 (9th Cir 1997) (rejecting defendants' claim that injunction would constitute a prior restraint in violation of the First Amendment).

Affirmed in part, reversed in part and remanded.

 ## NOTES AND QUESTIONS

1   It is important to note that the Ninth Circuit was simply reviewing the District Court decision for evidence of an abuse of discretion, or application of an erroneous point of law in the grant of an injunction.

2   Critically analyse the reasoning of the court. Do you agree with its findings?

3 After the above opinion was handed down, legal representatives of the plaintiffs suggested that Napster was both legally and morally wrong and that the decisions of the courts had confirmed this. Do you agree that Napster is morally wrong? If so, do you agree that the court affirmed this?

4 'Unlike King Canute, who knew his limitations, the recording industry has demonstrated its willingness to brace itself against the tide of digital music. These efforts, despite initial appearances, are destined to fail and record companies must embrace innovative solutions if they are to reap the rewards of the tidal change. They will achieve nothing unless they abandon their attachment to a copyright regime which simply cannot accommodate the digital age.' Critically analyse this statement with specific reference to the *Napster* decision.

5 In addition to Napster, there are a number of other peer-to-peer networks, such as Freenet and Gnutella, that have also received a lot of press attention. They have been said to pose a much more insidious threat to copyright owners. See further Andy Oram, 'The Value of Gnutella and Freenet', available at <http://www.praxagora.com/andyo/wr/gnutella_freenet_policy.html> 17 August 2006 and Andy Oram, 'Gnutella and Freenet Represent True Technological Innovation', available at <http://www.oreillynet.com/pub/a/network/2000/05/12/magazine/gnutella.html> 17 August 2006.

6 Following from the Napster decision, in 2002, the issue of P2P networks again reached the US Court of Appeals. The network in question in the 2002 dispute was the Aimster network.

In Re: Aimster Copyright Litigation, Appeal of: John Deep, Defendant

United States Court of Appeals for the Seventh Circuit, No 02-4125

Available at <http://www.ca7.uscourts.gov/tmp/SI01OI4Q.pdf> 28 April 2006

Before Posner, Ripple and Williams, Circuit Judges. Posner Circuit Judge:
Owners of copyrighted popular music filed a number of closely related suits, which were consolidated and transferred to the Northern District of Illinois by the Multi-district Litigation Panel, against John Deep and corporations that are controlled by him and need not be discussed separately. The numerous plaintiffs, who among them appear to own most subsisting copyrights on American popular music, claim that Deep's 'Aimster' Internet service (recently renamed 'Madster') is a contributory and vicarious infringer of these copyrights. The district judge entered a broad preliminary injunction, which had the effect of shutting down the Aimster service until the merits of the suit are finally resolved, from which Deep appeals. Aimster is one of a number of enterprises (the former Napster is the best known) that have been sued for facilitating the swapping of digital copies of popular music, most of it copyrighted, over the Internet.

Teenagers and young adults who have access to the Internet like to swap computer files containing popular music. If the music is copyrighted, such swapping, which involves making and transmitting a digital copy of the music, infringes copyright. The swappers, who are ignorant or more commonly disdainful of copyright and in any event discount the likelihood of being sued or prosecuted for copyright infringement, are the direct infringers. But firms that facilitate their infringement, even if they are not themselves infringers because they are not making copies of the music that is shared, may be liable to the copyright owners as contributory infringers. Recognizing the impracticability or futility of a copyright owner's suing a multitude of individual infringers ('chasing individual consumers is time consuming and is a teaspoon solution to an ocean problem,' Randal C Picker, 'Copyright as Entry Policy: The Case of Digital Distribution,' 47 *Antitrust Bull* 423, 442 (2002)), the law allows a copyright holder to sue a contributor to the infringement instead, in effect as an aider and abettor.

The Aimster system has the following essential components: proprietary software that can be downloaded free of charge from Aimster's Web site; Aimster's server (a server is a computer that provides services to other computers, in this case personal computers owned or accessed by Aimster's users, over a network), which hosts the Web site and collects and organizes information obtained from the users but does not make copies of the swapped files themselves and that also provides the matching service described below; computerized tutorials instructing users of the software on how to use it for swapping computer files; and 'Club Aimster,' a related Internet service owned by Deep that users of Aimster's software can join for a fee and use to download the 'top 40' popular-music files more easily than by using the basic, free service.

Someone who wants to use Aimster's basic service for the first time to swap files downloads the software from Aimster's Web site and then registers on the system by entering a user name (it doesn't have to be his real name) and a password at the Web site. Having done so, he can designate any other registrant as a 'buddy' and can communicate directly with all his buddies when he and they are online, attaching to his communications (which are really just emails) any files that he wants to share with the buddies. All communications back and forth are encrypted by the sender by means of encryption software furnished by Aimster as part of the software package downloadable at no charge from the Web site, and are decrypted by the recipient using the same Aimster-furnished software package. If the user does not designate a buddy or buddies, then *all* the users of the Aimster system become his buddies; that is, he can send or receive from any of them.

Users list on their computers the computer files they are willing to share. (They needn't list them separately, but can merely designate a folder in their computer that contains the files they are willing to share.) A user who wants to make a copy of a file goes online and types the name of the file he wants in his 'Search For' field. Aimster's server searches the computers of those users of its software who are online and so are available to be searched for files they are willing to share, and if it finds the file that has been requested it instructs the computer in which it is housed to transmit the file to the recipient via the Internet for him to download into his computer. Once he has done this he can if he wants make the file available for sharing with other users of the Aimster system by listing it as explained above. In principle, therefore, the purchase of a single CD could be levered into the distribution within days or even hours of millions of identical, near-perfect (depending on the compression format used) copies of the music recorded on the CD—hence the recording industry's anxiety about file-sharing services oriented toward consumers of popular music. But because copies of the songs reside on the computers of the users and not on Aimster's own server, Aimster is not a direct infringer of the copyrights on those songs. Its function is similar to that of a stock exchange, which is a facility for matching offers rather than a repository of the things being exchanged (shares of stock). But unlike transactions on a stock exchange, the consummated 'transaction' in music files does not take place in the facility, that is, in Aimster's server.

What we have described so far is a type of Internet file-sharing system that might be created for innocuous purposes such as the expeditious exchange of confidential business data among employees of a business firm ... The fact that copyrighted materials might sometimes be shared between users of such a system without the authorization of the copyright owner or a fair-use privilege would not make the firm a contributory infringer ... The Supreme Court made clear in the *Sony* decision that the producer of a product that has substantial non-infringing uses is not a contributory infringer merely because some of the uses actually made of the product (in that case a machine, the predecessor of today's videocassette recorders, for recording television programs on tape) are infringing. *Sony Corp of America, Inc v Universal City Studios, Inc,* 464 US 417, 78 L Ed 2d 574, 104 S Ct 774 (1984).

Sony's Betamax video recorder was used for three principal purposes, as Sony was well aware (a fourth, playing home movies, involved no copying). The first, which the majority opinion emphasized, was time shifting, that is, recording a television program that was being shown at a time inconvenient for the owner of the Betamax for later watching at a convenient time. The second was 'library building,' that is, making copies of programs to retain permanently. The third was skipping commercials by taping a program before watching it and then, while watching the tape, using the fast-forward button on the recorder to skip over the commercials. The first use the Court held was a fair use (and hence not infringing) because it enlarged the audience for the program. The copying involved in the second and third uses was unquestionably infringing to the extent that the programs copied were under copyright and the taping of them was not authorized by the copyright owners—but not all fell in either category ...

[We] reject the industry's argument that *Sony* provides no defense to a charge of contributory infringement when, in the words of the industry's brief, there is anything 'more than a mere showing that a product may be used for infringing purposes.' Although the fact was downplayed in the majority opinion, it was apparent that the Betamax was being used for infringing as well as noninfringing purposes—even the majority acknowledged that 25 percent of Betamax users were fast forwarding through commercials, *id* at 452 n 36—yet Sony was held not to be a contributory infringer. The Court was unwilling to allow copyright holders to prevent infringement effectuated by means of a new technology at the price of possibly denying noninfringing consumers the benefit of the technology. We therefore agree with Professor Goldstein that the Ninth Circuit erred in *A&M Records, Inc v Napster, Inc,* 239 F3d 1004, 1020 (9th Cir 2001), in suggesting that actual knowledge of specific infringing uses is a sufficient condition for deeming a facilitator a contributory infringer. 2 Paul Goldstein, *Copyright* s 6.1.2, p 6:12-1 (2d ed 2003).

Equally, however, we reject Aimster's argument that to prevail the recording industry must prove it has actually lost money as a result of the copying that its service facilitates. It is true that the Court in *Sony* emphasized that the plaintiffs had failed to show that they had sustained substantial harm from the Betamax. *Id* at 450-54, 456. But the Court did so in the context of assessing the argument that time shifting of television programs was fair use rather than infringement. One reason time shifting was fair use, the Court believed, was that it wasn't hurting the copyright owners because it was enlarging the audience for their programs. But a copyright owner who can prove infringement need not show that the infringement caused him a financial loss. Granted, without such a showing he cannot obtain compensatory damages; but he can obtain statutory damages, or an injunction, just as the owner of physical property can obtain an injunction against a trespasser without proving that the trespass has caused him a financial loss.

What is true is that when a supplier is offering a product or service that has noninfringing as well as infringing uses, some estimate of the respective magnitudes of these uses is necessary for a finding of contributory infringement. The Court's action in striking the cost-benefit trade-off in favor of Sony came to seem prescient when it later turned out that the principal use of video recorders was to allow people to watch at home movies that they bought or rented rather than to tape television programs.

We also reject Aimster's argument that because the Court said in *Sony* that mere 'constructive knowledge' of infringing uses is not enough for contributory infringement, 464 US at 439, and the encryption feature of Aimster's service prevented Deep from knowing what songs were being copied by the users of his system, he lacked the knowledge of infringing uses that liability for contributory infringement requires. Willful blindness is knowledge, in copyright law (where indeed it may be enough that the defendant *should* have known of the direct infringement, *Casella v Morris,* 820 F2d 362, 365 (11th Cir 1987); 2 Goldstein, *supra*, s 6.1, p 6:6), as it is in the law generally ... Our point is only that a service provider that would otherwise be a contributory infringer does not obtain immunity by using encryption to shield itself from actual knowledge of the unlawful purposes for which the service is being used.

We also do not buy Aimster's argument that since the Supreme Court distinguished, in the long passage from the *Sony* opinion that we quoted earlier, between actual and potential noninfringing uses, all Aimster has to show in order to escape liability for contributory infringement is that its file-sharing system *could* be used in noninfringing ways, which obviously it could be. Were that the law, the seller of a product or service used *solely* to facilitate copyright infringement, though it was capable in principle of noninfringing uses, would be immune from liability for contributory infringement. That would be an extreme result, and one not envisaged by the *Sony* majority. Otherwise its opinion would have had no occasion to emphasize the fact (at least the majority thought it a fact—the dissent disagreed, 464 US at 458-59) that Sony had not in its advertising encouraged the use of the Betamax to infringe copyright. *Id* at 438 ... To the recording industry, a single known infringing use brands the facilitator as a contributory infringer. To the Aimsters of this world, a single noninfringing use provides complete immunity from liability. Neither is correct.

To situate Aimster's service between these unacceptable poles, we need to say just a bit more about it. In explaining how to use the Aimster software, the tutorial gives as its *only* examples of file sharing the sharing of copyrighted music, including copyrighted music that the recording industry had notified Aimster was being infringed by Aimster's users. The tutorial is the invitation to infringement that the Supreme Court found was missing in *Sony*. In addition, membership in Club Aimster enables the member for a fee of $ 4.95 a month to download with a single click the music most often shared by Aimster users, which turns out to be music copyrighted by the plaintiffs. Because Aimster's software is made available free of charge and Aimster does not sell paid advertising on its Web site, Club Aimster's monthly fee is the only means by which Aimster is financed and so the club cannot be separated from the provision of the free software.

The evidence that we have summarized does not exclude the *possibility* of substantial noninfringing uses of the Aimster system, but the evidence is sufficient, especially in a preliminary-injunction proceeding, which is summary in character, to shift the burden of production to Aimster to demonstrate that its service has substantial noninfringing uses ... As it might:

1   Not all popular music is copyrighted.
2   A music file-swapping service might increase the value of a recording by enabling it to be used as currency in the music-sharing community, since someone who only downloads and never uploads, thus acting as a pure free rider, will not be very popular.
3   Users of Aimster's software might form select (as distinct from all-comers) 'buddy' groups to exchange non-copyrighted information about popular music, or for that matter to exchange ideas and opinions about wholly unrelated matters as the buddies became friendlier.
4   Aimster's users might appreciate the encryption feature because as their friendship deepened they might decide that they wanted to exchange off-color, but not copyrighted, photographs, or dirty jokes, or other forms of expression that people like to keep private, rather than just copyrighted music.
5   Someone might own a popular-music CD that he was particularly fond of, but he had not downloaded it into his computer and now he finds himself out of town but with his laptop and he wants to listen to the CD, so he uses Aimster's service to download a copy. This might be a fair use rather than a copyright infringement, by analogy to the time shifting approved as fair use in the *Sony* case.

All five of our examples of actually or arguably noninfringing uses of Aimster's service are possibilities, but as should be evident from our earlier discussion the question is how probable they are. It is not enough, as we have said, that a product or service be physically capable, as it were, of a noninfringing use. Aimster has failed to produce any evidence that its service has ever been used for a noninfringing use, let alone evidence concerning the frequency of such uses.

Even when there are noninfringing uses of an Internet file-sharing service, moreover, if the infringing uses are substantial then to avoid liability as a contributory infringer the provider of the service must show that it would have been disproportionately costly for him to eliminate or at least reduce substantially the infringing uses. Aimster failed to make that showing too, by failing to present evidence that the provision of an encryption capability *effective against the service provider itself* added important value to the service or saved significant cost. Aimster blinded itself in the hope that by doing so it might come within the rule of the *Sony* decision.

Turning to the second issue presented by the appeal, we are less confident than the district judge was that the recording industry would also be likely to prevail on the issue of vicarious infringement should the case be tried, though we shall not have to resolve our doubts in order to decide the appeal. 'Vicarious liability' generally refers to the liability of a principal, such as an employer, for the torts committed by his agent, an employee for example, in the course of the agent's employment. The teenagers and young adults who use Aimster's system to infringe copyright are of course not Aimster's agents. But one of the principal rationales of vicarious liability, namely the difficulty of obtaining effective relief against an agent, who is likely to be impecunious, Alan O Sykes, 'The Economics of Vicarious Liability,' *93 Yale LJ 1231*, 1241-42, 1272 (1984), has been extended in the copyright area to cases in which the only effective relief is obtainable from someone who bears a relation to the direct infringers that is analogous to the relation of a principal to an agent. See 2 Goldstein, *supra*, s 6.2, pp 6:17 to 6:18. The canonical illustration is the owner of a dance hall who hires dance bands that sometimes play copyrighted music without authorization. The bands are not the dance hall's agents, but it may be impossible as a practical matter for the copyright holders to identify and obtain a legal remedy against the infringing bands yet quite feasible for the dance hall to prevent or at least limit infringing performances. And so the dance hall that fails to make reasonable efforts to do this is liable as a vicarious infringer. *Dreamland Ball Room v Shapiro, Bernstein & Co, 36 F2d 354, 355 (7th Cir 1929)*, and other cases cited in *Sony Corp of America, Inc v Universal City Studios, Inc, supra,* 464 US at 437 n 18; 2 Goldstein, *supra*, s 6.2, pp 6:18 to 6:20. The dance hall could perhaps be described as a contributory infringer. But one thinks of a contributory infringer as someone who benefits directly from the infringement that he encourages, and that does not seem an apt description of the dance hall, though it does benefit to the extent that competition will force the dance band to charge the dance hall a smaller fee for performing if the band doesn't pay copyright royalties and so has lower costs than it would otherwise have.

We turn now to Aimster's defenses under the *Online Copyright Infringement Liability Limitation Act*, Title II of the *Digital Millennium Copyright Act* (DMCA), 17 USC s 512; see 2 Goldstein, *supra*, s 6.3. The DMCA is an attempt to deal with special problems created by the so-called digital revolution. One of these is the vulnerability of Internet service providers such as AOL to liability for copyright infringement as a result of file swapping among their subscribers. Although the Act was not passed with Napster-type services in mind, the definition of Internet service provider is broad ('a provider of online services or network access, or the operator of facilities therefor,' 17 USC s 512(k)(1)(B)), and, as the district judge ruled, Aimster fits it ... The common element of its safe harbors is that the service provider must do what it can reasonably be asked to do to prevent the use of its service by 'repeat infringers.' 17 USC s 512(i)(1)(A). Far from doing anything to discourage repeat infringers of the plaintiffs' copyrights, Aimster invited them to do so, showed them how they could do so with ease using its system, and by teaching its users how to encrypt their unlawful distribution of copyrighted materials disabled itself from doing anything to prevent infringement ...

 NOTES AND QUESTIONS

1   What was the significance of the encryption software in the Aimster software package? What were the Court's views on the tutorial for using Aimster?

2   How important to the Court's decision was Aimster's business model? Why?

3   How does the Court distinguish the facts in the *Sony* decision from the facts of the present case? What were some of the key facts that led the Court to decide as it did in *Aimster*?

4   Would it be fair to say that the decision in *Aimster* turned on the facts? Does the Court have a stance on P2P networks?

5   Napster and Aimster are representatives of the first-generation peer to peer network (P2P) networks. Despite being a P2P, they utilise the server–client structure for some tasks. Second-generation P2P networks are purer forms of the peer-to-peer concept with limited or no such use. The first major decision on these second-generation P2P networks came from the US Supreme Court in the following case.

Metro-Goldwyn-Mayer Studios Inc v Grokster Ltd

United States Supreme Court, 125 S Ct 2764 (2005)

Souter J delivered the opinion for the unanimous Court.

Souter J:

The question is under what circumstances the distributor of a product capable of both lawful and unlawful use is liable for acts of copyright infringement by third parties using the product. We hold that one who distributes a device with the object of promoting its use to infringe copyright, as shown by clear expression or other affirmative steps taken to foster infringement, is liable for the resulting acts of infringement by third parties.

Respondents, Grokster, Ltd, and StreamCast Networks, Inc, defendants in the trial court, distribute free software products that allow computer users to share electronic files through peer-to-peer networks, so called because users' computers communicate directly with each other, not through central servers.

A group of copyright holders (MGM for short, but including motion picture studios, recording companies, songwriters, and music publishers) sued Grokster and StreamCast for their users' copyright infringements, alleging that they knowingly and intentionally distributed their software to enable users to reproduce and distribute the copyrighted works in violation of the *Copyright Act*, 17 USC s 101 et seq (2000 ed and Supp II). MGM sought damages and an injunction.

Discovery during the litigation revealed the way the software worked, the business aims of each defendant company, and the predilections of the users. Grokster's eponymous software employs what is known as FastTrack technology, a protocol developed by others and licensed to Grokster. StreamCast distributes a very similar product except that its software, called Morpheus, relies on what is known as Gnutella technology. A user who downloads and installs either software possesses the protocol to send requests for files directly to the computers of others using software compatible with FastTrack or Gnutella.

The search results are communicated to the requesting computer, and the user can download desired files directly from peers' computers. As this description indicates, Grokster and StreamCast use no servers to intercept the content of the search requests or to mediate the file transfers conducted by users of the software, there being no central point through which the substance of the communications passes in either direction.

Although Grokster and StreamCast do not therefore know when particular files are copied, a few searches using their software would show what is available on the networks the software reaches. MGM commissioned a statistician to conduct a systematic search, and his study showed that nearly 90% of the files available for download on the FastTrack system were copyrighted works. Grokster and StreamCast dispute this figure ... They also argue that potential noninfringing uses of their software are significant in kind, even if infrequent in practice. Some musical performers, for example, have gained new audiences by distributing their copyrighted works for free across peer-to-peer networks, and some distributors of unprotected content have used peer-to-peer networks to disseminate files, Shakespeare being an example.

Grokster and StreamCast are not, however, merely passive recipients of information about infringing use. The record is replete with evidence that from the moment Grokster and StreamCast began to distribute their free software, each one clearly voiced the objective that recipients use it to download copyrighted works, and each took active steps to encourage infringement.

In addition to this evidence of express promotion, marketing, and intent to promote further, the business models employed by Grokster and StreamCast confirm that their principal object was use of their software to download copyrighted works. Grokster and StreamCast receive no revenue from users, who obtain the software itself for nothing. Instead, both companies generate income by selling advertising space, and they stream the advertising to Grokster and Morpheus users while they are employing the programs.

Finally, there is no evidence that either company made an effort to filter copyrighted material from users' downloads or otherwise impede the sharing of copyrighted files. Although Grokster appears to have sent e-mails warning users about infringing content when it received threatening notice from the copyright holders, it never blocked anyone from continuing to use its software to share copyrighted files ...

The Court of Appeals affirmed. 380 F3d 1154 (CA9 2004). In the court's analysis, a defendant was liable as a contributory infringer when it had knowledge of direct infringement and materially contributed to the infringement. But the court read *Sony Corp of America v Universal City Studios, Inc,* 464 US 417, 78 L Ed 2d 574, 104 S Ct 774 (1984), as holding that distribution of a commercial product capable of substantial noninfringing uses could not give rise to contributory liability for infringement unless the distributor had actual knowledge of specific instances of infringement and failed to act on that knowledge. The fact that the software was capable of substantial noninfringing uses in the Ninth Circuit's view meant that Grokster and StreamCast were not liable, because they had no such actual knowledge, owing to the decentralized architecture of their software.

The Ninth Circuit also considered whether Grokster and StreamCast could be liable under a theory of vicarious infringement. The court held against liability because the defendants did not monitor or control the use of the software, had no agreed-upon right or current ability to supervise its use, and had no independent duty to police infringement ...

The argument for imposing indirect liability in this case is, however, a powerful one, given the number of infringing downloads that occur every day using StreamCast's and Grokster's software. When a widely shared service or product is used to commit infringement, it may be impossible to enforce rights in the protected work effectively against all direct infringers, the only practical alternative being to go against the distributor of the copying device for secondary liability on a theory of contributory or vicarious infringement. See *In re Aimster Copyright Litigation*, 334 F3d 643, 645-646 (CA7 2003).

One infringes contributorily by intentionally inducing or encouraging direct infringement, see *Gershwin Pub Corp v Columbia Artists Management, Inc*, 443 F2d 1159, 1162 (CA2 1971), and infringes vicariously by profiting from direct infringement while declining to exercise a right to stop or limit it, *Shapiro, Bernstein & Co v H L Green Co*, 316 F2d 304, 307 (CA2 1963). Although 'the *Copyright Act* does not expressly render anyone liable for infringement committed by another,' *Sony Corp v Universal City Studios*, 464 US, at 434, 78 L Ed 2d 574, 104 S Ct 774 these doctrines of secondary liability emerged from common law principles and are well established in the law, *id, at* 486, 78 L Ed 2d 574, 104 S Ct 774 (Blackmun, J, dissenting); *Kalem Co v Harper Brothers*, 222 US 55, 62-63, 56 L Ed 92, 32 S Ct 20 (1911); *Gershwin Pub Corp v Columbia Artists Management, supra, at 1162*; 3 M Nimmer & D Nimmer, Copyright, 12.04[A] (2005) ...

The parties and many of the *amici* in this case think the key to resolving it is the *Sony* rule and, in particular, what it means for a product to be 'capable of commercially significant noninfringing uses.' *Sony Corp v Universal City Studios, supra, at* 442, 78 L Ed 2d 574, 104 S Ct 774. MGM advances the argument that granting summary judgment to Grokster and StreamCast as to their current activities gave too much weight to the value of innovative technology, and too little to the copyrights infringed by users of their software, given that 90% of works available on one of the networks was shown to be copyrighted. Assuming the remaining 10% to be its noninfringing use, MGM says this should not qualify as 'substantial,' and the Court should quantify *Sony* to the extent of holding that a product used 'principally' for infringement does not qualify. See Brief for Motion Picture Studio and Recording Company Petitioners 31. As mentioned before, Grokster and StreamCast reply by citing evidence that their software can be used to reproduce public domain works, and they point to copyright holders who actually encourage copying. Even if infringement is the principal practice with their software today, they argue, the noninfringing uses are significant and will grow.

We agree with MGM that the Court of Appeals misapplied *Sony*, which it read as limiting secondary liability quite beyond the circumstances to which the case applied ... The Ninth Circuit has read *Sony's* limitation to mean that whenever a product is capable of substantial lawful use, the producer can never be held contributorily liable for third parties' infringing use of it; it read the rule as being this broad, even when an actual purpose to cause infringing use is shown by evidence independent of design and distribution of the product, unless the distributors had 'specific knowledge of infringement at a time at which they contributed to the infringement, and failed to act upon that information.' 380 F3d at 1162

This view of *Sony*, however, was error, converting the case from one about liability resting on imputed intent to one about liability on any theory ... It is enough to note that the Ninth Circuit's judgment rested on an erroneous understanding of *Sony* and to leave further consideration of the *Sony* rule for a day when that may be required.

Sony's rule limits imputing culpable intent as a matter of law from the characteristics or uses of a distributed product. But nothing in *Sony* requires courts to ignore evidence of intent if there is such evidence, and the case was never meant to foreclose rules of fault-based liability derived from the common law. *Sony Corp v Universal City Studios,* 464 US, at 439, 78 L Ed 2d 574, 104 S Ct 774 ('If vicarious liability is to be imposed on *Sony* in this case, it must rest on the fact that it has sold equipment with constructive knowledge' of the potential for infringement). Thus, where evidence goes beyond a product's characteristics or the knowledge that it may be put to infringing uses, and shows statements or actions directed to promoting infringement, *Sony*'s staple-article rule will not preclude liability.

The classic case of direct evidence of unlawful purpose occurs when one induces commission of infringement by another, or 'entices or persuades another' to infringe, *Black's Law Dictionary* 790 (8th ed 2004), as by advertising …

The rule on inducement of infringement as developed in the early cases is no different today. Evidence of 'active steps . . . taken to encourage direct infringement,' *Oak Industries, Inc v Zenith Electronics Corp,* 697 F Supp 988, 992 (ND Ill 1988), such as advertising an infringing use or instructing how to engage in an infringing use, show an affirmative intent that the product be used to infringe, and a showing that infringement was encouraged overcomes the law's reluctance to find liability when a defendant merely sells a commercial product suitable for some lawful use, see, *eg, Water Technologies Corp v Calco, Ltd,* 850 F2d 660, 668 (CA Fed 1988) (liability for inducement where one 'actively and knowingly aids and abets another's direct infringement.' …

Accordingly, just as *Sony* did not find intentional inducement despite the knowledge of the VCR manufacturer that its device could be used to infringe, 464 US, at 439, n 19, 78 L Ed 2d 574, 104 S Ct 774, mere knowledge of infringing potential or of actual infringing uses would not be enough here to subject a distributor to liability. Nor would ordinary acts incident to product distribution, such as offering customers technical support or product updates, support liability in themselves. The inducement rule, instead, premises liability on purposeful, culpable expression and conduct, and thus does nothing to compromise legitimate commerce or discourage innovation having a lawful promise.

The only apparent question about treating MGM's evidence as sufficient to withstand summary judgment under the theory of inducement goes to the need on MGM's part to adduce evidence that StreamCast and Grokster communicated an inducing message to their software users. The classic instance of inducement is by advertisement or solicitation that broadcasts a message designed to stimulate others to commit violations. MGM claims that such a message is shown here. It is undisputed that StreamCast beamed onto the computer screens of users of Napster-compatible programs ads urging the adoption of its OpenNap program, which was designed, as its name implied, to invite the custom of patrons of Napster, then under attack in the courts for facilitating massive infringement. Those who accepted StreamCast's OpenNap program were offered software to perform the same services, which a factfinder could conclude would readily have been understood in the Napster market as the ability to download copyrighted music files. Grokster distributed an electronic newsletter containing links to articles promoting its software's ability to access popular copyrighted music. And anyone whose Napster or free file-sharing searches turned up a link to Grokster would have understood Grokster to be offering the same file-sharing ability as Napster, and to the same people who probably used Napster for infringing downloads; that would also have been the understanding of anyone offered Grokster's suggestively named Swaptor software, its version of OpenNap. And both companies communicated a clear message by responding affirmatively to requests for help in locating and playing copyrighted materials.

Three features of this evidence of intent are particularly notable. First, each company showed itself to be aiming to satisfy a known source of demand for copyright infringement, the market comprising former Napster users. StreamCast's internal documents made constant reference to Napster, it initially distributed its Morpheus software through an OpenNap program compatible with Napster, it advertised its OpenNap program to Napster users, and its Morpheus software functions as Napster did except that it could be used to distribute more kinds of files, including copyrighted movies and software programs. Grokster's name is apparently derived from Napster, it too initially offered an OpenNap program, its software's function is likewise comparable to Napster's, and it attempted to divert queries for Napster onto its own Web site. Grokster and StreamCast's efforts to supply services to former Napster users, deprived of a mechanism to copy and distribute what were overwhelmingly infringing files, indicate a principal, if not exclusive, intent on the part of each to bring about infringement.

Second, this evidence of unlawful objective is given added significance by MGM's showing that neither company attempted to develop filtering tools or other mechanisms to diminish the infringing activity using their software. While the Ninth Circuit treated the defendants' failure to develop such tools as irrelevant because they lacked an independent duty to monitor their users' activity, we think this evidence underscores Grokster's and StreamCast's intentional facilitation of their users' infringement.

Third, there is a further complement to the direct evidence of unlawful objective. It is useful to recall that StreamCast and Grokster make money by selling advertising space, by directing ads to the screens of computers employing their software. As the record shows, the more the software is used, the more ads are sent out and the greater the advertising revenue becomes. Since the extent of the software's use determines the gain to the distributors, the commercial sense of their enterprise turns on high-volume use, which the record shows is infringing. This evidence alone would not justify an inference of unlawful intent, but viewed in the context of the entire record its import is clear.

In addition to intent to bring about infringement and distribution of a device suitable for infringing use, the inducement theory of course requires evidence of actual infringement by recipients of the device, the software in this case. As the account of the facts indicates, there is evidence of infringement on a gigantic scale, and there is no serious issue of the adequacy of MGM's showing on this point in order to survive the companies' summary judgment requests. Although an exact calculation of infringing use, as a basis for a claim of damages, is subject to dispute, there is no question that the summary judgment evidence is at least adequate to entitle MGM to go forward with claims for damages and equitable relief.

In sum, this case is significantly different from *Sony* and reliance on that case to rule in favor of StreamCast and Grokster was error. *Sony* dealt with a claim of liability based solely on distributing a product with alternative lawful and unlawful uses, with knowledge that some users would follow the unlawful course. The case struck a balance between the interests of protection and innovation by holding that the product's capability of substantial lawful employment should bar the imputation of fault and consequent secondary liability for the unlawful acts of others.

The judgment of the Court of Appeals is vacated, and the case is remanded for further proceedings consistent with this opinion.

Justice Breyer, with whom Justice Stevens and Justice O'Connor join, concurring:

I agree with the Court that the distributor of a dual-use technology may be liable for the infringing activities of third parties where he or she actively seeks to advance the infringement. *Ante*, at 1. I further agree that, in light of our holding today, we need not now 'revisit' *Sony Corp of America v Universal City Studios, Inc,* 464 US 417, 78 L Ed 2d 574, 104 S Ct 774 (1984). *Ante*, at 17. Other Members of the Court, however, take up the *Sony* question: whether Grokster's product is 'capable of "substantial" or "commercially significant" noninfringing uses.' *Ante*, at 1 (Ginsburg, J, concurring) (quoting *Sony, supra,* at 442, 78 L Ed 2d 574, 104 S Ct 774). And they answer that question by stating that the Court of Appeals was wrong when it granted summary judgment on the issue in Grokster's favor. *Ante*, at 4. I write to explain why I disagree with them on this matter.

The Court's opinion in *Sony* and the record evidence (as described and analyzed in the many briefs before us) together convince me that the Court of Appeals' conclusion has adequate legal support.

(In *Sony*) the Court recognized the need for the law, in fixing *secondary* copyright liability, to 'strike a balance between a copyright holder's legitimate demand for effective—not merely symbolic—protection of the statutory monopoly, and the rights of others freely to engage in substantially unrelated areas of commerce.' *Id, at* 442, 78 L Ed 2d 574, 104 S Ct 774. It pointed to patent law's 'staple article of commerce' doctrine, *ibid*, under which a distributor of a product is not liable for patent infringement by its customers unless that product is 'unsuited for any commercial noninfringing use.' *Dawson Chemical Co v Rohm & Haas Co,* 448 US 176, 198, 65 L Ed 2d 696, 100 S Ct 2601 (1980). The Court wrote that the sale of copying equipment, 'like the sale of other articles of commerce, does not constitute contributory infringement if the product is widely used for legitimate, unobjectionable purposes. *Indeed, it need merely be capable of substantial noninfringing uses.*' *Sony,* 464 US, at 442, 78 L Ed 2d 574, 104 S Ct 774 (emphasis added). The Court ultimately characterized the legal 'question' in the particular case as 'whether [Sony's VCR] is *capable of commercially significant noninfringing uses*' (while declining to give 'precise content' to these terms). *Ibid* (emphasis added).

It then applied this standard. The Court had before it a survey (commissioned by the District Court and then prepared by the respondents) showing that roughly 9% of all VCR recordings were of the type—namely, religious, educational, and sports programming—owned by producers and distributors testifying on Sony's behalf who did not object to time-shifting.

The Court found that the magnitude of authorized programming was 'significant,' and it also noted the 'significant potential for future authorized copying.' 464 US, at 444, 78 L Ed 2d 574, 104 S Ct 774. The Court supported this conclusion by referencing the trial testimony of professional sports league officials and a religious broadcasting representative. *Id,* at 444, 78 L Ed 2d 574, 104 S Ct 774, and n 24.

When measured against *Sony's* underlying evidence and analysis, the evidence now before us shows that Grokster passes *Sony's* test—that is, whether the company's product is capable of substantial or commercially significant noninfringing uses. *Id,* at 442, 78 L Ed 2d 574, 104 S Ct 774. For one thing, petitioners' (hereinafter MGM) own expert declared that 75% of current files available on Grokster are infringing and 15% are 'likely infringing.' See App 436-439, PP6-17 (Decl of Dr Ingram Olkin); cf *ante*, at 4 (opinion of the Court). That leaves some number of files near 10% that apparently are noninfringing, a figure very similar to the 9% or so of authorized time-shifting uses of the VCR that the Court faced in *Sony* ...

Importantly, *Sony* also used the word 'capable,' asking whether the product is '*capable of*' substantial noninfringing uses. Its language and analysis suggest that a figure like 10%, if fixed for all time, might well prove insufficient, but that such a figure serves as an adequate foundation where there is a reasonable prospect of expanded legitimate uses over time. See *ibid* (noting a 'significant potential for future authorized copying'). And its language also indicates the appropriateness of looking to potential future uses of the product to determine its 'capability' ...

Here the record reveals a significant future market for noninfringing uses of Grokster-type peer-to-peer software. Such software permits the exchange of *any* sort of digital file—whether that file does, or does not, contain copyrighted material. As more and more uncopyrighted information is stored in swappable form, it seems a likely inference that lawful peer-to-peer sharing will become increasingly prevalent ...

There may be other now-unforeseen noninfringing uses that develop for peer-to-peer software, just as the home-video rental industry (unmentioned in *Sony*) developed for the VCR. But the foreseeable development of such uses, when taken together with an estimated 10% noninfringing material, is sufficient to meet *Sony*'s standard. And while *Sony* considered the record following a trial, there are no facts asserted by MGM in its summary judgment filings that lead me to believe the outcome after a trial here could be any different. The lower courts reached the same conclusion ...

The real question is whether we should modify the *Sony* standard, as MGM requests, or interpret *Sony* more strictly, as I believe Justice Ginsburg's approach would do in practice...

As I have said, *Sony* itself sought to 'strike a balance between a copyright holder's legitimate demand for effective—not merely symbolic—protection of the statutory monopoly, and the rights of others freely to engage in substantially unrelated areas of commerce.' *Id,* at 442, 78 L Ed 2d 574, 104 S Ct 774. Thus, to determine whether modification, or a strict interpretation, of *Sony* is needed, I would ask whether MGM has shown that *Sony* incorrectly balanced copyright and new-technology interests. In particular: (1) Has *Sony* (as I interpret it) worked to protect new technology? (2) If so, would modification or strict interpretation significantly weaken that protection? (3) If so, would new or necessary copyright-related benefits outweigh any such weakening?

The first question is the easiest to answer. *Sony*'s rule, as I interpret it, has provided entrepreneurs with needed assurance that they will be shielded from copyright liability as they bring valuable new technologies to market.

Sony's rule is clear ...

Sony's rule is strongly technology protecting ...

Sony's rule is forward looking. It does not confine its scope to a static snapshot of a product's current uses (thereby threatening technologies that have undeveloped future markets). Rather, as the VCR example makes clear, a product's market can evolve dramatically over time. And *Sony*—by referring to a *capacity* for substantial noninfringing uses—recognizes that fact. *Sony's* word 'capable' refers to a plausible, not simply a theoretical, likelihood that such uses will come to pass, and that fact anchors *Sony* in practical reality. Cf *Aimster, supra, at 651.*

Sony's rule is mindful of the limitations facing judges where matters of technology are concerned. Judges have no specialized technical ability to answer questions about present or future technological feasibility or commercial viability where technology professionals, engineers, and venture capitalists themselves may radically disagree and where answers may differ depending upon whether one focuses upon the time of product development or the time of distribution.

The second, more difficult, question is whether a modified *Sony* rule (or a strict interpretation) would significantly weaken the law's ability to protect new technology. Justice Ginsburg's approach would require defendants to produce considerably more concrete evidence—more than was presented here—to earn *Sony's* shelter. That heavier evidentiary demand, and especially the more dramatic (case-by-case balancing) modifications that MGM and the Government seek, would, I believe, undercut the protection that *Sony* now offers.

To require defendants to provide, for example, detailed evidence—say business plans, profitability estimates, projected technological modifications, and so forth—would doubtless make life easier for copyrightholder plaintiffs. But it would simultaneously increase the legal uncertainty that surrounds the creation or development of a new technology capable of being put to infringing uses. Inventors and entrepreneurs (in the garage, the dorm room, the corporate lab, or the boardroom) would have to fear (and in many cases endure) costly and extensive trials when they create, produce, or distribute the sort of information technology that can be used for copyright infringement. They would often be left guessing as to how a court, upon later review of the product and its uses, would decide when necessarily rough estimates amounted to sufficient evidence. They would have no way to predict how courts would weigh the respective values of infringing and noninfringing uses; determine the efficiency and advisability of technological changes; or assess a product's potential future markets. The price of a wrong guess—even if it involves a good-faith effort to assess technical and commercial viability—could be large statutory damages (not less than $750 and up to $30,000 *per infringed work*). 17 USC § 504(c)(1). The additional risk and uncertainty would mean a consequent additional chill of technological development.

The third question—whether a positive copyright impact would outweigh any technology-related loss—I find the most difficult of the three. I do not doubt that a more intrusive *Sony* test would generally provide greater revenue security for copyright holders. But it is harder to conclude that the gains on the copyright swings would exceed the losses on the technology roundabouts.

For one thing, the law disfavors equating the two different kinds of gain and loss; rather, it leans in favor of protecting technology. As *Sony* itself makes clear, the producer of a technology which *permits* unlawful copying does not himself *engage* in unlawful copying—a fact that makes the attachment of copyright liability to the creation, production, or distribution of the technology an exceptional thing. See 464 US, at 431, 78 L Ed 2d 574, 104 S Ct 774 (courts 'must be circumspect' in construing the copyright laws to preclude distribution of new technologies) ...

Will an unmodified *Sony* lead to a significant diminution in the amount or quality of creative work produced? Since copyright's basic objective is creation and its revenue objectives but a means to that end, this is the underlying copyright question. See *Twentieth Century Music Corp v Aiken,* 422 US 151, 156, 45 L Ed 2d 84, 95 S Ct 2040 (1975) ('Creative work is to be encouraged and rewarded, but private motivation must ultimately serve the cause of promoting broad public availability of literature, music, and the other arts'). And its answer is far from clear ...

Copyright holders at least potentially have other tools available to reduce piracy and to abate whatever threat it poses to creative production. As today's opinion makes clear, a copyright holder may proceed against a technology provider where a provable specific intent to infringe (of the kind the Court describes) is present. *Ante,* at 24 (opinion of the Court). Services like Grokster may well be liable under an inducement theory ...

Further, copyright holders may develop new technological devices that will help curb unlawful infringement. Some new technology, called 'digital "watermarking"' and 'digital fingerprinting,' can encode within the file information about the author and the copyright scope and date, which 'fingerprints' can help to expose infringers ...

Finally, as *Sony* recognized, the legislative option remains available. Courts are less well suited than Congress to the task of 'accommodating fully the varied permutations of competing interests that are inevitably implicated by such new technology.' *Sony,* 464 US, at 431, 78 L Ed 2d 574, 104 S Ct 774 ...

I do not know whether these developments and similar alternatives will prove sufficient, but I am reasonably certain that, given their existence, a strong demonstrated need for modifying *Sony* (or for interpreting *Sony*'s standard more strictly) has not yet been shown. That fact, along with the added risks that modification (or strict interpretation) would impose upon technological innovation, leads me to the conclusion that we should maintain *Sony,* reading its standard as I have read it. As so read, it requires affirmance of the Ninth Circuit's determination of the relevant aspects of the *Sony* question.

 # NOTES AND QUESTIONS

1   As mentioned above, the P2P network at issue in *Grokster* was a second-generation P2P network. No doubt the software designers planned the second-generation P2P architecture with a view to overcoming the legalities of the Napster-type networks. The Grokster network does not have a centralised system that catalogues all the files that are available for downloading. Instead, it is completely decentralised and uses its users' computers to store the files. In this way, Grokster (and StreamCast) were able to claim that they had no knowledge or control of what material was actually being transferred.

2   The action in *Grokster* began in the District Court which found in favour of Grokster. MGM appealed to the Ninth Circuit but was unsuccessful. In both lower court decisions, the *Sony* decision was applied and the court found that Grokster was not liable for secondary copyright infringement. Strictly speaking, the legal issue for the Supreme Court was whether the decision in *Sony* was properly applied by the lower courts. However, behind the legal arguments, the Supreme Court was urged to revisit the appropriateness of the *Sony* decision in the current digital environment. The *Sony* decision set a delicate balance and the issue was whether the balance should be recast more favourably towards copyright owners.

3   The Supreme Court decision distinguished *Sony* and hence there was no need to decide whether the balance set in *Sony* needed adjustment. On what basis did Justice Souter distinguish the facts from *Sony*? What role did unlawful intent and inducement play?

4   The judgment written by Breyer J examined the test in *Sony* more closely. What is the view put forward? According to Breyer J, should *Sony* continue to give broad protection to technology developers?

5   Justice Ginsburg also wrote a separate decision, as alluded to in Breyer J's judgment. Like Breyer J, her Honour also found herself with two other justices agreeing with her. That left the Court evenly split (3–3) on whether *Sony* should be read more narrowly.

6   It is important to note that the decision in *Grokster* does not condemn all P2P network operators to liability for secondary copyright infringement. The *Grokster* decision turned very much on its facts and it remains to be seen when a P2P network operator will be cleared of secondary copyright infringement.

7   In Australia, the relevant legal principle is the authorisation of copyright infringement (see further Y F Lim, 'Internet Service Providers and Liability for Copyright Infringement through Authorisation' (1997) 8 *Australian Intellectual Property Journal* 192-211). As discussed earlier, the word 'authorise' was held in the *Moorhouse* case to have its dictionary meaning of 'sanction, approve, countenance'. In 2000, s 36(1A) and s 101(1A) were inserted to generally codify the principles laid down in *Moorhouse*. These two sections require a court to consider the following factors when considering whether a person has authorised a primary act of infringement:

(a) the extent (if any) of the person's power to prevent the doing of the act concerned;

(b) the nature of any relationship existing between the person and the person who did the act concerned; and

(c) whether the person took any reasonable steps to prevent or avoid the doing of the act, including whether the person complied with any relevant industry codes of practice.

8   In one of the two major cases in Australia on the concept of authorisation as it applies to the Internet, it has been noted that these factors are not exhaustive. In *Universal Music Australia Pty Ltd v Cooper* [2005] FCA 972 ('*Cooper*'), Tamberlin J at [81] commented that s 101(1A) does not prevent the Court from taking into account other factors. This was referred to with approval by Wilcox J in the second major case *Universal Music Australia Pty Ltd v Sharman License Holdings* [2005] FCA 1242 ('*Sharman*'). These two cases will now be considered in turn.

9   The case of *Sharman* dealt with the Kazaa system, a P2P network similar to the P2P network in Grokster. Reference was made, however, to the concept of supernodes—argued to be more akin to the Napster type of network utilising some aspects of the client-server structure. This was not, however, ultimately crucial in the final decision.

10 The legal action was brought by 30 Australian and international record companies against numerous companies, their joint venture partners and four of the

executives. In addition to copyright infringement, the case was also argued on *Trade Practices Act* grounds as well as the tort of conspiracy. The central issue was whether the defendants authorised infringements of copyright by users of the Kazaa system.

Universal Music Australia Pty Ltd v Sharman License Holdings
Federal Court of Australia, [2005] FCA 1242

Wilcox J:

400 It is convenient to say immediately that I see no basis upon which it may be held that Sharman Holdings has authorised any infringements of copyright (or, indeed, committed any of the other infringements and breaches of duty alleged against it). The evidence provides little information about Sharman Holdings. All that is revealed is the date and place of the company's incorporation and the name of its sole director and sole shareholder. It is not shown to have done any particular act. It is possible that, as its name suggests, Sharman Holdings does no more than hold assets used by others. Insofar as it relates to Sharman Holdings, the proceeding must be dismissed.

401 The situation in relation to Sharman is different, at least in respect of authorisation. Sharman is the operator of the Kazaa system. As I have said, Sharman falls within s 112E. Sharman is not to be held to have authorised copyright infringement by Kazaa users merely because it provides the facilities they use in order to infringe the applicants' copyright. Something more is required. In evaluating the 'something more', regard must be paid to the factors listed in s 101(1A) of the Act, but bearing in mind Tamberlin J's observation in *Cooper*, that this is not an exhaustive list.

402 I accept that the intention behind the addition of s 101(1A) to the Act was to elucidate, rather than to vary, the pre-existing law about authorisation. I further accept, as did Bennett J in *Metro*, the continuing applicability of the *Moorhouse* test. A claim of authorisation can be made good only where it is shown that the person has sanctioned, approved or countenanced the infringement. It is not essential there be direct evidence of the person's attitude; as Gibbs J said in *Moorhouse*, inactivity or indifference, exhibited by acts of commission or omission, may reach such a degree as to support an inference of authorisation or permission.

403 Although s 112E provides that the provision of facilities is not enough to constitute authorisation, such provision is a matter relevant to 'the nature of [the] relationship' between Sharman and Kazaa users. If Sharman had not provided to users the facilities necessary for file-sharing, there would be no Kazaa file-sharing at all.

404 At all material times, it has been in Sharman's financial interest for there to be ever-increasing file-sharing, involving an ever-greater number of people. Sharman always knew users were likely to share files that were subject to copyright. At least since the Syzygy report in May 2003, Sharman, through Ms Hemming and Mr Morle, have been aware this was a major, even the predominant, use of the Kazaa system.

405 In the present case, the applicants are able to point to evidence of positive acts by Sharman that would have had the effect of encouraging copyright infringement. These acts include:

     (i) Sharman's website promotion of KMD as a file-sharing facility: see paras 68, 71, 73, 74, 78 and 79;

    (ii) Sharman's exhortations to users to use this facility and share their files: see paras 69, 77, 80 and 81;

   (iii) Sharman's promotion of the 'Join the Revolution' movement, which is based on file-sharing, especially of music, and which scorns the attitude of record and movie companies in relation to their copyright works: see paras 81-84 and 178. Especially to a young audience, the 'Join the Revolution' website material would have conveyed the idea that it was 'cool' to defy the record companies and their stuffy reliance on their copyrights.

406 Importantly, these acts took place in the context that Sharman knew the files shared by Kazaa users were largely copyright works.

407 It is true, as the respondents emphasised, that Sharman's promotional statements were made against the background that each page of the Kazaa website, contained a notice, albeit in small print, that Sharman does not 'condone activities and actions that breach the rights of copyright owners'. It is also true that users were told about the relevant EULA and made to click a box whereby they agreed to be bound by the EULA. It is difficult to believe those directing the affairs of Sharman, or any of the other respondents, ever thought these measures would be effective to prevent, or even substantially to curtail, copyright file-sharing. It would have been obvious to them that, were those measures to prove effective, they would greatly reduce Kazaa's attractiveness to users and, therefore, its advertising revenue potential. However, if any of those people did have such a view, it could not have survived receipt of the Syzygy report. That report showed the notices and EULA had had no effect on the behaviour of the focus group participants. As the participants were selected on the basis that they were representative of Kazaa users as a whole, or at least of young Kazaa users, those directing the affairs of Sharman (and Altnet) could not have done otherwise than appreciate that, notwithstanding what was on the website, copyright infringement was rife. Despite this, Sharman took no steps to include a filtering mechanism in its software, even in software intended to be provided to new users. There is no credible evidence that filtering was ever discussed. Sharman did not withdraw the 'Join the Revolution' material from its website. Rather, it included that material in the later version 3.0.

408 There is no evidence to suggest Ms Hemming, Mr Morle, Mr Bermeister or Mr Rose ever confronted the inconsistency between Sharman's website statements about not condoning copyright infringement and its conduct in the face of knowledge about what was actually happening.

409 Paragraphs (a) and (c) of s 101(1A) require consideration of the extent of Sharman's power to prevent copyright file-sharing and the steps it took to prevent or avoid that practice, including compliance with any relevant industry code of practice. There is no evidence of the existence of any such code.

410 The notices posted on Sharman's website about copyright infringement and the EULA are relevant to paras (a) and (c). However, the evidence shows that, to the knowledge of Sharman, they failed to prevent widespread copyright infringement.

411 If I am correct in my conclusions about keyword filtering (paras 254 to 294 above) and gold file flood filtering (paras 310 to 330 above), Sharman had power (in the case of

gold file flood filtering, in conjunction with Altnet) to prevent, or at least substantially to reduce, the incidence of copyright file-sharing. Yet Sharman did nothing; even when it introduced KMD v3 one week before commencement of the trial of this proceeding.

412 Counsel for the Sharman respondents argued that Kazaa users did not 'make a copy of the sound recording', within the meaning of s 85(1)(a) of the Act, merely by downloading a shared file into their computers. The argument was based on the proposition that the downloaded material would not fall within the definition of 'record' in s 10(1)(e) of the Act. I question whether that proposition is correct. However, it is not necessary to reach a conclusion about it. The function of s 10(1) is merely to indicate the meaning, in the Act, of particular words. The word 'record' is not used in s 85, so the defined meaning of that word is irrelevant to the interpretation of that section.

413 The word 'copy' is not relevantly defined by the Act. However, in normal parlance, it covers the digital transmission of the aggregate of sounds contained in a sound recording into a computer's data storage system, enabling those sounds to be reproduced at will or to be passed on to someone else.

414 Counsel for the Altnet respondents argued it would not be possible to find authorisation unless I was satisfied that Sharman was in a position to 'control' the file-sharing behaviour of Kazaa users. There may be room for debate as to whether it is desirable to continue to use the word 'control' in this context, having regard to the content of the new subs (1A) of s 101. However, it would not be inapt to use the word 'control' to describe Sharman's position. Sharman was not able to control the decisions of individual users as to whether or not they would engage in file-sharing and, if so, which particular works they would place into their 'My Shared Folder' file or download from other people. However, Sharman was in a position, through keyword filtering or gold file flood filtering, to prevent or restrict users' access to identified copyright works; in that sense, Sharman could control users' copyright infringing activities. Sharman did not do so; with the result that the relevant applicant's copyright in each of the Defined Recordings was infringed.

415 There is no evidence as to the identity of the particular Kazaa user or users who made available for sharing, or downloaded from another user, each of the Defined Recordings. However, somebody must have done so. Witnesses for the applicants gave uncontested evidence of being able to download each of these sound recordings as blue files.

416 Counsel for the Amici argued that to require software providers 'to monitor content for infringement would be wrong (because of eg ss 22(6) and 112E, evidencing Parliament's intent to "protect the messenger"), unrealistic and unfair.' Counsel said '[t]his would shift, without justification, the burden of enforcement away from the rights holder and onto unrelated third parties ... and remove from the rights holder any motivation to protect its own property ... and would fail to promote new technologies'.

417 The last point echoes a complaint of counsel for the Altnet respondents about the applicants' decision 'to release music on open CD format (in contrast with the secure DRM protected, gold files distributed by Altnet)' and the fact that some of the applicants, or their associates, market appliances that enable people to 'rip' CDs.

418 I accept that Parliament intended to 'protect the messenger', although only to the extent indicated by the Act; notably s 112E. However, on my findings, Sharman is and was more than a 'messenger'. Whether it is 'unrealistic and unfair' that a software provider

in Sharman's position should be held to have authorised copyright infringement by users of the software is a matter of opinion. The Court must take guidance from the Act, as elucidated by relevant judicial decisions. It is not for the Court to reject that guidance on the basis that the particular judge considers the result to be unrealistic and unfair. If Parliament thinks that is, indeed, the result of applying the Act, the remedy is in its hands.

419 The available evidence does not permit me to reach any clear conclusion as to the steps that might have been available to the applicants directly to protect their copyright in works reproduced in CDs distributed by them. The reason that evidence was not adduced, I surmise, is that all the respondents' counsel realised it is not a defence to an action for copyright infringement for a respondent to point to failings in self-protection by the copyright owner. Copyright law contains no equivalent of the doctrine of contributory negligence. If counsel are correct in asserting the applicants could have achieved some protection by adopting a DRM format, the applicants might do well to consider taking that course. However, neither the assertion nor the applicants' reaction to it can affect the legal issues now before the Court.

420 In my opinion, having regard to the whole of the relevant evidence, it should be held that Sharman infringed the applicants' copyright in their respective Defined Recordings by authorising Kazaa users to make copies of those sound recordings and to communicate those recordings to the public. By maintaining the Kazaa system in its present form, Sharman threatens to infringe the applicants' copyright in their other sound recordings in the same way ...

 NOTES AND QUESTIONS

1   Unlike the US law, the concept of authorisation in Australia does not have a *Sony* defence equivalent. The considerations for the head of liability are also different from the US principles of vicarious liability and contributory infringement. What are the similarities and what are the differences?

2   Under the concept of authorisation, is the defendant's attitude towards direct infringement important? Why and how? Is it important under the US law?

3   The US Supreme Court in *Grokster* distinguished the facts of *Grokster* from *Sony*. Are those considerations relevant in the Australian concept? Which of the factors in s 101(1A) would overlap with the facts considered by the US Supreme Court?

4   The recurring themes under the US and Australian Law would include power to prevent, ability to control, knowledge, inducement and direct financial interest. Do you see a merging of the concepts in the two jurisdictions?

5   The Court's ruling should not be seen as one that threatens the P2P technology. The decision allows the technology to continue to be used as long as it is used appropriately. Like *Grokster*, the *Sharman* decision turned very much on the facts and no broad sweeping position on the technology was taken by the Court. It should also be noted that three organisations were granted leave to intervene in the proceedings and their concerns represented the voice of consumers and civil libertarians.

6 The next decision we will consider is *Universal Music Australia Pty Ltd v Cooper* [2005] FCA 972. This case concerned a website operated by Cooper under the domain name of mp3s4free.net. The website contained, amongst other things, hyperlinks to music recordings in the mp3 file format. When Internet users clicked on those hyperlinks, the downloading of the files located on other servers would automatically occur. Cooper did not create the hyperlinks himself but his website was set up so that visitors to his website could post the hyperlinks without the need for Cooper to intervene and without Cooper's approval. A user could access Cooper's website without any payment and they could similarly download the mp3s for free. The website was hosted by an internet service provider (ISP) owned and run by E-Talk Communications Pty Ltd and Con-Cen Pty Ltd. Cooper and the ISP had an arrangement whereby Cooper did not pay a hosting fee, and in exchange, the ISP was permitted to place a logo and link to the ISP's home page from Cooper's website. It was in effect an advertising and traffic-sharing agreement. The issues raised in the case were direct copyright infringement, authorisation of copyright infringement, and violation of trade practices statutes. The trade practices claims were dismissed; thus our focus will be on the copyright claims.

Universal Music Australia Pty Ltd v Cooper

Federal Court of Australia, [2005] FCA 972

Tamberlin J:

77 Section 101(1) of the Act provides that copyright is infringed by a person who, not being the owner of the copyright, authorises the doing in Australia of any act that infringes the copyright ...

79 Justice Gibbs continued at 12–13:

> A person cannot be said to authorize an infringement of copyright unless he has some power to prevent it. Express or formal permission or sanction, or active conduct indicating approval, is not essential to constitute an authorization. ... However, the word 'authorize' connotes a mental element and it could not be inferred that a person had, by mere inactivity, authorized something to be done if he neither knew nor had reason to suspect that the act might be done.

The majority in *Moorhouse* stated at 21–2 that knowledge was not relevant where a general permission or invitation existed to perform the acts of infringement, however, it could become important if:

> the invitation were qualified in such a way as to make it clear that the invitation did not extend to the doing of acts comprised in copyright and if nevertheless it were known that the qualification to the invitation was being ignored and yet the University allowed that state of things to continue.

80 In each case, the question of whether the person has authorised the infringement of copyright is a question of fact: *Moorhouse* at 21 per Jacobs J. Express or formal permission or sanction is not essential to constitute an authorisation, however, as Sackville J

(Jenkinson and Burchett agreeing) said in *Nationwide News Pty Ltd v Copyright Agency Limited* (1996) FCR 399 at 422:

> Nonetheless a person does not authorise an infringement merely because he or she knows that another person might infringe the copyright and takes no steps to prevent the infringement.

In *Australasian Performing Right Association Ltd v Metro on George Pty Ltd* (2004) 61 IPR 575 at [18] *(Metro)*, Bennett J agreed that mere facilitation of infringing conduct and knowledge that there is a likelihood that there will be infringing use are insufficient to constitute authorisation. The element of control will be necessary to constitute authorisation to infringe copyright: see also *Nominet UK v Diverse Internet Pty Ltd* (2004) 63 IPR 543 at [129] per French J. However, as Gummow J stated in *Hanimex* at [48], the question remains open as to what degree of connection or control is necessary between the alleged authoriser and the primary infringer. Inactivity or indifference, exhibited by conduct, by acts of commission or omission, may reach a degree from which authorisation or permission may be inferred. The likelihood of the occurrence of the infringing act, as well as evidence of the degree of indifference displayed, will be relevant to a determination of whether the infringement of copyright has been authorised: *Metro* at [19]-[20] per Bennett J.

81 Subsection 101(1A) was introduced into the Act by the 2000 Amendment. This provision states that in deciding whether a person has authorised the doing in Australia of any act comprised in the copyright, the matters that must be taken into account by the Court include ...

These factors are not exhaustive and do not prevent the Court from taking into account other factors, such as the respondent's knowledge of the nature of the copyright infringement ...

84 The Cooper website is carefully structured and highly organised and many of its pages contain numerous references to linking and downloading. The website also provides the hyperlinks that enable the user to directly access the files on, and activate the downloading from, the remote websites. The website is clearly designed to, and does, facilitate and enable this infringing downloading. I am of the view that there is a reasonable inference available that Cooper, who sought advice as to the establishment and operation of his website, knowingly permitted or approved the use of his website in this manner and designed and organised it to achieve this result. In view of the absence of Cooper from the witness box, without any reasonable explanation apart from a tactical forensic suggestion that he was not a necessary or appropriate witness to be called in his own case, I am satisfied that the available inference of permission or approval by Cooper can more safely and confidently be drawn. Accordingly, I infer that Cooper has permitted or approved, and thereby authorized, the copyright infringement by internet users who access his website and also by the owners or operators of the remote websites from which the infringing recordings were downloaded.

85 The words 'sanction' and 'approve' are expressions of wide import. Cooper, in my view, could have prevented the infringements by removing the hyperlinks from his website or by structuring the website in such a way that the operators of the remote websites from which MP3 files were downloaded could not automatically add hyperlinks to the website without some supervision or control by Cooper. The evidence of Professor Sterling, who

was called on behalf of the applicants, is unchallenged to the effect that a website operator is always able to control the hyperlinks on his or her website, either by removal of the links or by requiring measures to be taken by the remote website operator prior to adding a hyperlink. A person cannot create a hyperlink between a music file and a website without the permission of the operator of the website because access to the code that is required to create the link must occur at level of the website. The Cooper website employed a 'CGI-BIN' script to accept hyperlink suggestions from visitors to the website. By virtue of this script, such suggestions were automatically added to the website without the intervention of Cooper. The evidence is that alternative software was in existence that would have enabled a third party to add a hyperlink to a website but which required the consent or approval of the website operator before such hyperlinks were added.

86 I note that Mr Speck, in cross-examination, agreed that Cooper could not control whether any particular sound recording remained on the internet or on a remote website, however, this is not the issue. The issue is whether Cooper had sufficient control of his own website to take steps to prevent the infringement. In my view, Cooper clearly did have sufficient control regarding both the user accessing his website and the remote operator placing hyperlinks on the website.

87 The Cooper website included a number of disclaimers indicating that MP3s could be both legal and illegal and that the downloading of MP3s would be legal only when the song's copyright owner had granted permission for the internet user to download and play the music sound recording. It is acknowledged by counsel for the first respondent that the disclaimers on the website inaccurately reflected copyright law in Australia. In my view, these statements do not, in the terms of s 101(1A)(c) of the Act, amount to reasonable steps to prevent or avoid the doing of the act. The disclaimers in fact indicate Cooper's knowledge of the existence of illegal MP3s on the internet and the likelihood that at least some of the MP3s to which the website provided hyperlinks constituted infringing copies of copyright music sound recordings. However, no attempt was made by Cooper, when hyperlinks were submitted to the website, to take any steps to ascertain the legality of the MP3s to which the hyperlinks related or the identity of the persons submitting the MP3s. In the words of Knox CJ in *Adelaide Corporation v Australasian Performing Right Association Ltd* (1920) 40 CLR 481 at 488, as approved by Gibbs CJ in *Moorhouse* at 13, Cooper 'abstained from action which under the circumstances then existing it would have been reasonable to take, or … exhibited a degree of indifference from which permission ought to be inferred.'

88 Accordingly, I find that Cooper has authorised the infringement of copyright in the music sound recordings, both by the internet users who downloaded the recordings and the operators of the remote websites …

89 Section 103 provides that copyright is infringed by a person who sells, lets for hire, or by way of trade offers, or exposes for sale, an article or exhibits an article in public. The applicant submits that Cooper has both sold or exposed for sale and exhibited by way of trade the music files on his website …

91 … I do not consider that he was exposing or offering for sale the sound recordings. There is no sale or trade between Cooper and the user or the owners or operators of the remote websites …

97   The 2000 Amendment provided for the protection of persons who make, or facilitate the making of, a communication. Section 39B applies to infringement of copyright in works and s 112E, which is in substantially similar terms, applies to infringement of copyright in subject matter other than works. Section 112E provides that a person, including a carrier or carriage service provider, who provides facilities for making, or facilitating the making of, a communication is not taken to have authorised any infringement of copyright in an audio-visual item merely because another person uses the facilities so provided to do something the right to do which is included in the copyright.

98   It is important to note that this provision has no application in relation to the applicants' claims of direct infringement pursuant to s 101 of the Act or the claims of secondary infringement pursuant to s 103 of the Act. The defence under s 112E applies only to infringement by authorisation. The 'Explanatory Memorandum' to the 2000 Amendment states that the:

> new clause 112E has the effect of expressly limiting the *authorisation liability* of persons who provide facilities for the making of, or facilitating the making of, communications. (Emphasis added)

99   The applicants emphasise the reference to the word 'merely' and say that the section has no application in the present case because the circumstances indicate that Cooper has been far more involved than just providing the facility that has been used to make the communication. In my opinion, the circumstances of this case are taken outside the protection afforded by s 112E of the Act because Cooper has offered encouragement to users to download offending material, as evidenced by the numerous references to downloading material on the website, and has specifically structured and arranged the website so as to facilitate this downloading …

110   Given my finding that Cooper did not 'make available online' or 'electronically transmit' the sound recordings, the applicants must also fail in their submission that E-Talk/Com-Cen directly infringed copyright by communicating the music sound recordings to the public.

111   It is common ground that Bal was the controlling mind of Com-Cen and E-Talk at all material times. Bal contends that he was not aware of the contents of the website prior to 17 October 2003, when *Anton Piller* orders were executed at the premises of E-Talk/Com-Cen Camperdown …

119   I do not accept that Bal and Takoushis were unaware of the contents of the site or that they failed to take any steps to inform themselves as to the volume of traffic that the website would be likely to attract…

121   Pursuant to s 101(1A) of the Act, in determining whether a person has authorised an infringement of copyright, the Court must take into account the extent of that person's power to prevent the doing of the act concerned and whether that person took any other reasonable steps to prevent or avoid the doing of the act. E-Talk/Com-Cen were responsible for hosting the website and providing the necessary connection to the internet and therefore had the power to prevent the doing of the infringing acts. They could have taken the step of taking down the website. Instead, they took no steps to prevent the acts of infringement …

126   I should add that even if the version of events provided by Takoushis and Bal was accepted (which it is not) to the effect that it was a practice of E-Talk/Com-Cen not to

make inquiries in relation to the contents of websites by reason of their title or name or other circumstances, this amounted to unreasonable conduct in relation to the provision of hosting services and to turning a blind eye to possible contraventions of copyright which could take place on the hosting site. Accordingly, within the meaning of s 112E it could not be said that they were doing no more than 'merely' hosting the website involved in the present circumstances. Where a host is on notice of an irregularity and deliberately elects not to investigate the operation and contents of a site and turns a blind eye to such indications, even having regard to the possible indication afforded by the title of the website, then, in my view, there are additional factors called into play beyond merely hosting the site ...

130 As Bal is the controlling mind of E-Talk/Com-Cen, I am satisfied on the evidence that E-Talk/Com-Cen authorised the infringing communication of the sound recordings to the public by the remote websites and the copying of the sound recordings by the internet users who downloaded the files.

 NOTES AND QUESTIONS

1   How different or similar is the facility in *Cooper* from the P2P file sharing facilities? Would Cooper have had more knowledge and control over the activities than the operators of the P2P networks? Why?

2   Does the decision in *Cooper* have any implications for the practise of hyperlink? Does this decision clarify the approach to be taken with respect to copyright liability for providing hyperlinks to material that is known to be or is likely to be infringing? See also discussion in Chapter 10 on deep linking.

3   The Court was also required to address the defence in s 112E. Why was the ISP not able to rely on this defence?

4   In *Nominet UK v Diverse Internet Pty Ltd* [2004] FCA 1244, the issue of authorisation was also considered by the Australian Federal Court. Diverse Internet and its officers were found to have infringed the copyright of a database containing domain names through its data mining activities in extracting and collating details from Nominet's database. The officers were found to have authorised copyright infringement as they had a degree of control or power. The activity of data mining has also raised other legal areas such as trespass and nuisance, but these have not been judicially considered in Australia.

5   It would appear that having a power to prevent is emerging to be a key consideration in cases on authorisation and the Internet. Consider the situation where an entity has the power to prevent through the total withdrawal of the facility. How would the Court deal with such a situation?

6   Two other key considerations have emerged from non-Internet cases on authorisation of copyright infringement over the decades. They are the right and ability to control and the ability to grant or purport to grant to a third person the right to do the act.

7   In the Singapore Court of Appeal case of *Ong Seow Pheng v Lotus Development* [1997] 3 SLR 137, it would appear that these two factors are paramount. The

case involved the appellant allegedly authorising another, Lur, to make 6706 infringing copies of software programmes. The only evidence came from Lur, who said Ong had told him to make copies to sell as he required. Lur would then make whatever copies he needed and sell them. The court stated:

33 We have the following observations on this evidence. Lur was a software pirate himself carrying on business under the name Xenix Trading and he hardly needed the appellants or anyone else to tell him to make any infringing copies for sale to his customers or otherwise. In so far as his evidence may be interpreted as meaning that he made the infringing copies of the respondents' programmes because he had been told to do so by Ong, we find it inherently incredible.

34 We accept that Ong supplied Lur with a copy of the programme together with the manuals. In doing so, he might well have suggested to Lur that copies of the programmes could be made. However, that is was a far cry from saying that the appellants thereby authorised Lur to make copies of the programme. He might have facilitated, and even incited, Lur's infringements, but as was held in *CBS Songs* and *Amstrad*, that is not the same thing as authorisation. As the learned judge held, and we agree with her, once the appellants had sold and delivered the infringing copies of the manuals or programmes to Lur, these copies were out of their hands and they had no control over what Lur would do with reference to them. Clearly, the *Moorhouse* case has no application here.

8 It would appear to be the case that under Singapore law, the concept of authorisation is interpreted to be considerably narrower than in Australia. However, another interpretation would be that where the facts indicate that the alleged authoriser has parted with the items or facilities in question, he or she will be regarded as no longer having any control over what the direct infringer chooses to do. Certainly, in the context of the Internet, it is doubtful if the facilitator will ever be in a position to be entitled to be regarded as having parted with any facility and hence be entitled to be regarded as no longer having any control over the direct infringer.

9 In December 2004, the Australian Parliament enacted the *Copyright Legislation Amendment Act 2004* which brings certain provisions of the Australian *Copyright Act 1968* into line with the Australia-US Free Trade Agreement. In particular, the *US Free Trade Agreement Implementation Act 2004* (Cth) inserted a new Division 2AA into the *Copyright Act 1968*. This new Division creates a 'safe harbour' for ISPs by setting out limitations on the remedies available against ISPs for copyright infringement relating to their on-line activities. However, before an ISP can take advantage of the safe harbour, it must satisfy certain criteria. The *Copyright Legislation Amendment Act 2004* added a condition that that an ISP must act expeditiously to remove or disable access to copyright material if the ISP becomes aware that the material is infringing or is likely to be infringing under the circumstances. This has raised questions of fairness and feasibility. It

would appear that take down notices could be issued to ISPs by people who are not the copyright owners. Second, the speed required by ISPs to act would mean that there would be little opportunity to investigate the validity of the copyright infringement claim. Lastly, it would appear that there are no mechanisms for people to object to their material from being removed by the ISP pursuant to a take down notice.

(f)　User rights

Copyright creates a regime in which certain acts may be carried out only with the permission of the copyright holder. However, as onerous as this may sound, the law also provides for a number of statutory defences. In addition, there may be an implied licence to do certain acts which do not require the permission of the copyright owner. These have been referred to by some as user rights, while others view them as exemptions rather than rights.

User rights: implied licence

Given the nature of the Internet, it could be argued that a copyright holder who deliberately places materials on a website without any security measures in place is consenting to its being accessed by users. Hence, it would nullify questions as to whether there is any infringement by transient reproduction, which would otherwise arise without such an implied consent. However, it is by no means clear that the same can be said with respect to caching of a website. Even if material is placed on the Internet to be used freely, there are no legal doctrines guaranteeing that an implied licence, in existence by virtue of the author's deliberate placement of the work onto the website, permits the process of caching.[21]

Another critical issue is whether the implied licence extends beyond access to cover other infringing acts, such as printing out or downloading materials. This is more contentious. However, there are strong grounds for an argument that where there is no express prohibition or security measures by the website operator, such activities should be treated as authorised. The case of *Trumpet Software Pty Ltd v OzE-mail Pty Ltd*[22] demonstrates the scope of implied licences. In that case, it was held that the defendants were entitled to bundle the plaintiffs' software with their own and distribute it commercially, against the wishes of the plaintiffs. The court held that because the software had been originally marketed as shareware—that is, as available for free use and reproduction—the defendants were entitled to bundle the software. However, the Federal Court did also hold that the redistribution must be of the entire software, without any adjustment to the original product. The clear implication is that while there

---

21　Some have suggested that s 43A could be used to cover caching, but much would depend on the definition of what is temporary and most caching currently being performed would probably not be considered temporary.

22　(1996) 34 IPR 481.

may be an implied licence to access, download, and print a website, the implied licence will not extend to dissemination of the materials in another form for commercial gain without clear statements permitting this.

User rights: fair dealing

The Australian *Copyright Act* contains a number of provisions by which various specified acts, which would otherwise fall within the scope of the infringement rules, are made lawful, thereby serving the interests of the public in enabling access to materials that would otherwise be unavailable. Sections 40 and 103C provide that a fair dealing with works and with audio-visual items (namely sound recordings, cinematograph films, broadcasts) for research or study does not constitute an infringement of copyright. Other exemptions in the Act include fair dealing for the purpose of criticism or review (s 41 and s 103A), or reporting news (s 42 and s 103B), or the giving of professional advice by a legal practitioner (s 43 and s 104). Under Australian copyright law, the fair dealing defences are specific defences. There is no general defence of fair dealing, similar to the US 'fair use' defence.

The USA provides a general fair use defence covering purposes such as criticism, comment, teaching, scholarship, and research. In determining whether the defence has been made out, a number of factors are to be taken into account, including whether the use is of a commercial nature or for non-profit educational purposes; the amount and substantiality of the portion used in relation to the whole work; and the effect of the use upon the market or the value of the copyright work. In the USA, there has also been debate as to whether fair dealing rules merely provide defences to claims of infringement or are free-standing user rights.

The two defences which will most likely be utilised in matters relating to the Internet are the research and study defence and the criticism or review defence. The research and study defence would probably be the most applicable to the average user who makes copies of websites, whether they be electronic or paper copies. The perennial issue regarding fair use for private study is the amount of the original material that can be legally copied. For example, s 40(3) of the *Copyright Act* allows the copying of the whole or part of an article in a periodical publication or the copying of not more than a 'reasonable portion' of a work. What is deemed to be a 'reasonable portion' of the work will vary according to the type of work under consideration. If the number of pages in a published edition of the work is ten or more pages, 10 per cent of the number of pages in that edition may be taken; or, where the work is divided into chapters, a whole or part of one chapter of the work may be taken. How rules such as these are translated into websites and web pages by the courts remain to be seen. Some websites could be considered as one whole work, while others can easily be categorised as comprising a number of works. The exact categorisation will determine the amount that can be copied. The defence of criticism or review will no doubt become a frequently used defence for defendants haled into court for copyright infringements. Many will try to cloak their infringements by some ostensible form of criticism or review. Whether or not they will succeed remains to be seen. In the US case of *BMG Music v Gonzalez* (US Court of Appeals 7th Cir No 05-1314, 9 Dec 2005), the defendant was found to have downloaded

1370 songs through the Kazaa P2P file-sharing system. The defendant argued the defence of fair use but it was rejected by the Court. The Court also held that the activities did not constitute either sampling or time shifting.

---

4   Online games

A craze that has hit many countries in Asia, as well as the USA, is the massively multiplayer on-line role-playing game. Players are not only the young; many adults are also attracted to the games. They offer not just entertainment but also an opportunity to make some money. Whether the profit-making is legally valid or not is another issue. These on-line games do raise many interesting property and intellectual property issues. The following article considers the copyright issues. The remainder of the intellectual property issues will be considered in later chapters.

Yee Fen Lim, 'Is It Really Just a Game? Copyright and Online Role-Playing Games'

(2006) 1(7) *Journal of Intellectual Property Law and Practice* 481

Introduction

Following the destruction and devastation caused by Hurricane Katrina, the operators of the 'EverQuest II' internet-based game made an announcement. It reassured 13,000 Gulf Coast subscribers to this online game, affected by Hurricane Katrina, that their virtual property would be protected until they could resume playing. The reaction to such an announcement was twofold. Either people thought, 'That's nice', or they thought 'Hang on, there's just been a huge hurricane, who cares about a game that's on the internet? Why does it matter if their 'property' is protected? It isn't even property.' Those falling into the second category were obviously unfamiliar with the enormously popular, highly lucrative, legally complex and global phenomenon of online gaming.

Massively multiplayer online role-playing games (MMORPGs or, for the purposes of this paper, online games) are a craze that has swept the globe faster than you can say 'Dark Age of Camelot', one of the most popular online games. Moore has succinctly noted the popularity of a new online game:

> Following the November 2004 launch of the MMORPG, World of Warcraft, the substantial network of US based game servers buckled under unprecedented demand. For the first time MMORPG users were forced to queue in their thousands, not to purchase the title, but to actually play the game once it was installed on the home PC. By July 2005 more than 2,000,000 gamers in the US, Europe and Australia, had signed up for the US$15 monthly subscription, on top of the retail price, to participate in the adventures of this online world. One month later another 500,000 players were added in the first week of the game's launch in China. The global subscription figures reached more than 4,000,000 in the first twelve

months of the game's release completely rewriting assumptions about the potential size of the MMORPG market. (citations omitted)

Being powered on the internet, with players from countries around the world, the games never stop. A player can go to bed at night and find a new ruler of an online kingdom by morning. On average, online gamers spend approximately 22 per hours per week online playing their favourite games. There have been reports of players spending up to 55 hours at a time playing and some Asian countries, where these games are enormously popular, have considered introducing laws designed to limit the number of hours children spend playing them on the internet.

The appeal of online games makes exciting video and computer games of the past, like Sonic the Hedgehog and Tomb Raider, look outdated. Online games allow users to create items and visual characters while playing the game. A player who subscribes to a game must first create an 'avatar'—a character that can have whatever features he chooses. Characters and other in-game items can take two forms: either text-based, literary characters or visual, animated, two-dimensional figures. The possibilities are endless—the avatar could be clothed in anything from a Santa Claus suit to a bikini, or have the abilities to become invisible or lift a car as though it were an apple. The character does not even need to resemble a human being. While playing the game, users can battle dragons, escape dungeons and rescue princesses (or handsome princes), acquiring abilities, swords, shields and coins (which can also be created). This heightened interactivity between the player and the game has been the major attraction of this phenomenon—and has arguably created the legal controversies surrounding online gaming.

In order to play an online game, a user must first either purchase a CD or download the game software from the website of the game provider for a flat fee. He must also pay a monthly subscription fee to access the game. The downloaded software allows the player to connect to the game server and play the game. Before a player commences the game, he must agree to the terms of an End User Licence Agreement (EULA) dictating the conditions for playing this game. A game provider

> can discipline players who violate the EULA, take away their privileges and powers, or even kick them out of the game space and eliminate their avatars.

EULAs have been praised for providing consumers with everything they need to know and the terms of the relationship between the player and the game provider. However, certain terms of these standard contracts, found among the billing arrangements and software requirements, often rob players of a number of rights too—most often, and most importantly, the intellectual property rights in any characters or items the user creates while playing the game.

The legal problems essentially begin here. Online gamers feel an almost passionate sense of 'entitlement' to ownership of the unique characters and items they create while playing the game. Most game developers feel the opposite: almost always the EULA states that the intellectual property rights of gamers vest with the game providers, depriving the player of any rights over the potential use of a character or item.

A further complication is that a lucrative online market has emerged for the sale of game characters and items. The value of this market has been estimated at approximately US$880 million. Whether sold on eBay or by private transaction, game items can fetch a fortune. In December 2004 University of Sydney graduate David Storey purchased an online island, complete with beaches and an abandoned castle, for AUS$35,000. In March 2005 a Chinese gamer sold a 'dragon sabre' sword in the game 'Legends of Mir 3' for AUS$1,129. Other items have sold for as much as US$3,000. On eBay a purchaser can buy a magic sword from the game 'Dark Age of Camelot' for $100. After sending one hundred real world dollars to the seller, the purchaser and seller will then meet inside the game so the seller can hand over the magic sword. Inside the game the purchaser can now defeat a dragon; outside the game the seller is $100 richer.

Game companies have been quick to crack down on this practice. While most EULAs state that players do not have the right to resell any items they create in the game, in most instances game companies have purported to rely on intellectual property law, in particular copyright, to stop such sales. As will be discussed, several companies have threatened online auction sites including Yahoo! and eBay with legal action, claiming that this practice infringes the intellectual property rights of the game provider. Players have complained, however, that it is not items that are being sold, but the fruits of the time players have invested in these games.

It will have become apparent to the reader that there are numerous legal issues arising in this area. Generally, these issues can be divided into three categories: copyright issues, other intellectual property regimes, and virtual property rights. This article will deal only with the copyright issues, focusing on the situation under US, Australia and Singapore laws.

Copyright Issues

(A) WHO OWNS THE COPYRIGHT IN IN-GAME CHARACTERS AND ITEMS?

You've made your online character. You can see him in all his two-dimensional glory in front of you. His name is Thor and he looks a lot like Brad Pitt but with larger arms, and he is a Knight of the Octagonal Table. You've also created a sword for Thor, called Swor, which cuts through iron bars as though they were string. Later, you decide to write a comic book. You've had a lot of fun with Thor during your online game-playing and decide you want to keep using him, so you decide to make him your main character. But you can't—you are infringing copyright and you did not read your EULA, because if you had, you would have seen that your game provider owns the intellectual property in all your creations. As Miller has noted, 'A subscriber creates. He is encouraged to create. However, he owns nothing but a good time.'

The first question to consider is whether copyright and other intellectual property rights exist in these online creations. The answer is yes. First, whether these characters are either visual or text-based, copyright subsists in them. Thus 'a visual similarity plus a similarity in character traits may be sufficient to establish copyright infringements where names of plaintiff's and defendant's characters differ.' Second, 'the IP law genie is already out of the bottle' as both game players and developers have sought to rely on copyright law in protecting their creations. However, whether copyright laws are the best, or even an adequate, method for protecting these virtual items is another matter.

Traditionally, an author is entitled to the copyright in any work or other subject matter that he creates. Copyright may be viewed as an incentive to authors to keep creating. The online gaming environment challenges these assumptions. It has been suggested that player/creators need no such incentive and therefore have no need for copyright protection for in-game characters and content, the rewards of the game being the main incentive for such creations. However, as Stephens has noted:

> Complex characters require hundreds of hours to create, and although the game developers have created the potential for these characters to exist by programming them into the software code, they do not actually appear in the game until a player has invested a significant amount of time in overcoming game obstacles to build the character. (citations omitted)

It is arguable that these 'rewards of the game' are not a good enough incentive for player/creators to devote their time to the game. There are numerous reasons outside the game as to why players devote great time and energy to the development of characters and content, including economic and creative reasons. Ownership of copyright in these characters and content is therefore important for any economic or creative aims of the individual player/creator to be achieved.

The fact that the game provider retains the copyright in the 'world' that the game provider has itself created, in which the game is played, is both understandable and undisputed. Many EULAs also forbid the preparation of derivative works, for example, comics or movies, based on the game worlds and under American law it is well within their intellectual property rights to do so.

Most complaints in this area, however, arise from the game provider asserting ownership over the intellectual property rights of gamers, with the use of EULAs being blamed for this injustice. Paragraph 8 of the 'EverQuest' EULA reads:

> We and our suppliers shall retain ownership of all intellectual property rights relating to or residing in the CD-ROM, the Software and the Game.

The online game 'Guild Wars' also contains a detailed EULA. This game, which the developer likes to term a 'Competitive Online Role-Playing Game', differs slightly from traditional MMORPGS as a player is given a private copy of an 'area' in which to complete a quest. The relevant provision of the EULA reads:

> 6. Content and Member Conduct
> (c) Member Content. Members can upload to and create content on our servers in various forms, such as in selections you make and characters and items you create for Guild Wars, and in bulletin boards and similar user-to-user areas ('Member Content'). By submitting Member Content to or creating Member Content on any area of the Service, you acknowledge and agree that such Member Content is the sole property of NC Interactive. To the extent that NC Interactive cannot claim exclusive rights in Member Content by operation of law, you hereby grant (or you warrant that the owner of such Member Content has expressly granted) to NC Interactive and its related Game Content Providers a non-exclusive, universal, perpetual, irrevocable, royalty-free, sublicenseable right to exercise all rights of any kind or nature associated with such Member Content, and all ancillary and subsidiary rights thereto, in any languages and media now known or not currently known.

Paragraph 8 of the 'Star Wars Galaxies: An Empire Divided' EULA reads:

For any of your Content that is not a Derivative Content, you hereby exclusively grant and irrevocably assign to our licensors and us all rights of any kind or nature throughout the universe to such Content (including all ancillary and subsidiary rights thereto which include, without limitation, merchandising and interactive media rights) in any languages and media now known or not currently known. To the extent that any of the rights assigned herein cannot presently be assigned under applicable law, you hereby exclusively grant to our licensors and us a universal, perpetual, irrevocable, royalty-free, sublicenseable (through multiple tiers) right to exercise all rights of any kind or nature associated with your Content, and all ancillary and subsidiary rights thereto, in any languages and media now known or not currently known.

Perhaps it was on the sage advice of Yoda that the lawyers enlisted to write this EULA included the term 'universe'.

Moore has described the sinister side of the EULA:

It is a legal device designed to limit the gamers' capacity for legitimate ownership when playing the game, but because installation of the game on the player's computer requires acknowledgement of the contract's terms, players are powerless to object.

Mathias Klang has made two noteworthy statements in relation to EULAs. First, in many cases the player must agree to the EULA after initially purchasing the game CD or downloading the game software from the internet. This being so, 'the actual terms that appear after the purchase of the CD should not be part of the contract and cannot be binding.' Such an argument, however, appears to be purely theoretical. Second:

Looking at EULAs today, we can see that many of the basic rules (of contracts) — which were created to ensure that adhesion contracts are not unduly onerous and surprising to one of the parties — are being ignored. Even a cursory survey among users will show that they do not read the contract terms. Those who read them find them confusing and, as the current situation with avatars shows, they are not in line with what the ordinary user feels to be correct.

Perhaps we are being too hard on EULAs and game providers. Most standard form EULAs are praised for offering 'efficiency, information and a variety of rights.' Until this point, this paper has taken the position that every EULA is a well-crafted piece of documentation, while in reality some game developers may have obtained poor legal advice that has resulted in a defective EULA. Dibbell has also suggested that game developers are 'caught between the demands of a not entirely captive customer base and the inefficiencies of trying to single-handedly manipulate a large, complex society.' In light of such a finding, Dibbell adds:

the end-user license agreement—that egregious tool of corporate tyranny over the defenseless, voiceless customer (or so I had painted it)—starts to look more like the place where a complicated give and take between designers and players is finally ratified, transformed from a murky power struggle into the legally binding rules of the game.

He is, however, quick to reaffirm his position that EULAs are in fact 'evil'.

Further, some game providers have defended EULAs and denial of players' copyrights on the basis that allowing player/creators to keep any intellectual property rights would allow the law into the game. This argument has not however stopped game companies from purporting to claim copyright infringements when they experience a problem, whether it be legal, commercial or economic.

Not all game providers impose such restrictions on players. 'Second Life' is an exception to this norm. In 2003 Linden Lab, owner of game service 'Second Life', announced that it had decided to allow players to retain all the intellectual property rights for content created while playing the game. This was seen as a bold move on the part of the company. Section 5.3 of the 'Second Life' Terms of Service now states:

> Linden acknowledges and agrees that, subject to the terms and conditions of this Agreement, including without limitation the limited licenses granted by you to Linden herein, you will retain any and all appli able copyright and/ or other intellectual property rights with respect to any Content you create using the Service.

Further, while EULAs may deprive players of their economic copyrights, many countries grant authors and creators moral rights in line with Article 6*bis* of the Berne Convention, these being personal rights belonging to creators that exist independently from economic rights. For example, in Australia, the *Copyright Act 1968* grants authors the right to be attributed as the author of one's work and the right of integrity, ie the right to object to distortions of a work or other modifications or derogatory actions. These rights are not assignable.

Part IX of the Singapore *Copyright Act* contains similar provisions. Under section 188, a person is under a duty not to falsely attribute authorship of a work. Section 189 states that, where a work has been altered by a person other than the author, that person is under a duty to not represent the work or a reproduction of it as being unaltered, if the person knows it is an altered work. However, under section 191, an action done by a person who owed a duty to another person will not constitute a breach of that duty if it is done outside Singapore, or with the express or implied permission of that other person.

Thus in jurisdictions such as Australia, even if a EULA states that the game provider retains ownership of all of a player's intellectual property rights, the moral rights will remain with him. Should the game provider infringe a moral right, the player would have an action. For example, if 'Thor' was transported from being a Knight of the Octagonal Table to being a guard in a game based on Holocaust concentration camps, Thor's creator would have an action against the game provider for infringing his right of integrity.

There are also arguments in favour of the concept of joint authorship between the player/creator and the game provider. While this argument has been rejected in an American context for failing to satisfy legislative requirements, it is worth considering from an Australian and Singaporean perspective. Section 10 of the *Copyright Act 1968* (Cth) defines 'work of joint authorship' as

> a work ... produced by the collaboration of two or more authors and in which the contribution of each author is not separate from the contribution of the other author or the contributions of the other authors.

Section 7 of the Singapore *Copyright Act* also contains the same definition.

The contributions of the game developers and player/creators are unlikely to satisfy this requirement as the sort of creations that we have considered thus far usually occur independently, whether they be the world in which the game is played, a character or a weapon. For example, when one person writes the lyrics to a song, and another person writes the music, the song is not a work of joint authorship. Rather, each person individually holds the copyright to the part of the song that was his responsibility. Similarly, in the online gaming context, the game provider is responsible for developing the initial world in which the game is played and providing the platform, but it is the individual players who create the characters that inhabit this world.

(B) THE OUT OF GAME SALE OF IN-GAME ITEMS AND COPYRIGHT

There are two methods for selling in-game items. The first is by selling an in-game item during the course of the game. For example, if a character needs a new sword, a player might approach another character and offer virtual coins in exchange for his sword. This allows the game itself to have its own 'virtual economy', a practice that 'can add greatly to game play'. Balkin has termed this 'in-game commodification.' The second method, 'real world commodification', is the out-of-game sale of in-game items. It is this practice that will now be considered.

Many EULAs state that the content creator has no right to sell any character or item created in the game. Players, however, have flagrantly ignored such provisions and the sale of in-game items and characters is thriving. This has led to numerous interventions by game companies in an attempt to stop the growing practice of what has been termed 'farming', where users solely play these games to acquire valuable in-game items and then sell any acquisitions. Many game companies have purported to rely on copyright law as a means of curbing this practice. However, as Ondrejka has noted, 'ironically, by attempting to use copyright to block sales, operators are simultaneously admitting IP law into their worlds, while choosing a fundamentally weak argument.' Sony, who until recently, has famously been anti-farming, used this argument in 2000 when it asked numerous internet auction sites to remove any in-game material displayed on that site for auction.

More illustrious, however, are the actions of Black Snow Interactive and the Mythic Entertainment. Black Snow Interactive, a farming company, which owned 'digital sweatshops' where online game players were employed to play the games to increase the going prices for virtual goods. Such 'sweatshops' are becoming increasingly common in Third World countries: Black Snow was based in Tijuana, Mexico. All players had accounts for and played the Mythic Entertainment-owned game 'Dark Age of Camelot'. Black Snow would then sell the in-game items and characters on eBay and other auction sites. Mythic Entertainment shut down the player's accounts, claiming this 'farming' infringed the company's intellectual property rights, and asked the online auctions sites to shut down any auctions of these items.

Black Snow Interactive initiated legal proceedings, filing a federal suit for unfair business practices. Black Snow claimed Mythic Entertainment was acting in an 'anti-competitive manner and was attempting to exert monopoly-like control over uncopyrightable material,' relying on an argument well-summarised by Klang: 'most players who want to trade their avatars claim that they are selling their time while the game manufacturers claim that they are selling the game manufacturers' own intellectual property.' Further, Black Snow partner Lee Caldwell stated in a press release that:

Mythic, in my opinion, and hopefully the court's, does not have the copyright ownership to regulate what a player does with his or her own time or to determine how much that time is worth on the free market.

Those questions were never answered. Black Snow Interactive ran out of funding for its mounting legal costs and the lawsuit apparently floundered (although Klang, uniquely, states that the judge found the provisions of the Mythic EULA valid and referred the case to arbitration.)

Game players and companies rely on the same arguments. When players are pursued for copyright or other intellectual property rights infringement, the in-game items and characters are not intellectual property but merely the fruits of an investment of time, while game providers claim that the items are intellectual property. However, when a game provider claims ownership over a player's character or another creation, the player will assert intellectual property rights: the game provider will either claim that the EULA the player agreed to provides that any and all property rights vest in the game provider, or that the characters or items in question do not qualify for individual intellectual property protection. In the second case, game owners have claimed that the characters are

> an intrinsic part of a virtual world, and that trying to separate them out as individual IP entities made about as much sense as taking every 50 word from a novel and splitting that off from the book as a whole.

Given, the convincing arguments already mentioned in favour of these characters and items being eligible for copyright protection, such a claim cannot succeed.

(C) IN-GAME COPYRIGHT INFRINGEMENT INFRINGEMENT BY PLAYERS WHILE PLAYING GAMES

When a user plays an online game, the copying of the games, its characters and its content arguably infringes copyright. Such infringement could either occur indirectly, for example through copying by a computer that is incidental to playing the game, or directly, for example through the transfer of digital items from player to player inside the game. The in-game practice of players purchasing items for virtual coins has already briefly been discussed. However the copying that occurs when players transfer an asset in the game is also arguably a form of copyright infringement. Stephens says:

> Object code represents every asset in the game, and courts have held that copying object code infringes the reproduction right (of the copyright owner). Infringement could occur if an asset transfer required the copying of the object code that represents the asset from one computer to another or from the computer's hard drive to its random access memory. For example, copying object code would occur if the server sent the player's computer a copy of the object code that represents the asset. The purchasing player would then be a direct infringer by making a copy of the object code, while the selling player would be the contributory infringer by inducing the purchasing player to make a copy of the code. (citations omitted)

Dibbell, however, disputes that such transfers amount to copyright infringement:

> To transfer a virtual sword or gold piece from one player to another is not to duplicate the item but to move it, as it were, from one file folder to another—a procedure involving trivial copying at most and none whatsoever for any economic purposes.

Such in-game trading, whether large-scale or trivial, is arguably one of the purposes of the game and is thus likely to occur in the ordinary course of play. Since the objective of these games is interaction between players and worlds, it is unlikely any copyright action would be brought if it were merely in the ordinary course of the game.

If, for example, a copy was made of the characters and content that was *not* in the ordinary course of the game, for example a screen capture of the game was taken, then the person who took that screenshot would be liable for copyright infringement. In *Micro Star v FormGen Inc*, the Court of Appeals for the Ninth Circuit held that 'screen shots violate the reproduction right and justify a preliminary injunction because screen shots are copies of game graphics.' Such an argument, however, brings us back to *whom* the person who took the screenshot is liable—the player who created the character or content in the screenshot, or the game provider. The answer is probably the game provider, except in 'Second Life' or other games where the EULA specifically states that copyright and other intellectual property rights vest in the player.

Contributory Infringement by Games Service Providers

Does any in-game content itself infringe any intellectual property rights existing outside the game (for example, what if Thor were based on Superman, sporting a tight blue outfit, red cape and a huge red 'T' on his chest)? Would the creator infringe copyright and be liable to the Superman copyright owner? The answer is yes. However, rather than pursue the individual players who create these characters, the copyright owners of popular comic and cartoon characters have instead pursued the game developers and providers.

In November 2004 Marvel Entertainment, the comic book conglomerate with the copyrights in comic gems including the Incredible Hulk, X-Men, Spiderman and the Fantastic Four, sued NCSoft, the company responsible for online game 'City of Heroes'. Marvel claimed that, as NCSoft game players both could and did create superhero characters that looked like, for example, the Incredible Hulk, NCSoft was liable for direct, contributory and vicarious copyright and trade mark infringement. NCSoft and the other defendants essentially had two defences under copyright law. The first was the 'substantial non-infringing use defence' of *Sony Corporation of America v University City Studios*. In that case, the US Supreme Court found that 'if a technology has a "significant, non-infringing use", then as a whole it is non-infringing and thus legal.' Dismissing a number of the plaintiff's trade mark claims, US District Court Judge R Gary Klausner stated that 'it is uncontested that Defendants' game has a substantial non-infringing use. Generally the sale of products with substantial non-infringing uses does not evoke liability for contributory copyright infringement.'

The second defence was the online service provider Safe Harbour provision of the *Digital Millennium Copyright Act*. If NCSoft could prove it was an online internet service provider (ISP) under the *Digital Millennium Copyright Act*, it would not be liable for contributory copyright infringement. Until this point, our discussion has been of players against game developers in a battle for rights. The question that arises here, however, is whether and/or when a game provider is liable for the actions of users who play the provider's game. Noveck has raised two possibilities: game providers can either be legally protected like ISPs, or the game provider will be held responsible as those involved in *Napster*. The availability of this defence, and the answer to this question, was aided when Judge Klausner refused to grant Marvel a judicial declaration that the game provider was not an online service provider within the meaning of the *Digital Millennium Copyright Act*.

The parties settled the case on 14 December 2005. However, the repercussions of this litigation have been numerous.

Both the media and internet-based organisations, including the Electronic Frontier Foundation, were intensely critical of Marvel's actions. Numerous cultural and legal scholars submitted an *amicus* brief to the Central District Court of California, appealing for the Court to grant summary judgment in favour of NCSoft. These *amici* included many major American names interested in online gaming and the law, including Edward Castronova, Julian Dibbell, Joshua Fairfield, Dan Hunter, Beth Simone Noveck and Lawrence Lessig. According to the brief:

> The players of NCSoft's *City of Heroes* are not represented in this lawsuit. Though Marvel brands them as 'direct infringers,' they are men and women, boys and girls who mix Marvel's cultural icons with their own self expresssion (sic) to create *personae* to participate in online communities. Their expressive conduct does not threaten Marvel's copyright privileges, but Marvel's lawsuit threatens to stifle their self-expression.

These interested parties based their submission on a *denial* that fictional characters were entitled to individual copyright protection. The brief further states:

> The avatars that one can find in Paragon City are not authorial works. Paragon City is populated by hundreds of thousands of non-fictional gamers engaged in expressive activities. It is therefore erroneous to equate individual avatars in Paragon City with fictional comic book or film 'characters.'

Such a suggestion illustrates the argument raised previously that, when it suits a situation, one may attempt to deny copyright protection on the basis that in-game characters are not entitled to individual copyright protection. Given, however, the expression of these 'avatars' as artistic, two-dimensional works, it is possible to claim that avatars are 'authorial works'. Indeed, Julian Dibbell has said, in relation to *Black Snow Interactive v Mythic Entertainment*: 'Mythic no doubt owned the copyright to its fictional swords and coins ...'

The point is this: if, as the *amicus* brief stated, 'the avatars that one can find in Paragon City are not authorial works', then how can one state that there is copyright in the swords and coins that these avatars use? Further, the view that these avatars are not characters worthy of individual copyright protection conflicts with submissions of NCSoft's own legal representation. A press statement released by Cooley Godward, attorneys for NCSoft and Cryptic Studios, reads:

> The parties' settlement allows them all to continue to develop and sell exciting and innovative products, but does not reduce the players' ability to express their creativity in making and playing original and exciting characters.

As noted in the *amicus* brief, real-world, flesh and bone, non-fictional gamers are engaging in expressive conduct—by authoring original and exciting characters. John Crittenden, attorney for NCSoft, also said that 'the settlement ensures that our clients' players can continue to express themselves creatively—which is the fundamental purpose of copyright law.'

Neither the Australian nor the Singapore *Copyright Act* deals with the term 'contributory infringement'. Rather, both Acts deal with the authorisation of infringing acts. Section 13(2) of the Australian *Copyright Act* states:

> ... the exclusive right to do an act in relation to a work, an adaptation of a work or any other subject-matter includes the exclusive right to authorize a person to do that act in relation to that work, adaptation or other subject-matter.

In Australia, copyright infringement also occurs when a person authorises another to do the primary infringing action. Thus, if the *Marvel* litigation were commenced in Australia, Marvel could have alleged that NCSoft infringed its copyright under section 36 of the *Copyright Act*, which includes a number of factors that aid determination of whether a person has authorised an infringement of copyright. These include the extent of a person's power to prevent the doing of the act of infringement, the nature of the relationship between the primary infringer and the person who allegedly authorised this infringement and whether the person took reasonable steps to prevent the doing of this infringement. These provisions were adopted for the purpose of codifying the principles set down by Justice Gibbs in *University of New South Wales v Moorhouse and Angus and Robertson,* the seminal Australian case dealing with authorisation of copyright. Thus, if we assess the actions of NCSoft against these provisions, NCSoft does not appear to escape lightly.

Section 9(2) of the Singapore *Copyright Act* ('Acts comprised in copyright') is identical to section 9(2) of the Australian Act.

Section 31(1) of the Singapore Act adds:

> ... the copyright in a literary, dramatic, musical or artistic work is infringed by a person who, not being the owner of the copyright, and without the licence of the owner of the copyright, does in Singapore, *or authorises the doing in Singapore of, any act comprised in the copyright.*

The main difference between the similar provisions of the Australian and Singaporean statutes is the factors set out in section 36(1A) of the Australian Act. Further, the Singapore and Australian Acts require a person to authorise the doing of an act in Singapore or Australia respectively. By merely allowing any direct copyright infringement to occur over the internet, by making the program for creating infringing characters available on the internet, this definition would be satisfied.

In an attempt to protect against future litigation of this kind, a number of EULAs and Terms of Service specifically deal with this issue. For example, Paragraph 4(d) of the 'Guild Wars' EULA reads:

> You may not select as your Character Name the name of another person, or a name which violates any third party's trademark right, copyright, or other proprietary right.

Paragraph 6(c) of the same EULA reads:

You shall indemnify and hold NC Interactive harmless from and against any claims by third parties that your Member Content infringes upon, violates or misappropriates any of their intellectual property or proprietary rights.

It remains to be resolved whether a court would uphold such a provision if the game developer was the provider of the means for a player to infringe the intellectual property rights of a third party.

In-Game 'Fakes'

Recently, game company Electronic Arts faced a problem that Louis Vuitton, Gucci and Chanel have been experiencing for years—the development and distribution of counterfeit in-game items. In 2004, internet hackers managed to make an unlimited number of counterfeit 'gold coins' that could be used to purchase items in popular online game 'Ultima Online'. Electronic Arts cancelled the game of the hackers and the counterfeit gold. No legal action was taken.

The incident raise the issue of counterfeit game characters and items, displaying another perspective of the out-of-game sale of in-game items issue. For example, if a person created an on-line character that looked exactly like a well-reputed, valuable character, then sold it to an unsuspecting player, what would be the legal consequences? Or, as in the Electronic Arts example, if counterfeit coins started to spread among a game, how could the game provider curb such an outbreak? One method could be an action for copyright infringement. In the coin example, if the game provider created these coins (or even if the game developer did not make these coins, given its EULA probably vested all player creation intellectual property rights in it), it could sue the offending player for copyright infringement. Further, if these in-game coins were branded with the game provider's logo, an action may also lie for trade mark infringement. Alternatively, there could be a criminal or property law response against the offender.

No Consensus

It would appear that there is still no general consensus on whether the creations by gamers in online games are afforded copyright protection. This article has argued that copyright subsists and that, since it does so, ownership of that intellectual property depends to a large extent on the wording of the individual EULA. It may be that through an inability to police and enforce the intellectual property rights, coupled with the hostile reactions from gamers, game developers may eventually change their policies and practices.

[Footnotes omitted]

----

5   Copyright reforms in Australia

On 14 May 2006, the Australian Federal Attorney-General Philip Ruddock announced significant copyright reforms which are aimed at making copyright laws fairer for consumers and tougher on copyright pirates. The proposals are to be applauded, but it remains to be seen how they will operate in practice. In some sense, the proposed amendments simply confirm basic copyright principles which have been overtaken by technology and subsequently, the strengthening of copyright protection for creators through the anti-circumvention provisions. At the time of writing, the draft exposure Bill for the reforms had not yet been released. A detailed press release of the reforms is available at: <http://www.ag.gov.au/agd/WWW/MinisterRuddockHome.nsf/Page/Media_Releases_2006_Second_Quarter_14_May_2006_-_Major_Copyright_Reforms_Strike_Balace_-_0882006>.

The proposed reforms cover a range of matters but the focus here will be on those that impact on copyright and the Internet. It is expected that two new exceptions for private use will be created. Firstly, consumers will be allowed to time-shift, an activity which has been held to be legal in the US since the US Supreme Court decision in *Sony v Universal City Studios*. This exception, however, will not allow a recording to be used over and over again or to be distributed by others.

The second exception will be interesting in terms of its implementation. It is proposed that 'format shifting' of material such as music, newspapers, books for personal use will be legalised. Consumers can transfer their CD collection onto IPods or MP3 players. This exception will only permit a person who has purchased a legitimate copy of some categories of copyright material to make a copy in a different format. In particular, the exception will allow individuals to store their personal music collection recorded on CDs, audio tapes or vinyl records on a MP3 player or a personal computer. The scanning of an article from a newspaper which one has purchased into the hard disk of a computer for personal use would also be allowed. Old VHS cassettes can be dubbed onto a DVD, but a film on a DVD will not be permitted to be transferred to a portable player. Under the proposed changes, it will not be legal to make a back-up copy of an audio CD or computer game. Further, a format-shift copy must be made by the owner of the original copy so it will not be possible for a business to make copies for a customer.

The most important aspect of the second exception is its inter-relationship with the anti-circumvention provision. While it may be grand to have the right or defence of format-shifting entrenched in the law, how will it actually operate? Many digital items have copy protection applied to them and under the *Copyright Act 1968*, the tools for circumvention are simply not accessible to the average consumer without breaching the Act. Indeed, in the *Consumer Q&A* attached to the press release, the question 'What if my CD has copy protection applied to it?' has a rather unhelpful answer: 'The Government is still considering this issue of copy protection'. It remains to be seen how this fundamental issue of statutory protection of technological protection measures will be tackled in the amendments.

Large-scale Internet piracy such as that effected through websites and via peer-to-peer file sharing networks will be tackled through the courts being given additional powers to award larger damages payouts or other remedies. This will apply where there have been multiple acts of infringement, but where it may not be practical for the copyright owner to prove every single act of infringement. Further, the definition of 'article' will be clarified and it will be confirmed that civil infringement proceedings will apply to copyright pirates who make electronic reproductions or copies of copyright material.

Other amendments are also proposed as a result of the Australian Government's review of the 2001 Digital Agenda copyright reforms. Most of the reforms are aimed at assisting libraries and archives to better serve the public in the on-line environment. In addition, the status of temporarily cached copies of materials used by educational institutions and the use of distributed technologies for classroom teaching will be clarified.

The press release also states that the scope of the communication right will also be clarified to overcome any doubt that Internet browsing is not part of the communication right, and will also confirm that statutory licences do not override the operation of other existing exceptions in the Act, including those allowing temporary copies to be made in the course of a communication.

Other reforms proposed include the introduction of:

- exceptions allowing schools, universities, libraries and other cultural institutions such as museums to use copyright material for non-commercial purposes. For example, this may allow a museum to include extracts of historical documents in materials for visitors; this may also allow a school to put an out-of-date VHS documentary onto DVD;
- an exception allowing non-commercial uses for the benefit of people with disabilities, for example, this may allow a person with a visual disability to convert a book they own into accessible text;
- a new exception for national cultural institutions to be able to more effectively preserve and provide public access to items in their collections of historical and cultural significance to Australia for future generations without breaching copyright;
- exceptions allowing the use of copyright material for parody or satire;
- new enforcement measures to combat copyright piracy including on-the-spot fines, proceeds of crime remedies, a change in presumptions in litigation to make it easier to establish copyright ownership and copyright piracy. For films, it is proposed that the Government will introduce an evidential presumption in civil cases that recognises the worldwide labelling practices of commercially released films. This will make it easier for copyright owners to prove their ownership of such films; and
- new offences for pay TV piracy.

----

6 Conclusion

The Internet has presented many new challenges to copyright law; indeed, it could be said that digital technology and the Internet have challenged the very core of copyright law. Copyright law had its beginnings centuries ago in a time where reproduction was difficult, yet it has survived into the twenty-first century where reproduction cannot be easier. Its resilience may well lie in its status as an economic right and the need to protect and reward intellectual creativity through economic channels.

Barlow and others suggested in the early 1990s that the battle was over for copyright holders and they should pack their bags and call it a day, as no law can compete with the technology. They were proven wrong. Today, the interests of copyright holders have not only been upheld and maintained, but they have also been strengthened—perhaps too much, according to some. Copyright has always aimed to balance the rights of users against the rights of copyright holders. The argument is that technology has tilted the balance so far from copyright holders that only a strong legal push can return the balance. However, this argument can only hold true when every user is regarded as a potential copyright infringer. When the average user is a law-abiding citizen who has no wish or inclination to infringe, then surely the equilibrium has not been maintained.

Trade Mark Law and the Internet

10

---

1 Trade marks explained

In order to demonstrate the significance of trade marks as they relate to the Internet, it is necessary to provide a basic outline of the trade marks regulatory regime as well as an outline of the peculiarities of the World Wide Web protocol and the Internet domain name system. Only after all of these preliminary materials have been examined can trade mark law be considered in the context of the Internet.

A trade mark is a sign that individually identifies a good or service and/or its source or origin and distinguishes it from other goods or services; it is a device of relationship. It need not provide an absolute, objective identification of a particular trader. It need only distinguish between the trade marked good or service from all other goods or services. Therefore, it could be a brand name or graphic rather than an identifying business name. There are two general types of trade marks: the registered trade mark, protected by legislation (see the Australian *Trade Marks Act 1995* (Cth) and Singapore's *Trade Mark Act 1998*), and the non-registered or common law trade mark, protected by the tort of passing off. The rights inherent in both types of trade marks are limited by two defining characteristics: domesticity and specificity. Domesticity is the notion that the trade mark will only be protected within the jurisdiction within which it operates, either through registration or the common law. Therefore, there is no such thing as an international trade mark. Specificity is the idea that protections are limited to the general sphere of business within which the goods or services are traded—that is, the protection is specific to a particular industry, product or service. This enables the use of one sign or mark by many owners while still ensuring that consumer confusion is prevented, which is the aim of the system in the first place. There are currently around 45 classes of goods and services in which trade marks can be registered.

Trade marks have a number of functions in addition to identifying or distinguishing the source or origin of goods or services. They can also indicate a standard of quality associated with a product or service as well as operating as an emblem of goodwill in the product or service. Most importantly, trade marks protect consumers from confusion and deception.

In the early 1990s, intellectual property was incorporated into the General Agreement on Tariffs and Trade (GATT) negotiations. This decision arose out of a perception that intellectual property required stronger and clearer protection due to its growing economic significance. The Uruguay Round of GATT encouraged protection for intellectual property in the belief that it would strengthen economic growth and encourage the global spread of technology. The TRIPS agreement triggered substantive and procedural changes to Australian trade mark law in order to enable compliance with the obligations under GATT and TRIPS. For example, the current definition of 'sign' represents a dramatic expansion of the definition of a trade mark. This is a result of the TRIPS agreement and accords with similar expansions in the USA and New Zealand. The definition covers any aspect of packaging, shape, colour, sound, or scent as a possible trade mark. It is so broad that almost anything could be capable of registration provided the 'sign' is capable of distinguishing the owner's goods or services from the goods or services of others. Sections 40 and 41 of the Australian *Trade Marks Act 1995*, extracted below, set out a number of requirements for the registration of a trade mark. Not only will trade mark registration be easier to obtain under the 1995 legislation compared with the earlier regime under the 1955 Act, but a much broader range of signs are eligible for registration. This expansion is largely a result of the TRIPS agreement and the fact that this agreement is contained within the trade liberalisation regimes of GATT administered by the WTO. That these regimes have pushed the regulation and institutionalisation of property rights to their limit is clearly evidenced by the new trade marks provisions.

Trade Marks Act 1995 (Cth) Part 2: Interpretation

6. DEFINITIONS
In this Act, unless the contrary intention appears: ...

sign includes the following or any combination of the following, namely any letter, word, name, signature, numeral, device, brand, heading, label, ticket, aspect of packaging, shape, colour, sound or scent

Trade Marks Act 1995 (Cth) Part 3: Trade marks and trade mark rights

17. WHAT IS A TRADE MARK?
A trade mark is a sign used, or intended to be used, to distinguish goods or services dealt with or provided in the course of trade by a person from goods or services so dealt with or provided by any other person.

40. TRADE MARK THAT CANNOT BE REPRESENTED GRAPHICALLY
An application for the registration of a trade mark must be rejected if the trade mark cannot be represented graphically.

41. TRADE MARK NOT DISTINGUISHING APPLICANT'S GOODS OR SERVICES

(1) For the purposes of this section, the use of a trade mark by a predecessor in title of an applicant for the registration of the trade mark is taken to be a use of the trade mark by the applicant.
(2) An application for the registration of a trade mark must be rejected if the trade mark is not capable of distinguishing the applicant's goods or services in respect of which the trade mark is sought to be registered (designated goods or services) from the goods or services of other persons.
(3) In deciding the question whether or not a trade mark is capable of distinguishing the designated goods or services from the goods or services of other persons, the Registrar must first take into account the extent to which the trade mark is inherently adapted to distinguish the designated goods or services from the goods or services of other persons.
(4) Then, if the Registrar is still unable to decide the question, the following provisions apply.
(5) If the Registrar finds that the trade mark is to some extent inherently adapted to distinguish the designated goods or services from the goods or services of other persons but is unable to decide, on that basis alone, that the trade mark is capable of so distinguishing the designated goods or services:

(a) the Registrar is to consider whether, because of the combined effect of the following:

(i) the extent to which the trade mark is inherently adapted to distinguish the designated goods or services;

(ii) the use, or intended use, of the trade mark by the applicant;

(iii) any other circumstances;

the trade mark does or will distinguish the designated goods or services as being those of the applicant; and

(b) if the Registrar is then satisfied that the trade mark does or will so distinguish the designated goods or services—the trade mark is taken to be capable of distinguishing the applicant's goods or services from the goods or services of other persons; and

(c) if the Registrar is not satisfied that the trade mark does or will so distinguish the designated goods or services—the trade mark is taken not to be capable of distinguishing the applicant's goods or services from the goods or services of other persons.

(6) If the Registrar finds that the trade mark is not inherently adapted to distinguish the designated goods or services from the goods or services of other persons, the following provisions apply:

(a) if the applicant establishes that, because of the extent to which the applicant has used the trade mark before the filing date in respect of the application, it does distinguish the designated goods or services as being those of the applicant—the trade mark is taken to be capable of distinguishing the designated goods or services from the goods or services of other persons;

(b) in any other case—the trade mark is taken not to be capable of distinguishing the designated goods or services from the goods or services of other persons.

 NOTES AND QUESTIONS

1   The 1955 Act stipulated that a mark would not be registered unless it was found to be 'inherently adapted to distinguish' those goods or services to which it was attached. This applied regardless of how effectively the mark did in fact distinguish the goods and services of the owner. This curiously artificial requirement is partially retained by the 1995 legislation. However, it is acknowledged in the new legislation that many highly distinctive marks do not satisfy this test. The single test under the 1995 Act is that the trade mark must be capable of distinguishing the applicant's goods and/or services. Give examples of how you might demonstrate that a mark was 'capable' of distinguishing a good or service from other, similar goods or services. Would marks that denote the kind, quality, value or purpose of goods or services be capable of distinguishing goods or services?

2   There are a number of other requirements, including the following: that the trade mark not be scandalous or its use be contrary to law (s 42); that the trade mark not be likely to deceive or cause confusion (s 43); and that the mark not be

substantially identical, or deceptively similar to another trade mark, or another mark with an application for trade mark pending (s 44).

3   Is the test for registration readily understandable? Explain in your own words exactly what is required in order to register a trade mark in Australia.

4   The Australian definition of 'sign' includes the term 'scent'. Section 40 states that '[a]n application for the registration of a trade mark must be rejected if the trade mark cannot be represented graphically'. Can a scent be represented graphically? Are these two provisions consistent? One of the first scent marks to be recognised was in the USA, where a scent, described as a high impact, fresh, floral fragrance reminiscent of plumeria blossoms, applied to sewing thread, was deemed a registrable trade mark (see *In re Clarke*, 17 USPQ2d 1238 (TTAB 1990)).

5   The Trade Marks Office maintains a register of trade marks that contains the particulars of all registered trade marks and any other relevant information on a single unified register.

6   It is important to note the distinction between business names and trade marks. Only limited protection accompanies a registered business name, due to the fact that the registration process prevents registration of any name identical or substantially similar to one already in existence. Critically analyse the importance of business name registration and trade mark registration in the context of the Internet. How might the goals for the registration regime, of both business names and trade marks, be circumvented by the Internet?

7   Once a mark has been registered, it operates to protect its owner from the use of that sign in the course of trade by any other person or business (see for example s 26 of the Singapore *Trade Marks Act 1998*). There are also exemptions from liability such as where the sign used is one's own name or the name of one's own place of business. See further, s 28 of the Singapore *Trade Marks Act 1998* and ss 122–124 of the Australian *Trade Marks Act 1995*. As such, the requirements for registration are very similar to the various elements of infringing conduct. Under the Singapore *Trade Marks Act 1998*, s 27(4) the use of a sign occurs when one:

(a)   applies it to goods or the packaging thereof;

(b)   offers or exposes goods for sale, puts them on the market or stocks them for those purposes under the sign, or offers or supplies services under the sign;

(c)   imports or exports goods under the sign;

(d)   uses the sign on an invoice, wine list, catalogue, business letter, business paper, price list or other commercial document, including any such document in any medium; or

(e)   uses the sign in advertising.

The Australian legislation is structured differently and s 7 includes aural representation as use of a mark. Section 7 defines the 'use of a trade mark in relation to' goods and services and it is broadly defined to mean use of the trade mark upon, or in physical or other relation to goods or services. The case law precedent does however cover most of the areas mentioned in s 27(4) of the Singapore statute.

8   In the decision of *Ward Group Pty Ltd v Brodie & Stone Plc* [2005] FCA 471, the Australian Federal Court held that the advertising of the UK Restoria product on the UK websites was not 'use' of the Restoria trade mark in Australia because the offers were not specifically targeted or directed at consumers in Australia. Justice Merkel noted at [43]: '...the use of a trade mark on the Internet, uploaded on a website outside of Australia, without more, is not a use by the website proprietor of the mark in each jurisdiction where the mark is downloaded. However, as explained above, if there is evidence that the use was specifically intended to be made in, or directed or targeted at, a particular jurisdiction then there is likely to be a use in that jurisdiction when the mark is downloaded. Of course, once the website intends to make and makes a specific use of the mark in relation to a particular person or persons in a jurisdiction there will be little difficulty in concluding that the website proprietor used the mark in that jurisdiction when the mark is downloaded'.

9   The statutory system of trade mark registration is designed to simplify and streamline trade mark regulation. Under the Act, if a trade mark is infringed, the owner of that mark need only show that the mark is registered. Once this has been demonstrated, there is no need to conduct the investigations required at common law as to whether the mark attracted and held any goodwill, or whether the mark is distinctive.

10   Under the Singapore *Trade Marks Act 1998*, a trade mark is defined in s 2 as 'any sign capable of being represented graphically and which is capable of distinguishing goods or services dealt with or provided in the course of trade by a person from goods or services so dealt with or provided by any other person'. A sign under the *Singapore Act* is also defined as broadly as the Australian Act.

Trade Marks Act 1995 (Cth) Part 2: Interpretation

10. DEFINITION OF DECEPTIVELY SIMILAR

For the purposes of this Act, a trade mark is taken to be deceptively similar to another trade mark if it so nearly resembles that other trade mark that it is likely to deceive or cause confusion.

Trade Marks Act 1995 (Cth) Part 12: Infringement of trade marks

120. WHEN IS A REGISTERED TRADE MARK INFRINGED?

(1) A person infringes a registered trade mark if the person uses as a trade mark a sign that is substantially identical with, or deceptively similar to, the trade mark in relation to goods or services in respect of which the trade mark is registered.

(2) A person infringes a registered trade mark if the person uses as a trade mark a sign that is substantially identical with, or deceptively similar to, the trade mark in relation to:

(a) goods of the same description as that of goods (registered goods) in respect of which the trade mark is registered; or

(b) services that are closely related to registered goods; or

(c) services of the same description as that of services (registered services) in respect of which the trade mark is registered; or

(d) goods that are closely related to registered services.

However, the person is not taken to have infringed the trade mark if the person establishes that using the sign as the person did is not likely to deceive or cause confusion.

(3) A person infringes a registered trade mark if:

(a) the trade mark is well known in Australia; and

(b) the person uses as a trade mark a sign that is substantially identical with, or deceptively similar to, the trade mark in relation to:

(i) goods (unrelated goods) that are not of the same description as that of the goods in respect of which the trade mark is registered (registered goods) or are not closely related to services in respect of which the trade mark is registered (registered services); or

(ii) services (unrelated services) that are not of the same description as that of the registered services or are not closely related to registered goods; and

(c) because the trade mark is well known, the sign would be likely to be taken as indicating a connection between the unrelated goods or services and the registered owner of the trade mark; and

(d) for that reason, the interests of the registered owner are likely to be adversely affected.

(4) In deciding, for the purposes of paragraph (3)(a), whether a trade mark is well known in Australia, one must take account of the extent to which the trade mark is known within the relevant sector of the public, whether as a result of the promotion of the trade mark or for any other reason.

NOTES AND QUESTIONS

1   Section 120(2) gives protection to similar goods or services in compliance with Art 16, Paragraph 1 of TRIPS. However, the words used to achieve this—'of the same description' and 'closely related to' other goods and services—will inevitably be the subject of contention. The US position protects trade mark owners against use of a mark on any product that would reasonably be thought by the buying public to come from the same source, or that would reasonably be thought to be affiliated with, connected with, or sponsored by, the trade mark owner. Which of these wordings do you find most understandable, practical, and useful? Why?

2   Which of the subsections contain a requirement of confusion on the part of the consuming public? What is the relevance of the requirement?

3   Subsection 3 gives protection for well-known trade marks and it fulfils Australia's obligations under Art 16, Para 3 of TRIPS. Do you think it is justifiable to include

a separate, broader protection for well-known marks? What does this suggest about the vested interests at play within trade marks regulation?

4   The *Trade Practices Act 1974* (Cth) also protects the distinctions created in the marketplace between various products by prohibiting misleading and deceptive conduct. Under s 52 of the *Trade Practices Act*, if an infringer uses a mark in trade or commerce and the use is misleading or deceptive or is likely to mislead or deceive, then the section would be breached. The *Trade Practices Act* will be discussed later in this chapter. A similar statute exists in Singapore, namely the *Consumer Protection (Fair Trading) Act 2003* where it is unfair practice for a supplier to do or say anything, or omit to do or say anything that would deceive or mislead consumers. The legislation provides remedies for consumers in such situations.

5   In contrast to the actions for infringement, a trade mark can be removed from the register on the grounds of non-use under s 92(4). An application for removal may be made by a person aggrieved by the fact that a trade mark is or may be registered. The onus of proof, however, rests with the defendant in this action, that is, the trade mark owner. This onus provision is significant and marks a shift from the 1955 Act. Can you provide any justifications for this reverse onus?

6   Infringement and defences will be covered in more detail later in this chapter.

7   Explain why a trade mark is a relative device, rather than an absolute label. Why is this important? What implications might it have for the conduct of business on the Internet?

8   At the beginning of this chapter it was noted that trade marks had traditionally received limited protection in the international sphere. The corollary of this is that trade marks are predominantly grounded in the legal systems of the nation state. What effect might the Internet have upon this grounding?

9   The infringement provisions contained in each of the subsections of s 120 of the Australian *Trade Marks Act 1995* are similar to the infringement provisions contained in s 27 of the Singaporean *Trade Marks Act* 1998 and s 10 of the UK *Trade Marks Act 1994*. In addition, a general concept of dilution was introduced into the Singapore *Trade Marks Act 1998* as a result of the Singapore–USA Free Trade Agreement. Section 2 defines dilution to mean the lessening of the capacity of the trade mark to identify and distinguish goods or services, regardless of whether there is any competition between the parties or whether there is any likelihood of confusion. Section 29(2)(b) then prohibits the use of the mark in relation to goods which have been placed on the market by the trade mark owner which causes dilution in an unfair manner of the distinctive character of the mark. The concept of dilution under US law will be considered below.

---

2   The World Wide Web protocol

It is generally possible to comprehend the legal implications of the Internet without becoming lost in a maze of technicalities. In the case of trade marks, however, the legal issues grow directly from the technological infrastructure of the Internet and, as such, a brief technical excursion is required.

Web pages are generally constructed using Hypertext Markup Language (HTML) which provides display instructions to web browser programs. The HTML commands enable the web browser to generate the appearance of web pages. Through these codes called 'tags', a web browser is instructed where to implement new paragraphs and line breaks, as well as other display format attributes such as font styles and sizes. HTML tags are hidden from normal view but most web browsers allow users to view the HTML source code through a viewing option.

The most highly used HTML tag is the hyperlink (or link), often represented as underlined text or as an image. By 'clicking' on a hyperlink using a pointing device such as a mouse, the contents of another web page referenced by the hyperlink are then displayed by the web browser. This 'jump' is the essence of hyperlinking, as it enables the user to connect to other web pages easily and quickly and retrieve information. It is these interconnections between web pages that have given the protocol its name as a web. A web page can contain many or no hyperlinks, but it is these branching mechanisms that have raised intellectual property questions.

Deep linking refers to linking to an internal or subsidiary page of a website that is located several levels down from the home page. A deep link takes the user directly to a particular web page, sometimes located many levels down from the home page. This allows the user to avoid having to look at or click through the home page and any other intervening pages.

The technique of framing allows the content of other linked websites to be displayed without completely leaving the site that was originally visited. The original website—the framing website—usually keeps its own borders or headings (more commonly known as banners), and the contents of the framed website (the second website) are displayed surrounded by the original website's banners and borders. The address shown on the browser software remains that of the framing website.

Frames can be used to frame more than one website at any one time. Often, the content of the framed web page cannot be completely displayed and scroll bars must be used to view the entire page of the framed web page.

Until recently, it was generally accepted that access to web pages and their content by linking was implicitly authorised by the mere fact of their presence on the Web. After all, why would anyone place any content on the Web if such content was not intended to be viewed by others? This assumption has been called into question in recent years as lawsuits have been brought under unfair competition laws, trade mark law and copyright law.

The final component in this most cursory of technical digressions is the role of the meta tag in HTML. Meta-tags are a type of HTML tag; however, they are not used to format the internal workings of a web document. Instead, meta-tags contain information about the web page such as the document title, the author's e-mail address, and, most importantly, keywords about the content of the web page or website. The meta-tags sit within the body of the website source code and are not visible when the site is loaded. The keywords contained in the meta-tags are the most commonly used aspect of meta-tags. Some search engines index websites by trawling the Internet using programs known as spiders. Spiders index pages either by searching through the contents of the web pages themselves, or by picking up the keywords in the meta-tags. Meta tag keywords therefore play a vital role in the accurate indexing of sites. When a search is requested, the index is consulted for sites that include information relevant to the search term that the user requested. By listing any number and variety of keywords, a website can increase its chance of being placed at the top of the list of search results. Each of these three technical features will now be examined in the context of their legal implications.

(a)   Linking, deep linking, and the law

There is very little settled law on linking and deep linking, but the early cases and commentary seem to suggest that linking to the home page of websites is legally permissible. It can be argued that the mere presence of a site on the web implicitly grants others permission to link to the home page of that website, and that is fundamental to the nature and operation of the Web.

Deep linking to a commercial website without permission raises numerous legal questions, and should be avoided. Linking to a home page is rarely objectionable. However, deep linking is objectionable because it allows the user to hop from the linking website straight to the best content and features of the website to which the original site is linked. The user can effectively bypass many other pages, including the home page, of the linked-to website and generally spend less time on it. What this means for the owner of the linked-to website is that there is less activity on his or her site: fewer 'hits' are generated. As there are fewer hits, the potential for advertising revenue also drops, as does the popularity of the site itself. However, can these objections be translated into the framework of existing trade mark law? It can generally be said that linking and deep linking are not likely to violate existing trade mark law, as long as the linking website does not suggest any nonexistent affiliation with the linked-to website, and the linking website does not tarnish the reputation of the linked-to website in any way. However, the cases discussed below indicate a developing legal argument that the practice of deep linking in and of itself might confuse consumers.

TicketMaster v Microsoft

One of the most famous disputes involving deep linking arose between TicketMaster and Microsoft.[1] Microsoft runs a site called 'Seattlesidewalk.com' which, as its name suggests, is focused on the city of Seattle. Microsoft also runs similar sites for other cities. The site lists current events around such as concerts, operas, movies, as well as the location of ticket outlets, and any other relevant information. For example, before the dispute began, the site provided a link from a Seattlesidewalk.com page to a TicketMaster page concerning the Dave Matthews concert that was coming to Seattle. The linked-to site was deep within the TicketMaster site and it enabled users to purchase tickets to the Seattle concert. TicketMaster objected to this deep link and started negotiations with Microsoft. TicketMaster's contention was that Microsoft should obtain a licence from

---

1   *Ticketmaster Corp v Microsoft Corp* [CV 97-3055RAP] (CD Cal, filed 28 April 28 1997). Case settled.

them for deep linking but Microsoft refused and sued TicketMaster in federal court in Los Angeles.

Microsoft's point in the litigation was that TicketMaster should have no objection to the linking because Microsoft was helping TicketMaster with ticket sales by directing its web visitors to TicketMaster's site. TicketMaster's complaint[2] was based upon trade mark dilution, and confusion as to source, sponsorship or affiliation as well as various state claims as to unfair competition and commercial misappropriation. At the heart of TicketMaster's claim was that users would be confused by the deep link as to the source and affiliations of the linked-to site. Unfortunately, this case did not provide any binding legal precedent. The lawsuit was eventually settled when Microsoft agreed to link to Ticketmaster's home page rather than providing deep links to individual events.

Shetland Times Ltd v Wills and Zetnews Ltd

This was a Scottish case initiated in 1996.[3] In this case, Lord Hamilton granted an interim interdict, similar to a injunction, to stop the *Shetland News* from making deep links to the *Shetland Times* website. The *Shetland Times*, a newspaper owned by the plaintiffs, carries local, national, and international news. The defendants provided a news reporting service called the *Shetland News*. Both parties operated websites based on their news reports.

The *Shetland News* website contained a number of headlines which also served as deep hyperlinks to articles on the *Shetland Times* website. Hence, readers could arrive at and read *Shetland Times* news articles without having to go through the plaintiff's home page. The plaintiffs argued that they planned to use advertising on their home page as a source of revenue. They claimed that due to the defendants' deep hyperlinks, the advertisements would never be seen by visitors arriving from the defendants' site, leading to a potential loss of revenue. The plaintiffs claimed that the deep linking caused readers to be misled into thinking that the news articles were part of *Shetland News* when in fact they were *Shetland Times* articles. Further, the plaintiffs also claimed that the linking also violated the copyright in their headlines. In granting the interim interdict, Lord Hamilton found that it was crucial that all access to the substantive material on the plaintiff's website should be obtained exclusively by accessing its website through the home page. In doing so, he also found that there was no substance to the defendants' defence that the plaintiff was benefiting from the greater public availability of its newspaper items, resulting from their presence on the defendants' website.

On 11 November 1997, the parties agreed to an out-of-court settlement. The terms of the agreement allowed *Shetland News* to link to stories on the *Shetland Times* website by the use of headlines, but the following rules must be observed. First, each hyperlink that goes to one of *Shetland Times'* stories must use the legend, 'A Shetland Times Story', which must appear under the headline and in the same size. Second, next to each headline there must be a button showing the *Shetland Times'* banner logo. And finally, these legends and buttons must be hyperlinks to the *Shetland Times* on-line headline page and not the articles themselves.

---

2   Text of complaint available at <http://www.jmls.edu/cyber/cases/ticket1.html> 29 May 2001.
3   *Shetland Times Ltd v Dr Jonathan Wills and Zetnews Ltd*, Scotland Court of Sessions (24 October 1996). Text of the settlement available at <http://www.jmls.edu/cyber/cases/shetld2.html> 29 May 2001.

It is important to note that the basis for the decision to grant the interim interdict was not actually based on any infringement of trade mark law, but rather, on a peculiar interpretation of the copyright cable programming law in Scotland.

TicketMaster Corp v Tickets.Com, Inc (2000) US Dist LEXIS 12987

This was a case in 2000 from the US District Court for the Central District of California. Tickets.Com, Inc was linking to Ticketmaster's subsidiary pages. Ticketmaster claimed that deep linking constituted both copyright infringement (because the information derived from Ticketmaster's website) and unfair competition (because customers would associate Tickets.com with Ticketmaster).

Tickets.com was deep-linking to Ticketmaster for events for which Tickets.com could not itself sell tickets. Tickets.com provided its customers with a 'Buy this ticket from another on-line ticketing company' link, which automatically transferred the customer to the relevant subsidiary page of Ticketmaster, bypassing the home page. The subsidiary page contained the Ticketmaster logo and trade mark, hence the court concluded that a customer must know he or she was dealing with Ticketmaster, not Tickets.com.

The Court decided that on the facts, there was no copyright infringement as Tickets. com copied facts and facts are not protected by copyright. The Court also found that merely posting a deep link itself does not constitute unfair competition but that deep linking with confusion of source can raise unfair competition issues. The facts indicated that there was no confusion of source. The Court refused to grant a preliminary injunction.

The lessons from *Ticketmaster Corp v Tickets.Com, Inc* are that one should indicate that the link is to another entity's website and if the linked to web page contains that entity's name, logo, trade mark and so on, it ought to be obvious to users that it is not the same organisation's website, and any indication of non-existent affiliation would be avoided. This dispute was also argued on other theories including breach of contract and trespass but these lacked sufficient proof.

Pacific Internet Ltd v Catcha.com Pte Ltd [2000] SLR 26

The Singapore High Court has had on one occasion considered the issue of deep linking. In the case of *Pacific Internet Ltd v Catcha.com*, the owner of a website in Singapore, whose competitor had deep linked to its website, sued on multiple grounds, including copyright infringement, passing off, and trespass. The defendant applied for an order to strike out the claim for trespass but the court refused, stressing the novelty of deep linking both in technology and law. On the trespass claim, the court indicated that it would fully entertain the theory that the plaintiff opened its site to the public for most purposes, but not for the purpose of allowing competitors to mine the site for deep links for inclusion on their sites. The Court also stressed the significant and creative damage claims made based on the deep linking. Among other things, the plaintiff claimed that the deep links to its site enhanced the value of the linking site, diminished the value of the plaintiff's site, and deprived the plaintiff of specific advertising revenue because of fewer 'eyeballs' being directed to its website. The court also accepted as plausible the plaintiff's theory that deep links to its site promoted customer loyalty with the defendant's site. The defendants' acts of alleged trespass by-passed the plaintiffs' home page and this created 'stickiness' within the defendants' websites so that it would be easier for web surfers to stay within the defendants' websites, notwithstanding that the content or search engine being viewed or used belonged to the plaintiffs. Following the High Court decision, the case eventually settled out of court.

TicketMaster Corp v Tickets.Com, Inc (2003) US Dist LEXIS 6483

This was a continuation of the dispute from 2000 already noted above. Following the District Court's refusal to grant preliminary injunction, the plaintiffs appealed unsuccessfully to the Ninth Circuit. The plaintiffs then narrowed its suit to three claims: trespass to chattel, copyright infringement and breach of contract. The defendants moved for summary judgment and the District Court granted summary judgment dismissing the trespass to chattel and copyright claims but found triable issues of fact on the contract theory.

The court rejected the trespass arguments because TicketMaster failed to show actual damage to its property. The copyright claim was mainly based on claiming copyright for the URLs and the temporary copies made when one accesses the website. Both these arguments were rejected with the court holding that the temporary copies were permitted under the fair use doctrine.

The claim based in contract was centred around the fact that the plaintiff imposed use restrictions on all users of its web pages. The licence stated that anyone visiting pages beyond the home page agreed not to deep link interior web pages, use automated programs like spiders on the site, or use information obtained from the site for commercial purposes. The evidence showed that the defendant had seen this licence several times on the website and had communicated about it with the plaintiff's representatives. Thus the plaintiff's contract claim was the only claim which survived summary judgment. While there was in existence some sort of 'browsewrap' licence, the facts showed that the defendants rejected the licence conditions but continued to access the plaintiff's website. There was no requirement on the plaintiff's website to positively require users to assent. The Court held that the browsewrap licence was unenforceable because the defendant did not consent to it. This raises the issue of whether website operators should place such a requirement as a matter of best practise.

Deep linking by search engines

If deep linking is objectionable for the reasons outlined above, where does deep linking by search engines stand? It has been argued that deep linking by search engines requires consideration of different issues, and this leads to different outcomes. First, the operators of linked-to websites generally have several techniques at their disposal to control deep linking by a search engine. Website operators often pay to be placed in a search engine's database, and can therefore decide whether search engines can locate particular pages on their sites.

Second, a list of deep links is produced by a search engine only after the user conducts a search. The process of searching indicates that the user is specifically looking for the page, and the inference to be drawn is that the target website has benefited, as the search engine has enabled the user to locate the website or web page. Third, websites can use advanced technology to block links from certain other websites, and hence they can block search engines from finding web pages located deep in their websites.

Deep linking by a search engine does not raise the confusion of source and unfair competition issues that are connected with commercial website deep linking. Deep linking by search engines may however raise issues connected with database protection under the EU Directive discussed in the previous chapter.

 ## NOTES AND QUESTIONS

1   In the *Shetland Times* case, the *Times* home page used the newspaper headlines as links to the materials deeper within their site. The headline texts were also taken by the *Shetland News* and used as hyperlinks to the *Times* stories. But, surprisingly, Lord Hamilton found that the headlines themselves had copyright, so the action of the *Shetland News* in copying them for use as hyperlinks on its own website was an infringement. In defence of Lord Hamilton's view, the creation of a headline does involve creativity in that information about the relevant item must be conveyed, the reader's attention needs to be attracted, and (at least in the case of the tabloid press, which much favours punning and humorous headlines) entertainment provided. However, the application of this decision is unlikely to be broad given the necessarily limited scope of the genre, and it is unlikely to extend to the typical hypertext link.

2   The Australian decision of *Universal Music Australia Pty Ltd v Cooper* [2005] FCA 972 discussed in the previous chapter in relation to copyright is also relevant here. When the decision in *Cooper* was handed down, it received much publicity in the popular press as being a decision against the practice of linking. As we have already seen, this is of course quite incorrect.

3   The oft-made argument against deep linking is the consumer confusion issue. Explain how owners of websites who wish to deep link to commercial sites can do so without triggering trade mark law issues.

4   In many of the cases concerning deep linking, the plaintiffs have used intellectual property law, namely trade mark law, as a weapon to combat the practice. Do you think trade mark law provides the appropriate solution? Why or why not?

(b)   Framing and the law

The practice of framing and its significant legal issues have led to more legal disputes than linking or deep linking. But as with linking and deep linking, there are very few precedents available. Framing is also generally regarded as objectionable for many of the same reasons as deep linking.

One of the first cases concerning framing was *Washington Post Co v Total News*,[4] involving a news directory that framed the contents of more than 1000 on-line news

---

4   No 97 Civ 1190 (PKL) (SDNY 28 February 1997). A copy of the complaint is available at <www.jmls.edu/cyber/cases/total1.html> 5 June 2001.

services from around the world. Washington Post Co was one of many news services that objected to Total News' practice of framing, which concealed the source of the content. The plaintiffs brought claims of, *inter alia*, trade mark dilution and unfair trade practices against Total News. The lawsuit was eventually settled out of court with Total News agreeing to stop its practice of framing. Trade mark dilution is an action available in the US for famous trade marks (similar in concept to s 120(3) under the Australian Act). It protects a strong mark from being 'whittled away' so that the trade mark selling power is reduced. It is usually sufficient to show either blurring or tarnishment. Blurring occurs when a connection is made in the mind of the consumer with the claimant's mark and such a connection weakens that brand. Tarnishment occurs when the infringer's use of another's mark is derisory or detrimental to the original mark, or that the original mark is intentionally linked to inferior products.

Framing often causes confusion as to the source of the content displayed in the browser and this would be the main basis for liability under trade mark law. If the viewer is confused or is likely to be confused about the source of any content including advertisements, then there is good cause for arguing an infringement of trade mark law. In any case, any trade mark infringement analysis is likely to be fact-specific, so if the framing website makes it clear that the user is viewing a different website and eliminates any confusion as to the source, then arguably there would be no trade mark infringement.

The remaining ground on which framing could offend trade mark laws is the concept of dilution, which is well-established in countries such as the USA. If the surrounding frame portrays the framed content or trade mark in an unfavourable light, the trade mark owner's reputation may be deemed to be tarnished. Alternatively, there may also be dilution if the surrounding frame blurs the distinctive quality of the framed content or trade mark.

(c)   Meta-tags and the law

The following article discusses the main issues with meta tagging and the abuse of meta-tags in the 1990s. These largely centred around search engines and the operation of search engines. Readers should take note of some of the developments since 2000 as highlighted in the Notes and Questions following the extract.

Andrew Murray, 'The Use of Trade Marks as Meta Tags: Defining the Boundaries'

(2000) 8(3) *International Journal of Law and Information Technology* 263

2. META TAGS AND TRADE MARKS

2.2. THE PRACTICE OF COMPETITIVE META TAGGING

... If we accept that most people navigate the Web in a similar manner to a library, with search engines fulfilling the function of a card catalogue, it is obviously to a site operator's advantage if they can promote their site through judicious keyword meta tagging. This is where, almost certainly, the growth of Internet trade marks disputes will occur in the coming years. The domain name/trade mark dichotomy may prove to be of little significance compared to the meta tag/trade mark disputes which will follow.

There have to date been no UK cases on the misuse of trade marks as meta tags, but there have been several US cases. Most of these cases have been relatively straightforward. From these cases, though, the first signs of possible loopholes are already emerging, and some meta tag disputes have ended in victory for the tagger rather than the trade mark owner.

The first reported meta tag case was *Insituform Technologies Inc v National Envirotech Group*. This case is an example of a 'classic' meta tag case. National Envirotech, a competitor of Insituform, embedded Insituform's trade marks 'Insituform' and 'Insitupipe' into the keyword meta tags of its web site. An action was raised on 1 July 1997 by Insituform, claiming that National Envirotech's actions amounted to unfair competition under the principle that one business may not pass off their goods or services as those of another or otherwise suggest a connection between them. The case was quickly settled upon agreement from National Envirotech that they would desist and would agree to a permanent injunction being entered. At a similar time to the *Insituform* case, several other instances of trade mark infringement in meta tags emerged. One of the first of these involved one of the leading experts in the field, Carl Oppedahl, a partner with New York attorneys Oppedahl and Larson. In *Oppedahl and Larson v Advanced Concepts*, the famous law firm was required to take action to protect their trade marks 'Oppedahl' and 'Larson'. The defendants, an unincorporated entity from Texas, had tagged these terms without any use of them on their web site. It appeared, and was claimed by Oppedahl and Larson, that the only reason the defendants had done so was to increase traffic to their web site. This is a particularly interesting early case for several reasons. Firstly, unlike the *Insituform* case, there was no visible use of the plaintiffs' trade mark on the defendants' web site; the only use was in the hidden source code. Second, Oppedahl and Larson actually allow (and apparently encouraged) the use of their trade marks on a parody page called 'This has nothing to do with Carl Oppedahl or Oppedahl and Larson'. It appears Carl Oppedahl was concerned that the actions of the defendants could have led surfers to assume the defendants were in some way linked to the famous firm, as there was no reference to Oppedahl and Larson in the text of their web page, a mistake which no visitor to the parody site could ever make. Again the plaintiffs were successful, with Oppedahl and Larson obtaining permanent injunctions against all defendants following agreed settlements finalised between December 1997 and February 1998.

Similar cases have been heard, some involving famous trade marks such as 'Playboy' and 'Playmate', and others, like the *Insituform* case, involving disputes between competitors. All have led to restraining orders being awarded. In each of these cases the infringer was attempting to increase traffic to their web site through the misuse of the trade mark in question. It is not clear, though that a UK court would take such a hard line with meta taggers, especially not in cases involving competitor meta tagging.

3. USING TRADE MARKS AS META TAGS

Despite the apparent acceptance of US defendants that their actions amount to a *prima facie* trade mark infringement, it may be contended that under UK law, use of a trade mark as a keyword meta tag is not a trade mark infringement. Instead of conceding the point, as in many of the US cases, a UK defendant may wish to claim that they have no case to answer.

In his work Professor Cornish identifies four types of infringement under the *Trade Marks Act 1994*. Type one infringement occurs when a sign or mark identical to that registered is used in relation to identical goods or services. With type one infringement Professor Cornish states that the trade mark holder is not required to demonstrate a likelihood of confusion. Type two infringement takes place when there is merely a similarity between the marks in question and/or the goods or services in issue. In such a case the plaintiff must establish there existed a 'likelihood of confusion'. Type three infringement is similar to the US concept of trade mark dilution. It occurs when the mark in question has a reputation in the UK and the infringer without due cause takes unfair advantage of, or is detrimental to the 'repute' of the trade mark. Finally Professor Cornish identifies a type four infringement under s 10(6) of the Act, where an unfair use of a trade mark has occurred in relation to a comparative advertisement.

Current meta tag disputes will usually fall into one of two categories: those disputes which occur between competitors (such as *Insituform Technologies Inc v National Envirotech Group* and *Niton Corporation v Radiation Monitoring Devices*), which may be categorised as type one/type two disputes; and disputes where a famous mark is in question (such as *Playboy Enterprises v AsiaFocus and Internet Promotions* and *Oppedahl and Larson v Advanced Concepts*), which may be categorised as type three disputes.

3.1. COMPETITOR INFRINGEMENT: TYPE ONE AND TWO CASES

Both type one and type two infringements require the defendant to have used 'in the course of trade a sign'. This offers our first potential defence. When a meta tagger makes use of a trade mark as a keyword meta tag, it is not clear they are using the sign in the course of trade. When the mark is tagged it may, at the option of the webmaster, be hidden in the code of the web page. This hidden code is then read by the spiders sent out by the search engine operators and is catalogued. The consumers may never see this code. All they know is that they have input 'Insituform' as a search term and in the returns they see listed the web site of National Envirotech. At no point has the customer seen National Envirotech make use of Insituform's trade mark. The question is, therefore, have National Envirotech made use of Insituform's trade mark in the course of trade?

The UK case law on use does not provide us with a clear answer on this question. This is perhaps to be expected, as previous case law has dealt with the use of a trade mark in the physical world where there is no way to bring the mark to the customer's attention without communicating the mark directly to the customer. Perhaps the case most analogous to the meta tag cases is *Trebor Basset v Football Association*. In this case the infringement complained of consisted of the inclusion of photographs of England footballers in packs of candy sticks produced by Trebor Basset. The Football Association claimed this was in breach of their registered trade mark (the three lions symbol), which was clearly visible on the shirts of the players in the photographs distributed by Trebor Basset. Mr Justice Rattee found there had been no infringement on the part of Trebor Basset. He relied upon the earlier judgment of Jacob J in *British Sugar plc v James Robertson & Sons Limited* in finding that the use of the sign complained of has to be used as a trade mark, by which it has to be used 'to identify the provenance of the relevant goods or services'. Here, as the photographs were contained inside the packet, this could not be the case. We can draw an analogy between the hidden use of a trade mark inside a packet of sweets and the hidden use of a trade mark in a line of code. The important difference between the two is the point at which the trade mark becomes apparent to the customer. With the trade mark inside the packet of sweets, it only is revealed to the customer after the product has been purchased, thereby reducing the likelihood of confusion as to the source of the product. The trade mark hidden in HTML code is, however, revealed to the customer, if we accept it is revealed at all, when the returns from the search engine are listed, which is before the point of access to the site in question.

There is evidence that the courts are willing to define 'use' more widely in cases where there is a risk that the mark's value as an indicator of origin may be adversely affected. Whether or not a UK court would define a hidden use of a trade mark as a keyword meta tag as 'use' may therefore depend upon whether a potential customer is likely to be confused as to the origin of the infringer's site, in the sense that they will incorrectly assume it is linked to the trade mark holder. To determine whether a meta tagger is making use of a trade mark in the course of trade, one therefore needs to determine the likelihood of confusion on the part of the customer. A likelihood of confusion on the part of the customer is therefore required for both type one and type two cases.

The European Court of Justice has provided guidance on the issue of confusion in the case of *Sabel v Puma*. The case, referred to the ECJ from the Bundesgerichtshof (German Federal Supreme Court), was a challenge on the part of Puma, the well-known sporting goods manufacturer, against the proposed registration as trade marks of a depiction of a 'bounding cheetah' and the word SABEL in relation to sports shoes. The ECJ considered the meaning of the term 'association' as set out in s 10(2) of the *Trade Marks Act*, and defined the term narrowly as a subset of confusion. Therefore, in the absence of possible confusion on the part of the consumer as to the possible source of the product, there can be no association even if the consumer could reasonably assume there was an associative relationship between the two suppliers. The Court then went on to provide guidance as to when confusion occurs. The test formulated is an objective standard where confusion is to be measured against the perception of the 'average consumer' who is deemed to perceive the mark as a whole and who does not analyse the detail of the mark. This is both an objective and measurably high standard. It is not enough for the consumer to create in his mind a loose association between the two products; he must think that, taken as a whole, the infringing mark indicates a connection with the trade mark holder.

Applying the principles of *Sabel v Puma* to a competitor meta tag dispute such as *Insituform v National Envirotech*, it is not clear there is a likelihood of confusion and therefore it may be argued that no infringement has occurred. In such cases the customer will input a search term (Insituform) and will find listed on the search return, among several other sites, the home page of National Envirotech. This return should not confuse the 'average consumer'. The courts must, in the interests of consistency, attribute to the average consumer a degree of understanding of advertising and promotional practices. Thus, just as the reasonable reader of a comparative advertisement is assumed to be knowledgeable about advertising practices, including puffery and selective comparisons, the average consumer of products offered over the Internet must be assumed to have a level of knowledge of advertising practices used in cyberspace such as stuffing and competitive tagging. Therefore it may be argued that in disputes between competitors the alleged infringer should not admit the infringement claim. At no point in the process will the average consumer be confused as to the content of the competitor sites, given the level of knowledge to be assumed and taking the use of the trade mark within the whole context in which it is being used. By focusing only on the use of the trade mark as a search term the courts would be erroneously focusing on the detail of the mark, not the perception of the mark as a whole in the context in which it is being used. Competitors may therefore argue that with an application of the *Sabel v Puma* standard, no infringement has occurred.

3.2. DILUTION: TYPE THREE CASES

It is more difficult to formulate a claim that no trade mark infringement has occurred in cases where the alleged infringer is taking advantage of a well-known trade mark such as Playboy. Section 10(3) provides a stronger protection to trade mark holders than the provisions of ss 10(1) and 10(2). This is due to the fact that s 10(3) does not require a likelihood of confusion on the part of the consumer. Although there are decisions of the UK courts which suggest that a likelihood of confusion is required under s 10(3), it can clearly be argued that whereas a likelihood of confusion may be required for the first level of protection under s 10(3) (where the mark is detrimental to the registered mark), such confusion is not required where the alleged infringer only takes unfair advantage of the mark. The taking of an unfair advantage is an act distinct from the standing of the registered trade mark. As such it does not require any loss or damage directly to the registered trade mark, rendering any likelihood of confusion redundant. On this basis any trade mark which has a reputation within the UK may rely upon the protection of s 10(3) where a meta tagger uses their trade mark as a keyword tag on a site offering dissimilar goods or services.

Although some may argue that this is an illogical conclusion, as it offers stronger protection to trade mark holders in relation to signs used for unrelated goods or services than it offers in relation to similar goods or services, the author would argue such a conclusion is not only logical but necessitated by the wording of s 10. If it was the intention of government to protect trade mark holders under s 10(3) only where there was a risk of confusion, this could have been expressly stated in the Act. The fact that s 10(3) remains silent on the issue of confusion indicates it is not required for a type three infringement. Additionally, s 10(3) is providing protection for a different aspect of the trade mark than that provided by sections 10(1) and 10(2).Whereas sections 10(1) and 10(2) are protecting the trade mark itself as a distinct piece of intangible property, section 10(3) is protecting the character or the repute of the trade mark. This is something quite different. With type one/type two infringement there must be damage to the mark itself. This is why under s 10(2) there must be likelihood of confusion. Under s 10(3) there is no requirement that the mark is damaged, merely its repute or character.

Character can be damaged without damage to the mark. Whereas the use of the Disney trade mark as a meta tag on a site offering pornographic material would not directly damage the Disney trade mark, as no one would be confused as to the source of the material and therefore would not be led to believe Disney had attached the trade mark to the site, it would certainly damage the character or repute of the Disney trade mark. Meta taggers who make use of a mark of some repute in relation to a site offering dissimilar goods or services will almost certainly fall foul of the provisions of s 10(3).

Part II—Defending your use of a registered trade mark

In the event the court finds the defendant/defender's use of a trade mark amounts to a *prima facie* infringement under s 10, the defendant/defender may wish to rely upon a fair use provision. There are two commonly used fair use defences. The first is a use of another's mark in a comparative advertisement under s 10(6) of the Act, and the second is the use of another's mark as an indicator of source or quality in relation to reselling the product, in accordance with the decision of the European Court of Justice in the case of *Parfums Christian Dior SA v Evora BV*. In the second part of this article both of these potential fair use defences will be analysed to determine their application to the practice of competitive meta tagging.

4. THE FAIR USE OF TRADE MARKS AS META TAGS

Both the US and the UK allow fair use defences to a claim of trade mark infringement. The defence under the *Lanham Act* may be found at s 33(b)(4) while the corresponding defence under the *Trade Marks Act 1994* may be found at ss 10(6) and 11(2). This section opens by analysing the decision in *Playboy Enterprises v Welles* and goes on to suggest how this decision may affect the development of UK law in this area. It concludes by suggesting a possible loophole in the law may be opened up should UK courts apply the reasoning of the *Welles* decision.

4.1. FAIR USE IN THE UNITED STATES: PLAYBOY ENTERPRISES v WELLES

Miss Welles was a former 'Playmate of the Year' who used this term, a registered trade mark of Playboy Enterprises, both on her web site and as a keyword meta tag. In February 1998 Playboy Enterprises raised an action against Miss Welles claiming five causes of action, including federal trade mark infringement and trade mark dilution. Miss Welles raised a 'fair use' defence: she contended that all the terms she used accurately described her and she was therefore entitled to use them. Miss Welles pointed to her prominent use of disclaimers as evidence that there was no likelihood of confusion, and claimed she was accurately describing herself as Playmate of the Year 1981 within the fair use provisions of the *Lanham Act*. The case was heard by Judge Judith Keep on 15 November 1999, and on 1 December she issued judgment in favour of Miss Welles, granting her motion for summary judgment and dismissing all eight of Playboy's claims. We now turn our attention to the key aspects of the judgment and the potential impact this judgment may have on the future use of trade marks as meta tags.

Playboy Enterprises based their claim on an earlier case, *Brookfield Communications Inc v West Coast Entertainment Corp*. In doing so, they claimed a web user who keyed the search term 'Playboy' into a search engine would be expecting results which would take him either to the official Playboy web site or to sites affiliated with Playboy Enterprises. On this basis, Playboy claimed, someone who found Miss Welles' site returned from such a search would assume her site was in some way linked to Playboy Enterprises, causing a 'likelihood of confusion on the basis of initial interest confusion'. Judge Keep had little difficulty in distinguishing the case before her from the *Brookfield* case. She pointed out that none of the previous meta tag cases had involved the fair use defence under the *Lanham Act* or a use of trade marks in meta tags which accurately and fairly describe the contents of the web page or web site. Judge Keep pointed out that if the consumer was searching for Miss Welles' web site, but could not remember her name, they would have to make use of key words describing Miss Welles, and that the key words that would identify Miss Welles to the public would be 'Playboy', 'Playmate' and 'Playmate of the Year'. As these keywords would be central to consumer access to Miss Welles' web site, and as Playboy Enterprises could not offer alternative search terms to the satisfaction of all parties and the court, Judge Keep dismissed Playboy's action saying:

> The World Wide Web is a commercial marketplace and a free speech marketplace. To give consumers access to it, the court must be careful to give consumers the freedom to locate desired names while protecting the integrity of trademarks and trade names. The court stresses that the underlying or foundational purpose of trademark protection is not to create a property interest in all words used in a commercial context, but rather, '[t]he policies of free competition and free use of language dictate that trademark law cannot forbid the commercial use of terms in their descriptive sense' (J McCarthy (1999), *Trademarks and Unfair Competition*, s 11.45 at 82). As Justice Holmes in *Prestonettes v Coty* 264 US 359 at 368 (1924) put more eloquently, '[w]hen a mark is used in a way that does not deceive the public we see no such sanctity in the word as to prevent its being used to tell the truth.'

The fair use defence under the *Lanham Act* states that 'the right to use the registered mark ... shall be subject to the ... defense that the use of the name, term or device charged to be an infringement is a use ... which is descriptive of and used fairly and in good faith only to describe the goods or services of such party'. To establish this defence, the defendant is required to prove three elements:

1   Their use of the term is not as a trade mark or service mark,
2   They use the term 'fairly and in good faith', and
3   They use the term only to describe their goods or services.

In addition to these three basic elements most US courts have accepted that an additional element, that of an absence of a likelihood of confusion on the part of the customer, is required for the fair use defence. This additional element is based on the view that it is inconsistent to find both a likelihood of confusion and a fair use. If the use being made of the trade mark is likely to confuse the customer then this is a breach of the basic purpose of a trade mark, an ability to identify the source or origin of the goods or service in question. The courts have therefore taken a view that a likelihood of confusion bars the defendant from relying upon the fair use defence.

The Ninth Circuit has put forward an eight-point test, called the 'Sleekcraft test', which may be used to determine when there is a likelihood of confusion. In the *Welles* case though, Judge Keep was keen not to adopt the Sleekcraft test in determining whether or not Miss Welles had made a fair use of the Playboy trade marks. She noted that the case was 'not a standard trade mark case and [did] not lend itself to the systematic application of the eight factors in Sleekcraft'. The major problems with applying the Sleekcraft test to meta tag disputes had been recognised in the earlier case of *Brookfield Communications Inc v West Coast Entertainment Corp*. The key difficulty the *Brookfield* court had found in applying the Sleekcraft test was the manner in which the confusion occurred with meta tag disputes. When a trade mark is used as a meta tag the result of this action is usually a 'hit' or return on a search engine when a keyword linked to that trade mark is entered as a search parameter. The result of this is the customer sees a list of potential web sites which will usually contain both the plaintiff's and the defendant's web sites. By reviewing this list the customer should then be able to identify the web site he is seeking, and even in the event he accidentally clicks onto the defendant's web site in error, any confusion is usually immediately rectified once the defendant's web site loads and the customer can see its content. Taking her lead from the reasoning of the court in the *Brookfield* case, Judge Keep decided the Sleekcraft test could not be applied to meta tag disputes and went on to analyse the likelihood of confusion in the instant case without reference to the eight factors listed in the Sleekcraft test.

Judge Keep then analysed the evidence in the case before her, applying what she called a 'common sense' approach. In particular she was keen to ensure that she remained flexible in applying traditional trade mark law to the question before her. In applying this common sense approach Judge Keep found that web users must utilise identifying words in their search for a web site. In the case of Miss Welles' web site a consumer who could not remember her name would use keywords such as 'Playboy' and 'Playmate' to search for her site, as these are her sources of public recognition. Miss Welles' use of these terms as keyword meta tags were therefore not only a fair use but one which in the interests of commerce were necessary, as without them some of Miss Welles' prospective customers would be unable to locate her site. On this basis Judge Keep ruled out Playboy Enterprises' claims of a likelihood of confusion on the part of the consumer and found that Miss Welles' use of the trademarks was a fair use.

Playboy argued there still remained a likelihood of confusion as there was a risk of 'initial interest confusion'. Initial interest confusion is the theory that the consumer will be temporarily confused by the misuse of a trade mark and as a result his or her attention will be drawn to the defendant's site even if this does not lead to a sale (or loss of a sale) once the confusion abates. The right to make an initial interest confusion claim can be found in the case of *Dr Seuss Enters v Penguin Books USA Inc*. Such a claim was allowed in the *Brookfield* case, the case upon which much of the Playboy Enterprises action was based.

Playboy Enterprises argued (supported by circumstantial evidence) that an 'appreciable number' of persons who enter the terms 'Playboy' or 'Playmate' into a search engine are looking for the official Playboy web site. This, they argued, showed initial interest confusion; meaning Miss Welles' use of their trade marks was not a fair use and entitling them to relief. Judge Keep, though, rejected this argument. She found that the *Dr Seuss* and *Brookfield* cases merely indicated that initial interest confusion was actionable under the *Lanham Act*. Neither case suggested that a finding of initial interest confusion compelled a finding of trade mark infringement or prevented a finding of 'fair use'. She pointed out that to the contrary, the decision in *Brookfield* made it clear that a finding of an initial interest confusion did not restrict the right of a defendant to make a fair use of a trade mark in accordance with the *Lanham Act*. On this basis, as the court found no evidence that Miss Welles had intended to divert customers of Playboy Enterprises to her web site by trading on Playboy's goodwill, Judge Keep determined that any initial interest confusion caused by Miss Welles' use of Playboy Enterprises trade marks was not such as to interfere with the finding that her use was a 'fair use', and the claim was dismissed. In reviewing all the evidence before her, Judge Keep found that Playboy Enterprises had failed to establish that Miss Welles' use of their trademarks was in any way unfair or confusing. The court found that Miss Welles was entitled to continue to use these terms as they were descriptive of the contents of her site and there was no evidence of an intent by her to trade off of the goodwill of Playboy enterprises. Playboy's claims were therefore dismissed: the trade mark holder had lost.

4.2. FAIR USE IN THE UNITED KINGDOM: COMPARATIVE ADVERTISING

As previously mentioned the *Trade Marks Act* also contains fair use provisions. The primary fair use provision in the UK is found in s 10(6) of the Act which states:

> Nothing in the preceding provisions of this section shall be construed as preventing the use of a registered trade mark by any person for the purpose of identifying goods or services as those of the proprietor or a licensee.
>
> But any such use otherwise than in accordance with honest practices in industrial or commercial matters shall be treated as infringing the registered trade mark if the use without due cause takes unfair advantage of, or is detrimental to, the distinctive character or repute of the trade mark.

This provision is designed to allow competitors to use the trade mark of another for the purposes of comparative advertising. It is generally felt that to allow traders to carry out such comparative advertising is good for the consumer in that such comparisons assist consumers in making choices. There is a counter-argument that such advertising should be prevented, as advertisers will be selective in the content of the advert and may therefore distort the facts. The risk of such adverts being so selective as to be distortive is, though, ameliorated by the requirement that the use made of the other party's trade mark must be 'in accordance with honest practices'; a distortional advert would not be found to be honest by the courts. The question of when a use of another's trade mark is fair has been examined several times since its introduction in 1994.

The first major analysis was that of Mr Justice Laddie in the case of *Barclays Bank v RBS Advanta*. In his analysis Laddie J concluded that a plaintiff could not succeed merely by showing that the defendant was taking an unfair advantage of the trade mark in question. This is because the section was clearly intended to allow comparative advertising to take place and all comparative advertising would contain elements of selective reporting and 'puffery'. All such advertisements would therefore run the risk of being found to be in breach of s 10(6) if all the plaintiff was required to demonstrate was an 'unfair advantage'. Instead, Laddie J felt that the plaintiff would have to make out a case for material dishonesty before the use of the trade mark would be found to be unfair.

This case and others which have followed have developed an objective standard to be applied when determining claims under s 10(6). This standard is tested with reference to a reasonable reader of the advertisement. The question posed is 'once the reader is given the full facts, would he say that the advertisement is not honest?' The reasonable reader of an advertisement is assumed to be knowledgeable about advertising practices. Therefore, he is expected to be aware of the use of advertising puffs and hyperbole in advertisements. Thus in the case of *Vodafone v Orange* it was expected that a reasonable reader of an advertisement which claimed, 'on average, Orange users save £20 every month' would assume this meant Orange users at the arithmetical mean, rather than all users of the service across all tariffs and services. The cases decided thus far all suggest that for an advertisement to be 'otherwise than in accordance with honest practices' in terms of s 10(6) it must be substantially misleading. This suggests that although we have no direct authority on the fair use of trade marks as meta tags in the UK, UK law on the fair use exception is broadly in line with the US position. A use will be fair unless it misleads the public or otherwise causes confusion which takes unfair advantage of or is detrimental to the mark.

4.3 FAIR USE IN THE UNITED KINGDOM: RESELLERS' RIGHTS

A second potential loophole which may be exploitable by web-based retailers is the resellers' right', illustrated in the case of *Parfums Christian Dior SA v Evora BN*. Evora are the operators of a chain of chemist shops in the Netherlands. They routinely import high-quality products via the grey market with the intention of selling them on to their customers at a reduced price. As part of their promotional literature they produced an advertising leaflet which pictorially reproduced the packaging of Dior products they had obtained in this manner. Dior claimed this reproduction infringed their trade marks in the products in question. Evora argued they were entitled to advertise the products in this manner, as the commercialisation of the product was a necessary implication of the exhaustion principle as demonstrated in cases such as *Centrafarm v Winthrop*. The Dutch courts found the type of advertising used by Evora, although down-market compared to that used by Dior, was of a kind customary in the sector in which Evora operated. The question remitted to the European Court of Justice by Hoge Raad was whether there were any circumstances in which a trade mark holder could interfere with the advertising of parallel imports, notwithstanding the principles of free movement of goods and exhaustion. The opinion of A-G Jacobs (supported by the Court) was that the principles of community law, which apply to the advertising of imported goods, are indistinguishable from the principles which apply to the marketing of such goods. This means that in determining whether or not the reseller is entitled to make use of the trade mark in this manner, domestic courts should apply the principles of *Bristol-Myers Squibb v Paranova*, which states that the trade mark holder may only object when their goods are being presented in a fashion that may damage the reputation of the trade mark.

The *Dior* principle has recently been applied in the UK in the case of *Zino Davidoff SA v A & G Imports Ltd*. In this case Mr Justice Laddie gave consideration to the principle of damage in relation to luxury goods, and guidance as to the application of the *Dior* principle in the UK. Although he had sympathy for the argument of Mr Michael Silverleaf QC that in relation to luxury goods 'sale at a low price, in large volume and through down-market outlets can be said to be the most effective way of detracting from the image of such goods', he emphasised that damage to the image of such goods caused merely by selling the goods more cheaply than the proprietor wishes is not a relevant consideration. Laddie J went to great length to attempt to draw a distinction between the right of the trade mark holder to impose restrictions on the further distribution of goods and the exhaustion principle. He pointed out that the application of such a right in cases of international exhaustion would 'come close to asserting a rule of community law that there is a presumption against consent to further exploitation in trade mark cases'. He felt such a position would 'bear little or no relationship to the proper function of the trade mark right' and in referring to a recent speech given by Jacob J at the University of Edinburgh, noted that the inimical use of a trade mark is as a marker of origin. Drawing from this he found that a reseller must therefore be entitled to make use of a supplier's trade mark, as it is the role of the trade mark to act as a badge of identity.

These decisions may prove to be of great import to web-based resellers. Both the *Dior* and *Davidoff* cases have illustrated that a re-importer may commercially exploit the attached trade mark of the goods in question provided the use made is not such as to damage the value of that mark. The same principle would extend to resellers who offer products via a web site. This would mean that a reseller offering a product such as Christian Dior perfume would be entitled to place a webvertisement on their site detailing the product and containing, among other things, the trade mark of the product in question. Applying the principles of the *Welles* decision in a similar manner to that described above in relation to comparative advertisements, the site operator may then fairly meta tag the trade mark in question as part of the content of their web site, allowing their site to be listed in returns against a search for the mark in question.

5. IS THERE A FAIR USE LOOPHOLE?

The application of the decision in the *Welles* case gives rise to the possibility of an interesting scenario. Potentially, it opens a loophole, which would allow web site operators to legally use their competitor's trade marks as meta tag keywords. As the *Welles* case has decided in the United States, it is legal within that jurisdiction to use a registered trade mark of another as a keyword meta tag if the defendant uses the mark in question to catalogue the content of their web site and they do so in such a manner which does not confuse users, and is not detrimental to the mark in question. It is the submission of the author, in the absence of authority, that the position in the UK, under both s 10(6) of the *Trade Marks Act* and the *Dior* principle, would be the same, provided the use of the mark was 'in accordance with honest practices' and did not without due cause take unfair advantage of, or be detrimental to, the distinctive character or repute of the trade mark'. The use of the trade mark of another as a keyword meta tag can therefore be inherently fair if you are genuinely cataloguing the content of your web site. Of course in most cases the operator of a web site would have no reason to include the trade mark of a competitor in the content of their web site. The issue of fair use meta tagging therefore does not arise. A potential loophole does emerge, though, if we fuse together the principle that you may make a fair use of a competitor's trade mark as a keyword meta tag, as described above, and the more traditional role of s 10(6) and the *Dior* principle: that is, to facilitate advertising. This creates the potential for a new trading practice, that of referring to, then meta tagging your competitors.

As s 10(6) allows the fair use of a competitor's trade mark for the purposes of comparative advertising, the first task the web site operator needs to carry out is the preparation of an online advertisement which complies with the objective fair use standard as defined in *Barclays Bank v RBS Advanta* and *Vodafone v Orange*. Once this advertisement is prepared the web site operator may then add this advertisement to their web site and then in accordance with the *Welles* decision they may fairly tag their competitor's trade mark as part of the content of their site. If there is no likelihood of confusion, and if their use of their competitor's trade mark is not detrimental to that mark, this should in theory be permissible. The question for any web site operator is how would the courts react to such a practice? Would the courts view this as being in accordance with honest practices, or would they view it as taking unfair advantage of the distinctive character or repute of the trade mark?

It may be assumed that the courts would instinctively move to prevent such a development, in much the same way as they moved quickly to prevent the practice of cybersquatting in the mid 1990s. The case in point here, though, would not be as clear-cut as with cybersquatting. With cybersquatting the courts could easily see an amoral, if not illegal, mischief occurring. Clearly the cybersquatters were appropriating valuable commercial assets to which they had no right or claim. In the event a web site operator carried out comparative content meta tagging in the manner described above, the question of whether or not this is immoral would be much less clear. A strong argument could be made for the morality (and legality) of acting in this way. If we return, for example, to the leading case of *Barclays Bank v RBS Advanta*, the advert in issue there was one prepared by the Royal Bank of Scotland, which claimed that the Royal Bank's credit card had 15 particular advantages over Barclay's Barclaycard and offered beneficial charges compared to the Barclaycard product. If the Royal Bank of Scotland were to repeat this advert on their web site and then meta tag the term 'Barclaycard', then obviously a search against Barclaycard would produce a return detailing the Royal Bank's web site. The customer could then access the Royal Bank's web site and read the advert before deciding for himself which credit card would be best for his particular circumstances. As Barclaycard is probably the best known credit card in the UK, this may be a popular search term entered by persons who are considering taking out a new credit card. The courts would find it very difficult to say that the Royal Bank was not simply assisting the consumer by making the comparisons available, this being, of course, one of the key reasons for the fair use exception in the first place.

In the event the courts were to accept this line of argument a new business opportunity would emerge. With the European Union predicting the value of global electronic commerce to have reached Euro200bn in the year 2000 and the Department of Trade and Industry predicting that the Internet will take 5–10% of all retail traffic in 2000, the Web is the world's fastest growing commercial marketplace. Being placed in the top 10 or 20 returns in search engines will be the digital equivalent of prime time television advertisements, and has the potential to be just as valuable. If courts were to rule that web site operators could legally make use of competitor's trade marks, as described, a new industry in comparative advertising specifically tailored to web sites could emerge. There is, though, one potential problem web site operators still must overcome before this industry in digital comparative advertising is established. This is the problem of the initial interest confusion.

Initial interest confusion is, as previously discussed, the theory that the consumer will be temporarily confused by the misuse of a trade mark. Judge Keep in the *Welles* case stressed the importance of flexibility in dealing with evolving cyberspace law. One aspect of the initial interest confusion claim she chose not to apply, as it was not in issue in the *Welles* case, was to test to see if there was evidence of whether the 'situation offers an opportunity for sale not otherwise available by enabling [the] defendant to interest prospective customers by confusion with the plaintiff's product'.

As a comparative advertisement by its nature is designed to offer an opportunity for sale, this may be seized upon by the courts as a reason to disallow the practice of comparatively advertising and then meta tagging a competitor's product. It is by no means certain, though, that the courts would act to prevent comparative advertisements being tagged in the manner described above if the web site operator acts in good faith.

This argument, it should be noted, cannot be levelled against resellers. In cases where resellers place an advert on a web site the product on offer remains that of the plaintiff. This means the plaintiff has still made the sale (although admittedly at an earlier stage in the supply chain). The plaintiff, it may be argued, has not lost a sale; they have just made a sale at a lower price than they otherwise would have done. Thus while the courts may move to exploit initial interest confusion to close the loophole in relation to comparative advertising, it would seem clear that web-based resellers are entitled to use as meta tags the trade marks of products in which they trade.

6. CONCLUSIONS

The Internet continually requires lawyers to re-examine the role of traditional legal frameworks as the free movement of information and globalisation it brings does not comply with traditional models of nation states, national governance and the traditional marketplace. The courts have been forced to adapt trade mark law to meet the challenges of cybersquatting and the role of domain names. The issue of meta tagging and trade marks is therefore just the latest in a long line of Internet-specific problems.

While it is arguable that the courts were required to take flexible and innovative interpretations of the law in relation to cybersquatting and protection of domain names, the issue of the fair use defence in relation to meta tags may provide the greatest challenge to date. As mentioned, it was always clear with cybersquatters that their actions were at the very least amoral, if not illegal, while cases involving domain names usually fell clearly into one of two categories, either the *bona fides* user or the *mala fides* user. The line between good and bad faith is, though, much narrower in the case of meta tagging. Although almost certainly the courts would move to prevent 'competitive meta tagging' carried out in the manner described above, the author suggests that such a practice is not only legal in terms of the *Trade Marks Act 1994* and the principle of exhaustion of rights within the EU, it is the application of these principles as was intended when they were developed. Competitor meta tagging is merely another method of advertising a product or service. Both s 10(6) and the *Dior* principle were developed to allow competitors/resellers to exploit a trade mark for the purpose of informing consumers of the existence of an alternative supplier for the same or similar product. Meta tags as an advertising medium must therefore benefit from such fair use provisions. It should not therefore be assumed that competitive meta taggers in the UK will fall foul of the provisions of the *Trade Marks Act*.

[Footnotes omitted]

NOTES AND QUESTIONS

1   Murray spends a considerable portion of the above extract discussing the various defences available to those accused of trade mark infringement. The reader is advised to return to this article when considering the general discussion of defences and domain names, below.

2   The focus throughout this book has been on the institutional responses to the challenges of the Internet. These institutions may be linked to the nation state, but need not be. In the case of meta-tags, an interesting customary institution is found in the policy of organisations that operate search engines. Search engines require websites to be registered to gain inclusion in their database. The engine operators now enforce a policy whereby a website will be rejected if it contains 'meta tag spam'. That is, if the meta tag repeats popular search terms with only partial or no relevance to their site in an attempt to increase traffic, some search engines will simply refuse to register the site. This is a good example of customary normative institutions that arise and operate independently of the law.

3   In *Brookfield Communications Inc v West Coast Entertainment Corp* 174 F 3d 1036 (9th Cir 1999), available at <http://laws.lp.findlaw.com/9th/9856918. html> 17 August 2006, the court found that use of the 'moviebuff' mark in meta-tags would cause prohibited 'initial interest confusion'. Initial interest confusion arises where a surfer, although not confused as to the source of any product at the time of purchase, is 'captured' by the infringing use of the plaintiff's mark. Use of the 'moviebuff' mark in a meta tag would cause the infringing site to be placed on a list of search results produced by search engines along with the trade mark holder. As a result, surfers originally seeking Brookfield by typing 'moviebuff' in a search engine might instead find West Coast's site. Once there, that surfer might make a purchase. Therefore, the court held, the defendant is improperly benefiting from the goodwill associated with the trade mark. Do you consider this an acceptable application of the law? Is this not the same as real life shopping?

4   Murray has canvassed the legal issues surrounding the use of trade marks in meta-tags. Would it be objectionable to have the name or mark of a competitor in the meta tag just once and no other reference or use of the name or mark anywhere else on the web page or website? Why, or why not? Would this fall foul of trade mark law?

5   In 2004, the England and Wales Court of Appeal handed down the decision of *Reed Executive Plc v Reed Business Information Ltd* [2004] EWCA Civ 159. Both parties had a legitimate claim to use the mark 'Reed'. Recruitment agency Reed Executive Plc sued publishers Reed Business Information Ltd and others (RBI). Reed Executive had registered the name 'Reed' as a trade mark in connection with employment agency services. RBI used the name 'Reed' in relation to their publishing business but had moved into the on-line recruitment market with the totaljobs.com venture. 'Reed' was used as a meta tag in the totaljobs website as well as in other parts of the website that were visible. Reed Executive argued that

RBI, a competitor, was using its mark, to direct traffic to RBI's site. However, the Appeal Court found no infringement.

6   The Court held that the sign 'Reed Business Information' was not identical to the registered trade mark 'Reed' and that the composite is not the same as use of the word 'Reed' in the sentence: 'Get business information from Reed.' The court found that the average consumer would recognise the additional words as serving to differentiate the defendant from Reeds in general. The Court also pointed out that 'Reed' is a common surname. One party calls itself 'Reed Business Information' because it supplies information to businesses and although both companies published job vacancies on-line, the Court found that they did not offer identical services.

7   Regarding the meta tag use issue, the Court found that the words 'Reed Business Information' used as a meta tag in the totaljobs site was not passing off and there was no confusion and hence no trade mark infringement. The Court acknowledged that whenever a user conducts a search, which includes a word in a metatag of a site, the search results will include that site along with all other sites which use that word, either in visible or hidden form and hence it is not unusual that when one conducts a search, some of the results appear to have nothing to do with the search term. A search under the phrase 'Reed jobs' always brought up a result list with totaljobs listed below the Reed Employment site so that anyone looking for Reed Employment would find them rather than totaljobs. No-one was likely to be misled and there was no misrepresentation and hence there was no passing off. In terms of trade mark infringement, the court was unable to find that there was any use of the sign to suggest a connection which did not exist. Causing a site to appear in a search result, without more, does not suggest any connection with anyone else.

8   The Reed dispute also concerned the purchase of the search term 'Reed' by the search engine Yahoo! to RBI. This will be considered in the next section.

(d)   Sale of keywords or search term associations by search engines

Search engines such as Google have in recent times profited by selling keywords or search term associations. Search engines sell advertising through selling keywords to customers who want to have their banner or pop-up advertising appear on any site retrieved when a user uses the purchased search term. It is in effect a form of contextual advertising. Sometimes the keywords sold are trade marks. Often, the price paid does not just trigger advertising but also the rank position in the search results. There have been numerous cases on the area in the US and in Europe and there is little agreement as to what the legal position is or should be. Certainly, in terms of Google's AdWords, at the time of writing, the debate continues to rage.

One of the earliest cases decided was *Playboy Enterprises, Inc v Netscape Comm Corp* (99-320 & 99-321, 2000 WL 1308815 (CD Cal Sept 13, 2000)) where the defendants sold the keywords 'playmate' and 'playboy' to advertisers whose banner ads linked to hard core pornographic sites. The plaintiffs owned trade marks reflecting these words. However, the request for an injunction was denied. The court found that the search term use of 'playboy' and 'playmate' involves only generic English language use and it cannot be presumed that those searching the Web using those keywords are necessarily looking for the Playboy Enterprises website. The case went on appeal (*Playboy Enterprises v Netscape Communications, et al*, 354 F3d 1020 (9th Cir 2004)). The court found that the marks were used 'in commerce' and that a likelihood of initial interest confusion existed. The case was remanded for further consideration, but the parties settled shortly afterward, with the terms of the settlement confidential.

Google has faced numerous lawsuits from trade mark owners in the USA and Europe. In the case of *Google v American Blinds & Wallpaper Factory, Inc*, No C 03-05340 JF (ND Cal Mar 30, 2005), the court followed *Playboy Enterprises v Netscape*, and the motion to dismiss was denied. The court rejected the argument that the sale of the trade mark terms as search terms did not constitute a 'use' of the trade marks.

In *Gov't Employees Ins Co v Google, Inc*, 330 F Supp 2d 700, 701 (ED Va 2004), Google was sued for both direct and contributory trade mark infringement. The direct infringement claims arose out of Google's sale of the plaintiff's trade mark as an adword. The plaintiff GEICO alleged that Google was using the mark in commerce in a way that was likely to confuse consumers. The indirect infringement claims were based on the infringing activities of the purchasers that had used the trade marks in their advertising. Google was alleged to have the ability to control the content of the advertisements. In August, the Eastern District of Virginia denied Google's motion to dismiss for failure to state a claim on both GEICO's trade mark infringement and contributory trade mark infringement claims.

When the dispute was heard, the District Court partially granted Google's motion for judgment as a matter of law (*Gov't Employees Ins Co v Google, Inc*, No 04-507 (ED Va Dec 15, 2004) ('GEICO II'). In *GEICO II*, the court distinguished between the sale of trade marked words to companies that made use of the marks in their ads and sales to companies that did not. The court held that there was insufficient evidence of consumer confusion over the 'sponsored links' that were triggered by trade marked adwords but which did not display the protected mark. However, the court reserved the question of Google's contributory liability for the actions of those who bought the adwords and used them to trigger ads containing the trade marked term.

In *Gov't Employees Ins. Co v Google, Inc*, 2005 US Dist LEXIS 18642; 77 USPQ2D (BNA) 1841 (ED Va Aug 8, 2005) ('GEICO III'), Judge Brinkema ruled that GEICO had established a likelihood of confusion, and therefore a violation of GEICO's trade mark, solely with regard to those sponsored links that use GEICO's trade marks in their headings or text. The court stayed the trial for 30 days to give the parties an opportunity to settle. The parties settled in September 2005.

At the time of writing in early 2006, CNG Financial Corp, which owns more than 1,300 Check 'n Go stores in 35 US states, is seeking an injunction preventing Google from selling ads linked to the Check 'n Go name.

The courts in France have ruled against the keyword sale by search engine operators numerous times. In February 2005, Google was fined €280,000 for use of Louis Vuitton's trade marks as keywords for sale (*Louis Vuitton Malletier v Google* Civil Court of Paris (TGI) February 4, 2005).

In the case of *Societe Des Hotels Meridien v SARL Google France*, (Nanterre Court (TGI) 16 December 2004), the court held that the use of 'le meridien' as a keyword violated the plaintiff's trade mark rights. The court also held that a user searching for 'meridien' or 'le meridien' was likely to be confused by a commercial link offering identical or similar services, and may believe that such services are of the same origin. Google was ordered to cease linking ads to the mark or face a 150 Euro per day fine. Google was also ordered to stop its Adwords Google Keywords Tool from suggesting, as keywords, the words 'meridien' or 'le meridien'.

In one of the earliest cases in France, Google was fined €75,000 for the sale to competitors of the trade marks 'bourse des vols' (airflight market) and 'bourse des voyages' (travel market) owned by Viaticum and Luteciel travel agencies, respectively. Google appealed the decision and lost its appeal in March 2005. The court in Versailles found that Google was guilty of 'trade mark counterfeiting' and ordered it to pay the damages originally awarded to French travel companies Luteciel and Viaticum. According to the decision, Google has no general obligation to monitor the keywords their customers choose, but Google must be able to prohibit the use of keywords such as those infringing trade marks. On the facts, the court held that Google knew or should have known the marks of the defendant companies. In any event, even if Google had legitimately not been aware of the fact that trade mark protected terms had been used, Google has been notified of the fraudulent use of the key words and had the duty to put an immediate stop to such infringement.

In February 2006, Google won its first Adwords case in France when a court in Nice ruled that sponsored links are not likely to confuse consumers, thus Google cannot be deemed liable for unfair competition (see <http://domaine.blogspot.com/2006/02/few-words-on-adwords.html>).

In contrast to the French courts, the German courts have reached decisions favourable to Google. In *Metaspinner Media v Google* (Az: 312 O 887/03; 312 O 324/04 Sep 2004), the Hamburg Court dismissed a trade mark infringement suit against Google based on the sale of plaintiff's *preispiraten* (price pirate) mark as a keyword to a competitor. The court held that there is neither trade mark infringement nor unfair competition as long as the trade mark does not appear in the text of the ad. In that case, the search engine can be held liable, but only after it has been informed about the infringement and does not stop the showing of the infringing ad. In this respect, the approach is similar to the US approach. See also *Nemetschek v Google*, (Az 33 O 21461/03) Munich Regional Court where it was held that Google was not responsible for third-party use of trade marks as keywords where it was unaware of any wrongdoing. However, the court also indicated that the sale and use of trade marks as keywords can be trade mark infringement, and that a search engine can be liable for trade mark infringement on the part of third parties if it was aware of the infringement, and if it was technically feasible and reasonable to expect that it could have prohibited such infringement.

In the UK case of *Reed v Reed* discussed above, the search term 'Reed' was used to trigger a Yahoo! Banner ad. This was not a case against a search engine operator but rather, the purchaser of the keyword. The court held that the banner ad itself referred only to totaljobs and there was no visible appearance of the word Reed at all. It found that users know that all sorts of banners appear when one executes a search and the ads may be triggered by something in the search term. The Court regarded users of search engines as somewhat savvy and found that users know that searches produce fuzzy results. Accordingly, the court found that a search for the term 'Reed' producing a totaljobs banner making no reference to the word 'Reed' and Reed Employment would not make anyone think there was a trade connection between the two. There would be no likelihood of confusion.

From the cases litigated thus far in the various jurisdictions, it would appear that the sale of trade marked words as keywords would be regarded as use in the course of trade as required under trade mark law. Whether or not there is confusion or likelihood of confusion is a point on which there is currently no consensus. Under Australian law s 120(2) and in the United Kingdom, s 10(2) and in Singapore, s 27(2), a likelihood of confusion is required before infringement can be established.

(e) Adware and pop-up advertising

A method of reaching potential consumers on the web that has surfaced in the past few years is pop-up advertising, another example of contextual advertising. Pop-up ads are advertisements that appear to Internet users generally within a new window, or web page, as they navigate websites. They are called 'pop-up' ads because while users surf the web, computer programs suddenly open new windows filled with advertising without any warning and without prompting by the user. There have been a number of cases in the US and most rely on some form of trade mark law and/or unfair competition violations.

In *Washington Post et al v The Gator Corporation*, 2002 US Dist Lexis 20879 (ED Va 2002), a group of publishers including the Washington Post, Newsweek Interactive, the New York Times and Dow Jones & Company filed a motion for preliminary injunction against the Gator Corporation (now called Claria). The software in question was the GAIN Adserver. This software determines a user's interests by recognising the Internet addresses which the user accesses and then it causes an advertisement to be displayed in a pop-up window on the user's computer screen. The software is usually bundled with one of the other popular applications offered by the Gator Corporation, such as eWallet. The court granted the preliminary injunction enjoining Gator from causing its pop-up advertisements to be displayed while users accessed the plaintiffs' websites. However, the court did not issue any findings of fact or conclusions of law.

Similarly, the company WhenU delivers contextual pop-up advertisements through its SaveNow software. The SaveNow software will trigger pop-up ads based on a number of events: the web address of the current web page, the overall content of the web page, or keywords typed into a search engine. The SaveNow software chooses which advertisements to trigger by comparing the above data with a directory of commonly used search phrases, commonly visited web addresses, and various keyword algorithms.

It is interesting to note that the WhenU's software does not store individual user information. In contrast, Claria's software tracks a user's long-term web surfing habits by collecting and storing anonymous data. We now turn to the three main cases involving WhenU in the US. The first of these is *U-Haul International v WhenU.com, Inc*, 279 F

Supp 2d 723 (ED Va 2003). Here, the court granted the defendant's motion for summary judgment. It was held that the inclusion of U-Haul's trade mark and URL in a fixed keyword list to generate contextual pop-up advertisements did not constitute 'use' of a mark in commerce within the meaning of the trade mark statute. The court further held that pop-up ads occurred as a result of a user's consensual download and installation of the software and that the software employed by WhenU was a 'pure machine-linking function' that did not interfere with U-Haul's website, and did not interact with U-Haul's server or systems. The plaintiff also claimed in copyright but the court found that there was no copyright infringement as there was no copying, displaying, altering.

The second litigation involving WhenU was *Wells Fargo & Co v WhenU.com, Inc*, 293, F Supp 2d 734 (ED Mich 2003) and it adopted the reasoning in *U-Haul International*. The WhenU ads did not use the plaintiff's trade marks or identify the plaintiff as the source. The court rejected the argument that WhenU's use of trade marked words in its proprietary directory constituted use 'in commerce'. The appearance of pop-up ads was a separate activity from the appearance of the plaintiff's website on the users' screens. The court was invited to analogise the use of the plaintiff's mark to the use of trade marks in metatags but it declined. The court found that a typical user would not perceive WhenU's pop-up as being sponsored by or affiliated with the plaintiff's website.

It would appear from these two cases that the court's decision on the 'use in commerce' requirement hinged on three factors. First, that WhenU.com did not explicitly market or sell the specific trade marks as keywords to advertisers, but instead included them in a fixed and proprietary keyword database. Second, the resulting matching trigger was an automated function that was not evident to the end user, irrespective of the appearance of branded competitive pop-up ads over the plaintiffs' websites. Lastly, the pop-up ads did not include the plaintiffs' trade marks. In the case of *1-800 Contacts, Inc v WhenU.com, et al*, 02 Civ 8043 (SDNY Dec 22, 2003), the plaintiff successfully obtained a preliminary injunction on nearly identical facts as the previous two cases. The court expressly rejected the holdings in *U-Haul* and *Wells Fargo*, and found that *1-800 Contacts* demonstrated that the defendant had used in commerce the plaintiff's mark in two ways. First, the inclusion of the defendant's mark in the directory of terms together with the purpose to advertise directly competing goods was a use in commerce. The court stressed that it was the added purpose of exhibiting directly competing goods that made the use a trade mark use. Second, the court found that using a consumer's prior knowledge of the plaintiff's trade mark to exhibit its own directly competing goods or services constituted trade mark use. The court emphasised that the defendant was capitalising on the plaintiff's reputation and goodwill. The court recognised the doctrine of initial interest confusion from the meta tag case of *Brookfield Communications v West Coast Entertainment Corp* and found a likelihood of source and initial interest confusion. This was despite the branding of WhenU's advertisements and despite the disclaimer.

WhenU appealed to the Second Circuit and the appeal was upheld (*1-800 Contacts, Inc v WhenU.com, Inc*, Docket Nos. 04-0026-cv and 04-0446-cv (2d Cir June 27, 2005)). A subsequent application to appeal to the US Supreme Court was denied.

The Second Circuit found that WhenU was not liable for trade mark infringement as a matter of law. The court held that WhenU does not 'use' 1-800's trade marks as a trade mark when it includes 1-800's website address, which is almost identical to 1-800's trade mark, in an unpublished directory of terms that trigger delivery of WhenU's contextually relevant advertising or when it causes separate, branded pop-up ads to appear on a user's computer screen either above, below, or along the bottom edge of the 1-800 website window. The rejection of any trade mark use, which is a precondition for any trade mark infringement liability, meant that it was not necessary for the court to consider other aspects of the trade mark case.

The court found that WhenU did not use 1-800 Contact's trade marks when it placed the term in its database of keywords that trigger ads. The court found that WhenU did not place 1-800 trade marks on any goods or services in order to pass them off as emanating from or authorised by 1-800. The court also pointed out that including the term into WhenU's database does not create the possibility of visual confusion with 1-800's mark. Regarding the placement of pop-up ads over the plaintiff's website, the court made an analogy to real-word trade mark 'adjacencies', such as how retail stores put different brands of products next to each other on the shelves. For example, it is quite common for different brands of colas such as Pepsi and Coca-Cola to be placed side by side on the supermarket shelf. This type of trade mark adjacencies according to the court is not use of the mark as a trade mark, and hence, the pop-up ad is just another form of adjacency.

It should be noted that WhenU and Claria rely on user consent to provide pop-up ads. They provide consumers with cost-free, proprietary software; in exchange, consumers install software that generates pop-up ads. Claria and WhenU bundle their cost-free software with the pop-up ad software so that a consumer cannot install one program without installing the other. In recent times, there have been organisations which have not sought the user's consent before installing such pop-up or advertising software on a user's computer. This lack of knowledge and consent have led to distinguishing this category of software as spyware. We will be considering spyware in a later chapter.

----

3   The domain name system

The domain name system essentially grew out of humans' ability to remember and recall words better than numbers. Domain names are often confused with electronic mail addresses and uniform resource locators (URLs). A domain name is actually a part of each of these. For example, in the e-mail address sam@mq.edu.au, the domain name is 'mq.edu.au'. Similarly, in the URL http://www.mq.edu.au/tour, the domain name is also 'mq.edu.au'. As far as computers on the Internet are concerned, Internet services are identified by Internet protocol addresses (IP addresses) which are four numbers from 0 to 255 separated by dots: 139.111.23.1 for example would be a valid IP address. E-mail and web addresses can operate by just using these numbers. Although the Internet can function perfectly well just by using these numbers, the domain name system was introduced for people's convenience and ease of memory. Not surprisingly, then, the domain name system provides a direct one-to-one mapping between the IP addresses and the domain names. And this has been the root of many problems. There can only be one 'mq.edu.au' or 'mcdonalds.com'. There can be subdomains such as 'law.mq.edu. au' or 'lib.mq.edu.au', but these belong to the holder of the domain.

Andrew Murray, 'Internet Domain Names: The Trade Mark Challenge'

(1998) 6 (3) *International Journal of Law and Information Technology* 285

1.4. The Domain Name System (DNS)

1.4.1. THE MECHANICS OF THE CURRENT DNS

… The domain name system, or DNS, is the system of global navigation within the Internet. Each page of information is given an 'address' called a Uniform Resource Locator (URL) which, like the address of every home, office or shop, must be unique if the user is to locate it. This address is made up of several sections. To illustrate how the DNS works, let's look at a typical URL:

> http://www.oup.co.uk/inttec/

This is the homepage of the *International Journal of Law and Information Technology* at Oxford University Press. The URL may be broken down as follows:

- **http:** This page uses hypertext transfer protocol. It is based on the software technology of Tim Berners-Lee.
- **www.** This page is found on the World Wide Web. The Web is now the dominant Internet format due to its user-friendliness.
- **oup.co.uk** The unique address of Oxford University Press. This is made up of two domain names: a top-level domain (TLD) and a second-level domain (SLD). Internet addresses are read right to left; the TLD is the .co.uk section of the domain. This tells the user the address is used by a UK registered commercial organization. (Note: the organization does not need to be registered in the UK, just the domain name.) The SLD comes to the left of the first period, ie oup. This is the identifier of the site operator. As a whole the domain name must be unique. There can be only one oup.co.uk address, although variations such as oup.com, or out.co.uk are possible. Before they can be used, second-level domains must be registered.
- **inttec/** This is a tertiary or third-level domain. Any text which follows the TLD is used to identify pages of information within the site managed by the domain name owner. Such tertiary domains do not require registration and will not be discussed further.

1.4.2. THE CURRENT REGISTRATION SYSTEM

… I will make reference to two varieties of top-level domain (TLD): the generic top-level domain (gTLD) and the national top-level domain (nTLD). Generic top-level domains have no affiliation to any particular nation. They are the .com, .org and .net domains. Applications to register a second-level domain within any of these gTLDs currently must be made to Network Solutions Inc (NSI) of Virginia. In effect NSI has a monopoly over gTLDs. Control over national top-level domains is devolved to national registrars. The UK registrar who controls all applications to register second-level domains within the .uk nTLD is Nominet UK Ltd of Abingdon, Oxfordshire. There are 239 recognized nTLDs listed in the International Standards Organization document ISO 3166.23. These reflect all possible permutations ranging from

.ac for Ascension Island to .zw for Zimbabwe. The list is periodically reviewed by the Maintenance Agency Secretariat to ensure that it takes account of political developments such as the emergence of the FYR of Macedonia. Not all countries are connected to the Internet, which means some codes are, as yet, unavailable for use ...

(a)   Top level domains

Previously, there were only six gTLDs: .gov (US government), .com, .org, .net, .edu (US educational institutions), and .mil. In November 2000, another seven were introduced into the infrastructure, .biz (businesses), .aero (air transport industry), .pro (credentialed professionals and related entities), .name (individuals), .museum (museums), .coop (cooperatives), .info (information). Between 2004 and 2005, the Internet Corporation for Assigned Names and Numbers (ICANN) considered a number of additional gTLDs. The following have been introduced: .travel (travel industry),[5] .jobs (human resource managers),[6] .mobi (consumers and providers of mobile phones),[7] .cat (Catalan linguistic and cultural community).[8] In addition to these generic top level domains, two others have been introduced: .arpa (used for technical infrastructure purposes)[9] and .int (registered organisations established by international treaties between governments).[10] ICANN is continuously considering new domains and readers should check ICANN's website for new domains that have been introduced. These recent additions will no doubt permeate general Internet parlance in the same manner as have other gTLDs.

The domain name system operates by a hierarchical system of name servers. At each domain level, a name server maintains a table of names and it points all enquiries to the name server registered for that name. Each name server in the hierarchy directs traffic through to the next level, which then selects the desired destination in the following level. Therefore, when a user requests www.mq.edu.au, the World Root will be consulted to establish the IP address of the .au name server, the .au name server will receive a query and will direct traffic to the .edu.au name server, which will then direct traffic to the .mq.edu.au name server. If any of the name servers do not maintain absolute integrity, the user will not be routed to the correct IP address as there is no other way of determining which domain name attaches to which IP address. It is this imperative which demands a rigorous system of verification, maintenance, and security of name servers.

---

5   See 'ICANN Officially Designates .JOBS and .TRAVEL', accessible at <http://www.icann.org/ announcements/announcement-08apr05.htm, last accessed 03/05/06>.

6   Ibid.

7   See dotmobi, 'What is dotmobi', accessible at <http://pc.mtld.mobi/mobilenet/index.html>, last accessed 03/05/06.

8   See .CAT, accessible at <http://www.domini.cat/en_index.php>, last accessed 03/05/06.

9   See ICANN—Top-Level Domains (gTLDs), accessible at <https://www.icann.org/tlds>, last accessed 30/04/06.

10   See IANA—.int Top-Level Domain, accessible at <http://www.iana.org/root-whois/int.htm>, last accessed 03/05/06.

Andrew Murray, 'Internet Domain Names: The Trade Mark Challenge'

(1998) 6 (3) *International Journal of Law and Information Technology* 285

4. A global problem, a global solution?

4.1. THE INTERNATIONAL AD HOC COMMITTEE REPORT

... The International Ad Hoc Committee (IAHC) was set up in November 1996 to review, and recommend improvements to, the domain name system (DNS). It comprised representatives of the Internet Architecture Board (IAB), Internet Assigned Numbers Authority (IANA), International Telecommunications Union (ITU), International Trademark Association (INTA), World Intellectual Property Organization (WIPO), and the Internet Society (ISOC). The IAHC charter stated that 'the DNS is an international resource and the IAHC will at all times operate with that perspective.' Despite this statement, it was a major criticism of the European Commission that there was no European representation on the IAHC, notwithstanding the fact that EU nations account for at least 15.6% of all host computers.

The recommendations of the committee were published in the *Final Report of the International Ad Hoc Committee: Recommendations for Administration and Management of gTLDs* on the 4th of February 1997, available from the IAHC web site. The report may be discussed in two distinct sections: (i) the creation of new gTLDs and (ii) the creation of new gTLD registrars. The following sections will discuss the proposals of the IAHC and evaluate their chances of solving the domain name/trade mark issue.

4.1.1. THE RECOMMENDATION TO CREATE EXTRA GTLDS

... In their report the committee discuss the pros and cons of creating extra gTLDs before recommending the creation of seven new gTLDs. The main reason given for the creation of extra gTLDs is the creation of alternative entry points into the DNS within the 'generic' field. The theory is that an increase in the number of gTLDs will create a naturally competitive market where registrars will compete for trade and in doing so will create a market in the new gTLDs, it being in their interest to promote their product. The main argument against the creation of extra gTLDs was that creation of extra gTLDs which overlap with the .com registry will not create alternative entry points for companies originally denied a .com registration; it will simply lead to duplication of registrations. The committee weighed the opposing arguments and decided in favour of the creation of extra gTLDs. In the author's opinion, they were mistaken in this decision and have made a recommendation which is in the interests of the few, rather than the many.

The argument against further gTLDs is threefold. Firstly there is the argument laid before IAHC that creation of extra gTLDs will lead to duplication of registration. This is a powerful argument: major companies already duplicate second-level domain names. Coca-Cola, for example, uses several domains, while Warner Brothers were willing to take action against Roadrunner Computer Systems for the 'roadrunner.com' domain while in possession of, among others, 'bugsbunny.com', 'wb.com' and 'looneytunes.com'. In all probability an increase in commercial gTLDs will not increase the number of individual trade mark holders, registered or unregistered, who make use of their trade mark on the Internet. Rather the effect of adding gTLDs such as .store and .firm to the list will be an increase in revenue for registrars. Commercial organizations will be forced to take out repeat registrations to protect their trade marks. The recommendation to increase the number of gTLDs will almost certainly not lead to improved access to the DNS for those companies who have missed out. Almost certainly the only winners are the registrars.

The second argument against simply increasing the number of gTLDs is the cachet of the .com domain. The .com domain has achieved a special status within the Internet community. The worth of other gTLDs must be evaluated with reference to this. There is no particular problem with getting your trade mark name on the Internet, as your domain name, if you are willing to compromise. Prince Sportswear, for example, could have used their registered trade mark had they registered their domain in Germany (prince.de) or Italy (prince.it). Neither domain name is currently taken. Prince Sportswear are, though, a US-based company who wished to use a US-recognized domain. The only practical option open to them was, therefore, the .com domain which, although generic, is the default address for US based commercial organizations. This is why the .com address has such cachet. The commercial Internet is dominated by American multinationals who all make use of the .com domain. In the virtual world of the Internet it is the neighbourhood to be in, the electronic equivalent of Rodeo Drive or Bond Street, and as the price is fixed at only $80 it is an exclusive address within the reach of all. Companies will always find ways into the exclusive .com neighbourhood rather than settling for the less salubrious surroundings of .firm or .store domains. Offering commercial organizations alternative addresses will not prevent disputes over the .com domain. In all likelihood such alternative addresses will be unacceptable alternatives. Companies instead will find other ways into the .com neighbourhood, as in the case of Prince Sportswear who found entry via a princetennis.com address. The .com address has been the focus of the vast majority of Internet trade mark disputes, and the creation of alternative gTLDs will do nothing to alleviate this.

The final argument against the introduction of further gTLDs is that there is no paucity of top-level domain names; rather, the shortage is to be found in second-level domains. Every country has its own national TLD (nTLD) assigned under ISO 3166, a total of 239 additional TLDs. It is understandable that businesses may not wish to register their domain in El Salvador (195 hosts) or Burkina Faso (45 hosts) but the majority of domestic registrars are happy to entertain applications from overseas and it is likely that whatever your trade mark you will be able to find at least one nTLD in which you will be able to register the second-level domain of your choice. Why do companies continue to seek registration in the .com domain at all costs? The reason is, as stated earlier, the .com domain is the pre-eminent commercial district of the virtual marketplace. Companies often, in a position to register their trade mark within another TLD, will settle for something lesser, such as princetennis.com or road-runner.com, simply to get the .com suffix. The creation of more TLDs is not the solution. There are already hundreds of available TLDs. What is required is a fairer method of distributing second-level domain names within the desirable neighbourhood of the .com domain.

NOTES AND QUESTIONS

1   In October 2001, the .info domain name became the first new gTLD to become operational in more than fifteen years.[11] The .info domain has the potential to become a Euro-centric rival to the US-centric .com domain. At this point, there have been 350000 registrations of .info names. Do you think that the problems of the original six domain names will simply be replayed in the realm of the new domains?

2   What is your reaction to the launch of the new names? Do you agree with Murray's criticism? Give reasons for your answer.

3   An argument in favour of adding new gTLDs is that it will allow multiple, almost identical domain names in a fashion very similar to the multiple traditional trade marks. Therefore, when a consumer makes a guess at an address businessname. biz and finds it to be a site unrelated to her target, she will simply move on and try businessname.pro and so on. Do you agree with this line of thinking?

(b) The institutional framework for the domain name system

To properly understand the Internet domain name system, it is important to consider the institutional structures which govern the domain name system and to understand the roles played by these organisations. Prior to 1999 the gTLDs were administered by a single registry and a single registrar, as were each of the nTLDs. For the gTLDs, this agency was called InterNIC. InterNIC was a cooperative of the National Science Foundation (NSF), AT&T, which bore responsibility for database integrity, and Network Solutions Incorporated (NSI). NSI was responsible for domain name registration services. The monopoly on registration was held by NSI until September 2000. In its place, a shared registry system (SRS) was developed and phased in, and officially started in April 1999. Until 2000, NSI also administered all of the gTLDs except .mil which was regulated by the US Department of Defence.

Until recently, the Internet Assigned Numbers Authority (IANA) was the central coordinator for the assignment of unique parameter values, that is, the domain names and their IP addresses. In 1998, the Internet Corporation for Assigned Names and Numbers (ICANN), a non-profit organisation, was formed for the purpose of taking over the domain name assignment function as well as the IP address allocation function and the general management of the domain name system, including root and name server management. In effect, ICANN took over many of the functions of InterNIC. It established the SRS system and controlled all Internet registry and registrar functions.

In Australia, Internet Names Australia, a division of Melbourne IT, which was handling domain name registration in the .com.au space, became one of five testbed registrars in 1999. INA then changed its name to Internet Names World Wide (INWW)

---

11   See <http://www.wired.com/news/business/0,1367,47227,00.html> 10 September 2001.

to reflect its new ability to register names in the .com, .net and .org domain name spaces. With the introduction of the seven new gTLDs in 2000, INWW, with a joint venture partner, Neustar, now has the exclusive right to operate the registry for the .biz domain name. Since 1999, the organisation .au Domain Administration Ltd (auDA) has been the policy authority and industry self-regulatory body for the .au domain space. Its functions include developing and implementing domain name policy, licensing registry operators, accrediting and licensing registrars such as Melbourne IT.

There is no directory of business addresses on the Internet. Therefore, businesses will often attempt to include their business name within their domain name. This allows potential customers to guess their address or use a search engine to find their website. The goal in this process is to register a domain name that will be as distinctive as the address or phone number used by the business, and which clearly identifies the business. As such, over time, domain names will increasingly come to represent a business in the course of its trade. However, we see here the uneasy combination of two normally distinct mechanisms. An address, although distinctive, does not identify a business and a business name will generally not provide enough detail to locate a business in the real world. Therefore, a problem arises in determining the point at which the domain name transcends its function as a mere address to become an identifying feature of the business. These issues go to the heart of the current trade mark controversies pertaining to domain names.

Real-world trade mark law contains two crucial limitations which in turn operate as the pillars of the legal regime: domesticity and specificity. Nothing in trade mark law prevents a person from registering an already registered sign in respect of different goods or services. In Australia, there are over 40 categories of goods and services within which a trade mark can be registered and, therefore, technically, there could be more than 40 marks that are similar but relate to different goods or services. Second, trade mark law is territorial and, as such, will only operate within the jurisdiction of the enacting state. The Internet respects neither of these limitations and herein lies the problem.

The Internet is global and, by design, no two domain names can be identical. Regardless of how distinct the fields of trade, and of how geographically separate the jurisdictions, no two websites can use the same domain name. Therefore there can only be one prince.com, one kodak.com, and so on. But there may be two or more businesses in the same country or in different countries equally entitled to the use of a name. Prince.com is one domain name that was the subject of a dispute between Prince plc in the United Kingdom and Prince Sportswear Inc in the USA. Prince plc registered the domain name first and was challenged by Prince Sportswear Inc.[12] This case, where both parties had real world rights attached to the disputed domain name, is discussed further in the extract below. This type of dispute might be viewed as 'domain name envy', whereby the cause of the grievance is the fact that the complainant did not register the domain name first.

Also, many cases have arisen when a registered domain name is the same as or very similar to the trading name or registered trade mark of a well-known company. These

---

12   *Prince plc v Prince Sportswear Group Inc* [1998] FSR 21.

domains are frequently offered to the owner of the registered trade mark or trading company in return for a high payment, or are used to draw people to the unrelated site. In this latter instance, there is not necessarily an attempt to confuse; rather, there is simply a desire to draw on the magnetism that attaches to the mark. This is called 'domain name hijacking' or more commonly 'cybersquatting'.

Finally, there are cases where the owners of well-known or famous marks have aggressively pursued policies to prevent others from using any rendition of a name that includes or alludes to their registered trade mark. These cases are sometimes labelled 'reverse domain name hijacking'.

Throughout this chapter, it is important to be aware of the distinction between a trade mark and a domain name. A domain name is an indicator of the address that locates a computer on the Internet. However, it does not necessarily function as a trade mark. Trade marks are generally viewed as indicia of source or origin, and must be used in the consumer marketplace to signify the source of goods or services. A trade mark cannot exist in a vacuum; it is a construct of relationship. A registered trade mark can be removed from the register for non-use and a particular sign will not function as a trade mark if it is used purely as an address of a particular trader. Sadly, there has been an unfortunate tendency in disputes to treat the two as synonymous, without the proper thought and discussion due.

Three main legal weapons have been used in these battles: the law of passing off, unfair competition laws, and trade mark law. Plaintiffs will often launch an action under as many heads as possible in order to maximise their chances of success.

 ## NOTES AND QUESTIONS

1   Write down a list of all the organisations and their acronyms that make up the institutional matrix at the heart of the domain name system.
2   What are the different types of use or misuse of domain names that have occurred thus far?

(c) The domain name system, passing off, and the *Trade Practices Act*

Although we commonly understand 'trade mark' to signify the rights in respect of a sign registered under the *Trade Marks Act 1995* (Cth), it can also signify common law rights attached to a sign. These rights can be protected irrespective of any registration through the tort of passing off. Passing off is a common law action available where a person or business is entitled to use a particular sign to the exclusion, at least, of the opposing parties in that action. By contrast, rights under the *Trade Marks Act* are granted to the registered owner of a mark upon registration and exist by virtue of the Act.

Alternatively, the rights to commercial independence and to operate free from any unintended commercial associations also come within the scope of the Australian *Trade Practices Act 1974* (Cth) and other unfair competition legislation. Section 52 of the

Trade Practices Act prohibits misleading or deceptive conduct or conduct that is likely to mislead or deceive in the course of trade. From the consumers' perspective, passing off and misleading and deceptive conduct are often almost indistinguishable.

In a non-Internet case, the Supreme Court of NSW, in *Fletcher Challenge Ltd v Fletcher Challenge Pty Ltd*[13] examined whether the law of passing off could apply to circumstances where the defendants claimed that there had not been any misrepresentation. It was held by Powell J that the tort of passing off could cover a defendant's false suggestions that its business was connected with the plaintiff's. It was further held that such a false suggestion would be capable of damaging the plaintiff's goodwill. Thus, if this case is taken to represent the current state of the law, the mere registration of a company name without more is enough to satisfy the requirements of the tort of passing off. Translating this to the Internet, the mere registration of a domain name which happens to be the trade mark of another might well be enough to satisfy the tort of passing off.

In *Capital Webworks Pty Ltd v Adultshop.com Ltd*,[14] Nicholson J dealt with the domain name adultshop.com.au. The applicant had previously been the registered holder of the domain name but due to an error, allowed the registration to lapse. The respondent then registered the domain name. The applicant's argument was based on the notion that there is goodwill vested in the domain name from its previous use of the mark. Nicholson J held that, regardless of the applicant's previous use of the domain name as a business website, there could be no goodwill vested in the domain name itself. In support of this, he found that the domain name, in itself, does not seek to refer to the business name but merely acts as an address. Goodwill can only subsist in a business name or trade mark which might then subsequently be incorporated into a domain name. Therefore, it is the business name or trade mark that generates goodwill, not the domain name. The fact that a domain name includes a business name does not necessarily mean that goodwill is vested in the domain name also.

In the *Adultshop* case, the applicant argued that the registration and use of the domain name by the defendant could be considered misleading and deceptive under s 52 of the *Trade Practices Act 1974* (Cth), as the applicant had previously used the domain name. The court held that the respondent had validly registered and used a domain name identical to its business name, and as such, it had made no misleading or deceptive representation to the public. This case should be contrasted with the case of *CSR Limited v Resource Capital Australia Pty Ltd*.[15] In this case, the court found that the defendant registered a few business names for the sole purpose of obtaining the relevant Internet domain names. The court held that the act of obtaining registration of the domain names constituted conduct that was misleading and deceptive or was likely to mislead and deceive persons and breached s 52 of the *Trade Practices Act 1974* (Cth). Alternatively, the conduct constituted a representation that the plaintiff and the defendant's company were affiliated.

The registration and use of a domain name similar to a trade mark owned by another may also raise issues related to confidential information. In the UK case of

---

13   [1981] NSWLR 196.
14   [2000] FCA 492.
15   [2003] FCA 279 (4 April 2003).

Global Projects Management Ltd v Citigroup Inc,[16] the plaintiff had registered a domain name incorporating the trade mark of the defendant. Even though the plaintiff was not actively attempting to misrepresent, as a result of owning the registration in the domain name, the plaintiff was in the position of receiving emails, some confidential and sensitive, addressed to the defendant but misdirected to the plaintiff as a result of the senders' mistaken beliefs about the defendant's correct domain name. In a relevant 12 month period, there were 4820 non-spam emails that reached the plaintiff and some of these emails contained confidential information concerning large transactions. Accordingly, the court held that the domain name in the hands of the plaintiff had caused or may cause loss to the defendant. On the facts, the court found that passing off was made out.

The use of unfair competition law and passing off as alternatives to trade mark law is also common practice in New Zealand. In the case of *New Zealand Post Ltd v Leng,*[17] the defendant maintained a predominantly pornographic website at the domain name nzpost.com. The plaintiff, NZ Post Ltd, is New Zealand's dominant postal provider and although it did not hold a registered trade mark, it held a common law trade mark and was entitled to protect its goodwill. Justice Williams found that the defendant had made a misrepresentation in the course of trade to prospective customers of the New Zealand postal service through operating the site at nzpost.com. The confusion which resulted, according to Williams J, was sufficient to demonstrate both passing off and misleading and deceptive conduct under the *Fair Trading Act 1986* (NZ).

 ## NOTES AND QUESTIONS

1 The decision in *Fletcher Challenge* is a dubious result. If mere registration of a business name is taken to satisfy the tort of passing off, there are likely to be innumerable unwitting tortfeasors registering business names every day. Can you suggest an amendment to this ruling which might render it less problematic? In particular examine the decisions of the WIPO dispute resolution bodies, below, and the effect of the concept of bad faith on the decision-making process.

2 Do you agree with the reasoning of Nicholson J in the *Adultshop* case?

3 Compare the reasoning in *Fletcher Challenge*, *Adultshop*, and *New Zealand Post*. Which of these three cases provides the most coherent result? Based on the brief discussion above, outline the strengths and weaknesses of each outcome.

The One in a Million litigation: England and Wales High Court

In the United Kingdom, a landmark domain name dispute, in which there were multiple plaintiffs, is *Marks & Spencer plc v One in a Million Ltd.*[18] This case, in the England and Wales High Court, dealt with trade mark law and the law of passing off.

---

16 [2005] EWHC 2663 (Ch).
17 [1999] 3 NZLR 219.
18 (1997) 42 IPR 309 also available at <http://www.bailii.org/cgi-bailii/disp.pl/ew/cases/EWHC/Patents/1997/357.html?query=%7e+fsr> 10 May 2001.

The *One in a Million* case involved a defendant who had registered a number of high-profile and commercially valuable domain names including marksandspencer.com, burger-king.com and buckinghampalace.org. The defendant admitted that his intention was not to use the domain names to host content, but to offer them up for sale. Indeed, the defendant had gone so far as to write to each of the plaintiffs offering to sell the relevant domain name for a substantial sum with a threat of sale to a third party if the offer was refused. As such, the case represents a prime example of 'cybersquatting' as described above.

Marks & Spencer plc, Ladbrokes plc, J Sainsbury plc, Virgin Enterprises Ltd, British Telecommunications plc, Telecom Securior Cellular Radio Ltd v One in a Million and Others

[1997] EWHC Patents 357 (28 November 1997)

High Court of Justice, Chancery Division, United Kingdom

Available at <http://www.bailii.org/ew/cases/EWHC/Patents/1997/357.html> 17 August 2006

Jonathon Sumption QC, sitting as a Deputy High Court Judge:

15 The Plaintiffs allege passing off and infringement of their trade marks. It is convenient to deal first with the case of Marks & Spencer.

16 The essence of the tort of passing off is a misrepresentation to the public (whether or not intentional) liable to lead them to believe that the goods and services offered by the representor are those of the Plaintiff. However, the tort is also committed by those who put or authorise someone to put an 'instrument of deception' into the hands of others. 'No man is permitted to use any mark, sign or symbol, device or other name whereby, without making a direct false representation himself to a purchaser who purchases from him, he enables such a purchaser to tell a lie or to make a false representation to somebody else who is the ultimate customer': *Singer v Loog* (1880) 18 Ch D 395 at 412, cited with approval by Lord Macnaughten in *Camel Hair Belting* [1896] AC 199 at 215–16.

17 In *Direct Line Group Limited v Direct Line Estate Agency* [1997] FSR 374 Laddie J granted an interlocutory injunction to the financial services group Direct Line against two individuals who had arranged the incorporation of a large number of companies under names comprising the names or trade marks of well-known enterprises, including three companies comprising the word 'Direct Line'. These facts he regarded as 'only reasonably consistent with an intention on their part to hitch themselves to other companies' reputations and make an illicit profit by doing so'. It was not clear whether the three companies in question had actually traded, and unnecessary for the judge to decide the point at the stage of granting interlocutory relief.

18 *Glaxo plc v Glaxowellcome Limited* [1996] FSR 388 was a rather similar case which came before Lightman J, also upon an application for an interlocutory injunction. The relevant

defendant was a company registration agent who registered the name Glaxowellcome Limited shortly after the announcement of Glaxo plc's intention to make a take-over bid for Wellcome and if it succeeded to rename itself Glaxo-Wellcome plc. The defendant subsequently offered to sell the company to Glaxo plc for an exorbitant price. In this case it was clear that the company had not traded, but the Judge considered it likely that it would. He appears to have formed this view on the basis that it was implicit in the demand for a high price for the company and that the Defendant was threatening that if it was not paid he would use or transfer the company to someone else who would use it to injure Glaxo's goodwill. The Judge granted a mandatory interlocutory injunction requiring the name of the company to be changed. In practice this amounted to final relief, because the object was to enable Glaxo themselves to change their name to Glaxo-Wellcome, thereby making a restoration of the original position virtually impossible. Lightman J said that 'the court will not countenance any such pre-emptive strike of registering companies with names where others have the goodwill in those names and the registering party demands a price for changing the names'.

19 The mere creation of an 'instrument of deception', without either using it for deception or putting it into the hands of someone else to do so, is not passing off. There is no such tort as going equipped for passing off. It follows that the mere registration of a deceptive company name or a deceptive Internet domain name is not passing off. In both of these cases the court granted what amounted to a *quia timet* injunction to restrain a threatened rather than an actual tort. In both cases, the injunctions were interlocutory rather than final, and the threat is no doubt easier to establish in that context. But even a final injunction does not require proof that damage will certainly occur. It is enough that what is going on is calculated to infringe the Plaintiff's rights in future.

20 In the case of Marks & Spencer, it is in my judgment beyond dispute that what is going on is calculated to infringe the Plaintiff's rights in future. The name *marksandspencer* could not have been chosen for any other reason than that it was associated with the well-known retailing group. There is only one possible reason why anyone who was not part of the Marks & Spencer plc group should wish to use such a domain address, and that is to pass himself off as part of that group or his products off as theirs. Where the value of a name consists solely in its resemblance to the name or trade mark of another enterprise, the Court will normally assume that the public is likely to be deceived, for why else would the Defendants choose it? In the present case, the assumption is plainly justified. As a matter of common sense, these names were registered and are available for sale for eventual use. Someone seeking or coming upon a web site called *http://marksandspencer.co.uk* would naturally assume that it was that of the Plaintiffs.

21 The only point made by the Defendants which is worthy of any attention is that there are uses to which they can put the domain name which would not involve passing off by them or any one else, namely (i) the sale of the domain name to Marks & Spencer themselves, and (ii) its simple retention with a view to blocking the use of the same name by Marks & Spencer in order to induce them to pay. I would accept that neither of these activities in themselves constitutes passing off. But that is not the point. The point is that the names are only saleable to Marks & Spencer and blocking their use by Marks & Spencer is only a useful negotiating tactic on the footing that they are names

which it is dangerous for Marks & Spencer to allow to remain out of their control. The danger arises from the risk of deception which their existence necessarily presents. The allegation that this was the Defendants' object in this case is fairly made, supported by overwhelming evidence, and is left wholly unanswered by the Defendants' affidavits. Any person who deliberately registers a domain name on account of its similarity to the name, brand name or trade mark of an unconnected commercial organisation must expect to find himself on the receiving end of an injunction to restrain the threat of passing off, and the injunction will be in terms which will make the name commercially useless to the dealer.

 ## NOTES AND QUESTIONS

1 Sumption QC, therefore, ruled that the tort had not itself been made out; however, there was sufficient threat of tortious injury in the future to warrant the granting of the injunction. In paragraph 20, he wrote: 'Someone seeking or coming upon a website called *http://marksandspencer.co.uk* would naturally assume that it was that of the Plaintiffs.' Do you think this is true? Would it be natural that such an assumption would be made by a user, regardless of the actual content of the site? What does this reveal about Sumption QC's view of the average Internet user?

2 The following extract is from the England and Wales Court of Appeal regarding the same matter. The Court of Appeal went further than Sumption QC in respect of the claim for passing off, holding that the tort itself had been sufficiently made out.

The One in a Million litigation: England and Wales Court of Appeal

---

British Telecommunications plc; Virgin Enterprises Ltd; J Sainsbury plc; Marks & Spencer plc and Ladbroke Group plc v One in a Million Ltd and Others

[1998] EWCA Civ 1272 (23 July 1998)

Available at <http://www.bailii.org/ew/cases/EWCA/Civ/1998/1272.html> 17 August 2006

Lord Justice Aldous:

50 In my view there can be discerned from the cases a jurisdiction to grant injunctive relief where a defendant is equipped with or is intending to equip another with an instrument of fraud. Whether any name is an instrument of fraud will depend upon all the circumstances. A name which will, by reason of its similarity to the name of another, inherently lead to passing off is such an instrument. If it would not inherently lead to passing off, it does not follow that it is not an instrument of fraud. The court

should consider the similarity of the names, the intention of the defendant, the type of trade, and all the surrounding circumstances. If it be the intention of the defendant to appropriate the goodwill of another or enable others to do so, I can see no reason why the court should not infer that it will happen, even if there is a possibility that such an appropriation would not take place. If, taking all the circumstances into account the court should conclude that the name was produced to enable passing off, is adapted to be used for passing off and, if used, is likely to be fraudulently used, an injunction will be appropriate.

51 It follows that a court will intervene by way of injunction in passing off cases in three types of case. First, where there is passing off established or it is threatened. Second, where the defendant is a joint tortfeasor with another in passing off either actual or threatened. Third, where the defendant has equipped himself with or intends to equip another with an instrument of fraud. This third type is probably mere *quia timet* action
    ...

71 It is accepted that the name Marks & Spencer denotes Marks & Spencer plc and nobody else. Thus anybody seeing or hearing the name realises that what is being referred to is the business of Marks & Spencer plc. It follows that registration by the appellants of a domain name including the name Marks & Spencer makes a false representation that they are associated or connected with Marks & Spencer plc. This can be demonstrated by considering the reaction of a person who taps into his computer the domain name marksandspencer.co.uk and presses a button to execute a 'whois' search. He will be told that the registrant is One in a Million Limited. A substantial number of persons will conclude that One in a Million Limited must be connected or associated with Marks & Spencer plc. That amounts to a false representation which constitutes passing off.

72 Mr Wilson submitted that mere registration did not amount to passing off. Further, Marks & Spencer plc had not established any damage or likelihood of damage. I cannot accept those submissions. The placing on a register of a distinctive name such as marksandspencer makes a representation to persons who consult the register that the registrant is connected or associated with the name registered and thus the owner of the goodwill in the name. Such persons would not know of One in a Million Limited and would believe that they were connected or associated with the owner of the goodwill in the domain name they had registered. Further, registration of the domain name including the words Marks & Spencer is an erosion of the exclusive goodwill in the name which damages or is likely to damage Marks & Spencer plc.

73 Mr Wilson also submitted that it was not right to conclude that there was any threat by the appellants to use or dispose of any domain name including the words Marks & Spencer. He submitted that the appellants, Mr Conway and Mr Nicholson, were two rather silly young men who hoped to make money from the likes of the respondents by selling domain names to them for as much as they could get. They may be silly, but their letters and activities make it clear that they intended to do more than just retain the names. Their purpose was to threaten use and disposal sometimes explicitly and on other occasions implicitly. The judge was right to grant *quia timet* relief to prevent the threat becoming reality.

74 I also believe that domain names comprising the name Marks & Spencer are instruments of fraud. Any realistic use of them as domain names would result in passing off and there was ample evidence to justify the injunctive relief granted by the judge to prevent them being used for a fraudulent purpose and to prevent them being transferred to others.

75 The other cases are slightly different. Mr Wilson pointed to the fact that there are people called Sainsbury and Ladbroke and companies, other than Virgin Enterprises Ltd, who have as part of their name the word Virgin and also people or firms whose initials would be BT. He went on to submit that it followed that the domain names which the appellants had registered were not inherently deceptive. They were not instruments of fraud. Further there had been no passing off and none was threatened and a transfer to a third party would not result in the appellants becoming joint tortfeasors in any passing off carried out by the person to whom the registrations were transferred. Thus, he submitted, there was no foundation for the injunctive relief in the actions brought by four of the respondents.

76 I believe that, for the same reasons I have expressed in relation to the Marks & Spencer plc action, passing off and threatened passing off has been demonstrated. The judge was right to conclude (page 273):

> The history of the defendants' activities shows a deliberate practice followed over a substantial period of time of registering domain names which are chosen to resemble the names and marks of other people and are plainly intended to deceive. The threat of passing off and trade mark infringement, and the likelihood of confusion arising from the infringement of the mark are made out beyond argument in this case, even if it is possible to imagine other cases in which the issue would be more nicely balanced.

77 I also believe that the names registered by the appellants were instruments of fraud and that injunctive relief was appropriate upon this basis as well. The trade names were well-known 'household names' denoting in ordinary usage the respective respondent. The appellants registered them without any distinguishing word because of the goodwill attaching to those names. It was the value of that goodwill, not the fact that they could perhaps be used in some way by a third party without deception, which caused them to register the names. The motive of the appellants was to use that goodwill and threaten to sell it to another who might use it for passing-off to obtain money from the respondents. The value of the names lay in the threat that they would be used in a fraudulent way. The registrations were made with the purpose of appropriating the respondents' property, their goodwill, and with an intention of threatening dishonest use by them or another. The registrations were instruments of fraud and injunctive relief was appropriate just as much as it was in those cases where persons registered company names for a similar purpose.

 ## NOTES AND QUESTIONS

1 This judgment has been criticised for extending the bounds of the tort of passing off too far[19] although it is still good law today. Do you agree with this? Critically analyse the reasoning of the two courts. Which do you prefer, and why?

---

19   Thorne and Bennett, 'Domain Names—Internet Warehousing: Has Protection of Well-Known Names on the Internet Gone too Far?' [1998] EIPR 468.

2 Explain all of the requisite elements in proving the tort of passing off. Do you think that the remedies attached to passing off are suitable in the Internet context? Give reasons for your answer and consider the judgment above as you do so.

(d) The domain name system and trade mark infringement

Andrew Murray, 'Internet Domain Names: The Trade Mark Challenge'

(1998) 6 (3) *International Journal of Law and Information Technology* 285

3. Trade marks in virtual reality

3.1. PROBLEMS WITH THE GLOBAL DOMAIN NAME SYSTEM (DNS)

… The commercialization of the Internet has created a new marketplace, a market within which companies, quite rightly, wish to exploit their trade marks. The problem is that shared interests in the same, or similar, trade marks may peacefully coexist in actual reality but not in the virtual marketplace. The major issue of the current domain name system is the paucity of second-level domain names. Whereas it is quite possible for two separate companies to use the trade mark Penguin for different goods, there is only one domain name 'penguin.com'. Although the proprietors of the above trade marks have not, to the author's knowledge, engaged in a dispute about who has the right to use the domain name penguin.com, several other parties who share trade marks, and who had peacefully coexisted in the actual world have engaged in high-profile domain name disputes.

3.2. SECOND-LEVEL DOMAINS AND TRADE MARK DISPUTES: A TRIO OF CASES

3.2.1. PITMAN TRAINING LTD v NOMINET UK

This dispute centred around the right to use the domain name 'pitman.co.uk', and the competing interests of two parties, Pitman Training Ltd and Pearson Professional Ltd. Both the training company and the publishing company had at one time been owned by a single company, but in 1985 they had demerged and Pearson Professional had bought the publishing business. As part of the demerger, Pitman Training Ltd agreed not to use the name Pitman, except in relation to their core business. The problem arose when the two companies, who had coexisted peacefully in the actual world for eleven years, tried to register their presence on the Internet. On the 15th of February 1996, Pearson registered the domain name 'pitman.co.uk', but took no action to develop their web presence. On the 15th of March 1996, Pitman Training Ltd also registered the domain name 'pitman.co.uk' with Nominet UK. They went on to establish a web presence in July 1996. Pearson had no knowledge of the Pitman Training web site until December 1996, but immediately upon discovering the Pitman Training web site they contacted both Pitman Training and Nominet UK, demanding that the right to use the pitman.co.uk domain name be reassigned to them. On the 4th of April 1997 Nominet, following threats of legal action from Pearson's lawyers, agreed to reassign the pitman.co.uk domain to Pearson, a transfer effected on the 7th of April. On the 9th of April, Pitman issued a writ against Pearson and Nominet requiring the immediate reinstatement of their rights to the pitman.co.uk domain. The problem for the judge was each party was entitled to make use of the Pitman trade name in their respective fields. Trade marks, registered or unregistered, benefit from specificity. Only where the marks are to be used in the same, or similar, field of business and there is a likelihood of confusion, will a potential breach of trade mark occur. In virtual reality, though, there is no specificity of domain names. There can be only one 'pitman.co.uk', and currently there is no method of differentiating between Pitman Training and Pitman Publishing. It was this lack of specificity which led to the dispute before the court.

The decision of the court was that the plaintiffs had no viable or reasonably arguable cause of action against the second defendant (Pearson) and the interim injunction was lifted, allowing Nominet to ratify the transfer of registration to Pearson. The impact of this case, for the present discussion, is twofold. First, the High Court was willing to uphold the policy of Nominet that registration of second-level domain names should be on a 'first come first served' basis. Secondly, and more importantly for present purposes, the fact the case came about at all is of significance. The parties to the action were closely linked. It had only been eleven years since the trade marks had been in the control of a single owner. They had peacefully traded alongside each other in accordance with their contractual undertakings. This was possible because each knew the other's business, and each knew its customer base. There was minimal risk of confusion on the part of this customer base because each operated in a separate market. The problem of a shared trade name only arose when each tried to gain entry to a single, global, market: the virtual market.

3.2.2. ROADRUNNER COMPUTER SYSTEMS INC v NETWORK SOLUTIONS INC

Roadrunner Computer Systems Inc ('Roadrunner') is an Internet access provider based in Santa Fe, New Mexico. In May 1994 they registered the domain name roadrunner.com in relation to their business. We are informed by Brunel & Laing that Roadrunner did not have a registered trade mark in its business name, but that thirty-eight other companies did have such a registration, including Warner Brothers. On the 13th of December 1995 Network Solutions Inc (NSI) informed Roadrunner that its right to use the roadrunner.com domain name had been challenged (by Warner Brothers) and that its registration would be put on hold after 30 days. NSI, like Nominet, operates a 'first come first served' policy for domain name allocation, but if a second party is able to demonstrate to the satisfaction of NSI that they have a prior registered trade mark in that name the original registration will be removed.

Roadrunner entered into negotiations with Warner Brothers; the Internet provider hoped to be able to reach agreement where it would be entitled to continue to use roadrunner.com, while Warner Brothers would use road-runner.com. According to Roadrunner, NSI proved to be the major protagonist in the dispute. In an attempt to strengthen their position against NSI, Roadrunner took out a Tunisian trade mark, but NSI refused to recognize it, saying it was 'out of time'. Roadrunner were left with no option but to litigate, and on the 26th of

March 1996 it filed an action with the District Court for the Eastern District of Virginia. The litigation was easily disposed of. Warner Brothers refused to state they were suffering legal harm, and as a result NSI were able to argue, successfully, that Roadrunner were no longer in danger of losing their domain name. The court agreed with this, said NSI no longer needed to invoke its dispute policy, and dismissed the case as moot.

Like the *Pitman* case, and the *Prince* case discussed below, the major impact of the *Roadrunner* case is not what it decided, but the issues it raised. Although Roadrunner did not have a registered trade mark, the registration of roadrunner.com could equally have been effected by any one of thirty-eight companies who have a registered federal or state trade mark. Each company is equally entitled to make use of their trade mark and, due to the concept of specificity of trade marks, in actual reality they all trade alongside one another. The problem for Warner Brothers was that when they entered the virtual marketplace, they found only one company was in a position to trade as roadrunner.com. This is a source of dispute which is certain to grow as commercialization of the Internet increases apace.

3.2.3. PRINCE PLC v PRINCE SPORTSWEAR GROUP INC

Prince plc is a UK-registered information technology company who specialize in desktop migration and IT training. Prince plc as a leading IT company developed their web presence at an early stage, and had since February 1995 been using the domain name 'prince.com'. Prince Sportswear is a US-registered sporting goods company who own the registered trade mark 'Prince' in relation to tennis and squash racquets and other items of sportswear. Prince Sportswear have registered trade marks with both the US and UK Patents Offices, and elsewhere.

On the 16th of January 1997 attorneys representing Prince Sportswear sent a letter to Prince plc indicating that in their opinion Prince plc's use of the prince.com domain name constituted infringement and dilution of their client's registered trade marks under the *Lanham Act*. In accordance with their dispute resolution policy NSI wrote to Prince plc on the 25th of February 1997. They indicated that unless Prince plc exhibited a trade mark registration of their own or they produced evidence they had 'filed a suit in any court of competent jurisdiction', their domain name registration would be suspended. Unable to exhibit the former, Prince plc were forced to follow the latter route. On the 28th of April they filed a suit in the High Court seeking declaration that their use of the prince.com domain name did not infringe Prince Sportswear's UK registered trade mark and an injunction to prevent Prince Sportswear from threatening further proceedings in relation to the prince.com domain name.

On the 30th of July Mr Justice Neuberger found in favour of Prince plc. The court had been asked to rule upon two distinct issues. Unfortunately, following the decision in the first issue, unwarranted threats of litigation in breach of s 21 of the *Trade Marks Act 1994*, Neuberger J felt it unnecessary to rule on the second issue, a declaration that the use of the domain name prince.com did not infringe Prince Sportswear's registered trade mark. On the question of unwarranted threats, Neuberger J found that Prince plc were entitled to protection under s 21. It had been argued by Prince Sportswear that s 21 did not apply to the case in issue as they were seeking only to protect US registered trade marks under the *Lanham Act*. The judge, though, disagreed, finding a reference to Prince Sportswear's UK registration in their initial letter to Prince plc to be proof of their intention to protect their UK trade mark. More interesting in relation to domain names was the judge's ruling on the claim of Prince Sportswear that the .com name reflects a US limited name. Neuberger J pointed out that Prince plc made use of the prince.com domain name from the UK and that Prince Sportswear were objecting to the use of the 'prince' name in a domain name 'in any country'; their objection was not limited to any individual market.

Like the *Pitman* and *Roadrunner* cases, the dispute in issue in the *Prince* case is as important as the decision of the court. In the *Prince* case both parties had carried on business in their respective fields for twelve years, relying upon specificity to distinguish themselves in the UK market. The interesting aspect of the *Prince* case, and what it adds to the evolving jurisprudence of Internet law, is its international dimension. Although the case came before an English court, and was decided on provisions of the UK *Trade Marks Act*, the issue for Prince Sportswear was access to the US marketplace. This was made clear by the initial letter to Prince plc which referred to their US registered trade marks, and sought to invoke the (American) *Lanham Act*. Although the existence of the prince.co.uk domain would have been a problem for Prince Sportswear's UK operation, it was the prince.com domain which they sought. The reason is the global nature of the .com domain, and its special place in relation to the US market. Prince Sportswear were forced into taking action because there was only one recognized domain name which suited their company, the prince.com domain. This issue is at the heart of the domain name/trade mark nexus. Like *Pitman*, like *Roadrunner*, the dispute in the *Prince* case arose because companies who had relied for years on specificity and domesticity of trade marks found the Internet to be the first truly global marketplace. For the first time, established businesses are finding they must compromise their interests. There can be only one registration of each trade mark, and with everyone competing for the .com registration that problem is exacerbated.

3.3. A SUMMARY OF THE 'ONE NAME ONE USER PROBLEM'

The cases discussed above, and others, indicate two difficulties for traditional trade mark law in relation to the Internet. First, trade marks are limited in their scope by both specificity and domesticity. The Internet does not respect national boundaries and, currently, has no capacity for differentiation of 'commercial' domain names. Traditional trade mark registers differentiate trade marks on the basis of the goods and/or services with which they are linked. All commercial entities, in the eyes of the Internet, are homogeneous. This creates a clash of cultures. Traditional trade mark lawyers used to dealing with the 'one mark, many owners' doctrine fail to grasp that their clients may 'lose' their cyberspace trade mark to another company. The shared rights of many can only be enjoyed by one, all too commonly the financially strongest. The Internet, more than any other technology, may concentrate intellectual property rights in the hands of a few corporations, and at a minimal cost of only $80 for worldwide protection.

The second effect is the 'globalization' of trade marks. Whereas traditionally each nation maintains its own trade mark register, allowing for at least 160 discrete national registers plus the community trade mark register in Alicante, there is currently one registry for the .com domain. Companies are finding their trademarks have been appropriated by others who operate without their jurisdiction. For these companies there is the alternative of national top-level domains (nTLDs) such as co.uk, which are maintained at a domestic level.

These domains, though, are perceived, correctly or incorrectly, as inferior to the .com domain. This is an issue which urgently requires to be addressed; nTLDs must not be seen to be inferior to gTLDs. It is this current misperception which has led to many disputes over second-level domains between parties who share an entitlement to use that name.

[Footnotes omitted]

 # NOTES AND QUESTIONS

1   In March 2001 at the Sixth Session of the WIPO Standing Committee on the Law
     of Trademarks, Industrial Designs and Geographical Indications in Geneva, *The
     Proposed Joint Recommendation Concerning the Protection of Marks, and Other
     Industrial Property Rights in Signs, on the Internet* was adopted. The Preamble
     to the document, available at <http://www.wipo.int/sct/en/documents/session_6/
     doc/sct6_7p.doc> 11 September 2001, states:

     > The present provisions are intended to be applied in the context of determining
     > whether, under the applicable law of a member state, use of a sign on the
     > Internet has contributed to the acquisition, maintenance or infringement of
     > a mark or other industrial property right in the sign, or whether such use
     > constitutes an act of unfair competition, and in the context of determining
     > remedies.

     > The WIPO document is yet to find regular use in national courts. Do you think
     > that the adoption of such international instruments is useful in the protection of
     > trade marks on the Internet? Would an international regime be more appropriate
     > to solving the problem than trade mark law?

2   Refer to the Pitman problem mentioned by Murray. Would a simple solution be
     for the two companies to share the same domain name, with links on the 'home'
     page linking users to the respective correct websites?

In Australia, there simply has not been as much litigation relating to trade marks and the Internet as in other common law jurisdictions, particularly the USA and the United Kingdom. The legislative frameworks in Australia and the United Kingdom are very similar. Therefore, the structure of the following sections will seek to combine the legislative provisions of the Australian *Trade Marks Act 1995* with some judicial consideration of general principles from the United Kingdom. There are some differences between the two Acts; however, the intention here is to provide a landscape of operative principles and attendant controversies. Singapore's trade mark provisions on infringement, as already mentioned, are also very similar.

As outlined in the introductory sections above, ss 120(1), (2), and (3), of the Australian *Trade Marks Act 1995* outline the conduct constituting infringement. Conveniently, in the United Kingdom the *Trade Marks Act 1994* includes its infringement provisions in subsections (1), (2), and (3) of s 10 and the Singaporean *Trade Marks Act 1998* provides for infringement in ss 27(1), (2) and (3). The content of these three subsections is substantially similar in the three jurisdictions and this facilitates the following parallel examination.

To briefly recap, subsection (1) provides for a very limited realm of infringement bounded by the 'goods or services in respect of which the trade mark is registered'. That is, unauthorised use of a registered mark in the same realm of trade as a registered mark is prohibited. Subsection (2) broadens the realm of infringement to include 'closely related' areas or areas of the same description, but adds the requirement that consumers must be confused or deceived. Lastly, subsection (3) expands the realm considerably to include goods or services that are not of the same description as or closely related to the original mark. However, there are two provisos here. Firstly, in Australia and Singapore, the mark must be 'well known' within the jurisdiction (in the United Kingdom, it must hold a 'reputation') and the unauthorised use must be likely to be taken as indicating a connection between the registered and unauthorised mark. Second, in Australia the use is likely to adversely affect the interests of the registered owner as a consequence of the first proviso; in Singapore, the use is likely to damage the interests of the owner; in Britain the mark must 'take unfair advantage of' or 'be detrimental to' the distinctive character or repute of the mark. For present purposes these differences in semantics will be ignored.

Therefore, broadly speaking, to establish infringement on the Internet, a trade mark owner must show that the trade mark is incorporated into the domain name, that the mark is being used in the course of trade and in relation to the same or similar goods or services as the registered mark, or for well-known marks, in unrelated goods or services, and that the domain name is being used to indicate origin in the goods and services. Whether the registration and posting of a domain name, in and of itself, amounts to use in the course of trade is a contentious issue. This issue was discussed directly in the *One in a Million* case which is extracted below.

Subsection (1)

For an infringement to be established under subsection (1), the domain name must be substantially identical or deceptively similar to the registered trade mark and must be used in relation to goods or services in respect of which the trade mark is registered. Although this may seem an onerous requirement, when you consider the breadth of categories for trade mark registration, the task of placing a domain in a different conceptual category from a registered trade mark is actually quite a simple task. The Internet muddies the waters, however. *Avnet Inc v Isoact Limited (Avnet)*[20] is a typical case of domain name envy and one of the earliest cases on domain names in the United Kingdom.

Avnet Inc is an American company that sells goods by catalogue. In so doing they carry advertisements for different manufacturers and hold the registered trade mark 'Avnet' in the United Kingdom in class 35 for advertising and promotional services. Isoact Limited is an Internet Service Provider with a particular focus on aviation and in the course of their business use the words 'Aviation Network' and 'Avnet'. Isoact Limited registered the domain name avnet.co.uk and allowed customers to display their own advertisements on their site.

---

20   [1998] FSR 16.

Avnet argued that Isoact infringed their registered trade mark by using the word 'avnet' in their domain name. Under s 10(1), they argued, the sign used by Isoact was identical to their registered mark and used in connection with identical goods and services. Therefore, looking to the specification of the goods and services, their registered trade mark had been infringed.

Avnet Incorporated v Isoact Limited

[1998] FSR 16

High Court of Justice, Chancery Division, United Kingdom, 28 July 1997

Jacob J:

[17] ... This is an application under Order 14 for summary judgment in a trade mark case. The plaintiffs put their case solely under section 10(1) of the *Trade Marks Act 1994* (identical marks and services). The plaintiffs' business consists of selling goods by catalogue: an actual, physical catalogue. They also have a Web page. The registered trade mark is the word 'Avnet' registered in class 35 under the following specification of goods:

> Advertising and promotional services; rental and leasing of advertising apparatus, hoardings, displays, screens and billboards; rental and leasing of electronic and computer-controlled advertising apparatus, displays, boards and screens; all included in class 35.

Argument has centred on the first part of the specification: 'Advertising and promotional services', which it is accepted must all 'be included in class 35'. I will come back to that second qualification in a moment. The defendants have a quite different business from that of the plaintiffs and it is not suggested that they are commercially in conflict. They are what is known as an Internet Service Provider (ISP). The particular interest of the defendants is in relation to aviation. The name which they use is Aviation Network, and they also use Avnet. They have a web site address: www.avnet.co.uk. To their customers they provide a service which consists, **[18]** among other things, of giving their customers an e-mail address and the customer's own web page. The promotional advertisement they put out themselves on the Internet says as follows (I concentrate on the two passages relied upon by the plaintiffs):

> You get your own Web space to publicise yourself, your ideas and your products.

Later on:

> Buy and sell your products and services.

The other things mentioned are important, however. The defendants say that you should subscribe to their service, you can ask the experts for solutions and opinions on any subject, you can get immediate answers to tough, technical questions, you can participate in the shaping and cutting edge of communications technology, and you get access to worldwide sources of information, including weather and other scientific research. Any other ISP will give you much the same sort of thing. Essentially, the plaintiffs sell technical goods via a physical catalogue and a web page, and the defendants provide Internet services. The conflict arises because of the coincidence of the use of the word 'Avnet'. The conflict happens to be in this country, because both parties are either within the jurisdiction or have activities within the jurisdiction, but the conflict could equally have been between two companies in wildly different parts of the world ...

I now turn to the facts of this case in a little more detail. What the defendant is doing is providing a facility for their customers to advertise on the customer's own web page. It follows, say the plaintiffs, that the 'defendants are providing advertising and promotional services'.

Mr Moody-Stuart for the defendant says that is not so. In argument, he drew an analogy of land, saying that the defendants were really providing land upon which their customer could build whatever they wanted to build, whether it be an advertising hoarding or a building or whatever. Another **[19]** way he put it was this: that a man who provides a facility for building a library is not a librarian. It is fair to say that this case invites one to think of analogies. Yet another analogy was the activity of a telephone company which provides a particular facility enabling the customer to do telesales. Is that telephone company really providing advertising and promotional services?

The answer I think depends on how widely one construes this expression 'advertising and promotional services'. It is not an unimportant question, because definitions of services, which I think cover six of the classifications in the respect of which trade marks can be registered, are inherently less precise than specifications of goods. The latter can be, and generally are, rather precise, such as 'boots and shoes'.

In my view, specifications for services should be scrutinised carefully and they should not be given a wide construction covering a vast range of activities. They should be confined to the substance, as it were, the core of the possible meanings attributable to the rather general phrase.

Here, 'advertising and promotional services' requires one to look at the essence of what the defendant is doing. The essence of what these defendants are doing is not providing advertising and promotional services in the way that, for example, an advertising agent does. They do no more than provide a place where their customers can put up whatever they like. They are not assisting the customers to write their copy; they suggest their customers can write their own copy if they want to. But they are not in any way even requiring their customers or expecting their customers to put up advertisements. The customers can put up whatever they like. I do not think that in substance what these defendants are doing is providing 'advertising and promotional services'.

Next, on the question of infringement, one asks whether, assuming I am wrong, what the defendants are doing constitutes advertising and promotional services included in class 35?

These words 'included in class X' in a specification of goods not infrequently cause difficulty. You have to look at the specification preceding these final words to see whether what the defendant is doing is within the scope of that, and then you have to ask the extra question: are they included in class X?

It is settled, at least at first instance, that to answer that second question one has to look at the Trademark Registry practice to see whether the Registrar in practice at the time of registration included the particular service or goods within that class (see *GE Trade Mark* [1969] RPC 418 at 458). This is not always easy, especially if the kind of goods or services did not exist at the time of registration.

Here, the defendants' solicitor has made enquiries of the Trademark Registry in an informal way by telephone. The officer concerned was asked about the provision of services to the advertising industry in the context of services provided by an ISP and she apparently said that if the ISP was actually renting out advertising space on a web site to customers, then it might possibly fall within class 35, but if it was just providing the usual **[20]** services of an ISP by providing the user with access to the Internet, then it would fall in class 42. She also indicated that she thought that advertising and promotional services in class 35 were the services an advertising agency provided, subject to production of advertising material, the rental of advertising space and the rental of hoardings and billboards.

This cannot be the last word on the subject (this is Order 14), but an advertising agency does not normally just hire a billboard; it normally hires a billboard for a particular advertisement. It advises its customers on how to advertise and where to advertise and where best to advertise at a given price. None of these things the defendants do.

I do not think that what the defendants do falls within class 35, as explained by the Registrar's officer. Certainly it is not shown to be within class 35 to Order 14 standard. So I do not think there is infringement of the mark established on that ground.

It is not necessary to go on further, but since the matter was argued, I will do so. The defendants counterclaim for rectification of the register or a declaration that the mark is invalid under section 46 and section 47 of the *Trademarks Act*. It is common ground that although two grounds are relied upon, they effectively boil down to the same thing: do the plaintiffs use the mark for services covered by the registration?

It seems to me that it is well arguable that they do not. What the plaintiffs do is to run a business of selling goods by catalogue—a catalogue equivalent of a retail business. In the course of that business they therefore carry advertisements of the goods of a variety of different manufacturers. In relation to those advertisements they enter into discussions with their suppliers, because it is important in a technical catalogue that the goods are described accurately. So they enter into discussions as to the precise description of the goods to be carried in their catalogue. That in itself I do not think could amount to the provision of advertising and promotional services. It is no different from a supermarket discussing and obtaining material for a special promotion of a particular manufacturer's goods.

However, the plaintiffs do more than that. They not only enter into discussions with their suppliers, but they charge the suppliers something for carrying the advertisement in their catalogue. Again, this is much the same as a supermarket proprietor going in for a special promotion of a manufacturer's goods and asking the manufacturer to contribute to the cost of the special promotion.

Essentially, though, these plaintiffs in their retail sales by catalogue and the supermarket in its retail sale from a shop are conducting the same function. They are conducting the business of retail sales. It has not been decided whether a specification of retail sales or the like is registrable under the current Act. It was not registrable under the old Act (see *Dee's Application* [1990] RPC 159). If it is registrable, it ought not to be registrable by a side wind of 'advertising and promotional services in class 35', when the real commercial activity is the sale of goods as such. I do not decide the point, however. It is manifest that this is not a case suitable for judgment under Order 14. I therefore reject the application.

NOTES AND QUESTIONS

1   Consider a scenario where the identity of a registered mark is called into question in relation to the Internet. Trade marks can be registered in a highly stylised form, or with a particular font, or in conjunction with a logo (the Coca-Cola dynamic ribbon device for example). It has already been accepted that identical does not mean absolutely identical and that external matters should be discounted in comparing a mark with a sign. At the moment, domain names come only in plain type. Therefore, for words that are registered trade marks, it is the word or words that should be considered, rather than the way in which they are presented. A case in point from the United States is *Jews for Jesus v Brodsky*.[21] Jews for Jesus was the registered owner of the phrase 'Jews for Jesus' but with the star of David in place of the 'O'. The court found that it had rights to the phrase on the Internet without the stylised 'O' because that was the current nature of the Internet. Is it possible that our courts would take a similar view in the event that the argument was over the identity of a trade mark? Are there any other solutions? What does this indicate to you about the appropriateness of applying trade mark law to domain names?

2   How did Jacob J come to the conclusion that the use was in a different class? Do you agree? Why, or why not?

3   What is the lesson that can be drawn from the above with respect to the application of subsection (1) to Internet domain names?

4   Consider the situation where a defendant registers a domain name that is similar to the plaintiff's trade mark. However, the defendant does not operate any content under the domain name, instead, users are immediately re-directed to the valid website of the plaintiff. Hence, the defendants do not sell any goods or services under the domain name. However, the defendant does obtain a financial benefit from capturing Internet traffic through 'fishing' for Internet users looking for the plaintiff's valid web address. Would the defendant be using a sign in the course of trade in relation to goods or services which are identical to the plaintiff's trade mark? See *Tesco Stores Ltd v Elogicom* [2006] EWHC 403.

Subsection (2)

The concept of the likelihood of confusion and deception is central to this subsection. Its presence is proscribed in the definition of 'deceptively similar' and its absence operates as a defence to conduct outlined in s 120(2).

Background on the interpretation of this subsection can be found in *British Sugar plc v James Robertson & Sons*,[22] which has been followed in Australia by *Ocean Spray Cranberries v Register of Trade Marks*.[23]

---

21   *Jews for Jesus v Brodsky* (DC NJ) Civil Action No 98-274 (AJL) 6 March 1998.
22   [1996] RPC 281.
23   (2000) 47 IPR 579; [2000] FCA 177 (25 February 2000).

British Sugar has also been followed by the High Court of Singapore in *Sime Darby Edible Products Ltd v Ngo Chew Hong Edible Oil Pte Ltd*[24] and *Richemont International SA v Goldlion Enterprise (Singapore) Pte Ltd*.[25] The test for infringement in *British Sugar* consisted of three parts. First, the court considered the similarity of the registered mark in relation to the infringing sign; second, the court analysed the similarity between the respective goods and services; and third, the court determined whether there was a likelihood of confusion because of any similarity that existed. In *British Sugar* the court decided that although the marks were identical, the goods were not similar, taking into account inter alia the uses of the products, their locations in supermarkets, and the respective food sectors into which they fell. As there was no infringement at the second stage, the third part of the test was not discussed in detail.

When this concept is applied to the Internet, issues of temporality become paramount. It is arguable that, even if Internet users arrive at a domain name that they mistakenly believe attaches to a particular business, a brief examination of the site should indicate that it is not what they sought. Therefore, if the law grants a leeway for cursory examination of home pages, there will be little likelihood of confusion, as long as the website owner does not deliberately set out to deceive. This relates to initial interest confusion which is discussed below.

Avnet Incorporated v Isoact Limited

[1998] FSR 16

High Court of Justice, Chancery Division, United Kingdom, 28 July 1997

[18] ... The plaintiffs' real concern is not that the defendants are going to compete with them in any way. The defendants do not. The concern is that there will be confusion over the word 'Avnet', that search engines and the like will produce the wrong Avnet and the man looking for them might either give up or somehow get himself into some other sort of muddle. It is difficult to see how the latter could occur, because he would see immediately that he is not getting advertisements for semiconductor chips and the like and things to do with aviation instead.

It is a general problem of the Internet that it works on words, and not words in relation to goods or services. So, whenever anyone searches for that word, even if the searcher is looking for the word in one context, he will, or may, find Web pages or data in a wholly different context.

That is the reason why the plaintiffs bring these proceedings. Of course, users of the Internet also know that that is a feature of the Internet and their search may produce an altogether wrong web page or the like. This may be an important matter for the courts to take into account in considering trade mark and like problems.

---

24   [2000] 4 SLR 360.
25   [2006] 1 SLR 401.

NOTES AND QUESTIONS

1   This raises the notion of 'initial interest confusion' which has been examined in the USA on a number of occasions. In particular, the case of *Brookfield*, mentioned above in relation to meta-tags, is instructive here. In that case the court enjoined the defendant from using a trade mark within the meta tag of a site unrelated to the mark. Is this reasoning transferable to the subject of domain names? What are the problems with the simple transposition of such a reasoning to domain name disputes? Refer to the facts in *Avnet*.

2   What level of knowledge does Jacob J attribute to Internet users? How might one use this to resolve the issue of initial interest confusion and domain names?

3   In *CSR Limited v Resource Capital Australia Pty Ltd* [2003] FCA 279 (4 April 2003), already discussed above, RCA registered some domain names that were similar to the trade marks owned by CSR. RCA did not actually engage in trade in the relevant industry although it purported to. The court found that there could be a threatened infringement of the trade mark if one were to take seriously the suggestion that RCA intended to engage in the sugar trade. However, that was not the real intention of RCA, who at no time used or intended to use the domain names as trade marks in relation to either goods or services. Hence the court had difficulty finding trade mark infringement.

4   Consider the facts of *Tesco Stores Ltd v Elogicom* [2006] EWHC 403 already referred to above. In relation to subsection (2) and the point of confusion, the court simply stated at [33]:

> In my judgment, the use of internet domain names is itself a service offered to the public, whereby the entry of such a name in the address bar of the computer of an individual browsing the internet will take them to a web site. In my view, by registering and making its 'tesco' related domain names available as pathways on the internet to Tesco web sites with a view to generating income for itself in the form of commission, Elogicom did use in the course of trade a series of signs (those domain names) which were each similar to the trade marks registered by Tesco and were each used in relation to services (the provision of internet access to Tesco web sites) identical with or similar to those for which the trade marks were registered, and in circumstances where there existed a likelihood of confusion on the part of the public, including the likelihood of association of Elogicom's service (the provision of internet access to Tesco web sites) with the trade marks. In the case of trade mark no 2321013, the service provided by Elogicom was identical to the service for which the trade mark was registered, since class 35 in that trade mark expressly includes 'assistance relating to all of the aforementioned services [ie including viewing and purchasing goods from a general merchandise Internet web site]', and I consider that the provision of domain names allowing speedy access to such a web site is itself a service in the form of provision of 'assistance' relating to the viewing and purchasing of goods on such a web site. Further, in relation to trade mark nos 2258927 and 2238995 (in which class 35 does not include express

reference to 'assistance' of the kind referred to in trade mark no 2321013, but does include reference to 'assistance in the selection of goods brought together'), I also conclude that the provision of domain names allowing speedy access to Tesco's internet web sites is itself a service in the form of provision of 'assistance in the selection of goods brought together'. In the case of all three trade marks, even if the service provided by Elogicom was not identical with services for which the trade marks were registered, the service provided by Elogicom would in my view be similar to those for which the trade marks were registered (namely, in broad terms, the provision of internet access to shopping services), within the meaning of section 10(2)(b) of the Act.

5   Do you agree with the characterisation that the use of a domain name is itself a service? It is through this device that the court was able to find the element of confusion. The defendant was not otherwise selling any goods or services and it would have been nearly impossible to find the required element of confusion because users, upon typing in the defendant's domain name in a web browser, would be immediately taken to the legitimate and valid website of the plaintiff. In a similar vein, the court also found the defendants liable for the tort of passing off.

Subsection (3)

The threshold requirement for this subsection to operate is that the trade mark infringed must be well-known or under the UK Act, a mark with a reputation. In addition, it must also be likely that the interests of the registered owner are adversely affected.

There appears to be only partial international agreement over the definition of a famous or well-known mark. In addition, terminology is used inconsistently. The Paris Convention, Article 6 *bis* refers to 'well known marks'. Section 10(3) of the UK Act refers to marks with a 'reputation'. Certain cases in the USA dealing with equivalent sections of the trade marks legislation have referred to 'famous' marks. Many jurisdictions have developed guidelines as to what constitutes a famous or well-known mark. In November 1999, the Paris Union Assembly and the General Assembly of WIPO adopted, on the basis of the recommendation of the Standing Committee on the Law of Trademarks, Industrial Design and Geographical Indications (the WIPO SCT), a *Joint Recommendation Concerning Provisions on the Protection of Well-Known Marks* which is a list of non-exhaustive criteria to be considered in determining whether a mark is well known.

Although one can try to identify the various marks that would fall into the category of being famous or well-known, the borderline cases are likely to be contentious. If famous or well-known marks are to get special protection, then there should be something very special that distinguishes them from others and different countries must agree to some extent on the criteria. A starting point might be that, because the Internet is accessible globally, only those marks that are known globally should be included, which may be only a very small number.

Although s 120(3) of the Australian Act refers to 'adversely affected' and s 10(3) of the UK Act refers to 'taking unfair advantage of' or 'detrimental to' the distinctive character or repute of the mark, in some jurisdictions such as the USA, the analogous concept of dilution is used. In none of these jurisdictions is there any requirement that the consumer be confused.

A trade mark can be diluted in two main ways: first, by blurring, and second, by tarnishing the reputation of a registered mark. Blurring results in an erosion of the distinctive quality of the mark, and therefore, of the mark's ability to call the product to the consumer's mind. For example, if the mark Volkswagen is well-known in connection with vehicles and related goods or services, and then is used without authorisation on a wide variety of dissimilar products, such as tennis racquets, its ability to call cars to the mind of consumers decreases. It has been held that use of a trade mark in an offensive or unsavoury context could tarnish the mark and reduce its capacity to call to mind positive associations with the goods or services. In some respects, the US anti-dilution law is broader than s 120(3). Under the US Act, there is no requirement of 'indicating a connection' with the registered goods or services, nor of an adverse affect. However, under the US Act, actual dilution is required and not the likelihood of dilution.

The key to dilution, or taking unfair advantage of or being detrimental to the character or repute of the mark lies in the concept of impairment. Subsection (3) is not concerned with confusion, but its focus is on the harm done to the registered mark. If these principles are applied to domain name disputes, the focus would be on the underlying goods and services for which the mark was registered, and not on the domain name itself as a trade mark. That is, rather than simply looking at how close the domain name is to the infringing mark, attention would be on the goods or services utilising the mark; the court would ask whether the use of the domain name would in any way adversely affect those goods or services.

In *One in a Million*, these terrestrial guidelines were not applied. The court spent considerable energy on the question of passing off, as extracted above. However, it did make some comments relevant to trade marks and subsection (3).

In dealing with s 10(3), Aldous LJ seems to have considered that the domain name itself was the trade mark, observing that the domain names were registered to take advantage of the distinctive character and reputation of the marks, an action which was both unfair and detrimental. According to this interpretation, s 10(3) was infringed. The court made clear its dislike of these practices. But the cursory examination of trade mark law has left a number of questions unanswered. More importantly, Aldous LJ seems to overlook the fact that a domain name can function as a trade mark if it is so used, but otherwise, the first and primary function of a domain name is as an address.

Marks & Spencer plc, Ladbrokes plc, J Sainsbury plc, Virgin Enterprises Ltd, British Telecommunications plc, Telecom Securior Cellular Radio Ltd v One in a Million and Others

[1997] EWHC Patents 357 (28 November 1997)

High Court of Justice, Chancery Division, United Kingdom

Available at <http://www.bailii.org/ew/cases/EWHC/Patents/1997/357.html> 17 August 2006

Jonathon Sumption QC, sitting as a Deputy High Court Judge:

22 I now turn to the cause of action based on trade mark infringement. Section 10(3) of the *Trade Marks Act 1994* provides:

> A person infringes a registered trade mark if he uses in the course of trade a sign which
>
> (a) is identical or similar to the trade mark, and
>
> (b) is used in relation to goods or services which are not similar to those for which the trade mark is registered, where the trade mark has a reputation in the United Kingdom and the use of the sign, being without due cause, takes unfair advantage of, or is detrimental to, the distinctive character or the repute of the trade mark.

23 Marks & Spencer is registered as a trade mark in connection with a variety of goods and services. The word marksandspencer, as part of a domain name, is not identical but is clearly similar to the trade mark. There is no requirement under section 10(3) that the goods or services should be similar to those for which the trade mark is registered. It is beyond argument that the trade mark Marks & Spencer has a reputation in the United Kingdom. It seems to me to be equally clear that the Defendant's use of it is detrimental to the trade mark, if only by damaging the Plaintiff's exclusivity.

24 What then are the issues which the defendants say should go to trial under this head? There appear to be two: (i) they deny that their use of it has been 'in the course of trade'; and (ii) they contend that it is an implicit requirement of section 10(3) that there should have been a likelihood of confusion on the part of the public, and there has been none.

25 The first of these points can be shortly dealt with. Use 'in the course of trade' means use by way of business. It does not mean use as a trade mark: *British Sugar plc v James Robertson & Sons Ltd* [1996] RPC 281, 290–2. The use of a trade mark in the course of the business of a professional dealer for the purpose of making domain names more valuable and extracting money from the trade mark owner is a use in the course of trade.

26 Turning to the second point, there is at the moment some uncertainty about whether it is the law that an infringing sign must for the purposes of section 10(3) be such as is likely to cause confusion. Some questions of law can appropriately be decided on an application for summary judgment. This one is, however, rather different. It is on the face of it strange that the likelihood of confusion should be required (as it expressly is) where the infringement consists in the use of an identical sign with similar goods or services, or a similar sign with identical or similar goods or services, but not where it consists of its use with goods which are not even similar. For substantially this reason, it has been decided on at least two occasions in England that section 10(3) does require proof that the use was such as was likely to cause confusion: see *BASF plc v CEP (UK) plc* [Knox J, 26 October 1995, unreported] and *Baywatch Production Co Inc v Home Video Channel* [1997] FSR 22. On the other hand, in a passing dictum in Case C-251/95

Sabel BV v Puma [unreported, 11 November 1997], the European Court of Justice has remarked that under the provision of the directive which permits Member States to include a provision such as section 10(3), no likelihood of confusion is required. This seems to me to be less than conclusive of an issue which raises important questions of principle, and requires fuller argument than can be appropriate on an application for summary judgment, and may ultimately require a reference to the European Court. I do not propose to resolve the question now. Nor do I need to, because even on the footing that the Plaintiffs must demonstrate a likelihood of confusion, they have done so. The test in this context depends not on the way the sign has been used but on whether a comparison between the sign and the trade mark shows an inherent propensity to confuse. There can, as it seems to me, be no doubt that this is the effect of the use by someone else of the domain name *marksandspencer*. The only basis on which the contrary has been suggested is that Internet users must be assumed to access sites by using search methods which will disclose their true owners. I am conscious of the heavy burden which lies on a Plaintiff seeking summary judgment when a question of fact is raised, but I regard this point as unarguable. Some people might access a site in that way. Plainly many would not. If the Defendants' submission had anything in it, they would not have thought it worth their while to register these names and attempt to sell them at a premium.

27 In the four other cases, the facts relevant to both causes of action are substantially the same in all relevant respects save one. The difference is that in the other four cases, it is somewhat less absurd for the Defendants to suggest the names which they have registered have an innocent use. It is impossible to imagine any unconnected party using the phrase 'Marks and Spencer' in his name or address if not to deceive, and the same may well be true of Cellnet. But the possibility is not so far-fetched in the case of the words 'Sainsbury', 'Ladbroke', 'Virgin', or 'BT'. The Defendants also say that in some cases the suffix (for example *.org* in the case of BT) serves to differentiate them from the trade marks. The Defendants make much of this point, but I am not impressed by it for the simple reason that although the words are probably capable of an innocent use, that is not the use that these Defendants intend. The history of the Defendants' activities shows a deliberate practice followed over a substantial period of time of registering domain names which are chosen to resemble the names and marks of other people and are plainly intended to deceive. The threat of passing off and trade mark infringement, and the likelihood of confusion arising from the infringement of the mark are made out beyond argument in this case, even in which it is possible to imagine other cases in which the issue would be more nicely balanced.

28 The result is that the Plaintiffs in all five actions are entitled to final injunctions *quia timet*. These will correspond substantially to paragraphs 1, 2, and 3 of the draft minutes of order attached to the summonses in the Marks & Spencer, Ladbrokes, Sainsbury, and Virgin actions. I accept that an order in the form of paragraph 2 (which requires the Defendants to take steps to have the disputed names assigned to the Plaintiffs) goes rather further than the negative form of injunctions normally appropriate *quia timet*. But it seems to me to be the most completely effective remedy, and one which does no injustice to the Defendants, for these names are of no value to them otherwise than as

a means of threatening unlawful acts. It is the equivalent, in this rather arcane context, of the delivery up of infringing goods. The Plaintiffs in the BT/Cellnet action will have orders substantially in the form of paragraphs 1 to 4 of their summons, plus orders in the form of paragraph 2 of the minutes of order in the other actions.

NOTES AND QUESTIONS

1   In comparison to the energy spent on the passing off aspects of the claim, there was only cursory analysis of s 10(3). Courts seem to dislike cybersquatting and take the view that where it appears there might have been some reprehensible practice, the cybersquatter is charged with creating an instrument of deception. This may present a number of problems when more difficult questions come before the courts.

2   On appeal, s 10(3) received only very brief treatment from Lord Justice Aldous:

> 83. I am not satisfied that section 10(3) does require the use to be trade mark use nor that it must be confusing use, but I am prepared to assume that it does. Upon that basis I am of the view that threats to infringe have been established. The appellants seek to sell the domain names which are confusingly similar to registered trade marks. The domain names indicate origin. That is the purpose for which they were registered. Further, they will be used in relation to the services provided by the registrant who trades in domain names.

> 84. Mr Wilson also submitted that it had not been established that the contemplated use would take unfair advantage of, or was detrimental to the distinctive character or reputation of the respondents' trade marks. He is wrong. The domain names were registered to take advantage of the distinctive character and reputation of the marks. That is unfair and detrimental.

> 85. I conclude that the judge came to the right conclusion on this part of the case for the right reasons.

Can the cursory nature of this treatment suggest anything about the utility of section 10(3)?

3   The Court in *One in a Million* took a flexible approach and held that use in the course of trade includes the mere registration of a trade mark as a domain name. This was followed by the New Zealand High Court in *DB Breweries Ltd v The Domain Name Company Ltd.*[26]

4   In the US case *Lockheed Martin Corp v Network Solutions, Inc,*[27] Network Solutions was sued for the mere registration of a trade mark as a domain name. The Ninth Circuit was reluctant to find any infringement of the *Lanham Act*, which is the relevant American unfair competition legislation. The court held:

---

26   (2000) 1 NZECC 70–009.
27   52 USPQ2d 181 (9th Cir 1999).

> When a domain name is used only to indicate an address on the Internet, the domain name is not functioning as a trade mark ... something more than the registration of the name is required before the use of a domain name is infringing.

5   As always, decisions in this area are highly fact-specific. The above decisions should be contrasted with another leading case in this area, *Panavision International LP v Toeppen*.[28] The respondent in this matter registered panavision. com, where he operated a non-commercial website that displayed photographs of his home town. The respondent argues that the domain name was used as an address to locate the website and was therefore not used commercially. The Court of Appeals, 9th Circuit, rejected this argument, holding that as long as Toeppen held the domain name, Panavision was prevented from exploiting the value of its marks. A crucial point in tipping the decision away from the respondent is the fact that he had attempted to sell the domain name to the corporation. Compare this reasoning with that applied in the WIPO dispute resolution proceedings below. Do you agree with the emphasis on the sale of the domain name?

6   In the UK case of *Tesco Stores Ltd v Elogicom* [2006] EWHC 403, already discussed above, the court concluded the following about the claim under subsection (3).

> ... I also consider that Elogicom's use of those domain names infringed Tesco's three trade marks, contrary to section 10(3) of the Act, in that Elogicom used the domain names in the course of its trade in relation to services, they were similar to Tesco's trade marks, Tesco's trade marks had a reputation in the United Kingdom and—subject to Elogicom's defences—its use of those domain names was 'without due cause' and took 'unfair advantage of' the distinctive character and the repute of Tesco's trade marks. In my view, Elogicom took unfair advantage of the Tesco brand, reflected in its trade marks, by using the word 'tesco' in its domain names specifically with the object of trading on and benefiting from Tesco's reputation with the general public, by capturing part of the traffic of persons browsing the internet and entering Tesco related names in the address bars on their computers in the hope of being taken to Tesco web sites, and then obtaining payment of commission from Tesco via TradeDoubler in relation to that traffic. Moreover, on the authority of the Court of Appeal's decision in *British Telecommunications Plc v One in a Million Ltd* [1999] FSR 1, it seems to me that the situation which Elogicom brought about would also fall to be regarded as detrimental to the distinctive character or the repute of Tesco's trade marks, within the meaning of section 10(3), since the following observation of Aldous LJ at p 25 would apply: 'The domain names were registered to take advantage of the distinctive character and reputation of the marks. That is unfair and detrimental.'

---

28   46 USPQ2d 1511 (9th Cir 1998).

The court focuses on the 'unfair advantage' rather than the 'detrimental' element of s 10(3). What does the court identify to be the 'unfair advantage'? Why is the advantage unfair?

7   The case of *Global Projects Management Ltd v Citigroup Inc* [2005] EWHC 2663 (Ch) discussed above also dealt with subsection (3). However, the court was swift in its discussion on the matter and simply rested on the declaration that it was bound by the decision in *One in a Million*.

Subsection (3): over-protection of well-known marks?

The reasoning in *One in a Million* brings into question the exact definition of a mark with a reputation, and therefore highlights the boundaries for determining the type of marks that would fall under this provision. Second, it questions what is meant by 'taking advantage of the distinctive character of a mark'. The wider the special protection given to these sort of marks, the more problematic it is for an individual or small business on the Internet to use any version of these marks, for what may be legitimate business or personal reasons, without fear of being challenged by the mark owner.

The danger in taking this wide approach to notions of dilution is that the focus of protection given shifts from the underlying goods and services to the domain name itself. A domain name can become a trade mark if it is used as a trade mark. However, when a domain name is used only to indicate an address on the Internet and not to identify the source of specific goods and services, the name is not functioning as a trade mark. It is imperative that the distinction between the two is maintained. In order to do so courts need only examine cases based on an assumption of the understanding held by the average Internet user regarding domain names and search engines. Too often courts have taken a condescending attitude to the ability of users to determine for themselves that the site they have entered is not what they were looking for. Granted, the realities of the Internet infrastructure create a peculiar set of trade mark circumstances; however, these circumstances do not always lead to infringement. See further Y F Lim, 'Internet Governance, Resolving the Unresolvable: Trade Marks Law and Internet Domain Names' (2002) 16 *International Review of Law Computers & Technology* 199–209.

Fuelling the uncertainties is many courts' lack of appreciation and/or acknowledgment of the domain name registration process, the common judicial misunderstanding of processes that have been customarily agreed upon within the Internet community, and the fact that the processes are unlikely to change. A more appropriate judicial stance would be to acknowledge that the process operates on a 'first come first served' basis and then proceed to publicise this fact. This approach would encourage general awareness of the fact that not every business will have an address that looks like www.businessname.com. This in turn would limit confusion and avoid or reduce the chances of trade mark infringement. Sadly, the present scenario serves only to perpetuate judicial, legal, and lay confusion.

NOTES AND QUESTIONS

1   The low threshold used in *Panavision* was apparently set deliberately to thwart those involved in domain name trading in circumstances where a fraudulent motive is readily apparent. There have been a number of cases in the USA where courts use similarly flexible interpretations of the commercial use requirement in situations where the conduct infringed some notion of business morality. Compare this approach with the result in *One in a Million*. How similar are the approaches taken on both sides of the Atlantic? What does this suggests about the relationship between semantics and principle in trade mark law?

2   Outline the ways in which trade mark infringements can be made out. Give an example from the Internet of circumstances that would fulfil the tests.

3   Do you think the standard rules of trade marks are demonstrably able to accommodate the challenges of the Internet?

4   'The trade mark regime cannot survive intact, as it is today, if courts do not heed the dangers of applying old principle to new circumstances. Consideration to the mechanics of the Internet must be given at every step. Further, courts must realise Internet users understand the ephemeral nature of the medium and understand the implicit normative code which accompanies the journey through cyberspace. This implicit code cannot be ossified through judicial pronouncement; it must be left to evolve with the Internet.' Critically analyse this passage with reference to trade mark law and the material above.

(e)   General defences

For any defendant haled into court for trade mark infringement, there are a number of defences available. It is not the aim here to canvass all of them; rather, it is the purpose of this section to highlight some of the more commonly used defences.

One of the first defences that was pleaded in the USA is that the domain name is not being used as a trade mark or in the course of trade. In order for the requirements such as those contained in s 120(1), (2) and (3) to be satisfied, the infringing sign must be used as a trade mark. The Singaporean and UK statutes are arguably slightly broader as the infringement provisions only require use of the sign in the course of trade, and not as a trade mark and this has been noted in cases such as *One in a Million*. Nevertheless, this defence was used in the context of the mere registration of a domain name without any use of the domain name. Unfortunately, courts in cases such as *Panavision v Toeppen* found that such registration could still be regarded as use in the course of trade and used as a trade mark, provided that there was an intention to seek commercial gain at some point in the future.

In sections 122 and 124 of the Australian Act, there are a number of situations where the use of a trade mark is not an infringement. Under s 122, it is acceptable to use a trade mark to identify the goods or services belonging to the trade mark owner. So for example, if a business advertises that it sells Mercedes automobile parts, the use of the Mercedes mark will not infringe the trade mark in it. In the USA, this issue was addressed in *Patmont Motor Works Inc v Gateway Marine*,[29] where the URL www. gateway.com/goped was used. This address directed Internet users to information about the 'Gopeds' sold by Gateway. However, the goped mark was held by Patmont. The court found that the use here of the mark was protected by the US fair use defence, which is similar to the Australian defence of using the mark to identify the goods. Further, the court found that the use of the mark not in the domain name part of the address but in the directory listing part of the URL in no way suggested any affiliations with the trade mark owner.

Section 122 of the Australian legislation provides:

(1) In spite of s 120, a person does not infringe a registered trade mark when:
(a) the person uses in good faith:
(i) the person's name or the name of the person's place of business; or
(ii) the name of a predecessor in business of the person or the name of the predecessor's place of business; or
(b) the person uses a sign in good faith to indicate:
(i) the kind, quality, quantity, intended purpose, value, geographical origin, or some other characteristic, of goods or services; or
(ii) the time of production of goods or of the rendering of services; or
(c) the person uses the trade mark in good faith to indicate the intended purpose of goods (in particular as accessories or spare parts) or services; or
(d) the person uses the trade mark for the purposes of comparative advertising; or
(e) the person exercises a right to use a trade mark given to the person under this Act; or
(f) the court is of the opinion that the person would obtain registration of the trade mark in his or her name if the person were to apply for it; or
(fa) both:
(i) the person uses a trade mark that is substantially identical with, or deceptively similar to, the first-mentioned trade mark; and
(ii) the court is of the opinion that the person would obtain registration of the substantially identical or deceptively similar trade mark in his or her name if the person were to apply for it; or
(g) the person, in using a sign referred to in subsections 120(1), (2) or (3) in a manner referred to in that subsection, does not (because of a condition or limitation subject to which the trade mark is registered) infringe the exclusive right of the registered owner to use the trade mark.
(2) In spite of s 120, if a disclaimer has been registered in respect of a part of a registered trade mark, a person does not infringe the trade mark by using that part of the trade mark.

Sections 122 and 124 of the Australian Act are mirrored in s 28 of the Singapore Act and in s 11 of the UK Act.

---

29   DC NCalif No C 96-2703 18 December 1997.

In cases involving real world situations, the use of registered marks for parody purposes has been held by courts to be an acceptable use of the marks. Some have even suggested that such parodies enhance consumer identification by increasing the scope of the mark and would, therefore, actually magnify the mark.[30] The use of parody on the Internet is well-known, well-established and generally well-accepted. Given the real world treatment of parodies and trade marks, it seems likely that the acceptance of the use of trade marks in parodies will also be transferred to Internet disputes when they arise.

The fourth defence is that of free speech as enshrined in the US constitution. In *Jews for Jesus*, discussed above, the defendant registered JewsforJesus.com but actually had no affiliation with the real world organisation of the same name. In fact, the defendant used the site to make disparaging points about the organisation. When challenged, he sought the protection of the First Amendment to the US Constitution by suggesting that he was merely using the domain name to criticise the policies and teachings of this organisation. The court rejected his argument, holding that he had done more than just register the name and use it in a non-commercial context. The facts showed that he used the site as a link to another site that sold merchandise and that his actions were in bad faith.

The crucial point here is that the court held that the domain name itself is not protected by the right to free speech, because it is not part of the communicative message. It was held, for example, that the defendant did not need to use the phrase 'Jews for Jesus' as or in a domain name in order to exercise free speech and make the criticisms. Therefore, to restrict his access to it does not restrict his right to free speech. A central aspect of free speech is the right to criticise. The Internet has presented unprecedented opportunities to criticise practically anyone and anything. More recently, the US courts have had the opportunity to consider situations where the website does not have any commercial element. In *Bosley Medical Institute v Kremer*, No 04-55962, 9th Cir Apr 4, 2005, the website generated no revenues and did not promote any goods or services. It did link to another website, which through a series of further links could lead to commercial advertisements. Although one could collapse this chain of links into a conclusion that the domain name use was commercial, the Ninth Circuit wisely rejected this reasoning.

In *Nissan Motor Co v Nissan Computer Co* 378 F 3d 1002, the US Court of Appeals for the Ninth Circuit upheld the rights of members of the public to criticise corporations without being deemed to have engaged in 'commercial speech' that can be enjoined under the trade mark laws.

The case involved Uzi Nissan who ran a computer business using his surname. He was sued by Nissan Motor, the giant automaker for trade mark infringement and dilution because he operated a website with the domain name nissan.com which he also used to criticise the car maker for suing him.

The trial court had found that Nissan was liable for both trade mark dilution and, to a limited extent, infringement, and consequently issued on order forbidding Nissan from using his website to criticise Nissan Motor in any way, even by linking to disparaging

---

30   See *Hormel Goods Corp v Jim Henson Productions* 73 F 3d 497 (2d Cir 1996).

websites. The trial judge reasoned that such criticism became 'commercial speech' and hence could be limited consistent with the First Amendment because it had the potential for injuring Nissan Motor's business.

In a unanimous opinion, the Ninth Circuit flatly rejected this reasoning and overturned the injunction and held that the injunction was an improper content-based restriction that is barred by the First Amendment. An application to appeal to the US Supreme Court was denied. The dilution claim was remanded for further proceedings and the trade mark infringement claim for car-related advertisements on nissan.com was upheld. Nissan.com was allowed to continue carrying advertisements that were not car-related.

One particular mechanism of criticism is the 'Sucks site'.[31] The ruling extracted below was handed down by the WIPO Arbitration and Mediation Centre, which will be examined below in more detail. Although the decision did not focus upon the defence of free speech, it provides a useful and succinct explanation of the 'Sucks site' concept.

The Leonard Cheshire Foundation v Paul Anthony Darke

WIPO Arbitration and Mediation Center, Administrative Panel Decision, Case No D2001-0131

Available at
<http://arbiter.wipo.int/domains/decisions/html/2001/d2001-0131.html> 17 August 2006

Registered use and bad faith

... The situation with regard to 'Sucks' sites is instructive. It is now well accepted that 'sucks' has entered the vernacular as a word loaded with criticism. There is reference to this in the 'wallmartcanadasucks.com' case (*Wal-Mart Stores, Inc v 'wallmartcanadasucks. com' and Kenneth J Harvey* (Case no D2000-1104). There was also the Panelist's comment, when looking at the legitimacy of the Respondent's site:

> Thus whether wallmartcanadasucks is effective criticism of Wal-Mart, whether it is in good taste, whether it focuses on the right issues, all are immaterial; the only question is whether it is criticism or parody rather than free-riding on another's trademark.

The American Restatement (Third—Unfair Competition) recognizes the balance that needs to be struck between the right of criticism and the rights of a trademark owner:

> One who uses a designation that resembles the trademark, trade name, collective mark or certification mark of another, not in a manner that is likely to associate the other's mark with the goods, services, or business of the actor, but rather to comment on, criticize, ridicule, parody, or disparage the other or the other's goods, services, business, or mark, is subject to liability without proof of the likelihood of confusion only if the actor's conduct meets the requirements of a cause of action for defamation, invasion of privacy, or injurious falsehood.

---

31   For further information on the 'Sucks site' phenomenon see <http://www.wired.com/news/politics/0,1283,38056,00.html> 11 September 2001.

The Respondent is entitled to a degree of personal freedom of expression, provided it is otherwise lawful and subject of course to the Complainant's legal right to seek to restrain such expression by other means. Once again however, we have to focus on the domain name issue and the wording of the Policy. As stated in the *Wal-Mart* case (*supra*): 'In domain name disputes it is critical whether the accused domain itself signifies parodic or critical purposes, as opposed to imitation of trademark.'

In the 'Sucks' type situations it is important to note that the domain name itself indicates that the domain name and the site resolved to is, in all probability, a criticism site ...

NOTES AND QUESTIONS

1   Do you agree with the reasoning in the *Patmont* case? Could the court's reasoning be extended to the domain part of the URL as well? Why, or why not? Why is there a natural tendency to give domain names such hallowed significance?

2   From the cursory look at parody and freedom of speech, how would you classify the relationship between the two? Would the defendant in the *Jews for Jesus* case have been better off registering the domain name jewsforjesussucks.com? What would this suggest about the state of the law in this area?

3   Section 122(1) might not be as clearly worded as it could be. What sort of use is it permitting?

4   Why do you think s 122(1)(a)(ii) is included? There are a number of significant differences across jurisdictions regarding both personal names as trade marks and personal names as domain names. In Australia and the United Kingdom one of the specific exceptions to trade mark infringement is the use by a person of his or her own name, even if it is a registered mark. So for example, a person named Mr Burger King could use his name in a domain name such as burgerking. net and it would be legal under the legislation (see the *Nissan* case discussed above). However, these rules are not consistently applied in all jurisdictions. In Germany there was a dispute over the domain name Krupp.de that was registered by Mr Krupp. The large and quite famous German steel company bearing the same name wanted the domain name handed over to them. The court held that a company with an outstanding reputation could prevent others from using the name. However, the court would not order the transfer of the domain name to the company; it only prevented Mr Krupp from using it. We will be returning to this issue of personal names and domain names later in the chapter.

(f)   Dispute resolution

From the foregoing, it seems that until a proper solution can be found to accommodate the use of trade marks in domain names, disputes will continue. As previously mentioned, ICANN administers the gTLDs. In October 1999, ICANN adopted a uniform dispute resolution policy ('UDRP') which applies to all domains registered in a number of these gTLDs. Under this policy, which is extracted in the next section, any dispute regarding a domain name must be initially submitted to an approved Dispute Resolution Service Provider. Currently there are four bodies who are approved to provide services under the dispute resolution policy: CPR Institute for Dispute Resolution (CPR, approved effective 22 May 2000); The National Arbitration Forum (NAF, approved effective 23 December 1999); World Intellectual Property Organisation (WIPO, approved effective 29 November 1999); Asian Domain Name Dispute Resolution Centre (ADNDRC, approved effective 28 February 2002).

An additional provider, eResolution (eRes), dealt with disputes from 1 January 2000 to 31 November 2001 but no longer handles these complaints. Each provider follows the Rules for Domain Name Dispute Resolution Policy as well as their own supplemental rules. See further <http://www.icann.org/udrp/approved-providers.htm.

auDA is responsible for facilitating dispute resolution for complaints involving .au websites. It has been responsible for the provision of this service since it entered into a formal agreement with ICANN giving it the right to administer the .au country code top level domain.[32] In 2002 an Australian domain name dispute resolution policy, auDRP, was established, as a national extension of the UDRP.

ICANN's Uniform Domain Name Dispute Resolution Policy set out the grounds for complaints and the relief available as well as the procedures the parties are to follow.

ICANN, Uniform Domain Name Dispute Resolution Policy

Adopted: 26 August 1999

Available at < http://www.icann.org/udrp/udrp-policy-24oct99.htm> 17 August 2006

Notes:

1   This policy is now in effect. See www.icann.org/udrp/udrp-schedule.htm for the implementation schedule.
2   This policy has been adopted by all accredited domain-name registrars for domain names ending in .com, .net, and .org. It has also been adopted by certain managers of country-code top-level domains (eg: .nu, .tv, .ws).
3   The policy is between the registrar (or other registration authority in the case of a country-code top-level domain) and its customer (the domain-name holder or registrant). Thus, the policy uses 'we' and 'our' to refer to the registrar and it uses 'you' and 'your' to refer to the domain-name holder.

1. Purpose

This Uniform Domain Name Dispute Resolution Policy (the 'Policy') has been adopted by the Internet Corporation for Assigned Names and Numbers ('ICANN'), is incorporated by

---

32   Owen Bradfield, 'Domain Names in Australia: Legal and Contractual Dispute Resolution' (2001) 12(2) *Journal of Law and Information Science* 231 at 232.

reference into your Registration Agreement, and sets forth the terms and conditions in connection with a dispute between you and any party other than us (the registrar) over the registration and use of an Internet domain name registered by you. Proceedings under Paragraph 4 of this Policy will be conducted according to the Rules for Uniform Domain Name Dispute Resolution Policy (the 'Rules of Procedure'), which are available at www.icann.org/udrp/udrp-rules-24oct99.htm, and the selected administrative-dispute-resolution service provider's supplemental rules.

2. Your representations

By applying to register a domain name, or by asking us to maintain or renew a domain name registration, you hereby represent and warrant to us that (a) the statements that you made in your Registration Agreement are complete and accurate; (b) to your knowledge, the registration of the domain name will not infringe upon or otherwise violate the rights of any third party; (c) you are not registering the domain name for an unlawful purpose; and (d) you will not knowingly use the domain name in violation of any applicable laws or regulations. It is your responsibility to determine whether your domain name registration infringes or violates someone else's rights.

3. Cancellations, transfers, and changes

We will cancel, transfer or otherwise make changes to domain name registrations under the following circumstances:

a   subject to the provisions of Paragraph 8, our receipt of written or appropriate electronic instructions from you or your authorized agent to take such action;
b   our receipt of an order from a court or arbitral tribunal, in each case of competent jurisdiction, requiring such action; and/or
c   our receipt of a decision of an Administrative Panel requiring such action in any administrative proceeding to which you were a party and which was conducted under this Policy or a later version of this Policy adopted by ICANN. (See Paragraph 4(i) and (k) below.)

We may also cancel, transfer or otherwise make changes to a domain name registration in accordance with the terms of your Registration Agreement or other legal requirements.

4. Mandatory administrative proceeding

This Paragraph sets forth the type of disputes for which you are required to submit to a mandatory administrative proceeding. These proceedings will be conducted before one of the administrative-dispute-resolution service providers listed at www.icann.org/udrp/approved-providers.htm (each, a 'Provider').

A. APPLICABLE DISPUTES

You are required to submit to a mandatory administrative proceeding in the event that a third party (a 'complainant') asserts to the applicable Provider, in compliance with the Rules of Procedure, that

(i)   your domain name is identical or confusingly similar to a trademark or service mark in which the complainant has rights; and

(ii) you have no rights or legitimate interests in respect of the domain name; and

(iii) your domain name has been registered and is being used in bad faith.

In the administrative proceeding, the complainant must prove that each of these three elements are present.

B. EVIDENCE OF REGISTRATION AND USE IN BAD FAITH

For the purposes of Paragraph 4(a)(iii), the following circumstances, in particular but without limitation, if found by the Panel to be present, shall be evidence of the registration and use of a domain name in bad faith:

(i)   circumstances indicating that you have registered or you have acquired the domain name primarily for the purpose of selling, renting, or otherwise transferring the domain name registration to the complainant who is the owner of the trademark or service mark or to a competitor of that complainant, for valuable consideration in excess of your documented out-of-pocket costs directly related to the domain name; or

(ii) you have registered the domain name in order to prevent the owner of the trademark or service mark from reflecting the mark in a corresponding domain name, provided that you have engaged in a pattern of such conduct; or

(iii) you have registered the domain name primarily for the purpose of disrupting the business of a competitor; or

(iv) by using the domain name, you have intentionally attempted to attract, for commercial gain, Internet users to your web site or other on-line location, by creating a likelihood of confusion with the complainant's mark as to the source, sponsorship, affiliation, or endorsement of your web site or location or of a product or service on your web site or location.

C. HOW TO DEMONSTRATE YOUR RIGHTS TO AND LEGITIMATE INTERESTS IN THE DOMAIN NAME IN RESPONDING TO A COMPLAINT

When you receive a complaint, you should refer to Paragraph 5 of the Rules of Procedure in determining how your response should be prepared. Any of the following circumstances, in particular but without limitation, if found by the Panel to be proved based on its evaluation of all evidence presented, shall demonstrate your rights or legitimate interests to the domain name for purposes of Paragraph 4(a)(ii):

(i)   before any notice to you of the dispute, your use of, or demonstrable preparations to use, the domain name or a name corresponding to the domain name in connection with a bona fide offering of goods or services; or

(ii) you (as an individual, business, or other organization) have been commonly known by the domain name, even if you have acquired no trademark or service mark rights; or

(iii) you are making a legitimate non-commercial or fair use of the domain name, without intent for commercial gain to misleadingly divert consumers or to tarnish the trademark or service mark at issue.

D. SELECTION OF PROVIDER

The complainant shall select the Provider from among those approved by ICANN by submitting the complaint to that Provider. The selected Provider will administer the proceeding, except in cases of consolidation as described in Paragraph 4(f).

E. INITIATION OF PROCEEDING AND PROCESS AND APPOINTMENT OF ADMINISTRATIVE PANEL

The Rules of Procedure state the process for initiating and conducting a proceeding and for appointing the panel that will decide the dispute (the 'Administrative Panel').

F. CONSOLIDATION

In the event of multiple disputes between you and a complainant, either you or the complainant may petition to consolidate the disputes before a single Administrative Panel. This petition shall be made to the first Administrative Panel appointed to hear a pending dispute between the parties. This Administrative Panel may consolidate before it any or all such disputes in its sole discretion, provided that the disputes being consolidated are governed by this Policy or a later version of this Policy adopted by ICANN.

G. FEES

All fees charged by a Provider in connection with any dispute before an Administrative Panel pursuant to this Policy shall be paid by the complainant, except in cases where you elect to expand the Administrative Panel from one to three panelists as provided in Paragraph 5(b)(iv) of the Rules of Procedure, in which case all fees will be split evenly by you and the complainant.

H. OUR INVOLVEMENT IN ADMINISTRATIVE PROCEEDINGS

We do not, and will not, participate in the administration or conduct of any proceeding before an Administrative Panel. In addition, we will not be liable as a result of any decisions rendered by the Administrative Panel.

I. REMEDIES

The remedies available to a complainant pursuant to any proceeding before an Administrative Panel shall be limited to requiring the cancellation of your domain name or the transfer of your domain name registration to the complainant.

J. NOTIFICATION AND PUBLICATION

The Provider shall notify us of any decision made by an Administrative Panel with respect to a domain name you have registered with us. All decisions under this Policy will be published in full over the Internet, except when an Administrative Panel determines in an exceptional case to redact portions of its decision.

K. AVAILABILITY OF COURT PROCEEDINGS

The mandatory administrative proceeding requirements set forth in Paragraph 4 shall not prevent either you or the complainant from submitting the dispute to a court of competent jurisdiction for independent resolution before such mandatory administrative proceeding is commenced or after such proceeding is concluded. If an Administrative Panel decides that your domain name registration should be cancelled or transferred, we will wait ten (10) business days (as observed in the location of our principal office) after we are informed by the applicable Provider of the Administrative Panel's decision before implementing that decision. We will then implement the decision unless we have received from you during that ten (10) business day period official documentation (such as a copy of a complaint, file-stamped by the clerk of the court) that you have commenced a lawsuit against the complainant in a jurisdiction to which the complainant has submitted under Paragraph 3(b)(xiii) of the Rules of Procedure. (In general, that jurisdiction is either the location of our principal office or of your address as shown in our Whois database. See Paragraphs 1 and 3(b)(xiii) of the Rules of Procedure for details.) If we receive such documentation within the ten (10) business day period, we will not implement the Administrative Panel's decision, and we will take no further action, until we receive (i) evidence satisfactory to us of a resolution between the parties; (ii) evidence satisfactory to us that your lawsuit has been dismissed or withdrawn; or (iii) a copy of an order from such court dismissing your lawsuit or ordering that you do not have the right to continue to use your domain name.

5. All other disputes and litigation

All other disputes between you and any party other than us regarding your domain name registration that are not brought pursuant to the mandatory administrative proceeding provisions of Paragraph 4 shall be resolved between you and such other party through any court, arbitration or other proceeding that may be available.

6. Our involvement in disputes

We will not participate in any way in any dispute between you and any party other than us regarding the registration and use of your domain name. You shall not name us as a party or otherwise include us in any such proceeding. In the event that we are named as a party in any such proceeding, we reserve the right to raise any and all defenses deemed appropriate, and to take any other action necessary to defend ourselves.

7. Maintaining the status quo

We will not cancel, transfer, activate, deactivate, or otherwise change the status of any domain name registration under this Policy except as provided in Paragraph 3 above.

8. Transfers during a dispute

A. TRANSFERS OF A DOMAIN NAME TO A NEW HOLDER

You may not transfer your domain name registration to another holder (i) during a pending administrative proceeding brought pursuant to Paragraph 4 or for a period of fifteen (15) business days (as observed in the location of our principal place of business) after such proceeding is concluded; or (ii) during a pending court proceeding or arbitration commenced regarding your domain name unless the party to whom the domain name registration is being transferred agrees, in writing, to be bound by the decision of the court or arbitrator. We reserve the right to cancel any transfer of a domain name registration to another holder that is made in violation of this subparagraph.

B. CHANGING REGISTRARS

You may not transfer your domain name registration to another registrar during a pending administrative proceeding brought pursuant to Paragraph 4 or for a period of fifteen (15) business days (as observed in the location of our principal place of business) after such proceeding is concluded. You may transfer administration of your domain name registration to another registrar during a pending court action or arbitration, provided that the domain name you have registered with us shall continue to be subject to the proceedings commenced against you in accordance with the terms of this Policy. In the event that you transfer a domain name registration to us during the pendency of a court action or arbitration, such dispute shall remain subject to the domain name dispute policy of the registrar from which the domain name registration was transferred.

9. Policy modifications

We reserve the right to modify this Policy at any time with the permission of ICANN. We will post our revised Policy at <URL> at least thirty (30) calendar days before it becomes effective. Unless this Policy has already been invoked by the submission of a complaint to a Provider, in which event the version of the Policy in effect at the time it was invoked will apply to you until the dispute is over, all such changes will be binding upon you with respect to any domain name registration dispute, whether the dispute arose before, on or after the effective date of our change. In the event that you object to a change in this Policy, your sole remedy is to cancel your domain name registration with us, provided that you will not be entitled to a refund of any fees you paid to us. The revised Policy will apply to you until you cancel your domain name registration.

 NOTES AND QUESTIONS

1   To which domains does this policy apply?
2   Consider the remedies available. What does this indicate about the nature of the procedure and the policy?
3   Critically analyse the policy. Do you agree that it grants significant rights to registered trade mark holders to the detriment of the small Internet users? In particular examine paragraphs 4(a), 4(b), and 4(c). Consider the legitimate interests provisions. Are they satisfactory?
4   Consider paragraph 4(b)(ii). How would this be interpreted? Would it be considered 'preventing' if the mark holder already held a domain name in one of the gTLDs which includes her mark? See *Bruce Springsteen v Jeff Burgar and Bruce Springsteen Club* WIPO Case No D2000-1532.

The following are decisions of the Administrative Panels of the WIPO Arbitration and Mediation Center which dealt with incidents where individuals had registered domain names that included the names of famous entertainers.

Madonna Ciccone, p/k/a Madonna v Dan Parisi and 'Madonna.com'

WIPO Arbitration and Mediation Center, Administrative Panel Decision, Case No D2000-0847

Available at
<http://arbiter.wipo.int/domains/decisions/html/2000/d2000-0847.html> 17 August 2006

1. The parties

The Complainant is Madonna Ciccone, an individual professionally known as Madonna. The Respondent is 'Madonna.com', the registrant for the disputed domain name, located in New York, New York, USA or Dan Parisi, the listed contact for the domain name.

2. The domain name(s) and registrar(s)

The disputed domain name is madonna.com.

The registrar is Network Solutions, Inc, 505 Huntmar Park Drive, Herndon, Virginia 20170, USA.

3. Procedural history

This action was brought in accordance with the ICANN Uniform Domain Name Dispute Resolution Policy, dated 24 October 1999 ('the Policy') and the ICANN Rules for Uniform Domain Name Dispute Resolution Policy, dated 24 October 1999 ('the Rules').

The Complaint was received by the WIPO Arbitration and Mediation Center on 21 July 2000 (e-mail) and on 24 July 2000 (hard copy). The Response was received on 23 August 2000 (e-mail) and on 28 August 2000 (hard copy). Both parties are represented by Counsel. There have been no further submissions on the merits.

Respondent elected to have the case decided by a three-member panel. David E Sorkin was appointed as the Respondent's nominee. James W Dabney was selected as the Complainant's nominee. Mark V B Partridge was appointed as presiding panelist.

It appears that all requirements of the Policy and the Rules have been satisfied by the parties, WIPO and the Panelists.

4. Factual background

Complainant is the well-known entertainer Madonna. She is the owner of US Trademark Registrations for the mark MADONNA for entertainment services and related goods (Reg No 1,473,554 and 1,463,601). She has used her name and mark MADONNA professionally for entertainment services since 1979. Complainant's music and other entertainment endeavors have often been controversial for featuring explicit sexual content. In addition, nude photographs of Madonna have appeared in Penthouse magazine, and Complainant has published a coffee-table book entitled *Sex* featuring sexually explicit photographs and text.

Respondent is in the business of developing web sites. On or about 29 May 1998, Respondent, through its business Whitehouse.com, Inc, purchased the registration for the disputed domain name from Pro Domains for $20,000. On 4 June 1998, Respondent registered MADONNA as a trademark in Tunisia. On or about 8 June 1998, Respondent began operating an 'adult entertainment portal web site'. The web site featured sexually explicit photographs and text, and contained a notice stating 'Madonna.com is not affiliated or endorsed by the Catholic Church, Madonna College, Madonna Hospital or Madonna the singer.' By 4 March 1999, it appears that Respondent removed the explicit sexual content from the web site. By 31 May 1999, it appears that the site merely contained the above notice, the disputed domain name and the statement 'Coming soon Madonna Gaming and Sportsbook'.

On 9 June 1999, Complainant, through her attorneys, objected to Respondent's use of the Madonna.com domain name. On 14 June 1999, Respondent through its counsel stated: 'As I assume you also know, Mr Parisi's website [*sic*] was effectively shut down before you sent your letter, and is now shut down altogether. He is in the process of donating his registration for the domain name.'

The word 'Madonna', which has the current dictionary definition as the Virgin Mary or an artistic depiction of the Virgin Mary, is used by others as a trademark, trade name and personal name. After Respondent's receipt of Complainant's objection, it appears that Respondent had communication with Madonna Rehabilitation Hospital regarding the transfer of the domain name to the Hospital. It further appears that Respondent has not identified all of its communications on this matter. Nevertheless, the transfer had not taken place at the time this proceeding was commenced.

By his own admission, Respondent has registered a large number of other domain names, including names that matched the trade marks of others. Other domain names registered by Respondent include <wallstreetjournal.com> and <edgaronline.com>. See Response, Exhibit A, paragraphs 30, 35.

5. Parties' contentions

A. COMPLAINANT

Complainant contends that the disputed domain name is identical to the registered and common law trade mark MADONNA in which complainant owns rights. She further contends that Respondent has no legitimate interest or rights in the domain name. Finally, Complainant contends that Respondent obtained and used the disputed domain name with the intent to attract Internet users to a pornographic web site for commercial gain based on confusion with Complainant's name and trade mark.

B. RESPONDENT

Respondent does not dispute that the disputed domain name is identical or confusingly similar to Complainant's trade mark. Respondent, however, claims that Complainant cannot show a lack of legitimate interest in the domain name because Respondent (a) made demonstrable preparation to use the domain name for a bona fide business purpose; (b) holds a bona fide trade mark in the word MADONNA; and (c) has attempted to make bona fide non-commercial use of the name by donating it to the Madonna Rehabilitation Hospital.

Respondent also contends that it has not registered and used the domain name in bad faith because (a) there is no evidence that its primary motivation was to sell the disputed domain name; (b) the domain name was not registered with an intent to prevent Complainant from using her mark as a domain name; (c) respondent is not engaged in a pattern of registering domain names to prevent others from doing so; (d) the use of a disclaimer on the web site precludes a finding that Respondent intentionally seeks to attract users for commercial gain based on confusion with Complainant's mark; and (e) the use of a generic term to attract business is not bad faith as a matter of law. Finally, Respondent claims that Complainant cannot legitimately claim tarnishment because she has already associated herself with sexually explicit creative work.

6. Discussion and findings

A. THE EVIDENTIARY STANDARD FOR DECISION

Paragraph 4(a) of the Policy directs that the complainant must prove each of the following:

(i)   that the domain name registered by the respondent is identical or confusingly similar to a trade mark or service mark in which the complainant has rights; and,

(ii) that the respondent has no legitimate interests in respect of the domain name; and,

(iii) that the domain name has been registered and used in bad faith.

A threshold question in proceedings under the Policy is to identify the proper standard for reaching a decision on each of these issues. The limited submissions allowed under the Policy make these proceedings somewhat akin to a summary judgment motion under the United States Federal Rules of Civil Procedure. On a summary judgment motion, the movant has the burden of showing that there are no disputes of material facts. All doubts are to be resolved in favor of the non-moving party. If there are material disputes of fact, the motion must be denied and the case will advance to a hearing before a trier of fact, either judge or jury.

Although the nature of the record is similar to that found on a summary judgment motion, our role is different to that of the Court on a summary judgment motion. Paragraph 15 of the Rules states that the 'Panel shall decide a complaint on the basis of the statements and documents submitted and in accordance with the Policy … '. Paragraph 10 of the Rules provides that the 'Panel shall determine the admissibility, relevance, materiality and weight of the evidence.' Paragraph 4 of the Policy makes repeated reference to the Panel's role in making findings of fact based on the evidence.

Based on the Policy and the Rules, we disagree with the view that disputes over material facts should not be decided in these proceedings. Rather, it is clear to us that our role is to make findings of fact as best we can based on the evidence presented, provided the matters at issue are within the scope of the Policy. There may be circumstances due to the inherent limitations of the dispute resolution process or for other reasons where it would be appropriate for a panel to decline to decide a factual dispute. However, the mere existence of a genuine dispute of material fact should not preclude a panel from weighing the evidence before it and reaching a decision.

Since these proceedings are civil, rather than criminal, in nature, we believe the appropriate standard for fact finding is the civil standard of a preponderance of the evidence (and not the higher standard of 'clear and convincing evidence' or 'evidence beyond a reasonable doubt'). Under the 'preponderance of the evidence' standard a fact is proved for the purpose of reaching a decision when it appears more likely than not to be true based on the evidence. We recognize that other standards may be employed in other jurisdictions. However, the standard of proof employed in the United States seems appropriate for these proceedings generally, and in particular for this proceeding which involves citizens of the United States, actions occurring in the United States and a domain name registered in the United States.

In this case, there are factual disputes over Respondent's intent in obtaining and using the disputed domain name. For the reasons just stated, these disputes do not preclude a decision. Instead, we reach a decision based on the preponderance of the evidence submitted by the parties on the basic issues under the Policy.

B. SIMILARITY OF THE DISPUTED DOMAIN NAME AND COMPLAINANT'S MARK

As noted above, Respondent does not dispute that its domain name is identical or confusingly similar to a trade mark in which the Complainant has rights. Accordingly, we find that Complainant has satisfied the requirements of Paragraph 4(c)(i) of the Policy.

C. LACK OF RIGHTS OR LEGITIMATE INTERESTS IN DOMAIN NAME

Complainant has presented evidence tending to show that Respondent lacks any rights or legitimate interest in the domain name. Respondent's claim of rights or legitimate interests is not persuasive.

First, Respondent contends that its use of the domain name for an adult entertainment web site involved prior use of the domain name in connection with a bona fide offering of goods or services. The record supports Respondent's claim that it used the domain name in connection with commercial services prior to notice of the dispute. However, Respondent has failed to provide a reasonable explanation for the selection of Madonna as a domain name. Although the word 'Madonna' has an ordinary dictionary meaning not associated with Complainant, nothing in the record supports a conclusion that Respondent adopted and used the term 'Madonna' in good faith based on its ordinary dictionary meaning. We find instead that name was selected and used by Respondent with the intent to attract for commercial gain Internet users to Respondent's web site by trading on the fame of Complainant's mark. We see no other plausible explanation for Respondent's conduct and conclude that use which intentionally trades on the fame of another can not constitute a 'bona fide' offering of goods or services. To conclude otherwise would mean that a Respondent could rely on intentional infringement to demonstrate a legitimate interest, an interpretation that is obviously contrary to the intent of the Policy.

Second, Respondent contends that it has rights in the domain name because it registered Madonna as a trade mark in Tunisia prior to notice of this dispute. Certainly, it is possible for a Respondent to rely on a valid trade mark registration to show prior rights under the Policy. However, it would be a mistake to conclude that mere registration of a trademark creates a legitimate interest under the Policy. If an American-based Respondent could establish 'rights' *vis-à-vis* an American complainant through the expedient of securing a trademark registration in Tunisia, then the ICANN procedure would be rendered virtually useless. To establish cognizable rights, the overall circumstances should demonstrate that the registration was obtained in good faith for the purpose of making bona fide use of the mark in the jurisdiction where the mark is registered, and not obtained merely to circumvent the application of the Policy.

Here, Respondent admits that the Tunisia registration was obtained merely to protect his interests in the domain name. Respondent is not located in Tunisia and the registration was not obtained for the purpose of making bona fide use of the mark in commerce in Tunisia. A Tunisian trade mark registration is issued upon application without any substantive examination. Although recognized by certain treaties, registration in Tunisia does not prevent a finding of infringement in jurisdictions outside Tunisia. Under the circumstances, some might view Respondent's Tunisian registration itself as evidence of bad faith because it appears to be a pretense to justify an abusive domain name registration. We find at a minimum that it does not evidence a legitimate interest in the disputed name under the circumstances of this case.

Third, Respondent claims that its offer to transfer the domain name to the Madonna Hospital in Lincoln, Nebraska, is a legitimate non-commercial use under Paragraph 4(c)(iii) of the Policy. We disagree. The record is incomplete on these negotiations. Respondent has failed to disclose the specifics of its proposed arrangement with Madonna Hospital. Complainant asserts that the terms of the transfer include a condition that Madonna Hospital not transfer the domain name registration to Complainant. It also appears that the negotiations started after Complainant objected to Respondent's registration and use of the domain name. These circumstances do not demonstrate a legitimate interest or right in the domain name, and instead suggest that Respondent lacks any real interest in the domain name apart from its association with Complainant. Further, we do not believe these circumstances satisfy the provisions of Paragraph 4(c)(iii), which applies to situations where the Respondent is actually making non-commercial or fair use of the domain name. That certainly was not the situation at the time this dispute arose and is not the situation now.

Respondent cites examples of other parties besides Complainant who also have rights in the mark Madonna, but that does not aid its cause. The fact that others could demonstrate a legitimate right or interest in the domain name does nothing to demonstrate that Respondent has such right or interest.

Based on the record before us, we find that Complainant has satisfied the requirements of Paragraph 4(a)(ii) of the Policy.

D. BAD FAITH REGISTRATION AND USE

Under Paragraph 4(b)(iv) of the Policy, evidence of bad faith registration and use of a domain name includes the following circumstances:

(iv) by using the domain name, you have intentionally attempted to attract, for commercial gain, Internet users to your web site or other online location, by creating a likelihood of confusion with the complainant's mark as to the source, sponsorship, affiliation, or endorsement of your web site or location or of a product or service on your web site or location.

The pleadings in this case are consistent with Respondent's having adopted <madonna. com> for the specific purpose of trading off the name and reputation of the Complainant, and Respondent has offered no alternative explanation for his adoption of the name despite his otherwise detailed and complete submissions. Respondent has not explained why <madonna. com> was worth $20,000 to him or why that name was thought to be valuable as an attraction for a sexually explicit web site. Respondent notes that the complainant, identifying herself as Madonna, has appeared in Penthouse and has published a '*Sex*' book. The statement that 'madonna' is a word in the English language, by itself, is no more of a defense than would be the similar statement made in reference to the word 'coke'. Respondent has not even attempted to tie in his web site to any dictionary definition of 'madonna'. The only plausible explanation for Respondent's actions appears to be an intentional effort to trade upon the fame of Complainant's name and mark for commercial gain. That purpose is a violation of the Policy, as well as US Trademark Law.

Respondent's use of a disclaimer on its web site is insufficient to avoid a finding of bad faith. First, the disclaimer may be ignored or misunderstood by Internet users. Second, a disclaimer does nothing to dispel initial interest confusion that is inevitable from Respondent's actions. Such confusion is a basis for finding a violation of Complainant's rights. See *Brookfield Communications Inc v West Coast Entertainment Corp*, 174 F 3d 1036 (9th Cir 1999).

The Policy requires a showing of bad faith registration and use. Here, although Respondent was not the original registrant, the record shows he acquired the registration in bad faith. The result is the equivalent of registration and is sufficient to fall within the Policy. Indeed, Paragraph 4(b)(i) of the Policy treats acquisition as the same as registration for the purposes of supporting a finding of bad faith registration. We therefore conclude that bad faith acquisition satisfies the requirement of bad faith registration under the Policy.

Respondent's reliance on a previous ICANN decision involving the domain name <sting. com> is misplaced. See *Gordon Sumner p/k/a/ Sting v Michael Urvan*, Case No 2000-0596 (WIPO 24 July 2000). In the *Sting* decision there was evidence that the Respondent had made bona fide use of the name Sting prior to obtaining the domain name registration and there was no indication that he was seeking to trade on the goodwill of the well-known singer. Here, there is no similar evidence of prior use by Respondent and the evidence demonstrates a deliberate intent to trade on the goodwill of Complainant. Where no plausible explanation has been provided for adopting a domain name that corresponds to the name of a famous entertainer, other Panels have found a violation of the Policy. See *Julia Fiona Roberts v Russell Boyd*, Case No D2000-0210 (WIPO 29 May 2000); *Helen Folsade Adu p/k/a Sade v Quantum Computer Services Inc*, Case No D2000-0794 (WIPO 26 September 2000).

There is also evidence in the record which tends to support Complainant's claim that Respondent's registration of the domain name prevents Complainant from reflecting her mark in the corresponding .com domain name and that Respondent has engaged in a pattern of such conduct. It is admitted that Respondent registers a large number of domain names and that some happen to correspond to the names or marks of others. We find, however, that the record is inconclusive on this basis for finding bad faith and do not rely on this evidence for our conclusion.

Respondent asserts that we should reject Complainant's claims because she has been disingenuous in claiming that her reputation could be tarnished by Respondent's actions. Respondent suggests that her reputation cannot be tarnished because she has already associated herself with sexually explicit creative work. That argument misses the point. Even though Complainant has produced sexually explicit content of her own, Respondent's actions may nevertheless tarnish her reputation because they resulted in association with sexually explicit content which Complainant did not control and which may be contrary to her creative intent and standards of quality. In any event, we do not rely on tarnishment as a basis for our decision.

Because the evidence shows a deliberate attempt by Respondent to trade on Complainant's fame for commercial purposes, we find that Complainant has satisfied the requirements of Paragraph 4(a)(iii) of the Policy.

7. Decision

Under Paragraph 4(i) of the Policy, we find in favor of the Complainant. The disputed domain name is identical or confusingly similar to a trademark in which Complainant has rights; Respondent lacks rights or legitimate interests in the domain name; and the domain name has been registered and used in bad faith. Therefore, we decide that the disputed domain name <madonna.com> should be transferred to the Complainant.

Gordon Sumner, p/k/a Sting v Michael Urvan

WIPO Arbitration and Mediation Center, Administrative Panel Decision, Case No D2000-0596

Available at
<http://arbiter.wipo.int/domains/decisions/html/2000/d2000-0596.html> 17 August 2006

1. The parties

1.1 The Complainant is Gordon Sumner, professionally known as 'Sting', a citizen of the United Kingdom who maintains a residence in the United States. The Respondent is Michael Urvan, of Marietta, Georgia, United States of America.

2. The domain names and registrar

2.1 The domain name the subject of this Complaint is 'sting.com'.

2.2 The Registrar of this domain name is Network Solutions, Inc of Herndon, Virginia, USA ('Registrar').

3. Procedural history

ISSUANCE OF COMPLAINT

3.1 The Complainant by e-mail and by courier submitted to the World Intellectual Property Organization Arbitration and Mediation Center ('WIPO Center') a Complaint made pursuant to the Uniform Domain Name Dispute Resolution Policy implemented by the Internet Corporation for Assigned Names and Numbers (ICANN) on 24 October 1999 ('Uniform Policy'), and under the Rules for Uniform Domain Name Dispute Resolution Policy implemented by ICANN on the same date ('Uniform Rules'). The e-mail copy of the Complaint was received by the WIPO Center on 13 June 2000, and the hard copy of the Complaint was received by the WIPO Center on 15 June 2000. An Acknowledgment of Receipt was sent by the WIPO Center to the Complainant, by e-mail dated 15 June 2000.

CONFIRMATION OF REGISTRATION DETAILS

3.2 A Request for Registrar Verification was dispatched by the WIPO Center to the Registrar by e-mail on 15 June 2000. By e-mail to the WIPO Center on 20 June 2000, the Registrar confirmed that it had received a copy of the Complaint from the Complainant; confirmed that it was the Registrar of the domain name the subject of the Complaint; confirmed that the current registrant of the domain name is the Respondent; informed that the administrative, and billing Contact for the domain names is the Respondent, and provided postal, telephone, facsimile and e-mail contact details for the administrative, technical, zone and billing Contact; and informed that the status of each of the domain names in issue is 'active'. The Registrar also confirmed that its 5.0 Service Agreement is in effect. Among other things, that agreement provides that the Respondent as registrant of the domain name agrees to be bound by the domain name dispute policy incorporated therein. The policy incorporated into the agreement is the Uniform Policy.

NOTIFICATION TO RESPONDENT

3.3 Having verified that the Complaint satisfied the formal requirements of the Uniform Policy and the Uniform Rules, and that payment of the filing fee had been properly made, the WIPO Center issued to the Respondent, and to the technical and zone contact for the domain name, a Notification of Complaint and Commencement of Administrative Proceeding, by e-mail on 20 June, and by courier and fax on 21 June, to the addresses provided by the Registrar. Copies of this Notification of Complaint were sent to the Complainant, the Registrar and ICANN by e-mail on 20 June.

3.4 This Administrative Panel finds that the WIPO Center has discharged its responsibility under Paragraph 2(a) of the Uniform Rules 'to employ reasonably available means calculated to achieve actual notice to Respondent'.

FILING OF RESPONSE

3.5 A Response was filed by the Respondent, and received by the WIPO Center by e-mail on 8 July, within the time specified in the Notification of Complaint. A hardcopy of the Response, with Exhibits, was subsequently received by the WIPO Center by courier.

CONSTITUTION OF ADMINISTRATIVE PANEL

3.6 Subsequent to receipt of the Response, and in accordance with the request in the Complaint, the WIPO Center proceeded to appoint a single Panelist, and invited Dr Andrew F Christie to so act. On 11 July 2000, Dr Christie indicated his ability to act as the sole Panelist in this case, and submitted to the WIPO Center a Statement of Acceptance and Declaration of Impartiality and Independence the following day. On 11 July 2000, the WIPO Center issued to both parties a Notification of Appointment of Administrative Panel and Projected Decision Date, informing of Dr Christie's appointment and that absent exceptional circumstances a decision would be provided by this Administrative Panel by 24 July 2000. The case before this Administrative Panel was conducted in the English language.

COMPLIANCE WITH THE FORMALITIES OF THE UNIFORM POLICY AND THE UNIFORM RULES

3.7 Having reviewed the Case File in this matter, this Administrative Panel concurs with the assessment by the WIPO Center that the Complaint complies with the formal requirements of the Uniform Policy and Uniform Rules.

INTERIM ORDERS

3.8 In response to certain procedural requests from the Complainant, this Administrative Panel issued an Interim Order on 19 July 2000, and a second Interim Order on 20 July 2000. The effect of the first Interim Orders was to deny the Complainant's request for a Stay, to rule invalid and disregard the Complainant's unsolicited submission of a Reply, and to extend to 26 July 2000, the date by which this Administrative Panel was required to forward a Decision in this case. The effect of the second Interim Order was to deny the Complainant's request to be allowed to submit a Reply. Copies of these interim orders are attached to this decision.

4. Factual background

COMPLAINANT'S ACTIVITIES AND TRADEMARKS

4.1 In his Complaint, the Complainant asserted the following in relation to his activities and trademarks. The Complainant is a world famous musician, recording and performing artist who has, for over twenty years, rendered high-quality musical services under his name, trade mark and service mark STING. Since at least as early as 1978, the Complainant has exclusively and continuously used the STING mark in connection with approximately twenty record albums, almost all of which have gone multi-platinum in the United States and enjoyed great commercial success worldwide. The Complainant has also used the STING mark in connection with innumerable worldwide concert tours involving venues with significant capacities, the majority of which sell out. The STING mark is internationally known and famous as a result of the Complainant's extensive, high-profile, and overwhelmingly commercially successful activities in the music industry. The Complainant is the owner of the STING mark as a trade mark and service mark. The name STING has become synonymous in the minds of the public with the Complainant and his activities in the music industry, and serves as a symbol of the goodwill and excellent reputation associated with Sting. The STING mark is famous and entitled to the widest scope of protection afforded by law, including protection against dilution.

4.2 In his Response, the Respondent asserted that there are 20 trade mark registrations of the word STING in the US, but none of them is registered by the Complainant. The word STING is a common word in the English language, and so registration of it as a domain name is not a violation of the Uniform Policy. The Respondent is not a competitor of the Complainant and the Respondent does not attempt to cause any confusion with him.

RESPONDENT'S ACTIVITIES

4.3 The Complainant asserted the following in relation to the Respondent's activities and use of the domain name. Until the Respondent was contacted by a representative of the Complainant, the Respondent made no use of the domain name. After being contacted by a representative of the Complainant, Respondent linked the domain name to another site called 'GunBroker.Com', which is a site that facilitates 'person to person' selling of guns. During or about February of 2000, and again during or about May of 2000, the Respondent offered to sell the domain name to the Complainant for $25,000. Since offering to sell the domain name to the Complainant for $25,000, the Respondent has frequently changed the web site identified by the domain name, usually with an 'under construction' message, and in some cases providing a link to a third-party operated unauthorized web site relating to the Complainant.

4.4 In his Response, the Respondent asserted that he has been using the nickname 'Sting' and more recently '=Sting=' publicly on the Internet for at least eight years. The Respondent registered the domain name in July 1995, approximately five years before this dispute was commenced. The Respondent did not register the domain name to sell it, nor did he register the domain to hold it hostage for any reason. The Respondent engaged in work on web site to which he intended the domain name 'sting.com' to resolve, prior to any notification of this dispute. The Respondent did not point the domain name 'sting.com' to the 'GunBroker.com' web site—this occurred for a short time as a result of an error on the part of the Respondent's web service provider. The Complainant's assertion that the Respondent initiated contact with the Complainant is false—the first contact was initiated by the Complainant on 16 May 2000.

5. Parties' contentions

THE COMPLAINT

5.1 The Complainant contends that each of the three elements specified in paragraph 4(a) of the Uniform Policy are applicable to the domain name the subject of this dispute.

5.2 In relation to element (i) of paragraph 4(a) of the Uniform Policy, the Complainant contends that the domain name is identical in its substantive part to the Complainant's unregistered trademark and service mark STING.

5.3 In relation to element (ii) of paragraph 4(a) of the Uniform Policy, the Complainant contends that the Respondent has no rights or legitimate interests in respect of the domain name in issue.

5.4 In relation to element (iii) of paragraph 4(a) of the Uniform Policy, the Complainant contends that evidence of bad faith registration and use is established by the following circumstances. First, the Respondent offered to sell the domain name to the Complainant for $25,000, an activity which corresponds to that listed in paragraph 4(b)(i) of the Policy as evidence of bad faith registration and use of a domain name. Secondly, the Respondent has used the domain name mark to link to the 'GunBrokers.com' web site, and as such is intentionally attempting to attract, for commercial gain, Internet users to an online location by creating a likelihood of confusion with the STING mark as to source, sponsorship, affiliation, or endorsement, being an activity which corresponds to that listed in paragraph 4(b)(iv) of the Policy as evidence of bad faith registration and use of a domain name. In addition, that site is personally offensive to the Complainant and contrary to his established reputation, and tarnishes the STING mark in violation of 15 USC s 1125(c). Thirdly, because the Complainant's STING mark has a strong reputation and is world famous, the Respondent can make no good faith use of the domain name, and 'it is not possible to conceive of any plausible actual or contemplated active use of the [D]omain [N]ame by the Respondent that would not be illegitimate, such as by being a passing off, an infringement of consumer protection legislation, or an infringement of the Complainant's rights under trade mark law'.

THE RESPONSE

5.5 The Respondent denies that each of the three elements specified in paragraph 4(a) of the Uniform Policy are applicable to the domain name the subject of this dispute.

5.6 In relation to element (i) of paragraph 4(a) of the Uniform Policy, the Respondent admits that he registered that domain name 'sting.com', and that the domain name is identical to the STING mark. However, the Respondent challenges the Complainant's claim to owning the STING mark, and the Complainant's claim that the STING mark is world famous and exclusively associated with the Complainant and so entitled to protection against dilution. In particular, the Respondent contends that the trademark STING has been the subject of 20 registrations in the United States, none of which has been granted to the Complainant. A list purporting to be a printout from an Internet search of the United States Patent and Trademark Office database of trade mark registrations for the word STING is Exhibit J to the Response.

5.7 In relation to element (ii) of paragraph 4(a) of the Uniform Policy, the Respondent contends that his use of the nickname 'Sting' and more recently '=Sting=' publicly on the Internet for at least 8 years has given him a legitimate interest in the domain name. The Respondent provided documentary evidence in Exhibits A, C, D, E and H to the Response, showing that for some years prior to this dispute he has used the domain name to point to a web site for e-mail purposes, he has used the nickname 'sting' or '=sting=' with global Internet gaming services, and he has had in development a web site intended to be located at the URL http://www.sting.com.

5.8 In relation to element (iii) of paragraph 4(a) of the Uniform Policy, the Respondent contends that his activities since registration of the domain name demonstrate that he did not register and has not been using the domain name in bad faith. In particular, the Respondent denies the Complainant's contention that the Respondent offered to sell the domain name to the Complainant for a sum greater than out of pocket expenses. Rather, the Respondent contends that it was the Complainant, through his attorney, who contacted him in relation to the domain name. The Respondent provides in Exhibit B to the Response a copy of an e-mail from the Complainant's attorney to him of 17 May 2000, initiating contact. The Respondent admits that upon solicitation from the Complainant's attorney he did make an offer to sell the domain name, but contends that this does not demonstrate his primary purpose in registering the domain name was to sell it to the Complainant.

5.9 In relation to the use of the domain name to point to the 'GunBrokers.com' web site, the Respondent contends that because this occurred due to a mistake by his web service provider, it is not evidence of bad faith use by him. Exhibit I of the Response contains a copy of a letter purporting to be from the Respondent's web service provider explaining how this mistake occurred. In addition, the Respondent contends that he had no knowledge of the Complainant's distaste for a web site selling guns.

5.10 The Respondent makes the further contention that it cannot be said he has engaged in a pattern of conduct of preventing trademark owners from reflecting their trademark in a corresponding domain name, because the other two domain names the Respondent owns have not been offered for sale to anyone.

6. Discussion and findings

DOMAIN NAME IDENTICAL OR CONFUSINGLY SIMILAR TO COMPLAINANT'S MARK

6.1 The relevant part of the domain name 'sting.com' is 'sting'. The Complainant asserts, the Respondent admits, and this Administrative Panel finds, that the domain name is identical to the word STING.

6.2 The Complainant is not the owner of a trade mark or service mark registration for the word STING. It is, however, clear that the Uniform Policy is not limited to a 'registered' mark; an unregistered, or common law, mark is sufficient for the purposes of paragraph 4(a)(i). The Complainant did not provide any documentary evidence in support of his assertion that he is the owner of the unregistered trademark and/or service mark STING. However, the Uniform Policy is not limited to trademarks or service marks 'owned' by the Complainant; it is sufficient for the purposes of paragraph 4(a)(i) that there be a trademark or service mark 'in which the Complainant has rights'. The Complainant asserted, and this Administrative Panel through the equivalent of taking judicial notice finds, that the Complainant is a world famous entertainer who is known by the name STING.

6.3 The question that arises is whether being known under a particular name is the same as having rights in that name as a 'trademark or service mark'. The answer to this question is not straightforward. On the one hand, there are a number of cases under the

Uniform Policy in which the Panel has treated the name of a famous or at least widely known person as constituting an unregistered trademark or service mark sufficient for the purposes of paragraph 4(a)(i) (eg *Julia Fiona Roberts v Russell Boyd* WIPO Case No D2000-0210; *Jeannette Winterson v Mark Hogarth* WIPO Case No D2000-0235; *Steven Rattner v BuyThisDomainName (John Pepin)* WIPO Case No D2000-0402).

6.4 On the other hand, the *Report of the WIPO Internet Domain Name Process* of 30 April 1999, on which ICANN based the Uniform Policy, at paragraphs 165–168, states as follows (footnote citations deleted, emphasis added):

> The preponderance of views, however, was in favor of restricting the scope of the procedure, at least initially, in order to deal first with the most offensive forms of predatory practices and to establish the procedure on a sound footing. Two limitations on the scope of the procedure were, as indicated above, favored by these commentators. The first limitation would confine the availability of the procedure to cases of deliberate, bad faith abusive registrations. The definition of such abusive registrations is discussed in the next section. The second limitation would define abusive registration by reference only to trademarks and service marks. *Thus, registrations that violate trade names, geographical indications or personality rights would not be considered to fall within the definition of abusive registration for the purposes of the administrative procedure.* Those in favor of this form of limitation pointed out that the violation of trademarks (and service marks) was the most common form of abuse and that the law with respect to trade names, geographical indications and personality rights is less evenly harmonized throughout the world, although international norms do exist requiring the protection of trade names and geographical indications. We are persuaded by the wisdom of proceeding firmly but cautiously and of tackling, at the first stage, problems which all agree require a solution. ... [W]e consider that it is premature to extend the notion of abusive registration beyond the violation of trademarks and service marks at this stage. After experience has been gained with the operation of the administrative procedure and time has allowed for an assessment of its efficacy and of the problems, if any, which remain outstanding, the question of extending the notion of abusive registration to other intellectual property rights can always be revisited.

It is clear from this statement that personality rights were not intended to be made subject to the proposed dispute resolution procedure. In adopting the procedure proposed in the WIPO Report, ICANN did not vary this limitation on its application. It must be concluded, therefore, that ICANN did not intend the procedure to apply to personality rights.

6.5 In the opinion of this Administrative Panel, it is doubtful whether the Uniform Policy is applicable to this dispute. Although it is accepted that the Complainant is world famous under the name STING, it does not follow that he has rights in STING *as a trademark or service mark*. Unlike the personal names in issue in the cases *Julia Fiona Roberts v Russell Boyd, Jeannette Winterson v Mark Hogarth, and Steven Rattner v BuyThisDomainName (John Pepin)*, the personal name in this case is also a common word in the English language, with a number of different meanings. The following are the entries for 'sting' from Merriam-Webster's Collegiate Dictionary:

sting *vb* stung; sting.ing [ME, fr. OE stingan; akin to ON stinga to sting and prob. to Gk stachys spike of grain, stochos target, aim] *vt* (bef. 12c) **1:** to prick painfully: as **a:** to pierce or wound with a poisonous or irritating process **b:** to affect with sharp quick pain or smart—'hail stung their faces' **2:** to cause to suffer acutely 'stung with remorse' **3:** overcharge, cheat *vi* **1:** to wound one with or as if with a sting **2:** to feel a keen burning pain or smart; also: to cause such pain—sting.ing.ly *adv* sting *n* (bef. 12c) **1 a:** the act of stinging; specif: the thrust of a stinger into the flesh **b:** a wound or pain caused by or as if by stinging **2:** stinger 2 **3:** a sharp or stinging element, force, or quality **4:** an elaborate confidence game; specif: such a game worked by undercover police in order to trap criminals

6.6 In light of the fact that the word 'sting' is in common usage in the English language, with a number of meanings, this case can be distinguished from the other cases cited above in which the Complainants' personal name was found also to be an unregistered trademark or service mark to which the Uniform Policy applies. This Administrative Panel is inclined to the view, therefore, that the Complainant's name STING is not a trademark or service mark within the scope of paragraph 4(a)(i) of the Uniform Policy. However, it is not necessary to reach a formal decision on this issue, because this Administrative Panel finds against the Complainant on other grounds, namely that the requirement of paragraph 4(a)(iii) is not met, as discussed below.

RESPONDENT'S RIGHTS OR LEGITIMATE INTERESTS IN THE DOMAIN NAME

6.7 The Respondent provided evidence of circumstances of the type specified in paragraph 4(c) of the Uniform Policy as giving rise to a right to or legitimate interest in the domain name. In particular, the Respondent provided in Exhibit C of the Response copies of various e-mail communications to him prior to the commencement of this dispute, showing that the 'UserName', the 'nickname', the 'Screen Name', or the 'Account PIC' under which the Respondent had registered for global Internet gaming services consisted of or included the word 'sting'. In Exhibit D to the Response, the Respondent provided copies of web page printouts from The Champions League of Quake, a service which monitors Quake servers and keeps track of the scores of registered players of this game. Those printouts show that the Respondent played this game using the player names 'sting' or '=sting='. In addition, the Respondent provided evidence in Exhibit E to the Response of preparations by him to establish a web site at the URL http://www. sting com.

6.8 Although this evidence is not irrelevant to the issue of whether or not the Respondent has a right to or a legitimate interest in the domain name, it is certainly at the weaker end of the spectrum of such evidence. The Respondent's use of the name 'sting' or '=sting=' for gaming does not establish that he has been 'commonly known' by the domain name as contemplated by paragraph 4(c)(ii). The word is undistinctive, and most likely is used by numerous people in cyberspace. In practice, this word provides the Respondent with anonymity rather than with a name by which he is commonly known. The Respondent's evidence of his preparations to establish a web site at the URL http://www.sting.com does not establish the circumstances contemplated by paragraph 4(c)(i), because there is no evidence that this proposed use of the domain name is in connection with a bona fide offering of goods or services.

6.9 In short, a more substantive use of the word 'sting' than that proven by the Respondent is required to show a right or legitimate interest in the domain name 'sting.com' (although this proven use is relevant to the issue of bad faith). On balance, therefore, this Administrative Panel finds that the Respondent does not have a right to or a legitimate interest in the domain name, in the sense in which that concept is used in paragraph 4(a)(ii) of the Uniform Policy.

DOMAIN NAME REGISTERED AND USED IN BAD FAITH

6.10 The Complainant has not satisfied this Administrative Panel that the Respondent registered and is using the domain name in bad faith. The Complainant asserted that the Respondent offered to sell the domain name to the Complainant for $25,000, but the Complainant provided no evidence in support of this assertion. In particular, the Complainant provided no evidence of the Respondent's alleged communications with the Complainant on this issue. The Respondent admitted that he offered to sell the domain name to the Complainant, but only after the Complainant solicited that offer. (The Respondent did not specify the price at which he offered to sell the domain name, but he did not dispute the Complainant's assertion of $25,000, so this Administrative Panel assumes the offered price was for that amount, or at least for an amount in excess of the Respondent's out-of-pocket expenses.) Although this evidence is *consistent* with the Complainant's contention that the Respondent acquired the domain name primarily for the purpose of selling it to the Complainant, as required by paragraph 4(b)(i), this evidence does not *prove* that. This evidence is equally consistent with the Respondent's contention that he acquired the domain name five years ago in good faith. In the absence of any evidence whatsoever from the Complainant going to the assertion of the Respondent's offer to sell the domain name, this Administrative Panel finds that the Complainant has not met the burden of proof on this issue.

6.11 This Administrative Panel does not accept the Complainant's contention that the linking of the domain name to the 'GunBroker.com' web site constituted intentionally attempting to attract, for commercial gain, Internet users to an online location by creating a likelihood of confusion with the STING mark as to source, sponsorship, affiliation, or endorsement, and so constitutes an activity which corresponds to that listed in paragraph 4(b)(iv) of the Uniform Policy as evidence of bad faith registration and use of the domain name. Again, the Complainant provided no evidence in support of this contention. In particular, the Complainant provided no evidence as to the contents of the 'GunBroker.com' site, and thus no evidence establishing that a likelihood of confusion with the STING mark was created as to source, sponsorship, affiliation or endorsement of the site. The Respondent admitted that the domain name did point to the 'GunBroker.com' site for a period of time, but provided evidence to the effect that this was due to an error on the part of the Respondent's web service provider. The evidence is therefore consistent with the Respondent's contention that there was no intentional attempt to attract Internet users for commercial gain. Once again, the Complainant has failed to satisfy its burden of proof on this point.

6.12 Finally, this Administrative Panel does not accept the Complainant's contention that 'it is not possible to conceive of any plausible actual or contemplated active use of the [D]omain [N]ame by the Respondent that would not be illegitimate, such as by being a passing off, an infringement of consumer protection legislation, or an infringement of the Complainant's rights under trademark law'. The words in quotation marks come from *Telstra Corporation Limited v Nuclear Marshmallows* WIPO Case No D2000-0003. In the *Telstra* case, the trademark in question was an invented word. In this case the mark in question is a common word in the English language, with a number of meanings. Unlike the situation in the *Telstra* case, therefore, it is far from inconceivable that there is a plausible legitimate use to which the Respondent could put the domain name. The Respondent has asserted a legitimate use to which he has put, and intends to put, the domain name. While the evidence provided in support of this assertion is not particularly strong, it is at least consistent with that assertion, and with his overall contention that he did not register and has not been using the domain name in bad faith. The Complainant has thus failed to satisfy the burden of proof on this point.

7. Decision

7.1 This Administrative Panel decides that the Complainant has not proven each of the three elements in paragraph 4(a) of the Uniform Policy in relation to the domain name the subject of the Complaint.

7.2 Pursuant to paragraph 4(i) of the Uniform Policy and paragraph 15 of the Uniform Rules, this Administrative Panel denies the request that the Registrar, Network Solutions, Inc, be required either to transfer to the Complainant, Gordon Sumner, p/k/a Sting, or to cancel, the domain name 'sting.com'.

 NOTES AND QUESTIONS

1 Compare and contrast the reasoning employed in *Sting* with that employed in the *Madonna* decision extracted above. Which do you find more persuasive?

2 Outline the central elements that a court will seek evidence of in order to transfer ownership of a domain name.

3 Examine the following two statements:

> *Bruce Springsteen v Jeff Burgar and Bruce Springsteen Club* WIPO Case No D2000-1532
>
> There is simply no evidence put forward by the Complainant that there has been any attempt by Mr Burgar to sell the domain name, either directly or indirectly.
>
> *Harrods Limited v Robert Boyd* WIPO Case No D2000-0060

It is also clear that the Respondent has no right or legitimate interest in respect of the domain normal name. He has since offered to sell it for a large sum of money.

Do you believe that the emphasis on commercial gain is an appropriate standard by which to judge the actions of registrants? How does this accord with the decisions discussed above? Why do these fora rely on this as a mark of bad faith?

4　Compare the reasoning in the above two decisions with the judicial decisions you have read throughout this chapter. In what respects do you find the two to be similar? In what respects do they differ?

5　In general, there are at least two distinctive approaches in panelists' application of the applicable rules. On the one hand, the approach in *Shirmax Shirmax Retail Ltd v CES Marketing Group Inc*, Case No AF0104, advocates strict construction of the Policy and the Rules, imposing on the complainant a considerable burden of proof before ordering a domain name's transfer. Alternatively, the approach in *Educational Testing Service v TOEFL*, WIPO Case No D2000-0044, emphasises the purpose of the Policy to be curbing abusive registration of domain names, an emphasis that influences the evaluation of evidence.

6　The UDRP has both been criticised and praised by commentators. Amongst the criticisms, it is said that the UDRP operates under a narrow paradigm where the complainant always has a 'legitimate interest' in the domain name, usually through a trade mark and it ignores situations where two organisations may have legitimate claims to the domain name.[33] From the foregoing disputes, do you agree with such a criticism?

7　It is true that complainants are likely to forum shop between approved providers, on the basis of differences in procedures, processes, and technologies used by each provider. However, unlike forum shopping across the legal processes of different jurisdictions, the set of rules that the complainant will be relying on are uniform no matter which provider is used.[34] In any event, the strength of the UDRP may lie in its very existence which serves as a deterrent to abuse of the domain name system. The UDRP is also inexpensive, fast, easy to use and, given it operates on the Internet, it is also highly accessible.

In the Report of the Second WIPO Process which was initiated to address certain intellectual property issues relating to Internet domain names, the issue of personal names when used in domain names was also dealt with.

33　Jacqueline D Lipton, 'Beyond Cybersquatting: Taking Domain Name Disputes Past Trademark Policy' (2005) 40 *Wake Forest Law Review* 1361 at 1377.

34　Jay P Kesan and Andres A Gallo, 'The Market for Private Dispute Resolution Services: An Empirical Reassessment of ICANN-UDRP Performance' (2005) 11 *Michigan Telecommunications and Technology Law Review* 285.

Report of the Second WIPO Internet Domain Name Process, 'The Recognition of Rights and the Use of Names in the Internet Domain Name System'

3 September 2001

Available at <http://arbiter.wipo.int/processes/> 17 August 2006

169 Identity is a fundamental attribute of 'the inherent dignity of the human person'. Many things are important in constituting a person's identity. The personal name is foremost among them and assists in creating distinctiveness or individuality, as well as serves as a succinct symbol pregnant with the associations that others have with that person. The importance of personal names to dignity is evident from the dark days of totalitarianism and nazism, when names were only numbers.

170 It has been often pointed out that the power and ubiquity of the technologies of communication and telecommunication have created greater opportunity for invasion of personal space and the use of attributes of personal identity in ways which are not approved by the person concerned. At the same time, these technologies have, in enhancing the visibility of public figures and leading business, sports and entertainment personalities, established the celebrity as a mundane feature of society.

171 The personal name is a difficult subject to treat. There is considerable diversity around the world in the way in which it is formulated and presented. These formulations and presentations (for example, which name, family or given, comes first, or whether the name consists of these two elements at all) are usually the result of the historical and cultural traditions of particular societies. Many sensitivities, including religious, political, historical, cultural and psychological, are touched by the subject of personal names.

The legal protection accorded to personal names

172 Personal names are rarely protected *as such* by the law. Their protection is usually a part of a broader legal principle or policy of which the misuse of personal names constitutes only one means of violation. Other means of violation include misuse of a person's likeness, image or voice.

173 Because of the diversity of interests affected by the treatment of personal names, the legal principles and policies that can be deployed to protect personal names are similarly diverse and vary, as might be expected, from country to country. These legal principles and policies include the right to publicity or the right to control the commercial use of one's identity, recognized in many states of the United States of America; the tort of unfair competition; the tort of passing off (conceptually treated, in many cases, as part of the law of unfair competition), recognized generally in common law countries; and the right to privacy.

174 It has not been possible to review in detail all the legal principles and policies that can be used for the protection of personal names in all of the countries of the world.

Nevertheless, it is possible to identify two main interests that underlie particular approaches adopted in a number of countries to the protection of personal names against misuse:

(i) A commonly expressed public policy for the protection of personal names against misuse is economic. This economic policy, in turn, has two bases. The first of those bases is the prevention of unjust enrichment through the unauthorized commercial use of another's identity. As stated by Kalven and quoted by the Supreme Court of the United States of America, 'The rationale for [protecting the right of publicity] is the straightforward one of preventing unjust enrichment by the theft of good will. No social purpose is served by having the defendant get free some aspect of the plaintiff that would have market value and for which he would normally pay.' The second basis of the economic interest underlying the protection of personal names against misuse is the prevention of deception and confusion on the part of consumers.

(ii) A social interest is also expressed as underlying legal principles protecting personal names against misuse. This interest is apparent in the right to privacy, or the qualified right to control exposure of oneself, where personal distress and anxiety are recognized as valid reasons to accord protection.

In a number of cases, both the economic and the social interests are recognized in the protection that law accords. Thus, in Switzerland, Article 29.2 of the Civil Code states that 'Where a person assumes the name of another to the latter's prejudice, the latter can apply for an injunction to restrain the continuation of this assumption, and can in addition claim damages if the act is proved to be wrongful, and moral compensation if this is justified by the nature of the wrong suffered.' And in Spain, Section 7.6 of the Law of 5 May 1982 provides that the unpermitted use of one's name, voice or likeness for *advertising or trade* purposes is an invasion of one's *personal* life.

175 The notoriety that attaches to certain persons can, in some countries, establish a basis for protection which is not available to ordinary persons. In other instances, notoriety can be a factor which can influence the extent of damages granted as a result of the wrongful use of the person's name, rather than a ground for establishing a separate form of protection from that available to non-famous persons.

176 In commerce, the protection that is recognized for personal names and other attributes of the personality is usually exploited through the vehicle of contract. Thus, by permitting, under contract (or license), another to use a person's name in association with products or services, the personal name becomes an asset.

177 The status of the personal name as a potential asset may be secured through the registration of a trademark (or service mark). Most national laws, and the Agreement on Trade-Related Aspects of Intellectual Property Rights (the TRIPS Agreement), explicitly recognize that personal names are eligible for registration as trademarks. While personal names are eligible for registration as trademarks, however, like any sign for which trademark registration is sought, they must be distinctive in order to be valid trademarks. Distinctiveness can be inherent, or can be acquired through use which causes consumers to identify the name with a particular source of goods or services.

178 While there are, as indicated in the preceding paragraphs, several different legal doctrines that apply on a widespread basis at the national level to protect personal names against misuse, there is no specific norm established at the international level for the protection of personal names. The absence of any such norm reflects the fact that there is a diversity of legal approaches to the protection of personal names at the national level.

Protection of personal names under the UDRP

179 As mentioned above, personal names may, in appropriate circumstances, be registered as trademarks and, in practice, many are. The protection of personal names as trademarks has provided a basis for the application of the Uniform Domain Name Dispute Resolution Policy (UDRP) to the protection of personal names against deliberate, bad faith registration as domain names in the gTLDs. While a few oppose this application of the UDRP, the clear weight of authority of many decisions is in favor of the application of the UDRP to the protection of personal names when they constitute trademarks. The present section of this Chapter outlines the main trends in this authority. Annex VI to this Report contains an indicative list of UDRP cases involving personal names that have been filed with the WIPO Arbitration and Mediation Center.

180 It is recalled that the UDRP provides that three conditions must be satisfied in order to establish that a domain name registration is abusive and that the complainant is entitled to relief:

(i)   the domain name is identical or confusingly similar to a trademark or service mark in which the complainant has rights;

(ii) the registrant of the domain name has no rights or legitimate interests in respect of the domain name; and

(iii) the domain name has been registered and is being used in bad faith.

The application of each of these conditions in the context of the protection of personal names is described in the ensuing paragraphs.

Trademark or service mark rights

181 The first condition requires that in each case the complainant must demonstrate that the personal name in question is protected as a trademark or service mark, in which that complainant has rights.

182 There have been a number of cases in which a complainant has demonstrated that it meets this requirement by submitting evidence that the personal name in question is registered as a trademark. The UDRP, however, does not require that a complainant must hold rights specifically in a *registered* trademark or service mark. Instead, it provides only that there must be 'a trademark or service mark in which the complainant has *rights*', without specifying how these rights are acquired. With this distinction in mind, many decisions under the UDRP have therefore determined that common law or unregistered trademark rights may be asserted by a complainant and will satisfy the first condition of the UDRP. In relation to personal names, in particular, numerous

UDRP decisions have relied upon a complainant's demonstration that it holds such common law rights in the disputed name. In making these decisions, panels have given attention to a number of factors, including:

(i) the distinctive character or notoriety of the name and the requirement that the domain name must be 'identical or confusingly similar' to it,

(ii) the relationship between this distinctive character and use of the name in connection with goods or services in commerce, and

(iii) the location of the parties and the bearing that this may have on the acquisition of unregistered trademark rights.

183 Regarding the distinctiveness of the name, panels have emphasized in many cases that the particular complainant's personal name, in the relevant field of commerce, enjoys widespread notoriety and fame. 'A claim based on an unregistered mark, including a personal name, requires that the claimant establish the distinctive character of the mark or name on which the claim is based.' Panels have also focused this analysis of distinctive character in relation to the second element mentioned above, 'whether or not the person in question is sufficiently famous in connection with the services offered by that complainant' in commerce. Using a personal name in association with certain goods or services can create distinctiveness and a secondary meaning in the name. With respect to similarity between the personal name in which trademark rights are held and the domain name registration, panels have found that small variations between the two (eg, such as removing the space between the first and last names), just as in cases involving words or terms other than personal names, are legally insignificant, so long as the registered domain name is 'confusingly similar' to the personal name.

184 The location of the parties can be significant for determining whether the complainant has trademark rights. Rule 15(a) of the Rules for Uniform Domain Name Dispute Resolution Policy (the 'Rules of Procedure') provides that the panel shall decide a complaint on the basis, *inter alia*, of '... any rules and principles of law that it deems applicable.' The applicable law will depend on the facts of the case, including the location of the parties. This Rule has allowed panels the flexibility to deal with disputes between parties with different national affiliations and concerning activity on a global medium. It is also a feature that has enabled complainants to seek protection for their names under trademark law, although they have not registered their names as a trademark or service mark in every country of the world.

The registrant has no rights or legitimate interests in the domain name

185 The second condition of the UDRP requires that there be no evidence that the domain name registrant has any rights or legitimate interests in the domain name that it has registered. Panels normally review the full record in a case to assess whether a respondent has any rights or interests in the domain name. Based on the distinctiveness of the personal name in question and certain facts indicating that (i) the domain name does not correspond to the respondent's own name, and (ii) the respondent has registered the names of many other celebrities, this determination in a number of cases has been

almost self-evident. In other cases, however, a more probing analysis has been called for. For example, the panel in one case found that, while the respondent's use of the name in question, 'sting', as a nickname on the Internet was *not* substantial enough to show any rights or legitimate interests in the domain name *sting.com*, the respondent's proven use was in fact relevant to the separate issue of bad faith. In another case, the panel disagreed with the respondent's argument that the domain name in question, *sade.com*, was being offered merely as a legitimate e-mail service. Instead, the panel found that, by placing the domain name in the music section of its web site and having registered it under the contact, 'The Sade Internet Fan Club', the respondent 'has set out to deliberately associate this service with the Complainant'. In a further case, the panel acknowledged that the respondent's contention was a serious one and that use of the domain name in question, *montyroberts.net*, was for legitimate non-commercial or fair use purposes. In balancing the rights of the complainant in its mark and the rights of the respondent to freely express its views about the complainant, however, the panel determined that:

> the right to express one's views is not the same as the right to use another's name to identify oneself as the source of those views. One may be perfectly free to express his or her views about the quality or characteristics of the reporting of *The New York Times* or *Time Magazine*. That does not, however, translate into a right to identify oneself as The New York Times or Time Magazine.

186 The panel found that, while the respondent's primary motive for establishing the web site might have been to criticize the complainant, this did 'not insulate Respondent from the fact that it is directly and indirectly offering products for sale on its web site, or at web sites hyperlinked to its site.'

The domain name has been registered and is being used in bad faith

187 The third condition that must be satisfied is evidence of bad faith. The UDRP sets forth four non-exhaustive examples of what may be considered 'evidence of the registration and use of a domain name in bad faith'. A review of the decisions concerning personal names indicates that each of these circumstances has been relied upon in one or more cases to support a determination that the registration and use of the domain name in dispute was in bad faith. Given the distinctive character of a number of the names in question and a consideration of other relevant facts, an underlying and consistent perception has been that the respondent, through the domain name registration, has clearly targeted the complainant's unique personal or professional name. Panels, however, have exercised caution in confirming that such parasitic practices relate to one of the illustrative bad faith factors listed in the UDRP or to a similar bad faith *commercial* exploitation of the complainant's name. Thus, in one case the panel ruled that, where the domain name was identical to the complainant's professional name but was connected to a *non-commercial* web site expressing criticism of the complainant (operated by a brother-in-law), the case involved alleged defamation and not infringement of a trademark right. Defamation, which goes to the reputation of an individual, does not have any necessary relationship to the commercial and infringing exploitation of a personal name used as a mark.

188 The UDRP has proven to be a useful tool for giving expression to the protection of personal names where trademark rights exist in those personal names, where the domain name holder has no right or legitimate interest and where there is evidence of bad faith in the registration and use of the domain name. However, it by no means affords comprehensive protection to personal names. For a start, the names of many persons, particularly ordinary persons, may have no distinctiveness attached to them, either inherently or as a result of use. Secondly, the names of political figures, religious leaders, scientists and historical persons may never have been used in commerce and, thus, are unlikely to have trademarks associated with them. Nevertheless, many sensitivities may attach to their use.

Analysis of comments and views expressed in response to the Interim Report

189 The Interim Report formulated three options with respect to the protection of personal names in the DNS and sought further comment on them. These options were:

(i)   The scope of the UDRP should not be broadened to cover personal names beyond those which are already protected under the current UDRP as trade or service marks.

(ii) The scope of the UDRP should be amended to encompass a new and narrow category of claims brought on the basis of a personality right in order to offer additional protection for personal names which do not qualify as trade or service marks under the current UDRP.

(iii) The amended UDRP, as proposed in (ii) above, should be introduced only in the forthcoming new gTLD .name, which is intended to serve individuals and allow them to create their own global digital identity.

190 Since the publication of the Interim Report, the registry of .names has developed an extensive rights protection scheme, including dispute resolution, the essential characteristics of which are reflected in the Appendices to the Registry Agreement which it has entered into with ICANN. Although the procedural and operational details of this scheme remain to be clarified at the time of the publication of this Report, it would appear from those Appendices that the .name protection mechanisms at least are intended to achieve the principal policy objectives underlying the third option proposed in the Interim Report. While only practical experience will demonstrate the effectiveness of those mechanisms, their application in .name will practically implement the third option mentioned above. The comments received on it in response to the Interim Report will not therefore be considered below.

191 The comments received were divided on whether the scope of the UDRP should be broadened to cover personal names that do not qualify as trade or service marks. While a significant number of commentators favored broadening the scope of the UDRP for purposes of protecting personal names, the majority believed that the protection offered by the UDRP in its present form is sufficient and that it should not be expanded to cover personality rights at this time.

192 Those who favor the inclusion of a form of personality right as a basis for formulating a complaint under the UDRP advance essentially two arguments in support of their position. First, they argue that, while the victims of abusive domain name registrations of personal names generally are famous persons, their celebrity status does not necessarily derive from any commercial activity. According to these commentators, there is no valid reason why famous persons whose reputation results from non-commercial activities, and who therefore would not normally qualify for protection under the current UDRP as holders of trade or service marks, should remain unprotected. They conclude that the UDRP should be amended in order to close what they perceive to be an unwarranted gap in the scope of protection that it offers to well-known individuals.

193 A second argument advanced in support of broadening the scope of the UDRP finds its origin in the discrepancies that exist between national laws of countries relating to unregistered trade or service marks. As is apparent from a review of the case law under the UDRP, many celebrities have not registered their personal names as marks, but have been found by panelists to be owners of unregistered marks, which equally qualify for protection under the UDRP. However, not all countries in the world offer protection to unregistered marks. Persons whose activities, even though clearly commercial in nature, are restricted to countries which protect only registered marks (eg, China, France, or Switzerland, among others), and who have not obtained any mark registrations corresponding to their personal names in those countries, would normally not benefit from the UDRP's protection. According to certain commentators, this reveals a bias, built into the UDRP, favoring parties from countries with legal systems protecting unregistered marks, typically (but not exclusively) countries with a common-law tradition. They argue that introducing the personality right as an additional basis for formulating a complaint under the UDRP would be an appropriate and reasonable means of rectifying what they perceive to be a form of discrimination between legal systems which has crept into the current procedure.

194 Those who favor broadening the scope of the UDRP to some form of personality right generally agree that protection should nonetheless be limited to abusive behavior on the part of registrants. Certain of these commentators believe that protection should be offered not only in relation to official personal names, but also to pseudonyms of famous persons (for instance, Kirk Douglas being the pseudonym of Issur Danielovitch Demsky).

195 Commentators who are opposed to broadening the scope of the UDRP to cover personality rights set out various reasons for their reluctance in this regard. Most importantly, they point out that there currently exist no internationally harmonized norms covering personality rights as such. While various forms of personality rights are recognized and protected in many jurisdictions throughout the world, this is achieved by relying on differing legal foundations, including common law principles, civil law provisions, statutory rights of publicity, privacy law and criminal law. In light of these various approaches to the problem, the nature and scope of protection granted to what is conveniently referred to as 'the personality right' varies from one jurisdiction to another. Commentators who resist expanding the scope of the UDRP to personality rights believe that any attempts to create additional protection under these circumstances will have substantial negative effects. They claim that panelists, faced with a void

of harmonized international rules, will be tempted to create new law offering greater protection to personality rights through the UDRP than that which is currently available under national laws. They warn that the UDRP thus would run the risk of developing into an illegitimate source of new and undesired regulation in the personality right arena. Furthermore, they believe that, in light of discrepancies between national laws, decisions granted under the UDRP would often be perceived as unfair, contested and ultimately invalidated at the national level. According to these commentators, this would be detrimental to the long-term credibility and viability of the UDRP as a consensus-based dispute resolution mechanism.

196 Most other arguments advanced against including some form of personality right as a basis for a complaint under the UDRP directly or indirectly flow from the fundamental difficulty set out in the previous paragraph. These arguments often are based on concerns that protecting personality rights under the UDRP would have a chilling effect on free speech and would unlawfully restrict the availability of names in the DNS. Furthermore, several commentators state that it would be exceedingly difficult to devise a uniform standard for determining who is sufficiently famous to benefit from protection and who is not, although other commentators argue that, to the extent the system would focus on abusive behavior, there would not be a need to limit the protection it offers to famous persons. Still others argue that it would be wholly inappropriate to expand the scope of the UDRP, be it the area of personality rights or in any other area, precisely at the time when preparations are being made to evaluate its operation.

197 Finally, those opposed to the expansion of the UDRP also argue that, as a practical matter, most persons whose personal names run the risk of being cybersquatted derive their celebrity status from commercial activities and therefore can claim the existence of at least an unregistered mark to benefit from the UDRP's protection. In other words, incorporating a personality right into the UDRP, according to this view, would introduce a host of complications for parties, ICANN, dispute resolution providers, and all others involved in the procedure which are unlikely to be in proportion to the magnitude of the problem that is to be addressed.

198 A few commentators have suggested that, if additional protection for personal names is to be incorporated into the UDRP, it should in any event be more narrowly drafted than the proposal reflected in the second option of the Interim Report. These commentators refer to a provision of the United States *Anticybersquatting Consumer Protection Act*, passed into law in November 1999, as a possible model in this connection. The provision in question provides for a cause of action against '[a]ny person who registers a domain name that consists of the name of another living person, or a name substantially and confusingly similar thereto, without that person's consent, with the specific intent to profit from such name by selling the domain name for financial gain to that person or any third party ...'.

Recommendation

199 It is clear that many sensitivities are offended by the unauthorized registration of personal names as domain names. It is clear also that UDRP does not provide solace for all those offended sensitivities, nor was it intended to do so, as originally designed.

The result is that there are some perceived injustices. Persons who have gained eminence and respect, but who have not profited from their reputation in commerce, may not avail themselves of the UDRP to protect their personal names against parasitic registrations. The UDRP is thus perceived by some as implementing an excessively materialistic conception of contribution to society. Furthermore, persons whose names have become distinctive in countries that do not recognize unregistered trademark rights are unlikely to find consolation in the UDRP in respect of bad faith registration and use of their personal names as domain names in those countries.

200 Nevertheless, we believe that the views expressed by the majority of commentators against the modification of the UDRP to meet these perceived injustices are convincing at this stage of the evolution of the DNS and the UDRP.

201 The most cogent of the arguments against modification of the UDRP is, we believe, the lack of an international norm protecting personal names and the consequent diversity of legal approaches deployed to protect personal names at the national level. We consider that this diversity would place parties and panelists in an international procedure in an untenable position and would jeopardize the credibility and efficiency of the UDRP.

202 It is recommended that no modification be made to the UDRP to accommodate broader protection for personal names than that which currently exists in the UDRP.

203 In making this recommendation, we are conscious of the strength of feeling that the unauthorized, bad faith registration and use of personal names as domain names engenders. We believe, however, that the most appropriate way in which the strength of this feeling should be expressed is through the development of international norms that can provide clear guidance on the intentions and will of the international community.

204 Insofar as ccTLDs are concerned, the lack of international norms is less significant. Clear law at the national level for the protection of personal names against abusive domain name registrations, if it exists, can be applied to registrations in the corresponding ccTLD.

 NOTES AND QUESTIONS

1   What rights are normally given to protect personal names? What about a person's face and image? What are personality rights?

2   Consider the options proposed in paragraph 189. Critique each of these options.

3   What solutions can you propose to deal with the challenges of personal names, trade marks and domain names? In your response, consider also the examples from the WIPO Administration and Mediation Center, extracted above, which deal with disputes over domain names and personal names.

(g) Cybersquatting

The proliferation of disputes over rights to domain names has led to widespread awareness and concern over the phenomenon termed 'cybersquatting'. In the USA the *Anticybersquatting Consumer Protection Act* (ACPA) was passed in 1999 specifically to outlaw the practice of cybersquatting. It prohibits conduct where a person has the intent, with bad faith, to profit from the goodwill of another's trade mark by registering or using a domain name that is identical with or similar to, or which dilutes a trade mark.

The most interesting aspect of this legislation is 15 USC s 1125(d)(2)(C). This rather obscure provision provides that domain names are property and can be subject to *in rem* actions that can be filed in the judicial district in which the registrar of the domain name is located. Actions *in rem* may proceed directly against the property itself, in this case the domain name, as opposed to *in personam* actions which must be directed against a legal person. In this event, the court's jurisdiction is limited to orders to delete or transfer the name. An *in rem* action may only be initiated when a plaintiff cannot locate the domain name registrant or cannot obtain personal jurisdiction over the registrant.[35]

The creation of an action *in rem* is possibly the first time that domain names have been regarded as property. In *Kremen v Stephen Michael Cohen, Network Solutions, et al*,[36] a dispute over sex.com, specifically ruled that a domain is not property and therefore could not be stolen. There have been quite a number of cases litigated under the ACPA which have been successful (see for example *Coca-Cola v Purdy* 382 F3d 774 (2004); *Mayflower Transit LLC v Prince* 314 F Supp 2d 362 (2004)). It is important to note however the requirement of profiting under the ACPA. In *TMI Inc v Maxwell* 368 F3d 433 (5th Cir 2004), the defendant was unhappy with the plaintiff and trade mark holder and he created a website to tell his story. The website contained a disclaimer that it was not the plaintiff's website and it contained a provision for readers to share information. There were no paid advertisements or links to other sites. On appeal, the Fifth Circuit reversed and held that the defendant's site was not a commercial use, which was required for liability. The site did not have a business purpose and the defendant was not engaged in the business of selling domain names. The defendant did not register domain names in order to sell them to the legitimate owners, which was the paradigmatic harm that the ACPA was enacted to eradicate. Hence, there was no bad faith intent to profit from the trade mark holder's mark.

In Australia, the domain name registration policy[37] of the .com.au domain goes some way towards preventing the practice of cybersquatting. The policy, administered by auDA, operates on the premise that the .com.au exists to enable commercial entities to register a domain name closely aligned with their commercial name. The policy states that the allocation of domain names is determined by a 'first come first served' system. However, the rules strictly require that the domain name be directly derived from the commercial name. To this end, only commercial entities registered and trading in Australia will be granted a .com.au. domain name. Indeed, the policy refers the applicant to state and federal regulations on the registration of business names and there is a requirement that they be registered commercial entities such as:

- companies (including foreign companies registered to trade in Australia)
- registered business names in any Australian State or Territory

---

35   See 15 USC § 1125(d)(2)(A)(ii)(II) and <http://www.worldweb-law.com/articles_5.html> and <http://www.gcwf.com/articles/interest/interest_42.html> 30 September 2001.

36   DC NCalif Case number C-98-20718 JW PVT.

37   See <http://www.auda.org.au/policies/auda-2005-01> 11 May 2006.

- incorporated associations in Australia, and
- Australian commercial statutory bodies.

Applicants can use either their complete commercial name, including trade mark, or an abbreviation in the domain name. When an abbreviation is requested there are three requirements:

- the domain name can only be derived from the characters in the business name
- characters can be removed from the business name but the sequence cannot be altered, and
- new characters cannot be introduced.

Once registered, the use of the name is by licence and this is not transferable. Therefore, even if a complainant wins, the court or panel cannot transfer the registration. The result is that upon successful challenge of a domain name, the complainant would then have to apply and pass through the necessary procedures in order to register the name. The policy also states that there are no proprietary rights in the domain name system.

The point of the system is to encourage registration by legitimate Australian companies and simplify the system of complaint. There are two alternative viewpoints on the merits of this system. On the one hand, in a commercial context, consumers can be assured that they are dealing with a legitimate business entity. Therefore, if a domain name is attached to a legitimate commercial entity the practice of cybersquatting can be largely eliminated. On the other hand, it could be argued that the ease of obtaining a registered business name in Australia and the lack of any thorough checks on the part of the accredited registrars mean that there are no substantial obstacles to registering a .com.au domain name in bad faith in Australia.

Generally speaking, dispute resolution panels aside, courts around the world have generally taken a dim view of cybersquatting activity. This is demonstrated in the United Kingdom with the *One in a Million* case and the New Zealand High Court cases of *DB Breweries Ltd v The Domain Name Co Ltd*[38] and *Qantas Airways Ltd v The Domain Name Company Ltd*.[39] These cases have highlighted the inter-relationship of causes of action in this area as well as demonstrating a distinct lack of judicial sympathy for 'cybersquatters'.

 NOTES AND QUESTIONS

1   Can you reconcile the decisions expressly declaring domain names not to be property with the creation of an *in rem* action? Are you comfortable with their coexistence? Will the jurisprudence be forced to change to accommodate the US legislation?

---

38   Before Randerson J, (2000) 1 NZECC 70–009.
39   Before Anderson J, (2000) 1 NZECC 70–005.

2 Litman[40] has suggested that, in the light of intellectual property owners' success in utilising standard legal protection on the Internet, the passing of the *Anticybersquatting Consumer Protection Act* (1999) grants another massive advantage to large corporations in the pursuit of their interests in domain names. Furthermore, it perpetuates the misconception that domain name space is and should be an extension of trade mark space, and encourages the notion that commercial interests should hold priority in the Internet. Critically analyse these statements in the light of the materials in this chapter.

3 Compare the decisions in the New Zealand cases with the decision in *Fletcher Challenge* in the New South Wales Supreme Court. The issue of when a domain name transcends its address function to become an identifying business feature is crucial to the Internet. If the domain name must be regarded solely as either address or identifier, which do you prefer? In your answer consider both the function of the domain name and the relationship between the domain name and the Internet protocol address. Consider also the fact that a registered trade mark is technically property, whereas a phone number is a service.

- -

4   Conclusion

The Internet is arguably the largest marketplace the world has ever seen. As such, laws to protect fair competition and to protect consumers are extremely important. Trade mark law is one branch of law which has acceptance in many jurisdictions; however, its acceptance worldwide as a branch of legal principles is distinct from its ability to operate worldwide. Trade mark law is designed to afford protection at the local or domestic level and not the international level. The Internet, however, is global, and therein lies the problem. The problem is further compounded by the peculiarities of the World Wide Web protocol, with the resulting need to transpose the existing trade mark law to the new setting. The moulding of the law to fit the new facts must be exercised with great care and without losing sight of the original rationales underlying the trade marks regime. Sadly, like copyright law, it seems trade mark law is on the march to giving trade mark holders even greater rights than ever. Trade mark holders' interests have been heard by the press and by the judiciary worldwide. However, the battle is not yet over. There is still hope, particularly in the ICANN Uniform Domain Name Dispute Resolution Policy and its refinement and further adoption.

---

40   J Litman, 'The DNS Wars: Trademarks and the Internet Domain Name System' 4 *Journal of Small & Emerging Business Law* 149 (2000).

11 Patents

----

1 Overview

In this chapter we will consider a particular type of patent that has been hotly debated in Australia, the USA, and many other parts of the world. Before we embark on that journey, we must first consider the patent system generally. A patent is a grant of monopoly power by the state to an inventor, who is given the exclusive right to commercially exploit his or her invention for a period of time. In return for stating the details of the invention in a public document, the inventor is given the power to control the market for the invention. The rationale for the patent system is that it provides an incentive to invent and innovate and to invest in processes that will lead to invention and innovation. Over time, this will yield high returns for society.

In Australia, patents are granted to inventors in accordance with the procedures established under the *Patents Act 1990* (Cth). To obtain a patent in Australia, an application must be made to the Patent Office within the organisation IP Australia. There are also equivalent bodies in other countries, established under the Patent Cooperation Treaty. The role of the Patent Office in Australia and the other equivalent bodies around the world is to scrutinise applications to ascertain whether the statutory requirements have been satisfied. In Australia and in many other countries, patents are awarded on a first-to-file basis, which means that the first applicant has a priority over those who file later. In the USA, a first-to-invent system is utilised.

----

2 Patentable inventions

The patent system in Australia provides for the protection of the standard patent. Until 24 May 2001, it also provided for a petty patent system. After that date, the petty patent system was replaced by the innovation patent system.

Section 18 of the *Patents Act* specifies the requirements for a device, substance, method, or process to qualify as a patent.

Patents Act 1990 (Cth) as Amended

18. PATENTABLE INVENTIONS
Patentable inventions for the purposes of a standard patent
(1) Subject to subsection (2), an invention is a patentable invention for the purposes of a standard patent if the invention, so far as claimed in any claim:

 (a) is a manner of manufacture within the meaning of section 6 of the Statute of Monopolies; and
 (b) when compared with the prior art base as it existed before the priority date of that claim:
  (i)   is novel; and
  (ii) involves an inventive step; and
 (c) is useful; and
 (d) was not secretly used in the patent area before the priority date of that claim by, or on behalf of, or with the authority of, the patentee or nominated person or the patentee's or nominated person's predecessor in title to the invention.

Patentable inventions for the purposes of an innovation patent

(1A) Subject to subsections (2) and (3), an invention is a patentable invention for the purposes of an innovation patent if the invention, so far as claimed in any claim:

 (a) is a manner of manufacture within the meaning of section 6 of the Statute of Monopolies; and
 (b) when compared with the prior art base as it existed before the priority date of that claim:
  (i)   is novel; and
  (ii) involves an innovative step; and
 (c) is useful; and
 (d) was not secretly used in the patent area before the priority date of that claim by, or on behalf of, or with the authority of, the patentee or nominated person or the patentee's or nominated person's predecessor in title to the invention.

(2) Human beings, and the biological processes for their generation, are not patentable inventions.

Certain inventions not patentable inventions for the purposes of an innovation patent

(3) For the purposes of an innovation patent, plants and animals, and the biological processes for the generation of plants and animals, are not patentable inventions.

(4) Subsection (3) does not apply if the invention is a microbiological process or a product of such a process.

7. NOVELTY AND INVENTIVE STEP

Novelty

(1) For the purposes of this Act, an invention is to be taken to be novel when compared with the prior art base unless it is not novel in the light of any one of the following kinds of information, each of which must be considered separately:

    (a) prior art information (other than that mentioned in paragraph (c)) made publicly available in a single document or through doing a single act;

    (b) prior art information (other than that mentioned in paragraph (c)) made publicly available in 2 or more related documents, or through doing 2 or more related acts, if the relationship between the documents or acts is such that a person skilled in the relevant art would treat them as a single source of that information;

    (c) prior art information contained in a single specification of the kind mentioned in subparagraph (b)(ii) of the definition of *prior art base* in Schedule 1.

Inventive step

(2) For the purposes of this Act, an invention is to be taken to involve an inventive step when compared with the prior art base unless the invention would have been obvious to a person skilled in the relevant art in the light of the common general knowledge as it existed in the patent area before the priority date of the relevant claim, whether that knowledge is considered separately or together with the information mentioned in subsection (3).

(3) The information for the purposes of subsection (2) is:

    (a) any single piece of prior art information; or

    (b) a combination of any 2 or more pieces of prior art information;

    being information that the skilled person mentioned in subsection (2) could, before the priority date of the relevant claim, be reasonably expected to have ascertained, understood and regarded as relevant and, in the case of information mentioned in paragraph (b), combined as mentioned in that paragraph.

Innovative step

(4) For the purposes of this Act, an invention is to be taken to involve an innovative step when compared with the prior art base unless the invention would, to a person skilled in the relevant art, in the light of the common general knowledge as it existed in the

patent area before the priority date of the relevant claim, only vary from the kinds of information set out in subsection (5) in ways that make no substantial contribution to the working of the invention.

(5) For the purposes of subsection (4), the information is of the following kinds:

    (a) prior art information made publicly available in a single document or through doing a single act;

    (b) prior art information made publicly available in 2 or more related documents, or through doing 2 or more related acts, if the relationship between the documents or acts is such that a person skilled in the relevant art would treat them as a single source of that information.

(6) For the purposes of subsection (4), each kind of information set out in subsection (5) must be considered separately.

 NOTES AND QUESTIONS

1   Compare the requirements for an innovative patent and a standard patent. How do they differ? Does one have a higher inventive threshold? Innovation patents are designed for lower-level inventions, and have a shorter life than standard patents (eight years compared with twenty). They are mainly aimed at domestic small-to-medium business enterprises to enable them to obtain protection for their inventions more quickly, without the hurdles of a standard patent.

2   Describe the criteria that a patent application must satisfy in order to fulfil the requirement of novelty.

3   Compare ss 7(2) and 7(4). Outline the substantive difference between these two provisions.

3 Unpatentable items

A patent cannot be granted for a mere discovery, idea, principle, or natural phenomenon. The leading Australian case on what inventions are patentable is the 1959 decision of the High Court in *NRDC v Commissioner of Patents*.[1] In the *NRDC* case, the High Court held that a process would be patentable if it offered some material advantage in the sense of being a useful art as distinct from a fine art, and was of economic value. Patents can therefore provide protection for technological developments. Patents can be granted over new machines, industrial methods, drugs, methods for making drugs, computer hardware, and even toys. But in many cases, one does not need to make a major breakthrough to be awarded a patent. Often, patented inventions are improvements to existing products or processes.

    Patent protection gives the inventor the exclusive right to commercially exploit the process or product described. The patent owner can sue any person who infringes his or her rights by making, selling, hiring, or using the patented invention during the term

---

1   (1959) 102 CLR 252.

of the patent. The patent owner may grant rights to others to 'exploit' the invention through licences. In exchange for this right, of course, the inventor must disclose his or her invention to the world.

4   Computer software

Patents have been granted for computer hardware for many years. Despite the *NRDC* decision, patent applications for computer software, on the other hand, were often rejected until the early 1990s. It was thought that computer software related to unpatentable subject matter as they involved abstract ideas, intellectual processes, and mathematical algorithms or schemes for operating machines. Cases decided during the 1990s in Australia and in the USA have made it clear that patents can be granted for innovations in computer software.

In Australia, the turning point was the 1991 case of *International Business Machines Corp v Commissioner of Patents*,[2] in which the Federal Court applied a broad test based on the principles established by the High Court in the *NRDC* case. In *International Business Machines Corp*, the patent was for the invention of a method and apparatus for producing a curve image in computer graphics displays. The method involved the use of mathematical algorithms in computing software. The use of mathematical algorithms was held in *International Business Machines Corp* to be analogous to the use of the compounds in *NRDC*. The court reasoned that there was nothing new about the mathematical algorithm, just as in the *NRDC* case, there was nothing new about the compounds. What was new, however, was the application of the selected mathematical methods to computers, and in particular, to the production of the desired curve images by the computer. This, it was said, involved inventive steps. The court did not give protection to a mathematical algorithm but to the application of the algorithm to achieve an end. Further, the court also held that the production of an improved curve image is a commercially useful effect in computer graphics and hence it belonged to the useful arts.

5   E-commerce patents

The rise of e-commerce has introduced a new kind of claim for patent protection—that of the on-line business method patent, or more simply e-commerce patent. An on-line business method is a business method directed to e-commerce, which uses the Internet as the vehicle for doing business. An e-commerce patent, then, is a patent to protect a method of doing business on the Internet. The two main objections that have been raised concerning such patents are first, they deal with computer software and second, they deal with business methods. The software debate has been settled in Australia and

---

2   (1991) 22 IPR 417. *CCOM Pty Ltd v Jie-jing Pty Ltd* (1994) 28 IPR 481. A decision of the Full Federal Court also found computer software patentable.

in other countries. It is the business method concern that we turn to for the remainder of this chapter.

Business methods can encompass a large variety of areas such as manufacturing, selling, and accounting. Manufacturing and accounting functions are primarily internal functions of the business, and with proper precaution and diligence, they can be protected as confidential information or trade secrets. By contrast, sales functions involve a large number of people outside the business who require access to information about the business's product or service in order to participate in the selling process and hence confidential information protection would not be appropriate. The Internet is undoubtedly an ideal medium for selling but the involvement of the many parties make protection of this form of business method under laws of confidentiality extremely difficult. Consequently, many organisations have been pursuing patent protection for their Internet sales-related business models.

State Street Bank and Trust Co v Signature Financial Group, Inc

United States Court of Appeals for the Federal Circuit, 96-1327

Available at

< http://www.ll.georgetown.edu/Federal/judicial/fed/opinions/97opinions/97-1327.html>
17 August 2006

Before Rich, Plager, and Bryson, Circuit Judges:

Background

Signature is the assignee of the '056 patent which is entitled 'Data Processing System for Hub and Spoke Financial Services Configuration'. The '056 patent was issued to Signature on 9 March 1993, naming R Todd Boes as the inventor. The '056 patent is generally directed to a data processing system ('the system') for implementing an investment structure which was developed for use in Signature's business as an administrator and accounting agent for mutual funds. In essence, the system, identified by the proprietary name Hub and Spoke®, facilitates a structure whereby mutual funds (Spokes) pool their assets in an investment portfolio (Hub) organized as a partnership. This investment configuration provides the administrator of a mutual fund with the advantageous combination of economies of scale in administering investments coupled with the tax advantages of a partnership ...

Discussion

... The following facts pertinent to the statutory subject matter issue are either undisputed or represent the version alleged by the nonmovant. See *Anderson v Liberty Lobby, Inc* 477 US 242 at 255 (1986). The patented invention relates generally to a system that allows an administrator to monitor and record the financial information flow and make all calculations necessary for maintaining a partner fund financial services configuration. As previously mentioned, a partner fund financial services configuration essentially allows several mutual funds, or 'Spokes', to pool their investment funds into a single portfolio, or 'Hub', allowing for consolidation of, *inter alia*, the costs of administering the fund combined with the tax advantages of a partnership. In particular, this system provides means for a daily allocation of assets for two or more Spokes that are invested in the same Hub. The system determines the percentage share that each Spoke maintains in the Hub, while taking into consideration daily changes both in the value of the Hub's investment securities and in the concomitant amount of each Spoke's assets.

In determining daily changes, the system also allows for the allocation among the Spokes of the Hub's daily income, expenses, and net realized and unrealized gain or loss, calculating each day's total investments based on the concept of a book capital account. This enables the determination of a true asset value of each Spoke and accurate calculation of allocation ratios between or among the Spokes. The system additionally tracks all the relevant data determined on a daily basis for the Hub and each Spoke, so that aggregate year end income, expenses, and capital gain or loss can be determined for accounting and for tax purposes for the Hub and, as a result, for each publicly traded Spoke.

It is essential that these calculations are quickly and accurately performed. In large part this is required because each Spoke sells shares to the public and the price of those shares is substantially based on the Spoke's percentage interest in the portfolio. In some instances, a mutual fund administrator is required to calculate the value of the shares to the nearest penny within as little as an hour and a half after the market closes. Given the complexity of the calculations, a computer or equivalent device is a virtual necessity to perform the task.

The '056 patent application was filed 11 March 1991. It initially contained six 'machine' claims, which incorporated means-plus-function clauses, and six method claims. According to Signature, during prosecution the examiner contemplated a s 101 rejection for failure to claim statutory subject matter. However, upon cancellation of the six method claims, the examiner issued a notice of allowance for the remaining present six claims on appeal. Only claim 1 is an independent claim.

The district court began its analysis by construing the claims to be directed to a process, with each 'means' clause merely representing a step in that process. However, 'machine' claims having 'means' clauses may only be reasonably viewed as process claims if there is no supporting structure in the written description that corresponds to the claimed 'means' elements. See *In re Alappat*, 33 F 3d 1526 at 1540–1, 31 USPQ 2d 1545 at 1554 (Fed Cir 1994) (*in banc*). This is not the case now before us.

When independent claim 1 is properly construed in accordance with s 112(6), it is directed to a machine, as demonstrated below, where representative claim 1 is set forth, the subject matter in brackets stating the structure the written description discloses as corresponding to the respective 'means' recited in the claims.

1   A data processing system for managing a financial services configuration of a portfolio established as a partnership, each partner being one of a plurality of funds, comprising:

    (a) computer processor means [a personal computer including a CPU] for processing data;

(b)   storage means [a data disk] for storing data on a storage medium;

(c)   first means [an arithmetic logic circuit configured to prepare the data disk to magnetically store selected data] for initializing the storage medium;

(d)   second means [an arithmetic logic circuit configured to retrieve information from a specific file, calculate incremental increases or decreases based on specific input, allocate the results on a percentage basis, and store the output in a separate file] for processing data regarding assets in the portfolio and each of the funds from a previous day and data regarding increases or decreases in each of the funds, [*sic*, funds'] assets and for allocating the percentage share that each fund holds in the portfolio;

(e)   third means [an arithmetic logic circuit configured to retrieve information from a specific file, calculate incremental increases and decreases based on specific input, allocate the results on a percentage basis and store the output in a separate file] for processing data regarding daily incremental income, expenses, and net realized gain or loss for the portfolio and for allocating such data among each fund;

(f)   fourth means [an arithmetic logic circuit configured to retrieve information from a specific file, calculate incremental increases and decreases based on specific input, allocate the results on a percentage basis and store the output in a separate file] for processing data regarding daily net unrealized gain or loss for the portfolio and for allocating such data among each fund; and

(g)   fifth means [an arithmetic logic circuit configured to retrieve information from specific files, calculate that information on an aggregate basis and store the output in a separate file] for processing data regarding aggregate year-end income, expenses, and capital gain or loss for the portfolio and each of the funds.

Each claim component, recited as a 'means' plus its function, is to be read, of course, pursuant to s 112(6), as inclusive of the 'equivalents' of the structures disclosed in the written description portion of the specification. Thus, claim 1, properly construed, claims a machine, namely, a data processing system for managing a financial services configuration of a portfolio established as a partnership, which machine is made up of, at the very least, the specific structures disclosed in the written description and corresponding to the means-plus-function elements (a)-(g) recited in the claim. A 'machine' is proper statutory subject matter under s 101. We note that, for the purposes of a s 101 analysis, it is of little relevance whether claim 1 is directed to a 'machine' or a 'process', as long as it falls within at least one of the four enumerated categories of patentable subject matter, 'machine' and 'process' being such categories.

This does not end our analysis, however, because the court concluded that the claimed subject matter fell into one of two alternative judicially-created exceptions to statutory subject matter. The court refers to the first exception as the 'mathematical algorithm' exception and the second exception as the 'business method' exception. Section 101 reads:

Whoever invents or discovers any new and useful process, machine, manufacture, or composition of matter, or any new and useful improvement thereof, may obtain a patent therefor, subject to the conditions and requirements of this title.

The plain and unambiguous meaning of s 101 is that any invention falling within one of the four stated categories of statutory subject matter may be patented, provided it meets the other requirements for patentability set forth in Title 35, ie, those found in ss. 102, 103, and 112(2).

The repetitive use of the expansive term 'any' in s 101 shows Congress's intent not to place any restrictions on the subject matter for which a patent may be obtained beyond those specifically recited in s 101. Indeed, the Supreme Court has acknowledged that Congress intended s 101 to extend to 'anything under the sun that is made by man' (*Diamond v Chakrabarty*, 447 US 303 at 309 (1980); see also *Diamond v Diehr*, 450 US 175 at 182 (1981)). Thus, it is improper to read limitations into s 101 on the subject matter that may be patented where the legislative history indicates that Congress clearly did not intend such limitations. See Chakrabarty, 447 US at 308 ('We have also cautioned that courts "should not read into the patent laws limitations and conditions which the legislature has not expressed."' (citations omitted)).

THE 'MATHEMATICAL ALGORITHM' EXCEPTION

The Supreme Court has identified three categories of subject matter that are unpatentable, namely 'laws of nature, natural phenomena, and abstract ideas' (*Diehr*, 450 US at 185). Of particular relevance to this case, the Court has held that mathematical algorithms are not patentable subject matter to the extent that they are merely abstract ideas. See *Diehr*, 450 US 175, *passim*; *Parker v Flook*, 437 US 584 (1978); *Gottschalk v Benson*, 409 US 63 (1972). In *Diehr*, the Court explained that certain types of mathematical subject matter, standing alone, represent nothing more than abstract ideas until reduced to some type of practical application, ie, 'a useful, concrete and tangible result' (*Alappat*, 33 F 3d at 1544, 31 USPQ 2d at 1557).

Unpatentable mathematical algorithms are identifiable by showing they are merely abstract ideas constituting disembodied concepts or truths that are not 'useful'. From a practical standpoint, this means that to be patentable an algorithm must be applied in a 'useful' way. In *Alappat*, we held that data, transformed by a machine through a series of mathematical calculations to produce a smooth waveform display on a rasterizer monitor, constituted a practical application of an abstract idea (a mathematical algorithm, formula, or calculation), because it produced 'a useful, concrete and tangible result'—the smooth waveform.

Similarly, in *Arrythmia Research Technology Inc v Corazonix Corp*, 958 F 2d 1053, 22 USPQ 2d 1033 (Fed Cir 1992), we held that the transformation of electrocardiograph signals from a patient's heartbeat by a machine through a series of mathematical calculations constituted a practical application of an abstract idea (a mathematical algorithm, formula, or calculation), because it corresponded to a useful, concrete or tangible thing—the condition of a patient's heart.

Today, we hold that the transformation of data, representing discrete dollar amounts, by a machine through a series of mathematical calculations into a final share price, constitutes a practical application of a mathematical algorithm, formula, or calculation, because it produces 'a useful, concrete and tangible result'—a final share price momentarily fixed for recording and reporting purposes and even accepted and relied upon by regulatory authorities and in subsequent trades.

The district court erred by applying the Freeman-Walter-Abele test to determine whether the claimed subject matter was an unpatentable abstract idea. The Freeman-Walter-Abele test was designed by the Court of Customs and Patent Appeals, and subsequently adopted by this court, to extract and identify unpatentable mathematical algorithms in the aftermath of *Benson* and *Flook*. See *In re Freeman*, 573 F 2d 1237, 197 USPQ 464 (CCPA 1978) as modified by *In re Walter*, 618 F 2d 758, 205 USPQ 397 (CCPA 1980). The test has been thus articulated:

First, the claim is analyzed to determine whether a mathematical algorithm is directly or indirectly recited. Next, if a mathematical algorithm is found, the claim as a whole is further analyzed to determine whether the algorithm is 'applied in any manner to physical elements or process steps', and, if it is, it 'passes muster under s 101': *In re Pardo*, 684 F 2d 912 at 915, 214 USPQ 673 at 675–6 (CCPA 1982) (citing *In re Abele*, 684 F 2d 902, 214 USPQ 682 (CCPA 1982)).

After *Diehr* and *Chakrabarty*, the Freeman-Walter-Abele test has little, if any, applicability to determining the presence of statutory subject matter. As we pointed out in *Alappat* 33 F 3d at 1543, 31 USPQ 2d at 1557, application of the test could be misleading, because a process, machine, manufacture, or composition of matter employing a law of nature, natural phenomenon, or abstract idea is patentable subject matter even though a law of nature, natural phenomenon, or abstract idea would not, by itself, be entitled to such protection. The test determines the presence of, for example, an algorithm. Under *Benson*, this may have been a sufficient indicium of nonstatutory subject matter. However, after *Diehr* and *Alappat*, the mere fact that a claimed invention involves inputting numbers, calculating numbers, outputting numbers, and storing numbers, in and of itself, would not render it nonstatutory subject matter, unless, of course, its operation does not produce a 'useful, concrete and tangible result' (*Alappat*, 33 F 3d at 1544, 31 USPQ 2d at 1557). After all, as we have repeatedly stated,

> every step-by-step process, be it electronic or chemical or mechanical, involves an algorithm in the broad sense of the term. Since s 101 expressly includes processes as a category of inventions which may be patented and s 100(b) further defines the word 'process' as meaning 'process, art or method, and includes a new use of a known process, machine, manufacture, composition of matter, or material', it follows that it is no ground for holding a claim is directed to nonstatutory subject matter to say it includes or is directed to an algorithm. This is why the proscription against patenting has been limited to *mathematical* algorithms ... (*In re Iwahashi*, 888 F 2d 1370 at 1374, 12 USPQ 2d 1908 at 1911 (Fed Cir 1989) (emphasis in the original)).

The question of whether a claim encompasses statutory subject matter should not focus on which of the four categories of subject matter a claim is directed to—process, machine, manufacture, or composition of matter—but rather on the essential characteristics of the subject matter, in particular, its practical utility. Section 101 specifies that statutory subject matter must also satisfy the other 'conditions and requirements' of Title 35, including novelty, non-obviousness, and adequacy of disclosure and notice. See *In re Warmerdam*, 33 F 3d 1354 at 1359, 31 USPQ 2d 1754 at 1757–8 (Fed Cir 1994). For the purpose of our analysis, as noted above, claim 1 is directed to a machine programmed with the Hub and Spoke software and admittedly produces a 'useful, concrete, and tangible result' (*Alappat*,

33 F 3d at 1544, 31 USPQ 2d at 1557). This renders it statutory subject matter, even if the useful result is expressed in numbers, such as price, profit, percentage, cost, or loss.

THE BUSINESS METHOD EXCEPTION
As an alternative ground for invalidating the '056 patent under s 101, the court relied on the judicially-created, so-called 'business method' exception to statutory subject matter. We take this opportunity to lay this ill-conceived exception to rest. Since its inception, the 'business method' exception has merely represented the application of some general, but no longer applicable legal principle, perhaps arising out of the 'requirement for invention'—which was eliminated by s 103. Since the 1952 *Patent Act*, business methods have been, and should have been, subject to the same legal requirements for patentability as applied to any other process or method.

The business method exception has never been invoked by this court, or the CCPA, to deem an invention unpatentable. Application of this particular exception has always been preceded by a ruling based on some clearer concept of Title 35 or, more commonly, application of the abstract idea exception based on finding a mathematical algorithm. Illustrative is the CCPA's analysis in *In re Howard*, 394 F 2d 869, 157 USPQ 615 (CCPA 1968), wherein the court affirmed the Board of Appeals' rejection of the claims for lack of novelty and found it unnecessary to reach the Board's section 101 ground that a method of doing business is 'inherently unpatentable' (*id* at 872, 157 USPQ at 617).

Similarly, *In re Schrader*, 22 F 3d 290, 30 USPQ 2d 1455 (Fed Cir 1994), while making reference to the business method exception, turned on the fact that the claims implicitly recited an abstract idea in the form of a mathematical algorithm and there was no 'transformation or conversion of subject matter representative of or constituting physical activity or objects' (22 F 3d at 294, 30 USPQ 2d at 1459 (emphasis omitted)).

State Street argues that we acknowledged the validity of the business method exception in *Alappat* when we discussed *Maucorps* and *Meyer*:

> *Maucorps* dealt with a business methodology for deciding how salesmen should best handle respective customers and *Meyer* involved a 'system' for aiding a neurologist in diagnosing patients. Clearly, neither of the alleged 'inventions' in those cases falls within any s 101 category (*Alappat*, 33 F 3d at 1541, 31 USPQ 2d at 1555).

However, closer scrutiny of these cases reveals that the claimed inventions in both *Maucorps* and *Meyer* were rejected as abstract ideas under the mathematical algorithm exception, not the business method exception. See *In re Maucorps*, 609 F 2d 481 at 484, 203 USPQ 812 at 816 (CCPA 1979); *In re Meyer*, 688 F 2d 789 at 796, 215 USPQ 193 at 199 (CCPA 1982).

Even the case frequently cited as establishing the business method exception to statutory subject matter, *Hotel Security Checking Co v Lorraine Co*, 160 F 467 (2d Cir 1908), did not rely on the exception to strike the patent. In that case, the patent was found invalid for lack of novelty and 'invention', not because it was improper subject matter for a patent. The court stated 'the fundamental principle of the system is as old as the art of bookkeeping, ie, charging the goods of the employer to the agent who takes them' (*id* at 469). 'If at the time of [the patent] application, there had been no system of bookkeeping of any kind in restaurants, we would be confronted with the question whether a new and useful system of cash registering and account checking is such an art as is patentable under the statute' (*id* at 472).

This case is no exception. The district court announced the precepts of the business method exception as set forth in several treatises, but noted as its primary reason for finding the patent invalid under the business method exception as follows:

> If Signature's invention were patentable, any financial institution desirous of implementing a multi-tiered funding complex modelled (*sic*) on a Hub and Spoke configuration would be required to seek Signature's permission before embarking on such a project. This is so because the '056 Patent is claimed [*sic*] sufficiently broadly to foreclose virtually any computer-implemented accounting method necessary to manage this type of financial structure (927 F Supp 502 at 516, 38 USPQ 2d 1530 at 1542 ...).

Whether the patent's claims are too broad to be patentable is not to be judged under s 101, but rather under ss 102, 103 and 112. Assuming the above statement to be correct, it has nothing to do with whether what is claimed is statutory subject matter.

In view of this background, it comes as no surprise that in the most recent edition of the *Manual of Patent Examining Procedures* ('MPEP') (1996), a paragraph of s 706.03(a) was deleted. In past editions it read:

> Though seemingly within the category of process or method, a method of doing business can be rejected as not being within the statutory classes. See *Hotel Security Checking Co v Lorraine Co*, 160 F 467 (2nd Cir 1908) and *In re Wait*, 24 USPQ 88, 22 CCPA 822 (1934) (MPEP s 706.03(a) (1994)).

This acknowledgment is buttressed by the US Patent and Trademark 1996 Examination Guidelines for Computer Related Inventions which now read:

> Office personnel have had difficulty in properly treating claims directed to methods of doing business. Claims should not be categorized as methods of doing business. Instead such claims should be treated like any other process claims (Examination Guidelines, 61 Fed Reg 7478 at 7479 (1996)).

We agree that this is precisely the manner in which this type of claim should be treated. Whether the claims are directed to subject matter within s 101 should not turn on whether the claimed subject matter does 'business' instead of something else.

Conclusion

The appealed decision is reversed and the case is remanded to the district court for further proceedings consistent with this opinion.

Reversed and remanded.

[Footnotes omitted]

NOTES AND QUESTIONS

1   Explain the US mathematical algorithm exception in your own words. How does it compare with the Australian position on mathematical algorithms as expounded in *International Business Machines Corp v Commissioner of Patents*, discussed above?

2   In the most basic sense, a business model is the method of doing business by which a company sustains itself. Some business models are quite simple. A company produces a good or service and sells it to customers. If the revenues from sales exceed the cost of operation, then the company realises a profit. Given this basic definition of a business model, why do you think there is strong opposition to the patenting of business models? Is it really protecting abstract ideas?

3   E-commerce will give rise to new kinds of business models, and it is this argument that some have used to support their protection through the patent system. However, the Web is also likely to reinvent tried-and-true models. Auctions are a perfect example. Auctions in the real world have been used to sell items from agricultural commodities to fine arts. On the Internet, companies like eBay have popularised the auction model and broadened its application to a wide variety of goods and services. However, auctions are only one example of the brokerage business model. The brokerage business model facilitates transactions by bringing buyers and sellers together. These can be business-to-business (B2B), business-to-consumer (B2C), or consumer-to-consumer (C2C). A broker makes its money by charging a fee for each transaction it enables. Brokerage models can take a number of forms. Firstly, they can be simple buy/sell execution facilitators like eTrade, where customers place orders to buy and sell. Second, they can be 'virtual malls' where a site hosts many on-line merchants and charges set-up, monthly listing, and/or fees for each transaction (examples are Yahoo!'s Store and Stuff.com). Third, they can be of the 'reverse auction' type, where a prospective buyer makes a final (sometimes binding) bid for a specified good or service, and the broker facilitates its acceptance and fulfilment (an example is Respond.com). Fourth, they can be in the form of classified ads, where a listing of items for sale or wanted for purchase is posted. Listing charges are incurred regardless of whether a transaction occurs. Finally, there is the 'search agent' form where an intelligent software agent or robot is used to seek out the best price for a good or service specified by the buyer; for example, an employment agency can act as a search agent broker, finding work for job-seekers or finding people to fill open positions listed by an employer.

In addition to the brokerage model, there are many other Internet business models, including, the advertising model, the infomediary model, the merchant model, the manufacturer model, the community model (based on user loyalty), the affiliate model, and the subscription model. Each of these models has numerous variants, which have manifested themselves on the Internet.

4   In *State Street*, the plaintiff argued that:

> if Signature's invention were patentable, any financial institution desirous of
> implementing a multi-tiered funding complex modelled (sic) on a Hub and
> Spoke configuration would be required to seek Signature's permission before
> embarking on such a project. This is so because the '056 Patent is claimed
> [sic] sufficiently broadly to foreclose virtually any computer-implemented
> accounting method necessary to manage this type of financial structure.

Do you agree? Could patents that are stated too broadly prevent others from conducting a business based on a similar business method? This lies at the heart of many debates on business model patents, whether they be Internet patents or not.

Welcome Real-Time SA v Catuity Inc

[2001] FCA 445 (17 May 2001)

Available at
< http://www.austlii.edu.au//cgi-bin/disp.pl/au/cases/cth/federal_ct/2001/445.html>
17 August 2006

Heerey J:

104 The respondents argued that the alleged invention the subject of the Patent covered material that had never been previously held to be within the concept of 'manner of manufacture' for the purposes of s 6 of the *Statute of Monopolies 1623*, which is adopted as part of the definition of 'patentable invention' by s 18(1)(a) of the Act.

105 Section 6 of the Statute of Monopolies provided that the invalidating of monopolies contained in preceding provisions of the statute

> shall not extend to any letters patents and grants of privilege for the term of fourteen
> years or under, hereafter to be made of the sole working or making of any manner of
> new manufactures within this realm, to the true and first inventor and inventors of
> such manufactures, which others at the time of making such letters patents and grants
> shall not use, so as also they be not contrary to the law or mischievous to the State
> by raising prices of commodities at home, or hurt of trade, or generally inconvenient.
> (Modern spelling)

106 The respondents argued that working directions and methods of doing things fell outside the concept. Directions as to how to operate a known article or machine or to carry out a known process so as to produce an old result were not patentable, even though they may be a different and more efficient method of doing things. An example was the rejection of a patent for operating a jet engine in a way so as to reduce noise during takeoff: *Rolls Royce Ltd's Application* [1963] RPC 251. Counsel referred to a number of earlier cases in which patents were refused for an improved method of preventing the fraudulent re-use of sales books dockets (*Re Brown* (1899) 5 ALR

81), improved methods for charcoal burning (*Commissioner of Patents v Lee* (1913) 16 CLR 138), improved methods for utilising an existing mechanism of septic tank purification (*Nielson v Minister for Public Works (NSW)* (1914) 18 CLR 423) and a method for felling trees by use of fire (*Rogers v Commissioner of Patents* (1910) 10 CLR 701.

107 Also rejected were patents for methods of calculation and theoretical schemes, plans and arrangements such as a stellar chart for ascertaining the position of an aircraft in flight (*Re Kelvin & Hughes Ltd's Application* (1954) 71 RPC 103), a plan relating to the layout of houses in a row or terrace so as to prevent overlooking (*ESP's Application* (1945) 62 RPC 87) and an arrangement of buoys for navigational purposes (*W's Application* (1914) 31 RPC 141).

108 In the present case it was said that the Patent was no more than a method or system for using well-known integers—a chip card, the memory space on that card, various computer programs, readers and printers—to operate familiar kinds of loyalty and incentive schemes for customers. Counsel argued that the recent Federal Court decisions in *International Business Machines Corporation v Commissioner of Patents* (1991) 33 FCR 218 (Burchett J) and *CCOM Pty Ltd v Jiejing Pty Ltd* (1994) 51 FCR 260 (Full Court) should be distinguished. Although like the present case in that they occurred in an environment of computing, in each case there was a physically observable effect that met the manner of manufacture requirement: the screen curve in *IBM* and the retrieval to graphical representations of desired characters for the assembly of text in *CCOM*.

109 As a variation of this argument it was also said that the invention fell within the principle stated in *Commissioner of Patents v Microcell Ltd* (1959) 102 CLR 232 at 249:

> Many valid patents are for new uses of old things. But it is not an inventive idea for which a monopoly can be claimed to take a substance which is known and used for the making of various articles, and make out of it an article for which its known properties make it suitable, although it has not in fact been used to make that article before.

2. PRINCIPLES

110 The leading authority in this area is the decision of the High Court in *National Research Development Corporation v Commissioner of Patents* (1959) 102 CLR 252 which has been described as a 'watershed' (*Joos v Commissioner of Patents* (1972) 126 CLR 611 at 616 per Barwick CJ) and a decision which 'changed the direction of the case law not only in Australia but also in the United Kingdom' (*CCOM* at 287). The case was an appeal from a rejection by the Deputy Commissioner of Patents of an application for a grant in respect of a herbicidal composition. The composition was effective against a number of common broad-leafed weeds, but did not harm certain broad-leafed crops, such as lucerne. So application of the composition to a weed-infested crop would kill the weeds but allow the crop to flourish. The Commissioner's grounds for rejection were that (i) this was merely a new use of a known substance and (ii) there was no manner of manufacture because the use of the composition did not result in a 'vendible product'; manufacture will ordinarily result in a physical or tangible object, but here all that happened was that the existing weeds were killed.

111 The Court (Dixon CJ, Kitto and Windeyer JJ) first held (at 264) that the application disclosed an invention since it claimed

> ... a new process for ridding crop areas of certain kinds of weeds, not by applying chemicals the properties of which were formerly well understood so that the idea of using them for this purpose involved no inventive step, but by applying chemicals which formerly were supposed not to be useful for this kind of purpose at all.

112 In turning to the question whether the process claimed was a 'manner of new manufacture' the Court pointed out that it was a mistake to treat the question as to whether a given process or product was within the term as if the question could be restated in the form: 'Is this a manner (or kind) of manufacture?' Their Honours said (at 269):

> It is a mistake which tends to limit one's thinking by reference to the idea of making tangible goods by hand or by machine, because 'manufacture' as a word of everyday speech generally conveys that idea. The right question is: 'Is this a proper subject of letters patent according to the principles which have been for the application of s 6 of the Statute of Monopolies?'

113 By 1842 it had been settled that 'manufacture' comprehended both a process and a product: *Crane v Price* (1842) 3 Man & G 580, 134 ER 239. But their Honours noted (at 270) that the question remained whether it was enough that a process produced a useful result or whether it was necessary that some physical thing was either brought into existence or so affected as the better to serve man's purposes. After discussing a number of authorities their Honours said (at 271):

> The truth is that any attempt to state the ambit of s 6 of the Statute of Monopolies by precisely defining 'manufacture' is bound to fail. The purpose of s 6, it must be remembered, was to allow the use of the prerogative to encourage national development in a field which already, in 1623, was seen to be excitingly unpredictable. To attempt to place upon the idea the fetters of an exact verbal formula could never have been sound. It would be unsound to the point of folly to attempt to do so now, when science has made such advances that the concrete applications of the notion which were familiar in 1623 can be seen to provide only the more obvious, not to say the more primitive, illustrations of the broad sweep of the concept.

114 Their Honours then discussed the proposition of Morton J in *Re GEC's Application* (1942) 60 RPC 1 which held that a method or process was a manufacture if it (i) resulted in the production of some vendible product or (ii) improved or restored to its former condition a vendible product or (iii) had the effect of preserving from deterioration some vendible product to which it is applied. In subsequent cases patents were upheld for a process of treating a stratum of subterranean soil (*Re Cementation Co Ltd's Application* (1945) 62 RPC 151) and a method of electrical transmission (*Rantzen's Case* (1946) 64 RPC 63). In discussing the last mentioned case their Honours said (at 275):

> The point is that a process, to fall within the limits of patentability which the context of the Statute of Monopolies has satisfied, must be one that offers some advantage which is material in the sense that the process belongs to a useful art as distinct from a fine art (see *Re Virginia-Carolina Chemical Corporation's Application* [1958] RPC 35 at 36)—that its value to the country is in the field of economic endeavour.

115 Their Honours' conclusion on this issue was as follows (at 277):

> ... the view which we think is correct in the present case is that the method the subject of the relevant claims has as its end result an artificial effect falling squarely within the true concept of what must be produced by a process if it is held to be patentable. This view is, we think, required by a sound understanding of the lines along which patent law has developed and necessarily must develop in a modern society. The effect produced by the appellant's method exhibits the two essential qualities upon which 'product' and 'vendible' seem designed to insist. It is a 'product' because it consists in an artificially created state of affairs, discernible by observing over a period the growth of weeds and crops respectively on sown land on which the method has been put into practice. And the significance of the product is economic; for it provides a remarkable advantage, indeed to the lay mind a sensational advantage, for one of the most elemental activities by which man has served his material needs, the cultivation of the soil for the production of its fruits. ... (The method) achieves a separate result and the result possesses its own economic utility consisting in an important improvement in the conditions in which the crop is to grow whereby it is afforded a better opportunity to flourish and yield a good harvest.

116 In *CCOM* a Full Court of this Court upheld a patent for an invention for a Chinese language word processor. The idea of the invention, in the Full Court's description (at 287), lay in the use of a particular method of characterisation of character strokes which is applied to an apparatus in such a way that operation of the keyboard will enable the selection through the computer, in a particular way, of the appropriate Chinese characters required for word processing. The primary judge had held that a manner of manufacture was not disclosed because there was no more than a procedure to organise and process the data; the other integers of programming and computer hardware were merely conventional means to produce the desired result.

117 In discussing this issue the Full Court noted (at 292) with apparent approval the observation of Professor James Lahore in (1978) 9 *Federal Law Review* at 22–3 that (*inter alia*) business, commercial and financial schemes had never been considered patentable. Also a distinction had been drawn between the discovery of laws or principles of nature and the application thereof to produce a particular practical and useful result.

118 Of particular importance for present purposes is the Full Court's discussion of English decisions concerning computer programs given after *NRDC* but before the United Kingdom Act of 1977. (The latter Act, unlike the Australian Act of 1990, expressly excluded business methods and computer programs from the ambit of patentability to the extent that the operation 'relates to that thing as such': *CCOM* at 288.)

119 In *Burroughs Corporation's Application* [1974] RPC 147 at 161 Graham and Whitford JJ had expressed the view that computer programs which have the effect of controlling computers to operate in a particular way, where such programs are embodied in physical form, are proper subject matter for letters patent. Their Lordships had also pointed out (at 158):

[I]t is not enough to take a narrow and confined look at the 'product' produced by a method. Of course, if a method is regarded purely as the conception of an idea, it can always be said that the product of such a method is merely intellectual information. If, however, in practice the method results in a new machine or process or an old machine giving a new and improved result, that fact should in our view be regarded as the 'product' or the result of using the method, and cannot be disregarded in considering whether the method is patentable or not.

120 This decision was followed by Burchett J in *International Business Machines Corporation v Commissioner of Patents* (1991) 33 FCR 218.

121 *International Business Machines Corporation's Application* [1980] FSR 564 (decided before the commencement of the 1977 Act) concerned a program designed to calculate automatically the selling price of shares by comparing a set of buying and selling orders. It was accepted that the scheme was not itself novel, and that a completely standard computer could be programmed to perform it. Nevertheless, Graham and Whitford JJ held that the patent was good. They said (at 572) that what the inventor sought to claim was a method involving the operation or control of a computer, such that it was programmed in a particular way to operate in accordance with the inventor's method. More than 'intellectual information' was involved because the method was involved in the program and in the apparatus in physical form.

122 The conclusion of the Full Court in CCOM on this issue was expressed in the following terms (at 295):

> The *NRDC* case at 275–7 requires a mode or manner of achieving an end result which is an artificially created state of affairs of utility in the field of economic endeavour. In the present case, a relevant field of economic endeavour is the use of word processing to assemble text in Chinese language characters. The end result achieved is the retrieval of graphic representations of desired characters, for assembly of text. The mode or manner of obtaining this, which provides particular utility in achieving the end result, is the storage of data as to Chinese characters analysed by stroke-type categories, for search including 'flagging' (and 'unflagging') and selection by reference thereto.

123 An issue analogous to that in the present case was considered by the United States Court of Appeals for the Federal Circuit in *State Street Bank and Trust Co v Signature Financial Group* 149 F 3d 1368 (1998). The relevant United States statute (35 USCA s 101) refers to four categories of statutory subject matter for patentability: 'Any new and useful process, machine, manufacture or composition of matter'. The case concerned a patent for a data processing system for implementing an investment structure. Mutual funds ('Spokes') pooled their assets in an investment portfolio ('Hub') organised as a partnership. This system allowed for consolidation of costs of administering the funds combined with the tax advantages of a partnership. In particular, it provided means for a daily allocation of assets for two or more Spokes that were invested in the same Hub. The system determined the percentage share that each Spoke maintained in the Hub, while taking into consideration daily changes both in value of the Hub's investment securities and the concomitant amount of each of Spoke's assets.

124 Previous decisions of the United States Supreme Court had held that mathematical algorithms are not patentable subject matter to the extent that they are merely abstract ideas. However, in *State Street* the Court of Appeals held (at 1373) that the transformation of data representing discrete dollar amounts by a machine through a series of mathematical calculations into a final share price constituted a practical application of a mathematical algorithm formula and calculation because it produced 'a useful, concrete and tangible result' in the form of a final share price momentarily fixed for recording and reporting purposes.

125 Reliance had been placed on the judicially created 'business method' exception to statutory subject matter. The Court's response (at 1375) was terse, to the point of brutality:

> We take this opportunity to lay this ill-conceived exception to rest.

126 Their Honours considered that business methods should be subject to the same legal requirements for patentability as applied to any other process or method.

3. CONCLUSION

127 In my opinion the Patent does produce an artificial state of affairs in that cards can be issued making available to consumers many different loyalty programs of different traders as well as different programs offered by the same trader. All this can be done instantaneously at each retail outlet. So what is involved here is not just an abstract idea or method of calculation. Moreover this result is beneficial in a field of economic endeavour—namely retail trading—because it enables many traders (including small traders) to use loyalty programs and thereby compete more effectively for business. Such competition is in turn beneficial to consumers, both in the general sense that competition is good and in the sense that they can obtain benefits in the form of discounts and free goods and services.

128 What is disclosed by the Patent is not a business method, in the sense of a particular method or scheme for carrying on a business—for example a manufacturer appointing wholesalers to deal with particular categories of retailers rather than all retailers in particular geographical areas, or Henry Ford's idea of stipulating that suppliers deliver goods in packing cases with timbers of particular dimensions which could then be used for floorboards in the Model T. Rather, the Patent is for a method and a device, involving components such as smart cards and POS terminals, *in* a business; and not just one business but an infinite range of retail businesses. *CCOM* and the English decisions referred to therein are in my opinion indistinguishable. The respondents' argument for distinguishing *CCOM*—the supposed lack of 'physically observable effect'—turns on an expression not found in *CCOM* itself. Nor does such a concept form part of the Full Court's reasoning. In any event, to the extent that 'physically observable effect' is required (and I do not accept that this is necessarily so) it is to be found in the writing of new information to the Behaviour file and the printing of the coupon.

129 The *State Street* decision is persuasive. It may be true, as the respondents argue, that United States patent law has a different historical source owing little or nothing to the Statute or Monopolies. The Constitution of the United States, Article 1, s 8, cl 8 confers

power on Congress 'To promote the Progress of Science and useful Arts, by securing for limited Times to Authors and Inventors the exclusive Right to their respective Writings and Discoveries'. But the social needs the law has to serve in that country are the same as in ours. In both countries, in similar commercial and technological environments, the law has to strike a balance between, on the one hand, the encouragement of true innovation by the grant of monopoly and, on the other, freedom of competition.

130 As to the *Microcell* point, it cannot amount to the *mere* new use of a known article in a manner for which the known properties of that article make it suitable to have devised a particular method of processing data using a chip card, the properties of which (particularly its limited memory space) presented difficulties which were overcome only after much time and effort.

VI. General inconvenience

131 The respondents argued that the Patent was, within the meaning of the Statute of Monopolies, generally inconvenient as it placed a restraint on traders in developing and operating loyalty and incentive schemes which were 'a commonplace way of doing business and had been so for many years in both the real and online worlds'. It was said that the applicant was seeking to monopolise a series of known integers for the purpose of a particular kind of loyalty scheme and was thereby preventing other traders from seeking to use those integers or the same composition of them in their own customer loyalty schemes.

132 But if an invention otherwise satisfies the requirement of s 18 it can hardly be a complaint that others in the relevant field will be restricted in their trade because they cannot lawfully infringe the patent. The whole purpose of patent law is the granting of monopoly …

 NOTES AND QUESTIONS

1 How does Justice Heerey come to the conclusion that the subject matter of the patent is not an abstract idea?

2 Does Justice Heerey believe the patent in question is a business method? Is he convincing?

3 Consider paragraph 131. This argument is often raised in e-commerce patent disputes. Does Justice Heerey resolve the issue, or avoid it?

4 Many have argued that it is not the patenting of business methods in e-commerce patents *per se* that is objectionable, but rather the broadness in which the patent claims are worded. How can this be overcome? Is it a legal issue, or rather a procedural issue related to the examination of patent applications?

- -

6 Litigation

Over the last five years, Internet patents have received a great deal of attention, in academic literature, case law, and the media. A number of high-profile Internet business method patents have been granted, including Amazon.com's 'One-Click' technique that allows 'for more efficiently ordering merchandise online'[3] and Priceline.com's patent 'on the reverse auction technique for buying airline techniques on the Internet.'[4] Both these patents, and Internet business method patents generally, have been greatly criticised, described as the 'mostly likely to cause harm if they are granted ... because of their potential for impending electronic commerce while it is still maturing.'[5]

In the USA, large and small firms alike have commenced legal action for infringement of their Internet business method patents. Indeed, according to *Time* magazine, patent lawsuits have soared over the past decade, up about 58 per cent since 1995.[6] In 2005, a number of business method and Internet patent cases have reached the US Supreme Court.[7] In addition to the criticism patent owners face for seeking and being granted an Internet patent, a number of criticisms have been made against both types of firms for bringing patent infringement claims. Larger firms—for example, Amazon.com, when it brought a claim in 1999 against Barnesandnoble.com for infringing its 'One-Click' patent—have been criticised for using litigation and an injunction as a means of gaining an edge over its competition. Smaller firms have faced a different type of criticism: that they are essentially 'patent trolls', described as small-time patent holders with dodgy claims and no actual businesses who are using the legal system to extract payments from firms with established operations and products.[8] The litigants are not the only ones who have drawn criticism: there have also been fears that the judges who hear Internet business method patent cases 'will patent what they do not understand ... [and] they are unlikely to understand in the Internet.'[9]

Amazon.com v Barnesandnoble.com,[10] one of the first Internet business method patent cases, involved two major on-line businesses that, when legal action commenced in 1999, were battling for domination of on-line book sales in the USA. Amazon alleged that Barnesandnoble.com's single click Express Lane web purchasing technique infringed on Amazon's 'one-click' checkout feature.[11] In response, Barnesandnoble.com claimed the 'invalidity defence', that is, that Amazon's 'one click' patent was invalid.[12] As one US legal commentator has explained succinctly, 'when a patent has allegedly been directly infringed there are several substantive defences that the alleged infringer may raise ... if upheld, the defence amounts to a judicial reevaluation of the validity of the patent.'[13]

---

3   John R Allison and Emerson H Tiller, 'The Business Method Patent Myth' (2003) 18 *Berkeley Technology Law Journal* 987 at 993.
4   Ibid.
5   Ibid at 989.
6   Daren Fonda, 'Patently Absurd', *Time* (New York), April 10 2006, Volume 167, Issue 15, 53.
7   Ibid.
8   Ibid at 54.
9   Rochelle Cooper Dreyfuss in Greg S Fine, 'To Issue or Not to Issue: Analysis of the Business Method Patent Controversy on the Internet' (2000/2001) 42 *Boston College Law Review* 1195 at 1203.
10   239 F3d 1343 (Fed Cir, 2001).
11   Greg S Fine, 'To Issue or Not to Issue: Analysis of the Business Method Patent Controversy on the Internet' (2000/2001) 42 *Boston College Law Review* 1195 at 1200.
12   *Amazon.com Inc v Barnesandnoble.com, Inc* 239 F3d 1343 at 1346 (Fed Cir, 2001).
13   Zhichong Gu, 'Note: *MercExchange v eBay: Should Newsgroup Postings Be Considered Printed Publications as a Matter of Law in Patent Litigation*' (2005) 35 *Golden Gate University Law Review* 228 at 242–3.

The 'invalidity defence' is a common defence in US patent litigation and has repeatedly been used throughout the numerous Internet business method patent cases to reach the courts.

The US District Court for the Western District of Washington found for Amazon. com and ordered a preliminary injunction preventing Barnesandnoble.com from using its Express Lane feature. The District Court's decision drew immense criticism and fueled calls to boycott Amazon because of its attempt to 'tax e-commerce through patents.'[14] The granting of the injunction was the major source of criticism and, even today, the granting of injunctions restraining companies from using features of patents that they have been found to infringe remains a contentious issue. Amazon was 'fortunate' to win its preliminary injunction against Barnesandnoble.com at the start of the 1999 Christmas shopping season.[15] It was not lifted until 14 months later, when the case came before the US Court of Appeals for the Federal Circuit.[16] However, during that 14 months Amazon was easily able to gain a competitive advantage over Barnesandnoble.com and the injunction provided 'a timely boost to Amazon.com in its quest to become a viable Internet business.'[17]

When Barnesandnoble.com appealed to the US Court of Appeals for the Federal Circuit, where Circuit Judge Clevenger found Barnesandnoble.com had mounted a substantial challenge to the validity of the patent, the injunction was lifted.[18] The Court found that the District Court had erred in its consideration of the validity of the patent, specifically, on the basis of its reading of the 'prior art references' cited by Barnesandnoble.com.[19] Circuit Judge Clevenger found that, in light of the prior art references Barnesandnoble.com had produced into evidence, there was a substantial question as to the validity of the Amazon patent that needed to be considered.[20] In light of this finding, the preliminary injunction should not have been granted and the court remanded the case for further proceedings.[21]

Prior art references is a key issue that continually arises in relation to Internet business method patents. As Allison and Tiller have noted, 'business method patents … have been repeatedly indicated for failing to cite sufficient prior art.'[22] One of the problems identified for this lack of prior art is 'the belief, true or not, that much evidence of prior business practices (are) unlikely to have found its way into written sources.'[23] The existence of prior art evidence, when the validity of a patent has been raised as a defence, can be a strong step towards victory for a defendant. This is true involving both Internet business method patents and patents for other Internet technologies.

14   Seth H Ostrow in Greg S Fine, 'To Issue or Not to Issue: Analysis of theBusiness Method Patent Contro-
      versy on the Internet' (2000/2001) 42 *Boston College Law Review* 1195 at 1201.
15   Zhichong Gu, above note 13 at 233, note 75.
16   Ibid.
17   Ibid.
18   *Amazon.com Inc v Barnesandnoble.com, Inc* 239 F3d 1343, at 1347 (Fed Cir, 2001).
19   *Amazon.com Inc v Barnesandnoble.com, Inc* 239 F3d 1343, at 1358 (Fed Cir, 2001).
20   *Amazon.com Inc v Barnesandnoble.com, Inc* 239 F3d 1343, at 1358 (Fed Cir, 2001).
21   *Amazon.com Inc v Barnesandnoble.com, Inc* 239 F3d 1343, at 1359-60 (Fed Cir, 2001).
22   John R Allison and Emerson H Tiller, 'The Business Method Patent Myth' (2003) 18 *Berkeley Technology
      Law Journal* 987 at 1015.
23   Ibid.

The continuing litigation involving Eolas Technologies and Microsoft indicates the importance of prior art evidence. This litigation has been running for a number of years, it was most recently considered by the US Court of Appeals for the Federal Circuit.[24] The case involved US Patent 5,838,906 (the 906 patent), which was owned by the Regents of the University of California and licensed by Eolas Technologies. The 906 patent was entitled 'distributed hypermedia method for automatically invoking external application providing interaction and display of embedded objects within a hypermedia document.'[25] The short-hand version of this description is that 'the claimed invention allows a user to use a web browser in a fully interactive environment ... for example, the invention enables a user to view news clips or play games across the Internet.'[26]

Previously, the District Court had found that Microsoft had infringed two claims of the 906 patent and had actively induced US users of Internet Explorer to infringe one of the patent claims. When the case came before the Court of Appeals for the Federal Circuit, one of the major issues for consideration was whether the District Court should have admitted certain prior art evidence submitted by the defendant. This was evidence of a web browser, Viola, that was both in existence and in public use before the University of California had registered its patent in October 1994.[27] The inventor, Pei-Yuan Wei, had created one version of Viola, titled DX34, and in May 1993 had demonstrated this version to Sun Microsystems, before making changes, which were reflected in a version referred to by the Court as DX37. However, the District Court found that DX34 did not constitute prior art because it was abandoned when Wei made the changes and hence, the demonstration to Sun Microsystems was not a public use.[28] The District Court found that Microsoft had failed to prove its invalidity defence and ordered Microsoft to pay Eolas a royalty of US$1.47 per 'infringing unit' of Internet Explorer, which amounted to damages totaling US$520,562,280.[29] However, the US Court of Appeals for the Federal Circuit reversed the decision of the lower court on the issue of whether DX34 constituted prior art. It found that 'creating an improved version of an invention does not in any sense abandon the original invention ... (therefore) the district court erroneously excluded DX34 as prior art.'[30] The admission of this prior art could have made an enormous difference in this case, and only adds more ammunition to those commentators who believe judges do not understand either patents or the Internet.[31]

A second recurring issue in Internet business method patent cases is whether or not injunctions, whether preliminary or permanent, should be granted. As the *Amazon.com* litigation indicates, there can be serious consequences for businesses which are ordered to refrain from using their method of doing business on the Internet if certain elements

24 *Eolas Technologies v Microsoft Corp* 399 F3d 1325 (Fed Cir, 2005), *certiorari denied Microsoft Corp v Eolas Technologies* 126 S Ct 568.
25 *Eolas Technologies v Microsoft Corp.* 399 F3d 1325, at 1328 (Fed Cir, 2005).
26 Ibid.
27 Ibid 1328 footnote 1 (Fed Cir, 2005).
28 *Eolas Technologies v Microsoft Corp* 399 F3d 1325, at 1333 (Fed Cir, 2005)
29 *Eolas Technologies v Microsoft Corp* 399 F3d 1325, at 1332 (Fed Cir, 2005)
30 *Eolas Technologies v Microsoft Corp* 399 F3d 1325, at 1333 (Fed Cir, 2005)
31 Above note 9 at 1203

are found to infringe a patent. Patent litigation tends to be long and costly, as illustrated by the *MercExchange v eBay* litigation, which will now be discussed. MercExchange commenced litigation in 2001; it reached the US District Court for the Eastern District of Virginia in 2003, the US Court of Appeal for the Federal Circuit in 2005, and finally the US Supreme Court in 2006. Fortunately for eBay, the District Court did not order a permanent injunction.

The *eBay* case is worthy of an extensive discussion for a number of reasons. First, many commentators believe it is a prime example of the previously mentioned, growing phenomenon of 'patent trolling.'[32] Simply put, this has been described as occurring when a patent holder that is not using the patented invention uses the threat of obtaining a permanent injunction against another business to obtain a large settlement.[33] Another aspect of patent trolling is where a small business that holds a patent seeks funds, whether from licence fees or litigation, from a bigger business. Indeed, while these may not all constitute examples, there have been a number of cases against big Internet businesses over the past few years, including *Pinpoint v Amazon.com*.[34] It is obviously attractive for a small business to sue a larger, well-reputed business for patent infringement—but, as has been noted, this can involve a lot of time and expense for all parties concerned.[35]

Even at the time of writing, when the US Supreme Court has just issued a ruling as to one issue of this case, it is likely that the litigation between eBay and MercExchange will continue. The facts of the case are simple. MercExchange was a website operated by Tom Woolston, who owned a number of auction-related business method patents. MercExchange had sought to licence its patents to eBay, but no agreement had been reached.[36] It is arguable that this licensing is a perfect example of patent trolling, a smaller business seeking a toll from a richer one with a great deal to lose. The 'innovative method' under issue was the fixed price purchasing feature of eBay's website, which allows customers to purchase items that are listed on eBay's website and also allows users to search for goods posted on other Internet websites and to purchase those goods.[37] In response, eBay claimed that the patents were invalid and presented evidence of a prior newsgroup posting that disclosed the invention in the MercExchange patent.[38] The invalidity defence failed and MercExchange succeeded, and eBay, as well its subsidiaries ReturnBuy and Half.com was found to have wilfully infringed a number of claims of two of the patents under consideration, and substantial damages were awarded to the plaintiff.[39] However, the District Court refused to order an injunction against eBay to restrain it from using certain elements of its auction method that infringed MercExchange's patents.[40]

---

32   Above note 6 at 54.
33   Susan R Miller, 'US Supreme Court Hears Argument in Case That Could Change the Face of Patent Law', *Lawyers Weekly USA*, Boston, March 27 2006, 1.
34   347 F Supp 2d 579 (ND Ill, 2004).
35   Above note 6 at 54.
36   *eBay v MercExchange*, 2006 US LEXIS 3872, May 15 2006, Supreme Court of the USA, at 3.
37   *MercExchange v eBay* 401 F3d 1323, 1325 (Fed Cir, 2005).
38   Zhichong Gu, 'Above note 13 at 227.
39   *MercExchange v eBay* 401 F3d 1323, 1326 (Fed Cir, 2005).
40   Ibid.

Both parties appealed the decision of the District Court. eBay appealed the denial of a motion for judgment as a matter of law on several issues and for a new trial regarding two of the three patents.[41] MercExchange cross-appealed, seeking the reversal of the District Court's denial of a permanent injunction.[42] Given that this issue went on to be considered by the Supreme Court, it is this aspect of the case that we now turn to. The Court of Appeals for the Federal Circuit found that the 'general rule is that a permanent injunction will issue once infringement and validity have been adjudged.'[43] As such, it found that the District Court erred in failing to award MercExchange a permanent injunction.[44] Interestingly, the Court of Appeals for the Federal Circuit noted that the District Court had said there was a public interest favouring 'the denial of a permanent injunction in view of a 'growing concern over the issuance of business-method patents which forced the PTO to implement a second level review policy and cause legislation to be introduced in Congress.'[45] However, the Court of Appeals found that 'a general concern regarding business method patents, however, is not the type of important public need that justifies the unusual step of denying injunctive relief.'[46]

Given the previous discussion of the devastating repercussions an injunction can have on an Internet business, this general rule could be a deciding factor in the success or failure of many Internet businesses. Thus it appears one of the most risky litigation an Internet business can be involved in is patent litigation. If the business is a defendant, apart from the enormous legal costs that it will face, the possibility of either a preliminary or permanent injunction could have a crushing effect on an Internet business. Internet patents thus appear to be a commodity: 'a simple, valid and broad business method patent claim can be a powerful weapon against business foes.'[47] However, it is a promising sign that such issues are reaching the courts, as evidenced by the District Court and Court of Appeals consideration of the controversy surrounding Internet business method patents.

When eBay successfully appealed to the US Supreme Court, the case created enormous interest. The short judgment handed down on 15 May 2006 focused on the issue of an injunction. The court decided, unanimously, that both courts had in fact erred, and it and stated that according to well-established principles of equity, a plaintiff seeking a permanent injunction must satisfy a 4-factor test before a court may grant such relief.[48] The court then went on to outline the test. The test is quite general, and not specific to the granting of injunctions in patent law. The Supreme Court further found that neither the District Court nor the Court of Appeals had considered these four factors and thus vacated the decisions.[49] The only reference made to the underlying controversy

---

41   Ibid.
42   Ibid.
43   *Richardson v Suzuki Motor Co* 868 F2d 1126, 1246-47 (Fed Cir, 1989) in *MercExchange v eBay* 401 F3d 1323, 1338 (Fed Cir, 2005).
44   *MercExchange v eBay* 401 F3d 1323, 1339 (Fed Cir, 2005).
45   Ibid.
46   Ibid.
47   Zhichong Gu, above note 13 at 233.
48   *eBay v MercExchange*, 2006 US LEXIS 3872, May 15 2006, Supreme Court of the USA, at 4–5.
49   *eBay v MercExchange*, 2006 US LEXIS 3872, May 15 2006, Supreme Court of the USA, at 8.

appeared in Justice Kennedy's judgment (with which Justices Stevens, Souter and Breyer concurred). Justice Kennedy stated:

> In cases now arising trial courts should bear in mind that in many instances the nature of the patent being enforced and the economic function of the patent holder present considerations quite unlike earlier cases. An industry has developed in which firms use patents not as a basis for producing and selling goods, but, instead, primarily for obtaining licensing fees ... For these firms, an injunction, and the potentially serious sanctions arising from its violation can be employed as a bargaining tool to charge exorbitant fees to companies that seek to buy licences to practice the patent ... When the patented invention is but a small component of the product the companies seek to produce and the threat of an injunction is employed simply for undue leverage in negotiations, legal damages may well be sufficient to compensate for the infringement and an injunction may not serve the public interest. In addition injunctive relief may have different consequences for the burgeoning number of patents over business methods, which were not of much economic and legal significance in earlier times. The potential vagueness and suspect validity of some of these patents may affect the calculus under the four-factor test.[50]

This may have been the only reference to the controversy in the decision of the court, but it would appear that the Supreme Court justices are cognisant of the practices of patent trolling.

----

7   Conclusion

There are sound reasons for the patenting of software. The problem with on-line business method patents lies perhaps in the scrutiny of the applications themselves. Many of the disputes have occurred as a result of applications being worded too broadly or an incomplete prior art base being consulted. In the USA, Robert Merges[51] has concluded that the rush to obtain e-commerce patents has pushed the patent system into crisis. The increased volume of patent applications that the Patent Office there has to consider has increased the error rate for issued patents and increased the number of invalid business concept patents that are actually issued. Merges advocates the adoption of a patent opposition system in the USA, much like the one currently in place in Europe. This, he argues, will lower the incidence of poor-quality patents. Perhaps Merges is right. The present system does not allow much room for public debate and scrutiny of patent applications and it may well be the solution to the problem.

---

50   Ibid at 14–15.
51   R P Merges, 'As Many as Six Impossible Patents Before Breakfast: Property Rights for Business Concepts and Patent System Reform' 14 *Berkeley Tech* LJ 577 (1999).

12 Online Role-playing Games: MMORPGs

----

1 Overview

In the chapter on Copyright and the Internet, we saw how Massively Multiplayer Online Role-Playing Games (MMORPGs) have raised issues in copyright law—and certainly copyright law has been the focus of these on-line games in the legal disputes that have arisen. This is not to suggest that the other branches of intellectual property law are irrelevant, indeed, both trade mark and patent laws have played, and will continue to play, major roles in the protection of rights in virtual space.[1] This chapter will turn to a discussion of how other intellectual property regimes affect on-line games, their developers and their players.

Returning to the example of Thor: after creating Thor, one agreed to the EULA in order to play the game. Assume that this EULA stated that all players retain any and all intellectual property rights, whether these be copyright, patent, design or trade

---

1   Daniel C Miller, 'Note: Determining Ownership in Virtual Worlds: Copyright and Licence Agreements' (2003) 22 *The Review of Litigation* 435 at 438.

mark rights.[2] By now, Thor has become quite famous as a sword maker, so much so that whenever anyone hears the word 'Thor' or sees a sword, they think of a Thor sword. In addition, after defeating an evil wizard called Larry Kotter, Thor claims Kotter's castle. All players must go through this castle to get to the next level. With the help of a computer programming book, a virtual obstacle course for the grounds of the castle is created. Since the opening of the obstacle course, Thor has received a lot of positive feedback on the obstacle course. Can Thor and the obstacle course be protected?

---

2 Trade mark protection

Stephens has suggested that, although no intellectual property regime provides a 'promising theory' for protecting in-game creations, game characters may qualify for either registered or unregistered trade mark protection.[3] Slavitt has made a similar suggestion. For a character to meet the requirements for a trade mark, it must be distinctive as trade mark protection will only be given for a name that can distinguish or identify the source of goods and services. However, Slavitt has also noted, a number of requirements must be met for a valid trade mark to exist—some of which may pose problems for the registration of on-line game characters.[4] In Australia, a 'trade mark' is defined as:

> a sign used, or intended to be used, to distinguish goods or services dealt with or provided in the course of trade by a person from goods or services so dealt with or provided by any other person.[5]

Section 6 of the *Trade Marks Act 1995* (Cth) provides a non-exhaustive list of features that can be considered as a 'sign' for the purposes of trade mark protection. These can include a name, a brand, a label, a colour, a sound or a shape, including two and three-dimensional shapes.[6]

In Singapore, a 'trade mark' is defined as:

> any sign capable of being represented graphically and which is capable of distinguishing goods or services dealt with or provided in the course of trade by a person from goods or services so dealt with or provided by any other person.[7]

Further, a sign is defined to include:

> any letter, word, name, signature, numeral, device, brand, heading, label, ticket, shape, colour, aspect of packaging or any combination thereof.[8]

---

2   While Thor is an original creation, these arguments are based on the suggestions of Kelly Slavitt in her article, 'Gabby in Wonderland—Looking Through The Internet Glass' (1998) 80 *Journal of Patent and Trademark Office Society* 611 at 618–19.

3   Molly Stephens, 'Note: Sales of In-Game Assets: An Illustration of the Continuing Failure of Intellectual Property Law to Protect Digital-Content Creators' (2002) 80 *Texas Law Review* 1513 at 1530–1.

4   Kelly M Slavitt, 'Gabby In Wonderland—Looking Through the Internet Glass' (1998) 80 *Journal of Patent & Trademark Office Society* 611 at generally 621–3.

5   See s 17, *Trade Marks Act 1995* (Cth).

6   See *Kenman Kandy Australia Pty Ltd v Registrar of Trade Marks* [2002] FCAFC 273.

7   Section 2, *Trade Marks Act 1998* (Cap 332) Singapore.

8   Section 2, *Trade Marks Act 1998* (Cap 332) Singapore.

A trade mark can be registered for any of the 34 classes of goods and 11 classes of services existing in Australia and Singapore. It is possible, therefore, that a person may wish to register his or her character or item as a trade mark in the goods or services provided, or under a more general category. For example, in both Australia[9] and Singapore,[10] Class 28 includes the registration of trade marks for 'games and playthings'.

Therefore, *prima facie*, it appears that graphically represented game characters may be eligible for trade mark registration and protection. Thor is a sword maker; he has a distinctive name and appearance, and a reputation among other players. Both he, and his creator, are therefore a reputable source of goods and services and other players in the game use Thor's name and appearance to identify Thor with the creator.[11] As Stephens has noted, 'a character may qualify for trademark protection if the players of the online game associate the character with a single, albeit anonymous player.'[12] Stephens has also stated that, in the case of many on-line games, players do come to identify a particular character with an individual player.[13]

The additional strength provided by trade mark protection cannot be overlooked. In addition to the right of the registered trade mark owner—whether this be the game developer or the player/creator—a number of national statutes also provide for trade mark infringement offences. For example, Part VI of the Singapore *Trade Marks Act* contains seven trade-mark related offences, including s 46, which deals with 'Counterfeiting a Trade mark'[14] and s 47, 'Falsely applying a registered trade mark to goods'.[15] The Australian *Trade Marks Act 1995* (Cth) also contains similar offences, including falsifying a registered trade mark,[16] falsely applying a registered trade mark[17] and selling goods with false marks.[18] Arguably, the type of behaviour that was discussed in relation to the production and distribution of in-game counterfeit items would fall under these provisions.

There are, however, a number of problems with this scenario. The first is that, despite Stephens' suggestion, it is arguable players are more likely to associate a particular character with a specific game rather than an individual player. Second, it may be difficult to convince either a trade mark registrar or a court, that what actually is going on in these games is 'trade'. Perhaps, if players retained not only full intellectual property rights for their creation and the right to sell their characters, both in and out of the game, this could be considered trade. This, however, creates a third problem: what happens when a player wants to sell the character. For example, in an American context, the goodwill

---

9   'Classes of Goods and Services', accessible at the IP Australia Trade Marks website, <http://www.ipaus-tralia.gov.au/trademarks/goods> last accessed 20/01/06.

10   'Trade Marks: Classification of Goods and Services', accessible at the IPOS—Intellectual Property Office of Singapore website, <http://www.ipos.gov.sg/main/aboutip/trademarks/classongoodsnsvcs.html>, last accessed 20/01/06.

11   Above note 3 at 1532.

12   Ibid.

13   Ibid.

14   Section 46 *Trade Marks Act 1998* (Cap 332) Singapore.

15   Section 47 *Trade Marks Act 1998* (Cap 332) Singapore.

16   Section 145 *Trade Marks Act 1995* (Cth).

17   Section 146 *Trade Marks Act 1995* (Cth).

18   Section 148 *Trade Marks Act 1995* (Cth).

created by a reputable trade mark comprises part of the selling price.[19] Maintaining this reputation may be impossible given 'transferring a character's associated goodwill because a more skilled player often transfers a character to a less skilled player who cannot maintain the character's reputation.'[20]

In addition, real-world trade mark protection problems also apply to an online game environment. Slavitt, in her example of online character 'Gabby', notes that she:

> may lose any trademark rights in the name Gabby if the word becomes generic, or if it acquires a secondary meaning, such that females who surf the Net are commonly referred to as 'Gabbys'. [21]

Such a problem may actually foster creativity. If players can satisfy the requirements for trade mark protection, then this may provide an incentive for developing more creative characters or in-game items.

----

3   Design registration

There has been little academic writing about the possibility of design registration for online gaming characters and items. It is a possibility, but, given the high threshold that must be met for registration, it is arguable few items or characters would be eligible for design registration. Most of the academic literature in this area has emanated from the USA. With that in mind, before proceeding, it is worth noting that in the US the intellectual property protection available for a design is called a 'design patent'. This is the US equivalent of the Australian 'design registration' system. There also exists a 'utility patent', the US equivalent of an Australian patent.

In the USA, a 'design consists of the visual ornamental characteristics embodied in, or applied to, an article of manufacture.'[22] Slavitt has suggested that an online gamer may be able to obtain a design patent on the 'ornamental graphical representation' of a character if that character is, as required for a design patent, 'new, original and non-obvious.'[23] This would allow a gamer a right to action against any other player, or, indeed, any other Internet user, who adopts a substantially similar graphic representation for infringement.[24] Further, according to Slavitt, and in an American context at least, an infringement action for a design patent can be brought even though, for example, other players were not confused about the similar character or the character has not been in continual use.[25]

---

19   Above note 3 at 1533–4.
20   Above note 3 at 1533.
21   Above note 4 at 621.
22   'A Guide to Filing a Design Patent Registration', US Patent and Trademark Office, accessible at the USTPO website, <http://www.uspto.gov/web/offices/pac/design/>, last accessed 17/01/06.
23   Above note 4 at 618–19.
24   Above note 4 at 619.
25   Above note 4 at 619.

In Australia, the term 'design,' 'in relation to a product, means the overall appearance of the product, resulting from one or more visual features of the product.'[26] The term 'visual feature' is further defined in the Australian *Designs Act 2003*, as 'in relation to a product, (including) the shape, configuration, pattern and ornamentation of the product.'[27] Given this definition, a two or three-dimensional game character may be covered by it. Pursuant to the Act, a design is only capable of registration if it is both new and distinctive when compared with the prior art base.[28]

In Singapore, the term is design is defined as:

'features of shape, configuration, pattern or ornament applied to an article by any industrial process, but does not include —

(a) a method or principle of construction; or
(b) features of shape or configuration of an article which —
    (i) are dictated solely by the function which the article has to perform;
    (ii) are dependent upon the appearance of another article of which the article is intended by the designer to form an integral part; or
    (iii) enable the article to be connected to, or placed in, around or against, another article so that either article may perform its function'[29]

Further, the Singapore *Registered Designs Act* provides a unique addition to our discussion as it deals with computers. Pursuant to s 4(6) of the Act, entitled 'Owner of the design', the Act deals with the situation where a design is generated by a computer in circumstances where there is no human designer.[30] This does not preclude registration of a design and, indeed, given our extensive discussion, it will be obvious that the creation of in-game characters and items do require human input. Further, s 7(1) of the Act states that computer games cannot be registered as designs. However, given that what game players or game developers are seeking to register are visual characters, this should not be a problem. Section 32 of the Singapore Act also provides that a registered design is to be treated as personal property.[31]

Thus, it would seem that, if one had a sword and wanted to register that design, it does seem possible.

- -

4 Patents

Bartle has given this example:

JackX spends two months programming a virtual pinball for VWX. VWX doesn't have any pinballs, and JackX isn't a great programmer, but he sticks at it and produces a serviceable model that meets with a warm reception from the other players. JillX sees

---

26   Section 5 *Designs Act 2003* (Cth).
27   Section 7(1) *Designs Act 2003* (Cth).
28   Section 15(1) *Designs Act 2003* (Cth).
29   Section 2 *Registered Designs Act 2000* (Cap 266) Singapore.
30   Section 4(6) *Registered Designs Act 2000* (Cap 266) Singapore.
31   Section 32 *Registered Designs Act 2000* (Cap 266) Singapore.

the pinball and thinks it's a great idea. She may not be as imaginative as JackX but she's a much better programmer, and within a week her mega-pinball hits the virtual streets. No one wants to play JackX's pinballs any more, they all want to play JillX's. JackX is not at all happy. He has another idea, for gravity-free 3D virtual pinballs, but doesn't want to be ripped off a second time. That's why he's going to patent it. In fact, he's so unhappy that he's going to patent it and only license it to other VWs (virtual worlds). See how many people stay with VWX playing stupid gravity-restricted pinballs when all their competitors have the new, exciting, gravity-free ones![32]

Patents are one of the strongest forms of intellectual property protection, giving the inventor the exclusive right to commercially exploit an invention for a limited period of time.[33] While patent protection might be useful for game developers, it is also arguably available to the gamer, to cement protection of the online obstacle course one has built. Unlike copyright, patents require formal registration, placing a burden of the gamer to seek out this type of protection. Further, if what a game developer or player/creator sought to patent was, for example, a computer program, then copyright would also subsist in that program. Generally speaking, then, patent registration and protection may be more useful for game providers and developers rather than players, as patents will protect the specific mechanics of an online game.[34]

Still, as Bartle has noted, there probably isn't any way in which a EULA could be worded to deny a player the right from selling a patent for a method, program or process within a game.[35] This would be akin to 'my demanding that if you play my virtual world, you're prohibited from selling a patent to someone else … thereby unfairly restricting free trade.'[36] However, EULAs can and do contain general statements about intellectual property which do cover a player's patent rights. As Appelcline has suggested, 'patents are the weapons of the rich … as cash-rich companies can spend time writing up patents, and prosecuting companies who violate them, and cash-poor companies have little recourse.'[37] The same analogy could be used for online gamers and game providers.

In Australia, standard patents, lasting twenty years, as well as innovation patents, lasting eight years, can be granted for computer programs.[38] For an innovation patent, which involves the lower-threshold test of the two, an 'invention' must be a manner of manufacture; new; innovative; useful and not previously used in secret.[39] In Singapore, for an invention to be patentable, the invention must be new, involve an inventive step

---

32   Richard A Bartle, 'Pitfalls of Virtual Property' (April 2004, The Themis Group), accessible on The Themis Group website,<http://www.themis-group.com/uploads/Pitfalls%20of%20Virtual%20Property.pdf> , last accessed 13/01/05, at 20.

33   Anne Fitzgerald and Brian Fitzgerald, *Intellectual Property in Principle* (2004, LawbookCo, NSW) at 258.

34   Shannon Appelcline, 'Trials, Triumphs and Trivialities—Online Games and the Law Part Three: Patents, Trade Secrets and Licences', 14th May 2005, accessible at the Skotos website, <http://www.skotos.net/articles/TTnT_148.phtml>, last accessed 17/01/06.

35   Above note 32 at 21.

36   Ibid.

37   Shannon Appelcline, 'Trials, Triumphs and Trivialities—Online Games and the Law Part Three: Patents, Trade Secrets and Licences', 14th May 2005, accessible at the Skotos website, <http://www.skotos.net/articles/TTnT_148.phtml>, last accessed 17/01/06.

38   See generally *IBM Corporation v Commissioner of Patents* (1991) 22 IPR 417 and *CCOM Pty Ltd v Jiejing Pty Ltd* (1994) 28 IPR 481.

39   Section 18(1A) *Patents Act 1990* (Cth).

and is capable of an industrial application.[40] Given both these definitions, it is likely that the online game programs as well as some of the player creations would qualify for a patent.

The existence of a patent also involves an interesting question of what happens when—much to the chagrin and unhappiness of players—an on-line game shuts down. This seems to raise as many legal questions as when the game was operating, and also serves as a reminder that the items being dealt with here are really businesses. Bartle has noted that when a virtual world closes down, players will sometimes try to buy the hardware and software and operate the VW themselves.[41] However, many game providers and developers often refuse, because that computer code is often patented software or a program that could be sold for the game developer's financial benefit elsewhere.[42]

----

5   Virtual property rights

Consider these two examples:

a)   Your favourite game is set in medieval England and based on the Robin Hood legend. You are a rich baron who has set up a large fortress to protect your wealth. You know of a band of players who have been robbing gamers and distributing their in-game items to newer players so that everyone will be on the same level—but that's the whole point of the game. One day, you are challenged to a duel. You leave your castle and, while you are gone, this band of merry players robs you and takes all your gold.

b)   You play the same favourite game. One night, after a successful day defending your fortress, you go to bed. The next morning, you log back into your account and discover that, due to a security failure on the part of your game provider, your account has been hacked and all your gold, plus your character and other items, have been taken.

In Example A, it is arguable that all these activities were part and parcel of the game and therefore within the rules of the game. As Balkin has noted, 'the ability to destroy or steal another's virtual possessions, or exterminate another character, is part of what it means to participate in the medium.'[43] In Example B, it is clear that hacking another player's account is not within the rules of the game. The question must therefore be asked what recourse, if any, does a player have and against whom. Certainly, the offending player (if the culprit is an player) may be excluded from the game pursuant to any

---

40   Section 13 *Patents Act 1994* (Cap 221) Singapore.
41   Above note 32 at 13.
42   Ibid.
43   Jack M Balkin, 'Institute for Information Law and Policy Symposium State of Play: I. Essay & Reflection: Law and Liberty in Virtual Worlds' (2004/2005) 49 *New York Law School Law Review* 63 at 72.

existing EULA.[44] However, in recent years, there has much been academic discussion of the possibility of recognising 'virtual property rights' that would allow legal recourse through the courts. Joshua Fairfield, for example, has pushed for the idea that computer code that is designed to act like real world property to be regulated and protected like real world property.[45] Such code, he has said, is 'designed to act more like land or chattel than ideas.'[46]

Generally, arguments for virtual property rights have taken two forms. First, there have been calls for existing criminal and property laws to apply to situations like Example B. In Australia, for example, the type of behaviour that occurred in Example B could possibly be caught under one of the provisions introduced by the Australian *Cybercrime Act 2001* (Cth). Second, there have also been calls for specific state regulation of in-game behaviour that has real-world effects.[47]

In both cases, the primary issue is recognising that in-game items are genuine property, as valuable as the computer that they are stored on, or the shares that one owns in a company. In their seminal article, *The Law of the Virtual Worlds*, Hunter and Lastowka note that virtual property is different from 'real property' in two ways. First, virtual property is intangible and second, virtual property is evanescent.[48] In the first instance, Hunter and Lastowka note that over the last 200 years, Western ideas of property have changed from the tangible to the intangible, so that 'the intangible problem of virtual property really (is) no problem at all.'[49] In the second case, Hunter and Lastowka note that 'objections to virtual property on the basis that it is ... impermanent are descriptively implausible ... (and) our property system cheerfully accommodates these characteristics.'[50] Therefore, if legal and political institutions, and the community at large, are able to accept that these in-game items are property, it is difficult to imagine that the law will not move to protect them.[51] Indeed, the development of any specific 'online gaming legislation' may currently be premature. As Hunter and Lastowka note:

> The battles fought over virtual property will involve claims sounding in property, contract, unfair competition, and other familiar real-world areas. At least initially, these claims should not pose too many problems for courts. Traditional approaches will work.[52]

In Western courts and legislatures, these issues have not been raised. However, a number of Asian nations—where on-line gaming is extremely popular, the theft of virtual property is increasingly common, and intellectual property laws somewhat lacking—have strongly supported the introduction of a separate category of virtual property rights.

---

44   Jack M Balkin, 'Virtual Liberty: Freedom to Design and Freedom to Play In Virtual Worlds' (2004) 90 *Virginia Law Review* 2043 at 2063.

45   Joshua Fairfield, 'Virtual Property' (2005) 85 *Boston University Law Review* 1047 at 1048.

46   Ibid at 1049.

47   Above note 32 at 73.

48   F Gregory Lastowka and Dan Hunter, 'The Law of the Virtual Worlds' (2004) (92) *California Law Review* 1 at 40.

49   Ibid at 40–2.

50   Ibid at 42.

51   Above note 44 at 2045.

52   Above note 48 at 72.

To date, none have been introduced, though this will undoubtedly change soon, for a number of reasons. The first is that in China, Taiwan, and South Korea, online gaming has become big business. In China, there already exist a number of professionals whose sole occupation is to trade in online gaming property.[53] Nice work if you can get it; according to Fairfield, in 2004 over 1000 professional sellers of virtual property made high-end salaries entirely from virtual worlds.[54]

The second reason is the willingness of the courts in Asian countries to recognise virtual property. With over 26.3 million gamers in China, it is unsurprising that the first, worldwide, virtual property decision was delivered by a Beijing court in late 2003.[55] In *Li Hongchen v Beijing Arctic Ice Technology Development Company*[56] (Beijing Arctic Ice), Li Hongchen commenced legal action against Beijing Ice, maker of the online game 'Hongyue', or 'Red Moon', following the theft of virtual property from his account by a hacker.[57] Li Hongchen had spent two years and more than $US1200 on the game and his property, but Beijing Arctic Ice claimed that 'the virtual properties were simply "piles of data" that had no real world value.'[58] It was held that Beijing Arctic Ice, as a result of problems with game security, had an obligation to restore the property, which included a number of virtual biological weapons.[59] The court decided mainly on principles of contract law, however, as Fairfield has noted, the court 'did so to protect a distinct property right—the right of the owner to control the property against the world, not merely as against the party who committed a wrongful action.'[60]

The third reason is that, while a number of gamers are attempting to enforce their virtual property rights in 'real world courts', for a number of players the violence of the games are beginning to spill over into reality. These highlight the need for proper methods of resolving virtual property incidents and disputes. Indeed, as Balkin stated:

> One of the most compelling reasons for state intervention is that the boundaries between the game space and real space are permeable. What happens to people (or their avatars) in the game space may have real world effects on them and on third parties who are not part of the game.[61]

Balkin's words were prophetic. In March 2005 Shanghai gamer Zhu Caoyuan was murdered by 41-year-old Qui Chengwei. Qui loaned Zhu a virtual sword from the game

---

53   Above note 45 at 1085.
54   Ibid.
55   Jay Lyman, 'Gamer Wins Lawsuit in Chinese Court Over Stolen Virtual Winnings', TechNews World, 19th December 2003, accessible on the TechNewsWorld website, <http://www.technewsworld.com/story/32441.html>, last accessed 18/01/06.
56   (2003). Joshua Fairfield lists the court as the Beijing Second Intermediate Court, while Jay Lyman lists the court as the Beijing Chaoyang District People's Court. See respectively Joshua Fairfield, 'Virtual Property' 85 *Boston University Law Review* 1047 at 1085 and Jay Lyman, 'Gamer Wins Lawsuit in Chinese Court Over Stolen Virtual Winnings', TechNews World, 19th December 2003, accessible on the TechNewsWorld website, <http://www.technewsworld.com/story/32441.html>, last accessed 18/01/06.
57   Above note 55.
58   Ibid.
59   Above note 55.
60   Above note 45 at 1085.
61   Above note 43 at 72.

'Legends of Mir 3'. Zhu then sold the sword for approximately $AUS1130.[62] When Qui discovered the sale he went to the police, who told him that the virtual weapon was not real property and was therefore not protected under law.[63] Although Zhu told Qui he would give him the money for the sword, Qui murdered Zhu. He was given a suspended death sentence in November 2005 and is expected to serve at least 15 years of a life sentence.[64]

This is undoubtedly an extreme example, but it does serve to illustrate the fact that it is naïve to suggest users merely play these games and create these characters and items for the 'rewards of the game'. Whether players create content for creative rewards, to build a reputation or to make a little real-world money, the issues that online gaming create need to be taken seriously.

All this is not to say that the Asian experience with virtual property has occurred flawlessly.[65] Consider the situation in South Korea, where, due to an increasingly common threat of virtual property theft, a section of the South Korean police force is now devoted to pursuing such crimes, to great success.[66] However, South Korea lacks any proper property rights law and this has resulted in a plethora of suits against game providers and injunctions against players attempting to sell virtual property.[67]

----

6   Online games and other legal issues

Questions have also been raised as to whether defamation, leading to a legal remedy in a real-world court, can occur in online games. As Balkin has noted:

> People can defame other people's real world identities in cyberspace, just as they can in real space. People can also defame players' in world identities, or avatars, for example, by falsely claiming that a particular character has cheated.[68]

It will have become apparent to the reader that online gamers invest significant time, money and resources into building up reputations in these games.[69] While gamers always have the option of simply joining another game should such slander occur, it is arguable that, where injury occurs to their in-game reputation, a person should have some kind of recourse, whether this be provided through a EULA or in a real world court of law.[70]

To many—particularly, for example, in the USA, where personal freedoms are so fiercely protected—the idea of the State legislating on what people can do in their spare

---

62   Amalie Finlayson and Reuters, 'Online Gamer Killed For Selling Virtual Weapon', 30th March 2005, at the Sydney Morning Herald website, accessible at <http://www.smh.com.au/news/World/Online-gamer-killed-for-selling-virtual-weapon/2005/03/30/1111862440188.html>.
63   Ibid.
64   'Chinese gamer sentenced to life' 8th June 2005, BBC News (UK), accessible at the BBC website, <http://news.bbc.co.uk/1/hi/technology/4072704.stm>, last accessed 13/01/06.
65   Above note 45 at 1088.
66   Ibid.
67   Ibid.
68   Above note 43 at 74.
69   Ibid.
70   Ibid.

time may seem somewhat questionable. However, a number of Asian countries have considered putting time limits on the number of hours users can spend playing online games per day. For example, in October 2005 Chinese authorities announced a plan to penalise online gamers who spent more than three hours playing a game, in an attempt to curb online gaming addiction.[71] If a player stays in the game for more than five hours, once the clock hits that time the game system cuts the ability level of the player and reduces it to zero.[72] However, quick-thinking gamers have started creating different accounts in games, so they can be switched to another account when the playing time on one gamer's account hits three hours.[73]

---

7   Conclusion

This chapter has examined some of the major non-copyright issues with MMORPGs, and no doubt, in the near future, there will be more litigation and more jurisprudence emerging on these on-line games. In the meantime, however, debate continues as to the proper scope of EULAs, and game developers are beginning to accede to pressures from gamers and commentators in terms of the enforcement of EULAs.

---

71   'Time Limits for Online Games Meant to Protect Children From Addiction', *Shanghai Daily* (China), 21st October 2005, accessible at the Shanghai Daily website, 'Time Limits For Online Games Meant to Protect Children From Addiction', *Shanghai Daily* (Shanghai) 21 October 2005, accessible on the Shanghai Daily website, <www.shanghaidaily.com/art/2005/10/21/206119/Time_limits_for_games_to_protect_children.htm>, last accessed 18/01/06.

72   Ibid.

73   Ibid.

Uninvited Material

1 Overview

In this chapter we will consider two specific areas of law which come loosely under the rubric of uninvited material. These are spam and spyware. Although they can be classed under the topics of content regulation, privacy, or crime, they have been given particular treatment because of the momentum evident in a number of jurisdictions in creating special statutes to handle the issues they raised. For example, in recent years, Australia, the USA,[1] the United Kingdom,[2] and South Korea[3] have all enacted laws combating spam.

2 Spam

Spam has been a growing problem for businesses and individuals over the last decade. Spam generally refers to unsolicited email, whether commercial or non-commercial, although the bulk of spam is commercial in nature. Initially, many regarded spam as

---

1   *Controlling The Assault of Non-Solicited Pornography And Marketing Act 2003.*
2   *Privacy and Electronic Communications (EC Directive) Regulations 2003.*
3   *Act on Promotion of Information & Communications & Communication Network Utilisation & Protection of 2001.* Revised on 18 December 2002 and entered into force on 19 January 2003. See further Professor David Sorkin's excellent website on spam laws: <http://www.spamlaws.com/>

being a minor nuisance, but it is now considered to be a major economic and social issue; there have been many reports of statistics of the prevalence of spam, with some showing that as much as 75 per cent of the Internet's email traffic consists of spam. MessageLabs reported that in 2004, on average, 73 per cent of all email traffic was spam (see <http://www.messagelabs.com>) and that in July 2004, 94.51 per cent of all email traffic in the world was spam.

Spam needs to be processed and managed, which translates into time and labour costs for individuals and businesses, not to mention the loss in access to legitimate Internet traffic and communications. The Radicati Group estimated that spam cost businesses US$20.5 billion in 2003. The single biggest issue with spam is that it costs the spammer virtually nothing to send spam; instead, the costs are borne by the recipients of spam.

----

3 Australian legislation on spam

In response to the spam problems faced by Australians, legislation was introduced in 2003 and came into effect on 10 April 2004. At the time, many commentators argued that it was pointless to pass legislation in Australia as studies showed that the majority of the spam originated from outside of Australia. Nevertheless, the legislation has served some purpose as a few prosecutions have been made under the Act.

The legislation is the *Spam Act 2003* (Cth). It introduced rules relating to electronic messages, which under s 5(1) includes not just email but also SMS and Multimedia Messaging Services (MMS). Under s 16, sending, without the express or implied consent of the recipient, a commercial electronic message that has an Australian link is prohibited unless it is a designated commercial message.

Schedule 2 defines the concept of consent. Consent includes consent that can reasonably be inferred from conduct and the business and other relationships of the individual or organisation concerned. The mere fact that an email address has been published does not amount to consent. The rationale underpinning the rules in Schedule 2 is that of 'reasonable expectation' that messages will be sent.

Designated commercial message is defined in Schedule 1. To qualify as a designated commercial message, the message must be primarily factual and not contain any commercial content. The message is permitted to contain certain information such as the sender's logo and employee name if applicable. Designated commercial electronic messages must comply with s 17, which requires commercial electronic messages to include certain information about the individual or organisation who authorised the sending of the message. Interestingly, any message sent or authorised by a government body, a registered political party, a religious organisation, or a charitable institution relating to goods or services supplied by the body is deemed a designated commercial electronic message.

Section 17 provides that all commercial electronic messages with an Australian link must set out clearly and accurately the identity of the sender who has authorised the message. The message must include accurate information about how the recipient can readily contact the sender, and the information must be reasonably likely to be valid for at least 30 days after the message is sent. The final requirement for commercial electronic messages is that they must include an unsubscribe facility. Section 18 provides that the message must contain a statement clearly and conspicuously advising the recipient of an electronic address that can be used to unsubscribe from future messages.

A review of the *Spam Act 2003* was carried out by the Department of Communications and Information, Information Technology and the Arts (DCITA) in late 2005, with the close of submissions on 1 February 2006. At the time of writing, a report has not yet been finalised for tabling in the Federal Parliament. See further <http://www.dcita.gov. au/ie/spam_home>.

Since the *Spam Act 2003* came into force, the regulator, Australian Communications and Media Authority, has fined a number of businesses. For example, in 2005, Global Racing Group Pty Ltd and Australian SMS Pty Ltd were fined $11,000 and $2200 respectively for sending out more than fifty thousand SMS messages to market software that provided horse racing tips. The first Australian case on the new spam laws concerned the company Clarity1 Pty Ltd. In 2005, the Federal Court issued interim injunctions against Clarity1 Pty Ltd and its managing director, Wayne Mansfield, restraining them from sending spam. The case was heard by the Federal Court in 2006; the defendants failed in their argument that they were entitled to rely on a number of defences, including that the emails had been consented to by the recipients.

Australian Communications and Media Authority v Clarity1

[2006] FCA 410 (13 April 2006)

Available at < http://www.austlii.edu.au/cgi-bin/disp.pl/au/cases/cth/federal_ct/2006/410. html> 17 August 2006

Nicholson J:

1   This is an application for orders under ss 24, 29 and 32 of the *Spam Act 2003* (Cth) ('the Spam Act') and declaratory relief under s 21 of the *Federal Court of Australia Act 1976* (Cth) in respect of alleged sending of unsolicited commercial electronic messages ('CEMs') and the use of harvested electronic addresses …

The pleadings

3   The first respondent ('Clarity1') is a company incorporated in Australia …
4   From 1 October 2003 Mr Mansfield has been the sole director of Clarity1. He supervises and is ultimately responsible for the business carried on by Clarity1. That business is carried on in each of the States and Territories of Australia.
5   The further amended statement of claim pleads that in the course of its business from 1 October 2003 to the present date, Clarity1 obtained a number of electronic addresses by one or several means …

7   Further it is pleaded that during the period from 1 October 2003 until approximately February 2005, Clarity1 obtained lists of electronic addresses harvested from the internet using address-harvesting software from organisations or persons selling such lists.

8   Then it is pleaded that when Clarity1 had obtained such electronic addresses, it immediately entered them into a series of databases ('the Databases') and text documents, being lists of electronic addresses ('the Lists').

9   The conduct which is pleaded in the further amended statement of claim is that during the period from 10 April 2004 until the present date Clarity1 periodically sent, or caused to be sent, CEMs to electronic addresses obtained in the Databases and the Lists. It is said that these were sent by using an internet carriage service or listed carriage service and were sent to an electronic address in connection with an email account. Further, it is pleaded that they contained statements which:

    1   offered to supply a good or service;
    2   advertised and/or promoted a good or service;
    3   advertised and/or promoted Clarity1 as a supplier, or prospective supplier, of certain goods or services under its own name or under the business names of Business Seminars Australia or ... Maverick Partnership.

    Therefore it is pleaded that at all material times Clarity1 used and continues to use harvested address lists obtained during the period in the manner and circumstances pleaded which form part of, and remain in, the Databases and Lists.

10 By reason of these matters it is pleaded the electronic messages referred to in [9] are CEMs within the meaning of s 6 of the *Spam Act*. Further, it is pleaded that they have an Australian link within the meaning of s 7 of that Act ...

12 The contraventions pleaded are that by sending, or causing to be sent, electronic messages without first obtaining the consent of the recipients, Clarity1 sent, or caused to be sent, CEMs with an Australian link in contravention of s 16(1) of the Spam Act. Further it is pleaded that by engaging in the conduct of use of harvested address lists, Clarity1 acted in contravention of s 22(1)(b) of the same Act.

13 In respect of each of these contraventions it is pleaded that Mr Mansfield was actively involved and knew the essential elements so that he was directly or indirectly, knowingly concerned in, or party to, each of those contraventions contrary to s 16(9) and s 22(3) respectively of the Spam Act.

14 In the respondents' defence it is asserted that at no time since the Spam Act became effective have either of them collected any email addresses by electronic harvesting software and further have not engaged any third party to create lists of email addresses that have been obtained by the use of electronic harvesting software. It is asserted any email address added to the Lists has been obtained by strict adherence to the provisions of the Spam Act. Likewise, it is asserted that at no time has any electronic message (including a CEM or email) been sent by them to any electronic address that does not comply with the necessary conditions regarding permission as set out in the Spam Act. It is asserted by the respondents that where such conduct occurred permission for the sending of the message was obtained prior to the 'implementation' of the Spam Act, complying with the conditions required by the relevant government regulations and guidelines in place at the relevant time when the electronic address was obtained.

15 Specifically it is asserted that each electronic message sent to any address complied with the Spam Act regarding having an unsubscribe facility. In the case of electronic messages being sent to an email address in the United Kingdom, it is asserted that the lists of email addresses used complied with the discretionary criteria of the Privacy and Electronics (EC Directive) Regulations 2003. There is also a denial that any email or electronic message with an Australian link has been sent to any email address other than those email addresses listed in Databases maintained by Clarity1 ...

Relevant legislation and regulations

17 The Spam Act has been amended by the *Australian Communications and Media Authority (Consequential and Transitional Provisions) Act 2005* (Cth), which principally relates to the naming of the applicant and otherwise does not affect the provisions here in issue.

Provisions relevant to sending commercial electronic messages

CONDITIONS APPLICABLE TO SENDING

18 Section 16 of the Spam Act deals with the sending of unsolicited CEMs. It relevantly provides:

16(1) A person must not send, or cause to be sent, a commercial electronic message that:
   (a) has an Australian link; and
   (b) is not a designated commercial electronic message.

(2) Subsection (1) does not apply if the relevant electronic account-holder consented to the sending of the message.
   Note: For the meaning of **consent**, see Schedule 2.

(3) Subsection (1) does not apply if the person:
   (a) did not know; and
   (b) could not, with reasonable diligence, have ascertained;
      that the message had an Australian link.

(4) Subsection (1) does not apply if the person sent the message, or caused the message to be sent, by mistake.

(5) A person who wishes to rely on subsection (2), (3) or (4) bears an evidential burden in relation to that matter ...

(9) A person must not:
   (a) aid, abet, counsel or procure a contravention of subsection (1) or (6); or
   (b) induce, whether by threats or promises or otherwise, a contravention of subsection (1) or (6); or
   (c) be in any way, directly or indirectly, knowingly concerned in, or party to, a contravention of subsection (1) or (6); or
   (d) conspire with others to effect a contravention of subsection (1) or (6).

(10) A person does not contravene subsection (9) merely because the person supplies a carriage service that enables an electronic message to be sent.

(11) Subsections (1), (6) and (9) are **civil penalty provisions**.'

19 The section is to be understood in relation to the definition of terms employed in it. Section 4 provides that 'send' includes attempt to send. Section 6 is titled 'Commercial electronic messages' and relevantly reads as follows:

> 6(1) For the purposes of this Act, a **commercial electronic message** is an electronic message, where, having regard to:
>
> (a) the content of the message; and
>
> (b) the way in which the message is presented; and
>
> (c) the content that can be located using the links, telephone numbers or contact information (if any) set out in the message;
>
> it would be concluded that the purpose, or one of the purposes, of the message is:
>
> (d) to offer to supply goods or services; or
>
> (e) to advertise or promote goods or services; or
>
> (f) to advertise or promote a supplier, or prospective supplier, of goods or services...

20 Section 7 provides the meaning (see s 4) for Australian link in the following terms:

> 7 For the purposes of this Act, a commercial electronic message has an Australian link if, and only *if:*
>
> (a) the message originates in Australia; or
>
> (b) the individual or organisation who sent the message, or authorised the sending of the message, is:
>
> (i) an individual who is physically present in Australia when the message is sent; or
>
> (ii) an organisation whose central management and control is in Australia when the message is sent; or
>
> (c) the computer, server or device that is used to access the message is located in Australia; or
>
> (d) the relevant electronic account-holder is:
>
> (i) an individual who is physically present in Australia when the message is accessed; or
>
> (ii) an organisation that carries on business or activities in Australia when the message is accessed; or
>
> (e) if the message cannot be delivered because the relevant electronic address does not exist—assuming that the electronic address existed, it is reasonably likely that the message would have been accessed using a computer, server or device located in Australia.

21 Section 18 of the Spam Act provides that CEMs must contain a functional unsubscribe facility as follows:

> 18(1) A person must not send, or cause to be sent, a commercial electronic message that:
>
> (a) has an Australian link; and
>
> (b) is not a designated commercial electronic message; unless:
>
> (c) the message includes:

(i) a statement to the effect that the recipient may use an electronic address set out in the message to send an unsubscribe message to the individual or organisation who authorised the sending of the first-mentioned message; or

(ii) a statement to similar effect; and

(d) the statement is presented in a clear and conspicuous manner; and

(e) the electronic address is reasonably likely to be capable of receiving:

(i) the recipient's unsubscribe message (if any); and

(ii) a reasonable number of similar unsubscribe messages sent by other recipients (if any) of the same message;

at all times during a period of at least 30 days after the message is sent; and

(f) the electronic address is legitimately obtained; and

(g) the electronic address complies with the condition or conditions (if any) specified in the regulations.

...

(9) For the purposes of the application of this section to a commercial electronic message, where the sending of the message is authorised by an individual or organisation, an **unsubscribe message** is:

(a) an electronic message to the effect that the relevant electronic account-holder does not want to receive any further commercial electronic messages from or authorised by that individual or organisation; or

(b) an electronic message to similar effect.

DESIGNATED COMMERCIAL ELECTRONIC MESSAGES

22 It will have been observed that the application of s 16 of the Spam Act requires reference to Sch 1 where the expression 'designated commercial electronic message' is defined in the following terms:

2(1) For the purposes of this Act, an electronic message is a **designated commercial electronic message** if:

(a) the message consists of no more than factual information (with or without directly-related comment) and any or all of the following additional information:

(i) the name, logo and contact details of the individual or organisation who authorised the sending of the message;

(ii) the name and contact details of the author;

(iii) if the author is an employee—the name, logo and contact details of the author's employer;

(iv) if the author is a partner in a partnership—the name, logo and contact details of the partnership;

(v) if the author is a director or officer of an organisation—the name, logo and contact details of the organisation;

(vi) if the message is sponsored—the name, logo and contact details of the sponsor;

      (vii) information required to be included by section 17;

      (viii) information that would have been required to be included by section 18 if that section had applied to the message; and

  (b) assuming that none of that additional information had been included in the message, the message would not have been a commercial electronic message; and

  (c) the message complies with such other condition or conditions (if any) as are specified in the regulations.

23 In relation to a charity or charitable institutions, cl 3 of Sch 1 provides:

  3 For the purposes of this Act, an electronic message is a **designated commercial electronic message** if:

    (a) the sending of the message is authorised by any by any of the following bodies: ...

      (iv) a charity or charitable institution; and

    (b) the message relates to goods or services; and

    (c) the body is the supplier, or prospective supplier, of the goods or services concerned.

24 In relation to educational institutions, cl 4 of Sch 1 reads:

  4 For the purposes of this Act, an electronic message is a **designated commercial electronic message** if:

    (a) the sending of the message is authorised by an educational institution; and

    (b) either or both of the following subparagraphs applies:

      (i) the relevant electronic account-holder is, or has been, enrolled as a student in that institution;

      (ii) a member or former member of the household of the relevant electronic account-holder is, or has been, enrolled as a student in that institution; and

    (c) the message relates to goods or services; and

    (d) the institution is the supplier, or prospective supplier, of the goods or services concerned.

25 Clause 5 of Sch 1 provides that the regulations may provide that a specified kind of electronic message is a designated CEM for the purposes of the Spam Act.

26 The Spam Regulations 2004 ('the Regulations') do not have any such relevant effect here. The Regulations commenced on the commencement of Pts 2–6 of the Spam Act (ss 15–40).

CONCEPT OF CONSENT AND THE EXCEPTION OF CONSPICUOUS PUBLICATION

27 Section 16 of the Spam Act also requires reference to Sch 2 where the concept of consent, of importance to this proceeding, is defined.

28 Clause 2 in Sch 2 contains the 'basic definition' of 'consent' as follows:

2   For the purposes of this Act, **consent** means:

   (a)   express consent; or

   (b)   consent that can reasonably be inferred from:

       (i)   the conduct; and

       (ii)   the business and other relationships;

       of the individual or organisation concerned.

29 Clause 4 of the same Schedule contains the following provisions on the issue of when consent may be inferred from the publication of an electronic address:

   4(1)   For the purposes of this Act, the consent of the relevant electronic account-holder may not be inferred from the mere fact that the relevant electronic address has been published.

   (2)   However, if:

       (a)   a particular electronic address enables the public, or a section of the public, to send electronic messages to:

           (i)   a particular employee; or

           (ii)   a particular director or officer of an organisation; or

           (iii)   a particular partner in a partnership; or

           (iv)   a particular holder of a statutory or other office; or

           (v)   a particular self-employed individual; or

           (vi)   an individual from time to time holding, occupying or performing the duties of, a particular office or position within the operations of an organisation; or

           (vii)   an individual, or a group of individuals, from time to time performing a particular function, or fulfilling a particular role, within the operations of an organisation; and

       (b)   the electronic address has been conspicuously published; and

       (c)   it would be reasonable to assume that the publication occurred with the agreement of:

           (i)   if subparagraph (a)(i), (ii), (iii), (iv) or (v) applies—the employee, director, officer, partner, office-holder or self-employed individual concerned; or

           (ii)   if subparagraph (a)(vi) or (vii) applies—the organisation concerned; and

       (d)   the publication is not accompanied by:

           (i)   a statement to the effect that the relevant electronic account-holder does not want to receive unsolicited commercial electronic messages at that electronic address; or

           (ii)   a statement to similar effect;

       the relevant electronic account-holder is taken, for the purposes of this Act, to have consented to the sending of commercial electronic messages to that address, so long as the messages are relevant to:

       (e)   if subparagraph (a)(i), (ii), (iii), (iv) or (v) applies—the work-related business, functions or duties of the employee, director, officer, partner, office-holder or self-employed individual concerned; or

    (f)   if subparagraph (a)(vi) applies—the office or position concerned; or

    (g)   if subparagraph (a)(vii) applies—the function or role concerned.

30 Section 4 of the Spam Act defines 'publish' to include publishing on the internet and publishing to the public or a section of the public.

31 Clause 5 of Sch 2 provides that the Regulations may provide that the consent of a relevant electronic account-holder may not be inferred in the circumstances specified in the Regulations or that the inference may be made in specified circumstances. The Regulations do not have any relevant effect here.

PROVISIONS RELEVANT TO ADDRESS-HARVESTING

32 Section 22 of the Spam Act is titled 'Address-harvesting software and harvested-address lists must not be used'. The description of 'address-harvesting software' is defined in s 4 as follows:

> **address-harvesting software** means software that is specifically designed or marketed for use for:
>
> (a)   searching the Internet for electronic addresses; and
>
> (b)   collecting, compiling, capturing or otherwise harvesting those electronic addresses.

33 The same section defines 'harvested-address list' as follows:

> **harvested-address list** *means:*
>
> (a)   a list of electronic addresses; or
>
> (b)   a collection of electronic addresses; or
>
> (c)   a compilation of electronic addresses;
>
> where the production of the list, collection or compilation is, to any extent, directly or indirectly attributable to the use of address-harvesting software.

34 In relation to the word 'use', s 4 provides it has a meaning affected by s 11. That latter section provides:

> 11   Unless the contrary intention appears, a reference in this Act to the **use** of a thing is a reference to the use of the thing either:
>
> (a)   in isolation; or
>
> (b)   in conjunction with one or more other things.

35 Section 22 reads:

> 22(1) A person must not use:
>
> (a)   address-harvesting software; or
>
> (b)   a harvested-address list;
>
> if the person is:
>
> (c)   an individual who is physically present in Australia at the time of the use; or
>
> (d)   a body corporate or partnership that carries on business or activities in Australia at the time of the use.

(2) Subsection (1) does not apply in relation to the use of address-harvesting software or a harvested-address list, if the use was not in connection with sending commercial electronic messages in contravention of section 16.

(3) A person must not:
    (a) aid, abet, counsel or procure a contravention of subsection (1); or
    (b) induce, whether by threats or promises or otherwise, a contravention of subsection (1); or
    (c) be in any way, directly or indirectly, knowingly concerned in, or party to, a contravention of subsection (1); or
    (d) conspire with others to effect a contravention of subsection (1).

(4) Subsections (1) and (3) are **civil penalty provisions**.

PROVISIONS FOR CIVIL PENALTIES

36 Civil penalties are provided for in Pt 4 of the Spam Act. Section 24 provides for pecuniary penalties for contravention of civil penalty provisions as follows:

24(1) If the Federal Court is satisfied that a person has contravened a civil penalty provision, the Court may order the person to pay to the Commonwealth such pecuniary penalty, in respect of each contravention, as the Court determines to be appropriate.

(2) In determining the pecuniary penalty, the Court must have regard to all relevant matters, including:
    (a) the nature and extent of the contravention; and
    (b) the nature and extent of any loss or damage suffered as a result of the contravention; and
    (c) the circumstances in which the contravention took place; and
    (d) whether the person has previously been found by the Court in proceedings under this Act to have engaged in any similar conduct; and
    (e) if the Court considers that it is appropriate to do so—whether the person has previously been found by a court in a foreign country to have engaged in any similar conduct.

37 Part 3 of the Regulations contains rules relating to unsubscribe facilities, none of which is at issue on this application.

Evidence

38 The applicant relies on 16 affidavits. Three of these are sworn by Mr Christopher Duffy, senior investigator of the applicant. The affidavit of Mr David Thompson, a partner of Deloitte Touche Tohmatsu ('Deloittes') was brought by way of expert evidence, as was the affidavit of Mr Benny Tak-Kuan Lee. The balance of the applicant's evidence comes from internet users.

39 Admitted into evidence on behalf of the respondents are eight affidavits. The applicant did not seek to cross-examine any of these deponents. Likewise, the applicant did not oppose the admission into evidence of the respondents' affidavits provided they were

subject to the applicant's objection based on lack of relevance. That objection will be determined as and when necessary in the light of the respondents' reliance on the affidavits in their submissions ...

49 As has been seen, s 16(5) of the Spam Act casts onto the respondents the evidential burden of proving that the relevant electronic account-holder consented to the sending of the CEM. This means that the respondents are obliged to show that there is sufficient evidence to raise an issue as to the existence or non-existence of a fact in issue, having regard to the civil standard of proof: JD Heydon, *Cross on Evidence*, 6th edn, Butterworths, Australia, 2000, at [7015].

50 In relation to this evidential burden it is to be noted that the respondents did not call the second respondent as a witness. Additionally, they were not prepared to open to cross-examination the affidavit of Mr Geoffrey Roland Pryde who was employed as the computer technician responsible for the maintenance of Clarity1's computer systems, including servers for the relevant periods. In consequence Mr Pryde's affidavit was not tendered into evidence.

51 This unexplained failure of the respondents to call Mr Mansfield or Mr Pryde as witnesses gives rise to the application of the rule in *Jones v Dunkel* (1959) 101 CLR 298. That is, it may lead to an inference that the uncalled evidence or missing material would not have assisted the respondents' case: JD Heydon, *Cross on Evidence* at [1215].

52 The applicant submits, correctly, that in the case of the failure to call Mr Mansfield '[C]onsiderable significance may attach if the absent witness is either the party or a senior executive of a corporate party closely engaged in the transactions in question and present in court during the hearing': JD Heydon, *Cross on Evidence* at [1215], citing *Dilosa v Latec Finance Pty Ltd* (1966) 84 WN (Pt 1) (NSW) 557 at 582 ...

Claim that first respondent unlawfully sent unsolicited commercial electronic messages

TERMS OF THE CLAIM

58 The applicant alleges that during the period from 10 April 2004 to the present date, Clarity1 contravened s 16(1) of the Spam Act by sending or causing to be sent the following:

1 at least 213 443 382 CEMs (of which 41 796 754 were successfully sent) to 5 664 939 unique electronic addresses; and

2 at least 56 862 092 CEMs (of which 33 199 806 were successfully sent) to 2 291 518 unique electronic addresses.

The first of these claims is based on an analysis of the 'Direct2' database and the second is based on an analysis of the 'success' and 'failed' text files contained in the System#11 by the expert witnesses, Mr Thompson and Mr Lee.

59 The evidence of Mr Thompson also establishes that of the emails referred to in the 'success' text files, 1 715 603 contained unique email addresses. Of the emails referred to in the 'failed' text files, 1 525 496 were sent to unique email addresses. That is, the total number of emails involved in successful sending was 3 241 099. The respondents accept that the evidence of Mr Thompson was that these were sent to Australian addresses.

The number is significant in the view of the respondents because they contend that the applicant has endeavoured to utilise the size of the data files to 'demonise' them.

60 Mr Thompson's report also identified a total of 1 558 557 email addresses in particular databases of Clarity1 related to the United Kingdom. Of these 799 375 were unique addresses. He was unable to identify the number of email messages sent to the United Kingdom. The respondents argue that the dispatch of such messages is permitted under the law applicable in the United Kingdom and does not attract the application of the Spam Act because they may not have had an Australian address. The submission overlooks that the definition of 'Australian link' in s 7 of that Act refers to much more than the having of such an address.

61 Mr Thompson's evidence requires consideration in the context of the further expert evidence of Mr Lee, a computer forensic specialist with Deloittes, specialising in network and systems security. He works under the guidance of Mr Thompson and assisted with the preparation of Mr Thompson's expert report. Following Mr Thompson having given his evidence, Mr Lee was requested by him to review certain data contained in the report. The result of his review was that Mr Lee testified that the number of unique email addresses in the success and failed lists totalled 2 291 518 compared to the figure of 3 241 099 given by Mr Thompson. The difference is 949 581.

62 Mr Lee also identified 161 852 harvested email addresses attached to emails. These totalled 161 852 unique addresses. From those, Mr Lee identified 10 519 unique addresses in the success file and 9499 in the failed file.

63 So far as some of these addresses were harvested after 10 April 2004 the respondents say this evidence is not relevant but the applicant contends it should be inferred they were utilised. As the evidence is not clear on this issue I do not place reliance upon it.

64 In any event, the respondents through their absence of response to the notice to admit facts, have admitted that at least 41 796 754 CEMs have been sent between 10 April 2004 and 7 April 2005 and this continued at the same rate until 24 October 2005.

65 Additionally, as the term 'send' in s 16(1) includes attempt to send (s 4) it is not material whether or not the respondents had 'successfully' sent the CEMs.

66 It follows that the applicant has proved these allegations, albeit with the necessary adjustment to the figures to accommodate the evidence of Mr Lee.

67 Nevertheless three additional facts must be borne in mind in that context. The first is that each CEM contained provision of a procedure stating what was required to remove the electronic address from the Lists. The second is that during the period from March 2001 to the hearing date, some 166 000 requests were made for removal from the Lists, all of which were acted upon. The third is that for a similar period only 79 complaints were made to the applicant concerning CEMs from Clarity1, and one from overseas. No complaint related to a failure to remove an electronic address from the database.

AUSTRALIAN LINK

68 The evidence brought by the applicant also establishes that the CEMs had an Australian link because either par (a), par (b) or par (c) of s 7 of the Spam Act is satisfied on that evidence. The weight of evidence, although lacking specificity with respect to each email, makes it more probable than not that all the emails sent to the United Kingdom

had an Australian link particularly because the sender or person authorising the sending was physically present or had its central management and control in Australia or the computer, server or device utilised for the sending was located in Australia.

DEFENCE OF DESIGNATED COMMERCIAL ELECTRONIC MESSAGE

CHARITY OR CHARITABLE INSTITUTION EXCEPTION

69 The respondents contend that the applicant has failed to take into account that the respondents had been contracted to provide services to registered charities so that the electronic messages were not 'commercial' and would be designated CEMs within cl 3 of Sch 1 of the Spam Act. Reliance is placed in support on p 89 of the Explanatory Memorandum to the Spam Act. In support reference is made by the respondents to the expert witness testimony of Deloittes which it is claimed, showed that email addresses identified as being 'harvested' prior to the implementation of the Spam Act were provided by Messrs Kelly and Parsons who were acknowledged by the applicant in correspondence and come within the description 'charity' or 'charitable organisation'. The difficulty for the respondents is that their case is devoid of any evidence to support this submission. The named individuals were not called. No evidence identifies which of the electronic messages come within this alleged category. On the contrary, the respondents' admission in the record of interview was that it was not a charity or charitable institution.

EDUCATIONAL INSTITUTION EXCEPTION

70 The respondents also contend it is relevant that at all times the messages sent by Clarity1 related to business education in the form of seminars and manuals, about which it was not said they were in some way misleading or deceptive or without merit. The latter facts are of no assistance to the respondents in respect of the claim of breach of s 16(1). So far as the preceding facts are an appeal to the application of cl 4 of Sch 1 whereby an electronic message is a designated commercial electronic message if sent to an educational institution, there is no evidence to satisfy the requirements of the clause, which has earlier been set out in these reasons.

DEFENCE OF CONSENT

INFERENCE OF CONSENT

71 In defence of the allegation, the respondents have sought to rely on s 16(2) of the Spam Act, that is, that the relevant electronic account-holder consented to the sending of the CEM. In this regard, the respondents have argued:
1. the CEMs sent by Clarity1 contained an 'unsubscribe facility'. As the recipients of the CEMs did not use the 'unsubscribe facility', the respondents are entitled to reasonably infer that the recipients consented to the sending of the CEMs;
2. the consent may also be inferred from the business relationship between Clarity1 and the individual or organisation concerned (cl 2(b)(ii) of Sch 2); and
3. the recipients published their electronic addresses on the internet.
72 Other than the eight affidavits for the respondents by deponents who have indicated that they are happy to receive CEMs from the respondents, the respondents have not advanced any evidence supporting any of those arguments. They rely upon inferences which they

say should be drawn in the circumstances. Even if the affidavits have relevance, they can do no more than establish the willingness of the deponents to receive CEMs, not that Clarity1 was aware of such consent prior to dispatching further CEMs.

PRESENCE OF ADDRESS ON INTERNET

73 The fact that an electronic address is published on the internet cannot support an inference of consent. This is because cl 4(1) of Sch 2 provides that 'for the purposes of this Act, the consent of the relevant electronic account-holder may not be inferred from the mere fact that the relevant electronic address has been published'.

UNSUBSCRIBE FACILITY

74 The starting point is the statutory provision relating to unsubscribe facilities contained in s 18 of the Spam Act. It is patent from the terms of that section that it is a provision directed to requiring the sender of a CEM with an Australian link and which is not a designated CEM to include an unsubscribe facility. It imposes an obligation on them to that effect. It does not impose any obligation upon a recipient of such a CEM to reply. It does not either expressly or by implication support an inference that a failure to use the unsubscribe facility implies consent.

75 The respondents place reliance on comments at pp 37-38 of the Office of the Federal Privacy Commissioner in 'Guidelines to the National Privacy Principles' issued in September 2001. There it was stated that 'it may be possible to infer consent from the individual's failure to opt out provided that the option to opt out was clearly and prominently presented and easy to take up'. However, that statement must be read against a further statement where, after listing a number of factors said likely to enhance the possibility of the drawing of an inference of consent, the passage concluded:

> It is unlikely that consent to receive marketing material on-line could be implied from a failure to object to it. This is because it is usually difficult to conclude that the message has been read and it is generally difficult to take up the option of opting out as it is commonly considered that there are adverse consequences to an individual from opening or replying to email marketing—such as confirming the individual's address exists. This may also apply where material is distributed using other automated processes. (This would not prevent an organisation from seeking opt in consent on-line if NPP 2.1 allowed it).

76 It is the case that such publications cannot control the interpretation of an Act of Parliament. The words of the Act must speak for themselves and be interpreted according to the normal rules of statutory construction. Nevertheless, where the respondents are self-represented and, in connection with the observance of a new Act, have relied upon statements in such publications, it appropriate to have regard to what they rely upon as having shaped their approach to the Spam Act.

77 If, as the respondents assert, there is to be an inference drawn of consent from the fact of a failure to reply to a CEM, the foundations for it must be found in the circumstances. There are powerful features of the evidence which are inconsistent with the drawing of any such inference and militate against it. They are also inconsistent with any inference being drawn from any prior business relationship constituted by the initial sending of an electronic message to a recipient.

78 First, the mere fact that Clarity1 sent a CEM to an electronic address and did not receive a response from the recipient does not provide a proper foundation for an inference of consent. From that factual foundation, no such inference is logically open.

79 Second, even less so is such inference likely to be open where the entire relationship between Clarity1 and the recipient is constituted in the absence of bilateral communication. There are no circumstances in such a case from which an inference can be drawn. The evidence shows this to be the case in the vast majority of the CEMs. It is compounded where the CEMs have been obtained by Clarity1 without the recipient's knowledge or participation. This is further considered below under the subheading 'Business or other relationships'.

80 Third, the mere presence of the unsubscribe facility does not provide the foundation for any inference. Many inferences are open to speculation and none are logically dictated by the circumstances. There are a variety of methods available to recipients to deal with unwanted CEMs. These include simply deleting the CEM without reading it and so being unaware of the unsubscribe facility; ignoring the CEM and/or reporting it to the applicant; utilising a filtering or blocking technique. The sender, in this case Clarity1, would have no way of knowing whether the CEM has been opened or read; it is equally open to inference that it may not have been so that the unsubscribe facility was unknown to the recipient.

81 The probability of this being the case was very substantially enhanced in the circumstances disclosed by the evidence in the case of Clarity1. It used Stealth Mail Master which has the functionality to randomise email header information, to use open proxies and to 'provide anonymity' and to hide the IP address (see the evidence of Mr Thompson). The CEMs were sent by utilising the process of 'rotating IPs' (see the evidence of Mr Timothy Villa and the record of interview). They were sent from a number of different 'yahoo.com' and 'yahoo.com.au' electronic addresses (see the evidence of Mrs Catherine Trudgeon and M/s Victoria Rollo). Substantially similar CEMs were sent in multiple copies to the same human recipient. The email header information was disguised and the IP address did not match the 'from' addresses. They were sent using overseas servers in the United States of America, Korea, China and elsewhere.

82 The view that the presence of the unsubscribe facility in these circumstances cannot give rise to the inference for which the respondents contend, is supported by the evidence which was given concerning the reluctance of users to activate an unsubscribe facility. Their evidence was that if they did so they would be confirming the existence of their email address and opening that address to spam: see the evidence of Mr Brett Watson; Mr Guy Miller; Mr John Bongiovanni; Mrs Trudgeon and Mr Christopher Rhodes as well as Mr Thompson.

83 The fact that the electronic unsubscribe facility offered by Clarity1 failed to identify Clarity1 or Business Seminars Australia makes it entirely unreasonable to expect unwilling recipients to use the unsubscribe facility. See the evidence of Mr Bongiovanni and Mr Villa.

84 Fourth, in the case of electronic addresses obtained by purchasing or leasing from external parties and using address-harvesting software, there is no evidence Clarity1 obtained or intended to obtain the consent of the relevant account-holders when it made the acquisitions.

85 Fifth, the respondents have not explained why so many CEMs were sent. The volume makes it improbable that the respondents could have been aware that consent was in place prior to the sending of the CEMs. It is antithetical to the drawing of the inference sought.

BUSINESS OR OTHER RELATIONSHIPS

86 The respondents contend that consent can be reasonably be inferred from the business relationships which Clarity1 has with the recipients of the CEMs. A further argument of the respondents is that neither the Spam Act nor the Explanatory Memorandum to it have addressed the use of email addresses which have been used over an extensive period, in many cases more than a year. It is said that in such instances the respondents can assert inferred consent because of the acceptance of messages over that period.

87 The reference to 'business relationships' in cl 2 of Sch 2 of the Spam Act must be understood in its immediate and surrounding context. The immediate context is one which conjoins the conduct of the individual or organisation who sent the CEM to the relationships as the factual foundation from which the inference may be drawn. It is not the business relationships alone which ground the inference. Additionally, the relevant relationships are not only business relationships; other relationships are equally relevant.

88 The phrase 'the business and other relationships' is not one which appears to have been regularly used so as to attract judicial consideration. 'Business' is defined in s 4 of the Spam Act, subject to appearance of contrary intention to include 'a venture or concern in trade or commerce, whether or not conducted on a regular, repetitive or continuous basis'. The reference to 'relationships' is to be taken to be a reference to a particular connection: *The Macquarie* Dictionary, 2ⁿᵈ edn, Macquarie University, New South Wales, 1991 at p 1484. 'Connection' means a 'relationship': *The Macquarie Dictionary* at p 381.

89 The applicant and others on behalf of the Australian Government issued a publication entitled '*Spam Act 2003*: A practical guide for business'. In addressing the issue of inferred consent at p 7 it states:

> You may be able to reasonably infer consent after considering both the conduct of the addressee and their relationship with you. For example, if the addressee has an existing relationship with you and has previously provided their address then it would be reasonable to infer that consent has been provided.

At p 8 the guide describes an 'existing relationship' in the following terms:

> It will be possible for you to infer consent based on the status of your relationship with the addressee, as long as it is consistent with the reasonable expectations of the addressee, and their conduct. The National Privacy Principles (available from www.privacy.gov.au), and particularly Privacy Principle 2, provides guidance on such communications. An existing business or other relationship may, for example, be a relationship that was initiated by a commercial activity (including provision, for a fee or free of charge, of information, goods, or of services) or other communication between you and potential addressee.

The following are examples that might suggest that a business, or other, relationship exists from which you may reasonably infer consent:

> persons who have purchased goods or services which involves ongoing warranty and service provisions; ...'

Privacy Principle 2 of the Principles provides in part:

2.1 An organisation must not use or disclose personal information about an individual for a purpose (the **secondary purpose**) other than the primary purpose of collection unless:

(a) both of the following apply:

(i) the secondary purpose is related to the primary purpose of collection and, if the personal information is sensitive information, directly related to the primary purpose of collection;

(ii) the individual would reasonably expect the organisation to use or disclose the information for the secondary purpose; or

(b) the individual has consented to the use or disclosure; or

(c) if the information is not sensitive information and the use of the information is for the secondary purpose of direct marketing:

(i) it is impracticable for the organisation to seek the individual's consent before that particular use; and

(ii) the organisation will not charge the individual for giving effect to a request by the individual to the organisation not to receive direct marketing communications; and

(iii) the individual has not made a request to the organisation not to receive direct marketing communications; and

(iv) in each direct marketing communication with the individual, the organisation draws to the individual's attention, or prominently displays a notice, that he or she may express a wish not to receive any further direct marketing communications; and

(v) each written direct marketing communication by the organisation with the individual (up to and including the communication that involves the use) sets out the organisation's business address and telephone number and, if the communication with the individual is made by fax, telex or other electronic means, a number or address at which the organisation can be directly contacted electronically; or

...

90 The applicant accepts that it is certainly possible that an organisation can comply with the *Privacy Act* and none the less contravene the Spam Act. Therefore the applicant submits that any particular advice concerning the *Privacy Act* or adherence to statements concerning the Principles, cannot assist the respondents in defending this proceeding.

91 The applicant's submissions also draw attention to the Explanatory Memorandum to the Spam Act which notes that:

At the present time there is no legislation specifically requiring a sender to obtain recipient's consent prior to sending spam to that individual, either initially or on an ongoing basis. Under the Privacy Act *1998* the collection of personal information from public sources may require an individual's explicit consent, but this aspect of the legislation has not yet been tested.

92 The receipt of electronic messages without more cannot give rise to the inference of consent because the receipt could be accounted for on many bases other than consent. I do not consider that such communication can properly come within the description of a 'business or other relationship'. There is no relationship when the communication is one sided. A relationship of the type referred to in Sch 2 implies a connection arising from mutuality. Communication from only one to another with no response from the other cannot properly be found to be a relationship, particularly in the context.

93 Additionally the respondents argue that consent may be inferred in the case of 'commercially available lists purchased, swapped or otherwise acquired prior to the implementation of the Spam Act in 2003'. The circumstances of the acquisition of lists so described is itself antithetical to the drawing of any inference that the lists were obtained with consent. The respondents did not seek to prove the existence of consent for such CEMs other than by inference.

94 The respondents also refer to the instance of an account-holder who has provided an electronic address such as by handing over a business card containing the address to a commercial entity, with the exception of circumstances which make apparent to a reasonable person that receipt of future messages is not expected. Again, no evidence has been brought to support a finding that such an occurrence affected the collection of any of the electronic addresses in issue.

95 In the respondents' final written submissions it is also contended that consent may be inferred where there is '[B]y the action of entering a competition or a request for information website maintained by the respondent or associated joint venture entities who displayed relevant Terms and conditions statements that allowed the use of the email address for promotional purposes'. It is further contended that the addresses are identified in the description of the various lists recorded in the evidence of Mr Duffy as 'JV' (joint ventures') or MainAU which total 929 200 separate email addresses. The applicant further objects on the ground that there is no evidence to support the primary submission. This objection is proper and I allow it.

96 There was evidence from Mr Duffy analysing 1 469 820 electronic addresses provided to him by the respondents. He concluded that of these, only 182 involved the placement of orders with the Maverick Partnership or Business Seminars Australia. The applicant submits that it does not follow even in these instances that the 182 purchasers of products thereby gave consent to the receipt of CEMs from Clarity1. Support for this submission is sought by the applicant in the Explanatory Memorandum at p 115. There it is said that consent will not always be inferred where there is a pre-existing relationship between a person and a business. The example is given of the purchase by a person of a t-shirt or groceries from a shop. In my view, the ordering of a product by email is in a different category than a relatively more casual purchase in a shop. The Memorandum accepts that the issue of consent is a question of fact to be considered according to each particular set of circumstances. The example of the t-shirt is also listed along with other casual types of purchase such as the purchase of a ticket to attend a concert or where a purchase is made anonymously.

97 What is required by cl 2 of Sch 2 of the Spam Act is that consent can reasonably be inferred from both the conduct and 'the business and other relationships' of the individual

or organisation concerned. Prima facie, the conclusion of a contract of purchase by an email order by an individual or organisation constitutes a 'business relationship' between the vendor and purchaser. In the absence of evidence to the contrary, it can be reasonably inferred that the recipient wishes to be kept aware of the business of the vendor, in this case Clarity1. It may be that such evidence could have been brought; for example that a particular purchaser wished only to have the relationship for the purchase of the particular product secured by the CEM. In the absence of such evidence, it is a reasonable inference that a person having displayed interest in the wares of the vendor on one occasion, wishes to be kept in touch with future opportunities for purchase of products marketed by the same vendor unless indicating to the contrary. To construe the reference to such relationships too strictly would not acknowledge commercial realities. Vendors would be left in doubt whether they could communicate with their clientele (that is, persons who have purchased goods from them) unless having from them express consent. I do not consider the provisions of the Spam Act are intended to bring about such a strict regime. The provision requires application with great regard to particular circumstances. The applicant not having brought evidence to rebut the prima facie evidentiary position raised by the evidence in the case of the 182 purchasers that they wished to trade with Clarity1, I do not consider it can be found that in those limited instances consent is not reasonably to be inferred. I infer the 182 purchasers gave their consent for the purposes of s 16(1) of the Spam Act.

98 The applicant also submits on this issue that Clarity1 has not presented any evidence or advanced any argument that it relied on a recipient's purchase of goods or services as the basis for making a reasonable inference of consent. In my view it was not necessary that it present such evidence given the prima facie position raised by the evidence of Mr Duffy. I consider that Clarity1 did advance argument that it had consent within cl 2 of Sch 2 of the Spam Act and hence consent reasonably is to be inferred from the business relationship constituted by the purchase of goods in the case of the 182 purchasers. That much was encompassed within the generality of the respondents' overall submissions.

DEFENCE OF AUTHORITY OF USER OF ACCOUNT TO GIVE CONSENT

99 The respondents' final written submissions also appeal to cl 3 of Sch 2. That provides that if a person other than the relevant electronic account-holder uses the relevant account to send an electronic message about consent, that person is taken to have been authorised to send that message on behalf of the relevant electronic account-holder. However, there is no evidence that consents were received under such circumstances and therefore no evidential foundation upon which to invoke the application of that clause.

DEFENCE OF CONSPICUOUS PUBLICATION

100 This defence is advanced in reliance upon cl 4 in Sch 2 of the Spam Act. For the exception to be applicable, a number of elements must be satisfied. First, there must be a particular electronic address enabling the public, or a section of the public, to send electronic messages to the person or holders of particular offices, positions, functions or roles specified in cl 4(2)(a)(i) to (vii) of Sch 2 of the Spam Act. Second,

the address must have been 'conspicuously published': cl 4(2)(b). Third, it must be 'reasonable to assume' that the publication occurred with the agreement of the person or organisation concerned: cl 4(2)(c). Four, it must be established that the publication was not accompanied by a statement to the effect that the relevant electronic account-holder does not want to receive unsolicited CEMs at that electronic address, or words to similar effect: cl 4(2)(d). Five, it must also be established that the CEM is relevant to the work-related business, functions or duties of the employee, director, officer, partner, office-holder or self-employed individual concerned; the office or position concerned; or the function or role concerned: cl 4(2)(e)–(g).

101 The term 'conspicuously published' is not defined in the Spam Act. The word 'conspicuous' means 'easy to be seen ... readily attracting the attention': *The Macquarie Dictionary* at p 384.

102 The applicant submits that in order to demonstrate that the conspicuous publication exception applies, the respondents must produce evidence which demonstrates, at the minimum where each electronic address has been published and obtained from; that the publication qualifies to be described as 'conspicuous publication' within the ordinary meaning of that term; that no statement against the sending of CEMs to the electronic address accompanies the publication of it; and how each CEM sent to the address relates to the matters set out in cl 4(2)(e)-(g) of Sch 2 of the Spam Act.

103 The respondents brought evidence to the following effect. Their witness Mr Allan Morgan deposes that his electronic address may have been found on the yellow pages or that he may have given it when replying to an advertisement. Mr Richard van Proctor deposes that he started receiving CEMs from Business Seminars Australia after 'signing up for a Platinum Privilege card'. Mr Anthony Paul deposes that his electronic address may have been obtained from the yellow pages, his website or trade directories. Mr Neill Ogge deposes that he believes Business Seminars Australia obtained his electronic address when he joined a trade exchange.

104 There is no further evidence from the respondents on this issue.

105 In their final submissions the respondents also assert they have consent where the addressee has either:

2.5.3.1 conspicuously published their email address—an active action, not a passive action as claimed by the applicant, or

2.5.3.2 subscribed to one or multiple websites that collect email addresses for marketing purposes.

2.5.3.3 each of these websites included a Terms and Conditions page that set out the use of the email address by the website on which it appeared and a network of websites that made use of the information collected.

2.5.3.4 samples of these terms and conditions are annexed to this Submission.

106 The applicant objects to 2.5.3.1 to 2.5.3.3 on the ground that the assertions the respondents there make are not supported by any evidence. It objects to 2.5.3.4 on the ground that the respondents are seeking to introduce new evidence after the close

of evidence. These objections are clearly proper and I allow them. Throughout the hearing the respondents understood that the purpose of adducing evidence was to open it, if required, to cross-examination. The respondents cannot in written submissions seek to follow a course in which such normal processes for the admission of evidence are bypassed.

107 The consequence is that no evidence of the type made requisite by the provisions of Sch 2 has been produced to support the respondents' contention that the defence is applicable. As the evidential burden falls on the respondents pursuant to s 16(5) of the Spam Act, they fail to make out the defence.

108 There is, in addition, evidence from some of the applicant's witnesses which demonstrates that the conspicuous publication exception cannot apply, at least in their cases. Mr Bongiovanni's electronic address was published on his academic website but the CEMs from Clarity1 do not relate to his academic activities. Likewise, in the case of Mr Andrew Cottas and Mr Miller, the CEMs did not relate to the relevant businesses. Mr Alexander Dawson and M/s Lesley La Coste only placed their addresses in limited non-conspicuous circumstances. The address of M/s Rollo was not advertised at all. In the case of Mr David Bromage, his website carried a disclaimer. Additionally, I accept that it may be inferred from the sheer volume of the electronic addresses contained in the Databases and Lists that, at the time of compilation, the respondents did not consider whether the publication of the electronic address on the internet was done in circumstances that met each the criteria set out in cl 4 of Sch 2 to the Spam Act.

109 In their final written submissions the respondents contend that the email address of the applicant's witness Mr Cottas is conspicuously displayed on a website without any limitation affecting spam so that it would be reasonable to assume/infer consent within the guidelines offered by the applicant's (and others') publication 'Spam Act 2003: A practical guide for business'. Such guidelines cannot govern the interpretation of the Spam Act. What has to be established is that the requirements of the Spam Act relating to conspicuous publication have been met. In any event, the guidelines accurately specify the requirement of that Act, in addition to conspicuous display and the absence of a spam deterrent, is that the message must relate to the addressee's published employment function or role. There is no evidence from the respondents that such is the case.

110 In relation to the evidence of Mrs Trudgeon, the respondents assert that because no incidence of the email addresses in question can be found by doing internet searches using various search engines, it is not possible that the email address came into possession of Clarity1 by the use of email address-harvesting software. Therefore, it is contended, at some time the account-holder entered her email address into a competition with conditions allowing for the subsequent use by Clarity1. Details of various competition and collection sites are annexed to the submissions. Assertions are also sought to be made of competitions conducted during the period 1998 to 2004. None of these matters is in evidence. It was not put to the witness that she may have entered a competition being one of the nominated competitions. No terms and conditions of such competitions were put into evidence. In the absence of appropriate proof, the inferences which the respondents seek to have drawn are not open.

OTHER DEFENCES

111 There is nothing in the case of the respondents seeking to invoke the defences in s 16(3) or s 16(4) of the Spam Act. In any event, there is nothing in the evidence which provides a foundation for reliance on those defences.

112 I therefore find that the claim under s 16(1) is made out.

Claim of use of harvested-address lists

113 The provisions of the Spam Act relevant to harvested-address lists—ss 4, 11 and 22—have been set out above. The prohibition in s 22(1) against the use of address-harvesting software or a harvested-address list is one which does not apply in the circumstances referred to in s 22(2). Those circumstances are where the use 'was not in connection with sending commercial electronic messages in contravention of section 16'. The consequence is that s 22(1) does apply where the use is in connection with sending CEMs in contravention of s 16.

114 The respondents have admitted that the principal methods used to obtain the electronic addresses contained in the Databases and Lists were by using address-harvesting software or by obtaining harvested-address lists from external parties. The admission is that the majority of such electronic addresses were obtained by one or other of those means. Apart from the admissions in the notice to admit facts, the affidavit of Mr Thompson supports this. Support is also found in the affidavit of Mr Duffy sworn on 18 July 2005. Additionally a number of the witnesses stated their belief that their electronic addresses were harvested from the internet and the assertion was not challenged by the respondents in cross-examination: see the evidence of Mr Villa, Mrs Trudgeon, Mr Dawson and M/s La Coste.

115 However, the respondents' case is and the evidence supports that the harvesting occurred prior to 10 April 2004 when the Spam Act relevantly came into operation. The act of harvesting is not alleged to have been contrary to the Spam Act. What is alleged against the respondents is that their usage of the harvested addresses after that date constitutes a contravention of s 22(1) because it was usage in connection with a contravention of s 16(1). The contravention of s 16(1) has been made out. It follows that in the majority of instances of contravention of s 16(1) Clarity1 used a harvested-address list in contravention of s 22(1) on each occasion.

116 The effect of the enactment of s 22(1) is to make illegal from the date of its application the usage to which it is directed. The fact that the address-harvesting may have occurred at a time when no such prohibition was in the law, does not prevent the application of the provision in its terms from the date it came into force. The provision is not simply concerned with how the list was obtained in the past. It is directed to the usage of the list in the circumstances of the prohibition.

117 I therefore find that the claim under s 22(1) is made out.

Accessorial liability

118 Since *Hamilton v Whitehead* (1988) 166 CLR 121 it is clear that the conduct of a person may result in liability being imposed on a company as the principal offender as

well as liability being imposed on that individual person as an accessory: see discussion in *Australian Competition and Consumer Commission v Black on White Pty Ltd* (2001) 110 FCR 1 at [17]–[19].

119 A person has aided or abetted a contravention if it can be shown that the person was aware of the essential elements of the contravention and intentionally participated in it. Similarly, a person is a 'party to a contravention' if the person has knowledge of the essential elements of, and participates in, or assents to, the contravention: see *Yorke v Lucas* (1985) 158 CLR 661 at 670; *Rural Press Ltd v Australian Competition and Consumer Commission* (2002) 193 ALR 399; *Australian Competition and Consumer Commission v Giraffe World Australia Pty Ltd (No 2)* (1999) 166 ALR 74.

120 A person is 'knowingly concerned' in a contravention if the person has something more than 'mere knowledge' of the subject of the contravention. The question is whether the person is implicated or involved in the offence and whether there is a practical connection between him and the offence: *Trade Practices Commission v Australia Meat Holdings Pty Ltd* (1988) 83 ALR 299.

121 It is admitted that Mr Mansfield, as the sole director of Clarity1, was at all relevant times fully aware and responsible for the business carried on by Clarity1. He intentionally participated in and knew the essential elements of each aspect of Clarity1's conduct, including the conduct which has been found to have contravened ss 16(1) and 22(1) of the Spam Act. It necessarily follows that he is liable under ss 16(9) and 22(3) of the Spam Act as a person who has been aiding, abetting, counselling or procuring a contravention, or directly or indirectly, knowingly concerned in, or party to, a contravention.

122 However, Mr Mansfield argues he has no case to answer, despite these provisions, because of s 8 of the Spam Act, which reads:

> 8(1) For the purposes of this Act (including subsection (2)), if:
> > (a) an individual authorises the sending of an electronic message; and
> > (b) the individual does so on behalf of an organisation;
> > then:
> > (c) the organisation is taken to authorise the sending of the electronic message; and
> > (d) the individual is taken not to authorise the sending of the electronic message.
>
> (2) For the purposes of this Act, if:
> > (a) an electronic message is sent by an individual or organisation; and
> > (b) the sending of the message is not authorised by any other individual or organisation;
> > the first-mentioned individual or organisation is taken to authorise the sending of the message.

123 There is no inconsistency between this section and the provisions of ss 16(9) and 22(3). Even if s 8(1) applies so as to result in the finding that Mr Mansfield did not authorise the sending of the electronic message, that cannot protect him against the application of the two subsections providing for accessorial liability. This is because the question raised by those two subsections is whether he was involved as an accessory in any of the ways stated in those subsections in the actions of Clarity1. The fact that s 8(1)

may have the consequence that he is not to be taken to have authorised the sending, does not answer the question raised by the two subsections whether he participated in the sending of the message in any of the relevant ways. *Hamilton v Whitehead* makes apparent that where liability is imposed on the company it is direct not vicarious, so that a person with knowledge of the material circumstances and who was the actor in the conduct constituting the circumstances will be 'knowingly concerned' in the commission of the offences committed by the company.

124   It follows also that there is no legal significance in Mr Mansfield's contention that at no time did he act in his own right or encourage the company. It is sufficient that he acted only as a director and the actor in the conduct. For him to be 'knowingly concerned' it is not necessary for him to be acting only 'in his own right'. The essential question in either case is whether he was on the evidence 'knowingly concerned' as that phrase and associated descriptions in the two subsections are understood at law.

Civil penalty

125   The issue of the appropriate civil penalty will be the subject of submissions at a hearing to be listed.

Orders

126   The above reasons entitle the applicant to declaratory relief in the form sought in the application, subject to any further submissions concerning the form of the orders in that respect. The making of such orders will be held over pending determination of the issues relating to civil penalty.

 NOTES AND QUESTIONS

1   This case illustrates neatly the application of the *Spam Act 2003* as well as the application of a number of the key defences. List all the defences raised and explain how the court dealt with each defence in applying the provisions of the *Spam Act 2003*.

2   How did the court decide the question of implied consent when dealing with business and other relationships? What were the facts in this case that swayed the court?

3   Explain the concept of harvesting email addresses. Why is it relevant to spam?

- -

4   Singapore legislation

Singapore has been dealing with the spam problem for some time.

In 2004, the Infocomm Development Authority of Singapore (IDA) worked closely with three ISPs to introduce a multi-pronged approach on email spam. The measures includes public education, industry self-regulation, a new legislative framework, and international cooperation. The first Consultation Paper outlining the proposed legislative framework was issued in May 2004; it sought feedback on the Proposed Legislative Framework for the Control of E-mail Spam. In September 2005, the Attorney-General's Chambers of Singapore and IDA issued a second public consultation paper on the proposed Spam Control Bill.[4] This second consultation exercise sought views on the draft Spam Control Bill for Singapore, which now includes mobile spam and proposes that civil rights and remedies be granted to any person who suffers loss or damage from non-compliant spam. At the time of writing, the Bill had not yet been enacted.

---

5 Spyware

Spyware was referred to in the discussion on trade mark law and pop-up advertising. Spyware is equally relevant to criminal law—indeed, it is a means by which much fraud and identity theft has been perpetrated on innocent and unsuspecting victims. The following article surveys the current legal landscape in Australia and the USA on spyware.

Kylie Howard & Yee Fen Lim, 'I Spy With My Little Eye —Taking a Closer Look at Spyware'

(2005) (2–3) *Journal of Information, Law and Technology*

<http://www2.warwick.ac.uk/fac/soc/law/elj/jilt/2005_2-3/howard-lim/> 17 August 2006

Spyware is a practical problem that can affect internet users everywhere. This article explains the problem of spyware, how it can affect users of PCs and the Internet and examines the legislative approach to spyware in both Australia and the US. Although spyware has recently received judicial and academic attention in many jurisdictions around the world, the actual effects of spyware are largely unknown by the everyday user of the Internet. And unfortunately, until there is a wide understanding of the nature and scope of spyware, it is unlikely that practical legal solutions will ever evolve. More importantly, if one does not know or understand a serious issue that could be impeaching upon their rights, one will never exercise the legal protections that exist (to the extent that they *do* exist). This article therefore, provides a detailed explanation of spyware, and how it can affect a user of the Internet. The article then focuses on two examples of how different jurisdictions have handled spyware—Australia and the US.

Introduction—What is Spyware?

> You are being watched. Monitored. Every move you make is being recorded, logged. Your personal tastes and desires, your friends, travel plans, favourite TV shows, and newspapers. Perhaps more disturbing, this information is stored into databases, sold and shared with nameless and countless others. And you have no idea ...[5]

---

4   See Press Release at <http://www.ida.gov.sg/idaweb/media/infopage.jsp?infopagecategory=telecoms. mr:media&versionid=2&infopageid=I3593> accessed 1 May 06.

5   Michael L Baroni, 'Spyware Beware' 47-APR Orange County Law 36.

The very problem with spyware is that it could never be the subject of an I spy game—it is invisible to the every day user of the Internet. Spyware is any form of technology that aids in gathering information about a person or an organisation without their knowledge or informed consent.[6] It is commonly referred to as 'snoopware' or 'trespassware' because the program snoops or trespasses into the private life of the user, sometimes to the extent of full identity theft.[7] A user of the Internet can sometimes play a part in downloading spyware, often without knowledge and by accident through downloading a spy-carrying email attachment, downloading 'free' software[8]. More often however, just simply using the Internet can result in spyware being placed on a user's computer as the spyware exploits vulnerabilities in the operating system of the user. Some examples of free software that have been known to be accompanied by spyware include browser toolbars and modifications, file transfer protocol, UnZip, PC clocks, personal organisers and Kazaa.[9] A user may or may not have consented to a 'monitoring' software as part of an end user licence agreement. Most would not be aware that the 'I agree' consented to involve having masses of personal information being collected (and even sold to third parties!). Problematically, firewalls or virus protecting software do not always prevent spyware downloads and often spyware is deliberately designed to be difficult or impossible to uninstall.

There are some very convincing reasons why Spyware should not be tolerated. The main arguments being security issues and the right to privacy. Regarding privacy, in the real world, would you agree to someone following you into shops, recording the purchases you make, looking at the types of books you read and then selling this information to a third party for marketing purposes? Probably not. In the virtual world, however, this is constantly happening to internet users everyday all over the world—and not just to home users, but to companies as well. Some marketing companies are making millions of dollars selling personal information to third parties.[10] It is not the intention of this article to explore all the data privacy issues that spyware present. It is acknowledged that spyware would infringe many of the protections enshrined in the EU Data Protection Directive however, the aim here is to focus on the security and fraudulent practices that spyware represent.

Specific concerns about spyware range from slowing down PCs to extreme theft of confidential information such as bank account details and passwords which can lead to identity theft and other forms of criminal activities. At its most innocuous level, the disruptive advertising pop-ups can consume significant resources on a PC.[11] Companies have reported that they are losing millions of dollars in down time and lost productivity and expect the issue to get worse.[12] Evidence of the worsening problem can be seen in a recent US survey (April, 2004)—over three months, some 30 million spyware programs had been installed

6   See <http://searchsmb.techtarget.com/> accessed 29 May 2005.

7   Commonwealth of Australia, Parliamentary Debates, *Hansard*, Second Reading Speech, 12 May 2005.

8   For example, the Kaaza file transfer program that was used by millons of people around the world to swap data also included another spyware software.

9   Hon Jefferson Lankford, 'Big Brother is Watching You' (2004) 40-AUG Ariz Att'y 8.

10   Commonwealth of Australia, Parliamentary Debates, *Hansard*, Second Reading Speech, 12 May 2005. 'Companies such as Doubleclick make millions of dollars each year from the sale of data and the target-ing of ads, yet their name is not often seen, other than in civil liberties courts.'

11   See <http://www.adwarereport.com> accessed 29 May 2005.

12   IDC, a company in the IT industry reported that $12 million was spent in 2003 on anti-spyware solu-tions. See <http://searchsmb.techtarget.com/> accessed 29 May 2005.

on approximately one million computers. The number of spyware programs installed on a similar number of computers is now at an alarming 85 million.[13]

The US seems to have given the issue of spyware considerable academic and judicial attention—as to whether the regime works in a practical sense is another question. As outlined in more detail below, there have been a number of cases brought under various legislative and common law regimes. The legislative approach in US, however, has proven to be problematic and unable to mould to the problem of spyware. Some states in the US have recognised this, and have moved toward introducing legislation to specifically deal with spyware. In Australia, although case law on this topic is scarce, we seem to be on track in terms of focussed attention on the issue. The Department of Communications, Information Technology and the Arts (DCITA) issued a discussion paper on the topic, with the purpose of seeking information and feedback from the Australian public to assist in developing a practical response that targets spyware that is not legitimately used. Responses from the public have now been received, and various strategies have been implemented to address the issue. The Australian Democrats have also shown interest in the issue and proposed a bill—the Spyware Bill 2005. However, as spyware is already present on millions of computers even if the bill is passed (which seems unlikely at this stage), it will be important to remember that some more general solutions will also be required before we can begin to confidently say that the issue is under control.

Legislative Review in Australia

It has been recognised that the availability of legal recourse against online offences increases the confidence of the public in using the Internet. In response to this, in 2004 the Minister for Communications, Information Technology and the Arts announced a review of the coverage of existing Australian laws in respect to the malicious use of spyware. DCITA began working with the Attorney-General's Department and law enforcement agencies to determine the adequacy of existing laws in combating spyware. DCITA found that existing legislation, such as the *Criminal Code Act 1995* (Cth), the *Privacy Act 1988* (Cth), *Telecommunications Act 1997* (Cth) and the *Trade Practices Act 1974* (Cth), covered many of the malicious behaviours associated with spyware[14] (this is explained in more detail below). The review covered behaviours such as deceptive conduct, unauthorised access, cyber-stalking, computer hijacking, theft of computer software, resources and bandwidth, denial of service attacks, damage to computer settings, identity theft, content modification, anti-competitive conduct and privacy impeachments.

For the purposes of the legislative review, spyware was defined as:

> any software application that is generally installed without the knowledge or consent of the user, to obtain, use or interfere with personal information or resources, content or settings for malicious or undesirable purposes.[15]

---

13   Commonwealth of Australia, Senate Parliamentary Debates, *Hansard*, Second Reading Speech, 12 May 2005.

14   See <http://www.choice.com.au/viewArticle.aspx?id=104706&catId=100245&tid=100008&p=1> accessed 5 June 2005.

15   <http://www.dcita.gov.au/__data/assets/pdf_file/24939/Outcome_of_Review.pdf> accessed 28 September 2005.

The table below outlines potential criminal offences that can be brought under existing legislation:

Legislation	Potential offence
Criminal Code Act 1995 (Cth)	Attempting to commit a serious offence (such as fraud) using a telecommunications network;
	Unauthorised access, modification or impairment of data, information or programs with intent to commit a serious offence;
	Causing unauthorised modification of data, information or programs to cause impairment— including the reliability, security or operation of data, information or programs;
	Unauthorised impairment of electronic communication;
	Unauthorised access to or modification of restricted data—data held on computer and to which access is restricted by an access control system (such as passwords etc) associated with the function of the computer;
	Possession or control of information with the intention to commit or facilitate a computer offence;
	Producing, supplying or obtaining data with intention committing or facilitating a computer offence;
	Dishonestly obtaining, possessing, supplying, using or dealing in personal financial information without consent; and
	Intentionally using a carriage service to menace, harass or cause offence.
Trade Practices Act 1974 (Cth)	Anti-competitive behaviour
	Misleading and deceptive conduct
Australian Securities and Investments Commission Act 2001 (Cth) and Corporations Act 2001 (Cth)	Misleading and deceptive conduct
Privacy Act 1988 (Cth)	Invasion of privacy
	Harvesting and collecting personal information
Criminal Law Consolidation Act 1935 (SA)	Identity theft
Telecommunications Act 1997 (Cth)	Applies to some use of personal information
Telecommunications (Interception) Act 1979 (Cth)	Collection of data and other information

As indicated above, the Australian Democrats are of a different view to DCITA—their view is that separate legislation is required to specifically deal with spyware and therefore introduced the Spyware Bill 2005—a proposed Act to regulate the unauthorised installation of computer software and require the clear disclosure to computer users of certain computer software features that may pose a threat to user privacy.

The objects of the proposed Act are to regulate the unauthorised or surreptitious installation of computer software and to require clear disclosure to computer users of certain computer software features that may pose a threat to a user's privacy or the speed or operation of their computer. The proposed Act aims to give computer users the right and capacity to know that software is being installed on their computer, refuse to have it installed and be able to uninstall any software.[16] Consent by a user to install the software was cleverly designed as a two-step process with the requirement of an 'affirmative consent' which is consent that is expressed through the action of a computer user and independent from any other consent solicited from the user during the installation process (for example, consent cannot be a broader consent for the installation of a separate software to which spyware is attached).[17] The first step of consent is to the general installation of the software.[18] Secondly, consent has to be obtained as to each individual information collection feature (and other features such as advertising, distributed computing feature and modification features) of the software. For example, if the spyware software once downloaded causes advertising pop-ups, collection of personal information and modifications to settings of the user's computer, the computer user must consent to each of these features before the software can be lawfully installed. This type of consent ensures that users are fully informed as to exactly how the software may affect them and their computer. Penalties under the proposed act are directed to the actual software developers rather than passive parties such as the host of a website through which software was made available.[19]

On 1 September 2005, the Minister for Communications, Information Technology and the Arts, Senator The Hon Helen Coonon, released a media statement indicating that malicious uses of spyware are already covered by existing laws with an emphasis on the need for the public to be aware of the threat of spyware.[20] To complement the need for public awareness, DCITA developed and released *Taking Care of Spyware*[21], a brochure designed to provide the public with information about spyware, how to remove it and how to prevent it. The brochure is supported by the Internet Industry Association's (IIA) national anti-spyware campaign[22] where the public can find more detailed information and sample the anti-spyware software that is available to use for a free trial period. Given this media release, it is unlikely that the Spyware Bill 2005 will receive sufficient support for it to be passed—perhaps this is the right approach as it is questionable, as suggested below, whether specific legislation is the solution to the growing spyware problem.

---

16   Clause 3, Spyware Bill 2005.
17   Clause 4 Spyware Bill 2005.
18   Clause 8(2)(a), Spyware Bill 2005.
19   See Clause 16, Spyware Bill 2005.
20   <http://www.minister.dcita.gov.au/media/media_releases/taking_care_of_spyware_-_protecting_con-
       sumers_on_the_net> accessed 28 September 2005.
21   <http://www.dcita.gov.au/__data/assets/pdf_file/30866/05020018_Spyware.pdf> accessed 28 Septem-
       ber 2005.
22   <www.nospyware.net.au> accessed 28 September 2005.

The Data Explosion—Can legislation fully cope with it?

As to whether legislation is an adequate mechanism to tackle spyware is a topic that is not just relevant to the jurisdictions that are considered in this article. All jurisdictions that are attempting to form a regime to limit certain uses of spyware need to carefully consider whether the legislative path is an effective or practical solution before utilising time and resource into developing such a regime.

Specific spyware legislation may not be the answer to the spyware problem:

(a) the very nature of spyware can make enforcement difficult because the presence of spyware can remain unknown. In other words, if a person does not know that they are being affected by spyware, legislation that prevents or limits such software is unlikely to be utilised. To summarise this point, legislation is not useful where it protects rights that people do not know are being put at risk and therefore shows that it is hardly adequate from a prevention point of view and education or public awareness is a more practical solution;

(b) evidence gathering is difficult for law enforcement agencies and may result in privacy implications—for example, a full copy of a person's hard disk may be needed to carry out a formal investigation. This may deter people from bring a complaint forward especially if there is anti-spyware software that is readily available—a non intrusive way to deal with spyware.

And some may argue that existing legislation is sufficient to deal with spyware. For instance, it is widely acknowledged that most jurisdictions in the developed world have extensive data protection and privacy legislation (and rights) to protect the privacy of individuals. However, even though privacy is one of the concerns of spyware, the privacy rights that already exist will not be utilised unless people *know* about the issue and *know* that it is effecting them in certain ways.

Many people would suggest that the solution of the knowledge issue is to obtain consent through contractual means. For instance, why can't it be included as part of an end user licence agreement? The answer is simply that if the spyware is disclosed to the user, it is unlikely that the average user would consent. It is our view that because of the extensive effects of spyware and its ability to gather substantial amounts of personal information without knowledge as to which person information is being gathered, consent through an end user licence agreement is inappropriate.

More generally, legislation has a limited geographical field of application, with physical frontiers. It should be kept in mind that most spyware does not originate in Australia—what happens for example, if a company in a jurisdiction other than Australia causes spyware to be installed without the relevant notices and consents that Australian law requires? It will all depend on whether Australia asserts jurisdiction over that company, and if it does, whether a judgment can be enforced in Australia. This very issue goes back to the widely debated topic of jurisdiction and the Internet. Existing legal regimes struggle to fit into the realm of the new internet medium, and there is really not much Australia can do except hope that other jurisdictions have legislative regimes (that are effective) to cope with the issue. Better still, we can hope that an international regime will come into play that brings consistency across the virtual world. Until then, understanding the existing legislative regimes is a useful start to combating the spyware phenomena.

The current situation in the US

Spyware has received more judicial attention in the US than in Australia, but still the number of spyware cases is low compared with the number of people potentially affected by spyware. One reason for this is because plaintiffs in the majority of cases, are forced to bring actions under existing legal regimes that are not entirely appropriate when applied to spyware actions. Three examples are the Consumer Fraud and Abuse Act, the Federal Trade Commission Act and the tort of trespass to chattels. Hopefully this trend will not extend to Australia given that the view in Australia is that existing legal regimes are sufficient to deal with malicious use of spyware.

The Consumer Fraud and Abuse Act and the Federal Trade Commission Act have been recognised as two federal statutes that can be used to bring an action against spyware. The Consumer Fraud and Abuse Act ('CFAA')[23] provides for a right to bring an action where there is damage caused to a computer system used by or for a government entity for administration of justice, national defence or national security.[24] It is recognised that the CFAA has potential (in limited situations) for those wishing to pursue an action against a spyware claim because it can be proven that spyware can cause quite a substantial amount of damage to a computer system.[25] The CFAA fails to combat the spyware issue in three main ways:

* it does not proscribe specific notice standards or require specific forms of consent before spyware is downloaded;
* it is limited in its application because it requires damage to be suffered to the computer system. This means that where spyware has only caused a massive impingement upon privacy, an action will not be successful; and
* it only applies where damage is caused to a government entity for administration of justice, national defence or national security.

The Federal Trade Commission Act ('FTCA')[26] has the power to prohibit 'unfair or deceptive' practices.[27] Section 13(b) of the statute grants the Federal Trade Commission ('FTC') the power to bring an action to obtain relief for false or deceptive advertising. Recently, the FTC has been using the power to prevent companies from deceptively collecting information from individuals—exactly one of the issues with spyware. For example, the FTC brought a successful action against Seismic Entertainment Productions Inc, who gained access to consumers' computers to advertise, by installing a software code without the consumers' knowledge or consent.[28] Although the FTCA has been used for spyware cases, like the CFAA, it has various limitations. The criticism is that there must be an element of deceptiveness before the FTC will bring a civil action and this may be difficult to prove. For example, companies could circumvent the FTC where they show that a consumer has consented to the download of 'other software' as part of the end user licence agreement. Most consumers would fail to realise that

---

23   18 USC §1030 (2004).
24   18 USC §1030 (2004) (g).
25   See Michael D Lane, 'Spies Among Us: Can New Legislation Stop Spyware From Bugging Your Computer?' (2005) 17 Loy Consumer L Rev 283 at 293.
26   15 USC § § 41-58 (2004).
27   15 USC § 45.
28   *Federal Trade Commission v Seismic Entertainment Productions Inc* No Civ 04-377-JD, 2004 WL 2403124.

'other software' could include spyware yet this could be enough to fail the 'deceptiveness' test. Therefore because the FTCA does not have particular notice requirements, consumers are not given the proper opportunity to provide informed consent.

The common law tort of trespass to chattels may also be relied on for spyware claims. Trespass to chattels includes the use of or the intentional bringing about of physical contact with a chattel owned by another person.[29] It has successfully been used for torts committed in cyberspace.[30] Courts have also started to award punitive damages for cyberspace cases where there has been wilful and wanton disregard for the property rights of others[31]—in some cases therefore, a plaintiff will not have to prove that it has suffered actual loss which may be difficult in spyware cases, where the loss that is suffered is not a calculated loss, but rather an extreme invasion of privacy. Where a court is unwilling to impose punitive damages however, many plaintiffs may be at odds in trying to show actual damage.

Although it is positive that existing legal regimes are attempting to accommodate the current issues of the virtual world, it is clear that there are various limitations with the existing regimes. The very issue is that until there are rigorous laws in place to combat the spyware phenomena, millions and millions of people will be at risk of the growing threat of spyware.

The only answer seems to be legislation that deals specifically with the spyware issue. Positively, some states in the USA have recently passed such legislation. Utah for example was the first state to formally recognise the issue by enacting the Spyware Control Act ('Utah Act')[32] which makes installing spyware or causing spyware to be installed on another person's computer illegal. California followed Utah by recently enacting the Consumer Protection Against Computer Spyware Act ('California Act') which became effective on 1 January 2005. The California Act makes it illegal to knowingly or wilfully cause the installation of software on a computer, where the software is used for 'wrongful' purposes.[33] There are a number of limitations to the California Act which may in reality result in little reduction of the widespread problem of spyware. These include[34]:

- the software that falls within the scope of the legislation must have a 'wrongful effect' (as defined by the legislation). This means that certain spyware may fall outside the provisions of the legislation;
- to be caught by the legislation it must be proven that there has been wilful or intentional deceptive actions.

---

29   Restatement (Second) of Torts §217 cmt.e (West 2005).
30   For example, *CompuServe Incorporated v Cyber Promotions Inc*, 962 F Supp 1015, 1015 (SD Ohio 1997); *eBay, Inc v Bidder's Edge, Inc* 100 F Supp dd 1058 (ND Cal 2000).
31   See *American Online Inc v National Healthcare Discount Inc* 174 F Supp 2d 890, 902 (MD Iowa 2001); *Tyco International (US) Inc, v John Does*, 1-3, No 01 Civ 3856, 2003 WL 21638205 (SDNY 2003).
32   *Spyware Control Act*, Utah Code Ann 2004.
33   'Wrongful' includes where the software damages a computer system; causes unauthorised financial charges to be made; opens multiple 'pop-up' ads that the user cannot close out of without closing out of their Internet browser or shutting down the computer altogether; modifies settings through intentionally deceptive means, or modifies security settings in any regard; collects personal information through 'intentionally deceptive' means (account balances, social security numbers, etc.); prevents the 'intentionally deceptive' installation or proper operation of anti-Spyware programs; or uses 'intentionally deceptive' means to induce an end-user into installing harmful programs, or deleting protective ones.
34   See Michael Baroni, 'Spyware Beware' (2005) 47-APR Orange County Law 36.

The Utah Act approach goes well beyond the Australian Democrat's Spyware Bill 2005 which does not go as far as banning spyware or other unauthorised installations of software. Instead, the Australian Democrat's approach is more in line with the California Act requiring that the owner of a computer consent to the download of software before that download actually occurs.

The blanket approach of Utah's Spyware Control Act has met obstacles and in June 2004, a federal district court in Utah granted a preliminary injunction ceasing enforcement of the statute on constitutional grounds.[35] The only way to truly combat the issue is the introduce federal legislation—an attempt to do this occurred after the leading case *In re Pharmatrack Inc Privacy* Litigation.[36] In that case, the defendant had employed a company named Pharmatrack to monitor their corporate web sties and provide them with a monthly analysis of web site traffic. Pharmatrack used 'NETcompare' a product designed to monitor clients' web pages and 'DRUGcompare' a product designed to monitor activity across disease categories and drug product pages. Using these products, Pharmatrack had collected names, addresses, telephone numbers, dates of birth, sex, insurance status, medical conditions, education levels and occupation. This resulted in detailed profiles of hundreds of individuals being collated without consent, authorisation or knowledge. Summary judgment was granted and upheld by the Third Circuit. Shortly after, the Spyware Control and Spyware Protection Bill 2001 was introduced in the 107th Congress. The stated purpose of the Bill was the requirement to disclose any surveillance capabilities contained within software, the nature of the information being collected and to whom the information would later be disclosed to. The bill never became law -perhaps this proves that historically many people were not particularly worried about spyware and as a result[37] Naturally, as the general population becomes more aware of spyware and its effects, many are pressuring the federal government to implement a hasty solution. And perhaps the federal government is finally listening.

A way forward in the US?

Recently, two promising US bills were introduced into Senate, both criminalising the illicit indirect use of protected computers. First, the *Enhanced Consumer Protection Against Spyware Act 2005* (s.1004) aims to provide the FTC with the resources necessary to protect users of the Internet from the unfair and deceptive acts of spyware. It has now been read twice and referred to the Committee on Commerce, Science and Transportation.[38] The summary statement of the bill has two clear messages[39]:

* Spyware should be a matter of high priority for FTC action; and
* The resources and tools available to the FTC should be enhanced to increase the vigour of the FTC's enforcement efforts.

---

35   *WhenU.com v Utah* No 040907578 (D Utah June 22 2004).
36   329 F3d 9 (1st Cir 5 September 2003).
37   See Mike Tonsing, 'The Battle Against Spyware is Just Beginning' (2004) 51-JUN Fed Law 16.
38   *Enhanced Consumer Protection Against Spyware Act 2005* (Introduced in Senate).
39   <http://www.geocities.com/edwardtjbrown/20052006.html> accessed 22 July 2005.

The bill gives authority to the FTC to seek an increased civil penalty (as determined by the FTC), of up to $3,000,000 where software is installed through deceptive acts or practices on protected computers.[40] The bill also gives the ability to the FTC to treble damages where there is pattern or practice of violation, and to disgorge any profits made.[41]

Secondly, the Software Principles Yielding Levels of *Consumer Knowledge Act* (or *Spyblock Act*) (s.687) was introduced into Senate on 20 March 2005. It has also been read twice and also referred to the Committee on Commerce, Science, and Transportation. The bill attempts to regulate the unauthorised installation of computer software, to require clear disclosure to computer users of certain computer software features that may pose a threat to user privacy. It aims to prohibit installing software on a computer without notice and consent and requires reasonable uninstall procedures for all downloadable software. It also authorises the FTC to issue rules as necessary to implement or clarify the provisions of the Act.

Conclusion

The unauthorised installation of spyware is rife, dangerously impinging on the privacy rights of Australians and all other users of the Internet throughout the world. The US has struggled to grapple with spyware by using the existing legal regimes. Does this show the importance and the real need to introduce legislation that specifically covers spyware? Possibly not, given the extensive review of Australian law recently undertaken by DCITA. We are yet to find out. Recently, two bills have been introduced into the US Senate which may be a move in the right direction—as to whether these are passed is another question. There has also been a bill that has been introduced in Australia by the Australian Democrats and a proactive move toward educating the public about the issues associated with spyware. It should be noted that even if none of these bills are passed, a jurisdictional issue will always exist—laws of a jurisdiction will generally only be enforced against those that send spyware within that jurisdiction. A final point of note needs to be made about the effectiveness of legislative regimes—although clarifying that legislation is adequate to cope with malicious use of spyware, the real burden of stopping the spread of spyware cannot rest entirely on the shoulders of legislation. The threats will only ever disappear with a widespread effort to educate and implement procedures to combat the ever-growing issue—this is only just starting to happen in Australia. As this article demonstrates, spyware is a global problem and will be difficult to completely eliminate. In practical terms therefore, we need to think about having broader approaches and procedures to handling the issue. Any rights given to computer users under legislation are only beneficial to the extent that the user knows that rights exist. Although spyware has been largely talked about by academics and those in the IT field, a recent National Cyber Security Alliance survey showed that even though more than 80% of computers are infected with spyware, only 10% of users actually knew what spyware was.[42] This is where awareness raising comes into play—and Australia is being proactive in

---

40   Section 5, *Enhanced Consumer Protection Against Spyware Act 2005* (Introduced in Senate).
41   Section 5(c), *Enhanced Consumer Protection Against Spyware Act 2005* (Introduced in Senate).
42   Byron Acohido & Jon Swartz, Market to Protect Consumer PCs Seems Poised for Takeoff; As Spyware, Viruses Spread, Threat to E-commerce Grows, USA Today, Dec 27, 2004, at B1.

this sense. Furthermore, before we can even begin to think that the spyware issue is under control there needs to be a set of procedures in place including an international complaints handling regime, a uniform approach to unauthorised installation of software and a guaranteed enforcement of penalties across the board. It is doubtful that all this can be achieved in the short term (or perhaps even the long term).

 NOTES AND QUESTIONS

1   What are the areas of existing Australian law that cover spyware? Are these areas of law appropriate to outlaw a novel technology such as spyware? Are additional sanctions necessary?

2   In Chapter 7, Internet Crime, we saw the Australian government introduce numerous provisions criminalising conduct on the Internet such as possessing certain types of pornography, publishing content inciting suicide, and so on. Is the Australian government inconsistent in enacting many specific Internet crimes and failing to enact specific laws on spyware?

3   A number of the states in the USA have enacted specific laws prohibiting spyware; an example is Washington's *Computer Spyware Act* (2005). At the time of writing, the US government still has not enacted any spyware laws. The Federal Trade Commission has, however, been successful in using consumer and fair trading provisions to prosecute instances of spyware use. See for example, *FTC v Seismic Entertainment Prods, Inc*, No 1:04-cv-00377-JD (2004).

Internet Taxation

1   Introduction

The Internet presents unique problems for the taxation of trade and commerce. Much debate has been generated as to the proper role of government intervention in private e-commerce through the levying of taxes on e-commerce. Second, it has spawned a variety of problems for the successful and effective administration of taxation. Finally, it has produced a number of reactionary responses, ranging from the declaration of broad and general principles to the enactment of specific legislative provisions.

This chapter will proceed by first examining the debate over whether the Internet should be taxed to begin with. It will then outline a number of challenges posed by the

Internet for the implementation of substantial taxing regime. Finally, it will detail some of the approaches taken by various domestic and international bodies in their attempts to bring order to present situation.

----

2 The Internet taxation debate

Before outlining the taxation challenges posed by e-commerce and discussing the several responses made to those challenges, one must appreciate the level of controversy concerning the appropriateness of taxing Internet activity and e-commerce in the first place. There is no clear consensus as to whether the Internet should, as a matter of policy, be taxed.[1] It is also critical to understand that much debate centres upon empirical arguments that are not necessarily supported by concrete data. For example, the debate as to whether Internet taxation would stifle Internet growth or maintain the government's tax base is limited by the lack of empirical evidence to compel the arguments on either side.[2]

(a) Arguments in favour of Internet taxation

The main argument in favour of taxing e-commerce is that failure to do otherwise would inevitably lead to an eroding government tax base, as businesses and consumers alike turn away from the traditional modes of trade in favour of a tax-free haven in cyberspace.[3] The taxation of goods and services provides governments with a vital source of revenue for the provision of public services and regulatory activities.[4] This means that the imposition of taxes in cyberspace is necessary to preserve the provision of the public benefit in the real world.

A secondary argument in favour taxing e-commerce is based on fairness and neutrality. A fundamental principle of taxation law is said to be that of neutrality.[5] Tax neutrality holds that a fair and equitable tax system must treat economically similar income equally.[6] In the context of emerging technologies such as the Internet, this means income earned through electronic commerce should be taxed similarly to that earned by more conventional modes of commerce.[7] There is no reason why what is effectively a 'tax subsidy' should be imposed on the Internet industry—especially when such an industry grows at the expense of conventional 'brick and mortar' retailers.[8] In essence,

---

1   Christopher J Schafer, 'Federal Legislation Regarding Taxation of Internet Sales Transactions' (2001) 16 *Berkley Technology Law Journal* 415 at 425.
2   Ibid at 426.
3   Ibid at 426–7; Blair Downey, 'E-Commerce: the Taxman's Nemesis' (2002) 53 at 56–7; John E Sununu, 'Policy Essay: The Taxation of Internet Commerce' (2002) 39 *Harvard Journal of Legislation* 325.
4   Sununu, ibid, 325.
5   Schafer, above n 1 at 427.
6   Clayton W Chan, 'Taxation of Global E-Commerce on the Internet: The Underlying Issues and Proposed Plans' (2000) 9 *Minnesota Journal of Global Trade* 233 at 248.
7   Ibid; Schafer, above n 1 at 427.
8   James J Jurinski, 'Federalism and State Taxation of E-Commerce: Is the End in Sight for State Sales Taxes?' (1999) 18 *Journal of State Taxation* 30 at 40–1.

commerce should take place on a level playing field, be it conducted electronically or conventionally.[9]

The final pro-taxation argument is perhaps more novel than the previous two. It has been argued that given the present chaotic state of taxation laws both domestically and internationally, the imposition of taxation in cyberspace, and thus across both national and international borders, would provide a much need 'jolt' for tax legislators, forcing a simplification of the tax system for all forms of commerce, not just the Internet.[10]

(b)   Arguments against Internet taxation

The first argument advanced against the imposition of Internet taxation is that it burdens the development and growth of the Internet and electronic commerce. The development of small Internet-based companies with little capital may be stifled, as they are unable to cope with tax burdens.[11] Indeed, it has been argued that the perils of taxing the Internet extend well beyond the small trader. It has been suggested that the Internet is so beneficial a technology that its growth and development should not be discouraged by the imposition of taxation.[12]

The problem with such arguments, however, is that they are not unique to the Internet.[13] The perils of taxation and the burden of tax liabilities are experienced by *all* traders—not just those who engage in e-commerce. It would seem to violate the principles of fairness and tax neutrality if people can avoid paying government dues simply by virtue of adopting a technological means of commerce.

A further argument advanced in opposition to Internet taxation is that the Internet is essentially a private realm that should be considered beyond the purview of government intervention in the form of taxation.[14] However, such arguments encounter criticism, particularly from the US government, when it is remembered that the Internet first developed as a government run Defence project in the 1960s and 1970s. Furthermore, this argument only really relates to the taxation of Internet use itself, rather than the taxation of income generated by conducting business via the Internet.

Indeed, to suggest that because what takes place over the Internet is in reality a private business matter and therefore beyond the reach of government taxation is again to suggest an Internet-specific argument that is not in fact unique to the Internet. The issue goes back to fairness, equality, and tax neutrality. It can be said of many private commercial transactions that they do not involve public or governmental dimensions; nevertheless, they, too are taxed on a par with other transactions.

Finally, it has been suggested that the most compelling argument against Internet taxation is that government tax laws are incapable of keeping pace with rapidly developing and emerging technologies.[15] The thrust of this argument seems to be that the Internet is

---

9   Sununu, above n 3 at 335.
10   Schafer, above n 1 at 427.
11   Downey, above n 3 at 56.
12   Schaffer, above n 1 at 427.
13   Downey, above n 3 at 56.
14   Ibid.
15   Downey, ibid.

such a complex and dynamic means of doing business that it is best to avoid the trouble of trying to tax it. The flaw in this argument is immediately apparent. Further, the idea that laws should be avoided because they are too difficult to maintain suggests a response favouring development of flexible and technology-neutral legislation.

----

3   The challenges for Internet taxation

The Internet generates several challenges for the administration and enforcement of tax laws and the collection of tax. Andrew Brian and Mark Hughes have comprehensively considered the issues and identified the major challenges faced by tax agencies in the face of emerging e-commerce and Internet technologies.[16] Theses challenges may be identified generally and grouped as: establishing transaction, identity, and location and overcoming lack of documentation; coping with dematerialisation of trade; meeting the increased burden on customs processes, and gaining easier access to tax havens.

(a)   Establishing transaction, identity and location

The collection of tax revenue requires recognition that a taxable transaction has occurred in the jurisdiction of the tax agency, and the subsequent identification of the person on whom that tax is to be levied. The Internet complicates the fulfilment of these requirements. First, it may be possible for those engaged in e-commerce to use an untraceable Internet site, so that neither their location nor their identity is discernible.[17] Second, the use of a foreign Internet server may compound the problem by locating an otherwise traceable transaction outside the taxing jurisdiction of the particular tax agency.[18] Finally, the traditional reliance on documentation for the purpose of tracing and evidencing transactions and imposing tax is no longer appropriate where Internet transactions do not leave a paper trail.[19]

The problem is compounded by the advance towards a 'cashless' society, which erodes tax authorities' ability to monitor transactions and levy taxation, as well as the disintermediation of commerce.[20] As buyers and sellers engage with each other directly, the need for processing of transactions through clearinghouses and other intermediaries results in the removal of a number of possible convenient taxing points in the goods cycle.[21]

The problem of establishing location is exacerbated by the fact that the most concrete and accepted principles of international taxation that have developed since the start of the 20th century are those of source and residence-based taxation rules.[22] Both these rules

---

16   Andrew Brian and Mark Hughes, 'Tax issues in cyberspace' (2001) 11(1) *Journal of Law and Information Science* 55.
17   Ibid; Chan, above n 6 at 252.
18   Ibid.
19   Ibid.
20   Ibid.
21   Ibid.
22   David L Forst, 'Old and New Issues in the Taxation of Electronic Commerce' (1999) 14 *Berkeley Technology Law Journal* 711 at 712; Chan, above n 6 at 248–9.

require that geographic criteria be satisfied before the imposition of tax. In the case of source-based taxation, a country may levy a tax on income once it is determined that the source of that income was within that country's borders. Residency rules meanwhile support the levy of a tax on a person's income once it is established that that person is a resident of the country imposing the tax. These principles, source and residency, comprise more detailed and complex rules for determination in any given case, however at their core, both of them rely upon principles of physical geography. That reliance breaks down in the context of Internet-based commerce where physical boundaries and borders mean very little. For example, in the context of residence-based rules, one issue that arises is whether it is possible for a company's website to constitute a 'permanent establishment' capable of satisfying the requisite criteria for levying a tax on that company.

(b)   Dematerialisation of trade

The surge in e-commerce has seen a shift away from trade of physical goods towards online goods available in digital form. This decrease in physical trade presents a problem as it becomes harder to identify when and where a transaction has taken place and assess the tax liability of traders based on a comparison of inputs and outputs.[23] This problem is particularly of issue to the imposition and collection of transaction-based taxes.[24] By making it possible for online goods (such as online music) to be delivered in digital, and therefore intangible form, the capacity to apply sales taxes, value added tax (VAT) and goods and services tax (GST) is greatly reduced.

(c)   Increased burden for customs

As the Internet breaks down the barriers to global commerce, increasing movement of consumers to purchase goods from overseas via the Internet will inevitably lead to a greater volume of goods ordered over the Internet passing through customs.[25] As the growth of e-commerce continues it will be necessary to ensure that customs are equipped to deal with this increased volume.[26]

(d)   Easier access to tax havens

The problem of taxpayers avoiding tax through resort to overseas tax havens has always been a problem for the administration of taxation.[27] With the advent of Internet banking, it has now become easier for taxpayers to set up accounts off shore in these tax havens.

---

23   Ibid.
24   Ibid; Kavita Panjratan, 'GST and electronic commerce: the great divide' (1999) 70(6) *Charter* 48, 49; Hal R Varian, 'Taxation of Electronic Commerce' (2000) 13 *Harvard Journal of Law and Technology* 639 at 649-50.
25   Ibid.
26   Ibid.
27   Ibid.

----

4 Responses to the challenges of Internet taxation

There have been a variety of responses to the problem posed by Internet taxation. Chief among these are the approaches of the OECD, the EU, and the USA.

(a) The OECD's Guiding Principles

The OECD agreed to a broad framework of key taxation principles in 1998—the Ottawa Taxation Framework.[28] The framework prescribes five guiding principles that are particularly relevant to the Australian situation following the endorsement by the ATO of the OECD framework.[29] The framework has also been adopted by international and domestic bodies in one form or another as part of an international effort to combat the problem of Internet taxation. It should be borne in mind, however, that the guiding principles are limited by the fact that they are, in essence, inspirational rather than substantial and prescriptive.

Neutrality

The first principle of Internet taxation is that of *neutrality*. By this, it is meant that taxation should be equitable between different types of e-commerce and between e-commerce and more conventional forms of commerce. This is arguably an extension of pro-Internet taxation arguments based upon the same underlying principle of equality and fairness outlined above. The thrust of the neutrality argument is an extension of existing tax laws to e-commerce.[30]

Neutrality is perhaps the single most important 'guiding principle' in the taxation of e-commerce.[31] Both the EU and the USA have emphasised the significance of a neutral approach to Internet taxation.[32] The United Kingdom, meanwhile, has taken the view that neutrality should focus upon the equal treatment of different form of technological commerce—proposing that the taxation of e-commerce be approached so that no particular form of commerce is advantaged or disadvantaged.[33]

Efficiency

The principle of efficiency refers to the minimisation of compliance costs for taxpayers and administrative costs for tax authorities. The thrust of the efficiency argument is the

---

28   Ottawa Ministerial Report on Electronic Commerce: Taxation Framework Conditions, OECD Centre for Tax Policy (1998) ('Ottawa Principles').

29   Duncan Bentley, 'The ATO, tax and the Internet: the emperor's new clothes?' (1999) 9 *Revenue Law Journal* 99 at 101.

30   Ibid at 103.

31   Ibid.

32   E-Commerce and Indirect Taxation, Com (98) Final, 17 June 1998 (European Union); *Internet Tax Freedom Act 1998* (US). The US Act prohibits the discriminatory taxation of e-commerce and has been extended until 2007.

33   Inland Revenue and HM Customs and Excise, *Electronic Commerce: the UK's Taxation Agenda* (1999) ('*UK Report*').

improvement of taxpayer services and tax administration generally.[34] The issue does not, however, appear to have engendered a great deal of international discussion.[35] Arguably, efficiency is not a goal specific to the Internet, but characteristic of taxation discourse generally.

Certainty and simplicity

It is argued that Internet tax rules should be clear and simple to understand so that tax liabilities and consequences can be predicted in advance and properly accounted for. Again, these are not uniquely Internet-focused principles, but are applicable to all instances of taxation. The aspirations of the OECD in this regard have been matched by the United Kingdom.[36]

It appears, however, that other players in the Internet taxation debate have resigned themselves to the inevitable fact that tax rules will never be simple and straightforward in their formulation. The EU has stated that it favours *certainty of rules* and *simplicity of compliance*.[37] Indeed, it is probably futile to attempt to make the rules of taxation substantively simple.[38]

Effectiveness and fairness

Taxation should produce the right amount of tax at the right time.[39] The importance of effectiveness and fairness is thus measured from the tax administrator's point of view.[40] Fairness also imports notions of proportionality between measures aimed at preserving the collection of taxation and the risks and potential for tax avoidance and evasion. Essentially, tax authorities should not exaggerate their responses to the challenge of Internet taxation.

Flexibility

Flexibility refers to the ability of a tax system to adapt to different commercial and technological developments. There is a substantial overlap between flexibility, the notion of neutrality as subscribed to by the UK approach to Internet taxation, and the desire for efficiency, certainty, and flexibility. Rules that can easily be adapted to changing technological and commercial realities require less in the way of administrative costs and will be easier to predict in application.

(b)   US *Internet Tax Freedom Act*

The key legislative enactment in the USA is the *Internet Tax Freedom Act* (1998). The title of the Act is at first deceptive: it does not propose a complete moratorium on all forms

---

34   Bentley, above n 29 at 106.
35   Ibid.
36   *UK Report*, above n 33 at 2.9.
37   Bentley, above n 29 at 106.
38   Ibid at 107.
39   Ottawa Principles, above n 28.
40   Bentley, above n 29 at 107.

of Internet taxation, but instead prohibits the imposition of three specific types of tax. It is seen as promoting the commercial potential of the Internet.

First, it prohibits the taxing of monthly access fees charged to customers for connecting to the Internet. This is arguably a response to criticisms that taxing the use of the Internet would diminish and stall the growth of Internet usage. Second, it prohibits double or multiple taxation of the Internet. This may be seen as an attempt to embody fairness within the taxation regime of e-commerce. Under the Act, one State cannot tax the same electronic transaction that has already been taxed by another jurisdiction without a credit for the tax paid to that other State. Finally, the Act proscribes the imposition of discriminatory taxes: a tax that singles out a particular group, item, or activity over others, such as e-commerce, is prohibited under the Act. This represents notions of fairness and neutrality in the Act.

The Act thus does not represent a comprehensive and substantial response to every dimension of the Internet taxation problem. Rather, it is aimed at combating specific problems identified as significant and capable of government response. The Act has a sunset provision set to expire in November 2007.

(c) The EU's VAT amendments for e-commerce

One solution proposed in response to the problem of Internet taxation in the context of sales based taxes such as GST or VAT has come from the EU. In 2002, the EU adopted changes to modify the rules for applying value added tax (VAT) to certain services supplied by electronic means as well as subscription-based and pay-per-view radio and television broadcasting (Council Directive 2002/38/EC). These changes took effect on 1 July 2003 and they affect products and services provided through digital download to consumers in the EU. These include services such as web hosting, sales of downloadable software and upgrades, the sale of electronic books, streaming music, digital movies, computer games, and even distance-learning services. The changes were aimed at addressing the disadvantage that European suppliers of electronic goods and services suffered compared with their US counterparts. An EU-based entity has always been required under EU law to collect taxes on all supplies of electronic goods and services, and this can put it at a disadvantage to its US counterparts, which do not operate under the same requirements. The VAT rates vary widely in the EU. For example, they are set at 15 per cent in Luxembourg and 25 per cent in Denmark and Sweden. Suppliers outside the EU will have to charge the VAT rate of the EU country where the consumer resides.

In May 2006, the European Commission produced a report to the EU Council in which it recommended that since the e-commerce VAT Directive has operated in a satisfactory manner and has achieved its objective of creating a level playing field for the taxation of electronic services, the period of application of the Directive should be extended until 31 December 2008 or until more permanent and wider measures are in place.[41]

---

41   *Report of the Commission of the European Communities to the Council on Council Directive 2002/38/WC of 7 May 2002* available at <http://ec.europa.eu/taxation_customs/resources/documents/taxation/vat/ COM(2006)210_en.pdf>.

(d)   The Australian experience

The problem experienced in the EU with respect to online delivery of intangibles such as software and services is also applicable in Australia. Goods and Services Tax (GST) is payable on most goods imported into Australia as a taxable importation. A person or entity must pay GST on a taxable importation irrespective of whether one is registered for GST. GST on a taxable importation is usually paid to the Australian Customs Service (Customs) before goods are released from Customs control. GST does not appear to be payable on services or intangibles delivered online.[42] Thus it is highly possible that for intangibles and services paid for and delivered online, it may cost the Australian consumer less to purchase over the Internet from a non-Australian business.

For tangible goods ordered on the Internet and delivered physically into Australia, the website of the Australian Customs Service advises that all goods (except for tobacco products and alcoholic beverages) may be imported duty and tax free if their value is $1000 or less.[43] This is irrespective of whether the goods are for personal use, as gifts or for business purposes. If their value is more than $1000, then duties and taxes are payable. The end result for the individual consumer is that if an item costs $1000 or less, the cost may be cheaper if bought over the Internet from a non-Australian business, but depending on the cost of postage, the overall cost of the item may not necessarily be cheaper.

The Australian Taxation Office (ATO) has made it clear that it subscribes to the OECD's broad principles.[44] This should come as no surprise, given Australia's role in developing these principles.[45] In particular, the ATO has stressed the importance of neutrality and efficiency as they appear in the OECD's guiding principles, together with a third key principle: that of balancing administration issues with taxpayer privacy.[46]

The importance of OECD developments to the progression of tax on e-commerce in Australia should not be underestimated. A substantial part of Australia's Double Taxation Agreements are based on the OECD's *Model Tax Convention* and Australian courts have held that, as such, OECD commentary on the OECD Model can be used to interpret Australian Double Taxation Agreements.[47]

The concept of 'permanent establishment' (PE) with respect to the Internet—and in particular, websites—is an interesting issue. Can a server located within a treaty country, used by a foreign enterprise for its homepage or website, constitute a permanent establishment? The OECD has attempted to clarify the meaning of PE in the context of computer equipment and websites. According to the OECD Working Party No 1 on Tax Conventions and Related Questions, 1999, the mere operation of a website or the presence of computer equipment within a jurisdiction does not of itself constitute a PE. However, computer equipment may constitute a PE even in the absence of personnel but a website cannot constitute a place of business. A server or other computer equipment

---

42   See generally the web site of the Australian Tax Office (ATO) at <http://www.ato.gov.au>.
43   See <http://www.customs.gov.au/site/page.cfm?u=5549>.
44   ATO, *Tax and the Internet: Second Report* (1999, AGPS), 1.3.1 ('*ATO Second Report*').
45   Peter Hill, 'Online Tax' (2001) 5 *E.Law Practice* 28.
46   Bentley, above n 29 at 111–12.
47   Ibid at 135; *Thiel v Federal Commissioner of Taxation* (1990) 171 CLR 338.

may be considered a PE. There is the further proviso that equipment will not constitute a PE unless its location is fixed for a sufficient period of time. Lastly, an ISP will not normally create a PE by agency for an enterprise whose website it hosts and a website will not create a PE by agency for the enterprise who owns it. These principles are generally accepted by the ATO, as can be seen from the following extract.

Australia Taxation Office, Taxation Determination TD 2005/2

<http://law.ato.gov.au/atolaw/view.htm?docid=TXD/TD20052/NAT/ATO/00001> 01 May 2006

Income tax: does a resident of a country with which Australia has a Tax Treaty, have a permanent establishment solely from the sale of trading stock through an internet website hosted by an Australian resident internet service provider?
FOI status: may be released

Preamble

The number, subject heading, date of effect and paragraph 1 to paragraph 2 of this document are a 'public ruling' for the purposes of Part IVAAA of the *Taxation Administration Act 1953* and are legally binding on the Commissioner.

1 No, where the internet service provider (ISP) is acting as a mere conduit, the Business Profits Article of the relevant Tax Treaty will apply. The non-resident will not, by virtue of the website alone, have a permanent establishment (PE) in Australia. The answer in this determination is provided on the basis of the assumptions in paragraph 2. If those assumptions are not fulfilled, the determination will not apply.

2 The following assumptions are made in this determination:

   (a) that the taxpayer, as a resident of the country with which Australia has a tax treaty, is entitled to the benefits of the relevant treaty;

   (b) that the ISP is carrying on a business as an ISP, is dealing at arm's length with the taxpayer and does not provide other services to the taxpayer in addition to the hosting arrangement which may give rise to a PE of the taxpayer; and

   (c) that any income from the sale is covered by the business profits article of the tax treaty and not some other article.

Domestic law

3 Subsection 6-5(3) of the *Income Tax Assessment Act 1997* (ITAA 1997) provides that the assessable income of a non-resident includes ordinary income derived directly or indirectly from all Australian sources as well as other ordinary income that a provision includes on a basis other than having an Australian source. In some circumstances, income derived by a non-resident from the sale of merchandise to Australian consumers through a website hosted by an Australian resident ISP may constitute assessable income of the non-resident under subsection 6-5(3). The income may also be assessable in

Australia under sections 38 to 43 of the *Income Tax Assessment Act 1936*, in which case the amount of profit to be included in the non-resident's assessable income is calculated under those provisions and not subsection 6-5(3) of the ITAA 1997.

Application of Tax Treaties

4   Where the tax position involves a resident of a country with which Australia has a Tax Treaty it is necessary to consider the application of the relevant articles in the Tax Treaty. Where there is inconsistency, the terms of the Tax Treaty effectively override those of Australia's domestic tax law. Profits from the sale of trading stock would constitute the profits of an enterprise carried on by a resident of the treaty partner country and would fall under the Business Profits Article. Under this article, Australia may not tax the business profits derived by an enterprise of the other contracting state unless those business profits are attributable to a permanent establishment situated in Australia through which the enterprise carries on business. Thus, the existence of a permanent establishment is central to the allocation of taxing rights under the Business Profits Article.

Definition of permanent establishment

5   The term 'permanent establishment' is defined in the Permanent Establishment Article in Australia's Tax Treaties, generally contained in Article 5. The term is defined in Article 5(1) to mean a:

fixed place of business through which the business of an enterprise is wholly or partly carried on.

6   Guidance on the application of this article to websites can be found in paragraphs 42.1 to 42.10 of the Commentary on Article 5 of the OECD Model Tax Convention on Income and on Capital (the Commentary). The Commentary discusses whether the use of computer equipment in electronic commerce operations in a country can constitute a permanent establishment under the Business Profits Article of the OECD Model.

7   A distinction is drawn between computer equipment and the data and software used by, or stored on, that equipment. A website is considered to be a combination of computer software and electronic data. The distinction between the website and the server on which the website is stored is important when, as in the case under consideration, the enterprise that operates the server is different from the enterprise that carries on business through the website. The server on which a website is stored is a piece of equipment with a physical location and may constitute a 'fixed place of business' of an enterprise which has that server at its disposal. However, the fact that an enterprise has a certain amount of space on the server of an ISP allocated for it to use to store software and data does not result in the server being at the disposal of the enterprise. The enterprise is not considered to have acquired a place of business by virtue of the hosting arrangements.

8   Where an ISP is only in the business of providing access to the internet it operates as a mere conduit for the business activities of the non-resident enterprise. The agreement with the ISP would not typically specify which server the website will be hosted on and the ISP may change the server used at their discretion. The space used for a specific

website on the server of the ISP is not at the disposal of the entity that owns the website. Thus, the enterprise does not have a fixed place of business in Australia.

9   Article 5(2) of Australia's Tax Treaties contains a list of examples each of which can be regarded as constituting a permanent establishment such as a place of management, an office, a branch, a factory or a workshop, or agricultural, pastoral or forestry property, etc. The website being a combination of software and data does not, of itself, fall within the list generally contained in Article 5(2).

10   Under Article 5(5) of Australia's Tax Treaties, an enterprise is deemed to have a permanent establishment where a person, other than an agent of an independent status, acts on behalf of an enterprise and habitually exercises an authority to substantially negotiate or conclude contracts on behalf of the enterprise. However, under Article 5(6) an enterprise will not be deemed to have a permanent establishment in Australia merely because that enterprise carries on business in Australia through a broker, general commission agent or any other agent of independent status, where the agent is acting in the ordinary course of their business.

11   In most cases, an ISP will not constitute a permanent establishment by virtue of it being a dependent agent, because the ISP is not an agent of the enterprise and would lack the authority to conclude, and would not regularly conclude contracts on behalf of the non-resident enterprise. The website itself does not constitute a dependent agent as it is not a 'person' as defined in Australia's tax treaties. Furthermore, the ISP could constitute an independent agent acting in the ordinary course of their business if, amongst other things, they host websites for a number of different enterprises.

Conclusion

12   Where the sole presence of an enterprise in Australia is a website hosted by an Australian ISP, the enterprise does not have a permanent establishment in Australia, subject to the assumptions in paragraph 2.

Date of effect

13   This Determination applies to years commencing both before and after its date of issue. However, it does not apply to taxpayers to the extent that it conflicts with the terms of settlement of a dispute agreed to before the date of the Determination (see paragraphs 21 and 22 of Taxation Ruling TR 92/20).

Commissioner of Taxation
9 March 2005
[footnotes omitted.]

 NOTES AND QUESTIONS

1   A distinction is drawn between computer equipment and the data and software used by, or stored on, that equipment. Explain the reasons for the distinction in the concept of PE.

2   This Determination will not apply in all circumstances; for example, if the taxpayer who owns the website does not qualify under a limitation of benefits article in a treaty or if the taxpayer is a dual resident and dual residents are excluded from the benefits of a treaty, then this determination will not apply.

3   The assumption in paragraph 2(b) is relevant to the law of agency. Explain the rationale given in the Determination for restricting the application of this Determination as set out under paragraph 2(b).

(e)   Singapore

Unlike the Australian approach, the authorities in Singapore have been active in dealing with the issue of tax and e-commerce. The Inland Revenue Authority of Singapore (IRAS) published the third edition of the *Income Tax Guide on E-Commerce* ('Guide') in 2001.[48] The Guide examines three main types of online operations for companies whose business operations are in Singapore:

(a) the company derives its income from EC activities through a website hosted in Singapore;

(b) the company derives its income from EC activities through a website and branch outside Singapore; and

(c) the company derives its income from EC activities through a website and branch in Singapore.

The first type of operation is fairly straightforward; all the company's operations would be subject to tax in Singapore, including income derived from business conducted through the website.

For the second type of operation, the assumption is that the company does not operate a branch in a foreign country, but hosts its website with a hosting service provider in a foreign country. For tangible goods, the income derived from its e-commerce business via a website hosted in a foreign country will be considered as income sourced in Singapore and will be subject to tax in Singapore. For intangible goods, if the company completes the obligation of its online activities largely through its operations in Singapore—such as sourcing for content, making promotion and advertising efforts, maintaining the currency of information for the website, responding to queries on its products and services, receiving due payments for purchases, and delivering products and services as well as providing after-sale services—then the income derived from the website will be considered as income sourced in Singapore and subject to tax in Singapore. If, however, the company has a branch and website hosted in a foreign country, much would depend on the activities of the branch. If the branch undertakes to market and sell the company's products and services electronically as well as complete the obligations arising from the online transactions, then the income arising from the online transactions through the website would be considered as income of the branch, and thus as taxable income of the branch—it would not be liable to tax in Singapore unless remitted back to Singapore.

---

48   Available at <http://www.iras.gov.sg/ESVPortal/resources/2001ec1.pdf> accessed 1/05/06.

For the last type of business operation, if the assumption is that the business only sets up a website hosted in Singapore without a branch, and for tangible goods, the website merely facilitates the conduct of e-commerce, with the substantial part of the business activities—such as manufacture of products, provision of product information for the website, and completion of obligations—made from the company outside Singapore. The company would not then be considered as having its business operations in Singapore. The income from the e-commerce transactions through the website is derived mainly from its operations outside Singapore, and such income would not be considered as sourced in Singapore, nor subject to tax in Singapore.

If the company is involved in intangible products, again, the income arising from the e-commerce transactions through the website in Singapore would not be considered as sourced in Singapore, and would not be subject to tax in Singapore as business income. However, although the company is not considered as trading in Singapore, withholding tax may still arise on the payments received by the company. If the payments are made by a resident or permanent establishment in Singapore for the use of, or right to use, the digitised products, withholding tax will arise. The customer in Singapore has to withhold the tax and pay it to the Comptroller out of the payments to be made to the company.

However, withholding of tax is not required for payments to non-residents for the following four categories of software: shrink-wrap software (for income accruing on or after 1 Jan 2001); downloadable software for the end user; site licences; and software bundled with computer hardware (the last three categories, for income accruing on or after 23 Feb 2001).[49]

The Guide also deals with the situation of an e-commerce intermediary—which includes not just ISPs, but also market-makers such as exchange platforms that bring together buyers and sellers. The intermediary income may be from commissions, service fees, subscription fees, registration fees, or advertising fees. The Guide provides that the intermediary will be liable to income tax in Singapore if its business operations are carried out in Singapore, but this is largely a question of fact and degree. If the intermediary has a substantial presence in Singapore, such as the presence of personnel and technical know-how, and it derives its income from the services provided through the personnel and know-how in Singapore, then income such as commissions and fees would be subject to tax in Singapore.

---

5   Concluding remarks

It is important to keep in mind that different international approaches to the problem of Internet taxation inevitably reflect the views of developed economies.[50] The limits of these approaches are perhaps best understood by awareness of the fact that Internet

---

49   See IRAS Circular, *Exemption of Software Payment from Tax* (Mar 2005) available at <http://www.iras.gov.sg/ESVPortal/resources/exemptionofsoftwarepaymentsfromtax.pdf> accessed 1/05/06.

50   Bentley, above n 29 at 108.

taxation presents a problem for both developed and developing economies.[51] Developing a substantial and comprehensive approach to Internet taxation will arguably take time and be the product of reactionary measures to identified instances of perceived Internet tax problems.[52]

---

51   Downey, above n 3 at 57.
52   Forst, above n 22 at 712.

15

The Way Ahead

It has become almost the norm to conclude publications in this field with a series of majestic statements waxing lyrical about the pervasive, persuasive, revolutionary, and unprecedented nature of the Internet. Although this allows the writer to make use of comfortable 'book-ends' in composition, it must also be acknowledged that these flourishes are, on the whole, accurate summations of the Internet and its influence on the development of the new global society.

There is no doubt that the Internet is the most exciting of all historical developments in communications media. Predictions inevitably lead to disappointment, and it would be unwise to chart an exact future course for the Internet. However, it is safe to say the Internet is most certainly still in its infancy. Yet in the infancy of all things we can identify character traits and features that will blossom as the subject grows.

Almost without exception, the chapters in this book introduced their subject matter with the observation: 'the Internet poses considerable challenges for this area of law'. Repetition arises, not through lack of creative inspiration, but through the simple fact that the Internet challenges many aspects of law. It is important to realise, however, that the challenge is far greater than merely to legal matters. In Chapter 8, Internet Content Regulation, the point was emphasised that legal questions must be placed in their social context in order to understand their structure fully and plan their amendment. In fact, this notion applies to all Internet-related legal challenges: the Internet does not merely challenge the way we regulate our lives; it changes the way we conduct our lives. It challenges the very fabric of our society by testing, for example, the extent to which we value our privacy, to which we worry about our children, to which intellectual property can be protected. Most of all, and most obviously, the Internet has changed the very structure of communication.

Some may lament the fact that activities once considered an exercise of the skills of social intercourse, such as discussing the weather with a stranger at a party, have been replaced by a medium in which the only contact occurs between the user and the keyboard. Some might also argue that the Internet has engendered an expectation of instant gratification that erodes important and valuable social interaction such as waiting in line or playing football in the backyard. In the face of this, it is useful, in this concluding chapter, to consider the extent to which the notion of the Internet has been romanticised by the aura of infinite possibilities that accompanies it. The response to the laments and critiques is the observation that change need not be destructive. The conversation between strangers at a function is no more valuable than that between strangers on ICQ, or in a chat room. Rather than pursuing these assertions and rebuttals here, it will suffice to say that, while the Internet does not herald the new dawn of global societal solidarity and communication nirvana, nor is it a harbinger of ill tidings and social decay.

In light of this, it will be clear to the reader that the range of topics covered by this work is not exhaustive. Nor is the treatment of each topic as deep as it might be. The goal was to sketch a landscape, and to introduce the themes that have come to identify the legal and institutional implications of the Internet.

The most significant recurring theme is the challenge to our concept of jurisdiction. Legal systems have created an enormous body of doctrine governing the relationship between the territory of the nation state and the legal right to exercise jurisdiction. Although the Internet has not rendered the concept of the nation state redundant, the fact that actions in the ether, of an unknown person in an unknown location, can bring about the most tangible of consequences, renders the connections between territory and jurisdiction less relevant than in the past. The difficulty lies not only in the fact that no solution has yet been found to this problem, but also in that no satisfactory solution has even appeared on the conceptual horizon.

Does the issue of jurisdiction hold more relevance for legal theory than practice? Legal theorists delight in musing over conundrums and technicalities. Often in practice, however, these intellectual puzzles rarely influence practical reality. Recent examples of international cooperation in law enforcement might demonstrate that, in some cases, the problems of jurisdiction are surmountable when needs be. However, for every high-profile case such as the Sasser Worm, there are innumerable cases of illegal or improper conduct which simply cannot, as yet, be regulated. Whether and how the global society solves the problems of jurisdiction will be a key element in the development of the true Internet jurisprudence.

The topic of jurisdiction leads directly to the drive for the harmonisation and globalisation of laws. All too often broad aspirations for harmonised laws are expressed in the hope that this might be the panacea for the Internet age. When examining this issue in the future, readers should be aware that espousing the rhetoric of harmonisation is much easier than achieving it. There are certainly benefits to be gained from international cooperation—indeed, to avoid such developments would be to take the stance of the ostrich. Many normative developments applicable to the Internet begin their journey to national implementation in the realm of international negotiations and policy discussion. Nevertheless, expressions of international cooperation and aspirational international instruments should be regarded with a healthy scepticism.

In turn, the drive for harmonisation highlights the increasing importance of international organisations, including the United Nations, the EU, the Organisation for Economic Cooperation and Development, and the World Trade Organisation, to name but a few. Each society's normative frameworks provide the benchmark for regulatory systems. In a large, representative democracy, these frameworks are often shaped by interest groups that lobby for the implementation of their preferred regulatory stance. The vector sum of various lobby groups produces the final outcome. As the subject of normative debate becomes increasingly international, so too do lobby groups. International organisations are frequently co-opted to represent the interests of large international players. These players might be governmental, corporate, or private. For example, it is clear that the US policy on encryption has influenced both the policies of other nation states and those of international organisations. Throughout this book, the role of international organisations in the development of institutional responses to the Internet has been constantly highlighted. The importance of international cooperation in the development of institutional responses to the Internet cannot be emphasised too strongly.

The penultimate point in this thematic reiteration has been implicit throughout this book: the dichotomy between developed and developing nations' participation in the Internet revolution. Even the most cursory glance at the materials herein reveals that the Internet is dominated by a trans-Atlantic intellectual duopoly. Europe and the USA are most certainly the two most powerful institutional structures at the dawn of the twenty-first century. If the Internet is to fulfil its potential, it is crucial that it does not become emblematic of the North–South dichotomy which has plagued so much of international relations to date. It is hoped, however, that with developments in some of the nations in Asia such as Singapore and China, which have been active in the area, the danger of this will be minimised.

Finally, whereas the Internet changes at a revolutionary pace, the law develops its responses at an evolutionary pace. The reader will undoubtedly be familiar with the comments frequently made regarding the dynamic nature of the Internet and the fact that change has never before been forced upon us so dramatically. Knee-jerk legal reactions will fail because, by definition, they do not allow sufficient time to examine the subtleties of choice and the implications of consequence. The law must not react impulsively, yet the alternative renders it obsolete as the world moves into uncharted territory. To address this dilemma, it may be useful to consider the institutional structures operative in the Internet context. These institutions might be legal—and indeed many were—but they may also be customary, contractual, or cooperative systems based far from the concept of nation state. Therefore, all is not lost if the law cannot lead the advance across the regulatory frontier.

The opening paragraphs of this book suggested that studies in this area would yield more questions than answers. The subsequent chapters confirmed this hypothesis, but, it is hoped, simultaneously provided some preliminary sketches of the new institutional landscape. As can be seen from the majority of the references used, the richest resource for cyberspace law materials is the Internet itself. Hence, this book is only a modest sketch. Each issue discussed herein would fill a volume of its own. Such detail would yield only more questions, conundrums and challenges along the road to the global Internet society.

Acknowledgments

The author and publisher would like to thank copyright holders for permission to reproduce copyright material. Sources are as follows.

Articles, reports, policies and directives

Australia Taxation Office, Taxation Determination TD 2005/2. Available at <http://law.ato.gov.au/atolaw/view.htm?docid=TXD/TD20052/NAT/ATO/00001> 1 May 2006.

Barlow, John Perry, 'The Economy of Ideas: Selling Wine Without Bottles on the Global Net'. Available at <http://www.eff.org/~barlow/EconomyOfIdeas.html> 1 October 2001.

Catchpole, James, 'The Regulation of Electronic Commerce: A Comparative Analysis of the Issues Surrounding the Principles of Establishment', *International Journal of Law and Information Technology 1*, (2000), 9(1), pp. 4–20 extracted), by permission of Oxford University Press.

Centre for Democracy and Technology, Initial CDT Analysis of the Clinton Administration's Proposed Cyberspace Electronic Security Act (CESA): Standards for Government Access to Decryption Keys, 23 September 1999. Available at <http://www.cdt.org/crypto/CESA/cdtcesaanalysis.shtml> 12 September 2001.

Cohen, William, Janet Reno, Jacob J Lew, and William Daley, *Preserving America's Privacy and Security in the Next Century: A Strategy for America in Cyperspace: A report to the President of the United States*, 16 September 1999. Available at <http://www.cdt.org/crypto/CESA/CESAwhitepaper.shtml>.

Debussere, Frederic, 'The EU E-Privacy Directive: A Monstrous Attempt to Starve the Cookie Monster?', *International Journal of Law and Information Technology 70 2 Cookie Technology in a Nutshell*, (2005), 13, by permission of Oxford University Press.

Debussere, Frederic, 'The EU E-Privacy Directive: A Monstrous Attempt to Starve the Cookie Monster?', *International Journal of Law and Information Technology 70*, (2005), 13, by permission of Oxford University Press.

Department of Commerce Bureau of Export Administration, 15 CFR Parts 732, 734, 740, 742, 744, 748, 770, 772, and 774 [Docket No. 001006282–0282–01] RIN 0694–AC32, *Revisions to Encryption Items.*

Federal Register/Vol 65, No 203/Thursday, 19 October 2000/Rules and Regulations p 62600. Available at <http://www.bxa.doc.gov/Encryption/pdfs/EncryptionRuleOct2K.pdf> 12 September 2001.

Directive 95/46/EC of the European Parliament and of the Council of 24 October 1995 on the Protection of Individuals with regard to the Processing of Personal Data and on the

Free Movement of Such Data. Available at <http://europa.eu.int/eur-lex/en/lif/dat/1995/en_395L0046.html> 10 September 2001. 'Only European Community legislation printed in the paper edition of the *Official Journal of the European Union* is deemed authentic.'

Directive 1999/93/EC of the European Parliament and of the Council of 13 December 1999 on a Community Framework for Electronic Signatures. Available at <http://europa.eu.int/eur-lex/en/lif/dat/1999/en_399L0093.html> 19 September 2001. 'Only European Community legislation printed in the paper edition of the *Official Journal of the European Union* is deemed authentic.'

Directive 96/9/EC of the European Parliament and of the Council of 11 March 1996 on the legal protection of databases. Available at <http://europa.eu.int/eur-lex/en/lif/dat/1996/en_396L0009.html> 4 September 2001. 'Only European Community legislation printed in the paper edition of the *Official Journal of the European Union* is deemed authentic.'

The Federal Trade Commission, Frequently Asked Questions about the Children's Online Privacy Protection Rule. Available at <http://www.ftc.gov/privacy/coppafaqs.htm> 19 September 2001.

Foss, Morten and Lee Belgrave, 'International Consumer Purchases through the Internet: Jurisdictional Issues Pursuant to European Law', *International Journal of Law and Information Technology 99*, (2000), 8(2), by permission of Oxford University Press.

Howard, Kylie and Yee Fin Lim, 'I Spy With My Little Eye—Taking a Closer Look at Spyware' (2005) (2-3) *The Journal of Information, Law and Technology*. Available at <http://www2.warwick.ac.uk/fac/soc/law/elj/jilt/2005_2-3/howard-lim/>.

ICANN, 'Uniform Domain Name Dispute Resolution Policy'. Adopted 26 August 1999. Available at < http://www.icann.org/udrp/udrp-policy-24oct99.htm> 8 May 2001. 'This material is subject to copyright and being used with ICANN's permission.'

Lim, Yee Fen, 'Is it really Just a Game? Copyright and Online Role-Playing Games' *(2006) 1(7) Journal of Intellectual Property Law and Practice 481.*

Litman, Jessica, 'The Exclusive Right to Read' 13 *Cardozo Arts and Entertainment Law Journal* 29 (1994). Available at <http://www.law.wayne.edu/litman/papers/read.htm> 4 June 2001.

Murray, Andrew, 'The Use of Trade Marks as Meta Tags: Defining the Boundaries', *International Journal of Law and Information Technology* 263, (2000), 8(3), by permission of Oxford University Press.

Murray, Andrew, 'Internet Domain Names: The Trade Mark Challenge', *International Journal of Law and Information Technology 285*, (1998), 6(3), by permission of Oxford University Press.

Organisation for Economic Cooperation and Development, Guidelines Governing the Protection of Privacy and Transborder Flows of Personal Data. © OECD. Available at <http://www.oecd.org//dsti/sti/it/secur/prod/PRIV-EN.HTM> 10 September 2001.

Post, David G, 'Personal Jurisdiction on the Internet: An Outline for the perplexed', *Temple University Law School/Cyberspace Law Institute, June 1998*. Available at <http://www.temple.edu/lawschool/dpost/outline.htm>.

Prepared Statement of the Federal Trade Commission on 'Self-Regulation and Privacy Online', before the Subcommittee on Communications of the Committee on Commerce, Science, and Transportation, United States Senate, 27 July 1999. Available at <http://www.ftc.gov/os/1999/9907/privacyonlinetestimony.pdf> 10 September 2001.

The President's Working Group on Unlawful Conduct on the Internet, The Electronic Frontier: The Challenge of Unlawful Conduct Involving the Use of the Internet, March 2000. Available at <http://www.cypercrime.gov/unlawful.htm> 24 September 2001.

Protecting Children, A Report from the Attorney General to the Vice President August 1999, Report on Cyberstalking: A New Challenge for Law Enforcement and Industry. Available at <http://www.cybercrime.gov/cyberstalking.htm> 25 September 2001.

Report of the Second WIPO Internet Domain Name Process, 'The Recognition of Rights and the Use of Names in the Internet Domain Name System', 3 September 2001. Available at <http://wipo2.wipo.int/process2/report/html/report.html> 30 September 2001. 'Material originally provided by the World Intellectual Property Organisation (WIPO). The Secretariat of WIPO assumes no liability or responsibility with regard to the transformation of this data.'

Rodriguez, Joseph C., 'A Comparative Study of Internet Content Regulations in the United States and Singapore: The Invincibility of Cyberporn' 1 *Asian-Pacific Law and Policy Journal* 9:1. Available at <http://www.hawaii.edu/aplpj/> 5 May 2006.

Smedinghoff, Thomas J. and Ruth Hill Bro, 'Moving with Change: Electronic Signature Legislation as a Vehicle for Advancing E-Commerce', *(1999) 17 John Marshall Journal of Computer and Information Law* 723. Available at <http://www.bmck.com/ecommerce/moveart.doc> 19 September 2001.

Sutter, Gavin, 'Nothing new under the Sun: Old Fear and New Media', *International Journal of Law and Information Technology* 338, (2000), 8, by permission of Oxford University Press.

Treaty on Certain Questions Concerning the Protection of Literary and Artistic Works (The Copyright Treaty) 1996. Available at <http://arl.cni.org/info/frn/copy/copytreaty.html> 5 August 2001. 'Material originally provided by the World Intellectual Property Organisation (WIPO). The Secretariat of WIPO assumes no liability or responsibility with regard to the transformation of this data.'

UNCITRAL Model Law on Electronic Signatures (2001). Available at <http://www.uncitral.org/english/texts/electcom/ml-elecsig-e.pdf> 19 September 2001.

United Nations Commission on International Trade Law (UNCITRAL) Model Law on Electronic Commerce, 1996 with additional article 5 bis as adopted in 1998.

United States Department of Commerce, *Safe Harbor Privacy Principles*, 21 July 2000. Available at <http://www.export.gov/safeharbor/SHPRINCIPLESFINAL.htm> 10 September 2001.

US Department of Justice, United States Attorney, Central District of California, Thom Mrozek, 'Five charged In Los Angeles with fraud in Internet auctions'. Available at <http://www.cybercrime.gov/mcclain.htm> 25 September 2001.

Vaver, David, 'Moral Rights Yesterday, Today and Tomorrow', *International Journal of Law and Information Technology* 271, (2000), 7(3), by permission of Oxford University Press.

- -

Cases

A & M Records, Inc., et al, v Napster, Inc, United States Court of Appeals for the Ninth Circuit, No. 00-16401 DC. Available at <http://laws.lp.findlaw.com/getcase/9th/case/0016401&exact=1> 4 May 2001.

American Civil Liberties Union, et al v Janet Reno, Attorney General of the United States 929 F Supp 824 (1996), The United States District Court for the Eastern District of Pennsylvania, Civil Action No 96-963, 11 June 1996.

Australian Communications and Media Authority v Clarity1 [2006] FCA 410 (13 April 2006). Available at <http://www.austlii.edu.au> 3 May 2006.

Australian Securities and Investments Commission v Matthews [2000] NSWSC 392 (4 May 2000), NSW Supreme Court. Available at <http://www.austlii.edu.au> 4 September 2001.

Australian Securities and Investments Commission v Matthews [1999] FCA 164 (19 February 1999), Federal Court of Australia. Available at <http://www.auslii.edu.au>.

Avnet Incorporated v Isoact Limited [1998] FSR 16, High Court of Justice, Chancery Division, United Kingdom, 28 July 1997.

Bernstein, Daniel J v United States Department of Justice et al, United States Court of Appeals for the Ninth Circuit, No 97-16686, DC No. CV-97-00582, 6 May 1999, at pp 4234–5. Available at <http://www.cdt.org/crypto/litigation/bernstein4.html> 13 September 2001.

Brinkibon Ltd v Stahag Stahl GmbH (1983) 2 AC 34, House of Lords, United Kingdom.

British Telecommunications plc; Virgin Enterprises Ltd; J Sainsbury plc; Marks & Spencer plc and Ladbroke Group plc v One in a Million Ltd and Others [1998] EWCA Civ 1272 (23 July 1998). Available at <http://www.bailii.org/ew/cases/EWCA/Civ/1998/1272.html> 15 April 2001.

Ciccone, Madonna, p/k/a Madonna v Dan Parisi and 'Madonna.com', WIPO Arbitration and Mediation Center, Administrative Panel Decision, Case No D2000-0847. Available at <http://arbiter.wipo.int/domains/decisions/html/2000/d2000-0847.html> 10 June 2001. 'Material originally provided by the World Intellectual Property Organisation (WIPO). The Secretariat of WIPO assumes no liability or responsibility with regard to the transformation of this data.'

Dow Jones & Co Inc v Gutnick [2002] HCA 56 (10 December 2002) High Court of Australia, Australia. Available at <http://www.austlii.edu.au/au/cases/cth/HCA/2002/56.html> 26 January 2006.

Eastern Power Ltd v Azienda Communale Energia and Ambiente [1999] OJ No 3275 Docket No C31224, Ontario Court of Appeal, Toronto, Ontario, Canada. Available at <http://www.ontariocourts.on.ca/decisions/OntarioCourtsSearch_VOpenFile.cfm?serverFilePath=d%3A%5Cusers%5Contario%20courts%5Cwww%5Cdecisions%5C1999%5CSeptember%5Ceastern%2Ehtm>.

Entores Ltd v Miles Far East Corporation [1955] 2 QB 327, Court of Appeal, United Kingdom.

Gutnick v Dow Jones & Co Inc [2001] VSC 305 (28 August 2001), Supreme Court of Victoria, Australia. Available at <http://www.austlii.edu.au/au/cases/vic/VSC/2001/305.html> 26 September 2001

In Re: Aimster Copyright Litigation. Appeal of: John Deep, Defendant, United States Court of Appeals for the Seventh Circuit, No 02-4125. Available at <http://www.ca7.uscourts.gov/tmp/SI01OI4Q.pdf> 28 April 2006.

Junger, Peter D v William Daley, United States Secretary of Commerce, et al, United States Court of Appeals for the Sixth Circuit, 4 April 2000, 2000 FED App 0117P (6th Cir). Available at <http://www.cdt.org/crypto/litigation/000404junger.shtml> 13 September 2001.

The Leonard Cheshire Foundation v Paul Anthony Darke, WIPO Arbitration and Mediation Center, Administrative Panel Decision, Case No D2001-0131. Available at <http://arbiter.wipo.int/domains/decisions/html/2001/d2001-0131.html> 10 September 2001. 'Material originally provided by the World Intellectual Property Organisation (WIPO). The Secretariat of WIPO assumes no liability or responsibility with regard to the transformation of this data.'

Macquarie Bank Limited and Anor v Berg [1999] NSWSC 526, NSW Supreme Court. Available at <http://www.austlii.edu.au> 03 September 2001.

Marks & Spencer plc, Ladbrokes plc, J Sainsbury plc, Virgin Enterprises Ltd, British Telecommunications plc, Telecom Securior Cellular Radio Ltd v One in a Million and Others [1997] EWHC Patents 357 (28 November 1997), High Court of Justice, Chancery Division, United Kingdom. Available at <http://www.bailii.org/ew/cases/EWHC/Patents/1997/357.html> 15 April 2001.

Metro-Goldwyn-Mayer Studios Inc v Grokster Ltd, United States Supreme Court, 125 S Ct 2764 (2005)

The People of the State of New York v World Interactive Gaming Corporation 714 NYS 2d 844 (NY County Sup Ct 1999) Supreme Court of the State of New York, County of New York: Commercial Part 53 Index No 404428/98. Available at <http://www.courts.state.ny.us/nycdlr/issue2-4/Internet.htm> 4 August 2001.

R v Stevens [1999] NSWCCA 69 (15 April 1999), NSW Criminal Court of Appeal. Available at <http://www.austlii.edu.au/> 16 September 2001.

State Street Bank and Trust Co v Signature Financial Group, Inc, United States Court of Appeals for the Federal Circuit, 96-1327. Available at <http://www.ll.georgetown.edu/Fed-Ct/Circuit/fed/opinions/97-1327.html> 6 June 2001.

Sumner, Gordon, p/k/a Sting v Michael Urvan, WIPO Arbitration and Mediation Center, Administrative Panel Decision, Case No D2000-0596. Available at <http://arbiter.wipo.int/domains/decisions/html/2000/d2000-0596.html> 10 June 2001. 'Material originally provided by the World Intellectual Property Organisation (WIPO). The Secretariat of WIPO assumes no liability or responsibility with regard to the transformation of this data.'

Universal Music Australia Pty Ltd v Sharman License Holdings, Federal Courts of Australia, [2005] FCA 1242.

Universal Music Australia Pty Ltd v Cooper, Federal Courts of Australia, [2005] FCA 972.

Welcome Real-Time SA v Catuity Inc [2001] FCA 445 (17 May 2001). Available at <http://www.austlii.edu.au> 30 September 2001.

Legislation

Australian Controls on the Export of Defence and Strategic Goods, Defence and Strategic Goods List.

Australian Controls on the Export of Defence and Strategic Goods, Defence and Strategic Goods List—Amendment No 1 of 1999 dated 23 June 1999.

Broadcasting Services Act as amended 1992.

Computer Misuse Act 1993 as amended (Singapore).

Copyright Act 1968 as amended.

Copyright Amendment (Digital Agenda) Act 2000.

Crimes Act 1900 as amended (NSW).

Customs Act 1901.

Customs (Prohibited Exports) Regulations 1958.

Electronic Transactions Act 1998 (Singapore).

Electronic Transactions Act 1999.

National Privacy Principles for the Fair Handling of Personal Information set out in Privacy Act
1988 as amended, Schedule 3.

Patents Act 1990.

Privacy Act 1988.

Trade Practices Act 1995.

Uniform Electronic Transactions Act 1999 (US).

Workplace Surveillance Act 2005 (NSW) as amended © State of New South Wales through the
Attorney General's Department of NSW

All legislative material herein is reproduced by permission but does not purport to
be the official or authorised version. It is subject to Commonwealth of Australia
copyright.

*Every effort has been made to trace the original source of copyright material contained in
this book. The publisher would be pleased to hear from copyright holders to rectify any
errors or omissions.*

Index